Gender Through the Prism of Difference

GENDER THROUGH THE PRISM OF DIFFERENCE

THIRD EDITION

Edited by

Maxine Baca Zinn
Michigan State University

Pierrette Hondagneu-Sotelo
University of Southern California

Michael A. Messner
University of Southern California

New York Oxford
OXFORD UNIVERSITY PRESS
2005

Oxford University Press

Oxford New York
Auckland Bangkok Buenos Aires Cape Town Chennai
Dar es Salaam Delhi Hong Kong Istanbul Karachi Kolkata
Kuala Lumpur Madrid Melbourne Mexico City Mumbai Nairobi
São Paulo Shanghai Taipei Tokyo Toronto

Published by Oxford University Press, Inc.
198 Madison Avenue, New York, New York 10016
www.oup.com

Library of Congress Cataloging-in-Publication Data

Gender through the prism of difference / edited by Maxine Baca Zinn, Pierrette Hondagneu-Sotelo, Michael A. Messner.—3rd ed.
p. cm.
Includes bibliographical references.
ISBN-13: 978-0-19-516764-1
ISBN-10: 0-19-516764-3
1. Sex role. I. Zinn, Maxine Baca, 1942- II. Hondagneu-Sotelo, Pierrette. III. Messner, Michael A.

HQ1075.G4666 2005
305.3—dc22

2004057573

Printing number: 9 8 7 6 5 4 3 2 1

Printed in the United States of America
on acid-free paper

CONTENTS

Preface ix

INTRODUCTION: Sex and Gender Through the Prism of Difference 1

I. PERSPECTIVES ON SEX, GENDER, AND DIFFERENCE 11

1. *Ann Fausto-Sterling,* The Five Sexes, Revisited 13
2. *Maxine Baca Zinn and Bonnie Thornton Dill,* Theorizing Difference from Multiracial Feminism 19
3. *Deniz Kandiyoti,* Bargaining with Patriarchy 26
4. *R. W. Connell,* Masculinities and Globalization 36
5. *Barbara Ehrenreich and Arlie Russell Hochschild,* Global Woman 49
6. *Chandra Talpade Mohanty,* Antiglobalization Pedagogies and Feminism 56

II. BODIES 63

Control and Resistance

7. *Jane Sprague Zones,* Beauty Myths and Realities and Their Impact on Women's Health 65
8. *Nomy Lamm,* It's a Big Fat Revolution 81
9. *Tamara Beauboeuf-Lafontant,* Strong and Large Black Women? Exploring Relationships Between Deviant Womanhood and Weight 86
10. *Jen'nan Ghazal Read and John P. Bartkowski,* To Veil or Not to Veil? A Case Study of Identity Negotiation Among Muslim Women in Austin, Texas 94
11. *Don Sabo,* Doing Time, Doing Masculinity: Sports and Prison 108
12. *Betsy Lucal,* What It Means to Be Gendered Me: Life on the Boundaries of a Dichotomous Gender System 113

Violence

13. *Cecilia Menjívar and Olivia Salcido,* Immigrant Women and Domestic Violence: Common Experiences in Different Countries 123
14. *Afroza Anwary,* Acid Violence and Medical Care in Bangladesh: Women's Activism as Carework 137
15. *Patricia Albanese,* Nationalism, War, and Archaization of Gender Relations in the Balkans 143
16. *Michael Kimmel,* Gender, Class, and Terrorism 154

III. SEXUALITIES 159

Sexual Relations, Intimacy, Power

17. *Karin A. Martin,* "I couldn't ever picture myself having sex . . .": Gender Differences in Sex and Sexual Subjectivity 161
18. *Matthew C. Gutmann,* Male Discretion and Sexual Indiscretion in Working Class Mexico City 177
19. *Kevin Bales,* Because She Looks like a Child 193
20. *Julia O'Connell Davidson,* The Sex Tourist, the Expatriate, His Ex-Wife, and Her "Other": The Politics of Loss, Difference, and Desire 203

Sexuality and Identity

21. *Dennis Altman,* The Globalization of Sexual Identities 216
22. *Michael A. Messner,* Becoming 100% Straight 227
23. *Yen Le Espiritu,* "Americans Have a Different Attitude": Family, Sexuality, and Gender in Filipina American Lives 233

IV. IDENTITIES 243

24. *Audre Lord,* Age, Race, Class, and Sex: Women Redefining Difference 245
25. *Elliott Femynye Bat Tzedek,* The Rights and Wrongs of Identity Politics and Sexual Identities 251
26. *Almas Sayeed,* Chappals and Gym Shorts: An Indian Muslim Woman in the Land of Oz 258
27. *Karen D. Pyke and Denise L. Johnson,* Asian American Women and Racialized Femininities: "Doing" Gender Across Cultural Worlds 263
28. Peggy McIntosh, White Privilege: Unpacking the Invisible Knapsack 278

V. FAMILIES 283

Motherhood, Fatherhood

29. *Patricia Hill Collins,* The Meaning of Motherhood in Black Culture and Black Mother–Daughter Relationships 285

30. *Lisa J. Udel,* Revision and Resistance: The Politics of Native Women's Motherwork 296

31. *Pierrette Hondagneu-Sotelo and Ernestine Avila,* "I'm Here but I'm There": The Meanings of Latina Transnational Motherhood 308

32. *Marcia C. Inhorn,* "The Worms are Weak": Male Infertility and Patriarchal Paradoxes in Egypt 323

Work and Families

33. *Pei-Chia Lan,* Maid or Madam? Filipina Migrant Workers and the Continuity of Domestic Labor 334

34. *M. Patricia Fernández Kelly,* Delicate Transactions: Gender, Home, and Employment Among Hispanic Women 347

35. *Elizabeth Higginbotham and Lynn Weber,* Moving Up with Kin and Community: Upward Social Mobility for Black and White Women 356

36. *Kathryn Edin,* What Do Low-Income Single Mothers Say About Marriage? 365

VI. CONSTRUCTING GENDER IN THE WORKPLACE 383

37. *Peter Levin,* Gendering the Market: Temporality, Work, and Gender on a National Futures Exchange 385

38. *Patti A. Giuffre and Christine L. Williams,* Boundary Lines: Labeling Sexual Harassment in Restaurants 392

39. *Karen J. Hossfeld,* "Their Logic Against Them": Contradictions in Sex, Race, and Class in Silicon Valley 407

40. *Pierrette Hondagneu-Sotelo,* Go Away . . . But Stay Close Enough 419

VII. EDUCATION AND SCHOOLS 437

41. *Ann Arnett Ferguson,* Naughty by Nature 439

42. *Julie Bettie,* How Working-Class Chicas Get Working-Class Lives 447

43. *Nancy Lopez,* Homegrown: How the Family Does Gender 465

44. *Yoshiko Nozaki* Feminism, Nationalism, and the Japanese Textbook Controversy over "Comfort Women" 481

VIII. POPULAR CULTURE 487

45. *Barry Glassner,* Black Men: How to Perpetuate Prejudice Without Really Trying 489
46. *Catherine A. Lutz and Jane L. Collins,* The Color of Sex: Postwar Photographic Histories of Race and Gender in *National Geographic Magazine* 497
47. *Susan Jane Gilman,* Klaus Barbie, and Other Dolls I'd Like To See 504
48. *Mimi Schippers,* Sexuality and Gender Maneuvering 508
49. *Lori Kendall,* "Oh No! I'm a Nerd!" Hegemonic Masculinity on an Online Forum 516

IX. CHANGE AND POLITICS 529

50. *King-To Yeung and Mindy Stombler,* Gay and Greek: The Identity Paradox of Gay Fraternities 531
51. *Mary Pardo,* Mexican American Women, Grassroots Community Activists: "Mothers of East Los Angeles" 541
52. *Radhika Gajjala and Annapurna Mamidipudi,* Cyberfeminism, Technology, and International "Development" 547
53. *Kevin Powell,* Confessions of a Recovering Misogynist 555

PREFACE

Over the past 30 years, texts and readers intended for use in women's studies and gender studies courses have changed and developed in important ways. In the 1970s and into the early 1980s, many courses and texts focused almost exclusively on women as a relatively undifferentiated category. Two developments have broadened the study of women. First, in response to criticisms by women of color and by lesbians that heterosexual, white, middle-class feminists had tended to "falsely universalize" their own experiences and issues, courses and texts on gender began in the 1980s to systematically incorporate race and class diversity. And simultaneously, as a result of feminist scholars' insistence that gender be studied as a relational construct, more concrete studies of men and masculinity began to emerge in the 1980s.

This book reflects this belief that race, class, and sexual diversity among women and men should be central to the study of gender. But this collection adds an important new dimension that will broaden the frame of gender studies. By including some articles that are based on research in countries outside the United States, in nonindustrial societies, and among immigrant groups, we hope that *Gender Through the Prism of Difference* will contribute to a transcendence of the often myopic, U.S.-based, and Eurocentric focus in the study of sex and gender. The inclusion of these perspectives is not simply useful for illuminating our own cultural blind spots: It also begins to demonstrate how, early in the twenty-first century, gender relations are increasingly centrally implicated in current processes of globalization.

Because the amount of high-quality research on gender has expanded so dramatically in the past decade, the most difficult task in assembling this collection was deciding *what* to include. The third edition, while retaining the structure of the previous edition, is different and improved. This edition includes material on gender issues relevant to the college-age generation including gender and popular culture, Islam, and men and war. Many of the new readings tend toward a more personal narrative style that students will find engaging.

We thank faculty and staff colleagues in the Department of Sociology and the Gender Studies program at the University of Southern California and in the Department of Sociology and the Julian Samora Research Institute at Michigan State University for their generous support and assistance. Other people contributed their labor to the development of this book. We are grateful to our research assistants, Genelle Gaudinez of the University of Southern California and Katie Thurman of Michigan State University, who contributed invaluable groundwork.

We acknowledge the helpful criticism and suggestions made by the following reviewers: Linda Grant, University of Georgia; Elizabeth B. Erbaugh, University of New Mexico; Jackie Eller, Middle Tennessee State University; Jean L. Potuchek, Gettysburg College; Joya Misra, University of Massachusetts; Janet Wirth-Cauchon, Drake University; and Kathryn B. Ward, Southern Illinois University. Our editor at Oxford University Press, Peter Labella, has been encouraging, helpful, and patient. We also thank Sean Mahoney and Celeste Alexander for their editorial assistance as the book moved into production.

Finally, we thank our families for their love and support as we worked on this book. Alan Zinn, Prentice Zinn, Gabrielle Cobbs, and Edan Zinn provide inspiration through their work for progressive social change. Miles Hondagneu-Messner and Sasha Hondagneu-Messner continually challenge the neatness of Mike and Pierrette's image of social life. Life with a fifteen-year-old and a twelve-year-old is less a neat rainbow shining through a stable prism than it is a kaleidoscope of constantly shifting moments and meanings. We do hope, though, that the kind of work that is collected in this book will eventually help them and their generation make sense of the world and move that world into more peaceful, humane, and just directions.

Gender Through the Prism of Difference

Introduction

Sex and Gender Through the Prism of Difference

"Men can't cry." "Women are victims of patriarchal oppression." "After divorces, single mothers are downwardly mobile, often moving into poverty." "Men don't do their share of housework and child care." "Professional women face barriers such as sexual harassment and a 'glass ceiling' that prevent them from competing equally with men for high-status positions and high salaries." "Heterosexual intercourse is an expression of men's power over women." Sometimes, the students in our sociology and gender studies courses balk at these kinds of generalizations. And they are right to do so. After all, some men are more emotionally expressive than some women, some women have more power and success than some men, some men do their share—or more—of housework and child care, and some women experience sex with men as both pleasurable and empowering. Indeed, contemporary gender relations are complex and changing in various directions, and as such, we need to be wary of simplistic, if handy, slogans that seem to sum up the essence of relations between women and men.

On the other hand, we think it is a tremendous mistake to conclude that "all individuals are totally unique and different," and that therefore all generalizations about social groups are impossible or inherently oppressive. In fact, we are convinced that it is this very complexity, this multifaceted nature of contemporary gender relations, that fairly begs for a sociological analysis of gender. In the title of this book, we use the image of "the prism of difference" to illustrate our approach to developing this sociological perspective on contemporary gender relations. The *American Heritage Dictionary* defines "prism," in part, as "a homogeneous transparent solid, usually with triangular bases and rectangular sides, used to produce or analyze a continuous spectrum." Imagine a ray of light—which to the naked eye appears to be only one color—refracted through a prism onto a white wall. To the eye, the result is not an infinite, disorganized scatter of individual colors. Rather, the refracted light displays an order, a structure of relationships among the different colors—a rainbow. Similarly, we propose to use the "prism of difference" in this book to analyze a continuous spectrum of people, in order to show how gender is organized and experienced differently when refracted through the prism of sexual, racial/ethnic, social class, physical abilities, age, and national citizenship differences.

EARLY WOMEN'S STUDIES: CATEGORICAL VIEWS OF "WOMEN" AND "MEN"

Taken together, the articles in this book make the case that it is possible to make good generalizations about women and men. But these generalizations should be drawn carefully, by always asking the questions "*which* women?" and "*which* men?" Scholars of sex and gender have not always done this. In the 1960s and 1970s, women's studies focused on the differences *between* women and men rather than *among* women and men. The very concept of gender, women's studies scholars demonstrated, is based on socially defined difference between women and men. From the macro level of social institutions such as the economy, politics, and religion, to the micro level of interpersonal relations, distinctions between women and men structure social relations. Making men and women *different* from one another is the essence of gender. It is also the basis of men's power and domination. Understanding this was profoundly illuminating. Knowing that difference produced domination enabled women to name, analyze, and set about changing their victimization.

In the 1970s, riding the wave of a resurgent feminist movement, colleges and universities began to develop women's studies courses that aimed first and foremost to make women's lives visible. The texts that were developed for these courses tended to stress the things that women shared under patriarchy—having the responsibility for housework and child care, the experience or fear of men's sexual violence, a lack of formal or informal access to education, and exclusion from high-status professional and managerial jobs, political office, and religious leadership positions (Brownmiller, 1975; Kanter, 1977).

The study of women in society offered new ways of seeing the world. But the 1970s approach was limited in several ways. Thinking of gender primarily in terms of differences *between* women and men led scholars to overgeneralize about both. The concept of patriarchy led to a dualistic perspective of male privilege and female subordination. Women and men were cast as opposites. Each was treated as a homogeneous category with common characteristics and experiences. This approach *essentialized* women and men. Essentialism, simply put, is the notion that women's and men's attributes and indeed women and men themselves are categorically different. From this perspective, male control and coercion of women produced conflict between the sexes. The feminist insight originally introduced by Simone De Beauvoir in 1953—that women, as a group, had been socially defined as the "other" and that men had constructed themselves as the subjects of history, while constructing women as their objects—fueled an energizing sense of togetherness among many women. As college students read books such as *Sisterhood Is Powerful* (Morgan, 1970), many of them joined organizations that fought—with some success—for equality and justice for women.

THE VOICES OF "OTHER" WOMEN

Although this view of women as an oppressed "other" was empowering for certain groups of women, some women began to claim that the feminist view of universal sisterhood ignored and marginalized their major concerns. It soon became apparent that treating women as a group united in its victimization by patriarchy was biased by too narrow a focus on the experiences and perspectives of women from more privileged social groups. "Gender" was treated as a generic category, uncritically applied to women. Ironically, this analysis, which was meant to unify women, instead produced divisions between and among them. The concerns projected as "universal" were removed from the realities of many women's lives. For example, it became a matter of faith in second-wave feminism that women's liberation would be accomplished by breaking down the "gendered public-domestic split." Indeed, the feminist call for women to move out of the kitchen and into the workplace resonated in the experiences of many of the college-educated white women who were inspired by Betty Friedan's 1963 book, *The Feminine Mystique*. But the idea that women's movement into workplaces was itself empowering or liberating seemed absurd or irrelevant to many working-class women and women of color. They were already working for wages, as had many of their mothers and grandmothers, and did not consider access to jobs and public life "liberating." For many of these women, liberation had more to do with organizing in communities and workplaces—often alongside men—for better schools, better pay, decent benefits, and other policies to benefit their neighborhoods, jobs, and families. The feminism of the 1970s did not seem to address these issues.

As more and more women analyzed their own experiences, they began to address the power relations that created differences among women and the part that privileged women played in the oppression of others. For many women of color, working-class women, lesbians, and women in contexts outside the United States (especially women in non-Western societies), the focus on male domination was a distraction from other oppressions. Their lived experiences could support neither a unitary theory of gender nor an ideology of universal sisterhood. As a result, finding common ground in a universal female victimization was never a priority for many groups of women.

Challenges to gender stereotypes soon emerged. Women of varied races, classes, national origins, and sexualities insisted that the concept of gender be broadened to take their differences into account (Baca Zinn ct. al., 1986; Hartmann, 1976; Rich, 1980; Smith, 1977). Many women began to argue that their lives were affected by their location in a number of different hierarchies: as African Americans, Latinas, Native Americans, or Asian Americans in the race hierarchy; as young or old in the age hierarchy; as heterosexual, lesbian, or bisexual in the sexual orientation hierarchy; and as women outside the Western industrialized nations, in subordinated geopolitical contexts. These arguments made it clear that women were not victimized by gender alone but by the historical and systematic denial of rights and privileges based on other differences as well.

MEN AS GENDERED BEINGS

As the voices of "other" women in the mid- to late 1970s began to challenge and expand the parameters of women's studies, a new area of scholarly inquiry was beginning to stir—a critical examination of men and masculinity. To be sure, in those early years of gender studies, the major task was to conduct studies and develop courses about the lives of women in order to begin to correct centuries of scholarship that rendered invisible women's lives, problems, and accomplishments. But the core idea of feminism—that "femininity" and women's subordination is a social construction—logically led to an examination of the social construction of "masculinity" and men's power. Many of the first scholars to take on this task were psychologists who were concerned with looking at the social construction of "the male sex role" (e.g., Pleck,

1981). By the late 1980s, there was a growing interdisciplinary collection of studies of men and masculinity, much of it by social scientists (Brod, 1987; Kaufman, 1987; Kimmel, 1987; Kimmel & Messner, 1989).

Reflecting developments in women's studies, the scholarship on men's lives tended to develop three themes : First, what we think of as "masculinity" is not a fixed, biological essence of men, but rather is a social construction that shifts and changes over time as well as between and among various national and cultural contexts. Second, power is central to understanding gender as a relational construct, and the dominant definition of masculinity is largely about expressing difference from—and superiority over—anything considered "feminine." And third, there is no singular "male sex role." Rather, at any given time there are various masculinities. R. W. Connell (1987; 1995; 2002) has been among the most articulate advocates of this perspective. Connell argues that hegemonic masculinity (the dominant form of masculinity at any given moment) is constructed in relation to femininities *as well as* in relation to various subordinated or marginalized masculinities. For example, in the United States, various racialized masculinities (e.g., as represented by African American men, Latino immigrant men, etc.) have been central to the construction of hegemonic (white middle-class) masculinity. This "othering" of racialized masculinities helps to shore up the privileges that have been historically connected to hegemonic masculinity. When viewed this way, we can better understand hegemonic masculinity as part of a system that includes gender as well as racial, class, sexual, and other relations of power.

The new literature on men and masculinities also begins to move us beyond the simplistic, falsely categorical, and pessimistic view of men simply as a privileged sex class. When race, social class, sexual orientation, physical abilities, immigrant, or national status are taken into account, we can see that in some circumstances, "male privilege" is partly—sometimes substantially—muted (Kimmel & Messner, 2004). Although it is unlikely that we will soon see a "men's movement" that aims to undermine the power and privileges that are connected with hegemonic masculinity, when we begin to look at "masculinities" through the prism of difference, we can begin to see similarities and possible points of coalition between and among certain groups of women and men (Messner, 1998). Certain kinds of changes in gender relations—for instance, a national family leave policy for working parents—might serve as a means of uniting particular groups of women and men.

GENDER IN INTERNATIONAL CONTEXTS

It is an increasingly accepted truism that late twentieth-century increases in transnational trade, international migration, and global systems of production and communication have diminished both the power of nation-states and the significance of national borders. A much more ignored issue is the extent to which gender relations—in the United States and elsewhere in the world—are increasingly linked to patterns of global economic restructuring. Decisions made in corporate headquarters located in Los Angeles, Tokyo, or London may have immediate repercussions on how women and men thousands of miles away organize their work, community, and family lives (Sassen, 1991). It is no longer possible to study gender relations without giving attention to global processes and inequalities. Scholarship on women in third world contexts has moved from liberal concerns for the impact of development policies on women (Boserup, 1970), to more critical perspectives that acknowledge how international labor and capital mobility are transforming gender and family relations (Fernández Kelly, this volume; Hondagneu-Sotelo and Avila, this volume), to theoretical debates on third world feminisms (Mohanty, 1991). The transformation of international relations from a 1990s "post–cold war" environment to an expansion of militarism and warfare in recent years has realigned international gender relations in key ways that call for new examinations of gender, violence, militarism, and culture (Enloe, 1993, 2000; Okin, 1999).

Around the world, women's paid and unpaid labor is key to global development strategies. Yet it would be a mistake to conclude that gender is molded from the "top down." What happens on a daily basis in families and workplaces simultaneously constitutes and is constrained by structural transnational institutions. For instance, in the second half of the twentieth century young, single women, many of them from poor rural areas, were (and continue to be) recruited for work in export assembly plants along the U.S.-Mexico border, in East and Southeast Asia, in Silicon Valley, in the Caribbean, and in Central America. While the profitability of these multinational factories depends, in part, on management's ability to manipulate the young women's ideologies of gender, the women—as suggested by various shop floor ethnographies and by Karen J. Hossfeld's article in this volume—do not respond passively or uniformly, but actively resist, challenge, and accommodate. At the same time, the global dispersion of the assembly line has concentrated corporate facilities in many U.S. cities, making available myriad managerial, administrative, and clerical jobs for college educated women. Women's paid labor is used at various points along this international system of production. Not only employment but also consumption embodies global interdependencies. There is a high probability that the clothing you are wearing and the computer you use originated in multinational corporate headquarters and in assembly plants scattered around third world nations. And if these items were actually manufactured in the United States, they were probably assembled by Latin American and Asian-born women.

Worldwide, international labor migration and refugee movements are creating new types of multiracial societies. While these developments are often discussed and analyzed with respect to racial differences, gender typically remains absent. As several commentators have noted, the white feminist movement in the United States has not addressed issues of immigration and nationality. Gender, however, has been fundamental in shaping immigration policies (Chang, 1994; Hondagneu-Sotelo, 1994). Direct labor recruitment programs generally solicit either male or female labor (e.g., Filipina nurses and Mexican male farm workers), national disenfranchisement has particular repercussions for women and men, and current immigrant laws are based on very gendered notions of what constitutes "family unification." As Chandra Mohanty suggests, "analytically these issues are the contemporary metropolitan counterpart of women's struggles against colonial occupation in the geographical third world" (1991:23). Moreover, immigrant and refugee women's daily lives often challenge familiar feminist paradigms. The occupations in which immigrant and refugee women concentrate—paid domestic work, informal sector street vending, assembly or industrial piece work performed in the home—often blur the ideological distinction between work and family and between public and private spheres (Hondagneu-Sotelo, 2001; Parrenas, 2001).

FROM PATCHWORK QUILT TO PRISM

All of these developments—the voices of "other" women, the study of men and masculinities, and the examination of gender in transnational contexts—have helped redefine the study of gender. By working to develop knowledge that is inclusive of the experiences of all groups, new insights about gender have begun to emerge. Examining gender in the context of other differences makes it clear that nobody experiences themselves as solely gendered. Instead, gender is configured through cross-cutting forms of difference that carry deep social and economic consequences.

By the mid-1980s, thinking about gender had entered a new stage, which was more carefully grounded in the experiences of diverse groups of women and men. This perspective is a general way of looking at women and men and understanding their relationships to the structure of society. Gender is no longer viewed simply as a matter of two opposite categories of people, males and females, but a range of social relations among differently situated people. Because centering on difference is a radical challenge to the conventional gender framework, it raises several concerns. If we think of all the systems that converge to simultaneously influence the lives of women and men, we can imagine an infinite number of effects these interconnected systems have on different women and men. Does the recognition that gender can be understood only contextually (meaning that there is no singular "gender" per se) make women's studies and men's studies newly vulnerable to critics in the academy? Does the immersion in difference throw us into a whirlwind of "spiraling diversity" (Hewitt, 1992:316) whereby multiple identities and locations shatter the categories "women" and "men"?

Throughout the book, we take a position directly opposed to an empty pluralism. Although the categories "woman" and "man" have multiple meanings, this does not reduce gender to a "postmodern kaleidoscope of lifestyles. Rather, it points to the *relational* character of gender" (Connell, 1992:736). Not only are masculinity and femininity relational, but different *masculinities* and *femininities* are interconnected through other social structures such as race, class, and nation. The concept of relationality suggests that "the lives of different groups are interconnected even without face-to-face relations (Glenn, 2002:14). The meaning of "woman" is defined by the existence of women of different races and classes. Being a white woman in the United States is meaningful only insofar as it is set apart from and in contradistinction to women of color.

Just as masculinity and femininity each depend on the definition of the other to produce domination, differences *among* women and *among* men are also created in the context of structured relationships. Some women derive benefits from their race and class position and from their location in the global economy, while they are simultaneously restricted by gender. In other words, such women are subordinated by patriarchy, yet their relatively privileged positions within hierarchies of race, class, and the global political economy intersect to create for them an expanded range of opportunities, choices, and ways of living. They may even use their race and class advantage to minimize some of the consequences of patriarchy and/or to oppose other women. Similarly, one can become a man in opposition to other men. For example, "the relation between heterosexual and homosexual men is central, carrying heavy symbolic freight. To many people, homosexuality is the *negation* of masculinity. . . . Given that assumption, antagonism toward homosexual men may be used to define masculinity" (Connell, 1992:736).

In the past decade, viewing gender through the prism of difference has profoundly reoriented the field (Acker, 1999; Glenn, 1999, 2002; Messner, 1996; West & Fenstermaker, 1995). Yet analyzing the multiple constructions of gender does not just mean studying groups of women and groups of men as different. It is clearly time to go beyond what we call the "patchwork quilt" phase in the study of women and men—that is, the phase in which we have acknowledged the importance of examining differences within constructions of gender, but do so largely by collecting together a study here on African American women, a study there on gay men, a study on working-class Chicanas, and so on. This patchwork quilt approach too often amounts to no more than "adding difference and stirring." The result may be a lovely mosaic, but like a patchwork quilt, it still tends to overemphasize boundaries rather than to highlight bridges of interdependency. In addition, this approach too often does not explore the ways that social constructions of femininities and masculinities are based on and reproduce relations of power. In short, we think that the substantial quantity of research that has now been done on various groups and subgroups needs to be analyzed within a framework that emphasizes differences and inequalities not as discrete areas of separation, but as interrelated bands of color that together make up a spectrum.

A recent spate of sophisticated sociological theorizing along these lines has introduced some useful ways to think about difference in relational terms. Patricia Hill Collins (1990, 1998, 2004) has suggested that we think of race, class, and gender as a socially structured "matrix of domination"; R. W. Connell has pressed us to think of multiple differences not in simple additive ways, but rather as they "abrade, inflame, amplify, twist, negate, dampen, and complicate each other" (Kessler et al., 1985). Similarly, Maxine Baca Zinn and Bonnie Thornton Dill (in this volume) have suggested that we consider a body of theory and practice they call "multiracial feminism" as a means of coming to grips with the relations between various systems of inequality. Such scholarship linking the interactive effects of race, class, gender, and sexuality has proliferated. Today, "intersectional" frameworks foster a more complete view of the different experiences of women and men across and within varied groups.

These are the kinds of concerns that we had in mind in putting together this collection. We sought individual articles that explored intersections or axes in the matrix of domination by comparing different groups. We brought together articles that explored the lives of people who experience the daily challenges of multiple marginality (e.g., black lesbians, immigrant women, etc.) or the often paradoxical realities of those who may identify simultaneously with a socially marginalized or subordinated identity (e.g., gay, poor, physically disabled, Latino, etc.) along with a socially dominant identity (e.g., man, white, professional class, etc.). When we could not find articles that directly compared or juxtaposed categories or groups, we attempted to juxtapose two or three articles that, together, explored differences and similarities between groups. To this end, we added a fifth dimension to the now commonly accepted "race/class/gender/sexuality" matrix: national origin. Reflecting a tendency in U.S. sociology in general, courses on sex and gender have been far too U.S.-focused and Eurocentric. Focusing on the construction of gender in industrializing societies or the shifting relations of gender among transnational immigrant groups challenges and broadens our otherwise narrow assumptions about the constraints and possibilities facing contemporary women and men. But it is not enough to remain within the patchwork quilt framework, to simply focus on women and men in other nations as though they were somehow separate from processes occurring in the United States. Again, the metaphor of the prism better illustrates the dual challenges we face in integrating analyses of national inequalities. A central challenge facing scholars today is to understand how constructions of masculinities and feminities move across national borders. In this regard, we need to acknowledge two distinct but interrelated outcomes. In the process of moving across national boundaries—through media images, immigration, or global systems of production—gender inequalities are reconstructed and take new shape. At the same time, global movements of gender transform the gendered institutions with which they come into contact. While it may seem ironic to focus on the nation in this era that some commentators have termed "postnational," we believe that we need to focus more on national difference precisely because of the increasing number and intensity of global connections and interdependencies.

The third edition of this book continues with all of these themes but adds attention to three arenas of gender to which previous editions of the book did not give sufficient attention: differences of generation, education and schools, and the images of gender promulgated by mass media and popular culture. In recent years, pundits have employed the term *Generation X* to refer to the vast and diverse group of the "twenty-something" (and by now "thirty-something") population. While celebrated by some as a new market for new products and condemned as spoiled slackers by others, Generation X is, in fact, more heterogeneous than the pundits would allow. In addition, boys, girls, and young women and men tend to relate to gender and sexuality issues in somewhat different ways than did the older generation of writers and activists who made up the "second wave" of feminism. "Third wave" feminism is a generational sensibility that is beginning to have an impact on college campuses and in popular culture in recent years (Heywood & Drake, 1997). The articles we have assembled on youth culture and generational differences are sprinkled throughout the various sections of this volume. The gendered character of these generational communities is, in many instances, defined by differences of race, class, sexuality, and nation. Yet these constituencies are also deliberately constructed by young people in ways that underline their distinctiveness, and sometimes oppositional stances, to other groups and older generations. The structuring of youth culture—and the agency of youth groups—can be seen in various contexts. In this third edition of the book, we add a new section that focuses on one key youth context: education and schools. The third edition also includes an expanded focus on popular culture and ideology. In recent years, the flourishing scholarship in cultural studies has shown that our experiences of gender are strongly shaped by mass media, advertisements, consumption, and leisure activities. Music, sports, and the marketing of difference through consumer goods, to cite a few examples, convey particular embodiments of gender. And yet, as much of the new scholarship on consumption suggests, people situated differently in a matrix of difference and inequality tend to interpret, use, and respond to popular culture and marketing messages in quite different ways.

We hope this book contributes to a new generation of scholarship in the study of sex and gender—one that moves beyond the patchwork quilt approach, which lists or catalogs difference, to an approach that takes up the challenge to explore the relations of power that structure these differences. The late Gloria Anzaldúa (1990), a Chicana lesbian and feminist, used the border as a metaphor to capture the spatial, ethnic, class, and sexual transitions traversed in one's lifetime. She states in a poem that "To survive the borderlands you must live *sin fronteras*" (without borders). Breaking down, reassessing, and crossing the borders that divide the patches on the quilt—both experientially and analytically—is key to the difficult task of transforming knowledge about gender. Looking at the various prisms that organize gender relations, we think, will contribute to the kind of bridge-building that will be needed for constructing broad-based coalitions to push for equality and social justice in the twenty-first century.

REFERENCES

Acker, Joan. 1999. "Rewriting Class, Race and Gender: Problems in Feminist Rethinking" Pp. 44–69 in Myra Marx Ferree, Judith Lorber, and Beth B. Hess (eds.), *Revisioning Gender.* Thousand Oaks, CA: Sage Publications.

Anzaldúa, Gloria. 1990. "To Live in the Borderlands Means You." Pp. 194–195 in Gloria Anzaldúa, *Borderlands La Frontera: The New Mestiza.* San Francisco, CA: Spinsters/Aunt Lute.

Baca Zinn, M., L., Weber Cannon, E., Higgenbotham, & B., Thornton Dill. 1986. "The Costs of Exclusionary Practices in Women's Studies," *Signs: Journal of Women in Culture and Society 11:* 290–303.

Boserup, Ester. 1970. *Woman's Role in Economic Development.* London: George Allen & Unwin.

Brod, Harry (ed.). 1987. *The Making of Masculinities: The New Men's Studies.* Boston: Allen & Unwin.

Brownmiller, Susan. 1975. *Against Our Will: Men, Women, and Rape.* New York: Simon & Schuster.

Chang, Grace. 1994. "Undocumented Latinas: The New 'Employable Mothers.'" Pp. 259–285 in Evelyn Nakano Glenn, Grace Chang, and Linda Rennie Forcey (eds.), *Mothering, Ideology, Experience, and Agency.* New York and London: Routledge.

Collins, Patricia Hill. 1990. *Black Feminist Thought: Knowledge, Consciousness, and the Politics of Empowerment.* Boston: Unwin Hyman.

Collins, Patricia Hill. 1998. *Fighting Words: Black Women and the Search for Justice.* Minneapolis: University of Minnesota Press.

Collins, Patricia Hill. 2004. *Black Sexual Politics: African Americans, Gender and the New Racism.* New York and London: Routledge.

Connell, R. W. 1987. *Gender and Power.* Stanford, CA: Stanford University Press.

Connell, R. W. 1992. "A Very Straight Gay: Masculinity, Homosexual Experience, and the Dynamics of Gender," *American Sociological Review 57:* 735–751.

Connell, R. W. 1995. *Masculinities.* Berkeley: University of California Press.

Connell, R. W. 2002. *Gender.* Cambridge: Polity.

De Beauvoir, Simone. 1953. *The Second Sex.* New York: Knopf.

Enloe, Cynthia. 1993. *The Morning After: Sexual Politics at the End of the Cold War.* Berkeley: University of California Press.

Enloe, Cynthia. 2000. *Maneuvers: The International Politics of Militarizing Women's Lives.* Berkeley: University of California Press

Glenn, Evelyn Nakano. 1999. "The Social Construction and Institutionalization of Gender and Race: An Integrative Framework." Pp. 3–43 in Myra Marx Ferree, Judith Lorber, and Beth B. Hess (eds.), *Revisioning Gender.* Thousand Oaks, CA: Sage Publications.

Glenn, Evelyn Nakano. 2002. *Unequal Sisterhood: How Race and Gender Shaped American Citizenship and Labor.* Cambridge, MA: Harvard University Press. 2002.

Hartmann, Heidi. 1976. "Capitalism, Patriarchy, and Job Segregation by Sex," *Signs: Journal of Women in Culture and Society 1:* (3), part 2, spring: 137–167.

Hewitt, Nancy A. 1992. "Compounding Differences," *Feminist Studies 18:* 313–326.

Heywood, L. & J. Drake (eds.). 1997. *Third Wave Agenda: Being Feminist, Doing Feminism.* Minneapolis: University of Minnesota Press.

Hondagneu-Sotelo, Pierrette. 1994. *Gendered Transitions: Mexican Experiences of Immigration.* Berkeley: University of California Press.

Hondagneu-Sotelo, Pierrette. 2001. *Domestica: Immigrant Workers Cleaning and Caring in the Shadows of Affluence.* Berkeley: University of California Press.

Kanter, Rosabeth Moss. 1977. *Men and Women of the Corporation.* New York: Basic Books.

Kaufman, Michael. 1987. *Beyond Patriarchy: Essays by Men on Pleasure, Power, and Change.* Toronto and New York: Oxford University Press.

Kessler, Sandra, Dean J. Ashendon, R. W. Connell, & Gary W. Dowsett. 1985. "Gender Relations in Secondary Schooling," *Sociology of Education 58:* 34–48.

Kimmel, Michael S. (ed.). 1987. *Changing Men: New Directions in Research on Men and Masculinity.* Newbury Park, CA: Sage.

Kimmel, Michael S. 1996. *Manhood in America: A Cultural History.* New York: Free Press.

Kimmel, Michael S. & Michael A. Messner (eds.). 1989. *Men's Lives.* New York: Macmillan.

Kimmel, Michael S. & Michael A. Messner (eds.). 2004. *Men's Lives,* 6th ed. Boston: Pearson A and B.

Lorber, Judith 1994. *Paradoxes of Gender.* New Haven: Yale University Press.

Messner, Michael A. 1996. "Studying Up on Sex," *Sociology of Sport Journal 13:* 221–237.

Messner, Michael A. 1998. *Politics of Masculinities: Men in Movements.* Thousand Oaks, CA: Sage Publications.

Mohanty, Chandra Talpade. 1991. "Cartographies of Struggle: Third World Women and the Politics of Feminism." Pp. 51–80 in Chandra Talpade Mohanty, Ann Russo, and Lourdes Torres, (eds.), *Third World Women and the Politics of Feminism.* Bloomington: Indiana University Press.

Morgan, Robin. 1970. *Sisterhood is Powerful: An Anthology of Writing from the Women's Liberation Movement.* New York: Vintage Books.

Okin, Susan Moller. 1999. *Is Multiculturalism Bad for Women?* Princeton: Princeton University Press.

Parrenas, Rhacel Salazar. 2001. *Servants of Globalization: Women, Migration and Domestic Work.* Stanford: Stanford University Press.

Pleck, J. H. 1976. "The Male Sex Role: Definitions, Problems, and Sources of Change," *Journal of Social Issues 32:* 155–164.

Rich, Adrienne. 1980. "Compulsory Heterosexuality and the Lesbian Experience," *Signs: Journal of Women in Culture and Society 5:* 631–660.

Sassen, Saskia. 1991.*The Global City: New York, London, Tokyo.* Princeton: Princeton University Press.

Smith, Barbara. 1977. *Toward a Black Feminist Criticism.* Freedom, CA: Crossing Press.

West, Candace & Sarah Fenstermaker. 1995. "Doing Difference," *Gender & Society 9:* 8–37.

PART I

Perspectives on Sex, Gender, and Difference

Are women and men or boys and girls really different, or do we just think and act as though they are different? In other words, are gender differences and inequalities rooted in biology, or are they socially constructed? Today, these questions are rarely answered with simplistic, pat answers. And the questions that gender scholars are asking have also grown more complex. Are these differences constant over time, historically invariant? If women and men are different, then are women—as a group—similar to one another? Do white women share similar experiences to those of women of color? Do women in various parts of the world share commonalities, or are their differences more important? The chapters in this opening section reflect a sampling of gender scholarship on the remarkable variability of gender. They tackle tricky questions of difference between women and men, as well as issues of difference among groups of women and among groups of men.

Difference has always preoccupied feminist thought. Not long ago, difference *between* women and men was a primary concern. "Difference feminism" rested on the notion that women's distinctive characteristics required a special approach to overcome discrimination. Unlike feminist demands that women and men receive "the same" treatment, difference feminists sought women's equality by appealing to the logic of a gender dichotomy. By acknowledging and sometimes even underscoring biological, emotional, and social differences between women and men, they argued that women should not rely on men's strategies to achieve equality.

Perspectives on difference have been transformed. Today, it is clear that although women and men everywhere are constructed in opposition to each other, the categories "women" and "men" have wide-ranging meanings. Gender is always complicated by complex stratification of intersecting power systems. More important, gender operates with and through other systems of opportunity and oppression, which give rise to vastly different gender experiences among women and among men. The chapters in this section move beyond dichotomous simplifications of women and men and show how gender is contingent on other dimensions of difference. Collectively, the chapters provide a foundation for seeing gender through a prism of difference.

In the first reading, Ann Fausto-Sterling takes up a subject of much current debate—the relationship between sex and gender. By deconstructing the "making" of dichotomous sexual identities of masculine and feminine, she disputes the division of the world into only two genders based simply on genital differences. This raises provocative questions about gender and about sex, and whether the relationship between them is a given. Our conceptions of gender begin to look very different if the human sexes are multiple. In the following reading, Maxine Baca Zinn and Bonnie Thornton Dill argue that a focus on race and class makes it clear that there can be no unitary analysis of women as a category. They analyze the development of multiracial feminism, noting both the tensions and the benefits, as they explore the theories and concepts in the growing body of scholarship on the intersections of race, class, and gender. A key insight here is recognition of the ways in which the differences among women are historically and socially constructed and grounded in diverse locations and interconnected inequalities.

Patriarchal systems are not monolithic and neither are women's responses to them. The reading by Deniz Kandiyoti is a classic study that examines different forms of patriarchy. Kandiyoti introduces the concept of "patriarchal bargains" to capture the ways in which women and men actively strategize, negotiate, and bargain within different economic and cultural contexts. The next three readings consider issues of gender and difference in relation to globalization. Exactly how is global restructuring affecting gender, and how is gender affecting global restructuring? In contrast to the common image of a homogenizing process sweeping the globe to make gender more uniform, global forces are, in fact, creating new gender hierarchies. R. W. Connell untangles the key strands in "the world gender order" to reveal how masculinities are being reconfigured by transnational power relations. Barbara Ehrenreich and Arlie Hochschild expose some of the contradictory demands globalization places on women in different parts of the world. They describe a global labor market in which much of the work associated with women's traditional roles—child care, homemaking, and sex—is being transferred from poor countries to rich ones. Much "care work" in the United States is becoming the domain of immigrant women of color who are driven from their countries, only to remain disenfranchised. This global transfer of services benefits many professional women and their careers, yet it rests on both global and intimate relations of dominance and subordination. As we broaden the lens through which we view gender relations and global diversity, we must guard against essentialist images of "local" women in different parts of the world. In the final reading, Chandra Mohanty reviews three strategies currently used to internationalize the women's studies curriculum. She calls for a comparative model that bridges the histories, experiences, and struggles of women in local communities and the effects of globalization on their differences, commonalities, and interconnections.

1

The Five Sexes, Revisited

ANNE FAUSTO-STERLING

As Cheryl Chase stepped to the front of the packed meeting room in the Sheraton Boston Hotel, nervous coughs made the tension audible. Chase, an activist for intersexual rights, had been invited to address the May 2000 meeting of the Lawson Wilkins Pediatric Endocrine Society (LWPES), the largest organization in the United States for specialists in children's hormones. Her talk would be the grand finale to a four-hour symposium on the treatment of genital ambiguity in newborns, infants born with a mixture of both male and female anatomy, or genitals that appear to differ from their chromosomal sex. The topic was hardly a novel one to the assembled physicians.

Yet Chase's appearance before the group was remarkable. Three and a half years earlier, the American Academy of Pediatrics had refused her request for a chance to present the patients' viewpoint on the treatment of genital ambiguity, dismissing Chase and her supporters as "zealots." About two dozen intersex people had responded by throwing up a picket line. The Intersex Society of North America (ISNA) even issued a press release: "Hermaphrodites Target Kiddie Docs."

It had done my 1960s street-activist heart good. In the short run, I said to Chase at the time, the picketing would make people angry. But eventually, I assured her, the doors then closed would open. Now, as Chase began to address the physicians at their own convention, that prediction was coming true. Her talk, titled "Sexual Ambiguity: The Patient-Centered Approach," was a measured critique of the near-universal practice of performing immediate, "corrective" surgery on thousands of infants born each year with ambiguous genitalia. Chase herself lives with the consequences of such surgery. Yet her audience, the very endocrinologists and surgeons Chase was accusing of reacting with "surgery and shame," received her with respect. Even more remarkably, many of the speakers who preceded her at the session had already spoken of the need to scrap current practices in favor of treatments more centered on psychological counseling.

What led to such a dramatic reversal of fortune? Certainly, Chase's talk at the LWPES symposium was a vindication of her persistence in seeking attention for her cause. But her invitation to speak was also a watershed in the evolving discussion about how to treat children with ambiguous genitalia. And that discussion, in turn, is the tip of a biocultural iceberg—the gender iceberg—that continues to rock both medicine and our culture at large.

Chase made her first national appearance in 1993, in these very pages, announcing the formation of ISNA in a letter responding to an essay I had written for *The Sci-*

Ann Fausto-Sterling, "The Five Sexes, Revisited," from *The Sciences,* July/August, 2000, Volume 40, Issue 4, pp. 18–24.

ences, titled "The Five Sexes" [March/April 1993]. In that article I argued that the two-sex system embedded in our society is not adequate to encompass the full spectrum of human sexuality. In its place, I suggested a five-sex system. In addition to males and females, I included "herms" (named after true hermaphrodites, people born with both a testis and an ovary); "merms" (male pseudohermaphrodites, who are born with testes and some aspect of female genitalia); and "ferms" (female pseudohermaphrodites, who have ovaries combined with some aspect of male genitalia).

I had intended to be provocative, but I had also written with tongue firmly in cheek. So I was surprised by the extent of the controversy the article unleashed. Right-wing Christians were outraged, and connected my idea of five sexes with the United Nations–sponsored Fourth World Conference on Women, held in Beijing in September 1995. At the same time, the article delighted others who felt constrained by the current sex and gender system.

Clearly, I had struck a nerve. The fact that so many people could get riled up by my proposal to revamp our sex and gender system suggested that change—as well as resistance to it—might be in the offing. Indeed, a lot has changed since 1993, and I like to think that my article was an important stimulus. As if from nowhere, intersexuals are materializing before our very eyes. Like Chase, many have become political organizers, who lobby physicians and politicians to change current treatment practices. But more generally, though perhaps no less provocatively, the boundaries separating masculine and feminine seem harder than ever to define.

Some find the changes underway deeply disturbing. Others find them liberating.

Who is an intersexual—and how many intersexuals are there? The concept of intersexuality is rooted in the very ideas of male and female. In the idealized, Platonic, biological world, human beings are divided into two kinds: a perfectly dimorphic species. Males have an X and a Y chromosome, testes, a penis and all of the appropriate internal plumbing for delivering urine and semen to the outside world. They also have well-known secondary sexual characteristics including a muscular build and facial hair. Women have two X chromosomes, ovaries, all of the internal plumbing to transport urine and ova to the outside world, a system to support pregnancy and fetal development, as well as a variety of recognizable secondary sexual characteristics.

That idealized story papers over many obvious caveats: some women have facial hair, some men have none; some women speak with deep voices, some men veritably squeak. Less well known is the fact that, on close inspection, absolute dimorphism disintegrates even at the level of basic biology. Chromosomes, hormones, the internal sex structures, the gonads and the external genitalia all vary more than most people realize. Those born outside of the Platonic dimorphic mold are called intersexuals.

In "The Five Sexes" I reported an estimate by a psychologist expert in the treatment of intersexuals, suggesting that some 4 percent of all live births are intersexual. Then, together with a group of Brown University undergraduates, I set out to conduct the first systematic assessment of the available data on intersexual birthrates. We scoured the medical literature for estimates of the frequency of various categories of intersexuality, from additional chromosomes to mixed gonads, hormones and genitalia. For some conditions we could find only anecdotal evidence; for most, however numbers exist. On the basis of that evidence, we calculated that for every 1,000 children born, seventeen are intersexual in some form. That number—1.7 percent—is a ballpark estimate, not a precise count, though we believe it is more accurate than the 4 percent I reported.

Our figure represents all chromosomal, anatomical and hormonal exceptions to the dimorphic ideal; the number of intersexuals who might, potentially, be subject to surgery as infants is smaller—probably between one in 1,000 and one in 2,000 live births. Furthermore, because some populations possess the relevant genes at high frequency, the intersexual birthrate is not uniform throughout the world.

Consider, for instance, the gene for congenital adrenal hyperplasia (CAH). When the CAH gene is inherited from both parents, it leads to a baby with masculinized external genitalia who possesses two X chromosomes and the internal reproductive organs of a potentially fertile woman. The frequency of the gene varies widely around the world: in New Zealand it occurs in only forty-three children per million; among the Yupik Eskimos of southwestern Alaska, its frequency is 3,500 per million.

Intersexuality has always been to some extent a matter of definition. And in the past century physicians have been the ones who defined children as intersexual—and provided the remedies. When only the chromosomes are unusual, but the external genitalia and gonads clearly indicate either a male or a female, physicians do not advocate intervention. Indeed, it is not clear what kind of intervention could be advocated in such cases. But the story is quite different when infants are born with mixed genitalia, or with external genitals that seem at odds with the baby's gonads.

Most clinics now specializing in the treatment of intersex babies rely on case-management principles developed in the 1950s by the psychologist John Money and the psychiatrists Joan G. Hampson and John L. Hampson, all of Johns Hopkins University in Baltimore, Maryland. Money believed that gender identity is completely malleable for about eighteen months after birth. Thus, he argued, when a treatment team is presented with an infant who has ambiguous genitalia, the team could make a gender assignment solely on the basis of what made the best surgical sense. The physicians could then simply encourage the parents to raise the child according to the surgically assigned gender. Following that course, most physicians maintained, would eliminate psychological distress for both the patient and the parents. Indeed, treatment teams were never to use such words as "intersex" or "hermaphrodite"; instead, they were to tell parents that nature intended the baby to be the boy or the girl that the physicians had determined it was. Through surgery, the physicians were merely completing nature's intention.

Although Money and the Hampsons published detailed case studies of intersex children who they said had adjusted well to their gender assignments, Money thought one case in particular proved his theory. It was a dramatic example, inasmuch as it did not involve intersexuality at all: one of a pair of identical twin boys lost his penis as a result of a circumcision accident. Money recommended that "John" (as he came to be known in a later case study) be surgically turned into "Joan" and raised as a girl. In time, Joan grew to love wearing dresses and having her hair done. Money proudly proclaimed the sex reassignment a success.

But as recently chronicled by John Colapinto, in his book *As Nature Made Him,* Joan—now known to be an adult male named David Reimer—eventually rejected his female assignment. Even without a functioning penis and testes (which had been removed as part of the reassignment) John/Joan sought masculinizing medication, and married a woman with children (whom he adopted).

Since the full conclusion to the John/Joan story came to light, other individuals who were reassigned as males or females shortly after birth but who later rejected their early assignments have come forward. So, too, have cases in which the reassignment has worked—at least into the subject's mid-twenties. But even then the aftermath of the surgery can be problematic. Genital surgery often leaves scars that reduce sexual sensitivity. Chase herself had a complete clitoridectomy, a procedure that is less frequently performed on intersexuals today. But the newer surgeries, which reduce the size of the clitoral shaft, still greatly reduce sensitivity.

The revelation of cases of failed reassignments and the emergence of intersex activism have led an increasing number of pediatric endocrinologists, urologists and psychologists to reexamine the wisdom of early genital surgery. For example, in a talk that preceded Chase's at the LWPES meeting, the medical ethicist Laurence B. McCullough of the Center for Medical Ethics and Health Policy at Baylor College of Medicine in Houston, Texas, introduced an ethical framework for the treatment of children with ambiguous genitalia. Because sex phenotype (the manifestation of genetically and embryologically determined sexual characteristics) and gender presentation (the sex role projected by the individual in society) are highly variable, McCullough argues, the various forms of intersexuality should be defined as normal. All of them fall within the statistically expected variability of sex and gender. Furthermore, though certain disease states may accompany some forms of intersexuality, and may require medical intervention, intersexual conditions are not themselves diseases.

McCullough also contends that in the process of assigning gender, physicians should minimize what he calls irreversible assignments: taking steps such as the surgical removal or modification of gonads or genitalia that the patient may one day want to have reversed. Finally, McCullough urges physicians to abandon their practice of treating the birth of a child with genital ambiguity as a medical or social emergency. Instead, they should take the time to perform a thorough medical workup and should disclose everything to the parents, including the uncertainties about the final outcome. The treatment mantra, in other words, should be therapy, not surgery.

I believe a new treatment protocol for intersex infants, similar to the one outlined by McCullough, is close at hand. Treatment should combine some basic medical and ethical principles with a practical but less drastic approach to the birth of a mixed-sex child. As a first step, surgery on infants should be performed only to save the child's life or to substantially improve the child's physical well-being. Physicians may assign a sex—male or female—to an intersex infant on the basis of the probability that the child's particular condition will lead to the formation of a particular gender identity. At the same time, though, practitioners ought to be humble enough to recognize that as the child grows, he or she may reject the assignment—and they should be wise enough to listen to what the child has to say. Most important, parents should have access to the full range of information and options available to them.

Sex assignments made shortly after birth are only the beginning of a long journey. Consider, for instance, the life of Max Beck: Born intersexual, Max was surgically assigned as a female and consistently raised as such. Had her medical team followed her into her early twenties, they would have deemed her assignment a success because she was married to a man. (It should be noted that success in gender assignment has traditionally been defined as living in that gender as a heterosexual.) Within a few years, however, Beck had come out as a butch lesbian; now in her mid-thirties, Beck has become a man and married his lesbian partner, who (through the miracles of modern reproductive technology) recently gave birth to a girl.

Transsexuals, people who have an emotional gender at odds with their physical sex, once described themselves in terms of dimorphic absolutes—males trapped in female bodies, or vice versa. As such, they sought psychological relief through surgery. Although many still do, some so-called transgendered people today are content to inhabit a more ambiguous zone. A male-to-female transsexual, for instance, may come out as a lesbian. Jane, born a physiological male, is now in her late thirties and living with her wife, whom she married when her name was still John. Jane takes hormones to feminize herself, but they have not yet interfered with her ability to engage in intercourse as a man. In her mind Jane has a lesbian relationship with her wife, though she views their intimate moments as a cross between lesbian and heterosexual sex.

It might seem natural to regard intersexuals and transgendered people as living midway between the poles of male and female. But male and female, masculine and feminine, cannot be parsed as some kind of continuum. Rather, sex and gender are best conceptualized as points in a multidimensional space. For some time, experts on gender development have distinguished between sex at the genetic level and at the cellular level (sex-specific gene expression, X and Y chromosomes); at the hormonal level (in the fetus, during childhood and after puberty); and at the anatomical level (genitals and secondary sexual characteristics). Gender identity presumably emerges from all of those corporeal aspects via some poorly understood interaction with environment and experience. What has become increasingly clear is that one can find levels of masculinity and femininity in almost every possible permutation. A chromosomal, hormonal and genital male (or female) may emerge with a female (or male) gender identity. Or a chromosomal female with male fetal hormones and masculinized genitalia—but with female pubertal hormones—may develop a female gender identity.

The medical and scientific communities have yet to adopt a language that is capable of describing such diversity. In her book *Hermaphrodites and the Medical Invention of Sex,* the historian and medical ethicist Alice Domurat Dreger of Michigan State University in East Lansing documents the emergence of current medical systems for classifying gender ambiguity. The current usage remains rooted in the Victorian approach to sex. The logical structure of the commonly used terms "true hermaphrodite," "male pseudohermaphrodite" and "female pseudohermaphrodite" indicates that only the so-called true hermaphrodite is a genuine mix of male and female. The others, no matter how confusing their body parts, are really hidden males or females. Because true hermaphodites are rare—possibly only one in 100,000—such a classification system supports the idea that human beings are an absolutely dimorphic species.

At the dawn of the twenty-first century, when the variability of gender seems so visible, such a position is hard to maintain. And here, too, the old medical consensus has begun to crumble. Last fall the pediatric urologist Ian A. Aaronson of the Medical University of South Carolina in Charleston organized the North American Task Force on Intersexuality (NATFI) to review the clinical responses to genital ambiguity in infants. Key medical associations, such as the American Academy of Pediatrics, have endorsed NATFI. Specialists in surgery, endocrinology, psychology, ethics, psychiatry, genetics and public health, as well as intersex patient-advocate groups, have joined its ranks.

One of the goals of NATFI is to establish a new sex nomenclature. One proposal under consideration replaces the current system with emotionally neutral terminology that emphasizes developmental processes rather than preconceived gender categories. For example, Type I intersexes develop out of anomalous virilizing influences; Type II result from some interruption of virilization; and in Type III intersexes the gonads themselves may not have developed in the expected fashion.

What is clear is that since 1993, modern society has moved beyond five sexes to a recognition that gender variation is normal and, for some people, an arena for playful exploration. Discussing my "five sexes" proposal in her book *Lessons from the Intersexed,* the psychologist Suzanne J. Kessler of the State University of New York at Purchase drives this point home with great effect:

> The limitation with Fausto-Sterling's proposal is that . . . [it] still gives genitals . . . primary signifying status and ignores the fact that in the everyday world gender attributions are made without access to genital inspection. . . . What has primacy in everyday life is the gender that is performed, regardless of the flesh's configuration under the clothes.

I now agree with Kessler's assessment. It would be better for intersexuals and their supporters to turn everyone's focus away from genitals. Instead, as she suggests, one should acknowledge that people come in an even wider assortment of sexual identities and characteristics than mere genitals can distinguish. Some women may have "large clitorises or fused labia," whereas some men may have "small penises or misshapen scrota," as Kessler puts it, "phenotypes with no particular clinical or identity meaning."

As clearheaded as Kessler's program is—and despite the progress made in the 1990s—our society is still far from that ideal. The intersexual or transgendered person who projects a social gender—what Kessler calls "cultural genitals"—that conflicts with his or her physical genitals still may die for the transgression. Hence legal protection for people whose cultural and physical genitals do not match is needed during the current transition to a more gender-diverse world. One easy step would be to eliminate the category of "gender" from official documents, such as driver's licenses and passports. Surely attributes both more visible (such as height, build and eye color) and less visible (fingerprints and genetic profiles) would be more expedient.

A more far-ranging agenda is presented in the International Bill of Gender Rights, adopted in 1995 at the fourth annual International Conference on Transgender Law and Employment Policy in Houston, Texas. It lists ten "gender rights," including the right to define one's own gender, the right to change one's physical gender if one so chooses and the right to marry whomever one wishes. The legal bases for such rights are being hammered out in the courts as I write and, most recently, through the establishment, in the state of Vermont, of legal same-sex domestic partnerships.

No one could have foreseen such changes in 1993. And the idea that I played some role, however small, in reducing the pressure—from the medical community as well as from society at large—to flatten the diversity of human sexes into two diametrically opposed camps gives me pleasure.

Sometimes people suggest to me, with not a little horror, that I am arguing for a pastel world in which androgyny reigns and men and women are boringly the same. In my vision, however, strong colors coexist with pastels. There are and will continue to be highly masculine people out there; it's just that some of them are women. And some of the most feminine people I know happen to be men.

2

Theorizing Difference from Multiracial Feminism

MAXINE BACA ZINN
BONNIE THORNTON DILL

Women of color have long challenged the hegemony of feminisms constructed primarily around the lives of white middle-class women. Since the late 1960s, U.S. women of color have taken issue with unitary theories of gender. Our critiques grew out of the widespread concern about the exclusion of women of color from feminist scholarship and the misinterpretation of our experiences,[1] and ultimately "out of the very discourses, denying, permitting, and producing difference."[2] Speaking simultaneously from "within and against" *both* women's liberation and antiracist movements, we have insisted on the need to challenge systems of domination,[3] not merely as gendered subjects but as women whose lives are affected by our location in multiple hierarchies.

Recently, and largely in response to these challenges, work that links gender to other forms of domination is increasing. In this article, we examine this connection further as well as the ways in which difference and diversity infuse contemporary feminist studies. Our analysis draws on a conceptual framework that we refer to as "multiracial feminism."[4] This perspective is an attempt to go beyond a mere recognition of diversity and difference among women to examine structures of domination, specifically the importance of race in understanding the social construction of gender. Despite the varied concerns and multiple intellectual stances which characterize the feminisms of women of color, they share an emphasis on race as a primary force situating genders differently. It is the centrality of race, of institutionalized racism, and of struggles against racial oppression that link the various feminist perspectives within this framework. Together, they demonstrate that racial meanings offer new theoretical directions for feminist thought.

TENSIONS IN CONTEMPORARY DIFFERENCE FEMINISM

Objections to the false universalism embedded in the concept "woman" emerged within other discourses as well as those of women of color.[5] Lesbian feminists and postmodern feminists put forth their own versions of what Susan Bordo has called "gender skepticism."[6]

Many thinkers within mainstream feminism have responded to these critiques with efforts to contextualize gender. The search for women's "universal" or "essential" characteristics is being abandoned. By examining gender in the context of other social divisions and

This article is reprinted from *Feminist Studies,* Volume 22, Number 2 (Summer 1996), pp. 321–331, by permission of the publisher, Feminist Studies, Inc.

perspectives, difference has gradually become important—even problematizing the universal categories, "women" and "men." Sandra G. Harding expresses the shift best in her claim that "there are no gender relations *per se,* but only gender relations as constructed by and between classes, races, and cultures."[7]

Many feminists now contend that difference occupies center stage as *the* project of women studies today.[8] According to one scholar, "difference has replaced equality as the central concern of feminist theory."[9] Many have welcomed the change, hailing it as a major revitalizing force in U.S. feminist theory.[10] But if *some* priorities within mainstream feminist thought have been refocused by attention to difference, there remains an "uneasy alliance"[11] between women of color and other feminists.

If difference has helped revitalize academic feminisms, it has also "upset the apple cart," and introduced new conflicts into feminist studies.[12] For example, in a recent and widely discussed essay, Jane Rowland Martin argues that the current preoccupation with difference is leading feminism into dangerous traps. She fears that in giving privileged status to a predetermined set of analytic categories (race, ethnicity, and class), "we affirm the existence of nothing but difference." She asks, "How do we know that for us, difference does not turn on being fat, or religious, or in an abusive relationship?"[13]

We, too, see pitfalls in some strands of the difference project. However, our perspectives take their bearings from social relations. Race and class difference are crucial, we argue, not as individual characteristics (such as being fat) but insofar as they are primary organizing principles of a society which locates and positions groups within that society's opportunity structures.

Despite the much-heralded diversity trend within feminist studies, difference is often reduced to mere pluralism; a "live and let live" approach where principles of relativism generate a long list of diversities which begin with gender, class, and race and continue through a range of social structural as well as personal characteristics.[14] Another disturbing pattern, which bell hooks refers to as "the commodification of difference," is the representation of diversity as a form of exotica, "a spice, seasoning that livens up the dull dish that is mainstream white culture."[15] The major limitation of these approaches is the failure to attend to the power relations that accompany difference. Moreover, these approaches ignore the inequalities that cause some characteristics to be seen as "normal" while others are seen as "different" and thus, deviant.

Maria C. Lugones expresses irritation at those feminists who see only the *problem* of difference without recognizing *difference.*[16] Increasingly, we find that difference *is* recognized. But this in no way means that difference occupies a "privileged" theoretical status. Instead of using difference to rethink the category of women, difference is often a euphemism for women who differ from the traditional norm. Even in purporting to accept difference, feminist pluralism often creates a social reality that reverts to universalizing women:

> So much feminist scholarship assumes that when we cut through all of the diversity among women created by differences of racial classification, ethnicity, social class, and sexual orientation, a "universal truth" concerning women and gender lies buried underneath. But if we can face the scary possibility that no such certainty exists and that persisting in such a search will always distort or omit someone's experiences, with what do we replace this old way of thinking? Gender differences and gender politics begin to look very different if there is no essential woman at the core.[17]

WHAT IS MULTIRACIAL FEMINISM?

A new set of feminist theories have emerged from the challenges put forth by women of color. Multiracial feminism is an evolving body of theory and practice informed by wide-ranging intellectual traditions. This framework does not offer a singular or unified feminism but a body of knowledge situating women and men in multiple systems of domination. U.S. multiracial feminism encompasses several emergent perspectives developed primarily by women of color: African Americans, Latinas, Asian Americans, and Native Americans, women whose analyses are shaped by their unique perspectives as "outsiders within"—marginal intellectuals whose social locations provide them a particular perspective on self and society.[18] Although U.S. women of color represent many races and ethnic backgrounds—with different histories and cultures—our feminisms cohere in their treatment of race as a basic social division, a structure of power, a focus of political struggle and hence a fundamental force in shaping women's and men's lives.

This evolving intellectual and political perspective uses several terms. While we adopt the label "multiracial," other terms have been used to describe this broad framework. For example, Chela Sandoval refers to "U.S. Third World feminisms,"[19] while other scholars refer to "indigenous feminisms." In their theory text-reader, Alison M. Jagger and Paula M. Rothenberg adopt the label "multicultural feminism."[20]

We use "multiracial" rather than "multicultural" as a way of underscoring race as a power system that interacts with other structured inequalities to shape genders. Within the U.S. context, race, and the system of meanings and ideologies which accompany it, is a fundamental organizing principle of social relationships.[21] Race affects all women and men, although in different ways. Even cultural and group differences among women are produced through interaction within a racially stratified social order. Therefore, although we do not discount the importance of culture, we caution that cultural analytic frameworks that ignore race tend to view women's differences as the product of group-specific values and practices that often result in the marginalization of cultural groups which are then perceived as exotic expressions of a normative center. Our focus on race stresses the social construction of differently situated social groups and their varying degrees of advantage and power. Additionally, this emphasis on race takes on increasing political importance in an era where discourse about race is governed by color-evasive language[22] and a preference for individual rather than group remedies for social inequalities. Our analyses insist upon the primary and pervasive nature of race in contemporary U.S. society while at the same time acknowledging how race both shapes and is shaped by a variety of other social relations.

In the social sciences, multiracial feminism grew out of socialist feminist thinking. Theories about how political economic forces shape women's lives were influential as we began to uncover the social causes of racial ethnic women's subordination. But socialist feminism's concept of capitalist patriarchy, with its focus on women's unpaid (reproductive) labor in the home failed to address racial differences in the organization of reproductive labor. As feminists of color have argued, "reproductive labor has divided along racial as well as gender lines, and the specific characteristics have varied regionally and changed over time as capitalism has reorganized."[23] Despite the limitations of socialist feminism, this body of literature has been especially useful in pursuing questions about the interconnections among systems of domination.[24]

Race and ethnic studies was the other major social scientific source of multiracial feminism. It provided a basis for comparative analyses of groups that are socially and legally subordinated and remain culturally distinct within U.S. society. This includes the systematic discrimination of socially constructed racial groups and their distinctive cultural arrangements. Historically, the categories of African American, Latino, Asian American, and Native American were constructed as both racially and culturally distinct. Each group has a distinctive culture, shares a common heritage, and has developed a common identity within a larger society that subordinates them.[25]

We recognize, of course, certain pitfalls inherent in an uncritical use of the multiracial label. First, the perspective can be hampered by a biracial model in which only African Americans and Whites are seen as racial categories and all other groups are viewed through the prism of cultural differences. Latinos and Asians have always occupied distinctive places within the racial hierarchy, and current shifts in the composition of the U.S. population are racializing these groups anew.[26]

A second problem lies in treating multiracial feminism as a single analytical framework, and its principle architects, women of color, as an undifferentiated category. The concepts "multiracial feminism," "racial ethnic women," and "women of color" homogenize quite different experiences and can falsely universalize experiences across race, ethnicity, sexual orientation, and age.[27] The feminisms created by women of color exhibit a plurality of intellectual and political positions. We speak in many voices, with inconsistencies that are born of our different social locations. Multiracial feminism embodies this plurality and richness. Our intent is not to falsely universalize women of color. Nor do we wish to promote a new racial essentialism in place of the old gender essentialism. Instead, we use these concepts to examine the structures and experiences produced by intersecting forms of race and gender.

It is also essential to acknowledge that race itself is a shifting and contested category whose meanings construct definitions of all aspects of social life.[28] In the United States it helped define citizenship by excluding everyone who was not a white, male property owner. It defined labor as slave or free, coolie or contract, and family as available only to those men whose marriages were recognized or whose wives could immigrate with them. Additionally, racial meanings are contested both within groups and between them.[29]

Although definitions of race are at once historically and geographically specific, they are also transnational, encompassing diasporic groups and crossing traditional geographic boundaries. Thus, while U.S. multiracial feminism calls attention to the fundamental importance of race, it must also locate the meaning of race within specific national traditions.

THE DISTINGUISHING FEATURES OF MULTIRACIAL FEMINISM

By attending to these problems, multiracial feminism offers a set of analytic premises for thinking about and theorizing gender. The following themes distinguish this branch of feminist inquiry.

First, multiracial feminism asserts that gender is constructed by a range of interlocking inequalities, what Patricia Hill Collins calls a "matrix of domination."[30] The idea of a matrix is that several fundamental systems work with and through each other. People experience race, class, gender, and sexuality differently depending upon their social location in the structures of race, class, gender, and sexuality. For example, people of the same race will experience race differently depending upon their location in the class structure as working class, professional managerial class, or unemployed; in the gender structure as female or male; and in structures of sexuality as heterosexual, homosexual, or bisexual.

Multiracial feminism also examines the simultaneity of systems in shaping women's experience and identity. Race, class, gender, and sexuality are not reducible to individual attributes to be measured and assessed for their separate contribution in explaining given social outcomes, an approach that Elizabeth Spelman calls "pop-bead metaphysics," where a woman's identity consists of the sum of parts neatly divisible from one another.[31] The matrix of domination seeks to account for the multiple ways that women experience themselves as gendered, raced, classed, and sexualized.

Second, multiracial feminism emphasizes the intersectional nature of hierarchies at all levels of social life. Class, race, gender, and sexuality are components of both social structure and social interaction. Women and men are differently embedded in locations created by these cross-cutting hierarchies. As a result, women and men throughout the social order experience different forms of privilege and subordination, depending on their race, class, gender, and sexuality. In other words, intersecting forms of domination produce *both* oppression *and* opportunity. At the same time that structures of race, class, and gender create disadvantages for women of color, they provide unacknowledged benefits for those who are at the top of these hierarchies—whites, members of the upper classes, and males. Therefore, multiracial feminism applies not only to racial ethnic women but also to women and men of all races, classes, and genders.

Third, multiracial feminism highlights the relational nature of dominance and subordination. Power is the cornerstone of women's differences.[32] This means that women's differences are *connected* in systematic ways.[33] Race is a vital element in the pattern of relations among minority and white women. As Linda Gordon argues, the very meanings of being a white woman in the United States have been affected by the existence of subordinated women of color; "They intersect in conflict and in occasional cooperation, but always in mutual influence."[34]

Fourth, multiracial feminism explores the interplay of social structure and women's agency. Within the constraints of race, class, and gender oppression, women create viable lives for themselves, their families, and their communities. Women of color have resisted and often undermined the forces of power that control them. From acts of quiet dignity and steadfast determination to involvement in revolt and rebellion, women struggle to shape their own lives. Racial oppression has been a common focus of the "dynamic of oppositional agency" of women of color. As Chandra Talpade Mohanty points out, it is the nature and organization of women's opposition which mediates and differentiates the impact of structures of domination.[35]

Fifth, multiracial feminism encompasses wide-ranging methodological approaches, and like other branches of feminist thought, relies on varied theoretical tools as well. Ruth Frankenberg and Lata Mani identify three guiding principles of inclusive feminist inquiry: "building complex analyses, avoiding erasure, specifying location."[36] In the last decade, the opening up of academic feminism has focused attention on social location in the production of knowledge. Most basically, research by and about marginalized women has destabilized what used to be universal categories of gender. Marginalized locations are well-suited for grasping social relations that remained obscure from more privileged vantage points. Lived experience, in other words, creates alternative ways of understanding the social world and the experience of different groups of women within it. Racially informed standpoint epistemologies have provided new topics, fresh questions, and new understandings of women and men. Women of color have, as Norma Alarcon argues, asserted ourselves as subjects, using our voices to challenge dominant conceptions of truth.[37]

Sixth, multiracial feminism brings together understandings drawn from the lived experiences of diverse and continuously changing groups of women. Among Asian Americans, Native Americans, Latinas, and Blacks are many different national cultural and ethnic groups. Each one is engaged in the process of testing, refining, and reshaping these broader categories in its own image. Such internal differences heighten awareness of and sensitivity to both commonalities and differences, serving as a constant reminder of the importance of comparative study and maintaining a creative tension between diversity and universalization.

DIFFERENCE AND TRANSFORMATION

Efforts to make women's studies less partial and less distorted have produced important changes in academic feminism. Inclusive thinking has provided a way to build multiplicity and difference into our analyses. This has lead to the discovery that race matters for everyone. White women, too, must be reconceptualized as a category that is multiple defined by race, class, and other differences. As Ruth Frankenberg demonstrates in a study of whiteness among contemporary women, all kinds of social relations, even those that appear neutral, are, in fact, racialized. Frankenberg further complicates the very notion of a unified white identity by introducing issues of Jewish identity.[38] Therefore, the lives of women of color cannot be seen as a *variation* on a more general model of white American womanhood. The model of womanhood that feminist social science once held as "universal" is also a product of race and class.

When we analyze the power relations constituting all social arrangements and shaping women's lives in distinctive ways, we can begin to grapple with core feminist issues about how genders are socially constructed and constructed differently. Women's difference is built into our study of gender. Yet this perspective is quite far removed from the atheoretical pluralism implied in much contemporary thinking about gender.

Multiracial feminism, in our view, focuses not just on differences but also on the way in which differences and domination intersect and are historically and socially constituted. It challenges feminist scholars to go beyond the mere recognition and inclusion of difference to reshape the basic concepts and theories of our disciplines. By attending to women's social location based on race, class, and gender, multiracial feminism seeks to clarify the structural sources of diversity. Ultimately, multiracial feminism forces us to see privilege and subordination as interrelated and to pose such questions as, How do the existences and experiences of all people—women and men, different racial-ethnic groups, and different classes—shape the experiences of each other? How are those relationships defined and enforced through social institutions that are the primary sites for negotiating power within society? How do these differences contribute to the construction of both individual and group identity? Once we acknowledge that all women are affected by the racial order of society, then it becomes clear that the insights of multiracial feminism provide an analytical framework, not solely for understanding the experiences of women of color but for understanding *all* women, and men, as well.

NOTES

1. Maxine Baca Zinn, Lynn Weber Cannon, Elizabeth Higginbotham, and Bonnie Thornton Dill, "The Costs of Exclusionary Practices in Women's Studies," *Signs* 11 (winter, 1986): 290–303.

2. Chela Sandoval, "U.S. Third World Feminism: The Theory and Method of Oppositional Consciousness in the Postmodern World," *Genders* (spring, 1991): 1–24.

3. Ruth Frankenberg and Lata Mani, "Cross Currents, Crosstalk: Race, 'Postcoloniality' and the Politics of Location," *Cultural Studies* 7 (May, 1993): 292–310.

4. We use the term "multiracial feminism" to convey the multiplicity of racial groups and feminist perspectives.

5. A growing body of works on difference in feminist thought now exists. Although we cannot cite all of the current work, the following are representative: Michèle Barrett, "The Concept of Difference," *Feminist Review* 26 (July, 1987): 29–42; Christina Crosby, "Dealing With Difference," in *Feminists Theorize the Political,* ed. Judith Butler and Joan W. Scott (New York: Routledge, 1992): 130–43; Elizabeth Fox-Genovese, "Difference, Diversity, and Divisions in an Agenda for the Women's Movement" in *Color, Class, and Country: Experiences of Gender,* ed. Gay Young and Bette J. Dickerson (London: Zed Books, 1994): 232–48; Nancy A. Hewitt, "Compounding Differences," *Feminist Studies* 18 (summer 1992): 313–26; Maria C. Lugones, "On the Logic of Feminist Pluralism," in *Feminist Ethics* ed. Claudia Card (Lawrence: University of Kansas Press, 1991), 35–44; Rita S. Gallin and Anne Ferguson, "The Plurality of Feminism: Rethinking 'Difference,' " in *The Woman and International Development Annual* (Boulder: Westview Press, 1993), 3: 1–16; and Linda Gordon, "On Difference," *Genders* 10 (spring, 1991): 91–111.

6. Susan Bordo, "Feminism, Postmodernism, and Gender Skepticism," in *Feminism/Postmodernism,* ed. Linda J. Nicholson (London: Routledge, 1990), 133–56.

7. Sandra G. Harding, *Whose Science? Whose Knowledge? Thinking from Women's Lives* (Ithaca: Cornell University Press, 1991), 179.

8. Crosby, 131.

9. Fox-Genovese, 232.

10. Faye Ginsberg and Anna Lowenhaupt Tsing, Introduction to *Uncertain Terms, Negotiating Gender in American Culture,* ed. Faye Ginsberg and Anna Lowenhaupt Tsing (Boston: Beacon Press, 1990), 3.

11. Sandoval, 2.

12. Sandra G. Morgan, "Making Connections: Socialist-Feminist Challenges to Marxist Scholarship," in *Women and a New Academy: Gender and Cultural Contexts,* ed. Jean F. O'Barr (Madison: University of Wisconsin Press, 1989), 149.

13. Jane Rowland Martin, "Methodological Essentialism, False Difference, and Other Dangerous Traps," *Signs* 19 (spring, 1994): 647.

14. Barrett, 32.

15. bell hooks, *Black Looks: Race and Representation* (Boston: South End Press, 1992), 21.

16. Lugones, 35–44.

17. Patricia Hill Collins, Foreword to *Women of Color in U.S. Society,* ed. Maxine Baca Zinn and Bonnie Thornton Dill (Philadelphia: Temple University Press, 1994), xv.

18. Patricia Hill Collins, "Learning from the Outsider Within: The Sociological Significance of Black Feminist Thought," *Social Problems* 33 (December, 1986): 514–532.

19. Sandoval, 1.

20. Alison M. Jagger and Paula S. Rothenberg, *Feminist Frameworks: Alternative Theoretical Accounts of the Relations between Women and Men.* 3d ed. (New York: McGraw Hill, 1993).

21. Michael Omi and Howard Winant, *Racial Formation in United States: From the 1960s to the 1980s,* 2d ed. (New York: Routledge, 1994).

22. Ruth Frankenberg, *The Social Construction of Whiteness: White Women, Race Matters* (Minneapolis: University of Minnesota Press, 1993).

23. Evelyn Nakano Glenn, "From Servitude to Service Work: Historical Continuities in the Racial Division of Paid Reproductive Labor," *Signs* 18 (autumn, 1992): 3. See also Bonnie Thornton Dill, "Our Mothers' Grief: Racial-Ethnic Women and the Maintenance of Families," *Journal of Family History* 13, no. 4 (1988): 415–31.

24. Morgan, 146.

25. Maxine Baca Zinn and Bonnie Thornton Dill, "Difference and Domination," in *Women of Color in U.S. Society,* 11–12.

26. See Omi and Winant, 53–76, for a discussion of racial formation.

27. Margaret L. Andersen and Patricia Hill Collins, *Race, Class, and Gender: An Anthology* (Belmont, Calif.: Wadsworth, 1992), xvi.

28. Omi and Winant.

29. Nazli Kibria, "Migration and Vietnamese American Women: Remaking Ethnicity," in *Women of Color in U.S. Society,* 247–61.

30. Patricia Hill Collins, *Black Feminist Thought: Knowledge, Consciousness, and the Politics of Empowerment* (Boston: Unwin Hyman, 1990).

31. Elizabeth Spelman, *Inessential Women: Problems of Exclusion in Feminist Thought* (Boston: Beacon Press, 1988).

32. Several discussions of difference make this point. See Baca Zinn and Dill, 10; Gordon, 106; and Lynn Weber, in the "Sym-

posium on West and Fenstermaker's 'Doing Difference,'" *Gender & Society* 9 (August 1995): 515–19.

33. Glenn, 10.

34. Gordon, 106.

35. Chandra Talpade Mohanty, "Cartographies of Struggle: Third World Women and the Politics of Feminism," in *Third World Women and the Politics of Feminism,* ed. Chandra Talpade Mohanty, Ann Russo, and Lourdes Torres (Bloomington: Indiana University Press, 1991), 13.

36. Frankenberg and Mani, 307.

37. Norma Alarcon, "The Theoretical Subject(s) of *This Bridge Called My Back* and Anglo American Feminism," in *Making Face, Making Soul, Haciendo Caras: Creative and Critical Perspectives by Women of Color,* ed. Gloria Anzaldua, (San Francisco: Aunt Lute, 1990), 356.

38. Frankenberg. See also Evelyn Torton Beck, "The Politics of Jewish Invisibility," *NWSA Journal* (fall 1988): 93–102.

3

Bargaining with Patriarchy

DENIZ KANDIYOTI

Of all the concepts generated by contemporary feminist theory, patriarchy is probably the most overused and, in some respects, the most undertheorized. This state of affairs is not due to neglect, since there is a substantial volume of writing on the question, but rather to the specific conditions of development of contemporary feminist usages of the term. While radical feminists encouraged a very liberal usage, to apply to virtually any form or instance of male domination, socialist feminists have mainly restricted themselves to analyzing the relationships between patriarchy and class under capitalism. As a result, the term *patriarchy* often evokes an overly monolithic conception of male dominance, which is treated at a level of abstraction that obfuscates rather than reveals the intimate inner workings of culturally and historically distinct arrangements between the genders.

It is not my intention to provide a review of the theoretical debates around patriarchy (Barrett 1980; Beechey 1979; Delphy 1977; Eisenstein 1978: Hartmann 1981; McDonough and Harrison 1978; Mies 1986; Mitchell 1973; Young 1981). Instead, I would like to propose an important and relatively neglected point of entry for the identification of different forms of patriarchy through an analysis of women's strategies in dealing with them. I will argue that women strategize within a set of concrete constraints that reveal and define the blueprint of what I will term the *patriarchal bargain*[1] of any given society, which may exhibit variations according to class, caste, and ethnicity. These patriarchal bargains exert a powerful influence on the shaping of women's gendered subjectivity and determine the nature of gender ideology in different contexts. They also influence both the potential for and specific forms of women's active or passive resistance in the face of their oppression. Moreover, patriarchal bargains are not timeless or immutable entities, but are susceptible to historical transformations that open up new areas of struggle and renegotiation of the relations between genders.

By way of illustration, I will contrast two systems of male dominance, rendered ideal-typical for the purposes of discussing their implications for women. I use these ideal types as heuristic devices that have the potential of being expanded and fleshed out with systematic, comparative, empirical content, although this article makes no pretense at providing anything beyond a mere sketch of possible variations. The two types are based on examples from sub-Saharan Africa, on the one hand, and the Middle East. South Asia, and East Asia on the other. My aim is to highlight a continuum ranging from less corporate forms of householding, involving the relative autonomy of mother-child units evidenced in sub-Saharan polygyny, to the more corporate male-headed entities prevalent in the regions identified by Caldwell (1978) as the "patriarchal belt." In the final section, I analyze the breakdown and transformation of patriarchal bargains and their relationship to women's consciousness and struggles.

AUTONOMY AND PROTEST: SOME EXAMPLES FROM SUB-SAHARAN AFRICA

I had one of my purest experiences of culture shock in the process of reviewing the literature on women in agricultural development projects in sub-Saharan Africa (Kandiyoti 1985). Accustomed as I was to only one type of patriarchy (which I shall describe in some detail later, under the rubric of classic patriarchy), I was ill prepared for what I found. The literature was rife with instances of women's resistance to attempts to lower the value of their labor and, more important, women's refusal to allow the total appropriation of their production by their husbands. Let me give some examples.

Wherever new agricultural schemes provided men with inputs and credit, and the assumption was made that as heads of household they would have access to their wives' unremunerated labor, problems seemed to develop. In the Mwea irrigated rice settlement in Kenya, where women were deprived of access to their own plots, their lack of alternatives and their total lack of control over men's earnings made life so intolerable to them that wives commonly deserted their husbands (Hanger and Moris 1973). In Gambia, in yet another rice-growing scheme, the irrigated land and credit were made available to men only, even though it was the women who traditionally grew rice in tidal swamps, and there was a long-standing practice of men and women cultivating their own crops and controlling the produce. Women's customary duties with respect to labor allocation to common and individual plots protected them from demands by their husbands that they provide free labor on men's irrigated rice fields. Men had to pay their wives wages or lend them an irrigated plot to have access to their labor. In the rainy season, when women had the alternative of growing their own swamp rice, they created a labor bottleneck for the men, who simply had to wait for the days women did not go to their own fields (Dey 1981).

In Conti's (1979) account of a supervised smallholder settlement project in Upper Volta, again, the men were provided with land and credit, leaving the women no independent resource base and a very inadequate infrastructure to carry out their daily household chores. The result was vocal protest and refusal to cooperate. Roberts (forthcoming) similarly illustrates the strategies used by women to maximize their autonomy in the African context. Yoruba women in Nigeria, for instance, negotiate the terms of their farm-labor services to their husbands while they aim to devote more time and energy to the trading activities that will enable them to support themselves and ultimately give up such services. Hausa women, whose observance of Islamic seclusion reduces the demands husbands can make for their services, allocate their labor to trade, mainly the sale of ready-cooked foodstuffs.

In short, the insecurities of African polygyny for women are matched by areas of relative autonomy that they clearly strive to maximize. Men's responsibility for their wives' support, while normative in some instances, is in actual fact relatively low. Typically, it is the woman who is primarily responsible for her own and her children's upkeep, including meeting the costs of their education, with variable degrees of assistance from her husband. Women have very little to gain and a lot to lose by becoming totally dependent on husbands, and hence they quite rightly resist projects that tilt the delicate balance they strive to maintain. In their protests, wives are safeguarding already existing spheres of autonomy.

Documentation of a genuine trade-off between women's autonomy and men's responsibility for their wives can be found in some historical examples. Mann (1985) suggests that despite the wifely dependence entailed by Christian marriage, Yoruba women in Lagos accepted it with enthusiasm because of the greater protection they thought they would receive. Conversely, men in contemporary Zambia resist the more modern ordinance marriage, as opposed to customary marriage, because it burdens them with greater obligations for their wives and children (Munachonga 1982). A form of conjugal union in which the partners may openly negotiate the exchange of sexual and labor services seems to lay the groundwork for more explicit forms of bargaining. Commenting on Ashanti marriage, Abu (1983, p. 156) singles out as its most striking feature "the separateness of spouses' resources and activities and the overtness of the bargaining element in the relationship." Polygyny and, in this case, the continuing obligations of both men and women to their own kin do not foster a notion of the family or household as a corporate entity.

Clearly, there are important variations in African kinship systems with respect to marriage forms, residence, descent, and inheritance rules (Guyer and Peters 1987). These variations are grounded in complete cultural and historical processes, including different modes of incorporation of African societies into the world economy (Mbilinyi 1982; Murray 1987; S. Young 1977). Nonetheless, it is within a broadly defined Afro-Caribbean pattern that we find some of the clearest instances of noncorporateness of the conjugal family both in ideology and practice, a fact that informs marital and marketplace strategies for women. Works on historical transformations (for example, Etienne and Leacock 1980) suggest that colonization eroded the material basis for women's relative autonomy (such as usufructary access to communal land or traditional craft production) without offering attenuating modifications in either marketplace or marital options. The more contemporary development projects discussed above also tend to assume or impose a male-headed corporate family model, which curtails women's options without opening up other avenues to security and well-being, The women perceive these changes, especially if they occur abruptly, as infractions that constitute a breach of their existing accommodations with the male-dominated order. Consequently, they openly resist them.

SUBSERVIENCE AND MANIPULATION: WOMEN UNDER CLASSIC PATRIARCHY

These examples of women's open resistance stand in stark contrast to women's accommodations to the system I will call *classic patriarchy.* The clearest instance of classic patriarchy may be found in a geographical area that includes North Africa, the Muslim Middle East (including Turkey, Pakistan, and Iran), and South and East Asia (specifically, India and China).[2]

The key to the reproduction of classic patriarchy lies in the operations of the patrilocally extended household, which is also commonly associated with the reproduction of the peasantry in agrarian societies (E. Wolf 1966). Even though demographic and other constraints may have curtailed the numerical predominance of three-generational patrilocal households, there is little doubt that they represent a powerful cultural ideal. It is plausible that the emergence of the patriarchal extended family, which gives the senior man authority over everyone else including younger men, is bound up in the incorporation and control of the family by the state (Ortner 1978), and in the transition from kin-based to tributary modes of surplus control (E. Wolf 1982). The implications of the patrilineal-patrilocal complex for women not only are remarkably uniform but also entail forms of control and subordination that cut across cultural and religious boundaries, such as those of Hinduism, Confucianism, and Islam.

Under classic patriarchy, girls are given away in marriage at a very young age into households headed by their husband's father. There, they are subordinate not only to all the men but also to the more senior women, especially their mother-in-law. The extent to which this represents a total break with their own kin group varies in relation to the degree of endogamy in marriage practices and different conceptions of honor. Among the Turks, there are lower rates of endogamy, and a husband is principally responsible for a woman's honor. Among the Arabs, there is much greater mutuality among affines, and a women's natal family retains both an interest and a say in protecting their married daughter's honor (Meeker 1976). As a result, a Turkish woman's traditional position more closely resembles the status of the "stranger-bride" typical of prerevolutionary China than that of an Arab woman whose position in the patriarchal household may be somewhat attenuated by endogamy and recourse to her natal kin.

Whether the prevalent marriage payment is dowry or bride-price, in classic patriarchy, women do not normally have any claim on their father's patrimony. Their dowries do not qualify as a form of premortem inheritance since they are transferred directly to the bridegroom's kin and do not take the form of productive property, such as land (Agarwal 1987; Sharma 1980). In Muslim communities, for a woman to press for her inheritance rights would be tantamount to losing her brothers' favor, her only recourse in case of severe ill-treatment by her husband or divorce. The young bride enters her husband's household as an effectively dispossessed individual who can establish her place in the patriliny only by producing male offspring.

The patrilineage totally appropriates both women's labor and progeny and renders their work and contribution to production invisible. Woman's life cycle in the patriarchally extended family is such that the deprivation and hardship she experiences as a young bride is eventually superseded by the control and authority she will have over her own subservient daughters-in-law. The cyclical nature of women's power in the household and their anticipation of inheriting the authority of senior women encourages a thorough internalization of this form of patriarchy by the women themselves. In classic patriarchy, subordination to men is offset by the control older women attain over younger women. However, women have access to the only type of labor power they can control, and to old-age security, through their married sons. Since sons are a woman's most critical resource, ensuring their life-long loyalty is an enduring preoccupation. Older women have a vested interest in the suppression of romantic love between youngsters to keep the conjugal bond secondary and to claim sons' primary allegiance. Young women have an interest in circumventing and possibly evading their mother-in-law's control. There are culturally specific examples of how this struggle works to the detriment of the heterosexual bond (Boudhiba 1985; Johnson 1983; Mernissi 1975; M. Wolf 1972), but the overall pattern is quite similar.

The class or caste impact on classic patriarchy creates additional complications. Among the wealthier strata, the withdrawal of women from nondomestic work is frequently a mark of status institutionalized in various seclusion and exclusion practices, such as the purdah system and veiling. The institution of purdah, and other similar status markers, further reinforces women's subordination and their economic dependence on men. However, the observance of restrictive practices is such a crucial element in the reproduction of family status that women will resist breaking the rules, even if observing them produces economic hardship. They forego economically advantageous options, such as the trading activities engaged in by women in parts of Africa, for alternatives that are perceived as in keeping with their respectable and protected domestic roles, and so they become more exploitable. In her study of Indian lacemakers in Narsapur, Mies (1982, p. 13) comments:

> Although domestication of women may be justified by the older forms of seclusion, it has definitely changed its character. The Kapu women are no longer *gosha*—women of a feudal warrior caste—but domesticated housewives and workers who produce for the world market. In the case of the lacemakers this ideology has become almost a material force. The whole system is built on the ideology that these women cannot work outside the house.

Thus, unlike women in sub-Saharan Africa who attempt to resist unfavorable labor relations in the household, women in areas of classic patriarchy often adhere as far and as long as they possibly can to rules that result in the unfailing devaluation of their labor. The cyclical fluctuations of their power position, combined with status considerations, result in their active collusion in the reproduction of their own subordination. They would rather adopt interpersonal strategies that maximize their security through manipulation of the affections of their sons and husband. As M. Wolf's (1972) insightful discussion of the Chinese uterine family suggests, this strategy can even result in the aging male patriarch losing power to his wife. Even though these individual power tactics do little to alter the structurally unfavorable terms of the overall patriarchal script, women become experts in maximizing their own life chances.

Commenting on "female conservatism" in China, Johnson (1983, p. 21) remarks: "Ironically, women through their actions to resist passivity and total male control, became participants with vested interests in the system that oppressed them." M. Wolf (1974) comments similarly on Chinese women's resistance to the 1950 Marriage Law, of which they were supposed to be the primary beneficiaries. She concludes, however, that despite their reluctance to totally transform the old family system, Chinese women will no longer be content with the limited security their manipulation of family relationships can provide.

In other areas of classic patriarchy, changes in material conditions have seriously undermined the normative order. As expressed succinctly by Cain et al. (1979, p. 410), the key to and the irony of this system reside in the fact that "male authority has a material base, while male responsibility is normatively controlled." Their study of a village in Bangladesh offers an excellent example of the strains placed by poverty on bonds of obligation between kin and, more specifically, on men's fulfillment of their normative obligations toward women. Almost a third of the widows in the villages were the heads of their own households, struggling to make a living through waged work. However, the labor-market segmentation created and bolstered by patriarchy meant that their options for work were extremely restricted, and they had to accept very low and uncertain wages.

Paradoxically, the risks and uncertainties that women are exposed to in classic patriarchy create a powerful incentive for higher fertility, which under conditions of deepening poverty will almost certainly fail to provide them with an economic shelter. Greeley (1983) also documents the growing dependence of landless households in Bangladesh on women's wage labor, including that of married women, and discusses the ways in which the stability of the patriarchal family is thereby undermined. Stacey's (1983) discussion of the crisis in the Chinese family before the revolution constitutes a classic account of the erosion of the material and ideological foundations of the traditional system. She goes on to explore how Confucian patriarchy was superseded by and transformed into new democratic and socialist forms. In the next section, I will analyze some of the implications of such processes of transformation.

THE DEMISE OF PATRIARCHAL BARGAINS: RETREAT INTO CONSERVATISM OR RADICAL PROTEST?

The material bases of classic patriarchy crumble under the impact of new market forces, capital penetration in rural areas (Kandiyoti 1984), or processes of chronic immiseration. While there is no single path leading to the breakdown of this system, its consequences are fairly uniform. The domination of younger men by older men and the shelter of women in the domestic sphere were the hallmarks of a system in which men controlled some form of viable joint patrimony in land, animals, or commercial capital. Among the propertyless and the dispossessed, the necessity of every household member's contribution to survival turns men's economic protection of women into a myth.

The breakdown of classic patriarchy results in the earlier emancipation of younger men from their fathers and their earlier separation from the paternal household. While this process implies that women escape the control of mothers-in-law and head their own households at a much younger age, it also means that they themselves can no longer look forward to a future surrounded by subservient daughters-in-law. For the generation of women caught in between, this transformation may represent genuine personal tragedy, since they have paid the heavy price of an earlier patriarchal bargain, but are not able to cash in on its promised benefits. M. Wolf's (1975) statistics on suicide among women in China suggest a clear change in the trend since the 1930s, with a sharp increase in the suicide rates of women who are over 45, whereas previously the rates were highest among young women, especially new brides. She relates this change explicitly to the emancipation of sons and their new possibility of escaping familial control in the choice of their spouse, which robs the older woman of her power and respectability as mother-in-law.

Despite the obstacles that classic patriarchy puts in women's way, which may far outweigh any actual economic and emotional security, women often resist the process of transition because they see the old normative order slipping away from them without any empowering alternatives. In a broader discussion of women's interest, Molyneux (1985, p. 234) remarks:

> This is not just because of "false consciousness" as is frequently supposed—although this can be a factor—but because such changes realized in a piecemeal fashion could threaten the short-term practical interests of some women, or entail a cost in the loss of

forms of protection that are not then compensated for in some way.

Thus, when classic patriarchy enters a crisis, many women may continue to use all the pressure they can muster to make men live up to their obligations and will not, except under the most extreme pressure, compromise the basis for their claims by stepping out of line and losing their respectability. Their passive resistance takes the form of claiming their half of this particular patriarchal bargain—protection in exchange for submissiveness and propriety.

The response of many women who have to work for wages in this context may be an intensification of traditional modesty markers, such as veiling. Often, through no choice of their own, they are working outside their home and are thus "exposed"; they must now use every symbolic means at their disposal to signify that they continue to be worthy of protection. It is significant that Khomeini's exhortations to keep women at home found enthusiastic support among many Iranian women despite the obvious elements of repression. The implicit promise of increased male responsibility restores the integrity of their original patriarchal bargain in an environment where the range of options available to women is extremely restricted. Younger women adopt the veil, Azari (1983, p. 68) suggests, because "the restriction imposed on them by an Islamic order was therefore a small price that had to be paid in exchange for the security, stability and presumed respect this order promised them."

This analysis of female conservatism as a reaction to the breakdown of classic patriarchy does not by any means exhaust the range of possible responses available to women. It is merely intended to demonstrate the place of a particular strategy within the internal logic of a given system, parallels to which may be found in very different contexts, such as the industrialized societies of Western Europe and the United States. Historical and contemporary analyses of the transformation of the facts and ideologies of Western domesticity imply changes in patriarchal bargains. Gordon's (1982) study of changing feminist attitudes to birth control in the nineteenth and twentieth centuries describes the strategy of voluntary motherhood as part of a broader calculus to improve women's situation. Cott's (1978) analysis of the ideology of passionlessness among Victorian women also indicates the strategic nature of women's choices.

For the modern era, Ehrenreich (1983) provides an analysis of the breakdown of the White middle-class patriarchal bargain in the United States. She traces the progressive opting out of men from the breadwinner role starting in the 1950s, and suggests that women's demands for greater autonomy came at a time when men's conjugal responsibility was already much diminished and alternatives for men outside the conjugal union had gained considerable cultural legitimacy. Despite intense ideological mobilization, involving experts such as doctors, counselors, and psychologists who tried to reinforce the idea of the responsible male breadwinner and the domesticated housewife, alternative trends started to emerge and to challenge the dominant normative order. Against this background, Ehrenreich evaluates the feminist and the antifeminist movements and says, "It is as if, facing the age-old insecurity of the family wage system, women chose opposite strategies: either to get out (figuratively speaking) and fight for equality of income and opportunity or to stay home and attempt to bind men more tightly to them" (1983, p. 151). The familism of the antifeminist movement could therefore be interpreted as an attempt to reinstate an older patriarchal bargain, with feminists providing a convenient scapegoat on whom to blame current disaffection and alienation among men (Chafetz and Dworkin 1987). Indeed, Stacey (1987, p. 11) suggests that "feminism serves as a symbolic lightning rod for the widespread nostalgia and longing for lost intimacy and security that presently pervade social and political culture in the United States."

However, the forms of consciousness and struggle that emerge in times of rapid social change require sympathetic and open minded examination, rather than hasty categorization. Thus Ginsburg (1984) evaluates antiabortion activism among women in the United States as strategic rather than necessarily reactionary. She points out that disengaging sexuality from reproduction and domesticity is perceived by many women as inimical to their best interests, since, among other things, it weakens the social pressure on men to take responsibility for the reproductive consequences of sexual activity. This concern and the general anxiety it expresses are by no means unfounded (English 1984) and speak to the current lack of viable alternatives for the emotional and material support of women with children. Similarly, Stacey (1987) identifies diverse forms of "postfeminist" consciousness of the postindustrial era. She suggests that a complex and often contradictory merging of depoliticized feminist attitudes to work and family and of personal strategies to enhance stability and intimacy in marriage are currently taking place.

At the ideological level, broken bargains seem to instigate a search for culprits, a hankering for the certainties of a more traditional order, or a more diffuse feeling that change might have gone either too far or badly wrong. Rosenfelt and Stacey's (1987) reflections on postfeminism and Stacey's (1986) discussion of conservative profamily feminism, although they criticize the alarmist premises of neoconservative discourse, take some of the legitimate concerns it expresses seriously.

CONCLUSION

Systematic analyses of women's strategies and coping mechanisms can help to capture the nature of patriarchal systems in their cultural, class-specific, and temporal concreteness and reveal how men and women resist, accommodate, adapt, and conflict with each other over resources, rights, and responsibilities. Such analyses dissolve some of the artificial divisions apparent in theoretical discussions of the relationships among class, race, and gender, since participants' strategies are shaped by several levels of constraints. Women's strategies are always played out in the context of identifiable patriarchal bargains that act as implicit scripts that define, limit, and inflect their market and domestic options. The two ideal-typical systems of male dominance discussed in this article provide different baselines from which women negotiate and strategize, and each affects the forms and potentialities of their resistance and struggles. Patriarchal bargains do not merely inform women's rational choices but also shape the more unconscious aspects of their gendered subjectivity, since they permeate the context of their early socialization, as well as their adult cultural milieu (Kandiyoti 1987a, 1987b).

A focus on more narrowly defined patriarchal bargains, rather than on an unqualified notion of patriarchy, offers better prospects for the detailed analysis of processes of transformation. In her analysis of changes in sexual imagery and mores in Western societies, Janeway (1980) borrows Thomas Kuhn's (1970) terminology of scientific paradigms. She suggests, by analogy, that widely shared ideas and practices in the realm of sexuality may act as sexual paradigms, establishing the rules of normalcy at any given time, but also vulnerable to change when "existing rules fail to operate, when anomalies can no longer be evaded, when the real world of everyday experience challenges accepted causality" (1980, p. 582). However, sexual paradigms cannot be fully comprehended unless they are inscribed in the rules of more specifically defined patriarchal bargains, as Janeway herself demonstrates in her discussion of the connection between the ideal of female chastity in Western societies and the transmission of property to legitimate heirs before the advent of a generalized cash economy.

To stretch the Kuhnian analogy even further, patriarchal bargains can be shown to have a normal phase and a crisis phase, a concept that modifies our very interpretation of what is going on in the world. Thus, during the normal phase of classic patriarchy, there were large numbers of women who were in fact exposed to economic hardship and insecurity. They were infertile and had to be divorced, or orphaned and without recourse to their own natal family, or unprotected because they had no surviving sons or—even worse—had "ungrateful" sons. However, they were merely considered "unlucky," anomalies and accidental casualties of a system that made sense otherwise. It is only at the point of breakdown that every order reveals its systemic contradictions. The impact of contemporary socioeconomic transformations upon marriage and divorce, on household formation, and on the gendered division of labor inevitably lead to a questioning of the fundamental, implicit assumptions behind arrangements between women and men.

However, new strategies and forms of consciousness do not simply emerge from the ruins of the old and smoothly produce a new consensus, but are created through personal and political struggles, which are often complex and contradictory (see Strathern 1987). The breakdown of a particular patriarchal system may, in the short run, generate instances of passive resistance among women that take the paradoxical form of bids for increased responsibility and control by men. A better understanding of the short- and medium-term strategies of women in different social locations could provide a corrective influence to ethnocentric or class-bound definitions of what constitutes a feminist consciousness.

NOTES

1. Like all terms coined to convey a complex concept, the term *patriarchal bargain* represents a difficult compromise. It is intended to indicate the existence of set rules and scripts regulating gender relations, to which both genders accommodate and acquiesce, yet which may nonetheless be contested, redefined, and renegotiated. Some suggested alternatives were the terms *contract, deal,* or *scenario;* however, none of these fully captured the fluidity and tension implied by bargain. I am grateful to Cynthia Cockburn and Nels Johnson for pointing out that the term *bargain* commonly denotes a deal between more or less equal participants, so it does not accurately apply to my usage, which clearly indicates an asymmetrical exchange. However, women as a rule bargain from a weaker position.

2. I am excluding not only Southeast Asia but also the Northern Mediterranean, despite important similarities in the latter regarding codes of honor and the overall importance attached to the sexual purity of women, because I want to restrict myself to areas where the patrilocal-patrilineal complex is dominant. Thus societies with bilateral kinship systems, such as Greece, in which women do inherit and control property and receive dowries that constitute productive property, do not qualify despite important similarities in other ideological respects. This is not, however, to suggest that an unqualified homogeneity of ideology and practice exists within the geographical boundaries indicated. For example, there are critical variations within the Indian subcontinent that have demonstrably different implications for women (Dyson and Moore 1983). Conversely, even in areas of bilateral kinship, there may be instances in which all the facets of classic patriarchy, namely, property, residence, and descent through the male line, may coalesce under specified circumstances (Denich 1974). What I am suggesting is that the most clear-cut and easily identifiable examples of classic patriarchy may be found within the boundaries indicated in the text.

REFERENCES

Abu, K. 1983. "The Separateness of Spouses: Conjugal Resources in an Ashanti Town." Pp. 156–68 in *Female and Male in West Africa,* edited by C. Oppong. London: George Allen & Unwin.

Agarwal, B. 1987. "Women and Land Rights in India." Unpublished manuscript.

Azari, F. 1983. "Islam's Appeal to Women in Iran: Illusion and Reality." Pp. 1–71 in *Women of Iran: The Conflict with Fundamentalist Islam,* edited by F. Azari. London: Ithaca Press.

Barrett, M. 1980. *Woman's Oppression Today.* London: Verso.

Beechey, V. 1979. "On Patriarchy." *Feminist Review* 3: 66–82.

Boudhiba, A. 1985. *Sexuality in Islam.* London: Routledge & Kegan Paul.

Cain, M., S. R. Khanan, and S. Nahar. 1979. "Class, Patriarchy, and Women's Work in Bangladesh." *Population and Development Review* 5:408–16.

Caldwell, J. C. 1978. "A Theory of Fertility: From High Plateau to Destabilization." *Population and Development Review* 4:553–77.

Chafetz, J. S. and A. G. Dworkin. 1987. "In Face of Threat: Organized Antifeminism in Comparative Perspective." *Gender & Society* 1:33–60.

Conti, A. 1979. "Capitalist Organization of Production Through Non-capitalist Relations: Women's Role in a Pilot Resettlement Project in Upper Volta." *Review of African Political Economy* 15/16:75–91.

Cott, N. F. 1978. "Passionlessness: An Interpretation of Victorian Sexual Ideology, 1790–1850." *Signs: Journal of Women in Culture and Society* 4:219–36.

Delphy, C. 1977. *The Main Enemy.* London: Women's Research and Resource Centre.

Denich, B. S. 1974. "Sex and Power in the Balkans." Pp. 243–62 in *Women, Culture and Society,* edited by M. Z. Rosaldo and L. Lamphere. Palo Alto, CA: Stanford University Press.

Dey, J. 1981. "Gambian Women: Unequal Partners in Rice Development Projects." Pp. 109–22 in *African Women in the Development Process,* edited by N. Nelson. London: Frank Cass.

Dyson, T. and M. Moore. 1983. "On Kinship Structures, Female Autonomy and Demographic Behavior." *Population and Development Review* 9:35–60.

Ehrenreich, B. 1983. *The Hearts of Men.* London: Pluto Press.

Eisensten, Z. 1978. "Developing a Theory of Capitalist Patriarchy and Socialist Feminism." Pp. 5–40 in *Capitalist Patriarchy and the Case for Socialist Feminism,* edited by Z. Eisenstein. New York: Monthly Review Press.

English, D. 1984. "The Fear That Feminism Will Free Men First." Pp. 97–102 in *Powers of Desire: The Politics of Sexuality,* edited by A. Snitow, C. Stansell, and S. Thompson. New York: Monthly Review Press.

Etienne, M. and E. Leacock (eds.). 1980. *Women and Colonization.* New York: Praeger.

Ginsburg, F. 1984. "The Body Politic: The Defense of Sexual Restriction by Anti-Abortion Activists." Pp. 173–88 in *Pleasure and Danger: Exploring Female Sexuality,* edited by C. S. Vance. London: Routledge & Kegan Paul.

Gordon, L. 1982. "Why Nineteenth Century Feminists Did Not Support (Birth Control) and Twentieth Century Feminists Do: Feminism, Reproduction and the Family." Pp. 40–53 in *Rethinking the Family: Some Feminist Questions,* edited by B. Thorne and M. Yalom. New York: Longman.

Greeley, M. 1983. "Patriarchy and Poverty: A Bangladesh Case Study." *South Asia Research* 3:35–55.

Guyer, J. I. and P. E. Peters. 1987. "'Introduction' to Conceptualizing the Household: Issues of Theory and Policy in Africa." *Development and Change* 18:197–213.

Hanger, J. and J. Moris. 1973. "Women and the Household Economy." Pp. 209–44 in *Mwea: An Irrigated Rice Settlement in Kenya,* edited by R. Chambers and J. Moris. Munich: Weltforum Verlag.

Hartmann, H. 1981. "The Unhappy Marriage of Marxism and Feminism: Towards a More Progressive Union." Pp. 40–53 in *Women and Revolution,* edited by L. Sargent. London: Pluto Press.

Janeway, E. 1980. "Who Is Sylvia? On the Loss of Sexual Paradigms." *Signs: Journal in Women in Culture and Society* 5:573–89.

Johnson, K. A. 1983. *Women, the Family and Peasant Revolution in China.* Chicago: Chicago University Press.

Kandiyoti, D. 1984. "Rural Transformation in Turkey and Its Implications for Women's Studies." Pp. 17–29 in *Women on the Move: Contemporary Transformations in Family and Society.* Paris: UNESCO.

———. 1985. *Women in Rural Production Systems: Problems and Policies.* Paris: UNESCO.

———. 1987a. "Emancipated but Unliberated? Reflections on the Turkish Case." *Feminist Studies* 13: 317–38.

———. 1987b. "The Problem of Subjectivity in Western Feminist Theory." Paper presented at the American Sociological Association Annual Meeting, Chicago.

Kuhn, T. 1970. *The Structure of Scientific Revolutions* (2nd ed.). Chicago: Chicago University Press.

Mann, K. 1985. *Marrying Well: Marriage, Status and Social Change Among the Educated Elite in Colonial Lagos.* Cambridge: Cambridge University Press.

Mbilinyi, M. J. 1982. "Wife, Slave and Subject of the King: The Oppression of Women in the Shambala Kingdom." *Tanzania Notes and Records* 88/89:1–13.

McDonough, R. and R. Harrison. 1978. "Patriarchy and Relations of Production." Pp. 11–41 in *Feminism and Materialism,* edited by A. Kuhn and A. M. Wolpe. London: Routledge & Kegan Paul.

Meeker, M. 1976. "Meaning and Society in the New East: Examples from the Black Sea Turks and the Levantine Arabs." *International Journal of Middle East Studies* 7:383–422.

Mernissi, F. 1975. *Beyond the Veil: Male-Female Dynamics in a Muslim Society.* New York: Wiley.

Mies, M. 1982. "The Dynamics of Sexual Division of Labour and the Integration of Women into the World Market." Pp. 1–28 in *Women and Development: The Sexual Division of Labour in Rural Societies,* edited by L. Beneria. New York: Praeger.

———. 1986. *Patriarchy and Accumulation on a World Scale: Women in the International Division of Labour.* London: Zed.

Mitchell, J. 1973. *Women's Estate.* New York: Vintage.

———. 1986. "Reflections on Twenty Years of Feminism." Pp. 34–48 in *What is Feminism?* edited by J. Mitchell and A. Oakley. Oxford: Basil Blackwell.

Molyneux, M. 1985. "Mobilization Without Emancipation? Women's Interests, the State and Revolution in Nicaragua." *Feminist Studies* 11:227–54.

Munachonga, M. L. 1982. "Income Allocation and Marriage Options in Urban Zambia: Wives Versus Extended Kin." Paper presented at the Conference on Women and Income Control in the Third World, New York.

Murray, C. 1987. "Class, Gender and the Household: The Developmental Cycle in Southern Africa." *Development and Change* 18:235–50.

Ortner, S. 1978 "The Virgin and the State." *Feminist Studies* 4:19–36.

Roberts, P. Forthcoming. "Rural Women in Western Nigeria and Hausa Niger: A Comparative Analysis," in *Serving Two Masters,* edited by K. Young. New Delhi: Allied Publishers.

Rosenfelt, D. and J. Stacey. 1987. "Second Thoughts on the Second Wave." *Feminist Studies* 13:341–61.

Sharma, U. 1980. *Women, Work and Property in North West India.* London: Tavistock.

Stacey, J. 1983. *Patriarchy and Socialist Revolution in China.* Berkeley: University of California Press.

———. 1986. "Are Feminists Afraid to Leave Home? The Challenge of Conservative Pro-Family Feminism." Pp. 219–48 in *What is Feminism?* edited by J. Mitchell and A. Oakley. Oxford: Basil Blackwell.

———. 1987. "Sexism by a Subtler Name? Postindustrial Conditions and Postfeminist Consciousness in the Silicon Valley." *Socialist Review* (Nov.): 7–28.

Strathern, M. 1987. "An Awkward Relationship: The Case of Feminism and Anthropology." *Sign Journal of Women in Culture and Society* 12:276–92.

Wolf, E. 1966. *Peasants.* Englewood Cliffs, NJ: Prentice-Hall.

———. 1982. *Europe and the People Without History.* Berkeley: University of California Press.

Wolf, M. 1972. *Women and the Family in Rural Taiwan.* Palo Alto, CA: Stanford University Press.

———. 1974. "Chinese Women: Old Skills in a New Context." Pp. 157–72 in *Women, Culture and Society,* edited by M. Z. Rosaldo and L. Lamphere. Palo Alto, CA: Stanford University Press.

———. 1975. "Woman and Suicide in China." Pp. 111–41 in *Women in Chinese Society,* edited by M. Wolf and R. Witke. Palo Alto, CA: Stanford University Press.

Young, I. 1981. "Beyond the Unhappy Marriage: A Critique of the Dual Systems Theory." Pp. 43–69 in *Women and Revolution,* edited by L. Sargent. London: Pluto Press.

Young, S. 1977. "Fertility and Famine: Women's Agricultural History in Southern Mozambique." Pp. 66–81 in *The Roots of Rural Poverty in Central and Southern Africa,* edited by R. Palmer and N. Parsons. London: Heinemann.

4

Masculinities and Globalization

R. W. Connell

The current wave of research and debate on masculinity stems from the impact of the women's liberation movement on men, but it has taken time for this impact to produce a new intellectual agenda. Most discussions of men's gender in the 1970s and early 1980s centered on an established concept, the male sex role, and an established problem: how men and boys were socialized into this role. There was not much new empirical research. What there was tended to use the more abstracted methods of social psychology (e.g., paper-and-pencil masculinity/femininity scales) to measure generalized attitudes and expectations in ill-defined populations. The largest body of empirical research was the continuing stream of quantitative studies of sex differences—which continued to be disappointingly slight (Carrigan, Connell, and Lee 1985).

The concept of a unitary male sex role, however, came under increasing criticism for its multiple oversimplifications and its incapacity to handle issues about power (Kimmel 1987; Connell 1987). New conceptual frameworks were proposed that linked feminist work on institutionalized patriarchy, gay theoretical work on homophobia, and psychoanalytic ideas about the person (Carrigan, Connell, and Lee 1985; Hearn 1987). Increasing attention was given to certain studies that located issues about masculinity in a fully described local context, whether a British printing shop (Cockburn 1983) or a Papuan mountain community (Herdt 1981). By the late 1980s, a genre of empirical research based on these ideas was developing, most clearly in sociology but also in anthropology, history, organization studies, and cultural studies. This has borne fruit in the 1990s in what is now widely recognized as a new generation of social research on masculinity and men in gender relations (Connell 1995; *Widersprueche* 1995; Segal 1997).

Although the recent research has been diverse in subject matter and social location, its characteristic focus is the construction of masculinity in a particular milieu or moment—a clergyman's family (Tosh 1991), a professional sports career (Messner 1992), a small group of gay men (Connell 1992), a bodybuilding gym (Klein 1993), a group of colonial schools (Morrell 1994), an urban police force (McElhinny 1994), drinking groups in bars (Tomsen 1997), a corporate office on the verge of a decision (Messerschmidt 1997). Accordingly, we might think of this as the "ethnographic moment" in masculinity research, in which the specific and the local are in focus. (This is not to deny that this work *deploys* broader structural concepts simply to note the characteristic focus of the empirical work and its analysis.)

The ethnographic moment brought a much-needed gust of realism to debates on men and masculinity, a corrective to the simplifications of role theory. It also provided a corrective to the trend in popular culture where vague discussions of men's sex roles were giving way to the mystical generalities of the mythopoetic movement and the extreme simplifications of religious revivalism.

Although the rich detail of the historical and field studies defies easy summary, certain conclusions emerge from this body of research as a whole. In short form, they are the following.

Plural Masculinities A theme of theoretical work in the 1980s, the multiplicity of masculinities has now been very fully documented by descriptive research. Different cultures and different periods of history construct gender differently. Striking differences exist, for instance, in the relationship of homosexual practice to dominant forms of masculinity (Herdt 1984). In multicultural societies, there are varying definitions and enactments of masculinity, for instance, between Anglo and Latino communities in the United States (Hondagneu-Sotelo and Messner 1994). Equally important, more than one kind of masculinity can be found within a given cultural setting or institution. This is particularly well documented in school studies (Foley 1990) but can also be observed in workplaces (Messerschmidt 1997) and the military (Barrett 1996).

Hierarchy and Hegemony These plural masculinities exist in definite social relations, often relations of hierarchy and exclusion. This was recognized early, in gay theorists' discussions of homophobia; it has become clear that the implications are far-reaching. There is generally a hegemonic form of masculinity, the most honored or desired in a particular context. For Western popular culture, this is extensively documented in research on media representations of masculinity (McKay and Huber 1992). The hegemonic form need not be the most common form of masculinity. Many men live in a state of some tension with, or distance from, hegemonic masculinity; others (such as sporting heroes) are taken as exemplars of hegemonic masculinity and are required to live up to it strenuously (Connell 1990a). The dominance of hegemonic masculinity over other forms may be quiet and implicit, but it may also be vehement and violent, as in the important case of homophobic violence.

Collective Masculinities Masculinities, as patterns of gender practice, are sustained and enacted not only by individuals but also by groups and institutions. This fact was visible in Cockburn's (1983) pioneering research on informal workplace culture, and it has been confirmed over and over: in workplaces (Donaldson 1991), in organized sport (Whitson 1990; Messner 1992), in schools (Connell 1996), and so on. This point must be taken with the previous two: institutions may construct multiple masculinities and define relationships between them. Barrett's (1996) illuminating study of hegemonic masculinity in the U.S. Navy shows how this takes different forms in the different subbranches of the one military organization.

Bodies as Arenas Men's bodies do not determine the patterns of masculinity, but they are still of great importance in masculinity. Men's bodies are addressed, defined and disciplined (as in sport; see Theberge 1991), and given outlets and pleasures by the gender order of society. But men's bodies are not blank slates. The enactment of masculinity reaches certain limits, for instance, in the destruction of the industrial worker's body (Donaldson 1991). Masculine conduct with a female body is felt to be anomalous or transgressive, like feminine conduct with a male body; research on gender crossing (Bolin 1988) shows the work that must be done to sustain an anomalous gender.

Active Construction Masculinities do not exist prior to social interaction, but come into existence as people act. They are actively produced, using the resources and strategies available in a given milieu. Thus the exemplary masculinities of sports professionals are not a product of passive disciplining, but as Messner (1992) shows, result from a sustained, active engagement with the demands of the institutional setting, even to the point of serious bodily damage from "playing hurt" and accumulated stress. With boys learning masculinities, much of what was previously taken as socialization appears, in close-focus studies of schools

(Walker 1988; Thorne 1993), as the outcome of intricate and intense maneuvering in peer groups, classes, and adult-child relationships.

Contradiction Masculinities are not homogeneous, simple states of being. Close-focus research on masculinities commonly identifies contradictory desires and conduct; for instance, in Klein's (1993) study of bodybuilders, the contradiction between the heterosexual definition of hegemonic masculinity and the homosexual practice by which some of the bodybuilders finance the making of an exemplary body. Psychoanalysis provides the classic evidence of conflicts within personality, and recent psychoanalytic writing (Chodorow 1994; Lewes 1988) has laid some emphasis on the conflicts and emotional compromises within both hegemonic and subordinated forms of masculinity. Life-history research influenced by existential psychoanalysis (Connell 1995) has similarly traced contradictory projects and commitments within particular forms of masculinity.

Dynamics Masculinities created in specific historical circumstances are liable to reconstruction, and any pattern of hegemony is subject to contestation, in which a dominant masculinity may be displaced. Heward (1988) shows the changing gender regime of a boys' school responding to the changed strategies of the families in its clientele. Roper (1991) shows the displacement of a production-oriented masculinity among engineering managers by new financially oriented generic managers. Since the 1970s, the reconstruction of masculinities has been pursued as a conscious politics. Schwalbe's (1996) close examination of one mythopoetic group shows the complexity of the practice and the limits of the reconstruction.

If we compare this picture of masculinity with earlier understandings of the male sex role, it is clear that the ethnographic moment in research has already had important intellectual fruits.

Nevertheless, it has always been recognized that some issues go beyond the local. For instance, mythopoetic movements such as the highly visible Promise Keepers are part of a spectrum of masculinity politics; Messner (1997) shows for the United States that this spectrum involves at least eight conflicting agendas for the remaking of masculinity. Historical studies such as Phillips (1987) on New Zealand and Kimmel (1996) on the United States have traced the changing public constructions of masculinity for whole countries over long periods; ultimately, such historical reconstructions are essential for understanding the meaning of ethnographic details.

I consider that this logic must now be taken a step further, and in taking this step, we will move toward a new agenda for the whole field. What happens in localities is affected by the history of whole countries, but what happens in countries is affected by the history of the world. Locally situated lives are now (indeed, have long been) powerfully influenced by geopolitical struggles, global markets, multinational corporations, labor migration, transnational media. It is time for this fundamental fact to be built into our analysis of men and masculinities.

To understand local masculinities, we must think in global terms. But how? That is the problem pursued in this article. I will offer a framework for thinking about masculinities as a feature of world society and for thinking about men's gender practices in terms of the global structure and dynamics of gender. This is by no means to reject the ethnographic moment in masculinity research. It is, rather, to think how we can use its findings more adequately.

THE WORLD GENDER ORDER

Masculinities do not first exist and then come into contact with femininities; they are produced together, in the process that constitutes a gender order. Accordingly, to understand the masculinities on a world scale, we must first have a concept of the globalization of gender.

This is one of the most difficult points in current gender analysis because the very conception is counterintuitive. We are so accustomed to thinking of gender as the attribute of an individual, even as an unusually intimate attribute, that it requires a considerable wrench to think of gender on the vast scale of global society. Most relevant discussions, such as the literature on women and development, fudge the issue.

They treat the entities that extend internationally (markets, corporations, intergovernmental programs, etc.) as ungendered in principle—but affecting unequally gendered recipients of aid in practice, because of bad policies. Such conceptions reproduce the familiar liberal-feminist view of the state as in principle gender-neutral, though empirically dominated by men.

But if we recognize that very large scale institutions such as the state are themselves gendered, in quite precise and specifiable ways (Connell 1990b), and if we recognize that international relations, international trade, and global markets are inherently an arena of gender formation and gender politics (Enloe 1990), then we can recognize the existence of a world gender order. The term can be defined as the structure of relationships that interconnect the gender regimes of institutions, and the gender orders of local society, on a world scale. That is, however, only a definition. The substantive questions remain: what is the shape of that structure, how tightly are its elements linked, how has it arisen historically, what is its trajectory into the future?

Current business and media talk about globalization pictures a homogenizing process sweeping across the world, driven by new technologies, producing vast unfettered global markets in which all participate on equal terms. This is a misleading image. As Hirst and Thompson (1996) show, the global economy is highly unequal and the current degree of homogenization is often overestimated. Multinational corporations based in the three major economic powers (the United States, European Union, and Japan) are the major economic actors worldwide.

The structure bears the marks of its history. Modern global society was historically produced as Wallerstein (1974) argued, by the economic and political expansion of European states from the fifteenth century on and by the creation of colonial empires. It is in this process that we find the roots of the modern world gender order. Imperialism was, from the start, a gendered process. Its first phase, colonial conquest and settlement, was carried out by gender-segregated forces, and it resulted in massive disruption of indigenous gender orders. In its second phase, the stabilization of colonial societies, new gender divisions of labor were produced in plantation economies and colonial cities, while gender ideologies were linked with racial hierarchies and the cultural defense of empire. The third phase, marked by political decolonization, economic neocolonialism, and the current growth of world markets and structures of financial control, has seen gender divisions of labor remade on a massive scale in the "global factory" (Fuentes and Ehrenreich 1983), as well as the spread of gendered violence alongside Western military technology.

The result of this history is a partially integrated, highly unequal and turbulent world society, in which gender relations are partly but unevenly linked on a global scale. The unevenness becomes clear when different substructures of gender (Connell 1987; Walby 1990) are examined separately.

The Division of Labor A characteristic feature of colonial and neocolonial economies was the restructuring of local production systems to produce a male wage worker–female domestic worker couple (Mies 1986). This need not produce a "housewife" in the Western suburban sense, for instance, where the wage work involved migration to plantations or mines (Moodie 1994). But it has generally produced the identification of masculinity with the public realm and the money economy and of femininity with domesticity, which is a core feature of the modern European gender system (Holter 1997).

Power Relations The colonial and postcolonial world has tended to break down purdah systems of patriarchy in the name of modernization, if not of women's emancipation (Kandiyoti 1994). At the same time, the creation of a westernized public realm has seen the growth of large-scale organizations in the form of the state and corporations, which in the great majority of cases are culturally masculinized and controlled by men. In *comprador* capitalism, however, the power of local elites depends on their relations with the metropolitan powers, so the hegemonic masculinities of neocolonial societies are uneasily poised between local and global cultures.

Emotional Relations Both religious and cultural missionary activity has corroded indigenous homosexual and cross-gender practice, such as the native American *berdache* and the Chinese "passion of the cut sleeve" (Hinsch 1990). Recently developed Western models of romantic heterosexual love as the basis for marriage and of gay identity as the main alternative have now circulated globally—though as Altman (1996) observes, they do not simply displace indigenous models, but interact with them in extremely complex ways.

Symbolization Mass media, especially electronic media, in most parts of the world follow North American and European models and relay a great deal of metropolitan content; gender imagery is an important part of what is circulated. A striking example is the reproduction of a North American imagery of femininity by Xuxa, the blonde television superstar in Brazil (Simpson 1993). In counterpoint, exotic gender imagery has been used in the marketing strategies of newly industrializing countries (e.g., airline advertising from Southeast Asia)—a tactic based on the long-standing combination of the exotic and the erotic in the colonial imagination (Jolly 1997).

Clearly, the world gender order is not simply an extension of a traditional European-American gender order. That gender order was changed by colonialism, and elements from other cultures now circulate globally. Yet in no sense do they mix on equal terms, to produce a United Colours of Benetton gender order. The culture and institutions of the North Atlantic countries are hegemonic within the emergent world system. This is crucial for understanding the kinds of masculinities produced within it.

THE REPOSITIONING OF MEN AND THE RECONSTITUTION OF MASCULINITIES

The positioning of men and the constitution of masculinities may be analyzed at any of the levels at which gender practice is configured: in relation to the body, in personal life, and in collective social practice. At each level, we need to consider how the processes of globalization influence configurations of gender.

Men's bodies are positioned in the gender order, and enter the gender process, through body-reflexive practices in which bodies are both objects and agents (Connell 1995)—including sexuality, violence, and labor. The conditions of such practice include where one is and who is available for interaction. So it is a fact of considerable importance for gender relations that the global social order distributes and redistributes bodies, through migration, and through political controls over movement and interaction.

The creation of empire was the original "elite migration," though in certain cases mass migration followed. Through settler colonialism, something close to the gender order of Western Europe was reassembled in North America and in Australia. Labor migration within the colonial systems was a means by which gender practices were spread, but also a means by which they were reconstructed, since labor migration was itself a gendered process—as we have seen in relation to the gender division of labor. Migration from the colonized world to the metropole became (except for Japan) a mass process in the decades after World War II. There is also migration within the periphery, such as the creation of a very large immigrant labor force, mostly from other Muslim countries, in the oil-producing Gulf states.

These relocations of bodies create the possibility of hybridization in gender imagery, sexuality, and other forms of practice. The movement is not always toward synthesis, however, as the race/ethnic hierarchics of colonialism have been recreated in new contexts, including the politics of the metropole. Ethnic and racial conflict has been growing in importance in recent years, and as Klein (1997) and Tillner (1997) argue, this is a fruitful context for the production of masculinities oriented toward domination and violence. Even without the context of violence, there can be an intimate interweaving of the formation of masculinity with the formation of ethnic identity, as seen in the study by Poynting, Noble, and Tabar (1997) of Lebanese youths in the Anglo-dominant culture of Australia.

At the level of personal life as well as in relation to bodies, the making of masculinities is shaped by global forces. In some cases, the link is indirect, such as the working-class Australian men caught in a situation of structural unemployment (Connell 1995), which arises from Australia's changing position in the global economy. In other cases, the link is obvious, such as the executives of multinational corporations and the financial sector servicing international trade. The requirements of a career in international business set up strong pressures on domestic life: almost all multinational executives are men, and the assumption in business magazines and advertising directed toward them is that they will have dependent wives running their homes and bringing up their children.

At the level of collective practice, masculinities are reconstituted by the remaking of gender meanings and the reshaping of the institutional contexts of practice. Let us consider each in turn.

The growth of global mass media, especially electronic media, is an obvious "vector" for the globalization of gender. Popular entertainment circulates stereotyped gender images, deliberately made attractive for marketing purposes. The example of Xuxa in Brazil has already been mentioned. International news media are also controlled or strongly influenced from the metropole and circulate Western definitions of authoritative masculinity, criminality, desirable femininity, and so on. But there are limits to the power of global mass communications. Some local centers of mass entertainment differ from the Hollywood model, such as the Indian popular film industry centered in Bombay. Further, media research emphasizes that audiences are highly selective in their reception of media messages, and we must allow for popular recognition of the fantasy in mass entertainment. Just as economic globalization can be exaggerated, the creation of a global culture is a more turbulent and uneven process than is often assumed (Featherstone 1995).

More important, I would argue, is a process that began long before electronic media existed, the export of institutions. Gendered institutions not only circulate definitions of masculinity (and femininity), as sex role theory notes. The functioning of gendered institutions, creating specific conditions for social practice, calls into existence specific patterns of practice. Thus, certain patterns of collective violence are embedded in the organization and culture of a Western-style army, which are different from the patterns of precolonial violence. Certain patterns of calculative egocentrism are embedded in the working of a stock market; certain patterns of rule following and domination are embedded in a bureaucracy.

Now, the colonial and postcolonial world saw the installation in the periphery, on a very large scale, of a range of institutions on the North Atlantic model: armies, states, bureaucracies, corporations, capital markets, labor markets, schools, law courts, transport systems. These are gendered institutions and their functioning has directly reconstituted masculinities in the periphery. This has not necessarily meant photocopies of European masculinities. Rather, pressures for change are set up that are inherent in the institutional form.

To the extent that particular institutions become dominant in world society, the patterns of masculinity embedded in them may become global standards. Masculine dress is an interesting indicator: almost every political leader in the world now wears the uniform of the Western business executive. The more common pattern, however, is not the complete displacement of local patterns but the articulation of the local gender order with the gender regime of global-model institutions. Case studies such as Hollway's (1994) account of bureaucracy in Tanzania illustrate the point; there, domestic patriarchy articulated with masculine authority in the state in ways that subverted the government's formal commitment to equal opportunity for women.

We should not expect the overall structure of gender relations on a world scale simply to mirror patterns known on the smaller scale. In the most vital of respects, there is continuity. The world gender order is unquestionably patriarchal, in the sense that it privileges men over women. There is a patriarchal dividend for men arising from unequal wages, unequal labor force participation, and a highly unequal structure of ownership, as well as cultural and sexual privileging. This has been extensively documented by feminist work on women's situation globally (e.g., Taylor 1985), though its implications for masculinity have mostly been ignored. The conditions thus exist for the production of a hegemonic masculinity on a world scale, that is to say, a dominant form of masculinity that embodies, organizes, and legitimates men's domination in the gender order as a whole.

The conditions of globalization, which involve the interaction of many local gender orders, certainly multiply the forms of masculinity in the global gender order. At the same time, the specific shape of globalization, concentrating economic and cultural power on an unprecedented scale, provides new resources for dominance by particular groups of men. This dominance may become institutionalized in a pattern of masculinity that becomes, to some degree, standardized across localities. I will call such patterns *globalizing masculinities,* and it is among them, rather than narrowly within the metropole, that we are likely to find candidates for hegemony in the world gender order.

GLOBALIZING MASCULINITIES

In this section, I will offer a sketch of major forms of globalizing masculinity in the three historical phases identified above in the discussion of globalization.

Masculinities of Conquest and Settlement

The creation of the imperial social order involved peculiar conditions for the gender practices of men. Colonial conquest itself was mainly carried out by segregated groups of men—soldiers, sailors, traders, administrators, and a good many who were all these by turn (such as the Rum Corps in early New South Wales, Australia). They were drawn from the more segregated occupations and milieu in the metropole, and it is likely that the men drawn into colonization tended to be the more rootless. Certainly the process of conquest could produce frontier masculinities that combined the occupational culture of these groups with an unusual level of violence and egocentric individualism. The vehement contemporary debate about the genocidal violence of the Spanish conquistadors—who in fifty years completely exterminated the population of Hispaniola—points to this pattern (Bitterli 1989).

The political history of empire is full of evidence of the tenuous control over the frontier exercised by the state—the Spanish monarchs unable to rein in the conquistadors, the governors in Sydney unable to hold back the squatters and in Capetown unable to hold back the Boers, gold rushes breaking boundaries everywhere, even an independent republic set up by escaped slaves in Brazil. The point probably applies to other forms of social control too, such as customary controls on men's sexuality. Extensive sexual exploitation of indigenous women was a common feature of conquest. In certain circumstances, frontier masculinities might be reproduced as a local cultural tradition long after the frontier had passed, such as the gauchos of southern South America and the cowboys of the western United States.

In other circumstances, however, the frontier of conquest and exploitation was replaced by a frontier of settlement. Sex ratios in the colonizing population changed, as women arrived and locally born generations succeeded. A shift back toward the family patterns of the metropole was likely. As Cain and Hopkins (1993) have shown for the British empire, the ruling group in the colonial world as a whole was an extension of the dominant class in the metropole, the landed gentry, and tended to reproduce its social customs and ideology. The creation of a settler masculinity might be the goal of state policy, as it seems to have been in late-nineteenth-century New Zealand, as part of a general process of pacification and the creation of an agricultural social order (Phillips 1987). Or it might be undertaken through institutions created by settler groups, such as the elite schools in Natal studied by Morrell (1994).

The impact of colonialism on the construction of masculinity among the colonized is much less documented, but there is every reason to think it was severe. Conquest and settlement disrupted all the structures of indigenous society, whether or not this was intended by the colonizing powers (Bitierli 1989). Indigenous gender orders were no exception. Their disruption could result from the pulverization of indigenous communities (as in the seizure of land in eastern North America and southeastern Australia), through gendered labor migration (as in gold mining with Black labor in South Africa; see Moodie 1994), to ideological attacks on local gender arrangements (as in the missionary assault on the *berdache* tradition in North America; see Williams 1986). The varied course of resistance to colonization is also likely to have affected the making of masculinities. This is clear in the region of Natal in South Africa, where sustained resistance to colonization by the Zulu kingdom was a key to the mobilization of ethnic-national masculine identities in the twentieth century (Morrell 1996).

Masculinities of Empire

The imperial social order created a hierarchy of masculinities, as it created a hierarchy of communities and races. The colonizers distinguished "more manly" from "less manly" groups among their subjects. In British India, for instance, Bengali men were supposed effeminate while Pathans and Sikhs were regarded as strong and warlike. Similar distinctions were made in South Africa between Hottentots and Zulus, in North America between Iroquois, Sioux, and Cheyenne on one side, and southern and southwestern tribes on the other.

At the same time, the emerging imagery of gender difference in European culture provided general symbols of superiority and inferiority. Within the imperial "poetics of war" (MacDonald 1994), the conqueror was virile, while the colonized were dirty, sexualized, and effeminate or childlike. In many colonial situations, indigenous men were called "boys" by the colonizers (e.g., in Zimbabwe; see Shire 1994). Sinha's (1995) interesting study of the language of political controversy in India in the 1880s and 1890s shows how the images of "manly Englishman" and "effeminate Bengali" were deployed to uphold colonial privilege and contain movements for change. In the late nineteenth century, racial barriers in colonial societies were hardening rather than weakening, and gender ideology tended to fuse with racism in forms that the twentieth century has never untangled.

The power relations of empire meant that indigenous gender orders were generally under pressure from the colonizers, rather than the other way around. But the colonizers too might change. The barriers of late colonial racism were not only to prevent pollution from below but also to forestall "going native," a well-recognized possibility—the starting point, for instance, of Kipling's famous novel *Kim* ([1901] 1987). The pressures, opportunities, and profits of empire might also work changes in gender arrangements among the colonizers, for instance, the division of labor in households with a large supply of indigenous workers as domestic servants (Bulbeck 1992). Empire might also affect the gender order of the metropole itself by changing gender ideologies, divisions of labor, and the nature of the metropolitan state. For instance, empire figured prominently as a source of masculine imagery in Britain, in the Boy Scouts, and in the cult of Lawrence of Arabia (Dawson 1991). Here we see examples of an important principle: the interplay of gender dynamics between different parts of the world order.

The world of empire created two very different settings for the modernization of masculinities. In the periphery, the forcible restructuring of economics and workforces tended to individualize, on one hand, and rationalize, on the other. A widespread result was masculinities in which the rational calculation of self-interest was the key to action, emphasizing the European gender contrast of rational man/irrational woman. The specific form might be local—for instance, the Japanese "salaryman," a type first recognized in the 1910s, was specific to the Japanese context of large, stable industrial conglomerates (Kinmonth 1981). But the result generally was masculinities defined around economic action, with both workers and entrepreneurs increasingly adapted to emerging market economies.

In the metropole, the accumulation of wealth made possible a specialization of leadership in the dominant classes, and struggles for hegemony in which masculinities organized around domination or violence were split from masculinities organized around expertise. The class compromises that allowed the development of the welfare state in Europe and North America were paralleled by gender compromises—gender reform movements (most notably the women's suffrage movement) contesting the legal privileges of men and forcing concessions from the state. In this context, agendas of reform in masculinity emerged: the temperance movement, compassionate marriage, homosexual rights movements, leading eventually to the pursuit of androgyny in "men's liberation" in the 1970s (Kimmel and Mosmiller 1992). Not all reconstructions of masculinity, however, emphasized tolerance or moved toward androgyny. The vehement masculinity politics of fascism, for instance, emphasized dominance and difference and glorified violence, a pattern still found in contemporary racist movements (Tillner 1997).

Masculinities of Postcolonialism and Neoliberalism

The process of decolonization disrupted the gender hierarchies of the colonial order and, where armed struggle was involved, might have involved a deliberate cultivation of masculine hardness and violence (as in South Africa; see Xaba 1997). Some activists and theorists of liberation struggles celebrated this, as a necessary response to colonial violence and emasculation; women in liberation struggles were perhaps less impressed. However one evaluates the process, one of the consequences of decolonization was another round of disruptions of community-based gender orders and another step in the reorientation of masculinities toward national and international contexts.

Nearly half a century after the main wave of decolonization, the old hierarchies persist in new shapes. With the collapse of Soviet communism, the decline of postcolonial socialism, and the ascendancy of the new right in Europe and North America, world politics is more and more organized around the needs of transnational capital and the creation of global markets.

The neoliberal agenda has little to say, explicitly, about gender: it speaks a gender-neutral language of "markets," "individuals," and "choice." But the world in which neoliberalism is ascendant is still a gendered world, and neoliberalism has an implicit gender politics. The "individual" of neoliberal theory has in general the attributes and interests of a male entrepreneur, the attack on the welfare state generally weakens the position of women, while the increasingly unregulated power of transnational corporations places strategic power in the hands of particular groups of men. It is not surprising, then, that the installation of capitalism in Eastern Europe and the former Soviet Union has been accompanied by a reassertion of dominating masculinities and, in some situations, a sharp worsening in the social position of women.

We might propose, then, that the hegemonic form of masculinity in the current world gender order is the masculinity associated with those who control its dominant institutions: the business executives who operate in global markets, and the political executives who interact (and in many contexts, merge) with them. I will call this *trans-national business masculinity.* This is not readily available for ethnographic study, but we can get some clues to its character from its reflections in management literature, business journalism, and corporate self-promotion, and from studies of local business elites (e.g., Donaldson 1997).

As a first approximation, I would suggest this is a masculinity marked by increasing egocentrism, very conditional loyalties (even to the corporation), and a declining sense of responsibility for others (except for purposes of image making). Gee, Hull and Lankshear (1996), studying recent management textbooks, note the peculiar construction of the executive in "fast capitalism" as a person with no permanent commitments, except (in effect) to the idea of accumulation itself. Transnational business masculinity is characterized by a limited technical rationality (management theory), which is increasingly separate from science.

Transnational business masculinity differs from traditional bourgeois masculinity by its increasingly libertarian sexuality, with a growing tendency to commodify relations with women. Hotels catering to businessmen in most parts of the world now routinely offer pornographic videos, and in some parts of the world, there is a well-developed prostitution industry catering for international businessmen. Transnational business masculinity does not require bodily force, since the patriarchal dividend on which it rests is accumulated by impersonal, institutional means. But corporations increasingly use the exemplary bodies of elite sportsmen as a marketing tool (note the phenomenal growth of corporate "sponsorship" of sport in the last generation) and indirectly as a means of legitimation for the whole gender order.

MASCULINITY POLITICS ON A WORLD SCALE

Recognizing global society as an arena of masculinity formation allows us to pose new questions about masculinity politics. What social dynamics in the global arena give rise to masculinity politics, and what shape does global masculinity politics take?

The gradual creation of a world gender order has meant many local instabilities of gender. Gender instability is a familiar theme of poststructuralist theory, but this school of thought takes as a universal condition a situation that is historically specific. Instabilities range from the disruption of men's local cultural dominance as women move into the public realm and higher education, through the disruption of sexual identities that produced "queer" politics in the metropole, to the shifts in the urban intelligentsia that produced "the new sensitive man" and other images of gender change.

One response to such instabilities, on the part of groups whose power is challenged but still dominant, is to reaffirm *local* gender orthodoxies and hierarchies. A masculine fundamentalism is, accordingly, a common response in gender politics at present. A soft version, searching for an essential masculinity among myths and symbols, is offered by the mythopoetic men's movement in the United States and by the religious revivalists of the Promise Keepers (Messner 1997). A much harder version is found, in that country, in the right-wing militia movement brought to world attention by the Oklahoma City bombing (Gibson 1994), and in contemporary Afghanistan, if we can trust Western media reports, in the militant misogyny of the Taliban. It is no coincidence that in the two latter cases, hardline masculine fundamentalism goes together with a marked anti-internationalism. The world system—rightly enough—is seen as the source of pollution and disruption.

Not that the emerging global order is a hotbed of gender progressivism. Indeed, the neoliberal agenda for the reform of national and international economics involves closing down historic possibilities for gender reform. I have noted how it subverts the gender compromise represented by the metropolitan welfare state. It has also undermined the progressive-liberal agendas of sex role reform represented by affirmative action programs, anti-discrimination provisions, child care services, and the like. Right-wing parties and governments have been persistently cutting such programs, in the name of either individual liberties or global competitiveness. Through these means, the patriarchal dividend to men is defended or restored, without an *explicit* masculinity politics in the form of a mobilization of men.

Within the arenas of international relations, the international state, multinational corporations, and global markets, there is nevertheless a deployment of masculinities and a reasonably clear hegemony. The transnational business masculinity described above has had only one major competitor for hegemony in recent decades, the rigid, control-oriented masculinity of the military, and the military-style bureaucratic dictatorships of Stalinism. With the collapse of Stalinism and the end of the cold war, Big Brother (Orwell's famous parody of this form of masculinity) is a fading threat, and the more flexible, calculative, egocentric masculinity of the fast capitalist entrepreneur holds the world stage.

We must, however, recall two important conclusions of the ethnographic moment in masculinity research: that different forms of masculinity exist together and that hegemony is constantly subject to challenge. These are possibilities in the global arena too. Transnational business masculinity is not completely homogeneous; variations of it are embedded in different parts of the world system, which may not be completely compatible. We may distinguish a Confucian variant, based in East Asia, with a stronger commitment to hierarchy and social consensus, from a secularized Christian variant, based in North America, with more hedonism and individualism and greater tolerance for social conflict. In certain arenas, there is already conflict between the business and political leaderships embodying these forms of masculinity: initially over human rights versus Asian values, and more recently over the extent of trade and investment liberalization.

If these are contenders for hegemony, there is also the possibility of opposition to hegemony. The global circulation of "gay" identity (Altman 1996) is an important indication that nonhegemonic masculinities may operate in global arenas, and may even find a certain political articulation, in this case around human rights and AIDS prevention.

REFERENCES

Altman, Dennis. 1996. Rupture or continuity? The internationalisation of gay identities. *Social Text* 48 (3): 77–94.

Barrett, Frank J. 1996. The organizational construction of hegemonic masculinity: The case of the U.S. Navy. *Gender Work and Organization* 3 (3): 129–42.

BauSteineMaenner, ed. 1996. *Kritische Maennerforschung* [Critical research on men]. Berlin: Argument.

Bitterli, Urs. 1989. *Cultures in conflict: Encounters between European and non-European cultures, 1492–1800,* Stanford, CA: Stanford University Press.

Bolin, Anne. 1988. *In search of Eve: Transexual rites of passage.* Westport, CT: Bergin & Garvey.

Bulbeck, Chilla. 1992. *Australian women in Papua New Guinea: Colonial passages 1920–1960.* Cambridge, U.K.: Cambridge University Press.

Cain, P. J., and A. G. Hopkins. 1993. *British Imperialism: Innovation and expansion, 1688–1914.* New York: Longman.

Carrigan, Tim, Bob Connell, and John Lee. 1985. Toward a new sociology of masculinity. *Theory and Society* 14 (5): 551–604.

Chodorow, Nancy. 1994. *Femininities, masculinities, sexualities: Freud and beyond.* Lexington: University Press of Kentucky.

Cockburn, Cynthia. 1983. *Brothers: Male dominance and technological change.* London: Pluto.

Cohen, Jon. 1991. NOMAS: Challenging male supremacy. *Changing Men* (Winter/Spring): 45–46.

Connell, R. W. 1987. *Gender and power.* Cambridge, MA: Polity.

———. 1990a. An iron man: The body and some contradictions of hegemonic masculinity. In *Sport, men and the gender order: Critical feminist perspectives,* edited by Michael A. Messner and Donald F. Sabo, 83–95. Champaign. IL: Human Kinetics Books.

———. 1990b. The state, gender and sexual politics: Theory and appraisal. *Theory and Society* 19:507–44.

———. 1992. A very straight gay: Masculinity, homosexual experience and the dynamics of gender. *American Sociological Review* 57 (6): 735–51.

———. 1995. *Masculinities.* Cambridge, MA: Polity.

———. 1996. Teaching the boys: New research on masculinity, and gender strategies for schools. *Teachers College Record* 98 (2): 206–35.

Cornwall, Andrea, and Nancy Lindisfarne, eds. 1994. *Dislocating masculinity: Comparative ethnographies.* London: Routledge.

Dawson, Graham. 1991. The blond Bedouin: Lawrence of Arabia, imperial adventure and the imagining of English-British masculinity. In *Manful assertions: Masculinities in Britain since 1800,* edited by Michael Roper and John Tosh, 113–44. London: Routledge.

Donaldson, Mike. 1991. *Time of our lives: Labour and love in the working class.* Sydney: Allen & Unwin.

———. 1997. Growing up very rich: The masculinity of the hegemonic. Paper presented at the conference Masculinities: Renegotiating Genders, June, University of Wollongong, Australia.

Enloe, Cynthia. 1990. *Bananas, beaches and bases: Making feminist sense of international politics.* Berkeley: University of California Press.

Featherstone, Mike. 1995. *Undoing culture: Globalization, postmodernism and identity.* London: Sage.

Foley, Douglas E. 1990. *Learning capitalist culture: Deep in the heart of Tejas.* Philadelphia: University of Pennsylvania Press.

Fuentes, Annette, and Barbara Ehrenreich. 1983. *Women in the global factory.* Boston: South End.

Gee, James Paul, Glynda Hall, and Colin Lankshear. 1996. *The new work order: Behind the language of the new capitalism.* Sydney: Allen & Unwin.

Gender Equality Ombudsman. 1997. *The father's quota.* Information sheet on parental leave entitlements, Oslo.

Gibson, J. William. 1994. *Warrior dreams: Paramilitary culture in post-Vietnam America.* New York: Hill and Wang.

Hagemann-White, Carol, and Maria S. Rerrich, eds. 1988. *FrauenMaennerBilder* (Women, Imaging, Men). Bielefeld: AJZ-Verlag.

Hearn, Jeff. 1987. *The gender of oppression: Men, masculinity and the critique of Marxism.* Brighton, U.K.: Wheatsheaf.

Herdt, Gilbert H. 1981. *Guardians of the flutes: Idioms of masculinity.* New York: McGraw-Hill.

———. ed. 1984. *Ritualized homosexuality in Melanesia.* Berkeley: University of California Press.

Heward, Christine. 1988. *Making a man of him: Parents and their sons' education at an English public school 1929–1950.* London: Routledge.

Hinsch, Bret. 1990. *Passions of the cut sleeve: The male homosexual tradition in China.* Berkeley: University of California Press.

Hirst, Paul, and Grahame Thompson. 1996. *Globalization in question: The international economy and the possibilities of governance.* Cambridge, MA: Polity.

Hollstein, Walter. 1992. *Machen Sie Platz, mein Herr! Teilen statt Herrschen* [Sharing instead of dominating]. Hamburg: Rowohlt.

Hollway, Wendy. 1994. Separation, integration and difference: Contradictions in a gender regime. In *Power/gender: Social relations in theory and practice,* edited by H. Lorraine Radtke and Henderikus Stam, 247–69. London: Sage.

Holter, Oystein Gullvag. 1997. Gender, patriarchy and capitalism: A social forms analysis. Ph.D. diss., University of Oslo, Faculty of Social Science.

Hondagneu-Sotelo, Pierrette, and Michael A. Messner. 1994. Gender displays and men's power: The "new man" and the Mexican immigrant man. In *Theorizing masculini-*

ties, edited by Harry Brod and Michael Kaufman, 200–218. Twin Oaks, CA: Sage.

Ito Kimio. 1993. *Otokorashisa-no-yukue* [Directions for masculinities]. Tokyo: Shinyo-sha.

Jolly, Margaret. 1997. From point Venus to Bali Ha'i: Eroticism and exoticism in representations of the Pacific. In *Sites of desire, economies of pleasure: Sexualities in Asia and the Pacific,* edited by Lenore Manderson and Margaret Jolly, 99–122. Chicago: University of Chicago Press.

Kandiyoti, Deniz. 1994. The paradoxes of masculinity: Some thoughts on segregated societies. In *Dislocating masculinity: Comparative ethnographies,* edited by Andrea Cornwall and Nancy Lindisfarne, 197–213. London: Routledge.

Kaufman, Michael. 1997. Working with men and boys to challenge sexism and end men's violence. Paper presented at UNESCO expert group meeting on Male Roles and Masculinities in the Perspective of a Culture of Peace, September, Oslo.

Kimmel, Michael S. 1987. Rethinking "masculinity": New directions in research. In *Changing men: New directions in research on men and masculinity,* edited by Michael S. Kimmel, 9–24. Newbury Park, CA: Sage.

———. 1996. *Manhood in America: A cultural history.* New York: Free Press.

Kimmel, Michael S., and Thomas P. Mosmiller, eds. 1992. *Against the tide: Pro-feminist men in the United States, 1776–1990, a documentary history.* Boston: Beacon.

Kindler, Heinz. 1993. *Maske(r)ade: Jungen- und Maennerarbeit fuer die Pratis* [Work with youth and men]. Neuling: Schwaebisch Gmuend und Tuebingen.

Kinmonth, Earl H. 1981. *The self-made man in Meiji Japanese thought: From Samurai to salary man.* Berkeley: University of California Press.

Kipling, Rudyard. [1901] 1987. *Kim.* London: Penguin.

Klein, Alan M. 1993. *Little big men: Bodybuilding subculture and gender construction.* Albany: State University of New York Press.

Klein, Uta. 1997. Our best boys: The making of masculinity in Israeli society. Paper presented at UNESCO expert group meeting on Male Roles and Masculinities in the Perspectives of a Culture of Peace, September, Oslo.

Lewes, Kenneth. 1988. *The psychoanalytic theory of male homosexuality.* New York: Simon & Schuster.

MacDonald, Robert H. 1994. *The language of empire: Myths and metaphors of popular imperialism, 1880–1918.* Manchester, U.K.: Manchester University Press.

McElhinny, Bonnie. 1994. An economy of affect: Objectivity, masculinity and the gendering of police work. In *Dislocating masculinity: Comparative ethnographies,* edited by Andrea Cornwall and Nancy Lindisfarne, 159–71. London: Routledge.

McKay, Jim, and Debbie Huber. 1992. Anchoring media images of technology and sport. *Women's Studies International Forum* 15 (2): 205–18.

Messerschmidt, James W. 1997. *Crime as structured action: Gender, race, class, and crime in the making.* Thousand Oaks, CA: Sage.

Messner, Michael A. 1992. *Power at play: Sports and the problem of masculinity.* Boston: Beacon.

———. 1997. *The politics of masculinities: Men in movements.* Thousand Oaks, CA: Sage.

Metz-Goeckel, Sigrid, and Ursula Mueller. 1986. *Der Mann: Die Brigitte-Studie* [The male]. Beltz: Weinheim & Basel.

Mies, Maria. 1986. *Patriarchy and accumulation on a world scale: Women in the international division of labour.* London: Zed.

Moodie, T. Dunbar. 1994. *Going for gold: Men, mines, and migration.* Johannesburg: Witwatersand University Press.

Morrell, Robert. 1994. Boys, gangs, and the making of masculinity in the White secondary schools of Natal, 1880–1930. *Masculinities* 2 (2): 56–82.

———. ed. 1996. *Political economy and identities in KwaZulu-Natal: Historical and social perspectives.* Durban, Natal: Indicator Press.

Nakamura, Akira. 1994. *Watashi-no Danseigaku* [My men's studies]. Tokyo: Kindaibugei-sha.

Oftung, Knut, ed. 1994. *Menns bilder og bilder av menn* [Images of men]. Oslo: Likestillingsradet.

Phillips, Jock. 1987. *A man's country? The image of the Pakeha male, a history.* Auckland: Penguin.

Poynting, S., G. Noble, and P. Tabar. 1997. "Intersections" of masculinity and ethnicity: A study of male Lebanese immigrant youth in Western Sydney. Paper presented at the conference Masculinities: Renegotiating Genders, June, University of Wollongong, Australia.

Roper, Michael. 1991. Yesterday's model: Product fetishism and the British company man, 1945–85. In *Manful assertions: Masculinities in Britain since 1800,* edited by Michael Roper and John Tosh, 190–211. London: Routledge.

Schwalbe, Michael. 1996. *Unlocking the iron cage: The men's movement gender politics, and the American culture.* New York: Oxford University Press.

Segal, Lynne. 1997. *Slow motion: Changing masculinities, changing men.* 2d ed. London: Virago.

Seidler, Victor J. 1991. *Achilles heel reader: Men, sexual politics and socialism.* London: Routledge.

Shire, Chenjerai. 1994. Men don't go to the moon: Language, space and masculinities in Zimbabwe. In *Dislocating masculinity: Comparative ethnographies,* edited by Andrea Cornwall and Nancy Lindisfarne, 147–58. London: Routledge.

Simpson, Amelia. 1993. *Xuxa: The mega-marketing of a gender, race and modernity.* Philadelphia: Temple University Press.

Sinha, Mrinalini. 1995. *Colonial masculinity: The manly Englishman and the effeminate Bengali in the late nineteenth century.* Manchester, U.K.: Manchester University Press.

Taylor, Debbie. 1985. Women: An analysis. In *Women: A world report,* 1–98. London: Methuen.

Theberge, Nancy. 1991. Reflections on the body in the sociology of sport. *Quest* 43:123–34.

Thorne, Barrie. 1993. *Gender play: Girls and boys in school.* New Brunswick. NJ: Rutgers University Press.

Tillner, Georg. 1997. Masculinity and xenophobia. Paper presented at UNESCO meeting on Male Roles and Masculinities in the Perspective of a Culture of Peace, September, Oslo.

Tomsen, Stephen. 1997. A top night: Social protest, masculinity and the culture of drinking violence. *British Journal of Criminology* 37 (1): 90–103.

Tosh, John. 1991. Domesticity and manliness in the Victorian middle class: The family of Edward White Benson. In *Manful assertions: Masculinities in Britain since 1800,* edited by Michael Roper and John Tosh, 44–73. London: Routledge.

United Nations Educational, Scientific and Cultural Organization (UNESCO). 1997. *Male roles and masculinities in the perspective of a culture of peace: Report of expert group meeting, Oslo, 24–28 September 1997.* Paris: Women and a Culture of Peace Programme, Culture of Peace Unit, UNESCO.

Walby, Sylvia. 1990. *Theorizing patriarchy.* Oxford, U.K.: Blackwell.

Walker, James C. 1988. *Louts and legends: Male youth culture in an inner-city school.* Sydney: Allen & Unwin.

Wallerstein, Immanuel. 1974. *The modern world-system: Capitalist agriculture and the origins of the European world-economy in the sixteenth century.* New York: Academic Press.

Whitson, David. 1990. Sport in the social construction of masculinity. In *Sport, men, and the gender order: Critical feminist perspectives,* edited by Michael A. Messner and Donald F. Sabo, 19–29. Champaign, IL: Human Kinetics Books.

Widersprueche. 1995. Special Issue: Maennlichkeiten. Vol. 56/57.

Williams, Walter L. 1986. *The spirit and the flesh: Sexual diversity in American Indian culture.* Boston: Beacon.

Xaba, Thokozani. 1997. Masculinity in a transitional society: The rise and fall of the "young lions." Paper presented at the conference Masculinities in Southern Africa, June, University of Natal-Durban, Durban.

5

Global Woman

BARBARA EHRENREICH
ARLIE RUSSELL HOCHSCHILD

"Whose baby are you?" Josephine Perera, a nanny from Sri Lanka, asks Isadora, her pudgy two-year-old charge in Athens, Greece.

Thoughtful for a moment, the child glances toward the closed door of the next room, in which her mother is working, as if to say, "That's my mother in there."

"No, you're *my* baby," Josephine teases, tickling Isadora lightly. Then, to settle the issue, Isadora answers, "Together!" She has two mommies—her mother and Josephine. And surely a child loved by many adults is richly blessed.

In some ways, Josephine's story—which unfolds in an extraordinary documentary film, *When Mother Comes Home for Christmas,* directed by Nilita Vachani—describes an unparalleled success. Josephine has ventured around the world, achieving a degree of independence her mother could not have imagined, and amply supporting her three children with no help from her ex-husband, their father. Each month she mails a remittance check from Athens to Hatton, Sri Lanka, to pay the children's living expenses and school fees. On her Christmas visit home, she bears gifts of pots, pans, and dishes. While she makes payments on a new bus that Suresh, her oldest son, now drives for a living, she is also saving for a modest dowry for her daughter, Norma. She dreams of buying a new house in which the whole family can live. In the meantime, her work as a nanny enables Isadora's parents to devote themselves to their careers and avocations.

But Josephine's story is also one of wrenching global inequality. While Isadora enjoys the attention of three adults, Josephine's three children in Sri Lanka have been far less lucky. According to Vachani, Josephine's youngest child, Suminda, was two—Isadora's age—when his mother first left home to work in Saudi Arabia. Her middle child, Norma, was nine; her oldest son, Suresh, thirteen. From Saudi Arabia, Josephine found her way first to Kuwait, then to Greece. Except for one two-month trip home, she has lived apart from her children for ten years. She writes them weekly letters, seeking news of relatives, asking about school, and complaining that Norma doesn't write back.

Although Josephine left the children under her sister's supervision, the two youngest have shown signs of real distress. Norma has attempted suicide three times. Suminda, who was twelve when the film was made, boards in a grim, Dickensian orphanage that forbids talk during meals and showers. He visits his aunt on holidays. Although the oldest, Suresh, seems to be on good terms with his mother, Norma is tearful and sullen, and Suminda does poorly in school, picks quarrels, and otherwise seems withdrawn from the world. Still, at the end of the film, we see Josephine once again leave her three children in Sri Lanka to return to Isadora in Athens. For Josephine can either live with her children in desperate poverty or make money by living apart from them. Unlike her affluent First World employers, she cannot both live with her family and support it.

Thanks to the process we loosely call "globalization," women are on the move as never before in history. In images familiar to the West from television commercials for credit cards, cell phones, and airlines, female executives jet about the world, phoning home from luxury hotels and reuniting with eager children in airports. But we hear much less about a far more prodigious flow of female labor and energy: the increasing migration of millions of women from poor countries to rich ones, where they serve as nannies, maids, and sometimes sex workers. In the absence of help from male partners, many women have succeeded in tough "male world" careers only by turning over the care of their children, elderly parents, and homes to women from the Third World. This is the female underside of globalization, whereby millions of Josephines from poor countries in the south migrate to do the "women's work" of the north—work that affluent women are no longer able or willing to do. These migrant workers often leave their own children in the care of grandmothers, sisters, and sisters-in-law. Sometimes a young daughter is drawn out of school to care for her younger siblings.

This pattern of female migration reflects what could be called a world-wide gender revolution. In both rich and poor countries, fewer families can rely solely on a male breadwinner. In the United States, the earning power of most men has declined since 1970, and many women have gone out to "make up the difference." By one recent estimate, women were the sole, primary, or coequal earners in more than half of American families (Gallinsky and Friedman 1995). So the question arises: Who will take care of the children, the sick, the elderly? Who will make dinner and clean house?

While the European or American woman commutes to work an average twenty-eight minutes a day, many nannies from the Philippines, Sri Lanka, and India cross the globe to get to their jobs. Some female migrants from the Third World do find something like "liberation," or at least the chance to become independent breadwinners and to improve their children's material lives. Other, less fortunate migrant women end up in the control of criminal employers—their passports stolen, their mobility blocked, forced to work without pay in brothels or to provide sex along with cleaning and child-care services in affluent homes. But even in more typical cases, where benign employers pay wages on time, Third World migrant women achieve their success only by assuming the cast-off domestic roles of middle- and high-income women in the First World—roles that have been previously rejected, of course, by men. And their "commute" entails a cost we have yet to fully comprehend.

The migration of women from the Third World to do "women's work" in affluent countries has so far received little scholarly or media attention—for reasons that are easy enough to guess. First, many, though by no means all, of the new female migrant workers are women of color, and therefore subject to the racial "discounting" routinely experienced by, say, Algerians in France, Mexicans in the United States, and Asians in the United Kingdom. Add to racism the private "indoor" nature of so much of the new migrants' work. Unlike factory workers, who congregate in large numbers, or taxi drivers, who are visible on the street, nannies and maids are often hidden away, one or two at a time, behind closed doors in private homes. Because of the illegal nature of their work, most sex workers are even further concealed from public view.

At least in the case of nannies and maids, another factor contributes to the invisibility of migrant women and their work—one that, for their affluent employers, touches closer to home. The Western culture of individualism, which finds extreme expression in the United States, militates against acknowledging help or human interdependency of nearly any kind. Thus, in the time-pressed upper middle class, servants are no longer displayed as status symbols, decked out in white caps and aprons, but often remain in the background, or disappear when company comes. Furthermore, affluent careerwomen increasingly earn their status not through leisure, as they might have a century ago, but by apparently "doing it all"—producing a fulltime career, thriving children, a contented spouse, and a well-managed home. In order to preserve this illusion, domestic workers and nannies make the house hotel-room perfect, feed and bathe the children, cook and clean up—and then magically fade from sight.

The lifestyles of the First World are made possible by a global transfer of the services associated with a wife's traditional role—child care, home-making, and sex—from poor countries to rich ones. To generalize and perhaps oversimplify: in an earlier phase of imperialism, northern countries extracted natural resources and agricultural products—rubber, metals, and sugar, for example—from lands they conquered and colonized. Today, while still relying on Third World countries for agricultural and industrial labor, the wealthy countries also seek to extract something harder to measure and quantify, something that can look very much like love. Nannies like Josephine bring the distant families that employ them real maternal affection, no doubt enhanced by the heartbreaking absence of their own children in the poor countries they leave behind. Similarly, women who migrate from country to country to work as maids bring not only their muscle power but an attentiveness to detail and to the human relationships in the household that might otherwise have been invested in their own families. Sex workers offer the simulation of sexual and romantic love, or at least transient sexual companionship. It is as if the wealthy parts of the world are running short on precious emotional and sexual resources and have had to turn to poorer regions for fresh supplies.

There are plenty of historical precedents for this globalization of traditional female services. In the ancient Middle East, the women of populations defeated in war were routinely enslaved and hauled off to serve as household workers and concubines for the victors. Among the Africans brought to North America as slaves in the sixteenth through nineteenth centuries, about a third were women and children, and many of those women were pressed to be concubines, domestic servants, or both. Nineteenth-century Irishwomen—along with many rural Englishwomen—migrated to English towns and cities to work as domestics in the homes of the growing upper middle class. Services thought to be innately feminine—child care, housework, and sex—often win little recognition or pay. But they have always been sufficiently in demand to transport over long distances if necessary. What is new today is the sheer number of female migrants and the very long distances they travel. Immigration statistics show huge numbers of women in motion, typically from poor countries to rich. Although the gross statistics give little clue as to the jobs women eventually take, there are reasons to infer that much of their work is "caring work," performed either in private homes or in institutional settings such as hospitals, hospices, child-care centers, and nursing homes.

The statistics are, in many ways, frustrating. We have information on legal migrants but not on illegal migrants, who, experts tell us, travel in equal if not greater numbers. Furthermore, many Third World countries lack data for past years, which makes it hard to trace trends over time; or they use varying methods of gathering information, which makes it hard to compare one country with another. Nevertheless, the trend is clear enough for some scholars . . . to speak of a "feminization of migration." From 1950 to 1970, for example, men predominated in labor migration to northern Europe from Turkey, Greece, and North Africa. Since then, women have been replacing men. In 1946, women were fewer than 3 percent of the Algerians and Moroccans living in France; by 1990, they were more than 40 percent. Overall, half of the world's 120 million legal and illegal migrants are now believed to be women.

Patterns of international migration vary from region to region, but women migrants from a surprising number of sending countries actually outnumber men, sometimes by a wide margin. For example, in the 1990s, women make up over half of Filipino migrants to all countries and 84 percent of Sri Lankan migrants to the Middle East. Indeed, by 1993 statistics, Sri Lankan women such as Josephine vastly outnumbered Sri Lankan men as migrant workers who'd left for Saudi Arabia, Kuwait, Lebanon, Oman, Bahrain, Jordan, and Qatar, as well as to all countries of the Far East, Africa, and Asia. About half of the migrants leaving Mexico, India, Korea, Malaysia, Cyprus, and Swaziland to work elsewhere are also women. Throughout the 1990s women outnumbered men among migrants to the United States, Canada, Sweden, the United Kingdom, Argentina, and Israel.

Most women, like men, migrate from the south to the north and from poor countries to rich ones. Typically, migrants go to the nearest comparatively rich country, preferably one whose language they speak or whose religion and culture they share. There are also local migratory flows: from northern to southern Thailand, for instance, or from East Germany to West. But of the regional or cross-regional flows, four stand out. One goes from Southeast Asia to the oil-rich Middle and Far East—from Bangladesh, Indonesia, the Philippines, and Sri Lanka to Bahrain, Oman, Kuwait, Saudi Arabia, Hong Kong, Malaysia, and Singapore. Another stream of migration goes from the former Soviet bloc to western Europe—from Russia, Romania, Bulgaria, and Albania to Scandinavia, Germany, France, Spain, Portugal, and England. A third goes from south to north in the Americas, including the stream from Mexico to the United States, which scholars say is the longest-running labor migration in the world. A fourth stream moves from Africa to various parts of Europe. France receives many female migrants from Morocco, Tunisia, and Algeria. Italy receives female workers from Ethiopia, Eritrea, and Cape Verde.

Female migrants overwhelmingly take up work as maids or domestics. As women have become an ever greater proportion of migrant workers, receiving countries reflect a dramatic influx of foreign-born domestics. In the United States, African-American women, who accounted for 60 percent of domestics in the 1940s, have been largely replaced by Latinas, many of them recent migrants from Mexico and Central America. In England, Asian migrant women have displaced the Irish and Portuguese domestics of the past. In French cities, North African women have replaced rural French girls. In western Germany, Turks and women from the former East Germany have replaced rural native-born women. Foreign females from countries outside the European Union made up only 6 percent of all domestic workers in 1984. By 1987, the percentage had jumped to 52, with most coming from the Philippines, Sri Lanka, Thailand, Argentina, Colombia, Brazil, El Salvador, and Peru.

The governments of some sending countries actively encourage women to migrate in search of domestic jobs, reasoning that migrant women are more likely than their male counterparts to send their hard-earned wages to their families rather than spending the money on themselves. In general, women send home anywhere from half to nearly all of what they earn. These remittances have a significant impact on the lives of children, parents, siblings, and wider networks of kin—as well as on cash-strapped Third World governments. Thus, before Josephine left for Athens, a program sponsored by the Sri Lankan government taught her how to use a microwave oven, a vacuum cleaner, and an electric mixer. As she awaited her flight, a song piped into the airport departure lounge extolled the opportunity to earn money abroad. The songwriter was in the pay of the Sri Lanka Bureau of Foreign Employment, an office devised to encourage women to migrate. The lyrics say:

After much hardship, such difficult times
How lucky I am to work in a foreign land.
As the gold gathers so do many greedy flies.
But our good government protects us from them.
After much hardship, such difficult times,
How lucky I am to work in a foreign land.
I promise to return home with treasures for everyone.

Why this transfer of women's traditional services from poor to rich parts of the world? The reasons are, in a crude way, easy to guess. Women in Western countries have increasingly taken on paid work, and hence need others—paid domestics and caretakers for children and elderly people—to replace them. For their part, women in poor countries have an obvious incentive to migrate: relative and absolute poverty. The "care deficit" that has emerged in the wealthier countries as women enter the workforce *pulls* migrants from the Third World and postcommunist nations; poverty *pushes* them.

In broad outline, this explanation holds true. Throughout western Europe, Taiwan, and Japan, but above all in the United States, England, and Sweden, women's employment has increased dramatically since the 1970s. In the United States, for example, the proportion of women in paid work rose from 15 percent of mothers of children six and under in 1950 to 65 percent today. Women now make up 46 percent of the U.S. labor force. Three-quarters of mothers of children eighteen and under and nearly two-thirds of mothers of children age one and younger now work for pay. Furthermore, according to a recent International Labor Organization study, working Americans averaged longer hours at work in the late 1990s than they did in the 1970s. By some measures, the number of hours spent at work have increased more for women than for men, and especially for women in managerial and professional jobs.

Meanwhile, over the last thirty years, as the rich countries have grown much richer, the poor countries have become—in both absolute and relative terms—poorer. Global inequalities in wages are particularly striking. In Hong Kong, for instance, the wages of a Filipina domestic are about fifteen times the amount she could make as a schoolteacher back in the Philippines. In addition, poor countries turning to the IMF or World Bank for loans are often forced to undertake measures of so-called structural adjustment, with disastrous results for the poor and especially for poor women and children. To qualify for loans, governments are usually required to devalue their currencies, which turns the hard currencies of rich countries into gold and the soft currencies of poor countries into straw. Structural adjustment programs also call for cuts in support for "noncompetitive industries," and for the reduction of public services such as health care and food subsidies for the poor. Citizens of poor countries, women as well as men, thus have a strong incentive to seek work in more fortunate parts of the world.

But it would be a mistake to attribute the globalization of women's work to a simple synergy of needs among women—one group, in the affluent countries, needing help and the other, in poor countries, needing jobs. For one thing, this formulation fails to account for the marked failure of First World governments to meet the needs created by its women's entry into the workforce. The downsized American—and to a lesser degree, western European—welfare state has become a "deadbeat dad." Unlike the rest of the industrialized world, the United States does not offer public child care for working mothers, nor does it ensure paid family and medical leave. Moreover, a series of state tax revolts in the 1980s reduced the number of hours public libraries were open and slashed school-enrichment and after-school programs. Europe did not experience anything comparable. Still, tens of millions of western European women are in the workforce who were not before—and there has been no proportionate expansion in public services.

Secondly, any view of the globalization of domestic work as simply an arrangement among women completely omits the role of men. Numerous studies, including some of our own, have shown that as American women took on paid employment, the men in their families did little to increase their contribution to the work of the home. For example, only one out of every five men among the working couples whom Hochschild interviewed for *The Second Shift* (Hochschild, 1989). In the 1980s shared the work at home, and later studies suggest that while working mothers are doing somewhat less housework than their counterparts twenty years ago, most men are doing only a little more. With divorce, men frequently abdicate their child-care responsibilities to their ex-wives. In most cultures of the First World outside the United States, powerful traditions even more firmly discourage husbands from doing "women's work." So, strictly speaking, the presence of immigrant nannies does not enable affluent women to enter the workforce; it enables affluent *men* to continue avoiding the second shift.

The men in wealthier countries are also, of course, directly responsible for the demand for immigrant sex workers—as well as for the sexual abuse of many migrant women who work as domestics. Why, we wondered, is there a particular demand for "imported" sexual partners? Part of the answer may lie in the fact that new immigrants often take up the least desirable work, and, thanks to the AIDS epidemic, prostitution has become a job that ever fewer women deliberately choose. But perhaps some of this demand grows out of the erotic lure of the "exotic." Immigrant women may seem desirable sexual partners for the same reason that First World employers believe them to be especially gifted as caregivers: they are thought to embody the traditional feminine qualities of nurturance, docility, and eagerness to please. Some men feel nostalgic for these qualities, which they associate with a bygone way of life. Even as many wage-earning Western women assimilate to the competitive culture of "male" work and ask respect for making it in a man's world, some men seek in the "exotic Orient" or "hot-blooded tropics" a woman from the imagined past.

Of course, not all sex workers migrate voluntarily. An alarming number of women and girls are trafficked by smugglers and sold into bondage. Because trafficking is illegal and secret, the numbers are hard to know with any certainty. Kevin Bales estimates that in Thailand alone, a country of 60 million, half a million to a million women are prostitutes, and one out of every twenty of these is enslaved (Bales 1999). Many of these women are daughters whom northern hill-tribe families have sold to brothels in the cities of the South. Believing the promises of jobs and money, some begin the voyage willingly, only to discover days later that the "arrangers" are traffickers who steal their passports, define them as debtors, and enslave them as prostitutes. Other women and girls are kidnapped, or sold by their impoverished families, and then trafficked to brothels. Even worse fates befall women from neighboring Laos and Burma, who flee crushing poverty and repression at home only to fall into the hands of Thai slave traders.

If the factors that pull migrant women workers to affluent countries are not as simple as they at first appear, neither are the factors that push them. Certainly relative poverty plays a major role, but, interestingly, migrant women often do not come from the poorest classes of their societies. In fact, they are typically more affluent and better educated than male migrants. Many female migrants from the Philippines and Mexico, for example, have high school or college diplomas and have held middle-class—albeit low-paid—jobs back home. One study of Mexican migrants suggests that the trend is toward increasingly better-educated female migrants. Thirty years ago, most Mexican-born maids in the United States had been poorly educated maids in Mexico. Now a majority have high school degrees and have held clerical, retail, or professional jobs before leaving for the United States. Such women are likely to be enterprising and adventurous enough to resist the social pressures to stay home and accept their lot in life.

Noneconomic factors—or at least factors that are not immediately and directly economic—also influence a woman's decision to emigrate. By migrating, a woman may escape the expectation that she care for elderly family members, relinquish her paycheck to a husband or father, or defer to an abusive husband. Migration may also be a practical response to a failed marriage and the need to provide for children without male help. In the Philippines, Rhacel Salazar Parreñas (2002) tells us, migration is sometimes called a "Philippine divorce." And there are forces at work that may be making the men of poor countries less desirable as husbands. Male unemployment runs high in the countries that supply female domestics to the First World. Unable to make a living, these men often grow demoralized and cease contributing to their families in other ways. Many female migrants, tell of unemployed husbands who drink or gamble their remittances away. Notes one study of Sri Lankan women working as maids in the Persian Gulf: "It is not unusual . . . for the women to find upon their return that their Gulf wages by and large have been squandered on alcohol, gambling and other dubious undertakings while they were away" (Gamburd, 2002).

To an extent then, the globalization of child care and housework brings the ambitious and independent women of the world together: the career-oriented upper-middle-class woman of an affluent nation and the striving woman from a crumbling Third World or postcommunist economy. Only it does not bring them together in the way that second-wave feminists in affluent countries once liked to imagine—as sisters and allies struggling to achieve common goals. Instead, they come together as mistress and maid, employer and employee, across a great divide of privilege and opportunity.

This trend toward global redivision of women's traditional work throws new light on the entire process of globalization. Conventionally, it is the poorer countries that are thought to be dependent on the richer ones—a dependency symbolized by the huge debt they owe to global financial institutions. What we explore, however, is a dependency that works in the other direction, and it is a dependency of a particularly intimate kind. Increasingly often, as affluent and middle-class families in the First World come to depend on migrants from poorer regions to provide child care, homemaking, and sexual services, a global relationship arises that in some ways mirrors the traditional relationship between the sexes. The First World takes on a role like that of the old-fashioned male in the family—pampered, entitled, unable to cook, clean, or find his socks. Poor countries take on a role like that of the traditional woman within the family—patient, nurturing, and self-denying. A division of labor feminists critiqued when it was "local" has now, metaphorically speaking, gone global.

To press this metaphor a bit further, the resulting relationship is by no means a "marriage," in the sense of being openly acknowledged. In fact, it is striking how invisible the globalization of women's work remains, how little it is noted or discussed in the First World. Trend spotters have had almost nothing to say about the fact that increasing numbers of affluent First World children and elderly persons are tended by immigrant care workers or live in homes cleaned by immigrant maids. Even the political groups we might expect to be concerned about this trend—antiglobalization and feminist activists—often seem to have noticed only the most extravagant abuses, such as trafficking and female enslavement. So if a metaphorically gendered relationship has developed between rich and poor countries, it is less like a marriage and more like a secret affair.

But it is a "secret affair" conducted in plain view of the children. Little Isadora and the other children of the First World raised by "two mommies" may be learning more than their ABC's from a loving surrogate parent. In their own living rooms, they are learning a vast and tragic global politics. Children see. But they also learn how to disregard what they see. They learn how adults make the visible invisible. That is their "early childhood education." . . .

The globalization of women's traditional role poses important challenges to anyone concerned about gender and economic inequity. How can we improve the lives and opportunities of migrant women engaged in legal occupations such as nannies and maids? How can we prevent trafficking and enslavement? More basically, can we find a way to counterbalance the systematic transfer of caring work from poor countries to rich, and the inevitable trauma of the children left behind? . . . Before we can hope to find activist solutions, we need to see these women as full human beings. They are strivers as well as victims, wives and mothers as well as workers—sisters, in other words, with whom we in the First World may someday define a common agenda.

REFERENCES

Bales, Kevin. 1999. *Disposable People: New Slavery in the Global Economy.* Berkeley: University of California Press.

Hochschild, Arlie Russell with Anne Machung. 1989. *The Second Shift.* New York: Viking Penguin.

Gallinsky, Ellen and Dana Friedman. 1995. *Woman: The New Providers.* Whirlpool Foundation Study, Part 1. New York: Families and Work Institute.

Gamburd, Michele. 2002. "Breadwinner No More," In *Global Woman.* Barbara Ehrenreich and Arlie Russell Hochschild (eds.), 190–206. New York: Metropolitan Books.

Parrenas, Rhacel Salazar. 2002. "The Care Crisis in The Philippines: Children and Transnational Families in the New Global Economy," In *Global Woman.* Barbara Ehrenreich and Arlie Russell Hochschild (eds.), 39–54. New York: Metropolitan Books.

6

Antiglobalization Pedagogies and Feminism

CHANDRA TALPADE MOHANTY

ANTIGLOBALIZATION STRUGGLES

. . . What does it mean to make antiglobalization a key factor for feminist theorizing and struggle? To illustrate my thinking about antiglobalization, let me focus on two specific sites where knowledge about globalization is produced. The first site is a pedagogical one and involves an analysis of the various strategies being used to internationalize (or globalize) the women's studies curriculum in U.S. colleges and universities. I argue that this move to internationalize women's studies curricula and the attendant pedagogies that flow from this is one of the main ways we can track a discourse of global feminism in the United States. Other ways of tracking global feminist discourses include analyzing the documents and discussions flowing out of the Beijing United Nations conference on women, and of course popular television and globalization scholarship I focus on is the emerging, notably ungendered and deracialized discourse on activism against globalization.

Antiglobalization Pedagogies

Let me turn to the struggles over the dissemination of a feminist cross-cultural knowledge base through pedagogical strategies "internationalizing" the women's studies curriculum. The problem of "the (gendered) color line" remains, but is more easily seen today as developments of transnational and global capital. While I choose to focus on women's studies curricula, my arguments hold for curricula in any discipline or academic field that seeks to internationalize or globalize its curriculum. I argue that the challenge for "internationalizing" women's studies is no different from the one involved in "racializing" women's studies in the 1980s, for very similar politics of knowledge come into play here.

So the question I want to foreground is the politics of knowledge in bridging the "local" and the "global" in women's studies. How we teach the "new" scholarship in women's studies is at least as important as the scholarship itself in the struggles over knowledge and citizenship in the U.S. academy. . . .

Chandra Talpade Mohanty, "Antiglobalization Pedagogies and Feminism," in *Feminism Without Borders: Decolonizing Theory, Practicing Solidarity,* pp. 237–251.

Drawing on my own work with U.S. feminist academic communities, I describe three pedagogical models used in "internationalizing" the women's studies curriculum and analyze the politics of knowledge at work. Each of these perspectives is grounded in particular conceptions of the local and the global, of women's agency, and of national identity, and each curricular model presents different stories and ways of crossing borders and building bridges. I suggest that a "comparative feminist studies" or "feminist solidarity" model is the most useful and productive pedagogical strategy for feminist cross-cultural work. It is this particular model that provides a way to theorize a complex relational understanding of experience, location, and history such that feminist cross-cultural work moves through the specific context to construct a real notion of universal and of democratization rather than colonization. It is through this model that we can put into practice the idea of "common differences" as the basis for deeper solidarity across differences and unequal power relations.

Feminist-as-Tourist Model This curricular perspective could also be called the "feminist as international consumer" or, in less charitable terms, the "white women's burden or colonial discourse" model. It involves a pedagogical strategy in which brief forays are made into non–Euro-American cultures, and particular sexist cultural practices addressed from an otherwise Eurocentric women's studies gaze. In other words, the "add women as global victims or powerful women and stir" perspective. This is a perspective in which the primary Euro-American narrative of the syllabus remains untouched, and examples from non-Western or Third World/South cultures are used to supplement and "add" to this narrative. The story here is quite old. The effects of this strategy are that students and teachers are left with a clear sense of the difference and distance between the local (defined as self, nation, and Western) and the global (defined as other, non-Western, and transnational). Thus the local is always grounded in nationalist assumptions—the United States or Western European nation-state provides a normative context. This strategy leaves power relations and hierarchies untouched since ideas about center and margin are reproduced along Eurocentric lines.

For example, in an introductory feminist studies course, one could include the obligatory day or week on dowry deaths in India, women workers in Nike factories in Indonesia, or precolonial matriarchies in West Africa, while leaving the fundamental identity of the Euro-American feminist on her way to liberation untouched. Thus Indonesian workers in Nike factories or dowry deaths in India stand in for the totality of women in these cultures. These women are not seen in their everyday lives (as Euro-American women are)—just in these stereotypical terms. Difference in the case of non–Euro-American women is thus congealed, not seen contextually with all of its contradictions. This pedagogical strategy for crossing cultural and geographical borders is based on a modernist paradigm, and the bridge between the local and the global becomes in fact a predominantly self-interested chasm. This perspective confirms the sense of the "evolved U.S./Euro feminist." While there is now more consciousness about not using an "add and stir" method in teaching about race and U.S. women of color, this does not appear to be the case in "internationalizing" women's studies. Experience in this context is assumed to be static and frozen into U.S.- or Euro-centered categories. Since in this paradigm feminism is always/already constructed as Euro-American in origin and development, women's lives and struggles outside this geographical context only serve to confirm or contradict this originary feminist (master) narrative. This model is the pedagogical counterpart of the orientalizing and colonizing Western feminist scholarship of the past decades. In fact it may remain the predominant model at this time. Thus implicit in this pedagogical strategy is the crafting of the "Third World difference," the creation of monolithic images of Third World/South women. This contrasts with images of Euro-American women who are vital, changing, complex, and central subjects within such a curricular perspective.

Feminist-as-Explorer Model This particular pedagogical perspective originates in area studies, where the "foreign" woman is the object and subject of knowledge and the larger intellectual project is entirely about countries other than the United States. Thus, here the local and the global are both defined as non–Euro-American. The focus on the international implies that it exists outside the U.S. nation-state. Women's, gender, and feminist issues are based on spatial/geographical and temporal/historical categories located elsewhere. Distance from "home" is fundamental to the definition of international in this framework. This strategy can result in students and teachers being left with a notion of difference and separateness, a sort of "us and them" attitude, but unlike the tourist model, the explorer perspective can provide a deeper, more contextual understanding of feminist issues in discretely defined geographical and cultural spaces. However, unless these discrete spaces are taught in relation to one another, the story told is usually a cultural relativist one, meaning that differences between cultures are discrete and relative with no real connection or common basis for evaluation. The local and the global are here collapsed into the international that by definition excludes the United States. If the dominant discourse is the discourse of cultural relativism, questions of power, agency, justice, and common criteriafor critique and evaluation are silenced.

In women's studies curricula this pedagogical strategy is often seen as the most culturally sensitive way to "internationalize" the curriculum. For instance, entire courses on "Women in Latin America" or "Third World Women's Literature" or "Postcolonial Feminism" are added on to the predominantly U.S.-based curriculum as a way to "globalize" the feminist knowledge base. These courses can be quite sophisticated and complex studies, but they are viewed as entirely separate from the intellectual project of U.S. race and ethnic studies. The United States is not seen as part of "area studies," as white is not a color when one speaks of people of color. This is probably related to the particular history of institutionalization of area studies in the U.S. academy and its ties to U.S. imperialism. Thus areas to be studied/conquered "out there," never within the United States. The fact that area studies in U.S. academic settings were federally funded and conceived as having a political project in the service of U.S. geopolitical interests suggests the need examine the contemporary interests of these fields, especially as they relate to the logic of global capitalism. In addition, as Ella Shohat argues, it is to "reimagine the study of regions and cultures in a way that transcends the conceptual borders inherent in the global cartography of the cold war" (2001, 1271). The field of American studies is an interesting location to examine here, especially since its more recent focus on U.S. imperialism. However, American studies rarely falls under the purview of "area studies."

The problem with the feminist-as-explorer strategy is that globalization is an economic, political, and ideological phenomenon that actively brings the world and its various communities under connected and interdependent discursive and material regimes. The lives of women are connected and interdependent, albeit not the same, no matter which geographical area we happen to live in.

Separating area studies from race and ethnic studies thus leads to understanding or teaching about the global as a way of not addressing internal racism, capitalist hegemony, colonialism, and heterosexualization as central to processes of global domination, exploitation, and resistance. Global or international is thus understood apart from racism—as if racism were not central to processes of globalization and relations of rule at this time. An example of this pedagogical strategy in the context of the larger curriculum is the usual separation of "world cultures" courses from race and ethnic studies courses. Thus identifying the kinds of representations of (non-Euro-American) women mobilized by this pedagogical strategy, and the relation of these representations to implicit images of First World/North women are important foci for analysis. What kind of power is being exercised in this strategy? What kinds of ideas of agency and struggle are being consolidated? What are the potential effects of a kind of cultural relativism on our understandings of the differences and commonalities among communities of women around the world? Thus the feminist-as-explorer model has its own problems, and I believe this is an inadequate way of building a feminist cross-cultural knowledge base because in the context of an interwoven world with clear directionalities of power and domination, cultural relativism serves as an apology for the exercise of power.

The Feminist Solidarity or Comparative Feminist Studies Model This curricular strategy is based on the premise that the local and the global are not defined in terms of physical geography or territory but exist simultaneously and constitute each other. It is then the links, the relationships, between the local and the global that are foregrounded, and these links are conceptual, material, temporal, contextual, and so on. This framework assumes a comparative focus and analysis of the directionality of power no matter what the subject of the women's studies course is—and it assumes both distance and proximity (specific/universal) as its analytic strategy.

Differences and commonalities thus exist in relation and tension with each other in all contexts. What is emphasized are relations of mutuality, co-responsibility, and common interests, anchoring the idea of feminist solidarity. For example, within this model, one would not teach a U.S. women of color course with additions on Third World/South or white women, but a comparative course that shows the interconnectedness of the histories, experiences, and struggles of U.S. women of color, white women, and women from the Third World/South. By doing this kind of comparative teaching that is attentive to power, each historical experience illuminates the experiences of the others. Thus, the focus is not just on the intersections of race, class, gender, nation, and sexuality in different communities of women but on mutuality and coimplication, which suggests attentiveness to the interweaving of the histories of these communities. In addition the focus is simultaneously on individual and collective experiences of oppression and exploitation and of struggle and resistance.

Students potentially move away from the "add and stir" and the relativist "separate but equal" (or different) perspective to the coimplication/solidarity one. This solidarity perspective requires understanding the historical and experiential specificities and differences of women's lives as well as the historical and experiential connections between women from different national, racial, and cultural communities. Thus it suggests organizing syllabi around social and economic processes and histories of various communities of women in particular substantive areas like sex work, militarization, environmental justice, the prison/industrial complex, and human rights, and looking for points of contact and connection as well as disjunctures. It is important to always foreground not just the connections of domination but those of struggle and resistance as well.

In the feminist solidarity model the One-Third/Two-Thirds paradigm makes sense. Rather than Western/Third World, or North/South, or local/global seen as oppositional and incommensurate categories, the One-Third/Two-Thirds differentiation allows for teaching and learning about points of connection and distance among and between communities of women marginalized and privileged along numerous local and global dimensions. Thus the very notion of inside/outside necessary to the distance between local/global is transformed through the use of a One-Third/Two-Thirds paradigm, as both categories must be understood as containing difference/similarities, inside/outside, and distance/proximity. Thus sex work, militarization, human rights, and so on can be framed in their multiple local and global dimensions using the One-Third/Two-Thirds, social minority/social majority paradigm. I am suggesting then that we look at the women's studies curriculum in its entirety and that we attempt to use a comparative feminist studies model wherever possible.

I refer to this model as the feminist solidarity model because, besides its focus on mutuality and common interests, it requires one to formulate questions about connection and disconnection between activist women's movements around the world. Rather than formulating activism and agency in terms of discrete and disconnected cultures and nations, it allows us to frame agency and resistance across the borders of nation and culture. I think feminist pedagogy should not simply expose students to a particularized academic scholarship but that it should also envision the possibility of activism and struggle outside the academy. Political education through feminist pedagogy should teach active citizenship in such struggles for justice.

My recurring question is how pedagogies can supplement, consolidate, or resist the dominant logic of globalization. How do students learn about the inequities among women and men around the world? . . .

After almost two decades of teaching feminist studies in U.S. classrooms, it is clear to me that the way we theorize experience, culture, and subjectivity in relation to histories, institutional practice, and collective struggles determines the kind of stories we tell in the classroom. If these varied stories are to be taught such that students learn to democratize rather than colonize the experiences of different spatially and temporally located communities of women, neither a Eurocentric nor a cultural pluralist curricular practice will do. In fact narratives of historical experience are crucial to political thinking not because they present an unmediated version of the "truth" but because they can destabilize received truths and locate debate in the complexities and contradictions of historical life. . . . These are the kinds of stories we need to weave into a feminist solidarity pedagogical model.

Antiglobalization Scholarship and Movements

> Women's and girls' bodies determine democracy: free from violence and sexual abuse, free from malnutrition and environmental degradation, free to plan their families, free to not have families, free to choose their sexual lives and preferences
>
> —*Zillah Eisenstein,* Global Obscenities, *1998*

There is now an increasing and useful feminist scholarship critical of the practices and effects of globalization. Instead of attempting a comprehensive review of this scholarship, I want to draw attention to some of the most useful kinds of issues it raises. Let me turn, then, to a feminist reading of antiglobalization movements and argue for a more intimate, closer alliance between women's movements, feminist pedagogy, cross-cultural feminist theorizing, and these ongoing anticapitalist movements.

I return to an earlier question: What are the concrete effects of global restructuring on the "real" raced, classed, national, sexual bodies of women in the academy, in workplaces, streets, households, cyberspaces, neighborhoods, prisons, and in social movements? And how do we recognize these gendered effects in movements against globalization? Some of the most complex analyses of the centrality of gender in understanding economic globalization attempt to link questions of subjectivity, agency, and identity with those of political economy and the state. This scholarship argues persuasively for a need to rethink patriarchies and hegemonic masculinities in relation to present-day globalization and nationalisms, and it also attempts to retheorize the gendered aspects of the refigured relations of the state, the market, and civil society by focusing on unexpected and unpredictable sites of resistance to the often devastating effects of global restructuring on women. And it draws on a number of disciplinary paradigms and political perspectives in making the case for the centrality of gender in processes of global restructuring, arguing that the reorganization of gender is part of the global strategy of capitalism.

Women workers of particular caste/class, race, and economic status are necessary to the operation of the capitalist global economy. Women are not only the preferred candidates for particular jobs, but particular kinds of women—poor, Third and Two-Thirds World, working-class, and immigrant/migrant women—are the preferred workers in these global, "flexible" temporary job markets. The documented increase in the migration of poor, One-Third/Two-Thirds World women in search of labor across national borders has led to a rise in the international "maid trade" (Parrefias 2001) and in international sex trafficking and tourism. Many global cities now require and completely depend on the service and domestic labor of immigrant and migrant women. The proliferation of structural adjustment policies around the world has reprivatized women's labor by shifting the responsibility for social welfare from the state to the household and to women located there. The rise of religious fundamentalisms in conjunction with conservative nationalisms, which are also in part reactions to global capital and its cultural demands, has led to the policing of women's bodies in the streets and in the workplaces.

Global capital also reaffirms the color line in its newly articulated class structure evident in the prisons in the One-Third World. The effects of globalization and deindustrialization on the prison industry in the One-Third World leads to a related policing of the bodies of poor, One-Third/Two-Thirds World, immigrant and migrant women behind the concrete spaces and bars of privatized prisons. Angela Davis and Gina Dent (2001) argue that the political economy of U.S. prisons, and the punishment industry in the West/North, brings the intersection of gender, race, colonialism, and capitalism into sharp focus. Just as the factories and workplaces of global corporations seek and discipline the labor of poor, Third World/South, immigrant/migrant women, the prisons of Europe and the United States incarcerate disproportionately large numbers of women of color, immigrants, and noncitizens of African, Asian, and Latin American descent.

Making gender and power visible in the processes of global restructuring demands looking at, naming, and seeing the particular raced, and classed communities of women from poor countries as they are constituted as workers in sexual, domestic, and service industries; as prisoners; and as household managers and nurturers. . . .

While feminist scholarship is moving in important and useful directions in terms of a critique of global restructuring and the culture of globalization, I want to ask some of the same questions I posed in 1986 once again. In spite of the occasional exception, I think that much of present-day scholarship tends to reproduce particular "globalized" representations of women. Just as there is an Anglo-American masculinity produced in and by discourses of globalization, it is important to ask what the corresponding femininities being produced are. Clearly there is the ubiquitous global teenage girl factory worker, the domestic worker, and the sex worker. There is also the migrant/immigrant service worker, the refugee, the victim of war crimes, the woman-of-color prisoner who happens to be a mother and drug user, the consumer-housewife, and so on. There is also the mother-of-the-nation/religious bearer of traditional culture and morality.

Although these representations of women correspond to real people, they also often stand in for the contradictions and complexities of women's lives and roles. Certain images, such as that of the factory or sex worker, are often geographically located in the Third World/South, but many of the representations identified above are dispersed throughout the globe. Most refer to women of the Two-Thirds World, and some to women of the One-Third World. And a woman from the Two-Thirds World can live in the One-Third World. The point I am making here is that women are workers, mothers, or consumers in the global economy, but we are also all those things simultaneously. Singular and monolithic categorizations of women in discourses of globalization circumscribe ideas about experience, agency, and struggle. While there are other, relatively new images of women that also emerge in this discourse—the human rights worker or the NGO advocate, the revolutionary militant and the corporate bureaucrat—there is also a divide between false, overstated images of victimized and empowered womanhood, and they negate each other. We need to further explore how this divide plays itself out in terms of a social majority/minority, One-Third/Two-Thirds World characterization. The concern here is with whose agency is being colonized and who is privileged in these pedagogies and scholarship. These then are my new queries for the twenty-first century.

Because social movements are crucial sites for the construction of knowledge, communities, and identities, it is very important for feminists to direct themselves toward them. The antiglobalization movements of the last five years have proven that one does not have to be a multinational corporation, controller of financial capital, or transnational governing institution to cross national borders. These movements form an important site for examining the construction of transborder democratic citizenship. But first a brief characterization of antiglobalization movements is in order.

Unlike the territorial anchors of the anticolonial movements of the early twentieth century, antiglobalization movements have numerous spatial and social origins. These include anticorporate environmental movements such as the Narmada Bachao Andolan in central India and movements against environmental racism in the U.S. Southwest, as well as the antiagribusiness small-farmer movements around the world. The 1960s consumer movements, people's movements against the IMF and World Bank for debt cancelation and against structural adjustment programs, and the antisweatshop student movements in Japan, Europe, and the United States are also a part of the origins of the antiglobalization movements. In addition, the identity-based social movements of the late twentieth century (feminist, civil rights, indigenous rights, etc.) and the transformed U.S. labor movement of the 1990s also play a significant part in terms of the history of antiglobalization movements.

While women are present as leaders and participants in most of these antiglobalization movements, a feminist agenda only emerges in the post-Beijing "women's rights as human rights" movement and in some peace and environmental justice movements. In other words, while girls and women are central to the labor of global capital, antiglobalization work does not seem to draw on feminist analysis or strategies. Thus, while I have argued that feminists need to be anticapitalists, I would now argue that antiglobalization activists and theorists also need to be feminists. Gender is ignored as a category of analysis and a basis for organizing in most of the antiglobalization movements, and antiglobalization (and anticapitalist critique) does not appear to be central to feminist organizing projects, especially in the First World/North. In terms of women's movements, the earlier "sisterhood is global" form of internationalization of the women's movement has now shifted into the "human rights" arena. This shift in language from "feminism" to "women's rights" has been called the mainstreaming of the feminist movement—a successful attempt to raise the issue of violence against women on to the world stage.

If we look carefully at the focus of the antiglobalization movements, it is the bodies and labor of women and girls that constitute the heart of these struggles. For instance, in the environmental and ecological movements such as Chipko in India and indigenous movements against uranium mining and breast-milk contamination in the United States, women are not only among the leadership: their gendered and racialized bodies are the key to demystifying and combating the processes of recolonization put in place by corporate control of the environment. . . .

Women have been in leadership roles in some of the cross-border alliances against corporate injustice. Thus, making gender, and women's bodies and labor visible, and theorizing this visibility as a process of articulating a more inclusive politics are crucial aspects of feminist anticapitalist critique. Beginning from the social location of poor women of color of the Two-Thirds World is an important, even crucial, place for feminist analysis. . . .

A transnational feminist practice depends on building feminist solidarities across the divisions of place, identity, class, work, belief, and so on. In these very fragmented times it is both very difficult to build these alliances and also never more important to do so. Global capitalism both destroys the possibilities and also offers up new ones. . . .

REFERENCES

Elsenstein, Zillah R. 1998. *Global Obscenities: Patriarchy, Capitalism, and the Lure of Cyberfantasy.* New York: New York University Press.

Davis, Angela, and Gina Dent. 2001. "Prison as a Border: A Conversation on Gender, Globalization, and Punishment." *Signs* 26, no. 4 (summer): 1235–42.

Parrenas, Rachel Salazar. 2001. "Transgressing the Nation-State: The Partial Citizenship and 'Imagined (Global) Community' of Migrant Filipina Domestic Workers." *Signs* 26, no. 4 (summer): 1129–54.

Shohat, Ella. 2001. "Area Studies, Transnationalism, and the Feminist Production of Knowledge." *Signs* 26, no. 4 (summer): 1269–72.

PART II

Bodies

What are we to make of the old Freudian dictum that "biology is destiny?" Are women's and men's different *social* positions and activities simply reflections of *natural* differences between the sexes? The articles in this section show that this belief does not stand up to critical scrutiny. First, even when we acknowledge the fact that there are some average differences between women's and men's bodies (for instance, on average, men are taller than women), average differences are not categorical differences (e.g., some women are taller than some men). Second, average bodily differences between women and men do not necessarily translate into particular social structures or practices. In fact, recent research in the sociology of the body shows a dynamic, reciprocal relationship between bodies and their social environments. For example, boys and men have been encouraged and rewarded for "building" muscular bodies, while girls and women have been discouraged or punished for this. Even among today's fitness-conscious young women, most feel that "too much muscle" is antithetical to attractiveness. These social beliefs and practices result in more muscular male bodies, and "slimmed or toned" female bodies that, together, appear to reflect "natural" differences.

In short, average bodily differences between women and men are at least as much a *result* of social beliefs and practices as they are a cause. In fact, since the early 1970s, many feminists have argued that patriarchal control over women's bodies (e.g., sexual control, rape, and other forms of violence, medical control of women's reproduction, the imposition of commercial fashions and narrow beauty standards, cultural beliefs about food and an obsession with thinness, etc.) is a major locus of men's control over women. This is a powerful observation that informed a great deal of fruitful feminist organizing around issues such as girls' and women's eating disorders, rape crisis centers, and women's shelters against domestic violence.

But as the articles in the first section of Part II demonstrate, the view of women as disempowered body-objects and men as empowered body-subjects tends to overgeneralize about a more complex reality. Jane Sprague Zones critically analyzes the cosmetics industry's suppression of diversity among women, and the ways that narrow bodily standards of beauty sometimes result in negative health consequences. Nomy Lamm offers a powerfully personal statement of resistance to the culture of thinness. Lamm discusses how her youthful "punk grrrl" feminism has provided her with a means of resisting the narrow mainstream media constructions of beauty, and for making the revolutionary assertion that her fat body is beautiful. Tamara Beauboeuf-Lafontant does not disagree that large women can be beautiful, but she questions the ways that culture has defined "strong and large black women" as independent. Beaubouef-

Lafontant asks whether the considerable weight that many black women carry on their bodies might sometimes be an unhealthy, embodied response to the multiple burdens imposed on them due to their position in a matrix of race, class, and gender domination. In the next chapter, Read and Bartkowski ask another question about the meanings of what women carry on their bodies: Is it empowering or is it oppressive for Muslim women living in a U.S. context to veil themselves? Or, perhaps, does veiling reveal the ways that women exercise agency within systems of gender, religion, and culture? Next, Don Sabo draws on his experience as an instructor in a maximum security men's prison to reflect on how, for survival reasons, male inmates tend to value and display a "hard" muscular masculinity and suppress any signs of softness. In a similar personal vein, Betsy Lucal closes this section with a fascinating essay on "gender bending." What is it like, Lucal asks, to be a person whose physical appearance does not seem to "fit" cleanly into one or the other of U.S. culture's two (male and female) sex categories?

Men's violence against other men on the streets and in wars has historically been more visible than men's violence against women. Only very recently are we beginning to understand the extent of men's violence against women and the more general implications of this violence for gender relations. Together, the articles in the second section explore several dimensions of the relationship between gender and violence. First, Menjivar and Salcido examine the experiences of immigrant women with domestic violence across a wide range of sending and receiving nations and communities. Next, Afroza Anwary describes how "acid violence" emerged in Bangladesh the 1990s as a chilling form of men's violence against women, and how international aid and medical agencies, coupled with local feminist organizations, combined to help the victims of this violence. In the next chapter, Patricia Albanese turns our attention to the coupling of war and rape in the Balkans. She argues that ethnic nationalism and militarization contributed to a "repatriarchalizing" of society, and that one enforcement mechanism of this reassertion of patriarchy was an escalation of men's violence against women. The 2001 terrorist attacks on the United States raised new questions about warfare and security in the twenty-first century. Michael Kimmel closes this section by asking some very provocative *gender* questions about terrorism. Both inside and outside the United States, Kimmel suggests, class factors may combine with particular forms of masculinity to contribute to the rise of terrorist violence.

7

Beauty Myths and Realities and Their Impact on Women's Health

JANE SPRAGUE ZONES

Of all the characteristics that distinguish one human being from the next, physical appearance has the most immediate impact. How a person looks shapes the kinds of responses she or he evokes in others. Physical appearance has similar effects on other social statuses. Those considered beautiful or handsome are more likely to accrue benefits such as attributions of goodness and better character, more desirability as friends and partners, and upward social mobility. Those considered unattractive receive less attention as infants, are evaluated more harshly in school, and earn less money as employees. The significance of physical appearance shifts in intensity as it interacts with other statuses, such as gender, race/ethnicity, age, class, and disability. For groups targeted for social mistreatment, such as women and racial or ethnic minorities, physical appearance has profound implications not only for the creation of first impressions but also for enduring influence on social effectiveness. The power of appearance pushes people to assimilate in order to avoid unwanted attention or to attract desired attention. The pushes and pulls to look "conventionally attractive" constitute assaults on diversity.

In this chapter, I describe and evaluate some of the ways that social concerns with women's appearance affect physical and emotional health status and limit the range of perceived and actual possibilities open to individuals and to groups. My particular focus is on how physical appearance is perceived by and affects women of color, those in various social classes, and women who are older or disabled. A review of research and literature that reflect women's personal experiences indicates that cultural preoccupation with how we look militates against the appreciation and expression of women's diversity.

I find two major bodies of research on this topic: the experimental social psychology and the body-image literatures. Much of what we know academically about appearance and its social effects is derived from experimental social psychology, mostly studies of the human face. This body of work generally neglects analyses of social status other than gender distinctions that affect interpersonal (usually romantic) attachment. This research, carried out mainly in university settings with primarily white undergraduate students, is paralleled by a smaller number of studies using other populations that yield comparable results. Global measures of physical attractiveness are employed, in which judges rate "stimulus persons" (either human confederates or photographic images of people with "normal" features) along a continuum ranging from very low to very high physical attractiveness (Patzer 1985). The body-image literature comes primarily from clinical psychology and feminist theory. Body-image scholars (Iazzetto 1988) typically cite historical evidence and open-ended interviews with informants to support their arguments. This school is much more attentive than are the experimentalists to the interaction of social statuses and physical appearance and to social and political contexts generally. Both approaches contribute to understanding the real effects of physical appearance. This chapter interweaves these two strands to show commonalities and differences between women in an attempt to understand the power of appearance in women's lives.

Although there have always been beauty ideals for women (Banner 1983), in modern times the proliferation of media portrayals of feminine beauty in magazines, billboards, movies, and television has both hastened and more broadly disseminated the communication of detailed expectations. There are increasingly demanding criteria for female beauty in western culture, and women are strongly pressured to alter their appearance to conform with these standards.

Naomi Wolf, in her book *The Beauty Myth* (1991), contends that the effect of widespread promulgation of womanly ideals of appearance perpetuates the myth that the "quality called 'beauty' objectively and universally exists. Women must want to embody it and men must want to possess women who embody it. This embodiment is an imperative for women and not for men, which situation is necessary and natural because it is biological, sexual, and evolutionary" (12). Wolf declares that this is all falsehood. Instead, beauty is politically and economically determined, and the myth is the "last, best belief system that keeps male dominance intact" (12). She argues that as women have emerged successfully in many new arenas, the focus on and demand for beauty has become more intense, attacking the private sense of self and creating new barriers to accomplishment. In Wolf's view, the increasing obsession with beauty is a backlash to women's liberation.

COMMONALTIES IN PERCEPTION OF BEAUTY

Many women concur that personal beauty, or "looking good," is fostered from a very early age. It is probably true that the ways in which people assess physical beauty are not naturally determined but socially and culturally learned and therefore "in the eye of the beholder." However, we tend to discount the depth of our *common* perception of beauty, mistakenly assuming that individuals largely set their own standards. At any period in history, within a given geographic and cultural territory, there are relatively uniform and widely understood models of how women "should" look. Numerous studies over time reinforce this notion (Iliffe 1960; Patzer 1985; Perrett, May, and Yoshikawa 1994).

BEAUTY'S SOCIAL SIGNIFICANCE FOR INDIVIDUALS

Much of the evidence from studies done by experimental social psychologists shows why people assign such importance to their appearance. They have found that people judged to be physically attractive, both male and female, are assumed to possess more socially desirable personality traits and expected to lead happier lives (Diori, Berscheid, and Walster 1972). Social science research shows that "cute babies are cuddled more than homely ones; attractive toddlers are punished less often. Teachers give special attention to better-looking pupils, strangers offer help more readily to attractive people, and jurors show more sympathy to good-looking victims" (Freedman 1986:7–8). This principle holds in virtually every aspect of our lives from birth to death and across racial and ethnic groups (Patzer 1985:232–33). The effects of these myriad positive responses to and assumptions about people who are considered attractive have self-fulfilling aspects as well. The expectations of others strongly shape development, learning, and achievement: people thought to be attractive become more socially competent and accomplished (Goldman and Lewis 1977).

Appearance-based discrimination targets women more than men. Women's self-esteem and happiness are significantly associated with their physical appearance; no such relationship exists for men as a group (Allgood-Merten, Lewinsohn, and Hops 1990; Mathes and Kahn 1975). Women's access to upward mobility is also greatly affected by physical appearance, which is a major determinant of marriage to a higher status man. By contrast, potential partners evaluate men more for intelligence or accomplishment. The significance of beauty in negotiating beneficial marriages is particularly true for White working-class women (Elder 1969; Taylor and Glenn 1976; Udry 1977; Udry and Eckland 1984). Banner (1983), who has traced the shifting models of beauty and fashion over two hundred years of American history, concludes that although standards of beauty may have changed, and women have greatly improved their access to social institutions, many females continue to define themselves by physical appearance and their ability to attract a partner.

The preoccupation with appearance serves to control and contain women's ambitions and motivations to gain power in larger political contexts. To the degree that many females feel they must dedicate time, attention, and resources to maintaining and improving their looks, they neglect activities to improve social conditions for themselves or others. Conversely, as women become increasingly visible as powerful individuals in shaping events, their looks become targeted for irrelevant scrutiny and criticism in ways with which men in similar positions are not forced to contend (Freedman 1986; Wolf 1991). For example, Marcia Clark, the lead prosecutor in the O. J. Simpson trial, was the focus of unremitting media attention for her dress, hairstyle, demeanor, and private life.

The major difference between discrimination based on appearance and mistreatment based on gender, race, or other social attributes is that individuals are legally protected against the latter (Patzer 1985:11). In an eye-opening review of legal cases related to appearance and employment, Wolf documents the inconsistencies that characterize decisions to dismiss women on the basis of their looks. "Legally, women *don't* have a thing to wear" (1991:42). Requirements of looking both businesslike and feminine represent a moving target that invites failure. In *Hopkins v. Price-Waterhouse,* a woman who brought in more clients than any other employee was denied a partnership because, her employers claimed, she did not walk, talk, or dress in an adequately feminine manner nor did she wear makeup. In another court case, it was ruled "inappropriate for a supervisor" of women to dress "like a woman" (Wolf 1991:39). If one appears businesslike, one cannot be adequately feminine; if one appears feminine, one cannot adequately conduct business.

BEAUTY MYTHS AND THE EROSION OF SELF-WORTH

Perhaps the biggest toll the "beauty myth" takes is in terms of women's identity and self-esteem. Like members of other oppressed groups of which we may also be part, women internalize cultural stereotypes and expectations, perpetuating them by enforced acceptance and agreement. For women, this is intensified by the interaction of irrational social responses to physical appearance not only with gender but with other statuses as well—race, class, age, disability, and the like. Continuous questioning of the adequacy of one's looks drains attention from more worthwhile and confidence-building pursuits.

A number of years ago, novelist Alice Walker was invited to speak at her alma mater, Spelman College, the highly regarded historically Black women's college in Atlanta. She used the opportunity to describe her experience of feeling as if she had reached the extent of her capacities for accomplishment a few years prior. "I seemed to have reached a ceiling in my brain," Walker recalled. She realized that "in my physical self there remained one last barrier to my spiritual liberation, at least in the present phase. My hair." Walker recognized it was not the hair itself but her relationship with it that was the problem. Months of experimentation with different styles followed. From childhood, her hair had endured domination, suppression, and control at the hands of outsiders. "Eventually I knew *precisely* what my hair wanted: . . . to be left alone by anyone, including me, who did not love it as it was" (Walker 1988:52–53). With that realization, the ceiling at the top of Walker's brain lifted, and her mind and spirit could continue to grow. Many African American women have sought just such a liberation from their hair, and others have celebrated its possibilities (Mercer 1990).

Glassner argues that the dramatically increased attention to fitness, diet, and physical well-being in recent years has been accompanied by a plummeting of satisfaction with our bodies (1988:246). There seems to be little relationship between actual physical attractiveness (conformance to culturally valued standards determined by judges) and individual women's satisfaction with their own appearance (Murstein 1972). Both men and women are unrealistic about how others perceive their bodies, but men tend to assume that people think they look better and women tend to assume that they look worse than they actually are perceived (Fallon and Rozin 1985). A recent poll of United States residents (Cimons 1990) found that fewer than a third of adults were happy with their appearance. Women were twice as likely as men to consider themselves to be fat.

Nagging self-doubts about weight emanate from the difference between projected images of women, many of which depict severely undernourished bodies, and our everyday reality. Half of the readers of *Vogue* magazine wear size 14 or larger (Glassner 1988:12), tormenting themselves with images of models with size 6 or smaller figures in every issue. Female models are 9 percent taller and 16 percent thinner than average women. Even the majority of women runners who are in good physical condition and fall within the ranges of weight and body fat considered desirable describe themselves as overweight (Robinson 1983). Research consistently shows that women not only overestimate their own size (Penner, Thompson, and Coovert 1991; Thompson and Dolce 1989) but they expect men to prefer thinner women than is the actual case (Rozin and Fallon 1988).

Internalizing the oppressive messages and images from outside has the effect of making the situation seem intractable. In Alice Walker's case, the distress that she had internalized from the ways in which people (or ads or media impressions) had communicated concern or distaste for her hair distracted her from her work, eroded her confidence, and slowed her progress. Competition between women is a prominent feature of internalized sexism, reflecting women's collusion with beauty expectations that are both limiting and unrealistically demanding. Women become each other's critics, keeping each other anxious and in line, thereby maintaining the status quo. In *Memoirs of an Ex-Prom Queen,* one of the enduring feminist novels of the 1970s, Alix Kates Shulman created a teenage protagonist so obsessed with and insecure about her looks that she realizes she actually is beautiful only after she learns that her closest friends hate her for it.

Internalized oppression causes additional harm by redirecting mistreatment from the dominant culture to other members of one's own group (Lipsky 1987). A transcript of a kitchen table conversation between two Black women illustrates how the preferential treatment of lighter-skinned slaves by their masters (who frequently fathered them) during the slavery era has produced continuing conflict among African Americans to the present day (Anderson and Ingram 1994). Tamara, a dark-skinned woman, recounts being ridiculed by family and neighbors as "ugly and black. . . . That's when I stopped liking black kids altogether. They hated me, and they made me hate my best friend [who was darker]. I remember everything about my childhood. It's like a diary. . . . I kept telling myself, 'There's got to be a way to get over this. One day this is going to stop.' But it never did. As I grew older, it just got worse. . . . To this day, I still find myself walking with my head down and trying to cover up my body" (358, 361). The preoccupation with skin color also had hurtful repercussions for Michele, a light-skinned Black woman. "Light-skinned blacks resent it when people say we are trying to be or act white. . . . On the other hand, society, both black and white, gives us these messages that we are 'better' than darker-skinned Blacks. It's sort of like we're in limbo" (359). The acting out of internalized oppression between members of a group creates additional pressures to assimilate or avoid visibility, and it disrupts the unity essential for social progress.

QUANTIFYING BEAUTY: CONVENTIONALITY AND COMPUTER ENHANCEMENT

The predominant, nearly universal standard for beauty in American society is to be slender, young, upper-class, and white without noticeable physical imperfections or disabilities. To the extent that a woman's racial or ethnic heritage, class background, age, or other social and physical characteristics do not conform to this ideal, assaults on opportunities and esteem increase. Physical appearance is at the core of racism and most other social oppressions, because it is generally what is used to classify individuals.

Although expectations relative to appearance vary in style and interpretation, there are commonalities in their effects on women. Bordo (1993) makes a strong philosophical case for examining the multiplicity of interpretations of the body. She cautions, however, that we must at the same time recognize the significant leveling effect of "the everyday deployment of mass cultural representations. . . . First, the representations *homogenize*. In our culture, this means that they will smooth out all racial, ethnic, and sexual 'differences' that disturb Anglo-Saxon, heterosexual expectations and identifications. . . . Second, these homogenized images *normalize*—that is, they function as models against which the self continually measures, judges, 'disciplines,' and 'corrects' itself" (24–25).

In a number of studies, conventionality has been found to be the most important component of beauty (Webster and Driskell 1983). Judith Langlois and colleagues used a computer to blend likenesses of individuals into composites, mathematically averaging out their features. Undergraduate students judged composites of sixteen or thirty-two faces to be significantly more attractive than individual faces for both male and female images. Composites made from blending thirty-two faces were judged more attractive than those composed of only sixteen (Langlois et al. 1990, 1991). A similar study, using Japanese and Caucasian judges and subjects found that "aesthetic judgements of face shape are similar across different cultural backgrounds" (Perrett, May, and Yoshikawa 1994: 239) and that the raters had the highest regard for a computerized caricature that exaggerated the ways that the fifteen most preferred faces differed from the average sixty.

This research is now being applied in the popular media. A computer-generated multiethnic supermodel cover face on a major women's magazine labeled "Who Is the Face of America?" accompanies a story lauding our "radically diversifying demographics" (Gaudoin 1994) when the image projected is one of convergence rather than diversity.

BEAUTY AND THE CHALLENGE OF SOCIAL DIVERSITY

Although significant beauty ideals appear to transcend cultural subgroup boundaries, appearance standards do vary by reference group. Clothing preferred by adolescents, for example, which experiences quick fashion turnover, is considered inappropriate for older people. Body piercing, a current style for young White people in urban areas of the United States, is repellant to most older adults and some ethnic minorities in the same age group. Religious and political ideologies are often identified through appearance. Islamic fundamentalist women wear clothing that covers body and face, an expression of religious sequestering; Amish women wear conservative clothing and distinctive caps; orthodox Jewish women wear wigs or cover their hair; African American women for many years wore natural hairdos to show racial pride; and Native American women may wear tribal jewelry and distinctive clothes that indicate their respect for heritage. In recent years, the disability rights movement has encouraged personal visibility to accompany the tearing down of barriers to access, resulting in a greater variety of appliances (including elegant streamlined wheelchairs) and functional clothing.

Although there are varying and conflicting standards of good looks and appropriate appearance that are held simultaneously by social subgroups, the dominant ideals prevail and are legitimated most thoroughly in popular culture. Webster and Driskell (1983) contend that physical appearance has effects similar to those of other social statuses such as gender, race, age, class, and so on, conferring superiority or inferiority in the social hierarchy. The implications of physical appearance gain in intensity when they are confounded with other statuses. Wendy Chapkis (1986) presents the perspectives of women from many groups—elderly, fat, Black, Asian, lesbian, disabled, and so on—who describe the injuries they have experienced as a result of their combined oppressions. To avoid social harassment and discrimination because of appearance, women frequently alter their looks to appear more conventional, an unwitting attack on diversity. Lisa Diane White, a leader in the Black Women's Health Project's self-help movement, addresses challenges involved in showing diversity. "With the recent upsurge of pride in our African heritage, we like to think that we as Black women feel better about ourselves today than our sisters did in the past. . . . But I think a lot of us are striving still for standards of beauty and acceptability that aren't our own, and we're suffering the pain inherent in this kind of quest" (quoted in Pinkney 1994:53).

One major way that dominant social forces have dealt with those who diverge is to remove these expressions from view—through ghettoization, anti-immigration policies, special education programs, retirement policies, and so on. The ultimate social insult is to render the oppressed invisible. Social barriers to visibility are expressed as well in pressures to avoid drawing attention to oneself. Those features that render us "different" are frequently the objects of harassment or unwanted attention. We learn to appear invisible. In the following sections, the gender effects of appearance in combination with other social statuses are described through personal accounts and social research.

Race and Ethnicity

In recent years, there has been a burgeoning of women's literature that provides a rich context for the significance of appearance in women's lives. Analyzing Toni Morrison's *The Bluest Eye,* a novel about a poor black family, Lakoff and Scherr describe how the author shows "ugliness seeping through the skin, becoming conviction." The dominant culture's imposition of white standards of beauty presents an added and impossible burden for women of color. Lakoff and Scherr's interviews with women of color found that as children they grew up feeling ugly and knowing that there was nothing they could do about it. "For these women the American Dream of beauty was a perpetual reminder of what they were not, and could never be" (Lakoff and Scherr 1984:252).

An examination by Patricia Morton (1991) of scholarly portrayals of Black women in American history and social science during this century showed persistent "shaping and endorsement of a distinctive and profoundly disempowering, composite image of Black womanhood . . . as a natural and permanent slave woman" (ix). The introduction of the black liberation movement with its slogan "Black Is Beautiful" meant to many African American women a welcome contradiction to the assorted ways in which racism had imposed feelings of ugliness. The impossibility of ever achieving the dominant culture's ideal, or even coming close, was deeply daunting. But ethnic pride movements also bring about pressures of their own for their constituents to look a particular way, fulfill a particular ideal (Mercer 1990).

Among White Americans who identify with ethnic minority groups, appearance plays a similar role, sometimes with frightening intensity. A Holocaust survivor continues to dye her hair blonde into old age because it was her light hair color that allowed her to pass as a non-Jew and avoid the Nazi death camps as a young adult. Her current feeling of security, unrelated to actual safety, remains bound up in her ability to pass.

A study of physical features of faces in photographs of "Miss Universe" contestants, half of whom were White, the others Black or Asian, found that Black and Asian beauty pageant contestants possessed most of the patterns of features associated with attractiveness in the white entrants (Cunningham 1986). Even though contestants were selected by their own nations, and judges for the international contest were from the Japanese contest site, the researcher suggests that both western and nonwestern national representatives were selected because they approximated western standards of beauty.

A comparison of U.S. women with women and girls in nonwestern countries shows that American females have a poorer self-image and diet more (Rothblum 1990). A parallel finding from a study by Aune and Aune (1994) found that White American women and men paid more attention to their appearance than African Americans and that, of the three groups, Asian Americans were the least concerned about personal appearance. Western beauty ideals have permeated the "global village," but their psychological effects appear to be greatest at the source. The pursuit of beauty has provided more and more commodities to offer on the world market, and in this industry, the United States is on the surplus side of the trade balance.

Age

Youthful appearance is a major feature of the beauty standard. In American society, peoples' worries about aging center around economic need disability, dependency, and death, all very significant and frightening issues. Consequently, visible signs of age on face and body often provoke dread. In *The Coming of Age* (1972:297), Simone de Beauvoir remarks that she has "never come across one single woman, either in life or in books, who has looked upon her own old age cheerfully. In the same way, no one ever speaks of 'a beautiful old woman.' "

Experimental studies corroborate the association of youthful features with attractiveness, Johnson (1985) points out that it is perceived age, not actual age, that is the decisive factor, and he concludes from his research on White women and men that "maintaining or recapturing youthful vigor is an important determinant of judged attractiveness" (160). However, gender differences appear to be related to age. In further studies, female judges found photos of men maintained their level of attractiveness across groups of increasing age, whereas male judges found photos of older women less attractive than those of younger women (Mathes et al. 1985).

Although there are limits to what an individual can do to stave off the physical effects of aging over a lifetime, many products and services claim to prolong youth. Raising fears about aging is a major tool in marketing cosmetics, hair coloring, and cosmetic surgery. Mary Kay Ash, addressing women who sell her cosmetic line, stated that "very young girls with perfect complexions can possibly be naturally beautiful, but at about age 25, things begin to happen. And senility begins at 28" (Rubenstein 1984). Of course, fostering the notion that young adults should begin to consider themselves beset by physical deterioration greatly extends the market for Mary Kay's products.

Wolf (1991:14) argues that aging in women is considered ugly because women become more powerful with age. Stronger attacks are required upon personal worth to undermine the threat posed by accumulation of experience and influence as we grow older.

Disability

Erving Goffman's classic studies of stigma (1963) provided the underpinnings for much of the research on physical appearance. His work focused on the negative social consequences of visible disability and other attributes that are socially devalued. To the extent that individuals have visible physical differences, they are at greater jeopardy of being perceived as and viewing themselves as unattractive.

Alice Walker wrote of being blinded in one eye by a BB pellet at age eight. She changed overnight from being a confident, cute whiz in school to a withdrawn and scared child who did not raise her head. She faced the unwanted curiosity of others because of the noticeable white scar tissue on the eye. At night she pleaded with the eye to clear up. "I tell it I hate and despise it. I do not pray for sight. I pray for beauty" (Walker 1990:284). After the scar tissue's removal at age fourteen, Walker emerged with greater confidence, but the inner scars of self-doubt remained to be battled into adulthood.

A survey of college students with disabilities indicates that they view their visible disabilities as being the primary referent in interactions with others. One student summed it up: "I think the visual impact of a person sitting in a chair with wheels on it is so great as to render all other impressions, such as dress or grooming, virtually insignificant" (Kaiser, Freeman, and Wingate 1984:6). Nevertheless, the authors conclude that people with physical disabilities respond to the labeling process by managing aspects of their appearance over which they can exert some control. Much of the effort goes toward "normalizing" appearance, attempting to make the disability less obvious.

In *Autobiography of a Face,* Lucy Grealy describes the effects of disfiguring cancer surgery that removed much of her jaw at age nine. In adolescence her face constitutes her identity, not unlike other girls her age, but because of the disfigurement, to an even greater extreme: "By equating my face with ugliness, in believing that without it I would never experience the deep, bottomless grief I called ugliness, I separated myself even further from other people, who I thought never experienced grief this deep" (Grealy 1994:180).

Class

Class status has a complex relationship to physical appearance, shaping standards of beauty that may be expensive and dysfunctional and requiring adherence to standards for class membership and identity. Similarly, physical beauty has ramifications for class status: people judged to be physically attractive stay in school longer, get better jobs, and have higher incomes—the three primary components of socioeconomic status.

Devotion of energy to "improvement" of appearance sometimes has dysfunctional results. Sociologist Thorstein Veblen noted a century ago in *The Theory of the Leisure Class* that the major characteristic of envied clothing is that it is impractical for any kind of work. Little did he anticipate the popularity of Levi's 501 denim jeans for people of all classes in the 1990s.

To generate continued profits, the fashion industry promotes frequent and dramatic changes in style that require investment in new clothing and "looks." These fashions come from many sources: media and sports stars (expensive high-top shoes, for example), the ghetto (cornrows, baggy pants, do-rags), as well as Paris fashions (ready-to-wear copies) (Davis 1992). Considerable resources are expended by people of all income levels to give the appearance of currency and affluence.

One researcher reports that appearance is more significant for African American women who are better educated than for those with less education (Udry 1977). Michele, a professional, who identifies herself as light-skinned, describes her repugnance at assumptions she feels Black men often make about her because of her skin color: "They think I'm attractive, some kind of 'catch.' . . . For instance, I went out with this dude recently. Mr. Fiction Writer, Would-be Lawyer, whatever. We met at a cafe. No sooner had we sat down than he puts his arm out and says, 'Umm, I like that. It's not often I get to go out with a person around the same shade as I am.' I thought, 'Oh, my God, this man is colorstruck.' All he could talk about was color, color, color. . . . I was so offended. We are just obsessed with shade" (Anderson and Ingram 1994:360).

Color is also used to make insidious class distinctions among Latinos. Richard Rodriguez, a California-raised Chicano, would incur his mother's wrath when he let himself be darkened by the summer sun as a boy. "You know how important looks are in this country. With *los gringos* looks are all that they judge on. But you! Look at you! You're so careless! . . . You won't be satisfied till you end up looking like *los pobres* who work in the fields, *los braceros* [physical laborers]" (Rodriguez 1990:265).

THE COMMERCIAL IMPERATIVE IN THE QUEST FOR BEAUTY

Standards of beauty are continually evolving and proliferating, and as new standards develop, "bodies are expected to change as well" (Freedman 1986:6). Unlike race, gender, or age, attractiveness may be considered to some extent an "achieved" characteristic subject to change through individual intervention (Webster and Driskell 1983). As Wolf puts it, "The beauty myth is always actually prescribing *behavior* and not appearance" (1991:14; emphasis added). In her study of black and white Baltimore women of various ages, both working class and middle class, Emily Martin found a common theme in ways that women discussed their health, which she summarized as "your self is separate from your body" (1989:77). Participants in Martin's study saw the body as something that must be coped with or adjusted to.

To accommodate expectations for physical appearance, women are exhorted to invest large amounts of time, money, and physical and emotional energy into their physical being. "The closer women come to power, the more physical self-consciousness and sacrifice are asked of them. 'Beauty' becomes the condition for a woman to take the next step" (Wolf 1991:28). Geraldine Ferraro, who was the first female candidate for vice president of the United States nominated by a major political party, noted in her autobiography that there were more reports on what she wore than on what she said.

Although there are many compelling theories about how the cultural preoccupation with feminine appearance evolved, it is clear that at present it is held in place by a number of very profitable industries. The average person is exposed to several hundred to several thousand advertisements per day (Moog 1990). To pitch their products, advertisers create messages that cannot immediately be recognized as advertising, selling images in the course of selling products. Two-thirds of the models who appear in magazine ads are teenagers or young adults. Although we are now seeing greater diversity in models, older people, low-income people, and people with disabilities rarely show up in advertisements because they do not project the image that the product is meant to symbolize (Glassner 1988:37). In numerous ways, advertising attacks women's self-esteem so they will purchase products and services in order to hold off bad feelings (Barthel 1988).

Most women's magazines generate much of their revenue from advertisers, who openly manipulate the content of stories. Wolf (1991:81–85) documents incidents in which advertisers canceled accounts because of editorial decisions to print stories unsupportive of their products. *Ms.* magazine, for example, reportedly lost a major cosmetics account after it featured Soviet women on the cover who were not wearing makeup.

Americans spend an estimated $50 billion a year on diets, cosmetics, plastic surgery, health clubs, and related gadgets (Glassner 1988:13). A review of costs of common beauty treatments itemized in a 1982 newspaper story found that a woman of means could easily rack up the bulk of an annual salary to care for her physical appearance. This entailed frequent visits to the hair salon, exercise classes, regular manicures, a home skin-care program with occasional professional facials, a monthly pedicure, professional makeup session and supplies, a trip to a spa, hair removal from various parts of the body, and visits to a psychiatrist to maintain essential self-esteem (Steger 1982). The list did not include the expense of special dietary programs, cosmetic surgery or dentistry, home exercise equipment, or clothing.

As new standards of beauty expectations are created, physical appearance becomes increasingly significant, and as the expression of alternative looks are legitimized, new products are developed and existing enterprises capitalize on the trends. Liposuction, developed relatively recently, has become the most popular of the cosmetic surgery techniques. Synthetic fats have been developed, and there is now a cream claimed to reduce thigh measurements.

Weight Loss

Regardless of the actual size of their bodies, more than half of American females between ages ten and thirty are dieting, and one out of every six college women is struggling with anorexia and bulimia (Iazzetto 1992). The quest to lose weight is not limited to White, middle-class women. Iazzetto cites studies that find this pervasive concern in black women, Native American girls (75 percent trying to lose weight), and high school students (63 percent dieting). However, there may be differences among adolescent women in different groups as to how rigid their concepts of beauty are and how flexible they are regarding body image and dieting (Parker et al. 1995). Studies of primary school girls show more than half of all young girls and close to 80 percent of ten- and eleven-year-olds on diets because they consider themselves "too fat" (Greenwood 1990; Seid 1989). Analyses of the origins, symbolic meanings, and impact of our culture's obsession with thinness (Chernin 1981; Freedman 1989; Iazzetto 1988; Seid 1989) occupy much of the body-image literature.

Concern about weight and routine dieting are so pervasive in the United States that the weight-loss industry grosses more than $33 billion each year. Over 80 percent of those in diet programs are women. These programs keep growing even in the face of 90 to 95 percent failure rates in providing and maintaining significant weight loss. Congressional hearings in the early 1990s presented evidence of fraud and high failure rates in the weight-loss industry, as well as indications of severe health consequences for rapid weight loss (Iazzetto 1992). The Food and Drug Administration (FDA) has reviewed documents submitted by major weight-loss programs and found evidence of safety and efficacy to be insufficient and unscientific. An expert panel urged consumers to consider program effectiveness in choosing a weight-loss method but acknowledged lack of scientific data for making informed decisions (Brody 1992).

Fitness

Whereas in the nineteenth century some physicians recommended a sedentary lifestyle to preserve feminine beauty, in the past two decades of the twentieth century, interest in physical fitness has grown enormously. Nowhere is this change more apparent than in the gross receipts of some of the major fitness industries. In 1987, health clubs grossed $5 billion, exercise equipment $738 million (up from $5 million ten years earlier), diet foods $74 billion, and vitamin products $2.7 billion (Brand 1988). Glassner (1989) identifies several reasons for this surge of interest in fitness, including the aging of the "baby boom" cohort with its attendant desire to allay the effects of aging through exercise and diet, and the institution of "wellness" programs by corporations to reduce insurance, absentee, and inefficiency costs. A patina of health, well-toned but skinny robustness, has been folded into the dominant beauty ideal.

Clothing and Fashion

For most of us, first attempts to accomplish normative attractiveness included choosing clothing that enhanced our self-image. The oppressive effects of corsets, clothing that interfered with movement, tight shoes with high heels, and the like have been well documented (Banner 1983, 1988). Clothing represents the greatest monetary investment that women make in their appearance. Sales for *exercise* clothing alone in 1987 (including leotards, bodysuits, warm-up suits, sweats, and shoes) totaled $2.5 billion (Schefer 1988). To bolster sales, fashion leaders introduce new and different looks at regular intervals, impelling women to invest in what is currently in vogue. Occasionally the designers' new ideas are rejected wholesale, but this is generally a temporary set-back. John Molloy's best-selling *Women's Dress for Success Book* (1977) attempted to resolve this problem for women by prescribing a skirted suit "uniform" that women could wear at work much like the standardized clothing that businessmen wear. He was able to demonstrate its utility in allowing women to project themselves as competent and effective in the workplace. Furthermore, to the extent that women who worked outside the home adopted this outfit, they would not become prey to the vagaries and expense of rapidly shifting fashion. The clothing industry orchestrated a wholesale attack on Molloy's strategy, labeling his uniform unfeminine, and another sensible strategy failed (Wolf 1991:43–45).

Cosmetics

The average person in North America uses more than twenty-five pounds of cosmetics, soaps, and toiletries each year (Decker 1983). The cosmetics industry produces over twenty thousand products containing thousands of chemicals, and it grosses over $20 billion annually (Becker 1991; Wolf 1991). Stock in cosmetics manufacturers has been rising 15 percent a year, in large part because of depressed petroleum prices. The oil derivative ethanol is the base for most products (Wolf 1991:82, 307). Profit margins for products are over 50 percent (McKnight 1989). Widespread false claims for cosmetics were virtually unchallenged for fifty years after the FDA became responsible for cosmetic industry oversight in 1938, and even now, the industry remains largely unregulated (Kaplan 1994). Various manufacturers assert that their goods can "retard aging," "repair the skin," or "restructure the cell." "Graphic evidence" of "visible improvement" when applying a "barrier" against "eroding effects" provides a pastiche of some familiar advertising catchphrases (Wolf 1991:109–10).

The FDA has no authority to require cosmetics firms to register their existence, to release their formulas, to report adverse reactions, or to show evidence of safety and effectiveness before marketing their products (Gilhooley 1978; Kaplan 1994). Authorizing and funding the FDA to regulate the cosmetics industry would allow some means of protecting consumers from the use of dangerous products.

Cosmetic Surgery

In interviews with cosmetic surgeons and users of their services, Dull and West (1991) found that the line between reconstructive plastic surgery (repair of deformities caused congenitally or by injury or disease) and aesthetic surgery has begun to blur. Doctors and their patients are viewing unimpaired features as defective and the desire to "correct" them as intrinsic to women's nature, rather than as a cultural imperative.

Because of an oversupply of plastic surgeons, the profession has made efforts to expand existing markets through advertising and by appeals to women of color. Articles encouraging "enhancement of ethnic beauty" have begun to appear, but they focus on westernizing Asian eyelids and chiseling African American noses. As Bordo (1993:25) points out, this technology serves to promote commonality rather than diversity.

Plastic surgery has been moving strongly in the direction of making appearance a bona fide medical problem. This has been played out dramatically in recent times in the controversy regarding silicone breast implants, which provides plastic surgeons with a substantial amount of income. Used for thirty years in hundreds of thousands of women (80 percent for cosmetic augmentation), the effects of breast implants have only recently begun to be studied to determine their health consequences over long periods (Zones 1992). In a petition to the FDA in 1982 to circumvent regulation requiring proof of safety and effectiveness of the implants, the American Society of Plastic and Reconstructive Surgeons stated, "There is a common misconception that the enlargement of the female breast is not necessary for maintenance of health or treatment of disease. There is a substantial and enlarging body of medical information and opinion, however, to the effect that these *deformities* [small breasts] are really a disease which in most patients result in feelings of inadequacy . . . due to a lack of self-perceived femininity. The enlargement of the underdeveloped female breast is, therefore, often very necessary to insure an improved quality of life for the patient" (Porterfield 1982:4–5; emphasis added).

Cosmetic surgeon James Billie of Arkansas, who claims to have operated on over fifteen thousand beauty contestants in the past ten years, maintains that three-quarters of Miss USA pageant contestants have undergone plastic surgery (Garchik 1992). Cosmetic surgery generates over a third of a billion dollars per year for practitioners, some of whom offer overnight household financing for patients. The hefty interest rates are returned in part to the surgeons by the finance corporation (Krieger 1989). Although cosmetic surgery is the biggest commercial contender in the medical realm, prescription drugs are increasingly lucrative ventures (such as Retin-A to reduce wrinkling skin, and hormones to promote growth in short boys and retard it in tall girls).

HEALTH RISKS IN QUEST OF BEAUTY

Physicians and medical institutions have been quoted as associating beauty with health and ugliness with disease. Dr. Daniel Tostesen of Harvard Medical School, whose research is supported by Shiseido, an expensive cosmetics line, claims that there is a "'subtle and continuous gradation' between health and medical interests on the one hand, and 'beauty and well-being on the other'" (Wolf 1991: 227). The imperative to look attractive, while promising benefits in self-esteem, often entails both serious mental and physical health risks.

Mental Health

For most women, not adhering to narrow, standardized appearance expectations causes insecurity and distraction, but for many, concerns about appearance can have serious emotional impact. Up until adolescence, boys and girls experience about the same rates of depression, but at around age twelve, girls' rates of depression begin to increase more rapidly. A study of over eight hundred high school students found that a prime factor in this disparity is girls' preoccupation with appearance. In discussing the study, the authors concluded that "if adolescent girls felt as physically attractive, effective, and generally good about themselves as their male peers did, they would not experience so much depression" (Allgood-Merten, Lewinsohn, and Hops 1990:61). Another study of the impact of body image on onset and persistence of depression in adolescent girls found that whereas a relatively positive body image does not seem to offer substantial protection against the occurrence of depression, it does seem to decrease the likelihood that depression will be persistent (Rierdan and Koff 1991; Rierdan, Koff, and Stubbs 1989).

Physical Health

Perceived or actual variation from society's ideal takes a physical toll, too. High school and college-age females who were judged to be in the bottom half of their group in terms of attractiveness had significantly higher blood pressure than the young women in the top half. The relationship between appearance and blood pressure was not found for males in the same age group (Hansell, Sparacino, and Ronchi 1982).

Low body weight has been heavily promoted as a life-prolonging characteristic. There is evidence to support this contention, but the effect of advocating low weight in collusion with the heavy cultural prescription for a very slender look has led people into cycles of weight loss and regained weight that may act as an independent risk factor for cardiovascular disease (Bouchard 1991). A recent review of the medical literature on weight fluctuation concludes that the potential health benefits of moderate weight loss in obese people, however, is greater than the known risks of "yo-yo dieting" (National Task Force 1994). Women constitute 90 percent of people with anorexia, an eating disorder that can cause serious injury or death. The incidence of anorexia has grown dramatically since the mid-1970s, paralleling the social imperative of thinness (Bordo 1986).

There are direct risks related to using commodities to alter appearance. According to the Consumer Products Safety Commission, more than 200,000 people visit emergency rooms each year as a result of cosmetics-related health problems (Becker 1991). Clothing has its perils as well. In recent years, meralgia paresthetica, marked by sciatica, pain in the hip and thigh region, with tingling and itchy skin, has made an appearance among young women in the form of "skin-tight jean syndrome" (Gateless and Gilroy 1984). In earlier times, the same problems have arisen with the use of girdles, belts, and shoulder bags. The National Safety Council revealed that in 1989 over 100,000 people were injured by their clothing and another 44,000 by their jewelry (Seligson 1992). These figures greatly underestimate actual medical problems.

Approximately 33 to 50 percent of all adult women have used hair coloring agents. Evidence over the past twenty-five years has shown that chemicals used in manufacturing hair dyes cause cancers in animals (Center 1979). Scientists at the National Cancer Institute (NCI) recently reported a significantly greater risk of cancers of the lymph system and of a form of cancer affecting bone marrow, multiple myeloma, in women who use hair coloring (Zahm et al. 1992). In the last twenty years, the incidence of non-Hodgkin's lymphoma in the United States increased by more than 50 percent largely as a result of immune deficiency caused by HIV. However, the NCI researchers conclude that, assuming a causal relationship, hair coloring product use accounts for a larger percentage of non-Hodgkin's lymphoma among women than any other risk factor. These conclusions have been challenged, however, by more recent research (Fackelmann 1994).

Because no cosmetic products require follow-up research for safety and effectiveness, virtually anything can be placed on the market without regard to potential health effects. Even devices implanted in the body, which were not regulated before 1978, can remain on the market for years without appropriate testing. During the decade of controversy over regulating silicone breast implants, the American Society of Plastic and Reconstructive Surgeons vehemently denied any need for controlled studies of the implant in terms of long-term safety. The society spent hundreds of thousands of dollars of its members' money in a public relations effort to avoid the imposition of requirements for such research to the detriment of investing in the expensive scientific follow-up needed (Zones 1992). Although case reports indicate a potential relationship between the implants and connective tissue diseases, recent medical reports discount the association. Definitive research will take more time to assuage women's fears.

Health consequences of beauty products extend beyond their impact on individuals. According to the San Francisco Bay Area Air Quality Management District, aerosols release 25 tons of pollution every day. Almost half of that is from hairsprays. Although aerosols no longer use chlorofluorocarbons (CFCs), which are the greatest cause of depletion of the upper atmosphere ozone layer, aerosol hydrocarbons in hairsprays are a primary contributor to smog and ground pollution.

THE BEAUTY OF DIVERSITY

Both personal transformation and policy intervention will be necessary to allow women to present themselves freely. Governmental institutions, including courts and regulatory agencies, need to accord personal and product liability related to appearance products and services the attention they require to ensure public health and safety. The legal system must develop well-defined case law to assist the court in determining inequitable treatment based on appearance discrimination.

Short of complete liberation from limitations imposed by appearance expectations, women will continue to attempt to "improve" appearance to better social relations. Ultimately, however, this is a futile struggle because of the depth and intensity of feelings and assumptions that have become attached to physical appearance. The predominant advice given to women in the body-image literature is to seek therapeutic assistance to transform damaged self-image into a more positive perspective on oneself. Brown (1985) recommends a social context in which such transformation can take place, as does Schwichtenberg (1989), who suggests that, failing women's unified rejection of costly and potentially dangerous beauty products and processes, women should band together into support networks. Lesbian communities have led the way, showing how mutual support can diminish the effects of the dominant society on women. By using supportive relationships as an arena to experiment with physical presence, women create a manageable and enjoyable social situation. The Black Women's Health Project has successfully modeled the formation of local support groups to encourage members to lead healthier lives. Having a small group as referents reduces the power of commercial interests to define beauty standards. Overweight women have created such resources in the form of national alliances (such as the National Association to Advance Fat Acceptance), magazines (such as *Radiance*), and regional support systems (Iazzetto 1992).

The personal solution to individual self-doubt or even self-loathing of our physical being is to continuously make the decision to contradict the innumerable messages we are given that we are anything less than lovely as human beings. Pinkney (1994) suggests several ways to reshape "a raggedy body image" by improving self-perception: respect yourself, search for the source of the distress, strut your strengths, and embrace the aging process. In a passage from *Beloved,* Toni Morrison demonstrates the way: "Love your hands! Love them. Raise them up and kiss them. Touch others with them, pat them together, stroke them on your face 'cause they don't love that either. *You* got to love it, *you!*" (1994:362).

REFERENCES

Allgood-Merten, Betty, Peter M. Lewinsohn, and Hyman Hops. (1990). "Sex differences and adolescent depression." *Journal of Abnormal Psychology* 99:55–63.

Anderson, Michele, and Tamara Ingram. (1994). "Color, color, color." Pp. 356–61 in Evelyn C. White (ed.), *The Black Women's Health Book,* rev. ed. Seattle: Seal Press.

Aune, R. Kelly, and Krystyna S. Aune. (1994). "The influence of culture, gender and relational status on appearance management." *Journal of Cross-Cultural Psychology* 25(2):258–72.

Banner, Lois W. (1983). *American Beauty.* Chicago: University of Chicago Press.

Barthel, Diane. (1988). *Putting on Appearances: Gender and Advertising.* Philadelphia: Temple University Press.

Beauvoir, Simone de. (1972). *The Coming of Age.* New York: Putnam.

Becker, Hilton. (1991). "Cosmetics: Saving face at what price? *Annals of Plastic Surgery* 26:171–73.

Bordo, Susan. (1986). "Anorexia nervosa: Psychopathology as the crystallization of culture." *Philosophical Forum* 17:73–104.

———. (1993). *Unbearable Weight: Feminism, Western Culture and the Body.* Berkeley: University of California Press.

Bouchard, Claude. (1991). "Is weight fluctuation a risk factor?" *New England Journal of Medicine* 324:1887–89.

Brand, David. (1988). "A nation of health worrywarts?" *Time,* 25 July, 66.

Brody, Jane E. (1992). "Panel criticizes weight-loss programs." *New York Times,* 2 April, A10.

Brown, Laura S. (1985). "Women, weight, and power: Feminist theoretical and therapeutic issues." *Women and Therapy* 4:61–71.

Chapkis, Wendy. (1986). *Beauty Secrets: Women and the Politics of Appearance.* Boston: South End Press.

Chemin, Kim. (1981). *The Obsession: Reflections on the Tyranny of Slenderness.* New York: Harper Colophon Books.

Cimons, Marlene. (1990). "Most Americans dislike their looks, poll finds." *Los Angeles Times,* 19 August, A4.

Cunningham, Michael R. (1986). "Measuring the physical in physical attractiveness: Quasi-experiments on the sociobiology of female facial beauty." *Journal of Personality and Social Psychology* 50:925–35.

Davis, Fred. (1992). *Fashion, Culture and Identity.* Chicago: University of Chicago Press.

Decker, Ruth. (1983). "The not-so-pretty risks of cosmetics." *Medical Self-Care* (Summer):25–31.

Dion, Karen, Ellen Berscheid, and Elaine Waister. (1972). "What is beautiful is good." *Journal of Personality and Social Psychology* 24:285–90.

Dull, Diana, and Candace West. (1991). "Accounting for cosmetic surgery: the accomplishment of gender." *Social Problems* 38:54–70.

Elder, Glen H., Jr. (1969). "Appearance and education in marriage mobility." *American Sociological Review* 34:519–33.

Fackelmann, K. A. (1994). "Mixed news on hair dyes and cancer risk." *Science News* 145 (5 Feb.):86.

Fallon, April E., and Paul Rozin. (1985). "Sex differences in perceptions of desirable body shape." *Journal of Abnormal Psychology* 94:102–5.

Freedman, Rita. (1986). *Beauty Bound.* Lexington, MA: Lexington Books.

———. (1989). *Bodylove.* New York: Harper and Row.

Garchik, Leah. (1992). "Knife tricks come to the rescue." *San Francisco Chronicle,* 1 September, C5.

Gateless, Doreen, and John Gilroy. (1984). "Tight-jeans meralgia: Hot or cold?" *Journal of the American Medical Association* 252:42–43.

Gaudoin, Tina. (1994). "Is all-American beauty un-American?" *Mirabella* (Sept.):144–46.

Gilhooley, Margaret. (1978). "Federal regulation of cosmetics: An overview." *Food Drug Cosmetic Law Journal* 33:231–38.

Glassner, Barry. (1988). *Bodies: Why We Look the Way We Do (and How We Feel about It).* New York: Putnam.

———. (1989). "Fitness and the postmodern self." *Journal of Health and Social Behavior* 30:180–91.

Goffman, Erving. (1963). *Stigma: Notes on the Management of Spoiled Identity.* Englewood Cliffs, NJ: Prentice-Hall.

Goldman, William, and Philip Lewis. (1977). "Beautiful is good: Evidence that the physically attractive are more socially skillful." *Journal of Experimental and Social Psychology* 13:125–30.

Grealy, Lucy. (1994). *Autobiography of a Face.* Boston: Houghton Mifflin.

Greenwood, M. R. C. (1990). "The feminine ideal: A new perspective." *UC Davis Magazine* (July):8–11.

Hansell, Stephen, J. Sparacino, and D. Ronchi. (1982). "Physical attractiveness and blood pressure: Sex and age differences." *Personality and Social Psychology Bulletin* 8:113–21.

Iazzetto, Demetria. (1988). "Women and body image: Reflections in the fun house mirror." Pp. 34–53 in Carol J. Leppa and Connie Miller (eds.), *Women's Health Perspectives: An Annual Review.* Volcano, CA: Volcano Press.

———. (1992). "What's happening with women and body image?" *National Women's Health Network News:* 1, 6, 7.

Iliffe, A. H. (1960). "A study of preferences in feminine beauty." *British Journal of Psychology* 51:267–73.

Johnson, Douglas F. (1985). "Appearance and the elderly." Pp. 152–60 in Jean Ann Graham and Albert M. Kligman (eds.), *The Psychology of Cosmetic Treatments.* New York: Praeger.

Kaiser, Susan B., Carla Freeman, and Stacy B. Wingate. (1984). "Stigmata and negotiated outcomes: The management of appearance by persons with physical disabilities." Annual meeting of the American Sociological Association, San Antonio, TX.

Kaplan, Sheila. (1994). "The ugly face of the cosmetics lobby." *Ms.* (Jan.–Feb.):88–89.

Krieger, Lisa M. (1989). "Fix your nose now, pay later." *San Francisco Examiner,* 30 October, 1.

Lakoff, Robin Tolmach, and Raquel L. Scherr. (1984). *Face Value: The Politics of Beauty.* Boston: Routledge and Kegan Paul.

Langlois, Judith H., Lori A. Roggman, and Loretta A. Rieser-Danner. (1990). "Infants' differential social responses to attractive and unattractive faces." *Developmental Psychology* 26:153–59.

Langlois, Judith H., Jean M. Ritter, Lori A. Roggman, and Lesley S. Vaughn. (1991). "Facial diversity and infant preferences for attractive faces." *Developmental Psychology* 27:79–84.

Lipsky, Suzanne. (1987). *Internalized Racism.* Seattle: Rational Island.

Martin, Emily. (1989). *The Woman in the Body: A Cultural Analysis of Reproduction.* Boston: Beacon Press.

Mathes, Eugene W., and Arnold Kahn. (1975). "Physical attractiveness, happiness, neuroticism, and self-esteem." *Journal of Psychology* 90:27–30.

Mathes, Eugene W., Susan M. Brennan, Patricia M. Haugen, and Holly B. Rice. (1985). "Ratings of physical attractiveness as a function of age." *Journal of Social Psychology* 125:157–68.

McKnight, Gerald. (1989). *The Skin Game: The International Beauty Business Brutally Exposed.* London: Sidgwick and Jackson.

Mercer, Kobena. (1990). "Black hair/style politics." Pp. 247–64 in Russell Ferguson, Martha Gever, Trinh T. Minh-ha, and Cornel West (eds.), *Out There: Marginalization and Contemporary Cultures.* Cambridge: MIT Press.

Molloy, John T. (1977). *The Woman's Dress for Success Book.* New York: Warner Books.

Moog, Carol. (1990). *Are They Selling Her Lips? Advertising and Identity.* New York: William Morrow.

Morrison, Toni. (1994). "We flesh." P. 362 in Evelyn C. White (ed.), *The Black Women's Health Book,* rev. ed. Seattle: Seal Press.

Morton, Patricia. (1991). *Disfigured Images: The Historical Assault on Afro-American Women.* New York: Praeger.

Murstein, Bernard I. (1972). "Physical attractiveness and marital choice." *Journal of Personality and Social Psychology* 22:8–12.

National Task Force on the Prevention and Treatment of Obesity. (1994). "Weight cycling." *Journal of the American Medical Association* 272(15):1196–1202.

Parker, Sheila, Mimi Nichter, Mark Nichter, Nancy Vuckovic, Colette Sims, and Cheryl Ritenbaugh. (1995). "Body image and weight concerns among African American and white adolescent females: Differences that make a difference." *Human Organization* 54(2): 103–13.

Patzer, Gordon L. (1985). *The Physical Attractiveness Phenomena.* New York: Plenum Press.

Penner, Louis A., J. Kevin Thompson, and Dale L. Coovert. (1991). "Size overestimation among anorexics: Much ado about very little?" *Journal of Abnormal Psychology* 100:90–93.

Perrett, D. I., K. A. May, and S. Yoshikawa. (1994). "Facial shape and judgments of female attractiveness." *Nature* 368:239–42.

Pinkney, Deborah Shelton. (1994). "Body check." *Heart and Soul* (Summer):50–55.

Porterfield, H. William. (1982). *Comments of the American Society of Plastic and Reconstructive Surgeons on the Proposed Classification of Inflatable Breast Prosthesis and Silicone Gel-Filled Breast Prosthesis,* submitted to the Food and Drug Administration. Washington, 1 July.

Rierdan, Jill, and Elissa Koff. (1991). "Depressive symptomatology among very early maturing girls." *Journal of Youth and Adolescence* 20:415–515.

Rierdan, Jill, Elissa Koff, and Margaret L. Stubbs. (1989). "Timing of menarche, preparation, and initial menstrual experience: replication and further analyses in a prospective study." *Journal of Youth and Adolescence* 18:413–26.

Robinson, Jennifer. (1983). "Body image in women over forty." *Melpomene Institute Bulletin* 2:12–14.

Rodriguez, Richard. (1990). "Complexion." Pp. 265–78 in Russell Ferguson, Martha Gever, Trinh T. Minhha, and Cornel West (eds.), *Out There: Marginalization and Contemporary Cultures.* Cambridge: MIT Press.

Rothblum, Esther. (1990). "Women and weight: Fad and fiction." *Journal of Psychology* 124:5–24.

Rozin, Paul, and April E. Fallon. (1988). "Body image, attitudes to weight, and misperceptions of figure preferences of the opposite sex: A comparison of men and women in two generations." *Journal of Abnormal Psychology* 97:342–45.

Rubenstein, Steve. (1984). "Cosmetic queen tells her women to think pink." *San Francisco Chronicle,* 3 February, 5.

Schefer, Dorothy. (1988). "Beauty: The real cost of looking good." *Vogue* (Nov.):157–68.

Schwichtenberg, Cathy. (1989). "The 'mother lode' of feminist research: Congruent paradigms in the analysis of beauty culture." Pp. 291–306 in Brenda Dervin, Lawrence Grossberg, Barbara J. O'Keefe, and Ellen Wartella (eds.), *Rethinking Communication.* Newbury Park, CA: Sage.

Seid, Roberta Pollack. (1989). *Never Too Thin: Why Women Are at War with Their Bodies.* New York: Prentice Hall.

Seligson, Susan. (1992). "The attack bra and other vicious clothes." *San Francisco Chronicle,* 13 January, D3–D4.

Shulman, Alix Kates. (1972). *Memoirs of an Ex-Prom Queen.* New York: Bantam Books.

Steger, Pat. (1982). "The making of a BP: How to diet, polish and pay your way to well-groomed perfection." *San Francisco Chronicle,* 3 August, 15.

Taylor, Patricia Ann, and Norval D. Glenn. (1976). "The utility of education and attractiveness for females' status attainment through marriage." *American Sociological Review* 41:484–98.

Thompson, J. Kevin, and Jefferey J. Dolce. (1989). "The discrepancy between emotional vs. rational estimates of body size, actual size, and ideal body ratings: Theoretical and clinical implications." *Journal of Clinical Psychology* 45:473–78.

Udry, J. Richard. (1977). "The importance of being beautiful: a reexamination and racial comparison." *American Journal of Sociology* 83:154–60.

Udry, J. Richard, and Bruce K. Eckland. (1984). "Benefits of being attractive: Differential payoffs for men and women." *Psychological Reports* 54:47–56.

Veblen, Thorstein. [1899] (1973). *The Theory of the Leisure Class.* Boston: Houghton Mifflin.

Walker, Alice. (1988). "Oppressed hair puts a ceiling on the brain." *Ms.* 16(6):52–53.

———. (1990). "Beauty: When the other dancer is the self." Pp. 280–87 in Evelyn C. White (ed.), *The Black Women's Health Book.* Seattle: Seal Press.

Webster, Murray, Jr., and James E. Driskell Jr. (1983). "Beauty as status." *American Journal of Sociology* 89:140–65.

Wolf, Naomi. (1991). *The Beauty Myth: How Images of Beauty Are Used against Women.* New York: William Morrow.

Zahm, Sheila Hoar, Dennis D. Weisenburger, Paula A. Babbitt, et al. (1992). "Use of hair coloring products and the risk of lymphoma, multiple myeloma, and chronic lymphocytic leukemia." *American Journal of Public Health* 82:990–97.

Zones, Jane Sprague. (1992). "The political and social context of silicone breast implant use in the United States." *Journal of Long-Term Effects of Medical Implants* 1:225–41.

8

It's a Big Fat Revolution

NOMY LAMM

I am going to write an essay describing my experiences with fat oppression and the ways in which feminism and punk have affected my work. It will be clear, concise and well thought-out, and will be laid out in the basic thesis paper, college essay format. I will deal with these issues in a mature and intellectual manner. I will cash in on as many fifty-cent words as possible.

I lied. (You probably already picked up on that, huh?) I can't do that. This is my life, and my words are the most effective tool I have for challenging Whiteboyworld (that's my punk-rock cutesy but oh-so-revolutionary way of saying "patriarchy"). If there's one thing that feminism has taught me, it's that the revolution is gonna be on my terms. The revolution will be incited through my voice, my words, not the words of the universe of male intellect that already exists. And I know that a hell of a lot of what I say is totally contradictory. My contradictions can coexist, cuz they exist inside of me, and I'm not gonna simplify them so that they fit into the linear, analytical pattern that I know they're supposed to. I think it's important to recognize that all this stuff does contribute to the revolution, for real. The fact that I write like this cuz it's the way I want to write makes this world just that much safer for me.

I wanna explain what I mean when I say "the revolution," but I'm not sure whether I'll be able to. Cuz at the same time that I'm being totally serious, I also see my use of the term as a mockery of itself. Part of the reason for this is that I'm fully aware that I still fit into dominant culture in many ways. The revolution could very well be enacted against me, instead of for me. I don't want to make myself sound like I think I'm the most oppressed, most punk-rock, most revolutionary person in the world. But at the same time I do think that revolution is a word I should use as often as I can, because it's a concept that we need to be aware of. And I don't just mean it in an abstract, intellectualized way, either. I really do think that the revolution has begun. Maybe that's not apparent to mainstream culture yet, but I see that as a good sign. As soon as mainstream culture picks up on it, they'll try to co-opt it.

For now the revolution takes place when I stay up all night talking with my best friends about feminism and marginalization and privilege and oppression and power and sex and money and real-life rebellion. For now the revolution takes place when I watch a girl stand up in front of a crowd of people and talk about her sexual abuse. For now the revolution takes place when I get a letter from a girl I've never met who says that the zine I wrote changed her life. For now the revolution takes place when the homeless people in my town camp out for a week in the middle of downtown.

For now the revolution takes place when I am confronted by a friend about something racist that I have said. For now the revolution takes place in my head when I know how fucking brilliant my girlfriends and I are.

And I'm living the revolution through my memories and through my pain and through my triumphs. When I think about all the marks I have against me in this society, I am amazed that I haven't turned into some worthless lump of shit. Fatkikecripplecuntqueer. In a nutshell. But then I have to take into account the fact that I'm an articulate, white, middle-class college kid, and that provides me with a hell of a lot of privilege and opportunity for dealing with my oppression that may not be available to other oppressed people. And since my personality/being isn't divided up into a privileged part and an oppressed part, I have to deal with the ways that these things interact, counterbalance and sometimes even overshadow each other. For example, I was born with one leg. I guess it's a big deal, but it's never worked into my body image in the same way that being fat has. And what does it mean to be a white woman as opposed to a woman of color? A middle-class fat girl as opposed to a poor fat girl? What does it mean to be fat, physically disabled and bisexual? (Or fat, disabled and *sexual at all?*)

See, of course, I'm still a real person, and I don't always feel up to playing the role of the revolutionary. Sometimes it's hard enough for me to just get out of bed in the morning. Sometimes it's hard enough to just talk to people at all, without having to deal with the political nuances of everything that comes out of their mouths. Despite the fact that I do tons of work that deals with fat oppression, and that I've been working so so hard on my own body image, there are times when I really hate my body and don't want to deal with being strong all the time. Because I am strong and have thought all of this through in so many different ways, and I do have naturally high self-esteem, I've come to a place where I can honestly say that I love my body and I'm happy with being fat. But occasionally, when I look in the mirror and I see this body that is so different from my friends', so different from what I'm told it should be, I just want to hide away and not deal with it anymore. At these times it doesn't seem fair to me that I have to always be fighting to be happy. Would it be easier for me to just give in and go on another diet so that I can stop this perpetual struggle? Then I could still support the fat grrrl revolution without having it affect me personally in every way. And I know I know I know that's not the answer and I could never do that to myself, but I can't say that the thought never crosses my mind.

And it doesn't help much when my friends and family, who all know how I feel about this, continue to make anti-fat statements and bitch about how fat they feel and mention new diets they've heard about and are just dying to try. "I'm shaped like a watermelon." "Wow, I'm so happy, I now wear a size seven instead of a size nine." "I like this mirror because it makes me look thinner."

I can't understand how they could still think these things when I'm constantly talking about these issues, and I can't believe that they would think that these are okay things to talk about in front of me. And it's not like I want them to censor their conversation around me. . . . I just want them to not think it. I know that most of this is just a reflection of how they feel about themselves and isn't intended as an attack on me or an invalidation of my work, but it makes it that much harder for me. It puts all those thoughts inside me. Today I was standing outside of work and I caught a glimpse of myself in the window and thought, "Hey, I don't look that fat!" And I immediately realized how fucked up that was, but that didn't stop me from feeling more attractive because of it.

I want this out of me. This is not a part of me, and theoretically I can separate it all out and throw away the shit, but it's never really gone. When will this finally be over? When can I move on to other issues? It will never be over, and that's really fucking hard to accept.

I am living out this system of oppression through my memories, and even when I'm not thinking about them they are there, affecting everything I do. Five years old, my first diet. Seven years old, being declared officially "overweight" because I weigh ten pounds over what a "normal" seven-year-old should weigh. Ten years old, learning to starve myself and be happy feeling constantly dizzy. Thirteen years old, crossing the border from being bigger than my friends to actually being "fat." Fifteen years old, hearing the boys in the next room talk about how fat (and hence unattractive) I am. Whenever I perform, I remember the time when my dad said he didn't like the dance I choreographed because I looked fat while I was doing it. Every time I dye my hair I remember when my mom wouldn't let me dye my hair in seventh grade because seeing fat people with dyed hair made her think they were just trying to cover up the fact that they're fat, trying to look attractive despite it (when of course it's obvious what they should really do if they want to look attractive, right?). And these are big memorable occurrences that I can put my finger on and say, "This hurt me." But what about the lifetime of media I've been exposed to that tells me that only thin people are lovable, healthy, beautiful, talented, fun? I know that those messages are all packed in there with the rest of my memories, but I just can't label them and their effects on my psyche. They are elusive and don't necessarily feel painful at the time. They are well disguised and often even appear alluring and romantic. (I will never fall in love because I cannot be picked up and swung around in circles. . . .)

All my life the media and everyone around me have told me that fat is ugly. Which of course is just a cultural standard that has many, many medical lies to fall back upon. Studies have shown that fat people are unhealthy and have short life expectancies. Studies have also shown that starving people have these same peculiarities. These health risks to fat people have been proven to be a result of continuous starvation—dieting—and not of fat itself. I am not fat due to lack of willpower. I've been a vegetarian since I was ten years old. Controlling what I eat is easy for me. Starving myself is not (though for most of my life I wished it was). My body is supposed to be like this, and I've been on plenty of diets where I've kept off some weight for a period of several months and then gained it all back. Two years ago I finally ended the cycle. I am not dieting anymore because I know that this is how my body is supposed to be, and this is how I want it to be. Being fat does not make me less healthy or less active. Being fat does not make me less attractive.

On TV I see a thin woman dancing with a fabulously handsome man, and over that I hear, "I was never happy until I went on [fill in the blank] diet program, but now I'm getting attention from men, and I feel so good! I don't have to worry about what people are saying about me behind my back, because I know I look good. You owe it to yourself to give yourself the life you deserve. Call [fill in the blank] diet program today, and start taking off the pounds right away!" TV shows me a close-up of a teary-eyed fat girl who says, "I've tried everything, but nothing works. I lose twenty pounds, and I gain back twenty-five. I feel so ashamed. What can I do?" The first time I saw that commercial I started crying and memorized the number on the screen. I know that feeling of shame. I know that feeling of having nowhere left to turn, of feeling like I'm useless because I can't lose all that "unwanted fat." But I know that the unhappiness is not a result of my fat. It's a result of a society that tells me I'm bad.

Where's the revolution? My body is fucking beautiful, and every time I look in the mirror and acknowledge that, I am contributing to the revolution.

I feel like at this point I'm expected to try to prove to you that fat can be beautiful by going into descriptions of "rippling thighs and full smooth buttocks." I won't. It's not up to me to convince you that fat can be attractive. I refuse to be the self-appointed full-figured porno queen. Figure it out on your own.

It's not good enough for you to tell me that you "don't judge by appearances"—so fat doesn't bother you. Ignoring our bodies and "judging only by what's on the inside" is not the answer. This seems to be along the same line of thinking as that brilliant school of thought called "humanism": "We are all just people, so let's ignore trivialities such as race, class, gender, sexual preference, body type and so on." Bullshit! The more we ignore these aspects of ourselves, the more shameful they become and the more we are expected to be what is generally implied when these qualifiers are not given—white, straight, thin, rich, male. It's unrealistic to try to overlook these exterior (and hence meaningless, right?) differences, because we're still being brainwashed with the same shit as everyone else. This way we're just not talking about it. And I don't want to be told, "Yes you're fat, but you're beautiful on the inside." That's just another way of telling me that I'm ugly, that there's no way that I'm beautiful on the outside. Fat does not equal ugly, don't give me that. My body *is* me. I want you to see my body, acknowledge my body. True revolution comes not when we learn to ignore our fat and pretend we're no different, but when we learn to use it to our advantage, when we learn to deconstruct all the myths that propagate fat-hate.

My thin friends are constantly being validated by mainstream feminism, while I am ignored. The most widespread mentality regarding body image at this point is something along these lines: Women look in the mirror and think, "I'm fat," but really they're not. Really they're thin.

Really they're thin. But really I'm fat. According to mainstream feminist theory, I don't even exist. I know that women do often look in the mirror and think that they are fatter than they are. And yes, this is a problem. But the analysis can't stop there. There are women who *are* fat, and that needs to be dealt with. Rather than just reassuring people, "No, you're not fat, you're just curvy," maybe we should be demystifying fat and dealing with fat politics as a whole. And I don't mean maybe, I mean it's a necessity. Once we realize that fat is not "inherently bad" (and I can't even believe I'm writing that—"inherently bad"—it sounds so ridiculous), then we can work out the problem as a whole instead of dealing only with this very minute part of it. All forms of oppression work together, and so they have to be fought together.

I think that a lot of the mainstream feminist authors who claim to be dealing with this issue are doing it in a very wrong way. Susie Orbach, for example, with *Fat Is a Feminist Issue.* She tells us: Don't diet, don't try to lose weight, don't feed the diet industry. But she then goes on to say: But if you eat right and exercise, you will lose weight! And I feel like, great, nice, it's so very wonderful that that worked for her, but she's totally missing the point. She is trying to help women, but really she is hurting us. She is hurting us because she's saying that there's still only one body that's okay for us (and she's the one to help us get it!). It's almost like that *Stop the Insanity* woman, Susan Powter. One of my friends read her book and said that the first half of it is all about fat oppression and talks about how hard it is to be fat in our society, but then it says: So use my great new diet plan! This kind of thing totally plays on our emotions so that we think, Wow, this person really understands me. They know where I'm coming from, so they must know what's best for me.

And there are so many "liberal" reasons for perpetuating fat-hate. Yes, we're finally figuring out that dieting never works. How, then, shall we explain this horrible monstrosity? And how can we get rid of it? The new "liberal" view on fat is that it is caused by deep psychological disturbances. Her childhood was bad, she was sexually abused, so she eats and gets fat in order to hide herself away. She uses her fat as a security blanket. Or maybe when she was young her parents caused her to associate food with comfort and love, so she eats to console herself. Or maybe, like with me, her parents were always on diets and always nagging her about what she was eating, so food became something shameful that must be hoarded and kept secret. And for a long, long time I really believed that if my parents hadn't instilled in me all these fucked-up attitudes about food, I wouldn't be fat. But then I realized that my brother and sister both grew up in exactly the same environment, and they are both thin. Obviously this is not the reason that I am fat. Therapy won't help, because there's nothing to cure. When will we stop grasping for reasons to hate fat people and start realizing that fat is a totally normal and natural thing that cannot and should not be gotten rid of?

Despite what I said earlier about my friends saying things that are really hurtful to me, I realize that they are actually pretty exceptional. I don't want to make them seem like uncaring, ignorant people. I'm constantly talking about these issues, and I feel like I'm usually able to confront my friends when they're being insensitive, and they'll understand or at least try to. Sometimes when I leave my insular circle of friends I'm shocked at what the "real world" is like. Hearing boys on the bus refer to their girlfriends as their "bitches," seeing fat women being targeted for harassment on the street, watching TV and seeing how every fat person is depicted as a food-obsessed slob, seeing women treated as property by men who see masculinity as a right to power. . . . I leave these situations feeling like the punk scene, within which most of my interactions take place, is so sheltered. I cannot imagine living in a community where I had nowhere to go for support. I cannot imagine living in the "real world."

But then I have to remember that it's still there in my community—these same fucked-up attitudes are perpetuated within the punk scene as well; they just take on more subtle forms. I feel like these issues are finally starting to be recognized and dealt with, but fat hating is still pretty standard. Of course everyone agrees that we shouldn't diet and that eating disorders are a result of our oppressive society, but it's not usually taken much further than that. It seems like people have this idea that punk is disconnected from the media. That because we are this cool underground subculture, we are immune to systems of oppression. But the punkest, coolest kids are still the skinny kids. And the same cool kids who are so into defying mainstream capitalist "Amerika" are the ones who say that fat is a symbol of capitalist wealth and greed. Yeah, that's a really new and different way of thinking: Blame the victim. Perpetuate institutionalized oppression. Fat people are not the ones who are oppressing these poor, skinny emo boys.

This essay is supposed to be about fat oppression. I feel like that's all I ever talk about. Sometimes I feel my whole identity is wrapped up in my fat. When I am fully conscious of my fat, it can't be used against me. Outside my secluded group of friends, in hostile situations, I am constantly aware that at any moment I could be harassed. Any slight altercation with another person could lead to a barrage of insults thrown at my body. I am always ready for it. I've found it doesn't happen nearly as often as I expect it, but still I always remain aware of the possibility. I am "the Fat Girl." I am "the Girl Who Talks About Fat Oppression." Within the punk scene, that's my security blanket. People know about me and know about my work, so I assume that they're not gonna be laughing behind my back about my fat. And if they are, then I know I have support from other people around me. The punk scene gives me tons of support that I know I wouldn't get elsewhere. Within the punk scene, I am able to put out zines, play music, do spoken-word performances that are intensely personal to me. I feel really strongly about keeping nothing secret. I can go back to the old cliché about the personal being political, and no matter how trite it may sound, it's true. I went for so long never talking about being fat, never talking about how that affects my self-esteem, never talking about the ways that I'm oppressed by this society. Now I'm talking. Now I'm talking. I'm talking all the time, and people listen to me. I have support.

And at the same time I know that I have to be wary of the support that I receive. Because I think to some people this is just seen as the cool thing, that by supporting me they're somehow receiving a certain amount of validation from the punk scene. Even though I am totally open and don't keep secrets, I have to protect myself.

This is the revolution. I don't understand the revolution. I can't lay it all out in black and white and tell you what is revolutionary and what is not. The punk scene is a revolution, but not in and of itself. Feminism is a revolution; it is solidarity as well as critique and confrontation. This is the fat grrrl revolution. It's mine, but it doesn't belong to me. Fuckin' yeah.

9

Strong and Large Black Women?

Exploring Relationships Between Deviant Womanhood and Weight

TAMARA BEAUBOEUF-LAFONTANT

Within the U.S. imagination, Black women have typically represented a "deviant womanhood" (Townsend Gilkes 2001) in terms of both physical and psychological characteristics. While white women have fought against assumptions of their passivity and weakness, Black women have had to contend with the myth of the strong Black woman, a historically complex distillation of images derived from two sources: the rationalizations of a white slave-holding society and Black culture's attempt to define womanhood for itself.

Understanding that societal and cultural images of Black womanhood too often have been rooted in "negative anti-woman mythology" (hooks 1981, 86), I draw on the work of Black and white feminists sensitive to the reality of multiple oppressions in Black women's lives. In particular, my analysis is rooted in Becky Thompson's (1992, 1994b) contention that eating problems—such as anorexia, bulimia, compulsive overeating and/or dieting—are common for diverse women given their origin as sensible "survival strategies" that use food to cope with experiences of oppression, trauma, and pain. Because eating problems are the embodiment of social inequalities, my analysis also extends recent work focused on the meaning of body image among Black women (Lovejoy 2001). In this article, however, I specifically examine how the presumption of strength and deviance may push Black women to develop eating problems—particularly compulsive overeating—that they and others are unable or unwilling to name as such. Thus, this article uses an oblique reading of much of the body image and Black feminist literature, bringing them in conversation to develop a new approach to examining Black women's weight and perceptions of their bodies. As a result, the following analysis focuses on two areas typically left out of body image discussions of Black women—a critical understanding of the particular social assumptions held of them and their own voices and reflections on their social realities. Drawing on a small yet currently undertheorized area of overlap between feminist and body image investigations of Black women's weight, I illuminate how the discourse of strength is a key oppressive experience that results in the genesis of eating problems among African American women as well as masks them.

To focus on Black women's social context and lived realities as a critical back-drop to discussions of their weight and body image, I organize the rest of the arti-

Tamara Beauboeuf-Lafontant, "Strong and Large Black Women? Exploring Relationships Between Deviant Womanhood and Weight," from *Gender & Society,* Volume 17/2003, p. 111–121.

cle around the following three themes: historical views of strength in Black women, contemporary Black feminist critiques of these images and their distortions of Black women's realities, and current research focused on eliciting Black women's actual voices on the subject of their bodies and lives.

MAMMY: A DISCOURSE OF DEVIANCE EMBODIED

A persistent "controlling image" of Black womanhood is that of the Mammy (Hill Collins 1991, 68). Designed to make the exploitation of Black women appear "natural, normal, and an inevitable part of everyday life" (Hill Collins 1991, 68), the large, dark-skinned, sexless Mammy was central to the rationalization of slavery as a "peculiar institution" of human bondage. A "passive nurturer, a mother figure who gave all without expectation of return, who not only acknowledged her inferiority to whites but who loved them" (hooks 1981, 84–85), Mammy was rewarded and elevated for being, simultaneously, a capable, domesticated woman and a dutiful, grateful slave. Physically removed and distinguished by her size, skin color and age from the ideals of true (white) womanhood, she embodied a deviance—a "dark heaviness" (Williamson 1998, 66)—that allowed a slaveholding society to see itself as "benign" in both its exploitation of Blacks and its domestication of women (White 1985, 58).

Physical deviance among Black women has been closely tied to perceptions of their emotional and spiritual strength (Townsend Gilkes 2001). A key example of such deviance exists in the appropriation of Sojourner Truth by nineteenth-century white feminists. Fabricated by Francis Dana Gage 12 years after the fact, the 1851 "Ain't I a woman?" soliloquy attributed to Truth was based on images of her as a deviant: "The weird, wonderful creature, who was at once a marvel and a mystery . . . this almost Amazon form, which stood nearly six feet high" whose performance of the speech had a "magical influence" on the audience and contributed greatly to the efforts of Gage and other reformers (Irvin Painter 1996, 165, 167, 168). While Truth's experiences as an enslaved woman are noted, the focus on her physical form and strength depicts structural oppression as having little real negative influence on her. She exists somehow outside of and in spite of slavery and sexism.

A modern-day example of attributions of strength based on perceptions of physical deviance is revealed in Retha Powers's (1989) account of her own battle with compulsive overeating and dieting. After admitting her struggle to a white high school counselor, she received the following response:

> You don't have to worry about feeling attractive or sexy because Black women aren't seen as sex objects, but as women. . . . Also, fat is more acceptable in the Black community—that's another reason you don't have to worry about it. (Powers 1989, 78, 134)

Despite the counselor's voiced desire to value Powers (1989) as a woman, her implicit view was of women as thin, white, and sexual. Furthermore, she viewed Powers's physical deviance from this norm as evidence of her emotional deviance—her stability and potential to help others "with more serious problems." In the process, the counselor revealed that her presumption of Black women's strength and physical deviance completely overshadows and rejects Powers's reality of having an eating problem. Resisting this image of deviance and the erasure of her reality, however, Powers titled her essay "Fat Is a Black Women's Issue" to point to this denial of both her eating problem and her humanity in a world that sees fat as an exclusively white feminist issue (Orbach [1978] 1988).

INVERSIONS OF OLD STEREOTYPES: FROM MAMMY TO THE STRONG BLACK WOMAN

While Powers (1989) focused on an oppressive societal image of Black womanhood, within African American culture, there are also troubling perceptions of Black women. Although most Black women would not see themselves as nor aspire to be Mammies, they do closely identify with the image of the strong Black woman—the African American woman who struggles to "make a way outa no way" (Reagon 1980, cited in

Thompson 1994b), who single-handedly raises her children, works multiple jobs, and supports an extended family. As Angela Mitchell and Kennise Herring (1998, 67) wrote, "If there's one prevailing image we have of ourselves, it's that we can survive anything. We get that image from our mothers, who frequently shield us from the truth of their feelings."

Rather than take care of her white owners like her Mammy predecessor, the Black superwoman now withstands adversity for the sake of her own family and community. However, many of the characteristics of fortitude and caretaking ascribed to strong Black women are an inversion of the Mammy myth and a continuation of the extreme selflessness that the Mammy role expected of Black women. Consistent in both stereotypes is the idea of a Black woman as a "longsuffering, religious, maternal figure," loved for "her self-sacrificing self-denial for those she loves" (hooks 1981, 66). While in some ways, an affirmation of women's capabilities, particularly within a society that associates femininity with passivity and weakness, the strength of Black women is often an ironic inversion of their deviance and a reflection of Black culture and white society's failure to take seriously Black women's oppression.

CONFLICTED INNER VISIONS AND THE MASK/ING OF STRENGTH

Black women's relationships to their bodies occur within overlapping cultural contexts that offer contradictory messages about their value and function (Lovejoy 2001). A self-described "dark, plump, African-American woman," sociologist, and ordained minister, Cheryl Townsend Gilkes (2001) wrote about the ambivalence, the "conflicted inner visions," that shaped her relationship to her own body during her youth:

> At the same time my peers and my mother impressed me with my visual deviance, my peers, my family, and my church encouraged me to occupy leadership roles and to excel in other ways. The negative voices about my size often came from the same chorus as the positive voices about other aspects of myself. (Townsend Gilkes 2001, 193)

The push-pull of criticism and then acceptance for her size seems to reflect what Townsend Gilkes (2001) also noted as the cultural reverence for the large Black woman:

> In spite of the high premium placed on culturally exalted images of white female beauty and the comedic exploitation that surrounds the large black woman, many African-American women know that *the most respected physical image of black women, within and outside of the community, is that of the large woman.* (Townsend Gilkes 2001, 183, emphasis added)

However, within the context of expectations for selflessness, the strength attributed to Black women is contradictory. As bell hooks (1981, 83) noted, "Much of what has been perceived by whites as an Amazonic trait in black women has been merely stoical acceptance of situations we have been powerless to change." Thus, rather than a reflection of agency and influence, the strength demonstrated by and seen in Black women is too often a sign of their resignation to the oppressiveness of their social context. That is, even within a culture that respects "large" Black women, the deviance "is not necessarily loved. It is an image of power in a community where women need to be fortified and empowered. Yet some of the most powerless women in the community struggle with overweight and its unhealthy consequences" (Townsend Gilkes 2001, 183).

Because the strong Black woman discourse is upheld both within and outside of the Black community, there is very little resonance for any African American woman who acknowledges or desires to speak about her weaknesses, pains, and frustrations. A clear example of this erasure and denial of pain is revealed in Meri Nana-Ama Danquah's (1998, 20) autobiographical account of depression. The incongruity of the "weakness" that depression suggests to many outsiders with the strength Danquah was assumed to embody meant that she could find "no acceptable ways, no appropriate words to begin a dialogue about this illness." In the words of a white woman speaking to Danquah (1998, 20), "It's just that when *black* women start going on Prozac, you know the whole world is falling apart." Furthermore, Danquah was vilified by members of her own culture as a race traitor who had forgotten the therapeutic aspects of religion and the cultural legacy of strength that runs through her blood: "Girl, you've been hanging out with too many white folk"; "What do you have to be depressed about? If our people could make it through slavery, we can make it through anything"; "Take your troubles to Jesus, not no damn psychiatrist" (Danquah 1998, 21). In such a context of pressure from both within and outside their communities to be strong, Black women suffering from depression often meet others' expectations of strength by engaging in "stoicism . . . denial . . . [and] a complete negation of their pain" (Danquah 1998, 277).

Based on their clinical work with Black women, Mitchell and Herring (1998) elucidated the behavioral consequences of such stoicism and of Black women's seeing themselves as the "mules of the world" (Neale Hurston 1937).

> Many Black women find it hard to admit they are overworked, overwhelmed, underloved, and depressed. . . . So instead of complaining or asking for help, many Black women try to keep on while they medicate their pain in self-destructive ways: by overeating, smoking, drinking, or using drugs. (Mitchell and Herring 1998, 67)

Two intriguing possibilities emerge from Mitchell and Herring's (1998) analysis: first, that Black women may unconsciously participate in their own dehumanization by seeing themselves through this discourse of deviance and strength as "mules of the world," rather than as human beings with capabilities as well as needs and vulnerabilities; and second, that overeating may be a form of self medication for women/mules who are overburdened and burden themselves with too much caring and responsibility for others. From a symbolic approach to the body and weight, we may view some overweight and obese Black women as literally carrying the weight of the world on their bodies. However, because overweight Black women are not as stigmatized by the larger society or by their own culture as are white women (Hebl and Heatherton 1998), a Black woman's "survival strategy" of overeating would remain invisible to many around her (Thompson 1994b). This is one potential connection between the higher weights observed among Black women and the emotional strain of having to minister to the needs of many. Furthermore, an uncritical acceptance of overweight as normative among Black women, as is currently found in much of the mainstream body image literature, may reflect research complicity in expecting Black women to represent a deviant, not fully human, womanhood, as well as a lack of interest in seeing Black women show a full range of emotions and needs that are not permitted by the stereotype of strength.

STRONG AND LARGE BLACK WOMEN SPEAKING OUT IN THE BODY IMAGE LITERATURE

Telling information about the presence of eating problems among Black women and the influence of discourses of strength and deviance on the interpretation of such problems is found largely in the few qualitative studies conducted on Black women and weight. In this research, we hear Black women, particularly those who are poor or struggling financially, facing societal and cultural expectations to be emotionally strong and physically large.

In their interviews with 36 college-educated Black women, Walcott-McQuigg et al. (1995) found that feelings of being overworked and depressed influenced women's eating patterns. In the words of one interviewee,

> I think overall weight management is not as important because we have too many other things that we have to worry about. . . . Many of us are managing homes as single parents, trying to raise children as single parents, and trying to make financial ends meet as single parents. I mean survival is what our concern is, not being the right size or weight. (Walcott-McQuigg et al. 1995, 513)

This woman's comments reflect the sense that strong Black women are given a cultural imperative that makes concern for self the equivalent of trivial self-indulgence—"I certainly have other things that preoccupy my mind as opposed to watching every pound I gain" (Walcott-McQuigg et al. 1995, 513). However, the fact that she is steadily gaining weight might reveal that she is barely surviving her responsibilities to others. As another interviewee noted, "food is a vehicle that is used to comfort us when we may not have much else" (Walcott-McQuigg et al. 1995, 512). Eating can also become a way of meeting social responsibilities and superficially taking care of oneself: "The only thing that I had time to do for myself socially to feel good was to eat" (Walcott-McQuigg et al. 1995, 507). And while overweight is caused by a combination of genetic, biological, and psychosocial factors, the concern we develop from a sensitivity to the discourses of strength and deviance is that the weight-related diseases that plague the Black female community (adult-onset diabetes, heart disease, hypertension) may be embodied manifestations of the contradictory distinction of being strong and powerless like a mule.

While individual Black women struggle with their myriad responsibilities to others, African American culture also assumes that substantial weight is an unremarkable, if not normative, aspect of Black women's lives. In their interviews with 24 lower-and middle-income rural Black women, Baturka, Hornsby, and Schorling (2000, 235) found common themes of personal dissatisfaction with weight as well as "strong cultural pressure to be self-accepting of their physical shape, to 'be happy with what God gave you,' and to make the most of their appearance." The researchers identified the existence of two voices among the women: cultural prescriptions to be self-accepting that clashed with their individual desires to manage their weight. The fact that 87.5 percent of the sample was either overweight or obese suggests that at least for these women, the weaker voice is their own. As the researchers noted, the influence of "significant male partners" to be self-accepting was considerable: "Half of the obese and one third of the overweight respondents reported that their husbands or boyfriends did not say anything about their weight. Another third of the overweight women said their male partners complimented them on their figures" (Baturka, Hornsby, and Schorling 2000, 238).

Although cultural variations in ideals of female physical attractiveness exist, that Black women prefer to be "thick" rather than "thin" is not simply their own construction of attractiveness or a reflection of their association of "positive characteristics, such as power and well-being, with heavy women" (Flynn and Fitzgibbon 1996, 627). Several studies reveal that Black women often explain and adjust their body sizes to meet the approval of Black men in their lives (Allan, Mayo, and Michel 1993; Ofosu, LaFreniere, and Senn 1998; Thomas 1989; Walcott-McQuigg et al. 1995). Unlike Black men, Black women describe beauty in psychological and attitudinal, rather than specific physical, traits (Gore 1999). For example, while Black adolescent girls identify style and attitude as key markers of beauty, they are simultaneously "aware that African American boys had more specific physical criteria for an 'ideal girl' than they had themselves" (Parker et al. 1995, 108). Thus, it seems that the physical traits that Black women embody and claim to prefer are often a reflection of Black men's desires. As one woman recalled, "[Black men] didn't want a neck bone. They liked a picnic ham" (Thompson 1994b, 30).

Among African American women who prefer to be "healthy" or "thick" in appearance, Allan, Mayo, and Michel (1993, 329) concluded that "'healthy' connotes solidness, stamina, attractiveness, and being well-nourished, or *a woman who can 'handle the rough times better'*" (emphasis added). However, the researchers also astutely remarked on a painful irony among the lower-income Black women who seem most supportive of a higher weight for themselves: Their association of size with stamina obscures the fact that many such women experience economic and social powerlessness (Allan, Mayo, and Michel 1993, 331; see also Flynn and Fitzgibbon 1996). Thus, a culture that prefers strong-looking, heavier women also seems to overlook the fact that such women, particularly those with lower incomes, have limited power in and over their lives.

Becky Thompson's (1994b) interview-based investigation of problem eating among 18 Black, Latina, and lesbian women found these women were living the contradictions of oppressive images of womanhood. While participants had problems with anorexia, bulimia, dieting, and compulsive eating, all 5 Black women in her sample were compulsive eaters and dieters, and none was anorexic (Thompson 1994a, 357).

As Thompson noted, precisely because Black women often "grow up amid positive messages about eating" (Thompson 1992, 554), compulsive eating may be a culturally acceptable way for these women to speak the unspeakable. Thompson's overall assertion that eating problems are not uncommon among Black women suggests to me that what may distinguish Black from white women is not their different levels of preoccupation with a culture of thinness but their expression of trauma and powerlessness in distinct, culturally influenced manners (Williamson 1998). That is, whether engaged in overeating or self-starvation, women with eating problems are clamoring for recognition within a society that systematically ignores, belittles, and violates them (Orbach [1978] 1988). This would explain the tentative finding that as Black women's socioeconomic status improves, the incidence of anorexia and bulimia among them increases (Abrams, Allen, and Gray 1993; Ofosu, LaFreniere, and Senn 1998; Wilfley et al. 1996). The appearance of these particular eating problems suggests that in contradiction to the discourse of strength and deviance, Black women are not impervious to socially induced eating problems. However, the presumption of an extraordinary strength renders this fact invisible to many around them, and it also makes Black women less likely to acknowledge their own vulnerabilities (Root 1990).

While the longings for power and validation among African American women are real, so are the systemic obstructions to their attainment. Could it be that Black women's bodies become the playing field for such contradictions between personal needs and cultural norms, between the desire for control and the persistence of oppression, between the voicing of pain and the denial of its existence? While such examples are far from conclusive, they do suggest that a necessary question to ask of Black women is not why they are overweight but what may be weighing them down. If we follow the feminist lead of taking a symbolic approach to weight (Chernin 1981), then we need to know the language of the weight, the voice of its hungers, and the tabooed conversations (cultural and societal) it attempts to hold. If we recognize that the strong Black woman stereotype is a mask, then we need to learn how it is hiding tears, projecting control and strength, and denying human pain in a way manifest by covering up a body in excess weight. In short, a focus on this stereotype of strength and deviance enables us to recognize how Black women's particular "multiple jeopardy" (King 1988) takes physical and emotional form.

CONCLUSION: MOVING BEYOND DENIAL AND DEVIANCE

Images of strength and deviance are myths that distort the reality of Black women's existence at the bottom of two patriarchies. In this article, I have maintained that what appears on the surface to be a protective factor may in fact be masking lives that are often exploited, unsatisfying, and overburdened—problems from which Black communities and the larger society do not protect African American women. Thus, it is both disingenuous and premature to extol the strengths and freedom of Black women with regard to their bodies. Rather, we need to prioritize research on how Black women understand their weight and their lives. If and when we ask Black women to speak with courage and honesty about their strengths and weaknesses, their dreams and disappointments, their loves and their angers, we may come to hear stories that are disturbing. Based on my reading of the discourses of strength and deviance, I believe it is unlikely that the predominant theme in conversations about weight will center on self-satisfaction, style, and looking good for Black men, as some studies have argued (Parker et al. 1995; Thomas 1989). We may find that rather than an assertion of agency and power, the weight that some Black women carry is a sign of dis-ease and un-ease, of problematic divisions of labor within Black families as well as between Black and non-Black communities.

Future studies, both quantitative and qualitative, are needed to distinguish Black women's individual choices about the size and shape of their bodies and their attempts to speak oppressive realities through their bodies. I am currently engaged in an interview study of Black women of varied weights to investigate the pressures they feel to embody their womanhood in particular physical forms and psychological traits. Exploring the thoughts and struggles of Black women clients of weight-reducing programs is another important avenue for research. Conducting such research will help generate more realistic standards of weight for all women so that health, rather than thinness or thickness, becomes a universal and attainable goal. My argument for such research centers not on committing Black women to a set of unhealthy weight norms, but on refashioning our approach to women's weight by illuminating, in the case of Black women, one of the most troubling discourses used to contain them as well as other women who are deemed their opposites. We cannot have realistic views of women's healthy weights until we acknowledge that many of our perceptions of women are based on flawed and controlling images of who they are expected to be and the physical forms that they are pressed to embody.

Finally, while I do not believe that every overweight Black woman has an eating problem, I do maintain that Black women's tendencies to mask their emotions, frustrations, angers, and fears, all in an attempt to live up to the image of the strong Black woman, contribute to some of the weight that individual Black women carry—through overeating, lack of regular exercise, or a general sense that focusing on their own health needs is trivial or selfish. As a result, I wonder if we change our cultural and societal expectations of Black womanhood, whether African American women will still be among the most overweight, obese, and prone to debilitating and fatal adult-onset diseases. When Black women feel empowered to enjoy their lives, to speak and be heard, and to choose their destinies, when they "learn *how* to put [their] needs first, [g]iving both Guilt and Struggle the finger" (Morgan 1999, 108), we may become compelled to adjust our cultural and societal expectations regarding weight and Black women.

REFERENCES

Abrams, Kay K., La Rue Allen, and James Gray. 1993. Disordered eating attitudes and behaviors, psychological adjustment, and ethnic identity: A comparison of Black and white female college students. *International Journal of Eating Disorders* 14:49–57.

Allan, Janet, Kelly Mayo, and Yvonne Michel. 1993. Body size values of white and Black women. *Research in Nursing and Health* 16:323–33.

Baturka, Natalie, Paige P. Hornsby, and John B. Schorling. 2000. Clinical implications of body image among rural African-American women. *Journal of General Internal Medicine* 15:235–41.

Chernin, Kim. 1981. *The obsession: Reflections on the tyranny of slenderness.* New York: Harper Colophon.

Danquah, Meri Nana-Ama. 1998. *Willow weep for me: A Black woman's journey through depression.* New York: One World.

Flynn, Kristin, and Marian Fitzgibbon. 1996. Body image ideals of low-income African American mothers and their preadolescent daughters. *Journal of Youth and Adolescence* 26:615–31.

Gore, Shirley. 1999. African-American women's perceptions of weight: Paradigm shift for advanced practice. *Holistic Nurse Practitioner* 13:71–79.

Hebl, Michelle, and Todd Heatherton. 1998. The stigma of obesity in women: The difference is black and white. *Personality and Social Psychology Bulletin* 24: 417–26.

Hill Collins, Patricia. 1991. *Black feminist thought.* New York: Routledge.

hooks, bell. 1981. *Ain't I a woman: Black women and feminism.* Boston: South End.

Irvin Painter, Nell. 1996. *Sojourner Truth: A life, a symbol.* New York: Norton.

King, Deborah K. 1988. Multiple jeopardy, multiple consciousness: The context of a Black feminist ideology. *Signs: Journal of Women in Culture and Society* 14:42–72.

Lovejoy, Meg. 2001. Disturbances in the social body: Differences in body image and eating problems among African American and white women. *Gender & Society* 15:239–61.

Mitchell, Angela, and Kennise Herring. 1998. *What the blues is all about: Black women overcoming stress and depression.* New York: Perigee.

Morgan, Joan. 1999. *When chickenheads come home to roost: My life as a hip-hop feminist.* New York: Touchstone.

Neale Hurston, Zora. 1937. *Their eyes were watching God.* Greenwich, CT: Fawcett.

Ofosu, Helen B., Kathryn D. LaFreniere, and Charlene Y. Senn. 1998. Body image perception among women of African descent: A normative context? *Feminism and Psychology* 8:303–23.

Orbach, Susie. [1978] 1988. *Fat is a feminist issue: The anti-diet guide to permanent weight loss.* New York: Berkley Books.

Parker, Sheila, Mimi Nichter, Mark Nichter, Nancy Vuckovic, Colette Sims, and Cheryl Ritenbaugh. 1995. Body image and weight concerns among African American and white adolescent females: Differences that make a difference. *Human Organization* 54:103–14.

Powers, Retha. 1989. Fat is a Black women's issue. *Essence,* October, 75, 78, 134, 136.

Root, Maria P. P. 1990. Disordered eating in women of color. *Sex roles* 22:525–36.

Thomas, Veronica G. 1989. Body-image satisfaction among Black women. *Journal of Social Psychology* 129: 107–12.

Thompson, Becky. 1992. "A way outa no way": Eating problems among African-American, Latina, and white women. *Gender & Society* 6:546–61.

———. 1994a. Food, bodies, and growing up female: Childhood lessons about culture, race, and class. In *Feminist perspectives on eating disorders,* edited by Patricia Fallon, Melanie A. Katzman, and Susan C. Wooley. New York: Guilford.

———. 1994b. *A hunger so wide and so deep: American women speak out on eating problems.* Minneapolis: University of Minnesota Press.

Townsend Gilkes, Cheryl. 2001. *If it wasn't for the women . . . : Black women's experience and womanist culture in church and community.* Maryknoll, NY: Orbis.

Walcott-McQuigg, Jacqueline, Judith Sullivan, Alice Dan, and Barbara Logan. 1995. Psychosocial factors influencing weight control behavior of African American women. *Western Journal of Nursing Research* 17: 502–20.

White, Deborah Gray. 1985. *Ar'n't I a woman? Female slaves in the plantation South.* New York: Norton.

Wilfley, Denise, George B. Schreiber, Kathleen M. Pike, Ruth H. Striegel-Moore, David J. Wright, and Judith Rodin. 1996. Eating disturbance and body image: A comparison of a community sample of adult Black and white women. *International Journal of Eating Disorders* 20:377–87.

Williamson, Lisa. 1998. Eating disorders and the cultural forces behind the drive for thinness: Are African American women really protected? *Social Work in Health Care* 28:61–73.

10

To Veil or Not To Veil?

A Case Study of Identity Negotiation Among Muslim Women in Austin, Texas

JEN'NAN GHAZAL READ

JOHN P. BARTKOWSKI

In light of expanded social opportunities for women in Western industrialized countries, scholars have turned their attention to the status of women in other parts of the world. This burgeoning research literature has given rise to a debate concerning the social standing of Muslim women in the Middle East. On one hand, some scholars contend that Muslim women occupy a subordinate status within many Middle Eastern countries. Some empirical evidence lends support to this view, as many researchers have highlighted the traditional and gendered customs prescribed by Islam—most notably, the veiling and shrouding of Muslim women (Afshar 1985; Fox 1977; Odeh 1993; Papanek 1973; see Dragadze 1994 for review).

On the other hand, a growing number of scholars now argue that claims about the oppression and subjugation of veiled Muslim women may, in many regards, be overstated (Brenner 1996; El-Guindi 1981, 1983; El-Solh and Mabro 1994; Fernea 1993, 1998; Gocek and Balaghi 1994; Hessini 1994; Kadioglu 1994; Kandiyoti 1991, 1992; Webster 1984). Scholars who have generated insider portraits[1] of Islamic gender relations have revealed that Muslim women's motivations for veiling can vary dramatically. Some Muslim women veil to express their strongly held convictions about gender difference, others are motivated to do so more as a means of critiquing Western colonialism in the Middle East. It is this complexity surrounding the veil that leads Elizabeth Fernea (1993, 122) to conclude that the veil (or *hijab*) "means different things to different people within [Muslim] society, and it means different things to Westerners than it does to Middle Easterners" (see also Abu-Lughod 1986; Walbridge 1997).

Our study takes as its point of departure the conflicting meanings of the veil among both Muslim religious elites and rank-and-file Islamic women currently living in the United States. In undertaking this investigation, we supplement the lone study (published in Arabic) that compares the gender attitudes of veiled and unveiled women (see L. Ahmed 1992 for review). That study, based largely on survey data collected from university women living in the Middle East, demonstrates that while veiled women evince some-

Jen'nan Ghazal Read and John P. Bartkowski, "To Veil or Not to Veil? A Case Study of Identity Negotiation Among Muslim Women in Austin, Texas," from *Gender & Society,* Volume 14/2000, p. 395–417.

what conservative gender attitudes, the vast majority of them support women's rights in public life and a substantial proportion subscribe to marital equality. We seek to extend these suggestive findings by using in-depth, personal interviews, because data from such interviews are more able to capture the negotiation of cultural meanings by veiled and unveiled respondents, as well as the nuances of these women's gender identities (Mishler 1986). . . .

THE LANDSCAPE OF ISLAM

. . . The most germane aspects of Muslim theology for this study concern two sets of Islamic sacred texts, the Qur'an and the hadiths (e.g., Munson 1988). The Qur'an is held in high esteem by virtually all Muslims. Not unlike the "high view" of the Bible embraced by various conservative Christian groups, many contemporary Muslims believe that the Qur'an is the actual Word of God that was ably recorded by Muhammad during the early portion of the seventh century. In addition to the Qur'an, many Muslims also look to the hadiths for moral and spiritual guidance in their daily lives. The hadiths, second-hand reports of Muhammad's personal traditions and lifestyle, began to be collected shortly after his death because of the difficulty associated with applying the dictates of the Qur'an to changing historical circumstances. The full collection of these hadiths has come to be known as the *sunna.* Along with the Qur'an, the hadiths constitute the source of law that has shaped the ethics and values of many Muslims.

Within Islam, the all-male Islamic clergy (variously called *faghihs, imams, muftis, mullahs,* or *ulumas*) often act as interpretive authorities who are formally charged with distilling insights from the Qur'an or hadiths and with disseminating these scriptural interpretations to the Muslim laity (Munson 1988). Given that such positions of structural privilege are set aside for Muslim men, Islam is a patriarchal religious institution. Yet, patriarchal institutions do not necessarily produce homogeneous gender ideologies, a fact underscored by the discursive fissures that divide Muslim religious authorities and elite commentators concerning the veil.

COMPETING DISCOURSES OF THE VEIL IN CONTEMPORARY ISLAM

Many Muslim clergy and Islamic elites currently prescribe veiling as a custom in which "good" Muslim women should engage (Afshar 1985; Al-Swailem 1995; Philips and Jones 1985; Siddiqi 1983). Proponents of veiling often begin their defense of this cultural practice by arguing that men are particularly vulnerable to corruption through unregulated sexual contact with women (Al-Swailem 1995, 27–29; Philips and Jones 1985, 39–46; Siddiqi 1983). These experts contend that the purpose of the hijab or veil is the regulation of such contact:

> The society that Islam wants to establish is not a sensate, sex-ridden society. . . . The Islamic system of *Hijab* is a wide-ranging system which protects the family and closes those avenues that lead toward illicit sex relations or even indiscriminate contact between the sexes in society. . . . To protect her virtue and to safeguard her chastity from lustful eyes and covetous hands, Islam has provided for purdah which sets norms of dress, social get-together . . . and going out of the four walls of one's house in hours of need. (Siddiqi 1983, vii–viii)

Many expositors of the pro-veiling discourse call attention to the uniquely masculine penchant for untamed sexual activity and construe the veil as a God-ordained solution to the apparent disparities in men's and women's sexual appetites. Women are therefore deemed responsible for the management of men's sexuality (Al-Swailem 1995, 29). Some contend that the Muslim woman who veils should be sure that the hijab covers her whole body (including the palms of her hands), should be monotone in color ("so as not to be attractive to draw the attentions to"), and should be opaque and loose so as not to reveal "the woman's shape or what she is wearing underneath" (Al-Swailem 1995, 24–25).

Pro-veiling Muslim luminaries also defend veiling on a number of nonsexual grounds. The veil, according to these commentators, serves as (1) a demonstration of the Muslim woman's unwavering obedience to the tenets of Islam; (2) a clear indication of the essential differences distinguishing men from women; (3) a reminder to women that their proper place is in the home rather than in pursuing public-sphere activities; and (4) a sign of the devout Muslim woman's disdain for the profane, immodest, and consumerist cultural customs of the West (e.g., Al-Swailem 1995, 27–29; Siddiqi 1983, 140, 156). In this last regard, veiling is legitimated as an anti-imperialist statement of ethnic and cultural distinctiveness.

Nevertheless, the most prominent justifications for veiling entail, quite simply, the idea that veiling is prescribed in the Qur'an (see Arat 1994; Dragadze 1994; Hessini 1994; Sherif 1987; Shirazi-Mahajan 1995 for reviews). Several Muslim clergy place a strong interpretive emphasis on a Qur'anic passage (S. 24:31) that urges women "not [to] display their beauty and adornments" but rather to "draw their head cover over their bosoms and not display their ornament." Many of these same defenders of the veil marshal other Qur'anic passages that bolster their pro-veiling stance: "And when you ask them [the Prophet's wives] for anything you want ask them from before a screen (*hijab*); that makes for greater purity for your hearts and for them" (S. 33:53); "O Prophet! Tell your wives and daughters and the believing women that they should cast their outer garments over themselves, that is more convenient that they should be known and not molested" (S. 33:59).

In addition to these Qur'anic references, pro-veiling Muslim clergy highlight hadiths intended to support the practice of veiling (see Sherif 1987 for review). Many pro-veiling Muslim clergy maintain that the veil verse was revealed to Muhammad at a wedding five years before the Prophet's death. As the story goes, three tactless guests overstayed their welcome after the wedding and continued to chat despite the Prophet's desire to be alone with his new wife. To encourage their departure, Muhammad drew a curtain between the nuptial chamber and one of his inconsiderate companions while ostensibly uttering "the verse of the hijab" (S. 33:53, cited above). A second set of hadiths claim that the verse of hijab was prompted when one of the Prophet's companions accidentally touched the hand of one of Muhammad's wives while eating dinner. Yet a third set of hadiths suggests that the verse's objective was to stop the visits of an unidentified man who tarried with the wives of the Prophet, promising them marriage after Muhammad's death.

In stark contrast to the pro-veiling apologias discussed above, an oppositional discourse against veiling has emerged within Islamic circles in recent years. Most prominent among these opponents of veiling are Islamic feminists (Al-Marayati 1995; Mernissi 1991; Shaheed 1994, 1995; see contributions in Al-Hibri 1982; Gocek and Balaghi 1994; see AbuKhalil 1993; An-Na'im 1987; Anees 1989; Arat 1994; Badran 1991; Fernea 1998 for treatments of Islamic feminism and related issues). Although Islamic feminists are marginalized from many of the institutional apparatuses available to the all-male Muslim clergy, they nevertheless exercise considerable influence via the dissemination of dissident publications targeted at Islamic women and through grassroots social movements (Fernea 1998; Shaheed 1994). Fatima Mernissi (1987, 1991), arguably the most prominent Muslim feminist, is highly critical of dominant gender conceptualizations that construe veiling as the ultimate standard by which the spiritual welfare and religious devoutness of Muslim women should be judged. In *The Veil and the Male Elite: A Feminist Interpretation of Women's Rights in Islam,* Mernissi (1991, 194) queries her readers:

> What a strange fate for Muslim memory, to be called upon in order to censure and punish [Islamic women]! What a strange memory, where even dead men and women do not escape attempts at assassination, if by chance they threaten to raise the *hijab* [veil] that covers the mediocrity and servility that is presented to us [Muslim women] as tradition. How did the tradition succeed in transforming the Muslim woman into that submissive, marginal creature who buries herself and only goes out into the world timidly and huddled in her veils? Why does the Muslim man need such a mutilated companion?

Mernissi and other Muslim commentators who oppose veiling do so on a number of grounds. First, Mernissi seeks to reverse the sacralization of the veil by linking the hijab with oppressive social hierarchies and male domination. She argues that the veil represents a tradition of "mediocrity and servility" rather than a sacred standard against which to judge Muslim women's devotion to Allah. Second, antiveiling Muslim commentators are quick to highlight the historical fact that veiling is a cultural practice that originated from outside of Islamic circles (see Schmidt 1989). Although commonly assumed to be of Muslim origin, historical evidence reveals that veiling was actually practiced in the ancient Near East and Arabia long before the rise of Islam (Esposito 1995; Sherif 1987; Webster 1984). Using this historical evidence to bolster their antiveiling stance, some Muslim feminists conclude that because the veil is not a Muslim invention, it cannot be held up as the standard against which Muslim women's religiosity is to be gauged.

Finally, Islamic feminists such as Mernissi (1991, chap. 5) point to the highly questionable scriptural interpretations on which Muslim clergy often base their pro-veiling edicts (see Hessini 1994; Shirazi-Mahajan 1995). Dissident Islamic commentators call attention to the fact that the Qur'an refers cryptically to a "curtain" and never directly instructs women to wear a veil. Although proponents of veiling interpret Qur'anic edicts as Allah's directive to all Muslim women for all time, Islamic critics of veiling counter this interpretive strategy by placing relatively greater weight on the "occasions of revelation" (*asbab nuzul al-Qur'an*)—that is, the specific social circumstances under which key Qur'anic passages were revealed (Mernissi 1991, 87–88, 92–93; see Sherif 1987). It is with this interpretive posture that many Islamic feminists believe the veil verse (S. 33:53) to be intended solely for the wives of Muhammad (Mernissi 1991, 92; see Sherif 1987). Muslim critics of veiling further counter many of the pro-veiling hadith citations by arguing that they are interpretations of extrascriptural texts whose authenticity is highly questionable (Mernissi 1991, 42–48; see Sherif 1987; Shirazi-Mahajan 1995). Finally, critics of hijab point to select verses in the Qur'an that invoke images of gender egalitarianism, including one passage that refers to the "vast reward" Allah has prepared for both "men who guard their modesty and women who guard their modesty" (S. 33:35).

THE VEIL AND GENDER IDENTITY NEGOTIATION AMONG MUSLIM WOMEN IN AUSTIN

To this point, we have drawn comparisons between pro-veiling edicts that link devout, desexualized Muslim womanhood to the practice of veiling and antiveiling discourses that reject this conflation of hijab and women's religious devotion. We now attempt to gauge the impact of these debates on the gender identities of a sample of 24 Muslim women—12 of whom veil, 12 of whom do not. All women in our sample define themselves as devout Muslims (i.e., devoted followers of Muhammad who actively practice their faith). These women were recruited through a combination of snowball and purposive sampling. Taken together, the respondents identify with a range of different nationalities (e.g., Iranian, Pakistani, Kuwaiti) and Muslim sects (e.g., Sunni, Shi'i, Ahmadia). Nineteen women have lived 10 or more years in the United States, while five women in our sample have immigrated in the past 5 years. Their ages range from 21 to 55 years old, and they occupy a range of social roles (e.g., college students, professional women, homemakers). Consistent with the demographic characteristics of U.S. Muslim immigrants at large (Haddad 1991b), our sample is composed of middle-class women with some postsecondary education (either a college degree or currently attending college). Class homogeneity among the respondents is also partly a product of the locale from which the sample was drawn, namely, a university town. Consequently, this study extends cross-cultural scholarship on the intersection of veiling, ethnicity, and nationality for middle-class Muslim women living in Western and largely modernized societies (e.g., Bloul 1997; Brenner 1996; Hatem 1994). . . .

Interview data collected from these women, identified below by pseudonyms, are designed to address several interrelated issues: What does the veil itself and the practice of veiling mean to these women? Among the women who veil, why do they do so? Among the women who do not veil, how have they arrived at the decision to remain unveiled? Finally, how does each group of our respondents feel about women who engage in the "opposite" cultural practice?

VEILED CONTRADICTIONS: PERCEPTIONS OF HIJAB AND GENDER PRACTICES AMONG VEILED MUSLIM WOMEN

Religious Edicts and Social Bonds

In several respects, the veiled respondents' accounts of wearing hijab conform to the pro-veiling gender discourse explicated above. Many of the veiled women invoke various sorts of religious imagery and theological edicts when asked about their motivations for veiling. One respondent in her early twenties, Huneeya, states flatly: "I wear the hijab because the Qur'an says it's better [for women to be veiled]." Yet another veiled woman, Najette, indicates that hijab "makes [her] more special" because it symbolizes her commitment to Islam. Mona says outright: "The veil represents submission to God," and Masouda construes the veil as a "symbol of worship" on the part of devout Muslim women to Allah and the teachings of the Prophet Muhammad. Not surprisingly, many veiled women contend that veiling is commanded in the Qur'an.

Of course, this abundance of theological rationales is not the only set of motivations that the veiled women use to justify this cultural practice. For many of the veiled respondents, the scriptural edicts and the religious symbolism surrounding the veil are given palpable force through their everyday gender practices and the close-knit social networks that grow out of this distinctive cultural practice. Indeed, narratives about some women's deliberate choice to begin veiling at a particular point in their lives underscore how religious edicts stand in tension with the women's strategic motivations. Several women recount that they began to veil because they had friends who did so or because they felt more closely connected to significant others through this cultural practice. Aisha, for example, longed to wear the veil while she attended high school in the Middle East approximately three decades ago. Reminiscent of issues faced by her teen counterparts in the United States, Aisha's account suggests that high school was a crucial time for identity formation and the cultivation of peer group relationships. The veil served Aisha as a valuable resource in resolving many of the dilemmas she faced 30 years ago as a maturing high school student. She decided to begin veiling at that time after hearing several prominent Muslim speakers at her school "talk[ing] about how good veiling is." The veil helped Aisha not only to form meaningful peer relationships at that pivotal time in her life (i.e., adolescence) but also continues to facilitate for her a feeling of connectedness with a broader religious community of other veiled Muslim women. During her recent trip to Egypt during the summer, Aisha says that the veil helped her "to fit in" there in a way that she would not have if she were unveiled.

Several other respondents also underscore the significance of Islamic women's friendship networks that form around the veil, which are particularly indispensable because they live in a non-Muslim country (i.e., the United States). In recounting these friendship circles that are cultivated around hijab in a "foreign" land, our veiled respondents point to an important overlay between their gender identities (i.e., good Muslim women veil) and their ethnic identities (i.e., as Middle Easterners). The common foundation on which these twin identities are negotiated is distinctively religious in nature. Hannan touts the personal benefits of veiling both as a *woman*—"the veil serves as an identity for [Islamic] women"—and as a *Muslim:* "[Because I veil,] Muslim people know I am Muslim, and they greet me in Arabic." This interface between gender and ethnicity is also given voice by Aisha, whose initial experiences with the veil were noted above. Aisha maintains, "The veil differentiates Muslim women from other women. When you see a woman in hijab, you know she's a Muslim." Much like the leading Muslim commentators who encourage Islamic women to "wear" their religious convictions (literally, via the veil) for all to see, these veiled respondents find comfort in the cultural and ethnic distinctiveness that the veil affords them. In this way, hijab is closely connected with their overlapping religious-gender-ethnic identities and links them to the broader community (*ummah*) of Islamic believers and Muslim women.

Gender Difference and Women's "Emancipation"

In addition to providing religious rationales for wearing the veil, many of the women who wear hijab also invoke the discourse of masculine-feminine difference to defend the merits of veiling. For several women, the idea of masculine hyper-sexuality and feminine vulnerability to the male sex drive is crucial to this essentialist rationale for veiling. Despite the fact that veiled women were rather guarded in their references to sex, their nods in that direction are difficult to interpret in any other fashion. In describing the veil's role in Islam and in the lives of Muslim men and women (such as herself), Sharadda states, "Islam is natural and men need some things naturally. If we abide by these needs [and veil accordingly], we will all be happy." She continues, "If the veil did not exist, many evil things would happen. Boys would mix with girls, which will result in evil things."

Similarly, Hannan describes what she perceives to be women's distinctive attributes and their connection to the veil: "Women are like diamonds; they are so precious. They should not be revealed to everyone—just to their husbands and close kin." Like Qur'anic references to women's "ornaments," Hannan is contrasting the "precious" diamond-like feminine character to the ostensibly less refined, less distinctive masculine persona. Interestingly, it is by likening women to diamonds that Hannan rhetorically inverts traditional gender hierarchies that privilege "masculine" traits over their "feminine" counterparts. In the face of those who would denigrate feminine qualities, Hannan reinterprets the distinctiveness of womanhood as more "precious" (i.e., more rare and valuable) than masculine qualities. Women's inherent difference from men, then, is perceived to be a source of esteem rather than denigration.

It is important to recognize, however, that the respondents who invoke this rhetoric of gender difference are not simply reproducing the pro-veiling discourse advanced by Muslim elites. Despite their essentialist convictions, many of the veiled respondents argue that the practice of wearing hijab actually liberates them from men's untamed, potentially explosive sexuality and makes possible for them various sorts of public-sphere pursuits. So, whereas pro-veiling Islamic elites often reason that women's sexual vulnerability (and, literally, their fragile bodily "ornaments") should restrict them to the domestic sphere, many of the veiled women in this study simply do not support this view of domesticized femininity. To the contrary, these women—many of whom are themselves involved in occupational or educational pursuits—argue that the veil is a great equalizer that enables women to work alongside of men. In the eyes of Hannan, women's "preciousness" should not be used to cajole them to remain in the home: "Women who wear the hijab are not excluded from society. They are freer to move around in society because of it."

Rabbab, who attends to various public-sphere pursuits, offers a similar appraisal. She argues that the face veil (hijab) is an invaluable aid for Muslim women who engage in extradomestic pursuits. In advancing this claim, Rabbab uses women who veil their whole bodies (such body garments are called *abaya*) as a counterpoint of excessive traditionalism. When asked what the veil means to her personally, as well as to Muslim women and Islamic culture at large, she says,

> It depends on the extent of the hijab [that is worn]. . . . Women who wear face veils and cover their whole bodies [with abaya] are limited to the home. They are too dependent on their husbands. How can they interact when they are so secluded? . . . [However,] taking away the hijab [i.e., face veil] would make women have to fight to be taken seriously [in public settings]. . . . With hijab, men take us more seriously.

This hijab-as-liberator rationale for veiling was repeated by many of the veiled women who pursued educational degrees in schools and on college campuses where young predatorial men ostensibly rove in abundance. Aisha, a 41-year-old former student, recounts how the veil emancipated her from the male gaze during her school years:

> There was a boy who attended my university. He was very rude to all of the girls, always whistling and staring at them. One day, I found myself alone in the hallway with him. I was very nervous because I had to walk by him. But because I was wearing the hijab, he looked down when I walked past. He did not show that respect to the unveiled girls.

Drawing on experiences such as these, Aisha concludes succinctly, "The veil gives women advantages. . . . They can go to coeducational schools and feel safe." A current student, Najette, says that the veil helps her to "feel secure" in going about her daily activities. Finally, the account of a young female student who is 22 years of age sheds further light on the hijab's perceived benefits in the face of men's apparent propensity to objectify women: "If you're in hijab, then someone sees you and treats you accordingly. I feel more free. Especially men, they don't look at your appearance—they appreciate your intellectual abilities. They respect you." For many of the veiled women in this study, the respect and protection afforded them by the hijab enables them to engage in extradomestic pursuits that would ironically generate sharp criticism from many pro-veiling Muslim elites.

The Discontents of Hijab and Tolerance for the Unveiled

While the foregoing statements provide clear evidence of these women's favorable feelings about hijab, many of the veiled women also express mixed feelings about this controversial cultural symbol. It was not uncommon for the veiled respondents to recount personal difficulties that they have faced because of their decision to wear hijab. Some dilemmas associated with the veil emanate from the fact that these women live in a secular society inhabited predominantly by Christians rather than Muslims. Najette, the same respondent who argued that veiling makes her feel "special," was quick to recognize that this esteem is purchased at the price of being considered "weird" by some Americans who do not understand her motivations for veiling. For women like her, engaging in a dissident cultural practice underscores Najette's cultural distinctiveness in a way that some people find refreshing and others find threatening.

Such points of tension surrounding the veil are evident not only in cross-cultural encounters such as that mentioned above. Even within Muslim circles, the practice of veiling has generated enough controversy to produce rifts among relatives and friends when some of the veiled respondents appear publicly in hijab. Huneeya, a student who veils because she wishes to follow Qur'anic edicts and enjoys being treated as an intellectual equal by her male peers, highlighted just this point of friction with her family members, all of whom except her are "against hijab. [My family members] think it is against modernity."

For some women, the tensions produced within intimate relationships by the veil move beyond the realm of intermittent family squabbles. One veiled respondent, Asma, revealed that extended family difficulties surrounding the veil have caused her to alter the practice of veiling itself, if only temporarily. Her recent experiences underscore the complex machinations of power involved in the contested arenas of family relations and friendships where veiling is concerned. Asma moved to the United States with her husband only two years ago. Asma was quite conscientious about veiling. She relished the sense of uniqueness and cultural distinctiveness afforded to her by the hijab while living in a non-Muslim country. Yet, recent summer-long visits from her mother-in-law presented her with a dilemma. Asma's mother-in-law had arranged the marriage between her son and daughter-in-law. At the time, the mother-in-law greatly appreciated the conservative religious values embraced by her future daughter-in-law, evidenced in Asma's attentiveness to wearing the veil. Yet, since that time, Asma's mother-in-law had undergone a conversion of sorts concerning the practice of veiling. Quite recently, Asma's mother-in-law stopped wearing the veil and wanted her daughter-in-law to follow suit by discarding the veil as well. Indeed, this mother-in-law felt that Asma was trying to upstage her by using the veil to appear more religiously devout than her elder. Asma's short-term solution to this dilemma is to submit to the wishes of her mother-in-law during her summer visits to the United States. Consequently, for two months each summer, Asma discards her veil. Yet, this solution is hardly satisfactory to her and does not placate Asma's veiled friends who think less of her for unveiling:

> I feel very uncomfortable without the veil. The veil keeps us [Muslim women] from getting mixed up in American culture. But I don't want to make my mother-in-law feel inferior, so I take it off while she is here. I know my friends think I am a hypocrite.

Although Asma is sanctioned by her friends for unveiling temporarily during her mother-in-law's visit, our interview data suggest that the preponderance of veiled women in this study harbor no ill will toward their Muslim sisters who choose not to veil. Despite these veiled women's enthusiastic defenses of hijab, they are willing to define what it means to be a good Muslim broadly enough to include Islamic women who do not veil. When asked, for instance, what she thought being a good Muslim entails, one of our veiled respondents (Najette) states simply: "You must be a good person and always be honest." Echoing these sentiments, Masouda suggests, "Your attitude towards God is most important for being a good Muslim—your personality. You must be patient, honest, giving." Even when asked point-blank if veiling makes a woman a good Muslim, another veiled respondent answers, "Hijab is not so important for being a good Muslim. Other things are more important, like having a good character and being honest." One respondent even took on a decidedly ecumenical tone in detaching veiling from Islamic devotion: "Being a good Muslim is the same as being a good Christian or a good Jew—treat others with respect and dignity. Be considerate and open-minded." In the end, then, these women in hijab are able to distinguish between what veiling means to them at a personal level (i.e., a sign of religious devotion) versus what the veil says about Muslim women in general (i.e., a voluntary cultural practice bereft of devotional significance). These veiled women's heterogeneous lived experiences with the hijab—both comforting and uncomfortable, affirming and tension producing, positive and negative—seem to provide them with a sensitivity to cultural differences that often seems lacking in the vitriolic debates about veiling currently waged by leading Muslims.

ISLAMIC FEMINISM MODIFIED: PERCEPTIONS OF HIJAB AND GENDER PRACTICES AMONG THE UNVEILED

Patriarchal Oppression and Religious Fanaticism

Just as veiled women draw on the pro-veiling discourse to defend the wearing of hijab, the unveiled women in this study often justify their abstention from this cultural practice by invoking themes from the antiveiling discourse. Several of these unveiled women argue quite straightforwardly that the veil reinforces gender distinctions that work to Muslim women's collective disadvantage. According to many of the unveiled women, the veil was imposed on Muslim women because of Middle Eastern men's unwillingness to tame their sexual caprice and because of their desire to dominate women. Rabeeya, for example, contends that Muslim women are expected to veil because "Middle Eastern men get caught up in beauty. The veil helps men control themselves." Offering a strikingly similar response, Najwa argues that "men can't control themselves, so they make women veil." Using the same critical terminology—that is, *control*—to make her point, Fozia has an even less sanguine view of the veil's role in Islam. When asked about the significance of the veil in Muslim societies, she states flatly: "The veil is used to control women." In short, many of the unveiled respondents view hijab in much the same way as elite Islamic feminists; that is, as a mechanism of patriarchal control.

Comments such as these suggest points of congruence between the veiled and unveiled respondents' understandings of hijab. Both groups of women seem to agree that hijab is closely related to men's sexuality. Recall that some of the veiled women contrast masculine hypersexuality to a desexualized view of femininity. Such women conclude that the veil is the God-ordained corrective for men's inability to control their own sexual impulses. Likewise, as evidenced in several statements from unveiled women, they link the veil to men's apparent inability (or, better, unwillingness) to contain their sexual desires. However, whereas several of the veiled women see masculine hypersexuality as natural and view the veil as a divine remedy for such sexual differences, many of the unveiled women reject these views. The unveiled respondents seem less willing to accept the notion that categorical gender differences should translate into a cultural practice that (literally and figuratively) falls on the shoulders of women. In a key point of departure from their sisters who wear hijab, the unveiled women in this study trace the origin of the veil not to God but rather to men's difficulties in managing their sexuality (again, "men can't control themselves, so they make women veil"). In men's attempt to manage their sexual impulses, so the account goes, they have foisted the veil on women. Very much in keeping with feminist discourses that take issue with such gendered double standards, the unveiled women conclude that it is unfair to charge women with taming men's sexuality.

Apart from these issues of social control and sexuality, several of the unveiled respondents also invoke themes of religious devotion and ethnic identity when discussing the significance of the veil for Muslims in general and for themselves (as unveiled Islamic women) in particular. Recall that leading Muslims who support veiling often highlight the religious and ethnic distinctiveness of hijab; however, prominent Muslim feminists counter that veiling did not originate with Islam and should not be understood as central to women's religious devoutness or ethnic identities (as non-Westerners). Echoing these Muslim feminist themes, several of the unveiled respondents seek to sever the veil from its religious and ethnic moorings. Fozia says that Muslim "women are made to believe that the veil is religious. In reality, it's all political," while Fatima asserts, "The veil is definitely political. It is used by men as a weapon to differentiate us from Westerners." Yet another respondent, Mah'ha, argues that it is only "fanatical" and "strict" Muslims who use the veil to draw sharp distinctions between Middle Easterners and Westerners. These remarks and others like them are designed to problematize the conflation of religious devotion, ethnic distinctiveness, and hijab evidenced in the pro-veiling discourse. Whereas the dominant discourse of veiling measures women's devotion to Islamic culture against hijab, many of the unveiled respondents imply—again, via strategic terms such as *political, fanatical,* and *strict*—that religious devotion and ethnic identification are good only in proper measure.

This rhetorical strategy allows these unveiled women to claim more moderate (and modern) convictions over and against those whose devotion to Allah has in their view been transmogrified into political dogmatism, religious extremism, and racial separatism. The unveiled women in our study do not eschew religious commitment altogether, nor are they in any way ashamed of their ethnic heritage. To the contrary, the unveiled respondents champion religious commitment (again, in good measure) and are proud to count themselves among the followers of Muhammad. Yet, they are quick to illustrate that their devotion to Allah and their appreciation of their cultural heritage are manifested through means that do not include the practice of veiling. Amna, for example, says, "Religious education makes me feel like a more pious Muslim. I read the Qur'an weekly and attend Friday prayer sermons," while Rabeeya states, "Being a good Muslim means believing in one God; no idolatry; following the five pillars of Islam; and believing in Muhammad." Concerning the issue of ethnoreligious identity, the basic message articulated by many of the unveiled women can be stated quite succinctly: A Muslim women can be true to her cultural and religious heritage without the veil. Samiya, a 38-year-old unveiled woman, says as much: "Muslim society doesn't exist on the veil. Without the veil, you would still be Muslim." Therefore, many of the unveiled women believe that the veil is of human (actually, male) origin rather than of divine making. And it is this very belief about the veil's this-worldly origins that enables many of the unveiled women to characterize themselves as devout followers of Muhammad who honor their cultural heritage even though they have opted not to veil.

Standing on Common Ground: Tolerance for the Other Among Unveiled Women

Finally, we turn our attention to the subjective contradictions that belie the prima facie critical reactions of our unveiled respondents toward the veil. Interestingly, just as the veiled women are reluctant to judge harshly their unveiled counterparts, these unveiled women who eschew hijab at a personal level nevertheless express understanding and empathy toward their Middle Eastern sisters who veil. At several points during interview encounters, the unveiled respondents escape the polemical hold of the antiveiling discourse by building bridges to their sisters who engage in a cultural practice that they themselves eschew.

First, several respondents imply that it would be wrong to criticize veiled women for wearing hijab when it is men—specifically, male Muslim elites—who are to blame for the existence and pervasiveness of the veil in Islamic culture. Amna, who does not veil, takes on a conciliatory tone toward women who do so by conceding that "the veil helps women in societies where they want to be judged solely on their character and not on their appearances." How is it that such statements, which sound so similar to the justifications for wearing hijab invoked by veiled women, emanate from the unveiled respondents? The strongly antipatriarchal sentiments of the unveiled women (described in the preceding section) seem to exonerate veiled women from charges of gender traitorism. Recall that many of the unveiled respondents, in fact, locate the origin of the veil in *men*'s sexual indiscretion and in *men*'s desire to control women: "Middle Eastern *men* get caught up in beauty. The veil helps *men* control *themselves*" (Rabeeya); "*Men* can't control *themselves,* so *they* make women veil" (Najwa); "The veil is *used to control women.* The women are *made to believe* that the veil is religious" (Fozia) (emphasis added). Ironically, it is the very antipatriarchal character of these statements that simultaneously enables the unveiled women to express their stinging criticism of the veil itself while proclaiming tolerance and respect for Islamic women who wear the veil. Indeed, since many of the unveiled respondents construe hijab to be a product of *patriarchal* oppression and assorted *masculine* hang-ups (e.g., struggles with sexuality, a preoccupation with domination and control), veiled women cannot legitimately be impugned for wearing hijab.

Second, many of the unveiled respondents are willing to concede that despite their own critical views of the veil, hijab serves an important cultural marker for Islamic women other than themselves. When asked about the role of the veil among Muslim women she knows in the United States, Rabeeya recognizes that many of her veiled Islamic sisters who currently live in America remain "very, very tied to their culture. Or they are trying to be. They [veil because they] want to feel tied to their culture even when they are far away from home." Because she herself is a devout Islamic woman living in a religiously pluralistic and publicly secularized society, Rabeeya is able to empathize with other Muslim women residing in the United States who veil in order to shore up their cultural identity. Similarly, Sonya draws noteworthy distinctions between her personal antipathy toward veiling and veiled women's attraction to hijab: "Some Muslim women need the veil to identify themselves with the Muslim culture. I don't feel that way."

Finally, several of the unveiled women in our study seem to express tolerance and empathy for their sisters in hijab because, at one time or another in the past, they themselves have donned the veil. Two of the unveiled respondents, for example, are native Iranians who are currently living in the United States. When these women return to Iran, they temporarily don the veil. Najwa, one of these women, explains, "As soon as we cross the Iranian border, I go to the bathroom on the airplane and put on the hijab." The experiences of our other native-born Iranian woman, Fatima, speak even more directly to the practical nuances that undergird unveiled women's tolerance for their veiled counterparts. On one hand, Fatima is highly critical of the veil, which has been the legally required dress for women in Iran during the past two decades. Referring to this fact, she impugns the veil as a "political . . . weapon" used by religious elites to reinforce invidious distinctions between Westerners and Middle Easterners. Yet, on the other hand, her personal experiences with hijab lead her to reject the stereotype that women who veil are "backward": "Progress has nothing to do with veiling. Countries without veiling can be very backwards . . . I have nothing against veiling. I feel very modern [in not veiling], but I respect those who veil." Like so many of her unveiled sisters, then, Rabeeya is critical of the veil as a religious icon but is unwilling to look down on Islamic women who wear hijab.

CONCLUSION AND DISCUSSION

This study has examined how a sample of Muslim women living in Austin, Texas, negotiate their gender identities in light of ongoing Islamic disputes about the propriety of veiling. Interview data with 12 veiled and 12 unveiled women reveal that many of them draw upon the pro-veiling and antiveiling discourses of Muslim elites, respectively, to justify their decisions about the veil. At the same time, the women highlight various subjective contradictions manifested in many of their accounts of veiling. Women who veil are not typically disdainful toward their unveiled Muslim sisters, and unveiled women in our sample seem similarly reluctant to impugn their veiled counterparts. Such findings were unanticipated in light of elite Muslim debates about the propriety of veiling.

What are we to make of the fact that the acrimony manifested between elite Muslim proponents and opponents of veiling is largely absent from these women's accounts of the veil? Several possible answers to this question emerge from our investigation. First, both the veiled and unveiled women in our study clearly exercise agency in crafting their gender identities. Drawing on themes of individualism and tolerance for diversity, the women are able to counterpose their own "choice" to veil or to remain unveiled on one hand with the personal inclinations of their sisters who might choose a path that diverges from their own. In this way, the respondents fashion gender identities that are malleable and inclusive enough to navigate through the controversy surrounding the veil. Second, the social context within which the women are situated seems to provide them with resources that facilitate these gender innovations. As noted above, our sample is composed of middle-class, well-educated Muslim women. We suspect that the progressive, multicultural climate of Austin and the human capital enjoyed by the women foster greater empathy between the veiled respondents and their unveiled counterparts. This degree of tolerance between veiled and unveiled Muslim women evinced in our study may be decidedly different for Islamic women living in other parts of the United States, other Western nations, or particular countries in the Middle East where the veil is a more publicly contested symbol.

Consequently, this study lends further credence to the insight that culture is not simply produced from "above" through the rhetoric of elites to be consumed untransformed by social actors who are little more than judgmental dopes. While the pro-veiling and entiveiling discourses have carved out distinctive positions for veiled Muslim women and their unveiled counterparts within the late twentieth century, the respondents in our study are unique and indispensable contributors to contemporary Islamic culture. It is these women, rather than the often combative elite voices within Islamic circles, who creatively build bridges across the contested cultural terrain of veiling; who forge ties of tolerance with their sisters, veiled and unveiled; and who help foster the sense of community (*ummah*) that is so esteemed by Muslims around the world. Convictions about Islamic culture and community take on new meaning as they are tested in the crucible of Muslim women's everyday experiences. . . .

NOTE

1. The merits of this insider or "emic" perspective are also clearly evidenced by a growing body of research that highlights the heterogeneous and contested character of gender relations among conservative Protestants (e.g., Bartkowski 1997a, 1997b, 1998, 1999, 2000; Gallagher and Smith 1999; Griffith 1997; Stacey 1990) and Orthodox Jews (Davidman 1993), an issue to which we return in the final section of this article.

REFERENCES

AbuKhalil, As'ad. 1993. Toward the study of women and politics in the Arab world: The debate and the reality. *Feminist Issues* 13:3–23.

Abu-Lughod, Lila. 1986. *Veiled sentiments.* Berkeley: University of California Press.

Acker, Joan. 1990. Hierarchies, jobs, bodies: A theory of gendered organizations. *Gender & Society* 4:139–58.

Afshar, Haleh. 1985. The legal, social and political position of women in Iran. *International Journal of the Sociology of Law* 13:47–60.

Ahmed, Gutbi Mahdi. 1991. Muslim organizations in the United States. In *The Muslims of America,* edited by Y. Y. Haddad. Oxford, UK: Oxford University Press.

Ahmed, Leila. 1992. *Women and gender in Islam: Historical roots of a modern debate.* New Haven, CT: Yale University Press.

Al-Hibri, Azizah, ed. 1982. *Women and Islam.* Oxford, UK: Pergamon.

Al-Marayati, Laila. 1995. Voices of women unsilenced—Beijing 1995 focus on women's health and issues of concern for Muslim women. *UCLA Women's Law Journal* 6:167.

Al-Swailem, Sheikh Abdullah Ahmed. 1995. Introduction. In *A comparison between veiling and unveiling,* by Halah bint Abdullah. Riyadh, Saudi Arabia: Dar-us-Salam.

Anees, Munawar Ahmad. 1989. Study of Muslim women and family: A bibliography. *Journal of Comparative Family Studies* 20:263–74.

An-Na'im, Abdullahi. 1987. The rights of women and international law in the Muslim context. *Whittier Law Review* 9:491.

Arat, Yesim. 1994. Women's movement of the 1980s in Turkey: Radical outcome of liberal Kemalism? In *Reconstructing gender in the Middle East: Tradition, identity, and power,* edited by F. M. Gocek and S. Balaghi. New York: Columbia University Press.

Badran, Margot. 1991. Competing agendas: Feminists, Islam and the state in 19th and 20th century Egypt. In *Women, Islam & the state,* edited by D. Kandiyoti. Philadelphia: Temple University Press.

Bartkowski, John P. 1997a. Debating patriarchy: Discursive disputes over spousal authority among evangelical family commentators. *Journal for the Scientific Study of Religion* 36:393–410.

———. 1997b. Gender reinvented, gender reproduced: The discourse and negotiation of spousal relations within contemporary Evangelicalism. Ph.D. diss., University of Texas, Austin.

———. 1998. Changing of the gods: The gender and family discourse of American Evangelicalism in historical perspective. *The History of the Family* 3:97–117.

———. 1999. One step forward, one step back: "Progressive traditionalism" and the negotiation of domestic labor within Evangelical families. *Gender Issues* 17:40–64.

———. 2000. Breaking walls, raising fences: Masculinity, intimacy, and accountability among the promise keepers. *Sociology of Religion* 61:33–53.

Bloul, Rachel A. 1997. Victims or offenders? "Other" women French sexual politics. In *Embodied practices: Feminist perspectives on the body,* edited by K. Davis. Thousand Oaks, CA: Sage.

Bozorgmehr, Mehdi, Claudia Der-Martirosian, and Georges Sabagh. 1996. Middle Easterners: A new kind of immigrant. In *Ethnic Los Angeles,* edited by R. Waldinger and M. Bozorgmehr. New York: Russell Sage Foundation.

Brasher, Brenda E. 1998. *Godly women: Fundamentalism and female power.* New Brunswick, NJ: Rutgers University Press.

Brenner, Suzanne. 1996. Reconstructing self and society: Javanese Muslim women and the veil. *American Ethnologist* 23:673–97.

Britton, Dana M. 1997. Gendered organizational logic: Policy and practice in men's and women's prisons. *Gender & Society* 11:796–818.

Currie, Dawn H. 1997. Decoding femininity: Advertisements and their teenage readers. *Gender & Society* 11:453–57.

Davidman, Lynn. 1993. *Tradition in a rootless world: Women turn to Orthodox Judaism.* Berkeley: University of California Press.

Davis, Kathy, ed. 1997. *Embodied practices: Feminist perspectives on the body.* Thousand Oaks, CA: Sage.

Dellinger, Kirsten, and Christine L. Williams. 1997. Makeup at work: Negotiating appearance rules in the workplace. *Gender & Society* 11:151–77.

Dragadze, Tamara. 1994. Islam in Azerbaijan: The position of women. In *Muslim women's choices: Religious belief and social reality,* edited by C. F. El-Solh and J. Mabro. New York: Berg.

El-Guindi, Fadwa. 1981. Veiling Infitah with Muslim ethic: Egypt's contemporary Islamic movement. *Social Problems* 28:465–85.

———. 1983. Veiled activism: Egyptian women in the contemporary Islamic movement. *Mediterranean Peoples* 22/23:79–89.

El-Solh, Camillia Fawzi, and Judy Mabro, eds. 1994. *Muslim women's choices: Religious belief and social reality.* New York: Berg.

Esposito, John L., ed. 1995. *The Oxford encyclopedia of the modern Islamic world.* New York: Oxford University Press.

———. 1998. Women in Islam and Muslim societies. In *Islam, gender, and social change,* edited by Y. Y. Haddad and J. L. Esposito. New York: Oxford University Press.

Fernea, Elizabeth W. 1993. The veiled revolution. In *Everyday life in the Muslim Middle East,* edited by D. L. Bowen and E. A. Early. Bloomington: Indiana University Press.

———. 1998. *In search of Islamic feminism: One woman's journey.* New York: Doubleday.

Fox, Greer L. 1977. "Nice girl": Social control of women through a value construct. *Signs: Journal of Women in Culture and Society* 2:805–17.

Gallagher, Sally K., and Christian Smith. 1999. Symbolic traditionalism and pragmatic egalitarianism: Contemporary Evangelicals, families, and gender. *Gender & Society* 13:211–233.

Gerami, Shahin. 1996. *Women and fundamentalism: Islam and Christianity.* New York: Garland.

Ghanea Bassiri, Kambiz. 1997. *Competing visions of Islam in the United States: A study of Los Angeles.* London: Greenwood.

Gocek, Fatma M., and Shiva Balaghi, eds. 1994. *Reconstructing gender in the Middle East: Tradition, identity, and power.* New York: Columbia University Press.

Griffith, R. Marie. 1997. *God's daughters: Evangelical women and the power of submission.* Berkeley: University of California Press.

Haddad, Yvonne Yazbeck. 1991a. American foreign policy in the Middle East and its impact on the identity of Arab Muslims in the United States. In *The Muslims of America,* edited by Y. Y. Haddad. Oxford, UK: Oxford University Press.

———. 1991b. Introduction. In *The Muslims of America,* edited by Y. Y. Haddad. Oxford, UK: Oxford University Press.

Hatem, Mervat F. 1994. Egyptian discourses on gender and political liberalization: Do secularist and Islamist views really differ? *Middle East Journal* 48:661–76.

Hermansen, Marcia K. 1991. Two-way acculturation: Muslim women in America between individual choice (liminality) and community affiliation (communitas). In *The Muslims of America,* edited by Y. Y. Haddad. Oxford, UK: Oxford University Press.

Hessini, Leila. 1994. Wearing the hijab in contemporary Morocco: Choice and identity. In *Reconstructing gender in the Middle East: Tradition, identity, and power,* edited by F. M. Gocek and S. Balaghi. New York: Columbia University Press.

Hollway, Wendy. 1995. Feminist discourses and women's heterosexual desire. In *Feminism and discourse,* edited by S. Wilkinson and C. Kitzinger. London: Sage.

Hunter, James Davison. 1994. *Before the shooting begins: Searching for democracy in America's culture war.* New York: Free Press.

Johnson, Steven A. 1991. Political activity of Muslims in America. In *The Muslims of America,* edited by Y. Y. Haddad. Oxford, UK: Oxford University Press.

Kadioglu, Ayse. 1994. Women's subordination in Turkey: Is Islam really the villain? *Middle East Journal* 48: 645–60.

Kandiyoti, Deniz. 1988. Bargaining with patriarchy. *Gender & Society* 2:274–90.

———. ed. 1991. *Women, Islam & the state.* Philadelphia: Temple University Press.

———. 1992. Islam and patriarchy: A comparative perspective. In *Women in Middle Eastern history: Shifting boundaries in sex and gender,* edited by N. R. Keddie and B. Baron. New Haven, CT: Yale University Press.

Mahoney, Maureen A., and Barbara Yngvesson. 1992. The construction of subjectivity and the paradox of resistance: Reintegrating feminist anthropology and psychology. *Signs: Journal of Women in Culture and Society* 18:44–73.

Mann, Susan A., and Lori R. Kelley. 1997. Standing at the crossroads of modernist thought: Collins, Smith, and the new feminist epistemologies. *Gender & Society* 11:391–408.

Manning, Cristel. 1999. *God gave us the right: Conservative Catholic, Evangelical Protestant, and Orthodox Jewish women grapple with feminism.* New Brunswick, NJ: Rutgers University Press.

Mernissi, Fatima. 1987. *Beyond the veil.* Rev. ed. Bloomington: Indiana University Press.

———. 1991. *The veil and the male elite: A feminist interpretation of women's rights in Islam.* Translated by Mary Jo Lakeland. New York: Addison-Wesley.

Mishler, Elliot G. 1986. *Research interviewing: Context and narrative.* Cambridge, MA: Harvard University Press.

Munson, Henry Jr. 1988. *Islam and revolution in the Middle East.* New Haven, CT: Yale University Press.

Odeh, Lama Abu. 1993. Post-colonial feminism and the veil: Thinking the difference. *Feminist Review* 43:26–37.

Papanek, Hanna. 1973. Purdah: Separate worlds and symbolic shelter. *Comparative Studies in Society and History* 15:289–325.

Philips, Abu Ameenah Bilal, and Jameelah Jones. 1985. *Polygamy in Islam.* Riyadh, Saudi Arabia: International Islamic Publishing House.

Schmidt, Alvin J. 1989. *Veiled and silenced: How culture shaped sexist theology.* Macon, GA: Mercer University Press.

Shaheed, Farida. 1994. Controlled or autonomous: Identity and the experience of the network, women living under Muslim laws. *Signs: Journal of Women in Culture and Society* 19:997–1019.

———. 1995. Networking for change: The role of women's groups in initiating dialogue on women's issues. In *Faith and freedom: Women's human rights in the Muslim world,* edited by M. Afkhami. New York: Syracuse University Press.

Sherif, Mostafa H. 1987. What is hijab? *The Muslim World* 77:151–63.

Shirazi-Mahajan, Faegheh. 1995. A dramaturgical approach to hijab in post-revolutionary Iran. *Journal of Critical Studies of the Middle East* 7 (fall): 35–51.

Siddiqi, Muhammad Iqbal. 1983. *Islam forbids free mixing of men and women.* Lahore, Pakistan: Kazi.

Smith, Dorothy E. 1987. *The everyday world as problematic: A feminist sociology.* Boston: Northeastern University Press.

Stacey, Judith, 1990. *Brave new families.* New York: Basic Books.

Stombler, Mindy, and Irene Padavic. 1997. Sister acts: Resisting men's domination in Black and white fraternity little sister programs. *Social Problems* 44:257–75.

Stone, Carol L. 1991. Estimate of Muslims living in America. In *The Muslims of America,* edited by Y. Y. Haddad. Oxford, UK: Oxford University Press.

Todd, Alexandra Dundas, and Sue Fisher, eds. 1988. *Gender and discourse: The power of talk.* Norwood, NJ: Ablex.

Walbridge, Linda S. 1997. *Without forgetting the imam: Lebanese Shi'ism in an American community.* Detroit, MI: Wayne State University Press.

Webster, Sheila K. 1984. Harim and hijab: Seclusive and exclusive aspects of traditional Muslim dwelling and dress. *Women's Studies International Forum* 7:251–57.

West, Candace, and Sarah Fenstermaker. 1995. Doing difference. *Gender & Society* 9:8–37.

Wodak, Ruth, ed. 1997. *Discourse and gender.* Thousand Oaks, CA: Sage.

11

Doing Time, Doing Masculinity

Sports and Prison

Don Sabo

I am a white, male college professor in my forties, hunched over a table in Attica Correctional Facility. My heart is pounding, my upper body is locked taut and shaking, and I am gazing into the eyes of an African American prisoner who, like so many of the men in this New York State prison, comes from what sociologists call the "underclass." We are different in most respects, but right now we are alike. Like me, he's puffing and straining, trying not to show it, sometimes cursing, and returning my gaze. We are arm wrestling, and in this case he puts me down in about two minutes, which in arm wrestling can be a long, long time.

I started arm wrestling in the joint about five years ago. I enjoy the physical connection that the contest brings. The participants initially stalk one another over a period of days or weeks, keeping their distance, evaluating each other's strengths and weaknesses. There may be some playful bad-mouthing or boasting that leads up to a bout. Eventually, they make the necessary moves that bring each to the table hand-in-hand, eye-to-eye. Even though arm wrestling is overtly combative, it can breed a closer connection with another man than is allowed for in most aspects of men's lives. It allows me to climb outside the bourgeois husk of my life and join with somebody in a way that temporarily suspends the hierarchical distinctions between free man and inmate, white and black, privileged and underprivileged, and teacher and student.

Arm wrestling also lets me pull my athletic past into the present, to enjoin youthful masculine spirits and facades. At the same time that these manly juices are resurrected, though, I try to tell myself and others that I don't take the competition so seriously. I want to learn the lesson that it is OK to be vulnerable to defeat.

Sometimes I win; sometimes I lose. It still matters to me whether I win or lose. I try hard to win, but, when I lose, I get over it quickly, accept it, and even welcome it as inevitable. Part of me is happy for the man who beat me. When I win, I savor the victories for a few days, bragging to myself, sometimes others, soothing my middle-aging ego with transparently masculine rationalizations that I am still strong, not over the bloody hill yet. Arm wrestlers understand that nobody wins all the time. Beneath the grit and show, we know there is more to it than winning or losing. We

---

also know that part of what makes arm wrestling more than just a contest or pastime is that it somehow speaks to our beliefs and feelings about being a man.

I have taught in prisons for fourteen years. My experiences, observations, and discussions with inmates have revealed that prison sports have different meanings for different men. I have learned that a great many motives, messages, and contradictions are crammed into the muscles and athletic pastimes of men in prison. Like men outside the walls, however, prisoners use sports as vehicles for creating and maintaining masculine identity.

DOING TIME, DOING SPORTS

Perhaps the most striking aspect of prison sports is their visibility. The yard is often a hub of athletic activity. Weight lifters huddle in small groups around barbells and bench press racks. Runners circle the periphery, while hoopsters spin and shoot on the basketball courts. There is the occasional volleyball game and bocce tournament. Depending on the facility and time of year, there may be football practices or games, replete with equipment and fans along the sidelines. Some prisons maintain softball leagues and facilities.

Inside the buildings, you will find a gym, basketball courts, and weight rooms. Power lifters struggle against gravity and insanity. Feats of strength produce heroes in the joint, sometimes even legends, or at least local legends. I have been told stories about Jihad Al-Sibbar, a man past his forties who weighs about 155 pounds. He is believed to be the strongest man in the New York State prison system, and I have heard it said more than once that, if given the opportunity, he could have competed at the Olympic level. I want and need to believe in these stories, not so much because they are tales of a strong man but because his triumphs say something about the potential of athletics to sustain sanity in an insane place.

Sports and fitness activities spill into the prison environment in other ways. An inmate may do daily calisthenics while in solitary. For example, Martin Sostre was an African American black power activist and inner-city bookstore owner who was framed by the police in 1967 and imprisoned for nine years. Sostre used physical exercise and yoga to survive long stints of solitary and to bolster his political struggles against prison and legal authorities (Copeland, 1970).

In almost any sector of the prison, fans may jabber about who will win the Super Bowl, the NBA finals, or the next heavyweight boxing match. The taunting, teasing, and betting that typify sports fans outside the walls are also rife among inmates and guards and other personnel. Some men gather in groups around television sets to watch the Final Four or "Monday Night Football," while others sit alone in their cells jabbing with George Foreman or soaring with Michael Jordan.

In short, sports and fitness activities in prison engage men's minds and bodies to varying degrees and, in the process, help them do their time. For some men, especially the young ones, athletics are no more than a fleeting pastime, a simple form of physical play, something to do to get to the end of another day. For others, sports and fitness activities are a crucial survival strategy, a life practice that is intended to create and maintain physical and mental health in a hostile, unhealthy place. For still others, working out or participating in sports helps them to displace anger and frustration, to get the rage out of their bodies and psyches before it explodes or turns in on them. And for some, the goal is to get big to be bad, to manufacture muscle and a jock presence in order to intimidate and dominate.

DOING MASCULINITY

The prison environment triggers a masculine awareness in me. I go on masculine alert. I don't walk around with biceps flexed and chest expanded, pretending to be a tough guy in front of anybody looking my way. That kind of suck-in-your-belly-and-lower-your-voice stuff faded away with my twenties. The masculinity that surfaces in the prison is more an attitude, a hazy cluster of concerns and expectations that get translated into emotion and physical movement in ways that never quite come clear. Though there are a few women around (for example, an occasional female guard, some women teachers), I see and smell the prison as an all-male domain. I sense a greater potential for danger and a heightened need to protect myself. I could get caught in a bad situation. I have been told not to trust anybody—prisoners, guards, or bureaucrats. Nobody. It sounds crazy, but the tinges of distrust and paranoia almost feel good. Indeed, there are parts of me, call them "threads" or "echoes" of a masculine identity, that embrace the distrust and welcome the presumed danger and potential for violence.

These masculine prompts are seldom uppermost in my mind. They do not emanate from inside of me; they are more like visitors that come and go, moving in and out of me like tap water gushing through an overfilled glass. Arm wrestling allows me to play out masculinity in tune with other elements of jailhouse jock culture. At the same time, the wrestling breeds familiarity with prisoners, pushes toward closeness and trust, and subverts hierarchical distinctions based on class, race, and professional status.

Like me, many men in prison deploy sports and fitness activities as resources to do masculinity—that is, to spin masculine identities, to build reputations, to achieve or dissolve status. For the men in prison, as elsewhere, masculine identity is earned, enacted, rehearsed, refined, and relived through each day's activities and choices. I'm not saying that the gender scripts that men follow in prison are reinvented each day, from moment to moment, man to man. Masculinity does not unfold inside us as much as it flows through us. It is not a strictly individual or psychological process. In doing gender, each individual participates in the larger prison culture, which scripts masculinity by supplying direction, role models, props, motivations, rewards, and values (Messerschmidt, 1993; West and Zimmerman, 1987). For many men, sports are a part of the formula for shaping gender identity.

SOFTNESS AND HARDNESS

In prison, the manly injunction to be strong is evident not only in the bulk or bearing of many men's bodies but in everyday speech as well. I have often heard prisoners describe other men as "hard" or "soft." Over the years, I have learned that there are many guises of hardness, which, inside and outside the prison culture, illustrate a variety of masculine expressions that stretch between the honorable and the perverse.

Being hard can mean that the individual is toned, strong, conditioned, or fit, rather than weak, flabby, or out of shape. A hard man cares for and respects his body. Life in prison is extremely oppressive, and it is extraordinarily difficult to eke out a healthy lifestyle. Cigarette smoke is everywhere. The noise on the blocks can jam the senses. Most inmates will tell you that the chow stinks, and, for those who think about such matters, a nutritionally sound diet is impossible to scrape together from the available cafeteria fare. For some men, then, the pursuit of sports and fitness activity is a personal quest to create a healthy body in an unhealthy environment. Those who succeed build a sense of accomplishment and garner the respect of others. Some men strive to be hard in order to build self-esteem. Being in prison is a colossal reminder of personal failure. A regular fitness regimen helps some men center mind and identity in the undeniably tangible locus of the body. For others, getting good at basketball or being recognized as a leading athlete earns the respect of peers. Damaged egos and healing psyches drink in the recognition and repair themselves.

Being hard can also be a defense against prison violence. The hard man sends the message that he is somebody to contend with, not a pushover, not somebody to "fuck with." The sexual connotations of this last phrase take on particular significance in the prison subculture, where man-on-man rape is part of life. The act of prison rape is tied to maintaining the status order among a maze of male groups. Blacks may rape whites or vice versa in order to establish dominant status. Older prisoners may use rape to enslave newcomers. Guards or prison administrators have been known to threaten to expose prisoners to greater threat of rape in order to evoke good behavior, to punish, or to squeeze out information. As Tom Cahill, himself a victim of prison rape, observed, "Once 'turned out'—prison parlance for raped—a survivor is caught in a bind. If an inmate reports a sexual assault, even without naming the assailant, he will be labeled a 'snitch,' a contract will automatically be placed on him, and his life expectancy will be measured in minutes from then" (1990:32).

Men's efforts to weave webs of domination through rape and physical intimidation *in prison* also reflect and reproduce men's domination of women in the social world beyond the walls. In the muscled, violent, and tattooed world of prison rape, woman is symbolically ever present. She resides in the pulpy, supple, and muted linguistic folds of the hardness/softness dichotomy. The prison phrase "make a woman out of you" means that you will be raped. Rape-based relationships between prisoners are often described as relationships between "men" and "girls" who are, in effect, thought of as "master" and "slave," victor and vanquished.

The hardness/softness split also echoes and fortifies stereotypes of masculinity and femininity (Bordo, 1999). To be "hard" means to be more manly than the next guy, who is said to be "soft" and more feminine. It is better to be hard than soft in prison. To be called hard is a compliment. To be labeled soft can be a playful rebuke or a serious put-down. The meanings around hardness and softness also flow from and feed homophobia, which is rampant in prison. The stigma of being labeled a homosexual can make a man more vulnerable to ridicule, attack, ostracism, or victimization.

CONCLUSION

Prison somehow magnifies the contradictions in men's lives, making them palpable, visible. For many prisoners, the pursuit of manhood was closely linked to their efforts to define masculine identity and worth—for example, robbing in order to be a good provider or husband, joining a gang in hopes of becoming a "big man" on the street, being a "badass" or "gangster" as a way of getting respect from peers, braving the violence of the drug trade, raping or beating on women in order prove manly superiority, or embezzling to achieve financial success and masculine adequacy. The irony here is that these scripted quests for manly power led, in part, to incarceration and loss of freedom and dignity. For lots of prisoners, and countless men on the outside, adherence to the traditional pathways to masculinity turned out to be a trap.

Men's participation in prison sports is fused with yet another contradiction. On one hand, sports and exercise provide prisoners with vehicles for self-expression and physical freedom. On the other hand, prison officials know that involvement in sports and exercise activities helps make inmates more tractable and compliant. Therefore, the cultivation of the body through sports and fitness activities is simultaneously a source of personal liberation and social control.

It is easy for men in prison or on the outside to get trapped by the cultural mandate of hardness. The image of the male athlete as a muscled, aggressive, competitive, and emotionally controlled individual dovetails the prevailing definition of masculinity in sexist culture. Conformity to this model for manliness can be socially and emotionally destructive. Muscles may remain "*the* sign of masculinity" (Glassner, 1988:192) in the male-dominated culture and the gender hierarchies that constitute the North American prison system. And yet my observations tell me that prisoners' relationships to muscle and masculinity are not simple or one-sided. Men cultivate their bodies in order to send a variety of messages about the meaning of masculinity to themselves and others. Whereas conformity to the credo of hardness for some men feeds the forces of domination and subordination, for others athletics and fitness are forms of self-care. Whereas many prison jocks are literally playing out the masculine scripts they learned in their youth, others are attempting to attach new meanings to sports and exercise that affirm health, sanity, and alternative modes of masculinity.

Perhaps the greatest contradiction pervading prison sports is that, despite the diversity of gendered meanings and practices that prisoners attach to their bodies through sports and exercise, the cultural mandate for hardness and toughness prevails. Men's soft sides remain hidden, suppressed, and underground. The punitive and often violent structures of prison hierarchies persist, breathing aggression and fear into men's bodies and minds. The same tragic contradiction informs men's lives in sports outside the prison walls, where structured gender inequality and sexism constrain efforts to reform gender relationships toward equity and healthful affirmation of the body.

Arm wrestling teaches me that the cages in men's lives can be made of iron bars, muscles, or myths. The harder I wrestle, the more I dream of escape.

REFERENCES

Bordo, S. 1999. *The Male Body: A New Look at Men in Public and in Private.* New York: Farrar, Straus and Giroux.

Cahill, T. 1990. "Prison Rape: Torture in the American Gulag." In *Men and Intimacy: Personal Accounts Exploring the Dilemmas of Modern Male Sexuality,* ed. Franklin Abbott. Freedom, Calif.: Crossing Press.

Copeland, V. 1970. *The Crime of Martin Sostre.* New York: McGraw Hill.

Glassner, B. 1988. *Bodies: Why We Look the Way We Do (and How We Feel about It).* New York: Putnam.

Messerschmidt, James W. 1993. *Masculinities and Crime: Critique and Reconceptualization of Theory.* Lanham, Md.: Rowman and Littlefield).

West, Candace, and Don H. Zimmerman. 1987. "Doing Gender." *Gender and Society* 1 (2):125–51.

12

What It Means to Be Gendered Me

Life on the Boundaries of a Dichotomous Gender System

BETSY LUCAL

I understood the concept of "doing gender" (West and Zimmerman 1987) long before I became a sociologist. I have been living with the consequences of inappropriate "gender display" (Goffman 1976; West and Zimmerman 1987) for as long as I can remember.

My daily experiences are a testament to the rigidity of gender in our society, to the real implications of "two and only two" when it comes to sex and gender categories (Garfinkel 1967; Kessler and McKenna 1978). Each day, I experience the consequences that our gender system has for my identity and interactions. I am a woman who has been called "Sir" so many times that I no longer even hesitate to assume that it is being directed at me. I am a woman whose use of public rest rooms regularly causes reactions ranging from confused stares to confrontations over what a man is doing in the women's room. I regularly enact a variety of practices either to minimize the need for others to know my gender or to deal with their misattributions.

I am the embodiment of Lorber's (1994) ostensibly paradoxical assertion that the "gender bending" I engage in actually might serve to preserve and perpetuate gender categories. As a feminist who sees gender rebellion as a significant part of her contribution to the dismantling of sexism, I find this possibility disheartening.

In this article, I examine how my experiences both support and contradict Lorber's (1994) argument using my own experiences to illustrate and reflect on the social construction of gender. My analysis offers a discussion of the consequences of gender for people who do not follow the rules as well as an examination of the possible implications of the existence of people like me for the gender system itself. Ultimately, I show how life on the boundaries of gender affects me and how my life, and the lives of others who make similar decisions about their participation in the gender system, has the potential to subvert gender.

Because this article analyzes my experiences as a woman who often is mistaken for a man, my focus is on the social construction of gender for women. My assumption is that, given the gendered nature of the gendering process itself, men's experiences of this phenomenon might well be different from women's.

Betsy Lucal, "What It Means to Be Gendered Me: Life on the Boundaries of a Dichotomous Gender System," from *Gender & Society,* Volume 13/1999, p. 781–797.

THE SOCIAL CONSTRUCTION OF GENDER

. . . We apply gender labels for a variety of reasons; for example, an individual's gender cues our interactions with her or him. Successful social relations require all participants to present, monitor, and interpret gender displays (Martin 1998; West and Zimmerman 1987). We have, according to Lorber, "no social place for a person who is neither woman nor man" (1994, 96); that is, we do not know how to interact with such a person. There is, for example, no way of addressing such a person that does not rely on making an assumption about the person's gender ("Sir" or "Ma'am"). In this context, gender is "omnirelevant" (West and Zimmerman 1987). Also, given the sometimes fractious nature of interactions between men and women, it might be particularly important for women to know the gender of the strangers they encounter, do the women need to be wary, or can they relax (Devor 1989)?

According to Kessler and McKenna (1978), each time we encounter a new person, we make a gender attribution. In most cases, this is not difficult. We learn how to read people's genders by learning which traits culturally signify each gender and by learning rules that enable us to classify individuals with a wide range of gender presentations into two and only two gender categories. As Weston observed, "Gendered traits are called attributes for a reason: People attribute traits to others. No one possesses them. Traits are the product of evaluation" (1996, 21). The fact that most people use the same traits and rules in presenting genders makes it easier for us to attribute genders to them.

We also assume that we can place each individual into one of two mutually exclusive categories in this binary system. As Bem (1993) notes, we have a polarized view of gender; there are two groups that are seen as polar opposites. Although there is "no rule for deciding 'male' or 'female' that will always work" and no attributes "that always and without exception are true of only one gender" (Kessler and McKenna 1978, 158, 1), we operate under the assumption that there are such rules and attributes. . . .

Not only do we rely on our social skills in attributing genders to others, but we also use our skills to present our own genders to them. The roots of this understanding of how gender operates lie in Goffman's (1959) analysis of the "presentation of self in everyday life," elaborated later in his work on "gender display" (Goffman 1976). From this perspective, gender is a performance, "a stylized repetition of acts" (Butler 1990, 140, emphasis removed). Gender display refers to "conventionalized portrayals" of social correlates of gender (Goffman 1976). These displays are culturally established sets of behaviors, appearances, mannerisms, and other cues that we have learned to associate with members of a particular gender. . . .

A person who fails to establish a gendered appearance that corresponds to the person's gender faces challenges to her or his identity and status. First, the gender nonconformist must find a way in which to construct an identity in a society that denies her or him any legitimacy (Bem 1993). A person is likely to want to define herself or himself as "normal" in the face of cultural evidence to the contrary. Second, the individual also must deal with other people's challenges to identity and status—deciding how to respond, what such reactions to their appearance mean, and so forth.

Because our appearances, mannerisms, and so forth constantly are being read as part of our gender display, we do gender whether we intend to or not. For example, a woman athlete, particularly one participating in a nonfeminine sport such as basketball, might deliberately keep her hair long to show that, despite actions that suggest otherwise, she is a "real" (i.e., feminine) woman. But we also do gender in less conscious ways such as when a man takes up more space when sitting than a woman does. In fact, in a society so clearly organized around gender, as ours is, there is no way in which to not do gender (Lorber 1994).

Given our cultural rules for identifying gender (i.e., that there are only two and that masculinity is assumed in the absence of evidence to the contrary), a person who does not do gender appropriately is placed not into a third category but rather into the one with which her or his gender display seems most closely to fit; that is, if a man appears to be a woman, then he will be categorized as "woman," not as something else. Even if a person does not want to do gender or would like to do a gender other than the two recognized by our society, other people will, in effect, do gender for that person by placing her or him in one and only one of the two available categories. We cannot escape doing gender or, more specifically, doing one of two genders. (There are exceptions in limited contexts such as people doing "drag" [Butler 1990; Lorber 1994].)

People who follow the norms of gender can take their genders for granted. Kessler and McKenna asserted, "Few people besides transsexuals think of their gender as anything other than 'naturally' obvious"; they believe that the risks of not being taken for the gender intended "are minimal for nontranssexuals" (1978, 126). However, such an assertion overlooks the experiences of people such as those women Devor (1989) calls "gender blenders" and those people Lorber (1994) refers to as "gender benders." As West and Zimmerman (1987) pointed out, we all are held accountable for, and might be called on to account for, our genders.

People who, for whatever reasons, do not adhere to the rules, risk gender misattribution and any interactional consequences that might result from this misidentification. What are the consequences of misattribution for social interaction? When must misattribution be minimized? What will one do to minimize such mistakes? In this article, I explore these and related questions using my biography.

For me, the social processes and structures of gender mean that, in the context of our culture, my appearance will be read as masculine. Given the common conflation of sex and gender, I will be assumed to be a male. Because of the two-and-only-two genders rule, I will be classified, perhaps more often than not, as a man—not as an atypical woman, not as a genderless person. I must be one gender or the other; I cannot be neither, nor can I be both. This norm has a variety of mundane and serious consequences for my everyday existence. Like Myhre (1995), I have found that the choice not to participate in femininity is not one made frivolously.

My experiences as a woman who does not do femininity illustrate a paradox of our two-and-only-two gender system. Lorber argued that "bending gender rules and passing between genders does not erode but rather preserves gender boundaries" (1994, 21). Although people who engage in these behaviors and appearances do "demonstrate the social constructedness of sex, sexuality, and gender" (Lorber 1994, 96), they do not actually disrupt gender. Devor made a similar point: "When gender blending females refused to mark themselves by publicly displaying sufficient femininity to be recognized as women, they were in no way challenging patriarchal gender assumptions" (1989, 142). As the following discussion shows, I have found that my own experiences both support and challenge this argument. . . .

GENDERED ME

Each day, I negotiate the boundaries of gender. Each day, I face the possibility that someone will attribute the "wrong" gender to me based on my physical appearance.

I am six feet tall and large-boned. I have had short hair for most of my life. For the past several years, I have worn a crew cut or flat top. I do not shave or otherwise remove hair from my body (e.g., no eyebrow plucking). I do not wear dresses, skirts, high heels, or makeup. My only jewelry is a class ring, a "men's" watch (my wrists are too large for a "women's" watch), two small earrings (gold hoops, both in my left ear), and (occasionally) a necklace. I wear jeans or shorts, T-shirts, sweaters, polo/golf shirts, button-down collar shirts, and tennis shoes or boots. The jeans are "women's" (I do have hips) but do not look particularly "feminine." The rest of the outer garments are from men's departments. I prefer baggy clothes, so the fact that I have "womanly" breasts often is not obvious (I do not wear a bra). Sometimes, I wear a baseball cap or some other type of hat. I also am white and relatively young (30 years old).[1]

My gender display—what others interpret as my presented identity—regularly leads to the misattribution of my gender. An incongruity exists between my gender self-identity and the gender that others perceive. In my encounters with people I do not know, I sometimes conclude, based on our interactions, that they think I am a man. This does not mean that other people do not think I am a man, just that I have no way of knowing what they think without interacting with them.

Living with It

I have no illusions or delusions about my appearance. I know that my appearance is likely to be read as "masculine" (and male) and that how I see myself is socially irrelevant. Given our two-and-only-two gender structure, I must live with the consequences of my appearance. These consequences fall into two categories: issues of identity and issues of interaction.

My most common experience is being called "Sir" or being referred to by some other masculine linguistic marker (e.g., "he," "man"). This has happened for years for as long as I can remember, when having encounters with people I do not know.[2] Once, in fact, the same worker at a fast-food restaurant called me "Ma'am" when she took my order and "Sir" when she gave it to me.

Using my credit cards sometimes is a challenge. Some clerks subtly indicate their disbelief, looking from the card to me and back at the card and checking my signature carefully. Others challenge my use of the card, asking whose it is or demanding identification. One cashier asked to see my driver's license and then asked me whether I was the son of the cardholder. Another clerk told me that my signature on the receipt "had better match" the one on the card. Presumably, this was her way of letting me know that she was not convinced it was my credit card.

My identity as a woman also is called into question when I try to use women-only spaces. Encounters in public rest rooms are an adventure. I have been told countless times that "This is the ladies' room." Other women say nothing to me, but their stares and conversations with others let me know what they think. I will hear them say, for example, "There was a man in there." I also get stares when I enter a locker room. However, it seems that women are less concerned about my presence there, perhaps because, given that it is a space for changing clothes, showering, and so forth, they will be able to make sure that I am really a woman. Dressing rooms in department stores also are problematic spaces. I remember shopping with my sister once and being offered a chair outside the room when I began to accompany her into the dressing room.

Women who believe that I am a man do not want me in women-only spaces. For example, one woman would not enter the rest room until I came out, and others have told me that I am in the wrong place. They also might not want to encounter me while they are alone. For example, seeing me walking at night when they are alone might be scary.[3]

I, on the other hand, am not afraid to walk alone, day or night. I do not worry that I will be subjected to the public harassment that many women endure (Gardner 1995). I am not a clear target for a potential rapist. I rely on the fact that a potential attacker would not want to attack a big man by mistake. This is not to say that men never are attacked, just that they are not viewed, and often do not view themselves, as being vulnerable to attack.

Being perceived as a man has made me privy to male-male interactional styles of which most women are not aware. I found out, quite by accident, that many men greet, or acknowledge, people (mostly other men) who make eye contact with them with a single nod. For example, I found that when I walked down the halls of my brother's all-male dormitory making eye contact, men nodded their greetings at me. Oddly enough, these same men did not greet my brother; I had to tell him about making eye contact and nodding as a greeting ritual. Apparently, in this case I was doing masculinity better than he was!

I also believe that I am treated differently, for example, in auto parts stores (staffed almost exclusively by men in most cases) because of the assumption that I am a man. Workers there assume that I know what I need and that my questions are legitimate requests for information. I suspect that I am treated more fairly than a feminine-appearing woman would be. I have not been able to test this proposition. However, Devor's participants did report "being treated more respectfully" (1989, 132) in such situations.

There is, however, a negative side to being assumed to be a man by other men. Once, a friend and I were driving in her car when a man failed to stop at an intersection and nearly crashed into us. As we drove away, I mouthed "stop sign" to him. When we both stopped our cars at the next intersection, he got out of his car and came up to the passenger side of the car, where I was sitting. He yelled obscenities at us and pounded and spit on the car window. Luckily, the windows were closed. I do not think he would have done that if he thought I was a woman. This was the first time I realized that one of the implications of being seen as a man was that I might be called on to defend myself from physical aggression from other men who felt challenged by me. This was a sobering and somewhat frightening thought.

Recently, I was verbally accosted by an older man who did not like where I had parked my car. As I walked down the street to work, he shouted that I should park at the university rather than on a side street nearby. I responded that it was a public street and that I could park there if I chose. He continued to yell, but the only thing I caught was the last part of what he said: "Your tires are going to get cut!" Based on my appearance that day—I was dressed casually and carrying a backpack, and I had my hat on backward—I believe he thought that I was a young male student rather than a female professor. I do not think he would have yelled at a person he thought to be a woman—and perhaps especially not a woman professor.

Given the presumption of heterosexuality that is part of our system of gender, my interactions with women who assume that I am a man also can be viewed from that perspective. For example, once my brother and I were shopping when we were "hit on" by two young women. The encounter ended before I realized what had happened. It was only when we walked away that I told him that I was pretty certain that they had thought both of us were men. A more common experience is realizing that when I am seen in public with one of my women friends, we are likely to be read as a heterosexual dyad. It is likely that if I were to walk through a shopping mall holding hands with a woman, no one would look twice, not because of their openmindedness toward lesbian couples but rather because of their assumption that I was the male half of a straight couple. Recently, when walking through a mall with a friend and her infant, my observations of others' responses to us led me to believe that many of them assumed that we were a family on an outing, that is, that I was her partner and the father of the child.

Dealing with It

Although I now accept that being mistaken for a man will be a part of my life so long as I choose not to participate in femininity, there have been times when I consciously have tried to appear more feminine. I did this for a while when I was an undergraduate and again recently when I was on the academic job market. The first time, I let my hair grow nearly down to my shoulders and had it permed. I also grew long fingernails and wore nail polish. Much to my chagrin, even then one of my professors, who did not know my name, insistently referred to me in his kinship examples as "the son." Perhaps my first act on the way to my current stance was to point out to this man, politely and after class, that I was a woman.

More recently, I again let my hair grow out for several months, although I did not alter other aspects of my appearance. Once my hair was about two and a half inches long (from its original quarter inch), I realized, based on my encounters with strangers, that I had more or less passed back into the category of "woman." Then, when I returned to wearing a flat top, people again responded to me as if I were a man.

Because of my appearance, much of my negotiation of interactions with strangers involves attempts to anticipate their reactions to me. I need to assess whether they will be likely to assume that I am a man and whether that actually matters in the context of our encounters. Many times, my gender really is irrelevant, and it is just annoying to be misidentified. Other times, particularly when my appearance is coupled with something that identifies me by name (e.g., a check or credit card) without a photo, I might need to do something to ensure that my identity is not questioned. As a result of my experiences, I have developed some techniques to deal with gender misattribution.

In general, in unfamiliar public places, I avoid using the rest room because I know that it is a place where there is a high likelihood of misattribution and where misattribution is socially important. If I must use a public rest room, I try to make myself look as nonthreatening as possible. I do not wear a hat, and I try to rearrange my clothing to make my breasts more obvious. Here, I am trying to use my secondary sex characteristics to make my gender more obvious rather than the usual use of gender to make sex obvious. While in the rest room, I never make eye contact, and I get in and out as quickly as possible. Going in with a woman friend also is helpful; her presence legitimizes my own. People are less likely to think I am entering a space where I do not belong when I am with someone who looks like she does belong.[4]

To those women who verbally challenge my presence in the rest room, I reply, "I know," usually in an annoyed tone. When they stare or talk about me to the women they are with, I simply get out as quickly as possible. In general, I do not wait for someone I am with because there is too much chance of an unpleasant encounter.

I stopped trying on clothes before purchasing them a few years ago because my presence in the changing areas was met with stares and whispers. Exceptions are stores where the dressing rooms are completely private, where there are individual stalls rather than a room with stalls separated by curtains, or where business is slow and no one else is trying on clothes. If I am trying on a garment clearly intended for a woman, then I usually can do so without hassle. I guess the attendants assume that I must be a woman if I have, for example, a women's bathing suit in my hand. But usually, I think it is easier for me to try the clothes on at home and return them, if necessary, rather than risk creating a scene. Similarly, when I am with another woman who is trying on clothes, I just wait outside.

My strategy with credit cards and checks is to anticipate wariness on a clerk's part. When I sense that there is some doubt or when they challenge me, I say, "It's my card." I generally respond courteously to requests for photo ID, realizing that these might be routine checks because of concerns about increasingly widespread fraud. But for the clerk who asked for ID and still did not think it was my card, I had a stronger reaction. When she said that she was sorry for embarrassing me, I told her that I was not embarrassed but that she should be. I also am particularly careful to make sure that my signature is consistent with the back of the card. Faced with such situations, I feel somewhat nervous about signing my name—which, of course, makes me worry that my signature will look different from how it should.

Another strategy I have been experimenting with is wearing nail polish in the dark bright colors currently fashionable. I try to do this when I travel by plane. Given more stringent travel regulations, one always must present a photo ID. But my experiences have shown that my driver's license is not necessarily convincing. Nail polish might be. I also flash my polished nails when I enter airport rest rooms, hoping that they will provide a clue that I am indeed in the right place.

There are other cases in which the issues are less those of identity than of all the norms of interaction that, in our society, are gendered. My most common response to misattribution actually is to appear to ignore it, that is, to go on with the interaction as if nothing out of the ordinary has happened. Unless I feel that there is a good reason to establish my correct gender, I assume the identity others impose on me for the sake of smooth interaction. For example, if someone is selling me a movie ticket, then there is no reason to make sure that the person has accurately discerned my gender. Similarly, if it is clear that the person using "Sir" is talking to me, then I simply respond as appropriate. I accept the designation because it is irrelevant to the situation. It takes enough effort to be alert for misattributions and to decide which of them matter; responding to each one would take more energy than it is worth.

Sometimes, if our interaction involves conversation, my first verbal response is enough to let the other person know that I am actually a woman and not a man. My voice apparently is "feminine" enough to shift people's attributions to the other category. I know when this has happened by the apologies that usually accompany the mistake. I usually respond to the apologies by saying something like "No problem" and/or "It happens all the time." Sometimes, a misattributor will offer an account for the mistake, for example, saying that it was my hair or that they were not being very observant.

These experiences with gender and misattribution provide some theoretical insights into contemporary Western understandings of gender and into the social structure of gender in contemporary society. Although there are a number of ways in which my experiences confirm the work of others, there also are some ways in which my experiences suggest other interpretations and conclusions.

WHAT DOES IT MEAN?

Gender is pervasive in our society. I cannot choose not to participate in it. Even if I try not to do gender, other people will do it for me. That is, given our two-and-only-two rule, they must attribute one of two genders to me. Still, although I cannot choose not to participate in gender, I can choose not to participate in femininity (as I have), at least with respect to physical appearance.

That is where the problems begin. Without the decorations of femininity, I do not look like a woman. That is, I do not look like what many people's commonsense understanding of gender tells them a woman looks like. How I see myself, even how I might wish others would see me, is socially irrelevant. It is the gender that I *appear* to be (my "perceived gender") that is most relevant to my social identity and interactions with others. The major consequence of this fact is that I must be continually aware of which gender I "give off" as well as which gender I "give" (Goffman 1959).

Because my gender self-identity is "not displayed obviously, immediately, and consistently" (Devor 1989, 58), I am somewhat of a failure in social terms with respect to gender. Causing people to be uncertain or wrong about one's gender is a violation of taken-for-granted rules that leads to embarrassment and discomfort; it means that something has gone wrong with the interaction (Garfinkel 1967; Kessler and McKenna 1978). This means that my nonresponse to misattribution is the more socially appropriate response; I am allowing others to maintain face (Goffman 1959, 1967). By not calling attention to their mistakes, I uphold their images of themselves as competent social actors. I also maintain my own image as competent by letting them assume that I am the gender I appear to them to be.

But I still have discreditable status; I carry a stigma (Goffman 1963). Because I have failed to participate appropriately in the creation of meaning with respect to gender (Devor 1989), I can be called on to account for my appearance. If discredited, I show myself to be an incompetent social actor. I am the one not following the rules, and I will pay the price for not providing people with the appropriate cues for placing me in the gender category to which I really belong.

I do think that it is, in many cases, safer to be read as a man than as some sort of deviant woman. "Man" is an acceptable category; it fits properly into people's gender worldview. Passing as a man often is the "path of least resistance" (Devor 1989; Johnson 1997). For example, in situations where gender does not matter, letting people take me as a man is easier than correcting them.

Conversely, as Butler noted, "We regularly punish those who fail to do their gender right" (1990, 140). Feinberg maintained, "Masculine girls and women face terrible condemnation and brutality—including sexual violence—for crossing the boundary of what is 'acceptable' female expression" (1996, 114). People are more likely to harass me when they perceive me to be a woman who looks like a man. For example, when a group of teenagers realized that I was not a man because one of their mothers identified me correctly, they began to make derogatory comments when I passed them. One asked, for example, "Does she have a penis?"

Because of the assumption that a "masculine" woman is a lesbian, there is the risk of homophobic reactions (Gardner 1995; Lucal 1997). Perhaps surprisingly, I find that I am much more likely to be taken for a man than for a lesbian, at least based on my interactions with people and their reactions to me. This might be because people are less likely to reveal that they have taken me for a lesbian because it is less relevant to an encounter or because they believe this would be unacceptable. But I think it is more likely a product of the strength of our two-and-only-two system. I give enough masculine cues that I am seen not as a deviant woman but rather as a man, at least in most cases. The problem seems not to be that people are uncertain about my gender, which might lead them to conclude that I was a lesbian once they realized I was a woman. Rather, I seem to fit easily into a gender category—just not the one with which I identify.

In fact, because men represent the dominant gender in our society, being mistaken for a man can protect me from other types of gendered harassment. Because men can move around in public spaces safely (at least relative to women), a "masculine" woman also can enjoy this freedom (Devor 1989).

On the other hand, my use of particular spaces—those designated as for women only—may be challenged. Feinberg provided an intriguing analysis of the public restroom experience. She characterized women's reactions to a masculine person in a public restroom as "an example of genderphobia" (1996, 117), viewing such women as policing gender boundaries rather than believing that there really is a man in the women's restroom. She argued that women who truly believed that there was a man in their midst would react differently. Although this is an interesting perspective on her experiences, my experiences do not lead to the same conclusion.[5] Enough people have said to me that "This is the ladies' room" or have said to their companions that "There was a man in there" that I take their reactions at face value.

Still, if the two-and-only-two gender system is to be maintained, participants must be involved in policing the categories and their attendant identities and spaces. Even if policing boundaries is not explicitly intended, boundary maintenance is the effect of such responses to people's gender displays.

Boundaries and margins are an important component of both my experiences of gender and our theoretical understanding of gendering processes. I am, in effect, both woman and not-woman. As a woman who often is a social man but who also is a woman living in a patriarchal society, I am in a unique position to see and act. I sometimes receive privileges usually limited to men, and I sometimes am oppressed by my status as a deviant woman. I am, in a sense, an outsider-within (Collins 1991). Positioned on the boundaries of gender categories, I have developed a consciousness that I hope will prove transformative (Anzaldua 1987).

In fact, one of the reasons why I decided to continue my nonparticipation in femininity was that my sociological training suggested that this could be one of my contributions to the eventual dismantling of patriarchal gender constructs. It would be my way of making the personal political. I accepted being taken for a man as the price I would pay to help subvert patriarchy. I believed that all of the inconveniences I was enduring meant that I actually was doing something to bring down the gender structures that entangled all of us.

Then, I read Lorber's (1994) *Paradoxes of Gender* and found out, much to my dismay, that I might not actually be challenging gender after all. Because of the way in which doing gender works in our two-and-only-two system, gender displays are simply read as evidence of one of the two categories. Therefore, gender bending, blending, and passing between the categories do not question the categories themselves. If one's social gender and personal (true) gender do not correspond, then this is irrelevant unless someone notices the lack of congruence.

This reality brings me to a paradox of my experiences. First, not only do others assume that I am one gender or the other, but I also insist that I *really am* a member of one of the two gender categories. That is, I am female; I self-identify as a woman. I do not claim to be some other gender or to have no gender at all. I simply place myself in the wrong category according to stereotypes and cultural standards; the gender I present, or that some people perceive me to be presenting, is inconsistent with the gender with which I identify myself as well as with the gender I could be "proven" to be. Socially, I display the wrong gender; personally, I identify as the proper gender.

Second, although I ultimately would like to see the destruction of our current gender structure, I am not to the point of personally abandoning gender. Right now, I do not want people to see me as genderless as much as I want them to see me as a woman. That is, I would like to expand the category of "woman" to include people like me. I, too, am deeply embedded in our gender system, even though I do not play by many of its rules. For me, as for most people in our society, gender is a substantial part of my personal identity (Howard and Hollander 1997). Socially, the problem is that I do not present a gender display that is consistently read as feminine. In fact, I consciously do not participate in the trappings of femininity. However, I do identify myself as a woman, not as a man or as someone outside of the two-and-only-two categories.

Yet, I do believe, as Lorber (1994) does, that the purpose of gender, as it currently is constructed, is to oppress women. Lorber analyzed gender as a "process of creating distinguishable social statuses for the assignment of rights and responsibilities" that ends up putting women in a devalued and oppressed position (1994, 32). As Martin put it, "Bodies that clearly delineate gender status facilitate the maintenance of the gender hierarchy" (1998, 495).

For society, gender means difference (Lorber 1994). The erosion of the boundaries would problematize that structure. Therefore, for gender to operate as it currently does, the category "woman" *cannot* be expanded to include people like me. The maintenance of the gender structure is dependent on the creation of a few categories that are mutually exclusive, the members of which are as different as possible (Lorber 1994). It is the clarity of the boundaries between the categories that allows gender to be used to assign rights and responsibilities as well as resources and rewards.

It is that part of gender—what it is used for—that is most problematic. Indeed, is it not *patriarchal*—or, even more specifically, *heteropatriarchal*—constructions of gender that are actually the problem? It is not the differences between men and women, or the categories themselves, so much as the meanings ascribed to the categories and, even more important, the hierarchical nature of gender under patriarchy that is the problem (Johnson 1997). Therefore, I am rebelling not against my femaleness or even my womanhood; instead, I am protesting contemporary constructions of femininity and, at least indirectly, masculinity under patriarchy. We do not, in fact, know what gender would look like if it were not constructed around heterosexuality in the context of patriarchy.

Although it is possible that the end of patriarchy would mean the end of gender, it is at least conceivable that something like what we now call gender could exist in a postpatriarchal future. The two-and-only-two categorization might well disappear, there being no hierarchy for it to justify. But I do not think that we should make the assumption that gender and patriarchy are synonymous. . . .

. . . In a recent book, *The Gender Knot*, Johnson (1997) argued that when it comes to gender and patriarchy, most of us follow the paths of least resistance, we "go along to get along," allowing our actions to be shaped by the gender system. Collectively, our actions help patriarchy maintain and perpetuate a system of oppression and privilege. Thus, by withdrawing our support from this system by choosing paths of greater resistance, we can start to chip away at it. Many people participate in gender because they cannot imagine any alternatives. In my classroom, and in my interactions and encounters with strangers, my presence can make it difficult for people not to see that there *are* other paths. In other words, following from West and Zimmerman (1987), I can subvert gender by doing it differently. . . .

NOTES

1. I obviously have left much out by not examining my gendered experiences in the context of race, age, class, sexuality, region, and so forth. Such a project clearly is more complex. As Weston pointed out, gender presentations are complicated by other statuses of their presenters: "What it takes to kick a person over into another gendered category can differ with race, class, religion, and time" (1996, 168). Furthermore, I am well aware that my whiteness allows me to assume that my experiences are simply a product of gender (see, e.g., hooks 1981; Lucal 1996; Spelman 1988; West and Fenstermaker 1995). For now, suffice it to say that it is my privileged position on some of these axes and my more disadvantaged position on others that combine to delineate my overall experience.

2. In fact, such experiences are not always limited to encounters with strangers. My grandmother, who does not see me often, twice has mistaken me for either my brother-in-law or some unknown man.

3. My experiences in rest rooms and other public spaces might be very different if I were, say, African American rather than white. Given the stereotypes of African American men, I think that white women would react very differently to encountering me (see, e.g., Staples [1986] 1993).

4. I also have noticed that there are certain types of rest rooms in which I will not be verbally challenged; the higher the social status of the place, the less likely I will be harassed. For example, when I go to the theater, I might get stared at, but my presence never has been challenged.

5. An anonymous reviewer offered one possible explanation for this. Women see women's rest rooms as their space; they feel safe, and even empowered, there. Instead of fearing men in such space, they might instead pose a threat to any man who might intrude. Their invulnerability in this situation is, of course, not physically based but rather socially constructed. I thank the reviewer for this suggestion.

REFERENCES

Anzaldua, G. 1987. *Borderlands/La Frontera.* San Francisco: Aunt Lute Books.

Bem, S. L. 1993. *The lenses of gender.* New Haven, CT: Yale University Press.

Butler, J. 1990. *Gender trouble.* New York: Routledge.

Collins, P. H. 1991. *Black feminist thought.* New York: Routledge.

Devor, H. 1989. *Gender blending: Confronting the limits of duality.* Bloomington: Indiana University Press.

Feinberg, L. 1996. *Transgender warriors.* Boston: Beacon.

Gardner, C. B. 1995. *Passing by: Gender and public harassment.* Berkeley: University of California.

Garfinkel, H. 1967. *Studies in ethnomethodology.* Englewood Cliffs, NJ: Prentice Hall.

Goffman, E. 1959. *The presentation of self in everyday life.* Garden City, NY: Doubleday.

———. 1963. *Stigma.* Englewood Cliffs, NJ: Prentice Hall.

———. 1967. *Interaction ritual.* New York: Anchor/Doubleday.

———. 1976. Gender display. *Studies in the Anthropology of Visual Communication* 3:69–77.

Howard, J. A., and J. Hollander. 1997. *Gendered situations, gendered selves.* Thousand Oaks, CA: Sage.

Kessler, S. J., and W. McKenna. 1978. *Gender: An ethnomethodological approach.* New York: John Wiley.

Johnson, A. G. 1997. *The gender knot: Unraveling our patriarchal legacy.* Philadelphia: Temple University Press.

Lorber, J. 1994. *Paradoxes of gender.* New Haven, CT: Yale University Press.

———. 1996. Beyond the binaries: Depolarizing the categories of sex, sexuality, and gender. *Sociological Inquiry* 66:143–59.

Lucal, B. 1997. "Hey, this is the ladies' room!": Gender misattribution and public harassment. *Perspectives on Social Problems* 9:43–57.

Martin, K. A. 1998. Becoming a gendered body: Practices of preschools. *American Sociological Review* 63:494–511.

Myhre, J. R. M. 1995. One bad hair day too many, or the hairstory of an androgynous young feminist. In *Listen up: Voices from the next feminist generation,* edited by B. Findlen. Seattle, WA: Seal Press.

West, C., and D. H. Zimmerman. 1987. Doing gender. *Gender & Society* 1:125–51.

Weston, K. 1996. *Render me, gender me.* New York: Columbia University Press.

13

Immigrant Women and Domestic Violence

Common Experiences in Different Countries

CECILIA MENJÍVAR
OLIVIA SALCIDO

. . . An assessment of the scholarship on domestic violence among immigrant women is necessary because it sets the stage for framing important theoretical questions, as well as informing policy. Although existing research on this subject matter is still limited in scope and relatively new, there have been recent calls to attend to this issue. One major effort was made at the United Nations Fourth World Conference on Women held in September 1995 in Beijing, which recognized violence against women as a violation of human rights, as set forth by the *Declaration on the Elimination of Violence against Women*. . . .

COMMON EXPERIENCES IN DOMESTIC VIOLENCE AMONG IMMIGRANT WOMEN

Studies of domestic violence have demonstrated that despite differences in language, religion, and custom, physical assaults on women occur at all social and economic levels.[1] But there has been a common tendency to stereotype domestic violence in some ethnic groups as an inherent part of their cultural repertoire. Nelson (1996) observed that the stigma of domestic violence and the fact that it usually occurs in the home makes accurate information on the magnitude of this problem scarce. Some studies have reported high rates of physical abuse among groups of women, reaching 60 percent or more in select populations in Latin America, Asia, and Africa. This information often reinforces the notion that gender-based abuse does not need the state's intervention because it is part of a group's culture and it takes place in the private realm. As Kofman et al. (2000, 101) observed, "The case of domestic violence exemplifies the tolerance of practices in the private sphere on grounds of nonintervention in the customs of others." Ferraro (1989) found that police officers viewed arrests in domestic violence situations among immigrants (as well as among other groups such as gays and Native Americans) as a waste of time because violence was supposed to be "a way of life for these people." Furthermore, such notions not only serve to substantiate host governments' perceptions that domestic violence among immigrants is inherently a part of their culture—and thus nothing can be done about it—but also that domestic violence is higher among immigrants because they import it with them.

However, our review of the scholarship shows that the incidence of domestic violence is not higher than it is in the native population but rather that the experiences of immigrant women in domestic violence situations are often exacerbated by their specific position as immigrants, including limited host-language skills, lack of access to dignified jobs, uncertain legal statuses, and experiences in their home countries, and thus their alternatives to living with their abusers are very limited (Hass, Dutton, and Orloff 2000). These factors are identified in studies of immigrant women and domestic violence to one degree or another, where it is argued that they serve to prevent early intervention and/or reinforce strategies used by the perpetrator for control (Bui and Morash 1999; Garcia 1993; Jang, Lee, and Morello-Frosch 1991; Kantor, Jasinski, and Aldarondo 1994; Mama 1993a, 1993b; Perilla, Bakeman, and Norris 1994). These immigrant-specific conditions are superimposed on other systems of oppression, such as class, race, and ethnicity, to further increase immigrant women's vulnerability to domestic violence.

Some scholars have observed that the incidence of domestic violence among immigrants may be attributed to specific circumstances that can be encapsulated as stressors. For instance, in explaining domestic abuse among Latinas in the United States, Perilla, Bakeman, and Norris (1994) found that, similar to the native U.S. population, stressors stemming from environmental sources (such as work, school, and finances) contributed to the occurrence of abuse among Latinas. These researchers also linked immigrant-specific contributing stressors, such as immigration status, lack of English proficiency, prejudice, and cultural variables, to the occurrence of abuse. Scholars in this tradition would argue that eliminating stressors would contribute to decreasing the incidence of domestic violence. However, other studies that focus on the batterers demonstrate that eliminating stress factors (e.g., alcoholism, drugs, financial problems) does not necessarily end domestic violence (see Ptacek 1988).

Immigrants face multiple challenges when they resettle in a foreign country. A number of factors influence their experience, including the resources they bring to the host country and those they find in the arriving context. These assets include their occupation, education, and, importantly, the social networks that await them in the host country (Menjívar 2000). In this respect, some studies find that immigrant women establish informal networks quite effectively (Hondagneu-Sotelo 1994; Kofman et al. 2000; Menjívar 2000). Others observe that immigrant women arrive with disadvantages in social status and basic human capital resources relative to immigrant men (Bui and Morash 1999) or cannot participate as actively in networks as their male counterparts do (Abraham 2000; Hagan 1998). In the latter instances, men are often the intermediaries between the women and community and state resources. Yet even when women are able to access services on their own, their partners may have a final say as to whether the women may access such resources. . . .

Language

Language is a factor that impedes women from learning and accessing services in receiving communities (Bui and Morash 1999; Garcia 1993; Goldman 1999; Nah 1993). Immigrants already fluent in the language of the host country, because they are well educated or the host and native languages are the same, remain the exception. Nah (1993) observed that the ability (or inability) to speak the host-country language greatly influences the process of resettlement and adaptation into the new culture. Immigrants with limited or no host-country language skills tend to live in communities with coethnics, who cater to their needs in their native language. But according to Merry (2000: 209), social and cultural differences, a lack of understanding of the legal process, and language differences disadvantage recent arrivals. Also, language skills and job opportunities go hand in hand. When lacking host-country language skills, most immigrants—male or female—are only able to find jobs in the lower echelons of the economy (Nah 1993). A professional woman who is not fluent in the host-country language may end up working in a factory or a restaurant, which poses negative consequences for her and her family in the long run as they often stay in those jobs for a long time. And for many immigrant women, language is a barrier in accessing and communicating their needs to community-service providers and in seeking protection from their abusers through the criminal justice system (Bui and Morash 1999; Jang, Lee, and Morello-Frosch 1991).

However, some women, in the absence of host-country language skills, become adept at networking informally in their communities. They manage to access information and services, often independent from their male partners or family members (Menjívar 2000). These women begin to gain "legal consciousness" (Merry 1990, 2000), that is, a realization and greater understanding of their rights as they spend more time in the host country. Nicollet (1998) observed the increased use of French custom and law where domestic violence occurred as women from Mauritania, Mali, Senegal, and Guinea-Bissau spent more time in France. Language can break barriers for immigrant women in domestic violence situations since women's language proficiency can reduce the batterer's ability to reinforce his power to control. However, it is important to note that the ability to speak (or learn) the host-country language does not always lead to an improvement for immigrant women in domestic violence situations, as a study conducted among Hindu Asian Indian women in the United States demonstrated (Mehrotra 1999). In fact, it may exacerbate the abusive behavior since male control and orthodox gender roles are contested. That being said, even though the evidence on language is uneven, we find that in general, language skills exert greater influence when combined with other limiting conditions, such as isolation, employment, and legal status.

Isolation from and Contact with Family and Community

Isolation may occur more easily for immigrant women as many have left behind families and loved ones. They enter a foreign environment where they may not know the language, culture, or physical geographic area and may recognize only a few familiar faces. In these situations, it is easier for men to control women's lives both emotionally and physically. Due to isolation, men are better able to gain sole control over resources that could offer legal, financial, and/or emotional support to the women. And conflicts often arise when women establish links in their communities. For instance, when Guatemalan and Salvadoran women in the United States obtained information on domestic violence and their rights at community organizations, their partners did not welcome such knowledge (Menjívar 1999, 2000).

Many immigrant women suffer from social isolation, and it can have fatal results. In a case of Tamil women in Canada, isolation—compounded with a feeling of powerlessness—led several Asian Indian women to jump from their apartment buildings to their deaths. In this study (Morrison, Guruge, and Snarr 1999, 156), one key informant explained,

> Yes, because they have no other way, they have nowhere to go. All they know is they [can jump] off their balcony. And it's very hard to get to them because they don't come out, they don't meet anybody and we don't know that these people exist until they commit suicide.

This case identifies dependency as the culprit working against immigrant women, as the abusive partner gains momentum in power and control after immigration, and women (often) no longer have the support of their sisters, cousins, and friends that they had back home, as a case of Ethiopians in Israel attests (Adelman 1997).[2] Of course, even when immigrant women live close to family members and friends (a situation related to language skills and economic opportunities), orthodox views about marriage and gender roles tend to take over. Such views may encourage the perception of domestic violence as acceptable behavior. For instance, Filipinas in Australia who suffered abuse and violence remained isolated geographically and also were subject to cultural stigmatization in their own community and in the larger society (Ang 1995, 44). Thus, women may be isolated even when surrounded by family, relatives, or extended family members. A Korean immigrant woman in Nah's (1993, 293) study demonstrated this in speaking of her difficulties with her extended family in New York, particularly with her mother-in-law:

> I live with my husband's parents and brother. Whatever my husband tells my mother-in-law, all the blame falls on me. They think I make him do it. Once my husband told his mother that he wanted to move out; all my in-laws accused me of inciting my husband.

And abusive or not, sometimes men are more apt to accept a woman's role change than are all other female extended-family members. As a Guatemalan woman in Mexico explained, "Sometimes it is easier to persuade a husband to accept the changed role than to convince his mother or sister" (Garcia 1993, 29). Thus, often, it is other women who uphold orthodox views.

Keeping the above in mind, should a woman decide to leave her abusive husband, her community and extended and immediate family may not be supportive, a situation not dissimilar from that encountered by native groups. However, it becomes more salient among immigrants as the extended family may be the only people they know in their new place of residence. Often, when a woman is involved in an abusive relationship, social service providers expect her to leave her home and ties to receive assistance at a shelter. But if she leaves the abusive partner, she runs the risk of being ostracized by her family because she left and thus could not possibly be a "good wife," and she feels profoundly guilty. These women face the difficulty of challenging traditional gender structures, where they usually hold a lower status, while at the same time trying to make use of the options that have become available to them through social service providers. Other factors may compound this lack of support, as when the abusive partner is the primary source of income for the extended family or when social norms exist that encourage women to sacrifice themselves for the sake of other family members.

Other orthodox views persist in the arena of arranged marriages, even when members of the communities where they are practiced migrate to industrialized countries. Among these groups, women who opt to marry outside of the practice of arranged marriage may find that they gain power in one arena but lose in the area of family support. In such cases, if they become victims of domestic violence, they are likely to be left to fend for themselves (Ang 1995; Mama 1993b). On the other hand, in cases of arranged marriages, the women's families frequently seek to maintain their status and respectability, often at the expense of the individual woman's security and safety.

In a study of Indian, Pakistani, and Korean women in Chicago, battered women confessed their shame over leaving their husbands (Supriya 1996). Immigrant communities may go so far as to deny that there are immigrant women's groups working to end domestic violence so as to avoid facing a problem that might prove embarrassing, as the case of South Asians in the United States attests (Dasgupta 2000). In Britain, the Southall Black Sisters organization has faced the community's hostility for their campaign against domestic violence in Asian families (Kofman et al. 2000, 180). Thus, women in domestic violence situations are well aware of their family's expectations and prefer to pretend that all is well. In the words of one woman, "To my parents I was playing happy families" (Mama 1993b, 105). In addition, Donnelly (1989) observed that among Hmong refugees in the United States, marital conflicts are resolved within the traditional clan structure, and it is acceptable to seek help from the American legal system only if this fails. Pleck (1983) observed that immigrant women fear seeking legal protection in dealing with abuse because letting the government interfere with what is supposed to be a family affair may undermine the traditional authority in the family. This reinforces the acceptability of domestic violence through the belief that it is a private matter, an idea exacerbated in the case of immigrants when it is reflected in laws that may allow justification for battering (Avni 1991; Bui and Morash 1999; Merry 2000).

The issue of isolation becomes more acute in cases of mail-order brides, a practice created by men in industrialized countries to marry docile and domesticated women from lands where more orthodox gender relations are still the norm. Men expect these women to accept a submissive and subordinate role in marriage. In addition, the bride is often on her own for the first time, in a foreign land where her support base is nonexistent, which increases her vulnerability and isolation. Many have documented situations where men have used the woman's immigrant condition to reinforce their control and abusive strategies (Erez 2000; Jang, Lee, and Morello-Frosch 1991; Mama 1993a, 1993b; Nayaran 1995). The number of studies concerning domestic violence among mail-ordered brides is limited, perhaps due to very low levels of reporting, and the few studies that do exist differ dramatically in the rates reported, ranging from 12 to 50 percent. According to one study, this rate is as high as 77 percent (Nayaran 1995, 106). In Australia, Filipina women married to Australian men acknowledged their isolation and marginalization during times of discord or relationship breaks (Ang 1995, 44).[3] In another study conducted in Australia, Easteal (1996) observed that victims and abusers are usually from the same ethnic group, with Asian women who have been sponsored for immigration by non-Asian partners as the exception. Australia's Filipino community's prejudice and stigmatization of mail-order brides compounds the limited assistance that native Australians and the legal system offer to these women. Woelz-Stirling, Kelaher, and Manderson (1998) observed that social disapproval and/or stereotyping of Filipina-Australian marriages (and the shame that women in these marriages often experience) has led to underreporting of emotional and physical abuse. Ang (1995, 43) quoted a Filipina referring to mail-order brides as saying, "I know a lot of Filipinas married to Caucasians . . . and all are professional and decent." Later, Ang mentioned that the very necessity of this qualifier indicated the negative associations with mail-order brides.

Changes in Economic Status

The scholarship that documents immigrant women's entry into paid employment in the destination country is extensive. In assessing the effects of women's labor force participation, some studies observe that employment can increase women's bargaining power and control over resources. In turn, this can be the basis for more personal freedom and egalitarian relationships within the home (Benería and Roldán 1987; Safa 1995). Other studies demonstrate that participation in the labor force does not always translate into increased status for women or, for that matter, a decrease in domestic violence (Bui and Morash 1999; Menjívar 1999). If the man's authority is reduced as a result of the woman's increased economic status, conflict could occur (Kibria 1994; Kudat 1982; Menjívar 1999). A Korean woman in Nah's study explained,

> I make more money than he does, and he is irascible these days. The other day I argued strongly back against his remarks. He blew up. . . . I now try to say I don't know and seek his opinion. [Another woman observed,] After long hours of work, I am too exhausted. My husband is selfish. Sitting on the couch, he orders me to do everything for him. (1993, 292)

In a study of Asian Indian women in the United States, Mehrotra (1999, 628) observed that the abusive behavior continues and also undermines the potential economic gains of immigrant working women. Mona, a study participant, explained,

> During my marriage the worst days were the days I would bring in the pay stub. I was getting yelled at so much. I would take my pay stub, go to my bedroom closet, close the closet and sit there and cry for two hours, three hours.

Mona's husband had established an account in which his access allowed him to monitor every expense, thus controlling her activities, including any attempts to access money, or for that matter, community resources.

In addition, immigrant women are usually required to work a double (even a triple) shift, contributing to reproductive tasks in the home as well as productive ones in the labor market, all the while making efforts to keep orthodox gender relations at home intact. For instance, Turkish women in Germany often made superhuman efforts to participate in both areas so as to not upset the delicate balance of power at home (Kudat 1982, 298). Many entered the labor force for the first time in Germany, and notably, many of these women migrated alone and were later followed by their husbands. In cases where women migrated with their husbands or were soon reunited with them, "[women were] not freed from kin controls to the same extent as women who had migrated alone" (Kudat 1982, 297).

Similarly, Nora, a Guatemalan immigrant in Los Angeles (Menjívar 1999), had to do all the household chores even though she was the sole breadwinner so as not to make her unemployed husband feel any loss of power.

Sometimes, the new financial power a woman feels can lead her to seek alternatives to the expected strict submission to her husband's authority (Kudat 1982). This newfound independence can also jump-start demands concerning money decisions and investments. Taken a step further, a woman may even boycott decisions made back home by refusing to remit her earnings. The authority of the husband is further threatened when he remains at home or his job is temporary and/or unstable (Menjívar 1999) because immigrant women often are able to find jobs more easily than men, especially work in domestic services or caring for children and the elderly. Thus, conflict—rather than equality—may be the result of a woman's greater independence and may lead to an increase in the rate of separation or divorce (and violence).

Should a woman decide to abandon her partner and go back to her country, there may not be any jobs for her there. At best, there will be very low-paying jobs in precarious environments where the women may find themselves stigmatized, affecting their chances of earning a decent living. For example, when the Turkish women mentioned earlier decided to return home, they could not re-create the changes in their roles they had gained abroad. Once again, they had to conform to traditional norms (i.e., not to work outside the home if it could be avoided) or return to the same social class from which they originated (Kudat 1982). It might not be a surprise then that generally, immigrant men are more inclined to return home than are the women. Many women experience tension on their return. While pressure swells to uphold their society's relatively more orthodox gender roles, economic conditions demand deviation from such culturally acceptable norms of behavior. Women who decide to stay in the receiving country after separation or divorce usually increase their prospects of becoming the head of the household and thus are likely to remain in the lower echelons of society. Thus, paid work does not lead to an advantage in domestic violence situations, because immigrant women's employment does not occur in isolation from sociocultural and gender ideologies and the structural constraints in the contexts where they live.

Legal Status

Theoretically gender-neutral, immigration laws affect men and women dissimilarly. For instance, Simons (1999) observed that foreign women who marry American men generally are more vulnerable than are foreign men who marry American women. Although immigrant women are already susceptible to battering, an irregular legal status compounds their vulnerability and isolation, as MacLeod and Shin (1990) demonstrated in a study of battered refugee women in Canada. Often, immigrant women fear contact with authorities in the destination country and underutilize or avoid the criminal justice system altogether (Erez 2000; Menjívar and Bejarano n.d.). Thus, they may be more reluctant to seek help or report abuse.

Immigrant women can be in vulnerable situations because the legality of their stay in the receiving country often is linked to their spouses (Bechtold and Dziewiecka-Bokun 1999). Family reunification laws, such as those in the United States and Europe, tend to make immigrant women rely on their partners as their sponsors for obtaining legal status (Kofman et al. 2000). Failure to report abuse stems from either fear of their spouse's finding out or procedures that state agencies, such as the U.S. Immigration and Naturalization Services, launch. For instance, about 300 men per year are deported as abusers after being reported, but their wives are deported with them as well (*Washington Post* cited in New rules 2001) because they have been claimed as dependants on their husband's applications (either for refugee status or regular admissions). In these cases, an abusive husband can use his wife's legal status as a form of blackmail, and the wife will avoid filing criminal charges against her husband because her own legal status will be jeopardized.[4]

In Europe and the United States, as well as in other receiving countries, immigration laws often require that couples remain married for a certain number of years for the union to be legally recognized. This requirement, along with others, is to show that the marriage is real and not a fictitious one created only to obtain legal status. But these requirements often translate into hurdles for immigrant women in situations involving domestic violence. If they are still awaiting their legal status (and must remain married the required number of years) and choose to leave their husbands because of abuse, they may never obtain legal status. In a study of domestic violence among immigrant women in Phoenix, Arizona, Salcido (2000) found that even when women seek social services assistance, their legal status makes it difficult to obtain help. Lorena, a 24-year-old Mexican immigrant, remained in an abusive marriage for five years. Her husband threatened her with taking away their three-year-old daughter and with deportation. He had permanent legal status, but she did not, and on several occasions he threatened to end the petition process for her legal residency. After she endured his abuse for several years, her husband took their three-year-old daughter with him to Los Angeles, and it was not until later that she found out he had filed for divorce. His abandonment initiated a long fight for her to regain custody of her daughter. She won the custody battle, but proof of her husband's abusive behavior in court to obtain her legal residency is still pending.

Lorena's doubts concerning the legal system are well founded. In the beginning, it was difficult for her to obtain help from community-based organizations to leave the abusive relationship. She was told by two different agencies specializing in domestic violence that they could not help her because she was not a legal resident. Lorena also had negative experiences in locating good legal representation:

> I didn't know where to go for help, so I went to a lawyer that does a lot of publicity in the community. He said he would take my case, but then he told me he only handled [auto] accident cases and he passed me on to another lawyer. I told this last lawyer all the problems that I had with my husband; how he had been abusive, but he never did anything with this information. I later found out that his license as a lawyer had been suspended and that this was why another lawyer who knew nothing about my case would show up during the hearings in court. (Salcido 2000, 29).

Even women who have lived in the United States longer and know that the legal system can protect them cannot always avail themselves of such assistance. Lorena stated,

> I'm not sure that I can prove that he [her husband] was abusive because I don't have any police records. I never called the police. My lawyer told me to write up a letter with dates and what happened in detail. But I'm not sure that this will work. (Salcido 2000, 29)

Lorena may be right. Studies indicate that court authorities favor primary evidence (i.e., police or medical records) over a victim's written account of the abuse (Goldman 1999). Thus, although Lorena could have qualified to self-petition under new regulations that allow women in domestic violence situations to do so (because she was married for more than three years), her case may be denied due to a lack of documents validating her account of the abuse.

Sara, another Phoenix woman described in Salcido's (2000, 22) study, was undocumented and was staying at a shelter. Odds were against her, but she seemed determined to change her current situation. Although she had a higher educational level than most women at the shelter, she was not sure it would make a difference in her income because of her undocumented status. In Sara's words, "My resources here are very limited because none of us [her children and herself] were born in the United States." Like many other women, Sara's possibility of gaining legal status in the United States remained slim. However, she kept optimistic: "Here I am lucky to have a job, I plan to take ESL classes and may even take the GED, and my children can later go on to school. I was very fortunate to have gotten in here [the shelter]."

In sum, when both women and men are undocumented, the women fear the security of their entire families will be at risk if they call attention to themselves (Crenshaw 1995). Under these circumstances, many women are reluctant to leave even the most abusive of partners. This situation becomes acute among refugee women because, as Morrison, Guruge, and Snarr (1999) pointed out, a husband who has sponsored his wife from a war-torn country holds untold power over that woman. Crenshaw (1995, 335) observed that these are the tragic consequences of the double subordination of immigrant (and refugee) women.

The Home Country as a Frame of Reference

In evaluating their situation, immigrants frame their current experiences using their home countries as a point of reference and assess their present situation in relation to what they left behind (Erez 2000; Menjívar 1999; Menjívar and Bejarano n.d.). Often, women arrive from countries where domestic violence simply is not reported because of a lack of legal protection or cultural prescriptions that prevent women from reporting violence. Resources for women in these situations are few and far between, leaving them to infer, initially, that the same applies in the destination countries. A Salvadoran woman in Phoenix, Arizona, laughed when asked if she ever thought of calling the police back home in the case of domestic violence (Menjívar and Bejarano n.d., 19). In her words,

> The police? Who would think of calling the police back there [in El Salvador]? If you called them they'd think it's a prank and they won't even bother coming! No one does that. Everyone will laugh if a woman calls for help if her husband is beating her.

A Salvadoran woman in San Francisco (Menjívar 2000, 170) echoed this response and also laughed when asked the same question, later adding, "As a woman, one has rights in this country." This perception was reinforced by the view of Marcos, a Guatemalan man (Menjívar and Bejarano n.d., 19) who said, "No, there's no way the police [in Guatemala] will come if a woman calls them. That [calling the police] wouldn't happen anyway, but I've heard it's different here." Whereas calling the police to intervene in a domestic violence case back home would seem ludicrous to these immigrants, the fact that women can do so in the United States—and get a response—does affect their perceptions of U.S. authorities.[5] But their experiences with authorities back home still linger in their minds, at least initially.

Therefore, immigrant women, and immigrants in general, tend to rely on this dual vision to assess their current situation, but as time elapses, they find that authorities pay relatively more attention to cases of domestic violence in the receiving countries (e.g., the United States, Canada, Australia, and Western Europe). Although this is not always the case, it nonetheless makes them feel a bit more secure and can make their partners think twice about what they do. For instance, Menjívar and Bejarano (n.d.) found that several Central American and Mexican women in Phoenix, Arizona, felt that if they ever needed to call the police for a domestic altercation, the police would be responsive, which made them feel "more secure." And in a study of Salvadorans in San Francisco (Menjívar 2000, 266), men agreed that as women become more informed about their rights in the host country, the men tend to think twice about "misbehaving at home." Thus, eventually, immigrant women learn about their new rights and about police protection in the destination country. This has had an impact on reporting domestic violence to local authorities, but it does not imply that immigrants' claims always will be treated fairly in the criminal justice systems of receiving countries (Menjívar and Bejarano n.d.).

RESPONSES IN THE HOST COUNTRIES

Until this point, we have focused on elements that we found present—with qualifications—in domestic violence situations across different groups in varying contexts. We now turn to various responses of the receiving countries, both at the national and at the local levels, to the issue of immigrant women and domestic violence.

This issue should be of interest to the receiving countries, as their foreign-born populations have greatly increased in the past two decades. Four out of every 10 Australians is an immigrant or first-generation child of immigrants, and half of them are from non–English-speaking backgrounds. About 70 percent of Australia's arrivals came from non–English-speaking countries in 1994 to 1995 (see the Australian Commerce and Industry Office Web site: http://www.Australia.org.tw). The Center for Immigration Studies indicates that 28.4 million immigrants live in the United States. As a percentage of the population, immigrants now account for 1 in every 10 residents, the highest percentage in 70 years (Camarota 2001), but still lower than the all-time high of 16 percent at the turn of the twentieth century. We turn first to governmental and then to nongovernmental responses.

Government-Level Legal Responses

There have been several types of government-level response to domestic violence among immigrants. In Canada, Australia, New Zealand, and Britain, efforts have been made to provide greater protection to battered women who file gender-based claims for asylum. The enactment of the Violence Against Women Act in the United States in 1994 was the first step by the U.S. Congress to protect immigrant women whose batterers took advantage of the women's undocumented status. Initially, this act stipulated that a woman in a domestic violence situation could obtain legal residence if she (1) entered her marriage in good faith, (2) resides in the United States, (3) was the victim of battery or extreme cruelty during her marriage, (4) would suffer extreme hardship if deported, (5) is a person of good moral character, and (6) lived in the United States with her citizen or legal permanent resident spouse (Goldman 1999, 381). The act was modified in 2000 to (1) allow women who are victims of domestic violence and are undocumented to self-petition and file for cancellation of deportation while their case is pending, (2) no longer require applicants to show proof of extreme hardship, and (3) include abuse inflicted outside of the United States.

Although this act signifies a victory for support groups of victims of domestic abuse, it is still relatively unknown, and there have been several problems with its implementation. Goldman (1999) noted that the courts have been ambiguous in determining what constitutes abuse and the process remains rigid and bureaucratic. Sometimes, it is the very involvement of the police and the law that may keep an immigrant woman in an abusive relationship. For instance, the law mandates that the husband and wife be arrested if they have a physical confrontation at the time the police arrive, even if the wife's actions were in self-defense. Second, she may also qualify, but not be allowed under the law, to accept government cash assistance because this may jeopardize her chances of obtaining legal residence. Arrest and/or government cash assistance could make it difficult to prove good moral character (another requirement for legal residence), since an immigration officer may view these as blemishes on a person's record. Coutin (2000, 189) also pointed out that women must be in a legal relationship to be able to apply for permanent residence under the act. Many women who are not legally married may stay in abusive situations in the hope that one day, their partners will marry them and then petition immigration for them. Critics of the act (mostly anti-immigrant groups) argue that this is an attempt to expand the definition of asylum, which will allow too many to enter (or stay) legally.

In addition to the Violence Against Women Act, on 7 December 2000, the U.S. Department of Justice and the U.S. Immigration and Naturalization Services put forward a proposal that would enable victims of domestic violence to be considered members of a special social group to apply for asylum. Together with political opinion, nationality, race, and religion, it is one of five protected categories in immigration law. The proposal would recognize women as capable of facing persecution because of their gender and make it easier for those who have been victims of domestic violence to gain asylum. This category has been extended to include gays and lesbians and women facing genital mutilation. But what the law says about claims based on gender is complex and contradictory (Einolf 2001, 10). For instance, the asylum petition of Roni Alvarado Peña, a Guatemalan woman who had been severely beaten, raped, and threatened with death by her husband, was denied because the Board of Immigration Appeals (an administrative court charged with interpreting immigration law) found that her case did not fit any of the five protected grounds for asylum. However, a Moroccan woman who requested asylum because her father, a conservative Muslim, abused her was approved because the Board of Immigration Appeals ruled that she had been persecuted on the basis of religion (Einolf 2001, 232–33). These cases demonstrate how legislative changes can benefit some women but not others because their potential benefit depends on their interpretation.

Ang (1995, 45) argued that despite the higher risk of domestic violence in the Filipino community in Australia—5.6 percent higher than any other group in

Australia including other ethnic minorities—the Australian government has yet to respond to the problem through legislation. The author claimed that legislation has either remained insensitive or detrimental to Filipinas, requiring proof of violent treatment before a case can be considered before the law. The Australian and the Philippine governments have jointly addressed some of these issues, such as a 1990 ban on mail-order brides from the Philippines, and have stipulated that Filipinas requesting permanent residence in Australia attend a mandatory orientation program by the Commission on Filipinos Overseas. The Australian Department of Immigration and Multicultural Affairs will not accept an applicant who has not attended the mandated counseling sessions (Woelz-Stirling, Kelaher, and Manderson 1998, 298). As of 1991, government regulations were altered for women applying for permanent residency, who must prove that their marriage is real (not only to gain permanent legal status).

If the woman is not married and separates before marriage, she will be required to leave Australia. However, in cases where the woman can provide evidence demonstrating that the termination of the relationship was due to domestic violence or that she has custody or joint custody of a child, residency may be granted. Although the Australian government provides limited English classes for all new immigrants, and women participate in an orientation program, they are not informed of available health services, social security entitlements, legal rights, or networks with other Filipinas living in Australia. Some of these women live in isolated areas such as Queensland, where services are restricted (e.g., lack of adequate emergency shelters). Also among these women, immigration laws can contribute to a belief that leaving an abusive relationship may jeopardize their immigration status (Woelz-Stirling, Kelaher, and Manderson 1998, 290). History reveals that racism and sexism are entrenched in immigration laws of the receiving countries. For example, U.S. immigration laws and policies have focused on keeping out the "illegals" instead of focusing on potential future citizens (see Chavez 1992).

Local Responses

Local-level responses include police intervention programs and nonprofit organizations that provide services that specifically target domestic violence among immigrant women. The Southall Black Sisters in Britain, composed of immigrant women, has been at the forefront of campaigning against domestic violence in Asian families and provides an example of these local-level organizations. There are several groups that provide shelter to women who are victims of domestic violence, but few do so for immigrants. In some cases, outreach efforts do not consider culturally appropriate ways of transmitting information, such as informal networks, and use mainstream forms of advertising for their services, such as newspapers. An informant in Salcido's (2000) study said that alternative forms of distributing information could be supermarkets, local Spanish radio stations, or simply word of mouth.

Regardless of the method used to transmit information about assistance, often, there is resistance by the immigrant community to those who attempt to provide support services to abused women (Crenshaw 1995, 341), mostly in fear about the "image" of the community (see South Asian cases described by Abraham 2000 and Dasgupta 2000). The reality is that in certain areas, such as Phoenix and other newer destination points, agencies providing services for the immigrant population have limited housing and staff resources, which greatly impedes outreach efforts. Furthermore, growing racism and anti-immigrant sentiment in different receiving contexts can pose a dilemma for immigrant women, who often must choose between their rights as women and their loyalties to their ethnic group (Kofman et al. 2000).

Research suggests that local authorities' intervention among immigrants is similar to intervention among native-born women, in the sense that the results vary from useful to damaging (Mama 1993a). Cultural sensitivity and immigrant-language skills among professionals in the community (e.g., the doctors, lawyers, and social workers) affect their ability to communicate in the victim's language (literally and culturally) and to understand domestic violence in a particular group, which shapes their ability to provide adequate information and, if applicable, take legal action. In the case of women who do not speak the language of the destination country, vulnerability, alienation, and ridicule reach higher levels. And if interpreters are used, the information given to a police officer may be filtered and distorted by an interpreter who may even favor the aggressor.

In addition, the language and framing that practitioners use to handle domestic violence cases is crucial. In a thorough review of research conducted in social work, psychology, psychiatry, and other helping professions working with batterers, Ptacek (1988, 54) found that the same language was being used by both the batterers and the social service providers. The discourse used to describe the batterers' actions justified, excused, and rationalized his actions as a loss of control that overpowered him and somehow was outside the realm of choice, portraying the batterer as temporarily insane.

A different problem occurs when police intervention increases the violence and exacerbates the women's vulnerability and alienation (Mama 1993a). This contradictory outcome of police intervention is similar to past studies of the efficiency of police intervention in domestic violence cases in general. Ferraro (1989) noted that even when policies instruct police to arrest, officers will rely on the victim's and the offender's characteristics to determine whether to arrest, a decision that also will be informed by legal, ideological, practical, and political considerations. For instance, Ferraro found that officers are less likely to make an arrest at the end of their shift since it takes at least an hour to process an arrest and officers receive no explicit incentives for complying with the policy and no penalties for evasion. Race, legality, and language further inform an officer's actions. Thus, as is the case in domestic violence generally, such attitudes on the part of authorities have deterred immigrant women from seeking formal interventions.

RECOMMENDATIONS FOR FUTURE RESEARCH AND POLICY

We have identified common elements present in the domestic violence experiences of immigrant women that are unique to their situation—language barriers, isolation, immigration-induced economic changes, legal status, and a cross-national comparative frame of reference. These factors, however, are not the only ones present in cases of domestic violence among immigrants. Kurz (1998) and O'Campo and Rojas-Smith (1998) observed that welfare reform in the United States has negatively affected the lives of poor women, including immigrant women, in domestic violence situations, and Rhee (1997) noted that a high cultural tolerance of men's heavy alcohol use can contribute to domestic violence. Furthermore, the factors we have identified do not exert their influence alone. Economic hardship can prevent women from leaving an abusive relationship, which is exacerbated when women either do not speak the language or are undocumented and do not know their options because they are isolated.

There have been different responses to domestic violence among immigrants both at the government and at the local level in receiving communities. Governments have enacted and amended immigration laws that are making it a little easier for immigrant women to find protection. At the local level, immigrants can access services directed to native-born women, but barriers such as language, cultural misunderstandings, and different perceptions in reporting prevent the immigrant women from efficiently using such services. Services that are similar to those provided to native-born women tend not to consider the specificities of immigrants' experiences and sociocultural practices. However, there are social service agencies that specifically assist immigrant women in domestic violence situations, and these tend to be linguistically and culturally appropriate, but there still are very few of them.

Far from exhausting the discussion, we hope our effort here will instigate future research. . . . Our exploration may have policy relevance as well. For instance, several studies recommended that community-based organizations operated by individuals of the same ethnic group as those receiving the services would work best at meeting the needs of immigrant communities (Nah 1993; Preisser 1999; Rhee 1995). The same researchers point out that mainstream institutions do not acknowledge the value of infusing other cultural models into existing programs that would enhance services to the immigrant community. Such recognition would provide services that are culturally sensitive and cater to the needs of women who would otherwise hesitate to seek formal interventions and also would make use of professional coethnics who are working in low-paid, low-skill jobs.

Therefore, to avoid the continued perpetration of physical, mental, emotional, and/or economic violence against immigrant women and their children, the courts, as well as other community agencies that are part of the formal system, need to recognize that immigrant women in domestic violence situations have needs that differ from those of the mainstream population. Rather than essentializing immigrant women's experiences, these need to be brought into mainstream discussions and policies. Thus, laws, definitions, and channels of information need to be adjusted to recognize the increasing presence of immigrant women. Importantly, studies need to be comprehensive, including the experiences of immigrant women who have entered through the formal system and through extralegal channels. In this way, immigrant women will be informed, in their own language, of community services that will educate them about their rights, empower them, and enable them to improve their immigrant-specific situation so that they can live dignified lives.

NOTES

1. See Ferraro and Johnson (1983) for an analysis of how (nonimmigrant) women experience abuse, how they rationalize it, and under what circumstances they leave abusive relationships.

2. Similarly, John Johnson pointed out to us that when people migrate, male control of violent males is also lessened because of the distance involved (personal communication 2001).

3. For instance, in 1982, Rodell estimated that 50 percent of Filipinas were living in the highly isolated area of Northern Queensland. Australia (Woelz-Stirling, Kelaher, and Manderson 1998, 295).

4. It would be erroneous to think that immigrant women do not attempt to improve their situation. For instance, women seeking refuge in Britain urged a local organization to help them maneuver the legal system to deport their abusive husbands (Griffin 1995 and Patel 1999, cited in Kofman et al. 2000).

5. Of course, the U.S. system has its flaws. Ferraro (1989) found that even though Arizona law mandated arrest for men who batter women, an arrest was made in only 18 percent of reported assaults. The comparisons that immigrant women make, therefore, are only relative.

REFERENCES

Abraham, Margaret. 2000. *Speaking the unspeakable: Marital violence among South Asian immigrants in the United States.* New Brunswick. NJ: Rutgers University Press.

Adelman, Madelaine Beth. 1997. Gender, law, and nation: The politics of domestic violence in Israel. Ph.D. diss., Duke University.

Ang, Maria Aliena. 1995. The Filipino settlement experience in Australia. *Asian Migrant* 8:42–46.

Avni, Noga. 1991. Battered wives: Characteristics of their courtship days. *Journal of Interpersonal Violence* 6(2): 232–39.

Bechtold, Brigitte H., and Ludmila Dziewiecka-Bokun. 1999. Social services for immigrant women in European nations; Including lessons from the Council of Europe's Project on Human Dignity and Social Exclusion. In *Gender and immigration,* edited by Gregory A. Kelson and Debra L. DeLaet. New York: New York University Press.

Benería, Lourdes, and Marta M. Roldán. 1987. *The crossroads of class and gender: Industrial homework, subcontracting, and household dynamics in Mexico City.* Chicago: University of Chicago Press.

Bui, Hoan N., and Merry Morash. 1999. Domestic violence in the Vietnamese immigrant community: An exploratory study. *Violence against Women* 5(7): 769–95.

Camarota, Steven A. 2001. *Immigrants in the United States—2000: A snapshot of America's foreign-born population.* Washington, DC: Center for Immigration Studies.

Campbell, Anne. 1993. *Men, women, and aggression.* New York: Basic Books.

Chavez, Leo R. 1992. *Shadowed lives: Undocumented immigrants in American society.* Fort Worth, TX: Harcourt Brace Jovanovich.

Coutin, Susan Bibler. 2000. *Legalizing moves: Salvadoran immigrants' struggle for U.S. residency.* Ann Arbor: University of Michigan Press.

Crenshaw, Kimberlé. 1995. Mapping the margins: Intersectionality, identity politics, and violence against women of color. In *After identity: A reader in law and culture,* edited by Dan Danielsen and Karen Engle. New York: Routledge.

Dasgupta, Shamita. 2000. Charting the course: An overview of domestic violence in the South Asian community in the United States. *Journal of Social Distress and the Homeless* 9:173–85.

Donnelly, Nancy Dorelle. 1989. The changing lives of refugee Hmong women. Ph.D. diss. University of Washington.

Esteal, Patricia. 1996. Double jeopardy: Violence against immigrant women in the home. *Family-Matters* 45:26–30.

Einolf, Christopher J. 2001. *The mercy factory: Refugees and the American asylum system.* Chicago: Ivan R. Dee.

Erez, Edna. 2000. Immigration, culture conflict and domestic violence/woman battering. *Crime Prevention and Community Safety: An International Journal* 2 (1): 27–36.

Ferraro, Kathleen. 1989. Policing battered women. *Social Problems* 36 (1): 61–74.

Garcia, Sandra. 1993. Outside, looking in. *Refugees* 2:27–30.

Goldman, Maurice. 1999. The Violence against Women Act: Meeting its goals in protecting battered immigrant women. *Family and Conciliation Courts Review* 37: 375–92.

Hagan, Jacqueline Maria. 1998. Social networks, gender, and immigrant incorporation: Resources and constraints. *American Sociological Review* 63:55–67.

Hass, Giselle Aguilar, Mary-Ann Dutton, and Leslye E. Orloff. 2000. Lifetime prevalence of violence against Latina immigrants: Legal and policy implications. *International Review of Victimology* 7:93–113.

Hondagneu-Sotelo, Pierrette. 1994. *Gendered transitions: Mexican experiences of immigration.* Berkeley: University of California Press.

Jang, Deeana, Debbie Lee, and Rachel Morello-Frosch. 1991. Domestic violence in the immigrant and refugee community: Responding to the needs of immigrant women. *Response to the Victimization of Women and Children* 13:2–7.

Kantor, Glenda Kaufman, Jana L. Jasinski, and Etiony Aldarondo. 1994. Sociocultural status and incidence of marital violence in Hispanic families. *Violence and Victims* 9 (3): 207–22.

Kofman, Eleonore, Annie Phizacklea, Parvati Raghuram, and Rosemary Sales. 2000. *Gender and international migration in Europe: Employment, welfare and politics.* London: Routledge.

Kudat, Aysc. 1982. Personal, familial and societal impacts of Turkish women's migration to Europe. In *Living in.two cultures: The socio-cultural situation of migrant workers and their families.* New York: Gower/UNESCO Press.

Kurz, Demie. 1998. Women, welfare, and domestic violence. *Social Justice* 25:105–22.

MacLeod, Linda, and Maria Shin. 1990. *Isolated, afraid and forgotten: The service delivery needs and realities of immigrant and refugee women who are battered.* Ottawa, Canada: National Clearing-house of Family Violence.

Mama, Amina. 1993a. Black women and police: A place where the law is not upheld. In *Inside Babylon: The Caribbean diaspora in Britain,* edited by Winston James and Clive Harris. New York: Verso.

———. 1993b. Woman abuse in London's Black communities. In *Inside Babylon: The Caribbean diaspora in Britain,* edited by Winston James and Clive Harris. New York: Verso.

Mehrotra, Meeta. 1999. The social construction of wife abuse: Experiences of Asian Indian women in the United States. *Violence against Women* 5 (6): 619–40.

Menjívar, Cecilia. 1999. The intersection of work and gender: Central American immigrant women and employment in California. *American Behavioral Scientist* 42 (4): 595–621.

———. 2000. *Fragmented ties: Salvadoran immigrant networks in America.* Berkeley: University of California Press.

Menjívar, Cecilia, and Cindy Bejarano. n.d. Latino immigrants' perceptions of crime and of police authorities: A case study from the Phoenix metropolitan area. Unpublished manuscript.

Merry, Sally Engle 1990. *Getting justice and getting even: Legal consciousness among working-class Americans.* Chicago: University of Chicago Press.

———. 2000. *Colonizing Hawaii: The cultural power of law.* Princeton, NJ: Princeton University Press.

Morrison, Lynn, Sepali Guruge, and Kymberly A. Snarr. 1999. Sri Lankan Tamil immigrants in Toronto: Gender, marriage patterns, and sexuality. In *Gender and immigration,* edited by Gregory A. Kelson and Debra L. DeLaet. New York: New York University Press.

Nah, Kyung-Hee. 1993. Perceived problems and service delivery for Korean immigrants. *Social Work* 38 (3): 289–96.

Nayaran, Uma. 1995. "Male-order" brides: Immigrant women, domestic violence and immigration law. *Hypatia* 10 (1): 104–19.

Nelson, Toni. 1996. Violence against women. *World Watch* 9 (4): 33–38.

New rules proposed by the Immigration and Naturalization Service would allow victims of domestic violence to apply for asylum in the U.S. 2001. *Off Our Backs* 31 (1):4.

Nicollet, Albert. 1998. Femmes d'Afrique noire sur les chemins d'Europe. *Cahiers-de-Sociologie Economique et Culturelle Ethnopsychologie* 29:81–99.

O'Campo, Patricia, and Lucia Rojas-Smith. 1998. Welfare reform and women' health: Review of the literature and implications for state policy. *Journal of Public Health Policy* 19:420–46.

Perilla, Julia, Roger Bakeman, and Fran H. Norris. 1994. Culture and domestic violence: The ecology of abused Latinas. *Violence and Victims* 9 (4): 325–39.

Pleck, Elizabeth. 1983. Challenges to traditional authority in immigrant families. In *The American family in social-historical perspective,* edited by Michael Gordon. New York: St. Martin's.

Preisser, Amita Bhandari. 1999. Domestic violence in South Asian communities in America: Advocacy and intervention. *Violence against Women* 5:684–99.

Ptacek, James. 1988. Why do men batter their wives? In *Feminist perspectives on wife abuse,* edited by Kersti Yllö and Michelle Bograd. Newbury Park, CA: Sage.

Rhee, Siyon. 1995. Domestic violence in the Korean immigrant family. *Journal of Sociology and Social Welfare* 24:63–77.

———. 1997. Domestic violence in the Korean immigrant family. *Journal of Sociology and Social Welfare* 24: 63–77.

Safa, Helen I. 1995. *The myth of the male breadwinner: Women and industrialization in the Caribbean.* Boulder, CO: Westview.

Salcido, Olivia. 2000. *The Wilson Community Project: Assessing domestic violence issues.* Tempe: Building Greater Communities Project, Arizona State University.

Simons, Lisa. 1999. Mail-order brides: The legal framework and possibilities for change. In *Gender and immigration,* edited by Gregory A. Kelson and Debra L. DeLaet. New York: New York University Press.

Supriya, K. E. 1996. Confessionals, testimonials: Women's speech in/and contexts of violence. *Hypatia* 11:92–106.

Woelz-Stirling, Nicole A., Margaret Kelaher, and Lenore H. Manderson. 1998. Power and the politics of abuse: Rethinking violence in Filipina-Australian marriages. *Health Care for Women International* 19:289–301.

14

Acid Violence and Medical Care in Bangladesh

Women's Activism as Carework

Afroza Anwary

This is a study of how carework for women victims of acid attacks has been developed since the 1980s. It is also a study of how feminist groups have generated regional as well as international support for victims. In other words, it is a study of activism as carework. I examine how women activists in Bangladesh amplify their concerns for acid victimization to reach the international arena and how they mobilize civil society toward its full potential as an agent of healing and health care. I also demonstrate how local and international organizations pressured the government of Bangladesh into providing necessary and crucial medical care for victims. This article illuminates the multiple sites of carework by highlighting the importance of international networks. I explain how people who care for a vulnerable group can promote gender justice in the context of a strong patriarchal society like Bangladesh.

Acid violence is a particularly vicious form of aggression against human beings. Sulfuric acid, thrown on a human body, causes skin tissue to melt, often exposing bones below the flesh, sometimes even dissolving the bones. Most attacks, made by men, are directed at the faces of young women to destroy their physical appearance (Swanson 2002). Recovering from the trauma takes considerable time and, because of the disfigurement, victims' psyches are debilitated, negatively affecting every aspect of their lives. Survivors of acid attacks experience social isolation, encounter great difficulty finding work, and if unmarried, lose the opportunity to marry.

Acid attacks are a classic example of how gender conditions the responses of civil society, especially private, voluntary, and nongovernmental organizations (NGOs). The world has shrunk due to globalization, allowing an instant flow of information between nations. Consequently, when human rights abuse is overlooked by a national government, an outcry from local activists who want to help the victims can be communicated globally, causing wide public awareness. When the government of Bangladesh failed to provide basic medical care to acid survivors, local activists were able to contact international activists using new technology and pressure the Bangladesh government into providing necessary and crucial medical care to victims. Interaction between the state and NGOs has made international resources available to acid survivors in domestic social struggles. I begin by considering the social contexts and meaning of acid at-

Afroza Anwary, "Acid Violence and Medical Care in Bangladesh: Women's Activism as Carework," from *Gender Society,* Volume 17/2003, p. 305–313.

tacks and explain why acid victimization has become highly sensationalized in a global world. Then I examine the effects of globalization on acid violence, demonstrate how existing gender divisions are contested by new labor demands embedded in globalization, and argue that this may precipitate a rise in acid attacks. Finally, I explain the importance of activism and international networks on social policy related to health care work.

ACID ATTACKS: SOCIAL CONTEXT AND MEANING

The Western world seems to hold a common myth that acid violence only occurs in the Third World and may be related to Islamic fundamentalist men's throwing acid in the faces of women who are not veiled. Historical and current evidence on acid attacks is inconsistent with this perception. Acid violence does not occur in Bangladesh alone. It occurs in Pakistan (A matter of honor 1999), China (Acid test 2000), Ethiopia (SWIPNET 1998), and historically, in Europe (Davis 1984). Poststructuralist feminists argue that such an image of the Third World, filtered through the Western media, makes the Third World culture accountable for women's subordination. Narayan (1997) argued that dowry death in India has been reframed in the United States. This reframing distorts the complexity of recent dowry-related deaths that are shaped by contemporary Indian national contextual factors, such as a market-dominated economy and an increasingly global and commercial culture. Likewise, recent Bangladeshi national complexity, not the Islamic culture of Bangladesh, is liable for acid attacks. Acid attacks are a modern problem partially related to global development. In Bangladesh, daily economic struggles take precedence over attempts to win legal rights for acid victims. The lack of medical care, the absence of alternative institutions for victims rejected by their families, the failure of the government to enforce laws against the attackers, and rapid globalization have facilitated local feminist groups' efforts to effectively publicize and sensationalize acid victimization. The publicity also created space for building political coalitions around concern for human rights among groups living in vastly different political and cultural conditions.

Obtaining accurate statistics on acid attacks is difficult because most Bangladeshis live in isolated rural communities and mechanisms to collect such information are weak. In addition, police reports significantly underrepresent the number of annual acid attacks. Many victims do not report attacks to police because they fear reprisals from offenders' friends and families (Nasreen Haq, personal communication, 3 March 2001). However, new evidence suggests that reported cases of attacks are increasing at an alarming rate. According to Swanson (2002), there are approximately 300 cases reported each year.

Motivated by a variety of situations, men throw acid on women much like men rape, to keep women in their place. As in many patriarchal cultures, masculinity in Bangladesh refers to the ability of men to protect, defend, and sustain their property, including their homes and families. Furthermore, recent high levels of poverty and unemployment in Bangladesh contribute to attacks on women because of family feuds over property. Destroying female relatives' faces is the worst type of humiliation performed by men. The following example of a young man named Kuddus illustrates this point. Kuddus's cousin, who claimed the ownership of a disputed fruit tree, attacked Kuddus's wife and sister. Earlier that day, Kuddus claimed his ownership of the tree (Acid attack on sister-in-laws 2002).

The tremendous emphasis on women's appearance is also responsible for acid attacks. Parents have a primary responsibility to protect their daughters from sexual temptations, thereby preserving their marriageability. In a society where marriage is the only way to maintain the social status of women and ensure their economic security, virginity and appearance are the only resources women have in the marriage market. Women are not expected to get involved in romantic relationships before marriage. Sometimes, men victimize women who reject their marriage proposals. The men know they can avoid direct responsibility for their acts because the government fails to prosecute acid attackers. By destroying women's appearance, attackers try to bolster the political power that they feel was threatened when the women rejected their proposals. The men use women's appearance and sexuality to mark the boundaries between themselves and the women. Therefore, appearance seems to be a map of power for men and women. The following case illustrates this point. Majeda's parents refused a marriage proposal for her from one man, and Majeda was married to someone else. The angry suitor attacked her. Her eyeballs were badly burnt and hung from their sockets. Her attacker is still at large (Help victims of acid violence 2001).

In summary, the national context of Bangladesh is partially responsible for acid attacks, and the devastating effects of acid attacks on the victims require emergency medical carework. In the next section, I explain how globalization may precipitate acid attacks in Bangladesh.

THE IMPACT OF GLOBALIZATION

The new labor demands embedded in globalization may precipitate a rise in acid attacks because they contest the existing gendered division of labor. Globalization of the national economy has had a significant effect on Bangladeshi government policy. To attract multinational corporations into taking advantage of cheap labor in Bangladesh, the government developed new policies that led to the growth of the export-oriented garment industry (Rozario 2001). However, the garment industry prefers to hire semiskilled or unskilled women, which has led to a dramatic increase in women's employment in the secondary sector of the economy.

Such encroachment from women into paid employment poses a challenge to male supremacy in Bangladesh, and women who achieve increased economic autonomy are apt to experience resistance and histility from men. Nonetheless, deteriorating economic conditions, high unemployment rates among male breadwinners, the increasing number of landless households, and the lack of agricultural work for male laborers has forced some men to allow their wives, daughters, and mothers to participate in the paid labor force. In urban centers, women are often the sole wage earners, and they are expected to take care of their household responsibilities as well (Rozario 2001).

Women who are burdened with both housework and paid labor and who fail to perform their traditional gender roles often are victimized by their husbands. For example, Ashma Begum worked in an export-oriented garment factory and was the sole breadwinner of the family. She returned home late from work. Her unemployed husband who gained some financial privilege from her income was irate because his dinner was not prepared by her. Later, he threw sulfuric acid on her face, disfiguring her (Acid attacks 1998a). Ashma Begum's victimization reflects a reactionary backlash against women's increasing autonomy caused partly by the process of globalization. It also reflects men's increasing insecurity about the erosion of patriarchal privilege in Bangladesh at the entrance to the twenty-first century.

In sum, globalization and the structural adjustment policies of the government of Bangladesh reinforce gender violence. In the next section, I show how globalization also initiated a new pattern of activism. I highlight the importance of international networks in helping to bring global resources to acid survivors and in pressuring the government of Bangladesh to provide medical care for them.

SOCIAL POLICY AND GENDER ACTIVISM

Acid attacks became a major issue of debate amid a resurgence of women's activism in the early 1980s. Early organized response to acid attacks stemmed from internal mobilization instigated by women's organizations such as Naripokkho, a national, voluntary membership organization working to build resistance to violence against women. Many staffers are university educated, having the ability and knowledge to interact with governmental, nongovernmental, and international agencies. Many have personal ties with local and global civil society organizations. The key resources of knowledge and know-how of the staff and the active participation of victims in programs like Naripokkho help activists link victims' experiences with all global injustice that women face. Naripokkho has four working groups: reproductive rights and women's health, violence against women and human rights, gender issues in the environment and development, and the representation of women in media and cultural politics (Nasreen Haq, personal communication, 3 March 2001). Programs and activities include research, campaigns, protest work, discussions, lobbying and advocacy, cultural events, alliance with other human rights organizations, and monitoring of state interventions to combat violence against women. The group organizes workshops for survivors and their families, helping to rebuild their confidence, returning them to an active life within their communities, and allowing victims to come together and realize that they are not alone (Asian Women's Resource Exchange 2002).

Many international organizations located in Bangladesh, such as the British Council (BC), responded to the call of women's groups to help the victims. The BC is the United Kingdom's international organization for educational and cultural relations. By using its global network of offices, the BC promotes, among other things, gender equality in a global world. The BC works closely with national governments, local NGOs, private agencies, and international organizations. The BC of Bangladesh formed Supporting Survivors of Acid Attacks, a project that helps survivors access quality medical care, legal assistance, rehabilitation, and education. Using posters, flyers, and stickers twice a year, the BC organizes weeklong festivals, seminars, and workshops, including drama related to women's issues and acid attacks (Farah Kabir, personal communication, 30 July 2002).

Naripokkho persuaded the United Nations Children's Fund (UNICEF) and Amnesty International to recognize the plight of the acid survivors. The group convinced UNICEF that most acid survivors are young girls, who should be considered children who need emergency health service from organizations like UNICEF (Naripokkho 2001). UNICEF works in close partnership with the Bangladesh government, the Ministry of Public Health, and other national and international NGOs to eliminate violence against women and girls. For example, with economic support from UNICEF's Bangladesh Child Protection Section, the Ministry of Women's and Children's Affairs made a video that documents case studies of men helping female survivors of violence to seek justice (Acid Survivors Foundation [ASF] 1999). UNICEF, with financial assistance from the Canadian International Development Agency, formed ASF. A board of 15 trustees representing national and international NGOs, international donors, and acid survivors governs ASF. The goal of ASF is to provide ongoing help in the treatment, rehabilitation, and reintegration of the victims of acid attacks. With the help of other NGOs, ASF ensures that victims receive treatment at the hospital within three days of their attacks, and it provides survivors with better access to legal justice systems (ASF 1999). ASF established Thikana House, which is the only health care facility service in the country for acid victims with less serious burns (Swanson 2002). The BC provided support for the positions of two case managers responsible for acid victims and supported transportation of victims to Tikhana House (Farah Kabir, personal communication, 30 July 2002).

The BC in Bangladesh showed a documentary called *Ayana,* which revealed that attacks did not stop victims and their families from surviving. Women's groups and national and international organizations used advocacy and lobbying to demand that the Bangladesh government provide necessary medical support for the victims and enforce laws against acid attacks (Farah Kabir, personal communication, 30 July 2002).

Activists also approached foreign NGOs worldwide. Italian NGOs Cooperazione Internationale and Associezone Onlus provided treatment for acid burn victims. Corporation Darmeyestekika, a Spanish NGO, funded the treatment of six survivors who were featured on television, which led to wide support from the Spanish society (Acid attacks 1998b). Two survivors were featured on the popular American television programs *20/20* and *Oprah.* These programs invoked hundreds of sympathetic Americans to help the survivors (Naripokkho 2001). British Airways worked closely with ASF to provide free roundtrip tickets for some survivors to travel abroad where they received reconstructive surgery (Faces of hope 1999).

In the early 1990s, newspapers reported a rash of disfigurement due to acid attacks on young women. By the mid-1990s, documentation of acid attacks recorded by activists and protests in Dhaka were followed by demands for better care for acid victims. Although the outside world was unaware of these acid attacks, knowledge started to spread outside Bangladesh after 1995. In 1999, the World Press Club gave an award to Shafiqul Alam for his photo of an acid survivor whose head, except for one eye, was completely covered by a veil. The victim was ashamed to show her face in public because of her severe scars. The award drew the attention of the Western world to acid attacks.

A few activists visited the United States to speak publicly about the plight of acid victims and to appeal to human rights organizations to provide medical care to the victims. In the United States, a Bangladeshi physician and an advocate for children's rights approached Healing the Children (HTC), a nonprofit organization that secures donated medical care for children around the world whose families cannot afford medical expenses. The doctor also requested that HTC sponsor acid survivors for reconstructive surgery (Naripokkho 2001). Friends and families of the advocates for children's rights in Bangladesh traced the young victims of acid attacks; then HTC approached the American embassy in Bangladesh to help with immigration-related issues for the victims (HTC 2002).

In 1999, two survivors of acid attacks were brought to the United States by HTC. HTC contacted Shriners Hospital, a 30-bed pediatric burn unit that provides cost-free acute care and reconstructive surgery to children having burns that cause deformity to their faces.

In 1999, the government of Bangladesh responded to the demands of the women's groups and national and international organizations by building a new 50-bed burn unit in Dhaka, Bangladesh. Until 1999, Dhaka Medical College Hospital was the only public hospital in the country that had a burn unit. Dhaka Medical College Hospital had only 8 beds for female patients, whereas 300 reported female victims needed urgent care each year (Swanson 2002).

In early 2001, HTC sent a medical team to Bangladesh to provide surgical services for victims of acid violence and to share skills and techniques with local physicians. With the help of local hospitals, HTC performed surgeries to excise scar tissue, release contracted skin, and graft skin to cover scarred areas. By 7 April 2001, 31 patients underwent surgery (HTC 2002).

In November 2001, two universities in Bangladesh and the University of North London jointly organized a two-day workshop on violence against women. An international seminar on violence against women was held in the BC auditorium in Dhaka in January 2002. The public was encouraged to participate in the seminars. Seminars and workshops provided an opportunity to promote networking among local organizations and between local and international organizations engaged in improving the status of women and their human rights (Farah Kabir, personal communication, 30 July 2002).

Now, because of assistance from national and international organizations, the spirit of cooperation and collegiality predominates among organizations and individuals providing medical care to acid survivors. In the center of this cooperation are women's groups that strategically mobilize information about acid attacks, successfully motivate different organizations to provide medical care to acid survivors, and gain some leverage over the much more powerful government that tries to ignore the human rights abuses in Bangladesh.

International networks also have affected the implementation of laws against acid attacks. The government of Bangladesh developed a law that legislated the death penalty as the maximum punishment for perpetrators of acid attacks. However, perpetrators largely go unpunished. Naripokkho has investigated 217 cases of acid attacks from October 1998 to September 2000. Of 217 cases, only 27 suits were filed against attackers, and only 18 cases were under investigation by the courts (Naripokkho 2000).

Recently, pressure from British dignitaries who attended meetings organized by the BC and pressure from the U.S. State Department, the U.S. Agency of International Development, and other international organizations have led high-ranking Bangladeshi officials and the prime minister of Bangladesh to direct the court to pay attention to acid attack cases that receive high international visibility (Swanson 2002).

In sum, international networks have been important in shaping the health care needs of acid survivors of Bangladesh. The role of women activists has been crucial in bringing international resources that help meet the physical and social needs of everyday life for acid survivors.

CONCLUSION

I have explored how the specific national context of Bangladesh has framed acid victimization, brought it onto the feminist agenda, and shaped the ways in which acid victimization is understood in a global world. I identified multiple sites of carework and argued that activism is a form of carework. I examined how feminist groups in Bangladesh, who cared for acid victims, contacted international activists using new technology, and I have shown the conditions that allowed international groups to respond to these local problems in Bangladesh. In particular, I have explained how local feminist groups successfully mobilized both local and international organizations to provide crucial medical care to victims of acid attacks.

Using dramatic personal testimonies of acid survivors, a network of women's groups was the first to broaden its concerns for acid victimization to reach the international arena by regular communication. It linked Bangladesh and international human rights activists through the frequent exchange of publications, visits, e-mails, letters, and postings on the Internet. New technology in a global world rapidly increases the number of individuals who are aware of the problems and strengthens the mobilization that is under way. A network of transnational human rights organizations then lobbied the government of Bangladesh and international organizations to provide medical care for victims. High visibility of acid victims in the international arena, protest in the cities, and pressure from international donor organizations to whom the government routinely turns for financial help forced the government to provide medical care to acid victims.

International organizations that work closely with local NGOs and other indigenous organizations sought appropriate and acceptable ways to provide medical care. In the absence of universal normative evaluations of acid victimization, international organizations provide universal normative evaluations of human rights abuses. Prestigious organizations such as UNICEF help build activists' credibility by publicly speaking on behalf of the victims. Such support is crucial for attracting public attention. In addition, support from international agencies is crucial because resources for the victims are shrinking significantly and assistance from outside organizations increases the resources of victims/local activists appreciably. On one hand, alignment with agencies has broadened the power base of local feminist groups and provided innovative tactics, which are particularly important for achieving the major goal of the victims: receiving medical care. On the other hand, by providing necessary medical care to the victims of acid attacks, local and international organizations met their social responsibilities.

REFERENCES

Acid attack on sister-in-laws. 2002. *Daily Ittefaq,* 13 July.

Acid attacks. 1998a. *Daily Star.* Retrieved 1 January 1998 from http://www.dailystarnews.com/200101/14/n1011410.htm.

———. 1998b. *Daily Star.* Retrieved 16 November 1998 from http://www.dailystarnews.com/200101/14/n1011410.htm.

Acid Survivors Foundation (ASF). 1999. Acid Survivors Foundation: An important new initiative Retrieved 16 October 1999 from http://www.bicn.com/ezino/features/lifeinbgd/htm.

Acid test. 2000. *Time,* 11 December.

Asian Women's Resource Exchange. 2002. National partners: Bangladesh. Retrieved 12 July 1997 from http://www.arrow.org.my/docs/partners.html.

Davis, Jennifer. 1984. A poor man's system of justice: The London police courts in the second half of the nineteenth century. *Historical Journal* 27:309–35.

Faces of hope: Teen launches crusade to stop acid attacks against women in Bangladesh. 1999. *20/20,* 1 November.

Healing the Children (HTC). 2002. Healing the Children: Bangladesh. Retrieved 23 July from http://www.htcne.org/Bangladesh.html.

Help victims of acid violence. 2001. *New Nation,* 4 January.

A matter of honor. 1999. *Nightline,* 16 February.

Narayan, Uma. 1997. *Dislocating cultures: Identities, traditions, and Third World feminism.* New York: Routledge.

Naripokkho. 2000. Brochure. 3 March.

———. 2001. Brochure. January–September.

Rozario, Santi. 2001. Claiming the campus for female students in Bangladesh. *Women's Studies International Forum* 24:157–66.

Swanson, Jordan. 2002. Acid attacks: Bangladesh's efforts to stop the violence. *Harvard Health Policy Review.* Retrieved 6 July 2002 from http://hcs.harvard.edu/~epihc/currentissue/swanson.php.

SWIPNET. 1998. Ethiopian woman victim of acid attack. Retrieved 28 November 1998 from http://home.swipnet.se/~w~26522/Home.

15

Nationalism, War, and Archaization of Gender Relations in the Balkans

PATRICIA ALBANESE

In the winter months of 1992 to 1993, the story broke. One headline read, "A Pattern of Rape: A Torrent of Wrenching First-Person Testimonies Tells of a New Serb Atrocity: Systematic Sexual Abuse" (Watson, Warner, & Barry, 1993). New charges of mass rape came on top of existing accusations of Serb atrocities. To this day no one knows exactly how many women were victims, but at the time estimates ranged from 30,000 to 50,000 (Watson et al., 1993). Testimonies tell of repeated rapes, violations by neighbors, gang rapes, and the existence of rape camps (Amnesty International, 1993). Although most abuses were said to have been committed by Serbs against Muslims, all sides claim to have been victims of abuse at the hands of enemy forces (Amnesty International, 1993). Investigation by the United Nations Commission of Experts revealed that more than 700 detention centers were operated by Bosnian Serbs (237 of them), the Muslim Army of Bosnia-Herzegovina (about 89), and Bosnian Croats (approximately 77) (Kaldor, 1999, p. 52). The Commission noted that the camps were the scene of numerous inhumane acts, including mass executions, torture, rape, and other forms of sexual assault; widespread rape had reportedly been used in the process of ethnic cleansing (Kaldor, 1999). In the years that followed the wars, numerous other sources documented the same. Although today we may have a clear(er) picture of what happened in the Balkans with the breakup of Yugoslavia, we are still left with the questions of why it occurred and how such abuse was at all possible.

The focus of this article is to address the questions of why and how such widespread abuse was not only possible but actually became quite common in ethnic conflicts and wars. . . .

I will emphasize the importance of context by concentrating on the role ethnic nationalism plays in not only perpetuating the conflict but also in repatriarchalizing society and gender relations in general. I will argue that with the rise of ethnic nationalism and militarization there are institutionalized attempts to revive traditional, authoritarian, and patriarchal social forms and relations, which I claim result in the creation of an archaized social environment or culture. This archaized environment includes a web of interrelated circumstances that place women, specifically women of a particular ethnic group, at an increased risk of violence. I will draw on global and historical examples

---

Patricia Albanese, "Nationalism, War, and Archaization of Gender Relations in the Balkans," from *Violence Against Women* Sept., pp. 999–1023.

of violence against women in war but focus on the case of the former Yugoslavia to show that as social conditions change with nationalism and militarization, the nexus of gender and ethnicity becomes significant and potentially deadly.

I will show that what we see in the Balkan conflicts, among other things, is an attempt to shift social values back to more patriarchal forms of authority. I will argue that the rise of nationalism often involves a revival of patriarchal values and attitudes that work to legitimize male control, sexual entitlement, and power. This may result not only in the rape of women by an ethnic Other during the conflict and in the battlefield but also in the increase of risk of domestic abuse by their intimate partners.

A BRIEF LOOK AT THEORIES OF WOMAN ABUSE

. . . I suggest that to understand why we are seeing the widespread sexual abuse of women in war, we must pay special attention to the context in which the violence takes place. In the case of the former Yugoslavia, we saw a rising tide of ethnic nationalism. This was followed by the breakup of the federation, which threw many of its former parts into crisis and some areas into violent ethnic clashes. Mass calls to arms and conscription brought together groups of men who, through formal and informal venues, formed ethnicized armies and paramilitary groups. In this environment, what was transmitted both on and off the battlefield were norms and values that celebrated male power and control. As a result, gendered power differentials that already existed in the societies were reinforced and institutionalized, particularly through nationalist propaganda. I suggest (and will explain in detail throughout the article) that what results are archaized environments that attempt to repatriarchalize social relations in a number of polities that emerged following the breakup of Yugoslavia.

ARCHAIZED ENVIRONMENTS

According to a number of researchers, changing rules threaten what some men consider to be their proprietary rights in marriage, resulting in increased reliance on violence (Sever, 1997). But what happens when the changing social rules actually attempt to repatriarchalize gender relations and institutionalize male control over women? I suggest that the blending of nationalism and militarism at the time of the breakup of the former Yugoslavia led to the revival and relegitimation of traditional gender relations, creating a broader archaized social environment. Nationalist propaganda on and off the battlefield played a key role in this. An archaized social environment, as I define it, refers to a culture that attempts to resurrect and institutionalize traditional gender relations and thereby relegitimize patriarchal domination. . . .

RISING TIDE OF NATIONALISM

Following the death of Yugoslavia's President Tito in 1980, nationalist movements started regaining political space in Yugoslav politics. First came Albanian uprisings in Kosovo in 1981 (Singleton, 1994). Not long after that, in 1983, Croatian historians began calling for the demystification of the Tito image and a reassessment of Yugoslavia's history (Singleton, 1994). This was followed by a rebirth of Serbian nationalism in the second half of the decade, which Slobodan Milosevic joined and superimposed himself. Economic resentment, which accompanied Yugoslavia's economic crisis, combined with this rise of nationalist consciousness. Many leaders quickly learned that they could help fill the leadership void left by Tito's death by using the nationalist card to garner popularity and power. Nationalist appeals provided the easiest route to political visibility for politicians without established constituencies (Woodward, 1995).

According to Michael Ignatieff (1993), nationalist politicians on both sides (Serb and Croat) took "the narcissism of minor difference" and turned it into a monstrous fable, in which their own people appeared as blameless victims and the other side as genocidal killers. Although it was never this homogenous or complete, extreme nationalist ideology promoted the idea that "all Croats became Ustashe assassins; all Serbs became Chetnik beasts" (p. 15). Needless to say, such rhetoric became an essential precondition of the bloodshed that followed.[1]

To an outsider, Serbs and Croats seem quite similar. In fact, both are said to speak the same language, with slight variations (Ignatieff, 1993).[2] Ignatieff claims that "it cannot be repeated too often that these peoples were neighbors, friends and spouses, not inhabitants of different ethnic planets" (p. 15). In fact, between 1977 and 1981, 13% of new marriages in Yugoslavia were ethnically mixed (Licht & Drakulic, 1996). Heterogamous Croats most often married Serbs (59.0% of all mixed marriages involving Croats), and 48% of heterogamous Muslims' marriages were with Serbs (Licht & Drakulic, 1996). Of course, heterogamy was among the first casualties of nationalism. Differences were accentuated and languages were divided and reinvented with the rise in nationalist sentiment and through nationalist propaganda. Nationalism refers to the belief that people are divided into nations and that each of these nations has the right to be a self-governing unit or nation state of its own (Gellner, 1983). Nationalism includes the claim that although men and women have many diverse identities, it is their national affiliation that provides them with their primary form of belonging (Ignatieff, 1993). In fact, the word *nationality* derives from the Latin *ratio* (to be born), implying a common racial or biological descent. In other words, nationalists view their ethnic group as a biological, self-perpetuating group (Calhoun, 1993), which receives its impress from an accumulation of remembered or imagined cultural and historical forces (Hayes, 1960). This often includes extolling the group's territorial and fighting past and its exploits of valor and prowess, whether victorious or vanquished (Hayes, 1960). . . .

In societies charged with ethnic nationalism, women are often seen as biological reproducers of the nation and carriers of culture. Thus, control over women in the domestic sphere becomes one of the prime ways of preserving cultural traditions that are perceived to be threatened in times of ethnic conflict.[3] So it follows, where men sacrifice their lives for their nation, how can women refuse to place themselves at the service and mercy of the nation's martyrs?

Such an ideology also places some women at risk of gender-based violence at the hands of the ethnic Other, as rape comes to be interpreted as a means of humiliating the Other and destroying a society's cultural, traditional, and religious integrity. In other words, some women become victims of gender-based violence not only because they are women, but also because they are female members of an ethnic group. In sum, nationalist ideology highlights the nexus of gender and ethnicity, whereas nationalist propaganda accentuates differences and promotes rivalry and violence.

ARCHAIZATION OF GENDER RELATIONS IN FORMER YUGOSLAVIA

A number of authors have noted that throughout the former Yugoslavia there has been what I have referred to as a social archaization, which has been characterized by a glorification of the past, a renewal of religious traditions, and a general rise in conservative, right-wing ideology (Ignatieff, 1993; Licht & Drakulic, 1996; Morokvasic, 1998; Slapsak, 1996; Ugresic, 1998). According to Susan Woodward (1995), in the republics of the former Yugoslavia, the political right provided a "ready-made receptacle for an anti-communist juggernaut against the existing regime" (p. 125). With the rise of nationalist sentiment, what resulted was an attempted archaization that included the reinforcement of traditional, conservative, and patriarchal relations in general and a renewal of traditional gender roles within the family (Tomanovic, 1994).

According to Serbian feminists women were glorified, but only in their role as mothers and parents of the nation (Prosic-Dvornic, 1994).[4] This was found to be true throughout Serbia, Croatia, and Bosnia. In Serbia, there were political campaigns to introduce into Serbian family law committees to scrutinize and restrict pregnant women's right to abortion. This would essentially spell the end of an exceptionally liberal law that had been in place since the 1950s (Licht & Drakulic, 1996).[5] Similarly, in Croatia, in the spring of 1992, the Ministry for Renewal established a Department for Demographic Renewal under the control of a Catholic priest (Albanese, 1996; B.a.B.e., 1995). Strategies were developed to raise an ethnically clean birth rate, and social support incentives were proposed for women who gave birth to more than four children (Albanese,

1996).[6] Muslims, too, "noticeably began to hark back to old values" (Zalihic-Kaurin, 1994, p. 173). For example, one Muslim spiritual leader proclaimed a fatwa. He said, "I have told my Muslim women: a minimum of five children! Two for themselves, three for Bosnia!" (Ugresic, 1998, p. 122). In daily political practice, women were exposed to discrimination while the "women's question" was pushed off the public scene as being of secondary importance (Prosic-Dvornic, 1994). As a result, a number of feminists from the former Yugoslavia argued that the nationalist politics and practices "have flung women backwards by at least half a century" (Ivekovic, 1995, p. 13).

These societies attempted to redefine the role of women as waves of largely patriarchal nationalism swept over them. It should be noted, however, that it was not like this before the wars. As with many East European countries, the emancipation of women in prewar Yugoslavia was at least in part ideological. The situation, in this respect, worsened with the arrival of nationalist governments. In prewar Yugoslavia, patriarchal attitudes persisted in everyday life in spite of the rhetoric of emancipation formally promoted by the state party system. Socialist rhetoric on the emancipation of women resulted in formal, institutionalized gender equality, although in practice they continued to be stuck with the double burden (Morokvasic, 1998). It should be said, however, that Yugoslav socialism had its own Marxist feminist tradition that experienced a strong and healthy renewal since the 1970s (Slapsak, 1996). Furthermore, women were often relatively equal in their pay and the type of work they performed, and their university enrollment rates and presence in other areas of social life gave women some grounds for having the impression that they were equal to men (Licht & Drakulic, 1996).

Feminist and activist Lepa Mladjenovic (1993) described how, for more than 12 years before the breakup of Yugoslavia, there was a network of feminist organizations from Zagreb (Croatia), Belgrade (Serbia), and Ljubljana (Slovenia) that met every year. She bewails women's current position, stating that "all that we had fought for and which was part of the rights of women during Communism was somewhat wiped out the minute the war started" (p. 6). I suggest this had much to do with the rise of nationalist sentiment.

When nationalists came to power, women became symbols of nationalist politics (Morokvasic, 1998; Yuval-Davis & Anthias, 1989) and more numerous victims of war and everyday violence (Djuric, 1995). Feminist groups were still quite strong but now fractured, divided by newly established national boundaries. At the time of the breakup of Yugoslavia, nationalistic governments of its former republics embarked on nationalist programs with traditionalist agendas. To promote popular devotion, their ideological discourses and propaganda celebrated the warrior who selflessly defends the nation's future and the mother who ensures its survival as the biological regenerator of the nation. Myths of the war hero were widespread in nationalist literature in Yugoslavia (Licht & Drakulic, 1996; Slapsak, 1996). This mythology was characterized by the willingness of devotees to lay down their lives on the battlefields—and many did.

MILITARISM, MASCULINITY, AND WAR

The Yugoslav federation came to an end in 1990 to 1991, when the newly elected nationalist governments of Croatia and Slovenia declared their sovereignty first and independence later (Woodward, 1995). In the early summer of 1991, an attempt to defend the territorial integrity of Yugoslavia resulted in a 10-day war between the Yugoslav People's Army and Slovenian territorial defense units. Armed hostilities meanwhile simmered between the Croatian nationalist government and the nationalist leadership of the Serbs of Croatia. Some argued that clashes occurred before the actual secession of Croatia, involving ethnic Croat police on one side and ethnic Serb police and armed civilians on the other in April and May of 1991. This ethnic division that cut through Croatia, separating most Croats from most Serbs, was duplicated—actually, in triplicate—in Bosnia, with three main ethnicities compared with Croatia's two. With the Yugoslav federal army increasingly becoming a Serbo-Montenegrin armed force, all troops in the field became (more or less) ethnically homogeneous. What resulted was that most armies and militias in the recent Balkan wars were ethnically specific. This set the stage for the ethnicized gender-based violence that resulted.

According to Susan Woodward (1995), the character of wars, particularly in the beginning, draws out patriarchal culture. Commonly, in war propaganda there is a reinforcement of patriarchal themes—for example, the obligation to protect family and community from the external threat, and the reassertion of manhood, heroism, and power. Many have noted that to this day, war remains a masculine pursuit (Ugresic, 1998). War is "predominantly, but by no means exclusively—and certainly not biologically—a masculine affair" (Licht & Drakulic, 1996, p. 112). Propaganda on all sides often projected war as an attractive and exciting male adventure. Ugresic reported that one soldier returning from the front announced that "war is shooting and shagging, screwing and killing" (p. 118). The hyper-masculinity promoted by the propaganda set fighting in war apart from and above other masculine pursuits at the time.

Military historian John Keegan (1993) noted that "as those who know soldiers as members of a military society recognize, such a society has a culture of its own akin to but different from the larger culture to which it belongs" (p. 226). Military culture is distinct, standing outside the bounds of society. It produces its own codes, more masculine and patriarchal than perhaps any others found in civil society. For example, one of the most cited Prussian generals and military theorists, Clausewitz (1832/1993), wrote that

> military virtues should not be confused with simple bravery, and still less with enthusiasm for a cause. Bravery is obviously a necessary component. But just as bravery, which is part of the natural make-up of a man's character, can be developed in a soldier—a member of an organization—it must develop differently in him than in other men. (p. 219)

Time and again, descriptions of ideal soldiers and exemplary armies highlight the difference between themselves and the average man. Clausewitz noted that "no matter how clearly we see the citizen and soldier in the same man, how strongly we conceive of war as the business of the entire nation . . . the business of war will always remain individual and distinct" (p. 219). In other words, militarism celebrates a form of hypermasculinity above and apart from the rest of society. "For as long as they practice this activity, soldiers will think of themselves as members of a kind of guild, in whose regulations, laws and customs the spirit of war is given pride of place" (Clausewitz, 1832/1993, p. 219).

Let us recap. What we find in parts of the former Yugoslavia is an attempted archaization of gender relations in everyday life that (re)institutionalizes patriarchal domination. On top of this, there is militarization and war, which celebrates hyper-masculinity and socially sanctions violence. What results is an enormously heightened sense of male empowerment and entitlement. The patriot and war hero is merely filling his socially prescribed gender role as defender of blood and soil. To protect his blood, he protects his women. By protecting women, he defends his blood. By cleansing the enemy, he defends and purifies his soil. To do both amounts to victory. To do neither may result in humiliation and defeat. Thus, sexual violence against their women is but one of the ways to destroy their national pride, manhood, and honor. What results is the commonly seen connection between sex and violence in war.

Historically, women have not only been treated as spoils of war, or booty, but have also been (ab)used by men to humiliate their opponents—deeming their opponents impotent in their inability to protect their women. Rape was quite consciously used this way when German soldiers raped Belgian and French women in World War I (Harris, 1993); Chinese women were raped by Japanese soldiers in 1937 in what came to be known as the Rape of Nanking (Chang, 1997). Countless other examples can be found throughout history.[7] . . .

Writing on the rapes in Bosnia, Amnesty International (1993) noted that in almost all reported or alleged cases of rape, the victims were of different nationality from the perpetrators. They were victims because they were women and members of their ethnic group. They were targets because they were viewed as possessions of other men and of other nations. One man's sexual potency became proof of another's impotence.[8] As a result, women were described as postboxes used to send messages to those other men (Ugresic, 1998). There were examples of how they were used as messengers to male kin in testimonies recorded by Amnesty International. In a number of cases, the rape victims were women whose sons or husbands were being sought by enemy soldiers. For example, one victim stated that her son, who was believed to have been involved in organized resistance, was mentioned as she was raped and sworn at (Amnesty International, 1993). In many cases, it appeared that women in the former Yugoslavia were raped with a political purpose: to intimidate, humiliate, and degrade women "and others affected by their suffering" (Helsinki Watch, 1993, p. 21).

Furthermore, in many cases, the rapes did not take place under a cloak of secrecy. Some men clearly wanted others to know what they were doing. It appeared that some did not fear retribution. Some women described how they were raped without regard for witnesses, and on occasion soldiers identified themselves to their victims (Helsinki Watch, 1993). There were also a number of cases in which the victim was raped by uniformed men whom she knew (see Amnesty International, 1993). Her rape signifies her ethnic group's inability to protect her, a sign of her nation's and her men's impotence against their rivals.[9]

According to nationalist sentiment, war rape not only disrupts or threatens the sanctity of family temporarily, but also permanently threatens the purity of the entire ethnic group. This leads to the perception that the rape by an ethnic Other puts into question the authenticity, legitimacy, and purity of the blood ties that bind that ethnic group, diluting its purity and ultimately even threatening it with annihilation. Such sentiments hinge on the notion that virtuous and pure virgins produce a nation (Koonz, 1981), which means that women raped by an ethnic enemy are damaged or tainted so that they may not be able to sustain the purity of the ethnic group. It follows that in peace, women are used to ensure the survival of their ethnic group. In war, women are sexually abused or misused by the ethnic Other bent on destroying the group. In a nationalist context, the rape calls into question the future of the nation and marks the defeat of the mythic warrior. Nationalist ideology, therefore, plays a role in making women vulnerable to violent sexual attacks while motivating men to exploit that vulnerability. Nationalism adds an appeal or motivation to rape while playing a role in the treatment of this issue and the rape victims by the ethnic groups involved—none of them sympathetic of women qua women, but only as ethnospecific females.

In peace, gender-biased and nationalist social norms champion chastity, at least in principle, whereas war suspends most sexually restrictive and other social mores. "Thou shalt not kill" becomes "kill or be killed," and coveting thy neighbor's wife is not only widespread as an ideology, but acted on. Despite all this, social norms continue to apply to rape victims in war. That is, women continue to be judged by their ability to maintain their chastity, despite the fact that they have no power to match that of their assailants. When all other traditional rules are stood on their heads, the rule governing female chastity is expected to remain intact, despite the complete inability of women to do so. The war-weary warrior can thus return to resume civilian life, regardless of his wartime behavior. A war-rape victim of such warriors is often blamed for her own victimization. For instance, some doctors who treated rape victims lamented that single women in traditional Muslim society "stigmatized by rape" will never marry (McKinsey, 1992). They were tainted, unpure, unworthy, and stigmatized because they could not fight off their attackers. Slavenka Drakulic (1993), who interviewed Muslim victims, maintains that women who have been raped have little or no prospect of a normal family life in the future. In spite of a fatwa issued by the highest Bosnian Muslim authority that men should marry these women and raise the children conceived in rape in a Muslim spirit, the women knew that this was unlikely to happen (Drakulic, 1993).

A victim's ethno-sexual impurity thus is her ethnic group's problem—and cause or call to arms—whereas her physical and psychological wounds are her own to deal with. This may have been the case when a women's group in Zagreb wanted to set up a special hostel where rape victims could receive long-term counseling. The community objected, believing that special hostels will identify and stigmatize women (Grant, 1993).

It is actually society in general and traditionalist nationalist ideology in particular, not hostels, that stigmatize women. By lifting the sexist nationalist double standard when it comes to women's purity or chastity, victims of violence could be given proper treatment. Instead, the women face the horror of sexualized violence and the subsequent burden of knowing that they will be rejected by their own men for something done to them by others. Doing away with nationalist ideology may also make women less likely to be seen as the prey of a group of men out to harm another.[10]

But the ordeal does not end on the battlefield. Reports reveal that women were raped and abused by men who returned from the front lines (Amnesty International, 1993). The nationalism and militarism that makes women vulnerable to abuse at the hands of their ethnic nemesis increases the risk of abuse off the battlefield as well.

MILITARIZATION OF EVERYDAY LIFE

Ethnic conflicts driven by nationalist interests, as was the case in parts of the former Yugoslavia, are extremely disruptive to everyday life. Yesterday's neighbor becomes an ethnic nemesis; in a day, childhood friends become hated enemies; social order turns into chaos. Overnight, there is a militarization of everyday life, with the most mundane things becoming connected to war issues. For example, it was not uncommon for shops that once displayed fancy handcrafted leather handbags in downtown shopping districts during peacetime to display handcrafted leather holsters for handguns during the war.[11] Guns became readily available, and machismo and bravado of war spilled in to replace civility.

All this occurred at the same time that governments in Croatia, Serbia, and Bosnia attempted to reinstitute patriarchal order and control in civil societies of the new republics. Nationalist propaganda proved to be highly instrumental, even within the ethnic group. Gendered nationalist propaganda granted men power and control over their women more than before the war. This was met with opposition by feminists in Croatia and Serbia, but they were met with a backlash of their own.

Nonnationalists, pacifists, and feminists who challenged the archaic new order were labeled the internal enemy. Feminists and women's groups were portrayed as subversive and were demonized by state-owned media (Albanese, 1996). For example, in Croatia there was a campaign against the five witches[12]—five Croatian feminist writers, political activists, and critics (Tax, 1993). These writers were labeled traitors and were intimidated and maligned by local newspapers (Albanese, 1996). One of the crimes against their ethnos that they were accused of was that (at least some of them) had ethnic Serb spouses or lovers. They were writing against the institutionalized attempts to return to traditional gender roles. They, and others like them, were writing about and against family relations that were becoming brutalized (Licht & Drakulic, 1996). In fact, many women's groups noted that the levels and forms of family violence intensified with the rise of nationalism and the outbreak of war (B.a.B.e., 1995; Licht & Drakulic, 1996; Morokvasic, 1998; Sander, 1994).

On a trip to Belgrade, Yugoslavia, in December 1996, I was taken to one of the feminist-run women's shelters (a secret location) where I interviewed women living in a privately run safehouse for women victims of male violence. One woman stood out in the group—her image and story remain vividly implanted in my mind. She was not much older than me (in her early 30s), a mother of three, but looking ancient. She was a Croatian Serb, living a fairly normal life in Croatia as a teacher, with her husband and children, before the war. He went off to fight and she stayed behind. When he returned he was violent, routinely abusing her and the children and threatening to shoot them all with his new revolver. In the chaos of Croatia's ethnic conflict, she fled with the children to Serbia. She joined a flood of Croatian Serb refugees making their way through war-tom Bosnia toward Belgrade. She was fleeing the Croat army and her abusive husband. She arrived in Belgrade bewildered by war, her skin blackened by bruises she received in beatings by her husband. She was in a catatonic state, unable to care for herself and her children. By some twist of fate, she found herself at the safehouse. It took her 3 months before she began combing her own hair. Slowly, she started caring for her children and earning some money making rugs out of rags, using a 200-year-old loom from Bohemia the women had at the house. Her peaceful life before the war was a distant memory. She did not blame her husband. He had been a victim, too, she told me. He was a victim of a war that sets neighbor against neighbor. He fought, he killed, he lost control.

According to Dobash and Dobash (1998), proprietary sexual inclinations toward wives act as ostensible motivating circumstances in cases of spousal violence. Nationalist propaganda and ideology openly and publicly granted men collective sexual proprietorship over their women. During the wars, the new states that had once formed Yugoslavia did not collect statistics on gender-based domestic violence, but several women's organizations, including the Autonomous Women's House, SOS Hotline, and B.a.B.e.[13] Legal Hotline in Croatia, reported sharp increases in the number of phone calls they received from battered women (B.a.B.e., 1995). Women's groups reported an increase in the use of weapons to threaten and control women. Women's shelters and hotlines in Zagreb, Croatia, reported more calls and requests for shelter, and courts recorded an increase in cases of domestic violence (B.a.B.e., 1995).

The same was true in Belgrade, the capital of Yugoslavia. Mirjana Morokvasic (1998) stated that "violence against women has increased everywhere" (p. 77) during these wars. The SOS Hotline for women and children victims of violence in Belgrade also registered more calls from battered women than ever before (Morokvasic, 1998). The hotline reported that the use of guns and other weapons among the civilian population in general, and in cases of violence against women, had dramatically increased during the war (Morokvasic, 1998).

Helke Sander (1994) wrote that according to women working in women's shelters in Serbia and Croatia, normal domestic violence is said to have risen 100% since the beginning of the war: "Nearly every man is armed and, if he is at home, sleeps with a weapon 'under his pillow.' Women, meanwhile, are not only beaten but also killed with these weapons" (p. xx). The possession of guns became a normal part of life.

One feminist activist I interviewed in Belgrade admitted to me in a whisper that even she carried a gun in her purse. She explained that her activism was not appreciated by some in her city. She had once been beaten up in the street and would not let it happen again. When she questioned her country's soldiers' violence against their wives, she was seen as a traitor. Many people believed that she had no right to question the actions of their war heroes, who risked or sacrificed their lives for their nation. To challenge their preeminence was seen as nothing short of treason. When she tried to protect her countrywomen from her countrymen, she was challenging men's (warriors') authority. To question or challenge a war hero was to challenge what gave him power in the first place, the nation he was fighting for.

A survey of 70 refugee women in Serbia revealed that war increased the imbalance of power between genders, with male power growing at the expense of female power (Nikolic-Ristanovic, Mrvic-Petrovic, Konstantinovic-Vilic, & Stevanovic, 1995). The study found that the state protection that women had in peacetime (albeit little) was completely absent during war. The study concluded that women were not only deprived of protection and left alone to face fear, destruction, and sexual, physical, and psychological violence at the hands of their ethnic rivals, but they were also mistreated and abused by those who, in a patriarchal society, were "traditionally expected to protect them"—their own husbands (Nikolic-Ristanovic et al., 1995, p. 199).[14]

CONCLUSION

In the Croatian and Bosnian wars of secession, women were subjected to violence, sexual double standards, and more. Gender-biased nationalism, in its fixated quest for an elusive ethno-biological purity, exposes women to sexual abuse. Ethnic hatred makes women attractive targets of sexual violence, with national and international political interests manipulating all this. Meanwhile, rape victims become a statistic, their human trauma an item in the national political cause, while they remain physically and emotionally scarred long after their ethnic group finally absolves them of their stigma—as the real political needs dictate, of course.

In war, a male victim becomes a hero, whereas a female victim becomes damaged goods, at least until it suits the nation to treat her otherwise. Rape in war is an accentuated extension of the powerlessness and subordination that women experience in peacetime. In the course of war, the raped women go from being virgins, to being victims, to being damaged goods, to being forgotten. Unless this is recognized as a recurrent pattern found in many ethnic conflicts the problem will not go away, and many more women will become cases in a war-rape statistic.

The misogyny of an embattled culture caught in war, existential uncertainty, the ubiquity of arms and violence in society, and an overarching nationalist ideology that attempts to archaize gender relations have joined to make women more vulnerable to gender-based violence, even in supposedly safe areas (B.a.B.e., 1995). In other words, there appears to be a link between abusive male behavior and the wider militarized culture that (perhaps inadvertently) legitimates all forms of violence (Enloe, 1993). That is why I suggest that it is the combination of nationalism and militarism that can help us begin to understand why such widespread gender-based violence plagued regions of the former Yugoslavia and other places at the same or other times.

The rise of nationalism and its amalgamation with militarism in the former Yugoslavia included attempts to revive and relegitimize traditional gender roles and relations. This created a broader, culturally archaized environment that attempted to revitalize and relegitimize patriarchal domination. To a certain extent it succeeded, at least temporarily and in some social circles. Some men felt they were given leave to protect (i.e., possess and control) their women. I suggest that what we witnessed in the former Yugoslavia was the result of at least three factors coalescing into a conducive situation: First, condoning of violence at the governmental or quasi-governmental level, which Straus (1977) suggests contributes to gender-based violence; second, militarization, which Bandura (1973) suggests contributes to gender-based violence; and third, subsequent interaction among soldiers, which DeKeseredy and Kelly (1993) suggest contributes to gender-based violence. Together, these helped the revival of patriarchal values, including a sense of collective sexual entitlement and collective proprietorship over women. Furthermore, at the broader societal level there was the intensification of traditional ideology, which Pagelow (1981) suggests contributes to gender-based violence, and nationalist propaganda, which appears to have resulted in an internalization and relegitimization of the patriarchal order. The war created a crisis situation, which Enarson (1999) believes increases the risk of gender-based violence. What results was an archaized environment that placed many women at an increased risk of violence. I propose that understanding the social context and a web of factors within which the wartime abuse of women took place helps us to understand why it was not only possible but widespread.

NOTES

1. According to the Aspen Institute's *Report of the International Commission on the Balkans*, the main causes of the war lie in the sparks of aggressive nationalism fanned into flames by those political leaders of the dissolving Yugoslav federation who have invoked the "ancient hatreds" to pursue their respective nationalist agendas and have deliberately used their propaganda machines to justify the unjustifiable: the use of violence for territorial conquest, expulsion of "other" peoples, and the perpetuation of authoritarian systems of power. (Tindemans, 1996, p. xiv)

2. At the University of Toronto, prior to the war, Serbo-Croatian was taught by one American-born professor. With the coming of the war, the same professor taught Serbian to half of the room and Croatian to the other half of the room. When I studied the language(s), Serbian and Croatian classes were being taught in adjoining classrooms by the same American-born professor. On the day when my class met the professor taught in one room, the teaching assistant taught the other class next door.

3. To question this order was seen as treasonous. How dare anyone, and perhaps especially women, question authority, domination, and discipline at a time when so many men are "offering their lives at the altar of the motherland" (McKinsey, 1992).

4. It should be said that many women's groups in the newly formed republics of the former Yugoslavia have not accepted this without a fight. Women's lobbies have formed throughout Croatia, Serbia, and other republics (see Licht & Drakulic, 1996; Morokvasic, 1998; Slapsak, 1996; Ugresic, 1998).

5. New feminist initiatives sprang forth during government campaigns to legally repatriarchalize gender relations. For example, when the Serbian parliament proposed a new family law, feminists demanded that a ministry for women be established. Furthermore, a Women's Parliament was founded on March 8, 1991 (Licht & Drakulic, 1996; A. Milic, personal communication, December 1996).

6. In Croatia, 4% of ministerial-level positions and 6.3% of subministerial positions were filled by women in 1994 (postwar and postsecession) (United Nations, 1995). This is far below the 15% of

parliamentary seats occupied by women in the former Yugoslavia in 1975 and 18.8% in 1987, just before the breakup and wars (United Nations, 1991). "When being presented to the Croatian public, one female member of the Croatian Assembly . . . listed three facts, in order of importance. First, she was the mother of five children; second, she was a Croat by nationality; third, she was a pharmacist" (Ugresic, 1998, p. 122).

7. Jewish women were abused and killed by German soldiers in Germany, Poland, and Russia during World War II; Vietnamese women were gang raped by American soldiers in the Vietnam war. Peter Arnett, Associated Press correspondent in Vietnam, believed that Americans participated in gang rape because Americans were trained in the buddy system for security against the dangers of individual fraternizing on operations (Brownmiller, 1975). Bengali women were abused at the hands of Pakistani soldiers in 1971 (Brownmiller, 1975).

8. Sex and war were often intertwined. Jokes, anecdotes, and images were commonly used to highlight the impotency of opponents and sexual potency of one's own forces. Ugresic (1998) noted that newspapers, such as *Hrvatski Vjesnik* (the *Croatian Herald*), were full of homosexual pornographic caricatures of Serb soldiers.

9. Ruth Harris (1993) described how French soldiers in the First World War felt psychologically emasculated when they were unable to protect their women and their right as *pere de famille* (father of the family) from the "barbarian's incursions" (German troops) (p. 199). French men were expected to destroy bastard children and reimpregnate French women to reappropriate them, the French family, and French national territory. It is perhaps because national identity is often linked to sexual reproduction and blood ties that it has been labeled as an eroticized identity.

10. Susan Brownmiller (1975) argued that "war provides men with the perfect psychological backdrop to give vent to their contempt for women. . . . A simple rule of thumb in war is that the winning side is the side that does the raping. . . . Rape by the conqueror is compelling evidence of the conquered's status of masculine impotence" (pp. 24–31). In other words, it is a battle between two (or more) groups of men.

11. This was seen by the author in Belgrade: fashionable lady's handbags flanked with armpit holsters, both made of the same leather (his and hers leather accessories).

12. The five witches were Rada Ivekovic (professor of philosophy and writer), Jelena Lovric (journalist), Slavenka Drakulic (writer and journalist), Dubravka Ugresic (writer), and Vesna Kesic (journalist and founding member of B.a.B.e.).

13. B.a.B.e. is a feminist group. In Serbo-Croatian, the word *babe* means old hags, and B.a.B.e. stands for Be Active, Be Emancipated.

14. Guatemalan indigenous women have reported that domestic violence increased during the years of civil war in their country (Enloe, 1993; see also Davies, 1994, p. 124). 19. According to Straus (1977), militaristic political ideologies validate the use of violence by powerful and respected citizens. This appears to be true in parts of the former Yugoslavia.

REFERENCES

Albanese, P. (1996). Leaders and breeders: The archaization of gender relations in Croatia. In B. Wejnert, M. Spencer, & S. Drakulic (Eds.), *Women in post-communism* (pp. 185–200). Greenwich, CT: JAI Press.

Amnesty International. (1993). *Bosnia-Herzegovina: Rape and sexual abuse by armed forces.* New York: Author.

B.a.B.e. (1995). *Status of women in Croatia.* Zagreb, Croatia: Author.

Bandura, A. (1973). *Aggression: A social learning analysis.* Englewood Cliffs, NJ: Prentice Hall.

Brownmiller, S. (1975). *Against our will: Men, women and rape.* New York: Fawcett Columbine.

Brownmiller, S. (1993, January 4). Making female bodies the battlefield. *Newsweek,* p. 37.

Calhoun, C. (1993). Nationalism and ethnicity. *Annual Review of Sociology,* 19, 211–239.

Chalk, F., & Jonassohn, K. (1990). *The history and sociology of genocide.* New Haven, CT: Yale University Press.

Chang, I. (1997). *The rape of Nanking.* New York: Basic Books.

Clausewitz, C. (1832/1993). *On war.* New York: Alfred A. Knopf.

Davies, M. (1994). *Women and violence.* London: Zed Books.

DeKeseredy, W., & Kelly, K. (1993). The incidence and prevalence of woman abuse in Canadian universities and college dating relationships. *Canadian Journal of Sociology,* 18,137159.

Djuric, T. (1995). From national economies to nationalist hysteria: Consequences for women. In H. Lutz, A. Phoenix, & N. Yuval-Davis (Eds.), *Crossfires: Nationalism, racism, and gender in Europe.* London: Pluto.

Dobash, R. E., & Dobash, R. P. (Eds.). (1998). *Rethinking violence against women.* Thousand Oaks, CA: Sage.

Drakulic, S. (1993). Women hide behind a wall of silence. In R. All & L. Litschultz (Eds.), *Why Bosnia? Writings on the Balkan wars* (pp. 116–121). Stony Creek, CT: Pamphleteer's Press.

Enarson, E. (1999). Violence against women in disasters: A study of domestic violence programs in the United States and Canada. *Violence Against Women,* 5, 742–768.

Enloe, C. (1993). *The morning after,* Berkeley: University of California Press.

Genes, R., & Straus, M. A. (1988). *Intimate violence: The causes and consequences of abuse in the American family.* New York: Touchstone.

Gellner, E. (1983). *Nations and nationalism.* Ithaca, NY: Cornell University Press.

Grant, L. (1993, August 8). Horror of rape. *Calgary Herald,* p. All.

Harris, R. (1993). The "child of the barbarian": Rape, race and nationalism in France during the First World War. *Past and Present,* 141, 170–206.

Hayes, C. (1926/1966). *Essays on nationalism.* New York: Russell & Russell.

Hayes, C. (1960). *Nationalism: A religion.* New York: Macmillan.

Helsinki Watch. (1993). *War crimes in Bosnia-Hercegovina* (Vol. 2). New York: Human Rights Watch.

Ignatieff, M. (1993). *Blood and belonging: Journeys into the new nationalism.* London: Viking.

Ivekovic, R. (1995). Women, democracy, and nationalism after 1989: The Yugoslav case. *Canadian Woman Studies, 16,* 10–13.

Kaldor, M. (1999). *New & old wars: Organized violence in a global era.* Stanford, CA: Stanford University Press.

Kane, T. A. (2000). Male domestic violence: Attitudes, aggression, and interpersonal dependency. *Journal of Interpersonal Violence, 15,* 16–29.

Keegan, J. (1993). *A history of warfare.* Toronto, Canada: Key Porter Books.

Koonz, C. (1981). *Mothers in the fatherland: Women, the family and Nazi politics.* New York: St. Martin's.

Licht, S., & Drakulic, S. (1996). When the word for peacenik was woman. In B. Wejnert & M. Spencer (Eds.), *Women in post-communism* (pp. 111–140). Greenwich, CT: JAI Press.

McKinsey, K. (1992, June 22). Croatia seeks ways to boost birthrate. *The Gazette* (Montreal), p. B1.

Mladjenovic, L. (1993, Summer). Serbian women unite against the war *Madre,* pp. 6–7.

Morokvasic, M. (1998). Nationalism, sexism and the Yugoslav war. In N. Charles & H. Hintjens (Eds.), *Gender, ethnicity and political ideologies* (pp. 65–90). London: Routledge.

Nikolic-Ristanovic, V., Mrvic-Petrovic, N., Konstantinovic-Vilic, S., & Stevanovic, I. (1995). *Zene, Nasilje I Rat* [Women, violence and war]. Belgrade, Yugoslavia: Soros Fund.

Okun, L. (1986). *Woman abuse.* Albany: State University of New York Press.

Pagelow, M. D. (1981). *Woman battering: Victims and their experiences.* Beverly Hills, CA: Sage.

Prebble, J. (1967). *Culloden.* Middlesex, UK: Penguin.

Prosic-Dvornic, M. (Ed.). (1994). *Cultures in transition.* Belgrade, Yugoslavia: Plato.

Sander, H. (1994). Prologue. In A. Stigimayer (Ed.), *Mass rape: The war against women in Bosnia-Herzegovina* (pp. xvii–xxiii). Lincoln: University of Nebraska Press.

Sever, A. (1997). Recent or imminent separation and intimate violence against women. *Violence Against Women, 3,* 566–589.

Singleton, F. (1994). *A short history of the Yugoslav peoples.* Cambridge, UK: Cambridge University Press.

Slapsak, S. (1996). Between the vampire husband and the mortal lover: A narrative for feminism in Yugoslavia. In B. Wejnert & M. Spencer (Eds.), *Women in post-communism* (pp. 201–224). Greenwich, CT: JAI Press.

Straus, M. A. (1977). Sociological perspective on the prevention and treatment of wifebeating. In M. Roy (Ed.), *Battered women.* New York: Van Nostrand Reinhold.

Tax, M. (1993). *The five Croatian "witches": A casebook on "Trial by public opinion" as a form of censorship and intimidation.* Paper presented at the International PEN Women Writers' Committee.

Tindemans, L. (1996). *Unfinished peace: Report of the International Commission on the Balkans.* Berlin, Germany: Aspen Institute (Carnegie Endowment for Peace).

Tomanovic, S. (1994). Socialization of the child under conditions of a changed everyday life of the family. *Sociologija, 36,* 483–493.

Ugresic, D. (1998). *The culture of lies.* London: Phoenix House.

United Nations. (1991). *The world's women, 1970–1990: Trends and statistics.* New York: Author.

United Nations. (1995). *The world's women, 1995: Trends and statistics.* New York: Author.

Watson, R., Warner, M. G., & Barry, J. (1993, January 4). A pattern of rape. Newsweek, p. 32.

Wilson, F., & Frederiksen, B. F (Eds.). (1995). *Ethnicity, gender, and subversion of nationalism.* London: Frank Cass.

Woodward, S. (1995). *Balkan tragedy: Chaos and dissolution after the cold war.* Washington, DC: The Brookings Institute.

Yuval-Davis, N., & Anthlas, F. (1989). *Woman-nation-state.* London: Macmillan.

Zalihic-Kaurin, A. (1994). The Muslim women. In A. Stigimayer (Ed.), *Mass rape: The war against women in Bosnia-Herzegovina* (pp. 170–173). Lincoln: University of Nebraska Press.

16

Gender, Class, and Terrorism

MICHAEL KIMMEL

The events of September 11 have sent scholars and pundits alike scrambling to make sense of those seemingly senseless acts. While most analyses have focused on the political economy of globalization or the perversion of Islamic teachings by Al Qaeda, several commentators have raised gender issues.

Some have reminded us that in our haste to lionize the heroes of the World Trade Center collapse, we ignored the many women firefighters, police officers, and rescue workers who also risked their lives. We've been asked to remember the Taliban's vicious policies toward women; indeed, even Laura Bush seems to be championing women's emancipation.

A few have asked us to consider the other side of the gender coin: men. Some have rehearsed the rather tired old formulae about masculine blood-lust or the drive for domination and conquest, with no reference to the magnificent humanity displayed by so many on September 11. In an article in *Slate,* the Rutgers anthropologist Lionel Tiger trotted out his old male-bonding thesis but offered no understanding of why Al Qaeda might appeal to some men and not others. Only the journalist Barbara Ehrenreich suggests that there may be a link between the misogyny of the Taliban and the masculinity of the terrorists.

As for myself, I've been thinking lately about a letter to the editor of a small, upstate-New York newspaper, written in 1992 by an American GI after his return from service in the gulf war. He complained that the legacy of the American middle class had been stolen by an indifferent government. The American dream, he wrote, has all but disappeared; instead, most people are struggling just to buy next week's groceries.

That letter writer was Timothy McVeigh from Lockport, N.Y. Two years later, he blew up the Murrah federal building in Oklahoma City in what is now the second-worst act of terrorism ever committed on American soil.

What's startling to me are the ways that McVeigh's complaints were echoed in some of the fragmentary evidence that we have seen about the terrorists of September 11, and especially in the portrait of Mohammed Atta, the suspected mastermind of the operation and the pilot of the first plane to hit the World Trade Center.

Looking at these two men through the lens of gender may shed some light on both the method and the madness of the tragedies they wrought.

McVeigh was representative of the small legion of white supremacists—from older organizations like the

---

Michael Kimmel, "Gender, Class, and Terrorism" from *The Chronicle of Higher Education* (February 8, 2002) B11–12.

John Birch Society, the Ku Klux Klan, and the American Nazi Party, to newer neo-Nazi, racist-skinhead, white-power groups like Posse Comitatus and the White Aryan Resistance, to radical militias.

These white supremacists are mostly younger (in their early 20s), lower-middle-class men, educated at least through high school and often beyond. They are the sons of skilled workers in industries like textiles and tobacco, the sons of the owners of small farms, shops, and grocery stores. Buffeted by global political and economic forces, the sons have inherited little of their fathers' legacies. The family farms have been lost to foreclosure, the small shops squeezed out by Wal-Marts and malls. These young men face a spiral of downward mobility and economic uncertainty. They complain that they are squeezed between the omnivorous jaws of global capital concentration and a federal bureaucracy that is at best indifferent to their plight and at worst complicit in their demise.

As one issue of *The Truth at Last,* a white-supremacist magazine, put it:

> Immigrants are flooding into our nation willing to work for the minimum wage (or less). Super-rich corporate executives are flying all over the world in search of cheaper and cheaper labor so that they can lay off their American employees. . . . Many young White families have no future! They are not going to receive any appreciable wage increases due to job competition from immigrants.

What they want, says one member, is to "take back what is rightfully ours."

Their anger often fixes on "others"—women, members of minority groups, immigrants, gay men, and lesbians—in part because those are the people with whom they compete for entry-level, minimum-wage jobs. Above them all, enjoying the view, hovers the international Jewish conspiracy.

What holds together these "paranoid politics"—antigovernment, anti-global capital but pro-small capitalist, racist, sexist, anti-Semitic, homophobic—is a rhetoric of masculinity. These men feel emasculated by big money and big government—they call the government "the Nanny State"—and they claim that "others" have been handed the birthright of native-born white men.

In the eyes of such downwardly mobile white men, most white American males collude in their own emasculation. They've grown soft, feminized, weak. White supremacists' Web sites abound with complaints about the "whimpering collapse of the blond male"; the "legions of sissies and weaklings, of flabby, limp-wristed, non-aggressive, non-physical, indecisive, slack-jawed, fearful males who, while still heterosexual in theory and practice, have not even a vestige of the old macho spirit."

American white supremacists thus offer American men the restoration of their masculinity—a manhood in which individual white men control the fruits of their own labor and are not subject to emasculation by Jewish-owned finance capital or a black- and feminist-controlled welfare state. Theirs is the militarized manhood of the heroic John Rambo, a manhood that celebrates their God-sanctioned right to band together in armed militias if anyone, or any government agency, tries to take it away from them. If the state and the economy emasculate them, and if the masculinity of the "others" is problematic, then only "real" white men can rescue America from a feminized, multicultural, androgynous melting pot.

Sound familiar? For the most part, the terrorists of September 11 come from the same class, and recite the same complaints, as American white supremacists.

Virtually all were under 25, educated, lower middle class or middle class, downwardly mobile. The journalist Nasra Hassan interviewed families of Middle Eastern suicide bombers (as well as some failed bombers themselves) and found that none of them had the standard motivations ascribed to people who commit suicide, such as depression.

Although several of the leaders of Al Qaeda are wealthy—Osama bin Laden is a multimillionaire, and Ayman al-Zawahiri, the 50-year-old doctor thought to be bin Laden's closest adviser, is from a fashionable suburb of Cairo—many of the hijackers were engineering students for whom job opportunities had been dwindling dramatically. (Judging from the minimal information I have found, about one-fourth of the hijackers had studied engineering.) Zacarias Moussaoui, who did not hijack one of the planes but is the first man to be formally charged in the United States for crimes related to September 11, earned a degree at London's

South Bank University. Marwan al-Shehhi, the chubby, bespectacled 23-year-old from the United Arab Emirates who flew the second plane into the World Trade Center, was an engineering student, while Ziad Jarrah, the 26-year-old Lebanese who flew the plane that crashed in Pennsylvania, had studied aircraft design.

Politically, these terrorists opposed globalization and the spread of Western values; they opposed what they perceived as corrupt regimes in several Arab states (notably Saudi Arabia and Egypt), which they claimed were merely puppets of American domination. "The resulting anger is naturally directed first against their rulers," writes the historian Bernard Lewis, "and then against those whom they see as keeping those rulers in power for selfish reasons."

Central to their political ideology is the recovery of manhood from the emasculating politics of globalization. The Taliban saw the Soviet invasion and westernization of Afghanistan as humiliations. Bin Laden's October 7 videotape describes the "humiliation and disgrace" that Islam has suffered "for more than 80 years." And over and over, Nasra Hassan writes, she heard the refrain: "The Israelis humiliate us. They occupy our land, and deny our history."

Terrorism is fueled by a fatal brew of antiglobalization politics, convoluted Islamic theology, and virulent misogyny. According to Ehrenreich, while these formerly employed or self-employed males "have lost their traditional status as farmers and breadwinners, women have been entering the market economy and gaining the marginal independence conferred by even a paltry wage." As a result, "the man who can no longer make a living, who has to depend on his wife's earning's, can watch Hollywood sexpots on pirated videos and begin to think the world has been turned upside down."

The Taliban's policies thus had two purposes: to remasculinize men and to refeminize women. Another journalist, Peter Marsden, has observed that those policies "could be seen as a desperate attempt to keep out that other world, and to protect Afghan women from influences that could weaken the society from within." The Taliban prohibited women from appearing in public unescorted by men, from revealing any part of their body, and from going to school or holding a job. Men were required to grow their beards, in accordance with religious images of Muhammad, yes; but also, perhaps, because wearing beards has always been associated with men's response to women's increased equality in the public sphere, since beards symbolically reaffirm biological differences between men and women, while gender equality tends to blur those differences.

The Taliban's policies removed women as competitors and also shored up masculinity, since they enabled men to triumph over the humiliations of globalization and their own savage, predatory, and violently sexual urges that might be unleashed in the presence of uncovered women.

All of these issues converged in the life of Mohammed Atta, the terrorist about whom the most has been written and conjectured. Currently, for example, there is much speculation about Atta's sexuality. Was he gay? Was he a repressed homosexual, too ashamed of his sexuality to come out? Such innuendoes are based on no more than a few circumstantial tidbits about his life. He was slim, sweet-faced, neat, meticulous, a snazzy dresser. The youngest child of an ambitious lawyer father and a pampering mother, Atta grew up shy and polite, a mama's boy. "He was so gentle," his father said. "I used to tell him, 'Toughen up, boy!' "

When such revelations are offered, storytellers seem to expect a reaction like "Aha! So that explains it!" (Indeed, in a new biography of Adolf Hitler, *The Hidden Hitler,* Lothar Machtan offers exactly that sort of explanation. He argues that many of Hitler's policies—such as the killing of longtime colleague and avowed homosexual Ernst Rohm, or even the systematic persecution and execution of gay men in concentration camps—were, in fact, prompted by a desire to conceal his own homosexuality.)

But what do such accusations actually explain? Do revelations about Hitler's or Atta's possible gay propensities raise troubling connections between homosexuality and mass murder? If so, then one would also have to conclude that the discovery of Shakespeare's "gay" sonnet explains the Bard's genius at explicating Hamlet's existential anguish, or that Michelangelo's sexuality is the decisive factor in his painting of God's touch in the Sistine Chapel.

Such revelations tell us little about the Holocaust or September 11. They do, however, address the consequences of homophobia—both official and informal—on young men who are exploring their sexual identities. What's relevant is not the possible fact of Hitler's or Atta's gayness, but the shame and fear that surround homosexuality in societies that refuse to acknowledge sexual diversity.

Even more troubling is what such speculation leaves out. What unites Atta, McVeigh, and Hitler is not their repressed sexual orientation but gender—their masculinity, their sense of masculine entitlement, and their thwarted ambitions. They accepted cultural definitions of masculinity, and needed someone to blame when they felt that they failed to measure up. (After all, being called a mama's boy, a sissy, and told to toughen up are demands for gender conformity, not matters of sexual desire.) Gender is the issue, not sexuality.

All three failed at their chosen professions. Hitler was a failed artist—indeed, he failed at just about every job he ever tried except dictator. McVeigh, a business-college dropout, found his calling in the military during the gulf war, where his exemplary service earned him commendations; but he washed out of Green Beret training—his dream job—after only two days. And Atta was the odd man out in his family. His two sisters both became doctors—one a physician and one a university professor. His father constantly reminded him that he wanted "to hear the word 'doctor' in front of his name. We told him, your sisters are doctors and their husbands are doctors and you are the man of the family."

Atta decided to become an engineer, but his degree meant little in a country where thousands of college graduates were unable to find good jobs. After he failed to find employment in Egypt, he went to Hamburg, Germany, to study architecture. He was "meticulous, disciplined, and highly intelligent, an ordinary student, a quiet, friendly guy who was totally focused on his studies," according to another student in Hamburg.

But his ambitions were constantly undone. His only hope for a good job in Egypt was to be hired by an international firm. He applied and was continually rejected. He found work as a draftsman—highly humiliating for someone with engineering and architectural credentials and an imperious and demanding father—for a German firm involved with razing low-income Cairo neighborhoods to provide more scenic vistas for luxury tourist hotels.

Defeated, humiliated, emasculated, a disappointment to his father and a failed rival to his sisters, Atta retreated into increasingly militant Islamic theology. By the time he assumed the controls of American Airlines Flight 11, he evinced a hysteria about women. In the message he left in his abandoned rental car, he made clear what mattered to him in the end. "I don't want pregnant women or a person who is not clean to come and say good-bye to me," he wrote. "I don't want women to go to my funeral or later to my grave." Of course, Atta's body was instantly incinerated, and no burial would be likely.

The terrors of emasculation experienced by lower-middle-class men all over the world will no doubt continue, as they struggle to make a place for themselves in shrinking economies and inevitably shifting cultures. They may continue to feel a seething resentment against women, whom they perceive as stealing their rightful place at the head of the table, and against the governments that displace them. Globalization feels to them like a game of musical chairs, in which, when the music stops, all the seats are handed to others by nursemaid governments.

The events of September 11, as well as of April 19, 1995 (the Oklahoma City bombing), resulted from an increasingly common combination of factors—the massive male displacement that accompanies globalization, the spread of American consumerism, and the perceived corruption of local political elites—fused with a masculine sense of entitlement. Someone else—some "other"—had to be held responsible for the terrorists' downward mobility and failures, and the failure of their fathers to deliver their promised inheritance. The terrorists didn't just get mad. They got even.

Such themes were not lost on the disparate bands of young, white supremacists. American Aryans admired the terrorists' courage and chastised their own compatriots. "It's a disgrace that in a population of at least 150 million White/Aryan Americans, we provide so few that are willing to do the same [as the terrorists]," bemoaned Rocky Suhayda, the chairman of the American Nazi Party. "A bunch of towel head/sand niggers put our great White Movement to shame."

It is from such gendered shame that mass murderers are made.

PART III

SEXUALITIES

Are sexual relations a realm of pleasure, of empowerment, of danger, or of oppression? Why is gender violence so often associated with sexual relations? The women's movement reawakened during the late 1960s and early 1970s during a sexual revolution that was telling youth "If it feels good, do it!" In this context an initial impulse of second-wave feminism was for women to reclaim sexual pleasure for themselves. But soon some feminists began to argue that "sexual liberation" had simply freed men to objectify and exploit women more. As studies began to illuminate the widespread realities of rape, sexual harassment in workplaces, and sexual exploitation of women in prostitution, it became clear that for women, sexuality was too often a realm of danger rather than pleasure. As a result, by the mid- to late 1970s, feminist activism focused more and more on antirape and antipornography efforts.

By the mid-1980s other feminists—often younger women, women of color, lesbian, and bisexual women—began to criticize radical feminists' preoccupation with the centrality of male heterosexuality and pornography in women's oppression. And in the 1990s many younger feminists sought to reclaim sexual pleasure as a realm of empowerment for women. Today, feminists tend to see sexuality in complicated ways—as a potential source of both pleasure *and* danger, both empowerment *and* oppression. Moreover, research now indicates that the experience of sexuality is not simply determined by gender—race, age, sexual orientation, religion, and culture and nationality also shape sexual experiences and attitudes. In the first article in this section, Karin A. Martin argues that cultural concerns over the dangers of U.S. adolescent girls' and boys' sexuality tend to divert them from discovering and using their sexual desires in empowering ways. A sexual double standard still exists in teen culture, Martin observes, and working-class youths tend to experience this double standard somewhat differently than middle-class youth. The next three articles examine sexuality in non-U.S. contexts. Matthew Gutmann's analysis of Mexican men's recent growth in "self consciousness about sexuality" offers a fascinating window into the complex interweavings of notions of "potency" with masculine identities and relationships. Next, Kevin Bales analyzes prostitution and sex slavery of girls and young women in Thailand. He offers a close-up look at the experience of Siri, a fifteen-year-old prostitute, while illustrating how the economy of Thailand, positioned in a growing world economy, creates the context for the growth of the sex trade within Thailand and across national borders. Finally Julia O'Connell Davidson examines the "demand side" of international sex tourism. "Sexpatriots" in the Dominican Republic, Davidson observes, are mostly middle-aged, white, heterosexual Euro-American men whose activities endanger the health and safety of Dominican women while partially shoring up the fragile identities of these privileged men.

Are gay men and lesbians clearly and categorically distinguishable from heterosexual men and women? The articles in the second part of this chapter explore the area of sexual identity. It is widely accepted among scholars today that the idea that there are distinct sexual "types" of people such as "the homosexual" and "the heterosexual" is a very modern construction. But it is also well known that social constructions have real consequences. Modern medical and scientific discourse may have created "the homosexual" with the goal of controlling "deviant" character types and normalizing "the heterosexual," but starting mostly in the 1970s men and women who identified as "gay" and "lesbian" drew strength from their shared identities. And from this strength, they challenged prevailing cultural attitudes, customs, and laws. But, as Dennis Altman points out in the first article in this section, this gay and lesbian movement was a particularly modern phenomenon, grounded mostly in the urban areas of wealthy, industrialized nations of the north. He warns that within the context of globalization, the emergence of modern gay and lesbian identities in the Southern Hemisphere's poorer nations could be as much a sign of new forms of neocolonial control as it is a sign of sexual liberation. Next, Michael Messner draws partly on autobiography to reflect on the social processes involved in a young male's construction of himself as "100% heterosexual." And finally, Yen Le Espiritu's study illustrates the ways that Filipina immigrants in the United States sometimes define themselves in opposition to their conception of white women as sexually "immoral." Espiritu's analysis reveals the complex interweavings of identities that are constructed in contexts of unequal power by race, gender, sexuality, and national origin.

17

"I couldn't ever picture myself having sex . . ."

Gender Differences in Sex and Sexual Subjectivity

KARIN A. MARTIN

> I think there are very few girls I know who are having sex and actually enjoying it, most say it hurts especially the first time. The guys who are being promiscuous are actually enjoying it.
>
> —*Middle-class 17-year-old girl*

Why do adolescents have sex? What kinds of internal and external factors influence their decisions to have sex? Is the experience of teenage sex different for boys and girls? These questions are left unanswered by much of the current research on teen sex. Chilman in describing teen sex research says that, "In general, many of the studies seem to be voyeuristic. Who does what, sexually, with whom, how, and when?"[1] She is right. Researchers have extensively studied the demographics of teenage sex[2] and sexual knowledge, attitudes, and behaviors.[3] Yet, there is little research about the experience of sex—if teens like it or not, how it makes them feel about themselves, if girls feel differently about it than boys do. "What sexuality means to adolescents, how it relates to other aspects of teenage life, and what strategies teens use to manage or incorporate it into their lives have not been studied in detail."[4] This chapter begins to fill this gap, again paying close attention to gender differences in agency and sexual subjectivity.

Throughout this chapter when I talk about "sex" I mean sexual intercourse because this is what teenagers mean when they talk about sex. There is a socially constructed line between all other forms of sexual petting and intercourse in teen culture. Intercourse is invested with more meaning and significance than any other act. I find that like puberty, first sexual experiences further solidify agency and sexual subjectivity in boys. Girls, however, feel less agentic and less sexually subjective after first sexual experiences.

In order to examine how teens further construct sexual subjectivity (or not), we need to understand why and how teens come to have sex, for the gender differences in the social and psychodynamic paths to first intercourse are telling. By paths to sex, I mean teens' interactions around, feelings about, expectations and knowledge about sex that cause teens to have sex. These include the meaning of dating or "going out" or having a boyfriend or girlfriend, expectations and experiences of sex, and the immediate social interaction between two teens, the "talk" or lack of it, that leads to sex.

IDEAL LOVE . . .

Dating, "seeing each other" (dating) and "going out" (having a long-term monogamous relationship, the step after "seeing each other")[5] are all important cross-gender relationships that organize teen social life. For the most part, these relations mimic those of teens' images of adulthood. In them, most teens practice traditional gender roles and heterosexuality. This is true for both class groups and both genders. But these relationships do not only mimic adult heterosexuality, they also mimic children's play. Thorne and Luria observe that kids often play games that are "girls against the boys."[6] This oppositional gender strategy is carried into early stories of romantic relationship. Whenever boys complained about girlfriends or girls about unfaithful boyfriends, their stories took on this tone of the girls against the boys. For example, the boys whom I interviewed complained about their girlfriends, commitment, and monogamy.[7] They said things like 19-year-old Paul did: "I'm trying not to attach myself right now, until I go away to school. I don't want to deal with anyone in high school. I don't want to carry any baggage." Boys freely admitted that one was not supposed to admit to liking his girlfriend in teenage boy culture. I asked Scott, a working-class 18-year-old, "Do guys talk about their girlfriends?"

> I don't ever talk to my guy friends about my girlfriend, except . . . well you never admit that you like her, never. You just say that she was a pain in the neck.

Girls, on the other hand, are immersed in romantic culture. They told stories of love . . .

> *Tell me about your boyfriend.*
> I love his personality. The way he treats me. The way he says he cares for me, it's really important to me. He's very outgoing. Umm, he's real funny, and he makes me laugh. Umm, he's, I think he's real nice lookin'. And he's not too tall. He's about 5′8″. So, he's just perfect. *(Valerie)*

. . . and sometimes of unfaithful boyfriends who betrayed them.

> He's really stubborn, and he didn't care about anything, and he lied, he lied all the time. He wasn't loyal at all or anything like that. *(Diana)*

. . . At adolescence, many girls, in the process of growing up and away from their families, shift their ideal love from their fathers to male peers. The project of ideal love and the shift of ideal love from fathers to male peers is simultaneously a social and a psychodynamic one. By shifting their ideal love to male peers instead of fathers, girls can be recognized as participating in the adult world of heterosexual romance. Adolescents usually want to be recognized as grown up, independent, and able to do things. I argue that many girls, especially working-class girls, find ideal love to be the only route (although often an alienated one) to attaining agency and sexual subjectivity, and it has a particularly strong force in girls' heterosexual relationships at this age.

Teen culture emphasizes compulsory heterosexuality and facilitates girls' move to ideal love with male peers. There are very few lesbian or gay teen romance novels and thousands of heterosexual ones. Television shows that are geared to teens, like *Beverly Hills 90210,* and soap operas, a favourite pastime of many teens, rarely have gay characters and never have regular gay characters. However, heterosexuality and the adventures it poses almost entirely comprise the plots of such shows. There is little room for gay or lesbian identity or desire in most of this adolescent pop culture. This may be part of the reason why establishing a gay or lesbian identity as a teen is a difficult and relatively new phenomenon, as well as why many gay and lesbian teens also have had heterosexual experience.[8] This emphasis on compulsory heterosexuality shapes all girls' and boys' (although boys are less caught up in romantic culture) fantasies and realities.

In early adolescence, girls, especially white working-class girls, become absorbed in teen idols, teen romances, and pop rock ballads about love.[9] Then, as teens, many girls acquire boyfriends and construct narratives about their boyfriends that cast them in the light of ideal love. Stories of ideal love are not stories of passion and sexuality but are stories of romance and what sociologist Arlie Hochschild calls magnified moments. A magnified moment is "a moment of heightened importance to the individual. This can be an epiphany, a moment of intense glee, or unusual insight. Within cautionary stories, it can be a moment of unusual despair."[10] First dates, first looks, first meetings, as well as break ups, all are or contain magnified moments for girls in ideal love. . . .

The best way to understand what ideal love is, is to hear girls describe it to you. They get excited, interested. Their stories become detailed, and these details, however insignificant and minor they may be to the listener, are clearly important to the narrator. Their stories also get infused with romantic language and romantic words—flowers, fairy tale, letters, swept off my feet, magic, flirting, intense, beach, cute, beautiful, secrets. Descriptions of ideal love also clearly have a story to them. The narrator has put the events together to make a "fairy tale sort of story" for herself. I asked Jill to tell me about her boyfriend (a question that was always met with enthusiasm and to which I always got a long answer).

> It's a fairy tale sort of a story. He's in the Marine Corps, and he was over in the Middle East during the war. And there were names in the newspaper you could write to, and I wrote to a Sergeant, and he'd just gotten married and felt really awkward writing, so he gave the letter to my boyfriend, Alan. Alan and I wrote and when he came back to the States he sent me flowers and asked if he could meet me, and once he came up to meet me we've been together ever since. That's last year. He's stationed in the south. I just came back from visitin' him. It's really far. He's getting out the end of May; so we won't have to do that any more. Anyway, he's wonderful. He's a spitting image, like inside, how he acts, of my dad. My father always said, like teasing me when I was little, wait, you'll find someone exactly like me. And it's true. He's quiet. He only speaks his mind when asked. He's very secretive about his feelings. I've just started tapping into them myself. He'll do anything to help anyone out. Our relationship is going well. We communicate really good. He can mumble on about something for five minutes and someone else would be truly lost but I'd know exactly what he's talking about. We really trust each other, and I don't trust really easily and he doesn't either. He's had a bad past, and I have a bad past, so. . . .

Kristen told a less complicated version of ideal love, and like Jill's military man, her ideal love is not an ordinary guy, but a reggae singer. He has special status. She told me about him at the beginning of our interview when I asked her what she day-dreamed about.

> I always think about this guy I met this summer. I wicked fell in love, wicked bad. I didn't just love him, but I wicked fell-in-love. You know, swept me off my feet. I just think about his face, the way he used to sing to me. He was wicked awesome. He used to like sing reggae to me. He was awesome. He was just one of a kind.

. . . First meetings with ideal loves are often magnified moments. Danielle described one of the most magnified moments I heard in all my interviews. Her first meeting with her boyfriend was a magnified moment in itself, yet within this general story, there was literally one specific moment that she magnified—when she and the boy turned to each other and said the exact same thing at the same time. It was clear to me as the listener that this was the moment that cinched the story that they were "right" for each other because she prefaced the moment in her telling with a breathless, giggling "I have to tell you this."

> *How did you meet your boyfriend?*
> We met in August of last year. We met on the beach! It was real cute. Me and my friends were walking down the beach and three guys kept driving by in this car, and they're always like, "Hey, State College" 'cause I had this State College shirt on. And umm, they're like "Do you want a ride?" They looked nice.

> They weren't dirty or anything. So I'm like "Sure!" Well, I waited for my friends to decide. And we got in and we hung out at the beach. And like he chased after me 'cause they were trying to pull us in the water. It was sooo fun! I'll never forget it. And then like . . . I have to tell you this! He chased after me, and like he grabbed me and started swinging me around and I'm like "Aaaah!" and I got a big mouth. He's going "Promise you're not gonna scream. Promise you're not gonna scream if I let you go. Come on, shhh. They're gonna think I'm raping you or something." So he let me go and then we're walking back to where my friends are and then we both look at each other and go "You run too fast." And it was so cute! Then that night he called me at like twelve o'clock and we talked 'til like five in the morning. And a couple of weeks later we started going out.

Over half of all the working-class girls in my sample told stories of ideal love as compared to one quarter of the middle-class girls. One reason for this is that working-class girls, who get little acknowledgment of their agency in other spheres, get recognition from others when they "accomplish" the task of acquiring a boyfriend. When I asked Linda, "What things make you feel good about yourself?" she replied, "When a guy calls me and asks me out on a date! Ahhh! That's the best. My mom can't believe I have so many dates." Esther, a working-class girl, said that she clearly got that message that boys, and especially a husband, were important accomplishments. They were things (among several others) that she and her mother fought about a lot.

> The most recent thing is I'm moving in with my boyfriend, and that's out of wedlock. She's a strict Catholic and that's a big thing, she wants me to get married ASAP, and she's bitching for more grandchildren, too. So she's really pushing that on me. We fight about my clothes, the way I act, how she doesn't like my way of reasoning or thinking. She thinks I'm too, I don't know, liberal, I guess maybe is the word. She thinks I'm just too outgoing for my own good. So she's always telling me about that, but the big thing is marriage right now.
>
> *So you don't want to get married.*
>
> No, No. I haven't even graduated from high school, and my big thing right now is just trying to start college.

Mothers, however, are not the only ones who think boyfriends are important for girls. Peers also see having a boyfriend as a sign of status and of accomplishment. Kendra claimed, "It's so important to have a boyfriend because it's really a sign . . . to have something saying you're really attractive to someone is really important."

Another reason for this class difference in ideal love is middle-class girls remain in ideal love with their fathers well into adolescence, in contrast to working-class girls who switch their allegiance quite early. Middle-class girls' ideal love of their fathers not only facilitates their feelings of agency but delays their sexual involvement with boyfriends. For, as we will see below, girls often have sex in order not to lose their ideal love.

The propensity toward ideal love in these working-class teenage girls does offer them one source of agency. Because of ideal love, working-class girls are more likely to break through the "tyranny of nice and kind" that Brown and Gilligan describe. Several working-class girls made it clear that they were not subjected to Brown and Gilligan's "tyranny of nice and kind." This group of working-class girls often said that they "had to" speak their mind or that they were "loud." Usually they were mean and unkind when fighting about boys or defending their own reputations with boys. For example, Amanda, a savvy 15-year-old who talked at length about her boyfriends and the "guys" she met at the mall, described how she stuck up for herself in a fight with another girl who thought Amanda was stealing her boyfriend, which Amanda was.

> Like the other night she called me and I was just so mad. I was like, "I'm just fucking friends with him!" And I was yelling 'cause I have a big mouth and then she said something, something . . . I can't remember but something "cunt" and then she was like, "I'm gonna nail you." And I was like. I'd kill her. She's so stupid, I could kill her. But like I wouldn't touch her unless she touched me first [points to her chest].

. . . Boyfriends are so important because a life organized around a man and mothering is many poor and working-class girls' only vision of the future.

But what about boys' roles in teenage love relationships? Boys do not usually reciprocate or lend support to girls' stories of ideal love. Take for example the boyfriend and girlfriend who told me how they met. The girl's story was full of the language of magnified moments and ideal love. The boy's story was very straightforward. He told me: "I think we met at the pool." She told me a much longer story. She said that they met at a party on Valentine's Day right after she had broken up with her last boyfriend. She had not wanted to go to the party, but her friends talked her into it. He had spent all night talking to her and teasing her, and then the next day he and his friends came in to where she worked. She was embarrassed because she charged him the wrong amount for something he bought, and she worried he would not like her anymore. She added at the end of her story that she had told him that he would never forget their anniversary, since it was Valentine's Day. Apparently, he had forgotten, or had not wanted to subscribe to such a romantic version of how they had met.

Boys rarely used the word love in discussing their feelings about their girlfriends or relationships. Love was something that they expressed to girls only reciprocally or out of awkwardness. Brent's story best exemplifies this phenomenon.

> I didn't think anything was going to happen between us, but she was spending the night at my house, well, she stayed in my room, so I was just like on the bed, and she was on the floor and she was telling me about everything that was going on. And like I went down to hug her and everything, and she wouldn't let go and so I don't know how long we were hugging or anything, but we started kissing and it . . . God it was so strange and she told me that she loved me in the middle of it all, and (laughs) I knew a little bit more about what it meant than I did in sixth grade, what was I gonna say "Oh thanks?" So I told her I loved her too, but I knew I didn't really, umm, I mean. . . .

Boys seem to be looking for a blend of friendship and sex in relationships with their girlfriends. They are not looking for romance or ideal love. Empirical research finds that men's friendships (and I suspect this is also true of teen boys' friendships) are based on doing things together rather than on talking or sharing emotions (as women's friendships are).[11] Talking, or having a "close" friend, is what some boys get and are looking for in relationships with their girlfriends. However, even boys who admit to wanting friendship, comment on the burden of commitment. Joe told me that he "went out with this girl for like a year, and I liked her a lot. We talked and went a lot of places together." Notice how brief his description of his girlfriend and their relationship is compared to girls' descriptions of their boyfriends. Since Joe did not seem very enthusiastic about his previous girlfriend I asked him, "Would you want to have a girlfriend now?" He replied, "Yeah, someone to talk to a lot. Like a good friend. Well, you also get too serious and get tied down a lot." I received this answer from many boys. They emphasized wanting a girlfriend, to have a friend, but not wanting too much commitment.

> *Would you want to have a girlfriend?*
> Yeah, well, I don't really have any real close friends, I have a lot of friends, but not really close, there's no one like close friend. The disadvantages would be that it's a lot of commitment, I think. *(Rick)*
> *Would you want to have a girlfriend?*
> It'd be someone to be with and talk to, but I feel that I wouldn't like, like, to feel that I have to devote a certain amount of time every night calling them. *(Eric)*

Given the short length of most teen relationships, boys' fears of and complaints about commitment seem unwarranted (or perhaps their fears of commitments are what cause such short relationships). I suspect that complaining about commitment and the amount of time one has to spend with a girlfriend has become part of establishing a sense of adult heterosexual masculinity. Finally, boys rarely express the feelings of romantic love that girls do. In particular, their stories have little of the romance, sadness, or melodrama that girls' stories have. There is little in boys' stories that suggest they are playing out a romantic narrative. Also, boys' stories, especially when they become stories of breaking up, often contain hostile feelings. I asked Paul why he started "going out" with his girlfriend.

> I think I liked her innocence. At first it was great. We could laugh and everything, but then we started to fight. I was like "forget it."

Why did you break up?
Well, put it this way. She has a wicked attitude, like and I was stupid. I ended it and she changed her attitude. Fine. I thought I'd give her a second chance this year, turned out she had the attitude again so I said goodbye.
What kind of attitude did she have?
Well, "I can't change" or "This is me, I'm sorry I can't be nicer." It's like, no! She still has the attitude. She has a mouth that I'd like to stick a bar of soap in for two hours. So I don't want to deal with that.

This story is very different from those we hear from girls, even girls who have broken up with their boyfriends. Finally, we will see below that sex, too, is less tied to love (as the old story goes) for boys than for girls.

EXPECTATIONS AND EXPERIENCES OF SEX . . .

Teenaged girls and boys have very different expectations and experiences of sex. Girls' expectations of sex range from romantic images portrayed by the media to fears that it will hurt, be painful, or scary, with the majority (well over half) falling in the latter category. There are no class differences or differences based on whether or not the girl had sex. I asked Tiffany about her first experience of sex, "Was it what you expected it to be like?" "No. Not at all. I expected the movie type thing." Erin had not yet had sex and thought,

> I think that when you love somebody a real lot, I think that it's gonna be great, and umm, just like everything that's going on like with AIDS and pregnancy. It's scary. So once you're like using birth control and you check for AIDS and things like that, other STDs, and you're not worried at all, then it's just like the only thing you're gonna be thinking about is that other person, and it's gonna be good, but if you're distracted by all those other things, I think it's gonna take away from it.

. . . Other girls' expectations were even more negative. Amy, like many girls, said, "I thought it was gonna hurt really, really bad. . . ." And Jill thought sex was "gross" when she was younger. . . .

Boys, on the other hand, had generally positive expectations about sex. They thought it would be pleasurable, and many said they looked forward to it or were curious about it. However, because boys are culturally supposed to think sex is good, it may have been more difficult for them to express negative expectations, although not impossible. Middle-class boys were able to express some of their anxieties about sex. They claimed a few more anxieties and were slightly less positive about their expectations than working-class boys, who were more invested in maintaining normative masculinity. Middle-class boys described expectations like Greg, a middle-class 16-year-old, and Dennis.

> I expect it to be good. I hope it's good. I know guys who have done it and just really regretted it afterwards. *(Greg)*

> I look forward to it. It's an experience I haven't had and I wonder what it's like, and I'll also be real nervous about how she feels and what it would be like and if I'd do it right, just basically that. *(Dennis)*

Dennis' admission that he worried whether or not he would "do it right" may be the most prevalent worry that boys have about sex. Laumann et al. found that young men (age 18–24) were most likely to have "anxiety about performance."[12]

Working-class boys, like Adam, Scott, and Rick, however, said they had few expectations about sex at all or only positive ones. They claimed respectively, "I'll just wait for the time to come. I'm not gonna worry about it"; "I thought it would be great. I couldn't wait to do it"; and "I think it'll be all right. I don't think it'll be scary or anything."

These expectations are in sharp contrast to girls'. No girl said that she looked forward to sex or that she expected it to be pleasurable.[13] Girls also have sex later than boys do, although girls more or less catch up in their late teens. In my sample about half of the girls (seventeen) and boys (ten) had had sex. However, according to Hayes, at age 15 only 5 percent of girls and 17 percent of boys have had sexual intercourse.[14] The percentage of both groups of teens who are sexually active increases as teens get older. By age 18 44 percent of girls and 64 percent of boys have had sexual intercourse. By age 20 most unmarried men and women are sexually active; over 80 percent of men and 70 percent of women have had sex once. (African-American teens and teens from lower socioeconomic class backgrounds have sex earlier than whites and those from higher socioeconomic class backgrounds.) This gender difference in age may be attributed to girls' more negative expectations of sex, as well as harsher proscriptions against sex for girls than boys. However, with such widely disparate expectations of sex, how do boys and girls decide to have sex, and why do teenage girls ever have sex given their negative expectations?

Although there is much research on which demographic factors may make teens more likely to have sex, there is little on how those decisions come about. There is no research that asks why boys have sex more than girls do and why they do so earlier. Teens do not add up their demographic variables to see if they should have sex. They have sex in the context of their lives and relationships. As Brooks-Gunn and Furstenberg (1989) note, "almost no information exists as to how teens initiate sexual activity."[15] From *their* perspective, how do teens decide to have sex?[16]

THE INTERACTIONAL PATHS TO SEX . . .

A girl's ideal love for a male peer *at adolescence* often adds a new dimension to ideal love—sex. However, this is not because the quality of girls' ideal love has changed or become more sexual, more passionate, or more desirous, but because male peers often insist on, provoke, or encourage girls to have sex. Several working-class girls said that the pattern in their high school was that many girls often had sex in their freshmen year because older boys saw them as easy targets, taught them how to party, and convinced them to have sex. The different paths that girls and boys take to having sex are generally that girls are pressured into sex, and boys do the pressuring. Both boys and girls see this as the pattern. Fourteen-year-old Adam said, "Well, I think the boys put a lot of pressure on the girls to do it." Girls acknowledge that boys pressure girls by using love. "Boys put so much pressure on you. It's just like TV—'But I love you,' and girls just giving it up, and they shouldn't." Tiffany, beginning in the language of ideal love, said,

> It's nice to lie there in their warm, comforting arms, and if you have feelings for them it's so hard to look in their eyes and say no. I could only do it if I was really angry. I mean if he was forcing me I could, he'd be in for a fight, but if it was just like "Oh please, come on baby" no way could I say no.

Not all boys, especially younger boys, seem to realize that they are pressuring girls. The boys I spoke with assumed that girls, usually anonymous, generic girls—their girlfriends were the exception—wanted to have sex as much as they did. Boys told me, "Girls want to have sex, too. It's pretty much the same as boys." Or "I think they [girls] think the same thing about sex and wonder about sex and wanting to do it." However, a few middle-class boys (three) acknowledged that sex, at least at first, was not as good for girls as for boys. For example, Rick, who is 15 and has not had sex, said, "It seems like for girls it would not be nearly as much fun, 'cause the first time is sort of nothing."

Older boys clearly do know that they are pressuring girls for sex. Anthropologist Peggy Reeve Sanday describes fraternity boys' common practice of "working a yes out." She recorded the following conversation between fraternity brothers:

> "Sometimes a woman has to resist your advances to show how sincere she is. And so, sometimes you've gotta help them along. You know she means no the first time, but the third time she could say no all night and you know she doesn't mean it."
>
> "Yeah, no always mean no at the moment, but there might be other ways of . . ."
>
> "Working a yes out?"
>
> "Yeah!"
>
> "Get her out on the dance floor, give her some drinks, talk to her for a while."
>
> "Agree to something, sign the papers . . ."
>
> "And give her some more drinks!"
>
> "Ply her with alcohol."[17]

The older boys I spoke with were not this explicit in indicating that they knew girls were sometimes reluctant. However, although both boys and girls often said that they "talked it over" with their partner before deciding to have sex, "talking it over" meant something different for boys and girls. Their descriptions of these "talks" and the tones of voices in which they spoke about them were quite different. Boys described things like middle-class 15-year-old, Craig did: "She was a little reluctant, but we just talked it over and decided it would be okay." Or like Scott did when I asked him, "How did you decide [to have sex]?" "It was easy after we talked it over," he replied.

Girls, however, were more reticent and much less likely to say it was easy when describing these conversations. For example, I asked the girls who had had sex the same question I asked Scott. "How did you decide to have sex?" Their answers were quite different from Scott's and most boys'. For example, Elaine and Diana replied in typical ways.

> It just happened really. I mean, I didn't want to 'cause I couldn't ever picture myself having sex, but umm, all my friends did, and umm, so it just happened and he was my first so . . . I thought it was right 'cause we were going out for two years before we did. *(Elaine)*

> *How did you decide to have sex?*
> I don't know. We like went out for three and a half months, and that's when we did it. We just talked about it and stuff that it was gonna hurt. And it did hurt! *(Diana)*

. . . Girls express their feelings of missing agency with their repeated phrase "it just happened."[18]

Cook, Boxer, and Herdt find that lesbian teens report sexual sequencing that is first heterosexual then homosexual, while gay male teens report the reverse. The girls in their study also say that heterosexual sex was something that *happened to them,* while it was something the gay boys sought out. The authors propose that "the greater likelihood of sexual pressure and coercion experienced by females from males predisposes girls to the heterosexual/homosexual sequence, not as a choice but as a consequence of growing up in a society where females encounter such experiences more than males."[19] I suggest that many lesbian teenagers and straight teenage girls have heterosexual sex for the same reasons—coercion.

Because the girls' answers to how they decided to have sex were often tinged with feelings of regret, shame, and hesitation, I became suspicious that many girls did not really *want* to have sex, and so I began asking boys and girls "Why do you think it is hard for some girls to say no if they really don't want to have sex?" Girls often answered this third person question in the first person or second person, moving the experience closer to themselves. Girls' answers, particularly working-class girls, reveal that their boyfriends often pressure them into sex. Notice the first- and second-person answers and the language of fear throughout girls' answers.

> Because they'll be *scared* like, that the guy will just say forget it, and he'll just probably go off to another girl and ask them the same question. And he'll just go to a person that says yes and stay with them, and then he'll probably just do it and then leave. *(Ellen)*

> 'Cause you're afraid that they're gonna leave you. *(Amanda)*

> 'Cause they're afraid the boy won't like them anymore or something would happen, you know, he'd get mad. *(Stephanie)* . . .

> [It's hard to say no] 'Cause they don't want the guy to think that she's a sissy, or she's, she's nothing, or she's not gonna be popular, or no one will think she's pretty anymore. Just for self-esteem reasons I think. *(Linda)*

Finally, Samantha said straightforwardly that it is hard for some girls to say no to boys "'Cause they're afraid of them."

Working-class girls openly discussed this pressure *and* the fact they often felt compelled to give in to it. A few even revealed such coercive pressure without being asked. For example, one girl told me she had sex with her boyfriend the first time when they were playing Truth or Dare with friends, and she "had to" do the dare. She was not physically forced to have sex, but goaded into it by her boyfriend (and presumably other friends who were present). The middle-class girls were more often able to say no to sex. For example, 17-year-old Heather told me confidently,

> That decision has definitely come up in the past two relationships I've had, because those people have been a lot older and umm, especially with Joey who

> was the last guy I went out with, umm. He sort of forced me to make that decision really early on, we had gone out for two weeks and all of sudden he was ready to have sex and that was a natural progression for him and he assumed that I'd you know. . . . I think that . . . to be in love with somebody probably comes once or twice or maybe three times in your life time and I don't believe my friends when they say they are in love with their boyfriends who they went out with for two weeks, umm, but I also don't know that you have to be *in* love with somebody, you know, to have sex with them. I think that if there's a potential for you to be in love with them and a really deep caring and definitely commitment and just feeling really comfortable with the person. Feeling like you could say anything to them, it's a pretty important prerequisite for having sex with them and I didn't feel like that with him after two weeks or after two months.

. . . Middle-class girls are better able than working-class girls to refuse sex that they do not want. . . . However, middle-class girls are not immune to giving in to their boyfriends' pressure to have sex. They are more reluctant to admit doing so than working-class girls are. They tell stories of pressure to have sex that disguise the pressure and the fact they gave in to it. Kendra, an opinionated middle-class girl, who prided herself on her self-confidence and assertiveness, reflected on her decision to have sex.

> How did I decide to? Umm, it just seemed kind of natural, I don't know. I mean I thought about it. It just seemed like it was right. I was fifteen. . . . He wanted to have sex with me and I had said no, I mean I didn't feel pressure and that's not why I said I would, but looking back I think it kind of took our relationship a step further and if I hadn't I don't know what we would have done. It would have been kind of stagnated I guess.

"The relationship will stagnate" is another version of "He'll break up with you if you say no." It is a story that can deny that a middle-class girl is really under pressure from boys and giving in to it. Middle-class girls are more invested in this disguise than working-class girls because they know from sex education and their knowledge of feminism that being "talked into it" is not the "right" reason for having sex. Regardless of how they discuss it, both middle- and working-class girls describe a variety of ways in which they are pressured or coerced into sex by their boyfriends. Such pressure clearly does not foster sexual subjectivity.

How does this gender dynamic of boys pressuring girls for sex and girls "giving in" get set up? I suggest that much of it is a result of the differing capacities for agency and sexual subjectivity that girls and boys have constructed up until this point. . . . Puberty . . . makes girls anxious about sex and their bodies and unsure of themselves and their abilities to act in the world. Puberty puts restrictions on girls' sexuality and self-confidence. Boys, on the other hand, come out of puberty feeling more grown up, more independent, and feeling generally positive about their bodies that are becoming more adult-like, and importantly, more masculine. When teens with these different capacities start dating each other, they have unequal abilities to negotiate for what they want; they have different wants: and the relationship means different things to them. Boys are more sure that they want sex, and as we have seen, they have higher expectations of sex. Girls, who are deeply invested in ideal love, are vague about when they will want sex and if they are "ready," especially since being ready rarely has anything to do with desire. . . .

These feelings of unsureness make sense given girls' low expectations of sex. This psychodynamic disparity in agency and sexual subjectivity, laid upon the cultural inequalities between the genders, gives boys a greater capacity to push for what they want, and leaves girls less able to articulate what they want for themselves *and* less able to claim it forcefully (or to articulate what they don't want and forcefully refuse it). I do not suggest girls are without any agency or without any sexual subjectivity. Rather, within the interactions with her boyfriend, within the "We talked it over," a girl finds it particularly hard to hold her own aganst a boy's assuredness and convincing reasons. This is especially true when a girl finds herself in ideal love with this boy. It is important not to underestimate the role and power of ideal love in adolescent girls' lives. As much as sex is not about passion and lust for teen girls, it *is* about ideal love and fear of losing one's ideal love, if one refuses sex. As we have seen above, many girls make this connection, saying "He'll break up with you if you say no."

There are exceptions to this pattern. Some boys do not want to have sex (yet), and certainly did not pressure girls to. In my sample they tend to be younger, Catholic boys, or boys who wanted to be in love first (which correlates with being younger). Jim, a working-class boy, told me a story about fears of guilt and pregnancy.

> I'd just say no to have sex. Being Catholic that's basically the only opinion I hear. But . . . I don't know. I wouldn't really feel comfortable buying a condom anyways, and I wouldn't have sex without a condom 'cause I'd feel guilty, and I'd help out with a kid, and so I just wouldn't have sex at all.

Similarly, Brent, a middle-class boy, also was not in a hurry to have sex, not because of fear or guilt but because he felt he was too young and "not ready." He was one of the only boys who used the term "ready."

> I'm definitely not ready to have sex yet . . . I'm not in control of my social life or academic life, and I'm not ready to start dealing with myself in that way. I'll be ready once I find somebody I love. I'm not gonna do it before that because, because my friends some of them have already done it and they feel real shitty about it if they did it with some random person just to try it or something.

Other teens in my sample also had decided to postpone sex. Some rationally thought about the decision, about their feelings, about themselves and their partners and decided not to have sex. These teens were few. More often the teens who decided not to have sex as teens (at least not up until the point at which I interviewed them) did so because of "morals," religion, and AIDS. For these teens the decision was usually more abstract than for those who decided to have sex, because they usually were teens who did not have "serious" girlfriends or boyfriends.

Several girls and boys also said that either because of their religion or "morals" they wanted to wait. One 17-year-old middle-class boy and one 16-year-old working-class girl who had each decided they did not want to have sex, said it was because they did not want to "get AIDS." . . . It is my impression that AIDS education has given teens who do not want to have sex, but do not want to be seen as "wimps" or "goody-goodies," an acceptable reason to decide against sex. It is more acceptable in teen culture to say one fears AIDS than to say one fears God, religion, parents, or pregnancy.

EXPERIENCES OF SEX . . .

As we would expect, given such different paths to sex, boys and girls have very different experiences of sex. The girls who did have sex found that it lived up to their negative expectations. They often described the experience as painful, scary, disappointing, or confusing.

> There was a couple of times that I thought I had decided and I was like "Okay, okay!" and then "No, I can't! I can't!" He was like "Okay, okay." And it was like the third time that I had said that. I'm like "Okay." I was real scared. I was afraid it would hurt. I cried and it did hurt. *(Valerie)* . . .
>
> Actually I was kind of happy, well, I don't know how to explain it. In a way I felt really good because I had shared this with somebody, but it was the most painful experience of my life. *(Tiffany)*

. . . As Thompson notes, it is ironic that "While girls hold their lovers responsible for virtually all the emotional pain they experience in relationships, they rarely blame them for sexual pain during first coitus. Instead they blame their own bodies."[20] Girls' experiences were not painful and scary because of some biological or natural necessity that first sex be bad for girls, but because girls often have sex when they do not physically or emotionally desire it, when they have little experiential knowledge about what sex will be like, how they will feel and how their bodies will feel. Girls' later and less frequent masturbation than boys contributes to their lack of subjective sexual body knowledge. Women who masturbate have better sex with their partners.[21] Finally, many girls move from kissing to intercourse in an extremely short period of time. Petting or "all the stuff that comes before" is often not a significant part of girls' sexual experiences. Jill said she was a tomboy and thought kissing was "gross" when she was 13 but she had sex when she was 14. This leaves little time to learn about sexual pleasure. As Erin told me,

> I think it's basically that guys think that . . . like that sex, is like the way to get . . . is like what you should do, you should have sex even if you haven't done everything else, even if you're not like totally comfortable, I think that they think that it's just like something they have to do. And you know, girls just like want to take their time and take it slowly and go for everything, like that leads up to sex and things like that.

Tolman finds that two thirds of her sample of thirty girls said that they "experienced sexual desire."[22] However, Tolman did not interview boys, and it is unclear if the extent of these girls' desires would be equal to that of boys similarly sampled. Would what "counts" as desire be more narrowly defined if researchers listened to boys as well? Also, we must distinguish between sexual desire and sexual pleasure. Although teen girls may desire, few find sexual pleasure. Thompson found that only one fourth of her sample of 400 girls were "pleasure narrators." "The pleasure narrators describe taking sexual initiative; satisfying their own sexual curiosity; instigating petting and coital relations."[23] Lesbian teens were more likely to be pleasure narrators (when discussing sex with girls) than heterosexual teens were in her sample. However, even they are rare as most lesbians do not come out until their late teens or early twenties.[24]

I did not find as many pleasure narrators as Thompson did, perhaps because my sample of girls was not as broad. Kristen who had waited a "long time" (until she was 16) before having sex said that she was "just a bundle of joy" afterward because she was "so excited to call [her best friend] and just so psyched." A few girls, especially those who were older and middle class, said that sex was "better" or a "little better" after the first few times. Fullilove et al. also find that sex gets better for girls as they get older. The authors found that among poor black women, age was related to having more power in sexual communication, in being clear about what one wants, and in getting it.[25] In my study, Jill, an 18-year-old working-class girl, described her current sex life as pleasurable, although her sex at ages 14 and 15 was not. However, she focused her discussion on the relationship rather than on desire or physical pleasure.

> It's gotten a lot better! It's good. Ummm, I don't really know how to say this. Sex is like a bonus, you know. It's another way of bringing us closer, but it's not in any way the center point or the main point of the relationship. We just consider it something extra special in the relationship.

Cherri, a middle-class 19-year-old, now had orgasms (she was one of only three girls who said she did), and she too attributed it to the fact of "love." Cherri said, "As soon as I began to relax and trust, it happened. We have a really open communication kind of relationship, and that makes all the difference. We're really close." . . .

Even these girls did not wholeheartedly embrace sexual experience and expressed a lot of ambivalence. For example, Audrey used an interesting strategy to resist having sex with her boyfriend. She decided that she and her boyfriend were going to have sex, and so wanting to be "responsible" she went to the doctor to get birth control pills. However, somewhere between starting the pills and sleeping with her boyfriend, she "cheated" on him. Cheating here means that she went out with another boy and kissed (and maybe petted), not that she had sex with him. Audrey then thought that since she had "cheated" on her boyfriend she must not be "ready" to have sex yet, and so decided not to. Kristen admitted to using the same strategy at one time as well. While strategies like "cheating" allow girls to assert control over their sexuality in an exciting way, they also express the ambivalence teenage girls, even girls who have "decided" to have sex, feel about sex.

Boys did not rave about their actual experiences of sex, but gave mild answers that claimed it was as they expected. They were much less negative and less ambivalent about their experiences than girls were, and they seemed less self-reflective. Scott said, "It was good. I was psyched to have done it." Craig only said, "I couldn't believe I saw a completely naked female body." Michael said with less confidence, "I felt okay.

I kind of hoped I did okay. I didn't really know, you know, if she thought it was [*okay*]." These answers were typical of boys in general and boys of their class. Middle-class boys' descriptions were slightly less confident and less positive. . . .

Boys in my sample said little about pleasure specifically, but also did not tell stories of pain or disappointment as girls did. Discussion of boys' pleasure from sex arose only in the context of discussions about condoms. Both boys and girls claimed that often boys did not want to use condoms because as one middle-class boy claimed, "You can't feel anything." In discussing with Amy whether students would use condoms if they were made available in school, she said sympathizing with the boys, "I don't know if they would [use condoms]. 'Cause a lot of guys, I know don't like them. 'Cause they don't get enough satisfaction off them." While boys and some girls expressed concern about boys' lack of or lessened pleasure, there was little concern about girls' lack of pleasure. It was expected that girls would not like sex as much as boys, especially first sex.

SEX AND SEXUAL SUBJECTIVITY . . .

What are the effects of first and early sexuality on teenage girls' and boys' selves? The sexual experiences that most boys have cause them to feel more subjective, agentic, and more like sexual subjects. The experience of girls "giving in" to boys solidifies boys' feelings of agency and sexual subjectivity. A boy now feels like he can will things and make them happen. He can do, and do sexually.

Boys feel grown up and more masculine as a result of having sex. Sex has often been seen as the test of masculinity for men, as a "mainstay of identity."[26] Heterosexual sex also facilitates bonds between men. Teenage boys know that having sex makes them more masculine. . . .

. . . Perhaps boys tell different stories about sex to each other, to men, than they do to women. However, their discussions, especially working-class boys', did indicate that sex made them feel grown-up, masculine, and bonded with other men, and they did indicate that bragging and boasting about sex was part of teenage boy culture.

Many boys described what happens after sex to be talking about it or in some way conveying it to other boys. When I asked Scott if he told anyone after he had sex he said, "You don't really have to come out and tell your friends, they just sort of know. You kinda just give the impression." Similarly, Jack said after sex boys tell others they "did it." . . .

> Boys do it so they can go tell their friends, "Yeah, Yeah!" You know. Although if it's your girlfriend you don't go tell your friends about it, but if it's like Sally off the Street then, yeah, you do. *(Jack)*

. . . For many boys, having sex may also relieve fears that they are not masculine enough, that they are a "faggot," a "wimp," a "sissy," a "baby," a "girl." No boy said this to me explicitly about himself, but many said sex was important for the masculinity of other boys. For example, Dennis, a middle-class 15-year-old, said, "I think for a lot of guys it looks macho and stuff to have, to be having sex." And recall Jack's comment which he made with swinging fists, that boys do it so they can tell their friends "Yeah! Yeah!" Having sex may be proof to oneself and others of masculinity. It is an accomplishment. . . .

By contrast, first and early experiences of sex generally lessen girls' feelings of subjectivity, agency, and sexual subjectivity. To restate: girls' first experiences of sex are usually negative. They say things like, "It was the most painful experience of my life." After sex girls often feel confused and unsure of themselves, their "decisions," their bodies, and sex. Many girls describe this confusion, which may take several forms, from fear of pregnancy, betrayal of friends and family, uncertainty about one's body. Kendra felt badly about herself for not having used contraception, and she was afraid she might be pregnant.

> *Did you use contraception the first time?*
> (Breathes in deeply.) No. Which is really bad, and I knew it, and I was just like praying 'cause I, I mean I had sex ed. since I was in like third grade, and I knew that . . . it's not like I thought "Oh, your first time you can't get pregnant." But I was just like . . . and I thought I was pregnant, but then I got my period, but that was very stressful. I was like ready to go buy one of those pregnancy tests. Or I was like, Sherri, one of my good friends, she was like, "Okay, we're going to

> the pharmacy," and I was like "No, I don't want to go." But I wasn't [pregnant].[27]

Tiffany was in the midst of her confusion about sex when we talked. She felt betrayed by her body, her family, and her friends. Her tone as she talked at length about her experience of sex moved between solemn and frustrated.

> We'd been going out a long time. And, we just felt that it was the right thing to do. We were gonna be responsible, definitely. And it was really a hard decision to make, because his parents are really Catholic, but they're not really much as Catholics—but like his mother, any girl that has a boyfriend, and she sleeps with him in her mind is a slut. And that's the way he's been brought up. He doesn't really agree with it. That made it really hard 'cause she was calling me a slut because I used a tampon. She found it in the garbage can and that made me so mad. I couldn't believe it. And that's so untrue and I don't know where she got that because you can still be a virgin and be using a tampon, and at that time I was. If she ever found out [that we were having sex now], I don't know what would really happen. We just made a decision because we felt that we love each other . . . I know I made the right decision. [But] it's really a hard test when you've got people saying well did you? Especially my mother, she goes and takes me to Planned Parenthood and then she says "I feel like shit for taking you there."She can't deal with the fact that I'm on the pill. I mean she knows this guy and she thinks he's really nice and all, and it's just that she can't cope with it. It's not the way she was brought up. I can understand that, but it's also hard when you've got his side of the family and getting that view. I think the worst part was when I didn't get my period on time, that was a major scare for me. That really hurt. [Unlike many girls this girl used foam and condoms when she first had sex.] I don't know what's worse, knowing that you could be pregnant or knowing that you could have an infection. Because it makes you think, did I make the right decision having sex? There are so many problems that come with it. You know my parents didn't know when I first started having sex and then they found out and at first they were really nice about it because we all thought that I was pregnant at that time, and they were like "No one should have to go through this." And after that it was just like, it was weird, it was kind of like this permission, and everything makes you second guess yourself. And now, I just had a period, a really long, horrible period, now I've got this other one that's just not going away, and now I think I've got some type of infection. Nobody knows, except a couple friends, and my parents don't know and it kind of makes everything so much more complicated. I wake up tired. It makes me feel in a way like a slut. I know that I shared something with somebody that I loved, but now, I feel so disgusting. I think that's what kids need to be told—it's not just STDs and everything, but all these things that go along with it, the mental stress, my mom told me, and I didn't really believe her. I wouldn't not do it again. I would do it again. I don't feel bad about that, but I never knew. It just makes it so horrible, it takes away from the actual act of sex. I don't think it's sex that's so bad, it's everything else that's horrible. If anything that would stop me from doing it again because the mental worry is so hard and you know, before I had sex I was thinking this is the last time this person is gonna see me as a virgin. I was like, what I was doing in my mind was horrible. It was hard 'cause my parents aren't liberal people, and I wish that most kids wouldn't have to go through that, and we wouldn't have to go sneaking around to some motel, we wouldn't have to lie about what you did that day. You wouldn't have to feel bad. All I want is for them to respect me. If I'm gonna feel good about myself I can't do it all on my own, and that's what I'm having trouble with right now.

Much of Tiffany's story reveals another longstanding complexity of sex for girls. If one has sex, does she become a "slut" or a " 'ho' "? The double standard in sex is still firmly rooted in teenage culture. . . .

Girls, as well as boys in my sample, subscribe to this double standard, although many middle-class girls did note that it exists and is unfair. Erin critically told me,

> It's very different for boys, it's like "a good job" if they have sex with somebody and then they're rewarded and stuff and all the guys are just like "That's great!" You have sex, and you're a girl and it's like "Slut!" That's how it is and you know guys can like sleep around and stuff, even if it's dangerous, but girls—you do that and it's just like, it's not accepted. I think that's really warped since it takes two people to have sex. It's very different.

In general, however, girls and boys distinguish between "Sally off the Street" and a "girlfriend" or between "the real cross-your-legs type girls and your so-called sluts," and there are no such distinctions made for boys. Although some girls are trying to create one by now referring to boys who treat girls badly and are only out for sex as "himbos," an alternative to bimbos. Many girls, like Tiffany, take the distinction of slut to heart and fear it. This is why ideal love is so important. If one has sex for love, she is not a slut, at least among these girls.

The meaning of slut, however, is highly variable and has changed somewhat in recent decades. Among the girls in my sample, simply having premarital sex was not enough to get labeled a slut, unless one was "too young" even in the eyes of peers to be having sex (consensus seemed to be that 12 or 13, pre-high school, was too young). Having multiple partners more often constitutes what one girl called "slut behavior." Similarly, Fullilove et al. (1990) in focus group discussions about sexuality with poor black women and teenage girls found that the definition of a "bad girl" was based on "sexual aggression; 'looseness,' that is giving sex in a casual manner without regard for who the partner was or requiring anything of the relationship; and 'tossing,' that is, giving sex in exchange for money or drugs."[28] Similarly, the girls whom I interviewed made distinctions between "regular" or "normal" girls and "girls who want it all the time," girls who "have it [sex] just to have it," and girls who "just do it to get in with the crowd, to be popular." Sociologist Ruth Horowitz in her study of urban Chicano youth found that girls who had sex before marriage were seen as "loose women," if they could not regain esteem by establishing themselves as mothers.[29] Regardless of its particular contextual meaning, the word slut holds a lot of power. Being called a slut or a ho—or feeling like one—is to feel degraded and dirty. Thus, this double standard adds to feelings of confusion after sex.

The feelings of confusion and uncertainty about sex span a wide range of time. Kendra and Tiffany describe these feelings in the weeks following sex. Elaine, on the other hand, felt confused and scared *immediately* after sex. I wondered if she had been more coerced than other girls or simply more willing to describe her feelings immediately following sex.

> I was kind of just like confused. I didn't know what to do. You know, I'd never had it so, I just, I was . . . I went to the bathroom. I didn't know what to do, I didn't know, you know, I was really scared. I didn't know what, I didn't know what was supposed to happen or anything like that so. . . . Now that he left I wish that we never did.

Later when I asked Elaine what advice she would give to a younger girl who was trying to decide whether or not to have sex she replied adamantly, "Don't have it! I'd just tell them to wait until they're ready, you know. Don't rush into anything 'cause once you do, it's like, it's gone, you don't have anything." This feeling that one has nothing left after sex, is one that several girls expressed. They seemed to have felt they had lost some part of their selves. This expression also suggests how much girls see sex as boys taking something from them and not as a give-and-take or a two-way interaction that should be enjoyable for both people.

Thus, as Kendra's, Tiffany's and Elanie's stories demonstrate, after sex, a girl often does not know if sex is something she willed and made happen, if it was something she wanted or not. She feels unsure about her role in its occurrence. Gavey finds that some adult women have sex under similar conditions because it is easier than continuing to say no or because they sometimes fear being raped.[30] Teen girls certainly do not call what happened to them rape. In fact they often have a hard time defining the pressure they felt. As seen above, they were more willing to talk about it in the third person than in the first person. For a girl, acknowledging the coercive context in which she had sex admits to her lack of agency and makes her feel bad, whereas claiming to have wanted sex denies her actual experience of coming to have sex and of the sex itself. On the other hand, saying she wanted to have sex might leave her labeled a slut. Thus, girls often reduced the story to "It just happened." . . .

NOTES

1. Chilman (1983) suggests that we need "somewhat open-ended, in-depth clinical studies that use both intensive interviews and appropriate tests that seek to understand more about the adolescent as a whole human being *who feels as well as thinks, values, and behaves*" (italics mine, p. 28). She goes on to say that with few exceptions "almost none of the research takes a developmental view of

adolescent sexuality in the context of the feelings of teenagers about themselves, their families, and their society" (p. 30).

2. Brooks-Gunn and Furstenberg (1989), Furstenberg et al. (1987), Hayes (1987), Hofferth and Hayes (1987), Zelnick and Kantner (1980).

3. Padilla and Baird (1991), Wright et al. (1990).

4. Brooks-Gunn and Furstenberg (1989:249)

5. These terms are probably specific to some subcultures of teenagers. The working-class teenagers used them more then the middle-class teenagers. Ruth Horowitz (1983) finds that urban Chicano youth in the midwest use these terms as well. Thorne's (1993) study (in Michigan and California) finds that children in early adolescence use the term "goin' with."

6. Thorne and Luria (1986).

7. Ward and Taylor (1994) also find white boys complain about their heterosexual relationships and give them very different meanings than girls do.

8. Raymond (1994), Cook, Boxer, and Herdt (1989).

9. Martin (1988).

10. Hochschild (1994).

11. Rubin (1985).

12. Laumann et al. (1994: 371).

13. Laumann et al. (1994) found that "only about 3 percent of women said that physical pleasure was their main reason for having first intercourse, compared to four times as many men who said this (12 percent)" (p. 329).

14. See Hayes (1987). However, I find these numbers for girls a bit low when comparing them to my sample in which, of girls who were an average age of about 16, half had sex. Many said they had sex at 14, 15, and 16 years old.

15. Brooks Gunn and Furstenberg (1989: 256)

16. Thompson (1994, 1990) has investigated this question, but she has only interviewed girls, and so her claims about gender differences in this decision making are weak.

17. Sanday (1990: 113).

18. Laumann et al. (1994) found that about one-fourth of all women reported that they did not want to have sex the first time (p. 328).

19. Cook, Boxer, and Herdt (1989: 26).

20. Thompson (1990: 345).

21. Hite (1976), Thompson (1990).

22. Tolman (1994).

23. Thompson (1990: 351).

24. Boys establish a sexual identity earlier, an average age of 15 (Anderson, 1990; Cook, Boxer, and Herdt 1989).

25. Fullilove et al. (1990).

26. Person (1980).

27. There is much research on teen contraceptive use. Some general findings are: the older an adolescent is the more likely she/he is to use contraception and to use it correctly (Zelnick, Kantner, and Ford 1981). Low income, low educational aspirations, troubled relationships with parents, no sex education (although this is debated) are all thought to lead teens to have sex at an earlier age and to make them less likely to use contraception (Brooks-Gunn and Furstenberg 1989; Brooks-Gunn 1992). Girls know more about specific contraceptives than boys do, and girls' contraceptive knowledge has been studied more frequently (Brooks-Gunn and Furstenberg 1989).

28. Fullilove et al. (1990: 52–3).

29. See Horowitz (1983).

30. Gavey (1993).

REFERENCES

Anderson, Dennis. (1990). Homosexuality in adolescence. *Atypical Adolescence and Sexuality,* Max Sugar, ed. New York: W. W. Norton.

Brooks-Gunn, Jeanne. (1992). The impact of puberty and sexual activity upon the health and education of adolescent girls and boys. In *Sex Equity and Sexuality in Education,* edited by Susan Shurberg Klein. Albany: State University of New York Press.

Brooks Gunn, Jeanne and Frank F. Furstenberg. (1989). Adolescent sexual behavior. Special issue: children and their development: knowledge base, research agenda, and social policy application. *American Psychologist* 44: 249–57.

Brown, Lyn Mikel and Carol Gilligan. (1992). *Meeting at the Crossroads: Women's Psychology and Girls' Development.* Cambridge, MA: Harvard University Press.

Chilman, Catherine S. (1983). *Adolescent Sexuality in a Changing American Society.* Bethesda MD: US Department of Health Education, and Welfare.

Cook, Judith, Andrew Boxer, and Gilbert Herdt. (1989). First homosexual experiences reported by gay and lesbian youth in an urban community. Presented at the Annual Meetings of the American Sociology Association.

Fullilove, Mindy Thompson, Robert E. Fullilove, Katherine Haynes, and Shirley Gross. (1990). Black women and aids prevention: a view toward understanding gender rules. *The Journal of Sex Research* 27: 1, 47–64.

Furstenberg, Frank F., S. Morgan, K. Moore, and J. Peterson. (1987). Race differences in the timing of adolescent intercourse. *American Sociological Review* 52: 511–18.

Gavey, Nicola. (1993). Technologies and effects of heterosexual coercion. In *Heterosexuality: A Feminism and Psychology Reader* edited by Sue Wilkinson and Celia Kitzinger. London: Sage Publications.

Hayes, C. D. (1987). *Risking the Future: Adolescent Sexuality, Pregnancy, and Childbearing, Volume II.* Washington, DC: National Academy of Science Press.

Hite, Shere. (1976). *The Hite Report: A Nationwide Study of Female Sexuality.* New York: Macmillan.

Hochschild, Arlie. (1994). The commercial spirit of intimate life and the abduction of feminism: signs from women's advice books. *Theory, Culture, and Society* 11: 2, 1–24.

Hoffereth, S. L. and C. D. Hayes. (1987). *Risking the Future: Adolescent Sexuality, Pregnancy, and Childbearing, Volume II.* Washington, DC: National Academy of Science Press.

Horowitz, Ruth. (1983). *Honor and the American Dream.* New Brunswick, NJ: Rutgers University Press.

Laumann, Edward O., John H. Gagnon, Robert T. Michael, and Stuart Michaels. (1994). *The Social Organization of Sexuality: Sexual Practices in the United States.* Chicago: University of Chicago Press.

Martin, Karin. (1988). Of romance and rock stars: teenage girls and the question of desire. Division Three Thesis, Hampshire College.

Moffatt, Michael. (1989). *Coming of Age in New Jersey: College and American Culture.* New Brunswick, NJ: Rutgers University Press.

Padilla, Amado and Traci Baird. (1991). Mexican-American adolescent sexuality and sexual knowledge: an exploratory study. *Hispanic Journal of Behavioral Sciences* 13: 95–104.

Person, Ethel. (1980). Sexuality as the mainstay of identity. *Signs* 5: 605–30.

Raymond, Diane. (1994). Homophobia, identity, and the meanings of desire: reflections on the cultural construction of gay and lesbian adolescent sexuality. In *Sexual Cultures and the Construction of Adolescent Identities,* edited by Janice Irvine. Philadelphia: Temple University Press.

Rubin, Lillian. (1985). *Just Friends.* New York: Harper and Row.

Sanday, Peggy Reeves. (1990). *Fraternity Gang Rape.* New York: New York University Press.

Thompson, Sharon. (1990). Putting a big thing into a little hole: teenage girls' accounts of sexual initiation. *Journal of Sex Research* 27: 3, 341–61.

——— (1994). What friends are for: on girls' misogyny and romantic fusion. In *Sexual Cultures and the Construction of Adolescent Identities,* edited by Janice Irvine. Philadelphia. Temple University Press.

Thorne, Barrie. (1993). *Gender Play.* New Brunswick, NJ: Rutgers University Press.

Thorne, Barrie and Zella Luria. (1986). Sexuality and gender in children's daily worlds. *Social Problems* 33: 176–90.

Tolman, Deborah. (1994). Daring to desire: culture and the bodies of adolescent girls. In *Sexual Cultures and the Construction of Adolescent Identities,* edited by Janice Irvine. Philadelphia: Temple University Press.

Ward, Janie Victoria and Jill McLean Taylor. (1994). Sexuality education for immigrant and minority students: developing a culturally appropriate curriculum. In *Sexual Cultures and the Construction of Adolescent Identities,* edited by Janice Irvine. Philadelphia: Temple University Press.

Wright, David, Lori Peterson, and Howard Barnes. (1990). The relation of parental employment and contextual variables with sexual permissiveness and gender role attitudes of rural early adolescents. *Journal of Early Adolescence* 10: 382–98.

Zelnick, M. and J. F. Kantner. (1980). Sexuality, contraception, and pregnancy among metropolitan area teenagers: 1971–1979. *Family Planning Perspectives* 12: 230–7.

Zelnick, M., J. F. Kantner, and K. Ford. (1981). *Sex and Pregnancy in Adolescence.* Beverly Hills: Sage Publications.

18

Male Discretion and Sexual Indiscretion in Working Class Mexico City

MATTHEW C. GUTMANN

SEX EDUCATIONS

Alfredo Pérez's wandering father, like many men of the older generations according to Alfredo, was absent for most of his son's life. Before his father died, however, Alfredo Pérez found him and, as he recounts,

"I took my wife and children to see him. He asked me to forgive him. I told him, 'Don't worry about it, Papa. I'm no one to judge you, only God.' A week later he died. I went to see him one Saturday, and by the next Saturday they told me he had died. When he died, well, we went to the burial and to the vigil. A lot of people began looking at me. I saw my sisters, and they said to me, 'Look, we want to introduce you to Papa's son.' So a man said to me, 'Glad to meet you, my name is Alfredo Pérez.' And then another, 'How are you, my name is Alfredo Pérez.' I met five Alfredos, all with the same last name, all my half brothers—Alfredo Pérez, Alfredo Pérez, Alfredo Pérez, each one."

Like his many namesake brothers, Alfredo Pérez was born in Mexico City, and he has lived there all his life. He describes himself as a carpenter, though like most men in the *clases populares* in Mexico, Alfredo counts carpentry as just one of many skills he has acquired over the years, and not one for which he has regularly found employment. Alfredo spent decades doing factory jobs, driving trucks, and occasionally hammering nails, and today he likes to look back on his working life and how he has kept trim over all these years. He had wild years with alcohol and affairs, he tells me, but those days are long past. Now his family is what counts.

"I've been married for thirty-two years, and we've had our ups and downs. I fight with her, we say things to each other. But she respects me, and I her. Even though we fight and we stop talking for a day or two, afterwards we're happy. And that's the way we will go through life, God willing. But the fine thing is to have some children who respect and admire you. I see now how they respect and admire and love me, and it's a *semilla* [seed] that I planted and taught to grow straight and tall." For Alfredo, one's self-identification as a man is closely connected with insemination, financial maintenance, and moral authority, all of which are in turn largely predicated on men's relationships with women.

People in Colonia Santo Domingo speak of men like Alfredo's father as more common in the past. If many Mexican male identities used to be wrapped up in adultery, polygamy, and siring many children, especially male children, today these are less central concerns. These issues are still important to varying degrees to some men, but in the *colonia* many younger men in particular have begun thinking more reflexively about their bodies than their fathers ever did, and today there is a growing sense that sexuality is as much a possibility as it is an ultimatum, that there are multiple sexualities—not just two—and that sexuality can and does change. In short, men in Santo Domingo are participants in what Sedgwick (1990:1) calls "the long crisis of modern sexual definition."

These men today express greater self-consciousness about sexuality, not in the sense that they talk more about sex, but that their manner of talking about sex is different. Two key factors have contributed to these transformations: one, the greater accessibility and widespread use of modern methods of birth control in the past twenty years in Mexico City; and two, in a less obvious but still significant fashion, the open challenge of homosexuality as a major form of sexual life and expression.[1] Both these factors have had direct and indirect ramifications on the construction of contemporary, modern sexualities in Mexican society.

Adult men have rarely died from childbirth in Mexico or anywhere else, of course, but the separation of sex from pregnancy, childbirth, and child rearing has had a profound impact on them as well as on women, and altered more than just fertility rates for men and women.[2] Sexuality increasingly has the ability to culturally transform personal and family life. And more than ever before, sexuality, potentially at least, can similarly be transformed, including sexuality in relation to romantic love.[3] Sexuality in this context is less and less tied to biological imperatives and more associated with desire, which is subjective and transitory. Yet this analysis of desire must always follow from its contextualization, because, as Lancaster (1992: 270) insists, "[d]esire is thus always part of the cultural, economic, and ideological world of social relations and social conflicts."[4] . . .

In my formal interviews with residents of Santo Domingo I asked men and women who was responsible for teaching their children about sexuality. After several interviews I also began asking people with whom they had discussed sex when they were young. Most had never discussed sexuality with either of their parents. All but a few said that they themselves felt a responsibility to teach their own children more about sex, though people differed, not clearly along gender lines, as to who should do it. Some thought both parents should handle the task together; others believed mothers should talk with their daughters and fathers with their sons. Several parents admitted that they preferred to wait until their children came to them with questions based on what they had heard or learned at school or elsewhere rather than initiate discussions on the topic.

In Santo Domingo mothers report that they do commonly talk with their daughters about menstruation. Sometimes in these discussions women explain that with their periods the girls have also reached an age when they can become pregnant, and mothers may impart to their daughters whatever they know about the functioning of the female reproductive system. Few fathers and fewer mothers, it seems, talk with their boys about these issues. Thus if there is great ignorance among all youth regarding sexuality, however uninformed girls may be about sex, it seems probable that boys know even less and have even fewer adults with whom they can discuss their concerns regarding their bodies and reproduction.

Based on interviews in Santo Domingo, on discussions with students at the José Vasconcelos Junior High School in the *colonia,* and on figures compiled in the 1988 (Mexican) *National Survey on Sexuality and the Family among Youth,*[5] most young men speak with male friends or with their fathers about sexuality. Around 40 percent of high school students, according to the *National Survey,* had spoken about the subject with male teachers. As for young women, most receive information about sexuality from their mothers and some from female friends and (for high school students) from female teachers.

At least some discussion about sex and bodies is beginning to occur—in contrast to what took place in earlier generations. This situation contributes to an expanding awareness of the distinctions between sex and procreation and a retreat from the perceived difference between what Adrienne Rich identifies as "fathering" and "mothering" (in the United States):

> To "father" a child suggests above all to beget, to provide the sperm which fertilizes the ovum. To "mother" a child implies a continuing presence, lasting at least nine months, more often for years. (1976:xi–xii)

While parenting and fathering practices vary significantly across space and time, in Mexico historically there has been a greater cultural significance for men than women regarding insemination, and therefore a closer identification for men than for women between the act of generative sex and social status. Recent studies have called attention to women's bearing and caring for children as distinguishing social markers in Mexico and have discussed how some women utilize the culturally esteemed status of motherhood to further their involvement in political activities (see Logan 1984; Nader 1986; and Martin 1990). But all this is a long way from identifying coitus with mothering.

Perhaps it is significant that there is no direct translation into Spanish for the English expressions *fathering* and *mothering*. Simply to render the former as *ser padre* clarifies nothing, since this phrase may be understood as either "to be a father" or "to be a parent." That is, even to state "to be a father" implies in Spanish (in its own linguistically biased manner) "to be a parent," just as being a parent in Spanish is lexically also being a father. This does not mean that Mexicans or other Spanish speakers are in any fundamental sense restricted in what they do by the peculiarities of their native tongue, but it does indicate that in Spanish some cultural concepts are expressed in more linguistically convoluted ways than are other concepts.[6]

PROCREATION

The importance of "blood ties" between parents and children came up unexpectedly in my discussion with the *muchachos* on the street one day. I happened to mention that one of my brothers had died fourteen years earlier. I told the youths that Andrew was not my brother by blood, but that nonetheless my mother continued to grieve for him, her stepson, as she would have for me. I told them that my mother still sometimes cried when she thought about my brother.

"I say if you had died instead," responded Esteban, "she would cry more because you were her son, right?"

"Maybe. I don't know."

"Sure, she loves your brother, but not like she loves you," said Celso.

"You can't compare a child born from your insides [*entrannas*], who you know is yours, who belongs to you," Jaime added.

I tried to take the discussion away from Andrew by saying, "If you have four children maybe you're going to love one more than the others."

"I think so," said Enrique.

"I don't think so," said Jaime.

"I say no, Mateo, because I have two children and I love them both the same," countered Celso.

Enrique, ever the diplomat, tried to resolve the debate, "What happens is that there are different factors. Maybe your mother cries for the boy because he spent a lot of time with her, he won her affection, he knew how to treat her with respect. Maybe the *muchacho* behaved better toward her than you did."

"That's what my mother sometimes says," I confided, and the *muchachos* smiled sympathetically.

Gabriel talked to me a lot about his four children. It was not until I'd known him for several months that I realized that the oldest two are step-children from his wife's previous marriage. Gabi says he loves each child equally and seeks love from each in return. For Gabi, ignoring the ties of blood is a point of pride.

In his late thirties, the skeptical Gabriel has worked for years as a skilled mechanic on the curb of the same side street in Santo Domingo. By fixing cars and *combis* on the street, Gabriel not only avoids costly garage rental but is also able to engage passersby in conversation. He is known among friends as a free spirit, and religion and spirituality are precisely the issues that animate him most. He is especially interested in the Aztecs and has a collection of posters and pamphlets about them. He has taken Nahuatl classes from time to time, and he uses Nahua names for his two youngest children. For Gabriel, it does not matter how children come into the world. When they come into his life, a man must relate to them as a father; this is what adults do, he says. It is of little consequence from whose loins or seed they come. Gabriel's ideas may be exceptional in the *colonia,* but they are not unique. . . .

I asked Toño, a single man of twenty-seven, about whether having children, especially boys, was important to him. "For me," he replied, "having a lot of kids to prove you're macho is *una chingadera* [equivalent to "a lot of bullshit"]. Those ideas are forty years old." Though not everyone would agree with Toño's assessment, he touches upon a sentiment that is more widespread than certain dominant images would lead us to believe: that Mexican men have to confirm their virility through fathering many children (in Rich's sense), especially male children.

Nor has the valorization of those who are fruitful and multiply been an issue solely for men as inseminators. Pronatal policies have been given boosts not only by Catholic Church doctrine, but also by the heart of the modern, liberal elite in Mexico. Following the lead of its not-so-distant neighbor to the north, on 13 April 1922 *Excelsior,* Mexico's newspaper of record, launched a campaign to celebrate the tenth of May every year as Mother's Day. Every year from 1922 until 1953, the newspaper awarded a prize to *la madre más prolífica,* the most prolific mother. Beginning in 1953, the Mexican widow who had made the most sacrifices to educate her children was honored. Mothers who had given birth to only girls were not allowed to compete. In 1968, the prize was given to the mother who since 1910 "had given more sons to the defense of the Fatherland, either as revolutionaries or as members of the National Army" (Acevedo 1982:60–62).

Efforts such as those by the publisher of *Excelsior* in 1922 may have been in part a response to popular will. Margarita Melville (personal communication) reports that her grandmother was active in a 1922 campaign to celebrate Mother's Day in Mexico City, and thus it is possible that the publisher was also supporting a preexisting demand. And, after all, if there were not a deep affection for mothers in Mexico, *Excelsior* never would have proposed celebrating Mother's Day, and the holiday never would have been accepted as it has been. Yet the more critical question would seem to be, how do ventures that are at least in part orchestrated by elite social classes create, reshape, and channel, and not simply reflect, the desires of so many nonelites? Returning to Gramsci's formulation of contradictory consciousness, the initiation of Mother's Day celebrations in Mexico provides one case of how uncritical consciousness came to be accepted and spread.

The other aspect of contradictory consciousness relates to consciousness that arises from and is reflected in the practical transformation of the real world.[7] If fatherhood in the minds of people in Santo Domingo is less associated with profligate behavior than the stereotypes would indicate, or at least if such behavior is becoming more proscribed, then these changes should be evident in the practical, everyday experiences of men in the *colonia.* . . .

The point was brought home to me when I went one day in early spring to the butcher shop on Huehuetzin Street to get some meat for Liliana. Although meat is a little more expensive there than it is in the supermarket, Guillermo and his brother always grind the beef twice when they know it will be fed to an infant. As I was leaving I thanked Guillermo and said something to the effect of "OK, gotta go cook this up with some pasta and—" Before I had time to add "vegetables," Guillermo interrupted me and said, "No, not pasta. That's just going to make her fat. *Sabes, el padre no sólo los engendra sino también tiene que atender a su alimentación* [You know, the father doesn't just procreate, he's also got to make sure they eat right]." Guillermo felt that since I was a new father he had the right and responsibility to give me advice when warranted. By wording his counsel of fatherly love and care in contrast to the familiar image of Man the Procreator, Guillermo was, probably consciously, positioning himself in opposition to a history, or at least a story, of Mexican men.

MALE POTENCY

> I would recommend that at least once a week men have sexual relations, since, for example in boxing, it stimulates masculine responses which are very necessary for combat. It's false that abstention is necessary or positive. If you have sexual contact, even twice, before the fight, you feel more like a man and your masculinity surges forth.
>
> *Bernardo Vargas, psychologist for the Pachuca* futbol *team (quoted in* Escenas de pudor y liviandad, *by Carlos Monsiváis)*

At least one history of Mexican men has told of them desiring not simply offspring in general but male heirs in particular, and of using their issue as irrefutable confirmation of the potency of their seed. In retrospect I realize that I sometimes baited men for statements that might confirm this "well-known" male cultural standard. I asked César one day, "Come on, tell the truth. Doesn't it bother you that you don't have a son?"

"No, I've never had a preference," he responded, content with his two teenage daughters.

"Because, that's the notion that—"

"Yeah, it's that machismo, that 'If it's not a boy, you leave the house.' No, no. I have always told my woman—she knows, my family knows—that whatever God brings us, great! I never asked for a boy, but there are a lot of folks who do prefer boys."

"Still?"

"Yes, still. I have a brother-in-law, and he just had a son. He told his woman that if it hadn't been a boy, she shouldn't have bothered to find him. I think that this kind of person is sick in the head, because we are already living in a modern age, and we should realize that it's not what one wants. Because if you want a boy, it's so easy to say, 'I want you to have a boy,' but then the whole world would be full of boys! It's like they say, 'Go to the corner, at an intersection, and when the moon is full, do this, and do that, so you'll get a boy.' That's a lie. Nature is so pretty that she provides us with everything we need. If she wants a boy, then a boy; if not, a girl."

I was determined, however, to find men who esteemed their male children more than their female, and were not too "modern" to say so. Elena told me that her husband, Carlos, had always wanted a boy, as did she, but that they had three girls. Yet when I talked to Carlos he said he was happier with girls, because they were easier to control. Then Diego Trujillo and his wife, both active in the Christian Base Communities, told me about their children: first a girl, the oldest, then another two girls, and then a boy. "Finally!" I exclaimed. Diego looked at me with a puzzled expression and politely responded, "No, we don't feel that way." Perhaps in my zeal to uncover the renowned preference for sons among Mexican men, I had left informants wondering instead, "Is this how they think in the United States?"[8]

In my own defense, I think that Diego probably understood just what I was getting at: an insulting image of Mexican men and their alleged need for male offspring. Therefore, I took his comments as more than a simple affirmation of his feelings and those of his wife about their personal situation. He was also attempting to refute inaccurate, idealized, and often racist beliefs held in the United States about Mexican men, at least the "traditional" ones.

Men and women speak easily of men who want to keep their wives pregnant all the time. But, curiously, among the people I know in Colonia Santo Domingo, no man wants to identify himself as such, nor does any woman want to label her husband in this way. (This is yet another instance of people approving stereotyped characterizations of others while insisting that those generalizations do not apply to themselves.) Referring to men other than her husband or brothers, Lupita the nurse summarized:

"The husbands who are Mexican machos say, 'I want to have children all the time.' And they want to have the woman pregnant while they are on the *otro lado* [other side—that is, the United States] doing whatever. And when women who have a lot of children, when they have a cesarean birth, they are asked if they want a tubal ligation. The woman who has a Mexican husband says, 'No, because my husband will get angry. Don't sterilize me until God lets me do it.' People get upset as well if you put in IUDs."

The impact of feminist ideas and practices is decidedly mixed in Colonia Santo Domingo, as was revealed in a seemingly exceptional story that Daniel told me about birth control and abortion. During his wife's second pregnancy, Dani told me, she wanted to get an abortion. Daniel was adamant that every life is sacred and that this one had already begun, despite the fact that he is an avowed agnostic and someone who openly ridicules the Catholic Church. On hearing Daniel's story, it was easy for me to conclude, "Here's a guy who's forcing his wife to bear his progeny." Before I had a chance to broach this idea with him, however, Daniel added slyly, "So you know what I did then? I went out and got myself cut"—that is, he got a vasectomy, something that puts him in a rather exclusive category among my friends in Santo Domingo. This was Dani's way of making short- and long-term deals with his wife. Dani's feelings and actions also illustrate that contradictory male identities—in this case, those relating to male sexualities—are to be found not only when comparing groups of men in the population as a whole, but within individual men as well.

URGES AND *AVENTURAS*

After I had spent several months in Mexico, my research suddenly assumed an explicitly sexual character in a very personal way when my wife and daughter returned to the United States for a couple of weeks. Before leaving, Michelle talked casually one day with Angela and Norma about her planned trip. Angela asked if she was worried about leaving me alone for so long, hinting not so subtly at the opportunity this would present me for *aventuras* (adventures)—in other words, adultery. When Michelle responded that she trusted me and was not concerned, Angela countered, "Well, sure, but do you trust the women?" Michelle had not understood the real threat, Angela counseled: men cannot help themselves when sexual opportunity presents itself.

The day after Michelle and Liliana left, I bumped into Norma and another neighbor, Lupita, at the *sobre ruedas* (open-air market) that is set up on Coyamel Street each Wednesday. After asking if Michelle and Liliana had gotten off all right, Norma turned to me and, forefinger pointing to her eye, said, "*¡Te estamos vigilando!* [We're keeping an eye on you!]". Lupita added, with the same gesture, that she too would mount a vigilant lookout. It was mainly a joke by these two married women who had already become like family. But it was also a warning to the husband of one of their absent friends that no fooling around would be tolerated—or go unreported. Implicit, again, was the message that men will try to get away with whatever they can sexually, unless they believe they might get caught.

What is interesting is not that the actual frequency of cheating is that high (or low, for that matter), but the insights all this provided into what many women and men in Santo Domingo view as an innate core of male sexuality. As Angela told me later when I asked about her comments to Michelle, "*¿A quién le dan pan que llore?* [Who cries (i.e., does something inappropriate) when they're given bread?]" Everyone knows what you do with bread: you eat it. The stereotype of men in Mexico being subject to uncontrollable bodily urges and needs is widely held in Santo Domingo—which just proves that some stereotypes about sexual identities in the region are shared by those living there.[9]

Many men tell of having had affairs with women other than their wives. "*No soy santo,*" confides Alfredo, "I'm no saint." The justification for adultery on the part of men is often that men have peculiar "natural desires." Further, men sometimes snickered to me that "*el hombre llega hasta donde la mujer lo diga* [men will get away with whatever women let them]." One of the most common expressions for an extramarital affair is *cana al aire*—literally, "a gray hair to the air," the image being that when you find a gray hair you pull it out quickly and fling it away; you do it, and it is over.

Such "flings" are said to be distinguished by their purely sexual as opposed to romantic content. One woman described to me how when her husband was younger he would often disappear on Friday night and not return until Sunday night. She would tell their children that he was working, to protect them, she said. Taxi drivers have an especially wide reputation for casual rendezvous with women fares. After waxing most poetic on the qualities of his wife, one *taxista* told me that he and she have an agreement that *aventuritas* are fine so long as they are not discussed between them later. "Twenty-one years is a long time to be married," he told me, suggesting that the underlying rationale was boredom in the marital bedroom. He also insisted that she has the same freedom to find lovers as he. After all, he reasoned to me, otherwise it would not be fair.

Affairs are discussed and joked about casually by many people in Santo Domingo. On boarding a *combi* driven by my friend Rafael, I asked how his infant son was doing. He said the boy of four months was doing great. There was one thing, though, that concerned my friend.

"What's bothering you?" I inquired. It was noisy on the minibus and we had to shout to make ourselves heard.

"Every day the boy looks more like people from the 'other side' [the United States]," he screamed.

"How?"

"He's got bright green eyes. I don't even think he's mine!"

He laughed heartily. The other passengers seemed oblivious to this self-disparaging and semilewd commentary. His was not the storybook image of a shamefaced and cuckolded husband.

Marcos told me that his wife, Delia, has been joking for years that Lolo, a neighborhood boy of fourteen, is her second husband. It all started when Delia's sister spread a rumor that Lolo had slept with Delia, Marcos related. "Sometimes I chew Lolo out," he continued, "telling him that I had to go to Tepito to buy my girls shoes when he should be the one doing it."

The documentary record leaves open to question the extent to which such banter is new. For example, the use of the term *cabrón,* which can figuratively refer to a cuckold, is widespread, but by no means necessarily tied to this one meaning or even to a negative quality.[10] Regardless of the history of jokes about infidelity, humorous quips about adultery today take place in a shifting context. Men continue to have affairs; this is nothing new. What has reportedly changed is the number of women who do so, and the fact that some are quite open about having lovers. A particularly promiscuous woman in Santo Domingo has even earned a nickname, La Tasqueña, for her amorous liaisons. La Tasqueña is married to a man who spends ten or eleven months a year in Detroit and returns for only short stays to Santo Domingo to visit her and their two children. Whenever her legal husband is in the United States, she has a series of men (one at a time) living with her, each of whom moves out temporarily when the legal husband returns to the *colonia.* Her nickname derives from an episode that occurred several years ago during one of her legal husband's infrequent visits. She was very late returning to the house one night, and when she finally arrived she complained that she had missed all the *combis* from the Tasqueña metro stop. The problem was that her neighbors had seen her elsewhere and knew this was a ruse to cover up her date that night.

Thus one of the creative responses of some women to men's adultery has been to take lovers of their own. Women's activities as varied as community organizing and paid work have led to far greater opportunities to meet other men and to have affairs with them. To whatever extent sexual "needs" were ever associated with men alone, this seems far less the case today in Santo Domingo.

In refutation of the commonplace that many or most Latin American men have their first sexual escapades with prostitutes, none of the men I interviewed from Colonia Santo Domingo save one admitted to ever having been to a prostitute. Nor had any men taken their sons to prostitutes "to become men." Once again, it is possible that my friends and informants were simply covering up sexual escapades from their pasts. More probable, I think, is that paying for sexual services is today more common in some areas of Mexico City—for instance, around the Centro Histórico—than it is in others. Then, too, it is possible that for many of my friends, paying for sex implies an unmanly inability to attract women sexually.

Going to prostitutes may be more of a tradition among young men from the middle and upper classes. In the survey on sexuality among high school students cited earlier, 20.5 percent of the well-to-do boys reported that their first sexual relation was with a prostitute (Consejo Nacional de Población 1988:120). Men from upper middle class homes also speak of the convention whereby the father hires a maid with whom his sons can have their first sexual encounters. Making caustic references to "the excesses of the feminist movement," one lawyer sarcastically told me that young men are often raped by these older and more sexually aggressive *muchachas,* adding, "I know this from personal experience." The lawyer's comments regarding feminism and rape bore witness to a defensive posture assumed by many men in his milieu today. Still, for this man and others of his class background and generation, it was taken for granted that males would lose their virginity prior to marrying whereas females should be virgins until their wedding night.

Female virginity continues to be an important issue for many men, but this double standard is far less an issue among younger men and women, especially as knowledge about and use of birth control by teens becomes more widespread. But the matter is contested—among teens, and between teens and their parents. As part of this gendered and generational confrontation over virginity, a particularly bizarre rumor about adolescent sexual behavior in the United States was making its way through the Pedregales in 1993. Some people had heard, and were convinced, that many girls in the United States have their hymens surgically removed so that the first time they have sexual intercourse they will not experience so much pain. This example, among others, was put forth to my wife, Michelle, to demonstrate that women in the United States have much more sexual freedom and know how to better enjoy themselves sexually.

NORTHERN PENETRATIONS

Due especially to factors such as migration and television, cultural boundaries that coincide with geographic divisions are far less prevalent today than at any time in the past. This is true both within Mexico and, of fundamental importance, across the international border with the United States. As Rouse notes,

> the growing institutionalization of migration to the United States . . . means that more of the Mexican population is oriented to developments outside the country and that this orientation is becoming steadily more pronounced. (1991:16)

The numbers of human beings involved in international migration is staggering. A recent study suggests that "14.8 percent of Mexico's labor force is, at one time or another, employed in the United States—legally or otherwise" (California Chamber of Commerce 1993:14). If these figures are correct, the experience of living and working in the United States is common to one out of every seven adult Mexicans. The impact of this transnational migration on cultural standards and manners within Mexico is evident in the realm of sexuality.

Because of migration and the fact that English has a certain cachet among youth throughout Mexico, and no doubt as a partial result of commercial dumping by the U.S. apparel industry, T-shirts with slogans in English are popular and commonly worn in Colonia Santo Domingo. Some merely appear bizarrely out of place, like one with the words "I love Ollie [North]!" over the Stars and Stripes. Others seem grotesque until you realize that surely most people haven't the foggiest idea what they mean. An eleven-year-old girl walking next to her older brother wears a T-shirt reading, "If I weren't giving head, I'd be dead. . . ."

According to recent figures, at least 3 million households in Mexico City have televisions (perhaps 95 percent of all homes), which are watched daily, and 59 percent of all families in Mexico City have videocassette recorders (García Canclini 1991:164). When we moved into Santo Domingo in mid-1992, in one neighboring household there were four televisions and four VCRs for seven adults and one child. Also of special relevance to the discussion of sexual practices and role models is the fact that every day in Mexico City and throughout the country new and old television programs originating in the United States and dubbed into Spanish are broadcast on major channels. During a random week (24–30 July 1993), the following U.S. television shows were seen: *Murphy Brown, Los años maravillosos (The Wonder Years), Beverly Hills 90210, Miami Vice, Los intocables (The Untouchables), Bonanza,* and *Alf,* as well as the cartoon shows *Los Simpsons, Las tortugas ninja ([Teenage Mutant] Ninja Turtles),* and *Los verdaderos casafantasmas (The Real Ghostbusters).* That same week, viewers of the major television stations could watch such classic cinematic fare as *Body Double, Absence of Malice, The Bigamist, My Man Godfrey, The Fugitive,* and *The Mummy.*

To call attention to the cultural, economic, and political power of the United States as well as the Catholic Church in Mexico, Arizpe (1993:378) refers to those bodies as the Regional Caciques. Most of my friends in Santo Domingo are acutely aware of how Mexican and other Latin American men and women are portrayed in U.S. television and cinema. Questions related to sexual roles and machismo, illegal immigrants and racism are noted and judged by audiences throughout Mexico. This does not mean, however, that all reactions are the same, as certain analysts of the "culture industry" would have it. Frequently there is debate over the meaning of episodes on the TV, as some more than others are able to transcend oversimplified representations and messages.

Regardless of the extent to which U.S. television and film do or do not accurately reflect aspects of sexual experiences occurring in the United States, they are reference points orienting international viewers' attention to alternate sexual lifestyles and relations. Following the opening in Mexico of the Hollywood movie *Pretty Woman* (released there as *La mujer bonita*), knee-high leather (or simulated leather) boots such as those worn by Julia Roberts in the film enjoyed enormous popularity for several years among young women in the *clases populares* in Mexico City. Whether or not these boots were directly associated with Roberts's occupation in the movie (she plays a prostitute) or with the story's outcome (she goes off with a handsome young billionaire), such highly gendered fashions are increasingly tied to direct U.S. influences.

Young women in Colonia Santo Domingo also began watching the Miami-based Spanish-language talk show *Cristina* as soon as it appeared on Mexico's Channel 2 at the end of 1992. "Look at what fifteen-year-old girls in the United States are talking about! They know it all!" seventeen-year-old Carmen exclaimed to me one day. Interestingly, Mexican intellectuals are likely to label *Cristina* a "U.S. program" or a "Cuban-American program," whereas young working class women, its main viewing audience in Santo Domingo, seldom care about where it comes from and simply refer to it as "my show."

As I was talking about witches one day with Martha, a friend who sells diapers in bulk in the open-air markets, she said to me, "You know what? There aren't as many witches in Mexico as there used to be. And do you know where they're coming from now? Your country." She smiled and related that she had seen a lot of (U.S.) witches on a *Cristina* program. I suggested that maybe they were part of the North American Free Trade Agreement.

WHEN THE MAN'S AN ASS

In Santo Domingo in the 1990s, if, with respect to women, virginity is less an issue and adultery more of one when compared with the situation twenty years earlier, divorce rates remain approximately the same. In Mexico City, 2 percent of women older than twelve reported their civil status as divorced in the 1990 census, whereas in the country overall the figure was 1 percent (INEGI 1992:22). The fact that of the women I know in Santo Domingo far more than one in fifty says she is divorced leads me to believe that many of these women had common-law marriages, and thus splitting up did not officially constitute divorce. Or perhaps some of them are still legally married yet call themselves divorced because they no longer live with their legal spouses. For whatever reasons, many of them have never gotten formally divorced.

Attitudes about divorce are changing, especially on the part of women, and in some instances this in turn has had dramatic effects on their men. In an interview in June 1991, Marco Rascón, president of the citywide Asamblea de Barrios, told me that divorces were on the rise among the influential organization's membership. He attributed the initiative in most cases to women militants who were no longer willing to tolerate husbands who opposed their wives' political efforts. Increasingly, according to Rascón, conflicts of this type were resolved either in divorce or in the husbands' following their wives and becoming Asamblea activists themselves. Nevertheless, the *muchachos* I talked with on the street were intrigued when they learned that my parents divorced when I was quite young, and they asked me a lot of questions about what it was like to grow up in that situation, indicating that divorce for them still carried a somewhat exotic flavor.

Rosa, a deeply religious and devout Catholic, repeated a story to me that her granddaughter had told her: "Oh, Grandma, in school they assigned us to write about the worst thing that has ever happened to us in our lives, and I put that for me the worst was my parents' divorce." But, Rosa confided to me, "I told her, 'Don't be an ass. It's the best thing that has ever happened to you.'" Rosa never thought highly of her former son-in-law, and for her, church stricture or not, there were some times when divorce was the best way out of a bad situation.

Men in Santo Domingo enjoy complaining about being married, some saying that marriage is to be endured (usually for the sake of the children). Numerous others, both newlyweds and those who have been married for many years, snipe at wives and marriage. But these attacks should not always be taken at face value. In many ways complaints of this kind by men in Santo Domingo are similar to *albures.* Ostensibly and superficially about sex, *albures* are more frequently double-entendre jokes and quips that use sex to comment on other topics and issues.

When they make wisecracks about the miseries of marriage, men likewise frequently use familiar codes, albeit often sexist ones, to vent their rage at life's iniquities and to blame especially loved ones for keeping them in their sorry state of affairs. If pressed on the issue, even some of the most ornery insulters of wives will tell you they pray they will die before their spouses, because they would not know how to live alone. Although male dependency upon wives to feed and clothe them doubtless focuses important aspects of women's subordination to men, such unvarnished sentiments on the part of men are not merely venal attempts at control, nor are they expressed without contradiction.

In the same way that men use *albures* and complain about marriage, those who are caught for their *aventuras* commonly raise the excuse that appearances can be deceptive and that extramarital flings do not necessarily mean what they might appear to mean. (And most of my male friends in Santo Domingo who admit to affairs say that they were eventually caught.) Needless to say, most of my male friends have a more difficult time sifting through the layers of meaning when a question of women's delinquencies arises. Juan came into the kitchen of his home one day as Angela and I were talking about adulterous friends and neighbors. Angela looked up and said to Juan, "Now, tell Mateo whether a man would forgive a woman for such an offense. Would you forgive her?"

"Men almost never forgive such women, and when they do it's because they really love them—" Juan started to respond.

"Or 'because he's an ass!' That's Juan's expression," Angela shot back.

"Men like it," Juan continued, "when their wives say to them, 'Look, I bought you this and—' "

"I bought you a sombrero!" Angela interrupted, making reference to covering the "horns" growing on a cuckolded man's head.

LA CASA CHICA

In Oscar Lewis's (1961) affectionate portrait of Mexican working class family life, *The Children of Sánchez,* he discusses many sexual practices in the capital in the 1950s. Overly confident in the resilience of cultural practices, I was sure when I began fieldwork in 1992 that one of these, *la casa chica* (the small house), was still an entrenched social institution. After all, Jesús Sánchez, whose children are the subject of Lewis's book, usually seemed to have a mistress or second wife, depending upon how you defined the relationship, whom he maintained in *la casa chica* (or *segundo frente* [second front]).

A concept and a practice regarding male gender identities in Mexico that social scientists have more often assumed than studied, *la casa chica* is usually thought of as the arrangement whereby a Mexican man keeps a woman other than his wife in a residence separate from his main (*casa grande*) household. It is generally discussed as a modern form of urban polygamy that is common in all social strata in Mexico and is by no means the prerogative of only wealthy men.[11]

Information on *la casa chica* was initially easy to come by. One man in a Christian Base Community in Colonia Ajusco spoke to me disparagingly of a brother of his who maintained *three* different households simultaneously, and did this on a factory worker's wages. A few weeks later, Luciano was welding a pipe in our apartment. Neighbors had already told me Luciano had a *casa chica,* so I was especially looking forward to talking with him. I asked Luciano about his family, and he told me that he and his wife were *separados* (separated). They had not lived together for years, he said. When I asked where he was living then, he replied, "Not far from here." But though he no longer shared a home with his "wife"—a couple of times Luciano fumbled over what to call her—because the house and the land were in his name, getting divorced was out of the question; in a divorce he would risk losing all the property.

On another occasion I mentioned to a friend, Margarita, that I was surprised I had not encountered the famous *casa chica* in Santo Domingo. Margarita paused a moment and then said to me carefully,

"*¿Sabes qué? Carmela es la casa chica.* [You know what? Carmela is *la casa chica.*]" Carmela, a woman in her late thirties whom I had previously met in the *colonia,* had lived for twelve years with the man she always referred to as her husband. But, it turned out, this man was legally married to (though separated from) another woman with whom he had four children, the youngest then thirteen. Carmela's "husband" had legally adopted her son from an earlier relationship, and she and this man later had a daughter who was then nine.

After a few months of fieldwork, I was getting quite wary of what *la casa chica* meant to different people, and how everyone referred to the "husbands" and "wives" of those involved in *las casas chicas.* By the time Rafael told me in December that his brother was living in their home with his *casa chica,* I had also grown a little weary of the term.

"Is he married to another woman?" I asked Rafael.

"Yes, he's been married for years," came the reply. "Of course, they haven't been together since he's been with this new woman, but he's still married to the first one."

Then a neighbor happened to mention a remarkable but more "classical" *casa chica* arrangement a couple of blocks from where we lived in Santo Domingo.

"You know the tire-repair place on the corner? Well, a guy used to live over it with two sisters. He lived with them both!"

"In the same house?" I asked suspiciously.

"No."

"But each sister knew about the other one?"

"They knew about it and each tried to outdo the other, trying to get him to realize that she was better. He lived with the two sisters, two days with one, two with the other."

"What were they thinking?"

"Their mother was the really stupid one. She used to say that he was her *doble yerno* [double son-in-law]. If the mother thought this, what could you expect from the daughters?"

Yet how the phrase *la casa chica* is used in daily discourse is often quite removed from such classical patterns. Rafael works in maintenance at the National University (UNAM), which borders Colonia Santo Domingo. He once told me that 60 percent of his fellow employees at the university have *casas chicas.* Astonished, I questioned him further. "Yes, I am talking about women as well as men." It soon became apparent that Rafael was talking about people having extramarital affairs; for him *casa chica* was a catchy analogue.

So too, although Margarita refers to Carmela as "*la casa chica,*" and although by Carmela's own account the man she lives with cheated on her early in their relationship, this man has been faithful to Carmela for seven years and he is her "husband." As for Luciano's arrangement, a few weeks after fixing our pipes, and after we had gotten to know each other better, he told me that for several years he had lived with a woman other than his "first wife." He and the second woman now have two children together. In responding to questions about "your spouse" in the survey I conducted, Luciano always answered with regard to this second woman.

Most of the *casas chicas* that I know of in Mexico City that conform to a pattern of urban polygamy—where a man shuttles between two (or more) households and the "wives" are often ignorant of each other—are maintained by well-paid workers or men from the middle and upper classes. Other than the rather extraordinary arrangement of the man married to two sisters, and the factory worker with three "wives," generally the only workers who can afford this kind of setup are truckers or migrants to the United States, or men who have high-paying jobs in the electrical, telephone, or petroleum industries.

So what, then, *is* the meaning of *la casa chica,* and what shape does it take in the lives of people in Colonia Santo Domingo? At least in some instances, rather than referring to urban polygamy, *la casa chica* is used to describe second (or later) marriages. In other words, it frequently refers to serial monogamy, and if adultery occasionally occurs, it does so within *this* context. The approach many people take to *la casa chica* is in part a product of Catholic doctrine and antidivorce sanctions. Mexican working class men as well as women have learned to manipulate the cultural rituals and social laws of machismo, not unlike the sixteenth-century rural French, who were, as Natalie Davis

(1983:46) writes, a people with "centuries of peasant experience in manipulating popular rituals and the Catholic law on marriage."

This is especially true for the poor, who cannot as easily arrange and afford church annulments of their marriages. Men are culturally expected to financially maintain their (first) "wives" forever, just as these women expect to be supported—not that this situation always obtains. That is, for many men and women *la casa chica* is the best resolution to a situation in which legal divorce is out of the question. It is the way serial monogamy is practiced by many people in a society in which one often must be "married" to one's first spouse for life. The fact that few women and men necessarily intend in this manner to subvert Catholic rules regarding marriage-for-life does not take away from the creative (and subversive) quality of their actions—one of the ways, to paraphrase Ortner (1989–90:79), in which arenas of nonhegemonic practice can become the bases of a significant challenge to hegemony.

In addition to prohibitions against divorce emanating from the Catholic Church, there are other factors that impinge on the situation. After divorce, first wives can more easily prevent fathers from seeing their children. And men such as Luciano can also lose property rights if their de facto divorces become de jure, and if they marry other women and end up living elsewhere.

The traditional *casa chica* arrangement in which one man lives simultaneously with more than one woman and "family" may or may not persist in the upper echelons of Mexican society. But it is not common in Colonia Santo Domingo, at least not in this sense of urban polygamy. At the same time, none of my analysis regarding serial monogamy minimizes the traumatic financial and emotional impact caused by men who do desert their wives and children, regardless of whether these men take up with other women.[12] My argument is instead threefold: first, that the expression *la casa chica* is used in a variety of ways in *colonias populares,* many of which have little to do with adultery as this latter term is defined by men and women involved in these unions; second, that these multiple meanings of *la casa chica* are illustrations of a cultural practice that has emerged in the context of Catholic laws on marriage; and third, that this cultural practice should be seen as part of a manipulative popular response to the church's ban on divorce.

Popular approaches to the *casa chica* in Santo Domingo are thus exemplary of Gramsci's notion of contradictory consciousness, as the unpredictable exigencies of the living enter into lively contest with the oppressive traditions and sycophantic bromides of dead generations. And, therefore, as Herzfeld (1987: 84) makes clear in another context, in instances such as the daily references and practices to the *casa chica* we should, rather than merely bearing witness to an "enforced passivity" induced from on high, especially and instead see "the quality of active social invention" in defiance of official discourse and control.

LOS SOLTEROS: MASTURBATION, CELIBACY, AND ASEXUALITY

During the same period in January when my wife and daughter were away and I was temporarily "*un hombre abandonado* [an abandoned man]," as some neighbors joked, I expected to hear comments from men about my temporary single status, opportunities for adultery, and much more. Reality proved not so much disappointing as unexpected.

During this time, I spent a Saturday afternoon, as I often did, having a couple of drinks on the corner with a few friends. Marcos, Gabriel, Marcial, Pablo, and Marcelo were all there drinking *anís,* on the rocks or straight, out of plastic cups. Eventually the discussion wound around to the fact that I was alone for a couple of weeks. There were initially some mild inquiries as to whether I would go out looking for some *jovencitas* (young women), but then the comments took an abrupt turn.

"You do know what we say about single guys, don't you?" asked Marcelo. "'*Los solteros son chaqueteros* [Single guys are meat beaters]' and '*No le aprietes el cuello al ganso* [Don't squeeze the goose's neck].'" Everyone laughed, especially when they made me repeat the phrases back to make sure I had learned them correctly. Then they insisted that I copy them down. "You should put them in your book," Marcos recommended.

Masturbating men may not conjure up as romantic an image as a *mujeriego* (womanizer). But I imagine this representation is infinitely more accurate, if mundane, in describing the sex lives of most single men in Santo Domingo than portraits of rapacious young Mexican men always on the prowl for female conquest.[13] Although I briefly hesitated to do so, I checked with Angela the next day to see if she was familiar with the expressions about masturbation I had heard and to make sure I had copied them correctly. She approved my transcriptions and then mentioned that she and her sisters often lament the bachelor status of a nephew by saying to each other, "*Le jala la cabeza al gallo* [He yanks the cock's head]." So much for my worry about embarrassing this grandmother.

Eventually I discovered that in Colonia Santo Domingo one of the most popular ways to describe a single man is to refer to him as a masturbating man. Roberto, a muffler repairman near where I lived, introduced me to his cousin Mario one day. Noting that his cousin was unmarried, Roberto added, "He's a *maraquero* [another slang expression for a man who masturbates]." No joke was made about the cousin being free to run around with a lot of women because of his single status. On another occasion, when we were discussing parents' roles in teaching their children about sexuality, Roberto told me that he and his wife both consider it important to teach their three boys about masturbation, so that they come to see it as part of a transitional stage and a good way to deal with "*estrés* [stress]." He did caution, however, that masturbation could be overdone and that it was only a stage through which one should pass in adolescence.

The assumption that all men love to have as many orgasms as possible is a view about male sexuality that is widely shared by men and women in Santo Domingo. This premise is basic to understanding the connections between men, masturbation, and womanizing, and to examining many of the sexual justifications and intimations heard in the *colonia.*

Héctor and I were walking through the famous La Merced market one overcast afternoon. We had already visited the Sonora market, where herbs, spices, Buddha statues, and love potions are sold. As we passed by a doorway marked "#4" leading to a series of indoor stalls, Héctor pulled my arm and said he wanted to show me something. He found a stall selling sweets made of squash, nuts, and other delicacies, and bought two pieces of *queso de tuna* (tuna-cactus cheese), a sweet made of the nopal cactus that looks like a light brown hockey puck, only smaller. I bit into one as we went back out on the street and continued walking.

After I had finished about half, Héctor smiled, pointed to the remaining portion, and mischievously informed me that *queso de tuna* has a marvelous side effect. About four the next morning, he told me, I would have an erection so hard that it would wake me up. Héctor must have also been sure that I would then want to wake Michelle and have the best sex of my life, because he added, "in the morning you can tell me if it worked." I asked him the obvious question: why hadn't he bothered to mention this little supposed attribute of *queso de tuna* before I ate it? He just laughed, sure that I was really grateful for having been given a food that would unleash my essential male sexual proclivities.

But the view that *all* men have the same sexuality fails to account for multiple sexualities—homosexual, heterosexual, bisexual—and it over-looks androgyny and *a*sexuality. It also overlooks changes in sexuality experienced throughout individuals' lives, from childhood through adolescence, early adulthood, middle age, and old age. And this outlook skirts around significant variations based on class, generation, and family histories.

After a man I know in Santo Domingo confessed to me, "I'll tell you honestly, sex has just never been as important to me as it seems to be for a lot of other guys," I decided to seek out a professional celibate, a Catholic priest, to talk more about male sexuality and asexuality. So I went back to see Padre Víctor Verdín of the Christian Base Communities, at the Iglesia de la Resurrección. I asked him, "For you, the church is your family in a way. But have you never thought that you might be missing something by not having a regular family? It's a naïve question, but a serious one."

"That's a little question, all right! Look, at the level of ideas, a lot of the time I have known that celibacy is right, in terms of leaving you time for others. You have to have a heart which is open to all, and your family is people and your personal relation is an intellectual one with God. But emotionally, in the heart and feelings, I lingered a long time and still I don't think I've got it, really experiencing with serenity and peace an acceptance that there will be tremendous incoherencies, a giant emptiness. It hasn't been easy. There are theories of Freudian sublimation, and in this sense, yes, you can cope. But one goes through various crises. Sometimes what hurts is parenthood. Sometimes it's the lack of tenderness. Sometimes you miss the sexual relation. Sometimes it's everything all at once."

Padre Víctor is a man nonetheless, by which I do not mean here simply that he is biologically male, but that he is a social male. Because of this fact, sexual tensions with women are not obviated by his office: "With women, you have to exercise certain obvious discretion, most of all so that no one misinterprets a certain closeness, or a certain friendliness. People are very sensitive, including in how you greet them, and you have to be careful to avoid ambiguous signs. In this culture, that's the way it is."[14]

Yet in the culture to which Padre Víctor refers, physical intimacy is "the way it is" for some more than others. And, really, there is only so much one man can do about the fact that men's and women's sexualities are increasingly open to ambiguity and misunderstanding. Sex is changing in important if uncalculated ways partly in response to pressures such as those the good padre and his iconoclastic church bring to bear on pregnant teenagers and their lovers. Throughout this Catholic land, youth continue to reach puberty knowing precious little about their and others' bodies. Yet birth control in some form is the standard procedure, albeit a women's procedure. Divorce restrictions remain in place, though they are routinely and creatively dodged, by some through *la casa chica.* Homophobia is a code of boyish insults, whereas sexual experimentation by young men with young men and by young women with young women is increasingly seen as legitimate. Though men are still acting like men, women too are experiencing urges and *aventuras.* The sexual contradictions of a generation have effectively transformed very little and quite a lot.

NOTES

1. I draw in this chapter on Giddens's (1992) insights regarding sexuality, love, and eroticism in modern societies. The term *homosexuality* is used guardedly here to refer to sex between men and sex between women. In Santo Domingo, however, unlike the United States, people usually mean by *homosexual* only the man who is penetrated by another (not necessarily "homosexual") man in anal intercourse. For more on these meanings and practices and certain similarities with regard to sex between men in different parts of Latin America and among Chicanos, see Lancaster 1992 and Almaguer 1991.

2. Unfortunately, no demographic studies have been conducted on fertility rates for men in Mexico. In fact, discussions are just now beginning in the field of demography worldwide as to what the concept of male fertility might even mean (Eugene Hammel, personal communication).

3. As Parker (1991:92) notes in his study of sexual culture in contemporary Brazil, "It is clear that in the modern period sexuality, focused on reproduction, has become something to be managed not merely by the Catholic church or by the state, but by individuals themselves."

4. Lancaster (1992:270) continues: "It is not simply that these relations and conflicts act on some interior and preexisting sexuality 'from the outside' but that they constitute it 'from the inside' as well. Which is to say (contrary to common sense): sexual history is possible only to the extent that desire is thoroughly historicized, and sexual anthropology only to the extent that its subject is effectively relativized."

5. The *National Survey* was compiled from 10,142 questionnaires completed by high school students, who in Mexico come overwhelmingly from middle and upper middle class backgrounds. See Consejo Nacional de Población 1988.

6. The notion of linguistic constraints on culture is given a classic expression in the Sapir-Whorf Hypothesis: "Human beings . . . are very much at the mercy of the particular language which has become the medium of expression for their society" (Sapir 1929 [1949]:162). See Tambiah (1990:111–39) for a recent and sensible effort to analyze the question of cross-cultural translation and the commensurability of cultures.

7. For a similar approach to questions of hegemony, borrowing from Giddens's formulation of "practical consciousness," see Cowan's (1990) nuanced development of Grimscian theories in her study of gender practices in a Greek Macedonian community.

8. In March 1993, on a beach at Puerto Escondido in Oaxaca, I finally met a man who in the course of a long conversation about his life told me, "I have five kids: four daughters and a baby—*un hijo* [a son]!" He shouted those last words, clearly delighted with the maleness of the new arrival. This man and I also talked about the coincidence of both of us having lived and worked in Chicago and Houston for many years. Might his experiences in the United States have made him especially "pro-boy," or was he simply happy for the

variation of a boy amid all those girls? My hunch is that the latter is closer to the truth.

9. Many other ethnographers who have worked in various regions of Mexico report similar sentiments regarding male sexuality. To evoke similar popular beliefs around San Luis Potosí, Behar (1993:290) writes that "men's need for sex is insatiable." Based on fieldwork in Oaxaca, Matthews (1987:228) calls attention to "an important female view of men as being, by nature, lustful, possessing an insatiable sexual appetite. They are like animals in that they seek their own satisfaction and are not concerned with the needs of others." At the same time, such opinions should not be taken to mean that women do not share similar urges. Matthews (1987:225) also speaks of "an important male view of women as being sexually uncontrolled." We may compare these last summations with Brandes's (1980:77) research in Andalusia, Spain, where "women are seductresses, possessed of insatiable, lustful appetites."

10. In this sense, *cabrón* has a usage similar to that of the U.S. English *son of a bitch;* they can be employed as both insults and compliments. For current usage by Mexicans of the term *Sancho,* a nickname for men being cuckolded, see Conover 1987:177–78.

11. For a recent mention of the practice, though not the name, of the *casa chica,* see Bossen 1988:272 on middle class households in Guatemala City. See also Diaz 1970:60 and Fromm and Maccoby 1970:149.

12. Given my interest in fathers and fathering, I was in contact with more men who lived with their families, even if they were not necessarily active in parenting, than I was with those who had abandoned their wives and children. Single mothers were nonetheless common enough in the *colonia.*

13. In my fieldwork in Santo Domingo I was privy to very few discussions about female masturbation.

14. Within the discipline of anthropology there has been an interesting and important dialogue regarding the possibility, and appropriateness, of male ethnographers working with women (see, for example, Gregory 1984; Herzfeld 1985:48; Brandes 1987; and Gilmore 1991:29, n. 2.). I believe that the anthropological study of male identities, of men *as men,* is considerably weakened when the only sources of information are men. In the same way that we have criticized as male bias an understanding of women of whatever culture that is based solely upon what men say about women (see Scheper-Hughes 1983), so too we must not depend on what only men say about themselves. Indeed, I found that on certain sensitive topics, such as domestic violence, rather than being more difficult to discuss these issues with women, it was often much easier to speak with them than it was to get men to think reflexively and report honestly about their experiences and ideas.

REFERENCES

Acevedo, Marta. 1982. *El 10 de mayo.* Mexico City: SEP.

Almaguer, Tomás. 1991. "Chicano Men: A Cartography of Homosexual Identity and Behavior." *differences* 3(2): 75–100.

Arizpe, Lourdes. 1993. "Una sociedad en movimiento." In *Antropologia breve de México.* Lourdes Arizpe, ed. Pp. 373–98. Mexico City: Academia de la Investigación Científica.

Behar, Ruth. 1993. *Translated Woman: Crossing the Border with Esperanza's Story.* Boston: Beacon.

Bossen, Laurel. 1988. "Wives and Servants: Women in Middle-Class Households, Guatemala City." In *Urban Life: Readings in Urban Anthropology.* 2nd edition. George Gmelch and Walter P. Zenner, eds. Pp. 265–75. Prospect Heights, IL: Waveland.

Brandes, Stanley. 1980. *Metaphors of Masculinity: Sex and Status in Andalusian Folklore.* Philadelphia: University of Pennsylvania Press.

———. 1987. "Sex Roles and Anthropological Research in Rural Andalusia." *Women's Studies* 13:357–72.

California Chamber of Commerce. 1993. *North American Free Trade Guide: The Emerging Mexican Market and Opportunities in Canada under NAFTA.* Sacramento: California Chamber of Commerce.

Conover, Ted. 1987. *Coyotes: A Journey through the Secret World of America's Illegal Aliens.* New York: Vintage.

Consejo Nacional de Población. 1988. *Encuesta nacional sobre sexualidad y familia en jóvenes de educación media superior, 1988. (Avances de investigación.)* Mexico City.

Cowan, Jane K. 1990. *Dance and the Body Politic in Northern Greece.* Princeton, NJ: Princeton University Press.

Diaz, May N. 1970. *Tonalá: Conservatism, Responsibility, and Authority in a Mexican Town.* Berkeley: University of California Press.

Fromm, Erich, and Michael Maccoby. 1970. *Social Character in a Mexican Village: A Sociopsychoanalytic Study.* Englewood Cliffs, NJ: Prentice Hall.

García Canclini, Néstor. 1991. "Conclusiones: ¿Para qué sirve el festival?" In *Públicos de arte y política cultural: Un estudio del II Festival de la ciudad de México.* Néstor Garcia Canclini et al., eds. Pp. 159–75. Mexico City: Universidad Autonóma Metropolitana.

Giddens, Anthony. 1992. *The Transformation of Intimacy: Sexuality, Love and Eroticism in Modern Societies.* Stanford, CA: Standford University Press.

Gilmore, David D. 1991. "Commodity, Comity, Community: Male Exchange in Rural Andalusia." *Ethnology* 30(1):17–30.

Gregory, James R. 1984. "The Myth of the Male Ethnographer and the Woman's World." *American Anthropologist* 86(2):316–27.

Herzfeld, Michael. 1985. *The Poetics of Manhood: Contest and Identity in a Cretan Mountain Village*. Princeton, NJ: Princeton University Press.

———. 1987. *Anthropology through the Looking-Glass: Critical Ethnography in the Margins of Europe*. Cambridge: Cambridge University Press.

Instituto Nacional de Estadística, Geografía e Informática. 1990. *Estados Unidos Mexicanos: Resumen general, XI censo general de población y vivienda*. Mexico City: INEGI.

———. 1992. *La mujer en México*. Mexico City: INEGI.

Lancaster, Roger. 1992. *Life Is Hard: Machismo, Danger, and the Intimacy of Power in Nicaragua*. Berkeley: University of California Press.

Logan, Kathleen. 1984. *Haciendo Pueblo: The Development of a Guadalajaran Suburb*. University: University of Alabama Press.

Martin, JoAnn. 1990. "Motherhood and Power: The production of a Woman's Culture of Politics in a Mexican Community." *American Ethnologist* 17(3):470–90.

Matthews, Holly F. 1987. "Intracultural Variation in Beliefs about Gender in a Mexican Community." *American Behavioral Scientist* 31(2):219–33.

Nader, Laura. 1986. "The Subordination of Women in Comparative Perspective." *Urban Anthropology* 15(3–4): 377–97.

Ortner, Sherry B. 1989–90. "Gender Hegemonies." *Cultural Critique* 14:35–80.

Rich, Adrienne. 1976. *Of Women Born: Motherhood as Experience and Institution*. New York: W. W. Norton.

Rouse, Roger. 1991. "Mexican Migration and the Social Space of Postmodernism." *Diaspora* 1(1):8–23.

Sapir, Edward. 1929. (1949) "The Status of Linguistics as a Science." In *Selected Writings of Edward Sapir*, David G. Mandelbaum, ed. Pp. 160–66. Berkeley: University of California Press.

Scheper-Hughes, Nancy. 1983. "Introduction: The Problem of Bias in Androcentric and Feminist Anthropology." *Women's Studies* 10:109–16.

Scheper-Hughes, Nancy. 1992. *Death without Weeping: The Violence of Everyday Life in Brazil*. Berkeley: University of California.

Schmidt, Henry C. 1978. *The Roots of* Lo Mexicano: *Self and Society in Mexican Thought, 1900–1934*. College Station: Texas A&M Press.

Schneider, David, and Raymond Smith. 1973. *Class Differences and Sex Roles in American Kinship and Family Structure*. Englewood Cliffs, NJ: Prentice-Hall.

Sedgwick, Eve Kosofsky. 1990. *Epistemology of the Closet*. Berkeley: University of California Press.

Tambiah, Stanley J. 1990. *Magic, Science, Religion, and the Scope of Rationality*. Cambridge: Cambridge University Press.

19

Because She Looks like a Child

KEVIN BALES

When Siri wakes it is about noon.[1] In the instant of waking she knows exactly who and what she has become. As she explained to me, the soreness in her genitals reminds her of the fifteen men she had sex with the night before. Siri is fifteen years old. Sold by her parents a year ago, she finds that her resistance and her desire to escape the brothel are breaking down and acceptance and resignation are taking their place.

In the provincial city of Ubon Ratchathani, in northeastern Thailand, Siri works and lives in a brothel. About ten brothels and bars, dilapidated and dusty buildings, line the side street just around the corner from a new Western-style shopping mall. Food and noodle vendors are scattered between the brothels. The woman behind the noodle stall outside the brothel where Siri works is also a spy, warder, watchdog, procurer, and dinner lady to Siri and the other twenty-four girls and women in the brothel.

The brothel is surrounded by a wall, with iron gates that meet the street. Within the wall is a dusty yard, a concrete picnic table, and the ubiquitous spirit house, a small shrine that stands outside all Thai buildings. A low door leads into a windowless concrete room that is thick with the smell of cigarettes, stale beer, vomit, and sweat. This is the "selection" room (*hong du*). On one side of the room are stained and collapsing tables and booths; on the other side is a narrow elevated platform with a bench that runs the length of the room. Spotlights pick out this bench, and at night the girls and women sit here under the glare while the men at the tables drink and choose the one they want.

Passing through another door, at the far end of the bench, the man follows the girl past a window, where a bookkeeper takes his money and records which girl he has selected. From there he is led to the girl's room. Behind its concrete front room, the brothel degenerates even further, into a haphazard shanty warren of tiny cubicles where the girls live and work. A makeshift ladder leads up to what may have once been a barn. The upper level is now lined with doors about five feet apart, which open into rooms of about five by seven feet that hold a bed and little else.

Scraps of wood and cardboard separate one room from the next, and Siri has plastered her walls with pictures of teenage pop stars cut from magazines. Over her bed, as in most rooms, there also hangs a framed portrait of the king of Thailand; a single bare lightbulb dangles from the ceiling. Next to the bed a large tin can holds water; there is a hook nearby for rags and towels. At the foot of the bed, next to the door, some clothes are folded on a ledge. The walls are very thin, and everything can be heard from the surrounding rooms; a shout from the bookkeeper echoes through all of them, whether their doors are open or closed.

After rising at midday, Siri washes herself in cold water from the single concrete trough that serves the brothel's twenty-five women. Then, dressed in a T-shirt and skirt, she goes to the noodle stand for the hot soup that is a Thai breakfast. Through the afternoon, if she does not have any clients, she chats with the other girls and women as they drink beer and play cards or make decorative handicrafts together. If the pimp is away the girls will joke around, but if not they must be constantly deferential and aware of his presence, for he can harm them or use them as he pleases. Few men visit in the afternoon, but those who do tend to have more money and can buy a girl for several hours if they like. Some will even make appointments a few days in advance.

At about five, Siri and the other girls are told to dress, put on their makeup, and prepare for the night's work. By seven the men will be coming in, purchasing drinks, and choosing girls; Siri will be chosen by the first of the ten to eighteen men who will buy her that night. Many men choose Siri because she looks much younger than her fifteen years. Slight and round faced, dressed to accentuate her youth, she could pass for eleven or twelve. Because she looks like a child, she can be sold as a "new" girl at a higher price, about $15, which is more than twice that charged for the other girls.

Siri is very frightened that she will get AIDS. Long before she understood prostitution she knew about HIV, as many girls from her village returned home to die from AIDS after being sold into the brothels. Every day she prays to Buddha, trying to earn the merit that will preserve her from the disease. She also tries to insist that her clients use condoms, and in most cases she is successful, because the pimp backs her up. But when policemen use her, or the pimp himself, they will do as they please; if she tries to insist, she will be beaten and raped. She also fears pregnancy, but like the other girls she receives injections of the contraceptive drug Depo-Provera. Once a month she has an HIV test. So far it has been negative. She knows that if she tests positive she will be thrown out to starve.

Though she is only fifteen, Siri is now resigned to being a prostitute. The work is not what she had thought it would be. Her first client hurt her, and at the first opportunity she ran away. She was quickly caught, dragged back, beaten, and raped. That night she was forced to take on a chain of clients until the early morning. The beatings and the work continued night after night, until her will was broken. Now she is sure that she is a very bad person to have deserved what has happened to her. When I comment on how pretty she looks in a photograph, how like a pop star, she replies, "I'm no star; I'm just a whore, that's all." She copes as best she can. She takes a dark pride in her higher price and the large number of men who choose her. It is the adjustment of the concentration camp, an effort to make sense of horror.

In Thailand prostitution is illegal, yet girls like Siri are sold into sex slavery by the thousands. The brothels that hold these girls are but a small part of a much wider sex industry. How can this wholesale trade in girls continue? What keeps it working? The answer is more complicated than we might think. Thailand's economic boom and its social acceptance of prostitution contribute to the pressures that enslave girls like Siri. . . .

ONE GIRL EQUALS ONE TELEVISION

The small number of children sold into slavery in the past has become a flood today. This increase reflects the enormous changes in Thailand over the past fifty years as the country has gone through the great transformation of industrialization—the same process that tore Europe apart over a century ago. If we are to understand slavery in Thailand, we must understand these changes as well, for like so many other parts of the world, Thailand has always had slavery, but never before on this scale.

The economic boom of 1977 to 1997 had a dramatic impact on the northern villages. While the center of the country, around Bangkok, rapidly industrialized, the north was left behind. Prices of food, land, and tools all increased as the economy grew, but the returns for rice and other agriculture were stagnant, held down by government policies guaranteeing cheap food for factory workers in Bangkok. Yet visible everywhere in the north is a flood of consumer goods—refrigerators, televisions, cars and trucks, rice cookers, air conditioners—all of which are extremely tempting. Demand for these goods is high as families try to join the ranks of the prosperous. As it happens, the cost of participating in this consumer boom can be met from an old source that has become much more profitable: the sale of children.

In the past, daughters were sold in response to serious family financial crises. Under threat of losing its mortgaged rice fields and facing destitution, a family might sell a daughter to redeem its debt, but for the most part daughters were worth about as much at home as workers as they would realize when sold. Modernization and economic growth have changed all that. Now parents feel a great pressure to buy consumer goods that were unknown even twenty years ago; the sale of a daughter might easily finance a new television set. A recent survey in the northern provinces found that of the families who sold their daughters, two-thirds could afford not to do so but "instead preferred to buy color televisions and video equipment."[2] And from the perspective of parents who are willing to sell their children, there has never been a better market.

The brothels' demand for prostitutes is rapidly increasing. The same economic boom that feeds consumer demand in the northern villages lines the pockets of laborers and workers in the central plain. Poor economic migrants from the rice fields now work on building sites or in new factories, earning many times what they did on the land. Possibly for the first time in their lives, these laborers can do what more well-off Thai men have always done: go to a brothel. The purchasing power of this increasing number of brothel users strengthens the call for northern girls and supports a growing business in their procurement and trafficking.

Siri's story was typical. A broker, a woman herself from a northern village, approached the families in Siri's village with assurances of well-paid work for their daughters. Siri's parents probably understood that the work would be as a prostitute, since they knew that other girls from their village had gone south to brothels. After some negotiation they were paid 50,000 baht (US$2,000) for Siri, a very significant sum for this family of rice farmers.[3] This exchange began the process of debt bondage that is used to enslave the girls. The contractual arrangement between the broker and the parents requires that this money be paid by the daughter's labor before she is free to leave or is allowed to send money home. Sometimes the money is treated as a loan to the parents, the girls being both the collateral and the means of repayment. In such cases the exorbitant interest charged on the loan means there is little chance that a girl's sexual slavery will ever repay the debt.

Siri's debt of 50,000 baht rapidly escalated. Taken south by the broker, Siri was sold for 100,000 baht to the brothel where she now works. After her rape and beating Siri was informed that the debt she must repay to the brothel equaled 200,000 baht. In addition, Siri learned of the other payments she would be required to make, including rent for her room, at 30,000 baht per month, as well as charges for food and drink, fees for medicine, and fines if she did not work hard enough or displeased a customer.

The total debt is virtually impossible to repay, even at Siri's higher rate of 400 baht. About 100 baht from each client is supposed to be credited to Siri to reduce her debt and pay her rent and other expenses; 200 goes to the pimp and the remaining 100 to the brothel. By this reckoning, Siri must have sex with three hundred men a month just to pay her rent, and what is left over after other expenses barely reduces her original debt. For girls who can charge only 100 to 200 baht per client, the debt grows even faster. This debt bondage keeps the girls under complete control as long as the brothel owner and the pimp believe they are worth having. Violence reinforces the control, and any resistance earns a beating as well as an increase in the debt. Over time, if the girl becomes a good and cooperative prostitute, the pimp may tell her she has paid off the debt and allow her to send small sums home. This "paying off" of the debt usually has nothing to do with an actual accounting of earnings but is declared at the discretion of the pimp, as a means to extend the brothel's profits by making the girl more pliable. Together with rare visits home, money sent back to the family operates to keep her at her job.

Most girls are purchased from their parents, as Siri was, but for others the enslavement is much more direct. Throughout Thailand agents travel to villages, offering work in factories or as domestics. Sometimes they bribe local officials to vouch for them, or they befriend the monks at the local temple to gain introductions. Lured by the promise of good jobs and the money that the daughters will send back to the village, the deceived families dispatch their girls with the agent, often paying for the privilege. Once they arrive in a city, the girls are sold to a brothel, where they are raped, beaten, and locked in. Still other girls are simply kidnapped. This is especially true of women and children who have come to visit relatives in Thailand from Burma or Laos. At bus and train stations, gangs watch for women and children who can be snatched or drugged for shipment to brothels.

Direct enslavement by trickery or kidnapping is not really in the economic interest of the brothel owners. The steadily growing market for prostitutes, the loss of girls to HIV infection, and the especially strong demand for younger and younger girls make it necessary for brokers and brothel owners to cultivate village families so that they can buy more daughters as they come of age. In Siri's case this means letting her maintain ties with her family and ensuring that after a year or so she send a monthly postal order for 10,000 baht to her parents. The monthly payment is a good investment, since it encourages Siri's parents to place their other daughters in the brothel as well. Moreover, the young girls themselves become willing to go when their older sisters and relatives returning for holidays bring stories of the rich life to be lived in the cities of the central plain. Village girls lead a sheltered life, and the appearance of women only a little older than themselves with money and nice clothes is tremendously appealing. They admire the results of this thing called prostitution with only the vaguest notion of what it is. Recent research found that young girls knew that their sisters and neighbors had become prostitutes, but when asked what it means to be a prostitute their most common answer was "wearing Western clothes in a restaurant."[4] Drawn by this glamorous life, they put up little opposition to being sent away with the brokers to swell an already booming sex industry.

By my own conservative estimate there are perhaps thirty-five thousand girls like Siri enslaved in Thailand. Remarkably, this is only a small proportion of the country's prostitutes. In the mid-1990s the government stated that there were 81,384 prostitutes in Thailand—but that official number is calculated from the number of registered (though still illegal) brothels, massage parlors, and sex establishments. One Thai researcher estimated the total number of prostitutes in 1997 to be around 200,000.[5] Every brothel, bar, and massage parlor we visited in Thailand was unregistered, and no one working with prostitutes believes the government figures. At the other end of the spectrum are the estimates put forward by activist organizations such as the Center for the Protection of Children's Rights. These groups assert that there are more than 2 million prostitutes. I suspect that this number is too high in a national population of 60 million. My own reckoning, based on information gathered by AIDS workers in different cities, is that there are between half a million and 1 million prostitutes.

Of this number, only about one in twenty is enslaved. Most become prostitutes voluntarily, though some start out in debt bondage. Sex is sold everywhere in Thailand: barbershops, massage parlors, coffee shops and cafés, bars and restaurants, nightclubs and karaoke bars, brothels, hotels, and even temples traffic in sex. Prostitutes range from the high-earning "professional" women who work with some autonomy, through the women working by choice as call girls or in massage parlors, to the enslaved rural girls like Siri. Many women work semi-independently in bars, restaurants, and night-clubs—paying a fee to the owner, working when they choose, and having the power to decide whom to take as a customer. Most bars and clubs cannot use an enslaved prostitute like Siri, as the women are often sent out on call and their clients expect a certain amount of cooperation and friendliness. Enslaved girls serve the lowest end of the market: the laborers, students, and workers who can afford only the 100 baht per half hour. It is low-cost sex in volume, and the demand is always there. For a Thai man, buying a woman is much like buying a round of drinks. But the reasons why such large numbers of Thai men use prostitutes are much more complicated and grow out of their culture, their history, and a rapidly changing economy.

"I DON'T WANT TO WASTE IT, SO I TAKE HER"

Until it was officially disbanded in 1910, the king of Thailand maintained a harem of hundreds of concubines, a few of whom might be elevated to the rank of "royal mother" or "minor wife." This form of polygamy was closely imitated by status-hungry nobles and emerging rich merchants of the nineteenth century. Virtually all men of any substance kept at least a mistress or a minor wife. For those with fewer resources, prostitution was a perfectly acceptable option, as renting took the place of out-and-out ownership.

Even today everyone in Thailand knows his or her place within a very elaborate and precise status system. Mistresses and minor wives continue to enhance any man's social standing, but the consumption of commercial sex has increased dramatically.[6] If an economic boom is a tide that raises all boats, then vast numbers of Thai men have now been raised to a financial position from which they can regularly buy sex. Nothing like the economic growth in Thailand was ever experienced in the West, but a few facts show its scale: in a country the size of Britain, one-tenth of the workforce moved from the land to industry in just the three years from 1993 to 1995; the number of factory workers doubled from less than 2 million to more than 4 million in the eight years from 1988 to 1995; and urban wages doubled from 1986 to 1996. Thailand is now the world's largest importer of motorcycles and the second-largest importer of pickup tricks, after the United States. Until the economic downturn of late 1997, money flooded Thailand, transforming poor rice farmers into wage laborers and fueling consumer demand.

With this newfound wealth, Thai men go to brothels in increasing numbers. Several recent studies show that between 80 and 87 percent of Thai men have had sex with a prostitute. Most report that their first sexual experience was with a prostitute. Somewhere between 10 and 40 percent of married men have paid for commercial sex within the past twelve months, as have up to 50 percent of single men. Though it is difficult to measure, these reports suggest something like 3 to 5 million regular customers for commercial sex. But it would be wrong to imagine millions of Thai men sneaking furtively on their own along dark streets lined with brothels; commercial sex is a social event, part of a good night out with friends. Ninety-five percent of men going to a brothel do so with their friends, usually at the end of a night spent drinking. Groups go out for recreation and entertainment, and especially to get drunk together. That is a strictly male pursuit, as Thai women usually abstain from alcohol. All-male groups out for a night on the town are considered normal in any Thai city, and whole neighborhoods are devoted to serving them. One man interviewed in a recent study explained, "When we arrive at the brothel, my friends take one and pay for me to take another. It costs them money; I don't want to waste it, so I take her."[7] Having one's prostitute paid for also brings an informal obligation to repay in kind at a later date. Most Thais, men and women, feel that commercial sex is an acceptable part of an ordinary outing for single men, and about two-thirds of men and one-third of women feel the same about married men.[8] . . .

MILLIONAIRE TIGERS AND BILLIONAIRE GEESE

Who are these modern slaveholders? The answer is anyone and everyone—anyone, that is, with a little capital to invest. The people who *appear* to own the enslaved prostitutes—the pimps, madams, and brothel keepers—are usually just employees. As hired muscle, pimps and their helpers provide the brutality that controls women and makes possible their commercial exploitation. Although they are just employees, the pimps do rather well for themselves. Often living in the brothel, they receive a salary and add to that income by a number of scams; for example, food and drinks are sold to customers at inflated prices, and the pimps pocket the difference. Much more lucrative is their control of the price of sex. While each woman has a basic price, the pimps size up each customer and pitch the fee accordingly. In this way a client may pay two or three times more than the normal rate, and all of the surplus goes to the pimp. In league with the bookkeeper, the pimp systematically cheats the prostitutes of the little that is supposed to be credited against their debt. If they manage the sex slaves well and play all of the angles, pimps can easily make ten times their basic wage—a great income for an ex-peasant whose main skills are violence and intimidation, but nothing compared to the riches to be made by the brokers and the real slaveholders.

The brokers and agents who buy girls in the villages and sell them to brothels are only short-term slaveholders. Their business is part recruiting agency, part shipping company, part public relations, and part kidnapping gang. They aim to buy low and sell high while maintaining a good flow of girls from the villages. Brokers are equally likely to be men or women, and they usually come from the regions in which they recruit. Some are local people dealing in girls in addition to their jobs as police officers, government bureaucrats, or even schoolteachers. Positions of public trust are excellent starting points for buying young girls. In spite of the character of their work, they are well respected. Seen as job providers and sources of large cash payments to parents, they are well known in their communities. Many of the women brokers were once sold themselves; some spent years as prostitutes and now, in their middle age, make their living by supplying girls to the brothels. These women are walking advertisements for sexual slavery. Their lifestyle and income, their Western clothes and glamorous, sophisticated ways promise a rosy economic future for the girls they buy. That they have physically survived their years in the brothel may be the exception—many more young women come back to the village to die of AIDS—but the parents tend to be optimistic.

Whether these dealers are local people or traveling agents, they combine the business of procuring with other economic pursuits. A returned prostitute may live with her family, look after her parents, own a rice field or two, and buy and sell girls on the side. Like the pimps, they are in a good business, doubling their money on each girl within two or three weeks; but also like the pimps, their profits are small compared to those of the long-term slaveholders.

The real slaveholders tend to be middle-aged businessmen. They fit seamlessly into the community, and they suffer no social discrimination for what they do. If anything, they are admired as successful, diversified capitalists. Brothel ownership is normally only one of many business interests for the slaveholder. To be sure, a brothel owner may have some ties to organized crime, but in Thailand organized crime includes the police and much of the government. Indeed, the work of the modern slaveholder is best seen not as aberrant criminality but as a perfect example of disinterested capitalism. Owning the brothel that holds young girls in bondage is simply a business matter. The investors would say that they are creating jobs and wealth. There is no hypocrisy in their actions, for they obey an important social norm: earning a lot of money is good enough reason for anything.

The slaveholder may in fact be a partnership, company, or corporation. In the 1980s, Japanese investment poured into Thailand, in an enormous migration of capital that was called "Flying Geese."[9] The strong yen led to buying and building across the country, and while electronics firms built television factories, other investors found that there was much, much more to be made in the sex industry. Following the Japanese came investment from the so-called Four Tigers (South Korea, Hong Kong, Taiwan, and Singapore), which also found marvelous opportunities in commercial sex. (All five of these countries further proved to be strong import markets for enslaved Thai girls, as discussed below.) The Geese and the Tigers had the resources to buy the local criminals, police, administrators, and property needed to set up commercial sex businesses. Indigenous Thais also invested in brothels as the sex industry boomed; with less capital, they were more likely to open poorer, working-class outlets.

Whether they are individual Thais, partnerships, or foreign investors, the slaveholders share many characteristics. There is little or no racial or ethnic difference between them and the slaves they own (with the exception of the Japanese investors). They feel no need to rationalize their slaveholding on racial grounds. Nor are they linked in any sort of hereditary ownership of slaves or of the children of their slaves. They are not really interested in their slaves at all, just in the bottom line on their investment.

To understand the business of slavery today we have to know something about the economy in which it operates. Thailand's economic boom included a sharp increase in sex tourism tacitly backed by the government. International tourist arrivals jumped from 2 million in 1981 to 4 million in 1988 to over 7-million in 1996.[10] Two-thirds of tourists were unaccompanied men; in other words, nearly 5 million unaccompanied men visited Thailand in 1996. A significant proportion of these were sex tourists.

The recent downturn in both tourism and the economy may have slowed, but not dramatically altered, sex tourism. In 1997 the annual illegal income generated by sex workers in Thailand was roughly $10 billion, which is more than drug trafficking is estimated to generate.[11] According to ECPAT, an organization working against child prostitution, the economic crisis in Southeast Asia may have increased the exploitation of young people in sex tourism:

> According to Professor Lae Dilokvidhayarat from Chulalongkorn University, there has been a 10 percent decrease in the school enrollment at primary school level in Thailand since 1996. Due to increased unemployment, children cannot find work in the formal sector, but instead are forced to "disappear" into the informal sector. This makes them especially vulnerable to sexual exploitation. Also, a great number of children are known to travel to tourist areas and to big cities hoping to find work.
>
> We cannot overlook the impact of the economic crisis on sex tourism, either. Even though travelling costs to Asian countries are approximately the same as before mid 1997, when the crisis began, the rates for sexual services in many places are lower due to increased competition in the business. Furthermore, since there are more children trying to earn money, there may also be more so called situational child sex tourists, i.e. those who do not necessarily prefer children as sexual partners, but who may well choose a child if the situation occurs and the price is low.[12]

In spite of the economic boom, the average Thai's income is very low by Western standards. Within an industrializing country, millions still live in rural poverty. If a rural family owns its house and has a rice field, it might survive on as little as 500 baht ($20) per month. Such absolute poverty means a diet of rice supplemented with insects (crickets, grubs, and maggots are widely eaten), wild plants, and what fish the family can catch. If a family's standard of living drops below this level, which can be sustained only in the countryside, it faces hunger and the loss of its house or land. For most Thais, an income of 2,500 to 4,000 baht per month ($100 to $180) is normal. Government figures from December 1996 put two-thirds of the population at this level. There is no system of welfare or health care, and pinched budgets allow no space for saving. In these families, the 20,000 to 50,000 baht ($800 to $2,000) brought by selling a daughter provides a year's income. Such a vast sum is a powerful inducement that often blinds parents to the realities of sexual slavery. . . .

BURMESE PROSTITUTES

The same economic boom that has increased the demand for prostitutes may, in time, bring an end to Thai sex slavery. Industrial growth has also led to an increase in jobs for women. Education and training are expanding rapidly across Thailand, and women and girls are very much taking part. The ignorance and deprivation on which the enslavement of girls depends are on the wane, and better-educated girls are much less likely to fall for the promises made by brokers. The traditional duties to family, including the debt of obligation to parents, are also becoming less compelling. As the front line of industrialization sweeps over northern Thailand, it is bringing fundamental changes. Programs on the television bought with the money from selling one daughter may carry warning messages to her younger sisters. As they learn more about new jobs, about HIV/AIDS, and about the fate of those sent to the brothels, northern Thai girls refuse to follow their sisters south. Slavery functions best when alternatives are few, and education and the media are opening the eyes of Thai girls to a world of choice.

For the slaveholders this presents a serious problem. They are faced with an increase in demand for prostitutes and a diminishing supply. Already the price of young Thai girls is spiraling upward. The slaveholders' only recourse is to look elsewhere, to areas where poverty and ignorance still hold sway. Nothing, in fact, could be easier: there remain large, oppressed, and isolated populations desperate enough to believe the promises of the brokers. From Burma to the west and Laos to the east come thousands of economic and political refugees searching for work; they are defenseless in a country where they are illegal aliens. The techniques that worked so well in bringing Thai girls to brothels are again deployed, but now across borders. . . .

Once in the brothels they are in an even worse situation than the enslaved Thai girls: because they do not speak Thai their isolation is increased, and as illegal aliens they are open to even more abuse. The pimps tell them repeatedly that if they set foot outside the brothel, they will be arrested. And when they are arrested, Burmese and Lao girls and women are afforded no legal rights. They are often held for long periods at the mercy of the police, without charge or trial. A strong traditional antipathy between Thais and Burmese increases the chances that Burmese sex slaves will face discrimination and arbitrary treatment. . . .

TO JAPAN, SWITZERLAND, GERMANY, THE UNITED STATES

Women and girls flow in both directions over Thailand's borders.[13] The export of enslaved prostitutes is a robust business, supplying brothels in Japan, Europe, and America. Thailand's Ministry of Foreign Affairs estimated in 1994 that as many as 50,000 Thai women were living illegally in Japan and working in prostitution. Their situation in these countries parallels that of Burmese women held in Thailand. The enticement of Thai women follows a familiar pattern. Promised work as cleaners, domestics, dishwashers, or cooks, Thai girls and women pay large fees to employment agents to secure jobs in rich, developed countries. When they arrive, they are brutalized and enslaved. Their debt bonds are significantly larger than those of enslaved prostitutes in Thailand, since they include airfares, bribes to immigration officials, the costs of false passports, and sometimes the fees paid to foreign men to marry them and ease their entry.

Variations on sex slavery occur in different countries. In Switzerland girls are brought in on "artist" visas as exotic dancers. There, in addition to being prostitutes, they must work as striptease dancers in order to meet the carefully checked terms of their employment. The brochures of the European companies that have leaped into the sex-tourism business leave the customer no doubt about what is being sold:

> Slim, sunburnt, and sweet, they love the white man in an erotic and devoted way. They are masters of the art of making love by nature, an art that we Europeans do not know. (Life Travel, Switzerland) [M]any girls from the sex world come from the poor north-eastern region of the country and from the slums of Bangkok. It has become a custom that one of the nice looking daughters goes into the business in order to earn money for the poor family . . . [Y]ou can get the feeling that taking a girl here is as easy as buying a package of cigarettes . . . little slaves who give real Thai warmth. (Kanita Kamha Travel, the Netherlands)[14]

In Germany they are usually bar girls, and they are sold to men by the bartender or bouncer. Some are simply placed in brothels or apartments controlled by pimps. After Japanese sex tours to Thailand began in the 1980s, Japan rapidly became the largest importer of Thai women. The fear of HIV in Japan has also increased the demand for virgins. Because of their large disposable incomes, Japanese men are able to pay considerable sums for young rural girls from Thailand. Japanese organized crime is involved throughout the importation process, sometimes shipping women via Malaysia or the Philippines. In the cities, the Japanese mob maintains bars and brothels that trade in Thai women. Bought and sold between brothels, these women are controlled with extreme violence. Resistance can bring murder. Because the girls are illegal aliens and often enter the country under false passports, Japanese gangs rarely hesitate to kill them if they have ceased to be profitable or if they have angered their slaveholders. Thai women deported from Japan also report that the gangs will addict girls to drugs in order to manage them more easily.

Criminal gangs, usually Chinese or Vietnamese, also control brothels in the United States that enslave Thai women. Police raids in New York, Seattle, San Diego, and Los Angeles have freed more than a hundred girls and women.[15] In New York, thirty Thai women were locked into the upper floors of a building used as a brothel. Iron bars sealed the windows and a series of buzzer-operated armored gates blocked exit to the street. During police raids, the women were herded into a secret basement room. At her trial, the brothel owner testified that she'd bought the women outright, paying between $6,000 and $15,000 for each. The women were charged $300 per week for room and board; they worked from 11:00 A.M. until 4:00 A.M. and were sold by the hour to clients. Chinese and Vietnamese gangsters were also involved in the brothel, collecting protection money and hunting down escaped prostitutes. The gangs owned chains of brothels and massage parlors, through which they rotated the Thai women in order to defeat law enforcement efforts. After being freed from the New York brothel, some of the women disappeared—only to turn up weeks later in similar circumstances three thousand miles away, in Seattle. One of the rescued Thai women, who had been promised restaurant work and then enslaved, testified that the brothel owners "bought something and wanted to use it to the full extent, and they didn't think those people were human beings."[16]

OFFICIAL INDIFFERENCE AND A GROWTH ECONOMY

In many ways, Thailand closely resembles another country, one that was going through rapid industrialization and economic boom one hundred years ago. Rapidly shifting its labor force off the farm, experiencing unprecedented economic growth, flooded with economic migrants, and run by corrupt politicians and a greedy and criminal police force, the United States then faced many of the problems confronting Thailand today. In the 1890s, political machines that brought together organized crime with politicians and police ran the prostitution and protection rackets, drug sales, and extortion in American cities. Opposing them were a weak and disorganized reform movement and a muckraking press. I make this comparison because it is important to explore why Thailand's government is so ineffective when faced with the enslavement of its own citizens, and also to remember that conditions *can* change over time. Discussions with Thais about the horrific nature of sex slavery often end with their assertion that "nothing will ever change this . . . the problem is just too big . . . and those with power will never allow change." Yet the social and economic underpinnings of slavery in Thailand are always changing, sometimes for the worse and sometimes for the better. No society can remain static, particularly one undergoing such upheavals as Thailand.

As the country takes on a new Western-style materialist morality, the ubiquitous sale of sex sends a clear message: women can be enslaved and exploited for profit. Sex tourism helped set the stage for the expansion of sexual slavery.

Sex tourism also generates some of the income that Thai men use to fund their own visits to brothels. No one knows how much money it pours into the Thai economy, but if we assume that just one-quarter of sex workers serve sex tourists and that their customers pay about the same as they would pay to use Siri, then 656 billion baht ($26.2 billion) a year would be about right. This is thirteen times more than the amount Thailand earns by building and exporting computers, one of the country's major industries, and it is money that floods into the country without any concomitant need to build factories or improve infrastructure. It is part of the boom raising the standard of living generally and allowing an even greater number of working-class men to purchase commercial sex.

Joining the world economy has done wonders for Thailand's income and terrible things to its society. According to Pasuk Phongpaichit and Chris Baker, economists who have analyzed Thailand's economic boom,

> Government has let the businessmen ransack the nation's human and natural resources to achieve growth. It has not forced them to put much back. In many respects, the last generation of economic growth has been a disaster. The forests have been obliterated. The urban environment has deteriorated. Little has been done to combat the growth in industrial pollution and hazardous wastes. For many people whose labour has created the boom, the conditions of work, health, and safety are grim.
>
> Neither law nor conscience has been very effective in limiting the social costs of growth. Business has reveled in the atmosphere of free-for-all. The machinery for social protection has proved very pliable. The legal framework is defective. The judiciary is suspect. The police are unreliable. The authorities have consistently tried to block popular organizations to defend popular rights.[17]

The situation in Thailand today is similar to that of the United States in the 1850s; with a significant part of the economy dependent on slavery, religious and cultural leaders are ready to explain why this is all for the best. But there is also an important difference: this is the new slavery, and the impermanence of modern slavery and the dedication of human-rights workers offer some hope.

NOTES

1. Siri is, of course, a pseudonym; the names of all respondents have been changed for their protection. I spoke with them in December 1996.

2. "Caught in Modern Slavery: Tourism and Child Prostitution in Thailand," Country Report Summary prepared by Sudarat Sereewat-Srisang for the Ecumenical Consultation held in Chiang Mai in May 1990.

3. Foreign exchange rates are in constant flux. Unless otherwise noted, dollar equivalences for all currencies reflect the rate at the time of the research.

4. From interviews done by Human Rights Watch with freed child prostitutes in shelters in Thailand, reported in Jasmine Caye, *Preliminary Survey on Regional Child Trafficking for Prostitution in Thailand* (Bangkok: Center for the Protection of Children's Rights, 1996), p. 25.

5. Kulachada Chaipipat, "New Law Targets Human Trafficking," Bangkok *Nation,* November 30, 1997.

6. Thais told me that it would be very surprising if a well-off man or a politician did not have at least one mistress. When I was last in Thailand there was much public mirth over the clash of wife and mistress outside the hospital room of a high government official who had suffered a heart attack, as each in turn barricaded the door.

7. Quoted in Mark Van Landingham, Chanpen Saengtienchai, John Knodel, and Anthony Pramualratana, *Friends, Wives, and Extramarital Sex in Thailand* (Bangkok: Institute of Population Studies, Chulalongkorn University, 1995), p. 18.

8. Van Landingham et al., 1995, pp. 9–25.

9. Pasuk Phongpaichit and Chris Baker, *Thailand's Boom* (Chiang Mai: Silkworm Books, 1996), pp. 51–54.

10. Center for the Protection of Children's Rights, *Case Study Report on Commercial Sexual Exploitation of Children in Thailand* (Bangkok, October 1996), p. 37.

11. David Kyle and John Dale, "Smuggling the State Back In: Agents of Human Smuggling Reconsidered," in *Global Human Smuggling: Comparative Perspectives,* ed. David Kyle and Rey Koslowski (Baltimore: Johns Hopkins University Press, 2001).

12. "Impact of the Asian Economic Crisis on Child Prostitution," *ECPAT International Newsletter* 27 (May 1, 1999), found at http://www.ecpat.net/eng/Ecpat.inter/IRC/articles.asp?articleID=143&NewsID=21.

13. *International Report on Trafficking in Women (Asia-Pacific Region)* (Bangkok Global Alliance Against Traffic in Women, 1996); Sudarat Sereewat, *Prostitution: Thai-European Connection* (Geneva: Commission on the Churches' participation in Development, World Council of Churches, n.d.). Women's rights and anti-trafficking organizations in Thailand have also published a number of personal accounts of women enslaved as prostitutes and sold overseas. These pamphlets are disseminated widely in the hope of making young women more aware of the threat of enslavement. Good examples are Siriporn Skrobanek *The Diary of Prang* (Bangkok: Foundation for Women, 1994); and White Ink (pseud.), *Our Lives, Our Stories* (Bangkok: Foundation for Women, 1995). They follow the lives of women "exported," the first to Germany and the second to Japan.

14. The brochures are quoted in Truong, *Sex, Money, and Morality: Prostitution and Tourism in Southeast Asia* (London: Zed Books, 1990), p. 178.

15. Carey Goldberg, "Sex Slavery, Thailand to New York," *New York Times* (September 11, 1995), p. 81.

16. Quoted in Goldberg.

17. Phongpaichit and Baker, 1996, p. 237.

20

The Sex Tourist, the Expatriate, His Ex-Wife, and Her "Other"

The Politics of Loss, Difference, and Desire

JULIA O'CONNELL DAVIDSON

> The English word 'desire' comes from the Latin *desiderare,* literally, to be away from the stars, whence to cease to see, regret the absence of, to seek. (Bishop and Robinson, 1998: 114)

> [W]e go to the exotic other to lose everything, including ourselves—everything that is but the privilege which enabled us to go in the first place. (Dollimore, 1991: 342)

In Western discourses on "racial" Otherness, the notion of "civilization" as the apex of an evolutionary process of social development has often been read as implying a radical separation from and/or a corruption of "nature," and thus involving a kind of loss, even as it confers intellectual supremacy upon the "civilized races." A number of authors have drawn attention to the relationship between this sense of loss and sexual desire for the Other (Bhatacharyya, 1997; Dollimore, 1991; Mercer, 1995; Said, 1978), and it is also highlighted in Bishop and Robinson's (1998) compelling analysis of the sex tourist industry in Thailand. Bishop and Robinson (1998) explore sex tourism in relation to discursive traditions which have constructed "Other cultures as qualitatively and quantitatively different with regard to sexual practices and mores" (1998: 114). One of the things their analysis of 18th-, 19th- and 20th-century western texts that eroticize Other cultures illuminates is the tension surrounding the idea of "civilization." Paying particular attention to the writings of Denis Diderot and, to a lesser extent Jean-Jacques Rousseau, Bishop and Robinson interrogate a discursive tradition wherein a vision of Other cultures as closer to "the state of nature" serves as a foil against which to critique certain aspects of European morality and social development. They show very clearly how contemporary accounts of sex tourism to Thailand (provided by sex tourists themselves as well as other commentators) resonate with these 18th-century representations of Other cultures' sexuality as in tune with "nature" and "untainted by European morality" (p. 114).

Whether and how these accounts of sex tourism resonate with post-Enlightenment representations of Eu-

"The Sex Tourist, the Expatriate, His Ex-Wife, and Her 'Other': The Politics of Loss, Difference, and Desire" in *Sexualities,* Volume 4, Number 1, pp 5–24.

ropean and North American "civilization" is less explicitly addressed in Bishop and Robinson's work, and these questions provide the starting point for this article. Drawing on an ethnographic study of sex tourism in the Dominican Republic,[1] this article explores the worldview of a group of white European and North American male heterosexual tourists and expatriates whose sexual desires are immediately and transparently linked to a set of political discontents with contemporary "civilization." Their desire for the Other does not express a wish to lose everything, so much as a wish to reclaim what they feel they have already lost. These are sexually hostile men, and my aim is not to suggest that they are somehow representative of *all* European and North American heterosexual men or even necessarily of *all* male sex tourists. What I do want to argue, however, is that the model of human sociality they use to make sense of their experience is informed by a mainstream political tradition within liberalism. The sense of loss which lies behind their desire is not extraordinary or unique to them as individuals, and an interrogation of that desire therefore sheds light on European/North American constructions of Self as well as of Other. Above all, the moral philosophy of these men reveals something of the whiteness, maleness and heterosexuality of classical liberalism's sovereign self and the tensions generated by its partial and exclusive universalism.

SEX TOURISM AND THE DOMINICAN REPUBLIC

The Dominican Republic, which occupies the eastern two-thirds of the island of Hispaniola, has a population of almost 8 million. Historically, the country's economy has been weakened by colonial neglect, Trujillo's 32-year dictatorship, foreign intervention and, above all in recent decades, by international debt. In the early 1980s, debt crisis and negotiations with the International Monetary Fund (IMF) led to the adoption of structural adjustment measures. These measures did little to improve the lot of the ordinary people (according to World Bank estimates in 1992, 60% of Dominicans were living in poverty, Howard, 1999: 33), but they did stimulate the expansion of tourism, a sector which the Dominican government had been promoting since the 1970s. The country now hosts around 1.8 million tourists annually, most of whom are North American or European (WTO, 1997).

Many, perhaps the majority, of these visitors are "ordinary" tourists seeking a cheap holiday or honeymoon in the Caribbean, but the country does also attract "sex tourists." Defined as those tourists who enter into some form of sexual-economic exchange with women, men or children resident in the host destination, sex tourists are a heterogeneous group. They vary in terms of nationality, gender, age, ethnicity and racialized identity, sexual orientation and socioeconomic background, as well as in terms of their sexual practices whilst abroad and the subjective meanings they attach to their sexual encounters (Clift and Carter, 2000; Kruhse-MountBurton, 1995; O'Connell Davidson, 1995; Pruitt and LaFont, 1995; Sanchez Taylor, 2000). They also differ as regards how central sex is to their travel experience.

For those to whom I shall refer to as "hardcore" sex tourists, however, the desire for particular kinds of sexual experience (generally those which are expensive, scarce or risky at home, such as sex with multiples of prostitute women or men, and/or with children, or transsexuals and/or with racialized Others) is a conscious and explicit part of the motivation to travel. Some hardcore sex tourists find the pleasures associated with a particular destination so great that they eventually decide to migrate and settle permanently in their chosen "sexual paradise." Such expatriates (or "sexpatriates") often play an active role in promoting sex tourism and organizing tourist-related prostitution in a given destination (see Ireland, 1993; O'Connell Davidson and Sanchez Taylor, 1996; Seabrook, 1996; Truong, 1990), and this is certainly the case in the Dominican Republic.

Many of the hotels, restaurants and bars that facilitate prostitute-use by tourists in Boca Chica, Puerto Plata and in Sosua (the country's three main sex tourist destinations) are owned or managed by North American or European expatriates. The more entrepreneurial amongst them have discovered that the internet offers excellent marketing opportunities, and their hotels and bars now feature on several websites that promote sex tourism. For instance, a number of American sexpatriates living in Boca Chica have established strong links with an American-based travel club, Travel and the Single Male (TSM), through which their businesses are advertised. The club, which is one of several similar organizations run by and for male sex tourists, boasts some 5000 members, most of whom are white Americans. TSM publishes a guidebook (Cassirer, 1992) and sells club membership for US$50 per annum. Members receive a quarterly newsletter, discounts in some hotels and brothels, and most importantly, are provided access to the TSM internet site. This provides information on travel and prostitution in various countries around the world, access to softcore pornographic photographs of female sex workers from those countries two message boards and a chat room for members to swap "sexperiences," views, news and handy travel tips.

As well as drawing on interviews with 31 sexpatriates and 30 hardcore sex tourists in the Dominican Republic, five of whom were members of TSM, this article makes fairly extensive use of materials published by TSM. The worldview of its members typifies that of hardcore male heterosexual sex tourists more generally (O'Connell Davidson, 1995, 1996, 1998), and their attitudes towards gender, "race" and sexuality are consistent with those expressed in other guidebooks and internet sites which promote this form of sex tourism (for instance, "Travel Philippines," "Brothels, Bordellos and Sinbins of the World)," and the "World Sex Guide," (see Bishop and Robinson, 1998; Hughes, 1998/9). The following extract from a posting on TSM's message board captures these attitudes well:

> Boca is a place of [European/North American] men's dreams and [European/North American] women's nightmares. It finds the heart of desire within all of us. Boca . . . is a place where sexual fantasies become commonplace. A place where you can go into your room with a pack of multi-colored girls and no one will blink twice. A place where an older man can convince himself that the young girl rotating on his lap cares for him and understands his needs more than the women from his homeland. It's a place where men come for lust and sometimes end up confusing it for love. It's where a man can be a star in his own adult videos. It's a place where a young pretty girl once offered me sex for a [plate of] lasagna. It's a place where every woman you see whether whore or maid or waitress, young or old, can be bought for a few hundred pesos. It's a place where you can have a girl, her sisters and her cousins. (TSM, posted 19 March 1998)

Though its organizers and members would not describe it as a political organization, the ethos of TSM is aggressively heterosexist, deeply misogynist and profoundly racist, and the club thus expresses and promotes a particular worldview, as well as a particular form of travel. Indeed, it implicitly, and sometimes explicitly, presents travel to "Third World" countries as a means of release from the restraints that are supposedly placed on the white male's self-sovereignty in the "First World." This form of sex tourism reflects a particular political vision of the West, then, as well as of the so-called "Third World." The following section considers this vision in relation to a mainstream discursive tradition of liberal political theory.

"NATURAL RIGHTS" AND SOCIAL CONTRACT

Classical political theory starts from the proposition that human beings are naturally competitive and self, interested and for this reason need safeguarding from each other. Hobbes (1968), for instance, holds that in a state of nature, each man would use all means available to him to possess, use and enjoy all that he would, or could, get. By agreeing (on condition that all men do the same) to a social contract that creates a political society or state, and by transferring rights of law-making and enforcement to that state, individuals can, it is argued, simultaneously retain powers of sovereignty over themselves, and be restrained from invading and destroying others. The legitimacy of the liberal democratic state hinges upon its role as enactor of laws that preserve and protect the "natural rights" of its citizens, "rights" which include possessing property, disposing of their own labour, exercising sovereignty over themselves, their own minds and bodies.

Carole Pateman (1988) has observed that missing from this story that social contract theorists tell about the origins of the liberal democratic state is the tale of the sexual contract. She argues that the pact through which powers of law-making and enforcement are transferred to the state is a pact between men, and is:

> a sexual as well as a social contract: it is sexual in the sense of patriarchal—that is, the contract establishes men's political right over women—and also sexual in the sense of establishing orderly access by men to women's bodies. (Pateman, 1988: 2)

Pateman's thesis thus suggests that the legitimacy of the liberal state actually rests on its role as enactor of laws which preserve and protect the "natural rights" of its *male* citizens, "rights" which are understood to include a right of access to women's bodies. Viewed in this way, it is possible to see how the extent and nature of such rights of access to female bodies, alongside the details of other "natural rights," can become the focus of political dispute. In other words, while in principle happy to enter into a pact with other men as regards access to women's bodies and other social arrangements, men might feel that the particular restraints imposed on male sexuality by a given state conflict with, rather than protect, the "natural rights" of its citizens. This was precisely the nature of Diderot's dispute with European moral and legal regulation of sexuality in the 18th century (for his criticisms of monogamy and the private ownership of women through the institution of marriage, see Bishop and Robinson, 1998: 120).

A similar case can be made in relation to "race," for as Mills (1998) and Puwar (1999) argue, the social contract is "raced" as well as gendered. In the sense that the myth of the original pact is a story about white men agreeing to transfer rights of law-making and enforcement to a political body, we can say that the legitimacy of the liberal democratic state is based upon and reinforces a particular racialized hierarchy. Again, the extent and precise details of white male rights over Others may be subject to dispute, even amongst those who are, in principle, reconciled to the liberal model of political contract.[2]

Here I want to suggest that hardcore sex tourists' political vision is informed by a classical liberal model of self, community and contract, within which naturally brutish men living in a "state of nature" are simultaneously free to conquer and at risk of invasion. They are "suspended between a fantasy of conquest and a dread of engulfment, between rape and emasculation" (McClintock, 1995: 27). The social contract of "civilization" is imagined as a release from this paranoiac paralysis, but only so long as it guarantees each man his "natural rights." If the "civilized" state comes to invade and deny individual men's "natural rights" over themselves, and over women and "racialized" Others, it loses legitimacy. This, I will argue, helps to explain the attraction that sites perceived as closer to "the state of nature" hold for hardcore male heterosexual sex tourists.

Rejecting the Authority of the "Civilized" State

In the course of interview work in the Dominican Republic, we have found that European and North American male sexpatriates and hardcore sex tourists are more than willing to hold forth on what is wrong with European/North American societies. The developments that trouble them most are those which they perceive to undermine a "natural" hierarchy that is classed, gendered and "faced." They rail against taxes, and most especially against tax-payers' money being spent on social welfare programmes for the undeserving poor (and more or less anyone who is poor in the West is deemed to be undeserving); they remonstrate against affirmative action programmes and/or equal opportunities legislation, as well as against divorce laws which empower women in relation to men, against women's entitlement to child support payments, and so on. Without prompting, they also bemoan the state's increasing incursion into spheres of life which they believe should be a matter of individual (white male) conscience, so that, for example, they take great exception to laws which compel them to wear seatbelts in cars and which prohibit drink-driving.

For all of the sexpatriates we have interviewed, the decision to migrate to the Dominican Republic was at least partially informed by their unwillingness to accept the authority of their home state, and in several cases, their move was urgently precipitated by their active refusal of this authority. Sometimes migration represented an attempt to escape prosecution for drugs or other offences, but more commonly sexpatriates are tax exiles from their own country (indeed, there is a

British-based organization called Scope, which provides members with information about tax avoidance schemes and tax havens as well as "sex havens"). A French-Canadian expatriate interviewed in Boca Chica is fairly typical of such men, if perhaps more unashamed than most about his desire to exercise white male privilege.

"Richard" worked as a real estate notary in Montreal until he pulled off a major deal in 1994. The Canadian government presented him with a tax bill for $200,000, so he put his money in a Swiss bank, bought a luxury yacht and left Canada for good. After cruising around the Caribbean for a couple of months, he ended up in the Dominican Republic, where he bought a bar. The bar he says, does not make money, "but I don't need money. It's just for fun." Richard loves the Dominican Republic:

> Here, the white man is king, everyone treats you like a king. You see, no one has forgotten Trujillo. It was a reign of terror, and everyone here, well, everyone over 60, they still tremble when a white man talks to them. . . . In Canada, we don't have so many blacks, but the Indians own the place. The whites are the second-class citizens in their own country because the Indians have all the rights now. Things are much better here, much better. This is really a racist country, everyone knows their place.

In his mid-50s, Richard is on his eighth wife, a Dominican woman in her 20s. This marriage will last he believes, because "In the Dominican Republic, women are slaves." They have to keep their husbands happy, or the men will beat them. So Richard is married, but free: "I can do what I want, and she can't say a thing. She doesn't have the right." Richard uses prostitutes and facilitates tourist-related prostitution by encouraging women and teenagers to solicit from his bar. He boasts that he is immune from prosecution by the Dominican authorities because he knows how to "do business" here:

> You have to understand it's corrupt from the top to the bottom. So you have to be in with the Dominicans, get a Dominican wife, make contacts, make some friends in the police and the military. You have to make your own security.

Richard's male bar staff are, he says, "fully armed," and this further adds to the impression that he views his bar as his own private fiefdom.

In interviews, hardcore male heterosexual sex tourists as well as sexpatriates emphasize contrasts between the burdens carried by the white male in "civilized" countries and the freedoms he enjoys in the Dominican Republic. A rather lengthy extract from an interview with an American sexpatriate and two of his sex-tourist friends (one of whom was a New Jersey police officer) shows how deeply disturbed such men are by legal and social changes which undermine what they see as their 'natural rights' in relation to women and racialized minority groups:

SEXPATRIATE: I'm 53 years old. Up in New York I've gotta screw 50-year-old women. Down here, 15 to 20 year olds, gorgeous women. . . . A friend of mine, he just threw out a 13-year-old girlfriend . . . [in the States] they've got laws. . . . I pay $1100 child support a month [to his American ex-wife] . . . 17 percent of your gross income for one child she gets, 25 percent for two, 33 percent for three. I've no idea what happens to men who have four kids. . . . Women's lib in America in the United States has killed marriage in America for any man who has brains. I wouldn't even marry a rich woman. . . . [Here] they're raised different. Women's lib hasn't hit here. . . .

SEX TOURIST A: In the States, [women] hire folks with cameras. They go to bed with cameras. If they wake up with a bruise, they take a picture of it. Call it abuse. Possible abuse.

SEXPATRIATE: In the United States, if you grab your wife like that, and you yell at her, put a little black blue mark, just a little one, she'll. . . .

SEX TOURIST A: When you've got a goddamn female announcing the NBA basketball game. These females go into the men's locker rooms, but the males cannot go into the ladies locker rooms. Most of these girls are dykes anyways. . . .

SEXPATRIATE: Oh yeah. She can call the police and say "He hit me. Didn't leave a bruise, but he hit me." And he never even punched her and he goes to jail. She can take a knife to him, and nothing.

SEX TOURIST B: Yeah, no marks, nothing. . . .

O'CD: Is it here like it was 40 years ago in the States?

SEX TOURIST A: 50 years ago. The worst thing that ever ever happened in the States was they gave women the right to vote.

SEXPATRIATE: The right to vote and the right to drive. . . .

O'CD: Is this what people mean when they talk about political correctness in America?

SEXPATRIATE: You can't use the N word, nigger. Always when I was raised up, the only thing was the F word, you can't use the F word. Now you can't say cunt, you can't say nigger. . . . There's just so many words I could use against women in the United States. I don't like white women. . . .

O'CD: What about black women in the States?

SEXPATRIATE: They're Americanized. They've all got their lawyer's number tattooed on their wrist just like the white women.

Read as a commentary on the social contract between the state and its citizens, this interview extract, as well as earlier quotes from Richard, suggest that hardcore sex tourists and sexpatriates are only really able to reconcile themselves to the authority of a state which is overtly patriarchal and white supremacist. Legal measures which accord even basic rights of self-sovereignty to women or non-whites are perceived as attacks upon the white male citizen's "natural rights," upon his selfhood, bodily integrity and honour. This response is clearly paranoid, but I do not think it can be dismissed as merely *individual* paranoia. Rather, I would argue that it has its basis in the contradictions of the liberal political theory that informs their worldview.

Bodies, "Natural Rights" and the "State of Nature"

Wellman (1997: 321) has commented on the increasing visibility of whiteness and maleness in the contemporary USA:

> Until recently, the categories "white" and "male" were taken for granted. . . . The taken for granted world of white male Americans, then, was their normalcy, not their whiteness or gender. As a result, the privileges that came with whiteness and masculinity were experienced as "normal," not advantages. But that is no longer possible. The normal has been made problematic by people of color and women, who have, through their visibility, challenged assumptions once taken for granted.

Similar developments are occurring in European societies, and are, at one level, a logical result of liberalism's rhetoric of universalism. Yet these developments also draw attention to the tension between that rhetoric of universal rights and liberalism's basis in a social contract that is gendered, classed and "raced." For many white European/North American men, the extension of universal rights to persons of colour and women is experienced as a loss of male sovereignty and selfhood. The sex tourists and sexpatriates under consideration here are certainly not alone in their disquiet, but they are distinguished by the fact that they attach such an immediate *erotic* significance to this sense of loss. This perhaps reflects their unusually intense anxiety about/fascination with matters corporeal (such as the ageing process, sexual functions and organs, phenotypical characteristics), something which may well be explained as a function of individual psychology and personal history.

At the same time, however, this anxiety/fascination resonates with the post-Enlightenment discourses about "nature" and "civilization" that perpetuated a Cartesian and Christian tradition which views the body as part of the physical world that must be controlled (see Seidler, 1987: 94). Where men are imagined as victims of biologically given heterosexual drives, control over male and female bodies can easily come to seem like a zero-sum game. Men can only control their own bodies if they can command control over women's bodies and access to women's bodies is thus one of the "natural" rights that the liberal state must guarantee men.

Equally, where a "racial" hierarchy is assumed to exist in nature, self-control over the white body entails dominance over Other bodies. The political and social order must ensure that Others pay white men their "natural" dues, not just by suffering themselves to be called "nigger," for example, but also by physically trembling when the white man speaks. Ferber (1999: 40) notes that under the Jim Crow system, it was commonly assumed that "a white boy doesn't become a man until he has had sexual relations with a black girl," and it seems to me that this too can be read as the physical exaction of a "natural" due. It is telling, therefore that the sexpatriate quoted above conjured with an image of equal rights as inscriptions on the body when he stated that black American women have "their lawyer's number tattooed on their wrist just like the white women."[3] Fantasies about the "Third World" as closer to a "state of nature" have to be understood in the context of these anxieties and discontents about the political order in the West. It is not a generalized nostalgia for a mythical past that informs these men's desires, but a wish to reclaim very specific powers. Hardcore sex tourists and sexpatriates see the Dominican Republic as a lawless and corrupt place ("There is no law here," they say), but it is simultaneously described as a place where "natural laws" operate. Thus, white men are feared, revered and obeyed by their "racial" and gender subordinates, while "naturally" promiscuous Dominican women and girls are available to meet the white man's "needs" uninhibited by European/North American codes of sexual morality, Here, then, white men can shed the burdens of First World "civilization," even as they retain all its economic and political privileges and collect their "natural" dues as "civilized" white men.

This leaves them in a position to make almost unlimited choices, and so to exercise quite extraordinary powers of sovereignty (their description of themselves as "kings" is, in this respect, not so very far-fetched). They are relieved of the burdens of civic responsibility beyond those that they choose for themselves. It is down to them to decide whether or not they provide economic support for the children they father, whether or not to beat their wives, or to leave bruises on women they sleep with, whether or not to mete out racist abuse, whether to pay prostitutes for the "services" they have "consumed" or to simply offer them a plate of lasagne, even whether or not to sexually abuse children. It is, in short, down to them to choose whether to harm or help their "natural" subordinates (Brace and O'Connell Davidson, 1996).

For these men, the exercise of power over "natural" subordinates does not appear to be simply an end in itself, however. As the following section will show, they are as concerned to establish and maintain "proper" relations among themselves as they are to reinstate traditional hierarchies of gender and "race." Again it will be argued that their preoccupations are perfectly consistent with traditional liberal discourses about selfhood and sovereignty.

SEX TOURISM AND THE "COMMUNITY"

In Sosua, Puerto Plata and Boca Chica, there are networks of European and North American heterosexual sexpatriates and sex tourists who visit regularly and/or for lengthy periods, whose ties to each other are both economic and social. They variously provide each other with custom, business, employment and/or services and enjoy a hard-drinking social life together. They "hang out" in bars, they gossip, they complain about the petty hardships they encounter in the Dominican Republic, give each other advice, reminisce together and generally enjoy a sense of collective inclusion in what would otherwise be an alien environment. These networks can loosely be termed "communities," and sexuality is pivotal to sex tourists' and sexpatriates' sense of collective inclusion. Rey Chow's (1999) discussion of community formation and the politics of admittance can be usefully applied here:

> As the etymological associations of the word 'community' indicate, community is linked to the articulation of commonality and consensus; a community is always based on a kind of collective inclusion. . . . At the same time, however, there is no community formation without the implicit understanding of who is and is not to be admitted. As the principle that regulates community formations, admittance operates in several crucial senses. There is first, admittance in the most physical sense of letting enter . . . to "let enter" is . . . closely connected with recognition and acknowledgement, which is the second major connotation of admittance. . . . Third, there is admittance in the sense of a confession—such as the admittance of a crime. Insofar as confession is an act of repentance, a surrender of oneself in reconciliation with the rules of society, it is also related to community. (1999: 35)

In the Dominican Republic, it is sexual contact with local women and teenagers which admits the male expatriate or tourist into the sex tourist "community" in the first two senses of admittance which Chow identifies. Take "Biggles," for example, a 52-year-old white Canadian sexpatriate living in Sosua. He first visited the country for a one-week holiday with a friend in 1990. At this point, he was not a habitual prostitute-user back home in Canada, nor did he travel to the Dominican Republic with the intention of sexually exploiting local women or children. Indeed, he had no particular desire to sexually experience the Other:

> I came down here . . . for a week and I stayed for a month. I came down with this guy, and as soon as we get down to the beach, he's got these two black girls, and I mean black. They weren't Dominican, they were Haitian. The blackest girls on the beach. And I said "no." I wasn't interested, I said I would never do that. . . . I'm not a bigot or anything but I just, I just don't, whatever, whatever. But hell, within the next couple of days I went with this girl and it was fantastic. . . . It was something I'd never done before. I don't know, I just thought, "Give it a try."

Biggles penetrated the "black girl" and entered the sex tourist "scene." So pleasing did he find the subculture of hardcore sex tourism that, over the next six years, he made repeated and regular visits to Sosua, always engaging in prostitute-use. In 1996, he decided to retire there, and his life now revolves entirely around this subculture.

Dominican women and girl's bodies are also often transacted between sexpatriates who own bar-brothels, or who make a living by procuring prostitutes for male tourists, and these exchanges also serve to establish and cement relationships between sexpatriates and sex tourists. Thus, for example, a 63-year-old white American expatriate who owns a beachside bar in Boca Chica explains that he gets "a lot of steady customers, a lot of guys that come here three, four, six, seven times a year." His bar, and photographs of its female bar staff, feature in the information on the Dominican Republic on TSM's website, and the owner is frequently referred to in the "chat" between members. He estimates that between 15 to 20 TSM members arrive at his bar each month and other American sex-patriates and sex tourists interviewed in Boca Chica described him as "the biggest pimp in town." In facilitating tourists' "entry" into Dominican women and teenagers, he simultaneously admits them to the sex tourist "community." They become "one of the guys."

Sexual contact with Dominican women and girls is also central to admittance in the sense that it provides the basis for recognition and acknowledgement between men. As one TSM member explains in a message board posting, he spent a great deal of time in his hotel bar in Boca Chica "bullshitting with guys" and "making friends":

> We are all there for the same carnal reason—[the] hotel is probably 95% single men—and a typical opening conversation would be—pointing at one of the girls—"have you been blown by her yet?"—"no, but I hear from so and so that she gives a great one." It makes for great comradery (TSM, posted 26 September 1997).

Another posting reads:

> Day 2. . . . I must comment on the fantastic camaraderie that was nurtured between Worm, Omega, Voodoo Chile and yours truly. It was just a whole lot of fun the whole time. And later we ran into Ronnie, Bogey, Pat, Newt, Jann, Digger, Woolf, JD and probably a couple more TSMers I can't remember. A quick breakfast . . . then down to . . . the beach . . . for a day in Paradise. Before I knew it, a large-breasted black woman in tight attire was grinning at me and massaging my back . . . At one point, I headed into the bathroom and before I knew it she was standing behind me at the toilet, trying to grab my dick. She wanted to suckee suckee me right then and there. (TSM, posted 11 January 1999)

And another:

> [The taxi] took me to the now infamous Ronnie's, upon entering I met some of the TSM crew. Omega (also known as Obi-wan, for his willingness to provide his invaluable wisdom to TSM newbies such as myself) . . . and of course Ronnie. After speaking to them for perhaps 5 minutes, I notice a cute girl enter the bar. She locked her gaze on me and promptly began to suck a bottle in a way not usually seen. Needless to say she had my undivided attention. I . . . inquire about her and whether Omega had any ad-

> vice . . . I proceeded to throw her over my shoulder and carry her out of the bar, [back] to the hotel, and . . . the fun was underway. (TSM, posted 10 January 1999)

In these and other similar postings, Boca Chica is constructed as a sexual playground for European/North American men, and Dominican women and girls as play-objects shared amongst them. The hardcore sex tourist's play-*mates,* that is, the subjects who give recognition and acknowledgement, are other European/North American men.

It is also worth noting that because admittance is predicated upon a common European/North American masculine identity and consensus about sexuality, it tends to nullify differences between sex tourists and sexpatriates in terms of age and class identity. Men in their 70s bond with men in their 20s and 30s; wealthier sexpatriates who own businesses socialize with the relatively poor sexpatriates who work for them; sex tourists who are police officers or scaffolders back home "have a whole lot of fun" with those who are senior accountants or company directors. The sense of group belonging comes from sharing the "natural" privileges of masculinity and whiteness, and sex tourists/sexpatriates enjoy the idea that they have secured a competitive advantage not just over local men, but also over the European/North American men who remain at home. As a 71-year-old American sex tourist told us:

> We all like to look like heroes. . . . Would I rather have a 70-year-old woman or an 18-year-old or a 25-year-old? Please. . . . You'll find very few men . . . that has done what I've done in the last 50 years. Right now they're all sitting in Hyde Park, feeding the pigeons.

This man is reliant on his sex tourist and sexpatriate friends to affirm this pleasing image. What good heroically fucking 18-year-olds while your contemporaries feed pigeons in a park if nobody of equal worth recognises this mark of your distinction?

Finally, I would argue that the hardcore sex tourist's impulse to divulge the details of his sexual experience (in conversations with other sex tourists/sexpatriates and in postings on internet sites) can be read as an attempt at group formation through admittance in Chow's third sense, that of confession:

> Little Ingris. . . . She isn't totally pro yet. I had her 3 times—my limit on a girl. . . . She is so tight that I broke 5 condoms on her and she was crying out something I've never heard before "*Tu Lance, ai ai*" over and over. . . . [Another] girl, broke 2 condoms on her. . . . After several screws I got her to do a posing session and used some of my toys with her, thank god 4 KY jelly. . . . I have some good poses of her for TSM.

I do not think such passages can be interpreted as acts of repentance, but they could be read as attempts at reconciliation with the rules of a subculture that bases membership and identity upon a shared willingness to reduce women and girls to sexual objects and to flout what are seen as repressive social strictures on heterosexual male sexuality (hardcore sex tourists fondly describe themselves as "bad boys"). In repeatedly confessing to his sexual transgressions, the sex tourist demonstrates himself to be "one of the guys." Homosexual acts cannot be confessed, of course, and male homosexuals are not admitted to the heterosexual male sex tourist "community." As one interviewee in Boca Chica put it, "Gays do come down here, but we don't have nothing to do with them."[4]

Thus far, I have been emphasizing the fact that "racially" Other female bodies serve as vehicles for relationships between European/North American male heterosexual sex tourists and sexpatriates in the Dominican Republic. Female bodies are exchanged, sometimes for money (as in the case of sexpatriates who organize prostitution), sometimes as free gifts (as in cases where sex tourists or sexpatriates "recommend" or share a woman/girl), and, as Rubin has observed, where "it is women who are being transacted, then it is the men who give and take them who are linked, the woman being a conduit of a relationship rather than a partner to it" (1975: 174).

It should also be clear that a hardcore sex tourist's worldview is nothing if not contradictory. They buy into overtly denigrating racisms, but women of colour are their chosen sexual objects. They say that women are the weaker sex, but berate them for the power they supposedly exercise over men. They are virulent homophobes, but are endlessly fascinated by the sex of other men. Let me now examine their urge to forge relationships with each other in relation to these contradictions and those implicit in the model of human sociality they accept.

DIFFERENCE AND INVASION

Late-19th-century and early-20th-century scientific discourses on race, gender and sexuality informed and buttressed one another (Somerville, 1997), and their legacy is conspicuous in overtly racist politics, which are invariably also sexist and homophobic politics. To the extent that biologically essentialist models of difference naturalize social and political inequalities based on gender and sexual orientation as well as "race," they can perhaps be said to inform an internally consistent worldview. But this *menage à trois* does not always appear to be a happy one. Indeed, essentialist understandings of gender and sexual difference seemingly pose huge problems for those whose imaginary communities are premised on notions of "race" sameness, problems which can become particularly acute during periods of social upheaval or change.[5]

The contradiction between men's perceived dependency upon women as mothers of "the race" and their dread of women's physical difference may be most visible in "racial" supremacist politics, but similar problems dog any model of community formation within which men establish links with each other through the exchange of women (see Chow, 1999). Wherever the traditional masculinist view that equates women with sex is accepted, women's relation to "the community" is necessarily difficult and ambiguous. Female sexuality and sexual difference is the key to maintaining the boundaries of community, not simply in the sense that women biologically reproduce its members, but also in the sense that, as objects of exchange between men, women serve to reproduce social links between the male members of the community. The ultimate taboo is thus the taboo against the sameness of men and women, for women's difference is vital to community formation (Chow, 1999; Freud, 1985; Rubin, 1975).

At the same time, however, female sexuality poses a profound threat to the boundaries of community. Since women are not actually objects, but only treated as such, their potential sexual agency is extremely dangerous. They could refuse:

> . . . their traditional position as "gifts," as the conduits and vehicles that facilitate social relations and enable group identity, [and] actually *give themselves.* By giving themselves, such women enter social relationships as active partners in the production of meanings rather than simply as the bearers of those meanings. (Chow, 1999:47–8)

If women break the taboo against the sameness of men and women by assuming sexual agency, they "no longer represent reliable conduits for men's relationships with each other and there is further a risk of boundary loss through acts of miscegenation" (Chow, 1999: 49). These anxieties are central to the worldview of hardcore male heterosexual sex tourists and sexpatriates. For these men, the legal construction of women as men's equals, combined with shifts to the traditional gendered division of labour, has broken this ultimate taboo. European/North American women claim male territory (they announce the NBA basketball game, they go into the men's locker rooms) and male rights (they call the police when beaten, they demand child support payments from absent fathers). They can no longer simply be treated as objects of exchange, and this has ramifications not just for European/North American men's relationships with European/North American women, but also for European/North American men's relationships with each other.

Without the certainty of sexual difference, all the laws and bonds of community that were based upon it are in jeopardy. As active agents in the production of community, women cannot be relied upon to reproduce a political order that these men are willing to contract into, indeed, they are likely to push for laws and law enforcement that conflict with, rather than protect, men's "natural rights." For hardcore sex tourists and sexpatriates, European/North American women's transgression of the fundamental taboo against the sameness of men and women also raises the spectre of another disastrous boundary loss, that between heterosexuality and homosexuality. Bishop and Robinson quote from a novel written by a Canadian expatriate who lives in Bangkok—"fucking a white woman is a step away from homosexuality" (Moore, 1993:107, cited in Bishop and Robinson, 1998: 167), and the same sentiment is reproduced in TSM postings on the subject of white women.

This draws attention to the relationship between taboos against the sameness of men and women and against homosexuality, and traditional liberal discourses about selfhood and sovereignty. Brace's (1997) discussion of Hobbes' vision of the "territorial" self is particularly useful here. Hobbes was preoccupied by the idea of a self that is vulnerable to invasion, a self "bounded by a hostile world it must seek to conquer and restrain":

> Hobbes encloses the self, the "rational inside" within a fortress, buttressed by our own sense of esteem and relating to others as outsiders or as absentees. Each person becomes a potential invader and a potential resistance fighter. We understand and experience our selfhood as enclosed, in need of protection against intrusion and invasion. . . . Each person may be a bounded sphere, but the boundary may prove fragile. Hobbes exhorts us to look at fully grown men "and consider how brittle the frame of our humane body is" . . . Hobbes's emphasis on the brittleness, the fragility of the human body is . . . central to male anxiety about boundary loss (1997: 143–4)

Brace goes on to note that the Hobbesian self, like McClintock's (1995) colonial self, is characterized by "dread of catastrophic boundary *loss* (implosion), associated with fears of impotence and infantalization and attended by an *excess* of boundary order and fantasies of unlimited power" (McClintock, 1995: 26). Imagining the self as territory and relations between selves in terms of invasion or conquest must, in sexual terms, translate into a fear of rape. If sex tourists imagine the Dominican Republic as close to a "state of nature," a space where fragile-bodied men are not constrained by any law, then their fantasies of conquest would simultaneously invoke the spectre of invasion and engulfment by other, stronger-bodied men. As well as shedding light on their obsessive fascination with each other as sexual beings, this, I believe, helps us to understand hardcore sex tourist/sexpatriates' impulse to forge links with each other in the Dominican Republic and other sites of sex tourism. The sexual objectification and exchange of women not only facilitates social relations and group identity, but also diffuses fears about homosexual invasion.

CONCLUSION

The subculture of male heterosexual sex tourism that has been considered in this article has grave consequences for the safety, health and well being of local women and girl children in the countries it targets. It also reveals something of the extent and chilling human consequences of global inequalities. Individual sexual agency is mediated through institutions of power, and the hardcore sex tourist's capacity to reclaim a particular vision of the European/North American Self through the sexual objectification of Others is predicated upon the existence of an equally particular economic, legal and political world order. And in terms of our understandings of the politics of "race," gender and sexuality in the West, the phenomenon of hardcore male heterosexual sex tourism sounds a warning bell, for the sense of loss which lies behind these sex tourists and sexpatriates' desires is not so very extraordinary. The same regrets, the same sense of being "away from the stars" can be found in speeches by right-wing politicians in North America and Europe and in the works of right-wing "think-tanks," newspaper editors and columnists and academics (for instance, Herrnstein and Murray, 1994; Murray, 1990), as well as in the publications of organizations like the UK Men's Movement (UKMM, 1999).

The men considered in this article are not differentiated from their more conventional right-wing compatriots by their preoccupation with European/North American notions of "civilization" and "nature," whiteness and blackness, maleness and femaleness, heterosexuality and homosexuality, merely by the fact that they seek to diffuse those tensions and reconcile contradictions through very specific sexual practices. Concluding her study of white supremacism in the USA, Ferber observes that "White supremacist discourse rearticulates dominant discourses on race and gender: therefore, any effective political response to the white supremacist movement must also attack these mainstream narratives" (1999: 156). The same point holds good in relation to the subculture of hardcore male heterosexual sex tourism.

NOTES

1. The interview data presented in this article was collected by Jacqueline Sanchez Taylor and the author in the course of ESRC funded research on tourist-related prostitution in the Caribbean.

2. See, for example, Hall's 1992 discussion of the debate between Thomas Carlyle and John Stuart Mill on Governor Eyre's reprisals against black Jamaicans following the 1865 Morant Bay riot, also Parekh, 1995.

3. See Elizabeth Grosz's discussion of Nietzsche and 'body inscription as the cultural condition for establishing social order and obedience' (1994: 129).

4. Men who seek sexual contact with boy children are the focus of particularly intense hostility from hardcore male heterosexual tourists, but the boundary between 'regular guys' and 'paedophiles' is less clear cut in relation to girl children.

5. See Theweleit's (1989) analysis of the writings of members of the German *Freikorps* in the 1920s, and Ferber's (1999) discussion of white supremacists in the contemporary USA.

REFERENCES

Bhattacharyya, G. (1997) 'The Fabulous Adventures of the Mahogany Princesses', in H. Mirza (ed.) *Black British Feminism.* London: Routledge.

Bishop, R. and Robinson, L. (1998) *Night Market: Sexual Cultures and the Thai Economic Miracle.* London: Routledge.

Brace, L. (1997) 'Imagining the Boundaries of a Sovereign Self', in L. Brace and J. Hoffman (eds) *Reclaiming Sovereignty,* pp. 137–54. London: Cassell.

Brace, L. and O'Connell Davidson, J. (1996) 'Desperate Debtors and Counterfeit Love: The Hobbesian World of the Sex Tourist', *Contemporary Politics* 2(3): 55–78.

Cassirer, B. (1992) *Travel & the Single Male.* Channel Island, CA: TSM.

Chow, R. (1999) 'The Politics of Admittance: Female Sexual Agency, Miscegenation, and the Formation of Community in Frantz Fanon', in A. Alessandrini (ed.) *Frantz Fanon: Critical Perspectives,* pp. 34–56. London: Routledge.

Clift, S. and Carter, S., eds (2000) *Tourism and Sex: Culture, Commerce and Coercion.* London: Pinter.

Dollimore, J. (1991) *Sexual Dissidence: Augustine to Wilde, Freud to Foucault.* Oxford: Clarendon Press.

Ferber, A. (1999) *White Man Falling: Race, Gender and White Supremacy.* New York: Rowman and Littlefield.

Freud, S. (1985 [1913]) 'Totem and Taboo', in Sigmund Freud *The Origins of Religion,* vol 13, pp. 43–224. Harmondsworth: Penguin.

Grosz, E. (1994) *Volatile Bodies: Toward a Corporeal Feminism.* Bloomington and Indianapolis: Indiana University Press.

Hall, C. (1992) *White, Male and Middle Class.* Cambridge: Polity.

Herrnstein, R. and Murray, C. (1994) *The Bell Curve: Intelligence and Class Structure in American Life.* New York: The Free Press.

Hobbes, T. (1968) *Leviathan.* Harmondsworth: Penguin.

Howard, D. (1999) *Dominican Republic.* London: Latin America Bureau.

Hughes, D. (1998/9) 'men@exploitation.com', *Trouble & Strife* 38: 21–27.

Ireland, K. (1993) *Wish You Weren't Here.* London: Save the Children.

Kruhse-MountBurton, S. (1995) 'Sex Tourism and Traditional Australian Male Identity', in M. Lanfant, J. Allcock and E. Bruner (eds) *International Tourism: Identity and Change.* London: Sage.

McClintock, A. (1995) *Imperial Leather: Race, Gender and Sexuality in the Colonial Contest.* London: Routledge.

Mercer, K. (1995) 'Busy in the Ruins of Wretched Phantasia', in R. Farr (ed.) *Mirage: Enigmas of Race, Difference and Desire.* London: ICA/Institute of International Visual Arts.

Mills, C. (1998) *The Racial Contract.* Ithaca: Cornell University Press.

Moore, C. (1993) *A Haunting Smile.* Bangkok: White Lotus Press.

Murray, C. (1990) *The Emerging British Underclass.* London: The IEA Health and Welfare Unit.

O'Connell Davidson, J. (1995) 'British Sex Tourists in Thailand', in M. Maynard and J. Purvis (eds), *(Hetero)sexual Politics,* pp. 42–64. London: Taylor & Francis.

O'Connell Davidson, J. (1996) 'Sex Tourism in Cuba', *Race & Class* 37(3): 39–48.

O'Connell Davidson, J. (1998) *Prostitution, Power and Freedom.* Cambridge: Polity.

O'Connell Davidson, J. and Sanchez Taylor, J. (1996) 'Child Prostitution and Sex Tourism', research papers 1–7. Bangkok: ECPAT.

Parekh, B. (1995) 'Liberalism and Colonialism: A Critique of Locke and Mill', in J. Nederveen and B. Parekh (eds) *The Decolonisation of Imagination: Culture, Knowledge and Power,* pp. 81–98. London: Zed.

Pateman, C. (1988) *The Sexual Contract.* Cambridge: Polity.

Pruitt, D. and LaFont, S. (1995) 'For Love and Money: Romance Tourism in Jamaica', *Annals of Tourism Research* 22(2): 422–40.

Puwar, N. (1999) 'Embodying the Body Politic: Race and Gender in the British State Elite', PhD thesis, University of Essex.

Rubin, G. (1975) 'The Traffic in Women: Notes on the "Political Economy" of Sex', in R. Reiter (ed.) *Toward an Anthropology of Women.* New York: Monthly Review Press.

Said, E. (1978) *Orientalism: Western Conceptions of the Orient.* Harmondsworth: Penguin.

Sanchez Taylor, J. (2000) 'Tourism and "Embodied" Commodities: Sex Tourism in the Caribbean', in S. Clift and S. Carter (eds) *Tourism and Sex: Culture, Commerce and Coercion,* pp. 41–53. London: Pinter.

Seabrook, J. (1996) *Travels in the Skin Trade: Tourism and the Sex Industry.* London: Pluto Press.

Seidler, V. (1987) 'Reason, Desire and Male Sexuality', in P. Caplan (ed.) *The Cultural Construction of Sexuality,* pp. 82–112. London: Routledge.

Somerville, S. (1997) 'Scientific Racism and the Invention of the Homosexual Body', in R. Lancaster and M. di Leonardo (eds) *The Gender/Sexuality Reader,* pp. 37–52. London: Routledge.

Theweleit, K. (1987) *Male Fantasies, Volume 1.* Cambridge: Polity.

Truong, T. (1990) *Sex, Money and Morality: Prostitution and Tourism in Southeast Asia.* London: Zed Books.

UKMM (1999) *UK Men's Movement Mission Statement* http://www.ukmm.org.net

Wellman, D. (1997) 'Minstrel Shows, Affirmative Action Talk, and Angry White Men: Marking Racial Otherness in the 1990s', in R. Frankenberg (ed.) *Displacing Whiteness,* pp. 311–331. London: Duke University Press.

WTO (World Tourism Organization) (1997) 'International Arrivals in the Americas 1996', cited in *Travel Weekly,* November 6.

21

The Globalization of Sexual Identities

DENNIS ALTMAN

Most of the literature about globalization and identity is concerned with the rebirth of nationalist, ethnic, and religious fundamentalism, or the decline of the labor movement.[1] (I am using "identity" to suggest a socially constructed myth about shared characteristics, culture, and history which comes to have real meaning for those who espouse it.)[2] Here I concentrate on the identity politics born of sexuality and gender, and the new social movements which arise from these. These new identities are closely related to the larger changes of globalization: consider the globalization of "youth," and the role of international capitalism in creating a teenage identity in almost every country, with specific music, language, fashion, and mores.[3] In recent years this is expressed in terms of "boy" and "girl" cultures, as in references to "boy bands" or "a booming girl culture worldwide,"[4] which suggests the invention of an intermediate generational identity between "children" and "youth."

Over the past decade I've been researching and thinking about the diffusion of certain sorts of "gay/lesbian" identities, trying to trace the connections between globalization and the preconditions for certain sexual subjectivities.[5] My examples are drawn predominantly from Southeast Asia because this is the part of the "developing" world I know best, but they could even more easily be drawn from Latin America, which has a particularly rich literature exploring these questions.[6] The question is not whether homosexuality exists—it does in almost every society of which we know—but how people incorporate homosexual behavior into their sense of self. Globalization has helped create an international gay/lesbian identity, which is by no means confined to the western world: there are many signs of what we think of as "modern" homosexuality in countries such as Brazil, Costa Rica, Poland, and Taiwan. Indeed the gay world—less obviously the lesbian, largely due to marked differences in women's social and economic status—is a key example of emerging global "subcultures," where members of particular groups have more in common across national and continental boundaries than they do with others in their own geographically defined societies.

It is worth noting that even within the "first world" there is a range of attitudes toward the assertion of gay/lesbian identities. While they have flourished in the English-speaking countries and in parts of northern Europe, there is more resistance to the idea in Italy and France, where ideas of communal rights—expressed through the language of multiculturalism in Australia and Canada, and through a somewhat different tradition of religious pluralism in the Netherlands and Switzerland—seem to run counter to a universalist rhetoric of rights, which are not equated with the recognition of separate group identities.[7] The United States shares both traditions, so that its gay and lesbian movement argues for recognition of "civil rights" on the basis of being just like everyone else, and in some cases deserving of special protection along the lines developed around racial and gender discrimination.

At the same time the United States has gone farthest in the development of geographically based gay and lesbian communities, with defined areas of its large cities—the Castro in San Francisco, West Hollywood, Halsted in Chicago, the West Village in New York—becoming urban "ghettos," often providing a base to develop the political clout of the community. (In almost all large American cities politicians now recognize the importance of the gay vote.) This model has been replicated in a number of western countries, whether it is the Marais in Paris or Darlinghurst in Sydney. There is some irony in the fact that, while homosexual rights have progressed much further in the countries of northern Europe, the United States remains the dominant cultural model for the rest of the world.

This dominance was symbolized in accounts in Europe of "gay pride" events in the summer of 1999, which often ignored national histories and attributed the origins of gay political activism to the Stonewall riots of 1969, ignoring the existence of earlier groups in countries such as Germany, the Netherlands, Switzerland, and France, and the radical gay groups which grew out of the 1968 student movements in both France and Italy. (Stonewall was a gay bar in New York City which was raided by the police, leading to riots by angry homosexuals and the birth of the New York Gay Liberation Front.) In cities as diverse as Paris, Hamburg, and Warsaw the anniversary of Stonewall was celebrated with Christopher Street Day, and the dominance of American culture is summed up by the press release from the Lisbon Gay, Lesbian, Bisexual, and Transgender Pride committee boasting of the performances of a "renowned DJ from New York City" and "Celeda—the Diva Queen from Chicago."

Thinking and writing about these questions, it became clear to me that observers, indigenous and foreign alike, bring strong personal investments to how they understand what is going on, in particular whether (in words suggested to me by Michael Tan) we are speaking of "ruptures" or "continuities." For some there is a strong desire to trace a continuity between precolonial forms of homosexual desire and its contemporary emergence, even where the latter might draw on the language of (West) Hollywood rather than indigenous culture. Such views are argued strenuously by those who cling to an identity based on traditional assumptions about the links between gender performance and sexuality, and deny the relevance of an imported "gay" or "lesbian" identity for themselves. Thus the effeminate *bakkla* in the Philippines or the *kathoey* in Thailand might see those who call themselves "gay" as hypocrites, in part because they insist on their right to behave as men, and to desire others like them.[8] For others there is a perception that contemporary middle-class self-proclaimed gay men and lesbians in, say, New Delhi, Lima, or Jakarta have less in common with "traditional" homosexuality than they do with their counterparts in western countries. As Sri Lankan author Shaym Selvadurai said of his novel *Funny Boy,* which is in part about "coming out" as gay: "The people in the novel are in a place that has been colonized by Western powers for 400 years. A lot of Western ideas—bourgeois respectability, Victorian morality—have become incorporated into the society, and are very much part of the Sri Lankan society."[9]

"Modern" ways of being homosexual threaten not only the custodians of "traditional" morality, they also threaten the position of "traditional" forms of homosexuality, those which are centered around gender nonconformity and transvestism. The title of the Indonesian gay/lesbian journal *Gaya Nusantara,* which literally means "Indonesian style," captures this ambivalence nicely with its echoes of both "traditional" and "modern" concepts of nation and sexuality, but at the same time it is clearly aimed at "modern" homosexuals rather than the "traditional" transvestite *waria.*[10]

It is often assumed that homosexuals are defined in most "traditional" societies as a third sex, but that too is too schematic to be universally useful. As Peter Jackson points out, the same terms in Thailand can be gender *and* sexual categories.[11] Here, again, we are confronted by considerable confusion, where similar phenomena can be viewed as either culturally specific or as universal. Insofar as there is a confusion between sexuality and gender in the "traditional" view that the "real" homosexual is the man who behaves like a woman (or, more rarely, vice versa) this is consistent with the dominant understanding of homosexuality in western countries during the hundred years or so before the birth of the contemporary gay movement. The idea of a "third sex" was adopted by people like Ulrichs and Krafft-Ebing as part of an apologia for homosexuality (giving rise to Carpenter's "intermediate sex").[12] In the 1918 novel *Despised and Rejected* the hero laments: "What had nature been about, in giving him the soul of a woman in the body of a man?"[13] Similar views can be found in Radclyffe Hall's novel *The Well of Loneliness* (1928), whose female hero calls herself Stephen. Today many people who experience homosexual desires in societies which do not allow space for them will see themselves as "men trapped in women's bodies" or vice versa.

In popular perceptions something of this confusion remains today—and persists in much popular humor, such as the remarkably successful play/film *La cage aux folles* (*The Birdcage*) or the film *Priscilla, Queen of the Desert.* George Chauncey argues that the very idea of a homosexual/heterosexual divide became dominant in the United States only in the mid-twentieth century: "The most striking difference between the dominant sexual culture of the early twentieth century and that of our own era is the degree to which the earlier culture permitted men to engage in sexual relations with other men, often on a regular basis, without requiring them to regard themselves—or be regarded by others—as gay. . . . Many men . . . neither understood nor organised their sexual practices along a hetero-homosexual axis."[14] John Rechy's landmark novel *City of Night* (1963) captures the transition to "modern" concepts: his world is full of "hustlers," "queens," "masculine" or "butch" homosexuals, whom he sometimes calls "gay."[15]

If one reads or views contemporary accounts of homosexual life in, say, Central America, Thailand, and Côte d'Ivoire,[16] one is immediately struck by the parallels. It is of course possible that the observers, all of whom are trained in particular ethnographic and sociological methods, even where, as in the case of Schifter they are indigenous to the country of study, are bringing similar—and one assumes unconscious—preconceptions with them. Even so, it is unlikely that this itself would explain the degree of similarity they identify. In the same way, the Dutch anthropologist Saskia Wieringa has pointed to the similarities of butch-femme role-playing in Jakarta and Lima, and how they echo that of preliberation western lesbian worlds.[17] In many "traditional" societies there were complex variations across gender and sex lines, with "transgender" people (Indonesian *waria,* Thai *kathoey,* Moroccan *hassas,* Turkish *kocek,* Filipino *bayot,* Luban *kitesha* in parts of Congo) characterized by both transvestite and homosexual behavior. These terns are usually—not always—applied to men, but there are other terms sometimes used of women, such as *mati* in Suriname, which also disrupt simplistic assumptions about sex and gender.[18] As Gilbert Herdt says: "Sexual orientation and identity are not the keys to conceptualizing a third sex and gender across time and space."[19] In many societies there is confusion around the terms—for example the *hijras* of India, who were literally castrated, are sometimes considered equivalent to homosexuals even though the reality is more complex.[20]

Different people use terms such as *bayot* or *waria* in different ways, depending on whether the emphasis is on gender—these are men who wish in some way to be women—or on sexuality—these are men attracted to other men. Anthropology teaches us the need to be cautious about any sort of binary system of sex/gender; Niko Besnier uses the term "gender liminality" to avoid this trap[21] and it should also alert us against the sort of romanticized assumptions that some Americans have brought to understanding the Native American *bedarche.*[22] Besnier also stresses that such "liminality" is not the same as homosexuality. "Sexual relations with men are seen as an optional consequence of gender liminality, rather than its determiner, prerequisite or primary attribute."[23] The other side of this distinction is that there are strong pressures to define *fa'afafine* (the Samoan term) or other such groups in Pacific countries as asexual, thus leading to a particular denial in which both Samoans and outsiders are complicit.[24]

Certainly most of the literature about Latin America stresses that a homosexual *identity* (as distinct from homosexual practices) is related to rejection of dominant gender expectations, so that "a real man" can have sex with other men and not risk his heterosexual identity. As Roger Lancaster put it: "Whatever else a *cochon* might or might not do, he is tacitly understood as one who assumes the receptive role in anal intercourse. His partner, defined as 'active' in the terms of their engagement, is not stigmatized, nor does he acquire a special identity of any sort."[25] Thus the *nature* rather than the *object* of the sexual act becomes the key factor. However, there is also evidence that this is changing, and a more western concept of homosexual identity is establishing itself, especially among the middle classes.

Sexuality becomes an important arena for the production of modernity, with "gay" and "lesbian" identities acting as markers for modernity.[26] There is an ironic echo of this in the Singapore government's bulldozing of Bugis Street, once the center of transvestite prostitution in the city—and its replacement by a Disneyland-like simulacrum where a few years ago I was taken to see a rather sanitized drag show presented to a distinctly yuppie audience.[27] There is an equal irony in seeing the decline of a homosexuality defined by gender nonconformity as a "modern" trend just when transsexuals and some theorists in western countries are increasingly attracted by concepts of the malleability of gender.[28] From one perspective the fashionable replica of the stylized "lipstick lesbian" or "macho" gay man is less "post-modern" than the *waria* or the Tongan *fakaleiti*.[29]

Perhaps the reality is that androgyny is postmodern when it is understood as performance, not when it represents the only available way of acting out certain deep-seated beliefs about one's sexual and gender identity. Even so, I remain unsure just why "drag," and its female equivalents, remains a strong part of the contemporary homosexual world, even where there is increasing space for open homosexuality and a range of acceptable ways of "being" male or female. Indeed there is evidence that in some places there is a simultaneous increase in both gay/lesbian identities *and* in transgender performance, as in recent developments in Taiwan where drag shows have become very fashionable, and some of the performers, known as "third sex public relations officers," insist that they are not homosexual even when their behavior would seem to contradict this.[30] Similar comments could probably be made about *onnabe,* Japanese women who dress as men and act as the equivalent of geishas for apparently heterosexual women, and Jennifer Robertson describes the incorporation of androgyny into the " 'libidinal' economy of the capitalist market" as "gender-bending" performers are turned into marketable commodities.[31] In the west it has become increasingly fashionable to depict transvestism in unmistakably heterosexual terms; what was daring (and possibly ambiguous) in the 1959 film *Some Like It Hot* becomes farce in the 1993 film *Mrs. Doubtfire.*[32] But at the same time there is, particularly in the United States, the emergence of a somewhat new form of transgender politics, in which the concern of an older generation to be accepted as the woman or man they "really" are is replaced by an assertion of a transgender identity and the malleability of gender.[33] (Western writers tend to be reasonably careful to distinguish between *transsexual* and *transvestite.* However, this distinction is often not made in parts of Asia and, I assume, other parts of the world.)

Speaking openly of homosexuality and transvestism, which is often the consequence of western influence, can unsettle what is accepted but not acknowledged. Indeed there is some evidence in a number of societies that those who proclaim themselves "gay" or "lesbian," that is, seek a public identity based on their sexuality, encounter a hostility which may not have been previously apparent. But there is a great deal of mythology around the acceptance of gender/sexual nonconformity outside the west, a mythology to which for different reasons both westerners and nonwesterners contribute. Romanticized views about homoeroticism in many nonwestern cultures, often based on travel experiences, disguise the reality of persecution, discrimination, and violence, sometimes in unfamiliar forms. Firsthand accounts make it clear that homosexuality is far from being universally accepted—or even tolerated—in such apparent "paradises" as Morocco, the Philippines, Thailand, or Brazil: "Lurking behind the Brazilians' pride of their flamboyant drag queens, their recent adulation of a transvestite chosen as a model of Brazilian beauty, their acceptance of gays and lesbians as leaders of the country's most widely practised religion and the constitutional protection of homosexuality, lies a different truth. Gay men, lesbians and transvestites face widespread discrimination, oppression and extreme violence."[34]

Just as the most interesting postmodern architecture is found in cities like Shanghai or Bangkok, so too the emphasis of postmodern theory on pastiche, parody, hybridity, and so forth is played out in a real way by women and men who move, often with considerable comfort, from apparent obedience to official norms to their own sense of gay community. The dutiful Confucian or Islamic Malaysian son one weekend might appear in drag at Blueboy, Kuala Lumpur's gay bar, the next—and who is to say which is "the real" person? Just as many Malaysians can move easily from one language to another, so most urban homosexuals can move from one style to another, from camping it up with full awareness of the latest fashion trends from Castro Street to playing the dutiful son at a family celebration.

To western gay liberationists these strategies might seem hypocritical, even cowardly (and some westerners expressed surprise at the apparent silence from Malaysian gay men after the arrest of Anwar on sodomy charges). But even the most politically aware Malaysians may insist that there is no need to "come out" to their family, while explaining that in any case their lover is accepted as one of the family—though not so identified. (The Malaysian situation is further complicated by the fact that Muslims are subject to both civil and *sharia* laws, and the latter have been used quite severely, against transvestites in particular.) Some people have suggested that everything is possible *as long as it is not stated,* but it is probably more complex than that. For many men I have met in Southeast Asia being gay does mean a sense of communal identity, and even a sense of "gay pride," but this is not necessarily experienced in the vocabulary of the west.

Middle-class English-speaking homosexuals in places like Mexico City, Istanbul, and Mumbai will speak of themselves as part of a gay (sometimes "gay and lesbian") community, but the institutions of such a community will vary considerably depending on both economic resources and political space. Thus in Kuala Lumpur, one of the richer cities of the "developing" world, there are no gay or lesbian bookstores, restaurants, newspapers, or businesses—at least not in the open way we would expect them in comparable American or European cities. There is, however, a strong sense of gay identity around the AIDS organization Pink Triangle—its name is emblematic—and sufficient networks for a gay sauna to open and attract customers. Yet when a couple of years ago I gave some copies of the Australian gay magazine *Outrage* to the manager of the Kuala Lumpur sauna, I was told firmly there could be no display of something as overtly homosexual as these magazines—which are routinely sold by most Australian newsagents. In the same way there is also a strong lesbian network in the city, and many women use office faxes and email to arrange meetings and parties.

At that same sauna I met one man who told me he had heard of the place through a friend now living in Sydney. In conversations I have had with middle-class gay men in Southeast Asia there are frequent references to bars in Paris and San Francisco, to Sydney's Gay and Lesbian Mardi Gras, to American gay writers. Those who take on gay identities often aspire to be part of global culture in all its forms, as suggested by this quote from a Filipino anthology of gay writing: "I met someone in a bar last Saturday . . . He's a bank executive. He's mestizo (your type) and . . . loves Barbra Streisand, Gabriel Garcia Marquez, Dame Margot Fonteyn, Pat Conroy, Isabel Allende, John Williams, Meryl Streep, Armistead Maupin, k. d. lang, Jim Chappell, Margaret Atwood and Luciano Pavarotti."[35]

Similarly magazines like *G & L* in Taiwan—a "lifestyle" magazine launched in 1996—mix local news and features with stories on international, largely American, gay and lesbian icons. As mobility increases, more and more people are traveling abroad and meeting foreigners at home. It is as impossible to prevent new identities and categories traveling as it is to prevent pornography traveling across the Internet.

As part of the economic growth of south and east Asia the possibilities of computer-based communications have been grasped with enormous enthusiasm, and have created a new set of possibilities for the diffusion of information and the creation of (virtual) communities. Whereas the gay movements of the 1970s in the west depended heavily on the creation of a gay/lesbian press, in countries such as Malaysia, Thailand, and Japan the Internet offers the same possibilities, with the added attraction of anonymity and instant contact with overseas, thus fostering the links with the diaspora already discussed. Work by Chris Berry and Fran Martin suggests that the Internet has become a crucial way for young homosexuals to meet each other in Taiwan and Korea—and in the process to develop a certain, if privatized, form of community.[36] In Japan the Internet has become a central aid to homosexual cruising.

It is precisely this constant dissemination of images and ways of being, moving disproportionately from north to south, which leads some to savagely criticize the spread of sexual identities as a new step in neocolonialism: "The very constitution of a subject entitled to rights involves the violent capture of the disenfranchised by an institutional discourse which inseparably weaves them into the textile of global capitalism."[37] This position is argued with splendid hyperbole by Pedro Bustos-Aguilar, who attacks both "the gay ethnographer . . . [who] kills a native with the charm of his camera" and "the union of the New World Order and Transnational Feminism" which asserts neocolonialism and western hegemony in the name of supposed universalisms.[38]

Bustos-Aguilar's argument is supported by the universalist rhetoric which surrounded the celebration of the twenty-fifth anniversary of Stone-wall, but he could have had great fun with a 1993 brochure from San Francisco which offered "your chance to make history . . . [at] the first ever gay & lesbian film festival in India & parallel queer tour"—and even more with the reporter from the *Washington Blade* who wrote of Anwar's "ostensibly being gay."[39] It finds a troubling echo in the story of an American, Tim Wright, who founded a gay movement in Bolivia, and after four years was found badly beaten and amnesiac: "And things have gone back to being what they were."[40]

A more measured critique comes from Ann Ferguson, who has warned that the very concept of an international lesbian *culture* is politically problematic, because it would almost certainly be based upon western assumptions, even though she is somewhat more optimistic about the creation of an international *movement,* which would allow for self-determination of local lesbian communities.[41] While western influences were clearly present, it is as true to see the emergence of groups in much of Latin America, in Southeast Asia, and among South African blacks as driven primarily by local forces.

It is certainly true that the assertion of gay/lesbian identity can have neocolonial implications, but given that many anti/postcolonial movements and governments deny existing homosexual traditions it becomes difficult to know exactly whose values are being imposed on whom. Both the western outsider and the local custodians of national culture are likely to ignore existing realities in the interest of ideological certainty. Those outside the west tend to be more aware of the difference between traditional homosexualities and contemporary gay identity politics, a distinction sometimes lost by the international gay/lesbian movement in its eagerness to claim universality.[42] New sexual identities mean a loss of certain traditional cultural comforts while offering new possibilities to those who adopt them, and activists in nonwestern countries will consciously draw on both traditions. In this they may be inconsistent, but no more than western gay activists who simultaneously deploy the language of universal rights and special group status.

In practice most people hold contradictory opinions at the same time, reminding us of Freud's dictum that "it is only in logic that contradictions cannot exist." There are large numbers of men and fewer women in non-western countries who will describe themselves as "gay" or "lesbian" in certain circumstances, while sometimes claiming these labels are inappropriate to their situation. It is hardly surprising that people want both to identify with and to distinguish themselves from a particular western form of homosexuality, or that they will call upon their own historical traditions to do so. This ambivalence is caught in this account by a Chinese-Australian: "[Chinese] gays were determined to advance their cause but in an evolutionary rather than revolutionary way. They seized on issues such as gayness, gay culture, gay lifestyle, equal rights for gays and so on. In romantic poems the gay dreams of our ancestors were represented by two boys sharing a peach and the emperor who cut his sleeves of his gown rather than disturb his lover sleeping in his arms. To revive this dream, and enable millions of Chinese-born gays to choose their lifestyle, is a huge task. But it has happened in Taiwan, as it did in Hong Kong, and so it will in China."[43]

There are of course examples of Asian gay groups engaging in political activity of the sort associated with their counterparts in the west. Indonesia has a number of gay and lesbian groups, which have now held three national meetings. The best-known openly gay figure in Indonesia, Dede Oetomo, was a candidate of the fledgling Democratic People's Party in the 1999 elections, which followed the overthrow of Suharto. There have been several small radical gay political groups established in the Philippines in recent years, and gay demonstrations have taken place in Manila. ProGay (the Progressive Organization of Gays in the Philippines), as its name suggests, is concerned to draw links between specifically gay issues and larger questions of social justice.[44] The first lesbian conference was held in Japan in 1985,[45] and there have been lesbian organizations in Taiwan since 1990 and the Philippines since 1992.[46] The international lesbigay press carried reports of a national conference of lesbians in Beijing in late 1998 and in Sri Lanka the following year. There have been several *tongzhi* gatherings in Hong Kong (a term adopted to cover "lesbians, bisexuals, gays and transgendered people"), and a manifesto adopted by the 1996 meeting argued that "[c]ertain characteristics of confrontational politics, such as through coming out and mass protests and parades may not be the best way of achieving *tongzhi* liberation in the family-centred, community-oriented Chinese societies which stress the importance of social harmony."[47] (An odd myth, given the revolutionary upheavals in twentieth-century China.) None of these groups have the history or the reach of gay/lesbian movements in Latin America, where Brazil, Argentina, Chile, and Mexico all have significant histories of a politicized homosexuality.

In many cases homosexual identities are asserted without an apparent gay/lesbian movement. In 1998 there was a move by bar owners in Kuala Lumpur to organize a gay-pride party which was canceled after a protest by the Malaysian Youth Council. The best example of a nonpolitical gay world can probably be found in Thailand, where there is a growing middle-class gay world, based neither on prostitution nor on traditional forms of gender non-conformity (as in the person of the *kathoey*), but only a small lesbian group, Anjaree, and no gay male groups at all since the collapse of a couple of attempts to organize around HIV in the late 1980s.[48] In late 1996 controversy erupted in Thailand after the governing body of the country's teacher-training colleges decreed that "sexual deviants" would be barred from entering the colleges. While there was considerable opposition to the ban (subsequently dropped), other than Anjaree most of this came from nongay sources. In the ensuing public debate one could see contradictory outside influences at work—both an imported fear of homosexuals and a more modern emphasis on how such a ban infringed human rights. As Peter Jackson concluded: "A dynamic gay scene has emerged . . . in the complete absence of a gay rights movement."[49]

Indeed it may be that a political movement is the least likely part of western concepts of homosexual identity to be adopted in many parts of the world, even as some activists enthusiastically embrace the mores and imagery of western queerdom. The particular form of identity politics which allowed for the mobilization of a gay/lesbian electoral pressure in countries like the United States, the Netherlands, and even France may not be appropriate elsewhere, even if western-style liberal democracy triumphs. The need of western lesbian/gays to engage in identity politics as a means of enhancing self-esteem may not be felt in other societies. Even so, one should read Jackson's comment about Thailand with some caution. Already when he wrote it there was an embryonic group in Bangkok around an American-owned and -run gay bookstore. At the end of 1999 one of the country's gay papers organized a gay festival and twilight parade in the heart of Bangkok, announcing it as "the first and biggest gay parade in Asia where Asian gay men have a basic human right to be who they want to be and love who they want to love."[50] Similarly, accounts of homosexual life in Japan alternate between assuming a high degree of acceptance—and therefore no reason for a political movement—and severe restrictions on the space to assert homosexual identity, though the gay group OCCUR has recently gained a certain degree of visibility.

The western gay/lesbian movement emerged in conditions of affluence and liberal democracy, where despite other large social issues it was possible to develop a politics around sexuality, which is more difficult in countries where the basic structures of political life are constantly contested.[51] Writing of contemporary South Africa Mark Gevisser notes: "Race-identification overpowers everything else—class, gender and sexuality."[52] In the same way basic questions of political economy and democratization will impact the future development of gay/lesbian movements in much of Asia and Africa. Yet in Latin America and eastern Europe gay/lesbian movements have grown considerably in the past decade, and there are signs of their emergence in some parts of Africa, for example in Botswana and in Zimbabwe, where President Mugabe has consistently attacked homosexuality as the product of colonialism.[53] Similar rhetoric has come from the leaders of Kenya,[54] Namibia, and Uganda, whose President Museveni has denounced homosexuality as "western"—using the rhetoric of the Christian right to do so.[55] Anglican bishops from Africa—though not South Africa—were crucial in defeating moves to change the Church of England's attitudes toward homosexuality at the 1998 decennial Lambeth Conference. South Africa is a crucial exception, perhaps because apartheid's denunciation of homosexuality made it easier for the African National Congress to develop a policy of acceptance as part of their general support for "a rainbow nation." Even so, some elements of the ANC are strongly homophobic, revealed in the rhetoric of many of Winnie Mandela's supporters.[56]

While many African officials and clergy maintain that homosexuality is not part of precolonial African culture, the evidence for its existence—and the slow acknowledgment of its role in African life—is emerging across the continent. One might speculate that the strong hostility from some African political and religious leaders toward homosexuality as a "western import" is an example of psychoanalytic displacement, whereby anxieties about sexuality are redirected to continuing resentment against colonialism and the subordinate position of Africa within the global economy. Western-derived identities can easily become markers of those aspects of globalization which are feared and opposed. Similarly, a 1994 conference for gay/MSMs (men who have sex with men) in Bombay was opposed by the National Federation of Indian Women, an affiliate of the Communist party of India, as "an invasion of India by decadent western cultures and a direct fall-out of our signing the GATT agreement."[57] Whether the federation was aware of how close its rhetoric was to right-wing Americans such as Patrick Buchanan is unknown.

Part of the appearance of modernity is the use of western languages. Rodney Jones has noted the importance of English as part of the cultural capital of Hong Kong homosexuals,[58] and when I attended an AIDS conference in Morocco in 1996 participants complained that despite an attempt to ensure equal use of Arabic it was "easier" to talk about sexuality in French. A similar emphasis on English is noted by James Farrar in presumably heterosexual discos in Shanghai, where ironically the Village People song "YMCA" has now become "a globalized dance ritual in which the dancers are encouraged to use their hands to make shapes of the English letters, identifying themselves momentarily with a boundless global ecumene of sexy happy youth 'at the YMCA.'"[59] One assumes the Shanghai dancers are unaware of the clearly gay overtones to both the song and the group. I admit to particular pleasure in reading this piece; an early proposal for my book *The Homosexualization of America* was rejected by an editor who complained (this was in 1982) that in a year no one would remember the Village People, the image with which I began that book.

A common language is essential for networking, and the past twenty years have seen a rapid expansion of networks among lesbian and gay groups across the world. In 1978 the International Lesbian and Gay Association (ILGA) was formed at a conference in Coventry, England.[60] While ILGA has largely been driven by northern Europeans, it now has member groups in more than seventy countries and has organized international meetings in several southern cities. Other networks, often linked to feminist and AIDS organizing, have been created in the past two decades, and emerging lesbian and gay movements are increasingly likely to be in constant contact with groups across the world. The inspiration from meeting with other lesbians at international women's conferences has been a powerful factor in the creation of lesbian groups in a number of countries. Thus the Asian Lesbian Network, which now includes women from twelve or thirteen countries, began at an International Lesbian Information Service conference in Geneva in 1986.[61]

In recent years there has been some attempt to promote international networking among transgendered people—or, as Americans now call them, transfolk—with both the British-based International Gender Transient Affinity and the U.S.-based Gender Freedom International lobbying to protect transgendered people across the world from what seems to be routine harassment and persecution. The paradox of globalization is played out in constructions of sex/gender which combine the premodern with the modern, so that people identifying with "traditional" forms of transgender identity will employ modern techniques of surgery and hormone therapy to alter their bodies.

The two largest international gay/lesbian institutions are probably those based around the Metropolitan Community Church and the Gay Games. The MCC is a Protestant sect founded by the Reverend Troy Perry in Los Angeles in 1968, whose congregations and ministers are largely homosexual, with an estimated congregation of more than 40,000 in some sixteen countries. Similar gay churches have emerged somewhat independently in several other societies such as South Africa and Mexico.[62] The Gay Games, modeled on the Olympics, which refused the use of its name, were first held in San Francisco in 1982, and have since become a major international event every four years, for which cities contend very bitterly. They also generate considerable international publicity, much of it of a somewhat voyeuristic nature.[63] Both of these "networks," it is worth stressing, originated in the United States.

Homosexuality becomes a particularly obvious measure of globalization, for the transformation of local regimes of sexuality and gender is often most apparent in the emergence of new sorts of apparently "gay" and "lesbian," even "queer," identities. Yet we must beware reading too much into these scripts. What is happening in Bangkok, Rio, and Nairobi is the creation of new forms of understanding and regulating the sexual self, but it is unlikely that they will merely repeat those forms which were developed in the Atlantic world. Walking through the "gay" area of Tokyo's Shinjuku you will see large numbers of young men in sneakers and baseball caps (or whatever happens to be the current "gay" look) but this does not mean they will behave or view themselves in the same way as equivalent young men in North America or northern Europe. . . .

NOTES

1. E.g., Frances Fox Piven, "Globalizing Capitalism and the Rise of Identity Politics," In L. Panitch, ed., *Socialist Register* (London: Merlin, 1995), 102–16; Leslie Sklair, "Social Movements and Global Capitalism," in F. Jameson and M. Miyoshi, eds., *The Cultures of Globalization* (Durham: Duke University Press, 1998), 291–311; Kaldor, *New and Old Wars,* 76–86.

2. For a clear exposition of this view of social constructionism see Jeffrey Weeks, *Sexuality and Its Discontents* (London: Routledge & Kegan Paul, 1985).

3. E.g., Beverley Hooper, "Chinese Youth: The Nineties Generation," *Current History* 90:557 (1991):264–69.

4. See Sherrie Inness, ed., *Millennium Girls* (Lanham, MD: Rowman & Littlefield, 1999); Marion Leonard, "Paper Planes: Travelling the New Grrrl Geographies," in T. Skelton and G. Valentine, eds., *Cool Places: Geographies of Youth Cultures* (London: Routledge, 1998), 101–18.

5. Much of this section draws on work originally published in the mid-1990s. See especially Dennis Altman, "Rupture or Continuity? The Internationalization of Gay Identities," *Social Text* 14:3 (1996): 77–94; Altman, "On Global Queering," *Australian Humanities Review,* no. 2, July 1996 (electronic journal, www.lib.latrobe.edu.au); Altman, "Global Gaze/Global Gays." *GLQ* 3 (1997): 417–36.

6. See the bibliography in Balderston and Guy, *Sex and Sexuality in Latin America,* 259–77; the chapters on Brazil and Argentina in B. Adam, J. W. Duyvendak, and A. Krouwel, eds., *The Global Emergence of Gay and Lesbian Politics* (Philadelphia: Temple University Press, 1999); and the special issue of *Culture, Health, and Society* (1:3 [1999]) on "alternative sexualities and changing identities among Latin American men," edited by Richard Parker and Carlos Carceres.

7. For a discussion of the French position see David Caron, "Liberté, Egalité, Sero-positivité: AIDS, the French Republic, and

the Question of Community," in Boule and Pratt, "AIDS in France," 281–93. On the Netherlands see Judith Schuyf and Andre Krouwel, "The Dutch Lesbian and Gay Movement: The Politics of Accommodation," in Adam, Duyvendak, and Krouwel, *Global Emergence of Gay and Lesbian Politics,* 158–83. On Australia see Dennis Altman, "Multiculturalism and the Emergence of Lesbian/Gay Worlds," in R. Nile, ed., *Australian Civilisation* (Melbourne: Oxford University Press, 1994), 110–24.

8. I owe thanks to a long list of people who over the years have discussed these issues with me, including Ben Anderson, Eufracio Abaya, Hisham Hussein, Lawrence Leong, Shivananda Khan, Peter Jackson, Julian Jayaseelan, Ted Nierras, Dede Oetomo, and Michael Tan.

9. Jim Marks, "The Personal Is Political: An Interview with Shaym Selvadurai," *Lambda Book Report* (Washington) 5:2 (1996): 7.

10. The original Indonesian term was *banci.* The term *waria* was coined in the late 1970s by combining the words for "woman" and "man." See Dede Oetomo, "Masculinity in Indonesia," in R. Parker, R. Barbosa, and P. Aggleton, eds., *Framing the Sexual Subject* (Berkeley: University of California Press, 2000), 58–59 n. 2.

11. See Peter Jackson, "Kathoey⟩⟨Gay⟩⟨Man: The Historical Emergence of Gay Male Identity in Thailand," in Manderson and Jolly, *Sites of Desire,* 166–90.

12. See Jeffrey Weeks, *Coming Out* (London: Quartet, 1977); John Lauritsen and David Thorstad, *The Early Homosexual Rights Movement* (New York: Times Change Press, 1974).

13. A. T. Fitzroy, *Despised and Rejected* (London: Gay Men's Press, 1988; originally published 1918), 223.

14. George Chauncey, *Gay New York* (New York: Basic Books, 1994), 65.

15. John Rechy, *City of Night* (New York: Grove, 1963).

16. E.g., Annick Prieur, *Mema's House, Mexico City* (Chicago: University of Chicago Press, 1998); Jacobo Schifter, *From Toads to Queens* (New York: Haworth, 1999); Peter Jackson and Gerard Sullivan, eds., *Lady Boys, Tom Boys, Rent Boys* (New York Haworth, 1999); *Woubi Cheri,* (1998), directed by Philip Brooks and Laurent Bocahul.

17. Saakia Wieringa, "Desiring Bodies or Defiant Cultures: Butch-Femme Lesbians in Jakarta and Lima," in E. Blackwood and S. Wieringa, eds., *Female Desires: Same-Sex Relations and Transgender Practices across Cultures* (New York: Columbia University Press, 1999), 206–29.

18. Gloria Wekker, "What's Identity Got to Do with It? Rethinking Identity in Light of the Mati Work in Suriname," in Blackwood and Wieringa, *Female Desires,* 119–38. Compare the very complex typologies of "same-sex" groups in Murray and Roscoe, *Boy-Wives and Female Husbands,* 279–82, and the chapter by Rudolph Gaudio on "male lesbians and other queer notions in Hausa," 115–28.

19. Herdt, *Third Sex, Third Gender,* 47.

20. See Serena Nanda, "The Hijras of India: Cultural and Individual Dimensions of an Institutionalized. Third Gender Role," in E. Blackwood, ed., *The Many Faces of Homosexuality* (New York: Harrington Park Press, 1986), 35–54. And read her comments in light of Shivananda Khan, "Under the Blanket: Bisexualities and AIDS in India," in Aggleton, *Bisexualities and AIDS,* 161–77.

21. See Niko Besnier, "Polynesian Gender Liminality through Time and Space," in Herdt, *Third Sex, Third Gender,* 285–328. Note that the subtitle of Herdt's book is "Beyond Sexual Dimorphism in Culture and History.".

22. See Ramon Gutierrez, "Must We Deracinate Indians to Find Gay Roots?" *Outlook* (San Francisco), winter 1989, 61–67.

23. Besnier, "Polynesian Gender Liminality," 300.

24. See Lee Wallace, "*Fa'afafine: Queens of Samoa* and the Elision of Homosexuality," *GLQ* 5:1 (1999): 25–39.

25. Roger Lancaster, "'That We Should All Turn Queer?' Homosexual Stigma in the Making of Manhood and the Breaking of Revolution in Nicaragua," in Parker and Gagnon, *Conceiving Sexuality,* 150.

26. See Henning Bech, *When Men Meet: Homosexuality and Modernity* (Chicago: University of Chicago Press, 1997); Kenneth Plummer, *The Making of the Modern Homosexual* (London: Hutchinson, 1981); Seidman, *Difference Troubles.*

27. See Laurence Wai-teng Leong, "Singapore," in West and Green, *Sociolegal Control of Homosexuality,* 134: and the remarkable Singapore film *Bugis Street* (1995), directed by Yon Fan—remarkable for having been made at all.

28. E.g., Sandy Stone, "The Empire Strikes Back: A Posttranssexual Manifesto," in P. Treichler, L. Cartwright, and C. Penley, eds., *The Visible Woman* (New York: New York University Press, 1998), 285–309.

29. See Niko Besnier, "Sluts and Superwomen: The Politics of Gender Liminality in Urban Tonga," *Ethnos* 62:1–2 (1997): 5 31.

30. Thanks to Arthur Chen of the AIDS Prevention and Research Center, Taipei, for this information.

31. Jennifer Robertson, *Takarazuka: Sexual Politics and Popular Culture in Modern Japan* (Berkeley: University of California Press, 1998), 207.

32. For some of the complications in reading cinematic versions of cross-dressing see Marjorie Garber, *Vested Interests* (New York: Routledge, 1992).

33. See Leslie Feinberg, *Transgender Warriors* (Boston: Beacon, 1996); Kate Bornstein, *Gender Outlaw* (New York: Routledge, 1993).

34. Sereine Steakley, "Brazil Can Be Tough and Deadly for Gays," *Bay Windows* (Boston), June 16, 1994.

35. Jerry Z. Torres, "Coming Out," in N. Garcia and D. Remoto, eds., *Ladlad: An Anthology of Philippine Gay Writing* (Manila: Anvil, 1994), 128.

36. Chris Berry and Fran Martin, "Queer'n'Asian on the Net: Syncretic Sexualities in Taiwan and Korean Cyberspaces," *Inqueeries* (Melbourne), June 1998, 67–93.

37. Pheng Cheah, "Posit(ion)ing Human Rights in the Current Global Conjuncture," *Public Culture* 9 (1997): 261.

38. Pedro Bustos-Aguilar, "Mister Don't Touch the Banana," *Critique of Anthropology* 15:2 (1995): 149–70.

39. Kai Wright, "Industrializing Nations Confront Budding Movement," *Washington Blade,* October 23, 1998.

40. Pedro Albornoz, "Landlocked State," *Harvard Gay and Lesbian Review* 6:1 (1999): 17.

41. Ann Ferguson, "Is There a Lesbian Culture?" in J. Allen, ed., *Lesbian Philosophies and Cultures* (Albany: State University of New York Press, 1990), 63–88.

42. See, e.g., the interview by William Hoffman with Mumbai activist Ashok Row Kavi, *Poz,* July 1998, which proclaims him "the Larry Kramer of India."

43. Bing Yu, "Tide of Freedom," *Capital Gay* (Sydney), May 1, 1998.

44. In July 1999 the paper ManilaOUT listed over twenty gay, lesbian, and "gay and lesbian-friendly" organizations in Manila.

45. Naeko, "Lesbian = Woman," in B. Summerhawk et al., eds., *Queer Japan* (Norwich, VT: New Victoria Publishers, 1998), 184–87.

46. Malu Marin, "Going beyond the Personal." *Women in Action* (ISIS International Manila) 1 (1996): 58–62.

47. Manifesto of Chinese Tongzhi Conference, Hong Kong, December 1996. Thanks to Graham Smith for providing this source.

48. See Andrew Matzner, "Paradise Not," *Harvard Gay and Lesbian Review* 6:1 (winter 1999): 42–44.

49. Peter Jackson, "Beyond Bars and Boys: Life in Gay Bangkok," *Outrage* (Melbourne), July 1997, 61–63.

50. Statement from *Male* magazine, quoted in *Brother/Sister* (Melbourne), September 16, 1999, 51.

51. There is a similar argument in Barry Adam, Jan Willem Duyvendak, and Andre Krouwel, "Gay and Lesbian Movements beyond Borders?" in Adam, Duyvendak, and Krouwel, *Global Emergence of Gay and Lesbian Politics,* 344–71.

52. Mark Gevisser, "Gay Life in South Africa," in Drucker, *Different Rainbows:* 116.

53. Dean Murphy, "Zimbabwe's Gays Go 'Out' at Great Risk," *Los Angeles Times,* July 27, 1998.

54. For one view of the situation in Kenya see Wanjira Kiama, "Men Who Have Sex with Men in Kenya," in Foreman, *AIDS and Men,* 115–26.

55. Chris McGreal, "Gays Are Main Evil, Say African Leaders." *Guardian Weekly,* October 7–13, 1999, 4.

56. See Carl Stychin, *A Nation by Rights* (Philadelphia: Temple University Press, 1998), chap. 3.

57. *Times of India.* November 9, 1994, quoted by Sherry Joseph and Pawan Dhall, "No Silence Please, We're Indians!" in Drucker, *Different Rainbows:* 164.

58. Rodney Jones, "'Potato Seeking Rice': Language, Culture, and Identity in Gay Personal Ads in Hong Kong," *International Journal of the Sociology of Language* 143 (2000): 31–59.

59. James Farrar, "Disco 'Super-Culture': Consuming Foreign Sex in the Chinese Disco," *Sexualities* 2:2 (1999): 156.

60. John Clark, "The Global Lesbian and Gay Movement," in A. Hendriks, R. Tielman, and E. van der Veen, eds., *The Third Pink Book* (Buffalo: Prometheus Books, 1993), 54–61.

61. "The Asian Lesbian Network," *Breakout* (newsletter of Can't Live in the Closet, Manila) 4:3–4 (1998): 13.

62. On South Africa see Graeme Reid, "'Going Back to God, Just as We Are': Contesting Identities in the Hope and Unity Metropolitan Community Church," *Development Update* (Johannesburg) 2:2 (1998): 57–65. For a discussion of a gay church in Azcapotzalco, on the outskirts of Mexico City, see "Living la Vida Local." *Economist,* December 18, 1999, 85–87.

63. Coverage of the 1994 games in New York by the Brazilian press is discussed in Charles Klein, "'The Ghetto Is Over, Darling': Emerging Gay Communities and Gender and Sexual Politics in Contemporary Brazil," *Culture, Health, and Society* 1:3 (1999): 239–41.

22

Becoming 100% Straight

MICHAEL A. MESSNER

In 1995, as part of my job as the President of the North American Society for the Sociology of Sport, I needed to prepare a one-hour long Presidential Address for the annual meeting of some 200 people. This presented a challenge to me: how might I say something to my colleagues that was challenging, at least somewhat original, and above all, not boring. Students may think that their professors are especially boring in the classroom, but believe me, we are usually much worse at professional meetings. For some reason, many of us who are able to speak to our students in the classroom in a relaxed manner, and using relatively jargon-free language, seem at these meetings to become robots, dryly reading our papers—packed with impressively unclear jargon—to our yawning colleagues.

Since I desperately wanted to avoid putting 200 sport studies scholars to sleep, I decided to deliver a talk which I entitled "studying up on sex." The title, which certainly did get my colleagues' attention, was intended as a play on words—a double entendre. "Studying up" has one, generally recognizable colloquial meaning, but in sociology, it has another. It refers to studying "up" in the power structure. Sociologists have perhaps most often studied "down"— studied the poor, the blue or pink-collar workers, the "nuts, sluts and perverts," the incarcerated. The idea of "studying up" rarely occurs to sociologists unless and until we are living in a time when those who are "down" have organized movements that challenge the institutional privileges of elites. So, for instance, in the wake of labor movements, some sociologists like C. Wright Mills studied up on corporate elites. And recently, in the wake of racial/ethnic civil rights movements, some scholars like Ruth Frankenberg have begun to study the social meanings of "whiteness." Much of my research, inspired by feminism, has involved a studying up on the social construction of masculinity in sport. Studying up, in these cases, has raised some fascinating new and important questions about the workings of power in society.

However, I realized, when it comes to understanding the social and interpersonal dynamics of sexual orientation in sport, we have barely begun to scratch the surface of a very complex issue. Although sport studies has benefited from the work of scholars like Helen Lenskyj, Brian Pronger and others who have delineated the experiences of lesbians and gay men in sports, there has been very little extension of these scholars' insights into a consideration of the social construction of heterosexuality in sport. In sport, just as in the larger society, we seem obsessed with asking "how do people become gay?" Imbedded in this question is the assumption that people who identify as heterosexual, or "straight," require no explanation, since they are simply acting out the "natural" or "normal" sexual orientation. It's the "sexual deviants" who require explanation, we seem to be saying, while the experience of heterosexuals, because we are considered normal, seems to require no critical examination or explanation. But I knew that a closer look at the development of sexual orientation or sexual identity reveals an extremely complex process. I decided to challenge myself and my colleagues by arguing that although we have begun to "study up" on corporate elites in sport, on whiteness, on masculinity, it is now time to extend that by studying up on heterosexuality.

But in the absence of systematic research on this topic, where could I start? How could I explore, raise questions about, and begin to illuminate the social construction of heterosexuality for my colleagues? Fortunately, I had for the previous two years been working with a group of five men (three of whom identified as heterosexual, two as gay) who were mutually exploring our own biographies in terms of our earlier bodily experiences that helped to shape our gender and sexual identities. We modeled our project after that of a German group of feminist women, led by Frigga Haug, who created a research method which they call "memory work." In short, the women would mutually choose a body part, such as "hair," and each of them would then write a short story, based on a particularly salient childhood memory that related to their hair (for example, being forced by parents to cut your hair, deciding to straighten one's curly hair, in order to look more like other girls, etc.). Then, the group would read all of the stories and discuss them one-by-one, with the hope of gaining some more general understanding of, and raising new questions about, the social construction of "femininity." What resulted from this project was a fascinating book called *Female Sexualization,* which my men's group used as an inspiration for our project.

As a research method, memory work is anything but conventional. Many sociologists would argue that this is not really a "research method" at all, because the information that emerges from the project can't be used very confidently as a generalizable "truth," and especially because in this sort of project, the researcher is simultaneously part of what is being studied. How, my more scientifically oriented colleagues might ask, is the researcher to maintain his or her objectivity in this project? My answer is that in this kind of research, objectivity is not the point. In fact, the strength of this sort of research is the depth of understanding that might be gained through a systematic group analysis of one's experience, one's *subjective* orientation to social processes. A clear understanding of the subjective aspect of social life—one's bodily feelings, emotions, and reactions to others—is an invaluable window that allows us to see and ask new sociological questions about group interaction and social structure. In short, group memory work can provide an important, productive, and fascinating insight into aspects of social reality, though not a complete (or completely reliable) picture.

So, as I pondered the lack of existing research on the social construction of heterosexuality in sport, I decided to draw on one of my own stories from my memory work men's group. Some of my most salient memories of embodiment are sports memories. I grew up the son of a high school coach, and I eventually played point guard on my dad's team. In what follows, I juxtapose one of my stories with that of a gay former Olympic athlete, Tom Waddell, whom I had interviewed several years earlier for a book that I wrote on the lives of male athletes.

TWO SEXUAL STORIES

Many years ago I read some psychological studies that argued that even for self-identified heterosexuals, it is a natural part of their development to have gone through "bisexual" or even "homosexual" stages of life. When I read this, it seemed theoretically reasonable, but it did not ring true in my experience. I have always been, I told myself, 100% heterosexual! The group process of analyzing my own autobiographical stories challenged this conception I had developed of myself, and also shed light on the way that the institutional context of sport provided a context for the development of my definition of myself as "100% straight." Here is one of the stories.

> When I was in the 9th grade, I played on a "D" basketball team, set up especially for the smallest of high

> school boys. Indeed, though I was pudgy with baby fat, I was a short 5′2″, still pre-pubescent with no facial hair and a high voice that I artificially tried to lower. The first day of practice, I was immediately attracted to a boy I'll call Timmy, because he looked like the boy who played in the Lassie TV show. Timmy was short, with a high voice, like me. And like me, he had no facial hair yet. Unlike me, he was very skinny. I liked Timmy right away, and soon we were together a lot. I noticed things about him that I didn't notice about other boys: he said some words a certain way, and it gave me pleasure to try to talk like him. I remember liking the way the light hit his boyish, nearly hairless body. I thought about him when we weren't together. He was in the school band, and at the football games, I'd squint to see where he was in the mass of uniforms. In short, though I wasn't conscious of it at the time, I was infatuated with Timmy—I had a crush on him. Later that basketball season, I decided—for no reason that I could really articulate then—that I hated Timmy. I aggressively rejected him, began to make fun of him around other boys. He was, we all agreed, a geek. He was a faggot.
>
> Three years later, Timmy and I were both on the varsity basketball team, but had hardly spoken a word to each other since we were freshmen. Both of us now had lower voices, had grown to around 6 feet tall, and we both shaved, at least a bit. But Timmy was a skinny, somewhat stigmatized reserve on the team, while I was the team captain and starting point guard. But I wasn't so happy or secure about this. I'd always dreamed of dominating games, of being the hero. Halfway through my senior season, however, it became clear that I was not a star, and I figured I knew why. I was not aggressive enough.
>
> I had always liked the beauty of the fast break, the perfectly executed pick and roll play between two players, and especially the long twenty-foot shot that touched nothing but the bottom of the net. But I hated and feared the sometimes brutal contact under the basket. In fact, I stayed away from the rough fights for rebounds and was mostly a perimeter player, relying on my long shots or my passes to more aggressive teammates under the basket. But now it became apparent to me that time was running out in my quest for greatness: I needed to change my game, and fast. I decided one day before practice that I was gonna get aggressive. While practicing one of our standard plays, I passed the ball to a teammate, and then ran to the spot at which I was to set a pick on a defender. I knew that one could sometimes get away with setting a face-up screen on a player, and then as he makes contact with you, roll your back to him and plant your elbow hard in his stomach. The beauty of this move is that your own body "roll" makes the elbow look like an accident. So I decided to try this move. I approached the defensive player, Timmy, rolled, and planted my elbow deeply into his solar plexus. Air exploded audibly from Timmy's mouth, and he crumbled to the floor momentarily.
>
> Play went on as though nothing had happened, but I felt bad about it. Rather than making me feel better, it made me feel guilty and weak. I had to admit to myself why I'd chosen Timmy as the target against whom to test out my new aggression. He was the skinniest and weakest player on the team.

At the time, I hardly thought about these incidents, other than to try to brush them off as incidents that made me feel extremely uncomfortable. Years later, I can now interrogate this as a *sexual* story, and as a *gender* story unfolding within the context of the heterosexualized and masculinized institution of sport. Examining my story in light of research conducted by Alfred Kinsey a half-century ago, I can recognize in myself what Kinsey saw as a very common **fluidity and changeability of sexual desire over the life-course.** Put simply, Kinsey found that large numbers of adult, "heterosexual" men had previously, as adolescents and young adults, experienced sexual desire for males. A surprisingly large number of these men had experienced sexual contact to the point of orgasm with other males during adolescences or early adulthood. Similarly, my story invited me to consider what is commonly called the **"Freudian theory of bisexuality."** Sigmund Freud shocked the post-Victorian world by suggesting that all people go through a stage, early in life, when they are attracted to people of the same sex. Adult experiences, Freud argued, eventually led most people to shift their sexual desire to what Freud called an appropriate "love object"—a person of the opposite sex. I also considered my experience in light of what lesbian feminist author Adrienne Rich called **institution of compulsory heterosexuality.** Perhaps the extremely high levels of homophobia that are often endemic in boys' and men's organized sports led me to deny and repress my own homoerotic desire through a direct and overt rejection of Timmy, through homophobic banter with male peers, and through the resultant stigmatization of the feminized Timmy. And eventually, I considered my experience in light of what the radical theorist Herbert Marcuse called the **sublimation of homoerotic desire** into an aggressive, violent act as serving to construct a clear line of demarcation between self-and-other. Sublimation, according to Marcuse, involves the driving underground, into the unconscious, of sexual desires that might appear dangerous due to their socially stigmatized status. But sublimation involves more than simple repression into the unconscious—it involves a transformation of sexual desire into something else—often into aggressive and violent acting out toward others, acts that clarify boundaries between one's self and others and therefore lessen any anxieties that might be attached to the repressed homoerotic desire.

Importantly, in our analysis of my story, my memory group went beyond simply discussing the events in psychological terms. My story did suggest some deep psychological processes at work, perhaps, but it also revealed the importance of social context—in this case, the context of the athletic team. In short, my rejection of Timmy and the joining with teammates to stigmatize him in ninth grade stands as an example of what sociologist R. W. Connell calls a **moment of engagement with hegemonic masculinity,** where I actively took up the male group's task of constructing heterosexual/masculine identities in the context of sport. The elbow in Timmy's gut three years later can be seen as a punctuation mark that occurred precisely because of my fears that I might be failing at this goal.

It is helpful, I think, to compare my story with gay and lesbian "coming out" stories in sport. Though we have a few lesbian and bisexual coming out stories among women athletes, there are very few gay male coming out stories. Tom Waddell, who as a closeted gay man finished sixth in the decathlon in the 1968 Olympics, later came out and started the Gay Games, an athletic and cultural festival that draws tens of thousands of people every four years. When I interviewed Tom Waddell over a decade ago about his sexual identity and athletic career, he made it quite clear that for many years sports *was* his closet. Tom told me,

> When I was a kid, I was tall for my age, and was very thin and very strong. And I was usually faster than most other people. But I discovered rather early that I liked gymnastics and I liked dance. I was very interested in being a ballet dance . . . [but] something became obvious to me right away—that male ballet dancers were effeminate, that they were what most people would call faggots. And I thought I just couldn't handle that . . . I was totally closeted and very concerned about being male. This was the fifties, a terrible time to live, and everything was stacked against me. Anyway, I realized that I had to do something to protect my image of myself as a male—because at that time homosexuals were thought of primarily as men who wanted to be women. And so I threw myself into athletics—I played football, gymnastics, track and field. . . . I was a jock—that's how I was viewed, and I was comfortable with that.

Tom Waddell was fully conscious of entering sports and constructing a masculine/heterosexual athletic identity precisely because he feared being revealed as gay. It was clear to him, in the context of the 1950s, that being revealed as gay would undercut his claims to the status of manhood. Thus, though he described the athletic closet as "hot and stifling," he remained in the closet until several years after his athletic retirement. He even knowingly played along with locker room discussions about sex and women, knowing that this was part of his "cover":

> I wanted to be viewed as male, otherwise I would be a dancer today. I wanted the male, macho image of an athlete. So I was protected by a very hard shell. I was clearly aware of what I was doing . . . I often felt compelled to go along with a lot of locker room garbage because I wanted that image—and I know a lot of others who did too.

Like my story, Waddell's story points to the importance of the athletic institution as a context in which peers mutually construct and re-construct narrow definitions of masculinity—and heterosexuality is considered to be a rock-solid foundation of this conception of masculinity. But unlike my story, Waddell's story may invoke what sociologist Erving Goffman called a "dramaturgical analysis": Waddell seemed to be consciously "acting" to control and regulate others' perceptions of him by constructing a public "front stage" persona that differed radically from what he believed to be his "true" inner self. My story, in contrast, suggests a deeper, less consciously strategic repression of my homoerotic attraction. Most likely, I was aware on some level of the dangers of such feelings, and was escaping the dangers, disgrace, and rejection that would likely result from being different. For Waddell, the decision to construct his identity largely within sport was a decision to step into a fiercely heterosexual/masculine closet that would hide what he saw to be his "true" identity. In contrast, I was not so much stepping into a "closet" that would hide my identify—rather, I was stepping out into an entire world of heterosexual privilege. My story also suggests how a *threat* to the promised privileges of hegemonic masculinity—my failure as an athlete—might trigger a momentary sexual panic that could lay bare the constructedness, indeed, the *instability* of the heterosexual/masculine identity.

In either case—Waddell's or mine—we can see how, as young male athletes, heterosexuality and masculinity were not something we "were," but something we were *doing*. It is very significant, I think, that as each of us was "doing heterosexuality," neither of us was actually "having sex" with women (though one of us desperately wanted to!). This underscores a point made by some recent theorists, that heterosexuality should not be thought of simply as sexual acts between women and men; rather, **heterosexuality is a constructed identity, a performance, and an institution** that is not necessarily linked to sexual acts. Though for one of us it was more conscious than for the other, we were both "doing heterosexuality" as an ongoing practice through which we sought (a) to avoid stigma, embarrassment, ostracism, or perhaps worse if we were even suspected of being gay; and (b) to link ourselves into systems of power, status, and privilege that appear to be the birthright of "real men" (i.e., males who are able to successfully compete with other males in sport, work, and sexual relations with women). In other words, each of us actively scripted our own sexual/gender performances, but these scripts were constructed within the constraints of a socially organized (institutionalized) system of power and pleasure.

QUESTIONS FOR FUTURE RESEARCH

As I prepared to tell my above sexual story publicly to my colleagues at the sport studies conference. I felt extremely nervous. Part of the nervousness was due to the fact that I knew some of my colleagues would object to my claim that telling personal stories can be a source of sociological insights. But a larger part of the reason for my nervousness was due to the fact that I was revealing something very personal about my sexuality in such a public way. Most of us aren't used to doing this, especially in the context of a professonal conference. But I had learned long ago, especially from feminist women scholars, and from gay and lesbian scholars, that biography is linked to history, and that part of "normal" academic discourse has been to hide "the personal" (including the fact that the researcher is himself or herself a person, with values, feelings, and, yes, biases) behind a carefully constructed facade of "objectivity." Rather than trying to hide—or be ashamed of—one's subjective experience of the world, I was challenging myself to draw on my experience of the world as a resource. Not that I should trust my experience as the final word on "reality"—white, heterosexual males like myself have made the mistake for centuries of calling their own experience "objectivity," and then punishing anyone who does not share their world view as "deviant." Instead, I hope to use my experience as an example of how those of us who are in dominant sexual/racial/gender/class categories can get a new perspective on the "constructedness" of our identities by juxtaposing our subjective experiences against the recently emerging world views of gay men and lesbians, women, and people of color.

Finally, I want to stress that, juxtaposed, my and Tom Waddell's stories do not shed much light on the question of why some individuals "become" gay while others "become" heterosexual or bisexual. Instead, I'd like to suggest that this is a dead-end question, and that there are far more important and interesting questions to be asked:

- How has heterosexuality, as an institution and as an enforced group practice, constrained and limited all of us—gay, straight, and bi?

- How has the institution of sport been an especially salient institution for the social construction of heterosexual masculinity?
- Why is it that when men play sports they are almost always automatically granted masculine status, and thus assumed to be heterosexual, while when women play sports, questions are raised about their "femininity" and their sexual orientation?

These kinds of questions aim us toward an analysis of the workings of power within institutions—including the ways that these workings of power shape and constrain our identities and relationships—and point us toward imagining alternative social arrangements that are less constraining for everyone.

REFERENCES

Haug, Frigga. 1987. *Female Sexualization: A Collective Work of Memory.* London: Verso.

Katz, Jonathan Ned. 1995. *The Invention of Heterosexuality.* New York: Dutton.

Messner, Michael A. 1992. *Power at Play: Sports and the Problem of Masculinity.* Boston: Beacon Press.

———. 1994. "Gay Athletes and the Gay Games: An interview with Tom Waddell," in M. A. Messner & D. F. Sabo (Eds.), *Sex, Violence and Power in Sports: Rethinking Masculinity* (pp. 113–119). Freedom, CA: The Crossing Press.

Pronger, Brian. 1990. *The Arena of Masculinity: Sports, Homosexuality, and the Meaning of Sex.* New York: St. Martin's Press.

23

"Americans Have a Different Attitude"

Family, Sexuality, and Gender in Filipina American Lives

YEN LE ESPIRITU

> I want my daughters to be Filipino especially on sex. I always emphasize to them that they should not participate in sex if they are not married. We are also Catholic. We are raised so that we don't engage in going out with men while we are not married. And I don't like it to happen to my daughters as if they have no values. I don't like them to grow up that way, like the American girls.
>
> —*Filipina immigrant mother*

> I found that a lot of the Asian American friends of mine, we don't date like White girls date. We don't sleep around like White girls do. Everyone is really mellow at dating because your parents were constraining and restrictive.
>
> —*Second generation Filipina daughter*

Drawing from my research on Filipino American families in San Diego, California, this paper explores the ways in which racialized immigrants claim through gender the power denied them through racism. Gender shapes immigrant identity and allows racialized immigrants to assert cultural superiority over the dominant group. For Filipino immigrants who come from a homeland that was once a U.S. colony, cultural reconstruction has been a way to counter the cultural Americanization of the Philippines, to resist the assimilative and alienating demands of U.S. society, and to reaffirm to themselves their self-worth in the face of colonial, racial, and gendered subordination.

The opening narratives above, made by a Filipina immigrant mother and a second generation Filipina daughter, suggest that the virtuous Filipina daughter is partially constructed on the conceptualization of white women as sexually immoral. They also reveal the ways in which women's sexuality—and their enforced "morality"—is fundamental to the structuring of social inequalities. Historically, the sexuality of racialized women has been systematically demonized and denigrated by dominant or oppressor groups to justify and bolster nationalist movements, colonialism, and/or racism. But as the above narratives indicate, racialized groups also castigate the morality of white women as a strategy of resistance—a means to assert a morally superior public face to the dominant society. But this strategy is not without costs. The elevation of Filipina chastity (particularly that of young women) has the effect of reinforcing masculinist and patriarchal power in the name of a greater ideal of national/ethnic self-respect. Because the control of women is one of the principal means of asserting moral superiority, young

Reprinted by permission of the author.

women in immigrant families face numerous restrictions on their autonomy, mobility, and personal decision making.

STUDYING FILIPINOS IN SAN DIEGO

The information on which this article is based come mostly from original research: in-depth interviews that I conducted with about one hundred Filipinos in San Diego. As in other Filipino communities along the Pacific Coast, the San Diego community grew dramatically in the twenty-five years following passage of the 1965 Immigration Act. In 1990, there were close to 96,000 Filipinos in San Diego County. Although they comprised only 4 percent of the county's general population, they constituted close to 50 percent of the Asian American population (Espiritu 1995). Many post-1965 Filipinos have come to San Diego as professionals—most conspicuously as health care workers. A 1992 analysis of the socio-economic characteristics of recent Filipino immigrants in San Diego indicated that they were predominantly middle class, college-educated, and English-speaking professionals who were much more likely to own rather than rent their homes (Rumbaut 1994).

Using the "snowball" sampling technique, I started by interviewing Filipino Americans whom I knew and then asking them to refer me to others who might be willing to be interviewed. In other words, I chose participants not randomly but rather through a network of Filipino American contacts whom the first group of respondents trusted. To capture as much as possible the diversity within the Filipino American community, I sought and selected respondents of different backgrounds and with diverse viewpoints. The interviews, tape-recorded in English, ranged from three to ten hours each and took place in offices, coffee shops, and homes. My questions were open-ended and covered three general areas: family and immigration history, ethnic identity and practices, and community development among San Diego's Filipinos. The interviewing process varied widely: some respondents needed to be prompted with specific questions, while others spoke at great length on their own. Some chose to cover the span of their lives; others focused on specific events that were particularly important to them.

CONSTRUCTING THE DOMINANT GROUP: THE MORAL FLAWS OF WHITE AMERICANS

In this section, I argue that female morality—defined as women's dedication to their families and sexual restraints—is one of the few sites where economically and politically dominated groups can construct the dominant group as "other" and themselves as superior. Because womanhood is idealized as the repository of tradition, the norms which regulate women's behaviors become a means of determining and defining group status and boundaries. As a consequence, the burdens and complexities of cultural (re)presentation fall most heavily on immigrant women and their daughters. Below, I show that Filipino immigrants claim moral distinctiveness for their community by (re)presenting "Americans" as morally flawed and themselves as family-oriented model minorities and their wives and daughters as paragons of morality.

Family-Oriented Model Minorities: "White Women Will Leave You . . ."

Many of my respondents constructed their "ethnic" culture as principled and the "American" culture as deviant. Most often, this morality narrative revolves around family life and family relations. When asked what set Filipinos apart from other Americans, my respondents—of all ages and class backgrounds—repeatedly contrasted the close-knit Filipino families to what they perceived to be the more impersonal quality of U.S. family relations. In the following narratives, "Americans" are characterized as lacking in strong family ties and collective identity, less willing to do the work of family and cultural maintenance, and less willing to abide by patriarchal norms in husband/wife relations:

> Our [Filipino] culture is different. We are more close-knit. We tend to help one another. Americans, ya know, they are all right, but they don't help each other that much. As a matter of fact, if the parents are old, they take them to a convalescent home and let them rot there. We would never do that in our culture. We would nurse them; we would help them until the very end (Filipino immigrant, 60 years old).

> Our (Filipino) culture is very communal. You know that your family will always be there, that you don't have to work when you turn 18, you don't have to pay rent when you are 18, which is the American way of thinking. You also know that if things don't work out in the outside world, you can always come home and mommy and daddy will always take you and your children in (second generation Filipina, 33 years old).

> Asian parents take care of their children. Americans have a different attitude. They leave their children to their own resources. They get baby sitters to take care of their children or leave them in day care. That's why when they get old, their children don't even care about them (Filipina immigrant, 46 years old).

Implicit in the negative depiction of U.S. families—as uncaring, selfish, and distant—is the allegation that White women are not as dedicated to their families as Filipina women. Several Filipino men who married White women recalled being warned by their parents and relatives that "White women will leave you." As one man related, "My mother said to me, 'Well, you know, don't marry a White person because they would take everything that you own and leave you.'" For some Filipino men, perceived differences in attitudes about women's roles between Filipina and non-Filipina women influenced their marital choice. A Filipino American navy man explained why he went back to the Philippines to look for a wife:

> My goal was to marry a Filipina. I requested to be stationed in the Philippines to get married to a Filipina. I'd seen the women here and basically they are spoiled. They have a tendency of not going along together with their husband. They behave differently. They chase the male, instead of the male, the normal way of the traditional way is for the male to go after the female. They have sex without marrying. They want to do their own things. So my idea was to go back home and marry somebody who has never been here. I tell my son the same thing: if he does what I did and finds himself a good lady there, he will be in good hands.

Another man who had dated mostly White women in high school recounted that when it came time for him to marry, he "looked for the kind of women that I'd met in the Philippines."

It is important to note the gender implications of these claims. That is, while both men and women identify the family system as a tremendous source of cultural pride, it is women—through their unpaid housework and kin work—who shoulder the primary responsibility for maintaining family closeness. Because the moral status of the community rests on women's labor, women, as wives and daughters, are not only applauded for but are expected to dedicate themselves to the family. Writing on the constructed image of ethnic family and gender, di Leonardo (1984) reminds us that "a large part of stressing ethnic identity amounts to burdening women with increased responsibilities for preparing special foods, planning rituals, and enforcing 'ethnic' socialization of children" (p. 222). A twenty-three-year-old Filipina spoke about the reproductive work that her mother performed and expected her to learn:

> In my family, I was the only girl, so my mom expected a lot from me. She wanted me to help her to take care of the household. I felt like there was a lot of pressure on me. It's very important to my mom to have the house in order: to wash the dishes, to keep the kitchen in order, vacuuming, and dusting and things like that. She wants me to be a perfect housewife. It's difficult. I have been married now for about four months and my mother asks me every now and then what have I cooked for my husband. My mom is also very strict about families getting together on holidays and I would always help her to organize that. Each holiday, I would try to decorate the house for her, to make it more special.

The burden of unpaid reproductive and kin work is particularly stressful for women who work outside the home. In the following narrative, a Filipina wife and mother described the pulls of family and work that she experienced when she went back to school to pursue a doctoral degree in nursing:

> The Filipinos, we are very collective, very connected. Going through the doctoral program, sometimes I think it is better just to forget about my relatives and just concentrate on school. All that connectedness, it steals parts of myself because all of my energies are devoted to my family. And that is the reason why I think Americans are successful. The majority of the

> American people they can do what they want. They don't feel guilty because they only have a few people to relate to. For us Filipinos, it's like roots under the tree, you have all these connections. The Americans are more like the trunk. I am still trying to go up to the trunk of the tree but it is too hard. I want to be more independent, more like the Americans.

It is important to note that this Filipina interprets her exclusion and added responsibilities as only racial when they are largely gendered. For example, when she says, "the American people they can do what they want," she ignores the differences in the lives of white men and white women—the fact that most white women experience similar pulls of family, education, and work.

Racialized Sexuality and (Im)morality: "In America . . . Sex Is Nothing"

Sexuality, as a core aspect of social identity, is fundamental to the structuring of gender inequality (Millett 1970). Sexuality is also a salient marker of Otherness and has figured prominently in racist and imperialist ideologies (Gilman 1985; Stoler 1991). Filipinas—both in the Philippines and in the United States—have been marked as desirable but dangerous "prostitutes" and/or submissive "mail order brides" (Halualani 1995; Egan 1996). These stereotypes emerged out of the colonial process, especially the extensive U.S. military presence in the Philippines. Until the early 1990s, the Philippines housed—at times unwillingly—some of the United States' largest overseas airforce and naval bases (Espiritu 1995, 14). Many Filipino nationalists have charged that "the prostitution problem" in the Philippines stemmed from U.S. and Philippine government policies that promoted a sex industry—brothels, bars, massage parlors—for servicemen stationed or on leave in the Philippines (Coronel and Rosca 1993; Warren 1993). In this context, *all* Filipinas were racialized to be sexual commodities, usable and expendable. The sexualized racialization of Filipina women is captured in Marianne Villanueva's short story "Opportunity" (1991). As the protagonist Nina, a "mail order bride" from the Philippines, enters the lobby to meet her American fiancé, the bellboys snicker and whisper *puta,* whore: a reminder that U.S. economic and cultural colonization of the Philippines always forms a backdrop to any relations between Filipinos and Americans (Wong 1993, 53).

In an effort to counter the pervasive hypersexualization of Filipina women, many of my respondents constructed American society—and White American women in particular—to be much more sexually promiscuous than Filipino. In the following narrative, a mother who came to the United States in her thirties contrasted the controlled sexuality of Filipinas in the Philippines with the perceived promiscuity of White women in the United States:

> In the Philippines, we always have chaperons when we go out. When we go to dances, we have our uncle, our grandfather, and auntie all behind us to make sure that we behave in the dance hall. Nobody goes necking outside. You don't even let a man put his hand on your shoulders. When you were brought up in a conservative country, it is hard to come here and see that it is all freedom of speech and freedom of action. Sex was never mentioned in our generation. I was thirty already when I learned about sex. But to the young generation in America, sex is nothing.

Similarly, another immigrant woman criticized the way young American women are raised, "Americans are so liberated. They allow their children, their girls, to go out even when they are still so young." In contrast, she stated that "the Filipino way, it is very important, the value of the woman, that she is a virgin when she gets married."

In this section on the "moral flaws of White Americans," I have suggested that the ideal "Filipina" is partially constructed on the community's conceptualization of White women. The former was everything which the latter was not: the one was sexually modest and dedicated to her family; the other sexually promiscuous and uncaring. Embodying the moral integrity of the idealized ethnic community, immigrant women, particularly young daughters, are expected to comply with male-defined criteria of what constitutes "ideal" feminine virtues. While the sexual behavior of adult women is confined to a monogamous and heterosexual context, that of young women is denied completely (c.f. Dasgupta and DasGupta 1996, 229–231). In the next section, I detail the ways in which Filipino immigrant parents, under the rubric of "cultural preservation," police their daughters' behaviors in order to safeguard their sexual innocence and virginity.

THE CONSTRUCTION(S) OF THE "IDEAL" FILIPINA: "BOYS ARE BOYS AND GIRLS ARE DIFFERENT . . ."

As the designated "keepers of the culture" (Billson 1995), the behaviors of immigrant women come under intensive scrutiny from both women and men of their own groups and from U.S.-born Americans (Gabbacia 1994, xi). In a study of the Italian Harlem community, 1880–1950, Robert Anthony Orsi (1985, 135) reports that "all the community's fears for the reputation and integrity of the domus came to focus on the behavior of young women." Because women's moral and sexual loyalties were deemed central to the maintenance of group status, changes in female behavior, especially of growing daughters, were interpreted as signs of moral decay and ethnic suicide, and were carefully monitored and sanctioned (Gabbacia 1994, 113).

Although immigrant families have always been preoccupied with passing on culture, language, and traditions to both male and female children, it is daughters who have the unequal burden of protecting and preserving the family name. Because sons do not have to conform to the image of an "ideal" ethnic subject as daughters do, they often receive special day-to-day privileges denied to daughters (Waters 1996, 75–76; Haddad and Smith 1996; 22–24). This is not to say that immigrant parents do not place undue expectations on their sons; it is rather that these expectations do not pivot around the sons' sexuality or dating choices. In contrast, parental control over the movement and action of daughters begins the moment she is perceived as a young adult and sexually vulnerable. It regularly consists of monitoring her whereabouts and rejecting dating (Wolf 1997). For example, the immigrant parents I interviewed seldom allowed their daughters to date, to stay out late, to spend the night at a friend's house, or to take an out-of-town trip.

Many of the second generation women I spoke to complained bitterly about these parental restrictions. They particularly resent what they see as gender inequity in their families: the fact that their parents place far more restrictions on their activities and movements than on their brothers. Some decried the fact that even their *younger* brothers had more freedom than they did. "It was really hard growing up because my parents would let my younger brothers do what they wanted but I didn't get to do what I wanted even though I was the oldest. I had a curfew and my brothers didn't. I had to ask if I could go places and they didn't. My parents never even asked my brothers when they were coming home."

When questioned about this "double standard," parents responded by pointing to the fact that "girls are different:"

> I have that Filipino mentality that boys are boys and girls are different. Girls are supposed to be protected, to be clean. In the early years, my daughters have to have chaperons and curfews. And they know that they have to be virgins until they get married. The girls always say that is not fair. What is the difference between their brothers and them? And my answer always is, "In the Philippines, you know, we don't do that. The girls stay home. The boys go out." It was the way that I was raised. I still want to have part of that culture instilled in my children. And I want them to have that to pass on to their children.

Even among self-described western-educated and "tolerant" parents, many continue to ascribe to "the Filipino way" when it comes to raising daughters. As one college-educated father explains:

> Because of my Western education, I don't raise my children the way my parents raised me. I tended to be a little more tolerant. But at times, especially in certain issues like dating, I find myself more towards the Filipino way in the sense that I have only one daughter so I tended to be a little bit stricter. So the double standard kind of operates: it's alright for the boys to explore the field but I tended to be overly protective of my daughter. My wife feels the same way because the boys will not lose anything, but the daughter will lose something, their virginity, and it can be also a question of losing face, that kind of thing.

Although many parents generally discourage dating or forbid their daughters to date, they still fully expect these young women to fulfill their traditional roles as women: to get married and have children. A young Filipina recounted the mixed messages she received from her parents:

> This is the way it is supposed to work. Okay, you go to school. You go to college. You graduate. You find a job. Then you find your husband, and you have children. That's the whole time line. But my question is, if you are not allowed to date, how are you supposed to find your husband? They say "no" to the whole dating scene because that is secondary to your education, secondary to your family. They do push marriage, but at a later date. So basically my parents are telling me that I should get married and I should have children but that I should not date.

The restrictions on girls' movement sometimes spill over to the realms of academics. Dasgupta and DasGupta (1996, 230) recount that in the Indian American community, while young men were expected to attend faraway competitive colleges, many of their female peers were encouraged by their parents to go to the local colleges so that they could live at or close to home. Similarly, Wolf (1997, 467) reports that some Filipino parents pursued contradictory tactics with their children's, particularly their daughters', education by pushing them to achieve academic excellence in high school, but then "pulling the emergency brake" when they contemplated college by expecting them to stay at home, even if it means going to a less competitive college, if at all.

The above narratives suggest that the process of parenting is gendered in that immigrant parents tend to restrict the autonomy, mobility, and personal decision making of their daughters more so than of their sons. I argue that these parental restrictions are attempts to construct a model of Filipina womanhood that is chaste, modest, nurturing, and family-oriented. This is not to say that parent-daughter conflicts exist in all Filipino immigrant families. Certainly, Filipino parents do not respond in a uniform way to the challenges of being racial-ethnic minorities. I met parents who have had to change some of their ideas and practices in response to their inability to control their children's movements and choices:

> I have three girls and one boy. I used to think that I wouldn't allow my daughters to go dating and things like that, but there is no way I could do that. I can't stop it. It's the way of life here in America. Sometimes you kind of question yourself, if you are doing what is right. It is hard to accept but you got to accept it. That's the way they are here.

> My children are born and raised here, so they do pretty much what they want. They think they know everything. I can only do so much as a parent. . . . When I try to teach my kids things, they tell me that I sound like an old record. They even talk back to me sometimes. . . .

These narratives, made by a professional Filipino immigrant father and a working-class Filipino immigrant mother respectively, call attention to the shifts in the generational power caused by the migration process and to the possible gap between what parents say they want for their children and their ability to control the young. On the other hand, the interview data do suggest that intergenerational conflicts are socially recognized occurrences in the Filipino community(ies). Even when respondents themselves had not experienced intergenerational tensions, they could always recall a cousin, a girlfriend, or a friend's daughter who had.

SANCTIONS AND REACTIONS: "THAT IS NOT WHAT A DECENT FILIPINO GIRL SHOULD DO . . ."

I do not wish to suggest that immigrant communities are the only ones who regulate their daughters mobility and sexuality. Feminist scholars have long documented the construction, containment, and exploitation of women's sexuality in various societies (Maglin and Perry 1996). We also know that the cultural anxiety over unbounded female sexuality is most apparent with regard to adolescent girls (Tolman and Higgins 1996, 206). The difference, I believe, is in the ways that immigrant and non- immigrant families sanction girls' sexuality. Non-immigrant parents rely on the gender-based good girl/bad girl dichotomy to control sexually assertive girls (Tolman and Higgins 1996,

206). In the dominant cultural accounts of women's sexuality, "good girls" are passive, threatened sexual objects while "bad girls" are active, desiring sexual agents (Tolman and Higgins 1996). As Dasgupta and DasGupta write (1996, 236), "the two most pervasive images of women across cultures are the goddess and whore, the good and bad women." This good girl/bad girl cultural story conflates femininity with sexuality, increases women's vulnerability to sexual coercion, and justifies women's containment in the domestic sphere.

Immigrant families, on the other hand, have an extra disciplining mechanism: they can discipline their daughters as racial/national subjects as well as gendered ones. That is, as self-appointed guardians of "authentic" cultural memory, immigrant parents can opt to regulate their daughters' independent choices by linking them to cultural ignorance or betrayal. As both parents and children recounted, young women who disobeyed parental strictures were often branded "non-ethnic," "untraditional," "radical," "selfish," and not "caring about the family." Parents were also quick to warn their daughters about "bad" Filipinas who had gotten pregnant outside of marriage. Filipina Americans who veered from acceptable behaviors were deemed "Americanized"—women who have adopted the sexual mores and practices of White women. As one Filipino immigrant father described the "Americanized" Filipinas: "They are spoiled because they have seen the American way. They go out at night. Late at night. They go out on dates. Smoking. They have sex without marrying."

From the perspective of the second generation daughters, these charges are stinging. Largely unacquainted with the "home" country, U.S.-born children depend on their parents' tutelage to craft and affirm their ethnic self and thus are particularly vulnerable to charges of cultural ignorance or betrayal (Espiritu 1994). The young women I interviewed were visibly pained—with many breaking down and crying—when they recounted their parents' charges. This deep pain—stemming in part from their desire to be validated as Filipina—existed even among the more "rebellious" daughters. As a 24-year-old daughter explained:

> My mom is very traditional. She wants to follow the Filipino customs, just really adhere to them, like what is proper for a girl, what she can and can't do, and what other people are going to think of her if she doesn't follow that way. When I pushed these restrictions, when I rebelled and stayed out later than allowed, my mom would always say, "That is not what a decent Filipino girl should do. You should come home at a decent hour. What are people going to think of you?" And that would get me really upset, you know, because I think that my character is very much the way it should be for a Filipina. I wear my hair long, I wear decent make-up. I dress properly, conservative. I am family oriented. It hurts me that she doesn't see that I am decent, that I am proper and that I am not going to bring shame to the family or anything like that.

This narrative suggests that even when parents are unable to control the behaviors of their children, their (dis)approval remained strong and powerful in shaping the emotional lives of their daughters (see Wolf 1997). Although better-off parents can and do exert greater controls over their children's behaviors than poorer parents (Wolf 1992; Kibria 1993), I would argue that *all* immigrant parents—regardless of class backgrounds—possess this emotional hold on their children. Therein lies the source of their power.

These emotional pains withstanding, many young Filipinas I interviewed contest and negotiate parental restrictions in their daily lives. Faced with parental restrictions on their mobility, young Filipinas struggle to gain some control over their own social lives, particularly over dating. In many cases, daughters simply misinform their parents of their whereabouts or date without their parents' knowledge. They also rebel by vowing to create more egalitarian relationships with their own husbands and children. A thirty-year-old Filipina who is married to a White American explained why she chose to marry outside her culture:

> In high school, I dated mostly Mexican and Filipino. It never occurred to me to date a white or black guy. I was not attracted to them. But as I kept growing up and my father and I were having all these conflicts, I knew that if I married a Mexican or a Filipino, they would be exactly like my father. And so I tried to date anyone that would not remind me of my dad. A lot of

> my Filipina friends that I grew up with had similar experiences. So I knew that it wasn't only me. I was determined to marry a white person because he would treat me as an individual.

Another Filipina who was labeled "radical" by her parents indicated that she would be more open-minded in raising her own children: "I see myself as very traditional in upbringing but I don't see myself as constricting on my children one day and I wouldn't put the gender roles on them. I wouldn't lock them into any particular way of behaving." It is important to note that even as these Filipinas desired new gender norms and practices for their own families, the majority hoped that their children would remain connected to the Filipino culture. My respondents also reported more serious reactions to parental restrictions, recalling incidents of someone they knew who had run away, joined gangs, or attempted suicide.

CONCLUSION

In this paper, I have shown that many Filipino immigrants use the largely gendered discourse of morality as one strategy to decenter Whiteness and to locate themselves above the dominant group, demonizing it in the process. Like other immigrant groups, Filipinos praise the United States as a land of significant economic opportunity but simultaneously denounce it as a country inhabited by corrupted and individualistic people of questionable morals. In particular, they criticize American family life, American individualism, and American women (c.f. Gabbacia, 1994, 113). Enforced by distorting powers of memory and nostalgia, this rhetoric of moral superiority often leads to patriarchal calls for cultural "authenticity" which locates family honor and national integrity in its female members. Because the policing of women's bodies is one of the main means of asserting moral superiority, young women face numerous restrictions on their autonomy, mobility, and personal decision making. This practice of cultural (re)construction reveals how deeply the conduct of private life can be tied to larger social structures.

The construction of White Americans as the "other" and American culture as deviant serves a dual purpose: It allows immigrant communities to reinforce patriarchy through the sanctioning of women's (mis)behavior *and* to present an unblemished, if not morally superior, public face to the dominant society. Strong in family values, heterosexual morality, and a hierarchical family structure, this public face erases the Filipina "bad girl" and ignores competing (im)moral practices in the Filipino communities. Through the oppression of Filipina women and the castigation of White women's morality, the immigrant community attempts to exert its moral superiority over the dominant Western culture and to reaffirm to itself its self-worth in the face of economic, social, political, and legal subordination. In other words, the immigrant community uses restrictions on women's lives as one form of resistance to racism. Though significant, this form of cultural resistance severely restricts women's lives, particularly those of the second generation, and casts the family as a site of potentially the most intense conflict and oppressive demands in immigrant lives.

REFERENCES

Billson, Janet Mancini. 1995. *Keepers of the Culture: The Power of Tradition in Women's Lives.* New York: Lexington Books.

Coronel, Sheila and Ninotchka Rosca. 1993. "For the Boys: Filipinas Expose Years of Sexual Slavery by the U.S. and Japan." *Ms.,* November/December p. 11+.

Dasgupta, Shamita Das and DasGupta, Sayantani. 1996. "Public Face, Private Face: Asian Indian Women and Sexuality." Pp. 226–243 in *Women, Sex, and Power in the Nineties,* edited by Nan Bauer Maglin and Donna Perry. New Brunswick, NJ: Rutgers University Press.

Di Leonardo, Micaela. 1984. *The Varieties of Ethnic Experience: Kinship, Class, and Gender among California Italian-Americans.* Ithaca and London: Cornell University Press.

Eastmond, Marita. 1993. "Reconstructing Life: Chilean Refugee Women and the Dilemmas of Exile." Pp. 35–53 in *Migrant Women: Crossing Boundaries and Changing Identities,* edited by Gina Buijs. Oxford: Berg.

Egan, Timothy. 1996. "Mail-Order Marriage, Immigrant Dreams and Death." *New York Times,* 26 May, p. 12+.

Espiritu, Yen Le. 1994. "The Intersection of Race, Ethnicity, and Class: The Multiple Identities of Second Generation Filipinos." *Identities* 1(2–3):249–273.

———. 1995. *Filipino American Lives.* Philadelphia: Temple University Press.

Gabbacia, Donna. 1994. *From the Other Side: Women, Gender, and Immigrant Life in the U.S., 1820–1990.* Bloomington and Indianapolis: Indiana University Press.

Gilman, Sander L. 1985. *Difference and Pathology: Stereotypes of Sexuality, Race, and Madness.* Ithaca: Cornell University Press.

Haddad Yvonne Y. and Jane I. Smith. 1996. "Islamic Values among American Muslims." Pp. 19–40 in *Family and Gender among American Muslims: Issues Facing Middle Eastern Immigrants and Their Descendants,* edited by Barbara C. Aswad and Barbara Bilge. Philadelphia: Temple University Press.

Halualani, Rona Tamiko. 1995. "The Intersecting Hegemonic Discourses of an Asian Mail-Order Bride Catalog: Philipina 'Oriental Butterfly' Dolls for Sale." *Women's Studies in Communication* 18(1):45–64.

Kibria, Nazli. 1993. *Family Tightrope: The Changing Lives of Vietnamese Immigrant Community.* Princeton, NJ: Princeton University Press.

Maglin, Nan Bauer and Donna Perry. 1996. "Introduction." Pp. xiii–xxvi in *"Bad Girls/Good Girls": Women, Sex, and Power in the Nineties,* edited by Nan Bauer Maglin and Donna Perry.

Millet, Kate. 1970. *Sexual Politics.* Garden City, NY: Doubleday.

Rumbaut, Ruben. 1994. "The Crucible Within: Ethnic Identity, Self-Esteem, and Segmented Assimilation Among Children of Immigrants." *International Migration Review,* 28(4):748–794.

Stoler, Ann Laura. 1991. "Carnal Knowledge and Imperial Power: Gender, Race, and Morality in Colonial Asia." Pp. 51–101 in *Gender at the Crossroads of Knowledge: Feminist Anthropology in the Postmodern Era,* edited by Micaela di Leonardo. Berkeley: University of California Press.

Tolman, Deborah L. and Tracy E. Higgins. 1996. "How Being a Good Girl Can Be Bad for Girls." Pp. 205–225 in *"Bad Girls/Good Girls": Women, Sex, and Power in the Nineties,* edited by Nan Bauer Maglin and Donna Perry. New Brunswick, NJ: Rutgers University Press.

Villanueva, Marianne. 1991. *Ginseng and Other Tales from Manila.* Corvallis, OR: Calyx.

Warren, Jenifer. 1993. "Suit Asks Navy to Aid Children Left in Philippines." *Los Angeles Times,* 5 March, p. A3+.

Waters, Mary C. 1996. "The Intersection of Gender, Race, and Ethnicity in Identity Development of Caribbean American Teens." Pp. 65–81 in *Urban Girls: Resisting Stereotypes, Creating Identities,* edited by Bonnie J. Ross Leadbeater and Niobe Way. New York and London: New York University Press.

Wolf, Diane L. 1992. *Factory Daughters: Gender, Household Dynamics, and Rural Industrialization in Java.* Berkeley: University of California Press.

———. 1997. "Family Secrets: Transnational Struggles among Children of Filipino Immigrants." *Sociological Perspectives* 40(3):457–482.

Wong, Sau-ling. 1993. *Reading Asian American Literature: From Necessity to Extravagance.* Princeton, NJ: Princeton.

PART IV

IDENTITIES

Our sense of who we are as women and men is not likely to remain the same over the span of our lives, but how are our identities formed and contested? How do our gendered identities change as they feed into our identities as members of religious groups, nations, or social movements? There is nothing automatic about identities. Identities are fluid rather than primordial, socially constructed rather than inherited, and they shift with changing social contexts. As the world grows more complex and interconnected, our identities, or self-definitions, respond to diverse and sometimes competing pulls and tugs.

Identities are both intensely private and vociferously public. Identities are also fundamentally about power and alliances. Racial-ethnic, religious, national, and sexual identities are at the core of many of today's social movements and political conflicts. Intertwined with these emergent and contested identities are strong ideas—stated or implicit—of what it is to be feminine and masculine. Most of the articles in this section rely on strong, first-person narratives as a vehicle to reflect how gender interacts with the creation and contestation of multifacted identities. Together, the authors suggest some of the ways that identities are actively shaped and defined in contradistinction to other identities, and the ways in which identities are sometimes imposed from above or resisted. In this view, identities involve a process of simultaneously defining and erasing difference, and of claiming and constructing spheres of autonomy.

In the first article, Audre Lorde draws on her own experience to argue that age, race, class, and sex are all simultaneous aspects of one's identity that cannot be easily separated out. Lorde argues that embracing these intertwined differences can offer opportunities for personal and collective growth and can point the way toward peaceful and just changes in the world. In the next article, Elliott Femynye Bat Tzedek echoes this concern, as she describes the limits and dangers that inhere when groups of people try to organize themselves based simply on one identity claim (such as "women," or "lesbians"). Tzedek states forcefully that "we are, all of us, so much bigger than the categories of identity politics."

Recent scholarship on immigrants has provided valuable insight into the ways that social contexts—and peoples' movement between and among different contexts—shape, constrain, and offer opportunities for the construction of identities. Immigrants are forced to more actively and consciously think about, strategize, and negotiate their identities within contradictory and shifting contexts. For instance, in the next selection, Almas Sayeed describes her struggles with negotiating and displaying her identity as a young Indian woman living in Kansas. Family, culture, and Islamic definitions of the female body collide with the local U.S. university town's culture of gender and sexuality, as Sayeed ruminates about the meanings of wearing (or not wearing) the *hijab,* the traditional Muslim headscarf. Similarly, Karen Pyke and Denise Johnson's article examines the lives of young Korean and Vietnamese immigrants in the United States. Pyke and Johnson illustrate the ways that these young women shape unique "femininities," as they negotiate the tensions between dominant forms of femininity in "mainstream White America," and their experience of gender in their more gender-dichotomous immigrant families and communities. Finally, this section concludes with a classic piece by Peggy McIntosh on white privilege. As McIntosh suggests, privileged identities—white, male, heterosexual, middle or upper class—are often invisible *as* identities. And this is a key way in which power operates, by rendering invisible the very mechanisms that create and perpetuate group-based inequities.

24

Age, Race, Class, and Sex

Women Redefining Difference

AUDRE LORDE

Much of western European history conditions us to see human differences in simplistic opposition to each other: dominant/subordinate, good/bad, up/down, superior/inferior. In a society where the good is defined in terms of profit rather than in terms of human need, there must always be some group of people who, through systematized oppression, can be made to feel surplus, to occupy the place of the dehumanized inferior. Within this society, that group is made up of Black and Third World people, working-class people, older people, and women.

As a forty-nine-year-old Black lesbian feminist socialist mother of two, including one boy, and a member of an interracial couple, I usually find myself a part of some group defined as other, deviant, inferior, or just plain wrong. Traditionally, in American society, it is the members of oppressed, objectified groups who are expected to stretch out and bridge the gap between the actualities of our lives and the consciousness of our oppressor. For in order to survive, those of us for whom oppression is as American as apple pie have always had to be watchers, to become familiar with the language and manners of the oppressor, even sometimes adopting them for some illusion of protection. Whenever the need for some pretense of communication arises, those who profit from our oppression call upon us to share our knowledge with them. In other words, it is the responsibility of the oppressed to teach the oppressors their mistakes. I am responsible for educating teachers who dismiss my children's culture in school. Black and Third World people are expected to educate White people as to our humanity. Women are expected to educate men. Lesbians and gay men are expected to educate the heterosexual world. The oppressors maintain their position and evade responsibility for their own actions. There is a constant drain of energy which might be better used in redefining ourselves and devising realistic scenarios for altering the present and constructing the future.

Institutionalized rejection of difference is an absolute necessity in a profit economy which needs outsiders as surplus people. As members of such an economy, we have all been programmed to respond to the human differences between us with fear and loathing and to handle that difference in one of three ways: ignore it, and if that is not possible, copy it if we think it is dominant, or destroy it if we think it is subordinate. But we have no patterns for relating across our human differences as equals. As a result, those differences have been misnamed and misused in the service of separation and confusion.

Certainly there are very real differences between us of race, age, and sex. But it is not those differences between us that are separating us. It is rather our refusal to recognize those differences, and to examine the distortions which result from our misnaming them and their effects upon human behavior and expectation.

Racism, the belief in the inherent superiority of one race over all others and thereby the right to dominance. Sexism, the belief in the inherent superiority of one sex over the other and thereby the right to dominance. Ageism. Heterosexism. Elitism. Classism.

It is a lifetime pursuit for each one of us to extract these distortions from our living at the same time as we recognize, reclaim, and define those differences upon which they are imposed. For we have all been raised in a society where those distortions were endemic within our living. Too often, we pour the energy needed for recognizing and exploring difference into pretending those differences are insurmountable barriers, or that they do not exist at all. This results in a voluntary isolation, or false and treacherous connections. Either way, we do not develop tools for using human difference as a springboard for creative change within our lives. We speak not of human difference, but of human deviance.

Somewhere, on the edge of consciousness, there is what I call a *mythical norm,* which each one of us within our hearts knows "that is not me." In America, this norm is usually defined as White, thin, male, young, heterosexual, Christian, and financially secure. It is with this mythical norm that the trappings of power reside within this society. Those of us who stand outside that power often identify one way in which we are different, and we assume that to be the primary cause of all oppression, forgetting other distortions around difference, some of which we ourselves may be practicing. By and large within the women's movement today, White women focus upon their oppression as women and ignore differences of race, sexual preference, class, and age. There is a pretense to a homogeneity of experience covered by the word *sisterhood* that does not in fact exist.

Unacknowledged class differences rob women of each others' energy and creative insight. Recently a women's magazine collective made the decision for one issue to print only prose, saying poetry was a less "rigorous" or "serious" art form. Yet even the form our creativity takes is often a class issue. Of all the art forms, poetry is the most economical. It is the one which is the most secret, which requires the least physical labor, the least material, and the one which can be done between shifts, in the hospital pantry, on the subway, and on scraps of surplus paper. Over the last few years, writing a novel on tight finances, I came to appreciate the enormous differences in the material demands between poetry and prose. As we reclaim our literature, poetry has been the major voice of poor, working class, and Colored women. A room of one's own may be a necessity for writing prose, but so are reams of paper, a typewriter, and plenty of time. The actual requirements to produce the visual arts also help determine, along class lines, whose art is whose. In this day of inflated prices for material, who are our sculptors, our painters, our photographers? When we speak of a broadly based women's culture, we need to be aware of the effect of class and economic differences on the supplies available for producing art.

As we move toward creating a society within which we can each flourish, ageism is another distortion of relationship which interferes without vision. By ignoring the past, we are encouraged to repeat its mistakes. The "generation gap" is an important social tool for any repressive society. If the younger members of a community view the older members as contemptible or suspect or excess, they will never be able to join hands and examine the living memories of the community, nor ask the all important question, "Why?" This gives rise to a historical amnesia that keeps us working to invent the wheel every time we have to go to the store for bread.

We find ourselves having to repeat and relearn the same old lessons over and over that our mothers did because we do not pass on what we have learned, or because we are unable to listen. For instance, how many times has this all been said before? For another, who would have believed that once again our daughters are allowing their bodies to be hampered and purgatoried by girdles and high heels and hobble skirts?

Ignoring the differences of race between women and the implications of those differences presents the most serious threat to the mobilization of women's joint power.

As White women ignore their built-in privilege of Whiteness and define *woman* in terms of their own experience alone, then women of Color become "other," the outsider whose experience and tradition is too "alien" to comprehend. An example of this is the signal absence of the experience of women of Color as a resource for women's studies courses. The literature of women of Color is seldom included in women's literature courses and almost never in other literature courses, nor in women's studies as a whole. All too often, the excuse given is that the literatures of women of Color can only be taught by Colored women, or that they are too difficult to understand, or that classes cannot "get into"them because they come out of experiences that are "too different." I have heard this argument presented by White women of otherwise quite clear intelligence, women who seem to have no trouble at all teaching and reviewing work that comes out of the vastly different experiences of Shakespeare, Molière, Dostoyefsky, and Aristophanes. Surely there must be some other explanation.

This is a very complex question, but I believe one of the reasons White women have such difficulty reading Black women's work is because of their reluctance to see Black women as women and different from themselves. To examine Black women's literature effectively requires that we be seen as whole people in our actual complexities—as individuals, as women, as human—rather than as one of those problematic but familiar stereotypes provided in this society in place of genuine images of Black women. And I believe this holds true for the literatures of other women of Color who are not Black.

The literatures of all women of Color recreate the textures of our lives, and many White women are heavily invested in ignoring the real differences. For as long as any difference between us means one of us must be inferior, then the recognition of any difference must be fraught with guilt. To allow women of Color to step out of stereotypes is too guilt provoking, for it threatens the complacency of those women who view oppression only in terms of sex.

Refusing to recognize difference makes it impossible to see the different problems and pitfalls facing us as women.

Thus, in a patriarchal power system where White-skin privilege is a major prop, the entrapments used to neutralize Black women and White women are not the same. For example, it is easy for Black women to be used by the power structure against Black men, not because they are men, but because they are Black. Therefore, for Black women, it is necessary at all times to separate the needs of the oppressor from our own legitimate conflicts within our communities. This same problem does not exist for White women. Black women and men have shared racist oppression and still share it, although in different ways. Out of that shared oppression we have developed joint defenses and joint vulnerabilities to each other that are not duplicated in the White community, with the exception of the relationship between Jewish women and Jewish men.

On the other hand, White women face the pitfall of being seduced into joining the oppressor under the pretense of sharing power. This possibility does not exist in the same way for women of Color. The tokenism that is sometimes extended to us is not an invitation to join power; our racial "otherness" is a visible reality that makes that quite clear. For White women there is a wider range of pretended choices and rewards for identifying with patriarchal power and its tools.

Today, with the defeat of ERA, the tightening economy, and increased conservatism, it is easier once again for White women to believe the dangerous fantasy that if you are good enough, pretty enough, sweet enough, quiet enough, teach the children to behave, hate the right people, and marry the right men, then you will be allowed to co-exist with patriarchy in relative peace, at least until a man needs your job or the neighborhood rapist happens along. And true, unless one lives and loves in the trenches it is difficult to remember that the war against dehumanization is ceaseless.

But Black women and our children know the fabric of our lives is stitched with violence and with hatred, that there is no rest. We do not deal with it only on the picket lines, or in dark midnight alleys, or in the places where we dare to verbalize our resistance. For us, increasingly, violence weaves through the daily tissues of our living—in the supermarket, in the classroom, in the elevator, in the clinic and the schoolyard, from the plumber, the baker, the saleswoman, the bus driver, the bank teller, the waitress who does not serve us.

Some problems we share as women, some we do not. You fear your children will grow up to join the patriarchy and testify against you, we fear our children will be dragged from a car and shot down in the street, and you will turn your backs upon the reasons they are dying.

The threat of difference has been no less blinding to people of Color. Those of us who are Black must see that the reality of our lives and our struggle does not make us immune to the errors of ignoring and misnaming difference. Within Black communities where racism is a living reality, differences among us often seem dangerous and suspect. The need for unity is often misnamed as a need for homogeneity, and a Black feminist vision mistaken for betrayal of our common interests as a people. Because of the continuous battle against racial erasure that Black women and Black men share, some Black women still refuse to recognize that we are also oppressed as women, and that sexual hostility against Black women is practiced not only by the White racist society, but implemented within our Black communities as well. It is a disease striking the heart of Black nationhood, and silence will not make it disappear. Exacerbated by racism and the pressures of powerlessness, violence against Black women and children often becomes a standard within our communities, one by which manliness can be measured. But these woman-hating acts are rarely discussed as crimes against Black women.

As a group, women of Color are the lowest paid wage earners in America. We are the primary targets of abortion and sterilization abuse, here and abroad. In certain parts of Africa, small girls are still being sewed shut between their legs to keep them docile and for men's pleasure. This is known as female circumcision, and it is not a cultural affair as the late Jomo Kenyatta insisted, it is a crime against Black women.

Black women's literature is full of the pain of frequent assault, not only by a racist patriarchy, but also by Black men. Yet the necessity for and history of shared battle have made us, Black women, particularly vulnerable to the false accusation that anti-sexist is anti-Black. Meanwhile, womanhating as a recourse of the powerless is sapping strength from Black communities, and our very lives. Rape is on the increase, reported and unreported, and rape is not aggressive sexuality, it is sexualized aggression. As Kalamu ya Salaam, a Black male writer points out, "As long as male domination exists, rape will exist. Only women revolting and men made conscious of their responsibility to fight sexism can collectively stop rape."[1]

Differences between ourselves as Black women are also being misnamed and used to separate us from one another. As a Black lesbian feminist comfortable with the many different ingredients of my identity, and a woman committed to racial and sexual freedom from oppression, I find I am constantly being encouraged to pluck out some one aspect of myself and present this as the meaningful whole, eclipsing or denying the other parts of self. But this is a destructive and fragmenting way to live. My fullest concentration of energy is available to me only when I integrate all the parts of who I am, openly, allowing power from particular sources of my living to flow back and forth freely through all my different selves, without the restrictions of externally imposed definition. Only then can I bring myself and my energies as a whole to the service of those struggles which I embrace as part of my living.

A fear of lesbians, or of being accused of being a lesbian, has led many Black women into testifying against themselves. It has led some of us into destructive alliances, and others into despair and isolation. In the White women's communities, heterosexism is sometimes a result of identifying with the White patriarchy, a rejection of that interdependence between women-identified women which allows the self to be, rather than to be used in the service of men. Sometimes it reflects a die-hard belief in the protective coloration of heterosexual relationships, sometimes a self-hate which all women have to fight against, taught us from birth.

Although elements of these attitudes exist for all women, there are particular resonances of heterosexism and homophobia among Black women. Despite the fact that woman-bonding has a long and honorable history in the African and African-American communities, and despite the knowledge and accomplishments of many strong and creative women-identified Black women in the political, social and cultural fields, heterosexual Black women often tend to ignore or discount the existence and work of Black lesbians. Part of this attitude has come from an understandable terror of

Black male attack within the close confines of Black society, where the punishment for any female self-assertion is still to be accused of being a lesbian and therefore unworthy of the attention or support of the scarce Black male. But part of this need to misname and ignore Black lesbians comes from a very real fear that openly women-identified Black women who are no longer dependent upon men for their self-definition may well reorder our whole concept of social relationships.

Black women who once insisted that lesbianism was a White woman's problem now insist that Black lesbians are a threat to Black nationhood, are consorting with the enemy, are basically un-Black. These accusations, coming from the very women to whom we look for deep and real understanding, have served to keep many Black lesbians in hiding, caught between the racism of White women and the homophobia of their sisters. Often, their work has been ignored, trivialized, or misnamed, as with the work of Angelina Grimke, Alice Dunbar-Nelson, and Lorraine Hansberry. Yet women-bonded women have always been some part of the power of Black communities, from our unmarried aunts to the amazons of Dahomey.

And it is certainly not Black lesbians who are assaulting women and raping children and grandmothers on the streets of our communities.

Across this country, as in Boston during the spring of 1979 following the unsolved murders of twelve Black women, Black lesbians are spear-heading movements against violence against Black women.

What are the particular details within each of our lives that can be scrutinized and altered to help bring about change? How do we redefine difference for all women? It is not our differences which separate women, but our reluctance to recognize those differences and to deal effectively with the distortions which have resulted from the ignoring and misnaming of those differences.

As a tool of social control, women have been encouraged to recognize only one area of human difference as legitimate, those differences which exist between women and men. And we have learned to deal across those differences with the urgency of all oppressed subordinates. All of us have had to learn to live or work or coexist with men, from our fathers on. We have recognized and negotiated these differences, even when this recognition only continued the old dominant/subordinate mode of human relationship, where the oppressed must recognize the masters' difference in order to survive.

But our future survival is predicated upon our ability to relate within equality. As women, we must root out internalized patterns of oppression within ourselves if we are to move beyond the most superficial aspects of social change. Now we must recognize differences among women who are our equals, neither inferior nor superior, and devise ways to use each others' difference to enrich our visions and our joint struggles.

The future of our earth may depend upon the ability of all women to identify and develop new definitions of power and new patterns of relating across difference. The old definitions have not served us, nor the earth that supports us. The old patterns, no matter how cleverly rearranged to imitate progress, still condemn us to cosmetically altered repetitions of the same old exchanges, the same old guilt, hatred, recrimination, lamentation, and suspicion.

For we have, built into all of us, old blueprints of expectation and response, old structures of oppression, and these must be altered at the same time as we alter the living conditions which are a result of those structures. For the master's tools will never dismantle the master's house.

As Paulo Freire shows so well in *The Pedagogy of the Oppressed,*[2] the true focus of revolutionary change is never merely the oppressive situations which we seek to escape, but that piece of the oppressor which is planted deep within each of us, and which knows only the oppressors' tactics, the oppressors' relationships.

Change means growth, and growth can be painful. But we sharpen self-definition by exposing the self in work and struggle together with those whom we define as different from ourselves although sharing the same goals. For Black and White, old and young, lesbian and heterosexual women alike, this can mean new paths to our survival.

We have chosen each other
and the edge of each others battles
the war is the same

if we lose
someday women's blood will congeal
upon a dead planet
if we win
there is no telling
we seek beyond history
for a new and more possible meeting.[3]

NOTES

1. From "Rape: A Radical Analysis, An African-American Perspective" by Kalamu ya Salaam in *Black Books Bulletin,* vol. 6, no. 4 (1980).

2. Seabury Press, New York, 1970.

3. From "Outlines," unpublished poem.

25

The Rights and Wrongs of Identity Politics and Sexual Identities

ELLIOTT FEMYNYE BAT TZEDEK

IDENTITY POLITICS: WHAT IT IS

Let me give you a vastly oversimplified, yet still basically true, version of how Identity Politics came to be. By the middle of the 1960s, the heady, heroic days of the Civil Rights movement were ending. Major battles had been won, territory had been granted, and the vast, multi-racial group of people who had won so much were faced with having to settle in for the long haul. Like all movements, there were splinters and splits and disagreements; the unity began to wear, as Black participants began to live the message of self-love and pride and grew weary of the continuing liberal racism of their white cohorts.[1] Black activists began to build Black Power, and women, who had had it with the macho posing, began to come to see themselves/ourselves as members of the group Women and break off in search of their/our own agendas. As the New Left reached its final days in the late 60s and early 70s, Identity Politics—that is, the direct association of one's membership in certain categories with one's political outlook and agenda—became the guiding philosophy of social-change groups and communities. IP is what I learned as Lesbian Feminist politics, learned so deeply and well, in fact, that reading and theorizing about its history sometimes shakes me up; for my first dozen years as a Feminist dyke, IP seemed not like a political theory, but a description of how the world actually is.

Like the permeations of New Left groups before it, Identity Politics is based in a search for "authenticity," meaning, and civil power. Within IP, each person's identity is based in membership in various social groups or categories, and that membership is seen as inherently politicized. Each identity group took from the Civil Rights victories the political stance that their identity is an inherent, immutable category. Because membership in this category is innate and not chosen, the argument went, full membership in Civil, democratic society must not be blocked. "This is who I am," the Civil Rights argument said, "and I didn't choose it and I can't change it, so you must give me rights based on this." The fallout of this choice of strategy is still with us in many ways, including the horrified proclamations by many Black clergy that the call for Gay and Lesbian civil rights is nothing like their own fight, for Blackness is immutable whereas "homosexuality" is chosen.[2]

Elliott Femynye Bat Tzedek, "The Rights and Wrongs of Identity Politics and Sexual Identities," from *Off Our Backs,* Volume 32, p. 8.

And before I go on to talk about the huge limitations that came with defining identity and politics in this way, I need to say that the version of Identity Politics I came into as a Feminist and Dyke has been of tremendous value to me. As only one example: going off to a middle-class college and learning to pass as middle-class was really destructive to me. I got a BA in literature, but lost my ability to write because I could not give voice to my now-silenced working-class life. Recognizing that I had been raised working-class and connecting with other working-class women gave me my life story back. It helped me identify and laugh at the shame I had internalized, helped me find pride and strength again, made space for me to write a story such as this. I don't think the questions IP asked, the positions it built or the answers it invented are at all silly or useless or wrong. I think they are limited by the nature of the political world around us, and by their own nature. The strategies, the activists, and the demonstrations accomplished a lot of change. The emphasis on cultural pride reconnected people to their lives, and encouraged the construction of historical narratives of resistance that greatly strengthened "identities" that had been devalued in the U.S., such as women, Chicanos/Latinos, lesbians, disabled people, and more. And, of course, the groups that invented the strategy which became IP, the Civil Rights and Black Power Movements, accomplished amazing things. As Paula Rust argues at length in *Bisexuality and the Challenge to Lesbian Politics,* the adaptation of IP (alongside Feminist politics) created space for lesbian identity to take shape and to become a social force, for "any group that could adapt the language of ethnic politics to its own ends could tap into a well-developed social change ideology."[3]

IDENTITY POLITICS: WHAT'S WRONG WITH IT

Yet—and a very large "yet" it is—from here and now, my mid-30's in the late 90's, I know this about Identity Politics (at least the versions I learned and lived within): we messed up, at the very beginning, first by choosing to reify identities as they were already defined in the world, and then by describing these identities as if they were inherent to us in some way instead of as descriptions of positions within extremely hierarchical, pre-existing social structures of power. "Woman," for example, was one of the main identities of IP, as a statement of biology. "Of color" was another main category, with groups dividing around the racial categories recognized within the United States at the time, as if those categories were physical features and not a colonial classification system. "Class" was another group, although its boundaries were never as tightly guarded because it couldn't be treated only as a physical or inherited "true" self. "Jewish" was a group; "Muslim" should have been, too, as people "oppressed by the tyranny of X-tianity," but there was only silence around the different but overlapping categories of Muslim and Arab women.[4] "Lesbian," as opposed to "heterosexual," was the other main identity of Feminist IP, although not until after years of skirmishes around defining "lesbian" as a statement of feminist politics, when it settled into being a "sexual orientation" or a "sexual identity" determined in early childhood or at birth.

So what was wrong with these categories, since all of them do describe who we are in the world? What they describe are places within a broader society which, at its very foundation, uses gender and racial categories to establish and maintain a small powerful elite. The problem with them is that simply restating the categories ignores the deeper truth that all of these categories are a creation and expression of social power. Race and gender aren't pre-existing reality; they are socially constructed categories.[5] By choosing to build identities around these constructions instead of choosing to attack the ways the categories had been constructed, IP created a position that was a strong base for fighting for civil and/or equal rights, including the right to live within one's own culture. But I think now that this base came at a tremendous price; we went to work building comfortable bases, but threw away our best weapons—questions. As long as we could ask questions about how power around us was constructed, we stood a chance of cracking open the foundation. But after we began to think of our social positions as identities that were "real" or "inherent," the question of how they were built, or why, became unnecessary, maybe even unthinkable.

Once Identity Politics became the organizing structure of our social change groups and communities, defining and defending our identity groups from challenges and threats, including being or feeling "silenced," became the main focus of our political lives. Sometimes I now look at myself in my 20s and think that I, and the lesbian and feminist world I moved and loved/love, were doing Feminist gangs, defining ourselves by what we wore and what words, phrases, and theories were in or out, "liberatory" or "tied into oppressive thinking." Don't get me wrong—we were also doing tremendously important work in the world staffing hot lines and book stores and lesbian concerts and protesting and spray painting, but we were also spent a huge amount of energy in fights over the boundaries of our identity groups. These border skirmishes, along with building cultural pride, seem to me now to be one of the defining characteristics of Identity Politics as we lived them. I don't necessarily think we were completely wrong, especially when the only alternative seemed to be a mushy, Love Everyone Without Distinction liberalism which was unwilling or unable to hold anyone or any system accountable for oppression. But when we reduced our lives to pre-existing, "by birth" categories, we created two major stumbling blocks. First, we created a huge contradiction in our own life stories, for most of us felt that "Feminist" and "Lesbian" were inherent parts of our identity, statements about our deepest selves, even while knowing none of us was born Feminist and that most of us didn't feel we were "bom" lesbian. Instead, we talked about choice, even while enshrining identity groups that were, supposedly, not chosen. Second, we lost, undervalued, or disappeared the richness of our life experiences, and too often threw out the chance to make profound connections around everything we've shared after the womb and early childhood. By embracing "by birth" identities, those of us using Identity Politics missed the chance to embrace the strength of groups based in the life experiences.[6] These groups, which have grown up around oppressions, goals, problems, and dreams that were shared, could well have done much more damage to the foundations of white/male/rich social power than reifying any pre-existing category.

As one example of the limits of an IP category, and of how an identity based in experience could have/might well yet create space for real social change (not just social adjustment), I want to explore the IP argument that reduces our "sexual identity" to a "sexual orientation" that we are born into. As a dyke and a Feminist, I've never been easy with the entire notion of "sexual orientation," which sounded more like needing a compass than anything else. Thinking about it now, in the context of looking back into IP, I can (more) clearly see why.

From here and now, in fact, I can without reservation say that I detest the definitions of lesbian and straight as "sexual identities," of continuing to label women by who we have sex with instead of by what sex means for us. And I hate defining lesbian as just one of many "sexual preferences." I hate it because it masks the social power of the institution of Heterosexuality. I hate it because it implies that, in a world in which nearly everything is connected to heterosexual power, choosing to live as a lesbian is merely a different but equivalent "choice" than "choosing" to live as a straight woman. I hate that "lesbian," which is my culture, my position as a social and political being, the speaking of my heart, the shape of my cornea, gets reduced to yet another identity by opposition: a lesbian is a woman who doesn't sleep with men. I hate it most when it is supported by the notion that "sexual identity" is about biology, about being "born that way," an argument that protects people who identify as heterosexuals from ever having to be accountable for choices they make about participating in the social institution of Heterosexuality.[7]

Thinking about how "sexual identity" used in this way hides and blurs a powerful social institution, I've found that there is no more space in my life for the idea of an inherent and nearly unalterable sexual identity. I know both men (a lot) and women (a few) who always "knew" they were sexually attracted only to members of their sex. I don't want to deny their knowledge or insight or feelings, but I do want to say that even this kind of knowledge can't justify the idea of a "sexual identity" built solely around which gender arouses one's sexual organs. Our identities are not just what we were born into, but are also, even more so, our experiences in the world, the understanding we create from those experiences, and the choices we make about enacting our understanding. When I consider these three aspects of identity, then "lesbian" is not the whole story of my sexual identity, no matter how young I was when I first wanted to kiss a certain female classmate. On days and months when I am overwhelmed by the sexual violence enacted on and in me, "victim/survivor of sexual violence" says much more about my sexual identity than does knowing the gender of my sex . . . partner/s.

What if I, what if we, as women, stopped defining our sexual identities around who we have sex with, and insisted instead on talking about what sex means for us? What if we, as Feminists, as a political strategy, began to define sexual identities around our experiences and those of other women? Instead of the gulf between those identified as "straight" and as "lesbian" (with bisexual women being marginal and perceived as a threat to both sides), what would an identity look like that includes the experience of these women:

- women for whom sex and violence have been the same
- women who are terrified of orgasm because they have been made to feel sexual excitement during torture
- women who would most like to not ever again have to think about sex
- women who completely understand Lorena Bobbitt

A NEW IDENTITY: WOMEN WHO HAVE BEEN HURT BY SEX

Imagine what this group, Women Who Have Been Hurt By Sex, would look and feel like. Imagine the numbers of women who could claim this Sexual Identity. Imagine the common experiences women within this group could identify around, the view of social power they would share. And when they/we spoke, imagine the truths that would be revealed, the very way speaking the group name would challenge embedded social power. Within U.S. culture, and the culture of IP that exists within it, sex carries a tremendous social, emotional and symbolic power. The truth about this power is disguised by a mythology that says sex is by definition good, that more sex is better, and that sexual experiences are always positive. The only allowable exception to this is if one participant came into the experience with clear and documentable criminal intent, clear enough that the encounter can be removed from the realm of sex into the realm of crime, thereby keeping the definition of sex as inherently good unchallenged.[8] This mythology is so necessary for maintaining male power and is so indoctrinated as to be unquestionable reality: the right of men to need and have orgasm is THE moral imperative of our society, for it is upheld at any cost and challenges to it are not allowed. The mythology of sex intentionally hides that fact that sexual experiences are not always positive even for people (especially women people) who choose to engage in them. The mythology also tells a grand lie about orgasms, proclaiming that their emotional and physiologic aspects are indivisible; there is, as Sheila Jeffreys points out, no word in English for having an orgasm from which one feels no pleasure and may even feel revulsion.[9] Yet this experience happens to many women, who find themselves being physically aroused by images of violence done to them,[10] and I've read accounts by Vietnam vets who now must live with tremendous shame that they were aroused by the violence they perpetrated.[11]

The identity Women Who Have Been Hurt By Sex would challenge this ruling mythology, would point out that the actual boundaries of "sex" include so much that is violent, coercive, and is not perceived (by the victim) as pleasurable. By making the boundaries obvious, we could open up space for discussion and change, space which is not addressed by reducing sexuality to "how we were born" or who we "prefer." By building any sexual identity based in experience, we could open up space for women to stop passively accepting sexuality as a given-at-birth declaration and begin to talk about what we want for ourselves, our communities, and our futures. As Joyce Trebilcot writes in *Taking Responsibility for Sexuality*.

> On this view [sexuality determined at birth], one's sexuality is clearly a given only; it is inherited, or acquired in childhood; it is something that happens to you. So this way of thinking about your sexuality tends to keep you docile: you are passive, submissive,

> with respect to it; [. . .] and there is no space in these causal accounts for women to participate in the creating of our own sexual identities.[12]

If we make identity groups from our lived experiences, we can begin to make a way out of the corner IP painted itself into. While I believe that the groups within Identity Politics were, at first, organized around shared experiences as women, lesbians, African Americans, and others, the adoption of the "ethnic" political stance had to reduce these complex experiences merely to expressions of pre-existing identity groups. By doing this, we surrendered the vast strength of our creativity and the tremendous sense of hopefulness about building new selves and a new world. But I can also see that basing identity in experience can have its own drawbacks and hazards, especially if the IP assumption that identity is inherent and unchanging is not challenged; if we see identity labels as a direct representation of our "true, deep" selves, any experience that is taken on as identity will also become frozen and determinist. I'm thinking in particular about three areas of danger in taking on experience as a way to create group identity: the risk of making everything merely personal and idiosyncratic; the risk of making ourselves nothing more than our experiences; and the tremendous violence we are likely to encounter if we advocate identities that do actually challenge the foundation of white/male/rich power.

Taking these in reverse order, how much do I need to say about the level of violence? Think of Martin Luther King, Jr. and of Malcom X, both killed not when pushing only for civil rights or Black self-power, but when each had come to a point in theory and organizing when he stood the chance of breaking down barriers between all poor people and so challenging economic power. Or think about the tiny ways we've been creating something like the identity Women Who Have Been Hurt By Sex, with sexual abuse survivor support groups and speak outs and microscopic legislative changes. Now think about the panic this has created within male power, producing some of the nastiest and most well-funded of the backlash groups, including the Fathers' Rights movements and the False Memory Syndrome Foundation. Both of these organizations are willing to state quite clearly that their agenda is to defend themselves against Feminism and Feminists, who they claim are attacking the Family because they attack male power. The Fathers' Rights activists are even quite clear about their plan to keep women and children legally bound to, dependent on, and available to men; their publicly stated strategy is to change custody laws, change divorce laws, and end welfare to single mothers and their children so that women can't afford to leave marriages, and are afraid to take their children out of an abusive home, especially their daughters.

This point is so important, for what the Fathers' Rights men and the False Memory Syndrome parents have in common is that they sprang up not when adult women were fighting only for ourselves, against rape and battering, but when we began to talk about holding men accountable for their attacks on girls, and about denying men further sexual access to their daughters and other girls. Why? From here and now, I think that male power realized that defending the identity "rapist" would expose too much of the foundation of their power, so instead concentrated on defending the boundaries of "father" and "family" so these could continue to hide and protect sex as a sheer statement of male power. Or maybe these men's identity as "men" is completely built on the right of ownership of women and children, and they are threatened by what makes the ownership explicit. In either case, I know that basing theory/identity in life as we live it, not as we're told life is, will always threaten hidden powers, and that we need to know this, daily, and plan for our safety in any way we can.

Another risk of building identity groups around experience is that identity could be easily reduced only to experience, the same way it was reduced within IP to inherency. For my example, Women Who Have Been Hurt By Sex, there looms the danger of being The Victim. Feminists and other groups fighting for social change, in part by listing the effects of the current world on their lives, have been accused of having a "victim mentality" for years now. Most of these attacks are just pure backlash strategy, trying to discredit uncomfortable truths. But I do have deep concerns about suggesting that women work within such an identity. I worry that organizing around what has happened to us will leave us stuck in place, able to say nothing after we say what has happened, reproducing the situation where we stand, staring into oncoming headlights, believing that if we can only explain clearly enough that being run down is painful, the power roaring down on us will brake in time and repent of its previously careless driving. How many women found out, with shock of betrayal so great that they left activism, that telling men that rape hurt us didn't stop them, and that, in fact, they had always known this and just didn't care? Telling those in power that we are victims of their power, or appealing to them for aid to mediate their ongoing violence against us, hasn't changed anything,[13] although revealing that their comfort relies upon our pain crosses a serious boundary, and may well move them to use any means necessary to silence us. If an identity such as I suggest were used only to plead with power, instead of challenge and undermine it, it would not be a useful identity statement. As bell hooks writes in "Refusing to Be a Victim," such a stance of pleading with those in power to stop hurting us creates a mindset in which the only power around is the power "they" have: "To name white males as all-powerful victimizers was to pay homage to their power, to see them as possessing the cure for all that ails."[14]

I worry, too, that if identity is organized around experience, we may repeat the mistake of solidifying experience into an unalterable trait of our "real" selves; the clearest example of this is our adoption of the phrase "battered woman" instead of saying "a woman who has been battered." "Battered woman" has two tragic flaws: the woman who has been battered has been reduced to a sub-category, verbally removed from "normal" women's "normal" experience; and "battered" has become an adjective, an agentless passive (to use its formal name within Linguistics), which serves to collapse both the agent (whom was she battered by?) and the action (she was beaten, terrorized, raped) into a quality of the woman herself.[15] If we begin to consciously build groups around shared experience, the labels we use will be important, will be part of our resistance.[16] We'll need a way to use language that, as bell hooks describes, "does not embrace the rhetoric of victimhood even as it vigilantly calls attention to actual victimization."[17]

The final pitfall of making identity groups from experience, a pit that is entirely too familiar to me, is the process of making an Identity out of even the most personal, isolated, and idiosyncratic life experience. We've all seen these little episodes of control: "None of you can sing/eat burritos in my presence, ever, because once a man who is a singer/Taco Bell employee hurt me, and your insistence on singing/eating burritos oppresses me." Taken out of context, such statements are laughable. But we brought these scenes on by seeing identity as inherent and unchanging, so that "who we are" is a little kingdom with vulnerable boundaries that must be defended if we are to survive, and by insisting on a link between the political/social and the personal. If some experiences are to be honored, why not all experiences? Toss in a little overdose of oversimplified therapy-speak ("when you, I feel, so you must not") and, whala, identity = experience = my right to defend myself = my right to exert total control in any situation. What can I say? We need to constantly explain to ourselves and each other that feelings are not the same as oppression, that painful experiences can be honored in ways other than group control, that Revolution is about creating justice, not about feeling safe.[18] And we need to wrestle with the painful truth that not all needs for physical and emotional safety can be met; no single space, for example, can be "safe" for both women with dangerous allergies to animals and women who move through the world with guide dogs.

Within the world of Identity Politics, where the "identity," the "self-hood" of both of the women living with these disabilities would be threatened by the need of the other to have access to any one Disability/Access area of event. That is, too often at our festivals and in our communities, this situation would lead to charges of abelism, of not caring about disability, even, in the occasional out-of-control argument, to charging that the organizers are fascists or nazis because the nazis also wanted to destroy people living with disabilities.[19] When identity is seen as both inherent and as the basis for political action and inclusion in community, I think that we all ultimately suffer. We are, all of us, so much bigger than the categories of Identity Politics. Yes, those words describe us, and say so much about what power, privilege and basic needs we have access to in the broader social world, but are they actually the only or the best way to choose those people with whom we want to build a future? Does who we were born to be determine more than our experiences? Does what has happened to us matter more than the choices we make from here forward about where we want to go? And if our "identities" aren't going to be the driving force of our political and community organizing, what will be?

NOTES

1. For more on the history of this, see Douglas Rossi now's book. *The Politics of Authenticity: Liberalism, Christianity and the New Left in America* (New York: Columbia University Press), 1998.

2. I saw this in particular here in Philadelphia when the city was debating a domestic benefits bill for city employees. One of the leading proponents of this line of argument was then-City Council President, now Mayor-elect John Street.

3. Paula Rust, *Bisexuality and the Challenge to Lesbian Politics: Sex Loyalty and Revolution* (New York: New York University Press), 1995, p. 173. In a very interesting discussion in the chapter "The Pink and Blue Herring." Rust explores the tensions within lesbian identity created when both "ethnic" discourse and feminist discourse were used to explain lesbian identities.

4. In her introduction to the anthology *Food for Our Grandmothers: Writings by Arab-American and Arab-Canadian Women* (Boston: South End Press), 1994, editor Joanna Kadi writes: ". . . after one particularly bad day, I coined this phrase for our community: The Most Invisibles of the Invisibles. [. . .] It raises questions about how the other invisibles are, and whether Arabs really are the most invisible. I believe we are. In the United States and Canada, it is not only white people who refuse to see us, it is other people of color—Latinos, Africans, Asians, Natives—who do not acknowledge our existence." (pp xix–xx)

5. This should not be read as saying categories of race, gender, and culture aren't socially real. People are discriminated against, tortured and killed every day because of belonging to these categories. We can't ignore social reality, but we also can not treat it as the only reality.

6. But wasn't Feminism exactly about women's shared life experiences as women" Well, yes and no. I think it started that way, but the pull of Identity Politics became so strong that membership in the category Women became far more important than understanding the commonality of our life experiences. IP, after all, taught us to focus on understanding all of the differences between us, in clear rebellion against a liberal view of Universal Woman-ness.

7. Until writing this essay, I would have said that "gay" people who argued "we were born this way" were a big problem in my understanding of sexuality and social power. Now, though, it's very clear that the most pressing problem is heterosexual people who believe they were "born that way." As usual, infighting among the oppressed group was keeping us away from the foundation of male power. Quel surprise.

8. Which is why, of course, only "violent" [sic] rapes by total, preferably darker-skinned, strangers stand a chance of being prosecuted in ways that don't destroy the victim's life. The courts and the media simply cannot handle something which may have been "just sex" to one of the participants.

9. Sheila Jeffreys, "Sexology and Anti-Feminism," in *The Sexual Liberals and the Attack on Feminism,* eds., Dorchen Leidholdt and Janice G. Raymond, The Athene Series, (Elmsford, NY: Pergamon Press, 1990), pp. 21–22.

10. Selma Miriam, of the BloodRoot Collective, hearing Sheila Jeffreys describe this absence in a speech at BloodRoot Restaurant, coined for it the concept of a "dis-rotic" experience. Thanks to Lierre Keith for telling me about the discussion that evening.

11. What do these two groups have in common" That they were quite consciously trained to be aroused by violence. So maybe we need this identity too—people who have been hurt by being trained to be turned on by violence. Imagine the size of this identity group, and the way it would bring together, around a common experience/problem, women and men (at least the ones who see being trained to be turned on by violence as a problem and could demonstrate to women's approval a desire to change).

12. Joyce Trebilcot, *Taking Responsibility for Sexuality* (Berkeley, CA: Acacia Books), 1983, pp. 6–9.

13. And we should keep in front of us our own wisdom: Don't Agonize, Organize!

14. bell hooks, "Refusing to Be a Victim: Accountability and Responsibility" in *Killing Rage* (Boston: South End Press, 1995), p. 56. Hooks is examining this situation as it plays out between African Americans and white power. Her strategy deeply influenced the shape of my thinking here.

15. I learned this from linguist Julia Penelope's amazing work on English, misogyny, and women's power in her book *Speaking Freely: Unlearning the Lies of the Fathers" Tongues,* The Athene Series, (Elmsford, NY: Pergamon Press, 1990), especially the chapter "The Agents Within." Anyone attempting to use English to describe power in society would be well advised (by me) to begin with this work.

16. Well, you may ask, why then do you call your example "Women Who Have Been Hurt By Sex" instead of naming the agent who did the hurting? A good question. Partly because agency is complicated, being both the people who do the hurting and the ideology they use to justify it. Maybe a better name would be "Women Who Have Been Hurt By People Using Sex and by the Ideology that Sex = Good for You." This, of course, would be immediately shortened in the media to "Women Who Have Been Hurt" or "Hurt Women." Or, even better, just to "Women," which is exactly where we are right now, with that label hiding all kinds of agents and actions.

17. hooks, p. 61.

18. For an excellent analysis of the role of therapy-speak and the tyranny of "I feel so you must," see Joan M. Ward, "Therapism and the Taming of the Lesbian Community," *Sinister Wisdom* 36 (Winter 1988/98): pp. 33–41.

19. And hey—the only women who can shake their heads about this are the ones who lived through a similar blow-up. We do this to each other, all the time.

26

Chappals and Gym Shorts

An Indian Muslim Woman in the Land of Oz

ALMAS SAYEED

It was finals week during the spring semester of my sophomore year at the University of Kansas, and I was buried under mounds of papers and exams. The stress was exacerbated by long nights, too much coffee and a chronic, building pain in my permanently splintered shins (left over from an old sports injury). Between attempting to understand the nuances of Kant's *Critique of Pure Reason* and applying the latest game-theory models to the 1979 Iranian revolution, I was regretting my decision to pursue majors in philosophy, women's studies *and* international studies.

My schedule was not exactly permitting much down time. With a full-time school schedule, a part-time job at Lawrence's domestic violence shelter and preparations to leave the country in three weeks, I was grasping to hold onto what little sanity I had left. Wasn't living in Kansas supposed to be more laid-back than this? After all, Kansas was the portal to the magical land of Oz, where wicked people melt when doused with mop water and bright red, sparkly shoes could substitute for the services of American Airlines, providing a quick getaway. Storybook tales aside, the physical reality of this period was that my deadlines were inescapable. Moreover, the most pressing of these deadlines was completely non–school related: my dad, on his way home to Wichita, was coming for a brief visit. This would be his first stay by himself, without Mom to accompany him or act as a buffer.

Dad visited me the night before my most difficult exam. Having just returned from spending time with his family—a group of people with whom he historically had an antagonistic relationship—Dad seemed particularly relaxed in his stocky six-foot-four frame. Wearing one of the more subtle of his nineteen cowboy hats, he arrived at my door, hungry, greeting me in Urdu, our mother tongue, and laden with gifts from Estée Lauder for his only daughter. Never mind that I rarely wore makeup and would have preferred to see the money spent on my electric bill or a stack of feminist theory books from my favorite used bookstore. If Dad's visit was going to include a conversation about how little I use beauty products, I was not going to be particularly receptive.

"Almas," began my father from across the dinner table, speaking in his British-Indian accent infused with his love of Midwestern colloquialisms, "You know that you won't be a spring chicken forever. While I was in Philadelphia, I realized how important it is for

Almas Sayeed, "Chappals and Gym Shorts: An Indian Muslim Woman in the Land of Oz," from Daisy Hernandez and Bushra Rehman, eds., *Colonize This!: Young Women of Color on Today's Feminism.* Copyright © 2002 Seal Press.

you to begin thinking about our culture, religion and your future marriage plans. I think it is time we began a two-year marriage plan so you can find a husband and start a family. I think twenty-two will be a good age for you. You should be married by twenty-two."

I needed to begin thinking about the "importance of tradition" and be married by twenty-two? This, from the only Indian man I knew who had Alabama's first album on vinyl and loved to spend long weekends in his rickety, old camper near Cheney Lake, bass fishing and listening to traditional Islamic Quavali music? My father, in fact, was in his youth crowned "Mr. Madras," weightlifting champion of 1965, and had left India to practice medicine and be an American cowboy in his spare time. But he wanted *me* to aspire to be a "spring chicken," maintaining some unseen hearth and home to reflect my commitment to tradition and culture.

Dad continued, "I have met a boy that I like for you very much. Masoud's son, Mahmood. He is a good Muslim boy, tells great jokes in Urdu and is a promising engineer. We should be able to arrange something. I think you will be very happy with him!" Dad concluded with a satisfied grin.

Masoud, Dad's cousin? This would make me and Mahmood distant relatives of some sort. And Dad wants to "arrange something"? I had brief visions of being paraded around a room, serving tea to strangers in a sari or a shalwar kameez (a traditional South Asian out-fit for women) wearing a long braid and chappals (flat Indian slippers), while Dad boasted of my domestic capabilities to increase my attractiveness to potential suitors. I quickly flipped through my mental Rolodex of rhetorical devices acquired during years of women's studies classes and found the card blank. No doubt, even feminist scholar Catherine MacKinnon would have been rendered speechless sitting across the table in a Chinese restaurant speaking to my overzealous father.

It is not that I hadn't already dealt with the issue. In fact, we had been here before, ever since the marriage proposals began (the first one came when I was fourteen). Of course, when they first began, it was a family joke, as my parents understood that I was to continue my education. The jokes, however, were always at my expense: "You received a proposal from a nice boy living in our mosque. He is studying medicine," my father would come and tell me with a huge, playful grin. "I told him that you weren't interested because you are too busy with school. And anyway you can't cook or clean." My father found these jokes particularly funny, given my dislike of household chores. In this way, the eventuality of figuring out how to deal with these difficult issues was postponed with humor.

Dad's marriage propositions also resembled conversations that we had already had about my relationship to Islamic practices specific to women, some negotiated in my favor and others simply shelved for the time being. Just a year ago, Dad had come to me while I was home for the winter holidays, asking me to begin wearing *hijab,* the traditional headscarf worn by Muslim women. I categorically refused, maintaining respect for those women who chose to do so. I understood that for numerous women, as well as for Dad, hijab symbolized something much more than covering a woman's body or hair; it symbolized a way to adhere to religious and cultural traditions in order to prevent complete Western immersion. But even my sympathy for this concern didn't change my feeling that hijab constructed me as a woman first and a human being second. Veiling seemed to reinforce the fact that inequality between the sexes was a natural, inexplicable phenomenon that is impossible to overcome, and that women should cover themselves, accommodating an unequal hierarchy, for the purposes of modesty and self-protection. I couldn't reconcile these issues and refused my father's request to don the veil. Although there was tension—Dad claimed I had yet to have my religious awakening—he chose to respect my decision.

Negotiating certain issues had always been part of the dynamic between my parents and me. It wasn't that I disagreed with them about everything. In fact, I had internalized much of the Islamic perspective of the female body while simultaneously admitting to its problematic nature (To this day, I would rather wear a wool sweater than a bathing suit in public, no matter how sweltering the weather). Moreover, Islam became an important part of differentiating myself from other American kids who did not have to find a balance between two opposing cultures. Perhaps Mom and Dad recognized the need to concede certain aspects of traditional Islamic norms, because for all intents and purposes, I had been raised in the breadbasket of America.

By the time I hit adolescence, I had already established myself outside of the social norm of the women in my community. I was an athletic teenager, a competitive tennis player and a budding weightlifter. After a lot of reasoning with my parents, I was permitted to wear shorts to compete in tennis tournaments, but I was not allowed to show my legs or arms (no tank tops) outside of sports. It was a big deal for my parents to have agreed to allow me to wear shorts in the first place. The small community of South Asian Muslim girls my age, growing up in Wichita, became symbols of the future of our community in the United States. Our bodies became the sites to play out cultural and religious debates. Much in the same way that Lady Liberty had come to symbolize idealized stability in the *terra patria* of America, young South Asian girls in my community were expected to embody the values of a preexisting social structure. We were scrutinized for what we said, what we wore, being seen with boys in public and for lacking grace and piety. Needless to say, because of disproportionate muscle mass, crooked teeth, huge Lucy glasses, and a disposition to walk pigeon-toed, I was not among the favored.

To add insult to injury, Mom nicknamed me "Amazon Woman," lamenting the fact that she—a beautiful, petite lady—had produced such a graceless, unfeminine creature. She was horrified by how freely I got into physical fights with my younger brother and armwrestled boys at school. She was particularly frustrated by the fact that I could not wear her beautiful Indian jewelry, especially her bangles and bracelets, because my wrists were too big. Special occasions, when I had to slather my wrists with tons of lotion in order to squeeze my hands into her tiny bangles, often bending the soft gold out of shape, caused us both infinite amounts of grief. I was the snot-nosed, younger sibling of the Bollywood (India's Hollywood) princess that my mother had in mind as a more appropriate representation of an Indian daughter. Rather, I loved sports, sports figures and books. I hated painful makeup rituals and tight jewelry.

It wasn't that I had a feminist awakening at an early age. I was just an obnoxious kid who did not understand the politics raging around my body. I did not possess the tools to analyze or understand my reaction to this process of social conditioning and normalization until many years later, well after I had left my parents' house and the Muslim community in Wichita. By positioning me as a subject of both humiliation and negotiation, Mom and Dad had inadvertently laid the foundations for me to understand and scrutinize the process of conditioning women to fulfill particular social obligations.

What was different about my dinner conversation with Dad that night was a sense of immediacy and detail. Somehow discussion about a "two-year marriage plan" seemed to encroach on my personal space much more than had previous jokes about my inability to complete my household chores or pressure to begin wearing hijab. I was meant to understand that that when it came to marriage, I was up against an invisible clock (read: social norms) that would dictate how much time I had left: how much time I had left to remain desirable, attractive and marriageable. Dad was convinced that it was his duty to ensure my long-term security in a manner that reaffirmed traditional Muslim culture in the face of an often hostile foreign community. I recognized that the threat was not as extreme as being shipped off to India in order to marry someone I had never met. The challenge was far more subtle than this. I was being asked to choose my community; capitulation through arranged marriage would show my commitment to being Indian, to being a good Muslim woman and to my parents by proving that they had raised me with a sense of duty and the willingness to sacrifice for my culture, religion and family.

There was no way to tell Dad about my complicated reality. Certain characteristics of my current life already indicated failure by such standards. I was involved in a long-term relationship with a white man, whose father was a prison guard on death row, an occupation that would have mortified my upper-middle-class, status-conscious parents. I was also struggling with an insurmountable crush on an *actress* in the Theater and Film Department. I was debating my sexuality in terms of cultural compatibility as well as gender. Moreover, there was no way to tell Dad that my social circle was supportive of these nontraditional romantic explorations. My friends in college had radically altered my perceptions of marriage and family. Many of my closest friends, including my roommates, were coming to terms with their own life-choices, having recently come out of the closet but unable to tell their families about their decisions. I felt inextricably linked to this group of women, who, like me, often had to lead double lives. The immediacy of fighting for issues such as queer rights, given the strength and beauty of my friends' romantic relationships, held far more appeal for me than the topics of marriage and security that my father broached over our Chinese dinner. There was no way to explain to my loving, charismatic, steadfastly religious father, who was inclined to the occasional violent outburst, that a traditional arranged marriage not only conflicted with the feminist ideology I had come to embrace, but it seemed almost petty in the face of larger, more pressing issues.

Although I had no tools to answer my father that night at dinner, feminist theory had provided me with the tools to understand *why* my father and I were engaged in the conversation in the first place. I understood that in his mind, Dad was fulfilling his social obligation as father and protector. He worried about my economic stability and, in a roundabout way, my happiness. Feminism and community activism had enabled me to understand these things as part of a proscribed role for women. At the same time, growing up in Kansas and coming to feminism here meant that I had to reconcile a number of different issues. I am a Muslim, first-generation Indian, feminist woman studying in a largely homogeneous white, Christian community in Midwestern America. What sacrifices are necessary for me to retain my familial relationships as well as a sense of personal autonomy informed by Western feminism?

The feminist agenda in my community is centered on ending violence against women, fighting for queer rights and maintaining women's reproductive choices. As such, the way that I initially became involved with this community was through community projects such as "Womyn Take Back the Night," attending pride rallies and working at the local domestic violence shelter. I am often the only woman of color in feminist organizations and at feminist events. Despite having grown up in the Bible belt, it is difficult for me to relate to stories told by my closest friends of being raised on cattle ranches and farms, growing up Christian by default and experiencing the strict social norms of small, religious communities in rural Kansas. Given the context of this community—a predominantly white, middle-class, college town—I have difficulty explaining that my feminism has to address issues like, "I should be able to wear *both* hijab *and* shorts if I chose to." The enormity of our agenda leaves little room to debate issues equality important but applicable only to me, such as the meaning of veiling, arranged marriages versus dating and how the north-south divide uniquely disadvantages women in the developing world.

It isn't that the women in my community ever turned to me and said, "Hey you, brown girl, stop diluting our priorities." To the contrary, the majority of active feminists in my community are eager to listen and understand my sometimes divergent perspective. We have all learned to share our experiences as women, students, mothers, partners and feminists. We easily relate to issues of male privilege, violence against women and figuring out how to better appreciate the sacrifices made by our mothers. From these commonalities we have learned to work together, creating informal social networks to complete community projects.

The difficulty arises when trying to put this theory and discussion into practice. Like last year, when our organization, the Womyn's Empowerment Action Coalition, began plans for the Womyn Take Back the Night march and rally, a number of organizers were eager to include the contribution of a petite, white belly dancer in the pre-march festivities. When I voiced my concern that historically belly dancing had been used as a way to objectify women's bodies in the Middle East, one of my fellow organizers (and a very good friend) laughed and called me a prude: "We're in Kansas, Almas," she said. "It doesn't mean the same thing in our culture. It is different here than over *there.*" I understood what she meant, but having just returned from seven months in the West Bank, Palestine two months before, for me over there *was* over here. In the end, the dance was included while I wondered about our responsibility to women outside of the United States and our obligation to address the larger social, cultural issues of the dance itself.

To reconcile the differences between my own priorities and those of the women I work with, I am learning to bridge the gap between the Western white women (with the occasional African-American or Chicana) feminist canon and my own experience as a first-generation Indian Muslim woman living in the Midwest. I struggle with issues like cultural differences, colonialism, Islam and feminism and how they relate to one another. The most difficult part has been to get past my myopic vision of simply laying feminist theory written by Indian, Muslim or postcolonial theorists on top of American-Western feminism. With the help of feminist theory and other feminists, I am learning to dissect Western models of feminism, trying to figure out what aspects of these models can be applied to certain contexts. To this end, I have had the privilege of participating in projects abroad, in pursuit of understanding feminism in other contexts.

For example, while living with my extended family in India, I worked for a micro-credit affiliate that advised women on how to get loans and start their own businesses. During this time I learned about the potential of micro-enterprise as a weapon against the feminization of poverty. Last year, I spent a semester in the West Bank, Palestine, studying the link between women and economics in transitional states and beginning to understand the importance of women's efforts during revolution. These experiences have been invaluable to me as a student of feminism and women's mobilization efforts. They have also shaped my personal development, helping me understand where the theoretical falls short of solving for the practical. In Lawrence, I maintain my participation in local feminist projects. Working in three different contexts has highlighted the amazing and unique ways in which feminism develops in various cultural settings yet still maintains certain commonalities.

There are few guidebooks for women like me who are trying to negotiate the paradigm of feminism in two different worlds. There is a delicate dance here that I must master—a dance of negotiating identity within interlinking cultural spheres. When faced with the movement's expectations of my commitment to local issues, it becomes important for me to emphasize that differences in culture and religion are also "local issues." This has forced me to change my frame of reference, developing from a rebellious tomboy who resisted parental imposition to a budding social critic, learning how to be a committed feminist and still keep my cultural, religious and community ties. As for family, we still negotiate despite the fact that Dad's two-year marriage plan has yet to come to fruition in this, my twenty-second year.

27

Asian American Women and Racialized Femininities

"Doing" Gender Across Cultural Worlds

KAREN D. PYKE
DENISE L. JOHNSON

The study of gender in recent years has been largely guided by two orienting approaches: (1) a social constructionist emphasis on the day-to-day production or doing of gender (Coltrane 1989; West and Zimmerman 1987) and (2) attention to the interlocking systems of race, class, and gender (Espiritu 1997; Hill Collins 2000). Despite the prominence of these approaches, little empirical work has been done that integrates the doing of gender with the study of race. A contributing factor is the more expansive incorporation of social constructionism in the study of gender than in race scholarship where biological markers are still given importance despite widespread acknowledgment that racial oppression is rooted in social arrangements and not biology (Glenn 1999). In addition, attempts to theoretically integrate the doing of gender, race, and class around the concept of "doing difference" (West and Fenstermaker 1995) tended to downplay historical macro-structures of power and domination and to privilege gender over race and class (Hill Collins et al. 1995). Work is still needed that integrates systems of oppression in a social constructionist framework without granting primacy to any one form of inequality or ignoring larger structures of domination.

The integration of gender and race within a social constructionist approach directs attention to issues that have been overlooked. Little research has examined how racially and ethnically subordinated women, especially Asian American women, mediate cross-pressures in the production of femininity as they move between mainstream and ethnic arenas, such as family, work, and school, and whether distinct and even contradictory gender displays and strategies are enacted across different arenas. Many, if not most, individuals move in social worlds that do not require dramatic inversions of their gender performances, thereby enabling them to maintain stable and seemingly unified gender strategies. However, members of communities that are racially and ethnically marginalized and who regularly traverse interactional arenas with conflicting gender expectations might engage different gender performances depending on the local context in which they are interacting. Examining the ways that such individuals mediate conflicting expectations would address several unanswered questions. Do marginalized women shift their gender performances across mainstream and subcultural settings in response to different gender norms? If so, how do they experience and ne-

Karen D. Pyke & Denise L. Johnson, "Asian American Women and Racialized Femininities," from *Gender & Society,* Volume 17/2003, p. 33–53.

gotiate such transitions? What meaning do they assign to the different forms of femininities that they engage across settings? Do racially subordinated women experience their production of femininity as inferior to those forms engaged by privileged white women and glorified in the dominant culture?

We address these issues by examining how second-generation Asian American women experience and think about the shifting dynamics involved in the doing of femininity in Asian ethnic and mainstream cultural worlds. We look specifically at their assumptions about gender dynamics in the Euro-centric mainstream and Asian ethnic social settings, the way they think about their gendered selves, and their strategies in doing gender. Our analysis draws on and elaborates the theoretical literature concerning the construction of femininities across race, paying particular attention to how controlling images and ideologies shape the subjective experiences of women of color. This is the first study to our knowledge that examines how intersecting racial and gender hierarchies affect the everyday construction of gender among Asian American women.

CONSTRUCTING FEMININITIES

Current theorizing emphasizes gender as a socially constructed phenomenon rather than an innate and stable attribute (Lorber 1994; Lucal 1999; West and Zimmerman 1987). Informed by symbolic interactionism and ethnomethodology, gender is regarded as something people do in social interaction. Gender is manufactured out of the fabric of culture and social structure and has little, if any, causal relationship to biology (Kessler and McKenna 1978; Lorber 1994). Gender displays are "culturally established sets of behaviors, appearances, mannerisms, and other cues that we have learned to associate with members of a particular gender" (Lucal 1999, 784). These displays "cast particular pursuits as expressions of masculine and feminine 'natures'" (West and Zimmerman 1987, 126). The doing of gender involves its display as a seemingly innate component of an individual.

The social construction of gender provides a theoretical backdrop for notions of multiple masculinities put forth in the masculinities literature (Coltrane 1994; Connell 1987, 1995; Pyke 1996). We draw on this notion in conceptualizing a plurality of femininities in the social production of women. According to this work, gender is not a unitary process. Rather, it is splintered by overlapping layers of inequality into multiple forms of masculinities (and femininities) that are both internally and externally relational and hierarchical. The concepts of hegemonic and subordinated masculinities are a major contribution of this literature. Hegemonic (also known as ascendant) masculinity is organized around the symbolic equation of masculinity and power. It is an ideal type that is glorified and associated with white men at the highest levels of society, although few actually possess the associated traits. Scholars have focused on how hegemonic masculinity legitimates men's domination of women as well as intramale hierarchies (Chen 1999; Connell 1987; Kendall 2000; Pyke 1996).

The concept of femininities has served mostly as a placeholder in the theory of masculinities where it remains undertheorized and unexamined. Connell (1987, 1995) has written extensively about hegemonic masculinity but offers only a fleeting discussion of the role of femininities. He suggested that the traits of femininity in a patriarchal society are tremendously diverse, with no one form emerging as hegemonic. Hegemonic masculinity is centered on men's global domination of women, and because there is no configuration of femininity organized around women's domination of men, Connell (1987, 183) suggested the notion of a hegemonic femininity is inappropriate. He further argued that women have few opportunities for institutionalized power relations over other women. However, this discounts how other axes of domination, such as race, class, sexuality, and age, mold a hegemonic femininity that is venerated and extolled in the dominant culture, and that emphasizes the superiority of some women over others, thereby privileging white upper-class women. To conceptualize forms of femininities that are subordinated as "problematic" and "abnormal," it is necessary to refer to an oppositional category of femininity that is dominant, ascendant, and "normal" (Glenn 1999, 10). We use the notion of hegemonic and subordinated femininities in framing our analysis.

Ideas of hegemonic and subordinated femininities resonate in the work of feminist scholars of color who emphasize the multiplicity of women's experiences. Much of this research has focused on racial and class variations in the material and (re)productive conditions of women's lives. More recently, scholarship that draws on cultural studies, race and ethnic studies, and women's studies centers the cultural as well as material processes by which gender and race are constructed, although this work has been mostly theoretical (Espiritu 1997; Hill Collins 2000; St. Jean and Feagin 1998). Hill Collins (2000) discussed "controlling images" that denigrate and objectify women of color and justify their racial and gender subordination. Controlling images are part of the process of "othering," whereby a dominant group defines into existence a subordinate group through the creation of categories and ideas that mark the group as inferior (Schwalbe et al. 2000, 422). Controlling images reaffirm whiteness as normal and privilege white women by casting them as superior.

White society uses the image of the Black matriarch to objectify Black women as overly aggressive, domineering, and unfeminine. This imagery serves to blame Black women for the emasculation of Black men, low marriage rates, and poverty and to control their social behavior by undermining their assertiveness (Hill Collins 2000). While Black women are masculinized as aggressive and overpowering, Asian women are rendered hyperfeminine: passive, weak, quiet, excessively submissive, slavishly dutiful, sexually exotic, and available for white men (Espiritu 1997; Tajima 1989). This Lotus Blossom imagery obscures the internal variation of Asian American femininity and sexuality, making it difficult, for example, for others to "see" Asian lesbians and bisexuals (Lee 1996). Controlling images of Asian women also make them especially vulnerable to mistreatment from men who view them as easy targets. By casting Black women as not feminine enough and Asian women as too feminine, white forms of gender are racialized as normal and superior. In this way, white women are accorded racial privilege.

The dominant culture's dissemination of controlling imagery that derogates nonwhite forms of femininity (and masculinity) is part of a complex ideological system of "psychosocial dominance" (Baker 1983, 37) that imposes elite definitions of subordinates, denying them the power of self-identification. In this way, subordinates internalize "commonsense" notions of their inferiority to whites (Espiritu 1997; Hill Collins 2000). Once internalized, controlling images provide the template by which subordinates make meaning of their everyday lives (Pyke 2000), develop a sense of self, form racial and gender identities, and organize social relations (Osajima 1993; Pyke and Dang in press). For example, Chen (1998) found that Asian American women who joined predominately white sororities often did so to distance themselves from images of Asian femininity. In contrast, those who joined Asian sororities were often surprised to find their ideas of Asian women as passive and childlike challenged by the assertive, independent women they met. By internalizing the racial and gendered myth making that circumscribes their social existence, subordinates do not pose a threat to the dominant order. As Audre Lorde (1984, 123) described, "the true focus of revolutionary change is never merely the oppressive situations which we seek to escape, but that piece of the oppressor which is planted deep within us."

Hegemonies are rarely without sites of resistance (Espiritu 2001; Gramsci 1971; Hill Collins 2000). Espiritu (1997) described Asian American writers and filmmakers whose portraits of Asians defy the gender caricatures disseminated in the white-dominated society. However, such images are often forged around the contours of the one-dimensional stereotypes against which the struggle emerges. Thus, controlling images penetrate all aspects of the experience of subordinates, whether in a relationship of compliance or in one of resistance (Osajima 1993; Pyke and Dang in press).

The work concerning the effects of controlling images and the relational construction of subordinated and hegemonic femininities has mostly been theoretical. The little research that has examined how Asian American women do gender in the context of racialized images and ideologies that construct their gender as "naturally" inferior to white femininity provides only a brief look at these issues (Chen 1998; Lee 1996). Many of the Asian American women whom we study here do not construct their gender in one cultural field but are constantly moving between sites that are guided by ethnic immigrant cultural norms and those of the Eurocentric mainstream. A comparison of how gender is enacted and understood across such sites brings the construction of racialized gender and the dynamics of hegemonic and subordinated femininities into bold relief. We examine how respondents employ cultural symbols, controlling images, and gender and racial ideologies in giving meanings to their experiences.

GENDER IN ETHNIC AND MAINSTREAM CULTURAL WORLDS

We study Korean and Vietnamese Americans, who form two of the largest Asian ethnic groups in southern California, the site of this research. We focus on the daughters of immigrants as they are more involved in both ethnic and mainstream cultures than are members of the first generation. Koreans and Vietnamese did not immigrate to the United States in substantial numbers prior to 1965 and 1975, respectively (Zhou 1999). Fully 80 percent of Korean Americans (Chang 1999) and 82 percent of Vietnamese Americans are foreign born (Zhou and Bankston 1998). The second generation, who are still mostly children and young adults, must juggle the cross-pressures of ethnic and mainstream cultures without the groundwork that a long-standing ethnic enclave might provide. This is not easy. Disparities between ethnic and mainstream worlds can generate substantial conflict for children of immigrants, including conflict around issues of gender (Kibria 1993; Zhou and Bankston 1998).

Respondents dichotomized the interactional settings they occupy as ethnic, involving their immigrant family and other coethnics, and mainstream, involving non-Asian Americans in peer groups and at work and school. They grew up juggling different cultural expectations as they moved from home to school and often felt a pressure to behave differently when among Asian Americans and non–Asian Americans. Although there is no set of monolithic, stable norms in either setting, there are certain pressures, expectations, and structural arrangements that can affect different gender displays (Lee 1996). Definitions of gender and the constraints that patriarchy imposes on women's gender production can vary from culture to culture. The Confucian moral code, which accords male superiority, authority, and power over women in family and social relations, has influenced the patriarchal systems of Korea and Vietnam (Kibria 1993; Min 1998). Women are granted little decision-making power and are not accorded an individual identity apart from their family role, which emphasizes their service to male members. A woman who violates her role brings shame to herself and her family. Despite Western observers' tendency to regard Asian families as uniformly and rigidly patriarchal, variations exist (Ishii-Kuntz 2000). Women's resistance strategies, like the exchange of information in informal social groups, provide pockets of power (Kibria 1990). Women's growing educational and economic opportunities and the rise of women's rights groups in Korea and Vietnam challenge gender inequality (Palley 1994). Thus, actual gender dynamics are not in strict compliance with the prescribed moral code.

As they immigrate to the United States, Koreans and Vietnamese experience a shift in gender arrangements centering on men's loss of economic power and increased dependency on their wives' wages (Kibria 1993; Lim 1997; Min 1998). Immigrant women find their labor in demand by employers who regard them as a cheap labor source. With their employment, immigrant women experience more decision-making power, autonomy, and assistance with domestic chores from their husbands. However, such shifts are not total, and male dominance remains a common feature of family life (Kibria 1993; Min 1998). Furthermore, immigrant women tend to stay committed to the ethnic patriarchal structure as it provides resources for maintaining their parental authority and resisting the economic insecurities, racism, and cultural impositions of the new society (Kibria 1990, 1993; Lim 1997). The gender hierarchy is evident in parenting practices. Daughters are typically required to be home and performing household chores when not in school, while sons are given greater freedom.

Native-born American women, on the other hand, are perceived as having more equality, power, and independence than women in Asian societies, reflecting differences in gender attitudes. A recent study of Korean and American women found that 82 percent of

Korean women agreed that "women should have only a family-oriented life, devoted to bringing up the children and looking after the husband," compared to 19 percent of U.S. women (Kim 1994). However, the fit between egalitarian gender attitudes and actual behavior in the United States is rather poor. Patriarchal arrangements that accord higher status to men at home and work are still the norm, with women experiencing lower job status and pay, greater responsibility for family work even when employed, and high rates of male violence. Indeed, the belief that gender equality is the norm in U.S. society obscures the day-to-day materiality of American patriarchy. Despite cultural differences in the ideological justification of patriarchy, gender inequality is the reality in both Asian and mainstream cultural worlds.

METHOD

Our sample ($N = 100$) consists of 48 daughters of Korean immigrants and 52 daughters of Vietnamese immigrants. Respondents ranged in age from 18 to 34 and averaged 22 years of age. Respondents either were U.S. born ($n = 25$) or immigrated prior to the age of 16 ($n = 74$), with 1 respondent having arrived at 18. Both parents of respondents were born in Korea or Vietnam. The data consist of 81 individual interviews and seven group interviews with 26 women—7 of whom were also individually interviewed. Data were collected in California between 1996 and 1999 using a convenience sample located through interviewers' networks and announcements posted at a university campus. We tried to diversify the sample by recruiting community college students and those who had terminated their education prior to receiving a college degree. College graduates or currently enrolled university and community college students compose 81 percent of the sample, and 19 percent are college dropouts or women who never attended college.

The data are part of a larger study of adaptation among second-generation Korean and Vietnamese Americans. These two groups were selected for study to enable a comparison of how their ethnic and socioeconomic distinctions affect different adaptation pathways. Vietnamese arrived as poorer, less-educated refugees than Koreans, who voluntarily immigrated. Among first-generation heads of households, only 19 percent of Vietnamese hold a college degree compared to 45 percent of Koreans (Oropesa and Landale 1995). However, analyses of these data have not produced the expected ethnic or class distinctions (Pyke 2000; Pyke and Dang in press). As the sample is mostly college educated, our data may not capture the economic distinctions of these two groups. Kibria (1997) found that the experience of growing up American in Asian immigrant families is similar, causing the rise of a panethnic Asian American identity. The young age of our sample can also explain the absence of class differences. Class distinctions might become more prominent when respondents move away from home, settle into careers, and marry. Furthermore, our respondents draw on larger societal definitions and ideologies that favor whiteness in giving meaning to their own experiences, which can obscure ethnic and class distinctions in their narratives.

As this is an interpretive study that emphasizes the meanings and understandings of respondents, we used a grounded theory method (Glaser and Straus 1967). This approach assumes that researchers should not define the areas of research interest and theoretical importance prior to data collection but rather should follow the issues and themes that respondents suggest are important, allowing theoretical explanation to emerge from the data. The emphasis is on the understandings of those being studied rather than the a priori assumptions of researchers. Data analysis involves a constant comparison of respondents' accounts so as to identify deep-seated themes. Questions are constantly adjusted to pursue emergent topics and issues. Hence, respondents are not asked standardized questions as occurs with quantitative research.

By employing this method, the theme concerning differential gender experiences in mainstream and ethnic interactional settings emerged from the data. During the initial stage of data collection, we asked 47 women and 26 men questions related to ethnic identity as well as about their experiences growing up in an immigrant family, relations with parents, reactions to parents' discipline, and desires for change within their families (Pyke 2000). Gender loomed large in the accounts of female respondents, who commonly complained about parents' gender attitudes, especially the stricter rules for girls than for boys. We noted that women tended to denigrate Asian ethnic realms and glorify mainstream arenas. They did so in ways both subtle and overt and typically focused on gender behavior, although not always. Some respondents described different behavior and treatment in settings with coethnics compared to those dominated by whites and other non-Asian Americans. We began asking about gender in ethnic and mainstream settings in later interviews. In addition to earlier questions about family dynamics and ethnic identity, we asked if respondents ever alter their behavior around people of different ethnicities, whether people of different ethnicities treat them differently, and if being American and Vietnamese or Korean were ever in opposition. When necessary to prompt a discussion of gender, we also asked respondents to describe any time someone had certain stereotypical expectations of them, although their responses often focused on gender-neutral racial stereotypes of Asians as good at math, bad drivers, or unable to speak English. A few were asked if others ever expected them to be passive or quiet, which several women had described as a common expectation they encountered. When respondents failed to provide examples of gender behavior, the topic was usually dropped and the interview moved to other areas of study not part of this analysis. We interviewed an additional 53 women for a total sample of 100. Trained assistants, most of whom are daughters of Asian immigrants, and the first author collected the data. Tape-recorded interviews and video-taped group interviews lasted from one to three hours.

The transcribed interviews were read closely, and recurring themes concerning gender dynamics and beliefs as well as changes in behavior across cultural settings were extracted for analysis. The sorted data were analyzed for underlying meanings and reread in the context of our emerging findings to ensure their validity (Glaser and Straus 1967). The analysis focused on two themes. The first concerned racialized beliefs about gender, which came in a variety of forms and recurred throughout the interviews. We use these data to describe the ways that respondents think about Asian and "American" (meaning white) femininity. The second theme concerns changes in gender behavior or treatment in ethnic and mainstream settings, with 44 of the 100 respondents (20 Korean Americans and 24 Vietnamese Americans) having provided clear examples. That 56 respondents did not provide data about changes in gender behavior across settings cannot be interpreted to mean that they do not have such experiences, particularly as the production of gender is not something about which one is usually highly aware. Some of these individuals were among the 47 women interviewed before questions about gender in different settings were posed, or they provided gender-neutral examples that were not useful to our analysis. Some claimed that they had too few encounters with coethnics or non-Asians to make comparisons. Others reported that they were not aware of being treated differently or changing their behavior across settings. There were also a few respondents who acknowledged that they change their behavior yet found it difficult to provide specific examples, which is not surprising given the nonconscious manner in which gender is generally produced. That nearly half of the sample provided descriptions of gender switching across settings indicates it is prominent enough to warrant our investigation. However, we cannot ascertain from our convenience sample how prominent this issue is for Asian American women in general, which is beyond the aim of our study. Our purpose is to describe these emergent themes and what they suggest about how racialized notions of gender are embedded in the construction of identity for second-generation Asian American women.

We present the emergent gender themes in three sections. The first focuses on the data from respondents who reported altering their behavior or being treated differently across cultural settings (including those who volunteered such information as well as those who provided examples in response to questions about cultural switching). We find a tendency to construct these worlds as monolithic opposites, with the mainstream regarded as a site of gender equity and ethnic arenas as gender oppressive. In the next section, we present data that contradict notions of ethnic and mainstream realms as uniformly distinct. Ethnic realms are not always sites of male dominance, and mainstream settings often are. We suggest that because gender is seen through a racialized lens, respondents often fail to recognize this diversity. In the final section, we draw on data from the entire sample to examine how the gendered behavior of Asian and non-Asian American women is narratively constructed as essentially and racially distinct, with white femininity regarded as superior. In presenting the data, we provide the respondent's age and ethnicity, using the abbreviations VA for Vietnamese American and KA for Korean American. Respondents used the term "American" to refer to non-Asian Americans, particularly whites. The use of "American" as a code for "white" is a common practice (Espiritu 2001; Pyke and Dang in press). This usage reflects the racialized bias of the dominant society, which constructs Asian Americans as perpetual foreigners and whites as the only true Americans. We stay close to this language so as to underscore our respondents' racialized assumptions.

GENDER ACROSS CULTURAL TERRAINS: "I'M LIKE A CHAMELEON. I CHANGE MY PERSONALITY"

The 44 respondents who were aware of modifying their gender displays or being treated differently across cultural settings framed their accounts in terms of an oppressive ethnic world and an egalitarian mainstream. They reaffirmed the ideological constructions of the white-dominated society by casting ethnic and mainstream worlds as monolithic opposites, with internal variations largely ignored. Controlling images that denigrate Asian femininity and glorify white femininity were reiterated in many of the narratives. Women's behavior in ethnic realms was described as submissive and controlled, and that in white-dominated settings as freer and more self-expressive.

Some respondents suggested they made complete personality reversals as they moved across realms. They used the behavior of the mainstream as the standard by which they judged their behavior in ethnic settings. As Elizabeth (19, VA) said,

> I feel like when I'm amongst other Asians . . . I'm much more reserved and I hold back what I think. . . . But when I'm among other people like at school, I'm much more outspoken. I'll say whatever's on my mind. It's like a diametric character altogether. . . . I feel like when I'm with other Asians that I'm the *typical* passive [Asian] person and I feel like that's what's expected of me and if I do say something and if I'm the *normal* person that I am, I'd stick out like a sore thumb. So I just blend in with the situation, (emphasis added)

Elizabeth juxtaposes the "typical passive [Asian] person" and the "normal," outspoken person of the mainstream culture, whom she claims to be. In so doing, she reaffirms the stereotypical image of Asians as passive while glorifying Americanized behavior, such as verbal expressiveness, as "normal." This implies that Asian ethnic behavior is aberrant and inferior compared to white behavior, which is rendered normal. This juxtaposition was a recurring theme in these data (Pyke 2000). It contributed to respondents' attempts to distance themselves from racialized notions of the typical Asian woman who is hyperfeminine and submissive by claiming to possess those traits associated with white femininity, such as assertiveness, self-possession, confidence, and independence. Respondents often described a pressure to blend in and conform with the form of gender that they felt was expected in ethnic settings and that conflicted with the white standard of femininity. Thus, they often described such behavior with disgust and self-loathing. For example, Min-Jung (24, KA) said she feels "like an idiot" when talking with Korean adults:

> With Korean adults, I act more shy and more timid. I don't talk until spoken to and just act shy. I kind of speak in a higher tone of voice than I usually do. But then when I'm with white people and white adults, I joke around, I laugh, I talk, and I communicate about how I feel. And then my voice gets stronger. But then when I'm with Korean adults, my voice gets really high. . . . I just sound like an idiot and sometimes when I catch myself I'm like, "Why can't you just make conversation like you normally do?"

Many respondents distanced themselves from the compliant femininity associated with their Asianness by casting their behavior in ethnic realms as a mere act not reflective of their true nature. Repeatedly, they said they cannot be who they really are in ethnic settings and the enactment of an authentic self takes place only in mainstream settings. Teresa (23, KA) provides an example. She said,

> I feel like I can be myself when I'm around white people or mixed people. The Korean role is forced on me; it doesn't feel natural. I always feel like I have to put on this act so that I can be accepted by Korean people. I think whites are more accepting of other people. Maybe that's why I feel more comfortable with them.

Similarly, Wilma (21, VA) states, "Like some Asian guys expect me to be passive and let them decide on everything. Non-Asians don't expect anything from me. They just expect me *to be me*" (emphasis added). Gendered behavior engaged in Asian ethnic settings was largely described as performative, fake, and unnatural, while that in white-dominated settings was cast as a reflection of one's true self. The femininity of the white mainstream is glorified as authentic, natural, and normal, and Asian ethnic femininity is denigrated as coerced, contrived, and artificial. The "white is right" mantra is reiterated in this view of white femininity as the right way of doing gender.

The glorification of white femininity and controlling images of Asian women can lead Asian American women to believe that freedom and equity can be acquired only in the white-dominated world. For not only is white behavior glorified as superior and more authentic, but gender relations among whites are constructed as more egalitarian. Katie (21, KA) explained,

> Like when I'm with my family and stuff, I'm treated like my ideas or feelings of things really don't make a difference. I have to be more submissive and quiet. I really can't say how I feel about things with guys if it goes against them in public because that is like disrespectful. With Caucasians, I don't quite feel that way. I feel my opinion counts more, like I have some pull. I think society as a whole—America—still treats me like I'm inferior as a girl but I definitely feel more powerful with other races than I do with my own culture because I think at least with Americans it's like [politically correct] to be equal between men and women.

Controlling images of Asian men as hypermasculine further feed presumptions that whites are more egalitarian. Asian males were often cast as uniformly domineering in these accounts. Racialized images and the construction of hegemonic (white) and subordinated (Asian) forms of gender set up a situation where Asian American women feel they must choose between white worlds of gender equity and Asian worlds of gender oppression. Such images encourage them to reject their ethnic culture and Asian men and embrace the white world and white men so as to enhance their power (Espiritu 1997). This was the basis on which some respondents expressed a preference for interacting with whites. As Ha (19, VA) remarked,

> Asians would expect me to be more quiet, shy . . . But with white friends, I can act like who I am. . . . With Asians, I don't like it at all because they don't take me for who I am. They treat me differently just because I'm a girl. And white. . . . I like the way they treat me because it doesn't matter what you do.

In these accounts, we can see the construction of ethnic and mainstream cultural worlds—and Asians and whites—as diametrically opposed. The perception that whites are more egalitarian than Asian-origin individuals and thus preferred partners in social interaction further reinforces anti-Asian racism and white superiority. The cultural dominance of whiteness is reaffirmed through the co-construction of race and gender in these narratives. The perception that the production of gender in the mainstream is more authentic and superior to that in Asian ethnic arenas further reinforces the racialized categories of gender that define white forms of femininity as ascendant. In the next section, we describe variations in gender performances within ethnic and mainstream settings that respondents typically overlooked or discounted as atypical.

GENDER VARIATIONS WITHIN CULTURAL WORLDS

Several respondents described variations in gender dynamics within mainstream and ethnic settings that challenge notions of Asian and American worlds as monolithic opposites. Some talked of mothers who make all the decisions or fathers who do the cooking.

These accounts were framed as exceptions to Asian male dominance. For example, after Vietnamese women were described in a group interview as confined to domesticity, Ngâ (22, VA), who immigrated at 14 and spoke in Vietnamese-accented English, defined her family as gender egalitarian. She related,

> I guess I grow up in a *different* family. All my sisters doesn't have to cook, her husbands cooking all the time. Even my oldest sister. Even my mom—my dad is cooking. . . . My sisters and brothers are all very strong. (emphasis added)

Ngâ does not try to challenge stereotypical notions of Vietnamese families but rather reinforces such notions by suggesting that her family is different. Similarly, Heidi (21, KA) said, "Our family was kind of *different* because . . . my dad cooks and cleans and does dishes. He cleans house" (emphasis added). Respondents often framed accounts of gender egalitarianism in their families by stating they do not belong to the typical Asian family, with "typical" understood to mean male dominated. This variation in gender dynamics within the ethnic community was largely unconsidered in these accounts.

Other respondents described how they enacted widely disparate forms of gender across sites within ethnic realms, suggesting that gender behavior is more variable than generally framed. Take, for example, the case of Gin (29, KA), a law student married to a Korean American from a more traditional family than her own. When she is with her husband's kin, Gin assumes the traditional obligations of a daughter-in-law and does all the cooking, cleaning, and serving. The role exhausts her and she resents having to perform it. When Gin and her husband return home, the gender hierarchy is reversed. She said,

> When I come home, I take it all out on him. "Your parents are so traditional, look what they are putting me through . . . ?" That's when I say, "You vacuum. [Laughing] You deserve it." And sometimes when I'm really mean, "Take me out to dinner. I don't want to cook for a while and clean for a while." So he tries to accommodate that. . . . Just to be mean I will say I want this, he will buy me something, but I will return it. I want him to do what I want, like I want to be served because I serve when I'm with them. . . . [It's] kind of like pay back time. It's [a] strategy, it works.

Gin trades on the subservience and labor she performs among her in-laws to boost her marital power. She trades on her subservience to her in-laws to acquire more power in her marriage than she might otherwise have. Similar dynamics were described by Andrea (23, VA). She remarked,

> When I'm with my boyfriend and we're over at his family's house or at a church function. I tend to find myself being a little submissive, kind of like yielding or letting him make the decisions. But we know that at home it ain't gonna happen. . . . I tend to be a strong individual. I don't like to conform myself to certain rules even though I know sometimes in public I have to conform . . . like being feminine and being submissive. But I know that when I get home, he and I have that understanding that I'm not a submissive person. I speak my own mind and he likes the fact that I'm strong.

Controlling images of Asian men as hyperdomineering in their relations with women obscures how they can be called on to compensate for the subservience exacted from their female partners in some settings. Although respondents typically offered such stories as evidence of the patriarchy of ethnic arenas, these examples reveal that ethnic worlds are far more variable than generally described. Viewing Asian ethnic worlds through a lens of racialized gender stereotypes renders such variation invisible or, when acknowledged, atypical.

Gender expectations in the white-dominated mainstream also varied, with respondents sometimes expected to assume a subservient stance as Asian women. These examples reveal that the mainstream is not a site of unwavering gender equality as often depicted in these accounts and made less so for Asian American women by racial images that construct them as compliant. Many respondents described encounters with non-Asians, usually whites, who expected them to be passive, quiet, and yielding. Several described non-Asian (mostly white) men who brought such expectations to their dating relationships. Indeed, the servile Lotus Blossom image bolsters white men's preference for Asian women (Espiritu 1997). As Thanh (22, VA) recounted,

> Like the white guy that I dated, he expected me to be the submissive one—the one that was dependent on the guy. Kind of like the "Asian persuasion," that's what he'd call it when he was dating me. And when he found out that I had a spirit, kind of a wild side to me, he didn't like it at all. Period. And when I spoke up—my opinions—he got kind of scared.

So racialized images can cause Asian American women to believe they will find greater gender equality with white men and can cause white men to believe they will find greater subservience with Asian women. This dynamic promotes Asian American women's availability to white men and makes them particularly vulnerable to mistreatment.

There were other sites in the mainstream, besides dating relationships, where Asian American women encountered racialized gender expectations. Several described white employers and coworkers who expected them to be more passive and deferential than other employees and were surprised when they spoke up and resisted unfair treatment. Some described similar assumptions among non-Asian teachers and professors. Diane (26, KA) related,

> At first one of my teachers told me it was okay if I didn't want to talk in front of the class. I think she thought I was quiet or shy because I'm Asian. . . . [Laughing.] I am very outspoken, but that semester I just kept my mouth shut. I figured she won't make me talk anyway, so why try. I kind of went along with her.

Diane's example illustrates how racialized expectations can exert a pressure to display stereotyped behavior in mainstream interactions. Such expectations can subtly coerce behavioral displays that confirm the stereotypes, suggesting a kind of self-fulfilling prophecy. Furthermore, as submissiveness and passivity are denigrated traits in the mainstream, and often judged to be indicators of incompetence, compliance with such expectations can deny Asian American women personal opportunities and success. Not only is passivity unrewarded in the mainstream; it is also subordinated. The association of extreme passivity with Asian women serves to emphasize their otherness. Some respondents resist this subordination by enacting a more assertive femininity associated with whiteness. Lisa (18, KA) described being quiet with her relatives out of respect, but in mainstream scenes, she consciously resists the stereotype of Asian women as passive by adjusting her behavior. She explained,

> I feel like I have to prove myself to everybody and maybe that's why I'm always vocal. I'm quite aware of that stereotype of Asian women all being taught to be submissive. Maybe I'm always trying to affirm that I'm not like that. Yeah, I'm trying to say that if anything. I don't fit into that image and I don't want that to be labeled on me.

Several respondents were aware that they are presumed to be "typical" Asian women, and thus compliant and quiet, in mainstream settings. They describe extra efforts they enlisted to disprove such assumptions. Katie, who said that she feels like her opinion counts more in mainstream settings, described a pressure from white peers to be more outspoken so as to demonstrate that she is not "really" Asian and is thus worthy of their company. She stated,

> When I'm with non-Asians and stuff, I feel as though I need to prove myself like they expect me to prove I'm worthy to be with them, and that even though I look Asian, I really am not. . . . Like I have to act like them—kind of loud, good at partying and stuff, just more outgoing . . . like if I stand out in a negative way, then I'm not cool to be with or something.

To act Asian by being reserved and quiet would be to "stand out in a negative way" and to be regarded as "not cool." It means one will be denigrated and cast aside. Katie consciously engages loud and gregarious behavior to prove she is not the typical Asian and to be welcomed by white friends. Whereas many respondents describe their behavior in mainstream settings as an authentic reflection of their personality, these examples suggest otherwise. Racial expectations exert pressure on these women's gender performances among whites. Some go to great lengths to defy racial assumptions and be accepted into white-dominated social groups by engaging a white standard of femininity. As they are forced to work against racial stereotypes, they must exert extra effort at being outspoken and socially gregarious. Contrary to the claim of respondents, gender production in the mainstream is also coerced and contrived. The failure of some respondents to recognize variations in gender behavior within mainstream and ethnic settings probably has much to do with the essentialization of gender and race. That is, as we discuss next, the racialization of gender renders variations in behavior within racial groups invisible.

THE RACIALIZATION OF GENDER: BELIEVING IS SEEING

In this section, we discuss how respondents differentiate femininity by race rather than shifting situational contexts, even when they were consciously aware of altering their own gender performance to conform with shifting expectations. Racialized gender was discursively constructed as natural and essential. Gender and race were essentialized as interrelated biological facts that determine social behavior.

Among our 100 respondents, there was a tendency to rely on binary categories of American (code for white) and Asian femininity in describing a wide range of topics, including gender identities, personality traits, and orientations toward domesticity or career. Racialized gender categories were deployed as an interpretive template in giving meaning to experiences and organizing a worldview. Internal variation was again ignored, downplayed, or regarded as exceptional. White femininity, which was glorified in accounts of gender behavior across cultural settings, was also accorded superiority in the more general discussions of gender.

Respondents' narratives were structured by assumptions about Asian women as submissive, quiet, and diffident and of American women as independent, self-assured, outspoken, and powerful. That is, specific behaviors and traits were racialized. As Ha (19, VA) explained, "sometimes I'm quiet and passive and shy. That's a Vietnamese part of me." Similarly, domesticity was linked with Asian femininity and domestic incompetence or disinterest, along with success in the work world, with American femininity. Several women framed their internal struggles between career and domesticity in racialized terms. Min-Jung said,

> I kind of think my Korean side wants to stay home and do the cooking and cleaning and take care of the kids whereas my American side would want to go out and make a difference and become a strong woman and become head of companies and stuff like that.

This racialized dichotomy was central to respondents' self-identities. Amy (21, VA) said, "I'm not Vietnamese in the way I act. I'm American because I'm not a good cook and I'm not totally ladylike." In fact, one's ethnic identity could be challenged if one did not comply with notions of racialized gender. In a group interview, Kimberly (21, VA) described "joking around" with coethnic dates who asked if she cooked by responding that she did not. She explained,

> They're like, "You're Vietnamese and you're a girl and you don't know how to cook?" I'm like, "No, why? What's wrong with that?" [Another respondent is laughing.] And they go, "Oh, you're not a Vietnamese girl."

Similarly, coethnic friends tell Hien (21, VA), "You should be able to cook, you are Vietnamese, you are a girl." To be submissive and oriented toward family and domesticity marks Asian ethnicity. Conformity to stereotypes of Asian femininity serves to symbolically construct and affirm an Asian ethnic identity. Herein lies the pressure that some respondents feel to comply with racialized expectations in ethnic settings, as Lisa (18, KA) illustrates in explaining why she would feel uncomfortable speaking up in a class that has a lot of Asians:

> I think they would think that I'm not really Asian. Like I'm whitewashed . . . like I'm forgetting my race. I'm going against my roots and adapting to the American way. And I'm just neglecting my race.

American (white) women and Asian American women are constructed as diametric opposites. Although many respondents were aware that they contradicted racialized notions of gender in their day-to-day lives, they nonetheless view gender as an essential component of race. Variation is ignored or recategorized so that an Asian American woman who does not comply is no longer Asian. This was also evident among respondents who regard themselves as egalitarian or engage the behavioral traits associated with white femininity. There was the presumption that one cannot be Asian and have gender-egalitarian attitudes. Asian American women can engage those traits associated with ascendant femininity to enhance their status in the mainstream, but this requires a rejection of their racial/ethnic identity. This is evident by the use of words such as "American," "whitewashed," or "white"—but not Asian—to describe such women. Star (22, KA) explained, "I look Korean but I don't act Korean. I'm whitewashed. [Interviewer asks, 'How do you mean you don't act Korean?'] I'm loud. I'm not quiet and reserved."

As a result, struggles about gender identity and women's work/family trajectories become superimposed over racial/ethnic identity. The question is not simply whether Asian American women like Min-Jung want to be outspoken and career oriented or quiet and family oriented but whether they want to be American (whitewashed) or Asian. Those who do not conform to racialized expectations risk challenges to their racial identity and charges that they are not really Asian, as occurs with Lisa when she interacts with her non-Asian peers. She said,

> They think I'm really different from other Asian girls because I'm so outgoing. They feel that Asian girls have to be the shy type who is very passive and sometimes I'm not like that so they think, "Lisa, are you Asian?"

These data illustrate how the line drawn in the struggle for gender equality is superimposed over the cultural and racial boundaries dividing whites and Asians. At play is the presumption that the only path to gender equality and assertive womanhood is via assimilation to the white mainstream. This assumption was shared by Asian American research assistants who referred to respondents' gender egalitarian viewpoints as evidence of assimilation. The assumption is that Asian American women can be advocates of gender equality or strong and assertive in their interactions only as a result of assimilation, evident by the display of traits associated with hegemonic femininity, and a rejection of their ethnic culture and identity. This construction obscures gender inequality in mainstream U.S. society and constructs that sphere as the only place where Asian American women can be free. Hence, the diversity of gender arrangements practiced among those of Asian origin, as well as the potential for social change within Asian cultures, is ignored. Indeed, there were no references in these accounts to the rise in recent years of women's movements in Korea and Vietnam. Rather, Asian ethnic worlds are regarded as unchanging sites of male dominance and female submissiveness.

DISCUSSION AND SUMMARY

Our analysis reveals dynamics of internalized oppression and the reproduction of inequality that revolve around the relational construction of hegemonic and subordinated femininities. Respondents' descriptions of gender performances in ethnic settings were marked by self-disgust and referred to as a mere act not reflective of one's true gendered nature. In mainstream settings, on the other hand, respondents often felt a pressure to comply with caricatured notions of Asian femininity or, conversely, to distance one's self from derogatory images of Asian femininity to be accepted. In both cases, the subordination of Asian femininity is reproduced.

In general, respondents depicted women of Asian descent as uniformly engaged in subordinated femininity marked by submissiveness and white women as universally assertive and gender egalitarian. Race, rather than culture, situational dynamics, or individual personalities, emerged as the primary basis by which respondents gave meaning to variations in femininity. That is, despite their own situational variation in doing gender, they treat gender as a racialized feature of bodies rather than a sociocultural product. Specific gender displays, such as a submissive demeanor, are required to confirm an Asian identity. Several respondents face challenges to their ethnic identity when they behave in ways that do not conform with racialized images. Indeed, some claimed that because they are assertive or career oriented they are not really Asian. That is, because they do not conform to the racialized stereotypes of Asian women but identify with a hegemonic femininity that is the white standard, they are different from other women of Asian origin. In this way, they manipulate the racialized categories of gender in attempting to craft identities that are empowering. However, this is accomplished by denying their ethnicity and connections to other Asian, American women and through the adoption and replication of controlling images of Asian women.

Respondents who claim that they are not really Asian because they do not conform with essentialized notions of Asian femininity suggest similarities to transgendered individuals who feel that underneath, they really belong to the gender category that is opposite from the one to which they are assigned. The notion that deep down they are really white implies a kind of transracialized gender identity. In claiming that they are not innately Asian, they reaffirm racialized categories of gender just as transgendered individuals reaffirm the gender dichotomy (Kessler and McKenna 1978; Lorber 1994). However, there are limitations to notions of a transracialized identity as racial barriers do not permit these women to socially pass into the white world, even though they might feel themselves to be more white than Asian. Due to such barriers, they use terms that are suggestive of a racial crossover, such as "whitewashed" or "American" rather than "white" in describing themselves. Such terms are frequently used among Asian Americans to describe those who are regarded as assimilated to the white world and no longer ethnic, further underscoring how racial categories are essentialized (Pyke and Dang in press). Blocked from a white identity, these terms capture a marginalized space that is neither truly white nor Asian. As racial categories are dynamic, it remains to be seen whether these marginalized identities are the site for new identities marked by hybridity (Lowe 1991) or whether Asian Americans will eventually be incorporated into whiteness. This process may be hastened by outmarriage to whites and high rates of biracial Asian Americans who can more easily pass into the white world, thereby leading the way for other Asian Americans. While we cannot ascertain the direction of such changes, our data highlight the contradictions that strain the existing racial and gender order as it applies to second-generation Asian American women.

While respondents construct a world in which Asian American women can experience a kind of transracial gender identity, they do not consider the same possibility for women of other races. A white woman who is submissive does not become Asian. In fact, there was no reference in these accounts to submissive white women who are rendered invisible by racialized categories of gender. Instead, white women are constructed as monolithically self-confident, independent, assertive, and successful—characteristics of white hegemonic femininity. That these are the same ruling traits associated with hegemonic masculinity, albeit in a less exaggerated, feminine form, underscores the imitative structure of hegemonic femininity. That is, the supremacy of white femininity over Asian femininity mimics hegemonic masculinity. We are not arguing that hegemonic femininity and masculinity are equivalent structures. They are not. Whereas hegemonic masculinity is a superstructure of domination, hegemonic femininity is confined to power relations among women. However, the two structures are interrelated with hegemonic femininity constructed to serve hegemonic masculinity, from which it is granted legitimacy.

Our findings illustrate the powerful interplay of controlling images and hegemonic femininity in promoting internalized oppression. Respondents draw on racial images and assumptions in their narrative construction of Asian cultures as innately oppressive of women and fully resistant to change against which the white-dominated mainstream is framed as a paradigm of gender equality. This serves a proassimilation function by suggesting that Asian American women will find gender equality in exchange for rejecting their ethnicity and adopting white standards of gender. The construction of a hegemonic femininity not only (re)creates a hierarchy that privileges white women over Asian-American women but also makes Asian American women available for white men. In this way, hegemonic femininity serves as a handmaiden to hegemonic masculinity.

By constructing ethnic culture as impervious to social change and as a site where resistance to gender oppression is impossible, our respondents accommodate and reinforce rather than resist the gender hierarchal arrangements of such locales. This can contribute to a self-fulfilling prophecy as Asian American women who hold gender egalitarian views feel compelled to retreat from interactions in ethnic settings, thus (re)creating Asian ethnic cultures as strongholds of patriarchy and reinforcing the maintenance of a rigid gender hierarchy as a primary mechanism by which ethnicity and ethnic identity are constructed. This marking of ethnic culture as a symbolic repository of patriarchy obscures variations in ethnic gender practices as well as the gender inequality in the mainstream. Thus, compliance with the dominant order is secured.

Our study attempts to bring a racialized examination of gender to a constructionist framework without decentering either race or gender. By examining the racialized meaning systems that inform the construction of gender, our findings illustrate how the resistance of gender oppression among our respondents draws ideologically on the denigration and rejection of ethnic Asian culture, thereby reinforcing white dominance. Conversely, we found that mechanisms used to construct ethnic identity in resistance to the proassimilation forces of the white-dominated mainstream rest on narrow definitions of Asian women that emphasize gender subordination. These findings underscore the crosscutting ways that gender and racial oppression operate such that strategies and ideologies focused on the resistance of one form of domination can reproduce another form. A social constructionist approach that examines the simultaneous production of gender and race within the matrix of oppression, and considers the relational construction of hegemonic and subordinated femininities, holds much promise in uncovering the micro-level structures and complicated features of oppression, including the processes by which oppression infiltrates the meanings individuals give to their experiences.

REFERENCES

Baker, Donald G. 1983. *Race, ethnicity and power.* Boston: Routledge Kegan Paul.

Chang, Edward T. 1999. The post-Los Angeles riot Korean American community: Challenges and prospects. *Korean American Studies Bulletin* 10:6–26.

Chen, Anthony S. 1999. Lives at the center of the periphery, lives at the periphery of the center: Chinese American masculinities and bargaining with hegemony. *Gender & Society.* 13:584–607.

Chen, Edith Wen-Chu. 1998. The continuing significance of race: A case study of Asian American women in white, Asian American, and African American sororities. Ph.D. diss., University of California, Los Angeles.

Coltrane, Scott. 1989. Household labor and the routine production of gender. *Social Problems* 36:473–90.

———. 1994. Theorizing masculinities in contemporary social science. In *Theorizing masculinities,* edited by Harry Brod and Michael Kaufman. Thousand Oaks, CA: Sage.

Connell, R. W. 1987. *Gender and power.* Stanford. CA: Stanford University Press.

———. 1995. *Masculinities.* Los Angeles: University of California Press.

Espiritu, Yen L. 1997. *Asian American women and men.* Thousand Oaks, CA: Sage.

———. 2001. "We don't sleep around like white girls do": Family, culture, and gender in Filipina American life. *Signs: Journal of Women in Culture and Society* 26:415–40.

Glaser, Barney G., and Anselm L. Straus. 1967. *The discovery of grounded theory.* New York: Aldine.

Glenn, Evelyn Nakano. 1999. The social construction and institutionalization of gender and race. In *Revisioning gender,* edited by Myra Marx Ferree, Judith Lober, and Beth B. Hess. Thousand Oaks, CA: Sage.

Gramsci, Antonio. 1971. *Selections from the prison notebooks of Antonio Gramsci,* edited and translated by Quintin Hoare and Geoffrey Nowell Smith. New York: International.

Hill Collins, Patricia. 2000. *Black feminist thought.* New York: Routledge.

Hill Collins, Patricia, Lionel A. Maldonado, Dana Y. Takagi, Barrie Thorne, Lynn Weber, and Howard Winant. 1995. Symposium: On West and Fenstermaker's "Doing difference." *Gender & Society* 9:491–513.

Ishii-Kuntz, Masako. 2000. Diversity within Asian American families. In *Handbook of family diversity,* edited by David H. Demo, Katherine Allen, and Mark A. Fine. New York: Oxford University Press.

Kendall, Lori. 2000. "Oh no! I'm a nerd!" Hegemonic masculinity on an online forum. *Gender & Society* 14: 256–73.

Kessler, Suzanne, and Wendy McKenna. 1978. *Gender: An ethnomethodological approach.* Chicago: University of Chicago Press.

Kibria, Nazli. 1990. Power patriarchy, and gender conflict in the Vietnamese immigrant community. *Gender & Society* 4:9–24.

———. 1993. *Family tightrope: The changing lives of Vietnamese Americans.* Princeton, NJ: Princeton University Press.

———. 1997. The construction of "Asian American": Reflections on intermarriage and ethnic identity among second generation Chinese and Korean Americans. *Ethnic and Racial Studies* 20:523–44.

Kim, Byong-suh. 1994. Value orientations and sex-gender role attitudes on the comparability of Koreans and Americans. In *Gender division of labor in Korea,* edited by Hyong Cho and Oil-wha Chang. Seoul, Korea: Ewha Women's University Press.

Lee, Jee Yeun. 1996. Why Suzie Wong is not a lesbian: Asian and Asian American lesbian and bisexual women and femme/butch/gender identities. In *Queer studies,* edited by Brett Beemyn and Mickey Eliason. New York: New York University Press.

Lim, In-Sook. 1997. Korean immigrant women's challenge to gender inequality at home: The interplay of economic resources, gender, and family, *Gender & Society* 11:31–51.

Lorber, Judith. 1994. *Paradoxes of gender.* New Haven, CT: Yale University Press.

Lorde, Audre. 1984. *Sister outsider.* Trumansberg, NY: Crossing Press.

Lowe, Lisa. 1991. Heterogeneity, hybridity, multiplicity: Marking Asian American differences. *Diaspora* 1: 24–44.

Lucal, Betsy. 1999. What it means to be gendered me: Life on the boundaries of a dichotomous gender system. *Gender & Society* 13:781–97.

Min, Pyong Gap. 1998. *Changes and conflicts.* Boston: Allyn & Bacon.

Oropesa, R. S., and Nancy Landale. 1995. *Immigrant legacies: The socioeconomic circumstances of children by ethnicity and generation in the United States.* Working paper 95-01R. State College: Population Research Institute, Pennsylvania State University.

Osajima, Keith. 1993. The hidden injuries of race. In *Bearing dreams, shaping visions: Asian Pacific American perspectives,* edited by Linda Revilla, Gail Nomura, Shawn Wong, and Shirley Hune. Pullman: Washington State University Press.

Palley, Marian Lief. 1994. Feminism in a Confucian society: The women's movement in Korea. In *Women of Japan and Korea,* edited by Joyce Gelb and Marian Lieff. Philadelphia: Temple University Press.

Pyke, Karen. 1996. Class-based masculinities: The interdependence of gender, class, and interpersonal power. *Gender & Society* 10:527–49.

———. 2000. "The normal American family" as an interpretive structure of family life among grown children of Korean and Vietnamese immigrants. *Journal of Marriage and the Family* 62:240–55.

Pyke, Karen, and Tran Dang. In press. "FOB" and "whitewashed": Intra ethnic identities and internalized oppression among second generation Asian Americans. *Qualitative Sociology.*

St. Jean, Yanick, and Joe R. Feagin. 1998. *Double burden: Black women and everyday racism.* Armonk. NY: M. E. Sharpe.

Schwalbe, Michael, Sandra Godwin, Daphne Holden, Douglas Schrock, Shealy Thompson, and Michele Wolkomir. 2000. Generic processes in the reproduction of inequality: An interactionist analysis. *Social Forces* 79: 419–52.

Tajima, Renee E. 1989. Lotus blossoms don't bleed: Images of Asian women. In *Making waves.* edited by Asian Women United of California. Boston: Beacon.

West, Candace, and Sarah Fenstermaker. 1995. Doing difference. *Gender & Society* 9:8–37.

West, Candace, and Don H. Zimmerman. 1987. Doing gender. *Gender & Society* 1:125–51.

Zhou, Min. 1999. Coming of age: The current situation of Asian American children. *Amerasia Journal* 25: 1–27.

Zhou, Min, and Carl L. Bankston III. 1998. *Growing up American.* New York: Russell Sage.

28

White Privilege

Unpacking the Invisible Knapsack

PEGGY MCINTOSH

Through work to bring materials from Women's Studies into the rest of the curriculum, I have often noticed men's unwillingness to grant that they are overprivileged, even though they may grant that women are disadvantaged. They may say they will work to improve women's status, in the society, the university, or the curriculum, but they can't or won't support the idea of lessening men's. Denials which amount to taboos surround the subject of advantages which men gain from women's disadvantages. These denials protect male privilege from being fully acknowledged, lessened or ended.

Thinking through unacknowledged male privilege as a phenomenon, I realized that since hierarchies in our society are interlocking, there was most likely a phenomenon of White privilege which was similarly denied and protected. As a White person, I realized I had been taught about racism as something which puts others at a disadvantage, but had been taught not to see one of its corollary aspects, White privilege, which puts me at an advantage.

I think Whites are carefully taught not to recognize White privilege, as males are taught not to recognize male privilege. So I have begun in an untutored way to ask what it is like to have White privilege. I have come to see White privilege as an invisible package of unearned assets which I can count on cashing in each day, but about which I was "meant" to remain oblivious. White privilege is like an invisible weightless knapsack of special provisions, maps, passports, codebooks, visas, clothes, tools and blank checks.

Describing White privilege makes one newly accountable. As we in Women's Studies work to reveal male privilege and ask men to give up some of their power, so one who writes about having White privilege must ask, "Having described it, what will I do to lessen or end it?"

After I realized the extent to which men work from a base of unacknowledged privilege, I understood that much of their oppressiveness was unconscious. Then I remembered the frequent charges from women of color that White women whom they encounter are oppressive. I began to understand why we are justly seen as oppressive, even when we don't see ourselves that way. I began to count the ways in which I enjoy unearned skin privilege and have been conditioned into oblivion about its existence.

My schooling gave me no training in seeing myself as an oppressor, as an unfairly advantaged person, or as a participant in a damaged culture. I was taught to see myself as an individual whose moral state depended on her individual moral will. My schooling followed the pattern my colleague Elizabeth Minnich has pointed out: Whites are taught to think of their lives as morally neutral, normative, and average, and also ideal, so that when we work to benefit others, this is seen as work which will allow "them" to be more like "us."

I decided to try to work on myself at least by identifying some of the daily effects of White privilege in my life. I have chosen those conditions which I think in my case *attach somewhat more to skin-color privilege* than to class, religion, ethnic status, or geographical location, though of course all these other factors are intricately intertwined. As far as I can see, my African American co-workers, friends and acquaintances with whom I come into daily or frequent contact in this particular time, place, and line of work cannot count on most of these conditions.

1. I can if I wish arrange to be in the company of people of my race most of the time.
2. If I should need to move, I can be pretty sure of renting or purchasing housing in an area which I can afford and in which I would want to live.
3. I can be pretty sure that my neighbors in such a location will be neutral or pleasant to me.
4. I can go shopping alone most of the time, pretty well assured that I will not be followed or harassed.
5. I can turn on the television or open to the front page of the paper and see people of my race widely represented.
6. When I am told about our national heritage or about "civilization," I am shown that people of my color made it what it is.
7. I can be sure that my children will be given curricular materials that testify to the existence of their race.
8. If I want to, I can be pretty sure of finding a publisher for this piece on White privilege.
9. I can go into a music shop and count on finding the music of my race represented, into a supermarket and find the staple foods which fit with my cultural traditions, into a hairdresser's shop and find someone who can cut my hair.
10. Whether I use checks, credit cards, or cash, I can count on my skin color not to work against the appearance of financial reliability.
11. I can arrange to protect my children most of the time from people who might not like them.
12. I can swear, or dress in second hand clothes, or not answer letters, without having people attribute these choices to the bad morals, the poverty, or the illiteracy of my race.
13. I can speak in public to a powerful male group without putting my race on trial.
14. I can do well in a challenging situation without being called a credit to my race.
15. I am never asked to speak for all the people of my racial group.
16. I can remain oblivious of the language and customs of persons of color who constitute the world's majority without feeling in my culture any penalty for such oblivion.
17. I can criticize our government and talk about how much I fear its policies and behavior without being seen as a cultural outsider.
18. I can be pretty sure that if I ask to talk to "the person in charge," I will be facing a person of my race.
19. If a traffic cop pulls me over or if the IRS audits my tax return, I can be sure I haven't been singled out because of my race.
20. I can easily buy posters, postcards, picture books, greeting cards, dolls, toys, and children's magazines featuring people of my race.
21. I can go home from most meetings of organizations I belong to feeling somewhat tied in, rather than isolated, out of place, outnumbered, unheard, held at a distance, or feared.
22. I can take a job with an affirmative action employer without having co-workers on the job suspect that I got it because of race.
23. I can choose public accommodation without fearing that people of my race cannot get in or will be mistreated in the places I have chosen.
24. I can be sure that if I need legal or medical help, my race will not work against me.

25. If my day, week, or year is going badly, I need not ask of each negative episode or situation whether it has racial overtones.
26. I can choose blemish cover or bandages in "flesh" color and have them more or less match my skin.

I repeatedly forgot each of the realizations on this list until I wrote it down. For me White privilege has turned out to be an elusive and fugitive subject. The pressure to avoid it is great, for in facing it I must give up the myth of meritocracy. If these things are true, this is not such a free country; one's life is not what one makes it; many doors open for certain people through no virtues of their own.

In unpacking this invisible knapsack of White privilege, I have listed conditions of daily experience which I once took for granted. Nor did I think of any of these perquisites as bad for the holder. I now think that we need a more finely differentiated taxonomy of privilege, for some of these varieties are only what one would want for everyone in a just society, and others give licence to be ignorant, oblivious, arrogant and destructive.

I see a pattern running through the matrix of White privilege, a pattern of assumptions which were passed on to me as a White person. There was one main piece of cultural turf; it was my own turf, and I was among those who could control the turf. *My skin color was an asset for any move I was educated to want to make.* I could think of myself as belonging in major ways, and of making social systems work for me. I could freely disparage, fear, neglect, or be oblivious to anything outside of the dominant cultural forms. Being of the main culture, I could also criticize it fairly freely.

In proportion as my racial group was being made confident, comfortable, and oblivious, other groups were likely being made inconfident, uncomfortable, and alienated. Whiteness protected me from many kinds of hostility, distress, and violence, which I was being subtly trained to visit in turn upon people of color.

For this reason, the word "privilege" now seems to me misleading. We usually think of privilege as being a favored state, whether earned or conferred by birth or luck. Yet some of the conditions I have described here work to systematically overempower certain groups. Such privilege simply *confers dominance* because of one's race or sex.

I want, then, to distinguish between earned strength and unearned power conferred systemically. Power from unearned privilege can look like strength when it is in fact permission to escape or to dominate. But not all of the privileges on my list are inevitably damaging. Some, like the expectation that neighbors will be decent to you, or that your race will not count against you in court, should be the norm in a just society. Others, like the privilege to ignore less powerful people, distort the humanity of the holders as well as the ignored groups.

We might at least start by distinguishing between positive advantages which we can work to spread, and negative types of advantages which unless rejected will always reinforce our present hierarchies. For example, the feeling that one belongs within the human circle, as Native Americans say, should not be seen as privilege for a few. Ideally it is an *unearned entitlement.* At present, since only a few have it, it is an *unearned advantage* for them. This paper results from a process of coming to see that some of the power which I originally saw as attendant on being a human being in the U.S. consisted in *unearned advantage* and *conferred dominance.*

I have met very few men who are truly distressed about systemic, unearned male advantage and conferred dominance. And so one question for me and others like me is whether we will be like them, or whether we will get truly distressed, even outraged, about unearned race advantage and conferred dominance and if so, what we will do to lessen them. In any case, we need to do more work in identifying how they actually affect our daily lives. Many, perhaps most, of our White students in the U.S. think that racism doesn't affect them because they are not people of color; they do not see "whiteness" as a racial identity. In addition, since race and sex are not the only advantaging systems at work, we need similarly to examine the daily experience of having age advantage, or ethnic advantage, or physical ability, or advantage related to nationality, religion, or sexual orientation.

Difficulties and dangers surrounding the task of finding parallels are many. Since racism, sexism, and heterosexism are not the same, the advantaging associated with them should not be seen as the same. In addition, it is hard to disentangle aspects of unearned advantage which rest more on social class, economic class, race, religion, sex and ethnic identity than on other factors. Still, all of the oppressions are interlocking, as the Combahee River Collective Statement of 1977 continues to remind us eloquently.

One factor seems clear about all of the interlocking oppressions. They take both active forms which we can see and embedded forms which as a member of the dominant group one is taught not to see. In my class and place, I did not see myself as a racist because I was taught to recognize racism only in individual acts of meanness by members of my group, never in invisible systems conferring unsought racial dominance on my group from birth.

Disapproving of the systems won't be enough to change them. I was taught to think that racism could end if White individuals changed their attitudes. (But) a "white" skin in the United States opens many doors for Whites whether or not we approve of the way dominance has been conferred on us. Individual acts can palliate, but cannot end, these problems.

To redesign social systems we need first to acknowledge their colossal unseen dimensions. The silences and denials surrounding privilege are the key political tool here. They keep the thinking about equality or equity incomplete, protecting unearned advantage and conferred dominance by making these taboo subjects. Most talk by Whites about equal opportunity seems to me now to be about equal opportunity to try to get into a position of dominance while denying that *systems* of dominance exist.

It seems to me that obliviousness about White advantage, like obliviousness about male advantage, is kept strongly inculturated in the United States so as to maintain the myth of meritocracy, the myth that democratic choice is equally available to all. Keeping most people unaware that freedom of confident action is there for just a small number of people props up those in power, and serves to keep power in the hands of the same groups that have most of it already.

Though systemic change takes many decades, there are pressing questions for me and I imagine for some others like me if we raise our daily consciousness on the perquisites of being light-skinned. What will we do with such knowledge? As we know from watching men, it is an open question whether we will choose to use unearned advantage to weaken hidden systems of advantage, and whether we will use any of our arbitrarily awarded power to try to reconstruct power systems on a broader base.

PART V

FAMILIES

In the late twentieth and early twenty-first century, major transformations in world economic and cultural systems have affected all families and households and given rise to new patterns of family living. Despite these changes, family life remains shrouded in myth. No matter how much families change, they remain idealized as natural or biological units based on the timeless functions of love, motherhood, and childbearing. "Family" evokes ideas of warmth, caring, and unconditional love in a refuge set apart from the public world. In this image, family and society are separate. Relations *inside* the family are idealized as nurturant, and those *outside* the family are seen as competitive. This ideal assumes a gendered division of labor: a husband/father associated with the public world and a wife/mother defined as the heart of the family. Although this image bears little resemblance to the majority of family situations, it is still recognizable in cultural ideals and public policies.

In the past three decades, feminist thought has been in the forefront of efforts to demythologize the family. Feminist thinkers have demonstrated that family forms are socially and historically constructed, not monolithic universals that exist across all times and all places or the inevitable result of unambiguous differences between women and men. Feminist thinkers have drawn attention to myths that romanticize "traditional" families in deference to male privilege and to the contradictions between idealized and real patterns of family life. They have directed attention to the close connections between families and other institutions in society. Early feminist critiques of the family characterized it as a primary site of women's oppression and argued in support of women's increased participation in the labor force as a means of attaining greater autonomy. But this analysis did not apply well to women of color or working-class women generally, because it falsely universalized the experiences of white middle-class women who had the option of staying home to raise their children.

More recently, feminist thought has begun to create a more complex understanding of the relationship between family and work by examining differences among women and taking men's experiences into account. The first four articles in this part of the book explore the symbolic meanings and lived realities of motherhood and fatherhood. They uncover experiences that are not simply gendered, but shaped by other lines of difference as well. First Patricia Hill Collins takes race, class, and history into account as she investigates mother–daughter relations among African Americans. In contrast to Eurocentric views of motherhood, she describes patterns of communal and collective mothering relations. Collins's concept of "other mothers" is adopted in the next reading by Lisa J. Udel as she explains why Native American women are loyal to cultural traditions that puzzle white U.S. feminists.

A growing U.S. market for domestic and child care workers is redefining motherhood for many Latinas. In the next article, Pierrette Hondagneu-Sotelo and Ernestine Avila reveal a family arrangement in which immigrant mothers work in the United States while their children remain in Mexico or Central America. Calling this adaptation "transnational mothering," their study shows how global patterns of family dispersal produce variations in the meanings and priorities of motherhood. Like motherhood, current scholarship on fatherhood opens the gender field to new kinds of questions. But as Martha Inhorn points out, our knowledge of fatherhood is typically uninformed by men's procreative issues, even though male infertility is a major global reproductive health problem. Inhorn's study of male infertility in Egypt highlights the patriarchal paradoxes posed by childlessness. Here, not only are women blamed for their husbands' infertility, but their gender identities suffer as well.

The second section takes up questions about work and family linkages and changing gender relations. Women's and men's new employment trends are transforming family realms. Yet the worldwide entrance of women into public sphere employment has not freed them from the demands of labor in the private sphere. Feminists have long argued that there are close connections between "outside" employment and "inside" family work. Pei-Chia Lan provides evidence for this claim in her study of domestic labor and global migration. She uses the example of Filipina domestic workers to reveal the connections between unpaid household labor and paid domestic work. Instead, she offers a fluid conception of feminized "domestic labor" that stretches across public and private spheres, with overlapping connotations of money and love.

By now, it is a truism that the movement of women into the workforce everywhere affects families. But work and family opportunities vary greatly because they are linked within a larger society that is stratified by class, race, and gender. The next three readings address the shaping power of larger economic forces on women's family roles. Patricia Fernández Kelly's comparison of industrial housework among Mexican American and Cuban women shows how the class context gives rise to different work and family patterns. While Cuban women's employment enhances their families' middle-class status, Mexican American women must rely on their work for survival. The reading by Elizabeth Higginbotham and Lynn Weber examines the role of the family in the achievements of black and white professional women. Their intersectional approach challenges conventional thinking about race, class, and the upward mobility of women and men. Finally, Kathryn Edin addresses the connections between economic marginality and marriage in the lives of low-income single mothers. Although the mothers in this study aspire to marriage, they think it is more risky than rewarding. Their stories provide an understanding of the retreat from marriage as it is conditioned by men's employment and women's desire for marriage with a measure of trust, respectability, and control.

29

The Meaning of Motherhood in Black Culture and Black Mother–Daughter Relationships

PATRICIA HILL COLLINS

"What did your mother teach you about men?" is a question I often ask students in my courses on African-American women. "Go to school first and get a good education—don't get too serious too young," "Make sure you look around and that you can take care of yourself before you settle down," and "Don't trust them, want more for yourself than just a man," are typical responses from Black women. My students share stories of how their mothers encouraged them to cultivate satisfying relationships with Black men while anticipating disappointments, to desire marriage while planning viable alternatives, to become mothers only when fully prepared to do so. But, above all, they stress their mothers' insistence on being self-reliant and resourceful.

These daughters, of various ages and from diverse social class backgrounds, family structures and geographic regions, had somehow received strikingly similar messages about Black womanhood. Even though their mothers employed diverse teaching strategies, these Black daughters had all been exposed to common themes about the meaning of womanhood in Black culture.[1]

This essay explores the relationship between the meaning of motherhood in African-American culture and Black mother–daughter relationships by addressing three primary questions. First, how have competing perspectives about motherhood intersected to produce a distinctly Afrocentric ideology of motherhood? Second, what are the enduring themes that characterize this Afrocentric ideology of motherhood? Finally, what effect might this Afrocentric ideology of motherhood have on Black mother–daughter relationships?

COMPETING PERSPECTIVES ON MOTHERHOOD

The Dominant Perspective: Eurocentric Views of White Motherhood

The cult of true womanhood, with its emphasis on motherhood as woman's highest calling, has long held a special place in the gender symbolism of White Americans. From this perspective, women's activities should be confined to the care of children, the nurturing of a husband, and the maintenance of the household. By managing this separate domestic sphere, women gain social influence through their roles as mothers, transmitters of culture, and parents for the next generations.[2]

While substantial numbers of White women have benefited from the protections of White patriarchy provided by the dominant ideology, White women themselves have recently challenged its tenets. On one pole lies a cluster of women, the traditionalists, who aim to retain the centrality of motherhood in women's lives. For traditionalists, differentiating between the experience of motherhood, which for them has been quite satisfying, and motherhood as an institution central in reproducing gender inequality, has proved difficult. The other pole is occupied by women who advocate dismantling motherhood as an institution. They suggest that compulsory motherhood be outlawed and that the experience of motherhood can only be satisfying if women can also choose not to be mothers. Arrayed between these dichotomous positions are women who argue for an expanded, but not necessarily different, role for women—women can be mothers as long as they are not *just* mothers.[3]

Three themes implicit in White perspectives on motherhood are particularly problematic for Black women and others outside of this debate. First, the assumption that mothering occurs within the confines of a private, nuclear family household where the mother has almost total responsibility for child-rearing is less applicable to Black families. While the ideal of the cult of true womanhood has been held up to Black women for emulation, racial oppression has denied Black families sufficient resources to support private, nuclear family households. Second, strict sex-role segregation, with separate male and female spheres of influence within the family, has been less commonly found in African-American families than in White middle-class ones. Finally, the assumption that motherhood and economic dependency on men are linked and that to be a "good" mother one must stay at home, making motherhood a full-time "occupation," is similarly uncharacteristic of African-American families.[4]

Even though selected groups of White women are challenging the cult of true womanhood and its accompanying definition of motherhood, the dominant ideology remains powerful. As long as these approaches remain prominent in scholarly and popular discourse, Eurocentric views of White motherhood will continue to affect Black women's lives.

Eurocentric Views of Black Motherhood

Eurocentric perspectives on Black motherhood revolve around two interdependent images that together define Black women's roles in White and in African-American families. The first image is that of the Mammy, the faithful, devoted domestic servant. Like one of the family, Mammy conscientiously "mothers" her White children, caring for them and loving them as if they were her own. Mammy is the ideal Black mother for she recognizes her place. She is paid next to nothing and yet cheerfully accepts her inferior status. But when she enters her own home, this same Mammy is transformed into the second image, the too-strong matriarch who raises weak sons and "unnaturally superior" daughters.[5] When she protests, she is labeled aggressive and unfeminine, yet if she remains silent, she is rendered invisible.

The task of debunking Mammy by analyzing Black women's roles as exploited domestic workers and challenging the matriarchy thesis by demonstrating that Black women do not wield disproportionate power in African-American families has long preoccupied African-American scholars.[6] But an equally telling critique concerns uncovering the functions of these images and their role in explaining Black women's subordination in systems of race, class, and gender oppression. As Mae King points out, White definitions of Black motherhood foster the dominant group's exploitation of Black women by blaming Black women for their characteristic reactions to their own subordination.[7] For example, while the stay-at-home mother has been held up to all women as the ideal, African-American women have been compelled to work outside the home, typically in a very narrow range of occupations. Even though Black women were forced to become domestic servants and be strong figures in Black households, labeling them Mammys and matriarchs denigrates Black women. Without a countervailing Afrocentric ideology of motherhood, White perspectives on both White and African-American motherhood place Black women in a no-win situation. Adhering to these standards brings the danger of the lowered self-esteem of internalized oppression, one that, if passed on from mother to daughter, provides a powerful mechanism for controlling African-American communities.

African Perspectives on Motherhood

One concept that has been constant throughout the history of African societies is the centrality of motherhood in religions, philosophies, and social institutions. As Barbara Christian points out, "There is no doubt that motherhood is for most African people symbolic of creativity and continuity."[8]

Cross-cultural research on motherhood in African societies appears to support Christian's claim.[9] West African sociologist Christine Oppong suggests that the Western notion of equating household with family be abandoned because it obscures women's family roles in African cultures.[10] While the archetypal White, middle-class nuclear family conceptualizes family life as being divided into two oppositional spheres—the "male" sphere of economic providing and the "female" sphere of affective nurturing—this type of rigid sex role segregation was not part of the West African tradition. Mothering was not a privatized nurturing "occupation" reserved for biological mothers, and the economic support of children was not the exclusive responsibility of men. Instead, for African women, emotional care for children and providing for their physical survival were interwoven as interdependent, complementary dimensions of motherhood.

In spite of variations among societies, a strong case has been made that West African women occupy influential roles in African family networks.[11] First, since they are not dependent on males for economic support and provide much of their own and their children's economic support, women are structurally central to families.[12] Second, the image of the mother is one that is culturally elaborated and valued across diverse West African societies. Continuing the lineage is essential in West African philosophies, and motherhood is similarly valued.[13] Finally, while the biological mother-child bond is valued, child care was a collective responsibility, a situation fostering cooperative, age-stratified, woman-centered "mothering" networks.

Recent research by Africanists suggests that much more of this African heritage was retained among African-Americans than had previously been thought. The retention of West African culture as a culture of resistance offered enslaved Africans and exploited African-Americans alternative ideologies to those advanced by dominant groups. Central to these reinterpretations of African-American institutions and culture is a re-conceptualization of Black family life and the role of women in Black family networks.[14] West African perspectives may have been combined with the changing political and economic situations framing African-American communities to produce certain enduring themes characterizing an Afrocentric ideology of motherhood.

ENDURING THEMES OF AN AFROCENTRIC IDEOLOGY OF MOTHERHOOD

An Afrocentric ideology of motherhood must reconcile the competing worldviews of these three conflicting perspectives of motherhood. An ongoing tension exists between efforts to mold the institution of Black motherhood for the benefit of the dominant group and efforts by Black women to define and value their own experiences with motherhood. This tension leads to a continuum of responses. For those women who either aspire to the cult of true womanhood without having the resources to support such a lifestyle, or who believe the stereotypical analyses of themselves as dominating matriarchs, motherhood can be oppressive. But the experience of motherhood can provide Black women with a base of self-actualization, status in the Black community, and a reason for social activism. These alleged contradictions can exist side by side in African-American communities, families, and even within individual women.

Embedded in these changing relationships are four enduring themes that I contend characterize an Afrocentric ideology of motherhood. Just as the issues facing enslaved African mothers were quite different from those currently facing poor Black women in inner cities, for any given historical moment the actual institutional forms that these themes take depend on the severity of oppression and Black women's resources for resistance.

Bloodmothers, Othermothers, and Women-Centered Networks

In African-American communities, the boundaries distinguishing biological mothers of children from other women who care for children are often fluid and changing. Biological mothers, or bloodmothers, are expected to care for their children. But African and African-American communities have also recognized that vesting one person with full responsibility for mothering a child may not be wise or possible. As a result, "othermothers," women who assist bloodmothers by sharing mothering responsibilities, traditionally have been central to the institution of Black motherhood.[15]

The centrality of women in African-American extended families is well known.[16] Organized, resilient, women-centered networks of bloodmothers and othermothers are key to this centrality. Grandmothers, sisters, aunts, or cousins acted as othermothers by taking on child care responsibilities for each other's children. When needed, temporary child care arrangements turned into long-term care or informal adoption.[17]

In African-American communities, these women-centered networks of community-based child care often extend beyond the boundaries of biologically related extended families to support "fictive kin."[18] Civil rights activist Ella Baker describes how informal adoption by othermothers functioned in the Southern, rural community of her childhood:

> My aunt who had thirteen children of her own raised three more. She had become a midwife, and a child was born who was covered with sores. Nobody was particularly wanting the child, so she took the child and raised him . . . and another mother decided she didn't want to be bothered with two children. So my aunt took one and raised him . . . they were part of the family.[19]

Even when relationships were not between kin or fictive kin, African-American community norms were such that neighbors cared for each other's children. In the following passage, Sara Brooks, a Southern domestic worker, describes the importance of the community-based child care that a neighbor offered her daughter. In doing so, she also shows how the African-American cultural value placed on cooperative child care found institutional support in the adverse conditions under which so many Black women mothered:

> She kept Vivian and she didn't charge me nothin either. You see, people used to look after each other, but now it's not that way. I reckon it's because we all was poor, and I guess they put theirself in the place of the person that they was helpin.[20]

Othermothers were key not only in supporting children but also in supporting bloodmothers who, for whatever reason, were ill-prepared or had little desire to care for their children. Given the pressures from the larger political economy, the emphasis placed on community-based child care and the respect given to othermothers who assume the responsibilities of childcare have served a critical function in African-American communities. Children orphaned by sale or death of their parents under slavery, children conceived through rape, children of young mothers, children born into extreme poverty, or children who for other reasons have been rejected by their bloodmothers have all been supported by othermothers who, like Ella Baker's aunt, took in additional children, even when they had enough of their own.

Providing as Part of Mothering

The work done by African-American women in providing the economic resources essential to Black family well-being affects motherhood in a contradictory fashion. On the one hand, African-American women have long integrated their activities as economic providers into their mothering relationships. In contrast to the cult of true womanhood, in which work is defined as being in opposition to and incompatible with motherhood, work for Black women has been an important and valued dimension of Afrocentric definitions of Black motherhood. On the other hand, African-American women's experiences as mothers under oppression were such that the type and purpose of work Black women were forced to do had a great impact on the type of mothering relationships bloodmothers and othermothers had with Black children.

While slavery both disrupted West African family patterns and exposed enslaved Africans to the gender ideologies and practices of slaveowners, it simultaneously made it impossible, had they wanted to do so for enslaved Africans to implement slaveowners' ideologies. Thus, the separate spheres of providing as a male domain and affective nurturing as a female domain did not develop within African-American families.[21] Providing for Black children's physical survival and attending to their affective, emotional needs continued as interdependent dimensions of an Afrocentric ideology of motherhood. However, by changing the conditions under which Black women worked and the purpose of the work itself, slavery introduced the problem of how best to continue traditional Afrocentric values under oppressive conditions. Institutions of community-based childcare, informal adoption, greater reliance on othermothers, all emerge as adaptations to the exigencies of combining exploitative work with nurturing children.

In spite of the change in political status brought on by emancipation, the majority of African-American women remained exploited agricultural workers. However, their placement in Southern political economics allowed them to combine child care with field labor. Sara Brooks describes how strong the links between providing and caring for others were for her:

> When I was about nine I was nursin my sister Sally—I'm about seven or eight years older than Sally. And when I would put her to sleep, instead of me goin somewhere and sit down and play, I'd get my little old hoe and get out there and work right in the field around the house.[22]

Black women's shift from Southern agriculture to domestic work in Southern and Northern towns and cities represented a change in the type of work done, but not in the meaning of work to women and their families. Whether they wanted to or not, the majority of African-American women had to work and could not afford the luxury of motherhood as a noneconomically productive, female "occupation."

Community Othermothers and Social Activism

Black women's experiences as othermothers have provided a foundation for Black women's social activism. Black women's feelings of responsibility for nurturing the children in their own extended family networks have stimulated a more generalized ethic of care where Black women feel accountable to all the Black community's children.

This notion of Black women as community othermothers for all Black children traditionally allowed Black women to treat biologically unrelated children as if they were members of their own families. For example, sociologist Karen Fields describes how her grandmother, Mamie Garvin Fields, draws on her power as a community othermother when dealing with unfamiliar children.

> She will say to a child on the street who looks up to no good, picking out a name at random, "Aren't you Miz Pinckney's boy?" in that same reproving tone. If the reply is, "No, ma'am, my mother is Miz Gadsden," whatever threat there was dissipates.[23]

The use of family language in referring to members of the Black community also illustrates this dimension of Black motherhood. For example, Mamie Garvin Fields describes how she became active in surveying the poor housing conditions of Black people in Charleston.

> I was one of the volunteers they got to make a survey of the places where we were paying extortious rents for indescribable property. I said "we," although it wasn't Bob and me. We had our own home, and so did many of the Federated Women. Yet we still fell like it really was "we" living in those terrible places, and it was up to us to do something about them.[24]

To take another example, while describing her increasingly successful efforts to teach a boy who had given other teachers problems, my daughter's kindergarten teacher stated, "You know how it can be—the majority of children in the learning disabled classes are *our children.* I know he didn't belong there, so I volunteered to take him." In these statements, both women invoke the language of family to describe the ties that bind them as Black women to their responsibilities to other members of the Black community as family.

Sociologist Cheryl Gilkes suggests that community othermother relationships are sometimes behind Black women's decisions to become community activists.[25] Gilkes notes that many of the Black women community activists in her study became involved in community organizing in response to the needs of their own children and of those in their communities. The following comment is typical of how many of the Black women in Gilkes' study relate to Black children: "There were a lot of summer programs springing up for kids, but they were exclusive . . . and I found that most of *our kids* (emphasis mine) were excluded."[26] For many women, what began as the daily expression of their obligations as community othermothers, as was the case for the kindergarten teacher, developed into full-fledged roles as community leaders.

Motherhood as a Symbol of Power

Motherhood, whether bloodmother, othermother, or community othermother, can be invoked by Black women as a symbol of power. A substantial portion of Black women's status in African-American communities stems not only from their roles as mothers in their own families but from their contributions as community othermothers to Black community development as well.

The specific contributions Black women make in nurturing Black community development form the basis of community-based power. Community othermothers work on behalf of the Black community by trying, in the words of late nineteenth-century Black feminists, to "uplift the race," so that vulnerable members of the community would be able to attain the self-reliance and independence so desperately needed for Black community development under oppressive conditions. This is the type of power many African-Americans have in mind when they describe the "strong, Black women" they see around them in traditional African-American communities.

When older Black women invoke this community othermother status, its results can be quite striking. Karen Fields recounts an incident described to her by her grandmother illustrating how women can exert power as community othermothers:

> One night . . . as Grandmother sat crocheting alone at about two in the morning, a young man walked into the living room carrying the portable TV from upstairs. She said, "Who are you looking for this time of night?" As Grandmother [described] the incident to me over the phone, I could hear a tone of voice that I know well. It said, "Nice boys don't do that." So I imagine the burglar heard his own mother or grandmother at that moment. He joined in the familial game just created: "Well, he told me that I could borrow it." "Who told you?" "John." "Um um, no John lives here. You got the wrong house."[27]

After this dialogue, the teenager turned around, went back upstairs and returned the television.

In local Black communities, specific Black women are widely recognized as powerful figures, primarily because of their contributions to the community's well-being through their roles as community othermothers. Sociologist Charles Johnson describes the behavior of an elderly Black woman at a church service in rural Alabama of the 1930s. Even though she was not on the program, the woman stood up to speak. The master of ceremonies rang for her to sit down but she refused to do so claiming, "I am the mother of this church, and I will say what I please." The master of ceremonies later explained to the congregation—"Brothers, I know you all honor Sister Moore. Course our time is short but she has acted as a mother to me. . . . Any time old folks get up I give way to them."[28]

IMPLICATIONS FOR BLACK MOTHER–DAUGHTER RELATIONSHIPS

In her discussion of the sex-role socialization of Black girls, Pamela Reid identifies two complementary approaches in understanding Black mother–daughter relationships.[29] The first, psychoanalytic theory, examines the role of parents in the establishment of personality and social behavior. This theory argues that the development of feminine behavior results from the girls' identification with adult female role models. This approach emphasizes how an Afrocentric ideology of motherhood is actualized through Black mothers' activities as role models.

The second approach, social learning theory, suggests that the rewards and punishments attached to girls' childhood experiences are central in shaping women's sex-role behavior. The kinds of behaviors that Black mothers reward and punish in their daughters are seen as key in the socialization process. This approach examines specific experiences that Black girls have while growing up that encourage them to absorb an Afrocentric ideology of motherhood.

African-American Mothers as Role Models

Feminist psychoanalytic theorists suggest that the sex-role socialization process is different for boys and girls. While boys learn maleness by rejecting femaleness via separating themselves from their mothers, girls establish feminine identities by embracing the femaleness of their mothers. Girls identify with their mothers, a sense of connection that is incorporated into the female personality. However, this mother-identification is problematic because, under patriarchy, men are more highly valued than women. Thus, while daughters identify with their mothers, they also reject them, since in patriarchal families, identifying with adult women as mothers means identifying with persons deemed inferior.[30]

While Black girls learn by identifying with their mothers, the specific female role with which Black girls identify may be quite different than that modeled by middle-class White mothers. The presence of working mothers, extended family othermothers, and powerful community othermothers offers a range of role models that challenge the tenets of the cult of true womanhood.

Moreover, since Black mothers have a distinctive relationship to White patriarchy, they may be less likely to socialize their daughters into their proscribed role as subordinates. Rather, a key part of Black girls' socialization involves incorporating the critical posture that allows Black women to cope with contradictions. For example, Black girls have long had to learn how to do domestic work while rejecting definitions of themselves as Mammies. At the same time they've had to take on strong roles in Black extended families without internalizing images of themselves as matriarchs.

In raising their daughters, Black mothers face a troubling dilemma. To ensure their daughters' physical survival, they must teach their daughters to fit into systems of oppression. For example, as a young girl in Mississippi, Black activist Ann Moody questioned why she was paid so little for the domestic work she began at age nine, why Black women domestics were sexually harassed by their White male employers, and why Whites had so much more than Blacks. But her mother refused to answer her questions and actually became angry whenever Ann Moody stepped out of her "place."[31] Black daughters are raised to expect to work, to strive for an education so that they can support themselves, and to anticipate carrying heavy responsibilities in their families and communities because these skills are essential for their own survival as well as for the survival of those for whom they will eventually be responsible.[32] And yet mothers know that if daughters fit too well into the limited opportunities offered Black women, they become willing participants in their own subordination. Mothers may have ensured their daughters' physical survival at the high cost of their emotional destruction.

On the other hand, Black daughters who offer serious challenges to oppressive situations may not physically survive. When Ann Moody became involved in civil rights activities, her mother first begged her not to participate and then told her not to come home because she feared the Whites in Moody's hometown would kill her. In spite of the dangers, many Black mothers routinely encourage their daughters to develop skills to confront oppressive conditions. Thus, learning that they will work, that education is a vehicle for advancement, can also be seen as ways of preparing Black girls to resist oppression through a variety of mothering roles. The issue is to build emotional strength, but not at the cost of physical survival.

This delicate balance between conformity and resistance is described by historian Elsa Barkley Brown as the "need to socialize me one way and at the same time to give me all the tools I needed to be something else."[33] Black daughters must learn how to survive in interlocking structures of race, class, and gender oppression while rejecting and transcending those very same structures. To develop these skills in their daughters, mothers demonstrate varying combinations of behaviors devoted to ensuring their daughters' survival—such as providing them with basic necessities and ensuring their protection in dangerous environments to helping their daughters go farther than mothers themselves were allowed to go.

The presence of othermothers in Black extended families and the modeling symbolized by community othermothers offer powerful support for the task of teaching girls to resist White perceptions of Black womanhood while appearing to conform to them. In contrast to the isolation of middle-class White mother/daughter dyads, Black women-centered extended family networks foster an early identification with a much wider range of models of Black womanhood, which can lead to a greater sense of empowerment in young Black girls.

Social Learning Theory and Black Mothering Behavior

Understanding this goal of balancing the needs of ensuring their daughters' physical survival with the vision of encouraging them to transcend the boundaries confronting them sheds some light on some of the apparent contradictions in Black mother–daughter relationships. Black mothers are often described as strong disciplinarians and overly protective parents; yet these same women manage to raise daughters who are self-reliant and assertive.[34] Professor Gloria Wade-Gayles offers an explanation for this apparent contradiction by suggesting that Black mothers "do not socialize their daughters to be passive or irrational. Quite the contrary, they socialize their daughters to be independent, strong and self-confident. Black mothers are suffocatingly protective and domineering precisely because they are determined to mold their daughters into whole and self-actualizing persons in a society that devalues Black women."[35]

Black mothers emphasize protection either by trying to shield their daughters as long as possible from the penalties attached to their race, class, and gender or by teaching them how to protect themselves in such situations. Black women's autobiographies and fiction can be read as texts revealing the multiple strategies Black mothers employ in preparing their daughters for the demands of being Black women in oppressive conditions. For example, in discussing the mother–daughter relationship in Paule Marshall's *Brown Girl, Brownstones,* Rosalie Troester catalogues some of these strategies and the impact they may have on relationships themselves:

> Black mothers, particularly those with strong ties to their community, sometimes build high banks around their young daughters, isolating them from the dangers of the larger world until they are old and strong enough to function as autonomous women. Often these dikes are religious, but sometimes they are built with education, family, or the restrictions of a close-knit and homogeneous community . . . this isolation causes the currents between Black mothers and daughters to run deep and the relationship to be fraught with an emotional intensity often missing from the lives of women with more freedom.[36]

Black women's efforts to provide for their children also may affect the emotional intensity of Black mother–daughter relationships. As Gloria Wade-Gayles points out, "Mothers in Black women's fiction are strong and devoted . . . but . . . they are rarely affectionate."[37] For far too many Black mothers, the demands of providing for children are so demanding that affection often must wait until the basic needs of physical survival are satisfied.

Black daughters raised by mothers grappling with hostile environments have to confront their feelings about the difference between the idealized versions of maternal love extant in popular culture and the strict, assertive mothers so central to their lives.[38] For daughters, growing up means developing a better understanding that offering physical care and protection is an act of maternal love. Ann Moody describes her growing awareness of the personal cost her mother paid as a single mother of three children employed as a domestic worker. Watching her mother sleep after the birth of another child, Moody remembers:

> For a long time I stood there looking at her. I didn't want to wake her up. I wanted to enjoy and preserve that calm, peaceful look on her face, I wanted to think she would always be that happy . . . Adline and Junior were too young to feel the things I felt and know the things I knew about Mama. They couldn't remember when she and Daddy separated. They had never heard her cry at night as I had or worked and helped as I had done when we were starving.[39]

Renita Weems's account of coming to grips with maternal desertion provides another example of a daughter's efforts to understand her mother's behavior. In the following passage, Weems struggles with the difference between the stereotypical image of the super strong Black mother and her own alcoholic mother, who decided to leave her children:

> My mother loved us. I must believe that. She worked all day in a department store bakery to buy shoes and school tablets, came home to curse out neighbors who wrongly accused her children of any impropriety (which in an apartment complex usually meant stealing), and kept her house cleaner than most sober women.[40]

Weems concludes that her mother loved her because she provided for her to the best of her ability.

Othermothers often play central roles in defusing the emotional intensity of relationships between bloodmothers and their daughters and in helping daughters understand the Afrocentric ideology of motherhood. Weems describes the women teachers, neighbors, friends, and other-mothers that she turned to for help in negotiating a difficult mother/daughter relationship. These women, she notes, "did not have the onus of providing for me, and so had the luxury of talking to me."[41]

June Jordan offers one of the most eloquent analyses of a daughter's realization of the high personal cost Black women have paid as blood-mothers and othermothers in working to provide an economic and emotional foundation for Black children. In the following passage, Jordan captures the feelings that my Black women students struggled to put into words:

> As a child I noticed the sadness of my mother as she sat alone in the kitchen at night. . . . Her woman's work never won permanent victories of any kind. It never enlarged the universe of her imagination or her power to influence what happened beyond the front door of our house. Her woman's work never tickled her to laugh or shout or dance. But she did raise me to respect her way of offering love and to believe that hard work is often the irreducible factor for survival, not something to avoid. Her woman's work produced a reliable home base where I could pursue the privileges of books and music. Her woman's work invented the potential for a completely different kind of work for us, the next generation of Black women: huge, rewarding hard work demanded by the huge, new ambitions that her perfect confidence in us engendered.[42]

Jordan's words not only capture the essence of the Afrocentric ideology of motherhood so central to the well-being of countless numbers of Black women. They simultaneously point the way into the future, one where Black women face the challenge of continuing the mothering traditions painstakingly nurtured by prior generations of African-American women.

NOTES

1. The definition of culture used in this essay is taken from Leith Mullings, "Anthropological Perspectives on the Afro-American Family," *American Journal of Social Psychiatry* 6 (1986): 11–16. According to Mullings, culture is composed of "the symbols and values that create the ideological frame of reference through which people attempt to deal with the circumstances in which they find themselves"(13).

2. For analyses of the relationship of the cult of true womanhood to Black women, see Leith Mullings, "Uneven Development: Class, Race and Gender in the United States Before 1900," in *Women's Work, Development and the Division of Labor by Gender,* ed. Eleanor Leacock and Helen Safa (South Hadley, MA: Bergin & Garvey, 1986), pp. 41–57; Bonnie Thornton Dill, "Our Mothers' Grief: Racial Ethnic Women and the Maintenance of Families," Research Paper 4, Center for Research on Women (Memphis, TN: Memphis State University, 1986); and Hazel Carby, *Reconstructing*

Womanhood: The Emergence of the Afro-American Woman Novelist (New York: Oxford University Press, 1987), esp. chapter 2.

3. Contrast, for example, the traditionalist analysis of Selma Fraiberg, *Every Child's Birthright: In Defense of Mothering* (New York: Basic Books, 1977) to that of Jeffner Allen, "Motherhood: The Annihilation of Women," in *Mothering, Essays in Feminist Theory,* ed. Joyce Trebilcot (Totawa, NJ: Rowan & Allanheld, 1983). See also Adrienne Rich, *Of Woman Born: Motherhood as Experience and Institution* (New York: Norton, 1976). For an overview of how traditionalists and feminists have shaped the public policy debate on abortion, see Kristin Luker, *Abortion and the Politics of Motherhood* (Berkeley, CA: University of California, 1984).

4. Mullings, "Uneven Development"; Dill. "Our Mother's Grief"; and Carby, *Reconstructing Womanhood.* Feminist scholarship is also challenging Western notions of the family. See Barrie Thorne and Marilyn Yalom, eds., *Rethinking the Family* (New York: Longman, 1982).

5. Since Black women are no longer heavily concentrated in private domestic service, the Mammy image may be fading. In contrast, the matriarch image, popularized in Daniel Patrick Moynihan's, *The Negro Family: The Case for National Action* (Washington, D.C.: U.S. Government Printing Office, 1965), is reemerging in public debates about the feminization of poverty and the urban underclass. See Maxine Baca Zinn, "Minority Families in Crisis: The Public Discussion," Research Paper 6, Center for Research on Women (Memphis, TN: Memphis State University, 1987).

6. For an alternative analysis of the Mammy image, see Judith Rollins, *Between Women: Domestics and Their Employers* (Philadelphia: Temple University, 1985). Classic responses to the matriarchy thesis include Robert Hill, *The Strengths of Black Families* (New York: Urban League, 1972); Andrew Billingsley, *Black Families in White America* (Englewood Cliffs, NJ: Prentice-Hall, 1968); and Joyce Ladner, *Tomorrow's Tomorrow,* (Garden City, NY: Doubleday, 1971). For a recent analysis, see Linda Burnham, "Has Poverty Been Feminized in Black America?" *Black Scholar* 16 (1985):15–24.

7. Mae King, "The Politics of Sexual Stereotypes," *Black Scholar* 4 (1973):12–23.

8. Barbara Christian, "An Angle of Seeing: Motherhood in Buchi Emecheta's *Joys of Motherhood* and Alice Walker's *Meridian,*" in *Black Feminist Criticism,* ed. Barbara Christian (New York: Pergamon, 1985), p. 214.

9. See Christine Oppong, ed., *Female and Male in West Africa* (London: Allen & Unwin, 1983); Niara Sudarkesa, "Female Employment and Family Organization in West Africa," in *The Black Woman Cross-Culturally,* ed. Filomina Chiamo Steady (Cambridge, MA: Schenkman, 1981), pp. 49–64; and Nancy Tanner, "Matrifocality in Indonesia and Africa and Among Black Americans," in *Woman, Culture, and Society,* ed. Michelle Rosaldo and Louise Lamphere (Stanford, CA: Stanford University Press, 1974), pp. 129–56.

10. Christine Oppong, "Family Structure and Women's Reproductive and Productive Roles: Some Conceptual and Methodological Issues," in *Women's Roles and Population Trends in the Third World,* ed. Richard Anker, Myra Buvinic, and Nadia Youssef (London: Croom Heim, 1982), pp. 133–50.

11. The key distinction here is that, unlike the matriarchy thesis, women play central roles in families and this centrality is seen as legitimate. In spite of this centrality, it is important not to idealize African women's family roles. For an analysis by a Black African feminist, see Awa Thiam, *Black Sisters, Speak Out: Feminism and Oppression in Black Africa* (London: Pluto, 1978).

12. Sudarkasa, "Female Employment."

13. John Mbiti, *African Religions and Philosophies* (New York: Anchor, 1969).

14. Niara Sudarkasa, "Interpreting the African Heritage in Afro-American Family Organization," in *Black Families,* ed. Harriette Pipes McAdoo (Beverly Hills, CA: Sage, 1981), pp. 37–53; and Deborah Gray White, *Ar'n't I a Woman? Female Slaves in the Plantation South* (New York: W. W. Norton, 1985).

15. The terms used in this section appear in Rosalie Riegle Troester's "Turbulence and Tenderness: Mothers, Daughters, and 'Othermothers' in Paule Marshall's *Brown Girl, Brownstones,*" *SAGE: A Scholarly Journal on Black Women* 1 (Fall 1984):13–16.

16. See Tanner, "Matrifocality"; see also Carrie Allen McCray, "The Black Woman and Family Roles," in *The Black Woman,* ed. LaFrances Rogers-Rose (Beverly Hills, CA: Sage, 1980), pp. 67–78; Elmer Martin and Joanne Mitchell Marlin, *The Black Extended Family* (Chicago: University of Chicago Press, 1978); Joyce Aschenbrenner, *Lifelines, Black Families in Chicago* (Prospect Heights, IL: Waveland, 1975); and Carol B. Stack, *All Our Kin* (New York: Harper & Row, 1974).

17. Martin and Martin, *The Black Extended Family;* Stack, *All Our Kin;* and Virginia Young, "Family and Childhood in a Southern Negro Community," *American Anthropologist* 72 (1970):269–88.

18. Stack, *All Our Kin.*

19. Ellen Cantarow, *Moving the Mountain: Women Working for Social Change* (Old Westbury, NY: Feminist Press, 1980), p. 59.

20. Thordis Simonsen, ed., *You May Plow Here, The Narrative of Sara Brooks* (New York: Touchstone, 1986), p. 181.

21. White, *Ar'n't I a Woman?;* Dill, "Our Mothers' Grief"; Mullings, "Uneven Development."

22. Simonsen, *You May Plow Here,* p. 86.

23. Mamie Garvin Fields and Karen Fields, *Lemon Swamp and Other Places, A Carolina Memoir* (New York: Free Press, 1983), p. xvii.

24. Ibid, p. 195.

25. Cheryl Gilkes, "'Holding Back the Ocean with a Broom,' Black Women and Community Work," in *The Black Woman,* ed. Rogers-Rose, 1980, pp. 217–31, and "Going Up for the Oppressed: The Career Mobility of Black Women Community Workers," *Journal of Social Issues* 39 (1983):115–39.

26. Gilkes, "'Holding Back the Ocean.'" p. 219.

27. Fields and Fields, *Lemon Swamp,* p. xvi.

28. Charles Johnson, *Shadow of the Plantation* (Chicago: University of Chicago Press, 1934, 1979), p. 173.

29. Pamela Reid, "Socialization of Black Female Children," in *Women: A Developmental Perspective,* ed. Phyllis Berman and Estelle Ramey (Washington, DC: National Institutes of Health, 1983).

30. For works in the feminist psychoanalytic tradition, see Nancy Chodorow, "Family Structure and Feminine Personality," in *Woman, Culture, and Society,* ed. Rosaldo and Lamphere, 1974; Nancy Chodorow, *The Reproduction of Mothering* (Berkeley, CA: University of California, 1978); and Jane Flax, "The Conflict Between Nurturance and Autonomy in Mother–Daughter Relationships and Within Feminism," *Feminist Studies* 4 (1978):171–89.

31. Ann Moody, *Coming of Age in Mississippi* (New York: Dell, 1968).

32. Ladner, *Tomorrow's Tomorrow;* Gloria Joseph, "Black Mothers and Daughters: Their Roles and Functions in American Society," in *Common Differences,* ed. Gloria Joseph and Jill Lewis (Garden City, NY: Anchor, 1981), pp. 75–126; Lena Wright Myers, *Black Women, Do They Cope Better?* (Englewood Cliffs, NJ: Prentice-Hall, 1980).

33. Elsa Barkley Brown, "Hearing Our Mothers' Lives," paper presented at fifteenth anniversary of African-American and African Studies at Emory College, Atlanta, 1986. This essay appeared in the Black Women's Studies issue of *SAGE: A Scholarly Journal on Black Women,* vol. 6, no. 1:4–11.

34. Joseph, "Black Mothers and Daughters"; Myers, 1980.

35. Gloria Wade-Gayles, "The Truths of Our Mothers' Lives: Mother–Daughter Relationships in Black Women's Fiction," *SAGE: A Scholarly Journal on Black Women* 1 (Fall 1984):12.

36. Troester, "Turbulence and Tenderness," p. 13.

37. Wade-Gayles, "The Truths," p. 10.

38. Joseph, "Black Mothers and Daughters."

39. Moody, *Coming of Age,* p. 57.

40. Renita Weems, "'Hush. Mama's Gotta Go Bye Bye': A Personal Narrative," *SAGE: A Scholarly Journal on Black Women* 1 (Fall 1984):26.

41. Ibid, p. 27.

42. June Jordan, *On Call, Political Essays* (Boston: South End Press, 1985), p. 145.

30

Revision and Resistance

The Politics of Native Women's Motherwork

LISA J. UDEL

Contemporary Native women of the United States and Canada, politically active in Indigenous rights movements for the past thirty years, variously articulate a reluctance to affiliate with white feminist movements of North America. Despite differences in tribal affiliation, regional location, urban or reservation background, academic or community setting, and pro- or anti-feminist ideology, many Native women academics and grassroots activists alike invoke models of preconquest, egalitarian societies to theorize contemporary social and political praxes. Such academics as Paula Gunn Allen, Rayna Green, and Patricia Monture-Angus, as well as Native activists Wilma Mankiller, Mary Brave Bird, and Yet Si Blue (Janet McCloud) have problematized the reformative role white feminism can play for Indigenous groups, arguing that non-Native women's participation in various forms of Western imperialism have often made them complicit in the oppression of Native peoples.[1] More important, Native women contend that their agendas for reform differ from those they identify with mainstream white feminist movements. The majority of contemporary Native American women featured in recent collections by Ronnie Farley, Jane Katz, and Steve Wall, for example, are careful to stress the value of traditional, precontact female and male role models in their culture.[2] One aspect of traditional culture that Native women cite as crucial to their endeavor is what Patricia Hill Collins calls "motherwork."[3] Many Native women valorize their ability to procreate and nurture their children, communities, and the earth as aspects of motherwork. "Women are sacred because we bring life into this world," states Monture-Angus. "First Nations women are respected as the centre of the nation for [this] reason."[4] Native women argue that they have devised alternate reform strategies to those advanced by Western feminism. Native women's motherwork, in its range and variety, is one form of this activism, an approach that emphasizes Native traditions of "responsibilities" as distinguished from Western feminism's notions of "rights."

Writing for an ethnically diverse feminist audience in the journal *Callaloo,* Clara Sue Kidwell (Choctaw/Chippewa) warns: "Although feminists might deny this equation of anatomy and destiny, the fact is that the female reproductive function is a crucial factor in determining a woman's social role in tribal societies. Women bear children who carry on the culture of the

Reprinted from *Frontiers: A Journal of Women Studies,* Volume 22, Number 2 (2001) by permission of the University of Nebraska Press.

group."[5] Mary Gopher (Ojibway) explains the analogy of woman/Earth inherent in philosophies of many tribes: "In our religion, we look at this planet as a woman. She is the most important female to us because she keeps us alive. We are nursing off of her."[6] Carrie Dann (Western Shoshone) adds: "Indigenous women, they're supposed to look at themselves as the Earth. That is the way we were brought up. This is what I try to tell the young people, especially the young girls."[7] Gopher and Dann invest motherwork with religious and cultural authority that they, as elders, must transmit to younger women in their communities. Many contemporary Native women argue that they must also educate white women in their traditional roles as women in order to safeguard the Earth, so that they will survive. Calling upon traditions of female leadership, Blue (Tulalip) contends:

> It is going to be the job of Native women to begin teaching other women what their roles are. Women have to turn life around, because if they don't, all of future life is threatened and endangered. I don't care what kind of women they are, they are going to have to worry more about the changes that are taking place on this Mother Earth that will affect us all.[8]

Blue, like many Native women activists, links women's authority as procreators with their larger responsibilities to a personified, feminized Earth.

Several Native women condemn Western feminism for what they perceive as a devaluation of motherhood and refutation of women's traditional responsibilities.[9] Paula Gunn Allen attributes the pronatalist stance articulated by so many Native women to the high incidence of coerced sterilization in Indian Health Service (IHS) facilities. An overpowering awareness of the government's abduction of Indian children, the nonconsensual sterilization of Native women, along with the nation's highest infant mortality rates, pervades the work of Native writers and activists.[10] American Indian Movement (AIM) veteran and celebrated author Mary Brave Bird, for instance, discusses the sterilization of her mother and sister, performed without their consent.[11] Many women told Jane Katz stories of the forced abduction of their children by social welfare agencies and mission schools that were published in *Messengers of the Wind.*[12] In her autobiography *Halfbreed,* Maria Campbell (métis) tells a similar story of the Canadian government placing her siblings in foster care when her mother died, despite the fact that her father—the children's parent and legal guardian—was still alive.[13]

Native women argue that in their marital contracts with Euramerican men they lost power, autonomy, sexual freedom, and maternity and inheritance rights, which precluded their ability to accomplish motherwork. Green observes, for example, that an eighteenth-century Native woman allied to a fur trader relinquished control over her life and the lives of the children she bore from her white partner. This lack of control was compounded by the fact that Native women married to white men gave birth to more children than those partnered with Native men. Furthermore, a Native woman lost the freedom to divorce of her own free will, and the "goods and dwelling that might have been her own property in Indian society became the possession of her white husband."[14] In contrast, within many Native traditions, notes Green:

> The children belonged entirely to women, as did the property and distribution of resources. Indian men abided by the rules of society. If a couple separated, the man would leave with only that which had belonged to him when he entered the relationship; if a woman formed an alliance with a European by choice, she had every reason to imagine that her society's rules would be followed. For Indians, a white man who married an Indian was expected to acknowledge the importance and status of women. . . . In some tribes, adult women were free to seek out sexual alliances with whomever they chose.[15]

In order to do motherwork well, Native women argue, women must have power.

Euramericans held different ideas about female sexuality and inheritance. Many white men married Indian women who owned land in order to acquire their inheritance. When conflict over property rights inevitably arose, European laws dominated, Native women lost ownership rights to their land and suffered diminished economic autonomy and political status. Examples of this phenomenon occurred in the early twentieth century when oil was discovered in Oklahoma; white men married into wealthy female-centered Osage families and inherited the family's property. "Under Osage practice, the oil revenues would have been reserved for the woman's family and controlled by her. Common property laws established by white men gave the husband control," explains Green. "In a number of notorious instances in Oklahoma, women were murdered so that their husbands could inherit their wealth."[16] Certainly the concept that Indian women suffer through sexual contact with non-Native men is evident in the works of Beth Brant, Green, and Mankiller, as well as in the story of the women of Tobique, who lost their Indian status once they married white men.

Native women also experienced the loss of economic and political power through diminished reproductive freedom. Christian ideology recast women's sexuality, emphasizing procreation, virtue, and modesty. Early records show missionaries' agitation over the sexual autonomy of most unmarried Native women. As Christian-based roles were asserted, Native traditions of birth control and population control were forgotten. For example, Cherokee women traditionally held the right to limit population through infanticide. Similarly, Seneca women were able to limit their families, starting childbearing early and ending it early. Seneca society also did not mandate marriage for legitimate childbearing.[17]

The involuntary sterilization of Native women (as well as Mexican American and African American women) is common knowledge among those communities affected but remains largely unknown to those outside the communities. A federal government investigation in 1976 discovered that in the four-year period between 1973 and 1976 more than three thousand Native women were involuntarily sterilized. Of the 3,406 women sterilized, 3,001 were between the ages of fifteen and forty-four.[18] A 1979 report revealed that six out of ten hospitals routinely sterilized women under the age of twenty-one, a clear violation of the 1974 Department of Health, Education, and Welfare (DHEW) guidelines prohibiting involuntary sterilization of minors.[19] According to Bertha Medicine Bull, a leader on the Montana Lame Deer Reservation, two local fifteen-year-old girls were sterilized when they had appendectomies, without their knowledge or consent.[20] Only four out of twelve IHS facilities were investigated; therefore, the estimated number of women sterilized either coercively (often through the illegal threat of withholding government aid or the removal of existing children), or without their knowledge, during this period is estimated at twelve thousand.[21]

Green writes that because of "sterilization and experimentation abuse on Native American women and men in Indian Health Service facilities, Native American people have been warier than ever of contraceptive technologies."[22] Many Native women, responding to the involuntary sterilization cases they have encountered directly and indirectly, blame the U.S. government for genocidal policies toward Native populations. Connie Uri (Choctaw), for example, observed in 1978: "We are not like other minorities. We have no gene pool in Africa or Asia. When we are gone, that's it."[23] Activist Barbara Moore (the sister Mary Brave Bird describes) links sterilization with genocide much more explicitly: "There are plans to get rid of Indians. They actually plan different kinds of genocide. One way to do that is through alcohol, another way is birth control, and one of the most cruel ways is to sterilize Indian women by force."[24] Moore recounts the story of her child's birth, delivered by Cesarean section and reported as a stillbirth, although the autopsy she demanded determined the cause of death as inconclusive. Moore states: "My child was born healthy. Besides this, they told me that I could not have any more children because they have had to sterilize me. I was sterilized during the operation without my knowledge and without my agreement."[25]

Native women thus value and argue for reproductive autonomy, which they link with empowered motherwork; but, they approach this autonomy from a perspective that they feel differs from mainstream feminism. Given the history of the IHS campaign to curtail Native women's reproductive capacity and thus Native populations, Native women emphasize women's ability, sometimes "privilege," to bear children. Within this paradigm, they argue, Native women's procreative capability becomes a powerful tool to combat Western genocide. Motherhood recovered, along with the tribal responsibility to nurture their children in a traditional manner and without non-Indigenous interference, assumes a powerful political meaning when viewed this way.[26]

WHITE FEMINISM AND REPRODUCTIVE AUTONOMY

The role of white feminism in the campaign for reproductive autonomy has been a sore point among many Native women who link the American eugenics movement with American birth control movements of the early twentieth century. Both movements, which involved the participation of white feminists of their time, began as an effort to grant women control over their fertility, and thus gain some measure of economic and political autonomy, but eventually gave way to eugenic and population control forces. The focus moved from "self determination" to the "social control" of immigrant and working classes by "the elite." As historian Linda Gordon explains, eugenics became a dominant aspect of the movement to legalize contraception and sterilization, and, eventually, "Birth controllers from the socialist-feminist revolution . . . made accommodations with eugenists."[27]

White-dominated feminism's historic failure to combat racist and classist ideologies, compounded by promotion of ideologies to gain suffrage in the past, has perpetuated the link between white mainstream feminism to eugenics. The resulting conflation of birth-control movements with eugenics and population control has had a negative impact both on disadvantaged people vulnerable to external social control and also on the feminist movement. Gordon argues that feminist birth control advocates accepted racist attitudes of the eugenicists and population controllers, even sharing anti–working-class, anti-immigrant sentiment.[28] The population control and eugenics movements dominated early and mid-twentieth-century white feminism, obfuscating the latter's agenda and efficacy. This history continues to influence theories of birth control today. According to Gordon, "Planned Parenthood's use of small-family ideology and its international emphasis on sterilization rather than safe and controllable contraception have far overshadowed its feminist program for women's self-determination."[29]

The public does not distinguish between birth control "as a program of individual rights" and population control as social policy that strips the individual of those very rights. It is this blurred distinction that Native women criticize. Brave Bird, for instance, points out the irrelevance of abortion rights to Indian women who see tribal repopulation as one of their primary goals. A self-identified Indian feminist, Brave Bird recognizes the value of reproductive rights for women whose bodies have been controlled by others; however, she objects to white feminists who would dictate an Indian feminist agenda to her.[30] In 1977 the Hyde Amendment withdrew federal funding for abortions but left free-on-demand surgical sterilizations funded by the DHEW; consequently some poor women were forced to choose infertility as their method of birth control because pregnancy prevention was also not funded.

Native women employ motherist rhetoric in their critiques of Western feminism as a response to their history of enforced sterilization and also as a defensive strategy crucial to marking women's dignity and contributions to Native cultures. Speaking to a predominantly white audience of feminists at the National Women's Studies Association meeting in 1988, Green explained that "models of kinship [mother, sister, grandmother, aunt] are used by Indian women to measure their capacity for leadership and to measure the success of their leadership."[31] Such kinship models of evaluation, however, are not to be read literally. These roles are *not* biologically determined, Green emphasized; they are symbolic:

> Women like me are going to blow it in the role of mother if left to the narrow, biological role. But in Indian country, that role was never understood necessarily only as a biological role; grandma was never understood as a biological role; sister and aunt were never understood in the narrow confines of genetic kinship.[32]

As leaders, Native women must oversee the survival of Native peoples, notes Green. While Green, like Blue and Carrie Dann, sees Native people as the primary redeemers of America, she emphatically refutes the appropriation of Native traditions to "heal" mainstream American culture. "We cannot do that," she explains.

> There has been so much abuse of this role that it's frightening. . . . *All* Indigenous people have that power, because we speak from the earth. . . . But we cannot heal you; only you can heal yourselves. . . . If we have any model to give, it is an aesthetic model, a cultural model, that works for us.

Green warns that Western appropriation of Indigenous traditions, rituals, and philosophies (made popular in the New Age Movement, for example) will not provide a "quick fix" for the problems of Western culture. Green's position is an attempt to clarify the role of Native traditions in the reformative enterprise. Native activists will not perform the service-work of healing Western cultures. Green points out that such expectations are embedded in colonial histories; they keep the "sick" Western subject at the center to be tended by the Native "other."[33]

Native women's strategic use of a motherist stance is a conscious act of separation from traditional feminists.[34] The women locate their activism not in feminist struggle, but in cultural survival, identifying themselves, as Anne Snitow explains, "not as feminists but as militant mothers, fighting together for [the] survival [of their children]." Women become motherists, Snitow writes, when "men are forced to be absent (because they are migrant workers or soldiers) or in times of crisis, when the role of nurturance assigned to women has been rendered difficult or impossible."[35] A motherist position would apply to Native women living on and off reservations where employment opportunities are scarce for men, as well as for women who lose their mothering capacity to sterilization or their living children to boarding schools. The motherists Snitow describes intuitively relied upon the presence of their female community because "crisis made the idea of a separate, private identity beyond the daily struggle for survival unimportant."[36]

White feminists and Native motherists endorsed divergent strategies, notes Snitow. Her model perfectly characterizes dichotomies between Native women's collective identifications—including their loyalties to traditions that puzzle white women—and non-Native feminists' individuating theories. "Collectivist movements are powerful, but they usually don't raise questions about women's work," she explains. "Feminism has raised the questions, and claimed an individual destiny for each woman, but remains ambivalent toward older traditions of female solidarity."[37] For example, traditional dichotomies of public and private domains, characteristic of much feminist writing of the 1970s and 1980s, does not work for women of color for whom "those domains are not separate or at least not separate in the same ways as for white women."[38] This is especially true with Native cultures, which are structured along collective rather than individual dynamics characteristic of Western cultures.[39] The separation of public and private spheres, along with "the primacy of gender conflict as a feature of the family, and the gender-based assignment of reproductive labor," constitute three concepts of traditional white feminist theory that ignore the interaction of race and gender and thus fail to account for Native women's experience of motherwork.[40]

Evelyn Nakano Glenn observes that for racial ethnic women, the concept of the "domestic" extends beyond the nuclear family to include broadly defined relations of kin and community. Often living in situations of economic insecurity and assault on their culture, racially ethnic women have not been able to rely solely on the nuclear family because it is not self-sufficient, but have relied upon and contributed to an extended network of family and community. Thus, work conducted in the domestic, hence "private," sphere includes contributions to the extended "public" network, where women care for each other's children, exchange supplies, and help nurse the sick. Racial ethnic women's work has simultaneously moved into the public sphere of the ethnic community, in support of the church, political organizing, and other activities on behalf of their collective. Glenn writes that racial ethnic women are "often the core of community organizations, and their involvement is often spurred by a desire to defend their children, their families, and their ways of life."[41]

Certainly Glenn's point is relevant to contemporary Native women living on and off the reservation. Focused on strengthening Native economies and traditions, contemporary Native women may engage in traditional skills of beadwork or quilting, for example, in order to earn money and prestige to benefit, feed, and educate their children. Women may engage in activities historically associated with men in order to revise and strengthen tribal culture. Such women drum at local powwows, or are political activists, such as Mary Brave Bird of AIM and, more recently, Winona LaDuke (White Earth Ojibwa), founder of the White Earth Land Recovery Project, cochair of the Indigenous Women's Network, and vice presidential candidate for the Green Party in the last two elections. Patricia Hill Collins notes that work and family do not function as separate, dichotomous spheres for women of color, but are, in fact, often overlapping. By linking individual and collective welfare, Collins neatly articulates the philosophy underlying most Native cultures. While individual achievement is sought and recognized, it is always within the context of the collective that such endeavors are valued. It follows that Wilma Mankiller became Principal Chief of the Cherokee to benefit the Cherokee.[42]

For women of color, then, motherwork involves working for the physical survival of children and community, confronting what Collins calls the "dialectical nature of power and powerlessness in structuring mothering patterns, and the significance of self-definition in constructing individual and collective racial identity." This type of motherwork, while ensuring individual and community survival, can result in the loss of individual autonomy "or the submersion of individual growth for the benefit of the group."[43] The deemphasis on individual autonomy proves troubling to white feminists who have sought to extricate the individual woman's identity from the debilitating influences of social expectation in order to articulate and celebrate her emergence into what has generally been viewed as a more liberated individual. Once again we experience the fallout of conflicting ideas between Western liberalism and Native collectivism.

When feminist theory posits "the family" as "the locus of gender conflict," focusing on the economic dependence of women and the inequitable division of labor, it inevitably draws upon models of the white, middle-class, nuclear family. Viewed thus, marriage within the white, middle-class, nuclear family oppresses women. In order to gain liberation, white feminists have argued, women must be free from the unequal balance of power marriage has conferred. In contrast, Glenn points out, women of color often experience their families as a "source of resistance to oppression from outside institutions." Within Glenn's construct, we see that women of color engage in activities to keep their families unified and teach children survival skills. This work is viewed as a method of resistance to oppression rather than gender exploitation. Unified in struggle against colonial oppression, family members focus on individual survival, maintenance of family authority, and the transmission of cultural traditions. Economically, Glenn notes, women of color remain less dependent upon men than white women because they must earn an income to support the family. Both incomes are necessary for a family's survival. Glenn writes that because the earning gap between women and men of color is narrower than that of whites, "men and women [of color have been] mutually dependent; dependence rarely ran in one direction." Such families may be sustained by members whose relationships are characterized by interdependence and gender complementarity.[44]

Glenn's paradigm of the family can be applied in a broader context in order to consider aspects of contemporary reservation and urban life. For example, Christine Conte's study of western Navajo women examines how they employ kin ties and cooperative networks to perform tasks, obtain resources, and acquire wealth. Such cooperation typically includes the exchange of labor, commodities, subsistence goods, information, cash, and transportation.[45] Similarly, women featured in Steve Wall's collection of interviews with tribal elders describe themselves as family leaders, intent on transmitting cultural traditions to the generation that follows them.[46] AIM schools of the 1970s, typically run by women, provide one example of offering Native children an alternative value system to the mission and boarding schools that many of their parents (such as Mary Brave Bird) experienced.

Like Glenn and Collins, Patricia Monture-Angus points to the differing roles that the family plays for Native women and non-Native women. Citing Marlee Kline, Monture-Angus notes that, while women of color and white women can both experience violence in the family, women of color look to their family as a system of support against violent racism from outside the family. Thus, while the Native family may "provide a site of cultural and political resistance to White supremacy,"[47] Native women can also experience contradictory relationships within their families, requiring that they also revise their families as they go along. Drawing upon networks of kin for support, survival, and pleasure, Native women also combat trends in domestic violence and prescribed gender roles that threaten and constrain them.[48]

Collins identifies three main themes that comprise ethnic women's struggles for maternal empowerment: 1) reproductive autonomy; 2) parental privileges; and 3) the threat of cultural eradication by the dominant culture.[49] Many women of color have not known the experience of determining their own fertility. For Native women sterilized without their consent, choosing to become a mother takes on political meaning, an act that challenges, as Angela Davis has said, "institutional policies that encourage white middle-class women to reproduce and discourage low-income racial ethnic women from doing so, even penalizing them."[50] Once a woman of color becomes a parent, she is threatened with the physical and/or psychological separation from her children "designed to disempower racial ethnic individuals and undermine their communities."[51] The Indian boarding and mission schools of the nineteenth and twentieth centuries serve as an example of this disempowerment, coupled, as they were, with "the pervasive efforts by the dominant group to control their children's minds" by forbidding any use of Native languages and the denigration of "the power of mothers to raise their children as they see fit."[52] For women of color, motherwork entails the difficult tasks of "trying to foster a meaningful racial identity in children within a society that denigrates people of color" and sustaining a form of resistance.[53]

For many Native women, motherwork is linked with the authority of leadership.[54] Discussing Western imperialism's degenerative effect on female leadership, Chief Wilma Mankiller contends:

> Europeans brought with them the view that men were the absolute heads of households, and women were to be submissive to them. It was then that the role of women in Cherokee society began to decline. One of the new values Europeans brought to the Cherokees was a lack of balance and harmony between men and women. It was what we today call sexism. This was not a Cherokee concept. Sexism was borrowed from Europeans.[55]

Mankiller characterizes the resistance she encountered to her campaign for the position of Principal Chief of the Cherokee as evidence of the erosion of traditional Native political structures under the onslaught of Western influence. Although traditionally matrilineal, the Cherokee adopted Western configurations of gender that favor patriarchal structures, notes Mankiller. Among recent Cherokee accomplishments, such as addressing issues of poverty and education reform, and the revitalization of cultural traditions, Mankiller includes revised gender roles and the reclamation of women's power.

The current status of Native women—both on and off the reservations involved in tribal political, cultural, and religious revitalization—drives many contemporary writers to emphasize the richness of traditional Native women's lives as models for reform. Just as Green insists on traditions that cultivate women's leadership, Lakota anthropologist Beatrice Medicine emphasizes the importance women play in Lakota ceremonial and artistic life, along with the status their work garners. Medicine contends that "the traditional woman was greatly respected and revered," that she hosted feasts and participated in sacred ceremonies, and that women's societies held competitions in the arts of sewing, beading, and other crafts that proved economically lucrative in trade and were thus prestigious for the winner. Contemporary life on the reservations is very different, Medicine notes. Lakota women suffer diminished prestige, and they are threatened by poor economic conditions, government usurpation of the functions traditionally provided by the family (such as welfare and education), and the loss of traditional values that unify kinship roles and obligations. Where Sioux women formerly used their artistic talents to make a respectable marriage and to earn prestige and wealth, they now continue their artistic work but with diminished economic return. At one time a woman might have earned one horse in exchange for a "skillfully decorated robe"; now she will earn approximately sixty cents an hour for a quilt.[56]

Many Native women agree with Allen, who contends, "The tradition of strong, autonomous, self-defining women comes from Indians. They [Euroamericans] sure didn't get it in sixteenth-century Europe."[57] Monture-Angus explains that the term "traditional" privileges neither "static" nor regressive perspectives, but embraces holistic approaches to reform. Monture-Angus points out that "traditional perspectives include the view that the past and all its experiences inform the present reality."[58] She advocates an interpretation of traditions that is fluid and adaptive, one that will enable Native societies to confront situations of contemporary life such as domestic violence, substance addiction, and youth suicide. Because many precontact cultures did not condone abuse of women, Monture-Angus argues, a literal interpretation of traditions will fail to provide a contemporary model of social reform. "What we can reclaim is the values [sic] that created a system where the abuses did not occur. We can recover our own system of law, law that has at its centre the family and our kinship relations. . . . We must be patient with each other as we learn to live in a decolonized way."[59] Monture-Angus articulates a belief in the beauty and efficacy of Native traditions shared by many Native women writing about strategies for battling colonialism and supporting tribal survival.

Part of the reclamation of cultural traditions involves the recognition of "responsibilities," a term many Native theorists distinguish from western notions of "rights." Native women thus articulate their responsibilities in terms of their roles as mothers and leaders, positing those roles as a form of motherwork. "Responsibility focuses attention not on what is mine, but on the relationships between people and creation (that is, both the individual and the collective)," writes Monture-Angus.[60] Native activists argue that rights-based theories predispose Western cultures to abuse the earth and to oppress other societies that value their relationship to the earth. Renee Senogles (Red Lake Chippewa) notes: "The difference between Native American women and white feminists is that the feminists talk about their rights and we talk about our responsibilities. There is a profound difference. Our responsibility is to take care of our natural place in the world."[61] Osennontion and Skonaganleh:rá concur, clarifying the emphasis of Haudenosaunee law on responsibilities within political and social realms, which include the observance of clan structure and communal ties, and a personal code of honor, integrity, compassion, and strength, linked to the maintenance of a relationship with the natural world.[62]

One primary goal of Native activists involves restructuring and reinforcing Indian families. This includes their reevaluation of both women's and men's roles. If Native women are to fulfill traditions of female leadership, they argue, Native men must reclaim their responsibilities so that the enterprise supporting Indigenous survival and prosperity can move forward. Native women repeatedly fault white feminists for the devaluation of men in their revisionary tactics. Part of a man's responsibility is to protect and provide for his family, as well as to expedite political and social duties. If a man fails in his responsibilities, it falls upon the society's women to instruct, reeducate, and remind him of his obligations. Native activists fault Western hegemony and capitalism as systems responsible for alienating so many Native men from their traditional responsibilities.

In the face of coerced agrarianism and the attending devaluation of hunting, and the consequences of forced removal and relocation, Native men have suffered a loss of status and traditional self-sufficiency even more extensive than their female counterparts, argue many Native women.[63] Women's traditional roles as procreator, parent, domestic leader, and even artisan have, to some extent, remained intact. For example, Clara Sue Kidwell observes that during early contact, women's "functions as childbearers and contributors to subsistence were not threatening to white society and were less affected than those of Indian men."[64] In situations of contact, Kidwell points out, women often became the custodians of traditional cultural values, engaging in reproductive labor and motherwork. In contrast, men suffer from an inability to fulfill traditional roles. On the Pine Ridge reservation of the Lakota, employment opportunities for Lakota men are practically nonexistent. Federal agencies, such as the BIA and IHS provide the majority of the employment available. Very few businesses are owned by the Lakota, and, because of the land allotment, less than 10 percent of reservation land is actually owned by Native Americans. Jobs available to men, such as construction, are project-oriented and thus sporadic, whereas job opportunities for women, such as nursing, teaching, clerical, and domestic work, are more consistently available.[65] Ramona Ford observes that contemporary Native women hold down more jobs than do Native men, although they earn inadequate wages.[66] It is evident that such cash-based, gender-delimited jobs keep the majority of Native people living below the poverty line in both the United States and Canada.[67]

Part of their responsibilities then, contend many Native women, is the restoration of traditional male roles, along with the selection and training of appropriate male leaders. Once installed in leadership roles, Osennontion and Skonaganleh:rá write, the men are responsible to the women who have empowered them, and the women ensure that their leaders remain "good men," mindful of the reciprocal relationship between leader and subject.[68] The definition of their responsibilities—their attendance to clan and communal structure through an investment in male esteem—coincides with the taxonomy I discuss in reproductive labor and motherwork.

While some Western feminists might recoil from such an investment in the restoration of male psyche, seeing it as a refined form of female abjection, it is important to remember that the majority of Native women writing and speaking today—who are political activists, feminist scholars, anthropologists, law professors, and grassroots organizers—all emphasize the importance of men to the revitalization of Native communities. Obviously then, these Native women do not prescribe female subjugation, but rather the solidification of a communal, extended network of support that acts as the family. This family takes many forms and rarely resembles the Western model of the nuclear, patriarch-led unit. For example, the two collections *Women of the Native Struggle* and *Wisdom's Daughters* feature vastly extended, matrilineal and matrilocal families, often with single, pregnant women as their members and leaders.[69] Such families seek to reintegrate men into communal life, but not within Western patriarchal paradigms. Osennontion and Skonaganleh:rá argue for the necessity of women's participation on the Band Council, the governing body for many East Coast Canadian tribes, including the Haudenosaunee: "Women have a responsibility to make sure that we don't lose any more, that we don't do any more damage, while we work on getting our original government system back in good working order."[70] As Monture-Angus notes, an emphasis on Native traditions does not preclude the integration of old and new. While recognizing the value of traditional culture and practice, Native activists and feminists do not blindly embrace behavior simply because it may be called "traditional," especially if it is oppressive to women. Just who determines what is to be called "traditional" and therefore valuable is also under scrutiny.

Indigenous women activists cite the difficulties that inform their theories and praxes of activism: the widespread violence committed against Native women; the common occurrence of rape; the murder of family members (Brave Bird, Campbell, and Lee Maracle, for instance, all recount such experiences); the murder and mutilation of leaders and friends (such as activist Annie Mae Aquash); the government's abduction of Indian children; and sterilization of Native women. It is vital that Native communities retrieve lost traditions of gender complementarity, they argue. The majority of Native American women involved in women's rights point to their own brand of feminism that calls on obscured traditions of women's autonomy and power. Such efforts, which are generally grassroots, reflect Native traditions of community-based activism comparable to the paradigm Snitow outlines.

In any discussion of possible coalition between contemporary Indigenous groups and white feminist groups, Native women insist that their prospective partners recognize Indigenous traditions of female autonomy and prestige, traditions that can provide models of social reform in white, as well as Native, America. This proposed coalition suggests a move beyond idealized appropriation, to a shared vision of political and cultural reform. In their eagerness to coalesce, white feminists have been rightly accused of ignoring or eliding differences between and among women. Native women resist reductionist impulses inherent in Western feminism, insisting that we examine the varying historical contingencies of each group that continue to shape feminist discourses into the next century.

NOTES

1. Examples include Paula Gunn Allen, *Off the Reservation: Reflections on Boundary-Busting, Border-Crossing, Loose Canons* (Boston: Beacon Press, 1998), *The Sacred Hoop: Recovering the Feminine in American Indian Traditions* (Boston: Beacon Press, 1986), and *Spider Woman's Granddaughters: Traditional Tales and Contemporary Writing by Native American Women* (Boston: Beacon Press, 1989); Jane Caputi, "Interview with Paula Gunn Allen," *Trivia*

16 (1990): 50–67, and "Interview" in *Backtalk: Women Writers Speak Out,* ed. Donna Perry (New Brunswick, N.J.: Rutgers University Press, 1993); Rayna Green, "American Indian Women: Diverse Leadership for Social Change," in *Bridges of Power: Women's Multicultural Alliances,* ed. Lisa Albrecht and Rose M. Brewer (Philadelphia: New Society Publishers, 1990), "Review Essay: Native American Women," *Signs: Journal of Women in Culture and Society* 6:2 (1980): 248–67, and *Women in American Indian Society* (New York: Chelsea House Publishers, 1992); Patricia A. Monture-Angus, *Thunder in My Soul: A Mohawk Woman Speaks* (Halifax: Fernwood Publishing, 1995); Patricia A. Monture, "I Know My Name: A First Nations Woman Speaks," in *Limited Edition: Voices of Women, Voices of Feminism,* ed. Geraldine Finn (Halifax: Fernwood Publishing, 1993); Wilma Mankiller and Michael Wallis, *Mankiller: A Chief and Her People* (New York: St. Martin's Press, 1993); Mary Brave Bird and Richard Erdoes, *Ohitika Woman* (New York: Harper Collins, 1993); Mary Crow Dog and Richard Erdoes, *Lakota Woman* (New York: Harper Collins, 1991); and Janet McCloud, in *Women of the Native Struggle: Portraits and Testimony of Native American Women,* ed. Ronnie Farley (New York: Orion Books, 1993).

2. Farley, *Women of the Native Struggle,* Jane Katz, ed., *Messengers of the Wind: Native American Women Tell Their Life Stories* (New York: Ballantine Books, 1995); and Steve Wall, ed., *Wisdom's Daughters: Conversations with Women Elders of Native America* (New York: Harper Perennial, 1993).

3. Patricia Hill Collins applies the term "motherwork" to the tasks engaged in by women/mothers of color. Collins contends that women of color recognize the embattled nature of their families and identify the most destructive forces as coming from outside their families rather than from within. Part of women's work, or motherwork, consists of maintaining "family integrity." The kind of motherwork Collins outlines, and many Native women describe, reflects the belief that "individual survival, empowerment, and identity require group survival, empowerment, and identity" ("Shifting the Center: Race, Class, and Feminist Theorizing About Motherhood," in *Representations of Motherhood,* ed. Donna Bassin, Margaret Honey, and Meryle Mahrer Kaplan [New Haven: Yale University Press, 1994], 59).

4. Monture-Angus, *Thunder in My Soul,* 49.

5. Clara Sue Kidwell, "What Would Pocahontas Think Now? Women and Cultural Persistence," *Callaloo* 17:1 (1994): 149.

6. Mary Gopher, in Farley, *Women of the Native Struggle, 77.*

7. Carrie Dann in Farley, *Women of the Native Struggle, 77.*

8. Yet Si Blue in Farley, *Women of the Native Struggle,* 83.

9. Monture-Angus, *Thunder in My Soul,* 210; Paula Gunn Allen, quoted in Caputi, "Interview," 8; and Ingrid Washinawatok-El Issa in Farley, *Women of the Native Struggle,* 48.

10. Allen, "Interview," in Perry, *Backtalk,* 17.

11. Mary Crow Dog and Richard Erdoes, *Lakota Woman* (New York: Harper-Perennial, 1991) 78–79.

12. Jane Katz, ed., *Messangers of the Wind: Native American Women Tell Their Life Stories* (New York: Ballantine Books, 1995), 35–37, 60, 80–81.

13. Maria Campbell, *Halfbreed* (Lincoln: University of Nebraska Press, 1973), 103–7.

14. Green, *Women in American Indian Society,* 37.

15. Green, *Women in American Indian Society,* 37–38.

16. Green, *Women in American Indian Society,* 38. Linda Hogan's *Mean Spirit* (New York: Ivy Books, 1990) is a fictionalized account of this gynocidal episode in Native-Euramerican history.

17. Ramona Ford, "Native American Women: Changing Statuses, Changing Interpretations," in *Writing the Range: Race, Class, and Culture in the Women's West,* ed. Elizabeth Jameson and Susan Armitage (Norman: University of Oklahoma Press, 1997), 58; and Nancy Shoemaker, "The Rise Or Fall of Iroquois Women," *Journal of Women's History* 2:3 (1991): 39–57, 51. For further discussion of gender in precontact cultures, see Evelyn Blackwood's "Sexuality and Gender in Certain Native American Tribes," *Signs: Journal of Women in Culture and Society* 10:1 (1984): 27–42.

18. Janet Karsten Larson, "And Then There Were None: Is Federal Policy Endangering the American Indian Species?" *Christian Century* 94, January 26, 1977, 61–63; and Mark Miller, "Native American Peoples on the Trail of Tears Once More: Indian Health Service and Coerced Sterilization," *America* 139 (1978): 422–25.

19. R. Bogue and D. W. Segelman, "Survey Finds Seven in 10 Hospitals Violate DHEW Guidelines on Informed Consent for Sterilization," *Family Planning Perspectives* 11:6 (1979): 366–67.

20. Miller, "Native American Peoples on the Trail of Tears," 424.

21. Charles R. England, "A Look at the Indian Health Service Policy of Sterilization, 1972–1976," *Native American Homepage,* October 10, 1997, 6. For a fuller discussion of this topic, see Myla F. Thyrza Carpio, "Lost Generation: The Involuntary Sterilization of American Indian Women" (master's thesis, Johns Hopkins, 1991).

22. Green, "Review Essay," 261.

23. Connie Uri, quoted in Miller, "Native American Peoples on the Trail of Tears," 423.

24. Barbara Moore quoted in Fee Podarski, "An Interview with Barbara Moore on Sterilization," *Akwesasne Notes* 11:2 (1979): 11–12.

25. Barbara Moore, quoted in Podarski, "An Interview with Barbara Moore," 11.

26. Indian status is another aspect of the eradication of Native populations. Both in Canada and the United States, entire tribes have lost their status as "Indian" or "Native" and are identified instead as "colored." For an example in early-twentieth-century Virginia see J. David Smith, *The Eugenic Assault on America: Scenes in Red, White, and Black* (Fairfax, Va.: George Mason University Press, 1993); and for a more recent example pertaining to the Tobique in Canada, see Tobique Women's Group, *Enough is Enough: Aboriginal Women Speak Out,* as told to Janet Silman, (Toronto: The Women's Press, 1987).

27. Linda Gordon, "Why Nineteenth-Century Feminists Did Not Support 'Birth Control' and Twentieth-Century Feminists Do:

Feminism, Reproduction, and the Family," in *Rethinking the Family: Some Feminist Questions,* ed. Barrie Thorne and Marilyn Yalom (Boston: Northeastern University Press, 1992), 149.

28. Linda Gordon, *Woman's Body, Woman's Right: A Social History of Birth Control in America* (New York: Grossman Publishers, 1976), 281.

29. Gordon, "Why Nineteenth-Century Feminists Did Not Support 'Birth Control,'" 150.

30. Mary Brave Bird and Richard Erdoes, *Ohitika Woman* (New York: Harper-Perennial, 1993), 58.

31. Green, "American Indian Women," 65.

32. Green, "American Indian Women," 66.

33. Green, "American Indian Women," 63, 64, 71.

34. Ironically, early feminists and advocates of "voluntary motherhood" proposed an agenda similar to Native women's. Both saw voluntary motherhood as part of a movement to empower women (Gordon, "Why Nineteenth-Century Feminists Did Not Support 'Birth Control,'" 145). Suffragists' desire to exalt motherhood was a way of creating a dignified, powerful position for women in contrast to popular notions of womanhood that connoted fragility and virtue. By evoking a powerful model, women responded to their sexual subjugation to men and created an alternate arena where they had authority (Gordon, *Woman's Body,* 133–34).

35. Ann Snitow, "A Gender Diary," in *Conflicts in Feminism,* ed. Mariann Hirsch and Evelyn Fox Keller (New York: Routledge, 1990), 20.

36. Snitow, "A Gender Diary," 20.

37. Snitow, "A Gender Diary," 22.

38. Quotation from in Bassin, Honey, and Kaplan, *Representations of Motherhood,* 5. See, for example, Jessica Benjamin, "Authority and the Family Revisted: Or, A World Without Fathers," *New German Critique* 4:3 (1978): 35–57; Nancy Chodorow, "Family Structure and Feminine Personality," in *Women, Culture, and Society,* ed. Michelle Zimbalist Rosaldo and Louise Lamphere (Stanford: Stanford University Press, 1974), 43–66; and Jean Bethke Elshtain, *Public Man, Private Woman: Women in Social and Political Thought* (Princeton: Princeton University Press, 1981).

39. For more detailed critiques of the limitations of dualistic separation of private and public sectors for gender analysis generally, see Susan Himmelweit, "The Real Dualism of Sex and Class," *Review of Radical Political Economics* 16:1 (1984): 167–83. For Native women more particularly, see Patricia Albers, "Sioux Women in Transition: A Study of Their Changing Status in a Domestic and Capitalist Sector of Production," in *The Hidden Half: Studies of Plains Indian Women,* ed. Patricia Albers and Beatrice Medicine (Latham MD: University Press of America, 1983), and Albers, "Autonomy and Dependency in the Lives of Dakota Women: A Study in Historical Change," *Review of Radical Political Economics* 17:3 (1985): 109–34.

40. Evelyn Nakano Glenn, "Racial Ethnic Women's Labor: The Intersection of Race, Gender and Class Oppression," *Review of Radical Political Economics* 17:3 (1985): 101; Patricia Hill Collins, "Shifting the Center"; and Bonnie Thornton Dill, "Our Mothers' Grief: Racial Ethnic Women and the Maintenance of Families," *Journal of Family History* 13:4 (1988): 415–31, use the term "reproductive labor" to refer to all of the work of women in the home. Dill describes reproductive labor to include "the buying and preparation of food and clothing, provision of emotional support and nurturance for all family members, bearing children, and planning, organizing, and carrying out a wide variety of tasks associated with the socialization" ("Our Mothers' Grief," 430).

I adopt Patricia Hill Collins's use of the term "motherwork," which she employs to "soften the dichotomies in feminist theorizing about motherhood that posit rigid distinctions between private and public, family and work, the individual and the collective, identity as individual autonomy and identity growing from the collective self-determination of one's group. Racial ethnic women's mothering and work experiences occur at the boundaries demarking these dualities" ("Shifting the Center," 59).

41. Glenn, "Racial Ethnic Women's Labor," 102, 103. Several recent studies of modern Native household units find that women often head extended families and kinship networks that resist capitalist models that marginalize them. See Albers, "Autonomy and Dependency in the Lives of Dakota Women," "From Illusion to Illumination: Anthropological Studies of American Indian Women," in *Gender and Anthropology. Critical Reviews for Research and Teaching,* ed. Sandra Morgan (Washington DC: American Anthropological Association, 1989), and "Sioux Women in Transition"; Martha C. Knack, *Life is With People: Household Organization of the Contemporary Southern Paiute Indians* (Socorro NM: Ballena Press, 1980); and Loraine Littlefield, "Gender, Class and Community: The History of Sne-Nay-Muxw Women's Employment" (Ph.D. diss., University of British Columbia, 1995).

42. Collins, "Shifting the Center," 58. Obviously, personal ambition is usually seen as selfish and suspect for women generally. Women have typically couched descriptions of their ambitions in terms of altruism and collective responsibility. My point here, however, is that leadership within Native paradigms embraces collective more than individual identity.

43. Collins, "Shifting the Center," 61, 62.

44. Glenn, "Racial Ethnic Women's Labor," 103–4. The high rate of single, female-headed households undermines Glenn conclusions somewhat. As seen in Wall's *Wisdom's Daughters,* for example, contemporary Native women may not "require" the income of Native men to survive at the subsistence level; however, they argue that women require men's economic contribution to live well, or above subsistence/poverty level. More important, Native women argue, they require men's social and cultural participation in tribal life in order to ensure survival of specific collective experiences and to perpetuate their traditions.

45. Christine Conte, "Ladies, Livestock, and Land and Lucre: Women's Networks and Social Status on the Western Navajo Reservation," *American Indian Quarterly* 6:1/2 (1982): 105, 116.

46. For example, Wall, *Wisdom's Daughters,* 169–70, 224–26.

47. Marlee Kline, cited in Monture-Angus, *Thunder in My Soul,* 42.

48. Not all Native women experience capitalism equally. Conte's study shows that while most Navajo women have been adversely affected by the forces of a market economy, several are able to manipulate elements of capitalism to benefit themselves and their households, while others experience diminished wealth ("Ladies, Livestock, and Land and Lucre," 120). Albers draws similar conclusions from her research on the Devil's Lake Sioux, particularly in "Autonomy and Dependency in the Lives of Dakota Women," 124–28.

49. Collins, "Shifting the Center," 65.

50. Angela Davis, quoted by Collins in "Shifting the Center," 65.

51. Collins, "Shifting the Center," 65.

52. Collins, "Shifting the Center," 66.

53. Collins, "Shifting the Center," 68.

54. See the proceedings from the United Nations Fourth World Conference on Women, Mothers of Our Nations, *Indigenous Women Address the World: Our Future—Our Responsibility* (Rapid City, S.D., 1995).

55. Mankiller and Wallis, *Mankiller,* 20.

56. Beatrice Medicine, "The Hidden Half Lives," in *Cante Ohitika Win (Brave-Hearted Women): Images of Lakota Women From the Pine Ridge Reservation South Dakota,* ed. Caroline Reyer (Vermillion: University of South Dakota Press, 1991), 5; and Albers and Medicine, *The Hidden Half,* 134–35. Nonetheless, Albers and Medicine contend that in contemporary life, star quilts remain one of the most prestigious items in the Sioux give-away system. Quilts are displayed or given at honoring ceremonies and when "Sioux return home from military service or college," at community events of importance such as memorial feasts and naming ceremonies, and during "donations of powwow officials" (Patricia Albers and Beatrice Medicine, "The Role of Sioux Women in the Production of Ceremonial Objects: The Case of the Star Quilt").

57. Allen, "Interview," in Perry, *Backtalk,* 10.

58. Monture-Angus, *Thunder in My Soul,* 244.

59. Monture-Angus, *Thunder in My Soul,* 258.

60. Monture-Angus, *Thunder in My Soul,* 28.

61. Renee Senogles, quoted in Farley, *Women of the Native Struggle,* 69.

62. Osennontion (Marlyn Kane) and Skonaganleh:rá (Sylvia Maracle), "Our World: According to Osennontion and Skonaganleh:rá," *Canadian Woman Studies/Les Cahiers de la Femme* 10:2/3 (1989): 7–19, 11.

63. Medicine, "Hidden Half Lives," 5; and Lindy Trueblood, "Interview," in Reyer, *Cante Ohitika Win,* 50.

64. Kidwell, "What Would Pocahontas Think Now?" 150.

65. Trueblood, "Interview," in Reyer, *Cante Ohitika Win,* 50.

66. Ford, "Native American Women," 59.

67. In Canada the 1986 average income for Aboriginal people was $12,899 compared to $18,188 earned by the average non-Native Canadian. The 1990 U.S. census reported the median household income of Indians living on a reservation was $19,865, compared with the U.S. median of $30,056. Thirty-five percent of U.S. Natives live below the federal poverty level (Jo Ann Kauffman and Yvette K. Joseph-Fox, "American Indian and Alaska Native Women," in *Race, Gender, and Health,* ed. Marcia Bayne-Smith [Thousand Oaks, California: Sage Publications, 1996], 71).

68. Osennontion and Skonaganleh:rá, "Our World," 14.

69. Katz, *Messengers of the Wind;* and Wall, *Wisdom's Daughters.*

70. Osennontion and Skonaganleh:rá, "Our World," 14.

31

"I'm Here, but I'm There"

The Meanings of Latina Transnational Motherhood

PIERRETTE HONDAGNEU-SOTELO
ERNESTINE AVILA

While mothering is generally understood as practice that involves the preservation, nurturance, and training of children for adult life (Ruddick 1989), there are many contemporary variants distinguished by race, class, and culture (Collins 1994; Dill 1988, 1994; Glenn 1994). Latina immigrant women who work and reside in the United States while their children remain in their countries of origin constitute one variation in the organizational arrangements, meanings, and priorities of motherhood. We call this arrangement "transnational motherhood," and we explore how the meanings of motherhood are rearranged to accommodate these spatial and temporal separations. In the United States, there is a long legacy of Caribbean women and African American women from the South, leaving their children "back home" to seek work in the North. Since the early 1980s, thousands of Central American women, and increasing numbers of Mexican women, have migrated to the United States in search of jobs, many of them leaving their children behind with grandmothers, with other female kin, with the children's fathers, and sometimes with paid caregivers. In some cases, the separations of time and distance are substantial; 10 years may elapse before women are reunited with their children. In this article we confine our analysis to Latina transnational mothers currently employed in Los Angeles in paid domestic work, one of the most gendered and racialized occupations.[1] We examine how their meanings of motherhood shift in relation to the structures of late-20th-century global capitalism.

Motherhood is not biologically predetermined in any fixed way but is historically and socially constructed. Many factors set the stage for transnational motherhood. These factors include labor demand for Latina immigrant women in the United States, particularly in paid domestic work; civil war, national economic crises, and particular development strategies, along with tenuous and scarce job opportunities for women and men in Mexico and Central America; and the subsequent increasing numbers of female-headed households (although many transnational

Pierrette Hondagneu-Sotelo and Ernestine Avila, "'I'm Here, but I'm There': The Meanings of Latina Transnational Motherhood," from *Doméstica: Immigrant Workers Cleaning and Caring in the Shadows of Affluence*.

mothers are married). More interesting to us than the macro determinants of transnational motherhood, however, is the forging of new arrangements and meanings of motherhood.

Central American and Mexican women who leave their young children "back home" and come to the United States in search of employment are in the process of actively, if not voluntarily, building alternative constructions of motherhood. Transnational motherhood contradicts both dominant U.S., White, middle-class models of motherhood, and most Latina ideological notions of motherhood. On the cusp of the millennium, transnational mothers and their families are blazing new terrain, spanning national borders, and improvising strategies for mothering. It is a brave odyssey, but one with deep costs. . . .

RETHINKING MOTHERHOOD

Feminist scholarship has long challenged monolithic notions of family and motherhood that relegate women to the domestic arena of private/public dichotomies and that rely on the ideological conflation of family, woman, reproduction, and nurturance (Collier and Yanagisako 1987, 36).[2] "Rethinking the family" prompts the rethinking of motherhood (Glenn 1994; Thorne and Yalom 1992), allowing us to see that the glorification and exaltation of isolationist, privatized mothering is historically and culturally specific.

The "cult of domesticity" is a cultural variant of motherhood, one made possible by the industrial revolution, by breadwinner husbands who have access to employers who pay a "family wage," and by particular configurations of global and national socioeconomic and racial inequalities. Working-class women of color in the United States have rarely had access to the economic security that permits a biological mother to be the only one exclusively involved with mothering during the children's early years (Collins 1994; Dill 1988, 1994; Glenn 1994). As Evelyn Nakano Glenn puts it, "Mothering is not just gendered, but also racialized" (1994, 7) and differentiated by class. Both historically and in the contemporary period, women lacking the resources that allow for exclusive, full-time, round-the-clock mothering rely on various arrangements to care for children. Sharing mothering responsibilities with female kin and friends as "other mothers" (Collins 1991), by "kin-scription" (Stack and Burton 1994), or by hiring child care (Uttal 1996) are widely used alternatives.

Women of color have always worked. Yet, many working women—including Latina women—hold the cultural prescription of solo mothering in the home as an ideal. We believe this ideal is disseminated through cultural institutions of industrialization and urbanization, as well as from preindustrial, rural peasant arrangements that allow for women to work while tending to their children. It is not only White, middle-class ideology but also strong Latina/o traditions, cultural practices, and ideals—Catholicism, and the Virgin Madonna figure—that cast employment as oppositional to mothering. Cultural symbols that model maternal femininity, such as *La Virgen de Guadalupe,* and negative femininity, such as *La Llorona* and *La Malinche,* serve to control Mexican and Chicana women's conduct by prescribing idealized visions of motherhood.[3]

Culture, however, does not deterministically dictate what people do.[4] Many Latina women must work for pay, and many Latinas innovate income-earning strategies that allow them to simultaneously earn money and care for their children. They sew garments on industrial sewing machines at home (Fernández Kelly and Garcia 1990) and incorporate their children into informal vending to friends and neighbors, at swap meets, or on the sidewalks (Chinchilla and Hamilton 1996). They may perform agricultural work alongside their children or engage in seasonal work (Zavella 1987); or they may clean houses when their children are at school or alternatively, incorporate their daughters into paid house cleaning (Romero 1992, 1997). Engagement in "invisible employment" allows for urgently needed income and the maintenance of the ideal of privatized mothering. The middle-class model of mothering is predicated on mother-child isolation in the home, while women of color have often worked with their children in close proximity (Collins 1994), as in some of the examples listed above. In both cases, however, mothers are with their children. The long distances of time and space that separate transnational mothers from their children contrast sharply to both mother-child isolation in the home or mother-child integration in the workplace.

Performing domestic work for pay, especially in a live-in job, is often incompatible with providing primary care for one's own family and home (Glenn 1986; Rollins 1985; Romero 1992, 1997).[5] Transnational mothering, however, is neither exclusive to live-in domestic workers nor to single mothers. Many women continue with transnational mothering after they move into live-out paid domestic work, or into other jobs. Women with income-earning husbands may also become transnational mothers.[6] The women we interviewed do not necessarily divert their mothering to the children and homes of their employers but instead reformulate their own mothering to accommodate spatial and temporal gulfs.

Like other immigrant workers, most transnational mothers came to the United States with the intention to stay for a finite period of time. But as time passes and economic need remains, prolonged stays evolve. Marxist-informed theory maintains that the separation of work life and family life constitutes the separation of labor maintenance costs from the labor reproduction costs (Burawoy 1976; Glenn 1986). According to this framework, Latina transnational mothers work to maintain themselves in the United States and to support their children—and reproduce the next generation of workers—in Mexico or Central America. One precursor to these arrangements is the mid-20th-century Bracero Program, which in effect legislatively mandated Mexican "absentee fathers" who came to work as contracted agricultural laborers in the United States. Other precursors, going back further in history, include the 18th- and 19th-centuries' coercive systems of labor, whereby African American slaves and Chinese sojourner laborers were denied the right to form residentially intact families (Dill 1988, 1994).

Transnational mothering is different from some of these other arrangements in that now women with young children are recruited for U.S. jobs that pay far less than a "family wage." When men come north and leave their families in Mexico—as they did during the Bracero Program and as many continue to do today—they are fulfilling familial obligations defined as breadwinning for the family. When women do so, they are embarking not only on an immigration journey but on a more radical gender-transformative odyssey. They are initiating separations of space and time from their communities of origin, homes, children, and—sometimes—husbands. In doing so, they must cope with stigma, guilt, and criticism from others. A second difference is that these women work primarily not in production of agricultural products or manufacturing but in reproductive labor, in paid domestic work, and/or vending. Performing paid reproductive work for pay—especially caring for other people's children—is not always compatible with taking daily care of one's own family. All of this raises questions about the meanings and variations of motherhood in the late 20th century.

TRANSNATIONAL MOTHERHOOD AND PAID DOMESTIC WORK

Just how widespread are transnational motherhood arrangements in paid domestic work? Of the 153 domestic workers surveyed, 75 percent had children. Contrary to the images of Latina immigrant women as breeders with large families—a dominant image used in the campaign to pass California's Proposition 187—about half (47 percent) of these women have only one or two children. More significant for our purposes is this finding: Forty percent of the women with children have at least one of their children "back home" in their country of origin.

Transnational motherhood arrangements are not exclusive to paid domestic work, but there are particular features about the way domestic work is organized that encourage temporal and spatial separations of a mother-employee and her children. Historically and in the contemporary period, paid domestic workers have had to limit or forfeit primary care of their families and homes to earn income by providing primary care to the families and homes of employers, who are privileged by race and class (Glenn 1986; Rollins 1985; Romero 1992). Paid domestic work is organized in various ways, and there is a clear relationship between the type of job arrangement women have and the likelihood of experiencing transnational family arrangements with their children. To understand the variations, it is necessary to explain how the employment is organized.

Although there are variations within categories, we find it useful to employ a tripartite taxonomy of paid domestic work arrangements. This includes live-in and live-out nanny-housekeeper jobs and weekly house-cleaning jobs.

Weekly house cleaners clean different houses on different days according to what Romero (1992) calls modernized "job work" arrangements. These contractual-like employee-employer relations often resemble those between customer and vendor, and they allow employees a degree of autonomy and scheduling flexibility. Weekly employees are generally paid a flat fee, and they work shorter hours and earn considerably higher hourly rates than do live-in or live-out domestic workers. By contrast, live-in domestic workers work and live in isolation from their own families and communities, sometimes in arrangements with feudal remnants (Glenn 1986). There are often no hourly parameters to their jobs, and as our survey results show, most live-in workers in Los Angeles earn below minimum wage. Live-out domestic workers also usually work as combination nanny-housekeepers, generally working for one household, but contrary to live-ins, they enter daily and return to their own home in the evening. Because of this, live-out workers better resemble industrial wage workers (Glenn 1986).

Live-in jobs are the least compatible with conventional mothering responsibilities. Only about half (16 out of 30) of live-ins surveyed have children, while 83 percent (53 out of 64) of live-outs and 77 percent (45 out of 59) of house cleaners do. As Table 1 shows, 82 percent of live-ins with children have at least one of their children in their country of origin. It is very difficult to work a live-in job when your children are in the United States. Employers who hire live-in workers do so because they generally want employees for jobs that may require round-the-clock service. As one owner of a domestic employment agency put it,

> They (employers) want a live-in to have somebody at their beck and call. They want the hours that are most difficult for them covered, which is like six thirty in the morning 'till eight when the kids go to school, and four to seven when the kids are home, and it's homework, bath, and dinner.

According to our survey, live-ins work an average of 64 hours per week. The best live-in worker, from an employer's perspective, is one without daily family obligations of her own. The workweek may consist of six very long workdays. These may span from dawn to midnight and may include overnight responsibilities with sleepless or sick children, making it virtually impossible for live-in workers to sustain daily contact with their own families. Although some employers do allow for their employees' children to live in as well (Romero 1996), this is rare. When it does occur, it is often fraught with special problems, and we discuss these in a subsequent section of this article. In fact, minimal family and mothering obligations are an informal job placement criterion for live-in workers. Many of the agencies specializing in the placement of live-in nanny-housekeepers will not even refer a woman who has children in Los Angeles to interviews for live-in jobs. As one agency owner explained, "As a policy here, we will not knowingly place a nanny in a live-in job if she has young kids here." A job seeker in an employment agency waiting room acknowledged that she understood this job criterion more broadly, "You can't have a family, you can't have anyone (if you want a live-in job)."

Table 1 Domestic Workers: Wages, Hours Worked and Children's Country of Residence

	Live-ins (n = 30)	Live-outs (n = 64)	House cleaners (n = 59)
Mean hourly wage	$3.79	$5.90	$9.40
Mean hours worked per week	64	35	23
Domestic workers with children	(n = 16)	(n = 53)	(n = 45)
All children in the United States (%)	18	58	76
At least one child "back home"	82	42	24

The subminimum pay and the long hours for live-in workers also make it very difficult for these workers to have their children in the United States. Some live-in workers who have children in the same city as their place of employment hire their own nanny-housekeeper—often a much younger, female relative—to provide daily care for their children, as did Patricia, one of the interview respondents whom we discuss later in this article. Most live-ins, however, cannot afford this alternative; ninety-three percent of the live-ins surveyed earn below minimum wage (then $4.25 per hour). Many live-in workers cannot afford to bring their children to Los Angeles, but once their children are in the same city, most women try to leave live-in work to live with their children.

At the other end of the spectrum are the house cleaners that we surveyed, who earn substantially higher wages than live-ins (averaging $9.46 per hour as opposed to $3.79) and who work fewer hours per week than live-ins (23 as opposed to 64). We suspect that many house cleaners in Los Angeles make even higher earnings and work more hours per week, because we know that the survey undersampled women who drive their own cars to work and who speak English. The survey suggests that house cleaners appear to be the least likely to experience transnational spatial and temporal separations from their children.

Financial resources and job terms enhance house cleaners' abilities to bring their children to the United States. Weekly housecleaning is not a bottom-of-the-barrel job but rather an achievement. Breaking into housecleaning work is difficult because an employee needs to locate and secure several different employers. For this reason, relatively well-established women with more years of experience in the United States, who speak some English, who have a car, and who have job references predominate in weekly housecleaning. Women who are better established in the United States are also more likely to have their children here. The terms of weekly housecleaning employment—particularly the relatively fewer hours worked per week, scheduling flexibility, and relatively higher wages—allow them to live with, and care for, their children. So, it is not surprising that 76 percent of house cleaners who are mothers have their children in the United States.

Compared with live-ins and weekly cleaners, live-out nanny-housekeepers are at an intermediate level with respect to the likelihood of transnational motherhood. Forty-two percent of the live-out nanny-housekeepers who are mothers reported having at least one of their children in their country of origin. Live-out domestic workers, according to the survey, earn $5.90 per hour and work an average workweek of 35 hours. Their lower earnings, more regimented schedules, and longer work-weeks than house cleaners, but higher earnings, shorter hours, and more scheduling flexibility than live-ins explain their intermediate incidence of transnational motherhood.

The Meanings of Transnational Motherhood

How do women transform the meaning of motherhood to fit immigration and employment? Being a transnational mother means more than being the mother to children raised in another country. It means forsaking deeply felt beliefs that biological mothers should raise their own children, and replacing that belief with new definitions of motherhood. The ideal of biological mothers raising their own children is widely held but is also widely broken at both ends of the class spectrum. Wealthy elites have always relied on others—nannies, governesses, and boarding schools—to raise their children (Wrigley 1995), while poor, urban families often rely on kin and "other mothers" (Collins 1991).

In Latin America, in large, peasant families, the eldest daughters are often in charge of the daily care of the younger children, and in situations of extreme poverty, children as young as five or six may be loaned or hired out to well-to-do families as "child-servants," sometimes called *criadas* (Gill 1994).[7] A middle-aged Mexican woman that we interviewed, now a weekly house cleaner, homeowner, and mother of five children, recalled her own experience as a child-servant in Mexico: "I started working in a house when I was 8 . . . they hardly let me eat any food. . . . It was terrible, but I had to work to help my mother with the rent." This recollection of her childhood experiences reminds us how our contemporary notions of motherhood are historically and socially circumscribed, and also correspond to the meanings we assign to childhood (Zelizer 1994).

This example also underlines how the expectation on the child to help financially support her mother required daily spatial and temporal separations of mother and child. There are, in fact, many transgressions of the mother-child symbiosis in practice—large families where older daughters care for younger siblings, child-servants who at an early age leave their mothers, children raised by paid nannies and other caregivers, and mothers who leave young children to seek employment—but these are fluid enough to sustain ideological adherence to the prescription that children should be raised exclusively by biological mothers. Long-term physical and temporal separation disrupts this notion. Transnational mothering radically rearranges mother-child interactions and requires a concomitant radical reshaping of the meanings and definitions of appropriate mothering.

Transnational mothers distinguish their version of motherhood from estrangement, child abandonment, or disowning. A youthful Salvadoran woman at the domestic employment waiting room reported that she had not seen her two eldest boys, now ages 14 and 15 and under the care of her own mother in El Salvador, since they were toddlers. Yet, she made it clear that this was different from putting a child up for adoption, a practice that she viewed negatively, as a form of child abandonment. Although she had been physically separated from her boys for more than a decade, she maintained her mothering ties and financial obligations to them by regularly sending home money. The exchange of letters, photos, and phone calls also helped to sustain the connection. Her physical absence did not signify emotional absence from her children. Another woman who remains intimately involved in the lives of her two daughters, now ages 17 and 21 in El Salvador, succinctly summed up this stance when she said, "I'm here, but I'm there." Over the phone, and through letters, she regularly reminds her daughters to take their vitamins, to never go to bed or to school on an empty stomach, and to use protection from pregnancy and sexually transmitted diseases if they engage in sexual relations with their boyfriends.

Transnational mothers fully understand and explain the conditions that prompt their situations. In particular, many Central American women recognize that the gendered employment demand in Los Angeles has produced transnational motherhood arrangements. These new mothering arrangements, they acknowledge, take shape despite strong beliefs that biological mothers should care for their own children. Emelia, a 49-year-old woman who left her five children in Guatemala nine years ago to join her husband in Los Angeles explained this changing relationship between family arrangements, migration, and job demand:

> One supposes that the mother must care for the children. A mother cannot so easily throw her children aside. So, in all families, the decision is that the man comes (to the U.S.) first. But now, since the man cannot find work here so easily, the woman comes first. Recently, women have been coming and the men staying.

A steady demand for live-in housekeepers means that Central American women may arrive in Los Angeles on a Friday and begin working Monday at a live-in job that provides at least some minimal accommodations. Meanwhile, her male counter-part may spend weeks or months before securing even casual day laborer jobs. While Emelia, formerly a homemaker who previously earned income in Guatemala by baking cakes and pastries in her home, expressed pain and sadness at not being with her children as they grew, she was also proud of her accomplishments. "My children," she stated, "recognize what I have been able to do for them."

Most transnational mothers, like many other immigrant workers, come to the United States with the intention to stay for a finite period of time, until they can pay off bills or raise the money for an investment in a house, their children's education, or a small business. Some of these women return to their countries of origin, but many stay. As time passes, and as their stays grow longer, some of the women eventually bring some or all of their children. Other women who stay at their U.S. jobs are adamant that they do not wish for their children to traverse the multiple hazards of adolescence in U.S. cities or to repeat the job experiences they themselves have had in the United States. One Salvadoran woman in the waiting room at the domestic employment agency—whose children had been raised on earnings predicated on her separation from them—put it this way:

> I've been here 19 years, I've got my legal papers and everything. But I'd have to be crazy to bring my children here. All of them have studied for a career, so why would I bring them here? To bus tables and earn minimum wage? So they won't have enough money for bus fare or food?

Who Is Taking Care of the Nanny's Children?

Transnational Central American and Mexican mothers may rely on various people to care for their children's daily, round-the-clock needs, but they prefer a close relative. The "other mothers" on which Latinas rely include their own mothers, *comadres* (co-godmothers) and other female kin, the children's fathers, and paid caregivers. Reliance on grandmothers and *comadres* for shared mothering is well established in Latina culture, and it is a practice that signifies a more collectivist, shared approach to mothering in contrast to a more individualistic, Anglo-American approach (Griswold del Castillo 1984; Segura and Pierce 1993). Perhaps this cultural legacy facilitates the emergence of transnational motherhood.

Transnational mothers express a strong preference for their own biological mother to serve as the primary caregiver. Here, the violation of the cultural preference for the biological mother is rehabilitated by reliance on the biological grandmother or by reliance on the ceremonially bound *comadres.* Clemencia, for example, left her three young children behind in Mexico, each with their respective *madrina,* or godmother.

Emelia left her five children, then ranging in ages from 6 to 16, under the care of her mother and sister in Guatemala. As she spoke of the hardships faced by transnational mothers, she counted herself among the fortunate ones who did not need to leave the children alone with paid caregivers:

> One's mother is the only one who can really and truly care for your children. No one else can. . . . Women who aren't able to leave their children with their mother or with someone very special, they'll wire money to Guatemala and the people (caregivers) don't feed the children well. They don't buy the children clothes the mother would want. They take the money and the children suffer a lot.

Both Central American and Mexican woman stated preferences for grandmothers as the ideal caregivers in situations that mandated the absence of the children's biological mother. These preferences seem to grow out of strategic availability, but these preferences assume cultural mandates. Velia, a Mexicana who hailed from the border town of Mexicali, improvised an employement strategy whereby she annually sent her three elementary school-age children to her mother in Mexicali for the summer vacation months. This allowed Velia, a single mother, to intensify her housecleaning jobs and save money on day care. But she also insisted that "if my children were with the woman next door (who babysits), I'd worry if they were eating well, or about men (coming to harass the girls). Having them with my mother allows me to work in peace." Another woman specified more narrowly, insisting that only maternal grandmothers could provide adequate caregiving. In a conversation in a park, a Salvadoran woman offered that a biological mother's mother was the one best suited to truly love and care for a child in the biological mother's absence. According to her, not even the paternal grandmother could be trusted to provide proper nurturance and care. Another Salvadoran woman, Maria, left her two daughters, then 14 and 17, at their paternal grandmother's home, but before departing for the United States, she trained her daughters to become self-sufficient in cooking, marketing, and budgeting money. Although she believes the paternal grandmother loves the girls, she did not trust the paternal grandmother enough to cook or administer the money that she would send her daughters.

Another variation in the preference for a biological relative as a caregiver is captured by the arrangement of Patricia, a 30-year-old Mexicana who came to the United States as a child and was working as a live-in, caring for an infant in one of southern California's affluent coastal residential areas. Her arrangement was different, as her daughters were all born, raised, and residing in the United States, but she lived apart from them during weekdays because of her live-in job. Her three daughters, ages 11/2, 6, and 11, stayed at their apartment near downtown Los Angeles under the care of their father and a paid nanny-housekeeper, Patricia's teenage cousin. Her paid caregiver was not an especially close relative, but she rationalized this arrangement by emphasizing that her husband, the girls' father, and therefore a biological relative, was with them during the week.

> Whenever I've worked like this, I've always had a person in charge of them also working as a live-in. She sleeps here the five days, but when my husband arrives he takes responsibility for them . . . When my husband arrives (from work) she (cousin/paid caregiver) goes to English class and he takes charge of the girls.

And another woman who did not have children of her own but who had worked as a nanny for her aunt stated that "as Hispanas, we don't believe bringing someone else in to care for our children." Again, the biological ties help sanction the shared child care arrangement.

New family fissures emerge for the transnational mother as she negotiates various aspects of the arrangement with her children, and with the "other mother" who provides daily care and supervision for the children. Any impulse to romanticize transnational motherhood is tempered by the sadness with which the women related their experiences and by the problems they sometimes encounter with their children and caregivers. A primary worry among transnational mothers is that their children are being neglected or abused in their absence. While there is a long legacy of child-servants being mistreated and physically beaten in Latin America, transnational mothers also worry that their own paid caregivers will harm or neglect their children. They worry that their children may not receive proper nourishment, schooling and educational support, and moral guidance. They may remain unsure as to whether their children are receiving the full financial support they send home. In some cases, their concerns are intensified by the eldest child or a nearby relative who is able to monitor and report the caregiver's transgression to the transnational mother.

Transnational mothers engage in emotion work and financial compensation to maintain a smoothly functioning relationship with the children's daily caregiver. Their efforts are not always successful, and when problems arise, they may return to visit if they can afford to do so. After not seeing her four children for seven years, Carolina abruptly quit her nanny job and returned to Guatemala in the spring of 1996 because she was concerned about one adolescent daughter's rebelliousness and about her mother-in-law's failing health. Carolina's husband remained in Los Angeles, and she was expected to return. Emelia, whose children were cared for by her mother and sister with the assistance of paid caregivers, regularly responded to her sister's reminders to send gifts, clothing, and small amounts of money to the paid caregivers. "If they are taking care of my children," she explained, "then I have to show my gratitude."

Some of these actions are instrumental. Transnational mothers know that they may increase the likelihood of their children receiving adequate care if they appropriately remunerate the caregivers and treat them with the consideration their work requires. In fact, they often express astonishment that their own Anglo employers fail to recognize this in relation to the nanny-housekeeper work that they perform. Some of the expressions of gratitude and gifts that they send to their children's caregivers appear to be genuinely disinterested and enhanced by the transnational mothers' empathy arising out of their own similar job circumstances. A Honduran woman, a former biology teacher, who had left her four sons with a paid caregiver, maintained that the treatment of nannies and housekeepers was much better in Honduras than in the United States, in part, because of different approaches to mothering:

> We're very different back there . . . We treat them (domestic workers) with a lot of affection and respect, and when they are taking care of our kids, even more so. The Americana, she is very egotistical. When the nanny loves her children, she gets jealous. Not us. We are appreciative when someone loves our children, and bathes, dresses, and feeds them as though they were their own.

These comments are clearly informed by the respondent's prior class status, as well as her simultaneous position as the employer of a paid nanny-housekeeper in Honduras and as a temporarily unemployed nanny-housekeeper in the United States. (She had been fired from her nanny-housekeeper job for not showing up on Memorial Day, which she erroneously believed was a work holiday.) Still, her comments underline the importance of showing appreciation and gratitude to the caregiver, in part, for the sake of the children's well-being.

Transnational mothers also worry about whether their children will get into trouble during adolescence or if they will transfer their allegiance and affection to the "other mother." In general, transnational mothers, like African American mothers who leave their children in the South to work up North (Stack and Button 1994), believe that the person who cares for the children has the right to discipline. But when adolescent youths are paired with elderly grandmothers, or ineffective disciplinary figures, the mothers may need to intervene. Preadolescent and adolescent children who show signs of rebelliousness may be brought north because they are deemed unmanageable by their grandmothers or paid caregivers. Alternatively, teens who are in California may be sent back in hope that it will straighten them out, a practice that has resulted in the migration of Los Angeles-based delinquent youth gangs to Mexican and Central American towns. Another danger is that the child who has grown up without the transnational mother's presence may no longer respond to her authority. One woman at the domestic employment agency, who had recently brought her adolescent son to join her in California, reported that she had seen him at a bus stop, headed for the beach. When she demanded to know where he was going, he said something to the effect of "and who are you to tell me what to do?" After a verbal confrontation at the bus kiosk, she handed him $10. Perhaps the mother hoped that money will be a way to show caring and to advance a claim to parental authority.

Motherhood and Breadwinning

Milk, shoes, and schooling—these are the currency of transnational motherhood. Providing for children's sustenance, protecting their current well-being, and preparing them for the future are widely shared concerns of motherhood. Central American and Mexican women involved in transnational mothering attempt to ensure the present and future well-being of their children through U.S. wage earning, and as we have seen, this requires long-term physical separation from their children.

For these women, the meanings of motherhood do not appear to be in a liminal stage. That is, they do not appear to be making a linear progression from a way of motherhood that involves daily, face-to-face caregiving toward one that is defined primarily through breadwinning. Rather than replacing caregiving with breadwinning definitions of motherhood, they appear to be expanding their definitions of motherhood to encompass breadwinning that may require long-term physical separations. For these women, a core belief is that they can best fulfill traditional caregiving responsibilities through income earning in the United States while their children remain "back home."

Transnational mothers continue to state that caregiving is a defining feature of their mothering experiences. They wish to provide their children with better nutrition, clothing, and schooling, and most of them are able to purchase these items with dollars earned in the United States. They recognize, however, that their transnational relationships incur painful costs. Transnational mothers worry about some of the negative effects on their children, but they also experience the absence of domestic family life as a deeply personal loss. Transnational mothers who primarily identified as homemakers before coming to the United States identified the loss of daily contact with family as a sacrifice ventured to financially support the children. As Emelia, who had previously earned some income by baking pastries and doing catering from her home in Guatemala, reflected,

> The money (earned in the U.S.) is worth five times more in Guatemala. My oldest daughter was then 16, and my youngest was 6 (when I left). Ay, it's terrible, terrible, but that's what happens to most women (transnational mothers) who are here. You sacrifice your family life (for labor migration).

Similarly, Carolina used the word *sacrifice* when discussing her family arrangement, claiming that her children "tell me that they appreciate us (parents), and the sacrifice that their papa and mama make for them. That is what they say."

The daily indignities of paid domestic work—low pay, subtle humiliations, not enough food to eat, invisibility (Glenn 1986; Rollins 1985; Romero 1992)—

means that transnational mothers are not only stretching their U.S.-earned dollars further by sending the money back home but also by leaving the children behind, they are providing special protection from the discrimination the children might receive in the United States. Gladys, who had four of her five children in El Salvador, acknowledged that her U.S. dollars went further in El Salvador. Although she missed seeing those four children grow up, she felt that in some ways, she had spared them the indignities to which she had exposed her youngest daughter, whom she brought to the United States at age 4 in 1988. Although her live-in employer had allowed the four-year-old to join the family residence, Gladys tearfully recalled how that employer had initially quarantined her daughter, insisting on seeing vaccination papers before allowing the girl to play with the employer's children. "I had to battle, really struggle," she recalled, "just to get enough food for her (to eat)." For Gladys, being together with her youngest daughter in the employer's home had entailed new emotional costs.

Patricia, the mother who was apart from her children only during the weekdays when she lived in with her employer, put forth an elastic definition of motherhood, one that included both meeting financial obligations and spending time with the children. Although her job involves different scheduling than most employed mothers, she shares views similar to those held by many working mothers:

> It's something you have to do, because you can't just stay seated at home because the bills accumulate and you have to find a way . . . I applied at many different places for work, like hospitals, as a receptionist—due to the experience I've had with computers working in shipping and receiving, things like that, but they never called me . . . One person can't pay all the bills.

Patricia emphasized that she believes motherhood also involves making an effort to spend time with the children. According to this criterion, she explained, most employers were deficient, while she was compliant. During the middle of the week, she explained, "I invent something, some excuse for her (the employer) to let me come home, even if I have to bring the (employer's) baby here with me . . . just to spend time with my kids."

Transnational mothers echoed these sentiments. Maria Elena, for example, whose 13-year-old son resided with his father in Mexico after she lost a custody battle, insisted that motherhood did not consist of only breadwinning: "You can't give love through money." According to Maria Elena, motherhood required an emotional presence and communication with a child. Like other transnational mothers, she explained how she maintained this connection despite the long-term geographic distance: "I came here, but we're not apart. We talk (by telephone) . . . I know (through telephone conversations) when my son is fine. I can tell when he is sad by the way he speaks." Like employed mothers everywhere, she insisted on a definition of motherhood that emphasized quality rather than quantity of time spent with the child: "I don't think that a good mother is one who is with her children at all times . . . It's the quality of time spent with the child." She spoke these words tearfully, reflecting the trauma of losing a custody battle with her ex-husband. Gladys also stated that being a mother involves both breadwinning and providing direction and guidance. "It's not just feeding them, or buying clothes for them. It's also educating them, preparing them to make good choices so they'll have a better future."

Transnational mothers seek to mesh caregiving and guidance with breadwinning. While breadwinning may require their long-term and long-distance separations from their children, they attempt to sustain family connections by showing emotional ties through letters, phone calls, and money sent home. If at all financially and logistically possible, they try to travel home to visit their children. They maintain their mothering responsibilities not only by earning money for their children's livelihood but also by communicating and advising across national borders, and across the boundaries that separate their children's place of residence from their own places of employment and residence.

Bonding with the Employers' Kids and Critiques of "Americana" Mothers

Some nanny-housekeepers develop very strong ties of affection with the children they care for during long workweeks. It is not unusual for nanny-housekeepers to be alone with these children during the workweek, with no one else with whom to talk or interact. The nannies, however, develop close emotional ties selectively, with some children, but not with others. For nanny-housekeepers who are transnational mothers, the loving daily caregiving that they cannot express for their own children is sometimes transferred to their employers' children. Carolina, a Guatemalan woman with four children between the ages of 10 and 14 back home, maintained that she tried to treat the employers' children with the same affection that she had for her own children "because if you do not feel affection for children, you are not able to care for them well." When interviewed, however, she was caring for two-year-old triplets—for whom she expressed very little affection—but she recalled very longingly her fond feelings for a child at her last job, a child who vividly reminded her of her daughter, who was about the same age:

> When I saw that the young girl was lacking in affection, I began to get close to her and I saw that she appreciated that I would touch her, give her a kiss on the cheek . . . And then I felt consoled too, because I had someone to give love to. But, I would imagine that she was my daughter, ah? And then I would give pure love to her, and that brought her closer to me.

Another nanny-housekeeper recalled a little girl for whom she had developed strong bonds of affection, laughingly imitating how the preschooler, who could not pronounce the "f" sound, would say "you hurt my peelings, but I don't want to pight."

Other nanny-housekeepers reflected that painful experiences with abrupt job terminations had taught them not to transfer mother love to the children of their employers. Some of these women reported that they now remained very measured and guarded in their emotional closeness with the employers' children, so that they could protect themselves for the moment when that relationship might be abruptly severed.

> I love these children, but now I stop myself from becoming too close. Before, when my own children weren't here (in the United States), I gave all my love to the children I cared for (then toddler twins). That was my recompensation (for not being with my children). When the job ended, I hurt so much. I can't let that happen again.

> I love them, but not like they were my own children because they are not! They are not my kids! Because if I get to love them, and then I go, then I'm going to suffer like I did the last time. I don't want that.

Not all nanny-housekeepers bond tightly with the employers' children, but most of them are critical of what they perceive as the employers' neglectful parenting and mothering. Typically, they blame biological mothers (their employers) for substandard parenting. Carolina recalled advising the mother of the abovementioned little girl, who reminded her of her own child, that the girl needed to receive more affection from her mother, whom she perceived as self-absorbed with physical fitness regimes. Carolina had also advised other employers on disciplining their children. Patricia also spoke adamantly on this topic, and she recalled with satisfaction that when she had advised her current employer to spend more than 15 minutes a day with the baby, the employer had been reduced to tears. By comparison to her employer's mothering, Patricia cited her own perseverance in going out of her way to visit her children during the week:

> If you really love your kids, you look for the time, you make time to spend with your kids . . . I work all week and for some reason I make excuses for her (employer) to let me come (home) . . . just to spend time with my kids.

Her rhetoric of comparative mothering is also inspired by the critique that many nanny-housekeepers have of female employers who may be out of the labor force but who employ nannies and hence do not spend time with their children.

> I love my kids, they don't. It's just like, excuse the word, shitting kids . . . What they prefer is to go to the salon, get their nails done, you know, go shopping, things like that. Even if they're home all day, they don't want to spend time with the kids because they're paying somebody to do that for them.

Curiously, she spoke as though her female employer is a wealthy woman of leisure, but in fact, both her current and past female employers are wealthy business executives who work long hours. Perhaps at this distance on the class spectrum, all class and racially privileged mothers look alike. "I work my butt off to get what I have," she observed, "and they don't have to work that much."

In some ways, transnational mothers who work as nanny-housekeepers cling to a more sentimentalized view of the employers' children than of their own. This strategy allows them to critique their employers, especially homemakers of privilege who are occupied with neither employment nor daily caregiving for their children. The Latina nannies appear to endorse motherhood as a full-time vocation in contexts of sufficient financial resources, but in contexts of financial hardship such as their own, they advocate more elastic definitions of motherhood, including forms that may include long spatial and temporal separations of mother and children.

As observers of late-20th-century U.S. families (Skolnick 1991; Stacey 1996) have noted, we live in an era wherein no one normative family arrangement predominates. Just as no one type of mothering unequivocally prevails in the White middle class, no singular mothering arrangement prevails among Latina immigrant women. In fact, the exigencies of contemporary immigration seem to multiply the variety of mothering arrangements. Through our research with Latina immigrant women who work as nannies, housekeepers, and house cleaners, we have encountered a broad range of mothering arrangements. Some Latinas migrate to the United States without their children to establish employment, and after some stability has been achieved, they may send for their children or they may work for a while to save money, and then return to their countries of origin. Other Latinas migrate and may postpone having children until they are financially established. Still others arrive with their children and may search for employment that allows them to live together with their children, and other Latinas may have sufficient financial support—from their husbands or kin—to stay home full-time with their children.

In the absence of a universal or at least widely shared mothering arrangement, there is tremendous uncertainty about what constitutes "good mothering," and transnational mothers must work hard to defend their choices. Some Latina nannies who have their children with them in the United States condemn transnational mothers as "bad women." One interview respondent, who was able to take her young daughter to work with her, claimed that she could never leave her daughter. For this woman, transnational mothers were not only bad mothers but also nannies who could not be trusted to adequately care for other people's children. As she said of an acquaintance, "This woman left her children (in Honduras) . . . she was taking care (of other people's children), and I said, 'Lord, who are they (the employers) leaving their children with if she did that with her own children!' "

Given the uncertainty of what is "good mothering," and to defend their integrity as mothers when others may criticize them, transnational mothers construct new scales for gauging the quality of mothering. By favorably comparing themselves with the negative models of mothering that they see in others—especially those that they are able to closely scrutinize in their employers' homes—transnational mothers create new definitions of good-mothering standards. At the same time, selectively developing motherlike ties with other people's children allows them to enjoy affectionate, face-to-face interactions that they cannot experience on a daily basis with their own children.

DISCUSSION: TRANSNATIONAL MOTHERHOOD

In California, with few exceptions, paid domestic work has become a Latina immigrant women's job. One observer has referred to these Latinas as "the new employable mothers" (Chang 1994), but taking on these wage labor duties often requires Latina workers to expand the frontiers of motherhood by leaving their own children for several years. While today there is a greater openness to accepting a plurality of mothering arrangements—single mothers, employed mothers, stay-at-home mothers, lesbian mothers, surrogate mothers, to name a few—even feminist discussions generally assume that mothers, by definition, will reside with their children.

Transnational mothering situations disrupt the notion of family in one place and break distinctively with what some commentators have referred to as the "epoxy glue" view of motherhood (Blum and Deussen 1996; Scheper-Hughes 1992). Latina transnational mothers are improvising new mothering arrangements that are borne out of women's financial struggles, played out in a new global arena, to provide the best future for themselves and their children. Like many other women of color and employed mothers, transnational mothers rely on an expanded and sometimes fluid number of family members and paid caregivers. Their caring circuits, however, span stretches of geography and time that are much wider than typical joint custody or "other mother" arrangements that are more closely bound, both spatially and temporally.

. . . Although not addressed directly in this article, the experiences of these mothers resonate with current major political issues. For example, transnational mothering resembles precisely what immigration restrictionists have advocated through California's Proposition 187 (Hondagneu-Sotelo 1995).[8] While proponents of Proposition 187 have never questioned California's reliance on low-waged Latino immigrant workers, this restrictionist policy calls for fully dehumanized immigrant workers, not workers with families and family needs (such as education and health services for children). In this respect, transnational mothering's externalization of the cost of labor reproduction to Mexico and Central America is a dream come true for the proponents of Proposition 187.

Contemporary transnational motherhood continues a long historical legacy of people of color being incorporated into the United States through coercive systems of labor that do not recognize family rights. As Bonnie Thornton Dill (1988), Evelyn Nakano Glenn (1986), and others have pointed out, slavery and contract labor systems were organized to maximize economic productivity and offered few supports to sustain family life. The job characteristics of paid domestic work, especially live-in work, virtually impose transnational motherhood for many Mexican and Central American women who have children of their own.

The ties of transnational motherhood suggest simultaneously the relative permeability of borders, as witnessed by the maintenance of family ties and the new meanings of motherhood, and the impermeability of nation-state borders. Ironically, just at the moment when free trade proponents and pundits celebrate globalization and transnationalism, and when "borderlands" and "border crossings" have become the metaphors of preference for describing a mind-boggling range of conditions, nation-state borders prove to be very real obstacles for many Mexican and Central American women who work in the United States and who, given the appropriate circumstances, wish to be with their children. While demanding the right for women workers to live with their children may provoke critiques of sentimentality, essentialism, and the glorification of motherhood, demanding the right for women workers to choose their own motherhood arrangements would be the beginning of truly just family and work policies, policies that address not only inequalities of gender but also in-equalities of race, class, and citizenship status.

NOTES

1. No one knows the precise figures on the prevalence of transnational motherhood just as no one knows the myriad consequences for both mothers and their children. However, one indicator that hints at both the complex outcomes and the frequencies of these arrangements is that teachers and social workers in Los Angeles are becoming increasingly concerned about some of the deleterious effects of these mother-child separations and reunions. Many Central American women who made their way to Los Angeles in the early 1980s, fleeing civil wars and economic upheaval, pioneered transnational mothering, and some of them are now financially able to bring the children whom they left behind. These children, now in their early teen years, are confronting the triple trauma of simultaneously entering adolescence—with its own psychological upheavals; a new society—often in an inner-city environment that requires learning to navigate a new language, place and culture; and they are also entering families that do not look like the ones they knew before their mothers' departure, families with new siblings born in the United States, and new step-fathers or mothers' boyfriends.

2. Acknowledgment of the varieties of family and mothering has been fueled, in part, by research on the growing numbers of women-headed families, involving families of all races and socioeconomic levels—including Latina families in the United States and elsewhere (Baca Zinn 1989; Fernández Kelly and Garcia 1990), and

by recognition that biological ties do not necessarily constitute family (Weston 1991).

3. *La Virgen de Guadalupe,* the indigenous virgin who appeared in 1531 to a young Indian boy and for whom a major basilica is built, provides the exemplary maternal model, *la mujer abnegada* (the self-effacing woman), who sacrifices all for her children and religious faith. *La Malinche,* the Aztec woman that served Cortes as a translator, a diplomat, and a mistress, and *La Llorona* (the weeping one), a legendary solitary, ghostlike figure reputed either to have been violently murdered by a jealous husband or to have herself murdered her children by drowning them, are the negative and despised models of femininity. Both are failed women because they have failed at motherhood. *La Malinche* is stigmatized as a traitor and a whore who collaborated with the Spanish conquerors, and *La Llorona* is the archetypal evil woman condemned to eternally suffer and weep for violating her role as a wife and a mother (Soto 1986).

4. A study comparing Mexicanas and Chicanas found that the latter are more favorably disposed to home-maker ideals than are Mexican-born women. This difference is explained by Chicanas' greater exposure to U.S. ideology that promotes the opposition of mothering and employment and to Mexicanas' integration of household and economy in Mexico (Segura 1994). While this dynamic may be partially responsible for this pattern, we suspect that Mexicanas may have higher rates of labor force participation because they are also a self-selected group of Latinas; by and large, they come to the United States to work.

5. See Romero (1997) for a study focusing on the perspective of domestic workers' children. Although most respondents in this particular study were children of day workers, and none appear to have been children of transnational mothers, they still recall significant costs stemming from their mothers' occupation.

6. This seems to be more common among Central American women than Mexican women. Central American women may be more likely than are Mexican women to have their children in their country of origin, even if their husbands are living with them in the United States because of the multiple dangers and costs associated with undocumented travel from Central America to the United States. The civil wars of the 1980s, continuing violence and economic uncertainty, greater difficulties and costs associated with crossing multiple national borders, and stronger cultural legacies of socially sanctioned consensual unions may also contribute to this pattern for Central Americans.

7. According to interviews conducted with domestic workers in La Paz, Bolivia, in the late 1980s, 41 percent got their first job between the age of 11 and 15, and one-third got their first job between the ages of 6 and 8. Some parents received half of the child-servant's salary (Gill 1994, 64). Similar arrangements prevailed in preindustrial, rural areas of the United States and Europe.

8. In November 1994, California voters passed Proposition 187, which legislates the denial of public school education, health care, and other public benefits to undocumented immigrants and their children. Although currently held up in the courts, the facility with which Proposition 187 passed in the California ballots rejuvenated anti-immigrant politics at a national level. It opened the door to new legislative measures in 1997 to deny public assistance to legal immigrants.

REFERENCES

Blum, Linda, and Theresa Deussen. 1996. Negotiating independent motherhood: Working-class African American women talk about marriage and motherhood. *Gender & Society* 10:199–211.

Burawoy, Michael. 1976. The functions and reproduction of migrant labor: Comparative material from Southern Africa and the United States. *American Journal of Sociology* 81:1050–87.

Chang, Grace. 1994. Undocumented Latinas: Welfare burdens or beasts of burden? *Socialist Review* 23:151–85.

Chinchilla, Norma Stoltz, and Nora Hamilton. 1996. Negotiating urban space: Latina workers in domestic work and street vending in Los Angeles. *Humbolt Journal of Social Relations* 22:25–35.

Collier, Jane Fishburne, and Sylvia Junko Yanagisako. 1987. *Gender and kinship: Essays toward a unified analysis.* Stanford, CA: Stanford University Press.

Collins, Patricia Hill. 1991. *Black feminist thought. Knowledge, consciousness, and the politics of empowerment.* New York: Routledge.

———. 1994. Shifting the center: Race, class, and feminist theorizing about motherhood. In *Mothering: Ideology, experience, and agency,* edited by Evelyn Nakano Glenn, Grace Chang, and Linda Rennie Forcey. New York: Routledge.

Dill, Bonnie Thornton. 1988. Our mothers' grief. Racial-ethnic women and the maintenance of families. *Journal of Family History* 13:415–31.

———. 1994. Fictive kin, paper sons and compadrazgo: Women of color and the struggle for family survival. In *Women of color in U.S. society,* edited by Maxine Baca Zinn and Bonnie Thornton Dill. Philadelphia: Temple University Press.

Fernández Kelly, M. Patricia, and Anna Garcia. 1990. Power surrendered, power restored: The politics of work and family among Hispanic garment workers in California and Florida. In *Women, politics & change,* edited by Louise A. Tilly and Patricia Gurin. New York: Russell Sage.

Gill, Lesley. 1994. *Precarious dependencies: Gender-class and domestic service in Bolivia.* New York: Columbia University Press.

Glenn, Evelyn Nakano. 1986. *Issei, Nisei, warbride: Three generations of Japanese American women in domestic service.* Philadelphia: Temple University Press.

———. 1994. Social constructions of mothering: A thematic overview. In *Mothering: Ideology, experience, and agency,* edited by Evelyn Nakano Glenn, Grace Chang, and Linda Rennie Forcey. New York: Routledge.

Griswold del Castillo, Richard. 1984. *La Familia: Chicano families in the urban Southwest, 1848 to the present.* Notre Dame, IN: University of Notre Dame Press.

Hondagneu-Sotelo, Pierrette. 1995. Women and children first: New directions in anti-immigrant politics. *Socialist Review* 25:169–90.

Rollins, Judith. 1985. *Between women: Domestics and their employers.* Philadelphia: Temple University Press.

Romero, Mary. 1992. *Maid in the U.S.A.* New York: Routledge.

———. 1996. Life as the maid's daughter: An exploration of the everyday boundaries of race, class and gender. In *Feminisms in the academy: Rethinking the disciplines,* edited by Abigail J. Steward and Donna Stanon. Ann Arbor: University of Michigan Press.

———. 1997. Who takes care of the maid's children? Exploring the costs of domestic service. In *Feminism and families,* edited by Hilde L. Nelson. New York: Routledge.

Ruddick, Sara. 1989. *Maternal thinking: Toward a politics of peace.* Boston: Beacon.

Scheper-Hughes, Nancy. 1992. *Death without weeping: The violence of everyday life in Brazil.* Berkeley: University of California Press.

Segura, Denise A. 1994. Working at motherhood: Chicana and Mexican immigrant mothers and employment. In *Mothering: Ideology, experience, and agency,* edited by Evelyn Nakano Glenn, Grace Chang, and Linda Rennie Forcey. New York: Routledge.

Segura, Denise A., and Jennifer L. Pierce. 1993. Chicana/o family structure and gender personality: Chodorow, familism, and psychoanalytic sociology revisited. *Signs: Journal of Women in Culture and Society* 19:62–79.

Skolnick, Arlene S. 1991. *Embattled paradise: The American family in an age of uncertainty.* New York: Basic Books.

Soto, Shirlene. 1986. Tres modelos culturales: La Virgin de Guadalupe, la Malinche, y la Llorona. *Fem* (Mexico City), no. 48:13–16.

Stacey, Judith. 1996. *In the name of the family: Retaining family values in the postmodern age.* Boston: Beacon.

Stack, Carol B., and Linda M. Burton. 1994. Kinscripts: Reflections on family, generation, and culture. In *Mothering: Ideology, experience, and agency,* edited by Evelyn Nakano Glenn, Grace Chang, and Linda Rennie Forcey. New York: Routledge.

Thorne, Barrie, and Marilyn Yalom. 1992. *Rethinking the family: Some feminist questions.* Boston: Northeastern University Press.

Uttal, Lynet. 1996. Custodial care, surrogate care, and coordinated care: Employed mothers and the meaning of child care. *Gender & Society* 10:291–311.

Weston, Kath. 1991. *Families we choose: Lesbians, gays, kinship.* New York: Columbia University Press.

Wrigley. 1995. *Other people's children.* New York: Basic Books.

Zavella, Patricia. 1987. *Women's work and Chicano families: Cannery workers of the Santa Clara Valley.* Ithaca, NY: Cornell University Press.

Zelizer, Viviana. 1994. *Pricing the priceless child: The social value of children.* Princeton, NJ: Princeton University Press.

Zinn, Maxine Baca. 1989. Family, race and poverty in the eighties. *Signs: Journal of Women in Culture and Society* 14:856–69.

32

"The Worms Are Weak"

Male Infertility and Patriarchal Paradoxes in Egypt

MARCIA C. INHORN

Worldwide, between 8 and 12 percent of couples suffer from infertility or the inability to conceive a child at some point during their reproductive lives (Reproductive Health Outlook 1999). However, in some non-Western societies, especially those in the "infertility belt" of Central and Southern Africa, rates of infection-induced infertility may be quite high, affecting as many as one-third of all couples attempting to conceive (Collet et al. 1988; Larsen 1994; Ericksen and Brunette 1996). Unfortunately, the new reproductive technologies that may provide solutions to infertility for many Western couples are often unavailable in these settings, and modern health care services may themselves be of abysmally poor quality (Inhorn 1994a; Sundby 2001). Thus, it is not surprising that the infertile often turn to traditional remedies and healers (Inhorn 1994b), a pattern found even in the West (Van Balen, Verdurmen, and Ketting 1995).

A growing ethnographic literature also demonstrates that women world-wide bear the major burden of infertility (Abbey, Andrews, and Halman 1991; Greil, Leitko, and Porter 1988; Inhorn 1994b; Inhorn and Van Balen 2001; Stanton et al. 1991; Van Balen and Trimbos-Kemper 1993). This burden may include blame for the reproductive failing; emotional distress in the forms of anxiety, depression, frustration, grief, and fear (Greil 1997); marital duress leading to abandonment, divorce, or polygamy; stigmatization and community ostracism; and, in many cases, bodily taxing, even life-threatening forms of medical intervention. . . .

MALE INFERTILITY IN GLOBAL PERSPECTIVE

Infertility, like most reproductive issues, seems to be a "woman's problem" and is thus conceptualized in indigenous systems of meaning and in global health policy discussions. However, the reality of infertility challenges this assertion because the biological etiology of infertility does not reside solely or even largely in the female reproductive tract. The most comprehensive epidemiological study of infertility to date—a World Health Organization–sponsored study of 5,800 infertile couples at thirty-three medical centers in twenty-two countries—found that men are the sole cause or a contributing factor to infertility in more than half of all

Marcia C. Inhorn, "'The Worms are Weak': Male Infertility and Patriarchal Paradoxes in Egypt," from *Men and Masculinities,* Volume 5/2003, p. 236–256.

couples around the globe (Cates, Farley, and Rowe 1985; Reproductive Health Outlook 1999). . . .

Given the various factors and the recalcitrance of male infertility to treatment, it is fair to say that men contribute significantly to global patterns of infertility.[1] It is surprising, then, that worldwide, men do not bear more of the social burden for infertility. The reasons appear obvious—women's bodies bear the "proof" of infertility through their failure to achieve pregnancy and childbirth, whereas men's bodies hide the evidence of reproductive defect. But a nuanced cultural analysis is required to account for this inequity, one that pays attention to patriarchy as a system of gender oppression (i.e., male domination/female subordination) and that implicates patriarchy in the gendered asymmetry that accompanies infertility worldwide. Although arguments for universal patriarchal oppression of women are difficult to sustain and have been rejected as ethnocentric in critiques of radical feminism (Elshtain 1981; Jaggar 1983; Tong 1989), it is clear that women's suffering over infertility is linked to patriarchal formations. Nonetheless, such patriarchal systems are often culturally diverse and locally informed; therefore, their expression is variable.

The case of male infertility in Egypt—where sperm are popularly referred to as "worms" and male infertility is glossed as "the worms are weak"—cannot be understood without reference to patriarchy in its local form. In Egypt, approximately 12 percent of all married couples experience difficulties conceiving (Egyptian Fertility Care Society 1995), but women are stigmatized for infertility—even in situations of confirmed male infertility—because of entrenched patriarchal gender ideologies and relations (Inhorn 1994a, 1996). Male infertility provides an excellent example of the ongoing nature of patriarchy in Egyptian social life and a lens through which patriarchal gender and conjugal relations may be viewed. Following a discussion of methodology, I describe two cases of infertility among men of different social classes, focusing on how the husbands' infertility affected their wives. Using this material and more general findings from two research projects on Egyptian infertility, I then analyze a series of patriarchal paradoxes whereby infertile husbands enjoy various forms of privilege in their marriages, social relations, and treatment experiences, often to the disadvantage of the wives who love and support them.

METHOD

This article's findings and arguments are based on two periods of field research in Egypt in which my focus of investigation was the problem of infertility. The first period lasted from October 1988 to December 1989 and involved mostly poor people living in and around Alexandria, Egypt's second largest city of more than 5 million inhabitants. Of the 190 women who formally participated in my study, 100 presented to the University of Alexandria's public obstetrics/gynecology teaching hospital for the treatment of infertility. There, I conducted in-depth, semistructured interviews in the Egyptian dialect, eventually making my way into women's homes and communities, where I was then introduced to their husbands.[2] Of the husbands in this study, 40 percent had a diagnosed infertility factor, and an additional 10 percent suffered from sexual dysfunction that had led, in most cases, to procreative difficulties.

Returning to Egypt in 1996, I spent three months conducting participant observation and in-depth semistructured interviewing in two private hospital-based in vitro fertilization (IVF) clinics located in elite suburbs of Cairo (Heliopolis and Maadi). In this study, involving sixty-six cases of infertility, most of my informants were educated, middle- to upper-class elites, who often presented to these IVF clinics as couples. Unlike my initial field-work, where women served as primary informants, the recent fieldwork involved male and female informants in nearly 40 percent of cases. Of the male partners among these sixty-six couples, 70 percent suffered from a diagnosed factor, including some severe cases (e.g., azoospermia).

This high percentage of male infertility cases in both studies reflects two sets of factors, one epidemiological and one clinical. With regard to epidemiological risk factors, Egyptian men are exposed to work and lifestyle factors linked to increased rates of infertility. Manual and lower-class agricultural laborers are often exposed to high heat, pesticides, and chemicals in their workplaces, all of which have been implicated in male infertility in Egypt (Inhorn and Buss 1994) and in other countries as well (Daniels 1997; Thonneau et al. 1998). Rural-born Egyptian men may also suffer the chronic effects of schistosomiasis, an endemic parasitic infection that affects reproductive function (Inhorn and Buss 1994; Yeboah, Wadhwani, and Wilson 1992). Finally, Egyptian men are heavy users of stimulants such as tea, Turkish coffee, high-nicotine cigarettes, and tobacco-filled waterpipes (Inhorn and Buss 1994), all of which have been implicated in a reduced likelihood of conception (Curtis, Savitz, and Arbuckle 1997). These high numbers reflect the changing clinical nature of male infertility treatment in Egypt. With the introduction of new reproductive technologies over the past decade, some male infertility cases are now treatable in urban IVF clinics in Alexandria and Cairo. Because my work was based in hospitals with IVF programs, the number of male infertility cases is probably overrepresented in my studies. . . .

TWO CASES OF MALE INFERTILITY

Madiha and Ahmed

Madiha[3] is a diminutive, attractive, and brave twenty-three-year-old, married to her infertile, twenty-eight-year-old husband, Ahmed, for five years. Both are uneducated and poor, as his carpenter's salary brings them only LE 40 a month.[4] Although Madiha worked in a textile factory before marriage and is willing to work again to improve their economic situation, Ahmed refuses this option, citing the problems of crowded transportation (with men who are "strangers") and Madiha's potential neglect of the housework.[5] Madiha has been seeking treatment for infertility since the third month of her marriage, when her mother- and sister-in-law insisted on taking her to a physician. Since then, she has endured countless "treatments," both ethnomedical and biomedical. Her mother-in-law has brought her vaginal suppositories of black glycerin to "bring out" any infection she might have in her vagina. Traditional healers and neighbors have performed painful "cupping" on her back to draw "humidity" out of her womb. Spiritist healers have said prayers over her and asked her to perform various rituals of circumambulation at religious sites. During one Friday noon prayer, she was asked by a female spiritist healer to urinate on top of an eggplant to "unbind" an infertility-producing condition known as *kabsa* or *mushahara.*[6]

Simultaneously, Madiha has pursued biomedical treatment at the urging of Ahmed and his relatives, with whom she has lived for most of her marriage. Two of the doctors she has visited have performed a procedure called tubal insufflation, in which carbon dioxide is pumped into the uterus without any anesthesia. One of the doctors told her that her cervix and uterus might be small and that "the smallest uterus can't get pregnant"; the procedure might "widen" or "dilate" her. The other physician offered no reason for performing the procedure. In fact, although tubal insufflation is widely practiced as a money-making procedure by Egyptian gynecologists with no specialized training in infertility, this technique, once used to diagnose tubal obstruction, has no therapeutic value and may actually produce infertility by forcing pathogenic bacteria from the lower into the upper genital tract (Inhorn 1994a; Inhorn and Buss 1993).

Madiha also underwent an operation under general anesthesia to correct a "folded" uterus. As she explained, "I didn't want this operation, but my in-laws pushed me and gave me the money." When the operation failed, the doctor asked Ahmed to go to a particular doctor for an "analysis." Ahmed complied and was asked to repeat the analysis twice and to take treatment.

According to Madiha, it was only then that "I knew I'm alright and something is wrong with my husband." Yet Ahmed refuses to believe he is the cause of the infertility and thus rejects treatment. His family, furthermore, refuses to believe that the first son in the family to marry is responsible for the infertility. As Madiha put it,

> Even my husband, when I tell him it's his problem, he doesn't answer me. When he went to the doctor for the first time, the doctor told him that he had pus and weakness in his *didan* [literally, "worms," i.e., sperm]. But he never goes for treatment, even though he knows I want him to. Every time I tell his family that it's "from him," they don't answer me. Instead, every time I tell them that I'm going to the doctor, they encourage me to, as if it's my problem. My family won't get involved. They know I'm not the reason

> and it's something wrong with Ahmed. They're "relaxed" because they know it's his problem.

Concerned about her ongoing childlessness, one of Madiha's paternal uncles, who had read about the University of Alexandria's new infertility program at Shatby Hospital, convinced her to go. At Shatby, Madiha underwent more tests, including laparoscopy, a surgical procedure to assess the condition of her fallopian tubes. There, the doctors told her that there was absolutely nothing wrong with her reproductive tract. Instead, another analysis showed Ahmed's sperm to be of "poor quality" in terms of count and motility. The physicians encouraged Madiha to undergo artificial insemination using her husband's sperm (so-called AIH, because "AID" using donor sperm is religiously prohibited). The first attempt failed, but at the time of my interview, she was mustering additional resources—and nerve—to try again.

She reported feeling sad and lonely not only because she has no children to care for but because she lacks support in her "search for children," either from her husband, his relatives, or her family—who do not want to make trouble as long as there is no threat of divorce. "One day," she said, "I got fed up. So I told him, 'If you want to get married again, just go! I don't want any more treatments.'" Although Ahmed does not admit to being infertile, she thinks some part of him must believe this, as he did not accept her offer of divorce and continues to be nice to her. Thus, even though Ahmed is a poor man, an unsatisfactory lover, and a traditional male who will not let Madiha work to fill her lonely days, Madiha believes that Ahmed loves her—more than she loves him—and that he will not divorce her, even if ongoing childlessness is "God's will." Madiha is literally *miskina*—"a poor miserable thing"—whose chances of becoming a mother remain slim because of the intractable infertility and truculent attitude of her husband.

Shahira, Mohammed, and Their Intracytoplasmic Sperm Injection (ICSI) Twins

Shahira is the twenty-five-year-old wife of Mohammed, a forty-three-year-old lawyer whose father was once a powerful politician. In addition to his legal practice, Mohammed rents a villa to a foreign embassy and owns a business center run by Shahira. She is Mohammed's second wife, married to him now for ten months. Before this, Mohammed was married for seventeen years to Hala, a woman now in her forties, whom he divorced two years ago because of their childlessness.

Early in his first marriage, physicians told Mohammed that he suffered from severe male-factor infertility, involving low sperm count and poor motility. He underwent repeated courses of hormonal therapy, none of which improved his sperm profile. Ultimately, he and Hala underwent several cycles of artificial insemination using concentrates of his sperm as well as five cycles of IVF, three times in Germany and twice in Egypt. Each trial was unsuccessful.

It was obvious to the Egyptian physicians who undertook one of the trials that Mohammed and Hala's marriage was deteriorating during the course of therapy—a deterioration they implied had something to do with Hala's "strong personality." Shahira seemed to agree:

> In Egypt, if a man knows he doesn't get his wife pregnant, he's always upset. And if you're pushing him all the time, and he's the reason for the problem, he feels like giving up [on the marriage], because there are no children to keep in the house. In my husband's case, he preferred to divorce her because their relationship became bad. They had different attitudes and behaviors, and the major reason for the divorce was that he knows he's the reason for no pregnancy. He's kind, and she's nervous and always asking too many questions.

Although Hala has not remarried, Mohammed remarried in little over a year. He chose Shahira, a Christian, after knowing her for five months. Mohammed was less interested in Shahira's "pedigree" (a college degree in tourism, with fluency in French and English) and in her religion (a Muslim man is allowed to marry a Christian woman) than in her youth, potential fecundity, acceptance of his infertility problem, and her willingness to try additional treatments with him. He told her, "I want to marry you, but you are a young lady, and I'm sure you want a baby." Shahira needed a "father figure" and felt that Mohammed could be "both a husband and a father." (Her father works in the United Arab Emirates, and she has not seen him for eight years. Her mother died when Shahira was ten, and she has "lived alone" with her younger brother and sister and two servants since their father emigrated in the early 1990s.) As Shahira stated,

> I need someone older, like a father, caring for me. And I'm sure he needs me, because he will think about pregnancy all the time, and he was bad, psychologically bad. And he needs someone to care for him as a wife. If I married a young man, he will ask first about himself. He wants to live with his wife alone. But my husband sees my case [i.e., she is like the "mother" to her younger siblings], and he accepts my case. But I accept his [infertility]. He's feeling for me—I can't separate from them [her siblings]—and he loves this in me. Because he says, "If you care for your sister and brother, you will care for me."
>
> I took my decision in two months, without love before marriage, but with my mind. But love has grown—100 percent. An important thing in marriage is understanding, feeling secure. That's more important than love. He's kind, and when I'm sick, he'll sit beside me and ask how I'm feeling. When I married him, I accepted 100 percent that I will not have children, and I wouldn't push him. But since I knew his case before marriage, I told him I'd be willing to try [IVF] more than once because he's kind. I was afraid, but I'll try.

A few months into their marriage, Shahira went to a gynecologist in Maadi, an elite suburb. The physician told her, "You are young and you haven't anything wrong, but the lab report of your husband is bad." She asked the physician about IVF, and he said, "No way, because your husband is a very bad case." Mohammed, meanwhile, underwent five months of drug therapy. His andrologist told him, "Your wife is young. ICSI may be successful, because she's young and has no problem. Don't hesitate. You should use any time you have."

Mohammed took Shahira to one of the two Egyptian IVF clinics where he had also taken his first wife. The physicians confirmed that because Shahira was young, with no known reproductive impairments, their chances of conceiving with ICSI, the newest variant of IVF, were greater than in Mohammed's previous attempts. With ICSI, as long as a single viable spermatozoon can be retrieved from a semen sample or directly from the testicles, it can be injected through so-called micromanipulation techniques into the ovum, thereby helping along the fertilization process. Thus, with ICSI, men with severe forms of infertility—for which all other forms of therapy, including standard IVF, are unsuccessful—are able to conceive biological off-spring. In other words, ICSI heralds a revolution in the treatment of male infertility, although it is accessible only to those who can afford it (at approximately LE 10,000, or U.S.$3,000, per trial).

Mohammed was delighted that Shahira and he were candidates for ICSI, but Shahira's reaction was different: "I'm afraid of any operation, or anything. I was so afraid, and I was not thinking it was going to be successful. But [the doctor] told me, 'Don't be afraid. It's easy. A small operation. It will be successful.' "

Shahira suffered uncomfortable side effects from the medications used to stimulate ovulation. Her gastric ulcer symptoms were exacerbated, and she felt abdominal cramping and pain throughout the treatment. "It's too difficult doing this ICSI," Shahira explained. "I take all these injections, I come to the hospital every day, I prepare for the operation, I see the anesthesia, the doctors. It's frightening. My husband—they just take the semen from him."

Once the ICSI procedure was completed, Shahira was still unconvinced of its efficacy. Thus, when she was scheduled for a blood test to determine her pregnancy status, she refused. She was so intransigent that Mohammed finally called the laboratory and had a doctor sent to their home to draw the sample. The next day, Mohammed and Shahira went to the laboratory, where the physician told them, "Congratulations. I wanted to tell you personally." Repeated pregnancy tests, along with three ultrasounds, confirmed that Shahira was pregnant—with twins in separate amniotic sacs.

Now Mohammed is in disbelief. Every day, he looks at Shahira's expanding belly and says, "Now I can't believe I will have children. I will believe it if I touch my son or daughter by myself." Shahira hopes that the birth of his twins will make Mohammed stop smoking three packs of cigarettes a day. Shahira is also concerned about the potential difficulties associated with a twin pregnancy and cesarean childbirth,[7] as well as the demands of taking care of two infants simultaneously. She hopes that at least one of the infants will be a girl, although Mohammed hopes for a son he can name Ahmed. If God wills, and the twins are born healthy, Shahira says she will not do ICSI again: "Once is enough. One operation, one delivery. It's too difficult and too frightening."

EGYPTIAN PATRIARCHY

The cases of Madiha and Ahmed and Shahira and Mohammed illustrate the relationship of male infertility to patriarchy in Egyptian culture. In Egypt, patriarchy involves relations of power and authority of men over women that are (1) learned through gender socialization within the family, where fatherhood gives men power; (2) manifested in intergender and intragender interactions within marriage, the family, and other interpersonal milieus; (3) engrained in pervasive ideologies of inherent male superiority; and (4) institutionalized on legal, political, economic, educational, and religious levels (Inhorn 1996; 3–4). Although I do not intend to suggest that Egypt is some-how more patriarchal than other societies, patriarchy operates on many levels in Egyptian society today. Furthermore, patriarchal ideologies cut across social classes, religious boundaries, and household types. However, as seen in the case of Madiha and Ahmed, manifestations of patriarchy are often more pronounced among the rural and urban lower classes living in extended family households.

Indeed, as suggested by other feminist scholars (Kandiyoti 1988, 1991; Joseph 1993, 1994), patriarchy in the Middle East is operationalized in the classic patrilineal, patrilocally extended family household. There, the senior male has total authority. For young women, subordination to both men and senior women (the latter of whom "buy into" patriarchy) is profound. This is particularly clear when young wives are unable to produce children, thereby threatening the social reproduction of the household and the husband's patrilineage at large. Exploring patriarchal relations in Middle Eastern households is thus crucial to understanding the social dimensions, intergender and intragender dynamics, and conjugal relations surrounding infertility. While it is clear why infertile women might suffer under such conditions of classic patriarchy, it is less clear what happens to women whose husbands are infertile. Yet, as shown in the case studies above, the condition of male infertility also threatens the happiness, health, security, and lives of Egyptian women. I argue that women suffer over men's infertility because of the nature of Egyptian patriarchy and the kind of patriarchal support Egyptian men receive in their family lives, even when they are infertile. Male infertility in Egypt creates four main patriarchal paradoxes: (1) who gets blamed for infertility in a marriage, (2) whose gendered identity is diminished by infertility, (3) who suffers in an infertile marriage, and (4) who pays the price for infertility treatment.

PATRIARCHY AND PROCREATIVE BLAME

The first paradox is seen in the realm of procreative theory, or how Egyptians conceive of the "coming into being" of human life (Delaney 1991; Inhorn 1994a). In contemporary Western reproductive biology,[8] procreation theories are "duogenetic," in that men and women are seen as contributing equally to the hereditary substance of the fetus, formed through the union of a woman's ovum and a man's spermatozoon. However, even with the widespread penetration of Western biomedicine and education around the world in the past half century, the globalization of such a duogenetic model is incomplete. Rather, in Egypt and in other parts of the Middle East (Crapanzano 1973; Delaney 1991; Good 1980; Greenwood 1981), lesser educated people believe procreation is "monogenetic," assigning men, the "givers of life," primary responsibility for procreation. Specifically, most poor urban Egyptians believe that men are the creators of preformed fetuses, which they carry in their sperm and which are then ejaculated and "caught and carried" by women's waiting wombs. In this scenario, women are not only marginalized as reproducers, but the products of their reproductive bodies, particularly menstrual blood, are seen as polluting to men and the fetuses they create. Although the notion of women's "eggs" is beginning to gain credence, even some educated Egyptians argue that men's sperm are reproductively dominant to women's eggs in terms of biogenetic input into the fetus.

Given this ideology of male procreation, it is a true patriarchal paradox that women, rather than men, are blamed for procreative failure. . . . Men, are seen as immune to infertility-producing bodily pathology. As long as a man can ejaculate his worm-borne fetuses into a woman's womb, he is deemed both virile and fertile.

With the advent of semen analysis in Egypt over the past three decades, however, the blame for infertility has shifted slightly. In fact, worm pathology is a titillating topic of conversation among poor urban Egyptians. Virtually every Egyptian has now heard of the problem of so-called weak worms. Weakness is a common cultural illness idiom in Egypt (DeClerque et al. 1986; Early 1993) and is rife in popular reproductive imagery. Most Egyptians now accept the idea that men, too, may be infertile because the worms are slow, sluggish, prone to premature death, or absent altogether. Because men's worms are considered living animals,[9] they are seen as suffering the problems of other animals, including excessive somnolence, natural death, and even murder (by other microbes or by some substance in the woman's body). The problem of not having enough worms is also recognized as important. Some men are seen as having no worms at all, a low percentage of worms, too few worms, or, in a fusion of popular and biomedical imagery, a low worm count.

But accepting male infertility in theory is not the same as accepting it in practice. Although Egyptians are willing to discuss the possibility of weak worms when a couple is childless, they are less willing to accept male infertility as the absolute cause of any given case. Even when men are acknowledged as having worm problems, such problems are seen as correctable through various medications thought to invigorate, even enliven, the most moribund of worms. The severity of many male infertility problems, which rarely respond well to drug therapy, remains unrecognized by most Egyptians. Rather, women are blamed for the failure to facilitate male procreation. . . .

PATRIARCHY AND MASCULINITY

This brings us to the second paradox: whereas infertility always mars a woman's femininity, no matter which partner is the cause of the problem, male infertility does not similarly redound on a man's masculinity. There are several reasons for this. First, there is widespread disagreement about the degree to which male infertility can be emasculating. The dominant view is that male infertility is profoundly emasculating, particularly given two major conflations: first, of infertility with virility or sexual potency and, second, of virility with manhood, the meanings of which are closely linked in North Africa (L. Ouzgane, personal communication, June 2001). In Egypt, infertile men are said to "not be good for women," to have their "manhood shaken," or to be "weak" and "incomplete," not "real men." Thus, infertility casts doubt on a man's sexual and gender identities—that is, whether he is a real man with the normal masculine parts, physiological processes, requisite strength of body and character, and appropriate sexual orientation. . . .

On the other hand, an alternative view voiced by many Egyptians of all social classes is that "a man is always a man," whether or not he is infertile, because having a child does not "complete a man as it does a woman." Indeed, whereas a woman's full personhood can be achieved only through attainment of motherhood, a man's sense of achievement has other potential outlets, including employment, education, religious/spiritual pursuits, sports and leisure, friendship groups, and the like. Egyptian men may delay marriage and parenting for many years as they pursue education, seek employment at home or abroad, and accrue resources to set up a household. Although more and more women in Egypt are entering the workforce (MacLeod 1991), the notion of a married career woman who remains childless by choice is unthinkable. Thus, while men and women in Egypt, almost without exception, eventually marry and expect to become parents, the truly mandatory nature of parenthood is experienced much more keenly by women, whose other avenues for self-realization are limited and who are judged harshly when they are unable to achieve motherhood early in their married lives.[10] . . .

Many women will go to great lengths to uphold their infertile husbands' reputations—literally shouldering the blame for the infertility in public—to avoid the stigma, psychological trauma, and possible marital disruptions such disclosure is likely to instigate. Egyptian women, understanding all too well the androcentric norms of their society, are not inclined to undermine their husbands' authority or standing as potential patriarchs, whose ability to produce children must remain unquestioned, particularly by other men. Indeed, masculinity in the Middle East is largely a homosocial enactment performed before and evaluated by other men. Thus, at the core of masculinity in the Middle East is homosocial competition and hierarchy—men's needs to prove themselves to other men (Ouzgane 1997:11–12). When male infertility does occur—literally wreaking havoc on a man's paternity and his ability to monogenetically procreate and prove his societal position as a patriarch or father figure to his biological children—then such infertility is rejected as implausible or hidden from public scrutiny by infertile men themselves and the women who share their secret. So stigmatizing is male infertility to prevailing "hegemonic masculinity" (Connell 1995, 76) that most Egyptian men would rather live a lie—enforcing or tacitly accepting a cover-up on the part of their wives and families—than risk exposure of their emasculating "defect" to their male peers. Themselves the victims of dominant masculinity norms, infertile Egyptian men thus pay the heavy price of diminished self-concept and profound psychic suffering over their secret stigma. But, I would argue, the burden may be even greater for such men's wives: by feeling compelled to shoulder the blame, they ensure that male infertility remains invisible and hegemonic masculinities remain intact. At the same time, such a "patriarchal bargain" (Kandiyoti 1988) means that wives of infertile men must endure the social ostracism that comes with this stigmatizing condition as well as the psychic and physical toll of medical treatment for a condition located outside their own bodies.

PATRIARCHY AND INFERTILE MARRIAGES

That such women's marriages are threatened points to a third paradox: infertility stemming from a husband rarely leads to wife-initiated divorce and may, in fact, strengthen marital bonds. Yet infertility may lead to husband-initiated divorce or polygamous remarriage, whether or not female infertility can be proved.

Egyptian men who acknowledge their infertility are unlikely to replace their wives in a futile attempt to prove their fertility. Knowledge of their secret failing often makes infertile men extremely solicitous of their wives, largely because of the guilt they feel over depriving their wives of children. In turn, wives of infertile men typically express profound sympathy and care and rarely deem the infertility a striking blow to their marriages. Indeed, marriages affected by male infertility are often some of the best. Infertile husbands are often reported by their wives to be exceptionally kind and loving. Women, for their part, often feel relief in knowing that their marriages are secure, and they generally (although not necessarily)[11] reciprocate their husbands' kindnesses with mutual affection and support, even "babying" their husbands in the ways mothers do their children. Furthermore, wives' willingness to accept the blame publicly is often impressive to their husbands, cementing the marital bonds further.

Egyptian women are socialized to be caregivers, and they often boast of the superior compassion that comes with being a woman. Given the opportunity, women will play this role with their husbands, even if a husband's condition leads to permanent childlessness in the marriage. When a man's condition seems hopeless, some men take pity on their wives and offer to free them from the childless union. However, unlike men known to leave their wives over childlessness, few women choose this route. Not only is a woman's decision to leave a marriage considered bad form, but many women feel profound sympathy for their husbands' plight and are even more loving as a result. . . .

When a wife is known to be infertile, on the other hand, men at least consider their Islamically condoned options of polygamous remarriage or divorce—even though most men ultimately reject this option (Inhorn 1996). Husbands in Egypt typically experience significant family pressure to replace their infertile wives and perpetuate the patrilineage. Thus, even when men choose not to divorce their infertile wives—thereby resisting the patriarchal scripts engendered by Egyptian family life—a wife's infertility still leads to marital disruption and insecurity. Many infertile women live in fear that their marriages will collapse, for Islamic personal status laws consider a wife's barrenness as grounds for divorce. Although Islam also allows women to divorce if male infertility can be proved, initiation of a divorce continues to be so stigmatizing that women rarely choose this option unless their marriages are truly unbearable. Thus, as seen in the case of Mohammed and his first wife. Hala herself did not initiate the divorce. It was Mohammed who left the marriage to try his reproductive luck with a younger, more sympathetic woman. Hala, meanwhile, was blamed for the divorce—by virtue of her strong (qua emasculating) personality, which further weakened Mohammed's psyche and his commitment to his marriage. Hala was deemed by all to have brought the divorce upon herself by reminding Mohammed too often of his diminished masculinity.

PATRIARCHY AND NEW REPRODUCTIVE TECHNOLOGIES

Mohammed and Hala's case also points to the fourth paradox: the new reproductive technologies to treat infertility have actually increased the potential for divorce in Egypt. Thus, the final paradox involves the ways in which reproductive technologies themselves may serve particular patriarchal ends in this cultural setting.

The newest reproductive technology known as ICSI has now entered the Egyptian landscape; with ICSI, cases of seemingly intractable male infertility can now be overcome, and the arrival of this revolutionary treatment has led to the flooding of Egyptian IVF clinics with male-infertility cases. But many of the wives who have stood by their infertile husbands for years arrive at Egyptian IVF centers as "reproductively elderly" women in their forties, too old to produce viable ova for the ICSI procedure. Unfortunately, because of declining success rates for IVF/ICSI in women aged forty and older, most Egyptian IVF centers refuse to accept these women into their patient populations. Some Egyptian IVF doctors argue that this is a compassionate restriction, since it prevents older women from suffering the economic, physical, and psychic hardships of likely futile attempts.

However, these age restrictions have proved devastating for Egyptian wives of infertile husbands. Because contemporary Islamic legal opinion forbids any kind of ova donation, as well as surrogacy and adoption, couples with a reproductively elderly wife face four difficult options: (1) to remain together permanently without children, (2) to raise orphaned foster children, (3) to divorce so that husbands can try their reproductive luck with younger women, or (4) to partake in a polygamous marriage. Polygamy is unacceptable to most Egyptian women today; yet the first and second options are unacceptable to a significant portion of Egyptian men, including the highly educated, upper-class men presenting themselves for male infertility treatment to IVF centers.[12] Thus, cases of male-initiated divorce—between infertile men in their forties and fifties and the once-fertile but now elderly wives who have stood by them for years—are beginning to grow. . . .

That more and more affluent, educated men are choosing this route—with little consideration of their first wives' feelings or futures—is the latest sad twist to the male infertility story in Egypt. Thus, the gendered dimensions of this new reproductive technology reveal the ongoing nature of Egyptian patriarchy and the ways in which cases of male infertility serve to expose it.

CONCLUSION

I have focused on male infertility in Egypt, highlighting the patriarchal paradoxes posed by this condition. I have sought to demonstrate how women living under a particular patriarchal regime suffer over men's infertility. Not only are they blamed for the infertility but their gender identities and marriages suffer as a result. Furthermore, women pay the price of male infertility treatment—not only the physically taxing embodiment of such treatment but actual abandonment by husbands when such treatment is no longer an option for elderly wives.

Other stories could be told of how male infertility plays out in men's and women's lives in Egypt. Such stories must attend to infertile men's perspectives on their marriages, identities, and experiences as members of a society in which men themselves are subject to stressful, competitive, hierarchical forms of hegemonic masculinity. Male infertility presents a crisis of masculinity for Egyptian men, one in which their manhood is shaken to its deepest core. But as demonstrated in this article, the effects of such masculine crises do not end there: they redound in multiple, often profoundly detrimental ways on the lives of the women who, by virtue of marriage, must share infertile men's secrets and uphold their masculinity at all costs.

NOTES

1. An ongoing debate in the clinical-epidemiological literature questions whether sperm concentrations have decreased globally over the past fifty years because of environmental toxins and global warming. While some investigators support the so-called big drop thesis, others do not.

2. For further details of the study methodology and sample, see the appendices in Inhorn (1994b).

3. Names used here are pseudonyms.

4. In 1988, this was the equivalent of a little more than U.S.$15, one of the lowest monthly household incomes in my sample of 100 women and their husbands.

5. Despite their poverty, many lower-class Egyptian men do not permit their wives to work. For a full explanation, see Inhorn (1996).

6. For full descriptions and interpretation of this cultural illness category, see Inhorn (1994a, 1994c).

7. Pregnancies with multiple fetuses are at greater risk of complications. In Egypt, all in vitro fertilization (IVF) and intracytoplasmic sperm injection pregnancies (ICSI) result in cesareans, or "surgical births."

8. Although contemporary Western biological models of procreation are duogenetic, monogenetic models, including notions of fetal preformation in male sperm, have a long intellectual history in the West, dating from the time of Aristotle to the 1800s (Inhorn 1994a; Laqueur 1990).

9. Egyptian physicians use an Arabic approximation for the English biomedical term *sperm;* they call sperm *hayawanat il-minawi,* literally, "spermatic animals," a term subsequently used by many educated patients. That sperm are living creatures—animals, in fact—has not been lost on the collective imagination of lesser educated Egyptians. Since spermatic animals are creatures so small that they can be seen only through a microscope (as in semen analysis), they then must resemble *didan,* literally, "worms" or "parasites," much like the schistosomiasis parasites that plague rural Egyptians and are known to be microscopic. Indeed, with the widespread knowledge of semen analysis and schistosomiasis (bilharziasis), the majority of poor urban Egyptians now equate sperm with worms.

10. Egyptian women may marry as early as their teens and usually by their twenties. Men often marry in their thirties, forties, or even later.

11. Some Egyptian IVF physicians have expressed concern that my research does not reflect well enough the ways in which elite women may exert psychological power over their infertile husbands and generally make their lives miserable.

12. The permanent fostering of orphans, tantamount to adoption in the West, is unpopular among Egyptians for several cultural reasons (Inhorn 1996). In my studies, middle-and upper-class Egyptians seemed less willing to entertain this possibility than did lower- and lower-middle class infertile couples.

REFERENCES

Abbey, A., F. M. Andrews, and L. J. Halman. 1991. Gender's role in responses to infertility. *Psychology of Women Quarterly* 15:295–316.

Becker, G. 2001. Deciding whether to tell children about donor insemination: An unresolved question in the United States. In *Infertility around the globe: New thinking on childlessness, gender, and reproductive technologies,* edited by M. C. Inhorn and F. van Balen. Berkeley: University of California Press.

Cates, W., T. M. N. Farley, and P. J. Rowe. 1985. Worldwide patterns of infertility: Is Africa different? *The Lancet* (September 14):596–98.

Collet, M., J. Reniers, E. Frost, F. Yvert, A. Leclerc, C. Roth-Meyer, B. Ivanoff, and A. Meheus. 1988. Infertility in Central Africa: Infection is the cause. *International Journal of Gynecology and Obstetrics* 26:423–28.

Connell, R. 1995. *Masculinities.* Berkeley: University of California Press.

Crapanzano, V. 1973. *The Hamadsha: A study in Moroccan ethnopsychiatry.* Berkeley: University of California Press.

Curtis, K. M., D. A. Savitz, and T. E. Arbuckle. 1997. Effects of cigarette smoking, caffeine consumption, and alcohol intake on fecundability. *American Journal of Epidemiology* 146:32–41.

Daniels, C. R. 1997. Between fathers and fetuses: The social construction of male reproduction and the politics of fetal harm. *Signs: Journal of Women in Culture and Society* 22:579–616.

DeClerque, J., A. O. Tsui, M. F. Abul-Ata, and D. Barcelona. 1986. Rumor, misinformation and oral contraceptive use in Egypt. *Social Science & Medicine* 23:83–92.

Delaney, C. 1991. *The seed and the soil: Gender and cosmology in Turkish village society.* Berkeley: University of California Press.

Early, E. A. 1993. *Baladi women of Cairo: Playing with an egg and a stone.* Boulder, CO: Lynne Rienner.

Egyptian Fertility Care Society. 1995. *Community-based study of the prevalence of infertility and its etiological factors in Egypt: (1) The population-based study.* Cairo: The Egyptian Fertility Care Society.

Elshtain, J. B. 1981. *Public man, private woman.* Princeton, NJ: Princeton University Press.

Ericksen, K., and T. Brunette. 1996. Patterns and predictors of infertility among African women: A cross national survey of 27 nations. *Social Science & Medicine* 42: 209–20.

Good, M.-J. D. 1980. Of blood and babies: The relationship of popular Islamic physiology to fertility. *Social Science & Medicine* 14B:147–56.

Greenwood, B. 1981. III(a) Perceiving systems: Cold or spirits? Choice and ambiguity in Morocco's pluralistic medical system. *Social Science & Medicine* 15B: 219–35.

Greil, A. L. 1997. Infertility and psychological distress: A critical review of the literature. *Social Science & Medicine* 45:1679–1704.

Greil, A. L., T. A. Leitko, and K. L. Porter. 1988. Infertility: His and hers. *Gender & Society* 2:172–99.

Inhorn, M. C. 1994a. *Quest for conception. Gender infertility, and Egyptian medical traditions.* Philadelphia: University of Pennsylvania Press.

———. 1994b. Interpreting infertility: Medical anthropological perspectives. *Social Science & Medicine* 39: 459–61.

———. 1994c. Kabsa (a.k.a. mushahara) and threatened fertility in Egypt. *Social Science & Medicine* 39:487–505.

———. 1996. *Infertility and patriarchy: The cultural politics of gender and family life in Egypt.* Philadelphia: University of Pennsylvania Press.

Inhorn, M. C., and K. A. Buss. 1993. Infertility, infection, and introgenesis in Egypt: The anthropological epidemiology of blocked tubes. *Medical Anthropology* 15:217–44.

———. 1994. Ethnography, epidemiology, and infertility in Egypt. *Social Science & Medicine* 39:671–86.

Inhorn, M., and F. Van Balen, eds., 2001. *Infertility around the globe: New thinking on childlessness, gender, and reproductive technologies.* Berkeley: University of California Press.

Irvine, D. S. 1998. Epidemiology and aetiology of male infertility. *Human Reproduction* 13 (Suppl. 1): 33–44.

Jaggar, A. M. 1983. *Feminist politics and human nature.* Totowa, NJ: Rowman & Allanheld.

Joseph, S. 1993. Connectivity and patriarchy among urban working-class Arab families in Lebanon. *Ethos* 21: 452–84.

———. 1994. Brother/sister relationships: Connectivity, love, and power in the reproduction of patriarchy in Lebanon. *American Ethnologist* 21:50–73.

Kandiyoti, D. 1988. Bargaining with patriarchy. *Gender & Society* 2:274–90.

———. 1991. Islam and patriarchy: A comparative perspective. In *Women in Middle Eastern history: Shifting boundaries in sex and gender,* edited by N. R. Keddie and B. Baron, 23–42. New Haven, CT: Yale University Press.

Laqueur, T. 1990. *Making sex: Body and gender from the Greeks to Freud.* Cambridge, MA: Harvard University Press.

Larsen, U. 1994. Sterility in sub-Saharan Africa. *Population Studies* 48:459–74.

MacLeod, A. E. 1991. *Accommodating protest: Working women, the new veiling, and change in Cairo.* New York: Columbia University Press.

Ouzgane, L. 1997. Masculinity as virility in Tahar Ben Jelloun's work. *Contagion: Journal of Violence, Mimesis, and Culture* 4:1–13.

Reproductive Health Outlook. 1999. *Infertility: Overview and lessons learned.* Available from www.rho.org.

Stanton, A. L., J. Tennen, G. Affleck, and R. Mendola. 1991. Cognitive appraisal and adjustment to infertility. *Women and Health* 17:1–13.

Sundby, J. 2001. Infertility and health care in countries with less resources: Case studies from sub-Saharan Africa. In *Infertility around the globe: New thinking on childlessness, gender, and reproductive technologies,* edited by M. C. Inhorn and F. van Balen. Berkeley: University of California Press.

Thonneau, P., L. Bujan, L. Multigner, and R. Mieusset. 1998. Occupational health exposure and male fertility: A review. *Human Reproduction* 13:2122–25.

Tong, R. 1989. *Feminist thought: A comprehensive introduction.* Boulder, CO: Westview.

Van Balen, F., and T. C. M. Trimbos-Kemper. 1993. Long-term infertile couples: A study of their well-being. *Journal of Psychosomatic Obstetrics and Gynaecology* 16:137–44.

Van Balen, F., J. E. E. Verdurmen, and E. Ketting. 1995. *Caring about infertility: Main results of the national survey about behavior regarding infertility.* Delft, the Netherlands: Eburon.

Yeboah, E. D., J. M. Wadhwani, and J. B. Wilson. 1992. Etiological factors of male infertility in Africa. *International Journal of Fertility* 37:300–307.

33

Maid or Madam?

Filipina Migrant Workers and the Continuity of Domestic Labor

PEI-CHIA LAN

Recently, feminist scholars have paid attention to the gendered division of house-work and domestic employment across class and racial lines. . . . These studies are divided into two distinct groups: Most studies of unpaid housework address only white, middle-class women, whereas the literature on domestic service is generally about women of color. To separate these two topics ignores their articulation and embeddedness. The gender battle over housework at home is influenced by the availability of domestic service in the market; those who offer domestic service are often wives and mothers who take care of their own families and households as well. A flawed dichotomy between the terms "maid" and "madam" blinds us to women's multiple roles and fluid trajectories. To explore women's agency in facing the complex organization of domestic labor, we need new ways of conceptualizing domestic labor that "transcend the constructed oppositions of public-private and labor-love" (Nakano Glenn 1994, 16).

. . . I view unpaid household labor and paid domestic work not as separate entities in an exclusive dichotomy but as structural continuities across the public/private divide. I develop the concept of the continuity of domestic labor to describe the feminization of domestic labor as multiple forms of labor done by women in both the public and private spheres. These labor activities, situated in different circumstances, are associated with shifting meanings (money/love) and fluid boundaries (maid/madam). I will elaborate this concept using the life experiences of Filipina migrant domestic workers in Taiwan. Some of these workers are housewives in the Philippines, but they, as overseas maids, become breadwinners, transnational mothers, and even domestic employers; the others are single women, who turn into old maids or foreign brides. The gendered as-

Pei-Chia Lan, "Maid or Madam? Filipina Migrant Workers and the Continuity of Domestic Labor," from *Gender & Society,* Volume 17/2003, p. 187–208.

signment of domestic labor has channeled these women's life chances in both the family and market and in the local as well as in the global context.

THE CONTINUITY OF DOMESTIC LABOR

Domestic labor, which refers to the labor activities that sustain the daily maintenance of a household, is accomplished by a variety of agents, with multiple formats, and in different settings. Family members, mostly women, carry out some household chores and caring labor themselves while transferring other parts of domestic labor to the market economy. For example, people purchase prepared-to-cook foods and mass-produced clothes, and they hire commercial services for duties like child care, cleaning, and gardening. These various arrangements of domestic labor are associated with different forms of compensation. Unpaid labor of female kin is considered a labor of love whose emotional value is related to the ideals of woman-hood, such as the cult of domesticity and intensive motherhood among white middle-class Americans (Hays 1996; Palmer 1989). In contrast, the value of domestic service done by nonfamily workers, predominantly minority women, is redeemed through wages.

Women in distinct social locations possess uneven resources to organize their own household labor and the market form of domestic service. Women who can afford the purchase of goods and services outsource a significant portion of their domestic responsibility to the market. They deliberate about what labor is socially acceptable to transfer to commercial agents without diminishing their status as "the lady of the house" (Kaplan 1987). The transfer of mothering labor permits these socially privileged women to enjoy the emotional value of motherhood, elevated to the status of "mother-manager" (Katz Rothman 1989). Those women who contribute paid domestic service are, however, forced to neglect their own families. Although receiving monetary rewards for their labor, these mother-domestics struggle to sustain family bonds and achieve motherhood with unpaid or underpaid assistance from their extended kin.

Despite the importance of identifying the opposition between maid and madam, in this article, I modify such dichotomous categorization by articulating a fluid, dynamic conception of domestic labor. I suggest that we analyze unpaid household labor and waged domestic work as structural continuities that characterize the feminization of domestic labor across the public and private spheres. . . .

I develop the concept of the continuity of domestic labor to describe the affinity between unpaid household labor and waged domestic labor—both are feminized work attached with moral merits and yet undervalued in cash. This concept especially sheds light on the life experiences of migrant domestic workers, who are situated in multiple, sometimes contradictory, locations, For them, taking care of the employer's family and taking care of their own family are interdependent activities, and the boundary between madam and maid is fluctuating and permeable. Migrant women may cross the madam/maid line through sequential movements in two opposite directions: First, migrant women who are homemakers in their home countries become breadwinners performing overseas waged domestic work. Second, single migrant women may seek international marriages as a path of social mobility, changing status from a maid who offers waged service for her foreign employers to a wife who offers unpaid household labor for her foreign husband.

The other experience that penetrates the maid/madam distinction is the simultaneous occupancy of domestic and labor force roles. Migrant women sell their domestic labor in the market but remain burdened with the gendered responsibilities in their own families. Although they consistently serve as providers of caring labor to others (their family as well as the employer), these labor activities are nevertheless conducted in segmented spatial settings. In reality, they experience a relation of conflict or disarticulation between these two simultaneous roles. While migrant women stay overseas to assist in the maintenance of another family, those who are mothers have to neglect their own children left behind, and those who are single sacrifice the prospect of starting their own families.

In this article, I illustrate the idea of the continuity of domestic labor with the case of Filipina migrant domestic workers in Taiwan. I divide my informants into two categories, migrant mothers and single migrants, who develop different experiences with motherhood and marriage, two major institutions that characterize the gendered division of domestic labor (Tung 1999). I ask the following questions: How does the structural continuity between unpaid domestic labor and paid domestic work affect the life trajectories of these women? How do they attempt to maintain or establish their own families while working overseas to take care of others' families? and How do they define their womanhood by negotiating the forms and meanings of their domestic labor?

DATA AND METHOD

. . . My research focuses on migrant domestic workers from the Philippines, which is now the world's second largest labor-exporting country (Asian Migrant Centre 2000). Filipino migrants possess a competitive advantage in the global labor market due to their adequate education and English proficiency. Their predominant destinations have recently switched from North America and Europe to the Middle East and East Asia. Taiwan has now become the fourth major host country, after Saudi Arabia, Hong Kong, and Japan. Domestic workers are a major part of the migrant labor force from the Philippines. Currently, more than half of Filipina overseas workers are placed in service occupations, mainly as cleaners, caretakers, and domestic helpers (National Statistics Office 2002).

This article is based on ethnographic data and in-depth interviews collected between July 1998 and July 1999. I did volunteer work in a church-based non-governmental organization in Taipei and frequently attended social outings with Filipina migrants on Sundays. I also conducted interviews with 56 Filipina domestic workers within and outside of this community. . . .

My analysis is divided into four sections that illustrate the experiences of migrant domestic workers in relation to the continuity of domestic labor. First, the feminization of domestic work allows Filipina housewives to have better opportunities than their husbands to land a job overseas and to become the primary breadwinner in the family. Second, migrant mothers play multiple roles to manage their paid and unpaid domestic labor at the same time. They are transnational mothers, substitute mothers, and even remote madams who hire maids in the Philippines. Third, single migrants experience the disarticulation of their paid and unpaid domestic labor—they face difficulties in building their own families when working overseas to maintain others' families. Last, some single migrants enter international marriage to escape the stigmatized status of (old) maid. The structural affinity between domestic work and household labor enhances their chances in the international marriage market.

FROM HOUSEWIFE TO BREADWINNER MAID

Despite the fact that a substantial number of married women hold waged jobs in the Philippines, the ideal Filipino family consists of a male breadwinner and a female housekeeper, and housework and child care are predominantly considered women's duties (Go 1993). The cultural heritages of the Spanish and American colonial regimes have inscribed male-centered gender relations that remain influential today (Illo 1995). Paradoxically, the patriarchal logic that governs as unequal division of household labor has created a niche for Filipina women in the global labor market. Women have even more advantages over their husbands in seeking jobs overseas. Most Filipino families in my study went through a similar migration pattern: During the 1980s, the husband left the wife and children at home to work in the Middle East. In the 1990s, it became the wife's turn to work abroad, and the husband stayed in the Philippines with the children. This transition happened due to the decline of male-oriented construction and manufacturing jobs in the Middle East during and after the Gulf War, in contrast to the growing demands for domestic workers in other host countries (Tarcoll 1996).

Roland Tolentino (1996, 58) described this transition for Filipina domestic workers: "Unpaid home labor in the domestic sphere becomes paid labor in international spaces." When these women shift their status from housewives to domestic workers, they perform similar duties but in geographically distinct settings. Their domestic labor, which was compensated by nothing but emotional value, is now paid for in cash when working overseas. Anamaria, a homemaker in the Philippines, points out the similarity and difference between her former work and her new job of cleaning and cooking for a Taiwanese family: "Working here is the same as working in my house in the Philippines," followed by a naughty smile, "but I get paid here!"

It is true that many migrant domestics suffer from endless requests from employers and long working hours in a live-in employment situation. But for women who were full-time employees in the Philippines, the workload in an overseas domestic job may be less than their double shifts at home. Says Vanessa, a former bookstore supervisor:

> In the Philippines, I am exhausted. I wake up early. I cook. I wash. When my children come home after school, I am still working. They heat the food I cook in the morning. Here, [the work is] easy. In the afternoon, I finish my work, I can just rest, watch HBO like this [crosses her legs and puts here feet on the table]. So look at me [points at her body], I have gained 10 pounds in the last six months!

Vanessa and many other Filipinas worked alone in Taiwan, separated from their husbands and children at home. Their migration pattern is different from the prevalent male-headed migration pattern, in which men's family authority and access to migrant network resources favor husbands' initial departure. Filipina workers in Taiwan and other Asian countries are independent migrants because contract-based employment excludes the options of permanent settlement and family reunification. Such a feminized migration pattern helps Filipina homemakers expand the scope of their lives and become the primary breadwinners in their families.

For example, Naomi and her husband, both in their mid-30s, own a chicken farm in the Philippines. The business is okay, but the household income seems modest considering their two-year-old son's future education. Hence, Naomi applied for jobs overseas, a decision made on her own: "I decided. My husband said OK. He will take care of our son with his parents. I have always wanted to work abroad when I was younger anyway." Naomi quit college and got married at the age of 18, and now she perceives working abroad as a belated chance for her to explore the world: "I want to see a different world. Before, I never had a chance to see different things. I got married too early."

Women's moves across borders and traditional gender roles result in drastic changes in their couple relations. Filipina migrants use the terms "houseband" or "huswife" to mock their "domesticated" husbands who stay home and perform most domestic tasks (Margold 1995). I frequently heard complaints that their husbands failed to adequately perform their new gender role, especially in the matter of household budgeting. Despite this, the shifting of social positions offers no guarantee that the husbands of migrant workers will take over domestic duties. Some of their husbands drink or gamble to excess when they are no longer in charge of the daily duty of breadwinning. In addition, another major concern troubles the minds of many Filipina migrants, as shown in this conversation I had with three Filipina migrants:

> HELEN: You remember Lisa? She went home for a vacation and came back again. She caught her husband with another wife. [Everybody sighs.]
>
> CLAUDIA: Many families are into trouble when one of them works abroad. Because the wife works abroad, she sends a lot of money to the husband. Every day is like his birthday. Then the man has a concubine, and the woman has a relationship abroad. Because they feel lonely!
>
> OLIVIA: When the wife is not there, the husband finds himself so miserable, and he thinks, "I earn less than my wife", so he finds another woman!

The Philippine media coined the term "Saudi Syndrome" to describe the anxieties of Filipino workers who were employed in the Middle East and were worried about their wives' infidelity at home (Arcinas, Banzon-Bautista, and David 1986). Filipina migrants harbor similar worries about their husbands left in the Philippines. The likelihood that a migrant woman's husband will have affairs is considered even higher than that for a migrant's wife. The rationale is described by Olivia—the "domesticated" husband feels "inferior" and "miserable" because his masculinity is "endangered" by a wife who makes more money than he does.

I interviewed Linda and her husband in the Philippine province where they lived. The husband used to work in Hong Kong as a construction worker but had been unemployed since his return. Linda then went to Taiwan as a domestic worker for two years. At the time of interview, the family income was earned exclusively by Linda, who sold snacks at street corners. As Linda's savings were being rapidly dissipated by supporting three children enrolled in expensive private schools, one of the parents would soon have to work abroad again. Linda talked about how they considered possible arrangements for the future:

AUTHOR: Would you like to go to Taiwan again?

LINDA: I don't know. He [my husband] said just stay home and sell *halo-halo* (a street dessert). He said he will go because Filipino men want to show they're macho macho [laughs]. I like life in Taiwan because so many money. Here? No! But here I can be with my children. This is the best.

AUTHOR: Who was taking care of your children?

LINDA: My husband. He said, "[it is] very hard to be a father and a mother at the same time." That's why he doesn't want to stay behind again. I asked my children, "Do you want me to work abroad again?" They said, "No, not you, papa." My husband didn't like me to go to Taiwan. He said. "It's not you, it's my responsibility to support the family." He feels ashamed.

AUTHOR: So you will not work abroad again?

LINDA: Well, if my husband cannot find a job, I will be forced to leave again.

Linda's husband "feels ashamed" about his wife's working abroad to support him and the children. He seeks a job overseas not only to regain the ideal masculine role of breadwinner but also to escape domestic burdens ("[It is] very hard to be a father and a mother at the same time"). In contrast, migrant women like Linda have no choice but to fulfill the double obligations. They are torn by the emotional strain of leaving children behind and the financial pressure of being "forced to leave again." The structural continuity between paid and unpaid labor facilitates these women's obtaining overseas jobs and financial rewards, but in the meantime, they pay the emotional cost of leaving their husbands and children and are stigmatized for their deviation from the ideal of domesticity and motherhood.

REMOTE MADAM, SUBSTITUTE MOTHER

While Filipina migrant workers are mothering others' children overseas, who is taking care of their children? Many rely on grandmothers, aunts, sisters, and other female kin to be substitute mothers; in some cases, the husbands quit their jobs and become full-time homemakers. There are also quite a few migrant mothers who seek non-family members to care for their children. Some consider hired help a better solution than kin caretakers as they find it emotionally difficult to evaluate or criticize the labor performance of relatives. Moreover, kin caregivers are not necessarily cheaper than waged workers because migrant parents are obligated to provide relatives with financial return under the cultural norm of *utang na loob* (debts of gratitude). These migrant domestic workers then become remote madams who hire local women to take care of their families while they are maintaining other households overseas.

Domestic service is one of the largest categories of waged work for women in the Philippines; by 1975, one out of five employed women was in domestic service (Eviota 1992, 88). Many domestics are rural women recruited by employers or recruiters from the city, and domestic work offers them a way to escape poverty in the provinces and access urban middle-class lives. Better-off households in the Philippines usually hire several domestic workers assigned specialized jobs. In addition to *yayas* (nannies) and helpers (household workers), they also hire liveout workers such as cooks and laundry women. The average wage of a live-in-helper or nanny in major cities is about Php 1,500 to Php2,000 (U.S.$30 to U.S.$40 in 2002) per month. The wage rate is even lower in the provinces. For example, I met a Filipina domestic worker whose wage was a meager Php500 (U.S.$17 in 1999) per month. When I asked her if she ever thought of working abroad, she answered me in broken English: "Me? No money!"

During interviews, several Filipina migrant domestic workers said to me, in a proud or embarrassed tone, "You know, I have a maid in the Philippines!" One of them is Christina, a college graduate and a former teacher. She hired a live-in domestic to take care of her children while she was working in Taiwan. Despite holding a similar occupation now, Christina drew a clear distinction between herself and her maid: "My sister was laughing, 'You have a maid in the Philippines, but you are a maid in Taiwan!' I said, 'It's different, They are undereducated. Not everyone can work abroad. You have to be very serious, very determined.' "

Migrant domestic workers' ambivalent status, being an overseas maid yet a remote madam, indicates their intermediate status in the multitiered "international division of reproductive labor" (Salazar Parreñas 2001, 72). On the top tier are middle- and upper-class women in advanced economies who hire migrant workers to mother their children; on the bottom are local women who pick up domestic duties transferred from migrant workers in the middle tier. Other studies have confirmed that the migratory flows from the Philippines are selective: The very poor and chronically unemployed seldom emigrate. The transnational recruitment process has a preference for applicants with high education, skills, working experience, ambition, and economic capital (Alegado 1992). Local domestic helpers are the women who possess less economic and cultural capital; they either are not sufficiently qualified or cannot afford the costs of seeking employment outside of the Philippines.

Migrant mothers received enhanced monetary value for their labor due to higher wage levels in foreign countries; their pecuniary gains enable them to transfer their household labor to poorer women in the Philippines. Becoming a madam at home marks their upgraded social status among village fellows and also brings in psychological compensation for migrants who suffer from class downgrading while working overseas as a maid. To some degree, the feminization of domestic labor has created opportunities for migrant women to improve their life chances, but for local helpers, domestic work remains a dead-end job with little economic value and social recognition.

Still, neither the monetary gains nor the social mobility acquired by migrant mothers cancels out their emotional costs in family separation. Their concurrent duties of unpaid motherhood and surrogate motherhood are segmented by geographic borders. Given the physical distance that hinders migrant mothers from performing their labor of love for their children, migrant mothers now display their love with letters, phone calls, and the money they earn in overseas domestic work. Previous studies have portrayed transnational motherhood with practices like sending children to private schools, purchasing expensive gifts, and remitting generous allowances (Hondagneu-Sotelo and Avila 1997; Salazar Pareñas 2001). Similarly, migrant mothers in Taiwan rely on the flow of remittances and packages to maintain emotional bonds on the basis of material dependency.

To equate love with money is fuzzy math, especially when one is faced with a shortage of cash. Evelyn, a single mother in her early 40s, has been doing part-time cleaning jobs after "running away" from her contract employer five years ago. Since then, she has not been able to visit her two children in the Philippines. Recently, she was diagnosed with a tumor but has no insurance to pay for further treatment. This physical condition has forced her to reduce her workload as well as the remittances sent to her children. Before I departed for my fieldtrip to the Philippines in 1999, Evelyn excitedly told me. "Maybe you can meet my children there!" During my stay in Manila, I did not get any messages from Evelyn's children but received a phone call from Evelyn one night. She was weeping on the phone:

> My children never called you, right? You know what day is today? It's Mother's Day! They don't remember this day or even my birthday! I am very sad, so I called you in the Philippines. I am not going to send them any more money. I'll see it they will think of me when they have no money.

Evelyn talked about her children in an earlier interview:

EVELYN: I feel very upset about my children. They don't talk to me. This one. . . . I left her studying in college, but now she got married and has a son already. . . . She never told me she got a [boy]friend! She never told me.

AUTHOR: Why don't they talk to you anymore? Are they mad at you or something?

EVELYN: I don't know. . . . Maybe because I don't send them money anymore. . . . I am sacrificing my life for *them!* I never never get involved with a man. I need a companion also, but I never think of that. I think only of my family. I don't want them to become like me. I am suffering for my marriage. But my children, they don't understand me. Sometimes I have no job! I have no money to give to my landlord. Sometimes I am hungry. I have no food. . . . I never ask them for help.

As Pierrette Hondagneu-Sotelo and Ernestine Avila (1997) have argued, migrant women, socially defined as primary caregivers, have to distinguish their transnational motherhood from an act of abandonment or disowning of their children. Deeply hurt by her children's suspicion that she had abandoned the family to enjoy life overseas, Evelyn defended herself by underscoring her practices of virtuous womanhood ("I never get involved with a man") and selfless motherhood ("I am sacrificing my life for them"). These practices accord with the cultural prescription of ideal womanhood in the Philippines—*mahinhin* (demure, virtuous, pious, or modest)—embodied by the Virgin Mary as well as the noble figures of Filipinas like the folklore character Maria Clara or the national mother Corazon Aquino (Siapno 1995). Despite Evelyn's efforts to be a virtuous transnational mother, over time, the physical separation obstructed her emotional connections with her children, and her illness hampered her ability to mother them with flows of remittances.

As ties with their children back home are loosening, migrant mothers may find emotional rewards in the job of surrogate motherhood. Scholars have named this situation "diverted mothering" (Wong 1994) or "displaced mothering" (Salazar Parreñas 2000). Rutchelle, a Filipina mother of two in her 30s, has been working for a Taiwanese household for more than two years. In the church, I frequently saw her along with two Taiwanese children, one girl of five and one boy of four. I assumed that their parents were busy at work, but Rutchelle corrected me: "No, the parents are at home. But the children want to be with me." I asked the boy, Tommy, what his parents were doing that day. He replied, "They're sleeping. Mommy was drinking last night." Rutchelle shook her head and said, "I don't understand why they sleep so much." . . .

Migrant caregivers are trapped in an emotional predicament at work: They have to assure their madams that their temporary presence will not shake the status of biological mothers, but they also feel traumatized if their emotional ties with the employers' children are only ephemeral. For instance, Rutchelle tried to comfort Tommy's mother, who sometimes feels jealous about the children's attachment to the migrant nanny: "I told her it's OK. I am only a housekeeper. I am here only temporary. The children have two Filipinas before. They forgot them. Helen, the last one, my boss showed him [Tommy] the picture. He doesn't know her." I checked with Tommy, asking, "Who is Helen?" Indeed, he shook his head. I joked with Tommy, "Helen would be upset if she knew you don't remember her." Rutchelle then grabbed the boy in her arms, saying with confidence, "But they will remember me forever!"

The establishment of emotional bonds with the children under their care is a double-edged sword for migrant caretakers. It provides when with some emotional rewards and social recognition for this undervalued carework, but it may also intensify their pain of separation from their own families and cause them additional emotional loss on termination of the job contract (Nelson 1990; Wrigley 1995). In addition, the emphasis on the emotional value in surrogate motherhood sometimes results in a reduction of monetary compensation received by careworkers. Some employers manipulate workers' attachment to the employers' children to extract additional unpaid labor, such as asking the workers to accompany the children on their days off or to give up annual vacations for the sake of the children.

This section has presented multiple roles taken by migrant mothers that cover a wide range of paid and unpaid domestic labor: They are remote madams who hire local helpers at home, they are transnational mothers who manage to deliver their love through overseas remittances, and they are substitute mothers who connect to the employers' children with a cash nexus as well as emotional ties. In all these circumstances, migrant mothers are engaged in a continual bargaining for money and love associated with their paid and unpaid mothering work. They have to pay certain emotional and monetary costs to be a good mother, either a transnational or a substitute one.

SINGLE MAID, OLD MAID

Most existing studies have focused on migrant workers who are mothers themselves, ignoring another significant group of single migrant women. Although these women are not yet tied to their own nuclear families, they are burdened with cultural expectations imposed on single daughters by their original families. Single adult daughters are expected to provide financial assistance to extended family members; the most common form is to sponsor education of younger siblings (Medina 1991). This section examines how single domestic workers negotiate their gendered responsibility to their families of origin and the possibilities of establishing their own families.

Nora, single in her late 30s, has a nursing degree from one of the most prestigious universities in the Philippines. She has been working overseas as a caretaker or domestic, first in Saudi Arabia and then in Taiwan, since the age of 24. Her father died a long time ago, and she is the only one in her family who is working overseas. She remits more than half of her monthly wage to her mother and younger sisters in the Philippines. From time to time, she sends money to other relatives in response to their requests to purchase appliances or to renovate their houses. Nora is also paying her youngest sister's tuition and other expenses in college. She tries to satisfy the sister's financial requests to protect her from the hardship of working overseas, as indicated by one dialogue I had with her:

AUTHOR: Will you encourage your sister to work abroad?

NORA: No the life working abroad is too hard. . . . And I know my sister, she cannot cook, cannot do any housework.

AUTHOR: Does she want to come?

NORA: Yes she wants to. I told her, "If you have a job there, a family there, [stay there and] I can buy you what you need." I just bought her a motorcycle. I told her, "Don't work abroad. It's too hard."

Jovita is another single Filipina who is in her late 20s and has been working overseas as a domestic worker for almost six years, One Sunday, I met her after she had just received a letter from her family. She showed no excitement and seemed upset. Amy, Jovita's best friend, tapped on her shoulder and said, "Well, they must have written to ask you for more money." Jovita nodded and said, "My mother, my sisters, they always ask me to send more money. They ask me why I don't send all the money home. I send NT $10,000 a month! I have to leave some for myself." After a deep sigh, she continued, "I told myself I will just stay to finish this contract because I am already old, feeling tired."

In addition to financial demands from her family, another thing that worries Jovita is the uncertain future after her contract in Taiwan. She wonders if she will be satisfied with the poor wage level in the Philippines. Also, she is concerned that she will not be able to find someone to mary if she continues to work abroad. Similar anxieties are shared by other Filipina single migrants. Rosemary told me the story of her friend, Manny, who is single in her late 20s. Manny's Taiwanese employers are so occupied by their multinational business that they leave Manny and the newborn baby alone at home most of the time. Rosemary described what happened to Manny:

> They [the employers] trust her very much. She's happy, because she loves the baby very much. It's like her own baby. When the mama comes home, the baby doesn't like her [the mama] and just cries. Manny's contract is going to finish soon, and the employer said, "We want you to stay forever." Manny said, "No! If I stay here forever, how can I get married and have my own baby?"

Manny's words indicate the conflict between assisting in the maintenance of the employer's family and the worker's desire to build a family of her own. Women's single status is usually associated with the social stigma of spinsterhood, whose equivalent term in Tagalog, *matandang dalaga,* figuratively means "womanhood partially fulfilled" (Hollnsteiner 1981). To ease the uncertainty regarding their marriage status, or the fulfillment of their womanhood, some Filipina single migrants imagine their future in the framework of the traditional ideals of housewifery and motherhood. For example, once Jovita told me, "I don't want to become my employer." When I asked what she meant, she answered, "They don't cook for their husbands. They don't take care of their own children. I don't want to become a wife like that. I want to cook a warm and nice dinner when he comes home after work." By criticizing her employer for failing to realize the domestic romance, Jovita establishes the moral superiority of traditional womanhood over her employer's career-oriented womanhood.

In fact, most migrant women are unable to achieve what Jovita perceives a good wife and a good mother should be. Some Filipina workers decide to remain single because of a perceived incompatibility between the life of working overseas and the traditional notion of family life. Fey has been working overseas for 11 years, since the age of 30. She talked about her perspective on marriage and her future plan:

> I saw my friends who leave their family and children to work abroad. That's not good. If you are alone, nothing worries you. So single is better. I want to work as long as I can, until 60 years old maybe. I will save some money, and I will save some money, and I will go back to the Philippines. I already bought a house there.

Some other Filipina workers refuse to enter a marriage for more radical reasons. Trina is a 38-year-old veteran domestic worker who has been in Singapore and Taiwan for more than 10 years. When I asked her if she was interested in marriage, she shook her head and said in a determined voice,

> No need [to get married]. I am a breadwinner now. I see my sister's life after getting married. I don't need that. She stays home, wasting her education. Her husband works oversea. She has to do cook, do wash, do everything! I don't want to marry, because after that you only stay home and cook food for her husband! Just like a maid! I am a maid. I know that! So why bother to marry!

Trina's remarks pinpoint the structural continuity between unpaid household labor and domestic work. She considers the social position of a housewife merely an unpaid version of maid, thus preferring her current economic independence and individual freedom as a single waged domestic worker. With the money earned overseas, she has purchased a piece of land on the outskirts of Manila and invested in a *sari-sari* (neighborhood grocery store) with sisters and cousins who are also single. Based on extended kin networks, these women create a community of mutual support, an alternative to the traditional nuclear family.

Migrant single daughters gain economic independence in overseas domestic employment but remain burdened with the financial responsibility to their original families. In addition, their temporary residency in foreign countries brings difficulty in settling down and building their own families, a situation that worries some women about their incomplete fulfillment of womanhood. Some single Filipinas seek international marriages to solve this predicament of the disarticulation between paid and unpaid domestic labor. The next section looks at this group of single Filipina migrants who alter their position from foreign maid to foreign bride.

FROM FOREIGN MAID TO FOREIGN BRIDE

After a Sunday mass, I found some Filipina workers in the backyard of the church secretly passing around a flyer, trying to avoid the attention of priests and nuns. The flyer, boldly titled "Heart of Asia: American and European Men Want To Write to You," started with this paragraph:

> Our international pen pal club gives you the chance to correspond with American and European men. These men have good jobs, nice homes, and higher education. But they are missing something in their lives. . . . They are looking for someone who is loyal, sensitive, and caring; someone who shares their traditional values about home, family, and relationships. They are seeking someone to respect and appreciate. They are seeking YOU.

This international pen pal club and many other similar agencies are based in Hong Kong, the city with the largest population of Filipina domestic workers in the world. The mushrooming phenomenon of mail-order brides—international marriages arranged through commercial agencies—usually happens between men from economically advanced countries and women from poorer countries. International marriage has a history in the Philippines due to the almost century-long U.S. army presence (Enloe 1989). Commercial agencies continue to target Filipina women who speak English and are familiar with Western lifestyles. The most popular destinations for Filipina brides are the United States, Australia, Germany, and England (Eviota 1992). Recently, the demand for female migrant spouses has come from men in wealthier Asian countries including Japan and Taiwan. A growing number of poor or widowed Taiwanese men have turned to Vietnam, Indonesia, China, and the Philippines for potential mates. The controversial nature and complex consequences of international marriages deserve in-depth analysis. My concern here is limited to the connection between overseas domestic employment and international marriages. . . .

. . . Some Filipina migrants marry Taiwanese men they meet through personal networks. Fey's sister worked in Taiwan as a domestic worker on a tourist visa in the 1980s. Through the referral of another Filipina bride, she later married a widowed Taiwanese man almost 20 years older than she. Fey commented on her sister's marriage:

FEY: This man told my sister, if you want to marry me, you can stay longer. I objected. I said, "You don't know what kind of person he is!" But my sister wanted to marry him because she wanted to stay in Taiwan.

AUTHOR: How's their marriage?

FEY: Not good! He keeps all the money. He has a pension from the government, but he only gives her a little allowance, so my sister has to do part-time [domestic] jobs. Now he's in the hospital. My sister is taking care of him. He has three children with the first wife. They seldom come to see him. But the father lets those children take care of his saving. My sister doesn't know how to read or write Chinese, so the children take all the money! So now, if he dies, my sister will have nothing!

HELEN: [overhears and comments] This is a waste of love!

FEY: [shakes her head] No, this is not love, just help.

The widely accepted myth that marriage is grounded solely on romantic love eads to an accusation that foreign spouses maneuver marriages to obtain citizenship. In fact, marriage has always been a social arrangement for mutual dependence and social exchange between two parties. This is especially true for people with limited social resources, whose marriages are often "not love, just help." Marriage in the Philippines is traditionally considered a path of social mobility for women; one of the measures of the desirability of the husband is the status upgrade he can offer (Medina 1991). Seen in this light, international marriage is a recent form of the old-fashioned tradition of "marrying up" (Cooke 1986). What is new is that the assurance of social mobility in an international marriage is grounded on the economic disparities between the countries of the groom and the bride.

In the eyes of Filipina migrants, Western and Taiwanese men become more lesirable mates when compared to Filipino men who are trapped in the poor homeland and offer little promise of economic stability and social mobility. The latter even present the risk of becoming demasculinized and domesticated husbands who depend on their wives working abroad. For example, 38-year-old Luisa, who was an entertainer in Japan before working in Taiwan, explained to me why she preferred marrying a foreigner to a Filipino:

> I don't want to marry a Filipino. They have no money, low salary. What if he says to me, "When will you go back to Taiwan? And send me money?" I will kill him! And it's not easy for me to find a Filipino. Because I have worked in Japan, in Taiwan, people think I am an urban, fashionable city girl. They think I must be materialistic, but I am not.

. . . International marriage indicates a crisis of masculinity not only for Filipinos but also for foreign grooms. These men, who are mostly widowed or divorced, lower class, and not preferred by women in their countries, attempt to regain their masculinity by rescuing Third World women from poverty. They fulfill their nostalgia for a prefeminist family romance by constructing an ideal domestic sphere sustained by the household labor of servile foreign wives (Tolentino 1996, 67–71). Unlike Taiwanese and Western women, who are liberated from the traditional gender roles, migrant women are considered better candidates for the ideal wife. The experience of overseas domestic work even becomes a positive qualification for women applicants in the international marriage market. This point was made clearly to me at one field moment. A group of Filipina migrants were reading and discussing an application form for an international pen pal club. Helen found a question embarrassing to answer and asked those who had applied before, "How did you answer this? What's your *profession?*" Luisa bluntly answered, "It's OK to say caretaker or domestic helper. They like that because they are all old and they like people who can take care of them."

The structural affinity between paid domestic worker and unpaid housewife, both socially defined as women's appropriate positions, is part of the driving force that facilitates migrant domestic workers' entrance into international marriages. This continuity is most explicit in those cases when a migrant domestic worker is married to her boss. It is not uncommon for Taiwanese middle-aged, divorced, or widowed men to propose to their migrant workers, usually hired to take care of their old or ill mothers. Nora, the nursing graduate I introduced earlier, received a marriage proposal from her Taiwanese employer right before her contract was about to finish. After Nora rejected this proposal, she and another Filipina, Rosemary, chatted about the proposal:

NORA: He [the boss] said, "You can stay here because my mother likes you and you like my mother."

ROSEMARY: They want to marry her because his mother likes her working here. So I told her, "No, this is a lifetime."

NORA: Right, if you get married, they will say, "You stay home, you don't go out."

ROSEMARY: And you don't get paid! [all laugh]

Most Filipina domestic workers, like Nora, are keenly aware that if they accept an employer's proposal, they will continue to perform similar domestic labor, only in the name of family obligation rather than employment. The workload placed on a wife may even be intensified since the labor of love offered by a family member is supposed to be incommensurable (thus unpaid) and incessant (no days off). Whenever a Filipina worker mentioned that her employer's relative was asking her for a date, I often heard responses from other Filipinas like this: "You have to be careful! Maybe they just want a free domestic helper and caretaker!" Helen pursued correspondence with an American man and received his proposal in a few months. She took some time to consider and finally turned it down for this reason: "When you have a husband, you have to provide all the service, cooking, cleaning, massage . . . for free! Being a DH [domestic helper], at least you got paid!"

Despite its monetary gains, waged domestic work is generally stigmatized as being unskilled, demeaning, and not a real job—recall Helen's embarrassment regarding how to indicate her profession when joining an international pen pal club. By contrast, unpaid household labor is granted more moral value and social recognition. This is why some Filipina migrants find more nonmaterial benefits in an international marriage than in waged domestic work. Luisa's American pen pal planned to visit Luisa and her family on her return to Manila for vacation, and they would discuss the possibility of marriage at that time. I told Luisa to be careful about marrying someone she barely knew. "I know," Luisa sighed deeply and said, "but I am tired of cleaning toilets!"

In fact, Luisa will not stop cleaning toilets after she gets married, but she will clean her own toilets instead of other people's toilets. Her housework will be socially labeled in the category of labor of love rather than that of waged labor; that is, she will lose monetary gains for her domestic labor but receive emotional value and social recognition instead. She will be able to detach herself from the stigma of maid and become a madam who can better approximate the dominant ideal of domesticity and motherhood. She enters an international marriage not only to seek social mobility in the uneven global village but also to pursue a romance with the elevated status of the lady of the house. . . .

CONCLUSION

In this article, I have sought to unravel the complexity of gendered domestic labor in the context of global migration. The feminization of domestic labor channels women's similar life chances in the family as well as the market. Individual women move across multiple positions involving different forms of domestic labor that are all defined as women's work. Taking on domestic work, a feminized occupation in both the local and global labor market, migrant women become transnational breadwinners but remain burdened by their gendered duties as mothers and wives back home. I underscore the continuity between household labor and waged domestic work to break down a dichotomous categorization between maid and madam. In actuality, women may shift between the status of maid and madam or occupy both positions at the same time. . . .

REFERENCES

Alegado, Dean Tiburcio. 1992. The political economy of international labor migration from the Philippines. Ph.D. diss., University of Hawaii, Manoa.

Arcinas, Fe R., Cynthia Banzon-Bautista, and Randolf S. David. 1986. *The odyssey of the Filipino migrant workers to the Gulf region.* Quezon City: University of the Philippines Press.

Asian Migrant Centre. 2000. *Asian migrant yearbook: Migration facts, analysis and issues in 1999.* Hong Kong: Asian Migrant Centre Ltd.

Cooke, Fadzilah M. 1986. *Australian Filipino marriages in the 1980s: The myth and the reality.* Research paper no. 37. Brisbane, Australia: School of Modern Asian Studies Centre for the Study of Australian Asian Relations, Griffith University.

Dumont, Jean-Paul. 2000. Always home, never home: Visayan "helper" and identities. In *Home and hegemony: Domestic service and identity politics in South and Southeast Asia,* edited by Kathleen M. Adams and Sara Dickey. Ann Arbor: University of Michigan Press.

Enloe, Cynthia. 1989. *Bananas, beaches, and bases.* Berkeley: University of California Press.

Eviota, Elizabeth Uy. 1992. *The political economy and gender, women and the sexual division of labor in the Philippines.* London: Zed Books.

Folbre, Nancy. 1991. The unproductive housewife: Her evolution in the 19th century economic thought. *Signs: Journal of Women in Culture and Society* 16(3): 463–84.

Go, Stella. 1993. *The Filipino family in the eighties.* Manila, Philippines: Social Development Research Center, De La Salle University.

Hays, Sharon. 1996. *The cultural constructions of motherhood.* New Haven, CT: Yale University Press.

Hollnsteiner, Mary R. 1981. The wife and the husband. In *Being Filipino,* edited by Gilda Fernando Cordero. Manila, Philippines: CCF Books.

Hondagneu-Sotelo, Pierrette. 1994. *Gendered transitions: Mexican experiences of migration.* Berkeley: University of California Press.

Hondagneu-Sotelo, Pierrette, and Ernestine Avila. 1997. "I am here, but I am there": The meanings of Latina transnational motherhood. *Gender & Society* 11 (5): 548–71.

Illo, Jean Frances. 1995. Redefining the Maybahay or housewife: Reflections on the nature of women's work in the Philippines. In *"Male" and "female" in developing Southeast Asia,* edited by Wazir Jahan Kavim. Oxford, UK: Berg.

Kaplan, Elaine. 1987. I don't do no windows: Competition between the domestic workers and the house-wife. In *Competition: A feminist taboo?* edited by Valerie Miner and Helen E. Longino. New York: Feminist Press.

Katz Rothman, Barbara. 1989. *Recreating motherhood: Ideology and technology in a patriarchal society.* New York: Norton.

Kibria, Nazli. 1993. *Family tightrope: The changing lives of Vietnamese Americans.* Princeton, NJ: Princeton University Press.

Lan, Pei-Chia. 2000. Global divisions, local identities: Filipina migrant domestic workers and Taiwanese employers. Ph.D. diss., Northwestern University, Evanston, IL.

Margold, Jane A. 1995. Narratives of masculinity and transnational migration: Filipino workers in the Middle East. In *Bewitching women, pious men: Gender and body politics in Southeast Asia,* edited by Aihwa Ong and Michael G. Peletz. Berkeley: University of California Press.

Medina, Belinda. 1991. *The Filipino family: A text with selected readings.* Quezon City: University of the Philippines Press.

Nakano Glenn, Evelyn. 1992. From servitude to service work: Historical continuities in the racial division of paid reproductive labor. *Signs: Journal of Women in Culture and Society* 18(1): 1–43.

———. 1994. Social constructions of mothering: A thematic overview. In *Mothering: Ideology, experience, and agency,* edited by Evelyn Nakano Glenn, Grace Chang, and Linda Rennie Forcey. New York: Routledge.

National Statistics Office. 2002. Press release of the 2001 survey on overseas Filipinos (SOF). Manila: National Statistics Office, the Philippine Government. Retrieved

24 September 2002 from http://www.census.gov.ph/data/pressrelease.

Nelson, Margaret K. 1990. *Negotiated care: The experiences of family day care providers.* Philadelphia: Temple University Press.

Palma-Beltran, Ruby. 1991. Filipino women domestic helpers overseas: Profile and implications for policy. *Asian Migrant* 4(2): 46–52.

Palmer, Phyllis. 1989. *Domesticity and dirt: Housewives and domestic servants in the United States, 1920–1940s.* Philadelphia: Temple University Press.

Salazar Parreñas, Rhacel. 2000. Migrant Filipina domestic workers and the international division of reproductive labor. *Gender & Society* 14(4): 560–80.

———. 2001. *Servants of globalization: Women, migration and domestic work.* Stanford, CA: Stanford University Press.

Siapno, Jacqueline. 1995. Alternative Filipina heroines: Contested tropes in leftist feminisms. In *Bewitching women, pious men: Gender and body politics in Southeast Asia,* edited by Aihwa Ong and Michael G. Peletz. Berkeley: University of California Press.

Taroll, Cecilla. 1996. Migrating "for the sake of the family?" Gender, life course and intra-household relations among Filipino migrants in Rome. *Philippine Sociological Review* 44(1–4): 12–32.

Tolentino, Roland B. 1996. Bodies, letters, catalogs: Filipinas in transnational space. *Social Text* 14(3): 49–76.

Tung, Charlene. 1999. The social reproductive labor of Filipina transmigrant workers in Southern California: Caring for those who provide elderly care. Ph.D. diss., University of California, Irvine.

Wang, Hong-Zen, and Shu-ming Chang. Forthcoming. The commodification of international marriages: Cross-border marriage business in Taiwan and Vietnam. *International Migration.*

Wong, Sau-Ling. 1994. Diverted mothering: Representations of caregivers of color in the age of "multi-culturalism." In *Mothering: Ideology, experience, and agency,* edited by Evelyn Nakano Glenn, Grace Chang, and Linda Rennie Forcey. New York: Routledge.

Wrigley, Julia. 1995. *Other people's children: An intimate account of the dilemmas facing middle-class parents and the women they hire to raise their children.* New York: Basic Books.

Yeoh, Branda S., and Shirlena Huang. 2000. "Home" and "away": Foreign domestic workers and negotiations of diasporic identity in Singapore. *Women's Studies International Forum* 23(4): 413–29.

34

Delicate Transactions

Gender, Home, and Employment Among Hispanic Women

M. PATRICIA FERNÁNDEZ KELLY

The days have vanished when scholars could comfortably speak about the roles of men and women as if they were immutable biological or temperamental traits. More than a decade of feminist thought and research in the social sciences has brought about a complex understanding of gender as a process reflecting political, economic, and ideological transactions, a fluid phenomenon changing in uneasy harmony with productive arrangements. The theoretical focus of this essay is on the way class, ethnicity, and gender interact.

I compare two groups of Hispanic women involved in apparel manufacturing: One includes native- and foreign-born Mexicans in Southern California; another, Cuban exiles in Southern Florida.[1] All the women have worked in factories at different stages in their lives, and they have also been involved in industrial work in the home. In a broad sense, women's incorporation into the work force is part and parcel of economic strategies that have allowed manufacturing firms to compete in domestic and international markets. From a more restricted perspective, it is also the result of personal negotiations between men and women in households and workplaces. Combining these perspectives, it is possible to compare the two groups of women to see the influence of economic resources and immigration histories on conceptions and institutions of gender. Despite sharing important characteristics, the two groups represent distinct economic classes and social situations. I use the cases to examine how economic and social factors can reinforce or undermine patriarchal values and affect women's attitudes toward and relationships with men.

A complex conceptualization of gender has emerged over the past two decades from the dialogue between Marxist and feminist scholars. In this dialogue, theorists have focused on the relationship between productive and reproductive spheres to uncover the varied content of gender relations under differing conditions of production and in different periods.[2] Here "gender" refers to meshed economic, political, and ideological relations. Under capitalism gender designates fundamental economic processes that determine the allocation of labor into remunerated and non-remunerated spheres of production. Gender also circumscribes the alternatives of individuals of different sexes in the area of paid employment. Women's specific socioeconomic experience is grounded in the contradiction that results from the wage labor/unpaid domestic labor split.

In addition, gender is political as it contributes to differential distributions of power and access to vital resources on the basis of sexual difference. The political asymmetry between men and women is played out both within and outside of the domestic realm. In both cases it involves conflict, negotiation, and ambivalent resolutions which are, in turn, affected by economic and ideological factors.

Finally, gender implicates the shaping of consciousness and the elaboration of collective discourses which alternatively explain, legitimate, or question the position of men and women as members of families and as workers. While all societies assign roles to individuals on the basis of perceived sexual characteristics, these roles vary significantly and change over time. Gender is part of a broader ideological process in constant flux. Moreover, adherence to patriarchal mores may have varying outcomes depending on their economic and political context.

This interplay of economic, political, and ideological aspects of gender is particularly evident in studying the relationship between women's paid employment and household responsibilities. Women's work—whether factory work, industrial homework, or unpaid domestic work—always involves negotiations of gendered boundaries, such as the line between wage labor and domestic responsibilities, and the arrangements that tie household organization and family ideals. Industrial homework, for example, both contradicts and complies with the ideological split between "work" and "family" as this sets standards for male-female differentiation; women who do homework work for wages but do not leave their homes and families.

Employers rely on homework to lower the wage bill, evade government regulations, and maintain competitiveness in the market;[3] none of these goals seem consistent with women's attempts to raise their economic status. Yet homework has been used by women to reconcile the responsibilities of domestic care with the need to earn a wage. Furthermore, women use and interpret homework as a strategy for bridging employment and family goals in a variety of ways. Women move between factory work, homework, and unpaid domestic labor on different trajectories, depending on both household organization and class-based resources.

Some conceptual clarification is needed for this analysis. It is necessary to distinguish "family" and "household." "Family" is an ideological notion that includes marriage and fidelity, men's roles as providers and women's roles as caretakers of children, and the expectation that nuclear families will reside in the same home. Rayna Rapp notes the prevalence of a family ideal shared by working- and middle-class people in the United States.[4] While "family" designates the way things should be, "household" refers to the manner in which men, women, and children actually join each other as part of domestic units. Households represent mechanisms for the pooling of time, labor, and other resources in a shared space. As households adjust to the pressures of the surrounding environment, they frequently stand in sharp, even painful, contrast to ideals regarding the family.

Class accounts largely for the extent to which notions about the family can be upheld or not. The conditions necessary for the maintenance of long-term stable unions where men act as providers and women as caretakers of children have been available among the middle and upper classes but absent among the poor. Nuclear households are destabilized by high levels of unemployment and underemployment or by public policy making it more advantageous for women with children to accept welfare payments than to remain dependent upon an irregularly employed man. The poor often live in highly flexible households where adherence to the norms of the patriarchial family are unattainable.

Class differences in the relation between household patterns and family ideals are apparent in women's changing strategies of factory work, homework, and unpaid labor. Homework, for example, can maintain family objectives or help compensate for their unattainability. In describing two contrasting ways women link household organization, paid employment, and gender and family ideals, my study creates a model for class and ethnic specific analyses of gender negotiations.

THE HISPANIC COMMUNITIES IN MIAMI AND LOS ANGELES

Although there are many studies comparing minorities and whites in the U.S., there have been few attempts to look at variations of experience within ethnic groups. This is true for Hispanics in general and for Hispanic women in particular; yet contrasts abound. For example, Mexicans comprise more than half of all Hispanics between eighteen and sixty-four years of age living in the U.S. Of these, approximately 70% were born in this country. Average levels of educational attainment are quite low with less than 50% having graduated from high school. In contrast, Cubans represent about 7% of the Hispanic population. They are mostly foreign-born; 58% of Cubans have 12 or more years of formal schooling.[5]

Both in Southern California and in Southern Florida most direct production workers in the garment industry are Hispanic. In Los Angeles most apparel firm operatives are Mexican women, in Miami, Cuban women.[6] The labor force participation rates of Mexican and Cuban women dispel the widespread notion that work outside the home is a rare experience for Hispanic women.[7] Yet the Los Angeles and Miami communities differ in a number of important respects. One can begin with contrasts in the garment industry in each area.

The two sites differ in the timing of the industry, its evolution, maturity, and restructuring. In Los Angeles, garment production emerged in the latter part of the nineteenth century and expanded in the 1920s, stimulated in part by the arrival of runaway shops evading unionization drives in New York. The Great Depression sent the Los Angeles garment industry into a period of turmoil, but soon fresh opportunities for the production of inexpensive women's sportswear developed, as the rise of cinema established new guidelines for fashion. During the 1970s and 1980s the industry reorganized in response to foreign imports; small manufacturing shops have proliferated, as has home production. In contrast, the apparel industry in Miami has had a shorter and more uniform history. Most of the industry grew up since the 1960s, when retired manufacturers from New York saw the advantage of opening new businesses and hiring exiles from the Cuban Revolution.

The expansion of the Los Angeles clothing industry resulted from capitalists' ability to rely on continuing waves of Mexican immigrants, many of whom were undocumented. Mexican migration over the last century ensured a steady supply of workers for the apparel industry; from the very beginning, Mexican women were employed in nearly all positions in the industry.[8] By contrast, the expansion of garment production in Miami was due to an unprecedented influx of exiles ejected by a unique political event. Cubans working in the Florida apparel industry arrived in the United States as refugees under a protected and relatively privileged status. Exile was filled with uncertainty and the possibility of dislocation but not, as in the case of undocumented Mexican aliens, with the probability of harassment, detention, and deportation.

Mexican and Cuban workers differ strikingly in social class. For more than a century, the majority of Mexican immigrants have had a markedly proletarian background. Until the 1970s, the majority had rural roots, although in more recent times there has been a growing number of urban immigrants.[9] In sharp contrast, Cuban waves of migration have included a larger proportion of professionals, mid-level service providers, and various types of entrepreneurs ranging from those with previous experience in large companies to those qualified to start small family enterprises. Entrepreneurial experience among Cubans and reliance on their own ethnic networks accounts, to a large extent, for Cuban success in business formation and appropriation in Miami.[10] Thus, while Mexican migration has been characterized by relative homogeneity regarding class background, Cuban exile resulted in the transposition of an almost intact class structure containing investors and professionals as well as unskilled, semi skilled, and skilled workers.

In addition to disparate class compositions, the two groups differ in the degree of their homogeneity by place of birth. Besides the sizable undocumented contingent mentioned earlier, the Los Angeles garment industry also employs U.S.-born citizens of Mexican heritage. First-hand reports and anecdotal evidence indicate that the fragmentation between "Chicana" and

"Mexicana" workers causes an unresolved tension and animosity within the labor force. Cubans, on the other hand, were a highly cohesive population until the early 1980s, when the arrival of the so-called "Marielitos" resulted in a potentially disruptive polarization of the community.

Perhaps the most important difference between Mexicans in Los Angeles and Cubans in Florida is related to their distinctive labor market insertion patterns. Historically, Mexicans have arrived in the U.S. labor market in a highly individuated and dispersed manner. As a result, they have been extremely dependent on labor market supply and demand forces entirely beyond their control. Their working-class background and stigma attached to their frequent undocumented status has accentuated even further their vulnerability vis-à-vis employers. By contrast, Cubans have been able to consolidate an economic enclave formed by immigrant businesses, which hire workers of a common cultural and national background. The economic enclave partly operates as a buffer zone separating and often shielding members of the same ethnic group from the market forces at work in the larger society. The existence of an economic enclave does not preclude exploitation on the basis of class; indeed, it is predicated upon the existence of a highly diversified immigrant class structure. However, commonalities of culture, national background, and language between immigrant employers and workers can become a mechanism for collective improvement of income levels and standards of living. As a result, differences in labor market insertion patterns among Mexicans and Cubans have led to varying social profiles and a dissimilar potential for socioeconomic attainment.

THE WOMEN GARMENT WORKERS

These differences between the two Hispanic communities have led to important differences between the two groups of women who work in the garment industry. For Mexican women in Southern California, employment in garment production is the consequence of long-term economic need. Wives and daughters choose to work outside the home in order to meet the survival requirements of their families in the absence of satisfactory earnings by men. Some female heads of household join the labor force after losing male support through illness, death, and, more often, desertion. In many of these instances, women opt for industrial homework in order to reconcile child care and the need for wage employment. They are particularly vulnerable members of an economically marginal ethnic group.

By contrast, Cuban women who arrived in Southern Florida during the 1960s saw jobs in garment assembly as an opportunity to recover or attain middle-class status. The consolidation of an economic enclave in Miami, which accounts for much of the prosperity of Cubans, was largely dependent upon the incorporation of women into the labor force. While they toiled in factories, men entered business or were self-employed. Their vulnerability was tempered by shared goals of upward mobility in a foreign country.

Despite their different nationalities, migratory histories, and class backgrounds, Mexicans and Cubans share many perceptions and expectations. In both cases, patriarchal norms of reciprocity are favored; marriage, motherhood, and devotion to family are high priorities among women, while men are expected to hold authority, to be good providers, and to be loyal to their wives and children. However, the divergent economic and political conditions surrounding Mexicans in Southern California and Cubans in Southern Florida have had a differing impact upon each group's ability to uphold these values. Mexican women are often thrust into financial "autonomy" as a result of men's inability to fulfill their socially assigned role. Among Cubans, by contrast, men have been economically more successful. Indeed, ideological notions of patriarchal responsibility have served to maintain group cohesion; that offers women an advantage in getting and keeping jobs within the ethnic enclave.

Cuban and Mexican women both face barriers stemming from their subordination in the family and their status as low-skilled workers in highly competitive industries. Nevertheless, their varying class backgrounds and modes of incorporation into local labor markets entail distinctive political and socioeconomic effects. How women view their identities as women is especially affected. Among Mexican garment workers disillusion about the economic viability of men becomes a desire for individual emancipation, mobility, and financial independence as women. However, these ideals and ambitions for advancement are most often frustrated by poverty and the stigmas attached to ethnic and gender status.

Cuban women, on the other hand, tend to see no contradiction between personal fulfillment and a strong commitment to patriarchal standards. Their incorporation and subsequent withdrawal from the labor force are both influenced by their acceptance of hierarchical patterns of authority and the sexual division of labor. As in the case of Mexicans in Southern California, Cuban women's involvement in industrial homework is an option bridging domestic and income-generating needs. However, it differs in that homework among them was brought about by relative prosperity and expanding rather than diminishing options. Women's garment work at home does not contradict patriarchal ideals of women's place at the same time as it allows women to contribute to the economic success that confirms gender stratification.

The stories of particular women show the contrasts in how women in each of these two groups negotiate the links among household, gender, and employment arrangements. Some of the conditions surrounding Mexican home workers in Southern California are illustrated by the experience of Amelia Ruíz.[11] She was born into a family of six children in El Cerrito, Los Angeles County. Her mother, a descendant of Native American Indians, married at a young age the son of Mexican immigrants. Among Amelia's memories are the fragmentary stories of her paternal grandparents working in the fields and, occasionally, in canneries. Her father, however was not a stoop laborer but a trained upholsterer. Her mother was always a homemaker. Amelia grew up with a distinct sense of the contradictions that plague the relationships between men and women:

> All the while I was a child, I had this feeling that my parents weren't happy. My mother was smart but she could never make much of herself. Her parents taught her that the fate of woman is to be a wife and mother; they advised her to find a good man and marry him. And that she did. My father was reliable and I think he was faithful but he was also distant; he lived in his own world. He would come home and expect to be served hand and foot. My mother would wait on him but she was always angry about it. I never took marriage for granted.

After getting her high school diploma, Amelia found odd jobs in all the predictable places: as a counter clerk in a dress shop, as a cashier in a fast-food establishment, and as a waitress in two restaurants. When she was 20, she met Miguel—Mike as he was known outside the barrio. He was a consummate survivor, having worked in the construction field, as a truck driver, and even as an English as a Second Language instructor. Despite her misgivings about marriage, Amelia was struck by Mike's penchant for adventure.

> He was different from the men in my family. He loved fun and was said to have had many women. He was a challenge. We were married when I was 21 and he 25. For a while I kept my job but when I became pregnant, Miguel didn't want me to work any more. Two more children followed and then, little by little, Miguel became abusive. He wanted to have total authority over me and the children. He said a man should know how to take care of a family and get respect, but it was hard to take him seriously when he kept changing jobs and when the money he brought home was barely enough to keep ends together.

After the birth of her second child, Amelia started work at Shirley's, a women's wear factory in the area. Miguel was opposed to the idea. For Amelia, work outside the home was an evident need prompted by financial stress. At first, it was also a means to escape growing disenchantment:

> I saw myself turning into my mother and I started thinking that to be free of men was best for women. Maybe if Miguel had had a better job, maybe if he had kept the one he had, things would have been different, but he didn't. . . . We started drifting apart.

Tension at home mounted over the following months. Amelia had worked at Shirley's for almost a year when, one late afternoon after collecting the three children from her parents' house, she returned to an empty home. She knew, as soon as she stepped inside, that something was amiss. In muted shock, she confirmed the obvious: Miguel had left, taking with him all personal possessions; even the wedding picture in the living room had been removed. No explanations had been left behind. Amelia was then 28 years of age, alone, and the mother of three small children.

As a result of these changes, employment became even more desirable, but the difficulty of reconciling home responsibilities with wage work persisted. Amelia was well regarded at Shirley's, and her condition struck a sympathetic chord among the other factory women. In a casual conversation, her supervisor described how other women were leasing industrial sewing machines from the local Singer distributor and were doing piecework at home. By combining factory work and home assembly, she could earn more money without further neglecting the children. Mr. Driscoll, Shirley's owner and general manager, made regular use of home workers, most of whom were former employees. That had allowed him to retain a stable core of about 20 factory seamstresses and to depend on approximately 10 home workers during peak seasons.

Between 1979, the year of her desertion, and 1985, when I met her, Amelia had struggled hard, working most of the time and making some progress. Her combined earnings before taxes fluctuated between $950 and $1,150 a month. Almost half of her income went to rent for the two-bedroom apartment which she shared with the children. She was in debt and used to working at least 12 hours a day. On the other hand, she had bought a double-needle sewing machine and was thinking of leasing another one to share additional sewing with a neighbor. She had high hopes:

> Maybe some day I'll have my own business; I'll be a liberated woman . . . I won't have to take orders from a man. Maybe Miguel did me a favor when he left after all. . . .

With understandable variations, Amelia's life history is shared by many garment workers in Southern California. Three aspects are salient in this experience. First, marriage and a stable family life are perceived as desirable goals which are, nonetheless, fraught with ambivalent feelings and burdensome responsibilities.

Second, tensions between men and women result from contradictions between the intent to fulfill gender definitions and the absence of the economic base necessary for their implementation. The very definition of manhood includes the right to hold authority and power over wives and children, as well as the responsibility of providing adequately for them. The difficulties in implementing those goals in the Mexican communities I studied are felt equally by men and women but expressed differently by each. Bent on restoring their power, men attempt to control women in abusive ways. Women often resist their husbands' arbitrary or unrealistic impositions. Both reactions are eminently political phenomena.

Third, personal conflict regarding the proper behavior of men and women may be tempered by negotiation. It can also result in the breach of established agreements, as in the case of separation or divorce. Both paths are related to the construction of alternative discourses and the redefinition of gender roles. Women may seek personal emancipation, driven partly by economic need and partly by dissatisfaction with men's performance as providers. In general, individuals talk about economic and political conflict as a personal matter occurring in their own homes. Broader contextual factors are less commonly discussed.

The absence of economic underpinnings for the implementation of patriarchal standards may bring about more equitable exchanges between men and women, and may stimulate women's search for individual well-being and personal autonomy as women. However, in the case at hand, such ideals remain elusive. Mexican garment workers, especially those who are heads of households, face great disadvantages in the labor market. They are targeted for jobs that offer the lowest wages paid to industrial workers in the United States; they also have among the lowest unionization rates in the country. Ironically, the breakdown of patriarchal norms in the household draws from labor market segmentation that reproduces patriarchal (and ethnic) stratification.

Experiences like the ones related are also found among Cuban and Central American women in Miami. However, a larger proportion have had a different trajectory. Elvira Gómez's life in the U.S. is a case in point. She was 34 when she arrived in Miami with her four children, ages three to twelve. The year was 1961.

> Leaving Havana was the most painful thing that ever happened to us. We loved our country. We would have never left willingly. Cuba was not like Mexico: we didn't have immigrants in large numbers. But Castro betrayed us and we had to join the exodus. We became exiles. My husband left Cuba three months before I did and there were moments when I doubted I would ever see him again. Then, after we got together, we realized we would have to forge ahead without looking back.
>
> We lost everything. Even my mother's china had to be left behind. We arrived in this country as they say, "covering our nakedness with our bare hands" (una mano delante y otra detrás). My husband had had a good position in a bank. To think that he would have to take any old job in Miami was more than I could take; a man of his stature having to beg for a job in a hotel or in a factory? It wasn't right!

Elvira had worked briefly before her marriage as a secretary. As a middle-class wife and mother, she was used to hiring at least one maid. Coming to the United States changed all that:

> Something had to be done to keep the family together. So I looked around and finally found a job in a shirt factory in Hialeah. Manolo (her husband) joined a childhood friend and got a loan to start an export-import business. All the time they were building the firm, I was sewing. There were times when we wouldn't have been able to pay the bills without the money I brought in.

Elvira's experience was shared by thousands of women in Miami. Among the first waves of Cuban refugees there were many who worked tirelessly to raise the standards of living of their families to the same levels or higher than those they had been familiar with in their country of origin. The consolidation of an ethnic enclave allowed many Cuban men to become entrepreneurs. While their wives found unskilled and semiskilled jobs, they became businessmen. Eventually, they purchased homes, put their children through school, and achieved comfort. At that point, many Cuban men pressed their wives to stop working outside of the home; they had only allowed them to have a job, in the first place, out of economic necessity. In the words of a prominent manufacturer in the area:

> You have to understand that Cuban workers were willing to do anything to survive. When they became prosperous, the women saw the advantage of staying at home and still earn additional income. Because they had the skill, owners couldn't take them for granted. Eventually, owners couldn't get operators anymore. The most skilled would tell a manager "my husband doesn't let me work out of the home." This was a worker's initiative based on the values of the culture. I would put ads in the paper and forty people would call and everyone would say "I only do homework." That's how we got this problem of the labor shortages. The industry was dying; we wouldn't have survived without the arrival of the Haitians and the Central Americans.

This discussion partly shows that decisions made at the level of the household can remove workers, actively sought and preferred by employers, from the marketplace. This, in turn, can threaten certain types of production. In those cases, loyalty to familial values can mitigate against the interests of capitalist firms. Interviews with Cuban women involved in homework confirm the general accuracy of this interpretation. After leaving factory employment, many put their experience to good use by becoming subcontractors and employing neighbors or friends. They also transformed so-called "Florida rooms" (the covered porches in their houses) into sewing shops. It was in one of them that Elvira Gómez was first interviewed. In her case, working outside the home was justified only as a way to maintain the integrity of her family and as a means to support her husband's early incursions into the business world:

> For many long years I worked in the factory but when things got better financially, Manolo asked me to quit the job. He felt bad that I couldn't be at home all the time with the children. But it had to be done. There's no reason for women not to earn a living when it's necessary; they should have as many opportunities and responsibilities as men. But I also tell my daughters that the strength of a family rests on the intelligence and work of women. It is foolish to give up your place as a mother and a wife only to go take orders from men who aren't even part of your family. What's so liberated about that? It is better to see your husband succeed and to know you have supported one another.

Perhaps the most important point here is the unambiguous acceptance of patriarchal mores as a legitimate guideline for the behavior of men and women. Exile did not eliminate these values; rather, it extended them in telling ways. The high labor force participation rates of Cuban women in the United States have been mentioned before. Yet, it should be remembered that, prior to their migration, only a small number of Cuban women had worked outside the home for any length of time. It was the need to maintain the integrity of their families and to achieve class-related ambitions that precipitated their entrance into the labor force of a foreign country.

In descriptions of their experience in exile, Cuban women often make clear that part of the motivation in their search for jobs was the preservation of known definitions of manhood and womanhood. Whereas Mexican women worked as a response to what they saw as a failure of patriarchal arrangements, Cuban women worked in the name of dedication to their husbands and children, and in order to preserve the status and authority of the former. Husbands gave them "permission" to work outside the home, and only as a result of necessity and temporary economic strife. In the same vein, it was a ritual yielding to masculine privilege that led women to abandon factory employment. Conversely, men "felt bad" that their wives had to work for a wage and welcomed the opportunity to remove them from the marketplace when economic conditions improved.

As with Mexicans in Southern California, Cuban women in Miami earned low wages in low-and semiskilled jobs. They too worked in environments devoid of the benefits derived from unionization. Nevertheless, the outcome of their experience as well as the perceptions are markedly different. Many Cuban women interpret their subordination at home as part of a viable option ensuring economic and emotional benefits. They are bewildered by feminist goals of equality and fulfillment in the job market. Yet, the same women have had among the highest rates of participation in the U.S. labor force.

CONCLUSIONS

For Mexican women in Southern California, proletarianization is related to a high number of female-headed households, as well as households where the earnings provided by women are indispensable for maintaining standards of modest subsistence. In contrast, Cuban women's employment in Southern Florida was a strategy for raising standards of living in a new environment. These contrasts in the relationship between households and the labor market occurred despite shared values regarding the family among Mexicans and Cubans. Both groups partake of similar mores regarding the roles of men and women; nevertheless, their actual experience has differed significantly. Contrasting features of class, educational background, and immigration history have created divergent gender and family dilemmas for each group.

This analysis underscores the impact of class on gender. Definitions of manhood and womanhood are implicated in the very process of class formation. At the same time, the norms of reciprocity sanctioned by patriarchal ideologies can operate as a form of social adhesive consolidating class membership. For poor men and women, the issue is not only the presence of the sexual division of labor and the persistence of patriarchal ideologies but the difficulties of upholding either.

Thus, too, the meaning of women's participation in the labor force remains plagued by paradox. For Mexican women in Southern California, paid employment responds to and increases women's desires for greater personal autonomy and financial independence. Ideally, this should have a favorable impact upon women's capacity to negotiate an equitable position within their homes and in the labor market. Yet these women's search for paid employment is most often the consequence of severe economic need; it expresses vulnerability, not strength within homes and in the marketplace. Indeed, in some cases, women's entry into the labor force signals the collapse of reciprocal exchanges between men and women. Women deserted by their husbands are generally too economically marginal to translate their goals of gender equality and autonomy into socially powerful arrangements. Conversely, Cuban women in Southern Florida have more economic power, but this only strengthens their allegiance to patriarchal standards. The conjugal "partnership for survival" Elvira Gómez describes is not predicated on the existence of a just social world, but rather an ideological universe entailing differentiated and stratified benefits and obligations for men and women.

NOTES

A different version of this essay appears in Women, Work, and Politics, *Louise Tilly and Patricia Guerin, eds. (New York: Russell Sage Foundation, 1990).*

1. This essay is based on findings from the "Collaborative Study of Hispanic Women in Garment and Electronics Industries" supported by the Ford Foundation under grant number 870 1149. Initial funding for the same project was also provided by the Tinker Foundation. The author gratefully acknowledges the continued encouragement of Dr. William Díaz from the Ford Foundation.

2. Joan W. Scott, "Gender: A Useful Category of Historical Analysis," *The American Historical Review,* 91, 5 (1986): 1053–75; Felicity Edholm, "Conceptualizing Women," *Critique of Anthropology,* 3, 9/10: 101–30. For a relevant analysis of class, see Michael Buroway, *The Politics of Production* (London: New Left Books, 1985).

3. M. Patricia Fernández Kelly and Anna M. García, "Informalization at the Core: Hispanic Women, Homework and the Advanced Capitalist State," in *The Informal Economy: Comparative Studies in Advanced and Third World Societies,* eds. Alejandro Portes, Manuel Castels, and Lauren Benton (Baltimore: Johns Hopkins University Press, 1989).

4. Rayna Rapp, "Family and Class in Contemporary America: Notes Toward an Understanding of Ideology," in *Rethinking the Family,* eds. Barrie Thorne and Marilyn Yalom (New York: Longman, 1982). See also Eli Zaretsky, *Capitalism, The Family and Personal Life* (New York: Harper and Row, 1976).

5. Frank D. Bean and Marta Tienda, *The Hispanic Population of the United States* (New York: Russell Sage Foundation, 1987). There are almost twenty million Hispanics in the United States, that is, 14.6% of the total population.

6. Approximately 75% and 67% of operatives in Los Angeles and Miami apparel firms are Mexican and Cuban women, respectively.

7. Note 54.2% of native-born and 47.5% of foreign-born Mexican women were employed outside the home in 1980. The equivalent figure for the mostly foreign-born Cuban women was almost 65%. Non-Hispanic white women's labor force participation in 1980 was assessed at 57.9% (U.S. Census of Population, 1980).

8. Peter S. Taylor, "Mexican Women in Los Angeles Industry in 1928," *Aztlán: International Journal of Chicano Studies Research,* 11, 1 (Spring, 1980): 99–129.

9. Alejandro Portes and Robert L. Bach, *Latin journey: Cuban and Mexican Immigrants in the United States* (Berkeley: University of California Press, 1985), 67.

10. Alejandro Portes, "The Social Origins of the Cuban Enclave Economy of Miami," *Pacific Sociological Review,* Special Issue on the Ethnic Economy. 30, 4 (October, 1987): 340–372. See also Lisandro Perez, "Immigrant Economic Adjustment and Family Organization: The Cuban Success Story Reexamined," *International Migration Review,* 20(1986):4–20.

11. The following descriptions are chosen from a sample of 25 Mexican and 10 Cuban women garment workers interviewed in Los Angeles and Miami Countries. The names of people interviewed, and some identifying characteristics, have been changed.

35

Moving Up with Kin and Community

Upward Social Mobility for Black and White Women

ELIZABETH HIGGINBOTHAM
LYNN WEBER

. . . When women and people of color experience upward mobility in America, they scale steep structural as well as psychological barriers. The long process of moving from a working-class family of origin to the professional-managerial class is full of twists and turns: choices made with varying degrees of information and varying options; critical junctures faced with support and encouragement or disinterest, rejection, or active discouragement; and interpersonal relationships in which basic understandings are continuously negotiated and renegotiated. It is a fascinating process that profoundly shapes the lives of those who experience it, as well as the lives of those around them. Social mobility is also a process engulfed in myth. One need only pick up any newspaper or turn on the television to see that the myth of upward mobility remains firmly entrenched in American culture: With hard work, talent, determination, and some luck, just about anyone can "make it." . . .

The image of the isolated and detached experience of mobility that we have inherited from past scholarship is problematic for anyone seeking to understand the process for women or people of color. Twenty years of scholarship in the study of both race and gender has taught us the importance of interpersonal attachments to the lives of women and a commitment to racial uplift among people of color . . .

. . . Lacking wealth, the greatest gift a Black family has been able to give to its children has been the motivation and skills to succeed in school. Aspirations for college attendance and professional positions are stressed as *family* goals, and the entire family may make sacrifices and provide support . . . Black women have long seen the activist potential of education and have sought it as a cornerstone of community development—a means of uplifting the race. When women of color or White women are put at the center of the analysis of upward mobility, it is clear that different questions will be raised about social mobility and different descriptions of the process will ensue. . . .

RESEARCH DESIGN

These data are from a study of full-time employed middle-class women in the Memphis metropolitan area. This research is designed to explore the processes of upward social mobility for Black and White women

---

Elizabeth Higginbotham and Lynn Weber, "Moving Up with Kin and Community: Upward Social Mobility for Black and White Women," from *Gender & Society*, Volume 6/1992, p. 416–440.

by examining differences between women professionals, managers, and administrators who are from working- and middle-class backgrounds—that is, upwardly mobile and middle-class stable women. In this way, we isolate subjective processes shared among women who have been upwardly mobile from those common to women who have reproduced their family's professional-managerial class standing. Likewise, we identify common experiences in the attainment process that are shared by women of the same race, be they upwardly mobile or stable middle class. Finally, we specify some ways in which the attainment process is unique for each race-class group . . .

. . . We rely on a model of social class basically derived from the work of Poulantzas (1974), Braverman (1974), Ehrenreich and Ehrenreich (1979), and elaborated in Vanneman and Cannon (1987). These works explicate a basic distinction between social class and social status. Classes represent bounded categories of the population, groups set in a relation of opposition to one another by their roles in the capitalist system. The middle class, or professional-managerial class, is set off from the working class by the power and control it exerts over workers in three realms: economic (power through ownership), political (power through direct supervisory authority), and ideological (power to plan and organize work; Poulantzas 1974; Vanneman and Cannon 1987).

In contrast, education, prestige, and income represent social statuses—hierarchically structured relative rankings along a ladder of economic success and social prestige. Positions along these dimensions are not established by social relations of dominance and subordination but, rather, as rankings on scales representing resources and desirability. In some respects, they represent both the justification for power differentials vested in classes and the rewards for the role that the middle class plays in controlling labor.

Our interest is in the process of upward social class mobility, moving from a working-class family of origin to a middle-class destination—from a position of working-class subordination to a position of control over the working class. Lacking inherited wealth or other resources, those working-class people who attain middle-class standing do so primarily by obtaining a college education and entering a professional, managerial, or administrative occupation. Thus we examine carefully the process of educational attainment not as evidence of middle-class standing but as a necessary part of the mobility process for most working-class people.

Likewise, occupation alone does not define the middle class, but professional, managerial, and administrative occupations capture many of the supervisory and ideologically based positions whose function is to control workers' lives. Consequently, we defined subjects as *middle class* by virtue of their employment in either a professional, managerial, or administrative occupation. . . . Classification of subjects as either professional or managerial-administrative was made on the basis of the designation of occupations in the U.S. Bureau of the Census's (1983) "Detailed Population Characteristics: Tennessee." Managerial occupations were defined as those in the census categories of managers and administrators; professionals were defined as those occupations in the professional category, excluding technicians, whom Braverman (1974) contends are working class.

Upwardly mobile women were defined as those women raised in families where neither parent was employed as a professional, manager, or administrator. Typical occupations for working-class fathers were postal clerk, craftsman, semiskilled manufacturing worker, janitor, and laborer. Some working-class mothers had clerical and sales positions, but many of the Black mothers also worked as private household workers. *Middle-class stable* women were defined as those women raised in families where *either* parent was employed as a professional, manager, or administrator. Typical occupations of middle-class parents were social worker, teacher, and school administrator as well as high-status professionals such as attorneys, physicians, and dentists. . . .

FAMILY EXPECTATIONS FOR EDUCATIONAL ATTAINMENT

Four questions assess the expectations and support among family members for the educational attainment of the subjects. First, "Do you recall your father or mother stressing that you attain an education?" Yes was the response of 190 of the 200 women. Each of the women in this study had obtained a college degree, and many have graduate degrees. It is clear that for Black and White women, education was an important concern in their families. . . .

The comments of Laura Lee,[1] a 39-year-old Black woman who was raised middle class, were typical:

> Going to school, that was never a discussable issue. Just like you were born to live and die, you were going to go to school. You were going to prepare yourself to do something.

It should be noted, however, that only 86 percent of the White working-class women answered yes, compared to 98 percent of all other groups. Although this difference is small, it foreshadows a pattern where White women raised in working-class families received the least support and encouragement for educational and career attainment.

"When you were growing up, how far did your father expect you to go in school?" While most fathers expected college attendance from their daughters, differences also exist by class of origin. Only 70 percent of the working-class fathers, both Black and White, expected their daughters to attend college. In contrast, 94 percent of the Black middle-class and 88 percent of the White middle-class women's fathers had college expectations for their daughters.

When asked the same question about mother's expectations, 88 percent to 92 percent of each group's mothers expected their daughters to get a college education, except the White working-class women, for whom only 66 percent of mothers held such expectations. In short, only among the White working-class women did a fairly substantial proportion (about one-third) of both mothers and fathers expect less than a college education from their daughters. About 30 percent of Black working-class fathers held lower expectations for their daughters, but not the mothers; virtually all middle-class parents expected a college education for their daughters.

Sara Marx is a White, 33-year-old director of counseling raised in a rural working-class family. She is among those whose parents did not expect a college education for her. She was vague about the roots of attending college:

> It seems like we had a guest speaker who talked to us. Maybe before our exams somebody talked to us. I really can't put my finger on anything. I don't know where the information came from exactly.

"Who provided emotional support for you to make the transition from high school to college?" While 86 percent of the Black middle-class women indicated that family provided that support, 70 percent of the White middle-class, 64 percent of the Black working class, and only 56 percent of the White working class received emotional support from family.

"Who paid your college tuition and fees?" Beyond emotional support, financial support is critical to college attendance. There are clear class differences in financial support for college. Roughly 90 percent of the middle-class respondents and only 56 percent and 62 percent of the Black and White working-class women, respectively, were financially supported by their families. These data also suggest that working-class parents were less able to give emotional or financial support for college than they were to hold out the expectation that their daughters should attend.

FAMILY EXPECTATIONS FOR OCCUPATION OR CAREER

When asked, "Do you recall your father or mother stressing that you should have an occupation to succeed in life?" racial differences appear: Ninety-four percent of all Black respondents said yes. In the words of Julie Bird, a Black woman raised-middle-class junior high school teacher.

> My father would always say, "You see how good I'm doing? Each generation should do more than the generation before." He expects me to accomplish more than he has.

Ann Right, a 36-year-old Black attorney whose father was a janitor, said:

> They wanted me to have a better life than they had. For all of us. And that's why they emphasized education and emphasized working relationships and how you get along with people and that kind of thing.

Ruby James, a Black teacher from a working-class family, said:

> They expected me to have a good-paying job and to have a family and be married. Go to work every day. Buy a home. That's about it. Be happy.

In contrast, only 70 percent of the White middle-class and 56 percent of the White working-class women indicated that their parents stressed that an occupation was needed for success. Nina Pentel, a 26-year-old white medical social worker, expressed a common response: "They said 'You're going to get married but get a degree, you never know what's going to happen to you.' They were pretty laid back about goals."

When the question focuses on a career rather than an occupation, the family encouragement is lower and differences were not significant, but similar patterns emerged. We asked respondents, "Who, if anyone, encouraged you to think about a career?" Among Black respondents, 60 percent of the middle-class and 56 percent of the working-class women answered that family encouraged them. Only 40 percent of the White working-class women indicated that their family encouraged them in their thinking about a career, while 52 percent of the White middle-class women did so. . . .

When working-class White women seek to be mobile through their own attainments, they face conflicts. Their parents encourage educational attainment, but when young women develop professional career goals, these same parents sometimes become ambivalent. This was the case with Elizabeth Marlow, who is currently a public interest attorney—a position her parents never intended her to hold. She described her parents' traditional expectations and their reluctance to support her career goals fully.

> My parents assumed that I would go college and meet some nice man and finish, but not necessarily work after. I would be a good mother for my children. I don't think that they ever thought I would go to law school. Their attitude about my interest in law school was, "You can do it if you want to, but we don't think it is a particularly practical thing for a woman to do."

Elizabeth is married and has three children, but she is not the traditional housewife of her parents' dreams. She received more support outside the family for her chosen lifestyle.

Although Black families are indeed more likely than white families to encourage their daughters to prepare for careers, like White families, they frequently steer them toward highly visible traditionally female occupations, such as teacher, nurse, and social worker. Thus many mobile Black women are directed toward the same gender-segregated occupations as White women. . . .

MARRIAGE

Although working-class families may encourage daughters to marry, they recognize the need for working-class women to contribute to family income or to support themselves economically. To achieve these aims, many working-class girls are encouraged to pursue an education as preparation for work in gender-segregated occupations. Work in these fields presumably allows women to keep marriage, family, and child rearing as life goals while contributing to the family income and to have "something to fall back on" if the marriage does not work out. This interplay among marriage, education, financial need, and class mobility is complex (Joslin 1979).

We asked, "Do you recall your mother or father emphasizing that marriage should be your primary life goal?" While the majority of all respondents did not get the message that marriage was the *primary* life goal, Black and White women's parents clearly saw this differently. Virtually no Black parents stressed marriage as the primary life goal (6 percent of the working class and 4 percent of the middle class), but significantly more White parents did (22 percent of the working class and 18 percent of the middle class).

Some White women said their families expressed active opposition to marriage, such as Clare Baron, a raised-working-class nursing supervisor, who said, "My mother always said, 'Don't get married and don't have children!'"

More common responses recognized the fragility of marriage and the need to support oneself. For example,

Alice Page, a 31-year-old White raised-middle-class librarian, put it this way:

> I feel like I am really part of a generation that for the first time is thinking, "I don't want to have to depend on somebody to take care of me because what if they say they are going to take care of me and then they are not there? They die, or they leave me or whatever." I feel very much that I've got to be able to support myself and I don't know that single women in other eras have had to deal with that to the same degree.

While White working-class women are often raised to prepare for work roles so that they can contribute to family income and, if necessary, support themselves, Black women face a different reality. Unlike White women, Black women are typically socialized to view marriage separately from economic security, because it is not expected that marriage will ever remove them from the labor market. As a result, Black families socialize all their children—girls and boys—for self-sufficiency (Clark 1986; Higginbotham and Cannon 1988). . . .

. . . Fairly substantial numbers of each group had never married by the time of the interview, ranging from 20 percent of the White working-class to 34 percent of the Black working-class and White middle-class respondents. Some of the women were pleased with their singlehood, like Alice Page, who said:

> I am single by choice. That is how I see myself. I have purposely avoided getting into any kind of romantic situation with men. I have enjoyed going out but never wanted to get serious. If anyone wants to get serious, I quit going out with him.

Other women expressed disappointment and some shock that they were not yet married. When asked about her feeling about being single, Sally Ford, a 32-year-old White manager, said:

> That's what I always wanted to do: to be married and have children. To me, that is the ideal. I want a happy, good marriage with children. I do not like being single at all. It is very, very lonesome. I don't see any advantages to being single. None!

SUBJECTIVE SENSE OF DEBT TO KIN AND FRIENDS

McAdoo (1978) reports that upwardly mobile Black Americans receive more requests to share resources from their working-class kin than do middle-class Black Americans. Many mobile Black Americans feel a "social debt" because their families aided them in the mobility process and provided emotional support. When we asked the White women in the study the following question: "Generally, do you feel you owe a lot for the help given to you by your family and relatives?" many were perplexed and asked what the question meant. In contrast, both the working- and middle-class Black women tended to respond immediately that they felt a sense of obligation to family and friends in return for the support they had received. Black women, from both the working class and the middle class, expressed the strongest sense of debt to family, with 86 percent and 74 percent, respectively, so indicating. White working-class women were least likely to feel that they owed family (46 percent), while 68 percent of white middle-class women so indicated. In short, upwardly mobile Black women were almost twice as likely as upwardly mobile White women to express a sense of debt to family.

Linda Brown, an upwardly mobile Black women, gave a typical response, "Yes, they are there when you need them." Similar were the words of Jean Marsh, "Yes, because they have been supportive. They're dependable. If I need them I can depend upon them."

One of the most significant ways in which Black working-class families aided their daughters and left them with a sense of debt related to care for their children. Dawn March expressed it thus:

> They have been there more so during my adult years than a lot of other families that I know about. My mother kept all of my children until they were old enough to go to day care. And she not only kept them, she'd give them a bath for me during the daytime and feed them before I got home from work. Very, very supportive people. So, I really would say I owe them for that.

Carole Washington, an upwardly mobile Black woman occupational therapist, also felt she owed her family. She reported:

> I know the struggle that my parents have had to get me where I am. I know the energy they no longer have to put into the rest of the family even though they want to put it there and they're willing. I feel it is my responsibility to give back some of that energy they have given to me. It's self-directed, not required.

White working-class women, in contrast, were unlikely to feel a sense of debt and expressed their feelings in similar ways. Irma Cox, part owner of a computer business, said, "I am appreciative of the values my parents instilled in me. But I for the most part feel like I have done it on my own." Carey Mink, a 35-year-old psychiatric social worker, said, "No, they pointed me in a direction and they were supportive, but I've done a lot of the work myself." Debra Beck, a judge, responded, "No, I feel that I've gotten most places on my own." . . .

COMMITMENT TO COMMUNITY

The mainstream "model of community stresses the rights of individuals to make decisions in their own self interest, regardless of the impact on the larger society" (Collins 1990, 52). This model may explain relations to community of origin for mobile White males but cannot be generalized to other racial and gender groups. In the context of well-recognized structures of racial oppression, America's racial-ethnic communities develop collective survival strategies that contrast with the individualism of the dominant culture but ensure the community's survival (Collins 1990, McAdoo 1978; Stack 1974; Valentine 1978). McAdoo (1978) argues that Black people have *only* been able to advance in education and attain higher status and higher paying jobs with the support of the wider Black community, teachers in segregated schools, extended family networks, and Black mentors already in those positions. This widespread community involvement enables mobile people of color to confront and challenge racist obstacles in credentialing institutions, and it distinguishes the mobility process in racial-ethnic communities from mobility in the dominant culture. For example, Lou Nelson, now a librarian, described the support she felt in her southern segregated inner-city school. She said:

> There was a closeness between people and that had a lot to do with neighborhood schools. I went to Tubman High School with people that lived in the Tubman area. I think that there was a bond, a bond between parents, the PTA . . . I think that it was just that everybody felt that everybody knew everybody. And that was special.

Family and community involvement and support in the mobility process means that many Black professionals and managers continue to feel linked to their communities of origin. Lillian King, a high-ranking city official who was raised working class, discussed her current commitment to the Black community. She said:

> Because I have more opportunities, I've got an obligation to give more back and to set a positive example for Black people and especially for Black women. I think we've got to do a tremendous job in building self-esteem and giving people the desire to achieve.

Judith Moore is a 34-year-old single parent employed as a health investigator. She has been able to maintain her connection with her community, and that is a source of pride.

> I'm proud that I still have a sense of who I am in terms of Black people. That's very important to me. No matter how much education or professional status I get, I do not want to lose touch with where I've come from. I think that you need to look back and that kind of pushes you forward. I think the degree and other things can make you lose sight of that, especially us Black folks, but I'm glad that I haven't and I try to teach that [commitment] to my son.

For some Black women, their mobility has enabled them to give to an even broader community. This is the case with Sammi Lewis, a raised-working-class woman who is a director of a social service agency.

She said, "I owe a responsibility to the entire community, and not to any particular group." . . .

CROSSING THE COLOR LINE

Mobility for people of color is complex because in addition to crossing class lines, mobility often means crossing racial and cultural ones as well. Since the 1960s, people of color have increasingly attended either integrated or predominantly White schools. Only mobile White ethnics have a comparable experience of simultaneously crossing class and cultural barriers, yet even this experience is qualitatively different from that of Black and other people of color. White ethnicity can be practically invisible to White middle-class school peers and co-workers, but people of color are more visible and are subjected to harsher treatment. Our research indicates that no matter when people of color first encounter integrated or predominantly White settings, it is always a shock. The experience of racial exclusion cannot prepare people of color to deal with the racism in daily face-to-face encounters with White people.

For example, Lynn Johnson was in the first cohort of Black students at Regional College, a small private college in Memphis. The self-confidence and stamina Lynn developed in her supportive segregated high school helped her withstand the racism she faced as the first female and the first Black to graduate in economics at Regional College. Lynn described her treatment:

> I would come into class and Dr. Simpson (the Economics professor) would alphabetically call the roll. When he came to my name, he would just jump over it. He would not ask me any questions, he would not do anything. I stayed in that class. I struggled through. When it was my turn, I'd start talking. He would say, "Johnson, I wasn't talking to you" [because he never said Miss Johnson]. I'd say, "That's all right, Dr. Simpson, it was my turn. I figured you just overlooked me. I'm just the littlest person in here. Wasn't that the right answer?" He would say, "Yes, that was the right answer." I drove him mad, I really did. He finally got used to me and started to help me.

In southern cities, where previous interaction between Black and White people followed a rigid code, adjustments were necessary on both sides. It was clear to Lynn Johnson and others that college faculty and students had to adapt to her small Black cohort at Regional College.

Wendy Jones attended a formerly predominantly White state university that had just merged with a formerly predominantly Black college. This new institution meant many adjustments for faculty and students. As a working-class person majoring in engineering, she had a rough transition. She recalled:

> I had never gone to school with White kids. I'd always gone to all Black schools all my life and the Black kids there [at the university] were snooty. Only one friend from high school went there and she flunked out. The courses were harder and all my teachers were men and White. Most of the kids were White. I was in classes where I'd be the only Black and woman. There were no similarities to grasp for. I had to adjust to being in that situation. In about a year I was comfortable where I could walk up to people in my class and have conversations.

For some Black people, their first significant interaction with White people did not come until graduate school. Janice Freeman described her experiences:

> I went to a Black high school, a Black college and then worked for a Black man who was a former teacher. Everything was comfortable until I had to go to State University for graduate school. I felt very insecure. I was thrown into an environment that was very different—during the 1960s and 1970s there was so much unrest anyway—so it was extremely difficult for me.

It was not in graduate school but on her first job as a social worker that Janice had to learn to work *with* White people. She said, "After I realized that I could hang in school, working at the social work agency allowed me to learn how to work *with* White people. I had never done that before and now I do it better than anybody."

Learning to live in a White world was an additional hurdle for all Black women in this age cohort. Previous generations of Black people were more likely to be educated in segregated colleges and to work within the confines of the established Black community. They taught in segregated schools, provided dental and medical care to the Black communities, and provided social services and other comforts to members of their own communities. They also lived in the Black community and worshiped on Sunday with many of the people they saw in different settings. As the comments of our respondents reveal, both Black and White people had to adjust to integrated settings, but it was more stressful for the newcomers.

SUMMARY AND CONCLUSIONS

Our major aim in this research was to reopen the study of the subjective experience of upward social mobility and to begin to incorporate race and gender into our vision of the process. In this exploratory work, we hope to raise issues and questions that will cast a new light on taken-for-granted assumptions about the process and the people who engage in it. The experiences of these women have certainly painted a different picture from the one we were left some twenty years ago. First and foremost, these women are not detached, isolated, or driven solely by career goals. Relationships with family of origin, partners, children, friends, and the wider community loom large in the way they envision and accomplish mobility and the way they sustain themselves as professional and managerial women.

Several of out findings suggest ways that race and gender shape the mobility process for baby boom Black and White women. Education was stressed as important in virtually all of the families of these women; however, they differed in how it was viewed and how much was desired. The upwardly mobile women, both Black and White, shared some obstacles to attainment. More mobile women had parents who never expected them to achieve a college education. They also received less emotional and financial support for college attendance from their families than the women in middle-class families received. Black women also faced the unique problem of crossing racial barriers simultaneously with class barriers.

There were fairly dramatic race differences in the messages that the Black and White women received from family about what their lives should be like as adults. Black women clearly received the message that they needed an occupation to succeed in life and that marriage was a secondary concern. Many Black women also expressed a sense that their mobility was connected to an entire racial uplift process, not merely an individual journey.

White upwardly mobile women received less clear messages. Only one-half of these women said that their parents stressed the need for an occupation to succeed, and 20 percent said that marriage was stressed as the primary life goal. The most common message seemed to suggest that an occupation was necessary, because marriage could not be counted on to provide economic survival. Having a career, on the other hand, could even be seen as detrimental to adult happiness.

Upward mobility is a process that requires sustained effort and emotional and cognitive, as well as financial, support. The legacy of the image of mobility that was built on the White male experience focuses on credentialing institutions, especially the schools, as the primary place where talent is recognized and support is given to ensure that the talented among the working class are mobile. Family and friends are virtually invisible in this portrayal of the mobility process.

Although there is a good deal of variation in the roles that family and friends play for these women, they are certainly not invisible in the process. Especially among many of the Black women, there is a sense that they owe a great debt to their families for the help they have received. Black upwardly mobile women were also much more likely to feel that they give more than they receive from kin. Once they have achieved professional managerial employment, the sense of debt combines with their greater access to resources to put them in the position of being asked to give and of giving more to both family and friends. Carrington (1980) identifies some potential mental health hazards of such a sense of debt in upwardly mobile Black women's lives.

White upwardly mobile women are less likely to feel indebted to kin and to feel that they have accomplished alone. Yet even among this group, connections to spouses and children played significant roles in defining how women were mobile, their goals, and their sense of satisfaction with their life in the middle class.

These data are suggestive of a mobility process that is motivated by a desire for personal, but also collective, gain and that is shaped by interpersonal commitments to family, partners and children, community, and the race. Social mobility involves competition, but also cooperation, community support, and personal obligations. Further research is needed to explore fully this new image of mobility and to examine the relevance of these issues for White male mobility as well.

NOTE

1. This and all the names used in this article are pseudonyms.

REFERENCES

Braverman, Harry. 1974. *Labor and monopoly capital.* New York: Monthly Review Press.

Carrington, Christine. 1980. Depression in Black women: A theoretical appraisal. In *The Black women,* edited by La Frances Rodgers Rose. Beverly Hills, CA: Sage.

Clark, Reginald. 1986. *Family life and school achievement.* Chicago: University of Chicago Press.

Collins, Patricia Hill. 1990. *Black feminist thought: knowledge, consciousness, and the politics of empowerment.* Boston: Routledge.

Ehrenreich, Barbara, and John Ehrenreich. 1979. The professional-managerial class. In *Between labor and capital,* edited by Pat Walker. Boston: South End Press.

Higginbotham, Elizabeth, and Lynn Weber Cannon. 1988. *Rethinking mobility: Towards a race and gender inclusive theory.* Research Paper no. 8. Center for Research on Women, Memphis State University.

Joslin, Daphne. 1979. Working-class daughters, middle-class wives: Social identity and self-esteem among women upwardly mobile through marriage. Ph.D. diss., New York University, New York.

McAdoo, Harriette Pipes. 1978. Factors related to stability in upwardly mobile Black families. *Journal of Marriage and the Family* 40:761–76.

Poulantzas, Nicos. 1974. *Classes in contemporary capitalism.* London: New Left Books.

U.S. Bureau of the Census. 1983. Detailed population characteristics: Tennessee. Census of the Population, 1980. Washington, DC: GPO.

Vanneman, Reeve, and Lynn Weber Cannon. 1987. *The American perception of class.* Philadelphia: Temple University Press.

36

What Do Low-Income Single Mothers Say about Marriage?

KATHRYN EDIN

When marriage rates among the poor plunged during the 1970s and 1980s, the American public began to blame welfare. During that time, an unmarried mother who had little or no income or assets could claim welfare until her youngest child aged out of the program (this was the case until 1996, when welfare became time-limited). If she were to marry, her access to welfare would be restricted. Up until the late 1980s, only about half of the states offered any benefits to married couples. By 1990, all states were required to offer welfare benefits to married couples with children who met certain income and eligibility criteria. Yet-these benefits were hard to claim because the husband's income and assets were counted in determining the family's ongoing eligibility for the program (all of his income if he was the children's father, and a portion of his income if he was not), and the couple had to prove the principal wage earner had a recent history of work. One study indicates that few welfare recipients understood these complex rules regarding marriage; they generally assumed that marrying would mean the loss of welfare, food stamp, and Medicaid benefits (Edin and Lein 1997).

Not surprisingly, the public viewed the program as one that discouraged the poor from marrying. The Personal Responsibility and Work Opportunity Reconciliation Act of 1996 (PRWORA) has many aims, but one is to increase the costs of non-marriage by decreasing the resources an unmarried mother can claim from the state (see Corbett 1998). To accomplish this goal, PRWORA mandates states to ensure that recipients comply with certain requirements and offers them new flexibility to go beyond these mandates and impose further requirements. At minimum, PRWORA requires that states limit cash benefit receipt to no more than five years in an adult recipient's lifetime. A second minimum requirement is that states must impose a 20-hour work requirement after two years of receipt. States can opt for other requirements such as school attendance for minor children and participation in "work-related activities" like job search or short-term training. Violations of these requirements can result in a full cut-off or a partial reduction of benefits (these are referred to as "sanctions"). These new time limits and participation requirements sharply limit (or make more costly) the resources that single mothers can claim from the state. Meanwhile, the welfare rolls have fallen to nearly half their early 1990s levels. Though some of the decline is a response to improving economic conditions, the decline is much greater than

Kathryn Edin, "What Do Low-Income Single Mothers Say About Marriage?" from *Social Problems,* Volume 47, Number 1, pp. 112–133.

the improvement in the economy would lead us to expect. Some scholars have claimed that the remainder is due to the "signaling effect" of welfare reform (e.g., that PRWORA has signaled to current and prospective clients that the rules have changed and that welfare is no longer an acceptable or feasible way of life), though there is little clear evidence in this regard.

. . . Yet despite this new world of welfare that confronts low-income adults, an analysis of ethnographic data from two cities suggests that the large majority of welfare recipients who are experiencing the changes with regard to welfare reform, are not planning on marrying in the near future. Furthermore, these recipients report that welfare reform has not changed their views on marriage. This is the case even though recipients said they believed welfare reform was "real" and would indeed be implemented (Edin, Scott, London, and Mazelis 1999).

. . . I utilize data drawn from in-depth, repeated ethnographic interviews with 292 low-income African American and white single mothers in three U.S. cities, to add qualitative grounding to our understanding of these trends. I seek to explicate the social role that marriage plays in the lives of low-income single mothers more fully. Drawing from these data, I show that though most low-income single mothers aspire to marriage, they believe that, in the short term, marriage usually entails more risks than potential rewards. Mothers say these risks may be worth taking if they can find the "right" man—and they define "rightness" in both economic and non-economic terms. They say they are willing, and even eager, to marry if the marriage represents an increase in their class standing and if, over a substantial period of time, their prospective husband's behavior indicates he won't beat them, abuse their children, refuse to share in household tasks, insist on making all the decisions, be sexually unfaithful, or abuse alcohol or drugs. However, many women also believe they can mitigate against these risks if they forgo marriage until the tasks of early child rearing are completed and they can concentrate more fully on labor market activities (e.g., holding a stable job). These women believe that by forgoing marriage until they can make regular and substantial contributions to the household economy, they can purchase the right to share more equally in economic and household decision-making within marriage. Additionally, an income of their own insures them against destitution if the marriage should fail. Mothers often say that they are hesitant to enter into marriage unless they have enough resources to legitimately threaten to leave the marriage if the previously mentioned behavioral criteria are violated. In this way, they believe they will have more control over a prospective husband's behavior and insurance against financial disaster should the marriage ultimately fail.

LITERATURE REVIEW

The median age at a first marriage is the highest it has been since the United States began keeping reliable statistics: twenty-four for women and twenty-six for men (U.S. Bureau of the Census 1991b). The propensity to remarry has also declined (Cherlin 1992). Furthermore, more women and men are choosing not to marry during the prime family-building years, and thus, more children are living with a single parent. Both non-marriage and single parenthood are particularly common among the poorest segments of American society (U.S. Bureau of the Census 1991a; Schoen and Owens, 1992:116). . . .

Both rates of entry into first marriage and remarriage are far lower for poor women than for their more advantaged counterparts (Bumpass and Sweet 1989). Once a woman has children, her chances of marrying are also lower than a childless woman's (Bennett, Bloom, and Craig 1991). There are also large differences by race (Bennett, Bloom and Craig 1990; 1989; Staples 1988). Yet it is poor women with children, a disproportionate share of whom are African Americans, on whom social welfare policy has focused.

Current theories that attempt to explain the decline in marriage have generally focused on four areas: women's economic independence; the inability of men (particularly minority men) to obtain stable family-wage employment; the role that welfare has played in creating marriage disincentives among the poor; and on what might be called cultural factors, such as the stalled revolution in gender roles (see Luker 1996: 158–160).

Many scholars argue that women's prospects for economic independence through work make it possible for them to raise their children apart from fathers who are wife beaters, child abusers, or otherwise difficult to live with (Becker 1981; South and Trent 1988; Teachman, Polonko, and Leìgh 1987; Trent and South 1989). In the classic version of this argument (Becker 1981), women who specialize in child rearing and household management, while their spouses specialize in market work, will find marriage very attractive. Women who combine such tasks with work will be less dependent on men to fulfill the bread-winning role. As wages rise, women's employment also rises, and the attractiveness of marriage declines. . . .

A second argument is that there is a shortage of marriageable men among some groups. Most work in this area has focused on African Americans, since it is among blacks that marriage rates are lowest. Some have addressed the question of whether this is due to an insufficient supply of marriageable black men, either because of rising unemployment and incarceration (Wilson 1996, 1987), declining earnings (Oppenheimer 1993), or sex-ratio imbalances (South and Lloyd 1992; Tucker and Mitchell-Kernan 1996). Most analyses show there is some evidence to support each of these variations on the male marriageable pool hypothesis, but the proportion of families headed by a single mother is simply much greater than this approach would predict (Fossett and Kielcolt 1993; Lichter, LeClere and McLaughlin 1991; South and Lloyd 1992).

Third, some have argued that the government may keep poor parents apart by making it more rewarding for the mother to collect welfare benefits than to marry a father with a menial job (Becker 1991; Murray 1984). According to this theory, welfare, rather than work, provides the economic independence that makes it possible, and even profitable, for mothers to eschew marriage. There is little evidence that out-of-wedlock birth rates are affected by either state variations in welfare levels or by changes in state benefits over time, though there is a modest negative effect for remarriage (Bane and Ellwood 1994; Hoffman 1997; Moffitt 1995).

Finally, some scholars argue that marriage decisions are influenced by what are generally termed "cultural" factors, even though these factors can sometimes be traced back to material realities. One argument points to the stalled revolution in sex roles. Although many men are earning less money than previously, and although wives are much more likely to work, few men truly share the household labor and childcare tasks (Hochschild 1989). Kristen Luker argues that when "men are increasingly less able to contribute financially to the household and when they show little willingness to do more work around the house, women will inevitably revise their thinking about marriage, work, and the raising of children" (1996:132). The gender gap in sex-role expectations has grown in recent decades. Scanzoni (1970:148) found that the divergence between husbands and wives over what constitutes legitimate male authority is widest at the lowest class levels. He also found that low status husbands exercised more power in conflict resolution than higher status husbands (1970:156). White women's views tend to be more egalitarian than white men's, both in terms of work and household duties. Black men and women both hold egalitarian views in terms of women's work, but black men lag behind their female counterparts (and white males) in their view of gender roles (Blee and Tickameyer 1995; Collins 1987). No study I know of estimates the strength of the relationship between the gender gap in sex role expectations and marriage rates. . . .

METHOD

I chose to study the social role of marriage among low-income single mothers for three reasons. First, they are the targets of recent legislation that attempts to encourage marriage. Second, the majority of low-income adult women, for whom the costs of non-marriage and child bearing are presumably the highest, are neither childless nor married (either because they never married or they divorced), and this trend appears to be growing stronger over time (U.S. Bureau of the Census 1993). . . . Third, it is most appropriate for the method I employ. Qualitative research designs typically focus on a single group or "case" and involve an in-depth investigation of the rich interplay of factors involved in some aspect of that group's shared experience (Becker 1992:209–210). . . .

These data consist of transcripts and field notes from in-depth, repeated, qualitative interviews with

292 low-income single mothers in three U.S. cities. In each city, my collaborators and I interviewed roughly 100 low-income single mothers: 87 in Charleston, South Carolina, 105 in Chicago, and 100 in Camden, New Jersey/Philadelphia, PA. In Chicago and Charleston, the sample was evenly divided between African Americans and whites. Interviews were conducted between 1989 and 1992. In Camden/Philadelphia, the sample is also predominately African American and white. These interviews were conducted between 1996 and 1999. About half of the respondents in each city and racial group relied on welfare, and about half worked at low wage jobs (they earned less than $7.50 per hour).

The cities vary in a number of interesting ways. Chicago offered average welfare benefits ($376 for a three-person family) and had an average labor market in the early 1990s, when we did most of our interviewing there. Charleston, South Carolina had very modest welfare benefits ($205 for a family of three) and a tight labor market. Camden, New Jersey is an industrial suburb of Philadelphia, Pennsylvania. In both states, residents received better-than-average welfare benefits in the mid- 1990s (roughly $420 for three persons) but the labor market in the Philadelphia region was quite slack. . . .

In all three cities, we scheduled conversations with each respondent at least twice to insure that there was sufficient time to develop adequate rapport. Within the context of these conversations, we addressed a predetermined set of topics, as well as additional topics brought up by the respondents. The order and precise wording of the questions regarding each topic was not prescribed, but followed the natural flow of conversation.

The primary goal of this analysis is to show what a relatively large, heterogeneous group of low-income single mothers say about the declining propensity of poor mothers and fathers to marry. The analysis is not meant to prove or disprove existing theories of family formation among the poor, but rather to give an in-depth account of the social role marriage plays in the lives of a relatively heterogeneous (in terms of city and race) groups of mothers within a single social category. The analysis will show that much of what poor mothers say supports existing theory, though mothers' accounts show a greater degree of complexity than these theories recognize. The reader will also see that poor mothers' accounts reveal motivations that existing approaches generally neglect. The result is a complex set of personal accounts that can lend crucial qualitative grounding to other representative studies of the retreat from marriage among the poor.

RESULTS

Analysis of the Chicago and Charleston low-income single mothers' accounts reveals five primary reasons why poor parents do not form or reform a legal union with a man (see Table 1). The first line of Table 1 shows the percentage of mothers whose transcripts re-

Table 1 Percent of Low-Income Single Mothers with Positive Views Regarding Marriage, Plans to Marry, and the Percent who Discussed the Importance of Various Factors on Marriage Attitudes by City and Race

	Chicago African American	Chicago White	Charleston African American	Charleston White	Sig. of F Race	Sig. of F City
Positive Orientation toward Marriage	46	60	41	62	*	
Affordability	79	66	55	39	*	***
Respectability	62	50	69	52	*	
Control	79	54	55	36	*	
Trust	66	94	44	60	**	***
Domestic violence	21	54	16	48	***	

Notes: *p < .10 **p < .05 ***p < .001

vealed positive views toward marriage and hoped to marry in the future. As is true in nationally representative surveys (South 1993), whites are somewhat more positively oriented toward marriage than are African Americans, particularly in our Southern site. There are no differences by city. Lines two through six show the five motivations the Chicago and Charleston women most often discussed when they talked about these views in depth. Since we asked all of the Camden/ Philadelphia mothers about each of these motivations, all talked about them, and nearly all felt they were relevant in mothers' decisions regarding marriage (even if they were not relevant to them personally).

Affordability

Men's income is an issue that matters enormously in poor parents' willingness and ability to stay together. Though the *total* earnings a father can generate is clearly the most important dimension for mothers, so is the *regularity* of those earnings, the *effort* men expend finding and keeping work, and the *source* of his income.

One African American mother in Chicago summed her views about contemporary marriage this way: "Men simply don't earn enough to support a family. This leads to couples breaking up." When we asked mothers specifically about their criteria for marriage, nearly every one told us the father would have to have a "good job." One reason was their recognition that the couple would probably not be able to sustain an independent household unless the father made a "decent" living. One African American Camden respondent told us:

> You can't get married and go on living with your mother. That's just like playing house. She expects your husband to be able to provide for you and if he can't, what is he doing marrying you in the first place! She's not going to put up with having him under her roof.

When mothers judge the merits of marriage, they worry a lot about the stability of men's earnings simply because they have to. At the bottom of the income distribution, single mothers who must choose between welfare or low-wage employment to pay their bills face a constant budget shortfall and thus, must continually find ways of getting extra money to pay their bills (Edin and Lein 1997). To generate extra cash, mothers must either find a side job or another adult who can provide regular and substantial economic support. Meanwhile, any given father or boyfriend is likely to have limited skills and a troubled employment history. In sum, while mothers have constant income needs, the men who father their children often cannot consistently meet these needs.

Mothers said their men often complained that women did not understand how difficult it was for men to find steady work. Yet, even mothers who were inclined to sympathize with men's employment difficulties were in a bind: they simply could not afford to keep an economically unproductive man around the house. Because of this, almost all of the low-income single mothers we interviewed told us that rather than marry the father of their children, they preferred to live separately or to cohabit. In cohabiting situations, mothers nearly always said they enforced a "pay and stay" rule. If a father quit his job or lost his job and did not (in the mother's view) try very hard to find another one, or drank or smoked up his paycheck, he lost his right to co-reside in the household. Since her name, not his, was generally on the lease, she had the power to evict him. A black mother from the Philadelphia area explained her practices in this regard:

> We were [thinking about marriage] for a while, but he was real irresponsible. I didn't want to be mean or anything, [but when he didn't work] I didn't let him eat my food. I would tell him, "If you can't put any food here, you can't eat here. These are your kids, and you should want to help your kids, so if you come here, you can't eat their food." Finally, I told him he couldn't stay here either. Right now, I think I would never [get tied to] a[nother] man who is irresponsible and without a job.

Keeping an unemployed man in the house puts a strain on a mother's, already overstrained, budget. It also precludes a woman's ability to offer co-residence to an alternative man who is employed. One African American mother from Charleston told us:

> I've been with my baby's father for almost 10 years, since high school graduation. He's talking marriage, but what I'm trying to do now is get away from him. He just lost his job [at the Naval base]. He worked there for 18 years. [Now] he's in work, out of work, then in work again. Right now he's just working part-time at McDonalds. I can do bad by myself, I don't need no one helping me [do bad]. I want somebody better, somebody [who can bring home] a regular paycheck. [So] I'm trying to get away from him right now.

If they are not married, she has the flexibility to lower her household costs by getting rid of him, and the possibility of replacing him with another more economically productive man (or at least one who is working at the time).

Women whose male partners couldn't, or wouldn't, find work, often lost respect for them and "just couldn't stand" to keep them around. A white Chicago divorcee told us:

> I couldn't get him to stay working. [T]he kids would be hungry and I'd throw a fit and he'd have a nerve to tell me, "Who cares? You're always over [at your mother's], why can't you ask her for some food?" Talk about a way [to lose someone's respect]. It's hard to love somebody if you lose respect. . . . [Finally, I couldn't take it and I made him leave].

As one can well imagine, men in this situation knew they were purchasing their place in the household and, to some extent, their hold on the woman's affections. The women we interviewed said this made men feel that their girlfriends "only want me for my money." They told us their children's fathers resented their girlfriends' "materialistic" attitudes. Holding fathers to these standards was often emotionally wrenching for mothers. One African American Camden mother expressed her emotional dilemma as follows:

> It was like there was a struggle going on inside of me. I mean, he lost his job at the auto body shop when they went [bankrupt] and closed down. Then he couldn't find another one. But it was months and months. I was trying to live on my welfare check and it just wasn't enough. Finally, I couldn't do it any more [because] it was just too much pressure on me [even though] he is the love of my life. I told him he had to leave, even though I knew it wasn't really his fault that [he wasn't working]. But I had nothing in the house to feed the kids, no money to pay the bills. Nothing. And he was just sitting there, not working. I couldn't take it, so I made him leave.

An African American mother from Charleston emphasized the fact that women not only value earnings, but respect a man who is making his best effort to support his family. She said, "Am I gonna marry him? Of course! If he didn't have a steady job? No, no. [But] If he's helping out the best he can, yeah, I would. He drives a truck [right now]." According to these mothers, a man who could not find work in the formal sector had two choices: he could stay home and wait for the children's mother to kick him out, or he could try to maintain his place in the family by finding work in the underground economy. Sometimes this technique worked, but more often, if backfired. Work in criminal trades was generally easier to get, but mothers said that fathers who engaged in crime for any length of time, generally lost their place in the family as well. When a father began to earn his living by selling drugs, a mother feared that he would bring danger into the household. Mothers worried that fathers' criminal companions might "come for them" at the house, or that fathers might store drugs, drug proceeds, or weapons in the house. Even worse, mothers feared that a father might start "using his product." Mothers also felt that a drug-dealing father would be a very poor role model for their children. Thus, mothers did not generally consider earnings from crime as legitimate earnings (they said they wouldn't marry such a man no matter how much he earned from crime).

Chicago respondents were more likely to discuss economic factors than Charleston mothers were. This difference could be due to the fact that, when the interviews took place, Chicago's unemployment rate was higher than Charleston's, or possibly due to more traditional values among Southerners regarding marriage. Blacks also discussed economic factors more often than whites. This is presumably because black men's earnings are lower than those of whites with similar skill levels.

Respectability

Even within very poor communities, residents make class-based distinctions among themselves. Most of our mothers' eventual goal was to become "respectable," and they believed that respectability was greatly enhanced by a marriage tie to a routinely employed partner earning wages significantly above the legal minimum. However, mothers said that they could not achieve respectability by marrying someone who was frequently out of work, otherwise underemployed, supplemented his income through criminal activity, and had little chance of improving his situation over time. Mothers believed that marriage to such a man would diminish their respectability, rather than enhance it.

Mothers seldom romanticized a father's economic prospects when it came to marriage (though they sometimes did so when conceiving the man's child [see Kefalas and Edin 2000]). They generally knew that if they entered into marriage with a lower-class man, the marriage was unlikely to last because the economic pressures on the relationship would simply be too great. Even if they had contemplated marriage to their children's father "for love" or "romantic feelings," their family members and friends generally convinced poor parents that such a marriage would collapse under economic strain (see also Stack 1974). For these mothers, marriage meant tying oneself to the class position of one's partner "for life." Even if a woman could afford to marry a man whose economic prospects were bleak, her decision would have signaled to her kin and neighbors that he was the best she could do. Mothers expected that marriage should pull them up the class ladder. Community notions of respectability help to explain sentiments like the one revealed by this African American mother in Charleston:

> I want to get married. I've always wanted to get married and have a family. [My baby's father,] he is doing pretty good, but I am not going to marry him until . . . we get some land. [We'll] start off with a trailer, live in that for about 10 years, and then build a dream house. But I am not going to get married and pay rent to someone else. When we save up enough money to [buy] an acre of land and [can finance] a trailer, then we'll marry.

Many mothers told us that their children's fathers also said that they planned to marry them, but wanted to "wait 'till we can afford a church wedding, not just a justice of the peace thing." Marriage made a statement to the larger community about each partner's current and prospective class standing. Thus, marriage could either confer respectability or deny it. If a low-income woman had a child with an erratically employed and unskilled man to whom she was not married, she had not tied herself in any permanent way to him or his class position. Most mothers weren't willing to sign an apartment lease with the man they were with, much less a marriage license. Mothers who remained unmarried were able to maintain their dream of upward mobility. "Marrying up" guaranteed the woman the respect of her community, while marrying at her own class level only made her look foolish in the eyes of her family and neighbors. When we asked mothers whether they would marry the erratic or low earners that had fathered their children, the most common response was "I can do bad by myself."

In addition to the importance women placed on respectability, they also had strong moral (and oftentimes religious) objections to marrying men whose economic situation would, in their view, practically guarantee eventual marital dissolution. Mothers often talked about the "sacred" nature of marriage, and believed that no "respectable" woman would marry under these circumstances (some spoke of such a marriage as a "sacrilege"). In interview after interview, mothers stressed the seriousness of the marriage commitment and their belief that "it should last forever." Thus, it is not that mothers held marriage in low esteem, but rather the fact that they held it in such high esteem that convinced them to forgo marriage, at least until their prospective marriage partner could prove himself worthy economically or they could find another partner who could. To these mothers, marriage was a powerful symbol of respectability, and should not be diluted by foolish unions.

Respectability was equally important for respondents in Chicago and Charleston, though it was somewhat more important for African Americans than for whites (and probably for the same reasons that affordability concerns were). Respondents' discourse in regard to respectability, however, varied quite dramatically by race (Bulcroft and Bulcroft 1993). Many African American respondents who claimed they wanted to marry "up or not at all" knew that holding to such standards might well mean not marrying at all. Whites had less of these anxieties. White respondents typically had sisters, other kin, and friends who had married men who earned a "decent" wage, and were somewhat more sanguine about their own chances of finding such a man than were blacks. A handful of white respondents even told us they planned to "marry out of poverty" so they could become housewives. Only one black respondent reported such plans.

Control and the Stalled Sex Role Revolution at Home

In a non-marital relationship, women often felt they had more control than they would have had if they married. Even if the couple cohabited, they nearly always lived with her mother or in an apartment with her name on the lease. Thus, mothers had the power to evict fathers if they interfered with child rearing, or tried to take control over financial decision-making. Mothers said that fathers who knew they were "on trial" could do little about this state of affairs, especially since they needed a place to live and could not generally afford one on their own. One African American Philadelphia-area respondent's partner quipped, "her attitude is like, 'it's either my way or the highway."

Why was control, not power, such an important issue for these women? Most mothers said they thought their children's fathers had very traditional notions of sex roles—notions that clashed with their more egalitarian views. One white cohabiting mother from Charleston said, "If we were to marry, I don't think it would be so ideal. [Husbands] want to be in charge, and I can't deal with that." Regardless of whether or not the prospective wife worked, mothers feared that prospective husbands would expect to be "head of the house," and make the "final" decisions about child rearing, finances, and other matters. Women, on the other hand, felt that since they had held the primary responsibility for both raising and supporting their children, they should have an equal say.

When we asked single mothers what they liked best about being a single parent, their most frequent response was "I am in charge," or "I am in control." Mothers seemed willing to take on the responsibilities of child rearing if they were also able to make and enforce the rules. In most mothers' views, the presence of fathers often interfered with their parental control, particularly if the couple married. Most women also felt that the presence of a husband might impede their efforts to discipline and spend time with their children. Mothers criticized men for being "too demanding" of their time and attention. A white Chicago mother answered the question, "What is it like being a single mother?" as follows: "It's great in terms of being independent. I'm just thrilled being away from my ex-husband. The joy of that hasn't worn off. I feel more freedom to be a parent how I want [to be]. We did not agree on parenting at all." A white Charleston respondent said, "[Marriage isn't an option] right now. I don't want any man thinking that he has any claim on my kids or on how I raise them."

Mothers were also concerned about losing control of the family's financial situation. One African American Chicago mother told us, "[I won't marry because] the men take over the money. I'm too afraid to lose control of my money again." Still another said, "I'm the head of the household right now, and I make the [financial] decisions. I [don't want to give that up]."

Finally, mothers often expressed the view that if they married, their men would expect them to do all of the household chores, plus "cook and clean" and otherwise "take care of" them. Some described their relationships with their ex-partners as "like having one more kid to take care of." We asked another divorced white Charleston mother whether she would ever consider marriage again. She answered,

> I don't know, I can't think that far ahead. I can't see it. This guy I'm with right now, I don't know. I like being by myself. The thought of having to cook and clean for somebody else? I'm like, "No." I'm looking for somebody who is going to cook and clean for me!

Concerns over control did not, however, mean that most women had abandoned their plans to marry. But they felt their own situations had to be such as to maximize their chances of exerting control in the marriage relationship. The primary way mothers who wanted to marry thought they could maintain power in a marriage relationship was by working and contributing to the family budget. One African American mother living in Charleston told me,

> One thing my mom did teach me is that you must work some and bring some money into the household so you can have a say in what happens. If you completely live off a man, you are helpless. That is why I don't want to get married until I get my own [career] and get off of welfare.

Mothers also wanted to get established economically prior to marriage because men had failed them in the past. This is why they often told us that if they did get married, they would make sure "the car is in my name, the house is in my name" and so on. They wanted to "get myself established first, and then get married" so if the marriage broke up, they wouldn't be "left with nothing." One African American Camden mother commented, "[I will consider marriage] one day when I get myself together. When I have my own everything, so I won't be left depending on a man."

The experience of breakup or divorce and the resulting financial hardship and emotional pain fundamentally transformed these women's relational views. I heard dozens of stories of women who had held traditional views regarding sex roles while they were younger and still in a relationship with their children's fathers. When the men for whom they sacrificed so much gave them nothing but pain and anguish, they felt they had been "duped." Their childhood fantasy of marriage was gone, as was their willingness to be dependent on or subservient to men.

Because of these painful experiences, formerly married white mothers generally placed as high priority on increasing their labor market skills and experience as their black never-married counterparts. They felt that a hasty remarriage might distract them from this goal (possibly because their husbands' income would make them too comfortable and tempt them to quit school or work). Like the African American mothers who had seldom been married, whites also said that once they remarried, they would keep working no matter what. The "little money of my own" both African American and white mothers spoke of was valued, not only for its contribution to the household economy, per se, but for the power it purchased them within the relationship, as well as its insurance value against destitution if the marriage should fail.

Mothers told us that the more established they became economically, the more bargaining power they believed they would have in a marital relationship. The mothers they knew who were economically dependent on men had to "put up with all kinds of behavior" because they could not legitimately threaten to leave without serious financial repercussions (due to the fact that they could not translate their homemaking skills into wages). Mothers felt that if they became more economically independent (had the car in their name, the house in their name, no common debts, etc.), they could legitimately threaten to leave their husbands if certain conditions (i.e., sexual fidelity) weren't met. These threats would, in turn they believed, keep a husband on his best behavior.

Taking on these attitudes of self-reliance and independence wasn't always easy. Some formerly married women whose partner failed them had never lived alone before, having gone straight from their parents' household to their husband's. In addition, some hadn't held a job in years, had no marketable skills, and had no idea about how to make their way in the world of employed women. One white Chicago resident was a full-time homemaker until her divorce. After getting no child support from her ex-husband for several months, this mother decided she had better get a job, but the best job she could find paid only minimum wage at the time. Her journey from her first job to her current position (which paid $7 an hour) was a painful one. Giving up this hard-won self-sufficiency for dependence on a man was simply too great a risk for her to take. She said, "I don't want to depend on nobody. It's too scary."

The often difficult life experiences of these mothers had convinced them of competencies they might not have known they had before single motherhood. Because of these experiences, their roles expanded to encompass more traditionally male responsibilities than before. The men, in their view, weren't respectful of these competencies. Instead, they expected them to revert to more traditional female roles. When we asked a white Chicago mother whether there were any advantages to being apart from the father of her children, she replied:

> You're the one in control. The good thing is that I feel good about myself. I feel more independent. Whereas when I was with Brian, I didn't. I had never been out on my own, but I took that step to move out and, since I did, I feel much better about myself as a person, that I can do it.

While it was true that some women were poorer financially than before their relationships ended, the increased pride they felt in being able to provide for themselves and their children partially compensated for economic hardship. Another white Chicago mother said "You know, I feel better [being alone] because I am the provider, I'm getting the things that I want and I'm getting them for myself, little by little."

Concerns about power might explain why childbearing and marriage have become separated from one another, particularly among the low-income population. Though we did not ask our Chicago and Charleston mothers questions about the ideal time to bear children and to marry, we did ask our Camden/Philadelphia mothers these questions. Most felt childbearing should ideally occur in a woman's early 20s, but that marriage should ideally occur in a woman's late 20s or early 30s. These answers are somewhat suspect because respondents might simply have been rationalizing past behavior (most hadn't been married when they had had their children, and half had never married). Even more confusing is the fact that these same respondents generally said that one should be married before having children. When interviewers probed deeper, respondents revealed that, though the goal of getting married first and having children second was indeed their ideal, it was hardly a practical choice given their economic situations and those of their partners.

Respondents' explanations of their views also revealed that many felt that childbearing required at least a temporary or partial withdrawal from the labor market. Childbearing within marriage and the labor market withdrawal it required, made women "dependent" and "vulnerable" and weakened their control. When mothers told us they wanted to wait to marry or remarry until their late 20s or early 30s, most assumed that, at this point, their youngest child would be in school. Thus, they would be free to more fully pursue labor market activities and, in this way, enhance their potential bargaining and decision-making role in any subsequent marital relationship. One African American Camden mother said.

> One guy was like, "marry me, I want a baby." I don't want to have to depend on anybody. No way. I [would rather] work. [If I married him and had his baby], I'd [have to quit work and] be dependent again. It's too scary.

There was no significant difference between cities in the salience of sex roles and power. Blacks were more concerned about these issues than whites, yet the differences are probably smaller than other studies of racial differences in sex role attitudes would suggest. Many of the white women we interviewed had been married in the past and most of them reported that they had begun their marriages thinking that they would stay at home or work part-time (at least while their children were young). Their husbands, they assumed, would be the primary breadwinners, while they specialized in household management and parenting. After the breakup of these relationships, white mothers were often shocked by how vulnerable their withdrawal from the labor market had made them. It was after learning these hard lessons that most white mothers developed the conviction that it was foolish to marry unless they had "established themselves" first.

Trust

For some mothers, the reaction of their partner to an unplanned pregnancy became their first hard lesson in "the way men are." Mothers said that fathers' responses ran the gamut from strong negative responses to strong positive ones, but some men were clearly panicked by the prospect of being responsible for a child—particularly those who feared a child support order. Some fathers denied paternity even when they had encouraged the mother to get pregnant and/or carry the child to term. In these situations, fathers often claimed that the child was not theirs because the mother was "a whore." One partner of a pregnant Camden mother told the interviewer (in the mother's presence), "how do I know the baby's mine? Who knows if she hasn't been stepping out on me with some other man and now she wants me to support another man's child!"

Subsequent hard lessons were learned when mothers' boyfriends or husbands proved unfaithful. This experience was so common among respondents that many simply did not believe men "could be faithful to only one woman." This "men will be men" belief did not mean that women were willing to simply accept infidelity as part of the natural course of a marriage. Most said they would rather never marry than to "let him make a fool out of me." One black Chicago resident just couldn't conceive of finding a marriageable man.

> All those reliable guys, they are gone, they are gone. They're either thinking about one of three things: another woman, another man, or dope. . . . [M]y motto is "there is not a man on this planet that is faithful." It's a man thing. I don't care, you can love your wife 'til she turns three shades of avocado green. A man is gonna be a man and it's not a point of a woman getting upset about it. It's a point of a woman accepting it. 'Cause a man's gonna do what a man's gonna do. . . . [Other] black women, they say "once you find a man that's gonna be faithful, you go ahead and get married to him." [They] got it all wrong. Then they gonna [be surprised when they find out] he ain't faithful. And the wife gonna end up in a nut house. It's better not to get married, so you don't get your expectations up.

A white mother from Charleston said, "I was married for three years before I threw him out after discovering that he had another woman. I loved my husband, but I don't [want another one]. This is a wicked world we are living in." A black Charlestonian said,

> I would like to find a nice man to marry, but I know that men cannot be trusted. That's why I treat them the way I do—like the dogs they are. I think that all men will cheat on their wives regardless of how much he loves her. And you don't ever want to be in that position.

Mother after mother told us cautionary tales of married couples they knew where either the man or the woman was "stepping out" on their spouse. They viewed the wounded spouse as either hopelessly naive (if they did not know) or without self-respect (if they did know). They did not want to place themselves in a similar position. Demands for sexual fidelity within marriage had a practical, as well as an emotional dimension. Women often gave examples of married men they knew who "spen[t] all his money on the little woman he [had] on the side." Mothers often feared that men would promise them and their children "the world" and then abandon them. One African American Camden mother summed up her views as follows: "Either they leave or they die. The first thing is, don't get close to them, 'cause they ain't no good from the beginning. When that man ain't doing right for me, I learn to dump [him]." A white mother from Chicago said: "I've been a single parent since the day my husband walked out on me. He tried to come back, but I am not one to let someone hurt me and my children twice. I am living on welfare [rather than living with him]."

Even the most mistrustful of our respondents generally held out some hope that they would find a man who could be trusted and who would stay around. One white Chicago mother said, "I want to meet a man who will love me and my son and want us to grow together. I just don't know if he exists." An African American mother living in Chicago said,

> Maybe I'll find a good person to get married to, someone to be a stepfather to my son. They're not all the same; they're not all bad. There are three things in my life: my school, my work, and my son. Not men. At first they love you, they think you're beautiful, and then they leave. When I got pregnant, he just left. My father is like that. He has kids by several different women. I hate him for it. I say, "I hate you. Why do you do that? Why?"

A white divorcee from Chicago explained her views of the differences between the sexes in this regard as follows:

> Men can say. "Well honey, I'm going out for the night." And then they disappear for two months.

> Whereas, the mother has a deeper commitment, conscience, or compassion. . . . If [women] acted like men, our kids would be in the park, left. We'd say "Oh, somebody else is going to take care of it." Everybody would be orphaned.

An African American mother from the Philadelphia area told us,

> I'm frustrated with men, period. They bring drugs and guns into the house, you take care of their kids, feed them, and then they steal your rent money out of your purse. They screw you if you put your self out for them. So now, I don't put myself out there any more.

Because their own experiences and the experiences of their friends, relatives, and neighbors has been so overwhelmingly negative, many women reduced the expressive value they placed on their relationships over time. Some instrumentalized their relationships with men to the point that they didn't "give it away anymore," meaning they no longer had sex without expecting something, generally something material, in return. A white Chicago mother put it this way: "Love is blind. You fall in love with the wrong one sometimes. It's easy to do. [Now] I am so mean . . . [when] I sleep with a guy I am like, 'Give me the money and leave me alone.'" Nonetheless, many of *these same women* often held out hope of finding a man who was "different," one who could be trusted.

Chicago mothers were significantly more likely to voice trust issues than their Charleston counterparts. This difference may reflect regional differences (Southerners may be more trusting than Northerners). It may also be true that trust issues are least salient in a tight labor market where jobs for unskilled men are more plentiful. Whites talked about the issue more than African Americans and could reflect differences in spontaneous self-reports of domestic abuse (discussed below).

Domestic Violence

In Chicago and Charleston, we did not ask directly about domestic abuse, yet, a surprisingly high number spontaneously spoke of some history of domestic violence in their childhood or adult lives. In Table 1, we include only those mothers for which the abuse had some bearing on marriage attitudes. We see no important differences across cities, but rather startling differences by race. One white mother living in Chicago decided to have her child with the assumption that she would marry the father, but after a series of physically abusive episodes triggered by arguments about his drinking and drug use, she changed her mind.

> The person I was with wasn't quite what I thought he was. We were going to get married, [but] I don't believe in making two mistakes. [There were about] four [big] blowouts before I finally actually [ended it]. The last one was probably the worst. We went to a friend's house [and] he started drinking, [doing] drugs, and stuff. I said, "please take me home now." So [we got in the car] and we started arguing about why he had to hang around people like that [who do] drugs and all that sort of stuff. One thing led to another and he kind of tossed me right out of the car.

Many women reported physical abuse during pregnancy. Several mothers reported having miscarriages because of such abuse. For others, the physical abuse began after the child was born. It was not uncommon for women to report injuries serious enough to warrant trips to the hospital emergency room. Two African American women from Charleston ended up in the emergency room following beatings from their boyfriends. One recounted:

> My daughter's father, we used to fight. I got to where nobody be punching on me because love is not that serious. And I figure somebody is beating on you and the only thing they love is watching you go the emergency room. That's what they love. A lot of these chicks, they think "he [hitting] me because [he loves me and] he don't want me looking at nobody [else]." Honey, he need help, and you need a little more help than he do because you stand there [and take it].

The other interjected: "Just leave him [if he abuses you], you get over [him]. You will be over [him eventually]."

The fact that women tended to experience repeated abuse from their children's fathers before they decided to leave attests to their strong desire to make things work with their children's fathers. Many women finally left when they saw the abuse beginning to affect their children's well-being. One white Charleston mother explained:

> . . . it was an abusive situation. It was physical. . . . [My daughter] saw us fighting a lot. The minute she would see us fighting, she would go into hysterics. It would turn into an all-out brawl. She was terrified. And this was what that did to her and I thought. "I've got to get out of here."

But the economic pressures associated with leaving sometimes propelled mothers into another harmful relationship. One white Chicago mother explained:

> I married [my first husband] a month after I had [our son]. And I married him because I couldn't afford [to live alone]. Boy, was that stupid. And I left him [two years after that] when our daughter was five months old. I got scared. I was afraid because my kids were starting to get in the middle. [My son] still to this day, when he thinks someone is hurting me, he'll start screaming and crying and beating on him. He had seen his father [beat me up]. I didn't want him to see that. I remarried six months later because I couldn't make it [financially]. And I got into another abusive marriage. And we got separated before the year was even up. He would burn me [with cigarettes]. He was an alcoholic. He was a physical abuser, mental [too]. I think he would have killed me [if I had stayed].

Another white Chicagoan said, "after being abused, physically abused, by him the whole time we were married, I was ready to [kill him]. He put me in the hospital three times. I was carrying our child four and a half months, he beat me and I miscarried." A white Charlestonian said, "I was terrified to leave because I knew it would mean going on welfare. . . . But that is okay. I can handle that. The thing I couldn't deal with is being beat up." When we asked one black Charleston woman if there were any advantages to being a single mom, she replied, "not living with someone there to abuse you. I'm not scared anymore. I'm scared of my bills and I'm scared of I get sick, what's going to happen to my kids, but I'm not afraid for my life."

We are not sure why there is so much domestic violence among poor parents, but our interviews with mothers give us a few clues. First, mothers sometimes linked episodes of violence to fathers' fears about their ability to provide, especially in light of increased state efforts toward child support enforcement. This explanation was most often invoked in reference to the beatings women received when they were pregnant. Second, some mothers living in crime-ridden, inner-city neighborhoods talked about family violence as a carryover from street violence. The Camden/Philadelphia mothers talked at length about the effect this exposure had had on their children's fathers' lives (and their own), and some even described the emotional aftermath of this exposure as "Post-Traumatic Stress Syndrome."

DISCUSSION

Since the 1970s, a sharply declining proportion of unskilled men have been able to earn enough to support a family (U.S. House of Representatives 1997). These trends clearly have had a profound influence on marriage among low-income men and women. But even when a marriage might be affordable, mothers might judge the risks marriage entails as too great for other reasons, some of which reflect changes in the economy, but are not economic *per se*.

In these mothers' view, wives still borrow their class standing from their husbands. Since a respectable marriage is one that lasts "forever," mothers who marry low-skilled males must themselves give up their dreams of upward mobility. In the interim, single motherhood holds a somewhat higher status than a "foolish" marriage to a low-status man. . . .

Beyond affordability and respectability concerns, these interviews offer powerful evidence that there has been a dramatic revolution in sex-role expectations among women at the low end of the income distribution, and that the gap between low-income men's and women's expectations in regard to gender roles is wide. Women who have proven their competencies through the hard lessons of single parenthood aren't generally willing to enter subservient roles—they want to have substantial control and bargaining power in subsequent relationships. Some mothers learned the dangers of economic dependence upon men through the pain and financial devastation that accompanied a separation and divorce. Others were schooled by their profound disappointment at their baby's father's reaction to the pregnancy and his failure to live up to the economic and emotional commitments of fatherhood. Both groups of mothers equate marital power with economic power, and believe that the emotional and financial risk that marriage entails is only sustainable when they themselves have reached some level of economic self-sufficiency.

The data also show that, though a small number of women want to marry and become housewives, the overwhelming majority want to continue working during any subsequent marriage. Since these mothers generally believe that childbearing and rearing young children necessitate a temporary withdrawal from the labor market, many place the ideal age at which to marry in the late 20s (when their youngest child is school age) and the ideal age to bear children in the early 20s—the age they say is the "normal" time for women to have children. Delaying marriage until they can concentrate more fully on labor market activity maximizes their chances of having a marriage where they can have equal bargaining power. The income from work also allows them to legitimately threaten to leave the husband if certain behavioral standards are not met and many women believe that such threats will serve to keep husbands in line. These data suggest that the bargaining perspective, which many studies of housework currently employ, may be useful in understanding marriage attitudes and non-marital relational dynamics, as well.

Mothers believe that marital power is crucial, at least partially, because of their low trust of men. I know of no data that demonstrate that gender mistrust has grown over time, but certainly the risk of divorce, and the economic destitution for women that so often accompanies it, has grown. Trust issues are exacerbated by the experience of domestic violence. Many mothers told interviewers that it was these experiences that taught them "not to have any feeling for men." National-level data show that violence is more frequent among those with less income (Ptacek 1998). Presumably, such violence, along with the substance abuse that frequently accompanics it, is a way of "doing gender" for men who cannot adequately fulfill the breadwinner role. Though women's accounts did not always allow me to establish the sequence of events leading up to episodes of violence, many of those that did showed that violence followed job loss or revelation of a pregnancy. Both are sources of economic stress.

These data also reveal some interesting differences by city and by race, though the sample size is small. Charleston mothers worried less about affordability and trust issues than Chicago mothers. The first difference could result from the differences in local labor markets (tight versus somewhat slack) which disproportionately affect the employment of unskilled and minority men (Jencks 1992), or regional differences (Southerners might be more traditional than Northerners). The second difference is harder to explain, though regional differences and economic differences between the cities may also play a role. If men behave in an untrustworthy manner (i.e., "unfaithful") in order to compensate for their inability to fulfil the provider role, we would expect that women in tight labor markets might find it easier to trust male partners than women in slack labor markets. The impact of labor market conditions and regional variations on the marriage attitudes and rates for low-skilled men and women would be fruitful topics for further study across a wider range of labor markets and regions.

The analysis also revealed some interesting race difference. In both Charleston and Chicago, African Americans were more likely to name affordability, respectability, and control concerns, while whites mentioned trust and domestic violence more often. Affordability and respectability might be more salient for blacks because their chances of finding a marriage partner with sufficient economic resources to satisfy such concerns are lower than for whites. The salience of trust for whites might reflect higher rates of domestic violence, though these figures reflect spontaneous comments and probably underestimate the actual rate of violence for women in the sample. They may also reflect the fact that whites who elaborated on these experiences generally stayed with the violent partner (to whom they were often married) longer than African Americans. Whites' living arrangements might also have afforded less protection from violent men than blacks' in that whites were more likely to cohabit with their partner, while blacks were more likely to live in an extended-kin household. Nationally representative data also show that low-income whites cohabit significantly more often than comparable African Americans (Harris and Edin 1996).

In relation to theories of the retreat from marriage, there is no doubt that economic factors are necessary, though not sufficient, criteria for marriage among most low-income women interviewed. Theories that posit the importance of the stalled revolution of sex roles and Wilson's argument that non-marriage among blacks results from very low levels of trust, were both strongly supported, though our analysis revealed that trust was even more important for whites. Drake and Cayton and Rainwater's notions of instrumentality in male-female relationships also received support. I will say more about the economic independence and welfare disincentives arguments below.

In sum, the mothers we spoke to were quite forthcoming about the fact that the men who had fathered their children often weren't "worth a lifetime commitment" given their general lack of trustworthiness, the traditional nature of their sex-role views, the potential loss of control over parental and household decisions, and their risky and sometimes violent behavior. While mothers maintained hopes of eventual marriage, they viewed such hopes with some level of skepticism. Thus, they devoted most of their time and energy toward raising their children and "getting it together financially" rather than "waiting on a man." Those that planned on marrying, generally assumed they would put off marriage until their children were in school and they were able to be fully engaged in labor market activity. By waiting to marry until the tasks associated with early child-rearing and the required temporary withdrawal from the labor market were completed, mothers felt they could enhance their bargaining power within marriage.

This complex set of motivations to delay marriage or remarriage (or less frequently, to avoid them altogether) has interesting implications for welfare reform. The authors of PRWORA explicitly sought to encourage marriage among the poor by increasing the cost of non-marriage (e.g., reducing the amount of resources an unmarried mother can claim from the state). Put in the language of the welfare disincentives argument, PRWORA decreases the disincentives to marry, or, according to the economic independence theory, limits one source of financial independence for women who forgo marriage. If single mothers have fewer resources from the state, it is reasonable to argue that they might become more dependent on men and men's income. This may seem particularly likely given the fact that unskilled and semiskilled ex-welfare recipients will probably not be able to make enough money in the low-wage sector to meet their monthly expenses (Edin and Lein 1997) and that the gap between their income and expenses is likely to grow as they move from welfare to work (at least after the increased earned-income disregards some states offer elapse at the five year point or sooner). To make matters worse, unless the labor market remains extremely tight, low-skilled mothers' wages are not likely to increase over time because of a lack of premium on experience in the low-wage sector (Blank 1995; Burtless 1995; Harris and Edin 1996).

If PRWORA is fully implemented, these new financial realities might well encourage some couples to marry. However, if men's employment opportunities and wages do not increase dramatically, these data suggest that mothers might continue to opt for boyfriends (cohabiting or not), who can be replaced if they do not contribute, rather than husbands who cannot be so easily traded for a more economically productive man. Even if mothers believed that they would be no worse off, or even slightly better off, by marrying than by remaining single, these data show that marriage is far more complicated that a simple economic cost-benefit assessment. The women's movement has clearly influenced what behaviors (i.e., infidelity) women are willing to accept within a marital relationship, and the level of power they expect to be able to exert within the relationship. Given the low level of trust these mothers have of men—often times rooted in the experience of domestic violence—and given their view that husbands want more control than the women are willing to give them, women recognize that any marriage that is also economically precarious, might well be conflict-ridden and short lived. Interestingly, mothers say they reject entering into economically risky marital unions out of respect for the institution of marriage, rather than because of a rejection of the marriage norm.

In the light of PRWORA and the new set of financial incentives and disincentives and disincentives it provides, it is likely that cohabitation will increase, given the fact that cohabitation nearly always allowed the mothers interviewed to make a substantial claim on the male cohabiter's income. However, increased cohabitation might put women and children at greater risk if their partner is violent. In these situations, a separate residence may be a protective factor, as the race differences in the experience of domestic abuse I report here may indicate.

CONCLUSIONS

In short, the mothers interviewed here believe that marriage will probably make their lives more difficult than they are currently. They do not, by and large, perceive any special stigma to remaining single, so they are not motivated to marry for that reason. If they are to marry, they want to get something out of it. If they cannot enjoy economic stability and gain upward mobility from marriage, they see little reason to risk the loss of control and other costs they fear marriage might exact from them. Unless low-skilled men's economic situation improve and they begin to change their behaviors toward women, it is quite likely that most low-income women will continue to resist marriage even in the context of welfare reform. Substantially enhanced labor market opportunities for low-skilled men would address both the affordability and respectability concerns of the mothers interviewed. But other factors, such as the stalled sex-role revolution at home (control), the pervasive mistrust of men, and the high probability of domestic abuse, probably mean that marriage rates are unlikely to increase dramatically.

REFERENCES

Bane, Mary Jo, and David T. Ellwood. 1994. *Welfare Realities. Cambridge,* MA: Harvard University Press.

Becker, Gary S. 1981. *A Treatise on the Family.* Cambridge, MA: Harvard University Press.

Becker, Howard S. 1992. "Cases, causes, conjectures, stories, and imagery." In *What is a case?,* eds. Charles C. Ragin and Howard S. Becker, 205–216. New York: Cambridge University Press.

Bennett, N. C., D. E. Bloom, and P. H. Craig. 1990. "American marriage patterns in transition." Paper presented at the Conference on Demographic Perspective on the American Family, April, Albany, New York.

Blank, Rebecca M. 1995. "Outlook for the U.S. labor market and prospects for low-wage entry jobs." In *The work Alternative,* eds. Demetra Smith Nightingale and Robert H. Haveman. Washington, DC: The Urban Institute Press; Cambridge, MA: Harvard University Press.

Blee, Kathleen M., and Ann R. Tickameyer. 1995. "Racial differences in men's attitudes about women's gender roles." *Journal of Marriage and the Family* 57:21–30.

Bulcroft, Richard A., and Kris A. Bulcroft. 1993. "Race differences in attitudinal and motivational factors in the decision to marry." *Journal of Marriage and the Family* 55:338–355.

Bumpass, Larry., and James A. Sweet. 1989. "Children's experience in single parent families: Implications of cohabitation and marital transitions." *Family Planning Perspectives* 61(6):256–260.

Burtless, Gary. 1995. "Employment prospects of welfare recipients." In *The Work Alternative,* eds Demetra Smith Nightingale and Robert H. Haveman. Washington, DC: The Urban Institute Press; Cambridge, MA: Harvard University Press.

Cherlin, Andrew. 1992. *Marriage, Divorce, Remarriage. Cambridge,* MA: Harvard University Press.

Collins, Patricia H. 1987 "The meaning of motherhood in black culture and black mother/daughter relationships." *Signs* 4:3–10.

Corbett, Thomas. 1998. "Reallocation, redirection, and reinvention: Assessing welfare reform in an era of discontinuity." Unpublished manuscript.

Edin, Kathryn, and Laura Lein. 1997. *Making Ends Meet: how Single Mothers Survive Welfare and Low Wage Work.* New York: Russell Sage Foundation.

Fossett, Mark A., and K. Jill Kielcolt 1993 "Mate availability and family structure among African Americans in U.S. metropolitan areas." *Journal of Marriage and the Family* 55:302–331.

Harris, Kathleen Mullan, and Kathryn Edin. 1996. "From welfare to work and back again." Unpublished manuscript.

Hochschild, Arlie 1989 *The Second Shift.* New York: Viking.

Hoffman, Saul. 1997. "Could it be true after all? AFDC benefits and non-marital births to young women." *Poverty Research News.* Chicago: Joint Center for Poverty Research, 1(2):1–3.

Hoffman, Saul D., and Greg Duncan. 1994. "The role of incomes, wages, and AFDC benefits on marital disruption." *The Journal of Human Resources* 30(10):19–41.

Jencks, Christopher 1992 *Rethinking Social Policy.* Cambridge, MA: Harvard University Press, 120–142.

Kefalas, Maria, and Kathryn Edin. 2000. "The meaning of motherhood." Unpublished manuscript.

Lichter, Daniel T., F. B. LeClere. and Diane K. McLaughlin. 1991. "Local marriage market conditions and the marital behavior of black and white women." *American Journal of Sociology* 96:843–867.

Luker, Kristin 1996 *Dubious Conceptions: The Politics of Teenage Pregnancy.* Cambridge. MA: Harvard University Press.

Moffitt, Robert A. 1995. "The effect of the welfare system on non-marital childbearing." *Report to Congress on Out of Wedlock Childbearing.* Department of Health and Human Services. Washington, DC: U.S. Government Printing Office, 167–173.

Murray, Charles. 1984. *Losing Ground.* New York: Basic Books.

Nelson, Timothy, Kathryn Edin, and Susan Clampet-Lundquist. 1999. "Doing the best I can: How low-income non-custodial fathers talk about their families." Unpublished manuscript.

Oppenheimer, Valerie K. 1993. "Women's rising employment and the future of the family in industrial societies." *Population and Development Review* 20(2): 293–342.

Ptacek, James. 1988. "Why do men batter wives." In *Feminist Perspectives on Wife Abuse,* eds, K. Yllo and M. Bograd. Thousand Oaks: Sage Publications.

Raphael, Jody, and Richard D. Tolman. 1997. *Trapped by Poverty, Trapped by Abuse.* Chicago, IL: The Taylor Institute.

Scanzoni, John H. 1970. *Opportunity and the Family.* New York: Free Press.

Schoen, Robert, and Dawn Owens 1992 "A further look at first unions and fist marriages," In *In The Changing American Family,* eds. Scott J. South and steward E. Tolnay. Boulder, CO: Westview Press.

South, Scott J. 1992. "For love or money? Sociodemographic determinants of the expected benefits from marriage." In *The Changing American Family: Sociological and Demographic Perspectives,* eds. S. J. South and S. E. Tolnay. Boulder, CO: Westview, 171–194.

———. 1993. "Racial and ethnic differences in the desire to marry." *Journal of Marriage and the Family* 55:357–370.

South, Scott J., and Kim M. Lloyd. 1992. "Marriage opportunities and family formation: Further implications of imbalanced sex ratios." *Journal of Marriage and the Family* 54:440–451.

Stack, carol B. 1974. *All Our Kin.* New York: Harper and Row.

Staples, Robert. 1988. "An overview of race and marital status." In *Black Families,* ed. H. P. McAdoo, 187–189. Newbury Park, CA: Sage.

Teachman, Jay D., Karen A. Polonko, and Geoffrey K. Leigh. 1987. "Marital timing: Race and sex comparisons." *Social Forces* 66:239–268.

Trent, Katherine, and Scott J. South. 1989. "Structural determinants of the divorce rate: A cross-societal comparison." *Journal of Marriage and the Family* 51:391–404.

Tucker, Belinda B., and Claudia Mitchell-Kernan. 1996. *The Decline in Marriage Among African Americans: Causes, Consequences, and Policy Implications.* New York: Russell Sage Foundation.

U.S. Bureau of the Census. 1993. *Poverty in the United States: 1992. Current Population Reports,* Series P60, No. 185, Washington, DC: U.S. Government Printing Office.

——— . 1991a. "Marital status and living arrangements, 1990." *Current Population Reports,* Series P-20, No. 450:1, Table A. Washington DC: U.S. Government Printing Office.

——— . 1991b. "Marital status and living arrangements, 1990." *Current Population Reports,* Series P-20, No. 461. Washington DC: U.S. Government Printing Office.

U.S. House of Representatives, Committee on Ways and Means. 1997. *Overview of Entitlement Programs (Greenbook)* Washington DC: U.S. Government Printing Office.

Wilson, William J. 1996. *When Work Disappears.* New York: Alfred A. Knopf.

——— . 1987. *The Truly Disadvantaged.* Chicago: University of Chicago Press.

PART VI

CONSTRUCTING GENDER IN THE WORKPLACE

How much does gender influence one's status at work? Does the feminization of paid labor around the world place women on a more equal footing with men? Or is paid labor another arena that intensifies women's disadvantages? Is it an arena that intensifies *some* women's disadvantages more than others? *Why* is gender inequality such a pervasive feature of work? Is it built into the workplace, or is it the outcome of differences in women and men themselves, their socialization, their behaviors, and their interactions? The readings in this part rely on studies of women and men in different work settings to address these questions. They show how the societal patterns of gender, race, class, sexuality, and immigrant status shape the work experiences of different groups.

Paid workers are increasingly diverse. Today's average worker in the global economy may be either a man or a woman and of any age, race, class, sexual orientation, or nationality. The average worker in the global economy may labor virtually unseen inside the home or may work in a public workplace as an assembler, teacher, secretary, or restaurant worker. Yet whatever the average worker does for a living, she or he is very likely to work at a job assigned on the basis of gender. Everywhere, gender organizes workplaces. Even five-year-olds can readily identify what is a "man's job" and what is a "woman's job." Women's jobs and men's jobs are structured with different characteristics and different rewards. Seldom do women and men do the same jobs in the same place for the same pay. In every society we find a familiar pattern: women earn less than men, even when they work in similar occupations and have the same level of education. But exactly *how* does work become so dramatically divided? How is workplace inequality maintained? Can gender boundaries be dismantled? The first reading speaks to these questions. Peter Levin's study of workplace practices on the trading floor of the American Commodities Exchange shows how masculinity is built into the structure of work *and* reinforced by workplace interactions. However, he finds that gender is articulated differently depending on the pace of work. Temporal rhythms are the key to understanding the distinctive gender patterns that emerge as women and men relate to each other in busy times and quiet times.

The experience of workers is further complicated by the interplay of gender and other power systems. Women and men of different races, national origins, and immigrant groups become clustered in certain kinds of work. Job opportunities are shaped by *who* people are—by their being women or men, educated or uneducated, of a certain race, sexual orientation, and residents of specific geopolitical settings—rather than their skills or talents. These hierarchies also define what constitutes acceptable behavior on the job. In their study of restaurant workers, Patti A. Giuffre and Christine L. Williams discover that the definition of sexual harassment depends on *who* the perpetrator is and *who* the victim is. Double standards of race, class, and sexual orientation mask a good deal of sexual discrimination in workplaces.

The next two readings consider some of the complex matters related to the effects of globalization on women's work. Both studies examine control and resistance in the global workplace, where gender relations can be friction-filled rather than harmonious. Karen Hossfeld's study of assembly workers in the widely acclaimed Silicon Valley illustrates how race and gender can also be used by workers themselves to resist coercive measures in the work place. Pierrette Hondagneu-Sotelo's study of Latina domestics and their employers uncovers a form of labor embedded in intricate power relations among women. Domestic labor is isolated and devalued labor. It takes place in the confines of employers' homes, where employers and domestics each use strategies that are potentially at odds. Hondagneu-Sotelo reveals how most employers prefer distant, impersonal relations with their domestic employees, while their Latina domestic workers want employers who give them recognition and respect. The outcome is a unique and often contentious gender arrangement, raising difficult questions about the organization of work based on divisions of race, class, and nationality in the global era.

37

Gendering the Market

Temporality, Work, and Gender on a National Futures Exchange

PETER LEVIN

On the often-chaotic trading floor of the American Commodities Exchange(ACE),[1] time matters. In the world of organized commodity futures trading, both gender and the markets themselves are organized temporally. Scholars have long argued that gender is not a quality inherent to individuals but rather it consists of a set of socially produced, hierarchically organized relations between men and women (Connell, 1987, 1995: Stacey & Thorne, 1985; West & Zimmerman, 1987). Men and women face differential conditions in the context of organizations and in labor markets more broadly (Epstein, 1970; Hartmann, 1976; Kanter, 1977). Furthermore, a number of scholars have documented how bureaucracies as well as the microlevel processes of workplaces are also "gendered" (Acker, 1990; Britton, 1997; Ferguson, 1984; Hall, 1993; Leidner, 1991, 1994; Pringle, 1989; Salzinger, 1997). Increasingly detailed evidence shows how gender changes across factory settings and management strategies so that gendered meanings "take place within the framework of local, managerial subjectivities and strategies" (Salzinger, 1997, p. 550). With variations in factory-level labor processes, gender takes on different subjective meanings and varies in distributional effects.

Perhaps less noted and less studied are the effects of temporal variations on gender. For many occupations and in many organizations, the pacing of work significantly affects both the subjective understanding and the structural arrangement of gender. Temporality complements studies of gender variation across spatial locales. The ACE is not a continuous or homogeneous work environment. Rather, the temporal shifts in market activity shape the ways men and women understand and constitute gender.

The ACE floor operates within two distinct gender repertoires, one of *competence* and the other of *sexualized difference*. In the modality of work, gender is constituted within a language of competence, which constructs the trading floors as gender neutral even as it privileges a particular form of dominant masculinity. During slower times of play, gender reemerges in a more overtly sexualized form. These two repertoires can shift abruptly; men on the floor refer to women's bodies as suitable for sexual objectification in one moment and unsuitable for handling the physicality of the

Peter Levin, "Gendering the Market: Temporality, Work, and Gender on a National Futures Exchange," from *Work & Occupations,* Volume 28/2001, p. 112–130.

market in the next. In this article, I show the ways in which gender vacillates between these two repertoires.

AT WORK AND PLAY

My work confirms Baker's (1984) analysis of trading patterns at a U.S. stock options market, identifying the market as diurnally curvilinear, with heightened activities in the morning and afternoon and a slow, nonactive midday period. Investor orders build up overnight and are released as the market opens, providing a spurt of trading in the early part of the morning. Furthermore, economic data is often released within the first hour of trading, providing additional impetus for speculative market activity. This was readily apparent to me while I was working as a clerk during the market's opening. As the clock ticks toward the opening bell, there emerges an almost palpable sense of expectation and excitement. Cordiality and muted greetings to colleagues and competitors turn to intermittent shouts about "the call," the anticipated opening range based upon overnight market activity. In the moments before the bell rings to announce the opening of trading, the volume can climb to a loud, continuous shout. It is what many respondents called "electric.". . . .

Similarly, activity picks up again as traders make their final trades of the day. There are categories of trades made explicitly during the market's closing range. Furthermore, the Exchange sounds a bell for the last minute, last 10 seconds, and the end of trading, creating a heightened sense of urgency.

Participants anticipate other busy times as well—the release of economic data, meetings of the federal reserve board, and planned political speeches. During these spells, lasting anywhere from moments to hours, traders and employees adopt a triage mentality. When the boards posting market prices go "fast market," indicating an inability of the electronic boards to keep up with the pace of changes in trading prices, the most important thing to do is minimize errors, stay controlled, and remain alert for unanticipated market movements and customer responses. Breaks for lunch or coffee are shortened or cancelled. Because it is impossible to predict what will happen when the market moves, all participants remain in a state of high readiness. . . .

The market does slow down, particularly in the middle of the day. When trading diminishes, a different set of rules applies. The pace and intensity of actual working time ranges from day to day. As one respondent said, "You could be for 20 minutes under an unbearable amount of stress, and then once that 20 minutes is over, you could have 2 hours of doing nothing" (24-year-old male pit clerk). During slow periods, traders would leave the pits or stand around waiting for something to happen. People on the floor amused themselves by telling jokes, goofing around, doing crossword puzzles, reading newspapers, or standing around engaging in idle conversation.

Fieldwork observations distinguishing the ACE as two distinct modalities depending on the amount of market activity were confirmed in focused interviews. Respondents routinely distinguished the exchange's fast and slow periods. A 28-year-old female trade checker described it in the following manner, typical of my respondents:

> When it's fast, it's all about business, it's like you're in an accounting firm during tax time, and it is all business, nobody smiling . . . you might not be pleasant, some of them are fighting; as you know, they get upset. And then when it's slow, it's laid back, people are smuggling in food, they're doing the stupid little sharking,[2] which I think is so, it's hilarious . . . and then, the wrestling between the boys. . . . It's like kindergarten, when it's slow, and you're looking for something to do. . . .

At Work: Gender as Competence

These fast and slow periods provide the temporal context for distinguishing the two gender repertoires operating on the ACE floor. Although men and women did not physically change during work and play periods, the "constituting narratives" (Salzinger, 1997) of gender as a set of social relations between men and women varied widely within these two contexts. These temporal shifts and the different gender repertoires operating during work and play reveal the localized content of gender on the trading floor. During work, men on the floor rarely noted women as women. Instead, men gauged women's success and failure in the pits with seemingly gender-neutral criteria. Although women were somewhat more likely to see the different application of these criteria to men and women (e.g., in the different meanings of aggressiveness assigned to men and women), they too were as likely as men to accept competence as gender neutral.

Thus, men and women insisted that gender itself was not the cause of success or failure on the trading floor. Instead of pointing to gender, participants would talk about competence as being able to "get the job done," particularly under the heavy stress of a fast market. Gender, however, did not disappear during work times. Competence, though imbued with a gender-neutral veneer, smuggled in a distinctively "gendered logic" (Acker, 1990; Smith, 1987). Rather than being subsumed or displaced by competence, gender operated through it. Within this logic, competence and masculinity coincided considerably. Enacting a hegemonic masculinity coincided with proving oneself to be an aggressive, assertive participant in the market. Because the components of competence were interpreted as masculine, women were often put in positions where they were forced to compromise between being competent and distancing themselves from conventional ideals of femininity. The operation of this gender repertoire is illustrated in three key facets of competence on the trading floor: handling stress, being aggressive, and being physical.

One element of competence at the ACE is the ability to handle stress under fast market conditions. The fact that the markets potentially change very quickly creates specific challenges for working on the floor. For example, at the height of trading in 1994, contracts traded hands at a rate averaging 50 per second. Incremental changes in the price of a contract, known as a tick, range between $12.50 and $32 per tick. For a 100-contract order, a single tick is often worth more than $2,000; a 1,000-contract order can be worth $25,000.

Although participants talked about handling stress as a universal activity, interviews with participants showed how they linked stress management to distinctly masculine attributes. Often, clerks and traders coped with stressful, mistake-laden days by trying to deliberately forget about errors made under pressure:

> It's like when you make an error when you're playing baseball. I played sports my whole life, and whenever you made an error, you sat there and moped about it, chances were the next time . . . the ball was hit to you, you're going to make an error again. So you, it's like, so key to just forget about it. And how weird is that, that you say to yourself, O.K., forget about the fact that I just lost $12,000 for that guy, let's go back to work. That's challenging. (24-year-old male pit clerk)

Sports metaphors are a significant and often pervasive component of accounts of the market, and, in fact, a number of former athletes actually work on the floor. Linking competence to sports allowed men to interpret their experiences in the context of a competitive masculinity unavailable to women (Hearn & Parkin, 1987; Messner, 1992; pp. 17–19). Metaphors such as sports and battle were often used to describe the pressures of a fast-moving market. Women do participate in both athletics and armed service, but for men, the metaphor of sports denoted manliness as much as masculinity. Without explicit reference to gender, these narratives nevertheless tied together masculinity and the ability to handle pressure.

Because handling pressure acts explicitly as a gender-neutral concept but was implicitly constituted as a masculine ideal, women who do excel under pressure are in a position where their success must be explained. Under these circumstances, men grudgingly acknowledged successful women as competent but not also as women. That is, women traders could be respected as a trader or treated as a woman but rarely both. A handful of female brokers, and clerks on the floor were identified as competent in this manner, as this 54-year-old male trader made clear:

> Take Susan, that's a perfect example. Now there's a person. There's a player, there's a market maker, and so for her, you have to respect her. Forget about the fact that she's a woman. You have to respect her as a person, because she was in there, was constantly in the market. I think you just know that there's a person that I can go to with a 50 [contract order] and know that it's going to clear the next day at that price.

In this trader's account, the example of a successful woman who could handle the pressure served to downplay gender as a constituent element of competence, focusing instead on the importance of being reliable under pressure. But later in the same interview, this same trader remarked that Susan's ability to compete "maybe makes her less of a woman." Despite the rhetoric of gender neutrality, high-status women often compromised their femininity. Successful male traders, by contrast, were held in higher esteem through their abilities to "step up" in fast markets.

The second element of competence as a gender repertoire is the ability to be aggressive. In an active market, clerks compete with each other to get orders from customers, and traders compete with each other to buy and sell contracts at the best possible prices. Almost 80% of my respondents (15 of 19) explicitly listed aggressiveness as an important element of competence. The imagery that respondents used to describe aggressiveness was vivid, often sexual or violent, and revealed its gendered character: "You have to want to cut someone's balls off" (54-year-old male); "From 7:20 to 2:00, I turn it on" (35-year-old male); "I'm trying to buy 1,000 at a better price, we're not going to sit there and discuss it over a cup of tea" (25-year-old female); "It's survival of the fittest. It's a war" (26-year-old male).

Although both women and men considered themselves aggressive traders, gender again operated through, rather than instead of, competence. Most women on the floor described themselves as aggressive, a quality heightened by the work environment. A 25-year-old female pit clerk, proud of her ability to "hold her own" in a male-dominated environment, conceptualized aggressiveness as universally practiced and at the same time highly defeminizing:

> Everything about the pit goes against what would be, I think, considered feminine. You're yelling, you're screaming, you're spitting, the guys fart and burp all day long, the place smells, it's sweaty, the language is foul, it's aggressive, you're competing aggressively for business. Whether you're a clerk or if you're in the pit as a broker, you're competing aggressively to get your order filled ahead of the next guy. I don't think it's a very feminine environment.

With respect to the actual practices of being aggressive, women were virtually indistinguishable from their male counterparts in their ability and willingness to get in the face of a recalcitrant clerk or trader who was not allowing them to get their orders filled.

Nevertheless, aggressiveness continued to be coded as an eminently masculine characteristic. Women on the floor were often considered "bitchy," a term applied widely to women in men's worlds (see Kanter, 1977; Williams, 1989). For instance, this same woman, when I asked if people called her Deborah or Debbie, replied that "they mostly just call me 'bitch.'" By contrast, men were often criticized for not being aggressive enough. Nonaggressive men were considered ineffective: they did not command enough attention, fill their orders, or get good trades.

Being physical is the third element of competency on the floor. In one respect, the job is in fact physically demanding. The exchange requires all floor participants to remain standing while on the floor, which often means that people stand on their feet for hours at a time. Yelling is an integral part of the labor process, and some traders go to voice therapists to strengthen their voices to be heard. Finally, particularly during busier times on the floor, there is quite a bit of physical jostling as traders struggle to execute their orders and clerks attempt to get the attention of both traders and their customers.

Working on the ACE floor highlights the importance of physical size and space. Depending on the day, there were anywhere between 400 and 1,000 people standing in the trading area where I worked. Clerks often observed that the amount of space that was "theirs" during the day is roughly the space of their body: "The space of my body, pretty much. I mean, I stand, I just stand there, and that's my office. You know, I just stand in a little spot, like the area of a floor tile, all day long" (24-year-old male pit clerk). The press of bodies on the floor emphasizes physical size and floor presence, especially height. Large physical size, being both big and tall, is an advantage in this environment.

Being physical is the component of competence that most closely dovetails with connotations of gender as a reference to male and female bodies. Not surprisingly, physical differences became a locus for discussion about women on the floor. Respondents assumed that most women were at a disadvantage due to the physical nature of the floor. Women's voices are "not as heavy" and seemingly not able to carry as well as men's. Women are also seen as less physically able to hold their own. In addition, many of the respondents pointed out that even for the women who could "hack it," the floor would not be a desirable work environment:

> With girls, and being in the pits, you're like this [claps his hands together]. You're pancaked, man. Some women don't feel comfortable with that, probably. You know, having a guy pressed right up, you know, you're pressed up against a guy, and having a guy pressed up against you from behind. All day long. I would think that'd be uncomfortable for a woman. (39-year-old male clerk)

Invoking women's perceived inability to be as physical as necessary to hold their own in the pits cast gender language of competence yet attributed this difficulty to the characteristics of women's bodies.

The definition of competency that emerges from the discussion of work is a gender repertoire that constructs in masculine, and often sexual, terms while at the same time maintaining a veneer of gender neutrality. Language, even when sexualized, was likely to be directed at the market itself rather than at women as women. Traders often spoke in quite coarse manners about getting "fucked" by the market or accidentally "screwing" a customer, but these constituting discourses were captured in competence rather than in sexualized difference. In periods of work, gender is not made less salient, instead, masculinity is codified in ways that give shape to ACE work activities.

At Play: Gender as Sexualized Difference

If during the period of work, gender is interpreted as a form of competence, during play periods, gender becomes much more directly tied to sex and heterosexual imagery. Here women's bodies became objects for heterosexual masculinity. I focus on joking and getting along as important mechanisms through which the informal social structure of the floor is maintained in gender-dichotomous ways. When the market is less active, a dominant part of the exchange's atmosphere or cultural context consists largely of risque storytelling, practical-joke playing, and joke telling. Masculinity becomes more explicitly sexualized and women more fully excluded from the men's world of trading.

In addition to acting as a stress reliever, as in classical accounts of humor at work (Haas, 1972; Radcliffe-Brown, 1965; Wilson, 1979), joking acts as a primary language through which group solidarity is formed and maintained (Hughes, 1958, p. 109; Lyman, 1987; Norman, 1994). As such, jokes act as a key element of the constituting discourse of gender. Kanter's (1977) study of a large, male-dominated corporation treated joking as a part of corporate culture where men would use off-color or sexual jokes to emphasize women's differences from their male counterparts (pp. 225–226). In my setting, many women did attempt to participate in the joking culture. They spoke about "playing the game" or being able to joke without being offended by the men's apparently juvenile and sexualized behavior. Many women on the floor stress their thick skins and their aptitude for taking a joke. Despite these seemingly "honorary men"—women who could be expected to laugh at jokes and listen to ongoing banter—the repertoire of sexual joking during times of play highlighted rather than minimized the differences between men and women and created visible in-groups and out groups.

The sexual content of the trading floor corresponds to other accounts of merchant bankers (McDowell & Court, 1994) and bond traders (Lewis, 1989). In my observations, joking often had very explicit sexual connotations. In one typical example, after an altercation between two male clerks, one said to the other, "You weigh 100 pounds more than me, you could probably beat up my sister too." The second clerk's response, both to the clerk and laughing onlookers, was "Yeah, I could, but I'd fuck her first. Up the ass!" Violent and sexually aggressive jokes in particular facilitate the identification of the ACE as a man's world. These jokes are ubiquitous. They include reworking comic strips in sexually suggestive ways, alluding to the sexual practices of coworkers (and their relatives), putting sexual spins on current events, and making jokes about individual women on the floor.

The *hetero*-sexualization of jokes in this male bonding precludes women from being able to be, as in McDowell's (1995) characterization of British merchant bankers, "honorary big swinging dicks" during these periods of play (see also Acker, 1990, regarding "honorary men" in organizations). Although many of the women on the floor did swear and occasionally act sexually coarse with men, their status as women made it difficult for them to be sexual subjects; men continued to see women, as a group, as sexual objects. For instance, although some women considered themselves one of the guys, this did not preclude them from being sexually objectified. Women on the floor who told dirty jokes were seen as having their femininity eroded, and participants spoke of this erosion as "not very delicate" or "unladylike," and such women were said to "talk like a truck driver." The contradiction lies in the fact that for a woman to be one of guys, she has to stop being feminine. For men on the floor, discursively constructing even unladylike women as potential sexual objects maintains their ability to assert themselves as masculine men. . . .

With some exceptions—there was one female phone clerk who was jokingly sharing pictures from *Playgirl* to a disgusted audience of men—there is little opportunity for women to joke as sexual aggressors.

Men used joking and sexual banter about women as a way to reinforce a highly gendered group solidarity. This took place particularly during play periods. Talk about sexual exploits over the weekends was pervasive, graphically describing receiving oral sex from a date, picking up women and taking them home from a bar, or paying for prostitutes to come to a party. Comments and joking stories told throughout the less active moments of the trading day provided a way for the men on the floor to communicate their manliness to each other. . . .

CONCLUSION

The primary claim I make is that attention to temporality on the ACE floor highlights different gender repertoires that serve as the constituting discourse of gender, that gender actually operates differently according to the temporal rhythms of the market. When the market is active, gender is articulated through the language of competence. The components of competence—handling stress, being aggressive, being physical—are understood as gender neutral on their face but at the same time obscure highly gendered logics of action. This explains why both men and women perceived women as having to fit in a man's world by getting in people's faces, shouting, pushing, and shoving. This construction of competence is hegemonic: It postures as gender neutral but actually tilts the playing field in favor of men.

When the market is less active, the more overtly sexualized repertoire of joking and getting alone emerges. Men and women use jokes to pass time, fit in, and relieve tension, but a direct result of men's sexual banter is to facilitate group solidarity among men to the exclusion of women. Strong heterosexual joking is predicated on men being the sexual agents of jokes and women being the objects. Although a few long-tenured women were able to joke with the men, for most, this was not the case. Women could not easily participate in these jokes precisely because the concept of women as agents disrupts the normal pattern of female objectification. If both men and women were able to be subjects of sexual banter, who would be left to be the objects?

My second, more general claim is that temporal rhythms are a key to understanding variations in gendered work practices. Salzinger (1997), for example, makes a convincing argument that the meaning of gender can vary greatly at the shop-floor level depending on such local conditions as management attitudes and labor processes. My argument is that even at the local level, gender changes dramatically depending on the pace of work. Particularly in workplaces characterized by lots of temporal variation in the workday—hospital emergency rooms, police departments, restaurants—time matters a great deal with regard to how gender is articulated. In most workplaces, there are lunch hours, coffee breaks, speedups, or slowdowns, all of which have important consequences for the study of gender. . . .

NOTES

1. The ACE, and all names of participants, are pseudonyms.

2. "Shark fins" are trading cards ripped into the shape of a fin. These fins are then surreptitiously attached to an unaware person's jacket collar, and the "sharked" individual is then often sent on a bogus errand. As he or she passes along the lines of clerks and run-

ners, people will scream out "Shark!" until the individual, often turning red in embarrassment or anger, notices he or she has been tagged.

REFERENCES

Acker, J. (1990). Hierarchies, jobs, bodies: A theory of gendered organization. *Gender and Society, 4,* 139–158.

Baker, W. E. (1984). The social structure of a national securities market. *American Journal of Sociology, 89,* 775–811.

Britton, D. M. (1997). Gendered organizational logic: Policy and practice in men's and women's prisons. *Gender and Society, 11,* 796–818.

Connell, R. W. (1987). *Gender and power.* Cambridge, MA: Polity Press.

Connell, R. W. (1995). *Masculinities,* Berkeley: University of California Press.

Epstein, C. F. (1970). *Woman's place: Options and limits in professional careers,* Berkeley: University of California Press.

Ferguson, K. (1984). *The feminist case against bureaucracy,* Philadelphia: Temple University Press.

Haas, J. (1972). Binging: Educational control among high steel ironworkers. *American Behavioral Scientist 16,* 27–34.

Hall. E. J. (1993). Waitering/waitressing: Engendering the work of table servers. *Gender and Society, 7,* 329–346.

Hartmann, H. (1976). Capitalism patriarchy, and job segregation by sex. In M. Blaxall & B. Reagan (Eds.). *Women and the workplace: The implications of occupational segregation* (pp. 137–169). Chicago: University of Chicago Press.

Hearn, J., & Parkin, P. W. (1987). Gender and organizations: A selective review and critique of a neglected area. *Organization Studies, 4,* 219–242.

Hughes, E. (1958). *Men and their work,* Glencoe. IL: Free Press.

Kanter, R. M. (1977). *Men and women of the corporation.* New York: Basic Books.

Leidner, R. (1991). Serving hamburgers and selling insurance: Gender, work, and identity in interactive service jobs. *Gender and Society, 5,* 154–177.

Leidner, R. (1994). *Fast food, fast talk: Service work and the routinization of everyday life.* Berkeley: University of California Press.

Lewis, M. (1989). *Liar's poker: Two cities, true greed.* New York: Norton.

Lyman, P. (1987). The fraternal bond as a joking relationship: A case study of the role of sexist jokes in male group bonding. In M. Kimmel (Ed.). *Changing men: New directions in research on men and masculinity* (pp. 148–163). Newbury Park, CA: Sage.

McDowell, L. (1995). Body work: Heterosexual gender performances in city workplaces. In D. Bell & G. Valentine (Eds.). *Mapping desire: Geographics of sexualities* (pp. 75–95). New York: Routledge.

McDowell. L., & Court, G. (1994). Missing subjects: Gender, power, and sexuality in merchant banking. *Economic Geography, 70,* 229–251.

Messner, M. A. (1992). *Power at play: Sports and the problem of masculinity.* Boston, MA: Beacon.

Norman, K. (1994). The ironic body: Obscene joking among Swedish working-class women. *Ethnos, 59,* 187–211.

Pringle, R. (1989), *Secretaries talk: Sexuality, power, and work.* London: Verso.

Radcliffe-Brown. A. R. (1965). *Structure and function in primitive society.* New York: Free Press.

Salzinger, L. (1997). From high heels to swathed bodies: Gendered meanings under production in Mexico's export-processing industry. *Feminist Studies, 28,* 549–574.

Smith, D. E. (1987). *The everyday world as problematic: A feminist sociology.* Boston: Northeastern University Press.

Stacey, J., & Thorne, B. (1985). The missing feminist revolution in sociology: *Social Problems, 32,* 301–316.

West. C., & Zimmerman, D. (1987). Doing gender. *Gender and Society, 1,* 125–151.

Williams, C. L. 1989, *Gender differences at work: Women and men in nontraditional occupations.* Berkeley: University of California Press.

Wilson, C. (1979). *Jokes: Form, content, use and function.* New York: Academic Press.

38

Boundary Lines

Labeling Sexual Harassment in Restaurants

PATTI A. GIUFFRE

CHRISTINE L. WILLIAMS

Sexual harassment occurs when submission to or rejection of sexual advances is a term of employment, is used as a basis for making employment decisions, or if the advances create a hostile or offensive work environment (Konrad and Gutek 1986). Sexual harassment can cover a range of behaviors, from leering to rape (Ellis, Barak, and Pinto 1991; Pryor 1987; Reilly et al. 1992; Schneider 1982). Researchers estimate that as many as 70 percent of employed women have experienced behaviors that may legally constitute sexual harassment (MacKinnon 1979; Powell 1986); however, a far lower percentage of women claim to have experienced sexual harassment. Paludi and Barickman write that "the great majority of women who are abused by behavior that fits legal definitions of sexual harassment—and who are traumatized by the experience—do not label what has happened to them 'sexual harassment'" (1991, 68).

Why do most women fail to label their experiences as sexual harassment? Part of the problem is that many still do not recognize that sexual harassment is an actionable offense. Sexual harassment was first described in 1976 (MacKinnon 1979), but it was not until 1986 that the U.S. Supreme Court included sexual harassment in the category of gender discrimination, thereby making it illegal (Paludi and Barickman 1991); consequently, women may not yet identify their experiences as sexual harassment because a substantial degree of awareness about its illegality has yet to be developed.

Many victims of sexual harassment may also be reluctant to come forward with complaints, fearing that they will not be believed, or that their charges will not be taken seriously (Jensen and Gutek 1982). As the Anita Hill-Clarence Thomas hearings demonstrated, women who are victims of sexual harassment often become the accused when they bring charges against their assailant.

There is another issue at stake in explaining the gap between experiencing and labeling behaviors "sexual harassment": many men and women experience some sexual behaviors in the workplace as pleasurable. Research on sexual harassment suggests that men are more likely than women to enjoy sexual interactions at work (Gutek 1985; Konrad and Gutek 1986; Reilly et al. 1992), but even some women experience sexual overtures at work as pleasurable (Pringle 1988). This attitude may be especially strong in organizations that

Patti A. Giuffre and Christine L. Williams, "Boundary Lines: Labeling Sexual Harassment in Restaurants," from *Gender & Society,* Volume 8/1994, p. 378–401.

use and exploit the bodies and sexuality of the workers (Cockburn 1991). Workers in many jobs are hired on the basis of their attractiveness and solicitousness—including not only sex industry workers, but also service sector workers such as receptionists, airline attendants, and servers in trendy restaurants. According to Cockburn (1991), this sexual exploitation is not completely forced: many people find this dimension of their jobs appealing and reinforcing to their own sense of identity and pleasure; consequently, some men and women resist efforts to expunge all sexuality from their places of work.

This is not to claim that all sexual behavior in the workplace is acceptable, even to some people. The point is that it is difficult to label behavior as sexual harassment because it forces people to draw a line between illicit and "legitimate" forms of sexuality at work—a process fraught with ambiguity. Whether a particular interaction is identified as harassment will depend on the intention of the harasser and the interpretation of the interchange by the victim, and both of these perspectives will be highly influenced by workplace culture and the social context of the specific event.

This article examines how one group of employees—restaurant workers—distinguishes between sexual harassment and other forms of sexual interaction in the workplace. We conducted an in-depth interview study of waitpeople and found that complex double standards are often used in labeling behavior as sexual harassment: identical behaviors are labeled sexual harassment in some contexts and not others. Many respondents claimed that they enjoyed sexual interactions involving coworkers of the same race/ethnicity, sexual orientation, and class/status backgrounds. Those who were offended by such interactions nevertheless dismissed them as natural or inevitable parts of restaurant culture.[1] When the same behavior occurred in contexts that upset these hegemonic heterosexual norms—in particular, when the episode involved interactions between gay and heterosexual men, or men and women of different racial/ethnic backgrounds—people seemed willing to apply the label sexual harassment

We argue that identifying behaviors that occur only in counterhegemonic contexts as sexual harassment can potentially obscure and legitimate more insidious forms of domination and exploitation. As Pringle points out, "Men control women through direct use of power, but also through definitions of pleasure—which is less likely to provoke resistance" (1988, 95). Most women, she writes, actively seek out what Rich (1980) termed "compulsory heterosexuality" and find pleasure in it. The fact that men and women may enjoy certain sexual interactions in the workplace does not mean they take place outside of oppressive social relationships, nor does it imply that these routine interactions have no negative consequences for women. We argue that the practice of labeling as "sexual harassment" only those behaviors that challenge the dominant definition of acceptable sexual activity maintains and supports men's institutionalized right of sexual access and power over women.

METHODS

The occupation of waiting tables was selected to study the social definition of sexual harassment because many restaurants have a blatantly sexualized workplace culture (Cobble 1991; Paules 1991). According to a report published in a magazine that caters to restaurant owners, "Restaurants . . . are about as informal a workplace as there is, so much so as to actually encourage—or at the very least tolerate—sexual banter" (Anders 1993, 48). Unremitting sexual banter and innuendo, as well as physical jostling, create an environment of "compulsory jocularity" in many restaurants (Pringle 1988, 93). Sexual attractiveness and flirtation are often institutionalized parts of a waitperson's job description; consequently, individual employees are often forced to draw the line for themselves to distinguish legitimate and illegitimate expressions of sexuality, making this occupation an excellent context for examining how people determine what constitutes sexual harassment. In contrast, many more sexual behaviors may be labeled sexual harassment in less highly sexualized work environments.[2]

Eighteen in-depth interviews were conducted with male and female waitstaff who work in restaurants in Austin, Texas. Respondents were selected from restaurants that employ equal proportions of men and women on their wait staffs. Overall, restaurant work is highly sex segregated: women make up about 82 percent of all waitpeople (U.S. Department of Labor 1989), and it is common for restaurants to be staffed only by either waitresses or waiters, with men predominating in the higher-priced restaurants (Cobble 1991; Hall 1993; Paules 1991). We decided to focus only on waitpeople who work in mixed-sex groups for two reasons. First, focusing on waitpeople working on integrated staffs enables us to examine sexual harassment between co-workers who occupy the same position in an organizational hierarchy. Co-worker sexual harassment is perhaps the most common form of sexual harassment (Pryor 1987; Schneider 1982); yet most case studies of sexual harassment have examined either unequal hierarchical relationships (e.g., boss-secretary harassment) or harassment in highly skewed gender groupings (e.g., women who work in nontraditional occupations) (Benson and Thomson 1982; Carothers and Crull 1984; Gruber and Bjorn 1982). This study is designed to investigate sexual harassment in unequal hierarchical relationships, as well as harassment between organizationally equal co-workers.

Second, equal proportions of men and women in an occupation implies a high degree of male-female interaction (Gutek 1985). Waitpeople are in constant contact with each other, help each other when the restaurant is busy, and informally socialize during slack periods. In contrast, men and women have much more limited interactions in highly sex-segregated restaurants and indeed, in most work environments. The high degree of interaction among the wait staff provides ample opportunity for sexual harassment between men and women to occur and, concomitantly, less opportunity for same-sex sexual harassment to occur.

The sample was generated using "snowball" techniques and by going to area restaurants and asking waitpeople to volunteer for the study. The sample includes eight men and ten women. Four respondents are Latina/o, two African American, and twelve White. Four respondents are gay or lesbian; one is bisexual; thirteen are heterosexual. (The gay men and lesbians in the sample are all "out" at their respective restaurants.) Fourteen respondents are single; three are married; one is divorced. Respondents' ages range from 22 to 37.

Interviews lasted approximately one hour, and they were tape-recorded and transcribed for this analysis. All interviews were conducted by the first author, who has over eight years' experience waiting tables. Respondents were asked about their experiences working in restaurants; relationships with managers, customers, and other co-workers; and their personal experiences of sexual harassment. Because interviews were conducted in the fall of 1991, when the issue was prominent in the media because of the Hill-Thomas hearings, most respondents had thought a lot about this topic.

FINDINGS

Respondents agreed that sexual banter is very common in the restaurant: staff members talk and joke about sex constantly. With only one exception, respondents described their restaurants as highly sexualized. This means that 17 of the 18 respondents said that sexual joking, touching, and fondling were common, everyday occurrences in their restaurants. For example, when asked if he and other waitpeople ever joke about sex, one waiter replied, "about 90 percent of [the jokes] are about sex." According to a waitress, "at work . . . [we're] used to patting and touching and hugging." Another waiter said, "I do not go through a shift without someone . . . pinching my nipples or poking me in the butt or grabbing my crotch. . . . It's just what we do at work."

These informal behaviors are tantamount to "doing heterosexuality," a process analogous to "doing gender" (West and Zimmerman 1987).[3] By engaging in these public flirtations and open discussions of sex, men and women reproduce the dominant cultural norms of heterosexuality and lend an air of legitimacy—if not inevitability—to heterosexual relationships. In other words, heterosexuality is normalized and naturalized through its ritualistic public display. Indeed, although most respondents described their workplaces as highly sexualized, several dismissed the constant sexual innuendo and behaviors as "just joking," and nothing to get upset about. Several respondents claimed that this is simply "the way it is in the restaurant business," or "just the way men are."

With only one exception, the men and women interviewed maintained that they enjoyed this aspect of their work. Heterosexuality may be normative, and in these contexts, even compulsory, yet many men and women find pleasure in its expression. Many women—as well as men—actively reproduce hegemonic sexuality and apparently enjoy its ritual expression; however, in a few instances, sexual conduct was labeled as sexual harassment. Seven women and three men said they had experienced sexual harassment in restaurant work. Of these, two women and one man described two different experiences of sexual harassment, and two women described three experiences. Table 1 describes the characteristics of each of the respondents and their experiences of sexual harassment.

We analyzed these 17 accounts of sexual harassment to find out what, if anything, these experiences shared in common. With the exception of two episodes (discussed later), the experiences that were labeled "sexual harassment" were not distinguished by any specific words or behaviors, nor were they distinguished by their degree of severity. Identical behaviors were considered acceptable if they were perpetrated by some people, but considered offensive if perpetrated by others. In other words, sexual behavior in the workplace was interpreted differently depending on the context of the interaction. In general, respondents labeled their experiences sexual harassment only if the offending behavior occurred in one of three social contexts: (1) if perpetrated by someone in a more powerful position, such as a manager; (2) if by someone of a different race/ethnicity; or (3) if perpetrated by someone of a different sexual orientation.

Our findings do not imply that sexual harassment did not occur outside of these three contexts. Instead, they simply indicate that our respondents *labeled* behavior as "sexual harassment" when it occurred in these particular social contexts. We will discuss each

Table 1 Description of Respondents and Their Reported Experiences of Sexual Harassment at Work

Pseudonym	Age	Race[a]	SO[b]	MS[c]	Years In Restaurant[d]	Sexualized Environment[e]	Sexually Harassed[f]
Kate	23	W	H	S	1	yes	yes (1)
Beth	26	W	H	S	5	yes	yes (1)
Ann	29	W	H	S	1*	yes	yes (2)
Cathy	29	W	H	S	8 mos.*	yes	yes (3)
Carla	22	W	H	M	5 mos.*	yes	yes (3)
Diana	32	L	H	M	6	no	no
Maxine	30	L	H	M	4	yes	no
Laura	27	W	B	S	2*	yes	yes (1)
Brenda	23	W	L	S	3	yes	yes (2)
Lynn	37	B	L	D	5*	yes	no
Jake	22	W	H	S	1	yes	yes (1)
Al	23	W	H	S	3	yes	no
Frank	29	W	H	S	8	yes	yes (1)
John	31	W	H	S	2	yes	no
Trent	23	W	G	S	1*	yes	no
Rick	24	B	H	S	1.5	yes	yes (2)
David	25	L	H	S	5	yes	no
Don	24	L	G	S	1*	yes	no

a. Race: B = Black, L = Latina/o, W = White.
b. SO = sexual orientation: B = bisexual, G = gay, H = heterosexual, L = lesbian.
c. MS = marital status: D = divorced, M = married, S = single.
d. Years in restaurant refers to length of time employed in current restaurant. An asterisk indicates that respondent has worked in other restaurants.
e. Whether or not the respondent claimed sexual banter and touching were common occurrences in their restaurant.
f. Responded yes or no to the question: "Have you ever been sexually harassed in the restaurant?" Number in parentheses refers to number of incidents described in the interview.

of these contexts and speculate on the reasons why they were singled out by our respondents.

Powerful Position

In the restaurant, managers and owners are the highest in the hierarchy of workers. Generally, they are the only ones who can hire or fire waitpeople. Three of the women and one of the men interviewed said they had been sexually harassed by their restaurants' managers or owners. In addition, several others who did not personally experience harassment said they had witnessed managers or owners sexually harassing other waitpeople. This finding is consistent with other research indicating people are more likely to think that sexual harassment has occurred when the perpetrator is in a more powerful position (e.g., Ellis et al. 1991).

Carla describes being sexually harassed by her manager:

> One evening, [my manager] grabbed my body, not in a private place, just grabbed my body, period. He gave me like a bear hug from behind a total of four times in one night. By the end of the night I was livid. I was trying to avoid him. Then when he'd do it, I'd just ignore the conversation or the joke or whatever and walk away.

She claimed that her co-workers often give each other massages and joke about sex, but she did not label any of their behaviors sexual harassment. In fact, all four individuals who experienced sexual harassment from their managers described very similar types of behavior from their co-workers, which they did not define as sexual harassment. For example, Cathy said that she and the other waitpeople talk and joke about sex constantly: "Everybody stands around and talks about sex a lot. . . . Isn't that weird? You know, it's something about working in restaurants and, yeah, so we'll all sit around and talk about sex." She said that talking with her co-workers about sex does not constitute sexual harassment because it is "only joking." She does, however, view her male manager as a sexual harasser:

> My employer is very sexist. I would call that sexual harassment. Very much of a male chauvinist pig. He kind of started [saying] stuff like, "You can't really wear those shorts because they're not flattering to your figure. . . . But I like the way you wear those jeans. They look real good. They're right." It's like, you know [I want to say to him], "You're the owner, you're in power. That's evident. You know, you need to find a better way to tell me these things." We've gotten to a point now where we'll joke around now, but it's never ever sexual ever. I won't allow that with him.

Cathy acknowledges that her manager may legitimately dictate her appearance at work, but only if he does so in professional—and not personal—terms. She wants him "to find a better way to tell me these things," implying that he is not completely out-of-line in suggesting that she wear tight pants. He "crosses the line" when he personalizes his directive, by saying to Cathy "*I like* the way you wear those jeans." This is offensive to Cathy because it is framed as the manager's personal prerogative, not the institutional requirements of the job.

Ann described a similar experience of sexual harassment from a restaurant owner:

> Yeah, there's been a couple of times when a manager has made me feel real uncomfortable and I just removed myself from the situation. . . . Like if there's something I really want him to hear or something I think is really important there's no touching. Like, "Don't touch me while I'm talking to you." You know, because I take that as very patronizing. I actually blew up at one of the owners once because I was having a rough day and he came up behind me and he was rubbing my back, like up and down my back and saying, you know, "Oh, is Ann having a bad day?" or something like that and I shook him off of me and I said, "You do not need to touch me to talk to me."

Ann distinguishes between legitimate and illegitimate touching: if the issue being discussed is "really important"—that is, involving her job status—she insists there be no touching. In these specific situations, a back rub is interpreted as patronizing and offensive because the manager is using his powerful position for his *personal* sexual enjoyment.

One of the men in the sample, Frank, also experienced sexual harassment from a manager:

> I was in the bathroom and [the manager] came up next to me and my tennis shoes were spray-painted silver so he knew it was me in there and he said something about, "Oh, what do you have in your hand there?" I was on the other side of a wall and he said, "Mind if I hold it for a while?" or something like that, you know. I just pretended like I didn't hear it.

Frank also described various sexual behaviors among the waitstaff, including fondling, "joking about bodily functions," and "making bikinis out of tortillas." He said, "I mean, it's like, what we do at work. . . . There's no holds barred. I don't find it offensive. I'm used to it by now. I'm guilty of it myself." Evidently, he defines sexual behaviors as "sexual harassment" only when perpetrated by someone in a position of power over him.[4]

Two of the women in the sample also described sexual harassment from customers. We place these experiences in the category of "powerful position" because customers do have limited economic power over the waitperson insofar as they control the tip (Crull 1987). Cathy said that male customers often ask her to "sit on my lap" and provide them with other sexual favors. Brenda, a lesbian, described a similar experience of sexual harassment from women customers:

> One time I had this table of lesbians and they were being real vulgar towards me. Real sexual. This woman kind of tripped me as I was walking by and said, "Hurry back." I mean, gay people can tell when other people are gay. I felt harassed.

In these examples of harassment by customers, the line is drawn using a similar logic as in the examples of harassment by managers. These customers acted as though the waitresses were providing table service to satisfy the customers' private desires, instead of working to fulfill their job descriptions. In other words, the customers' demands were couched in personal—and not professional—terms, making the waitresses feel sexually harassed.

It is not difficult to understand why waitpeople singled out sexual behaviors from managers, owners, and customers as sexual harassment. Subjection to sexual advances by someone with economic power comes closest to the quid pro quo form of sexual harassment, wherein employees are given the option to either "put out or get out." Studies have found that this type of sexual harassment is viewed as the most threatening and unambiguous sort (Ellis et al. 1991; Fitzgerald 1990; Gruber and Bjorn 1982).

But even in this context, lines are drawn between legitimate and illegitimate sexual behavior in the workplace. As Cathy's comments make clear, some people accept the employers' prerogative to exploit the workers' sexuality, by dictating appropriate "sexy" dress, for example. Like airline attendants, waitresses are expected to be friendly, helpful, and sexually available to the male customers (Cobble 1991). Because this expectation is embedded in restaurant culture, it becomes difficult for workers to separate sexual harassment from the more or less accepted forms of sexual exploitation that are routine features of their jobs. Consequently, some women are reluctant to label blatantly offensive behaviors as sexual harassment. For example, Maxine, who claims that she has never experienced sexual harassment, said that customers often "talk dirty" to her:

> I remember one day, about four or five years ago when I was working as a cocktail waitress, this guy asked me for a "Slow Comfortable Screw" [the name of a drink]. I didn't know what it was. I didn't know if he was making a move or something. I just looked at him. He said, "You know what it is, right?" I said, "I bet the bartender knows!" (laughs). . . . There's another one, "Sex on the Beach." And there's another one called a "Screaming Orgasm." Do you believe that?

Maxine is subject to a sexualized work environment that she finds offensive; hence her experience could fit the legal definition of sexual harassment. But because sexy drink names are an institutionalized part of restaurant culture, Maxine neither complains about it nor labels it sexual harassment: Once it becomes clear that a "Slow Comfortable Screw" is a legitimate and recognized restaurant demand, she accepts it (albeit reluctantly) as part of her job description. In other words, the fact that the offensive behavior is institutionalized seems to make it beyond reproach in her eyes. This finding is consistent with others' findings that those who work in highly sexualized environments may be less likely to label offensive behavior "sexual harassment" (Gutek 1985; Konrad and Gutek 1986).

Only in specific contexts do workers appear to define offensive words and acts of a sexual nature as sexual harassment—even when initiated by someone in a more powerful position. The interviews suggest that workers use this label to describe their experiences only when their bosses or their customers couch their requests for sexual attentions in explicitly personal terms. This way of defining sexual harassment may obscure and legitimize more institutionalized—and hence more insidious—forms of sexual exploitation at work.

Race/Ethnicity

The restaurants in our sample, like most restaurants in the United States, have racially segregated staffs (Howe 1977). In the restaurants where our respondents are employed, men of color are concentrated in two positions: the kitchen cooks and bus personnel (formerly called busboys). Five of the White women in the sample reported experiencing sexual harassment from Latino men who worked in these positions. For example, when asked if she had ever experienced sexual harassment, Beth said:

> Yes, but it was not with the people . . . it was not, you know, the people that I work with in the front of the house. It was with the kitchen. There are boundaries or lines that I draw with the people I work with. In the kitchen, the lines are quite different. Plus, it's a Mexican staff. It's a very different attitude. They tend to want to touch you more and, at times, I can put up with a little bit of it but . . . because I will give them a hard time too but I won't touch them. I won't touch their butt or anything like that.
>
> [Interviewer: So sometimes they cross the line?]
>
> It's only happened to me a couple of times. One guy, like, patted me on the butt and I went off. I lost my shit. I went off on him. I said, "No. Bad. Wrong. I can't speak Spanish to you but, you know, this is it." I told the kitchen manager who is a guy and he's not . . . the head kitchen manager is not Hispanic. . . . I've had to do that over the years only a couple of times with those guys.

Beth reported that the waitpeople joke about sex and touch each other constantly, but she does not consider their behavior sexual harassment. Like many of the other men and women in the sample, Beth said she feels comfortable engaging in this sexual banter and play with the other waitpeople (who were predominantly White), but not with the Mexican men in the kitchen.

Part of the reason for singling out the behaviors of the cooks as sexual harassment may involve status differences between waitpeople and cooks. Studies have suggested that people may label behaviors as sexual harassment when they are perpetrated by people in lower status organizational positions (Grauerholz 1989; McKinney 1990); however, it is difficult to generalize about the relative status of cooks and waitpeople because of the varied and often complex organizational hierarchies of restaurants (Paules 1991, 107–10). If the cook is a chef, as in higher-priced restaurants, he or she may actually have more status than waitpeople, and indeed may have the formal power to hire and fire the waitstaff. In the restaurants where our respondents worked, the kitchen cooks did not wield this sort of formal control, but they could exert some informal power over the waitstaff by slowing down food orders or making the orders look and/or taste bad. Because bad food can decrease the waitperson's tip, the cooks can thereby control the waitperson's income; hence servers are forced to negotiate and to some extent placate the wishes and desires of cooks to perform their jobs. The willingness of several respondents to label the cooks' behavior as sexual harassment may reflect their perception that the cooks' informal demands had become unreasonable. In such cases, subjection to the offensive behaviors is a term of employment, which is quid pro quo sexual harassment. As mentioned previously, this type of sexual harassment is the most likely to be so labeled and identified.

Because each recounted case of sexual harassment occurring between individuals of different occupational statuses involved a minority man sexually harassing a White woman, the racial context seems equally important. For example, Ann also said that she and the other waiters and waitresses joke about sex and touch each other "on the butt" all the time, and when asked if she had ever experienced sexual harassment, she said,

> I had some problems at [a previous restaurant] but it was a communication problem. A lot of the guys in the kitchen did not speak English. They would see the waiters hugging on us, kissing us and pinching our rears and stuff. They would try to do it and I couldn't tell them, "No. You don't understand this. It's like we do it because we have a mutual understanding but I'm not comfortable with you doing it." So that was really hard and a lot of times what I'd have to do is just sucker punch them in the chest and just use a lot of cuss words and they knew that I was serious. And there again, I felt real weird about that because they're just doing what they see go on everyday.

Kate, Carla, and Brenda described very similar racial double standards. Kate complained about a Mexican busser who constantly touched her:

> This is not somebody that I talk to on a friendly basis. We don't sit there and laugh and joke and stuff. So, when he touches me, all I know is he is just touching me and there is no context about it. With other people, if they said something or they touched me, it would be funny or . . . we have a relationship. This person and I and all the other people do not. So that is sexual harassment.

And according to Brenda:

> The kitchen can be kind of sexist. They really make me angry. They're not as bad as they used to be because they got warned. They're mostly Mexican, not even Mexican-American. Most of them, they're just starting to learn English.
>
> [Interviewer: What do they do to you?]
>
> Well, I speak Spanish, so I know. They're not as sexual to me because I think they know I don't like it. Some of the other girls will come through and they will touch them like here [points to the lower part of her waist]. . . . I've had some pretty bad arguments with the kitchen.
>
> [Interviewer: Would you call that sexual harassment?]
>
> Yes, I think some of the girls just don't know better to say something. I think it happens a lot with the kitchen guys. Like sometimes, they will take a relleno in their hands like it's a penis. Sick!

Each of these women identified the sexual advances of the minority men in their restaurants as sexual harassment, but not the identical behaviors of their white male co-workers; moreover, they all recognize that they draw boundary lines differently for Anglo men and Mexican men: each of them willingly participates in "doing heterosexuality" only in racially homogamous contexts. These women called the behavior of the Mexican cooks "sexual harassment" in part because they did not "have a relationship" with these men, nor was it conceivable to them that they *could* have a relationship with them, given cultural and language barriers—and, probably, racist attitudes as well. The white men, on the other hand, can "hug, kiss, and pinch rears" of the white women because they have a "mutual understanding"—implying reciprocity and the possibility of intimacy.

The importance of this perception of relationship potential in the assessment of sexual harassment is especially clear in the cases of the two married women in the sample, Diana and Maxine. Both of these women said that they had never experienced sexual harassment. Diana, who works in a family-owned and -operated restaurant, claimed that her restaurant is not a sexualized work environment. Although people occasionally make double entendre jokes relating to sex, according to Diana, "there's no contact whatsoever like someone pinching your butt or something." She said that she has never experienced sexual harassment:

> Everybody here knows I'm married so they're not going to get fresh with me because they know that it's not going to go anywhere, you know so . . . and vice versa. You know, we know the guys' wives. They come in here to eat. It's respect all the way. I don't think they could handle it if they saw us going around hugging them. You know what I mean? It's not right.

Similarly, Maxine, who is Colombian, said she avoids the problem of sexual harassment in her workplace because she is married:

> The cooks don't offend me because they know I speak Spanish and they know how to talk with me because I

> set my boundaries and they know that. . . . I just don't joke with them more than I should. They all know that I'm married, first of all, so that's a no-no for all of them. My brother used to be a manager in that restaurant so he probably took care of everything. I never had any problems anyway in any other jobs because, like I said, I set my boundaries. I don't let them get too close to me.
>
> [Interviewer, You mean physically?]
>
> Not physically only. Just talking. If they want to talk about, "Do you go dancing? Where do you go dancing?" Like I just change the subject because it's none of their business and I don't really care to talk about that with them . . . not because I consider them to be on the lower levels than me or something but just because if you start talking with them that way then you are just giving them hope or something. I think that's true for most of the guys here, not just talking about the cooks. . . . I do get offended and they know that so sometimes they apologize.

Both Maxine and Diana said that they are protected from sexual harassment because they are married. In effect, they use their marital status to negotiate their interactions with their co-workers and to ward off unwanted sexual advances. Furthermore, because they do not view their co-workers as potential relationship "interests," they conscientiously refuse to participate in any sexual banter in the restaurant.

The fact that both women speak Spanish fluently may mean that they can communicate their boundaries unambiguously to those who only speak Spanish (unlike the female respondents in the sample who only speak English). For these two women, sexual harassment from co-workers is not an issue. Diana, who is Latina, talks about "respect all around" in her restaurant; Maxine claims the cooks (who are Mexican) aren't the ones who offend her. Their comments seem to reflect more mutual respect and humanity toward their Latino co-workers than the comments of the white waitresses. On the other hand, at least from Maxine's vantage point, racial harassment is a bigger problem in her workplace than is sexual harassment. When asked if she ever felt excluded from any groups at work, she said:

> Yeah, sometimes. How can I explain this? Sometimes, I mean, I don't know if they do it on purpose or they don't but they joke around you about being Spanish . . . Sometimes it hurts. Like they say, "What are you doing here? Why don't you go back home?"

Racial harassment—like sexual harassment—is a means used by a dominant group to maintain its dominance over a subordinated group. Maxine feels that, because she is married, she is protected from sexual harassment (although, as we have seen, she is subject to a sexualized workplace that is offensive to her); however, she does experience racial harassment where she works, and she feels vulnerable to this because she is one of very few nonWhites working at her restaurant.

One of the waiters in the sample claimed that he had experienced sexual harassment from female coworkers, and race may have also been a factor in this situation. When Rick (who is African American) was asked if he had ever been sexually harassed, he recounted his experiences with some White waitresses:

> Yes. There are a couple of girls there, waitpeople, who will pinch my rear.
>
> [Interviewer: Do you find it offensive?]
>
> No (laughs) because I'm male. . . . But it is a form of sexual harassment.
>
> [Interviewer: Do you ever tell them to stop?]
>
> If I'm really busy, if I'm in the weeds, and they want to touch me, I'll get mad. I'll tell them to stop. There's a certain time and place for everything.

Rick is reluctant about labeling this interaction "sexual harassment" because "it doesn't bother me unless I'm, like, busy or something like that." In those cases where he is busy, he feels that his female co-workers are subverting his work by pinching him. Because of the race difference, he may experience their behaviors as an expression of racial dominance, which probably influences his willingness to label the behavior as sexual harassment.

In sum, the interviews suggest that the perception and labeling of interactions as "sexual harassment" may be influenced by the racial context of the interaction. If the victim perceives the harasser as expressing a potentially reciprocal relationship interest they may be less likely to label their experience sexual harassment. In cases where the harasser and victim have a different race/ethnicity and class background, the possibility of a relationship may be precluded because of racism, making these cases more likely to be labeled "sexual harassment."

This finding suggests that the practices associated with "doing heterosexuality" are profoundly racist. The White women in the sample showed a great reluctance to label unwanted sexual behavior sexual harassment when it was perpetrated by a potential (or real) relationship interest—that is, a White male co-worker. In contrast, minority men are socially constructed as potential harassers of White women: any expression of sexual interest may be more readily perceived as nonreciprocal and unwanted. The assumption of racial homogamy in heterosexual relationships thus may protect White men from charges of sexual harassment of White women. This would help to explain why so many White women in the sample labeled behaviors perpetrated by Mexican men as sexual harassment, but not the identical behaviors perpetrated by White men.

SEXUAL ORIENTATION

There has been very little research on sexual harassment that addresses the sexual orientation of the harasser and victim (exceptions include Reilly et al. 1992; Schneider 1982, 1984). Surveys of sexual harassment typically include questions about marital status but not about sexual orientation (e.g., Fain and Anderton 1987, Gruber and Bjorn 1982; Powell 1986). In this study, sexual orientation was an important part of heterosexual men's perceptions of sexual harassment. Of the four episodes of sexual harassment reported by the men in the study, three involved openly gay men sexually harassing straight men. One case involved a male manager harassing a male waiter (Frank's experience, described earlier). The other two cases involved co-workers. Jake said that he had been sexually harassed by a waiter:

> Someone has come on to me that I didn't want to come on to me. . . . He was another waiter [male]. It was laughs and jokes the whole way until things got a little too much and it was like, "Hey, this is how it is. Back off. Keep your hands off my ass." . . . Once it reached the point where I felt kind of threatened and bothered by it.

Rick described being sexually harassed by a gay baker in his restaurant:

> There was a baker that we had who was really, really gay. . . . He was very straightforward and blunt. He would tell you, in detail, his sexual experiences and tell you that he wanted to do them with you. . . . I knew he was kidding but he was serious. I mean, if he had a chance he would do these things.

In each of these cases, the men expressed some confusion about the intentions of their harassers—"I knew he was kidding but he was serious." Their inability to read the intentions of the gay men provoked them to label these episodes sexual harassment. Each man did not perceive the sexual interchange as reciprocal, nor did he view the harasser as a potential relationship interest. Interestingly, however, all three of the men who described harassment from gay men claimed that sexual banter and play with other *straight* men did not trouble them. Jake, for example, said that "when men get together, they talk sex," regardless of whether there are women around. He acceded, "people find me offensive, as a matter of fact," because he gets "pretty raunchy" talking and joking about sex. Only when this talk was initiated by a gay man did Jake label it as sexual harassment.

Johnson (1988) argues that talking and joking about sex is a common means of establishing intimacy among heterosexual men and maintaining a masculine identity. Homosexuality is perceived as a direct challenge and threat to the achievement of masculinity and consequently, "the male homosexual is derided by other males because he is not a real man, and in male logic if one is not a real man, one is a woman" (p. 124). In Johnson's view, this dynamic not only sustains masculine identity, it also shores up male dominance over women; thus, for some straight men, talking about sex with other straight men is a form of reasserting masculinity and male dominance, whereas talking about sex with gay men threatens the very basis for their masculine privilege. For this reason they may interpret the sex talk and conduct of gay men as a form of sexual harassment.

In certain restaurants, gay men may in fact intentionally hassle straight men as an explicit strategy to undermine their privileged position in society. For example, Trent (who is openly gay) realizes that heterosexual men are uncomfortable with his sexuality, and he intentionally draws attention to his sexuality in order to bother them:

> [Interviewer: Homosexuality gets on whose nerves?]
>
> The straight people's nerves. . . . I know also that we consciously push it just because, we know, "Okay. We know this is hard for you to get used to but tough luck. I've had my whole life trying to live in this straight world and if you don't like this, tough shit." I don't mean like we're shitty to them on purpose but it's like, "I've had to worry about being accepted by straight people all my life. The shoe's on the other foot now. If you don't like it, sorry."
>
> [Interviewer: Do you get along well with most of the waitpeople?]
>
> I think I get along with straight women. I get along with gay men. I get along with gay women usually. If there's ever going to be a problem between me and somebody it will be between me and a straight man.

Trent's efforts to "push" his sexuality could easily be experienced as sexual harassment by straight men who have limited experience negotiating unwanted sexual advances. The three men who reported being sexually harassed by gay men seemed genuinely confused about the intentions of their harassers, and threatened by the possibility that they would actually be subjected to and harmed by unwanted sexual advances. But it is important to point out that Trent works in a restaurant owned by lesbians, which empowers him to confront his straight male co-workers. Not all restaurants provide the sort of atmosphere that makes this type of engagement possible; indeed, some restaurants have policies explicitly banning the hiring of gays and lesbians. Clearly, not all gay men would be able to push their sexuality without suffering severe retaliation (e.g., loss of job, physical attacks).

In contrast to the reports of the straight men in this study, none of the women interviewed reported sexual harassment from their gay or lesbian co-workers. Although Maxine was worried when she found out that one of her co-workers was lesbian, she claims that this fact no longer troubles her:

> Six months ago I found out that there was a lesbian girl working there. It kind of freaked me out for a while. I was kind of aware of everything that she did towards me. I was conscious if she walked by me and accidently brushed up against me. She's cool. She doesn't bother me. She never touches my butt or anything like that. The gay guys do that to the [straight] guys but they know they're just kidding around. The [straight] guys do that to the [straight] girls, but they don't care. They know that they're not supposed to do that with me. If they do it, I stop and look at them and they apologize and they don't do it anymore. So they stay out of my way because I'm a meanie (laughs).

Some heterosexual women claimed they feel *more* comfortable working with gay men and lesbians. For example, Kate prefers working with gay men rather than heterosexual men or women. She claims that she often jokes about sex with her gay co-workers, yet she does not view them as potential harassers. Instead, she feels that her working conditions are more comfortable and more fun because she works with gay men. Similarly, Cathy prefers working with gay men over straight men because "gay men are a lot like women in that they're very sensitive to other people's space." Cathy also works with lesbians, and she claims that she has never felt sexually harassed by them.

The gays and lesbians in the study did not report any sexual harassment from their gay and lesbian co-workers. Laura, who is bisexual, said she preferred to work with gays and lesbians instead of heterosexuals because they are "more relaxed" about sex. Brenda said she feels comfortable working around all of her male and female colleagues—regardless of their sexual orientation:

> The guys I work with [don't threaten me]. We always run by each other and pat each other on the butt. It's no big deal. Like with my girlfriend [who works at the

> same restaurant], all the cocktailers and hostesses love us. They don't care that we're gay. We're not a threat. We all kind of flirt but it's not sexual. A lesbian is not going to sexually harass another woman unless they're pretty gross anyway. It has nothing to do with their sexuality; it has to do with the person. You can't generalize and say that gays and lesbians are the best to work with or anything because it depends on the person.

Brenda enjoys flirtatious interactions with both men and women at her restaurant, but distinguishes these behaviors from sexual harassment. Likewise, Lynn, who is a lesbian, enjoys the relaxed sexual atmosphere at her workplace. When asked if she ever joked about sex in her workplace, she said:

> Yes! (laughs) All the time! All the time—everybody has something that they want to talk about on sex and it's got to be funny. We have gays. We have lesbians. We have straights. We have people who are real Christian-oriented. But we all jump in there and we all talk about it. It gets real funny at times. . . . I've patted a few butts . . . and I've been patted back by men, and by the women, too! (laughs)

Don and Trent, who are both gay, also said that they had never been sexually harassed in their restaurants, even though both described their restaurants as highly sexualized.

In sum, our interviews suggest that sexual orientation is an important factor in understanding each individual's experience of sexual harassment and his or her willingness to label interactions as sexual harassment. In particular, straight men may perceive gay men as potential harassers. Three of our straight male respondents claimed to enjoy the sexual banter that commonly occurs among straight men, and between heterosexual men and women, but singled out the sexual advances of gay men as sexual harassment. Their contacts with gay men may be the only context where they feel vulnerable to unwanted sexual encounters. Their sense of not being in control of the situation may make them more willing to label these episodes sexual harassment.

Our findings about sexual orientation are less suggestive regarding women. None of the women (straight, lesbian, or bisexual) reported sexual harassment from other female co-workers or from gay men. In fact, all but one of the women's reported cases of sexual harassment involved a heterosexual man. One of the two lesbians in the sample (Brenda) did experience sexual harassment from a group of lesbian customers (described earlier), but she claimed that sexual orientation is not key to her defining the situation as harassment. Other studies have shown that lesbian and bisexual women are routinely subjected to sexual harassment in the workplace (Schneider 1982, 1984); however, more research is needed to elaborate the social contexts and the specific definitions of harassment among lesbians.

The Exceptions

Two cases of sexual harassment were related by respondents that do not fit in the categories we have thus far described. These were the only incidents of sexual harassment reported between co-workers of the same race: in both cases, the sexual harasser is a white man, and the victim, a white woman. Laura—who is bisexual—was sexually harassed at a previous restaurant by a cook:

> This guy was just constantly badgering me about going out with him. He like grabbed me and took me in the walk-in one time. It was a real big deal. He got fired over it too. . . . I was in the back doing something and he said, "I need to talk to you," and I said. "We have nothing to talk about." He like took me and threw me against the wall in the back. . . . I ran out and told the manager, "Oh my God. He just hit me," and he saw the expression on my face. The manager went back there . . . and then he got fired.

This episode of sexual harassment involved violence, unlike the other reported cases. The threat of violence was also present in the other exception, a case described by Carla. When asked if she had ever been sexually harassed, she said,

> I experienced two men, in wait jobs, that were vulgar or offensive and one was a cook and I think he was a rapist. He had the kind of attitude where he would rape a woman. I mean, that's the kind of attitude he had. He would say totally, totally inappropriate [sexual] things.

These were the only two recounted episodes of sexual harassment between "equal" co-workers that involved white men and women, and both involved violence or the threat of violence.[5]

Schneider (1982, 1991) found the greatest degree of consensus about labeling behavior sexual harassment when that behavior involves violence. A victim of sexual harassment may be more likely to be believed when there is evidence of assault (a situation that is analogous to acquaintance rape). The assumption of reciprocity among homogamous couples may protect assailants with similar characteristics to their victims (e.g., class background, sexual orientation, race/ethnicity, age)—*unless* there is clear evidence of physical abuse. Defining only those incidents that involve violence as sexual harassment obscures—and perhaps even legitimatizes—the more common occurrences that do not involve violence, making it all the more difficult to eradicate sexual harassment from the workplace.

DISCUSSION AND CONCLUSION

We have argued that sexual harassment is hard to identify, and thus difficult to eradicate from the workplace, in part because our hegemonic definition of sexuality defines certain contexts of sexual interaction as legitimate. The interviews with wait-people in Austin, Texas, indicate that how people currently identify sexual harassment singles out only a narrow range of interactions, thus disguising and ignoring a good deal of sexual domination and exploitation that take place at work.

Most of the respondents in this study work in highly sexualized atmospheres where sexual banter and touching frequently occur. There are institutionalized policies and practices in the workplace that encourage—or at the very least tolerate—a continual display and performance of heterosexuality. Many people apparently accept this ritual display as being a normal or natural feature of their work; some even enjoy this behavior. In the in-depth interviews, respondents labeled such experiences as sexual harassment in only three contexts: when perpetrated by someone who took advantage of their powerful position for personal sexual gain; when the perpetrator was of a different race/ethnicity than the victim—typically a minority man harassing a white woman; and when the perpetrator was of a different sexual orientation than the victim—typically a gay man harassing a straight man. In only two cases did respondents label experiences involving co-workers of the same race and sexual orientation as sexual harassment—and both episodes involved violence or the threat of violence.

These findings are based on a very small sample in a unique working environment, and hence it is not clear whether they are generalizable to other work settings. In less sexualized working environments, individuals may be more likely to label all offensive sexual advances as sexual harassment, whereas in more highly sexualized environments (such as topless clubs or striptease bars), fewer sexual advances may be labeled sexual harassment. Our findings do suggest that researchers should pay closer attention to the interaction context of sexual harassment taking into account not only gender but also the race, occupational status, and sexual orientation of the assailant and the victim.

Of course, it should not matter who is perpetrating the sexually harassing behavior: sexual harassment should not be tolerated under any circumstances. But if members of oppressed groups (racial/ethnic minority men and gay men) are selectively charged with sexual harassment, whereas members of the most privileged groups are exonerated and excused (except in cases where institutionalized power or violence are used), then the patriarchal order is left intact. This is very similar to the problem of rape prosecution: minority men are the most likely assailants to be arrested and prosecuted, particularly when they attack white women (LaFree 1989). Straight white men who sexually assault women (in the context of marriage, dating, or even work) may escape prosecution because of hegemonic definitions of "acceptable" or "legitimate" sexual expression. Likewise, as we have witnessed in the current debate on gays in the military, straight men's fears of sexual harassment justify the exclusion of gay men and lesbians, whereas sexual harassment perpetrated by straight men against both straight and lesbian women is tolerated and even endorsed by the military establishment, as in the Tailhook investigation (Britton and Williams, forthcoming). By singling out these contexts for the label "sexual harassment," only marginalized men will be prosecuted, and the existing power structure that guarantees privileged men's sexual access to women will remain intact.

Sexual interactions involving men and women of the same race and sexual orientation have a hegemonic status in our society, making sexual harassment difficult to identify and eradicate. Our interviews suggest that many men and women are active participants in the sexualized culture of the workplace, even though ample evidence indicates that women who work in these environments suffer negative repercussions to their careers because of it (Jaschik and Fretz 1991; Paludi and Barickman 1991; Reilly et al. 1992; Schneider 1982). This is how cultural hegemony works—by getting under our skins and defining what is and is not pleasurable to us, despite our material or emotional interests.

Our findings raise difficult issues about women's complicity with oppressive sexual relationships. Some women obviously experience pleasure and enjoyment from public forms of sexual engagement with men; clearly, many would resist any attempt to eradicate all sexuality from work—an impossible goal at any rate. Yet it is also clear that the sexual "pleasure" many women seek out and enjoy at work is structured by patriarchal, racist, and heterosexist norms. Heterosexual, racially homogamous relationships are privileged in our society: they are institutionalized in organizational policies and job descriptions, embedded in ritualistic workplace practices, and accepted as legitimate normal, or inevitable elements of workplace culture. This study suggests that only those sexual interactions that violate these policies, practices, and beliefs are resisted and condemned with the label "sexual harassment."

We have argued that this dominant social construction of pleasure protects the most privileged groups in society from charges of sexual harassment and may be used to oppress and exclude the least powerful groups. Currently, people seem to consider the gender, race, status, and sexual orientation of the assailant when deciding to label behaviors as sexual harassment. Unless we acknowledge the complex double standards people use in "drawing the line," then sexual domination and exploitation will undoubtedly remain the normative experience of women in the workforce.

NOTES

1. It could be the case that those who find this behavior extremely offensive are likely to leave restaurant work. In other words, the sample is clearly biased in that it includes only those who are currently employed in a restaurant and presumably feel more comfortable with the level of sexualized behavior than those who have left restaurant work.

2. It is difficult, if not impossible, to specify which occupations are less highly sexualized than waiting tables. Most occupations probably are sexualized in one way or another; however, specific workplaces may be more or less sexualized in terms of institutionalized job descriptions and employee tolerance of sexual banter. For example, Pringle (1988) describes some offices as coolly professional—with minimal sexual joking and play—whereas others are characterized by "compulsory jocularity." Likewise, some restaurants may de-emphasize sexual flirtation between waitpeople and customers, and restrain informal interactions among the staff (one respondent in our sample worked at such a restaurant).

3. We thank Margaret Andersen for drawing our attention to this fruitful analogy.

4. It is also probably significant that this episode of harassment involved a gay man and a heterosexual man. This context of sexual harassment is discussed later in this article.

5. It is true that both cases involved cooks sexually harassing waitresses. We could have places these cases in the "powerful position" category, but did not because in these particular instances, the cooks did not possess institutionalized power over the waitpeople. In other words, in these particular cases, the cook and waitress had equal organizational status in the restaurant.

REFERENCES

Anders, K. T. 1993. Bad sex: Who's harassing whom in restaurants? *Restaurant Business,* 20 January, pp. 46–54.

Benson, Donna J., and Gregg E. Thomson. 1982. Sexual harassment on a university campus: The confluence of authority relations, sexual interest and gender stratification. *Social Problems* 29:236–51.

Britton, Dana M., and Christine L. Williams. Forthcoming. Don't ask, don't tell, don't pursue: Military policy and the construction of heterosexual masculinity. *Journal of Homosexuality.*

Carothers, Suzanne C., and Peggy Crull. 1984. Contrasting sexual harassment in female- and male-dominated occupations. In *My troubles are going to have trouble with me: Everyday trials and triumphs of women workers,* edited by K. B. Sacks and D. Remy. New Brunswick, NJ: Rutgers University Press.

Cobble, Dorothy Sue. 1991. *Dishing it out: Waitresses and their unions in the twentieth century.* Urbana: University of Illinois Press.

Cockburn. Cynthia. 1991. *In the way of women.* Ithaca, NY: I.L.R. Press.

Crull, Peggy. 1987. Searching for the causes of sexual harassment: An examination of two prototypes. In *Hidden aspects of women's work,* edited by Christine Bose, Roslyn Feldberg, and Natalie Sokoloff. New York: Praeger.

Ellis, Shmuel, Azy Barak, and Adaya Pinto. 1991. Moderating effects of personal cognitions on experienced and perceived sexual harassment of women at the workplace. *Journal of Applied Social Psychology* 21: 1320–37.

Fain, Terri C., and Douglas L. Anderton. 1987. Sexual harassment: Organizational context and diffuse status. *Sex Roles* 17: 291–311.

Fitzgerald, Louise F. 1990. Sexual harassment: The definition and measurement of a construct. In *Ivory power: Sexual harassment on campus,* edited by Michele M. Paludi. Albany: State University of New York Press.

Grauerholz, Elizabeth. 1989. Sexual harassment of women professors by students: Exploring the dynamics of power, authority, and gender in a university setting. *Sex Roles* 21:789–801.

Gruber, James E., and Lars Bjorn. 1982. Blue-collar blues: The sexual harassment of women auto workers. *Work and Occupations* 9:271–98.

Gutek, B. A. 1985. *Sex and the workplace.* San Francisco: Jossey-Bass.

Hall, Elaine J. 1993. Waitering/waitressing: Engendering the work of table servers. *Gender & Society* 7:329–46.

Howe, Louise Kapp. 1977. *Pink collar workers: Inside the world of women's work.* New York: Avon.

Jaschik, Mollie L., and Bruce R. Fretz. 1991. Women's perceptions and labeling of sexual harassment. *Sex Roles* 25:19–23.

Jensen, Inger W., and Barbara A. Gutek. 1982. Attributions and assignment of responsibility in sexual harassment. *Journal of Social Issues* 38: 122–36.

Johnson, Miriam. 1988. *Strong mothers, weak wives.* Berkeley: University of California Press.

Konrad, Alison M., and Barbara A. Gutek. 1996. Impact of work experiences on attitudes toward sexual harassment. *Administrative Science Quarterly* 31:422–38.

LaFree, Gary D. 1989. *Rape and criminal justice: The social construction of sexual assault.* Belmont, CA: Wadsworth.

MacKinnon, Catherine A. 1979. *Sexual harassment of working women: A case of sex discrimination.* New Haven, CT: Yale University Press.

McKinney, Kathleen. 1990. Sexual harassment of university faculty by colleagues and students. *Sex Roles* 23: 421–38.

Paludi, Michele, and Richard B. Barickman. 1991. *Academic and workplace sexual harassment.* Albany: State University of New York Press.

Paules, Greta Foff. 1991. *Dishing it out: Power and resistance among waitresses in a New Jersey restaurant.* Philadelphia. Temple University Press.

Powell, Gary N. 1986. Effects of sex role identity and sex on definitions of sexual harassment. *Sex Roles* 14:9–19.

Pringle, Rosemary. 1988. *Secretaries talk: Sexuality, power and work.* London: Verso.

Pryor, John B. 1987. Sexual harassment proclivities in men. *Sex Roles* 17:269–90.

Reilly, Mary Ellen, Bernice Lott, Donna Caldwell, and Luisa DeLuca. 1992. Tolerance for sexual harassment related to self-reported sexual victimization. *Gender & Society* 6:122–38.

Rich, Adrienne, 1980. Compulsory heterosexuality and lesbian existence. *Signs* 5:631–60.

Schneider, Beth E. 1982. Consciousness about sexual harassment among heterosexual and lesbian women workers. *Journal of Social Issues* 38:75–98.

———. 1984. The office affair. Myth and reality for heterosexual and lesbian women workers. *Sociological Perspectives* 27:443–64.

———. 1991. Put up and shut up: Workplace sexual assaults. *Gender & Society* 5:533–48.

U.S. Department of Labor, Bureau of Labor Statistics. 1989, January. *Employment and earnings.* Washington, DC: Government Printing Office.

West, Candace, and Don H. Zimmerman. 1987. Doing gender. *Gender & Society* 1:125–51.

39

"Their Logic Against Them"

Contradictions in Sex, Race, and Class in Silicon Valley

KAREN J. HOSSFELD

> The bosses here have this type of reasoning like a seesaw. One day it's "you're paid less because women are different than men," or "immigrants need less to get by." The next day it's "you're all just workers here—no special treatment just because you're female or foreigners."
>
> Well, they think they're pretty clever with their doubletalk, and that we're just a bunch of dumb aliens. But it takes two to use a seesaw. What we're gradually figuring out here is how to use their own logic against them.
>
> —*Filipina circuit board assembler in Silicon Valley (emphasis added)*

This chapter examines how contradictory ideologies about sex, race, class, and nationality are used as forms of both labor control and labor resistance in the capitalist workplace today. Specifically, I look at the workplace relationships between Third World immigrant women production workers and their predominantly White male managers in high-tech manufacturing industry in Silicon Valley, California. My findings indicate that in workplaces where managers and workers are divided by sex and race, class struggle can and does take gender-and race-specific forms. Managers encourage women immigrant workers to identify with their gender, racial, and national identities when the managers want to "distract" the workers from their class concerns about working conditions. Similarly, when workers have workplace needs that actually are defined by gender, nationality, or race, managers tend to deny these identities and to stress the workers have learned to redeploy their managers' gender and racial tactics to their own advantage, however, in order to gain more control over their jobs. As the Filipina worker quoted at the beginning of the chapter so aptly said, they have learned to use managers' "own logic against them." . . .

This chapter draws from a larger study of the articulation of sex, race, class, and nationality in the lives of immigrant women high-tech workers (Hossfeld 1988b). Empirical data draw on more than two hundred interviews conducted between 1982 and 1986 with Silicon Valley workers; their family members, employers, and managers; and labor and community organizers. Extensive in-depth interviews were conducted with eighty-four immigrant women, represent-

---

Karen J. Hossfeld, "'Their Logic Against Them': Contradictions in Sex, Race, and Class in Silicon Valley," in *Women Workers and Global Restructuring,* edited by Kathryn Ward.

ing twenty-one Third World nationalities, and with forty-one employers and managers, who represented twenty-three firms. All but five of these management representatives were U.S.-born White males. All of the workers and managers were employed in Santa Clara County, California, firms that engaged in some aspect of semiconductor "chip" manufacturing. I observed production at nineteen of these firms. . . .

SILICON VALLEY

"Silicon Valley" refers to the microelectronics-based high-tech industrial region located just south of San Francisco in Santa Clara County. California.[1] . . .

Class Structure and the Division of Labor

Close to 200,000 people—one out of every four employees in the San Jose Metropolitan Statistical Area labor force—work in Silicon Valley's micro-electronics industry. There are more than 800 manufacturing firms that hire ten or more people each, including 120 "large" firms that each count over 250 employees. An even larger number of small firms hire fewer than ten employees apiece. Approximately half of this high-tech labor force—100,000 employees—works in production-related work: at least half of these workers—an estimated 50,000 to 70,000—are in low-paying, semiskilled operative jobs (Siegel and Borock 1982; *Annual Planning Information* 1983).[2]

The division of labor within the industry is dramatically skewed according to gender and race. Although women account for close to half of the total paid labor force in Santa Clara County both inside and outside the industry, only 18 percent of the managers, 17 percent of the professional employees and 25 percent of the technicians are female. Conversely, women hold at least 68 percent and by some reports as many as 85 to 90 percent of the valley's high-tech operative jobs. In the companies examined in my study, women made up and average of 90 percent of the assembly and operative workers. Only rarely do they work as production managers or supervisors, the management area that works most closely with the operatives.

Similar disparities exist vis-à-vis minority employment. . . . Within the microelectronics industry, 12 percent of the managers, 16 percent of the professionals, and 18 percent of the technicians are minorities—although they are concentrated at the lower-paying and less powerful ends of these categories. An estimated 50 to 75 percent of the operative jobs are thought to be held by minorities.[3] My study suggests that the figure may be closer to 80 percent.

Both employers and workers interviewed in this study agreed that the lower the skill and pay level of the job, the higher the percentage of Third World immigrant women who were employed. Thus assembly work, which is the least skilled and lowest-paying production job, tends to be done predominantly by Third World women. . . .

This occupational structure is typical of the industry's division of labor nationwide. The percentage of women of color in operative jobs is fairly standardized throughout various high-tech centers; what varies is *which* minority groups are employed, not the job categories in which they are employed.[4]

Obviously, there is tremendous cultural and historical variation both between and within the diverse national groups that my informants represent. Here I emphasize their commonalities. Their collective experience is based on their jobs, present class status, recent uprooting, and immigration. Many are racial and ethnic minorities for the first time. Finally, they have in common their gender and their membership in family households.

LABOR CONTROL ON THE SHOP FLOOR

Gender and Racial Logic

In Silicon Valley production shops, the ideological battleground is an important arena of class struggle for labor control. Management frequently calls upon ideologies and arrangements concerning sex and race, as well as class, to manipulate worker consciousness and to legitimate the hierarchical division of labor. Management taps both traditional popular stereotypes about the presumed lack of status and limited abilities of women, minorities, and immigrants and the workers' own fears, concerns, and sense of priorities as immigrant women.

But despite management's success in disempowering and devaluing labor, immigrant women workers have co-opted some of these ideologies and have developed others of their own, playing on management's prejudices to the workers' own advantage. In so doing, the workers turn the "logic" of capital against managers, as they do the intertwining logics of patriarchy and racism. The following section examines this sex- and race-based logic and how it affects class structure and struggle. I then focus on women's resistance to this manipulation and their use of gender and racial logics for their own advantage.

From interviews with Silicon Valley managers and employers, it is evident that high-tech firms find immigrant women particularly appealing workers not only because they are "cheap" and considered easily "expendable" but also because management can draw on and further exploit pre-existing patriarchal and racist ideologies and arrangements that have affected these women's consciousness and realities. In their dealings with the women, managers fragment the women's multifaceted identities into falsely separated categories of "worker," "ethnic," and "woman." The effect is to increase and play off the workers' vulnerabilities and splinter their consciousness. But I also found limited examples of the women drawing strength from their multifaceted experiences and developing a unified consciousness with which to confront their oppressions. These instances of how the workers have manipulated management's ideology are important not only in their own right but as models. To date, though, management holds the balance of power in this ideological struggle.

I label management's tactics "gender-specific" and "racial-specific" forms of labor control and struggle, or gender and racial "logic." I use the term *capital logic* to refer to strategies by capitalists to increase profit maximization. Enforcement by employers of a highly stratified class division of labor as a form of labor control is one such strategy. Similarly, I use the terms *gender logic* and *racial logic* to refer to strategies to promote gender and racial hierarchies. Here I am concerned primarily with the ways in which employers and managers devise and incorporate gender and racial logic in the interests of capital logic. Attempts to legitimate inequality form my main examples.

I focus primarily on managers' "gender-specific" tactics because management uses race-specific (il)logic much less directly in dealing with workers. Management clearly draws on racist assumptions in hiring and dealing with its work-force, but usually it makes an effort to conceal its racism from workers. Management recognizes, to varying degrees, that the appearance of blatant racism against workers is not acceptable, mainly because immigrants have not sufficiently internalized racism to respond to it positively. Off the shop floor, however, the managers' brutal and open racism toward workers was apparent during "private" interviews. Managers' comments demonstrate that racism is a leading factor in capital logic but that management typically disguises racist logic by using the more socially acceptable "immigrant logic." Both American and immigrant workers tend to accept capital's relegation of immigrants to secondary status in the labor market.

Conversely, "gender logic" is much less disguised: management uses it freely and directly to control workers. Patriarchal and sexist ideology is *not* considered inappropriate. Because women workers themselves have already internalized patriarchal ideology, they are more likely to "agree" with or at least accept it than they are racist as assumptions. This chapter documents a wide range of sexist assumptions that management employs in order to control and divide workers.

Gender Ideology

A growing number of historical and contemporary studies illustrate the interconnections between patriarchy and capitalism in defining both the daily lives of working women and the nature of work arrangements in general. Sallie Westwood, for example, suggests that on-the-job exploitation of women workers is rooted in part in patriarchal ideology. Westwood states that ideologies "play a vital part in calling forth a sense of self linked to class and gender as well as race. Thus, a patriarchal ideology intervenes on the shop floor culture to make anew the conditions of work under capitalism" (1985:6).

One way in which patriarchal ideology affects workplace culture is through the "gendering" of workers—what Westwood refers to as "the social construction of masculinity and femininity on the shop floor" (page 6). The forms of work culture that managers encourage, and that women workers choose to develop, are those that reaffirm traditional forms of femininity. This occurs in spite of the fact that, or more likely because, the women are engaged in roles that are traditionally defined as nonfeminine: factory work and wage earning. My data suggest that although factory work and wage earning are indeed traditions long held by working-class women, the dominant *ideology* that such tasks are "unfeminine" is equally traditional. For example I asked one Silicon Valley assembler who worked a double shift to support a large family how she found time and finances to obtain elaborate manicures, makeup, and hair stylings. She said that they were priorities because they "restored [her] sense of femininity." Another production worker said that factory work "makes me feel like I'm not a lady, so I have to try to compensate."

This ideology about what constitutes proper identity and behavior for women is multileveled. First, women workers have a clear sense that wage earning and factory work in general are not considered "feminine." This definition of "feminine" derives from an upper-class reality in which women traditionally did not need (and men often did not allow them) to earn incomes. The reality for a production worker who comes from a long line of factory women does not negate the dominant ideology that influences her to say, "At work I feel stripped of my womanhood. I feel like I'm not a lady anymore. It makes me feel . . . unattractive and unfeminine."

Second, women may feel "unwomanly" at work because they are away from home and family, which conflicts with ideologies, albeit changing ones, that they should be home. And third, earning wages at all is considered "unwifely" by some women, by their husbands, or both because it strips men of their identity as "breadwinner."

One the shop floor, managers encourage workers to associate "femininity" with something contradictory to factory work. They also encourage women workers to "compensate" for their perceived loss of femininity. This strategy on the part of management serves to devalue women's productive worth.

Under contemporary U.S. capitalism, ideological legitimation of women's societal roles and of their related secondary position in the division of labor is already strong outside the workplace. Management thus does not need to devote extreme efforts to developing new sexist ideologies within the workplace in order to legitimate the gender division of labor. Instead, managers can call on and reinforce preexisting ideology. Nonetheless, new forms of gender ideology are frequently introduced. These old and new ideologies are disseminated both on an individual basis, from a manager to a worker or workers, and on a collective basis, through company programs, policies, and practices. Specific examples of informal ways in which individual managers encourage gender identification, such as flirting, dating, sexual harassment, and promoting "feminine" behavior, are given below. The most widespread company practice that encourages engenderment, of course, is hiring discrimination and job segregation based on sex.

An example of a company policy that divides workers by gender is found in a regulation one large firm has regarding color-coding of smocks that all employees in the manufacturing division are required to wear. While the men's smocks are color-coded according to occupation, the women's are color-coded by sex, regardless of occupation. This is a classic demonstration of management's encouragement of male workers to identify according to job and class and its discouragement of women from doing the same. Regardless of what women do as workers, the underlying message reads, they are nevertheless primarily women. The same company has other practices and other practices and programs that convey the same message. Their company newsletter, for example, includes a column entitled "Ladies' Corner" which runs features on cooking and fashion tips for "the working gal." A manager at this plant says that such "gender tactics," as I call them, are designed to "boost morale by reminding the gals that even though they do unfeminine work, they really are still feminine." But although some women workers may value femininity, in the work world, management identifies feminine traits as legitimation for devaluation.

In some places, management offers "refeminization" perks to help women feel "compensated" for their perceived "defeminization" on the job. A prime example is the now well-documented makeup sessions and beauty pageants for young women workers sponsored by multinational electronics corporations at their Southeast Asian plants (Grossman 1979; Ong 1985). While such events are unusual in Silicon Valley, male managers frequently use flirting and dating as "refeminization" strategies. Flirting and dating in and of themselves certainly cannot be construed as capitalist plots to control workers; however, when they are used as false compensation for and to divert women from poor working conditions and workplace alienation, they in effect serve as a form of labor control. In a society where women are taught that their femininity is more important than other aspects of their lives—such as how they relate to their work—flirting can be divisive. And when undesired, flirting can also develop into a form of sexual harassment, which causes further workplace alienation.

One young Chinese production worker told me that she and a co-worker avoided filing complaints about illegal and unsafe working conditions because they did not want to annoy their White male supervisor, whom they enjoyed having flirt with them. These two women would never join a union, they told me, because the same supervisor told them that all women who join unions "are a bunch of tough, big-mouthed dykes." Certainly these women have the option of ignoring this man's opinions. But that is not easy, given the one-sided power he has over them not only because he is their supervisor, but because of his age, race, and class.

When women workers stress their "feminine" and female characteristics as being counter to their waged work, a contradictory set of results can occur. On one hand, the women may legitimate their own devaluation as workers, and, in seeking identity and solace in their "femininity," discard any interest in improving their working conditions. On the other hand, if turning to their identities as female, mother, mate, and such allows them to feel self-esteem in one arena of their lives, that self-esteem in one arena of their lives, that self-esteem may transfer to other arenas. The outcome is contingent on the ways in which the women define and experience themselves as female or "feminine." Femininity in White American capitalist culture is traditionally defined as passive and ineffectual, as Susan Brownmiller explores (1984). But there is also a female tradition of resistance.

The women I interviewed rarely pose their womanhood or their self-perceived femineity as attributes meriting higher pay or better treatment. They expect *differential* treatment because they are women, but "differential" inevitably means lower paid in the work world. The women present their self-defined female attributes as creating additional needs that detract from their financial value. Femininity, although its definition varies among individuals and ethnic groups, is generally viewed as something that subtracts from a woman's market value, even though a majority of women consider it personally desirable.

In general, both the women and men I interviewed believe that women have many needs and skills discernible from those of male workers, but they accept the ideology that such specialness renders them less deserving than men of special treatment, wages, promotions, and status. Conversely, both the men and women viewed men's special needs and skills as rendering men more deserving. Two of the classic perceived sex differentials cited by employers in electronics illustrate this point. First, although Silicon Valley employers consistently repeat the old refrain that women are better able than men to perform work requiring manual skills, strong hand-eye coordination, and extreme patience, they nonetheless find it appropriate to pay workers who have these skills (women) less than workers who supposedly do not have them (men). Second, employers say that higher entry-level jobs, wages, and promotions rightly belong to heads of households, but in practice they give such jobs only to men, regardless of their household situation, and exclude women, regardless of theirs.

When a man expresses special needs that result from his structural position in the family—such as head of household—he is often "compensated," yet when a women expresses a special need resulting from her traditional structural position in the family-child care or her position as head of household—she is told that such issues are not of concern to the employer or, in the case of child care, that it detracts from her focus on her work and thus devalues her productive contribution. This is a clear illustration of Heidi Hartmann's definition of patriarchy: social relationships between men, which, although hierarchical, such as those between employer and worker, have a material base that benefits men and oppresses women (1976).

Definitions of femininity and masculinity not only affect the workplace but are in turn affected by it. Gender is produced and reproduced in and through the workplace, as well as outside it. Gender identities and relationships are formed on the work floor both by the labor process organized under capitalism and by workers' resistance to that labor process. "Femininity" in its various permutations is not something all-bad and all-disempowering: women find strength, pride, and creativity in some of its forms. . . . I turn now to one of the other tenets of women worker's multitiered consciousness that employers find advantageous: gander logic that poses women's work as "secondary."

THE LOGIC OF "SECONDARY" WORK

Central to gender-specific capital logic is the assumption that women's paid work is both secondary and temporary. More than 70 percent of the employers and 80 percent of the women workers interviewed stated that a woman's primary jobs are those of wife, mother, and homemaker, even when she works full time in the paid labor force. Because employers view woman's primary job as in the home, and they assume that, prototypically, every woman is connected to a man who is bringing in a larger paycheck, they claim that women do not need to earn a full living wage. Employers repeatedly asserted that they believed the low-level jobs were filled only by women because men could not afford to or would not work for such low wages.

Indeed, many of the women would not survive on what they earned unless they pooled resources. For some, especially the nonimmigrants, low wages did mean dependency on men—or at least on family networks and household units. None of the women I interviewed—immigrant or nonimmigrant—lived alone. Yet most of them would be financially better off without their menfolk. For most of the immigrant women, their low wages were the most substantial and steady source of their family's income. *Eighty percent of the immigrant women workers in my study were the largest per annum earners in their households.*

Even when their wages were primary—the main or only family income—the women still considered men to be the major bredwinners. The women considered their waged work as secondary, both in economic value and as a source of identity. Although most agreed that women and men who do exactly the same jobs should be paid the same, they had little expectation that as women they would be eligible for higher-paying "male" jobs. While some of these women—particularly the Asians—believed they could overcome racial and class barriers in the capitalist division of labor, few viewed gender as a division that could be changed. While they may believe that hard work can overcome many obstacles and raise their *families'* socioeconomic class standing, they do not feel that their position in the gender division of labor will change. Many, of course, expect or hope for better jobs for themselves—and others expect or hope to leave the paid labor force altogether—but few wish to enter traditional male jobs or to have jobs that are higher in status or earnings than the men in their families.

The majority of women who are earning more than their male family members view their situation negatively and hope it will change soon. They do not want to earn less than they currently do; rather, they want their menfolk to earn more. This was true of women in all the ethnic groups. . . .

As in the rest of America, in most cases, the men earned more in those households where both the women and men worked regularly. In many of the families, however, the men tended to work less regularly than the women and to have higher unemployment rates. While most of the families vocally blamed very real socioeconomic conditions for the unemployment, such as declines in "male" industrial sector jobs, many women also felt that their husbands took out their resentment on their families. A young Mexicana, who went to a shelter for battered women after her husband repeatedly beat her, described her extreme situation:

> He knows it's not his fault or my fault that he lost his job: they laid off almost his whole shift. But he acts like I keep my job just to spite him, and it's gotten so I'm so scared of him. Sometimes I think he'd rather

> kill me or have us starve than watch me go to work and bring home pay. He doesn't want to hurt me, but he is so hurt inside because he feels he has failed as a man.

Certainly not all laid-off married men go to the extreme of beating their wives, but the majority of married women workers whose husbands had gone through periods of unemployment said that the men treated other family members significantly worse when they were out of work. When capitalism rejects male workers, they often use patriarchal channels to vent their anxieties. In a world where men are defined by their control over their environment, losing control in one arena, such as that of the work world, may lead them to tighten control in another arena in which they still have power—the family. This classic cycle is not unique to Third World immigrant communities, but as male unemployment increases in these communities, so may the cycle of male violence.

Even some of the women who recognize the importance of their economic role feel that their status and identity as wage earners are less important than those of men. Many of the women feel that men work not only for income but for respect and dignity. They see their own work as less noble. Although some said they derive satisfaction from their ability to hold a job, none of the women considered her job to be a primary part of her identity or a source of self-esteem. These women see themselves as responsible primarily for the welfare of their families: their main identity is as mother, wife, sister, and daughter, not as worker. Their waged work is seen as an extension of caring for their families. It is not a question of *choosing* to work—they do so out of economic necessity.

When I asked whether their husbands' and fathers' waged work could also be viewed as an extension of familial duties, the women indicated that they definitely perceived a difference. Men's paid labor outside the home was seen as integral both to the men's self-definition and to their responsibility vis-à-vis the family; conversely, women's labor force participation was seen as contradictory both to the women's self-image and to their definitions of female responsibility.

Many immigrant women see their wage contribution to the family's economic survival not only as secondary but as *temporary,* even when they have held their jobs for several years. They expect to quit their production jobs after they have saved enough money to go to school, stay home full time, or open a family business. In actuality, however, most of them barely earn enough to live on, let alone to save, and women who think they are signing on for a brief stint may end up staying in the industry for years.

That these workers view their jobs as temporary has important ramifications for both employers and unions, as well as for the workers themselves. When workers believe they are on board a company for a short time, they are more likely to put up with poor working conditions, because they see them as short term. . . .

Employers are thus at an advantage in hiring these women at low wages and with little job security. They can play on the women's *own* consciousness as wives and mothers whose primary identities are defined by home and familial roles. While the division of labor prompts the workers to believe that women's waged work is less valuable than men's, the women workers themselves arrive in Silicon Valley with this ideology already internalized.

A young Filipina woman, who was hired at a walk in interview at an electronics production facility, experienced a striking example of the contradictions confronting immigrant women workers in the valley. Neither she nor her husband, who was hired the same day, had any previous related work experience or degrees. Yet her husband was offered an entry-level job as a technician, while she was offered an assembly job paying three dollars per hour less. The personnel manager told her husband that he would "find [the technician job] more interesting than assembly work." The woman had said in the interview that she wanted to be considered for a higher-paying job because she had two children to support. The manager refused to con sider her for a different job, she said, and told her that "it will work out fine for you, though, because with your husband's job, and you *helping out* [emphasis added] you'll have a nice little family income."

The same manager told me on a separate occasion that the company preferred to hire members of the same families because it meant that workers' relatives would be more supportive about their working and the combined incomes would put less financial strain on individual workers. This concern over workers and their families dissipated, however, when the Filipino couple split up, leaving the wife with only the "helping-out" pay instead of the "nice little family income." When the woman requested a higher-paying job so she could support her family, the same manager told her that "family concerns were out of place at work" and did not promote her. . . .

RESISTANCE ON THE SHOP FLOOR

There is little incidence in Silicon Valley production shops of *formal* labor militancy among the immigrant women, as evidenced by either union participation or collectively planned mass actions such as strikes. Filing formal grievances is not common in these workers' shop culture. Union activity is very limited, and both workers and managers claim that the incidence of complaints and disturbances on the shop floor is lower than in other industries. Pacing of production to restrict output does occur, and there are occasionally "informal" incidents, such as spontaneous slowdowns and sabotage. But these actions are rare and usually small in scale. Definitions of workplace militancy and resistance vary, of course, according to the observer's cultural background, but by their *own* definitions, the women do not frequently engage in traditional forms of labor militancy.

There is, however, an important, although often subtle, arena in which the women do engage in struggle with management; the ideological battleground. Just as employers and managers harness racist, sexist, and class-based logic to manipulate and control workers, so too workers use this logic against management. In the ideological arena, the women do not merely accept or react to the biased assumptions of managers: they also develop gender-, class-, and race-based logic of their own when it is to their advantage. The goal of these struggles is not simply ideological victory but concrete changes in working conditions. Further, in Silicon Valley, immigrant women workers have found that managers respond more to workers' needs when they are couched in ethnic or gender terms, rather than in class and labor terms. Thus, class struggle on the shop floor is often disguised as arguments about the proper place and appropriate behavior of women, racial minorities, and immigrants.

When asked directly, immigrant women workers typically deny that they engage in any form of workplace resistance or efforts to control their working conditions. This denial reflects not only workers' needs to protect clandestine activities, but also their consciousness about what constitutes resistance and control. In their conversations with friends and co-workers, the women joke about how they outfoxed their managers with female or ethnic "wisdom." Yet most of the women do not view their often elaborate efforts to manipulate their managers' behavior as forms of struggle. Rather, they think of their tactics "just as ways to get by," as several workers phrased it. It is from casual references to these tactics that a portrait of worker logic and resistance emerges. . . .

The vast majority of these women clearly wish to avoid antagonizing management. Thus, rather than engaging in confrontational resistance strategies, they develop less obvious forms than, say, work stoppages, filing grievances, and straight-forwardly refusing to perform certain tasks, all of which have frequently been observed in other industrial manufacturing sectors. Because the more "quiet" forms of resistance and struggle for workplace control engaged in by the women in Silicon Valley are often so discrete and the workers are uncomfortable discussing them, it is probable that there are more such acts and they are broader in scope than my examples imply. As a Chinese woman in her forties who has worked as an operative in the valley for six years explained:

> Everybody who does this job does things to get through the day, to make it bearable. There are some women who will tell you they never do anything unproper or sneaky, but you are not to believe them. The ones that look the most demure are always up to something. . . . There's not anybody here who has never purposefully broken something, slowed down work, told fibs to the supervisor, or some such thing. And there's probably no one but me with my big mouth who would admit it! . . .

The most frequently mentioned acts of resistance against management and work arrangements were ones that played on the White male managers' consciousness—both false and real—about gender and ethnic culture. Frequently mentioned examples involved workers who turned management's ideologies against them by exploiting their male supervisors' misconceptions about "female problems." A White chip tester testified:

> It's pretty ironic because management seems to have this idea that male supervisors handle female workers better than female supervisors. You know, we're supposed to turn to mush whenever he's around and respect his authority or something. But this one guy we got now lets us walk all over him. He thinks females are flighty and irresponsible because of our hormones—so we make sure to have as many hormone problems as we can. I'd say we each take hormone breaks several times a day. My next plan is to convince him that menstrual blood will turn the solvents bad, so on those days we have to stay in the lunchroom!

A Filipina woman production worker recounted another example:

> The boss told us girls that we're not strong enough to do the heavy work in the men's jobs—and those jobs pay more, too. So, I suddenly realized that gosh, us little weak little things shouldn't be lifting all those heavy boxes of circuit board parts we're supposed to carry back and forth all the time—and I stopped doing it.
>
> The boss no longer uses that "it's too heavy for you girls" line anymore . . . but I can tell he's working on a new one. That's okay; I got plenty of responses.

A Mexican wafer fabricator, whose unit supervisor was notorious for the "refeminization" perks discussed above, told of how she manipulated the male supervisor's gender logic to disguise what was really an issue of class struggle:

> I was getting really sick from all the chemicals we have to work with, and I was getting a rash from them on my arms. [The manager] kept saying I was exaggerating and gave the usual line about you can't prove what caused the rash. One day we had to use an especially harsh solvent, and I made up this story about being in my sister's wedding. I told him that the solvents would ruin my manicure, and I'd be a mess for the wedding. Can you believe it? He let me off the work! This guy wouldn't pay attention to my rash, but when my manicure was at stake, he let me go!

Of course, letting this worker avoid chemicals for one day because of a special circumstance is more advantageous to management than allowing her and others to avoid the work permanently because of health risks. Nonetheless, the worker was able to carve out a small piece of bargaining power by playing off her manager's gender logic. The contradiction of these tatics that play up feminine frailty is that they achieve short-term, individual goals at the risk of reinforcing damaging stereotypes about women, including the stereotype that women workers are not as productive as men. From the workers' point of view, however, the women are simply using the prejudices of the powerful to the advantages of the weak.

Another "manicure" story resulted in a more major workplace change at one of the large plants. Two women fabricator operatives, one Portuguese and one Chicana, applied for higher-paying technician jobs whereupon their unit supervisor told them that the jobs were too "rough" for women and that the work would "ruin their nails." The women's response was to pull off their rubber gloves and show him what the solvents and dopants had done to their nails, despite the gloves. (One of the most common chemicals used in chip manufacturing is acetone, the key ingredient in nail polish removal. It also eats right through "protective" rubber gloves.) After additional goading and bargaining, the supervisor provisionally let them transfer to technician work.

Although the above are isolated examples, they represent tactics that workers can use either to challenge or play off sexist ideology that employers use to legitimate women's low position in the segregated division of labor. Certainly there are not enough instances of such behavior to challenge the inequality between worker and boss, but they do demonstrate to managers that gender logic cannot always be counted on to legitimate inequality between male and female workers. And dissloving divisions between workers is a threat to management hegemony.

RACIAL AND ETHNIC LOGIC

Typically, high-tech firms in Silicon Valley hire production workers from a wide spectrum of national groups. If their lack of a common language (both linguistically and culturally) serves to fragment the labor force, capital benefits. Conversely, management may find it more difficult to control workers with whom it cannot communicate precisely. Several workers said they have feigned a language barrier in order to avoid taking instructions; they have also called forth cultural taboos—both real and feigned—to avoid undesirable situations. One Haitian woman, who took a lot of kidding from her employer about voodoo and black magic, insisted that she could not work the night shift because evil spirits were out then. Because she was a good worker, the employer let her switch to days. When I tried to establish whether she believed the evil spirits were real or imagined, she laughed and said, "Does it matter? The result is the same: I can be home at night with my kids."

Management in several plants believed that racial and national diversity minimized solidarity. According to one supervisor, workers were forbidden from sitting next to people of their own nationality (i.e., language group) in order to "cut down on the chatting." Workers quickly found two ways to reverse this decision, using management's own class, racial, and gender logic. Chinese women workers told the supervisor that if they were not "chaperoned" by other Chinese women, their families would not let them continue to work there. Vietnamese women told him that the younger Vietnamese women would not work hard unless they were under the eyes of the older workers and that a group of newly hired Vietnamese workers would not learn to do the job right unless they had someone who spoke their language to explain it to them. Both of these arguments could also be interpreted as examples of older workers wanting to control younger ones in a generational hierarchy, but this was not the case. Afterwards both the Chinese and the Vietnamese women laughed among themselves at their cleverness. Nor did they forget the support needs of workers from other ethnic groups: they argued with the supervisor that the same customs and needs held true for many of the language groups represented, and the restriction was rescinded.

Another example of a large-scale demonstration of interethnic solidarity on the shop floor involved workers playing off supervisors' stereotypes regarding the superior work of Asians over Mexicans. The incident was precipitated when a young Mexicana, newly assigned to an assembly unit in which a new circuit board was being assembled, fell behind in her quota. The supervisor berated her with racial slurs about Mexicans' "laziness" and "stupidity" and told her to sit next to and "watch the Orientals." As a group, the Asian women she was stationed next to slowed down their production, thereby setting the average quota on the new boards at a slower than usual pace. The women were in fits of laughter after work because the supervisor had assumed that the speed set by the Asians was the fastest possible, since they were the "best" workers.

Hispanic workers also turn management's anti-Mexican prejudices against them, ash Salvadorean woman explained:

> First of all, the bosses think everyone from Latin American is Mexican, and they think all Mexicans are dumb. So, whenever they try to speed up production, or give us something we don't want to do, we just act dumb. It's not as if you act smart and you get a promotion or a bonus anyway.

A Mexicana operative confided, "They [management] assume we don't understand much English, but we understand when we want to."

A Chinese woman, who was under five feet tall and who identified her age by saying she was a "grandmother," laughingly told how she had her White male supervisor "wrapped around [her] finger." She consciously played into his stereotype that Asian women are small, timid, and obedient by frequently smiling at and bowing to him and doing her job carefully. But when she had a special need, to take a day or a few hours off, for example, she would put on her best guileless, ingratiating look and, full of apologies, usually obtained it. She also served as a voice for co-workers whom the supervisor considered more abrasive. On one occasion, when three White women in her unit complained about poor lighting and headaches, the supervisor became irritated and did not respond to their complaint. Later that week the Chinese "grandmother" approached him, saying that she was concerned that poor lighting was limiting the workers' productivity. The lighting was quickly improved. This incident illustrates that managers can and do respond to workers' demands when they result in increased productivity.

Some workers see strategies to improve and control their work processes and environments as contradictory and as "Uncle Tomming." Two friends, both Filipinas, debated this issue. One argued that "acting like a China doll" only reinforced white employers' stereotypes, while the other said that countering the stereotype would not change their situation, so they might as well use the stereotype to their advantage. The same analysis applies to women workers who consicously encourage male managers to view women as different from men in their abilities and characteristics. For women and minority workers, the need for short-term gains and benefits and for long-term equal treatment is a constant contradiction. And for the majority of workers, short-term tactics are unlikely to result in long-term equality.

POTENTIAL FOR ORGANIZING

Obviously, the lesson here for organizing is contradictory. Testimonies such as the ones given in these pages clearly document that immigrant women are not docile, servile people who always follow orders, as many employers interviewed for this study claimed. Orchestrating major actions such as family migration so that they could take control of and better their lives has helped these women develop leadership and survival skills. Because of these qualities, many of the women I interviewed struck me as potentially effective labor and community organizers and rank-and-file leaders. Yet almost none of them were interested in collective organizing, because of time limitations and family constraints and because of their lack of confidence in labor unions, the feminist movement, and community organizations. Many were simply too worn out from trying to make ends meet and caring for their families. And for some, the level of inequality and exploitation on the shop floor did not seem that bad, compared to their past experiences. . . .

Nonetheless, their past torment does not reduce the job insecurity, poor working conditions, pay inequality, and discrimination so many immigrant workers in Silicon Valley experience in their jobs. In fact, as informants' testimonies suggest, in many cases, past hardships have rendered them less likely to organize collectively. At the same time, individual acts of resistance do not succeed on their own in changing the structured inequality of the division of labor. Most of these actions remain at the agitation level and lack the coordination needed to give workers real bargaining power. And, as mentioned, individual strategies that workers have devised can be contradictory. Simultaneous to winning short-run victories, they can also reinforce both gender and racial stereotypes in the long run. Further, because many of these victories are isolated and individual, they can often be divisive. For workers to gain both greater workplace control *and* combat sexism and racism, organized *collective* strategies hold greater possibilities. . . .

My findings indicate that Silicon Valley's immigrant women workers have a great deal to gain from organizing, but also a great deal to contribute. They have their numeric strength, but also a wealth of creativity, insight, and experience that could be a shot in the arm to the stagnating national labor movement. They also have a great deal to teach—and learn from—feminist and ethnic community movements. But until these or new alternative movements learn to speak and listen to these women, the women will continue to struggle on their own, individually and in small groups. In their struggle for better jobs and better lives, one of the most effective tactics they have is their own resourcefulness in manipulating management's "own logic against them."

NOTES

1. For a comprehensive analytical description of the development of Silicon Valley as a region and an industry, see Saxenian 1981.

2. These production jobs include the following U.S. Department of Labor occupational titles: semiconductor processor; semiconductor assembler; electronics assembler, and electronics tester. Entry-level wages for these jobs in Silicon Valley in 1984 were $4.00 to $5.50; wages for workers with one to two years or more ex-

perience were $5.50 to $8.00 an hour, with testers sometimes earning up to $9.50.

3. "Minority" is the term used by the California Employment Development Department and the U.S. Department of Labor publications in reference to people of color. The statistics do not distinguish between immigrants and nonimmigrants within racial and ethnic groupings.

4. In North Carolina's Research Triangle, for example, Blacks account for most minority employment, whereas in Albuquerque and Texas, Hispanics provide the bulk of the production labor force. Silicon Valley has perhaps the most racially diverse production force, although Hispanics—both immigrant and nonimmigrant—still account for the majority.

REFERENCES

Annual Planning Information: San Jose Standard Metropolitan Statistical Area, 1983–1984. 1983. Sacramento: California Department of Employment Development.

Brownmiller, Susan. 1984. *Femininity.* New York: Simon and Schuster.

Grossman, Rachel. 1979. "Women's Place in the Integrated Circuit." *Southeast Asia Chronicle 66—Pacific Research* 9:2–17.

———. 1980. "Bitter Wages: Women in East Asia's Semiconductor Plants." *Multinational Monitor* 1 (March): 8–11.

Hartmann, Heidi. 1976. "Capitalism, Patriarchy, and Job Segregation by Sex." In *Women in the Workplace,* ed. Martha Blaxall and Barbara Reagan, 137–70. Chicago: University of Chicago Press.

Hossfeld Karen. 1988a. "Divisions of Labor, Divisions of Lives: Immigrant Women Workers in Silicon Valley." Ph.D. diss., University of California, Santa Cruz.

———. 1988b. "The Triple Shift: Immigrant Women Workers and the Household Division of Labor in Silicon Valley." Paper presented at the annual meetings of the American Sociological Association, Atlanta.

Ong, Aihwa. 1985. "Industrialization and Prostitution in Southeast Asia." *Southeast Asia Chronicle* 96:2–6.

Saxenian, Annalee. 1981. *Silicon Chips and Spatial Structure: The Industrial Basis of Urbanization in Santa Clara County, California.* Working Paper no. 345. Berkeley: Institute of Urban and Regional Planning, University of California.

Siegel, Lenny, and Herb Borock. 1982. *Background Report on Silicon Valley.* Prepared for the U.S. Commission on Civil Rights. Mountain View, Calif: Pacific Studies Center.

Westwood, Sallie. 1985. *All Day, Every Day: Factory and Family in the Making of Women's Lives.* Champaign: University of Illinois Press.

40

Go Away . . . But Stay Close Enough

PIERRETTE HONDAGNEU-SOTELO

. . . Scholarly research on U.S. paid domestic work in the late nineteenth and throughout the twentieth century has generally seen close, personal relations between employer and employee as a key mechanism of oppression and labor control. According to this line of thinking, the employer's maternalism mandates the employee's rituals of deference, which reinforce inequality and hierarchy. For example, maternalism often imposes heavy quid pro quo obligations on paid domestic workers, blurring the distinction between paid work and unpaid favors. Employers may require from their employees deference, gratitude, and perhaps extra hours on duty. In the process, they gain not only unpaid services but also a sense of superiority and enhanced racial, class, and gender status. Moreover, employers may hold the domestic workers' personalities to be as important as, and sometimes more important than, their competence at the job itself.

Other observers have argued that close employer-employee relations can help empower domestic workers. As the sociologist Bonnie Thornton Dill notes, "The intimacy which can develop between an employer and employee, along with the lack of job standardization may increase the employee's leverage in the relationship and give her some latitude within which to negotiate a work plan that meets her own interests and desires." Accordingly, close personal relationships with their employers may make it possible for some paid domestic workers to win more favorable job terms.

In contemporary Los Angeles, domestic employer-employee relations do not follow any one pattern. Many of the Latina immigrants doing domestic work are relatively new to the occupation, as are a number of their employers. But a couple of trends are clear: maternalism among employers has declined, and most Latina employees say they prefer employers who interact more personally with them. In this chapter, I try to make sense of these preferences by distinguishing between *maternalism*—which I see as a unilateral positioning of the employer as a benefactor who receives personal thanks, recognition, and validation of self from the domestic worker—and *personalism,* a bilateral relationship that involves two individuals recognizing each other not solely in terms of their role or office (such as clerk or cleaner) but rather as persons embedded in a unique set of social relations, and with particular aspirations. Many Latina domestic workers today want more closeness and consideration of their personhood from their employers, who, for

Pierrette Hondagneu-Sotelo "Go Away . . . But Stay Close Enough," from *Doméstica: Immigrant Workers Cleaning and Caring in the Shadows of Affluence.* Copyright © 2001, The Regents of the University of California Press. Reprinted by permission.

various reasons, are reluctant to engage in these exchanges.

These desires by both parties seem to contradict the conclusions of researchers who have concentrated on domestic work in previous eras: they are new social patterns that demand sociological explanations. Such explanations lie in the employers' and employees' social locations, their identities as women in contemporary society, the domestic job tasks involved, and the ways in which paid domestic work is organized. I begin by discussing those who have greater power in determining the quality of the relationship, the women who are employers.

EMPLOYERS AND PERSONALISM

Employed Employers and the Time Bind: "My Time, or Her Time?"

Karla Steinheimer, a talkative, fast-thinking thirty-six-year-old, drank a lot of coffee and worked in a fast-track office. Her quick-mindedness and determination had helped her land a job as a manager in a film production company, a job with considerable responsibility and always-looming deadlines; her husband Bob was a self-employed accountant. Both had extremely demanding schedules, and each worked at least fifty or fifty-five hours a week. Neither one had taken any time off from work since immediately after the birth of their two-year-old son. Consequently, their live-out nanny/housekeeper, Filomina, worked eleven hours a day, Monday through Friday, taking care of the Steinheimers' toddler. She had not taken a vacation since beginning the job two years prior to our interview.

A harried working mother cannot simply turn over her toddler to a nanny/housekeeper; she must spend some of her precious and limited time with her employee, and time was already in short supply for this quintessentially harried working mom. Karla had come to resent the time and emotional energy given to Filomina, but increasingly she saw it as a "necessary evil"—a view shared by many in her circle of busy working women. "I think it's always an issue—everyone I know faces this," she explained. "It's a lonely job, so when we are home Filomina will follow us around and you know, will talk because she's alone in the house all day. But we're usually in a hurry to get out the door or otherwise. So, there's always that issue."

With a previous housekeeper, Karla had found such demands for conversation easier to ignore. Now, she felt obliged to reciprocate with Filomina because of the child. "I think it's very important to spend the time talking to your child care provider because if you don't, you don't know what's going on," she reasoned. "I always have a lot of questions I want to ask Filomina about how the day went. What did he [the baby] have to eat, you know, was he constipated . . . you know, all those issues; but then it always turns into a whole thing about Filomina's cousin's friend's brother who did this and on and on and on."

"So, how do you deal with that when it gets into the cousin's friend's brother?" I asked.

"Just, the best I can. I don't mean to be ungracious or unkind but I try to limit it if I'm running out the door to an appointment or have things that I need to do in the house." To minimize these annoying verbal interruptions to their own work, employers like Karla may shift their schedules, rearrange their furniture, and even momentarily confine themselves to one part of the house—all tactics that Karla herself had tried. Most recently, she had moved her home office into her small bedroom, because "that's an area that I can be shut off from Filomina. The desk was set up in the baby's room, but if I went in there, then she was going in and out all the time. So now if I have to work and make phone calls I go in my bedroom and shut the door and then there's no disturbance." Instead of the domestic worker, as is traditional, being relegated to invisibility and confined to the "backroom" kitchen of a large home, the employer, now in a much smaller house, seeks to establish privacy by sequestering herself in a makeshift bedroom office. Both arrangements reflect the employer's privilege to search for and maintain her own privacy; but in this contemporary example, it is the employer who is spatially confined.

Instrumental personalism, of the type that the sociologist Jennifer Bickham Mendez observed in the cleaning agencies she studied, characterized Karla and Bob Steinheimer's relationship with their nanny/housekeeper. To ensure good care for her son, Karla felt obliged to participate in some personal conversations with Filomina. She contrasted these interactions to the "nonrelationship" she and her husband had maintained with a housecleaner who worked for them for approximately ten years, before the birth of their son. Karla recalled literally fleeing the housecleaner, whom they perceived as overly chatty and needy. "If we were at home by any chance with our cleaning lady, who used to absolutely follow us around, you know, it was impossible to do anything when she was there. When I was in my first trimester of pregnancy and I was feeling so sick, come hell or high water, I was out of that door at eight o'clock because I didn't want to run into her or her incessant questions." The housecleaner often asked for advice on how to deal with credit problems, but Karla and her husband preferred "very little contact." "To be honest," she confided, "we would try to stay out of the house, because you know, she would drive us crazy—talk, talk, talk."

The Steinheimers were dissatisfied with Filomina's cleaning, or, as they put it, the lack of it: "It got to the point where you could swipe your finger and write your name in the dust." But rather than losing a trusted, patient, and loving nanny, they accepted her poor cleaning and had recently hired a Latina housecleaner to come in and clean once every three weeks. When that woman, accompanied by her daughter, arrived on Saturday mornings, the Steinheimers promptly scooped up their son and departed to the corner café for cappuccino and croissants: "We just make it a point to never be home on those Saturday mornings." Once again, the Steinheimers are able to avoid time-consuming and awkward personal interactions. They thus maintain the type of anonymous, contractual relations with the housecleaner that they are prevented from having with their nanny/housekeeper.

Women engaged in full-time employment just don't have the time to establish personalistic or maternalistic relations with their domestic employees. With demanding careers and work schedules, they are too busy to cultivate such personal relationships. . . .

These employers may also be less interested than homemakers in establishing close, personalistic relations with their domestic employees. Working women who pay someone to work in their home derive their own identity largely from their jobs and careers, while the lives of homemakers often revolve around school, home, and family activities. Working women are therefore less likely than homemakers to view a domestic employee as a personal assistant or an extension of themselves. As Mary Romero has observed, "A homemaker who has her identity tied up in the home and family cannot simply hire another women to care for her family's needs without threatening her self-image. Thus, when private household workers are hired to maintain a particular life-style, many homemakers feel obligated to retain control even though they do not actually perform the work." For working women who pay nanny/housekeepers and cleaners, the organization and rapid pace of their life—what Hochschild calls the "Taylorization of home life"—often lead to their viewing a personalistic relationship with the nanny/housekeeper not as a means to gain personal satisfaction or a feeling of superiority, but rather as one more time-consuming burden. They wish to minimize or, if possible, avoid altogether such interchanges.

Many women find the pace required to maintain both their career and family life unbearable. Even well-to-do women who can afford private nanny/housekeepers find it hard to keep up, and many women with young children opt out of the rat race entirely. Others, like Ellen Maxson, choose to work part-time. She had earned a J.D. and a Ph.D. in art history from Ivy League universities; but while her children were young, she had decided to work limited hours as a museum and art gallery consultant, enjoying, she said, "the best of both worlds."

When I interviewed her, she reflected on her strained relations with the many nanny/housekeepers who briefly cycled through her home. Ellen attributed these "failed relationships" to her assumption that they could be covered by a "business contract." Indeed, unlike most employers, she had developed a systematic hiring strategy that included a job application form and a typed list detailing the employee's hours and pay, her own expectations for cleaning, and rules for the children's television viewing, meal preparation, and park excursions. While she had recently become slightly less controlling, the change had barely salvaged a sour relationship with her current nanny/housekeeper, a young white woman from Louisiana who tried to quit after ten days on the job. The Guatemalan woman she had employed previously left after two months. Ellen recognized that in order to minimize employee turnover and to establish more satisfactory domestic relations in the future, she would need "to spend more time on, you know, the human dynamic."

Still, she had trouble finding the time required for a more personalistic relationship. "When she [the nanny/housekeeper] comes [to work], I'm ready to get going with my own work. When I'm taking over from her, she's ready to get on with her own life, and so whose time do you spend developing the relationship? My time in the morning when she gets here? Or her time when she's leaving and she's ready to get on with her stuff?" Ellen tried to remedy the situation by scheduling her nanny/housekeeper to work four and a half hours a day, rather than only four hours, thereby buying herself an extra half hour to chat. "I found that I need to be a little bit freer with a few dollars here and there," she confided sheepishly, "for the long-term investment." When I asked if she had approached the relationship with her employee in such a businesslike manner because of her background in law, she said no, instead attributing it partly to her desire to replicate the reserve that her upper-class mother had maintained with household servants and partly to "just being busy and in not wanting to put time into what might feel like an unpredictable friendship." For Ellen Maxson, time was the major consideration. Employed parents who hire a part-time nanny/housekeeper may see developing a satisfactory relationship with the employee as taking too many of the total hours of employment.

Major gender inequities with her husband were also part of Ellen's problem. Her husband, who worked as a museum curator, encouraged her to invest more time cultivating a personalistic relationship with the nanny; yet even though he was sometimes home during the day, he refused to participate in fostering that relationship. "He wasn't going to spend it [time] on getting to know her. He thought this was important and wanted me to do it . . . for maybe a longer child care relationship with her." Both she and her husband rationalized giving her the responsibility by pointing to their different employment statuses: she worked part-time, while her husband worked full-time. But even when both husband and wife work full-time, the wife, as a rule, handles all transactions with the domestic worker. Of the thirty-nine employers I interviewed, thirty-two were married; and in only one instance did the husband take responsibility for hiring, communicating with, and paying the domestic employee.

Working women who employ domestic workers in their home sometimes complained to one another about the burdens of personalism, as Ellen Maxson did with her friends: "A friend of mine up the street," she said, "has someone who worked for her mom and now works for her, and she said, 'Oh, I'm just spending so much energy in this friendship relationship. I wish I could just have a business relationship.'" For these women, employing a nanny/housekeeper solved the problems of how to care for their children and clean a dirty house, but it simultaneously pressured them to take on not just a second but a third shift—the work of building and maintaining a relationship with the women who cared for their children and their homes. The cost of being relieved of household duties involves not only money but time, spent building a personal relationship with the woman who does their domestic work. . . .

Employed Employers and Housecleaners: Fleeting Greetings

Unlike their peers who hire nannies, employers who hire someone to clean their homes need not invest much time or emotional energy in the employer-employee relationship. Employed women typically maintain fairly distant relations with their weekly or biweekly housecleaners. Since they themselves are generally at their office during the day, their interactions with the housecleaners tend to be brief and businesslike.

Tess Miller, a single professional, had a Salvadoran woman clean her house biweekly. She described her relationship with the cleaner as consisting of a fleeting, twice-monthly greeting, made stilted by the language barrier: "She comes, she says hello, I say hello. I try to remember," she chuckled, "how to say something else [in Spanish]. A lot of times I just say, 'Hello, I'm going to work, good-bye, the money is on the table.'" Although Tess's job as a magazine editor allowed her to work at home a good deal of the time, she intentionally left when the housecleaner arrived—because, she explained, "I like not having to figure out what to do with myself while someone is in the house [cleaning]."

Many employers feel awkward, even guilty, about having a poorer Latina immigrant cleaning around them while they themselves appear to sit idly; Tess was no exception. Part of her job entailed reading popular magazines, but she did not want the cleaner to misinterpret that work as leisure activity. Her modest-sized home—approximately 900 square feet, with no hallways—made it impossible for her to hide away in the study while the housecleaner was there. Regardless of whether employers' work responsibilities or their desire to avoid social awkwardness pulls them out of the home, the upshot is the same: little contact between employer and employee. Other employers who occasionally work at home described similar efforts to minimize social interactions. A writing instructor reported, "I'd call it a kind of touching-base kind of conversation . . . a few, health things . . . the mechanics of rearranging the day [for cleaning]. . . . I'm usually out. I don't like to feel like I'm in her way." A business consultant echoed this sentiment: "I don't like being home because I feel like I'm in the way. I think it's easier [for them] to come in and do what they have to do without stepping over me." A busy physician and mother of two school-age children, accustomed to only greeting her weekly housecleaner as she leaves for her office, lamented dryly, "Every time that I'm so sick that I have to stay home, it's always a Tuesday that she's here. It never fails." Employed employers who hire weekly cleaners tend to shun personalistic relations.

Homemakers and Housecleaners: Generational Divides and Distances

Well-to-do homemakers who have weekly cleaners generally have more discretionary time than do employed women. Even if they are busy buying food, chauffeuring children to their various activities and appointments, and volunteering at charities, they are more likely to be home and have the time to casually stop and chat with the housecleaner or the nanny/housekeeper. But the personalism exhibited by today's homemaker employers varies considerably, depending on life stage and generation. Women in their thirties and forties seem to feel the tug of personalistic domestic relations less strongly than do homemakers in their late fifties and sixties. The older women, whose children are now grown, often seek close relations with their housecleaners, although they are not always able to achieve them.

It is not clear whether the younger homemakers' preference for stricter limits on personalism is due to their absorption in their children and family lives, generational differences, or their own prior experience in the workforce. Compared to their harried employed peers, however, they had more time and personal energy to spare in talking with their domestic workers. Tara Mostrianni, who had formerly worked as a stockbroker but was now at home caring for her two preschoolers, clearly exemplifies this pattern. She had hired a Mexican housecleaner to come once a week, and a Guatemalan woman watched the children on Mondays, Wednesdays, and Fridays while she ran errands and did volunteer work at her son's preschool. "Yeah, we've gotten friendly and that's fine," she commented. "I mean, I don't want to hear if she's having marital problems or whatever. She would never burden me with that." Tara reported discussing topics such as children, neighborhoods, crime, and safety, but she did not wish to delve too deeply into the lives of her domestic workers. She did not know, for example, who cared for the children of her weekly housecleaner or of her three-day-a-week nanny while they were working for her. At the same time, however, she spoke disapprovingly of the very distanced relationship that a career-oriented friend of hers had established with a nanny.

Similarly, Beverly Voss, who had worked for fifteen years as a midlevel manager and was now the stay-at-home mother of two young daughters, reported that she preferred not having a close relationship with the live-in nanny/housekeeper. "It's kind of distant, which is probably better than getting too involved. She kind of has her life and we have ours, and obviously I know about some of what she does on the weekends, but I don't pry very much and she doesn't disclose a lot." Beverly said there was nothing about the relationship she would like to change. "I don't want it any closer than it is. There should be a certain amount of distance, because she is working for us, yet she is part of our family." Unless Beverly's husband, a prominent attorney, was absent, the nanny/housekeeper ate her evening meals apart from the family, and Beverly emphasized that the nanny/housekeeper was an employee, a subordinate: "We're not at home kind of equals. She *is* working for us." Yet at the same time, she insisted on their interdependence, saying, "I think she knows that we're there for her, and she's there for us, like a family." Like other younger baby boomer women, she preferred distance to personalism and intimacy.

Maternalistic Desires: Denial and Fulfillment

Older homemakers, who were born prior to the end of World War II and who were in their fifties and sixties with their children already grown, generally preferred closer relations with their paid domestic workers. In some ways, they attempted to use their housecleaners to fill their "empty nests." Such was the case with Evelyn Potts, a fifty-eight-year-old who had recently retired from teaching and was now devoting more of her time to making and trying to sell ceramic sculptures. When her housecleaner arrived, she told me, they often sat down to chat. "If it looks like something has happened in either of our families in the last two weeks that we've been apart, we will spend some time before she gets started talking about that. Sometimes I'll insist that she have a cup of coffee and something to eat with me to go over that. . . . Our conversations usually revolve around family, around difficulties that she may be having in making her way in Los Angeles." Family conflicts, medical and financial problems, and immigration issues were common topics. While many employers dwell only on the travails and hardships of the housecleaner, Evelyn reported that they also discussed the housecleaner's children and their successes. "I think she's enormously proud of them," she noted.

The relationship went far beyond conversation; Evelyn Potts watched out for her employee's health by prohibiting the use of certain chemical cleaning products, and she even took the housecleaner, Mrs. Gonzalez, to her own doctor to prevent her from having an unnecessary hysterectomy. When Evelyn's husband asked Mrs. Gonzalez to iron his shirts, she intervened to put that onerous task off-limits. She enjoyed her intimate relationship with the housecleaner; and unlike most employers who have engaged in this sort of maternalistic involvement, she did not call the housecleaner by her first name, preferring a more formal and respectful address. She also expressed surprise at the extent of her involvement: "I did not expect to form a personal attachment with Mrs. Gonzalez. I did not expect I would know her whole family, and I did not expect that I would ultimately sponsor her for her green card, and in fact, the whole family."

Despite their greater power, employers cannot force their employees to accept personalistic relations. Several homemakers fondly recalled relationships they had had with previous domestic workers, and they spoke with some frustration about their inability to foster closer relationships with their current weekly housecleaners. Laura Jaspers, a retired schoolteacher who had worked only after her children started going to school, retained a very strong homemaking sensibility, as the wall of family photos in her suburban family room suggested. She had established very maternalistic relations with her previous housecleaners, who had reciprocated by showing personal interest in aspects of her own life, especially the celebrations surrounding the weddings of her three children. She recalled one woman who had cleaned her house for five years, who would "get excited with all that stuff. She really liked seeing the wedding dresses." The interest went both ways, as Laura inquired into the personal and family matters of the housecleaners. Yet they shared portions of their lives asymmetrically. What Laura remembered most vividly about her previous housecleaners was the voyeuristic pleasure she herself had derived from observing the "soap opera" quality of the housecleaners' lives. "They were always," she told me, "putting everything in my lap."

"What kinds of things would they tell you?"

"Oh, all their problems with their marriages and their husbands getting in jail and their kids getting in trouble, and you know, all those kinds of things. And the gossip about their sisters and their sisters-in-law." She listened to "all of this chaos" not simply because she enjoyed the drama but because she also became quite involved in responding to these personal crises. Perhaps acting as a personal benefactor enabled her to experience herself simultaneously as superior, altruistic, and benevolent; much previous scholarship has emphasized this function of employers' benevolent maternalism Laura Jaspers sometimes went to considerable effort to help them. She once offered her home as temporary refuge to a housecleaner and her children who were escaping a violent, battering husband and father. Another housecleaner had a chronically ill, disabled child, and she had, on many occasions, driven them around Los Angeles to various medical clinics. In both instances, Laura's husband raised objections to her "getting too involved personally," but she had ignored him.

Although Laura preferred this type of closeness, she had been unable to foster it with her current housecleaner. "She really holds me at arm's length, and I know almost as little about her three years later as I did the first two weeks that I had met her. It's just become more of a business thing than the other ones were." Initially, she was bothered by this and tried to get closer. "I'd be blabbing away and she'd just nod and say yes, no, and you know, that kind of thing." While Laura used to enjoy working alongside the other housecleaners, she now deliberately left the house while the cleaning was performed. She had become more reserved and less intrusive. "When the other gals were here, they were dusting, I'd be putting the books back in the cupboards or jabbering away or something or changing sheets together. Now, I must say, I do try to stay away from her more than the others. It's just a different person." Laura reports that she was "much more comfortable with the ones who I was closer to," but she has adapted. When she drives the current housecleaner down the hill from her canyon home to the bus stop, she has learned to keep conversation to a minimum.

Similarly, Norine Christophe, a fifty-eight-year-old affluent homemaker with three grown children, longed for the type of close, personalistic relationships she had established with several previous housecleaners. In particular, she fondly recalled her chatty relationship with Elena, a Mexican woman who had cleaned her house weekly for seven years. When she met her, Elena was single and worked as a live-in for a neighbor. Over time, Elena built up a weekly route of houses, had four children—with three different fathers, as Norine emphasized—married, and ultimately withdrew from employment to raise her children. Yet they continued to stay in touch. Elena remained poor, needy, dependent, and demonstrative with Norine, who responded by giving her advice, used household items, and once even an old car. "She has the need, so I still save my old clothes," she explained. "Last time Elena came it was Easter, and I had box after box. . . . And I'll be darned, they took every one of those boxes!" Elena had always reciprocated with gratitude, affection, and appreciation, and though she no longer worked for Norine Christophe, she still telephoned her and sent holiday cards.

When I interviewed her, Norine was employing Marta, whom she described as a very "self-sufficient" woman who had no need for used items, unsolicited advice, or excessive chitchat. Norine missed the open, loquacious ease with which Elena had discussed her boy-friends, her pregnancies, and other personal matters. Now, when she asked Marta a question—about her mother's health or her daughter's progress in school—"Well, she'll just give me minimal answers and then I assume that she doesn't want to talk." Contrasting the two, she said, "I had a real personal relationship with Elena. Marta is pretty much very businesslike." When I asked which she preferred, she quickly retorted, "Oh, Elena, hands down. Because I know to this day—she cares for me, and I care for her, so it went beyond the employer-employee thing."

At the end of our interview, Norine Christophe asked if I didn't know of a poor, needy family looking for a personal patron such as herself. She told me about how her friend Diane, "who is very, I mean, really very wealthy," had through her church befriended a single black mother and begun helping her. "Diane has almost adopted them," she pouted, "and I'm just so envious! Don't you know of a little family that I could get to know, that I could visit?" She stipulated the type of involvement she imagined, noting that she would act "sort of like I did with Elena":

> Of course, it couldn't be on a regular basis. Since we travel so much, I wouldn't be a good member of anything anyway, but maybe someone that I just care for, and think of in the holidays, and sort of like I did with Elena. If you know of anyone like that, maybe, say, a single mom with some kids and she's struggling . . . just that I could know on a personal basis—I am on a nonscheduled basis, this wouldn't be two o'clock

> every Tuesday kind of thing, so I could be flexible with my schedule. But I think I could really offer someone some caring and time and love and help and money too . . . so I could have the fun of seeing the kids go through school.

I responded by telling her about Mission Dolores, the activist Catholic parish located in Boyle Heights, in East Los Angeles. I knew they operated, among other programs, a soup kitchen, a shelter for homeless women and children, and classes for gang youth. "Oh," she gasped, "but wouldn't I have to actually go there? Isn't it very dangerous?"

As other observers of paid domestic work have pointed out, maternalistic employers of paid domestic workers may become accustomed to helping the poor without the discomfort of leaving their own safe, affluent neighborhoods. Instead of a benefactor like Norine Christophe transporting used clothing to the ghetto or the barrio, the needy come to her garage. There are other benefits to this maternalistic approach to charity. While employers may offer care and demonstrate affection, they do so on their own time, when they feel like it. The employer may get satisfaction from her intimate view of the private tribulations of a woman whose life is so unlike anything she knows that it might seem to have come from a novel—a woman who is poor, who lives in a crime-ridden neighborhood, who is raising children without the financial support of a husband, who is Latina and perhaps lacks U.S. citizenship or legal papers. Moreover, for her offered guidance and care, the employer receives personal recognition and appreciation.

In this scenario, the maternalistic homemaker employer gets more from her employee than better job performance or loyalty. She derives pleasure both from her voyeurism and from perceiving herself as kind and altruistic. Unlike someone who, say, writes a check to a charity organization, she can directly view the benefits of her contributions and "have the fun of seeing the kids." In fact, she need never see where they live, only what she gives them. Without leaving her affluent neighborhood or following anyone else's schedule, such an employer can construct a sense of herself as generous, altruistic, and kind—key attributes of the ideal bourgeois feminine personality.

Several caveats must be inserted into this discussion of homemaker employers and employed employers. The distinctions between the two groups are not absolute. These are not static characteristics: some woman have shifted from domesticity to full-time employment, and vice versa. After these transitions, their attitude toward personalism with their domestic workers may change. . . .

Finally, even though employers hold the upper hand, there are always two parties to a relationship. As we have seen, employers cannot unilaterally determine the quality of the relationship with their paid domestic workers. Homemakers are not able to impose close, intimate relations, though they may try; and harried working women who won't make time to talk with their nanny/housekeepers are sometimes forced to do so. Even paying employers can't always get what they want.

Class Distinctions: Upstairs, Downstairs, or All in the Family?

Class is a slippery concept in the United States, where nearly everybody, from warehouse loaders to millionaire entrepreneurs, is likely to identify as middle class. Distinctions between the middle class and the upper class, like those between homemakers and employed women, are often blurry. Moreover, even though class reproduces itself with remarkable consistency, some individuals move sharply up or down the social scale. For example, Carolyn Astor, the daughter of a waitress and a used car salesman, had recently married into a prominent, wealthy philanthropic family. When I met her, she was already, without irony, a diligent student of upper-class life, eagerly calling on her mother-in-law and her in-law's family friends to receive guidance on being the employer of a three-day-a-week nanny/housekeeper. Carolyn was openly affectionate with the Oaxacan nanny, who happened to unexpectedly arrive with flowers, hugs and birthday wishes for her on the morning I interviewed her. Along with picking up pointers on noblesse oblige, Carolyn was learning how to rule with authority. When her nanny/housekeeper had missed work to attend prenatal medical appointments, she had consulted her mother-in-law's friend; thereafter, she began paying the nanny daily instead of biweekly, to ensure, as she put it, "no work, no pay."

In general, very high income employers tend to favor more distant relations with their domestic employees than do middle-class and upper-middle-class employers. They prefer an American version of the "upstairs, downstairs" segregation of master and servant. In part, this physical separation is encouraged by their palatial, mansionsized homes. Spatial distance appears to facilitate emotional distance between employer and employee. The telephone systems with which these large homes are equipped hint at the physical obstacles to easy conversation. In each room, an office telephone with an elaborate array of push buttons sits on a table. When a call comes in, it can be transferred to any of about a dozen phone extensions located in other rooms throughout the house. Upper-class employers often hire a small staff of domestic workers; they may trade confidences with a primary housekeeper but retain greater distance from the others. Hierarchies of job tasks also affect personalistic relations; like the less-wealthy employers described above, those in the upper class may have closer relationships with employees who care for their young children than with those who do only cleaning. Yet I found that in these homes, there are limits—not always well-defined, but present nonetheless—on how informally and intimately employees may interact with employers.

When I interviewed Jenna Proust, the wife of a Hollywood agent, she was employing four women of color to ensure that her household ran smoothly. One Guatemalan woman performed most of the cleaning Monday through Friday from 8 A.M. until 2 P.M.; on weekdays at noon, a young Salvadoran woman arrived to clean, cook, shop for groceries, drive the children home from elementary school or to appointments, and look after the children until 8 P.M. On Saturday evenings, an African American woman served as the babysitter for the two children; and on Tuesday evenings and Sunday afternoons, a young Chicana—who had previously worked as their live-in—came to work as a nanny. Jenna Proust and her husband paid approximately $4,000 a month for these women to take care of their 6,700-square-foot home and their two children.

As we sat down in her cavernous living room, Jenna propped her feet up on the distressed, antique coffee table and told me, "I think I've gotten to the point where I'm hiring more passive people." She was referring to Latina immigrants, whom she saw as reserved and demure, as opposed to Martha, the U.S.-born Chicana whom she had previously hired as a live-in and now had working only two days a week, or to the European au pairs that she had employed in the past. Although she perceived Ronalda, the young Salvadoran woman who worked from noon until 8 P.M., to be barely competent at her usual tasks and totally at sea in interactions outside the family, such as with the children's orthodontist or with the plumber, she was, for the time, willing to overlook these failings because of Ronalda's quiet, deferential manner. By contrast, she had complete confidence in the abilities and judgment of Martha, a Chicana from the rural area of Oxnard, California. Martha could be counted on to purchase the right kind of coffee filters when she did the shopping, or to know that a child should not have an allergy shot while on antibiotics, but Jenna Proust found her loud, brash, and too familiar.

"For instance," she explained, "I've been trying to lose weight this year and exercising a lot, and Martha has trouble with weight too. I don't want to share that with her but she has taken it upon herself to burst onto the scene, like last night telling me exactly how many pounds she lost, like a child almost, and more like a close friend. This is where I would like a little distance." Martha had not only incorrectly assumed that Jenna would be interested in reciprocal exchanges on dieting successes and struggles, ones that perhaps highlighted the employer's failures, but she had also refused to act submissively. This too bothered Jenna: "She'll say, 'Don't say anything to me or I'll bite your head off, I have PMS!' And that to me is just well, I just don't like living with someone who's put me on notice especially someone who works for me and I won't pull the class thing, but excuse me, I'm the one who is paying the bills here." Although Jenna believed that when hiring someone to care for children, it is important "to know who this person is a little bit," she also found herself preferring to keep relations with the domestic workers more distant, "more businesslike than previous relationships. My children are older, and I think I am getting to be less interested in the level of involvement I had because I'm asking the people to be less involved in our family life now." In the past, she had taken several sick live-in nanny/housekeepers to doctors, but she no longer wanted to engage in this sort of maternalistic assistance.

At the same time, she remained ambivalent about these choices. She emphasized to me that as a "child of the sixties," she didn't require the same type of deference, distance, and formality that her mother had. The daughter of a corporate attorney and, as she put it, a "charity ball mother," she recalled growing up in elite enclaves of Los Angeles with a uniformed maid ringing a bell for dinner. "I dislike the bell. I really dislike treating someone like a servant," she murmured in a hushed voice. Jenna Proust did not identify with that kind of formality—she herself dressed in jeans and sneakers—yet she wanted distance and personal privacy from the domestic employees. Martha was her main negative example, and she commented, "She gets a little too close. . . . I really don't want to be on intimate terms with my workers. At the same time, I like being on a very comfortable and causal basis with them. You're raising kids together, how can it not be?"

Bonnie Feinstein, a part-time interior decorator and wife of a Hollywood director, employed three domestic employees at a cost of $3,000 a month to manage her large, rambling home and her three elementary school-age children. A Salvadoran woman worked as the full-time, live-out nanny/housekeeper from Monday through Friday, a Filipina woman worked Saturday morning through Sunday, and another Salvadoran woman cleaned the 5,700-square-foot house two days a week. Both Bonnie and her husband were so bothered by the familiarity exhibited by Sarita, the two-day-a-week cleaner, and by the Filipina nanny that they had discussed firing them.

Bonnie described how Sarita had cheerfully greeted her husband, an Academy Award-winning director, with a teasing, affectionate, "Hello handsome!" Irritated by the lack of deference but, like many husbands, unwilling to speak to the domestic employee himself, he had passed the problem to his wife. Uncertain of what to do, she said nothing to Sarita. . . .

Female upper-class employers such as these generally don't work, so they may spend considerable time together with the domestic workers in these large homes. Despite the size of the homes, contact with round-the-clock help is unavoidable, increasing the possibility of misunderstandings and potentially explosive contacts. These employers therefore find it particularly important to hire employees who will gauge and maintain just the right measure of distance.

EMPLOYEES: "I WANT THEM TO KNOW WHO I AM"

> My ideal employer? Someone who would talk with me about her family, who would ask questions about mine, about what I did in Mexico before I came here. Someone who would be considerate of my time.
>
> —*Marisela Ramírez*

As the epigraph suggests, there is a dramatic mismatch in what employers and employees desire from their relationship. Employers who hire someone to clean and look after their children at home generally want some distance from the women who do the work. They are often too pressed for time because of their work and family schedules; they may feel it is beneath them or a waste of time to personally interact with subordinates; or they simply feel too awkward about having someone taking care of their home and children to establish personal bonds. They want some breathing space—but the women they hire want more intimacy.

The structure of the job, the extent to which care work (and not just cleaning) is involved, and the organization of the lives of the domestic workers as newly arrived immigrant women prompt many Latina domestic workers in Los Angeles to prefer personalistic employer-employee relations. These are women who have left their homes, jobs, friends, and family members in Mexico, Guatemala, and El Salvador. Many of them have young children of their own, left behind in their countries of origin, whom they have not seen for years. Some had been born into middle-class lives, complete with social recognition and public status, and perhaps homes with their own domestic help. Now, they may spend very long days and even nights on the job, giving intimate care; some hold down second jobs on weekends or evenings. When they do have time off, it is filled with their own household chores, with visits to the coin-operated laundry, or with English classes. Their many personal sacrifices leave little time for human contact as they try to establish themselves on secure financial ground. The relative anonymity of their lives, the quality of their jobs, the larger political context of racialized nativism, and the rushed pace of life in Los Angeles leave many domestic workers without any sense of belonging and aching for some personal recognition. In addition, they have cultural expectations for everyday social interactions that clash with what they find on the job. Latin Americans are a good deal more likely to emote, hug, and verbally express affection than are typical Anglo-Americans. This *cultura de cariño,* or culture of affection, also contributes to the mismatched expectations of domestic workers and their employers.

Latina immigrants who do domestic work for pay are not, of course, a homogeneous group. Among the factors distinguishing them is their relative degree of social incorporation in the United States. At one extreme are recently arrived immigrant women, who lack nearby family and close friends and indeed may have only a handful of acquaintances in Los Angeles, who do not speak any English, who do not drive, and who do not know their way around downtown's *el centro,* the swap meets, or other commercial centers. At the other extreme are women with well-established local ties, who navigate easily about the city either on the bus or in their own cars, who have their families and strong social circles surrounding them, and who may participate in church or community organizations. The former are more likely to be employed in live-in nanny/housekeeper jobs, and the latter in weekly housecleaning. Not only job arrangements but also the level of social incorporation determine how personalistic they expect relations to be. Recently arrived women working in live-in jobs are generally more eager for personalistic employer-employee relations—and more critical of their employers who deny them this closeness—than are more established women working as housecleaners. Still, both groups of women express a preference for personalism with their employers.

Nanny/Housekeepers Versus Housecleaners

Women who strictly do housecleaning expect less personalism than do their nanny/housekeeper peers, in part because of the nature of their work. Those women who care for children on their jobs feel that their employers have a duty to acknowledge the intimate care they provide. Nanny/housekeepers who care for young children feel most poignantly the inherent contradiction between their tasks and their treatment. They work in the midst of a family; and unlike their housecleaning peers, they are paid for activities—nurturing, singing songs and reciting nursery rhymes, coaxing children to bathe, nap, or eat—that are emotional, intimate, and particularly tailored to each child. They often become genuinely attached to the children as they perform these tasks day in and day out. When they are treated coldly or as if they were invisible by their employers, who may be standing right next to them, they find such actions insulting and alienating. As one nanny put it, "Here I am caring for their children, and look at how they treat me!" Some nannies point out that self-interest should persuade employers to change this behavior, observing that employers who treat their employees well can expect those employees to provide better care for the children and remain in the job longer.

In short, because their work engages so intimately with the children, the Latina women who work as nanny/housekeepers want verbal, personalistic recognition from their employers. Deborah Stone, who has examined caring work in institutional contexts, argues that what is produced in caring work is a *relationship* between the giver and recipient of care. Thus to improve poor quality care, we must valorize caregiving as relationship building. The problem in managed elder care, the area on which she focuses, is that caregivers are discouraged from "caring about" or showing favoritism to the recipients. Private nanny/housekeepers appear to have the opposite problem: while these caregivers are expected to care about their charges, the employers do not seem to personally recognize them or find value in building a relationship with them.

While Latina domestic workers do not desire personalistic relations with their employers in lieu of decent pay or fair job terms, many of them prefer an employer who takes personal interest in them to an employer who pays more and treats them disrespectfully and coldly. They want to keep their dignity on the job, and thus they want employers to talk to them and listen when they speak. As Stone observes, talking and listening are key components of caregiving, so it should be no surprise that caregivers want their employers to listen to their own concerns and even aspirations. They don't necessarily want or expect gifts and advice (although many are grateful for these gestures). And they don't, of course, want interference—as we have seen, for a Latina domestic worker, the ideal employer is one who is out of the home for most of the day, not monitoring her and issuing ad hoc orders. But caregivers do want employers who will talk with them in an open and respectful manner—employers who will listen to and respect them as persons.

Job Structures

Live-in and live-out nanny/housekeepers find that the spatial and social isolation of the job intensifies their craving for personal contact. Typically they work for only one employer, and spend each day at the home of the same family. With the exception of those hired by very high income families who simultaneously employ several domestic workers, they generally have no co-workers with whom to speak. The job is, as one employer conceded, "a lonesome one." Nanny/housekeepers may be alone for most of the day, or they may spend the entire day with infants. If they are lucky, they may meet up for an hour or two with a group of nannies at a public park, or on arranged play dates.

Nanny/housekeepers with live-in jobs are the most isolated. They work long hours—on average, more than sixty hours a week—leaving the employer's home only on Saturday afternoons, when they retreat to a shared apartment or a rented room until Monday morning. During the rest of the week, they remain confined to their work site. Without anyone to speak with day after day, many of them become emotionally distraught and depressed. It is little wonder that they often seek more personalistic relations with the only adults they see, their employers.

Erlinda Castro, a middle-aged Guatemalan woman and mother of five, had spent three years working as a live-in housekeeper in three different households before finally establishing her route of weekly housecleaning jobs. In the first of her live-in jobs, she worked for a family whom she described as good employers, because they paid her what she had expected to earn and because they did not pile on an unreasonable number of duties. The school-age children were gone for most of the day, and her job tasks seemed fair and physically manageable. The employers did not criticize her work and they never insulted or yelled at her. Unlike many other live-ins, she had her own room and there was food for her to eat. Yet Erlinda found her employers cold and impersonal, unresponsive to her attempts to engage them in conversation; and she told me that their aloofness drove her out of the job.

"I would greet the *señora,* 'Good morning, *señora* Judy,'" she recalled. "They spoke a little Spanish, but the *señor* never spoke. If I greeted him, maybe in between his teeth he would mutter, 'Heh,' just like that. That's how one is often treated, and it feels cruel. You leave your own home, leaving everything behind only to find hostility. You're useful to them only because you clean, wash, iron, cook—that's the only reason. There is no affection. There is nothing." She expected some warmth and affection, but instead she found a void. Erlinda Castro entered the home of these employers directly after leaving her home and five children in Guatemala. On weekends she visited with her husband, whom she had joined in Los Angeles. It was her first experience with paid domestic work, and although she was not put off by the pay, the job tasks, or the low status of the job, the impersonal treatment became intolerable. "I felt bad, really bad. I couldn't go on with that, with nothing more than, 'Good morning, *señora*' and, 'Good night, *señora.*' Nothing else. They would say nothing, nothing, absolutely nothing to me! They would only speak to me to give me orders." Erlinda stayed on that job for approximately one year, leaving it for another live-in job that a friend had told her about.

Being treated as though one is invisible is a complaint commonly voiced by domestic workers of color working for white employers. As the historian David Katzman has noted in his study of the occupation in the South, "One peculiar and most degrading aspect of domestic service was the requisite of invisibility. The ideal servant . . . would be invisible and silent[,] . . . sensitive to the moods and whims of those around them, but undemanding of family warmth, love or security." In her early 1980s ethnographic research, for which she posed as a housecleaner, Judith Rollins revealed a telling moment: an employer and her teenage son conducted an entire conversation about personal issues in her presence. "This situation was," Rollins wrote in her field notes,"the most peculiar feeling of the day: being there and not being there." At different times, African American, Japanese American, and Chicana domestic workers in the United States have had the same disturbing experience.

Some domestic workers see personalism as the antidote to these indignities and humiliations. Verbal interaction affords them respect and recognition on the job. Elvira Areola, a Mexicana, had worked for eleven years for one family. I interviewed her several days after an acrimonious fight with her employer—a disagreement that became physical—had left her jobless and without an income. As a single mother, she found herself in a frightening position. Still, she expressed no regrets, partly because the almost completely nonverbal relationship that she had maintained for several years with the *patrona* had been so strained. Her female employer had not worked and was physically present in the home, yet they hardly interacted "I would arrive [in the morning] and sometimes she wouldn't greet me until two in the afternoon. . . . I'd be in the kitchen, and she'd walk in but wouldn't say anything. She would ignore me, as if to say, 'I'm alone in my house and there's no one else here.' Sometimes she wouldn't speak to me the whole day . . . she'd act as if I was a chair, a table, as if her house was supposedly all clean without me being there." Her dissatisfaction with the lack of appreciation and verbal recognition was echoed in the accounts of many other women.

Domestic workers tend to accept much more readily the minimal verbal exchanges they often experience with male employers. Ronalda Saavedra described her male employers' blur of unchanging monosyllabic greetings: "In the morning they say 'Hi!' and then 'Bye!' Then in the evenings they come around again with that same old 'Hi!' and then 'Bye!' " Similarly, while Maribel Centeno often enjoyed conversing with her female employer, she noted that "the husband is different. He sometimes doesn't greet me, and sometimes I want to think it's just because he is so into his profession." Fears of sexual harassment may help explain the domestic workers' different responses to the same behavior.

Downward Class Mobility

Prior class status plays an important role in fueling an expectation for personalism. In contemporary Los Angeles, Latina nanny/housekeepers who in their countries of origin had enjoyed middle-class status and jobs that brought them into contact with the public are acutely sensitive to their employers' failure to recognize them as people. Sometimes they suffer depression and low self-esteem as a result. Twenty-five-year-old Maribel Centeno, a former university student, worked as a live-out nanny/housekeeper. Although she was happier in that job than in her former position as a live-in in her first few years in the United States, she cited as one of its biggest disadvantages the *bloqueo* that it had produced in her—a kind of emotional and communicative wall that had developed because she lacked daily interaction with others. She now found it hard to speak with other people in informal social gatherings. In Guatemala, she had been surrounded by friends, family, co-workers, and student peers. She had attended university, worked part-time as a radio operator and in her parents' general store, and frequently socialized with friends. The daily monotony and loneliness she endured as a nanny/housekeeper provided a stark contrast to her former life. Exaggerating only slightly, she said, "Sometimes I go for days, and then I realize I haven't heard myself talk."

Nanny/housekeepers try to address these problems as best they can. Despite owning a car, Maribel sometimes deliberately took the bus so that she could enjoy the company of other domestic workers on her way to work. Even though she found their discussions rather dull, uninformed, and uncultured, she welcomed the personal contact. She lived with two of her cousins and had a steady boyfriend; but as new Guatemalan immigrants, they too were busy, working long hours and attending ESL classes. Maribel's female employer did not work, so she was usually present when Maribel was cleaning the house and looking after a hyperactive adolescent boy when he arrived home from school. Although their relationship was rife with tensions—over wages, time off, and the employer's underestimation of her—Maribel cited the conversation and personalism she had with her employer as one of the best things about her job. "She always greets me and gives me a kiss, and when I leave, it's the same. She asks after my parents, for my sister, she asks how I'm doing in school. . . . At noon, maybe I'll be upstairs and she'll call out that she's making a turkey sandwich. 'Do you want one?' "

Maribel deliberately initiated conversations with her employer designed to showcase her considerable knowledge and curiosity about politics, music, and history. In fact, she believed that her employer usually showed respect and interest in her precisely because she had proven herself to be well-educated and informed about current events. There was a genuine warmth between the two, which I witnessed when we gathered at a hotel to celebrate Maribel's graduation from a U.S. high school. The employer beamed at Maribel's accomplishments and applauded her goal to move out of domestic work and into cosmetology or teaching. Describing their relationship, Maribel said, "I feel that she's, ah, not really my friend, but there is a certain kind of respect. I think that's because I study, because if it wasn't for that, well I don't know." Yet tensions between the two remained. Maribel also reported that during the day, her employer often ignored her, spending most of her time holed up in the pool cabana smoking, talking on the phone, or paying bills. Moreover, the employer did not always show her respect, and Maribel resented these indignities.

Maribel recounted a number of painful incidents that demonstrated her employer's tendency to objectify and underestimate her. On one occasion the employer, assuming that Maribel had never heard of a submarine sandwich, condescendingly explained how to assemble one out of bread, mayonnaise, and sliced meats. "At first I didn't say anything, I just looked at her. How could she think I didn't know what a submarine is!" Maribel told me that she had then launched into a speech that Guatemalans enjoyed the same modern technology as Americans, and that in fact, Guatemalans had much more, as their Mayan civilization had developed advanced mathematics and the concept of zero years before they were in use in Europe. On another occasion, the employer allowed a friend to drop off children for Maribel to watch—creating extra work without extra pay. The employer assured her friend not to worry: "Maribel knows how to dial 911 and she has attended university." The other woman had exclaimed, "Oh, really?" Maribel mimicked the look of disbelief by raising her eyebrows and added, "and she looked at me like I was an animal in the zoo!"

Such incidents highlighted the employer's (and her friend's) view of Maribel as backward, inferior, and ignorant. For a number of reasons, Maribel saw her job as less than perfect. She wanted higher pay and the assurance that it would continue when the employers vacationed or had the house remodeled, and she disapproved of the employer's liberal child-rearing style. Yet more objectionable than these more material drawbacks was her employer's insinuation that she and other Latinas and Latinos were inferior, which hurt her deeply. "She's even made comments like, 'Did you see the housekeeper across the street? She has seven children! Now *you* must know how to think. You don't come here just to have children!' Of course, she'll never say, 'Oh, you're all a burden on the state,' but that's what she means." In Maribel Centeno's relationship with her employer, respectful warmth coexisted along with deep antagonism rooted in inequalities of class, citizenship status, and race, and both found daily expression.

Domestic workers who prefer personalistic relations with their employers are looking for some recognition of their humanity. Yet personalistic relations, as Maribel's case illustrates and as previous literature argues, can also emphasize the employees' inferiority and the employers' sense of superiority. Although domestic workers differ on how much of their private lives they wish to share with their employers—and many of them have learned that intimate details are best kept to themselves—all object to being treated as invisible non-persons or as replaceable cogs. Certainly they want fair pay and decent working conditions, but they also want to be treated as more than just generic employees. Many of them say they prefer personalism because it recognizes their own needs, preferences, and feelings.

While the literature on paid domestic work has stressed how employers deploy personalism as a mechanism of control, contemporary Latina domestic workers in Los Angles see nonpersonalistic employers as potentially more exploitative. For the most part, these women had no illusions that a personalistic relationship with their employers signified the friendship of equals; but they saw personalism as an avenue through which employers could show respect for them as people. Without it, a domestic worker loses all individual identity. Several of the women used words such as "robot" or "disposable" to describe how employers view them. They assume that employers cannot fully subordinate or manipulate someone seen instead as a person.

Maura de la Covarrubia, who had worked as an attorney in Peru, had an unusual arrangement: she worked as a nanny for several different families, visiting each one day a week, and for another family as a nanny/housekeeper only on the weekends. She had established fairly close relations with most of her female employers, and she used her educational and class background to her advantage. Maura held very clear ideas on what constituted a desirable employer. "An ideal employer," she offered, "is a friendly person, someone who pays well, and above all, who thinks that the person who works for her, whether as a 'housekeeper' or as a 'baby-sitter,' or whatever, is a human being. I think there are some people who don't see us as human beings, but rather we're just, just some *thing* that works there, some *thing* that if you get tired of, you just exchange it for another, for another, and for another! It's as if we're disposable!" . . .

Other Latina nanny/housekeepers contrasted their dehumanizing treatment by some employers with recognition as persons by others. Patricia Paredes, a very savvy Mexican live-in nanny/housekeeper whose job required that she live across town from her husband and three young daughters during the week, said, "I like it when people treat you right, when they know you are human and have feelings. I like being treated like a human, not a robot." She went even further, praising her employer for treating her "as family . . . that's how I like to be treated. I'm never humiliated or put down."

Paid domestic workers seek a personalism that goes beyond superficial cordiality to recognition that their health, well-being, and personal circumstances affect their ability to work. They want employers who don't simply ask how they feel but adjust the job to take into account illness or a personal crisis. . . .

Social Incorporation

Recently arrived women who work as nanny/housekeepers are often bereft of family and community, in a sense out of necessity. Forty percent of the 153 domestic workers surveyed who were mothers reported that they had left at least one child "back-home," in their countries of origin, and that this was much more likely to be true of live-in nanny/housekeepers, least likely of weekly housecleaners. While some Latina domestic workers in Los Angeles have rich social networks of friends, kin, and community, others are basically on their own.

At one end of continuum might be someone like Lupe Vélez, who is firmly entrenched in her own family and community life. A Mexicana, Lupe entered the United States when her father, a contract laborer who came to California in the bracero era, brought the family in the late 1960s. She had married in the 1970s; and when I interviewed her, she and her husband, a welder, had two cars, owned a house on the east side of Los Angeles, and had five U.S.-born children, including two who were already attending state colleges. Lupe cleaned about nine houses a week, driving to them in her Toyota. She also kept busy with her teenage children and Latina social circles, with *comadres,* sister-in-law, neighbors, and church life. I spoke with her one hot, summer evening in her tiny, neatly furnished living room, where family photos adorned nearly every available space, a group of teenage boys socialized on the front porch, and the phone rang often. With all the activity surrounding her, Lupe didn't have a great need to receive personalistic treatment from her employers. As a weekly housecleaner, she saw many of them only fleetingly, and she clearly understood her job as a money-earning activity. Yet she too desired employer appreciation, reporting that it felt good when an employer sometimes called her at home to simply thank her for her excellent cleaning. When I asked what she liked best about her job, she said with an easy laugh, "Well, the pay is important—but especially that they treat me well!" But because Lupe Vélez had a full life with family and friends, she was not as concerned about employer personalism as were some Latina immigrants who had arrived more recently.

At the other end of the continuum is Carmen Velasquez, a thirty-nine-year-old Mexican woman. She had worked at live-in jobs for ten years in the United Statas, and had no complaints about her current job. In fact, when I asked her to describe an ideal employer, she replied, "The ones I have." She currently worked for an attorney and a schoolteacher, caring for their toddler and living in their home. They treated her with respect, paid her on time, acted friendly, and were not too demanding in their expectations. Unlike many other live-in nanny/housekeepers, she ended her workday when the female employer returned home at 5 P.M. Yet her longing for more personalistic, familylike relations with her employers was revealed when I asked her what she might do differently if she herself were to employ a domestic worker. "If I had lived through all of this," she reflected, "I would try to make sure that person felt as though she wasn't a stranger to my family, so that she would feel like part of my family and that of my children. [I'd make sure] that she could share those moments when I was there—not as a maid or employee but rather as a friend."

More than any cultural explanation, the social conditions of Carmen's life explain her preference for personalism. Carmen, a single mother, had no family life of her own in Los Angeles. She had left her three children in Mexico ten years earlier, when they were four, five, and seven years old. She sent money to the children and communicated with them and her *comadres,* who cared for the children in Mexico; she had not seen them for a decade. A series of traumatic events had left her completely estranged from the father of the children, her parents, and her siblings. In spite of these familial hard-ships, Carmen maintained a warm, loving, upbeat personality. Whenever I saw her around young children—the children of other domestic workers, or my own three-year-old—she could scarcely contain her affection, extending her arms to embrace them or give their chubby arms a squeeze.

Although she had been in the United States for ten years, she was still working as a live-in nanny/housekeeper, with no residence of her own. Unlike many live-in employees who share an apartment or at least rent a room to which they can retreat on weekends, Carmen stayed at her employer's house. This enabled her to send a larger portion of her earnings to her children in Mexico, but it also kept her isolated from Latino community life. Her Anglo employer's home was located in a secluded canyon neighborhood, home mostly to Anglos and Armenians. The nearby streets had no sidewalks, no pedestrians, and no commercial life. On weekdays, Carmen sometimes took the toddler to the park, where she met with two other Latina nannies; during the evenings, she attended English classes, joining a small group of Latino students within a largely Armenian student body. In her room she studied English and enjoyed reading self-help books that focus on self-esteem. "I always try to stay positive," she told me. One Sunday afternoon each month, she attended a meeting of the Domestic Workers' Association, but she spent many weekends riding aimlessly around on public buses, just to get out of the employer's house.

DISTINGUISHING MATERNALISM FROM PERSONALISM

In the large and theoretically sophisticated literature on paid domestic work, employer maternalism is roundly, and rightly, condemned as a principal source of exploitation. One alternative, most forcefully advocated by the sociologist Mary Romero, is to maintain businesslike, contractual relations concerned specifically and exclusively with job tasks and schedules. The contractual ideal may be realizable in housecleaning work—which is, not coincidentally, the form of paid domestic work on which Romero's primary research has focused. When care work is involved, however, emotional connection is an integral part of the job and a clear-cut relation between client and customer is far rarer.

More important, as we saw in this chapter, both Latina nanny/housekeepers and housecleaners report that when employer-employee relations remain devoid of personalistic interactions, they feel ignored and disrespected. While it might be tempting to dismiss their statements as exemplifying what Marxists would denounce as false consciousness, we should take seriously what they say about their work and how it makes them feel. To understand why these Latina domestic workers want more affinity and personal connection with their employers, we must distinguish between maternalism and personalism. Employer maternalism is a one-way relationship, defined primarily by the employer's gestures of charity, unsolicited advice, assistance, and gifts. The domestic employee is obligated to respond with extra hours of service, personal loyalty, and job commitment. Maternalism underlines the deep class inequalities between employers and employees. More problematically, because employer maternalism positions the employee as needy, deficient, and childlike, it does not allow the employee any dignity and respect. Personalism, by contrast, is a two-way relationship, albeit still asymmetrical. It involves the employer's recognition of the employee as a particular person—the recognition and *consideración* necessary for dignity and respect to be realized. In the absence of fair wages, reasonable hours, and job autonomy, personalism alone is not enough to upgrade domestic work; but conversely, its absence virtually ensures that the job will be experienced as degrading.

To be sure, employers can use personalistic relations as a strategy to mask low salaries, lack of benefits, and long hours of work with out overtime pay, but for the most part, Latina housecleaners and nanny/housekeepers see cold, impersonal employer-employee relations as blatant reminders of the low regard in which society holds them. They experience this on-the-job treatment as continuous with the various anti-immigrant, and particularly anti-Latino, campaigns in California during the 1990s, Racialized nativism sets the stage on which these relationships or nonrelationships acquire meaning.

For their part, many employers would prefer to have more distant, impersonal relationships with their domestic workers, not because they wish to rationalize labor practices but because personalism obligates them to care about their employees. As their time becomes increasingly scarce, they resist spending time and emotional energy even on talking with their domestic workers. As we have seen, many contemporary American employers are not quite comfortable with having someone do domestic work in their home. Though they may not voice or even feel class or racial guilt, they are still made profoundly uneasy by the darker, poorer, Spanish-speaking women toiling away in their homes, making them masters and mistresses—an image that doesn't fit their view of themselves, or their sense of the United States as a modern, democratic, classless, and color-blind society. Finally, personalism implicitly limits employers' power flexibility to control their employees.

Yet despite what they might prefer, and despite their greater power, employers must still negotiate their relationships with their employees; compromises are often necessary on both sides. As we have seen, the social characteristics of employers and employees, as well as the structure of domestic jobs, affect the degree of personalism in employer-employee relations more than individual wishes do.

PART VII

EDUCATION AND SCHOOLS

In the United States education is heralded as the great leveler of class, racial, and gender inequalities, promising social mobility to working-class and nonwhite youth, and to women and girls. The reality often falls short, as social inequalities are often reproduced within schools. But while holding out the promise of upward social mobility, what do schools teach about gender? As all of the articles in the section attest, schools teach far more than the standard curriculum.

What do schools teach children about themselves? Popular culture and educational institutions are imbued with gendered images of "nice girls" and "naughty boys." Boys in our culture are thought of as naughty and rambunctious, but innocent. When they commit minor transgressions, they are frequently let off the hook by the idea that "boys will be boys," and that their natural development entails mischievous tumbles with "snakes and snails and puppy dog tails." This, afterall, is seen as preparation for manhood. But as Ann Ferguson's research, based on a detailed ethnographic study in Oakland schools and neighborhoods, shows, boys' special dispensation for transgressive behavior comes packaged with white racial privilege. When inner-city African Americans misbehave, they do not receive the protection of acceptable labels such as "naughty boys." Rather, they are seen as "willfully bad," and Ferguson compellingly argues that this particular sort of interpretive framing of gender is the result of "adultification." In other words, poor, inner-city black children are denied the protections of childhood. African American elementary school boys are routinely perceived to be hyperdangerous and plain old bad, and this has serious repercussions in many arenas, including education.

In the next chapter, sociologist Julie Bettie raises similar questions about the intersections of race, class, gender, and public education. Based on her ethnographic study of girls in a high school located in the central valley of California, Bettie shows us the ways in which these teenage girls' gendered performances are race and class specific. For high school girls, feminine identities are constructed and conveyed through the adoption of distinctive styles and bodily adornment that reflect class and race. White prep school girls favor light pastels and pink nail polish, while the non–prep school Chicana girls adopt darker colors as badges of a "dissident femininity."

Can double-standards rooted in family life wind up helping girls and hindering boys in education and work outcomes? This is suggested by Nancy Lopez in her study of West Indian and Dominican second-generation youth in New York City. These girls generally grow up weighted down with more family domestic responsibilities than do their brothers, but these obligations wind up enhancing the girls' self-esteem, and when coupled with the role models of their independent mothers and grandmothers, this helps the young women in their future endeavors. Meanwhile, their male peers suffer from racial discrimination and neglect from family and school, and they often develop gender identities that hinge less on responsibility and more on "hanging out" as "streetboys." The final chapter in this section examines competing curricular standards and shows how progressive teachers in Japan have challenged Japanese masculinist and racist narratives by introducing into the curriculum a topic previously silenced, that of the Korean "comfort women" who were institutionally raped by Japanese soldiers during the Asia-Pacific War. As Yoshiko Nozaki shows, antisexist, anti-imperialist education is not a given, but an achievement that is fought for, in this case by South Korean and Japanese feminists.

41

Naughty by Nature

Ann Arnett Ferguson

Two representations of black masculinity are widespread in society and school today. They are the images of the African American male as a criminal and as an endangered species. These images are routinely used as resources to interpret and explain behaviour by teachers at Rosa Parks School when they make punishment decisions. An ensemble of historical meanings and their social effects is contained within these images.

The image of the black male criminal is more familiar because of its prevalence in the print and electronic media as well as in scholarly work. The headlines of newspaper articles and magazines sound the alarm dramatically as the presence of black males in public space has come to signify danger and a threat to personal safety. But this is not just media hype. Bleak statistics give substance to the figure of the criminal. Black males are disproportionately in jails: they make up 6 percent of the population of the United States, but 45 percent of the inmates in state and federal prisons: they are imprisoned at six times the rate of whites.[1] In the state of California, one-third of African American men in their twenties are in prison, on parole, or on probation, in contrast to 5 percent of white males in the same age group. This is nearly five times the number who attend four-year colleges in the state.[2] The mortality rate for African American boys fourteen years of age and under is approximately 50 percent higher than for the comparable group of white male youth, with the leading cause of death being homicide.[3]

The second image, that of the black male as an endangered species, is one which has largely emanated from African American social scientists and journalists who are deeply concerned about the criminalization and high mortality rate among African American youth.[4] It represents him as being marginalized to the point of oblivion. While this discourse emanates from a sympathetic perspective, in the final analysis the focus is all too often on individual maladaptive behavior and black mothering practices as the problem rather than on the social structure in which this endangerment occurs.

These two cultural representations are rooted in actual material conditions and reflect existing social conditions and relations that they appear to sum up for us. They are lodged in theories, in commonsense understandings of self in relation to others in the world as well as in popular culture and the media. But they are condensations, extrapolations, that emphasize certain elements and gloss over others. They represent a narrow selection from the multiplicity, the heterogeneity of actual relations in society.

Since both of these images come to be used for identifying, classification, and decision making by teachers at Rosa Parks School, it is necessary to analyze the manner in which these images, or cultural representations of difference, are produced through a racial discursive formation. Then we can explain how they are utilized by teachers in the exercise of school rules to produce a context in which African American boys become more visible, more culpable as "rule-breakers."

A central element of a racist discursive formation is the production of subjects as essentially different by virtue of their "race." Historically, the circulation of images that represent this difference has been a powerful technique in this production.[5] Specifically, blacks have been represented as essentially different from whites, as the constitutive Other that regulates and confirms "whiteness." Images of Africans as savage, animalistic, subhuman without history or culture—the diametric opposite of that of Europeans—rationalized and perpetuated a system of slavery. After slavery was abolished, images of people of African descent as hypersexual, shiftless, lazy, and of inferior intellect, legitimated a system that continued to deny right of citizenship to blacks on the basis of race difference. This regime of truth about race was articulated through scientific experiments and "discoveries," law, social custom, popular culture, folklore, and common sense. And for three hundred years, from the seventeenth century to the middle of the twentieth century, this racial distinction was policed through open and unrestrained physical violence. The enforcement of race difference was conscious, overt, and institutionalized.

In the contemporary period, the production of a racial Other and the constitution and regulation of racial difference has worked increasingly through mass-produced images that are omnipresent in our lives. At this moment in time it is through culture—or culturalism[6]—that difference is primarily asserted. This modern-day form for producing racism specifically operates through symbolic violence and representations of Blackness that circulate through the mass media, cinematic images and popular music, rather than through the legal forms of the past. The representational becomes a potent vehicle for the transmission of racial meanings that reproduce relations of difference, of division, and of power. These "controlling images" make "racism, sexism, and poverty appear to be natural, normal, and an inevitable part of everyday life."[7]

CULTURAL REPRESENTATIONS OF "DIFFERENCE"

The behavior of African American boys in school is perceived by adults at Rosa Parks School through a filter of overlapping representations of three socially invented categories of "difference": age, gender, and race. These are grounded in the commonsense, taken-for-granted notion that existing social divisions reflect biological and natural dispositional differences among humans: so children are essentially different from adults, males from females, blacks from whites.[8] At the intersection of this complex of subject positions are African American boys who are doubly displaced: as black children, they are not seen as childlike but adultified; as black males, they are denied the masculine dispensation constituting white males as being "naturally naughty" and are discerned as willfully bad. Let us look more closely at this displacement.

The dominant cultural representation of childhood is as closer to nature, as less social, less human. Childhood is assumed to be a stage of development: culture, morality, sociability is written on children in an unfolding process by adults (who are seen as fully "developed," made by culture not nature) in institutions like family and school. On the one hand, children are assumed to be dissembling, devious, because they are more egocentric. On the other hand, there is an attribution of innocence to their wrongdoing. In both cases, this is understood to be a temporary condition, a stage prior to maturity. So they must be socialized to fully understand the meaning of their acts.

The language used to describe "children in general" by educators illustrates this paradox. At one districtwide workshop for adult school volunteers that I attended, children were described by the classroom teacher running the workshop as being "like little plants, they need attention, they gobble it up." Later in the session, the same presenter invoked the other dominant representation of children as devious, manipulative, and powerful. "They'll run a number on you. They're little lawyers, con artists, manipulators—and they usually win. They're good at it. Their strategy is to get you off task. They pull you into their whirlwind."

These two versions of childhood express the contradictory qualities that adults map onto their interactions with children in general. The first description of children as "little plants," childhood as identical with nature, is embedded in the ideology of childhood. The second version that presents children as powerful, as self-centered, with an agenda and purpose of their own, arises out of the experience adults have exercising authority over children. In actual relations of power, in a twist, as children become the objects of control, they become devious "con artists" and adults become innocent, pristine in relation to them. In both instance, childhood has been constructed as different in essence from adulthood, as a phase of biological, psychological, and social development with predictable attributes.

Even though we treat it this way, the category "child" does not describe and contain a homogeneous and naturally occurring group of individuals at a certain stage of human development. The social meaning of childhood has changed profoundly over time.[9] What it means to be a child varies dramatically by virtue of location in cross-cutting categories of class, gender, and race.[10]

Historically, the existence of African American children has been constituted differently through economic practices, the law, social policy, and visual imagery. This difference has been projected in an ensemble of images of black youth as not childlike. In the early decades of this century, representations of black children as pickaninnies depicted them as verminlike, voracious, dirty, grinning, animal-like savages. They were also depicted as the laugh-provoking butt of aggressive, predatory behavior; natural victims, therefore victimizable. An example of this was their depiction in popular lore as "alligator bait." Objects such as postcards, souvenir spoons, letter-openers and cigar-box labels were decorated with figures of half-naked black children vainly attempting to escape the open toothy jaws of hungry alligators.[11]

Today's representations of black children still bear traces of these earlier depictions. The media demonization of very young black boys who are charged with committing serious crimes is one example. In these cases there is rarely the collective soul-searching for answers to the question of how "kids like this" could have committed these acts that occurs when white kids are involved. Rather, the answer to the question seems to be inherent in the disposition of the kids themselves.[12] The image of the young black male as an endangered species revitalizes the animalistic trope. Positioned as part of nature, his essence is described through language otherwise reserved for wildlife that has been decimated to the point of extinction. Characterized as a "species," they are cut off from other members of family and community and isolated as a form of prey.

There is continuity, but there is a significant new twist to the images. The endangered species and the criminal are mirror images. Either as criminal perpetrator or as endangered victim, contemporary imagery proclaims black males to be responsible for their fate. The discourse of individual choice and responsibility elides the social and economic context and locates predation as coming from within. It is their own maladaptive and inappropriate behavior that causes African Americans to self-destruct. As an endangered species, they are stuck in an obsolete stage of social evolution, unable to adapt to the present. As criminals, they are a threat to themselves, to each other, as well as to society in general.

As black children's behavior is refracted through the lens of these two cultural images, it is "adultified." By this I mean their transgressions are made to take on a sinister, intentional, fully conscious tone that is stripped of any element of childish naïveté. The discourse of childhood as an unfolding developmental stage in the life cycle is displaced in this mode of framing school trouble. Adultification is visible in the way African American elementary school pupils are talked about by school adults.

One of the teachers, a white woman who prided herself on the multicultural emphasis in her classroom, invoked the image of African American children as "looters" in lamenting the disappearance of books from the class library. This characterization is especially meaningful because her statement. which was made at the end of the school year that had included the riots in Los Angeles, invoked that event as a framework for making children's behavior intelligible.

> I've lost so many library books this term. There are quite a few kids who don't have any books at home, so I let them borrow them. I didn't sign them out because I thought I could trust the kids. I sent a letter home to parents asking them to look for them and turn them in. But none have come in. I just don't feel the same. *It's just like the looting in Los Angeles.*

By identifying those who don't have books at home as "looters," the teacher has excluded the white children in the class, who all come from more middle-class backgrounds so, it is assumed, "have books at home." In the case of the African American kids, what might be interpreted as the careless behavior of children is displaced by images of adult acts of theft that conjure up violence and mayhem. The African American children in this teacher's classroom and their families are seen not in relation to images of childhood, but in relation to the television images of crowds rampaging through South Central Los Angeles in the aftermath of the verdict of the police officers who beat Rodney King. Through this frame, the children embody a willful, destructive, and irrational disregard for property rather than simple carelessness. Racial difference is mediated through culturalism: blacks are understood as a group undifferentiated by age or status with the proclivity and values to disregard the rights and welfare of others.

Adultification is a central mechanism in the interpretive framing of gender roles. African American girls are constituted as different through this process. A notion of sexual passivity and innocence that prevails for white female children is displaced by the image of African American females as sexual beings: as immanent mothers, girlfriends, and sexual partners of the boys in the room.[13] Though these girls may be strong, assertive, or troublesome, teachers evaluate their potential in ways that attribute to them an inevitable, potent sexuality that flares up early and that, according to one teacher, lets them permit men to run all over them, to take advantage of them. An incident in the Punishing Room that I recorded in my field notes made visible the way that adult perceptions of youthful behavior were filtered through racial representations. African American boys and girls who misbehaved were not just breaking a rule out of high spirits and needing to be chastised for the act, but were adultified, gendered figures whose futures were already inscribed and foreclosed within a racial order:

> Two girls, Adila and a friend, burst into the room followed by Miss Benton a black sixth-grade teacher and a group of five African American boys from her class. Miss Benton is yelling at the girls because they have been jumping in the hallway and one has knocked down part of a display on the bulletin board which she and her class put up the day before. She is yelling at the two girls about how they're wasting time. This is what she says: "You're doing exactly what they want you to do. You're playing into their hands. Look at me! Next going to be tracking you."
>
> One of the girls asks her rather sullenly who "they" is.
>
> Miss Benton is furious. "Society, that's who. You should be leading the class, not fooling around jumping around in the hallway. Someone has to give pride to the community. All the black men are on drugs, or in jail, or killing each other. Someone has got to hold it together. And the women have to do it. And you're jumping up and down in the hallway."
>
> I wonder what the black boys who have followed in the wake of the drama make of this assessment of their future, seemingly already etched in stone. The teacher's words to the girls are supposed to inspire them to leadership. The message for the boys is a dispiriting one.

Tracks have already been laid down for sixth-grade girls toward a specifically feminized responsibility (and, what is more prevalent, blame) for the welfare of the community, while males are bound for jail as a consequence of their own socially and self-destructive acts.

There is a second displacement from the norm in the representation of black males. The hegemonic, cultural image of the essential "nature" of males is that they are different from females in the meaning of their acts. Boys will be boys: they are mischievous, they get into trouble, they can stand up for themselves. This vision of masculinity is rooted in the notion of an essential sex difference based on biology, hormones, uncontrollable urges, true personalities. Boys are naturally more physical, more active. Boys are naughty by *nature*. There is something suspect about the boy who is "too docile," "like a girl." As a result, rule breaking on the part of boys is looked at as something-they-can't-help, a natural expression of masculinity in a civilizing process.

This incitement of boys to be "boylike" is deeply inscribed in our mainstream culture, winning hearts and stirring imaginations in the way that the pale counterpart, the obedient boy, does not. . . .

African American boys are not accorded the masculine dispensation of being "naturally" naughty. Instead the school reads their expression and display of masculine naughtiness as a sign of an inherent vicious, insubordinate nature that as a threat to order must be controlled. Consequently, school adults view any display of masculine mettle on the part of these boys through body language or verbal rejoinders as a sign of insubordination. In confrontation with adults, what is required from them is a performance of absolute docility that goes against the grain of masculinity. Black boys are expected to internalize a ritual obeisance in such exchanges so that the performance of docility appears to come naturally. According to the vice principal, "These children have to learn not to talk back. They must know that if the adult says you're wrong, then you're wrong. They must not resist, must go along with it, and take their punishment," he says.

This is not a lesson that all children are required to learn, however. The disciplining of the body within school rules has specific race and gender overtones. For black boys, the enactment of docility is a preparation for adult racialized survival rituals of which the African American adults in the school are especially cognizant. For African American boys bodily forms of expressiveness have repercussions in the world outside the chain-link fence of the school. The body must be taught to endure humiliation in preparation for future enactments of submission. The vice principal articulated the racialized texture of decorum when he deplored one of the Troublemakers, Lamar's, propensity to talk back and argue with teachers.

Lamar had been late getting into line at the end of recess, and the teacher had taken away his football. Lamar argued and so the teacher gave him detention. Mr. Russell spelled out what an African American male needed to learn about confrontations with power.

> Look, I've told him before about getting into these show-down situations—where he either has to show off to save face, then if he doesn't get his way then he goes wild. He won't get away with it in this school. Not with me, not with Mr. Harmon. But I know he's going to try it somewhere outside and it's going to get him in *real* trouble. He has to learn to ignore, to walk away, not to get into power struggles.

Mr. Russell's objective is to hammer into Lamar's head what he believes is the essential lesson for young black males to learn if they are to get anywhere in life: to act out obeisance is to survive. The specter of the Rodney King beating by the Los Angeles Police Department provided the backdrop for this conversation, as the trial of the police officers had just begun. The defense lawyer for the LAPD was arguing that Rodney King could have stopped the beating at any time if he had chosen.

This apprehension of black boys as inherently different both in terms of character and of their place in the social order is a crucial factor in teacher disciplinary practices. . . .

Let us examine now more closely some widespread modes of categorizing African American boys, the normalizing judgments that they circulate, and the consequences these have on disciplinary intervention and punishment.

BEING "AT-RISK": IDENTIFYING PRACTICE

The range of normalizing judgments for African American males is bounded by the image of the ideal pupil at one end of the spectrum and the unsalvageable student who is criminally inclined at the other end. The ideal type of student is characterized here by a white sixth-grade teacher:

> Well, it consists of, first of all, to be able to follow directions. Any direction that I give. Whether it's get this out, whether it's put this away, whether it's turn to this page or whatever, they follow it, and they come in and they're ready to work. It doesn't matter high skill or low skill, they're ready to work and they know that's what they're here for. Behaviorally, they're ap-

> propriate all day long. When it's time for them to listen, they listen. The way I see it, by sixth grade, the ideal student is one that can sit and listen and learn from me—work with their peers, and take responsibility on themselves and understand what is next, what is expected of them.

This teacher, however, drew on the image of the Good Bad Boy when she described the qualities of her "ideal" male student, a white boy in her class. Here the docility of the generic ideal student becomes the essentially naughty-by-nature male:

> He's not really Goody Two-shoes, you know. He's not quiet and perfect. He'll take risks. He'll say the wrong answer. He'll fool around and have to be reprimanded in class. There's a nice balance to him.

The modal category for African American boys is "at-risk" of failure. The concept of "at-riskness" is central to a discourse about the contemporary crisis in urban schools in America that explains children's failure as largely the consequence of their attitudes and behaviors as well as those of their families. In early stages of schooling they are identified as "at-risk" of failing, as "at-risk" of being school drop-outs. The category has been invested with enormous power to identify, explain, and predict futures. For example, a white fifth-grade teacher told me with sincere concern that as she looked around at her class, she could feel certain that about only four out of the twenty-one students would eventually graduate from high school. Each year, she said, it seemed to get worse.

Images of family play a strong role in teacher assessments and decisions about at-risk children. These enter into the evaluative process to confirm an original judgment. Families of at-risk children are said to lack parental skills; they do not give their children the kind of support that would build "self-esteem" necessary for school achievement. But this knowledge of family is superficial, inflamed by cultural representations and distorted through a rumor mill.

The children themselves are supposed to betray the lack of love and attention at home through their own "needy" behavior in the classroom. According to the teachers, these are pupils who are always demanding attention and will work well only in one-to-one or small-group situations because of this neglect at home. They take up more than their share of time and space. Donel, one of the African American boys who has been identified as at-risk by the school, is described by his teacher:

> He's a boy with a lot of energy and usually uncontrolled energy. He's very loud in the classroom, very inappropriate in the class. He has a great sense of humor, but again its inappropriate. I would say most of the time that his mouth is open, it's inappropriate, it's too loud, it's disrupting. But other than that [dry laugh] he's a great kid. You know if I didn't have to teach him, if it was a recreational setting, it would be fine.

So Donel is marked as"inappropriate" through the very configuration of self that school rules regulate: bodies, language, presentation of self. The stringent exercise of what is deemed appropriate as an instrument of assessment of at-riskness governs how the behavior of a child is understood. The notion of appropriate behavior in describing the ideal pupil earlier, and here as a way of characterizing a Troublemaker, reveals the broad latitude for interpretation and cultural framing of events. For one boy, "fooling around" behavior provides the balance between being a "real" boy and being a "goody-goody," while for the other, the conduct is seen through a different lens as "inappropriate," "loud," "disruptive."

Once a child is labeled "at-risk," he becomes more visible within the classroom, more likely to be singled out and punished for rule-breaking activity. An outburst by an African American boy already labeled as "at-risk" was the occasion for him to be singled out and made an example of the consequences of bad behavior before an audience of his peers; this was an occasion for a teacher to (re)mark the identity of a boy as disruptive. . . .

. . . Once a reputation has been established, the boy's behavior is usually refigured within a framework that is no longer about childish misdemeanors but comes to be an ominous portent of things to come. They are tagged with futures: "He's on the fast track to San Quentin Prison," and "That one has a jail-cell with his name on it." For several reasons, these boys are more likely to be singled out and punished than other children. They are more closely watched. They are more likely to be seen as intentionally doing wrong than a boy who is considered to be a Good Bad Boy. Teachers are more likely to use the "moral principle" in determining whether to call attention to misdemeanors because "at-risk" children need discipline, but also as an example to the group, especially to other African American boys who are "endangered." The possibility of contagion must be eliminated. Those with reputations must be isolated, kept away from the others. Kids are told to stay away from them: "You know what will happen if you go over there." In the case of boys with reputations, minor infractions are more likely to escalate into major punishments.

UNSALVAGEABLE STUDENTS

In the range of normalizing judgments, there is a group of African American boys identified by school personnel as, in the words of a teacher, "insalvageable." This term and the condition it speaks to is specifically about masculinity. School personnel argue over whether these unsalvageable boys should be given access even to the special programs designed for those who are failing in school. Should resources, defined as scarce, be wasted on these boys for whom there is no hope? Should energy and money be put instead into children who can be saved? I have heard teachers argue on both sides of the question. These "boys for whom there is no hope" get caught up in the school's punishment system: surveillance, isolation, detention, and ever more severe punishment.

These are children who are not children. These are boys who are already men. So a discourse that positions masculinity as "naturally" naughty is reframed for African American boys around racialized representations of gendered subjects. They come to stand as if already adult, bearers of adult fates inscribed within a racial order.

NOTES

1. *New York Times,* September 13, 1994, 1.

2. *Los Angeles Times,* November 2, 1990, 3.

3. G. Jaynes and R. Williams Jr., eds., *A Common Destiny: Blacks in American Society* (Washington, D.C.: National Academic Press, 1989), 405, 498.

4. See, for example, Jewelle Taylor Gibbs, "Young Black Males in America: Endangered, Embittered, and Embattled," in Jewelle Taylor Gibbs et al., *Young, Black, and Male in America: An Endangered Species* (New York: Auburn House, 1988); Richard Majors and Janer Mancini Billson, *Cool Pose: The Dilemmas of Black Manhood in America* (New York: Lexington Press. 1992); Jawanza Kunjufu, *Countering the Conspiracy to Destroy Black Boys,* 2 vols. (Chicago: African American Images, 1985).

5. See, for example, W. E. B. Du Bois, *Souls of Black Folk* (1903); reprint, New York: Bantam, 1989): Frantz Fanon, *Black Skins, White Masks,* trans. Charles Lam Markmann (New York: Grove Press, 1967): Stuart Hall, "The Rediscovery of 'Ideology': Return of the Repressed in Media Studies." in *Culture, Society, and the Media,* ed. Michael Gurevitch et al. (New York: Methuen, 1982); Leith Mullings, "Images, Ideology, and Women of Color," in *Women of Color in U.S. Society,* ed. Maxine Baca Zinn and Bonnie Thornton Dill (Philadelphia: Temple University Press, 1994); Edward Said, *Orientalism* (New York: Vintage, 1978).

6. Gilroy, *Small Acts,* 24, argues that "the culturalism of the new racism has gone hand in hand with a definition of race as a matter of difference rather than a question of hierarchy."

7. Collins, *Black Feminist Thought,* 68.

8. While many of the staff at Rosa Parks School would agree at an abstract level that social divisions of gender and race are culturally and historical produced, their actual talk about these social distinctions as well as their everyday expectations, perceptions, and interactions affirm the notion that these categories reflect intrinsic, *real* differences.

9. See, for example, Phillipe Ariès, *Centuries of Childhood: A Social History of Family Life* (New York: Vintage, 1962).

10. Thorne, *Gender Play;* and Valerie Polakow, *Lives on the Edge: Single Mothers and Their Children in the Other America* (Chicago: University of Chicago Press, 1993).

11. Patricia Turner, *Ceramic Uncles and Celluloid Mammies: Black Images and Their Influence on Culture* (New York: Anchor, 1994), 36.

12. A particularly racist and pernicious example of this was the statement by the administrator of the Alcohol, Drug Abuse, and Mental Health Administration. Dr. Frederick K. Goodwin, who stated without any qualms: "If you look, for example, at male monkeys, especially in the wild, roughly half of them survive to adulthood. The other half die by violence. That is the natural way of it for males, to knock each other off and, in fact, there are some interesting evolutionary implications. . . . The same hyper aggressive monkeys who kill each other are also hyper sexual, so they copulate more and therefore they reproduce more to offset the fact that half of them are dying." He then drew an analogy with the "high impact [of] inner city areas with the loss of some of the civilizing evolutionary things that we have built up. . . . Maybe it isn't just the careless

use of the word when people call certain areas of certain cities, jungles." Quoted in Jerome G. Miller, *Search and Destroy: African American Males in the Criminal Justice System* (New York: Cambridge University Press, 1996), 212–13.

13. The consensus among teachers in the school about educational inequity focuses on sexism. Many of the teachers speak seriously and openly about their concern that girls are being treated differently than boys in school: girls are neglected in the curriculum, overlooked in classrooms, underencouraged academically, and harassed by boys. A number of recent studies support the concern that even the well-intentioned teacher tends to spend less classroom time with girls because boys demand so much of their attention. These studies generally gloss over racial difference as well as make the assumption that *quantity* rather than *quality* of attention is the key factor in fostering positive sense of self in academic setting. See, for example, Myra Sadker and David Sadker, *Failing at Fairness: How America's Schools Cheat Girls* (New York: C. Scribner's Sons, 1994). Linda Grant looks at both race and gender as she examines the roles that first- and second-grade African American girls play in desegregated classrooms. She finds that African American girls and white girls are positioned quite differently vis-à-vis teachers. In the classrooms she observed, white girls were called upon to play an academic role in comparison with African American girls, who were cast in the role of teacher's helpers, in monitoring and controlling other kids in the room, and as intermediaries between peers. She concluded that black girls were encouraged in stereotypical female adult roles that stress service and nurture, while white girls were encouraged to press toward high academic achievement. Most important for this study, Grant mentions in passing that black boys in the room receive the most consistent negative attention and were assessed as having a lower academic ability than any other group by teachers. See Linda Grant, "Helpers, Enforcers, and Go-Betweens: Black Females in Elementary School Classrooms, " in *Women of Color in U.S. Society,* ed. Maxine Baca Zinn and Bonnie Thornton Dill (Philadelphia: University of Pennsylvania Press, 1994).

42

How Working-Class Chicas Get Working-Class Lives

JULIE BETTIE

Since I spent my first days at Waretown High in a college-preparatory class (a class that fulfills a requirement for admission to either California State University or University of California institutions), the first students I met were college bound. Later I came to know these girls through the eyes of non-college-preparatory students as "the preps." They were mostly white, but included a handful of Mexican-American girls. Some of the white girls were also known as "the 90210s," after the popular television show about wealthy high schoolers, *Beverly Hills 90210*. The preps eagerly volunteered to help me out with what they saw as my "school project," relating easily to the concept, and they were ready and willing to talk at length about themselves and others. Displaying both social and academic skills, they were, in short, "teacher's pets" (Luttrell 1993) or the "rich and populars" (Lesko 1988).

I soon began wandering the halls of the school in search of a nonprep class where I might find girls who seemed more like I was in high school. The memory of my own gender-specific high school experience led me to the business building, where unthinkingly I looked for a roomful of typewriters and girls with steno pads. Of course, I found neither, but rather rooms full of computers on which some students were practicing their word-processing skills while others were learning computer programming.

Looking for help connecting with non-college-prep girls, I visited the faculty room in the business department, which offers primarily vocational track classes, to recruit the aid of teachers and ask whose class I might visit. When I told these teachers that I wanted to talk to some of their girl students about their aspirations beyond high school, teachers shook their heads and laughed together in a knowing way, one man joking that "They'll all be barefoot and pregnant." While the other teachers expressed discomfort with his way of making the point, they did acknowledge that their students did not have high aspirations and often were "trouble." They told me that one student, Yolanda, would be happy to give me "a piece of her mind," noting further that "if she doesn't like your survey, she'll tell you." They shook their heads about another, Christina, who had recently "told off her employer," and they explained that it would be very difficult to interview any of these girls, because they would fail to show up or I would be able to keep their attention only for a short time. Nonetheless, I was invited to attend their classes and attempt to recruit girls to talk with.

The first day I attended Ms. Parker's business skills class was characteristic of my future visits to non-prep classes. On this particular day, there was a substitute teacher taking her place. The differences between the girls from the college-prep class and these girls were immediately noticeable. The latter wore more makeup and tight-fitting clothing, and seemed to have little interest in the classroom curriculum. In fact, the class was out of the teacher's hands. The girls, mostly Mexican-American, were happy to have me as a distraction. One, whom I came to know later as Lorena, said loudly (Lorena was always loud), "Oh, we heard you might be coming. What do you want to know? I'll tell you." Completely ignoring the substitute, who had clearly given up on having any control over the class, they invited me to play cards. I hesitated, asking what would happen if the vice principal, whom students refered to as "Mr. D," were to come by.

LORENA: Oh, he never does; besides [flirtatiously] he *likes* me.

BECKY: He doesn't like me. He's always callin' me into his office for something.

LORENA: He'll just ask me where's the other half of my shirt.

Lorena was referring to the short crop top she was wearing, which was fashionable at the moment, but was against school dress codes because it revealed her bare midriff. Pointing to the man behind the teacher's desk, Lorena went on:

> That's "Mr. H." He's our sub. Don't you think he's attractive? He's from the university too.

She called him over to ask a question, and when he arrived, Lorena opened her book and pointed entirely randomly at a paragraph on the page saying coyly, "I don't understand *this*." He tried to respond appropriately by explaining the course material, but when it became clear to him that her question was not serious, he turned to me and politely asked about my "study":

MR. H: What's your focus?

LORENA: [interrupting] You mean what's your *phone number?*

This brought rounds of laughter from the girls. It became obvious to the sub that Lorena was playing, and he wandered away a bit red in the face. She turned to me:

> Did you check him out? You should go on a date with him.

I wasn't sure what to make of this incident for a while, wondering if the girls, whose affectionate self-referent was "las chicas," were "othering" him (as a sub) or me (as the outsider/researcher/white girl) or both of us (as adults) by making one or both of us the target of their humor. As it turned out, this practice of trying to set me up with substitute teachers became almost a hazing ritual. Whenever the girls saw me on a day they knew they were going to have a substitute teacher in class, they asked me to come visit them in class. Not wanting to decline any opportunity to spend time with them, I would always respond to their invitations, stopping in to chat with them for the few minutes before the bell rang and class officially began. Over several weeks, they began to accept and befriend me as I began to respond to the setting-me-up ritual without embarrassment, and I engaged (somewhat reluctantly) in their playful attempts to humiliate the sub, othering him as the sub, as an adult, and as a man; in the process I became less of an other to the girls.

I came to see the ritual of setting me up as one element of a larger theme among las chicas. Bored with their vocational schooling, las chicas often brought heterosexual romance and girl culture into the classroom as a favorite form of distraction. They regularly brought photo albums to look through during class; these contained pictures of a weekend event like homecoming, a prom, a wedding, a quinceañera,[1] or sometimes a new baby. On this day in the business skills class, Imelda had brought a framed college photo collection of her and Christina, best friends. She had written sentimental words of friendship on the spaces in between the pictures in Spanish. She read them aloud and, then after an awkward moment, read them again, but this time in English for the sake of Blanca, who, wearing a long face, had silently tugged on Christina's sleeve to indicate that she didn't understand.

The conversation turned, and they began talking about a girl they didn't like, one who had been "talking shit about Lorena." They took turns telling whom they would most like to fight. Flor declined her turn, "If I say, I'm afraid her girls will jump me." Bored with this conversation, Christina pulled a folded up newspaper page out of her purse and began reading people's horoscopes out loud. In the background the sub made a useless plea, "Okay, whoever's listening, you need to do chapter five today." On other days the topics of our conversations included fashion, shopping, and recent events on the television soap opera *Days of Our Lives*. Near the end of each period, girls would stop their work early, if they were doing it at all, to pull out compacts, powder their faces, and check their lipstick and liner, reapplying when necessary.

These elements of "girl culture" were notably missing from the college-prep classrooms I had been visiting. It is not, of course, that gender display was altogether absent in prep classrooms, but where las chicas could be found blatantly using class time to primp, applying makeup and adjusting hair, in prep classrooms a girl might secretively slip a powder compact out of her backpack and turn her back away from the teacher to powder her face before the bell rang and the walk between classes, where social life happens, was to begin. For preps the overt use of class time for such an activity was recognized as inappropriate. Moreover, the "natural" look adopted by preps suggests one is not really wearing makeup and to pull this off means application of it must be done in secret.

Las chicas, having "chosen" and/or been tracked into non college prep courses, showed little interest in the formal curriculum offered at the school, finding a variety of ways to kill time. They employed rituals of girl culture as an alternative to and refusal of official school activities, including the kind of classroom learning that prep students embraced. Like their male counterparts, las chicas, along with most other students at the school, have had their dignity wounded through exposure to preps who, with the complicity of teachers, routinely and unknowingly inflicted class- and race-based injuries. But, unlike the boys, las chicas' strategy of rejecting schooling, and prep values by association, is usually less violent and less confrontational, and perhaps easily overlooked, often naturalized as heterosexual interest and dismissed.

As Penelope Eckert (1989) explains, middle-class performers embrace adult (and I would add middle-class) norms for the adolescent life stage, and this means preparing to enter another institution similar to high school. Non-preps, on the other hand, violate these norms by laying claims to adult status before middle-class adults think they should. Where middle-class-performing girls (both white and Mexican-American) chose academic performance and the acceptance and praise of teachers' and parents' as signs of achieving adult status, non-prep girls earned and wore different "badges of dignity" (Sennett and Cobb 1972; MacLeod 1995). They rejected school-sanctioned notions of proper femininity. For them, expressions of sexuality, and by extension motherhood, operated as a sign of adult status and served to reject teachers' and parents' methods of keeping them childlike.

There were many occasions on which this difference in orientation between working- and middle-class performers was made clear. When I met Mariana, a Mexican-American middle-class performer and told her I was at the school to study girls, she immediately presumed my interest would be in those "at risk." I sat with her in the library where she worked on a report for her "Transition to College English" class. As she meticulously assembled the planning calendar of her report on the college of her choice, her comments parroted adult and middle-class morality: "There are a lot of teen pregnancies here. It is real sad. Girls whose futures are ruined. It's sad. And there's gang violence." Alternatively, a white working class performer named Brenda, who approached me from the back of the room at an Future Homemakers of America (FHA) meeting where she had been sitting with a group of friends, asked bluntly, "Who are you?" I began to explain, but she interrupted, "Oh, never mind. We know. We've been talking about you back there," Then jutting out her hip, placing her hand on it, and batting her heavily mascara'd eyes, she said mockingly, "Are you here to study our *promiscuity?*" in full recognition of the fact that adult school personnel perceived her sexualized femininity as a violation of adolescence, and she expected me to do the same.

THE SYMBOLIC ECONOMY OF STYLE

There was, at the school, a symbolic economy of style that was the ground on which class and racial/ethnic relations were played out. A whole array of gender-specific commodities were used as markers of distinction among different groups of girls, who performed race-class-specific versions of femininity. Hairstyles, clothes, shoes, and the colors of lipstick, lip liner, and nail polish, in particular, were key markers in the symbolic economy that were employed to express group membership as the body became a resource and a site on which difference was inscribed.[2] For example, las chicas preferred darker colors for lips and nails in comparison to preps, who either went without or wore clear lip gloss, pastel lip and nail color or French manicures (the natural look). Each group was fully aware of the other's stylistic preference and knew that their own style was in opposition. In short, girls created and maintained symbolic opposition, where "elements of behavior that come to represent one category [are] rejected by the other, and . . . may be exploited by the other category through the development of a clearly opposed element" (Eckert 1989, 50).

The association of light with prep girls and dark with non-prep girls may be arbitrary, but the association of pastels with "youth, innocence, and gaiety" and darker colors with "somberness, age, and sophistication" does happen to coincide with middle- and working-class life stage trajectories (Eckert 1989, 50). Where middle-class performers experience an extended adolescence by going to college, working-class performers across race/ethnicity begin their adult lives earlier. The importance of colors as a tool of distinction was evident one day before business skills class when I complimented Yolanda on her nail color, and the girls clustered around her desk to compare colors. Bianca felt the need to apologize for hers. Displaying her hand on the table with others, she explained, "Mine is too pink, but it's my grandma's. I was at her house last night and she offered it, and I didn't want to hurt her feelings."

Further, las chicas explained to me that the darker colors they chose and the lighter colors preps wore were not simply related to skin color. As Lorena explained, "It's not that, 'cause some Mexican girls who look kinda white, they wear real dark lip color" so no one will mistake them as white. And when I mentioned that I rarely saw white girls in dark lipstick, Lisa, a white prep, explained, scoffing and rolling her eyes,

> Oh, there are some, but they're girls who are trying to be hardcore [meaning these were white girls who were performing chola identity]. And those hick girls [white working-class], some of them wear that bright pink crap on their lips and like *ba-loo* eye shadow!

The dissident femininity performed by both white and Mexican-American working-class girls were ethnic-specific styles, but nonetheless both sets of girls rejected the school-sanctioned femininity performed by college prep students.[3] Working-class performers across race were perceived similarly by preps as wearing too much makeup.

Girls often expressed disdain for one another's style or at least were perplexed by preferences other than their own. Lorena, describing the difference between las chicas and preps, said:

> Well, those prep girls, they wear their hair real straight and then sometimes just curl it at the end, either this way or that way [motioning a flipped-up or turned-under curl with her hands].

When I asked about makeup, she said:

> Natural! Barely any. Maybe pink or something. Like that ugly girl who got homecoming queen. You know how *we* do our hair right? We put stuff [gel] in it and then scrunch it like this [demonstrating]. Well, some of us wear our hair straight. But then it's real long and no curl at the end.

Leticia gave a lucid accounting of the typography of subculture and style and was very clear in her recognition that preps were the norm from which all others deviated.

LETICIA: Well, the preps they usually wear their jeans regular, you know, normal, like how pants are *supposed* to fit. We wear our pants either too big and baggy or at least big at the bottom but tight at the top [bell bottoms], depends on your figure. Those hicks they wear their pants, those ones, umm . . .

JULIE: Wranglers?

LETICIA: Yeah, they wear 'em way too tight. And big belts too, I don't know what their shoes are called.

JULIE: What about the smokers, what do they look like?

LETICIA: Tore up! They have holes in their pants, and they are all ripped at the bottom. And they wear a lotta black. Heavy metal T-shirts and chains. They dye their hair weird colors.

In spite of the meanings that working-class girls themselves gave to their gender-specific cultural markers— a desire to remain differentiated from preps— their performances were overdetermined by broader cultural meanings that code women in heavy makeup and tight clothes as low class and oversexed, in short, cheap. In other words, class differences are often understood as sexual differences, as Sherry Ortner usefully explains, where "the working class is cast as the bearer of an exaggerated sexuality, against which middle-class respectability is defined" (1991, 177). Among women, "clothing and cosmetic differences are taken to be indexes of the differences in sexual morals" between classes (178).[4] And indeed, this was the case, as middle-class performing prep girls (both white and Mexican-American) perceived las chicas, as well as working-class performing white girls, as overly sexually active. But non-prep Mexican-American girls were seen as especially so because, although there was no evidence that they were more sexually active, they were more likely to keep their babies if they became pregnant, so there was more often a visible indicator of their sexual activity.

BOYS ARE "BUGGIN"

Las chicas' gender performance and girl culture worked, whether by intent or not, as a strategy to reject the prep version of schooling but, despite appearances, were not necessarily designed to culminate in a heterosexual relationship. Some of the girls whose feminine performance appeared the most sexualized were actually the least interested in heterosexual relations, marriage, or children. Despite what appeared to be an obsession with heterosexual romance, a "men are dogs" theme was prevalent among them. They knew men could not be counted on to support them and any children they might have, and they desired economic independence.

And so their girl culture was less often about boys at all than about sharing in rituals of traditional femininity as a kind of friendship bonding among girls. As Angela McRobbie (1991) describes, although the overt concern in girl culture is with boys and romance, girls often set themselves physically apart from boys. Lorena made this clear one day.

LORENA: Well, when we go out, to the clubs or someplace, we all get a bunch of clothes and makeup and stuff and go to one person's house to get ready. We do each other's hair and makeup and try on each other's clothes. It takes a long time. It's more fun that way. [Thoughtfully, as if it just occurred to her] Sometimes, I think we have more fun getting ready to go out than we do going out—'cause when we go out, we just *sit* there.

JULIE: So then the clothes and makeup and all aren't for the men or about getting their attention?

LORENA: Well, we like to see how many we can *meet*. But, well, you know, I don't fall for their lines. We talk to them, but when they start buggin', then we just go.

In short, non-preps had no more or less interest in heterosexual romance than did girls who performed prep or school-sanctioned femininity. Nonetheless, teachers and preps often misread the expression of class and race differences in style among working-class performers as evidence of heterosexual interest. They failed to perceive girls' class and racial/ethnic selves and so unknowingly reproduced the commonsense belief that what is most important about girls, working-class performers in particular, is their girlness. Las chicas' style was not taken as a marker of race/ethnicity and class distinction but was reduced to gender and sexuality.

Not only has girl culture as a method to refuse schooling been missed by androcentric social science, but teachers too tended to naturalize gender and heterosexuality, treating girls' strategies as harmless. Although I once saw a teacher take a magazine away from a boy in class because it was distracting him from the assignment, no teacher ever told the girls to put away their photo albums, although they were at least as much a distraction. Girls across race and class performance were aware of their ability to violate rules without consequence as a result of teachers', and in particular male teachers', view of boys as troublemakers and girls as harmless. Girls told stories of getting out of gym class by faking menstrual cramps, of cheating on laps by doing one and then panting and exclaiming to the coach that they'd done thirteen. Lisa told how a boy who said "fuck" was put in detention all day, but "a girl who was yellin' it in the office, nothin' happened ta her. I counted, and she said it thirteen times!" . . .

ROUTES TO ADULTHOOD

Sensitive to the fact that girls were aware of the current moral panic over teen pregnancy and anticipated that adults were interested in their sexuality, I generally avoided the topic, letting girls bring it up themselves, then proceeding cautiously with my questions. Often girls preferred to begin talking in the third person about sexuality, describing friends' views and practices, before (sometimes but not always) shifting to their own. Most of the girls I spoke with, across all social groupings, reported that they were sexually active. It was understood that most girls who were in "serious" relationships were probably having sex with their boyfriends, and this was acceptable. Some girls suggested that it was not taboo for girls to have sex outside of relationships, although girls had to be much more careful than boys about their frequency here for fear of being labeled. Girls agreed that there was still a double standard: boys could be sexually active with multiple partners without consequence, while girls were called sluts for the same behavior. What is important to recognize here is that girls' interest in sex was not *always* embedded in a narrative of romance.

In short, there were girls who did and girls who didn't across all group categories, but the race and class injury that occurred was in the perception of who was *too* sexually active. While many prep girls, whose presentation of self was squeaky clean, were sexually active, they were secretive about this violation of adolescence and used birth control pills, often without parents' knowledge (but sometimes with). White middle-class performers were more likely than other girls to have abortions if they became pregnant, as a way of ensuring the life stages that they and their parents had in mind for them. One girl explained, "My friend had an abortion and got her parents' insurance to pay for it without her parents even knowing that was the procedure she had done."

Stories of abortion were almost nonexistent among Mexican-American girls, and Mexican-American girls were less likely than white middle- or working-class girls to use birth control regularly.[5] Girls became pregnant for a variety of reasons. Blanca explained that she lacked information about birth control—"My parents, they didn't tell me nothing about birth control"—and wrongly believed myths like "you can't get pregnant your first time." Mexican-American girls often said they knew about, but didn't believe in, the use of birth control or in abortion. Christina explained, "Having something growing inside you is a spiritual thing. If it happens, then God meant for it to happen. You just have to deal with it." But some were willing to consider birth control, suggesting that abortion was the worse of two evils. The most common explanation given for pregnancies was "it just happened," which seemed most often to mean that girls were unprepared and had no birth control plan, either because they didn't know they were going to have sex or because they were uncomfortable planning ahead to use birth control, as this compromised their belief system or suggested to themselves and others that they were too willing. Sometimes this situation was combined with stories of boys who refused to use condoms:

> YOLANDA: Well one reason it happens is that guys don't wanna use condoms. And then you just get caught up in the moment.

While girls did too often say they "felt a lotta pressure" and had sex before they were ready, they also often acknowledged their willing participation. But teen sexuality (and pregnancy) cannot be wholly explained either by girls' victimization or by their desire.[6] The most popular discourse at the school among adults was one of female victimization, where girls became pregnant after being pressured by boys to have sex when they were not yet ready. Consequently, in the face of adult authority and public discourse on teen sexuality, the safest narrative for a girl to give is one of victimization, because it evades her responsibility. Less acceptable would be to acknowledge her desire, which is still, it seems, considered taboo for girls even as it is expected among boys. Indeed, any discourse on female desire or recognition that girls may be willing and interested in sex was largely missing among adults with whom I spoke at the school.[7] But the worst possible thing for a girl to admit to is an intentional pregnancy, and only one girl I spoke, with suggested this:

LETICIA: Well some girls want kids. You go through that phase you know. I did a year or two ago. I wanted, one. You want to be a young mother. Don't want to be an old parent cause then [if you are young] you'll understand them better.

Regardless of how a girl becomes pregnant (which occurs for a variety of reasons, including the use of birth control that fails), after the fact, having a baby can be a marker of adult status (just as sexuality was), and girls recognize it as such. For non-prep girls who do not have college and career to look forward to as signs of adulthood, motherhood and the responsibility that comes with it can be employed to gain respect, marking adult status. Teachers often expressed surprise at the degree of casualness among students about pregnancies and babies at school, one saying with ambivalence, "Babies are really celebrated here among girls; they are not ashamed. They bring them to class." Another teacher was more clearly sympathetic about babies in class:

> It's a bit awakward because you don't want to seem to support it [teen pregnancy], but the pregnancy and the baby already happened, so it makes no sense to shun them [girls] either. One baby was fussy, so I had to teach while bouncing him on my hip. It's as if the girls are saying, this is my life, this is what happened, don't punish me for it.

In the end, however, girl's overt claim to adulthood startles adult and middle-class sensibility.

Pregnancy and babies became an extension of the girl culture that was present in non-prep classrooms. Talk of baby clothes and the anticipation of delivery were further ways girls overtly expressed their boredom with their vocational schooling and their sense of its irrelevance. About a month before school ended, Elvira gave birth to a baby girl. Either because she had no child-care options or because she was simply excited about her newborn, she brought the baby to school with her several days during the last few weeks of school. The baby became a great distraction in the classroom, and the teacher dealt with it by asking Elvira to move to another room, allowing girls to go visit her there and see the baby two at a time. Eventually she and another girl who were both failing the class, totally uninvested in the work, and distracting other students who did have a chance of passing, were kicked out of the class. Most girls with babies eventually chose to finish their schooling at an alternative community school where they could graduate with fewer credit hours and where classes ended at one o'clock, making day care arrangement less complicated.

Girls' orientation to early maternity is not necessarily linked to an ideology of romance. Girls know from each other's experience that boys should not be relied upon. Sometimes girls believe they are an exception to this rule, one suggesting, for example, that because her boyfriend did not want her to have an abortion, this was a sign that he really loved her. I had this conversation with Yolanda about her friend Bianca.

YOLANDA: Well, she should've protected herself. But since she didn't, she should have just had the baby but not get married. It isn't gonna work. He's not gonna stick around. I mean that's the only reason they got married, even though they say they "wanted to anyway." [rolling her eyes]

JULIE: What would you do?

YOLANDA: I ain't never gettin' married. But I looove babies!

For the most part, girls were very cynical about boys. They felt that men could not be counted on for economic support or as co-parents, or to meet the girls' ideals of romance and intimacy. One teacher, commenting on conversations among girls that he routinely overheard in his class noted,

> You know, they don't talk about the fathers much. They are pretty irrelevant to them.

In short, working-class performers were more willing to consider parenthood and sometimes marriage as an appropriate next life stage after high school (and sometimes during, which usually meant continuing to live with her parent[s]). While these girls knew that "college" was a necessity to insure a living wage, it was something they would more often consider doing simultaneously with other adult roles. The "going away to college" experience was decidedly a prep one, while working-class performers were likely to attend the local community college and begin their adult lives as workers, parents, and spouses at the same time. They saw no convincing reason to postpone parenthood. Pregnancy is not the cause of their vocational schooling, the cause of their ending up in a low-wage job, or the cause of their poverty, thought that myth continues to circulate in public discourse legitimating anti-welfare sentiment and justifying punitive policies (Luker 1996).

For the most part las chicas' girl culture was interpreted as harmless, thought of as natural heterosexual interest, and therefore not negatively sanctioned. But when this girl culture was extended to include maternity, which school personnel saw as too adult and thus found unacceptable, they responded. During a year's end awards ceremony, I sat on the bleachers at the end of the gym near the lunchroom doors among students who were required to attend but had not interest in the ceremony. In the group of Mexican-American students I sat behind, one young mother had a toddler with her who was being passed around, and two young men in particular were competing over who got to hold the child. As one young man made silly faces and got the baby to smile, the group began to laugh, getting louder as they became more and more involved in the baby's play. As the unit administrator and master of the ceremony announced which students had perfect school attendance, had GPAs above 3.5, and were receiving university scholarships, a teacher angrily stomped over to the group of students, chiding them, "You could at least be polite and pay attention when someone is talking." The mother haughtily picked up her toddler and, head held high, walked out of the gym with four girlfriends following in solidarity.

Working-class performers across race shared the resentful view of the ceremony as an imposed glorification of prep students. The teachers and administrators did have some awareness of the way in which celebrating the successes of some made others look and feel like failures. They tried to finesse this by making attendance at such an event optional, where each teacher could decide whether or not to bring her/his class. But if a teacher chose to attend, which most teachers did, every student in that class was required to be either in the gym or in the adjoining lunchroom during this time. Added to the injury of being forced to attend a ceremony celebrating students who were able to achieve "success" by the standards of the institution, adults, and middle-class norms, the teacher's punitive attitude toward the baby's presence was a further insult that put non-prep students "back in their place" by trying to recenter attention on the success of students who could and did follow the institutional ideals.

Although las chicas were no more sexually active than other girls at the school, they suffered the consequences of their sexual activity in ways that middle-class performers did not. (White working-class girls were also more likely to keep babies than their middle-class counterparts, but still not at as high a rate as Mexican-American girls.) The presence of more babies among Mexican-American girls than any other group of girls was wrongly perceived by white preps (and some school personnel) as a difference of sexual morals between racial/ethnic groups. But the deeper injury is that those who have babies will experience the punishment of a gender regime, which blames women who become single moms for their own poverty by suggesting sexual immorality, especially if they are young. This logic fails to recognize that teen pregnancy is highly correlated with class and race: most of these young women were working-class or poor before they became mothers (Luker 1996). Their continued (or increased) impoverishment is a consequence of their vocational curriculum, low-wage jobs, and lack of affordable child care. Further, their potential heterosexual partners are working-class men of color who are also less likely to be able to earn wages that can support families. These young moms don't have and, for good reasons, don't want to rely on male support. They want and need to be able to support themselves and any children they might have. They want economic equality outside of heterosexual relationships.

POST–HIGH SCHOOL TRACKS

Once a year, a nearby vocational business school invited students to come tour their facility, paying the school for the use of a bus and treating the students to a pizza lunch. Most of las chicas signed up to go. We piled into the bus on a rainy December morning. Girls paired off in twos, sets of best friends sharing a seat near the middle of the bus, while boys moved to the back, each occupying a seat by himself, head against the bus window and legs extended to take up the whole space. Given the purpose of the trip, I presumed this would be a good opportunity to talk to girls about their plans beyond high school. But, as usual, this was of little interest. In fact, it was a topic that I saw clearly caused the girls to feel uncertainty and a related stress, so they changed the conversation to music and fashion. . . .

At the school we were taken to a classroom and seated in desks. The environment felt school-like and familiar, but in fact this was deceptive, since the woman speaking at the front of the room, a Ms. Laney, was actually giving a sales pitch under the guise of teaching and advising us about the expenses of life and job opportunities. She began by asking how much we thought it cost to live on your own and how much per hour one would need to earn. . . .

She knew her audience well, asking them rhetorically, "How many of you want to continue to live at home with your parents after graduation?" No one did, of course, and yet these were students who did not have the option of going off to college to escape parental authority. She worked to convince them that their lifestyles would change. She explained that they would want more than Burger King and a movie. They would want weekend trips, concerts, sports events. They would have roommate problems. They would not want to settle for the old Pinto or station wagon grandma was planning to give them. She told them about taxes and insurance, things they might not have thought of before. She joked that for some it was not a problem, because they have rich parents. To the girls she said, "Some of you will marry someone really rich." Addressing the boys in the back of the room, "Some of you will go into crime because you already know it pays more."

She exploited their sense of filial piety, suggesting that the sooner they begin working, the sooner they would stop being an economic burden to their parents. "Wouldn't you like to be able to help your parents out? Maybe even buy them something nice for their anniversary? Send them on a cruise?" She told them there is a difference between education and skills, arguing that going thirty thousand dollars into debt with a student loan for four to six years of college and then coming out with a bachelor's degree in history and therefore no job is impractical. Further, she went on, "Junior college takes twice as long as business school because of crowded classrooms and general education courses which are not necessary." Aware of students' knowledge that junior colleges have open admission and are understood by high schoolers to be the bottom rung, the place for those who can't go anywhere else, she said, "We don't accept just anyone. You have to have a high school diploma. You have to dress professionally here. No jeans. We'll help you understand which clothes are professional clothes and which are not. And you cannot be late. You must be serious about it." But aware of their academic insecurity, she added, "You don't have to have a high GPA, and you don't even have to know how to turn on a computer." She showed them a framed diploma like the one they would receive upon graduation and then brought in Mike, one of their students, a young Latino who had gone to high school in a town near Waretown, to give his personal testimonial.

Mike was wearing a suit and tie and began, "I was a slacker big time in high school."

Ms. Laney chimed in, "You can see the transformation."

Ana asked Mike if it was hard to work a job while he went to school, and he responded, "Yeah, but it's all up to you."

Ms. Laney stated, "The effort you put in here is directly related to the money you earn when you get out. Now he is disciplined and goal oriented."

Ana asked Mike why he didn't go to college, and Ms. Laney interrupted, "That would have taken him seven years."

Mike said, "Yeah, this is a lot more better."

After the sales pitch ended, we were taken to the lounge. The girls rushed to the table where boxes of pizza were waiting, saying, "Hurry, before the guys get there. They'll eat it all." Over pizza the girls discussed the merits of the business school. The tidiness of the package presented to them was quite appealing. In just a year or so one could have accomplished a goal, completed a program quickly, unlike the eternity that four years of high school felt like, and unlike the four or more years college would take. This sounded doable. You could begin in the summer to get schooling out of the way early, and in the end you could have a job where you dressed nicely, maybe sat at your own desk, lived away from parents, did not get married right away. The focus on individual initiative was convincing, causing girls to temporarily believe that they had the power to rise above the constraints against them. When I mentioned to the girls that at no time during the presentation or in any of the written material we had been given were we told how much it would cost to attend, Yolanda immediately put down her pizza and marched across the room to ask a staff member about cost. She returned, "It's kinda a lot—eighteen thousand dollars for a sixteen-month program. But the lady said that in the long run that's cheaper than college. And she said not to worry 'cause they give you scholarships and loans and stuff. And you can pay it back real slow over time, after you get a good job."

Flor wasn't with us that day because she had gone on the tour the year before as a junior and had already made up her mind that she would attend the business school. About two weeks before high school graduation she went to the school to arrange payment, planning to begin her course work in the summer. She came back astounded. "Do you know how much it costs!? They'll give you loans, but you have to pay all that back! What am I gonna do? To apply to junior college now means that I'd have ta pay another fifty dollars for another placement test. My mom is gonna start crying if I tell her that." As we headed toward the counseling office to find applications for junior college, Flor wailed, "I don't know how to do this. No one in my family's ever gone to college." In the end, none of las chicas would attend the business school.

Michelle Fine (1991) provides a critique of proprietary schools (private profit-making institutions) that offer curricula in such areas as business, computing, secretarial skills, travel agent skills, and cosmetology and present themselves as alternatives to the public sector. Such schools advertise far and wide, make appealing promises, and deploy deceptive techniques to recruit the most vulnerable youth. Students in these institutions are disproportionately low-income and from populations of color.[8]

I and many of my Midwestern high school friends attended such an institution after high school, where we chose from impressive programs with titles such as Private Executive Secretarial Science and Fashion Merchandising, then landed jobs doing clerical and retail work. This school indirectly acknowledged that students might be placed in low-level jobs upon graduation, but worked to convince us that the difference between those of us with a certificate and those without was the opportunity for mobility. The fashion merchandising certificate, in particular, held out the promise of mobility at a major department store after "getting one's foot in the door." The brochure and the faculty instilled the hope that after a short time doing retail, one could expect to become a buyer for a department store and have a cosmopolitan life flying about to major world cities, attending fashion shows. Fine names this the "folklore of glamour and success," which students find so compelling in these schools' unethical recruitment techniques.

Most importantly, as Fine found at the high school she studied, I never heard students at Waretown High informed of or protected from the questionable recruitment practices of such schools that disseminate misleading information. When no critique is offered to assist students in their decision making, high schools "perpetuate the prevailing belief in their economic utility" (1991, 93). Though these students think they are making a wise choice in seeking a two-year certificate instead of a four-year degree, since two years is all the time and money they can afford, they will still probably not end up with jobs that pay them enough to support themselves and will quite likely go into debt as a consequence of attending.

HIGH SCHOOL TRACKS

Some girls felt tracked into a vocational curriculum. When I asked Yolanda about tracking, she'd never heard of it. But after I explained the concept to her, she said:

> Oh, yeah. That happened to me. This counselor told me to take all the non-required classes. Now I'm way behind in English and math, so that is why I can't go to a state school. The counselor said I wasn't ready. I heard she got fired for that.

Blanca also hadn't heard of tracking but recognized it upon explanation:

> Oh, is that discrimination? 'Cause then I have experienced discrimination.

. . . Other girls felt they had more actively chosen their course work. Christina explained that her vocational curse work began in ninth grade when students were first allowed to choose an elective course. She chose a vocational elective work-experience "class" that allowed her to do clerical work in the attendance office at the junior high for one class period a day, with her aunt, a school employee. Overhearing me ask Celia and Ramona if they recalled how they came to take vocational courses instead of college-prep ones, Lucia asked, "What are prep classes?" When I explained these were the classes that people who want to get into state school or universities have to take, Ramona chimed in, "Oh, the hard ones, the ones you don't wanna take. Like chemistry," at which all three cringed. Likewise, Marycruz said, "I guess I just always liked business classes. They were something I could do, really easy. I just like the basic stuff."

When I asked Leticia her plan and how she felt about being in the vocational curriculum, she said:

> Well, it's okay, because I just plan to go to the JC for a couple years for general education courses. And then I wanted to go into law. But I found out that law taked too long of schooling. I don't have enough money to go to school that long. So I checked out paralegal, but didn't like that as much. I'll just go to the JC now and decide later.

Now that they were in their senior year, las chicas recognized that it was too late to make up for the consequences of being in the vocational curriculum. Consequently, their primary focus was on graduating from high school, regardless of grades. If it was not necessary to pass a particular class to graduate, then little effort was invested. ("Oh, is there a test in this class today?") Girls experienced class-time assignments as busywork, swapping their papers regularly in class, trading the calculations from each other's cash flow charts in an accounting class and answers on how to select, thaw, and cook meats from a nutrition class assignment, for example. ("It's not copying, it's sharing.") If class was inconvenient, it was skipped. "Well we're packin' 'em in today," the teacher noted during a sixth period class that was half-empty. Blanca had caught a ride home with Yolanda, who, with school permission, left every day after fifth period to go to work. Without a car, Blanca would have had to walk home if she didn't leave early with Yolanda. And Leticia, who hadn't been in school at all the day before, explained, "My mom needed the car yesterday 'cause she had to do something, and I didn't want to walk."

Sometimes girls dealt with their anxiety about the future with a certain denial of the facts, a refusal to believe that things would not work out for them, a tone of self-determination. At one point Vince, a friend, tried to talk Lorena out of going to the business school, saying, "What are you going there for? That won't do you no good. Look at my brother. He went there, and look what he's doin' [warehouse work]. Trying to get out of debt."

Lorena argued back, "Uh uh, they said they place 95 percent of their students. He musta not done well."

Vince argued, "He graduated with an A."

But she replied defiantly, "Then it's his fault for studying the wrong thing. You can't prove me wrong, I'm Lorena."

During other moments when girls stopped the fun to talk about their futures, they became somber, anxious, and depressed. This happened more frequently as graduation approached. Occasionally, girls were able to articulate their dilemma. Yolanda, for example, explained that she had wanted to go into law or international business.

YOLANDA: But I know I won't really do that. I mean, the girls and I were talking the other day. We all listed the things we wanted to do. And I said, it's all bullshit. You guys know we ain't really gonna do any a that.

JULIE: What are you going to do?

YOLANDA: I don't know. I don't want to work as hard as my aunt [who worked two retail sales jobs] to make enough money. I don't have to have a fancy job like a lawyer. I just want a simple life. An okay car. I want just a pretty good life. No guys, on one controlling me. But [asking sincerely] what kinda job like that is there?

Yolanda implicitly recognized that there is no middle-income, non-college-educated, working-class location for her to occupy, which leaves her in a precarious situation. But given that school culture equates success with college attendance and that failure to do well enough to go to college is readily understood as an individual failure, las chicas were often left with no one to blame but themselves.

Differential skills are learned across academic and vocational curriculums. Where college-prep students learn "critical thinking, problem solving, drawing conclusions, making generalizations, or evaluating or synthesizing knowledge . . . [i]n vocational track classes students are required to learn only simple memory tasks or comprehension" (Oakes 1985, 77; and see Persell 1977). Many of las chicas were, in fact, good students, earning high grades, but in a vocational curriculum. It is working-class students and students of color who are tracked into the vocational curriculum, thus institutionalizing race and class inequalities. . . .

Both the school's own internal discourse on race and ethnicity and the wider social discourse on education in general suggest that there are structural reasons why Mexican-American students don't do as well as their white counterparts, but las chicas were not always able to apply this idea to themselves. In comparison to immigrant students who were struggling to learn English and whose parents worked the worst jobs in the community, las chicas seemed well-off. Further injury was inflicted by the occasional poor and/or immigrant Mexican-American student who did particularly well at school and therefore was a mystifying source of confusion. School culture, and society more generally, loves stories of exception, of people who defy the odds. These students are held up as models to which all should aspire, and so much attention is paid to exceptions that it is easy to forget those who make up the rule. At times las chicas were proud that "one of ours" had done well, adding to the collective self-esteem of the community, but at other times the success of such a student was detrimental to the esteem of individuals. . . .

Getting a high school diploma, not to mention a year of junior college, deceptively suggests mobility to las chicas and possibly to their parents. But most girls wind up in low-wage clerical or retail jobs. In comparison to mothers (and fathers) whose work was less than glamorous and sometimes dirty (cannery, factory, fields), working in an office or behind a cash register in retail can indeed appear as mobility. It has been suggested that women who work in clean jobs, indoors, near management, wearing "dress up" clothes, have perhaps always been wrongly perceived as middle-class by working-class standards (Willis 1977; Ortner 1991). This confusion was made clear one day when I asked Flor what she wanted to do for work after high school, and she said:

> I don't know. Maybe be a lawyer or a receptionist or something like that. Somethin' in an office.

Given the historic meanings of the category "working class," as predominantly masculine manual labor, postindustrialism does make a U.S. working class hard to locate, especially when so many women fill the ranks.

Girls vacillated between understanding their dilemma, the circumstances of their lives that were resulting in precarious futures, and denial about it. Most of the time they avoided talking about it, distracting themselves with the details of girl culture. The face-saving game non-preps played throughout senior year was to suggest that they were going to business school so they could get done quickly and get a good job, which they would then work while attending college. Or they would say that they would go to the JC, just for a while, and then transfer to college. While JCs are promoted by the school as a route to what students understand as "real" college for those not on the college-prep track in high school, this longer, more circuitous route was a difficult one to follow. There were few to no stories of older siblings or friends who had actually done either route. Going away to college is not a possibility for most of these girls, and attending the local community college is infantalizing, for it means continuing to live at home, continuing to attend school in the town in which they grew up. In short, it doesn't feel much different from high school; hence the expression that "junior college is high school with ashtrays." Most girls told stories of friends and siblings who attended junior college for a year or so before giving it up and settling into a low-wage job.

ON ACTING WHITE

Mexican-American students did have a way in which they simultaneously recognized and displaced class, at times explaining differences among themselves in racial/ethnic terms as "acting white" versus acting "the Mexican role." The class coding of these descriptions is revealed when the categories are pushed only slightly. When I asked Lorena what she meant by "acting white," she gave an animated imitation of a girl she'd met at a Future Business Leaders of America (FBLA) meeting, affecting a stereotypical "valley girl" demeanor and speech pattern:

> Ohmigod, like I can't believe I left my cell phone in my car. It was so nice to meet you girls, do keep in touch.

Lorena perceived this sentiment as quite disingenuous since they had just met. Indeed, part of working-class girls' interpretation of preps was that they were "fake"; their friendships were considered phony and insincere, always working in the interests of social ambition. Lorena went on.

> I'm going to play volleyball for Harvard next year.

Clearly "Harvard" was an exaggeration on Lorena's part, but for her any university may as well have been Harvard, as it was just as distant a possibility. When I pointed out to her that she was using a "valley girl" accent, she explained:

> But it's not just how they talk, it's what they talk about. Like "Let's go shopping at Nordstrom's." They brag about their clothes and cars.

I pushed for whether she thought preps really were purposefully bragging or were just unaware of how their talk affected others around them. She was convinced it was intentional: "They know. They brag."

Erica, a Filipina-American girl who had been befriended by and accepted as one of las chicas confided to me, "There's a lot of trashing of white girls really, and Mexican girls who act white." When I asked her what she meant by "acting white," her answer was straightforward:

> ERICA: The preps.
>
> JULIE: Not the smokers or the hicks or—
>
> ERICA: Oh, no, never smokers, basically preps.

At some level, the girls knew that "acting white" didn't refer to whites generally, but to preps specifically (that is, a middle-class version of white), but class as a way of making distinctions among whites was not (easily articulated.[9] The whites most visible to them were those who inflicted the most class injuries, the preps. In fact, working-class whites were invisible in their talk, unless I asked specifically about them. The most marginalized, hard-living, working-class whites, known as the smokers, were either unknown or perplexing to most Mexican American students. As Mariana, a Mexican-American middle-class performer, said to me, almost exasperated:

> I mean, they're white. They've had the opportunity. What's wrong with them?

The utility or necessity of describing class performances in racial terms as "acting white" is found in the difficulty all students had coming up with a more apt way of describing class differences in a society in which class discourse as such is absent. It is also found in the reality of the lives of Mexican-American students for whom the fact that race and class correlate (that people of color are overrepresented among the poor) was highly visible. This is not to say that there is nothing racial/ethnic-specific that might be named "acting white" outside of middle-classness, but it was not made clear in girls' talk what that might be.[10]

In popular discourse, class is often not a present category of thought at all or is considered temporary (a condition of immigration) and not institutionalized. As a result, categories like race and gender, which appear to be essentially there, fixed, and natural, readily take the place of class in causal reasoning rather than being understood as intertwined with one another (for example, when class difference is read as sexual morality). In other words, class appears in popular discourse, "just not in terms we recognize as 'about class'" (Ortner 1991, 170). Read through gender and through race, class meaning is articulated in other terms.

At times, race/ethnicity was understood and explained by students in performance terms, as when whites were said to act Mexican and Mexicans to act white. Girls were able to delineate the contents of those categories and the characteristics of the performances, which were class coded. But, alternatively, one's race performance was *expected* to correspond to a perceived racial "essence," marked by color and surname. Understandings of race as a performance and as an essence existed simultaneously. Consequently, middle- or working-class performances were perceived and read differently, depending on the race/ethnicity of the performer and the reader. This is because class performances have race-specific meanings linked to notions of "authentic" racial/ethnic identity, where white is high or middle and brown is low. As one Mexican-American girl said, "The cholos play the Mexican role."

The common-sense way class and race codings work together is seen when comparing the styles of working-class performers across race/ethnicity. White working-class youth expressed their overt rejection of prep norms by dressing down. They wore torn-up jeans and anything they could find that seemed to oppositionally confront middle-class performers' ideals of appropriate presentation of oneself, taking the fact that they didn't have the money to meet the ideal to an extreme. In contrast, Mexican-American students employed a different oppositional strategy. Since brown is always already a code for low economic status, dressing down was not part of their defiant style. Cholos' clean look, their crisp and perfectly ironed Dickie brand work clothing and starched white T-shirts, and cholas' perfect hair and makeup represented an effort to defy the color/poverty link at the same time that it refused white middle-class norms by rejecting the prep version.[11]

The notion of racial/ethnic authenticity is a discursive resource mobilized to perform the work of constructing racial/ethnic boundaries, boundaries that are inevitably class coded. In short, race and class are always already mutually implicated and read in relationship to one another. But when class is couched in race and ethnicity, and vice versa, it impairs our understanding of *both* social forces. Not only do we fail to learn something about class as a shaper of identity, but further, because of the conflation, we fail to learn much about the existence of racial/ethnic cultural forms and experience *across* class categories.

MIDDLE-CLASS CHOLA PERFORMANCES

This leads me to the examples of Ana and Rosa and their friends, who were exceptions to the class-origin-equals-class-performance rule. When students perform class identities that do not correspond with those of their families of origin, there is a negotiation between their inherited identity from home and their chosen public identity at school. For Mexican-American girls this negotiation was quite complicated. They struggled with the meanings of and links between class mobility, assimilation, and racial politics or identification where income, what kind of work parents did (such as agricultural or warehouse work), generation of immigration, skin color, and Spanish fluency were key signifiers that then became the weapons of identity politics, used to make claims to authenticity and accusations of inauthenticity.

Friendship groups were clearly shaped by class and race performance. While girls were largely unable to articulate their performance in race-class terms, they knew that each group preferred different styles and that friendships were organized around presentation of physical self. The class origin/class performance correlation existed with few exceptions. A handful of girls were outliers, third-generation Mexican-American, from professional middle-class families, whose style and presentation of self were consistent with las chicas, even though they attended college-prep classes and planned to go to state schools. They were differentiated from another small group, college-prep Mexican-American girls who, like white preps, wore little or no makeup, whose dress was less gender-coded, and who were heavily involved in school activities. These Mexican-American college-prep girls rejected chola style as "trouble." They perceived las chicas as too allied to boys in gangs; las chicas perceived them as too nerdy and straight.

Ana and Rosa's small crowd were transgressors of a kind. They had each individually struggled to find their place in this race-class meaning system. They had grown up in white neighborhoods and gone to elementary schools that were primarily white and where, as Rosa explained, "I knew I was different, because I was brown." In junior high, which was less segregated, some of them began performing chola style and were "jumped in" to a gang. When I asked Ana why, she explained that she hated her family.

> ANA: My mom wanted this picture perfect family, you know. And I just hated it.
>
> JULIE: What do you mean by a perfect family?
>
> Ana: You know, we had dinner at night together, and everything was just okay. She was so *happy.* And I hated that. My life was sad; my friends' lives were sad.
>
> Julie: Why were they sad?
>
> ANA: One friend's mom was on welfare, the other didn't know who her dad was. Everything was wrong in their families.

As she described class differences between herself and her friends, she struggled for the right words to describe it. And as Lorena sought to describe the difference between herself and her friend Ana, she too searched for words:

> Well, in junior high she was way downkind a low, she got in with the bad crowd. But in high school she is higher up kinda. I mean not as high as Patricia is [another middle-class performer] but she's not as low as she used to be.

Lorena's perception of Ana as high-but-low was shaped by Ana's crossover style and the fact that in some sense she had earned her low. Status by performing chola identity and gang-banging. Although by the time I had met Ana, Rosa, an Patricia, they had accepted the cultural capital their parents had to give them, were now college-prep, and had been admitted to four-year colleges, they were still friends with las chicas and still dressed and performed the kind of race-class femininity that las chicas did. In this way they distanced themselves from preps and countered potential accusations of acting white. In short, their style confounded the race-class equation and was an intentional strategy. By design, they had middle-class aspirations without assimilation to prep, which for them meant white, style. It went beyond image to politics, as they participated in MEChA (Movimiento Estudiantil Chicano de Aztlán) and tried to recruit las chicas to participate too. In fact, when I went along on the bus ride to tour the business school with las chicas, I was surprised to find that Ana, Rosa, and Patricia came along. I asked why they had come along since they had already been accepted to four-year schools. Rosa responded, "Because we're with the girls, you know; we have to be supportive, do these things together."

Mexican-American girls' friendships crossed class performance boundaries more often than white girls' did because there was a sense of racial alliance that drew them together, both in an oppositional relation to white students at school and through activities outside of the school in the Mexican-American community. Further, Mexican American girls were also far more pained by the divisions among themselves than white girls ever were (an aspect of whiteness that can seem invisible). There was a recognition among Mexican-American girls of the need to present a united front, and this was particularly acute among girls who were politicized about their racial/ethnic identity and participated in MEChA. For white girls, competition among them (over heterosexual relationships or class performance or whatever issue) did not threaten them as a racial/ethnic minority community; there was (usually) no superordinate goal or outside threat they could see that would necessitate their solidarity on racial grounds. For the most part, their whiteness was invisible to them, though, as we will see, there were times when whiteness, like brownness, functioned as a source of implied solidarity.

In spite of the fact that cross-class friendship were more likely, still class differences were salient among Mexican-American girls, as evidenced in Lorena's description of Ana, and in descriptions working-class performers gave to MEChA, if they knew what it was at all, as "for brainy types," since it was understood as a college-prep activity. Some of las chicas did join MEChA, but they typically played inactive roles. When I asked Yolanda about it, she had this to say:

> Well, we joined, but it's not the same for me as it is for Patricia 'cause her mom is educated and all. She's real enthusiastic about it. You know, she's going to college and will do it there. But like Lorena and me, we can't always make it to the meetings. They're at lunch time, and I have to go to work then, or I want to at least get some lunch before I go to work.

Yolanda and Lorena both had vocational work-experience "class" the last two periods of school, which allowed them to leave school early and receive school credit for working. Patricia expressed some frustration with las chicas' failure to be very involved, as she and the other college-prep MEChA members struggled to find ways to reach *la raza,* to get the people to come to the functions they organized.

Further, the politicized racial/ethnic identity MEChA offered allowed Ana, Rosa, Patricia, and their friends to be middle-class performers and not deracinate. MEChA offers bicultural identity by making it possible for middle-class performers to do well in school and yet maintain a political-cultural racial/ethnic identity Ironically, although MEChA, at least as it existed at Waretown High, embraced a working-class, community-based agenda, it served middle-class performers, those who were already tracked upward, more than it did a working-class base. It appealed less to working-class performers whose racial identity was more secure and who were less vulnerable to accusations of acting white. Because it was understood as a college-prep activity (originating in the university and promoting higher education), MEChA was therefore intimidating to working-class performers, who experienced class-injury in relationship to it. Class difference stood in the way of the racial alliance MEChA students desired, but it was not understood as such. . . .

EDUCATED IN ROMANCE?

Overall, las chicas' race-class performance of femininity was read by their peers, and at times by their teachers, as a marker of heterosexual interest and sexual practice. It is an easy equation to assume that las chicas' girl culture, lack of interest in schooling, and poor school performance are a consequence of the fact that as girls they have been "educated in romance," that potentially higher aspirations were sidetracked by girls' socialization in romance and relationship (Holland and Eisenhart 1990).

But this suggested sequence of causality is, once again a consequence of envisioning girls as only gendered, failing to see their gender performances as race- and class-specific. Rather, their working-class location, informed by racial formation, leads them to a vocational track, and their rejection of middle-class prep norms takes a gender-specific form. Ironically, the tendency to see working-class girls as shaped most by gender may occur precisely because of the particular working-class racialized version of femininity they are performing. We will see that working-class white girls as well are perceived as sexualized; thus class differences, performed in race-specific ways, are often wrongly understood as primarily about gender and a difference of sexual morality between "good girls" and "bad girls," Instead, choices about appearance, girls' use of gender-specific commodities, are one way they negotiate meanings and construct distinction among themselves in a race- and class-stratified society. . . .

NOTES

1. A quinceaãera is a celebration of a girl's fifteenth birthday, thought to signal the time when she enters adulthood and becomes a woman, has reached sexual maturity, and/or is ready for marriage.

2. For a parallel kind of analysis see Banks 2000 on black women and the cultural politics of hair.

3. The distinction I make here between dissident and school-sanctioned femininity is an oversimplification.

4. See also Enstad 1999.

5. See Blake 1997; Zavella 1997; and Hurtado 1998, among many others, for discussions of Chicana sexuality. It is certainly the case that my status as a cultural outsider shaped the conversations I had with Mexican-American girls on the topic of sexuality. There were no particular incidents or remarks that made a lack of intersubjectivity or girls' discomfort apparent to me, but nonetheless I want to acknowledge here this likelihood.

6. See S. Thompson 1995 for a sophisticated account of "teenage girls' tales of sex, romance and pregnancy." See also Tolman 1994.

7. See Fine 1988 for a fuller discussion of the "missing discourse of desire" in sex education courses and how anti-sex rhetoric arrests the development of sexual responsibility among adolescents.

8. Fine summarizes the status of proprietary schools in the state of New York, where the State Department of Education's 1985 report "found that proprietary schools [were] involved in violation of entry requirements; questionable recruitment practices; high dropout rates; less than quality standards; inadequate record keeping:; and failure to offer instructional programs approved by the State Department of Education" (19991, 91).

9. Fordham and Ogbu (1986) and Fordham (1996, 1999) address the meanings of the phrase "acting white" among black students. The content of "acting white" in their subjects' accounts is often (but not always) coded middle class (e.g., attending the Smithsonian or the symphony, playing golf, going to the country club, and doing volunteer work). Fordham and Ogbu show that academic success is equated with whiteness and that the fear of being accused of "acting white" can lead to underachievement and various other strategies that are employed to "cope with the burden of acting white." See also Cousins 1999 and Mature-Bianchi 1991, who discusses "acting Anglo" among Mexican-American students. Setting aside the students' meanings, when I refer to a student as "acting white" here I do not, of course, mean that they are really Mexican-American in a modernist, realist, essentialist way. Rather, white and Mexican-American are historically constructed, racialized subjectivities that are only temporarily fixed categories of identity, in that social actors embrace them as real and they are real in their consequences. Likewise, there is no "authentic" racial/ethnic self, but only an ideology of essentialized authenticity that is mobilized by actors to achieve various effects.

10. It is not apparent what the content of whiteness as a cultural identity is in social science discourse either. For many writers on whiteness (Roediger 1991, 1994; Allen 1994, 1997; Lipsitz 1998), whiteness is conceptualized as a system of domination, where whiteness is described as a politicized racial positioning in the struggle over resources. When whiteness is viewed as nothing more than an oppressive ideology, it is seen as culturally bereft. Whiteness as a *cultural* identity is less explored in whiteness studies, but notable exceptions include Hartigan who, pointing to regional and class differences among whites, argues that "while whiteness may be fixed as a unified or unifying phenomenon when regarded ideologically at the national level, on the ground that unity quickly becomes illusory" (1997b, 180).Twine (1997) also points to white cultural identity as the product of everyday negotiations in her interviews with multiracial women of known African descent who acquired a white cultural identity in childhood. Activities such as family conversations and silences, dating, consumerism, and friendships were central to the shifting racial identities of these women. See also P. Cohen 1997 and Perry 2001. Whiteness as an identity outside of middle-classness is discussed again in chapter 6.

11. Vigil (1988) explains the link between pachuco style and low income, noting that starched and creased khaki pants, for example, originated in military and penal institutions, sites central to working-class life. Likewise, Dickie is a brand of work clothing, which has been appropriated and has come to signify group membership.

REFERENCES

Allen, Theodore W. 1994. *The Invention of the White Race.* Vol 1, *Racial Oppression and Social Control.* London and New York: Verso.

———. 1997. *The Invention of the White Race.* Vol. 2, *The Origin of Racial Oppression in Anglo America.* London and New York; Verso.

Banks, Ingrid. 2000. *Hair Matters: Beauty, Power, and Black Women's Consciousness.* New York: New York University Press.

Blake, Debra J. 1997. *The Right to Passion: Chicana Sexuality Refigured.* PhD.diss., University of Iowa.

Cohen, Phil. 1997. "Laboring under Whiteness." In *Displacing Whiteness: Essays in Social and Cultural Criticism,* edited by Ruth Frankenberg, 244–82. Durham, N.C.: Duke University Press.

Cousins, L. H. 1999. "Playing between Classes: America's Troubles with Class, Race, and Gender in a Black High School and Community." *Anthropology and Education Quarterly* 30, no. 3 (Sept.):294–316.

Eckert, Penelope. 1989. *Jocks and Burnouts: Social Categories and Identity in the High School.* New York: Teachers College Press.

Enstad, Nan. 1999. *Ladies of Labor, Girls of Adventure: Working Women, Popular Culture, and Labor Politics at the End of the Twentieth Century.* New York: Columbia University Press.

Fine, Michelle. 1988. "Sexuality, Schooling, and Adolescent Females: The Missing Discourse of Desire." *Harvard Educational Review,* 58, no. 1: 29–53.

———. 1991. *Framing Dropouts: Notes on the Politics of an Urban Public High School.* Albany: State University of New York Press.

Fordham, Signithia. 1996. *Blacked Out: Dilemmas of Race, Identity, and Success at Capital High.* Chicago: University of Chicago Press.

———. 1999. "Dissin' the Standard: Ebonics as Guerrilla Warfare at Capital High." *Anthropology and Education Quarterly* 30, no. 3 (Sept.): 272–93.

Fordham, Signithia, and John Ogbu. 1986. "Black Students' School Success: Coping with the Burden of 'Acting White.'" *Urban Review* 18, no. 3: 176–206.

Hartigan, John, Jr. 1997b. "Locating White Detroit." In *Displacing Whiteness: Essays in Social and Cultural Criticism,* edited by Ruth Frankenberg, 180–213. Durham, N.C.: Duke University Press.

Holland, Dorothy C., and Margaret Eisenhart. 1990. *Educated in Romance: Women, Achievement, and College Culture.* Chicago: University of Chicago Press.

Horowitz, Ruth. 1983. *Honor and the American Dream: Culture and Identity in a Chicano Community.* New Brunswick, N.J.: Rutgers University Press.

Hurtado, Aida. 1998. "The Politics of Sexuality in the Gender Subordination of Chicanas." In *Living Chicana Theory,* edited by Carla Trujillo, 383–428. Berkeley, Calif.: Third Woman Press.

Lesko, Nancy. 1988. "The Curriculum of the Body: Lessons From a Catholic High School." In *Becoming Feminine: The Politics of Popular Culture,* edited by Leslie G. Roman, Linda K. Christian-Smith, and Elizabeth Ellsworth, 123–42. Philadelphia: The Falmer Press.

Lipsitz, George. 1998. *The Possessive Investment in Whiteness: How White People Profit from Identity Politics.* Philadelphia: Temple University Press.

Luker, Kristin. 1996. *Dubious Conceptions: The Politics of Teenage Pregnancy.* Cambridge, Mass: Harvard University Press.

MacLeod, Jay. 1995. *Ain't No Makin' It: Aspirations and Attainment in a Low-Income Neighborhood.* 2nd ed. Boulder,Colo.: Westview Press.

Matute-Bianchi, Maria Eugenia. 1991. "Situational Ethnicity and Patterns of School Performance among Immigrant and Nonimmigrant Mexican-Descent Students." In *Minority Status and Schooling: A Comparative Study of Immigrant and Involuntary Minorities,* edited by Margaret A. Gibson and John U. Ogbu, 205–48. New York: Garland Publishing.

McRobbie, Angela. 1991. *Feminism and Youth Culture.* London: Macmillan.

Oakes, Jeannie. 1985. *Keeping Track: How Schools Structure Inequality.* New Haven: Yale University Press.

Ortner, Sherry. 1991. "Reading America: Preliminary Notes on Class and Culture." In *Recapturing Anthropology: Working in the Present,* edited by Richard G. Fox, 73–42. Santa Fe: School of American Research Press.

Oulette, Laurie. 1999. "Inventing the Cosmo Girl: Class Identity and Girl-Style American Dreams." *Media, Culture, and Society* 21, no. 3 (May): 359–83, 428.

Perry, Pamela. 2001. "White Means Never Having to Say You're Ethnic: White Youth and the Construction of 'Cultureless' Identities." *Journal of Contemporary Ethnography* 30, no. 1 (Feb.): 56–91.

Persell, Caroline. 1977. *Education and Inequality: A Theoretical and Empirical Synthesis.* New York: Free Press.

Roediger, David R. 1991. *The Wages of Whiteness: Race and the Making of the American Working Class.* New York: Verso.

———. 1994. *Towards the Abolition of Whiteness: Essays on Race, Politics and Working Class History.* New York: Verso.

Sennett, Richard, and Jonathan Cobb. 1972. *The Hidden Injuries of Class.* New York: Vintage Books.

Thompson, Sharon. 1994. "What Friends Are For: On Girls' Misogyny and Romantic Fusion." In *Sexual Cultures and the Construction of Adolescent Identities,* edited by Janice Irvine, 228–49. Philadelphia: Temple University Press.

———. 1995. *Going All the Way: Teenage Girls' Tales of Sex, Romance, and Pregnancy.* New York: Hill and Wang.

Tolman, Deborah L. 1994."Daring to Desire: Culture and the Bodies of Adolescent Girls." In *Sexual Cultures and the Construction of Adolescent Identities,* edited by Janice Irvine, 250–84. Philadelphia: Temple University Press.

Twine, France Winddance. 1997. "Brown-skinned White Girls: Class, Culture, and the Construction of White Identity in Suburban Communities." In *Displacing Whiteness: Essays in Social and Cultural Criticism,* edited by Ruth Frankenberg, 214–43. Durham, N.C.: Duke University Press.

Vigil, James Diego. 1988. *Barrio Gangs: Street Life and Identity in Southern California.* Austin: University of Texas Press.

Willis, Paul. 1977. *Learning to Labour: How Working Class Kids Get Working Class Jobs.* Farnborough, U.K.: Saxon House.

Zavella, Patricia. 1997. "Playing with Fire: The Gendered Construction of Chicana/Mexicana Sexuality." In *The Gender/Sexuality Reader,* edited by Roger N. Lancaster and Micaela di Leonardo. New York: Routledge.

43

Homegrown

How the Family Does Gender

NANCY LOPEZ

> In a relationship, the man has to work as equally hard as the woman does in order for it to work. And that's the way I see it. Because there is no man on this earth that's going to tell me, "Go, get up and cook dinner for me, woman!" I'd be like, "Please!" Because whoever my husband was going to be, I'm not cooking for him. If he wants food, let him go cook! Because of the type of career that I'm going to be in, I'm not going to have time to go make some gourmet dish for some man who's sitting down doing nothing! I want to finish school. I want to be financially stable.
>
> —*Nicole, 18-year-old West Indian woman*

INTRODUCTION

Although Nicole was only 18 years old and still in high school, she articulated a biting feminist critique that was rooted in the lived experiences of her mother. Nicole's visceral commitment to her independence as a woman was a lesson learned from her mother, who had emigrated to the United States from Jamaica when she separated from her husband, whom she described as "lazy." The fact that Nicole's mother left Nicole with her grandmother in Jamaica, emigrated by herself to the United States, found a job as a home attendant, and then brought Nicole to the United States as the head of her household left a lasting impression on Nicole about what it means to be a woman. Independence from men was the lesson second-generation women gleaned from their mothers' experiences.

In this chapter I explored the ways in which women and men fashion their gender identities and how these identities are tied to their understanding of the role of education in their lives. Feminist articulations among second-generation women were part and parcel of gender role transformations that are occurring across the globe, including Latin American and Caribbean nations.[1] The emergence of a feminist critique among second-generation Caribbean women was linked to the historical development of feminism among Caribbean women, which resulted from the increased labor-force participation of Caribbean women, both in their home countries and in the United States. Second-generation women created their gender identities against the backdrop of their immigrant mothers' struggles. The gendered division of labor in immigrant households played an important role in shaping men and women's outlooks toward education. In due course women fash-

---

ioned feminist outlooks and practices, which led them to define education as the route to independence.

Conversely, men's exemption from the adult responsibilities imposed on their female counterparts left them deprived of the emotional supports readily available to women. Men actually occupied rather precarious positions within the family structure. Most second-generation men spent much of their leisure time outside of the home or engaged in sports. Men seemed preoccupied with establishing a firm gender identity. Men did not necessarily perceive their masculinity as their education. Men established their sense of manhood by becoming preoccupied with asserting their masculinity through work, dating, and distancing themselves from home life. The first part of the chapter details the distinct *lived experiences* of women, and the next section highlights men's gendering processes.

WOMEN'S GENDER(ING)

Working Mothers = Adult Girls

The globalization of the economy has brought about striking changes in traditional gender roles and family structures.[2] As more and more women have entered the paid work force, men are no longer necessarily the breadwinners in their households.[3] The restructuring of labor markets and concomitant changes in gender and family ideologies have resulted in a large increase in the number of female-headed households across the globe.[4] Women constitute the majority of immigrants from the Caribbean. In a quest to establish financial independence and provide a better future for their families, many Caribbean mothers emigrated to the United States, with or without their spouses and families. During the 1960s and 1970s, as many as 70% of Anglophone Caribbean and 54% of Dominican and Haitian immigrants were women.[5] Since women were often the first to migrate, Caribbean families were reconfigured with mothers as the sole economic providers for their families. In New York City women headed 50% percent of Dominican households, 44% percent of Trinidadian households, and over 33% of Haitian households.[6] These patterns were mirrored in our survey sample: 45% of the women and 54% of the men had grown up in households headed by women. Since the 1960s, Caribbean immigrant women have been concentrated into the lowest echelons of the declining sectors of manufacturing, especially in the garment industry, and in low-level service sector jobs, such as home attendant and nurse's aide.[7] Thirty-three percent of Dominicans, 21% of Haitians, and 11% of Jamaicans in the United States lived in poverty.[8]

Caribbean mothers' entry into the paid labor force had a palpable effect on the lives of their daughters. While their mothers worked, women served as surrogate mothers to their siblings at a very young age. Marie, a 19-year-old Haitian woman who had grown up in Crown Heights, Brooklyn, was attending a community college. Over her kitchen table, Marie giggled as she reflected on the adult responsibilities she juggled when she was just a girl:

> I was nine and my brothers were eight. We used to stay home by ourselves because my mother had to go to work and she didn't have any money for a babysitter. My obligation was to make sure that all my brothers and sisters met in front of the school and waited for each other. Then we used to walk home. My mother was very strict. She would tell us that she was going to call us to make sure that we were home safe. And then I would get dinner started, clean the house and that was how it was.

Like many other Caribbean women, Marie's mother worked long hours as a nurse's assistant and was seldom home. Because gender role expectations assigned women to the domestic sphere, Marie, who was only a year older than her twin brothers, was made responsible for household chores and child rearing.[9] Indeed, during interviews, women were usually busy preparing meals, washing dishes, or feeding and diapering younger siblings. One lesson the gender-biased division of labor at home taught women was that homemaking is hard work.

A fundamental difference between the immigrant mothers of the second generation and European American mothers was their relationship to power structures. European American mothers have spouses who earn "family" wages.[10] However, regardless of whether or not there is a working spouse present in the household, working-class women who are members of racially stigmatized groups have always had to work in the paid labor force to provide for their families.[11] Ironically,many Caribbean women and other racially stigmatized low-income mothers toil as childcare providers and housekeepers for affluent families, most of whom are European American, yet they may be labeled "bad" mothers because they cannot afford childcare for their own children.[12] Middle-class European American mothers enjoy the luxury of choosing whether to remain at home with their children.

Katia, a 19-year-old Dominican woman who had grown up in Flatbush and Canarsie, Brooklyn, was attending a community college in the Bronx. Katia laughed when discussing the differences she noticed between Dominican families in the United States and other American families:

> For Dominican girls, by the age of twelve, you know how to cook, clean and wash by hand. We had no washing machine, back then. It seems to me that in an American [White] home, a typical one, the mother does everything, while the daughter is out shopping at the mall after school. And she has her own car and everything.

As Katia pointed out, working-class Caribbean young women cannot count on middle-class luxuries, such as washing machines,cars, credit cards, and stay-at-home mothers. Although Katia's mother and father both worked—her mother in the garment industry and her father as a repairman—their household income with two workers was only $10,000. As members of the working class, women clearly differentiated their home experiences from those of middle-class European Americans, who did not have to worry about their livelihood, as they were not expected to be the breadwinners of their households.

Because women's gender roles scripted them to assume adult responsibilities at an early age, they were also more likely than men to have served as institutional brokers for their families.[13] Ofelia, a 20-year-old Dominican woman who had been raised by her aunt in Corona, Queens, after her mother had passed away, spoke at length about translating for her family:

> When my aunt went to unemployment, anything that she needed, I read the letters that came through the mail and stuff like that. For me it was a source of pride because she used to say, my niece reads in English, look she knows. I felt bad and proud at the same time because she would compare me to my brothers and she would ask them while they watched television what are they saying, and my brothers couldn't tell her. Yeah. I felt like an adult. That is one thing but I wasn't embarrassed about it. As a matter of fact, we did it so much that my Mom [aunt] would not go out by herself. Even if they spoke Spanish, you were not allowed to go out. One of us had to go with my Mom all the time.

At an early age women learned how to navigate a maze of institutions that were unfamiliar to their parents.[14]

Familism, a sense of affinity, obligation, and closeness to the family, permeated the narratives of the women. Cassandra, a 27-year-old Dominican woman who had grown up in Washington Heights, Manhattan, and earned a BA in psychology, echoed women's sentiments:

> Translating for my parents made me feel like an English-speaking brain. It felt good to know that I knew a lot of English. . . . Whenever my mom had to go to any office or hospital, I just had to go because if I didn't go they're going to treat my Mom differently. They are going to make her wait and if I went they're were going to take care of her right away.

Although both men and women viewed translating for their parents as an obligation, gender differences emerged in relation to their feelings about it. Women reported not only feeling proud of these responsibilities; they felt a deep sense of respect for their mothers in particular. These types of experiences were significant not only because they helped women enhance and maintain their bilingual skills, but also because they helped them foster a sense of competence and efficacy in the outside world. In due course, women matured more quickly than their male counterparts and simultaneously cultivated a sense of pride and appreciation for the struggles of their immigrant families, particularly those of their mothers.

Dual Frame of Reference

Women narrated stories that depicted their mothers as the most important figure in their lives and spoke about their own growth process, occurring against the backdrop of their mothers' experiences.[15] Maryse, a 21-year-old Haitian woman, had grown up in a mother-headed household in Crown Heights, Brooklyn, and was attending a vocational training school for computer programming. Maryse voiced the dual frame of reference experienced by women:

> In Haiti, you didn't have that much education. I mean, the education there was not as much as over here. Therefore, my mother's goal was for us to get all the education there was out there. . . . I would never disrespect my mother because I know how hard she works for us. There were times when she would break her back for us.

Maryse's deep respect for her mother, who labored as a home attendant to provide for her family, had a strong impact on her views about the role of education in her life. Maryse viewed education as a way of showing respect to her mother and bringing honor to her family.

Yvelise was a 24-year-old Dominican woman who had grown up in Washington Heights, Manhattan, and had dropped out of high school but had eventually earned a GED and attended postsecondary vocational training in computer technology. When asked about what kinds of things she was proud of in her life, Yvelise did not hesitate:

> My mother. She has been there. She understands. She is my best friend. My mother. I call her for everything.
>
> [So you can always count on her?]
>
> Yes. I have a mother. Some people don't have a mother.
>
> [Besides your family, are there any other important people or events that have influenced you either in a positive or a negative way?]
>
> Definitely, my grandmother, in a positive way, because when I have a problem, she tells me not to feel bad and she talks to me a lot. She supports me a lot. And she was the one who pushed me to "Go to church." So she pushed me into going to church and I feel better. I see her weekly. Every week. When you go to church, when you're Catholic and you go to church, you feel better about yourself. You will get more strength to want to do anything. If you don't go to church, you don't anything, just lay around. You don't want to do anything. I go every week.

Yvelise beamed as she described how her relationships with her mother and her grandmother were fountains of emotional support for her during difficult times. The significance of these "home spaces" is that they may provide women with support to succeed in spite of daunting obstacles. Pastor et al. (1996) posit that "home spaces" that provide emotional support are not limited to homes, but may include other social spaces found in schools and churches. Growing evidence suggests that spirituality is yet another space in which women cultivate webs of social support.[16]

Yvelise connected her deep commitment to her mother to the importance of pursuing a college education:

> I want to go, not really for myself but for my mother. I really want to finish for my mother, maybe become a teacher or something for my mother because she would feel proud of me. She would say, my daughter, the one who finished college, she's a teacher, she's this, she's that, whatever.

Expressing a deep feeling of love and respect for her mother, Cassandra, a 27-year-old Dominican woman who had grown up in Washington Heights, Manhattan, explained what propelled her to pursue her education:

> I see my mother. She always wanted to get a better job, but she didn't speak English. She couldn't read. She couldn't write. So, to me, that was a push for me. I have to do better than that. Not that I didn't want to become my mother, because to me, my mother was the most wonderful person. But, because I didn't want to go through all the obstacles she went through. Right now, I am definitely planning to go back for my master's degree.

Women consistently assessed their educational and employment aspirations against the backdrop of the hardships their mothers had endured because they had not had opportunities to further their education.

Yvonne, a 22-year-old Dominican woman who had grown up in Williamsburg and Bushwick, Brooklyn, and was attending a community college in Manhattan, recalled that her outlook on education crystallized when she learned about her mother's past hardships:

> What really influenced me was my mother. She was the oldest of the eight children who came to the United States. She was 16 and all the other ones were much younger, so they went through elementary school and high school here; so they basically grew up knowing more English than Spanish. Then my grandmother and grandfather were working, so it was basically upon my mother to come home, cook, clean and help with the raising of the children. My aunts they got more of an advantage than my mother did and my aunts and uncles have very good jobs today. My aunts have very good jobs. They've gone to college. They've had more opportunities than my mother did. I remember being very young and my aunts would take me to their jobs and I would love the offices. The truth was that's what motivated me.

Women's decisions about their futures were etched against the backdrop of a self-sacrificing mother, as well as other women in their families. Through assessing their mothers' situations, women were able to evaluate their options regarding marriage, education, family, and career plans. Women's views about the role of education in their lives were intimately tied to their status as women. Suarez-Orozco (1987) found that Salvadoran youth maintained a dual frame of reference in which they contrasted their present situation with that which their parents had left in the home country. An intense feeling of guilt and obligation toward a sacrificing mother, along with the dream of ending family hardship, led these young people to emphasize academic success as a means of bringing honor to their families.[17]

Familism and Social Support

Janet, a 26-year-old Dominican woman who had grown up in Washington Heights, Manhattan, had earned a BA in psychology. Janet explained nostalgically the nurturing she received in her family:

> In some ways, I think, Hispanics, in general, tend to be a little bit more on top of their children than white Americans. White Americans tend to be more individualistic. I don't see them having the heart-to-heart talks. In Hispanic families and in my family, if one of us did something, immediately someone would be calling an aunt to tell her. It didn't matter if it was just a bad report card; everybody knew your business. Whereas, I find that in white American families it was a little different. I think there was probably a little bit more affection in Dominican families. We were more touchy, feely—you get hugged a lot more. But I think you also get a lot more sheltering sometimes and you feel caught between two worlds. You have that very strong Dominican heritage and that family influence, but then there was also this very independent, be-on-your-own mentality.

Janet's assertions that Caribbean families are "touchy, feely [spaces] were you get hugged" pointed to the high levels of familism present in these homes. "Home" was a place where women felt the strong hand of social control and bore the brunt of a gender-biased division of labor, but it was also a "safe space" in which women sought support through woman-centered social relations.[18]

Family gatherings provided another space in which women wove close ties to their family members, particularly other female kin. Marie recalled the gendering processes that took place during family get-togethers:

> When we used to go out to a family party, my brothers would just run away and start playing with each other, or they would start playing ball and they did not really talk to the grown-ups. So my brothers were really shoddy when it comes to speaking Haitian Creole. They try, but they don't speak it because they always avoided family members. Meanwhile, we [the sisters] were always talking with the grown-ups.

Research has shown that second-generation women are more likely to be bilingual than men.[19] Second-generation women literally spend more time in their homes, interacting with older adult relatives who may not speak English.[20] In part because gender roles prescribed women to interact more regularly with their extended kin by helping their mothers prepare meals and entertain family members during special occasions, women were more likely to forge relationships with these women and thereby have more opportunity to retain their mother tongue.

Aunts, godmothers, grandmothers, and mothers were the nodes in the woman-centered webs of emotional support that second-generation Caribbean women were able to draw upon during difficult times. During moments of family crisis, Caribbean women took the lead in solving problems. Marie reminisced about the special relationship she had had with her godmother:

> When we lived in Crown Heights, I remember my godmother. She was my second mother. My godmother would come over, she had five children of her own, and every weekend she would come with a big bag of clothes for us. Of course they were hand-me-downs, but they were already washed so we just picked out the clothes we could wear. Sometimes on our birthday we would get some money. I just love my godmother!

Marie explained that she had a very close relationship with her godmother, such that she felt comfortable talking to her about sex and other personal issues. Marie, who planned to pursue a career in the health industry, also spoke fondly of an aunt whom she admired because she had struggled in college to become a registered nurse. For women, talking with older family members often grew into close familial bonds and lasting relationships.

On Cloistering and Sexual Policing

One common thread in women's stories about their childhood was that they grew up sequestered in their homes. Despite the familism that permeated their narratives, women spoke about the cloistering and sexual policing they were subjected to in family life. Cassandra, the 27-year-old Dominican woman had grown up in Washington Heights, Manhattan, explained that while her brothers were allowed to go to baseball games, she was not given the same liberties:

> I had to come home straight from school. Some of my friends were in young adults clubs, but my mother didn't believe in that. Oh, no! Like my brother was allowed to go out to the movies, go outside. I was not allowed. Even in high school I wasn't allowed to go out. It was not fair. My brother was allowed to go out with his friends and party. My brother went to the prom. I didn't because I was a girl. My mother didn't trust the school. I didn't go. I remember that night. I cried so much. I was so embarrassed. And I bragged to everybody that I went. "Where are the pictures?" "Oh, I didn't take pictures." . . .

. . . In a study of second-generation Vietnamese students' social adaptation to the United States, Zhou and Bankston (1998) found that young women, unlike young men, were subjected to strict social control, and they were responsible for more household work than their male counterparts. However, they concluded that strict social control of young women had a positive influence on their education, in that it actually propelled them into academic achievements.[21] Young women growing up in such controlled social environments may come to view schools as the only way to achieve some degree of independence. Zhou and Bankston concluded that traditional Vietnamese culture may have been conservative in intent, however, in practice, it had a positive effect on the education of young women in these communities.

Parents further "protected" their daughters by limiting the amount of time they could spend socializing outside the home in the company of young men. Mothers and fathers often warned their daughters that they needed to pursue their education because of their subordinate gender position. Margaret, a 21-year-old West Indian woman of Antiguan ancestry who had grown up in Springfield Gardens, Queens, and had earned a bachelor of arts degree in psychology, reflected on her parents' advice:

> My parents would tell me, "You have to work twice as hard because you are Black and you have it even worse because you are a woman." And, I guess it kind of made me want to be one of those women that can be independent without depending on somebody.

Mothers, in particular, warned their daughters about the perils of depending upon a man for economic support.[22] Rosy, a 19-year-old West Indian college student of Trinidadian ancestry, who had grown up in Flatbush and Bedford Stuyvesant, Brooklyn, remarked that neither of her parents approved of her dating during high school:

> My father personally doesn't want any guys around me because he knows how he was when he was younger and he thinks that every male was like that. And my mother, she doesn't want me to get tied down because of what happened to her when she was younger. She doesn't want me to go through the same thing. She had her first child when she was fifteen and married when she was twenty-something. So she didn't get a chance to do anything. So she was putting all of that on me.

Interestingly, Rosy's mother's fundamental concern was for her daughter's long-term independence and happiness, whereas her father was more interested in Rosy's immediate safety and in protecting her from the sexual advances of young men. Nonetheless, Rosy took her mother's advice and planned to pursue a Ph.D. in psychology.

Avoiding premature childbearing was a theme that emerged in the narratives of women in this study, but not in those of men. Women spoke about deliberately avoiding sexual activity and self-policing their sexual desires to ensure that they achieved their educational goals.[23] Nicole, the 18-year-old West Indian woman of Jamaican ancestry, quoted in the introduction, aspired to become a medical doctor. While we sat at her kitchen table Nicole prepared food, cleaned the kitchen, and played intermittently with her baby sister, Lisa, who marveled over my tape recorder and occasionally approached Nicole to play with the microphone pinned on her shirt. Although Lisa was a toddler, Nicole boasted that she had taught her the alphabet, as well as addition and subtraction. When queried about her plans for marriage and children, Nicole asserted passionately that she did not plan to get married any time soon: "I have no intentions of letting men screw up my life! I have to finish school. Definitely. Once I'm through with school, I'll be in my thirties. Then, I can think about having a child." Among women, the intention to delay marriage and child rearing was always discursively linked to the stigmatization of their sexuality and the importance of acquiring educational credentials for dismantling these stereotypes. Although Nicole was still enrolled in high school, she had an A average. When asked about her grades Nicole insisted that she was not going to become another "teenage mother statistic." These findings contrast sharply with other studies that suggest that upon reaching adolescence women lose self-esteem and become embedded in a culture of romance.[24] . . .

"Homegrown" Feminism

While women spoke appreciatively of their mothers' sacrifices and courageous efforts to provide for their families in the face of daunting obstacles, they also criticized the double standard that marked the difference between acceptable behavior for men and women. Marie, a 19-year-old Haitian woman, had some sharp comments about her mother's gender-biased child-rearing practices:

> Of course, the guys could get away with it. They didn't want to do their homework, they didn't want to do the dishes and they could get away with it. But let me and my sisters decide one day that we didn't want to do it, she will talk to us all night long. My mother would say: "You'll not get married and no man was going to want you." I remember one time my sister didn't do the dishes. It was 2:00 in the morning! My mother went and woke her up! She said: "Get up and go do the dishes!" My sister was dead sleeping and she had to get up and do the dishes.

When asked to describe how she felt about this double standard Marie elaborated:

> In one way, it was kind of unfair because my brothers always got away with stuff, but in another instance, I can't really blame my mother because I see where she grew up.

Women often emphathized with their mother's struggles. Although Marie criticized her mother's double standard regarding household duties, she still expressed a deep respect for her mother and did not blame her for her gender-biased child-rearing practices.

How can second-generation women critique the double standard in their homes, while at the same time remaining firmly committed to their families and their communities? In *The Color of Privilege: Three Blasphemies on Race and Feminism,* Aida Hurtado (1996) sheds light on this apparently contradictory phenomenon. According to Hurtado blasphemy involves confronting unpleasant, unvoiced, and often ignored social relations that have been suspended for the sake of group survival. The Chicano movement during the 1960s took on the progressive political agenda of promoting voter registration, prison reform, and the unionization of farm workers, yet it had not confronted the issue of sexism within the Chicano community. Hurtado explained that in bringing attention to issues of sexism, Chicanas sought to dismantle gender oppression in their homes by embracing their families and cultural heritage, not by divorcing themselves from the men in their communities.[25] Hurtado argued that these efforts were not condoning male domination, but rather served as bridges in bringing about the important work of community-building and social change.[26] In this light, the effervescent feminist critique among second-generation Caribbean women is blasphemous because it grows out of a deep love and respect for their community.

Some scholars have suggested that the development of a feminist consciousness among Caribbean immigrant women is a simple by-product of assimilation into the American mainstream.[27] However, the development of feminist practices among second-generation Caribbean women in the United States is a messy and complex process with historical origins and cannot be explained solely as a function of assimilation. Multiple generations of Caribbean women have historically engaged in feminist practices that have challenged male domination. Feminist rumblings are rooted in global structural changes in the economy, family structures, and culture.[28]

Jahaira, a 30-year-old Dominican woman who had grown up in Bush-wick, Brooklyn, and earned a B.A. in public administration, talked about how she learned her feminist practices:

> We didn't grow up with that big a male dominance. My mom was always the person that you asked permission to and the person who said whether you can go or not. Or you can have this or not. Even though my father was there at times, she was always the steady person there so she was the one who said what to do and when to go. In my family we're strange because we tend, now in our relationships, to be dominant.

Jahaira, clearly did not envision being taken care of by a man. Divorced and raising two children, Jahaira was in no rush to marry the father of her children:

> You mean like get married? No. I'm not rushing to do it because a lot of marriages are failing. I don't see these children's father and I being the perfect, ideal couple that will last untold years. So, if we get married that's okay. But it's not something I have to do. I am self-sufficient. A lot of people get married and it is out of love and stuff but sometimes it is convenient and it is economically sane to do. I take care of myself.

Given that many second-generation Caribbean women had mothers who were the first in their families to emigrate, it was not surprising that they articulated a homegrown feminist discourse rooted in their mother's actions. Multiple generations of strong women who headed their households both in the Caribbean and in the Diaspora were inspirations to second-generation women.

Cassandra, who had grown up in a two-parent household, remembered that as a child she was extremely critical of her father's authoritarian behavior in the family:

> My father never learned how to cook. My father doesn't even know how to boil an egg! He was so demanding! "The food was too hot! It's too cold! My clothes were wrinkled!" I would say to myself, "Why can't you do it? You're a person too." We were always upset about it. I remember when he used to come from work, oh my God! We had to have his sandals waiting for him. All he had to do was give us the look.

Cassandra's reaction to her home life was imbued with anxiety, anger, fear, and love. Although she resented her father's behavior as a *caudillo* (the strongman of the household), Cassandra also noted that her mother, despite her wifely submissiveness, resisted her husband's social control and was not completely dependent on him for financial support:

> My mother always used to put in an equal share of the household money because even though she was at home raising us, she never sat down in the house. She was never home waiting for my father to bring the check. My mother was making more money than my Dad. We used to go out and clean apartments together and we used to baby-sit. I used to go and help her out. She was always doing something. She used to bring in more money than he did. My father never even knew how much.

Cassandra's mother probably did not view herself as a "feminist"; however, her behavior can be described as feminist because it was aimed at producing some degree of self-determination.[29] It was her mother's resistance to male domination that provided Cassandra with the vantage point from which she made decisions regarding marriage, work, education, and career. Among many working-class and third-world women, adherence to a feminist identity is not a prerequisite for feminist practices. Even in patriarchal homes, women carved out their own autonomy.

Cassandra divorced because she found her husband to be too domineering. When I asked her if she was considering remarrying, Cassandra remarked:

> I'm just waiting for the right thing to happen. I'm not in a rush, but at the same time I haven't found the adequate partner for me, somebody who has gone to school, like me. Somebody that has gone through school; that's what I want because I'm not just going to pick any guy from the street just to know that I have a man. No. I can take care of my child. My child and I, we're doing fine. It's rough being a single parent, especially since I grew up with my mom and my dad, they married for so many years, that for me it is very hard to put myself in this situation. But I'm not just going to take anybody. No way! To me, success means having stability financially, having a house, being self-sufficient.

Women's commitment to independence and egalitarian gender roles was always defined with reference to their mother's hardships. In due course, women wove a "homegrown" feminist standpoint that was anchored in the lessons they had gleaned from their mothers' perseverance in the face of daunting obstacles.[30] In a study of Mexican immigrants in California, Hondagneu-Sotelo (1994) posited that "it is not feminist ideology but structural rearrangements that promote social change in spousal relations."[31] Likewise, in a study of women's labor-market participation in the Dominican Republic, Puerto Rico, and Cuba, Safa (1995) found that women's entry into the paid labor force has translated into greater autonomy within the household. However, she also cautioned that the micro-level gains in terms of gender equality at the household level were undermined at the macro level. This was due to the fact that Dominican, Puerto Rican, and Cuban women toiled in low-wage manufacturing industries that were infamous for their labor abuses and exploitative wages. Thus, while women's entry into the labor force has allowed them more freedom to challenge male hegemony within their homes, it has not automatically translated into an improved living standard for women at the macro level. . . .

MEN'S GENDER(ING)

The Absence of a Dual Frame

Men were absolved from the adult responsibilities imposed on their female counterparts. When asked about his household responsibilities while growing up, Andrés, a 24-year-old Dominican man who had grown up in Corona, Queens, and who was enrolled in the police academy, explained that he was not responsible for housework while growing up:

> We were boys. We didn't have to do many chores around the house. My mother used to take care of the house and do the cooking. When my mother was working she used to have a neighbor come over and stay with us until she returned.

As Andrés explained, in a household where there were no girls, in the mother's absence, another woman, usually a relative or friend, assumed the domestic chores. Regardless of their age, men were rarely expected to assume childcare responsibilities, perform domestic duties, or assume other family obligations. . . .

Since men were absolved from chores, they did not compare their present situation with that of their parents, even when their fathers were present. John, a 25-

year-old Dominican man who had grown up in Washington Heights, Manhattan, and had dropped out of school but eventually earned a GED, chuckled when recalling the gendered division of housework in his family: "I never washed dishes. I was never expected to wash dishes. But my sisters, my mother showed them to cook. She showed them how to clean the house." Because mothers excused their sons from the responsibilities automatically assigned to their daughters, young men growing up in these households did not personally identify with their mothers' struggles as parents who were often the heads of their households. In essence, men's lived experiences with the gendered division of labor in Caribbean households did not provide them with a dual frame of reference from which to evaluate their choices about marriage, education, and career, as it did for women.

The gender(ing) that took place within Caribbean homes reinforced men's traditional views on gender roles and family ideologies. Rodrigo was a 23-year-old Dominican man who had grown up with both of his parents on the Lower East Side of Manhattan. Rodrigo had dropped out of high school in the tenth grade, but he had eventually earned a GED. When asked about the differences between how boys and girls were raised, Rodrigo justified his lack of participation in household responsibilities: "My sisters had to clean the house and stuff like that. Me, I just had to stay and watch TV. I didn't really have that much responsibility. I'm not good at housework." Not surprisingly, Rodrigo smirked when I asked him about his views on gender roles and family ideologies. While he agreed that in a marriage the husband and wife should work and contribute to the household expenses, he still felt that childcare responsibilities were primarily the responsibility of the wife. Rodrigo's sentiments were echoed in a survey: twice as many men as women indicated that in a marriage housework and childcare were primarily the woman's responsibility.[32]

Men also did not serve as institutional brokers for their families. Indeed, several men mentioned that during the few times they translated for their parents, they felt somewhat embarrassed. Rodrigo remarked:

> Translating? Well, when I was growing up that was usually my sisters. That was usually their forté. Now that I'm the only one at home, if they have a phone call or anything that they needed me to help them out with, then I do it. . . . It feels OK. But, I mean, they've been here for so many years; I wish they would have learned English by now.

The meanings men assigned to the task of translating for their families contrasted sharply with women's affirmations that they felt "smart" and "proud" that they were able to help their parents. Moreover, another consequence of men's lack of responsibilities in the family was that men did not maintain close relationships with their family members.

Streetboys

In spite of the brisk March breezes, Rodrigo, who shared a one-bedroom dilapidated Lower East Side tenement apartment with his mother, father, and sister, insisted that we conduct the interview outside, saying "I hate being upstairs cramped up with my parents. I'd rather conduct the interview downstairs in the park." So we headed downstairs to a park bench not far from his home. While we spoke Rodrigo kept an eye on his motorcycle and greeted his neighborhood friends as they walked by. While most of the interviews with women took place in their homes, I often conducted interviews with men outside of the home: in parks, in fast-food restaurants, on the street, or on the run in a car.

Despite parental efforts to protect both daughters and sons from the vices of the street, in practice men were given more liberties. Another case in point was Denzel; he was an 18-year-old West Indian man who was born in Trinidad and Tabago, but whose parents were from Grenada. He had grown up in Flatbush, Brooklyn. Denzel had a C average in high school and was still enrolled in the eleventh grade. As with the other men in the study, scheduling an interview with Denzel was a challenge, as he was never home. According to Serena, his 15-year-old sister, who always answered the phone, Denzel was outdoors playing basketball and only returned home in the late evening. When asked whether concerns about crime ever kept him from going out, Denzel instead described his family's efforts to safeguard his teenage sister:

> My mom tries to keep her safe. Told her she shouldn't talk to boys. My mom makes sure that if a boy calls and my sister stays on the phone too long, my mom tells her: "Get off my phone and do your work because I don't want you talking to boys who can screw up your life." So my sister is protected from "the boys element." When I see her talking to a boy, I say: "Let me talk to you for a minute. I think you were talking to a bad person." She might give you a hard time but afterwards she leaves him alone and goes about her business. [So your mom was basically very protective of your sisters, more than with the boys?] Yeah, because she knows we can take care of ourselves. But with her, she makes sure my sister doesn't get caught up with the boys. My sister, she goes to my high school and has a 93 something average, so right now she can get into any college she wants.

Serena attended the same high school as Denzel, but unlike her brother she was an exemplary student who was on the honor roll. Before dashing off to his game, Denzel proceeded to tease his younger sister, Serena, for being a feminist. Serena shared a poem she had written for her English class, which essentially spoke about how men were "dogs" and women could not count on men these days—a lesson she had learned from her mother, who was head of the household with four children. Freed from the onerous domestic tasks required of their sisters, men had much more leisure time on their hands. At the end of the interview, Denzel and his older brother were off to play basketball with the makeshift milk-crate hoops that lined the neighborhood streets. Meanwhile, Serena was confined to the home, playing the role of surrogate mother, taking care of their baby sister, cleaning, and cooking.

Unlike women's narrative about having close relationships with their families, men's childhood stories were peppered with episodes of spending time "in the streets," playing basketball, and "hanging out," usually with other young men. Men justified their preference for the street by pointing to their overcrowded apartments. Severe overcrowding in many working-class and poor Caribbean homes was often resolved by transforming the living room into a substitute bedroom. In accordance with the principle of maintaining the privacy of the women in the home, the sole bedroom in the apartment often became a de facto woman's space, while the more public living room quarters were designated a male space, while the more public living room quarters were designated a male space. Young men growing up in overcrowded homes may not want to stay home all day because they lacked any private space—their bedrooms were public spaces during the daytime. This was the case in the homes of Peter, Joaquín, Richard, Perry, and Denzel. Denzel and his older teenage brother shared a sofa bed in the living room, while his mother and two sisters shared the only bedroom in the apartment. In spite of the greater freedom men enjoyed in comparison with their sisters, they occupied rather marginal spaces within their families. . . .

Becoming a Man

Steven, a 23-year-old West Indian man, had grown up in a two-parent household in East Flatbush, Brooklyn; his mother was from St. Vincent and his father was from Grenada. Steven, who was enrolled in CUNY and had a D+ average, described why he had looked forward to work after school throughout his high school years:

> I didn't want to be home. I didn't want to be there cramped inside the house. That's one of the reasons I always worked. I didn't want to be there with my mom. I wanted to be out! Being at work was like freedom, even though you had to take crap. That's why I always worked.

As described by Steven one aspect of men's quest to fashion a gender identity was actively distancing themselves from their mothers. The quest to establish a firm sense of gender identity—a deep seated sense of self as "masculine" or "feminine"—became a project that occupied much of men's free time.[33] Regardless of whether their fathers were present, young men had a more formidable task before them than their female counterparts. . . .

Another aspect of proving one's "manhood" was engaging in fights. Men narrated many instances of "testing," particularly in junior high school, where young men were compelled to prove their manliness by physically defending themselves. Denzel, an 18-

year-old West Indian man, described some of the male hazing rituals he underwent during his preadolescent years:

> It was rough! Because in junior high school kids try to play hard rocks. They try to act like big men and do bad and stuff. The first day I was in that school, this kid I knew said something that got him in trouble and I tried to stick up for him and he put the whole thing on me so then I had to fight five guys.

Of course episodes in which men had to demonstrate their virility by engaging in fights often translated into problems at school. Haitian men, in particular, recalled many violent incidents at school. Perry, an 18-year-old Haitian man who had grown up in Prospect Heights, Brooklyn, was still enrolled in high school, with a C average. Perry's sense of manhood was intimately tied to defending his blemished ethnic identity:

> The thing I didn't like was why some Haitians would lie and say they're Jamaican. I'd look at them and say that's your country, why were you putting yourself down because people call you names? It's important for me to let people know that I'm Haitian. I don't care if they don't want to be my friend.

Men saw ethnic teasing as a direct assault on their masculinity and responded by engaging in fights. Fine and Weis (1998) used Benamayor's (1992:72) concept of cultural citizenship to explain how Puerto Rican men's sense of ethnic pride was intimately tied to their notions of what it means to be a man who defends his race. Cultural citizenship is a process through which an oppressed people arrive at a common identity and establish solidarity. In this light, men's attempts to defend their ethnicity can also be understood as intimately tied to notions of hegemonic masculinity.

Instead of focusing on postsecondary eduction, men sometimes turned to a time-honored bastion of maleness—the military—to establish their sense of manhood. Reynaldo was an 18-year-old Dominican man who was born and raised in Inwood, Manhattan, and had grown up with both parents. Reynaldo, who was still enrolled in high school with a C average, mentioned that he did not plan to go to college:

> I'm going to the military to see if I can make a man of myself because I like to chill too much. I didn't like school that much. I barely made it through high school because I like chilling too much. You know, like hanging out with your friends playing basketball and stuff.

For Reynaldo, joining the military was the first step in becoming a man and feeling like an adult. It was striking that several men mentioned joining the armed services as a career path, but none of the women did so. While, at an early age, women already felt like women because they had assumed many adult responsibilities in the home, men struggled to achieve a secure sense of gender identity. In the end, men had to actively seek spaces where they could establish their sense of manhood, such as sports, and workplace, or the military.

Yet another space in which men attempted to construct their masculinity was romantic relationships with women. Men's narratives were peppered with references to many episodes of "chasing girls" throughout their adolescence.[34] When asked about the most important aspect of high school, many of the men, especially those who had not done well in school, responded with "Chilling, talking to the girls." Steven, a 23-year-old West Indian, joked about how he decided to attend college: "I was following a girl. . . . Do not let my name be known that I went to college to follow a girl. Everyone knew this. All my friends, they knew this because they knew the girl." Now that Steven was older, in retrospect he came to the conclusion that "it was stupid" to attend college because he wanted to chase after one particular woman.

Some of the men indicated that they sometimes skipped classes during high school to follow "girls." Sam, a 26-year-old Haitian man who had grown up in Flushing, Queens, admitted that his biggest flaw in life was that he was only interested in women and openly bragged that he was a "ladies' man." Sam remembered that he had actually transferred to a high school that offered a nursing program because he wanted to attend a high school that had more girls. In a study of African Americans enrolled in a public high school in Washington, DC, Fordham (1996) found that low-achieving men were also preoccupied with their masculinity. These young men measured their manhood in terms of having sexual freedom and not committing themselves to any particular women. In contrast, high-achieving men tended to have only one serious girlfriend.

When queried about why they thought that more women in their communities graduated high school than men, José, a 25-year-old Dominican man, chuckled:

> We were *tigueres* [tigers]. We were chilling in the street all the time. You won't see girls in the corner, especially in Dominican families. They lock down. Then, the only thing the girls can do is open a book and read.

In Dominican culture, a *tiguere* is a male cultural form. A *tiguere,* like a tiger, is a man who is quick on his feet and is usually hanging out in the street; he is witty, can fend for himself against insurmountable odds, and is deemed to be a maverick in the art of persuasion. The *tiguere* is also known for his sexual prowess.

Men felt that women's higher educational attainment was related to the different ways in which men and women evaluated their futures. Deren, an 18-year-old West Indian who had grown up in Corona, Queens, explained:

> Girls are more serious than guys are. Guys, we just want to hang out and do other things, but girls are more studious. Girls mature faster than guys do. When guys still want to play around, girls are already mature. They want to go to school more. They want to learn and they have the idea to look in the future.

Although Deren did not explain why "girls are more serious" about their education than young men, seemingly home life is an important part of the reason. Whereas women were expected to be serious and responsible in family affairs at a very early age, men were not. In essence, the gender-biased division of labor in family life contributed to the different ways in which men and women were gendered and evaluated their futures.

Men even defended the double standard, boasting that they took an active role in keeping their sisters away from the "boys element." Otherwise, according to Denzel, your sisters away from the "boys element." Otherwise, according to Denzel, your sisters might come home "with a belly right in front of you." While men reported that their parents warned them about "getting a girl pregnant," they did not share any of these worries themselves.[35] Since men did not see themselves as responsible for childcare, they expressed little concern about becoming parents. Unlike women, who did not want men "screwing up" their lives, men did not talk about delaying sexual activities as a way of securing their future educational opportunities.

CONCLUSION

This chapter began with the question of how changing gender roles influence the outlooks of women and men toward the role of education in their lives. I found that gender-biased child-rearing practices within the home setting have an important influence. At a young age, second-generation women assumed adult responsibilities and in some cases become surrogate mothers to their younger siblings. This led them to have closer ties to the family and develop a strong gender identity as women. In spite of the social supports available to women in their homes, they were also subjected to stricter social control than their male counterparts. Women also became institutional brokers for their families and felt pride in being able to assist their parents in this capacity. In due course, women developed a dual frame of reference in which they contrasted their own situation with that of their mothers. Women's narratives were marked by the assumption that they would assume full responsibility for the well-being of their families. These experiences provided women with an important vantage point from which to evaluate their decisions regarding their futures, leading them to reject early childbearing and to define education as a way of achieving independence. The challenges of the gender-biased division of labor in the household provided women with a critical consciousness from which to understand the role of education in their lives.[36]

The feminist outlooks and practices articulated by women were not simply by-products of assimilation into U.S. society; they were part and parcel of the lived feminist legacies of strong foremothers, including mothers, grandmothers, and great-grandmothers.[37]

Notwithstanding the fact that the legacy of the women's movement has left an indelible imprint on the outlooks of young women growing up in the United States, women's dreams of an education and financial independence were also an extension of the lived experiences of their immigrant mothers. Rather, they represented the historical legacy of Caribbean women who have headed their households both in their home countries as well as in the Diaspora and could be described as manifesting *transnational feminism(s)* that originated in the sending society and was rearticulated in the Caribbean Diaspora.[38]

For several reasons, men did not articulate a dual frame of reference. First of all, gender-biased childbearing practices generally absolved men from many of the adult responsibilities imposed on their sisters. Men also spent much of their time during their childhood and adolescent years outside their homes, usually playing sports. This led them to have very weak ties to their extended kin. In short, the webs of family ties that women maintained with other family members provided them with emotional supports that perhaps were unavailable to the men. At the same time, it was clear that for men achieving gender identity was fraught with problems. While women's narratives tied notions of womanhood and independence to education, men discursively linked their feelings of independence to education, men discursively linked their feelings of independence and masculinity to hanging out, working, and establishing romantic relationships with women. Whereas women expressed deep concern about the consequences of premature childbearing, men did not articulate any of these worries.

NOTES

1. For a review of the literature documenting these patterns, see Tiano (2001), Safa (1995), and Hondagneu-Sotelo (1994, 2003).

2. Contrary to the popular perception that only women possess "gender," at any historical point, both men and women are gendered in relationship to one another (see Hondagneu-Sotelo, 1994, 1999).

3. Safa (1995).

4. Milkman (1987), Hondagneu-Sotelo (1994), Espiritu (1997), Mahler (1997), Lopez-Springfield. (1997), Baca-Zinn and Thorton-Dill (1994), Safa (1995), Hernandez and Lopez (1997).

5. Hernandez et al. (1995), Kasinitz (1992), Zephir (1996), Laguerre (1984), Pessar (1987).

6. City University of New York (1995).

7. Kasinitz (1992), Pessar and Grasmuck (1991), Foner (1987).

8. Grasmuck and Grosfuguel (1997).

9. Valenzuela, Angela (1999).

10. Hurtado (1996), Ammot and Matthaei (1991).

11. In a study of childcare practices among elite White women in New York City and Los Angeles, Wrigley (1995) found that there is little pressure for high-quality government-monitored daycare because the privileged class has a choice. Wrigley (1992) warned that private solutions to larger public issues cannot solve social problems.

12. Wrigley (1995), Roberts (1997).

13. Valenzuela (1999).

14. Valenzuela, Abel (1999), hooks (1981), Pastor et al. (1996), Stanton-Salazar (1997).

15. See Hidalgo (2000), Rolón (2000).

16. Hurtado (1996), Fine and Weis (1998), Pastor et al. (1996).

17. Suarez-Orozco (1987) did not discuss gender differences, if any, between men and women's dual frame of reference. See Suarez-Orozco and Suarez-Orozco (1995).

18. Pastor et al. (1996), Zhou and Bankston (1998).

19. See Portes and Schauffler (1996).

20. Zhou and Bankston (1998), Perez (1996).

21. Zhou and Bankston (1998:184).

22. Washington and Newman (1991).

23. Tolman (1996).

24. Thorne (1993).

25. Hurtado (1996:79).

26. Anzaldua (1987).

27. Pessar and Grasmuck (1991), Georges (1990), Gil and Vasquez (1996).

28. Hernandez and López (1997).

29. Hondagneu-Sotelo (1994:196).

30. Momsen (1993), Senior (1991), Verene-Shepherd et al. (1995).

31. Hondagneu-Sotelo (1994:196).

32. In the survey, 44% of the men compared with 21% of the women felt that in a marriage the wife should be primarily responsible for housework.

33. As explained by Anzaldua (1987:84), "men, even more than women, are fettered to gender roles."

34. Fordham (1996).

35. Vera et al. (1996).

36. Pastor (1996).

37. Paravisini-Gebert (1997), Lopez-Springfield (1997).

38. Hondagneu-Sotelo (1994), Baca-Zinn and Thorton-Dill (1994), Lopez-Springfield (1997), Glick-Schiller et al. (1992), Moraga and Anzaldua (1983).

REFERENCES

Ammot, Teresa, and Julie Matthaei. 1991. Race, Gender and Work: *A Multicultural Economic History of Women in the United States.* Boston: South End Press.

Anzaldua, Gloria, 1987. *Borderlands: La Frontera, The New Mestiza.* San Francisco: Aunt Lute.

Baca-Zinn, Maxine, and Bonnie Thorton-Dill. 1994. "Difference and Domination." In *Women of Color in United States Society,* edited by Maxine Baca-Zinn and Bonnie Thorton-Dill. Philadelphia: Temple University Press.

Benmayor, Rina. 1992. *Responses to Poverty among Puerto Rican Women: Identity, Community and Cultural Citizenship.* New York: Centro de Estudios Puertorriquenos, Hunter College, City University of New York.

City University of New York. 1995. "Immigration and the CUNY Student of the Year 2000." New York: CUNY.

Espiritu, Yen Le. 1997. *Asian American Men and Women: Labor, Law and Love.* Thousand Oaks, CA:Sage Publications.

Fine, Michelle, and Lois Weis. 1998. *The Unknown City: Lives of Poor and Working-Class Young Adults.* Boston: Beacon Press.

Foner, Nancy, editor. 1987. "The Jamaicans: Race and Ethnicity among Migrants in New York City." In *New Immigrants in New York.* New York: Columbia University Press.

Fordham, Signithia. 1996. *Blacked Out: Dilemmas of Race, Identity, and Success at Capital High.* Chicago: University of Chicago Press.

Georges, Eugenia. 1990. *The Making of a Transnational Community: Migration, Development and Cultural Change in the Dominican Republic.* New York: Columbia University Press.

Gil, Rosa Maria, and Carmen Inoa Vazquez. 1996. *La Paradoja de Maria.* New York: Putnam.

Grasmuck, Sherri, and Ramon Grosfuguel. 1997. "Geopolitics, Economic Niches, and Social Capital Among Recent Caribbean Immigrants in New York City: Neglected Dimensions of Assimilation Theory." Transnational Communities and the Political Economy of New York City in the 1990s, Conference, February 21–22, Robert J. Milano Graduate School of Management and Urban Policy, New School for Social Research.

Hernandez, Ramona, and Nancy Lóopez. 1997. "Yola and Gender: Dominican Women's Unregulated Migration." In *Dominican Studies: Resources and Research Questions.* Dominican Research Monographs. New York: Dominican Studies Institute at City University of New York (reprinted in *Documents of Dissidence: Selected Writings by Dominican Women,* edited by Daisy Cocco De Filippis. New York: Dominican Studies Institute at City University of New York).

Hernandez, Ramona, Francisco Rivera-Batiz, and Roberto Agodini. 1995. *Dominican New Yorkers: A Socioeconomic Profile, 1990.* New York: Dominican Studies Institute at City University of New York.

Hildalgo, Nitza. 2000. "Puerto Rican Mothering Strategies: The Role of Mothers and Grandmothers in Promoting School Success." In *Puerto Rican Students in U.S. Schools,* edited by Sonia Nieto. Mahwah, NJ: Lawrence Erlbaum Associates.

Hondagneu-Sotelo, Pierrette. 1999. "Gender and Contemporary U.S. Immigration." *American Behavioral Scientist* 42(4):565–576.

———. 1994. *Gendered Transitions: Mexican Experiences of Migration.* Berkeley: University of California.

———. 2003. *Gender and U.S. Immigration: Contemporary Trends,* edited by Pierrette Hondaganeu-Sotelo. University of California Press.

hooks, bell. 1981. *Ain't I a Women? Black Women and Feminism.* Boston: South End Press.

Hurtado, Aida. 1996. *The Color of Privilege: Three Blasphemies on Race and Feminism.* Ann Arbor, MI: University of Michigan.

Kasinitz, Philip. 1992. *Caribbean New York: Black Immigrants and the Politics of Race.* Ithaca, NY: Cornell University Press.

Laguerre, Michael. 1984. *American Odyssey: Haitians in New York City.* Ithaca, NY: Cornell University Press.

Lopez-Springfield, Consuelo, editor. 1997. *Daughters of the Caliban: Caribbean Women in the Twentieth Century.* Indianapolis: Indiana University Press.

Mahler, Sarah. 1997. "Bringing Gender to a Transnational Focus: Theoretical and Empirical Ideas." Presentation at the Latin American Studies Association Annual Meeting.

Milkman, Ruth. 1987. *Gender at Work.* Chicago: University of Illinois Press.

Momsen, Janet. 1993. *Women and Change in the Caribbean: A Pan-Caribbean Perspective.* Bloomington, IN: Indiana University Press.

Paravisini-Gebert, Lizabeth. 1997. "Decolonizing Feminism: The Home-Grown Roots of Caribbean Women's Movement." In *Daughters of the Caliban: Caribbean Women in the Twentieth Century,* edited by Consuelo Lopez-Springfield. Indianapolis: Indiana University Press.

Pastor, Jennifer, Jennifer McCormick, and Michelle Fine. 1996. "Makin Homes: An Urban Girl Thing." In *Urban Girls: Resisting Stereotypes, Creating Identities,* edited by Bonnie Leadbeater and Niobe Way. New York: New York University Press.

Perez, Lizandro. 1996. "The Households of Children of Immigrants in South Florida: An Exploratory Study of Extended Family Arrangements." In *The New Second Generation,* edited by Alejandro Portes. New York: Russell Sage Foundation.

Pessar, Patricia. 1987. "The Linkage Between the Household and Workplace of Dominican Women in the U.S." In *Caribbean Life in New York City: Sociocultural Dimensions,* edited by Constance R. Sutton and Elsa M. Chancy. New York: Center for Migration Studies.

Pessar, Patricia, and Sherri Grasmuck. 1991. *Between Two Islands: Dominican International Migration.* Berkeley: University of California Press.

Portes, Alejandro, and Richard Schauffler. 1996. "Language and the Second Generation: Bilingualism Today and Yesterday." In *The New Second Generation,* edited by Alejandro Portes. New York: Russell Sage Foundation.

Roberts, Dorothy. 1997. *Killing the Black Body: Race, Reproduction, and the Meaning of Liberty.* New York: Pantheon.

Rolón, Carmen. 2000. "Puerto Rican Female Narratives About Self, School and Success." In *Puerto Rican Students in U.S. Schools,* edited by Sonia Nieto. Mahwah, NJ: Lawrence Erlbaum Associates.

Safa, Helen. 1995. *The Myth of the Male Breadwinner: Women and Industrialization in the Caribbean.* New York: Westview.

Senior, Olive. 1991. *Working Miracles: Women's Lives in the English-Speaking Caribbean.* Bloomington, IN: Indiana University Press.

Stanton-Salazar, Ricardo. 1997. "A Social Capital Framework for Understanding the Socialization of Racial Minority Children and Youths." *Harvard Educational Review* 67(1):1–40.

Suarez-Orozco, Marcelo. 1987. "'Becoming Somebody' Central American Immigrants in U.S. Inner-City Schools." *Anthropology and Education Quarterly* 18(4):287–299.

Suarez-Orozco, Marcelo, and Carola Suarez-Orozco. 1995. *Transformations: Immigration, Family Life, and Achievement Motivation Among Latino Adolescents.* Stanford, CA: Stanford University Press.

Thorne, Barrie. 1993. *Gender Play: Girls and Boys in School.* New Brunswick, NJ: Rutgers University Press.

Tiano, Susan. 2001. "From Victims to Agents: A New Generation of Literature on Women in Latin America." *Latin American Research Review* 36(3):183–203.

Tolman, Deborah. 1996. "Adolescent Girls' Sexuality: Debunking the Myth of the Urban Girl." In *Urban Girls: Resisting Stereotypes, Creating Identities,* edited by Bonnie Leadbeater and Niobe Way. New York: New York University Press.

Valenzuela, Abel. 1999. "Gender Roles and Settlement Activities among Children and Their Immigrant Families." *American Behavioral Scientist* 42(4):720–742.

Valenzuela, Angela. 1999. *Subtractive Schooling: The Politics of Schooling in a U.S. Mexican High School.* Albany, NY: State University of New York Press.

Vera, Elizabeth, Le'Roy Reese, Roberta Paikoff, and Robin Jarrett. 1996. "Contextual Factor of Sexual Risk-Taking in Urban African American Preadolescent Children." In *Urban Girls: Resisting Stereotypes, Creating Identities,* edited by Bonnie Leadbeater and Niobe Way. New York: New York University Press.

Verene-Shepherd, Bridget, et al. 1995. *Engendering History: Caribbean Women in Historical Perspective.* New York: St. Martin's Press.

Washington, Valora, and Joanna Newman. 1991. "Setting Our Own Agenda: Exploring the Meaning of Gender Disparities among Blacks in Higher Education." *Journal of Negro Education* 60(1):19–35.

Wrigley, Julia. 1995. *Other People's Children.* New York: Basic Books.

Wrigley, Julia. 1992. "Gender, Education and the Welfare State." In *Education and Gender Inequality,* edited by Julia Wrigley. New York: Falmer Press.

Zephir, Flore. 1996. *Haitian Immigrants in Black America.* Westport, CT: Bergin and Garvey.

Zhou, Min, and Carl Bankston. 1998. *Growing Up American: How Vietnamese Children Adapt to Life in the United States.* New York: Russell Sage Foundation.

44

Feminism, Nationalism, and the Japanese Textbook Controversy over "Comfort Women"

YOSHIKO NOZAKI

In 1993, "women's human rights" were recognized at the World Conference on Human Rights in Vienna, resulting in the "Declaration of the Elimination of Violence against Women." In 1994, the International Conference on Population and Development in Cairo recognized the reproductive rights of women, and the 1995 World Conference on Women in Beijing included the issue of sexual rights of women in its report. At these UN conferences, the wartime rape and abuse of women was viewed as constituting (sexual) war crimes. The participants of these conference were well aware of what was happening in places such as Bosnia and Rwanda, and it was in that connection that the issue of "comfort women" became a constant focus of discussion.[1]

The existence of comfort facilities and comfort women during the Asia-Pacific War (1931–1945) has not been a secret. In fact, at the end of the war the Allied Forces, led by the United States, took many comfort women into custody as POWs. However, although the Allied Forces knew that many of the women had been forced to work in the comfort facilities, they did not view the matter as a war crime requiring the prosecution of the Japanese involved. (Except for two cases-one involving Dutch women in Indonesia, and the other Guam female residents, no further investigation was conducted.)[2] The issue remained by and large unrecognized in postwar Japan, in spite of a hard-fought struggle over the national memory—in particular, "the official wartime history" as taught to Japanese schoolchildren—for many years.[3]

Many Japanese writings on war memories referred to comfort women, known as *ianfu* in Japanese. They were Japanese and non-Japanese women who "comforted" Japanese officers and soldiers on the front as well as in occupied territories during the Asia-Pacific War. Some comfort facilities were privately run (and supervised by the military), others built and directly managed by the military.[4] In his memoirs, Japan's former prime minister Yasuhiro Nakasone, a political ally of Ronald Reagan, mentioned his involvement in building comfort facilities in Borneo when he was a young navy officer. He wrote about it rather proudly:

> [The troop I commanded was] a big one consisting of three thousand men. Soon [after the occupation of the island it turned out that] there were some who raped

Yoshiko Nozaki, "Feminism, Nationalism, and the Japanese Textbook Controversy over 'Comfort women,'" p. 170–189. France Winddance Twine and Kathleen M. Blee, eds., *Feminism and Antiracism: International Struggles for Justice.*

> the native women and some who indulged in gambling. In some cases I built comfort facilities for these men, with considerable effort.[5]

In the 1990s the Japanese military comfort women system came to be seen as one of Japan's major war crimes. The issue became a major site of political as well as educational struggle, as feminists and progressives put the question of Japanese imperialism, particularly as expressed in the military's sexual slavery, on the national and international agenda. In this chapter I examine how South Korean and Japanese feminists as well as teachers engaged in peace and justice education (who did not necessarily self-identify as feminists) challenged nationalist narratives of the nation.[6] . . .

GENDER AND JAPAN'S PEACE AND JUSTICE EDUCATION

Since the early 1990s, a number of books and education journals have featured the reports of progressive teachers from a range of backgrounds who have attempted to include the issue of comfort women in their classrooms. A major group that has taken up the issue has been that of progressive social studies teachers. . . .

Interestingly, even among these teachers, there were some initial reservations regarding the need to include the issue of comfort women in their curriculum. Social studies teaching has been a male-dominated profession in Japan and the leaders of various study groups have more often than not been men.[7] While progressive in terms of race and ethnicity, they have been rather conservative with respect to gender. For example when Kiyoko Ihara, a junior high social studies teacher, reported her teaching about the issue in 1993 at a regional study meeting, she received largely negative comments, including statements such as "[The comfort women issue] brings up the issue of sex [and sexual relations], which is difficult to deal with" and "The feeling of a woman teacher is not sufficient reason for venturing to include the topic."[8]

Male teachers have been more reluctant to address the issue of sex—perhaps because it forces them to confront an issue that would inevitably question their own sexism. Furniko Kawada, a feminist writer who has written extensively on the comfort women issue, recalls her experience of joining a teachers' study group:

> After two junior high social studies teachers presented their reports on wrestling with [the issue of] "comfort women" in their classrooms, the participants were asked to give their thoughts and opinions in turn. [One of the male teachers said,] "My school is a boys' school, so . . ." [What he meant was] he was reluctant to deal with the issue of "comfort women" in his classes. . . . Why is there resistance to addressing the issue of "comfort women" [among teachers] in a boys' school? . . . That male teacher must be a conscientious teacher, since he joined the voluntary group for the study of teaching. Even so, though, he does not directly face up to the issues concerning sex, but seals them in a dark place, and leaves them there.[9]

This attitude has begun to change as the right-wing attack on textbook has intensified. More and more teachers, both men and women, have begun to consider this subject an important step in their decades-long effort to address Japanese colonialism and war crimes. They have come to feel the need to overcome their reluctance and address the issue of sex and sexism, in order to promote peace and justice education.[10] By the mid-1990s, teaching about military sexual slavery had become not only legitimate, but was considered an ideal approach to peace and justice education. . . .

CLASSROOM APPROACHES AND STUDENT RESPONSES

Curriculum planning is the selection of knowledge. Teachers, with little official support, usually develop their own curriculum and materials when teaching about comfort women. Their materials may consist of excerpts from books, slides, or videos. However, some teachers go beyond that. For example, when Tsuzuki, a teacher discussed above, began to teach about the issue, she used excerpts of Kim Hak-soon's testimony in newspapers and books. But as she taught her classes, she kept asking herself questions such as, "How did the former comfort women feel when they were coming out?" "What do they think of Japan now?" and "What are their lives like now?" She decided to visit and hear them directly. Since then she has visited former comfort women in South Korea several times, and has gradually come to feel closer to them, and has found them to be more and more important to her. She uses her first-hand knowledge of being with them in her classes.[11] Although Tsuzuki's case is perhaps unique, it is not uncommon among teachers with this level of commitment to participate in study meetings and tours, to which some former comfort women are invited.

The inclusion of a new topic inevitably requires the modification off the existing curriculum. Tsuzuki views the issue of comfort women as one that needs to be examined at least in terms of ethnic and gender relations. Ideally, she states, the topic should be taught in different classes: in social studies, in relation to the Asia-Pacific War and Japan's war crimes in health education, in relation to sex education; and in homeroom classes, in relation to human rights and peace education. In her view, it is extremely important for teachers to accumulate a sufficient variety of teacher-planned curricula examples. The health education curriculum she has developed (with other teachers) for grades seven through nine includes sex education in each grade. The curriculum includes topics such as the development of the body, sex and reproduction, pregnancy and delivery, abortion and contraception, sexual diseases, AIDS, sexual relationships and abuse, the commodification of sex, and sexual violence in war. Her students spend two hours on the last topic, examining it through the experience(s) of comfort women.[12]

Curriculum decision making also involves the allocation of time. When social studies teachers attempt to teach about comfort women, they usually find little room for the subject in the existing curriculum. Tadaaki Suzuki, a junior high social studies teacher, sees the existing curriculum as failing to meet the demands of his students, who wish to know Japan's wartime history in greater depth. The curriculum of his school (drawn up in accordance with the *Instructional Guidelines* written and published by the Ministry of Education) suggests that eight hours of teaching be allocated to the invasion of China, and events leading up to World War II. Suzuki has developed his own plan, which allows him to use twenty hours for the entire unit, by reducing the allocation of hours here and there in other units. In particular, his plan enables him to spend four hours on the war atrocities Japan committed in China and other Asian countries, including the Nanjing Massacre, Unit 731, the massacre of the Chinese population in Singapore, forced labor, and comfort women.[13]

Nontraditional instructional methods are also used. Takuji Yoshida, a high school politics and economics teacher, supplements his traditional mass teaching methods with a theme-learning approach in which he lists fifteen themes, from which he asks his twelfth-grade students to choose one. Within the theme of their choice students are expected to find a specific topic to study and present to their class. Every year, in Yoshida's experience, students who choose the theme of "Japan and Asia" present the comfort women issue in about half the classes he teaches (another topic that appears often is the Nanjing Massacre). Presentations are followed by a discussion session. Presenters usually come prepared with answers to questions they anticipate will be raised.[14]

In terms of their students' responses, teachers for the most part have reported good results. Their reports indicate that some common reactions and views have emerged among students working through the issue: first, the students were greatly shocked by the stories and testimony of comfort women and by the fact that the perpetrators were the wartime Japanese government and military (and in a broader sense Japanese soldiers, that is, ordinary Japanese). Second, they soon came to understand the issue as one that remains unresolved, and for that reason an important contemporary matter about which they have to think. After five hours of classes on the subject, for example, a sixth-grader in Masao Yamada's class stated:

> I had thought that we [the younger generation] were not involved, since the people of the old days were the ones who did it, but [after the class] I thought we were involved since we [belonged to] the same [group], Japanese.[15]

Many students also recognize the need for an apology and compensation from the Japanese government, and further, they feel the issue needs to be included in school textbooks, wishing to know more about the facts. For example, a junior high school student in Suzuki's class (discussed above) stated:

> What the Japanese government should do now is first to disclose all the data and sources concerning the war comfort women, and then apologize, . . . Japan has given economic aid and so on [to Asian countries], but I want it to do this [the disclosure and apology] first. The other day, there was a minister who said "there was no Nanjing Massacre." [This] is very disappointing to me.[16]

In a survey Suzuki conducted after implementing his lesson plan, many of his students singled out Japan's war atrocities as the topic about which they desired to learn more.

CONCLUSION

The Japanese imperial project involved a myth of Japanese racial superiority over the Asians they colonized. To this extent, education remains central to overcoming of racialist and masculinist narratives of the Japanese nation. While some Japanese teachers initially resisted including the topic of comfort women in teaching their courses, the nationalist attacks on peace and justice education and school textbooks motivated reluctant teachers to confront their own sexism, and to transform the school curriculum by teaching wartime history that sometimes centered on the experiences of Korean women suffering under Japanese imperialism. The struggle over Japanese national narratives exemplifies one way that feminist and nonfeminist teachers can be included in projects that can be considered feminist and antiracist in their objectives.

In the 1990s, the appearance and voice(s) of former comfort women shot through the imaginary national unity of both South Korea and Japan and led us to inevitable intersections of nationalism and feminism. A new meaning associated with the issue of comfort women—which represented the matter as one of many Japanese war crimes and human rights violations during the war years—clearly pointed to the gendered and ethnicized construction of "nation." As its new significance came to gain some legitimacy, however, Japanese right-wing nationalists, including politicians, journalists, and scholars, launched a series of counteroffensives. What Joan Wallach Scott calls the "politics of history"—that is, the play of forces involved in the construction and implementation of meaning associated with past events—has intensified.[17]

Japanese politics and policies of the 1990s on unresolved issues of the war have been the products of compromise, and therefore remain contradictory at best. How one evaluates the politics and policies of the period depends on how one assesses such compromise and contradiction. Interestingly, those at both ends of the political spectrum—nationalists and critical leftists (including many feminists) who did not move to the center—have been the most incisive critics of the current policies. Although the critical left has a valid point in my view when it contends that the important principles underlying Japan's war responsibility and official compensation should not be sacrificed to practical political compromise, it is also clear that the nationalists have been taking advantage of the confusing situation. Japanese feminists—activists or academics—need to find ways to participate fully in the process of compromise, while honoring our commitment to bringing justice to the unresolved issues of war, including the issue of comfort women.

Despite the great advances made by teachers in the 1990s concerning the subject of comfort women, the major problem they face has remained—the Japanese government's lack of real interest in teaching about the issue. While maintaining its position for the inclusion of the topic in history textbooks, the government has done very little to promote and support the kinds of teaching efforts discussed above. For example, had it been serious, the government could have suggested several substantial changes in the existing preservice and in-service teacher training programs, and in the existing social studies and history education curricula. However, almost no such suggestion has been made in either area (or in the related areas of educational and curriculum policy).

The majority of new teachers, including social studies teachers, enter the field without sufficient training to confront unresolved issues of war, including that of military sexual slavery. For those who are already in the profession and wish to include these issues in classrooms, their school districts typically offer no in-service training, or if they do, such training sometimes adopts a nationalist or militarist perspective. Moreover, the existing curricula are already packed and leave little room for the incorporation of new topics of any kind. Many concerned teachers have revised their curses in order to include the subject of comfort women (and other war-related topics), even though schools and school districts do not always welcome the modification of traditional curricula.[18]

NOTES

1. The term "sexual slavery" would be more accurate than "comfort women." In this paper, however, I generally employ the latter term because it has been the one most often used. The terminology has been controversial in Japan. The term *jugun-ianfu* ("war comfort women") was once used commonly, but recently the term *gun-ianfu* ("military comfort women") has come to be seen as more suitable. These terms also appear in this chapter, depending on the context.

2. Toshiyuki Tanaka, "Naze Beigun wa Jugun Ianfu Mondai o Mushi Shitanoka" (Why Did the U.S. Forces Ignore the Issue of War Comfort Women?), *Sekai*, no. 627 (1996): 174–83, and no. 628 (1996): 270–79.

3. Yoshiko Nozaki and Hiromitsu Inokuchi, "Japanese Education, Nationalism, and Ienaga Saburo's Court Challenges," *Bulletin of Concerned Asian Scholars*, vol. 30, no. 2 (1998): 37–46. See also Yoshiko Nozaki, "Textbook Controversy and the Production of Public Truth: Japanese Education, Nationalism, and Saburo Ienaga's Court Challenges." Ph.D. dissertation, University of Wisconsin, 2000.

4. Some women were paid, others were not. A clear distinction between the two is problematic, however, since in either case women experienced severe gender and sexual oppression.

5. Yasuhiro Nakasone, "Nijusansai de Sanzen'nin no Soshikikan" (The General Commander of Three Thousand Men at the Age of Twenty-Three), in Takanori Matsuura, *Owarinaki Kaigun* (The Navy That Never Ends) (Tokyo: Bunkahoso Kaihatsu Senta, 1978), 98.

6. This chapter can only refer to a few of the great number of volumes and articles on the subject. See the *Bulletin of Concerned Asian Scholars*, vol. 36, no. 4 (1994), for a list of publications dealing with this topic and the featured article, Kazuko Watanabe, "Militarism, Colonialism, and the Trafficking of Women: 'Comfort Women' Forced into Sexual Labor for Japanese Soldiers." See also *positions east asia cultural critique*, vol. 5, no. 1 (1997), which is a special issue entitled "The Comfort Women: Colonialism, War, and Sex." Recent significant publications include: Laura Hein, "Savage Irony: The Imaginative Power of the Military Comfort Women in the 1990s," *Gender and History*, vol. 11, no. 2 (1999): 336–72; Maria Henson, *Comfort Woman* (Lanham: Rowman and Littlefield, 1999); Yuki Tanaka, *Comfort Women: What Our Fathers Did Not Tell Us* (New York: Routledge, forthcoming); and Yoshiaki Yoshimi, *Military Comfort Women*, trans. Suzanne O'Brien (New York: Columbia University Press, forthcoming).

7. For example, as of 1998, approximately 31,500 teachers teach social studies at junior high schools (grades 7–9), and approximately 82 percent of them are men. See Monbusho (Ministry of Education, Japan), "Heisei 10-nendo Gakko Kyoin Tokei Chose Hokokusho," in *Report on Statistical Research of Schoolteachers in the 1998–1999 Fiscal Year* (Tokyo: Okurasho Insstusukyoku, 1999), 8, 90.

8. Kiyoko Ihara, "Jugonen Senso: Jugun Ianfu wo Toriagete" (The Fifteen-year War: Teaching about the War Comfort Women), *Rekishi Chiri Kyoiku*, no. 506 (1993): 89.

9. Fumiko Kawada, "Jyo: Chugakusei ni koso Oshietai 'Ianfu' Mondai" (Introduction: The Comfort Women We Would Like to Teach Especially to Junior High School Students), in Fumiko Kawada, ed., Jugyo *"Jugun Ianfu": Rekishi Kyoiku to Sei Kyoiku karano Apurochi* (Teaching about "War Comfort Women": Approaches from History Education and Sex Education) (Tokyo: Kyoikushiryo Shuppankai, 1998), 10–11.

10. Hajime Sato, "'Ai, Jugun Ianfu' Hi no Sakebi" (The Cry of the Monument of Grief for "War Comfort Women"), *Rekishi Chiri Kyoiku*, no. 524 (1994): 120.

11. Sumie Tsuzuki, "Heiwa Gakushu to Sei Kyoiku no Tsumikasane no nakade" (Through the Accumulation Peace Education and Sex Education), in Kawada, Jugyo "Jugun Ianfu," 48–49.

12. Tsuzuki, "Heiwa Gakushu to Sei Kyoiku," 50–59.

13. Tadaaki Suzuki, "Junanassi no Haru o Kaeshite: Jugonen Senso to 'Jugun Ianfu' Mondai" (Return the Spring of Life of Seventeen-Year-Olds: The Fifteen-Year War and the Issue of "War Comfort Women"), in Kawada, Jugyo *"Jugun Ianfu,"* 63–70.

14. Takuji Yoshida, "Kokosei ga Tsukuru 'Jugun Ianfu' Gakushu" (Learning of "War Comfort Women" Developed by High School Students), in Kawata, *Jyugyo Jugun Ianfu*, 146–55.

15. Masso Yamada, "Sei Kyoiku wo Dodai nisuete" (Based on Sex Education), in Norio Ishide et al., eds., *"Nihongun Ianfu" wo do Oshieruka* (How to Teach about "Japanese Military Comfort Women") (Tokyo: Nashinokisha, 1997), 35

16. Suzuki, "Junanasai no Haru o Kaeshite," 77.

17. Joan Wallach Scott, *Gender and the Politics of History* (New York: Columbia University Press, 1988), 5.

18. Unfortunately, since the late 1990s a right-wing nationalist backlash has taken place, which is important to be reported internationally. I would, however, like to leave it for my future work. See also Yoshiko Nozaki, Japanese Politics and the History Textbook Controversy, 1982–2001. *International Journal of Educational Research*, 37.6&7 (2002): 603–622.

PART VIII

POPULAR CULTURE

Most of the chapters in this book have examined gender and other relations of inequality primarily in terms of peoples' lived experiences within social institutions such as families, workplaces, and schools. However, the arena of beliefs and values is also of crucial importance. Take, for example, the recent debates about sexual violence in media, about sex education in schools, about "family values," and about same-sex marriages. To be sure, the results of these debates will have a real impact on peoples' lives within social institutions. But the terrain of these debates is largely the arena of ideas, values, and symbols. And one of the most dynamic places in which people learn, contest, and forge values and beliefs is in the vast arena of popular culture. In this part, the articles reflect on how the magazines we read, the music we listen to, and the internet sites that we frequent are cultural creations through which dominant values are often imposed on people. But they may also become arenas in which these values are contested and new values forged.

Dominant cultural beliefs about and media images of subordinated groups—be they women, racialized or colonized "others," working-class people, or sexual minorities—tend to obscure, and thus legitimize, the privileges of dominant groups. In the first article in this section, Barry Glassner shows how widespread media-driven fears of black men in the United States tend to obscure the actual dangers that are faced *by* black boys and men. Glassner examines the public furor over violence in "gangsta rap" music, and concludes that "fear mongers project onto black men precisely what slavery, poverty, educational deprivation, and discrimination have ensured that they do not have—great power and influence." In the next article, Catherine A. Lutz and Jane L. Collins argue that for white U.S. readers, *National Geographic* has provided an opportunity to gaze upon the bodies and lives of non-Western women in ways that reveal white middle-class women's ambivalence about motherhood, sexuality, and wage labor. Although millions of readers might think of *National Geographic* as their window on the world, Lutz and Collins suggest that the ways the magazine presents non-Western women may tell us more about ourselves than about the "other."

Dominant imagery and symbols that are continually reiterated in popular culture—think, for instance, of the powerful, avenging white male soldier in movies, or the familiar tropes of heterosexual romance in popular music—are powerful in the ways they shape and constrain our thoughts, desires, fears, and identities. In recent years it has become commonplace among those who study popular culture to argue that we need to go beyond simply analyzing and criticizing the apparently sexist, racist, and/or homophobic *content* of media texts and to look also at what people *do* with popular culture. People are not automatons; we do not all respond to popular culture images in uniform ways. Susan Jane Gilman draws on her own childhood memories of playing ambivalently with Barbie and other dolls to level a stinging critique on the ways these dolls "quickly become the defining criteria" for beauty and for little girls' sense of status and worth. Gilman notes that the pain that accompanies this realization can be more acute for "other" girls like she and her friends—urban, Jewish, black, Asian, and Latina girls. But she notes that many girls develop their own modes of playing with Barbie—including decapitation! And she ends with a humorous list of Barbie dolls that she would like to see—dolls that speak to a spectrum of girls' body types, sexualities, ethnicities, and religions. Next, Mimi Schippers draws on her research in alternative hard rock youth subcultures to reflect on how different kinds of music constrain or enable different expressions of gender and sexuality. Mainstream rock music, Schippers argues, tends to structure conventional relations of heterosexuality and gender. Alternative hard rock is a context that facilitates "gender maneuvering," characterized by broader and more fluid relations of gender and sexuality. Finally, Lori Kendall examines an online community, and she argues convincingly that this is an emergent context for new forms of gender maneuvering for white men who define themselves as "nerds." While these men rail about, and often reject, the dominant form of masculinity performed by more "successful" (non-nerdy) men, they continue to construct their identities in terms of heterosexuality and talk of women "as foreign beings who like abuse." Through ironic humor, these men create a culture that distances them both from other men and from women.

45

Black Men

How to Perpetuate Prejudice Without Really Trying

BARRY GLASSNER

Journalists, politicians, and other opinion leaders foster fears about particular groups of people both by what they play up and what they play down. Consider Americans' fears of black men. These are perpetuated by the excessive attention paid to dangers that a small percentage of African-American men create for other people, and by a relative *lack* of attention to dangers that a majority of black men face themselves.

The dangers to black men recede from public view whenever people paint color-blind pictures of hazards that particularly threaten African-American men: discussions of disease trends that fail to mention that black men are four times more likely to be infected with the AIDS virus and twice as likely to suffer from prostate cancer and heart disease than are white men; reports about upturns in teen suicide rates that neglect to note evidence that the rate for white males crept up only 22 percent between 1980 and 1995 while the rate for black males jumped 146 percent; or explorations of the gap between what middle class Americans earn and the expenses of maintaining a middle-class lifestyle that fail to point out that the problem is more acute for black men. (College-educated black men earn only as much as white men with high school diplomas.)[1]

The most egregious omissions occur in the coverage of crime. Many more black men are casualties of crime than are perpetrators, but their victimization does not attract the media spotlight the way their crimes do. Thanks to profuse coverage of violent crime on local TV news programs, "night after night, black men rob, rape, loot, and pillage in the living room," Caryl Rivers, a journalism instructor at Boston University, has remarked. Scores of studies document that when it comes to *victims* of crime, however, the media pay disproportionately more attention to whites and women.[2]

On occasion the degree of attention becomes so skewed that reporters start seeing patterns where none exist—the massively publicized "wave" of tourist murders in Florida in the early 1990s being a memorable example. By chance alone every decade or two there should be an unusually high number of tourists murdered in Florida, the statistician Arnold Barnett of MIT demonstrated in a journal article. The media uproar was an "overreaction to statistical noise," he wrote. The upturn that so caught reporters' fancy—ten tourists killed in a year—was labeled a crime wave because the media chose to label it as such. Objectively speaking, ten murders out of 41 million visitors did not even constitute a ripple, much less a wave, especially considering that at least 97 percent of all victims of crime in Florida are Floridians. Although the Miami area had the highest crime rate in the nation during this period, it was not tourists who had most cause for worry. One study showed that British, German, and Canadian tourists who flock to Florida each year to avoid winter weather were more than 70 times more likely to be victimized at home. The typical victim of crime in Florida, though largely invisible in the news, was young, local, and black or Hispanic.[3] . . .

Drug violence, like almost every other category of violence, is not an equal opportunity danger. It principally afflicts young people from poor minority communities, and above all, young black men. But reporters and politicos never seem to lack for opportunities to perpetuate the myth of indiscriminate victimization. "Random Killings Hit a High—All Have 'Realistic' Chance of Being Victim, Says FBI," read the headline in *USA Today*'s story in 1994 about a government report that received big play that year. Had the academics and elected officials who supplied reporters with brooding comments about the report looked more closely at its contents, however, they would have learned that it was misleading. As Richard Moran, a sociology professor at Mount Holyoke College, subsequently pointed out in a commentary on National Public Radio, the FBI report made random killings seem more prevalent than they are by lumping together two distinct categories of murders: those that remained unsolved, and those committed by strangers. Many an unsolved murder later turns out to have been committed by a relative or other acquaintance of the victim.[4]

To suggest that all Americans have a realistic chance of being a victim of homicide is to heighten already elevated anxieties among people who face little risk. In spite of the impression given by stories like the one in *Time* titled "Danger in the Safety Zone: As Violence Spreads into Small Towns, Many Americans Barricade Themselves," which focused on random murders in several hamlets throughout the country, tens of millions of Americans live in places where there hasn't been a murder in years, and most of the rest of us live in towns and neighborhoods where murder is a rare occurrence.[5]

Who *does* stand a realistic chance of being murdered? You guessed it: minority males. A black man is about eighteen times more likely to be murdered than is a white woman. All told, the murder rate for black men is double that of American soldiers in World War II. And for black men between the ages of fifteen and thirty, violence is the single leading cause of death.[6]

OF DOGS AND MEN

David Krajicek, a journalism instructor at Columbia University, recalls a term that he and his editor used when he worked as a crime reporter for the *New York Daily News* in the 1980s. The term was *unbless*—unidentified black males. "Unbless," Krajicek notes, "rarely rated a story unless three or four turned up at the same location. We paid little attention to these routine murders because the police paid little attention."[7]

Police inattention is one of several factors that journalists accurately cite to account for why white crime victims receive more media attention than black victims. Journalists also cite complaints from African-American leaders about the press paying too much attention to problems and pathologies in black communities. But are crime victims the best candidates to overlook in the service of more positive coverage? A host of studies indicate that by downplaying the suffering of victims and their families the media do a disservice to minority neighborhoods where those victims live. Criminologists have documented that the amount of coverage a crime victim receives affects how much attention police devote to the case and the willingness of prosecutors to accept plea bargains. As a rule, the more coverage, the more likely that an assailant will be kept behind bars, unable to do further harm to the victim or community. In addition, when a neighborhood's crime victims are portrayed *as* victims—sympathetically and without blame, as humans rather than as statistics—people living in other parts of the city are more inclined to support improved social services for the area, which in turn can reduce the crime rate.[8]

Underreporting of black victims also has the effect of making white victims appear more ubiquitous than they are, thereby are, thereby fueling whites' fears of black criminals, something that benefits neither race. Helen Benedict, a professor of journalism at Columbia University, has documented that rapes of white women by black men—which constitute a tiny proportion of all rapes—receive considerable media attention. In a separate study of women's concerns about crime Esther Madriz, a sociology professor at Hunter College, discovered that stories in the news media "reinforce a vision of society in which black men are foremost among women's fears."[9]

Another explanation journalists and editors give for their relative neglect of black victims might be called the Journalism 101 defense. Those of us who took an introductory journalism course in college remember the teacher pounding into our cerebrums the famous dictate attributed to John Bogart, city editor of the *New York Sun* in the 1880s: "When a dog bites a man that is not news, when a man bites a dog, that is news." Everyone *expects* black crime victims, the argument goes, so their plight isn't newsworthy. Here is how a writer for the *Los Angeles Times,* Scott Harris, characterized the thoughts that go through reporters' and editors' minds as they ponder how much attention, if any, to accord to a city's latest homicide: "Another 15-year-old shot to death? Ho hum. Was he an innocent bystander? What part of town? Any white people involved?"[10]

As heartless and bigoted as this reasoning may sound, actually there would be nothing objectionable about it if news organizations applied the man-bites-dog principle universally. Obviously they do not; otherwise, there would never be stories about crimes committed by black men, since no one considers black perpetrators novel or unexpected.[11]

My friend David Shaw, media critic at the *Los Angeles Times,* offers a simpler explanation for the scant attention to black victims. To stay in business newspapers must cater to the interests of their subscribers, few of whom live in inner-city minority neighborhoods. The same market forces result in paltry coverage of foreign news in most American newspapers, Shaw suggests.[12]

Now *there's* a study someone should do: compare the amount of attention and empathy accorded by the U.S. press during the 1990s to black men shot down in American cities to, say, Bosnians killed in that country's civil war. I wouldn't be surprised if the Bosnians fared better. The tendency to slight black victims extends even to coverage of undeniably newsworthy crimes such as shootings of police by fellow officers. In 1996, after a white New York City police officer, Peter Del-Debbio, was convicted of shooting Desmond Robinson, a black plainclothes transit officer in the back, wounding his kidneys, liver, lungs, and heart, reporters and columnists evidenced great sympathy for Del-Debbio. They characterized him as having made an innocent mistake and suffering overwhelming remorse. The agony of Robinson and his family, by contrast, received more modest attention. Few reporters seriously questioned—and some overtly endorsed—the official spin from the district attorney, mayor, and defense attorneys that the shooting had nothing to do with race and was largely the victim's fault—even though in testimony Del-Debbio recalled having reacted not to seeing just any man with a gun but "a male black with a gun."[13]

While some writers made note of the fact that black officers say their white colleagues are quick to fire at African Americans working undercover because they view them as suspects, no reporter, the best I can determine, investigated the issue. When Richard Goldstein, a media critic for the *Village Voice,* reviewed the coverage of the shooting he found that only the *Daily News*—not the *Times* or *Post*—made note of the fact that, since 1941, twenty black police officers in New York had been shot by white colleagues. During that time not a single white officer had been shot by a black cop. "Imagine," wrote Goldstein, "the shock-horror if 20 female officers had been shot by male cops. But when it comes to race, the more obvious the pattern the more obscure it seems."[14] . . .

MAKERS OF THE NATION'S MOST HAZARDOUS MUSIC

Fear mongers project onto black men precisely what slavery, poverty, educational deprivation, and discrimination have ensured that they do not have—great power and influence.

After two white boys opened fire on students and teachers at a schoolyard in Jonesboro, Arkansas, in

1998 politicians, teachers, and assorted self-designated experts suggested—with utter seriousness—that black rap musicians had inspired one of them to commit the crime. A fan of rappers such as the late Tupac Shakur, the thirteen-year-old emulated massacrelike killings described in some of their songs, we were told. Never mind that, according to a minister who knew him, the Jonesboro lad also loved religious music and sang for elderly residents at local nursing homes. By the late 1990s the ruinous power of rap was so taken for granted, people could blame rappers for almost any violent or misogynistic act anywhere.[15]

So dangerous were so-called gangsta rappers taken to be, they could be imprisoned for the lyrics on their albums. Free speech and the First Amendment be damned—when Shawn Thomas, a rapper known to his fans as C-Bo, released his sixth album in 1998 he was promptly arrested and put behind bars for violating the terms of his parole for an earlier conviction. The parole condition Thomas had violated required him not to make recordings that "promote the gang lifestyle or are anti-law enforcement."

Thomas's new album, "Til My Casket Drops," contained powerful protest lyrics against California governor Pete Wilson. "Look how he did Polly Klaas/Used her death and her family name/So he can gain more votes and political fame/It's a shame that I'm the one they say is a monster." The album also contained misogynistic and antipolice lyrics. Thomas refers to women as whores and bitches, and he recommends if the police "try to pull you over, shoot 'em in the face."[16]

Lyrics like these have been the raw material for campaigns against rappers for more than a decade—campaigns that have resulted not only in the incarceration of individual rappers but also in commitments from leading entertainment conglomerates such as Time Warner and Disney, as well as the state of Texas, not to invest in companies that produce gangsta albums. William Bennett and C. Delores Tucker, leaders of the antirap campaigns, have had no trouble finding antipolice and antiwomen lyrics to quote in support of their claim that "nothing less is at stake than civilization" if rappers are not rendered silent. So odious are the lyrics, that rarely do politicians or journalists stop to ask what qualifies Bennett to lead a moralistic crusade on behalf of America's minority youth. Not only has he opposed funding for the nation's leader in quality children's programming (the Public Broadcasting Corporation), he has urged that "illegitimate" babies be taken from their mothers and put in orphanages.[17]

What was Delores Tucker, a longtime Democratic party activist, doing lending her name as coauthor to antirap articles that Bennett used to raise money for his right-wing advocacy group, Empower America? Tucker would have us believe, as she exclaimed in an interview in *Ebony,* that "as a direct result" of dirty rap lyrics, we have "little boys raping little girls." But more reliable critics have rather a different take. For years they have been trying to call attention to the satiric and self-caricaturing side of rap's salacious verses, what Nelson George, the music critic, calls "cartoon machismo."[18]

Back in 1990, following the release of *Nasty As They Wanna Be,* an album by 2 Live Crew, and the band's prosecution in Florida on obscenity charges, Henry Louis Gates confided in an op-ed in the *New York Times* that when he first heard the album he "bust out laughing." Unlike *Newsweek* columnist George Will, who described the album as "extreme infantilism and menace . . . [a] slide into the sewer," Gates viewed 2 Live Crew as "acting out, to lively dance music, a parodic exaggeration of the age-old stereotypes of the oversexed black female and male." Gates noted that the album included some hilarious spoofs of blues songs, the black power movement, and familiar advertising slogans of the period ("Tastes great!" "Less filling!"). The rap group's lewd nursery rhymes were best understood, Gates argued, as continuing an age-old Western tradition of bawdy satire.[19]

Not every informed and open-minded follower of rap has been as upbeat as Gates, of course. Some have strongly criticized him, in fact, for seeming to vindicate performers who refer to women as "cunts," "bitches," and "hos," or worse, who appear to justify their rape and murder, as did a track on the 2 Live Crew album that contained the boast, "I'll . . . bust your pussy then break your backbone."

Kimberlé Williams Crenshaw, a professor of law at UCLA, wrote in an essay that she was shocked rather than amused by *Nasty As They Wanna Be.* Black women should not have to tolerate misogyny, Crenshaw argued, whether or not the music is meant to be laughed at or has artistic value—both of which she granted about *Nasty.* But something else also concerned Crenshaw: the singling out of black male performers for vilification. Attacks on rap artists at once reflect and reinforce deep and enduring fears about the sexuality and physical strength of black men, she suggests. How else, Crenshaw asks, can one explain why 2 Live Crew were the first group in the history of the nation to be prosecuted on obscenity charges for a musical recording, and one of only a few ever tried for a live performance? Around this same time, she observes, Madonna acted out simulated group sex and the seduction of a priest on stage and in her music videos, and on Home Box Office programs the comic Andrew Dice Clay was making comments every bit as obscene and misogynistic as any rapper.[20]

The hypocrisy of those who single out rap singers as especially sexist or violent was starkly—and comically—demonstrated in 1995, when presidential candidate Bob Dole denounced various rap albums and movies that he considered obscene and then recommended certain films as wholesome, "friendly to the family" fare. Included among the latter was Arnold Schwarzenegger's *True Lies,* in which every major female character is called a "bitch." While in real life Arnold may be a virtuous Republican, in the movie his wife strips, and he puts her through hell when he thinks she might be cheating on him. In one gratuitous scene she is humiliated and tortured for twenty minutes of screen time. Schwarzenegger's character also kills dozens of people in sequences more graphically violent than a rapper could describe with mere words.[21]

Even within the confines of American popular music, rappers are far from the first violently sexist fictional heroes. Historians have pointed out that in country music there is a long tradition of men doing awful things to women. Johnny Cash, in an adaptation of the frontier ballad "Banks of the Ohio" declares, "I murdered the only woman I loved/Because she would not marry me." In "Attitude Adjustment" Hank Williams Jr. gives a girlfriend "adjustment on the top of her head." Bobby Bare, in "If That Ain't Love," tells a woman, "I called you a name and I gave you a whack/Spit in your eye and gave your wrist a twist/And if that ain't love what is."

Rock music too has had its share of men attacking women, and not only in heavy metal songs. In "Down By the River" amiable Neil Young sings of shooting his "baby." And the song "Run for Your Life," in which a woman is stalked and threatened with death if she is caught with another man, was a Beatles hit.[22]

JUST A THUG

After Tupac Shakur was gunned down in Las Vegas in 1996 at the age of twenty-five much of the coverage suggested he had been a victim of his own raps—even a deserving victim. "Rap Performer Who Personified Violence, Dies," read a headline in the *New York Times.* " 'What Goes 'Round . . .': Superstar Rapper Tupac Shakur Is Gunned Down in an Ugly Scene Straight Out of His Lyrics," the headline in *Time* declared. In their stories reporters recalled that Shakur's lyrics, which had come under fire intermittently throughout his brief career by the likes of William Bennett, Delores Tucker, and Bob Dole, had been directly implicated in two previous killings. In 1992 Vice President Dan Quayle cited an antipolice song by Shakur as a motivating force behind the shooting of a Texas state trooper. And in 1994 prosecutors in Milwaukee made the same claim after a police officer was murdered.[23]

Why, when white men kill, doesn't anyone do a *J'accuse* of Tennessee Ernie Ford or Johnny Cash, whose oddly violent classics are still played on country music stations? In "Sixteen Tons" Ford croons, "If you see me comin'/Better step aside/A lotta men didn't/A lotta men died," and in "Folsom Prison Blues" Cash crows, "I shot a man in Reno just to watch him die." Yet no one has suggested, as journalists and politicians did about Shakur's and 2 Live Crew's lyrics, that these lines overpower all the others in Ford's and Cash's songbooks.[24]

Any young rap fan who heard one of Shakur's antipolice songs almost certainly also heard one or more of his antiviolence raps, in which he recounts the horrors of gangster life and calls for black men to stop killing. "And they say/It's the white man I should fear/But it's my own kind/Doin' all the killin' here," Shakur laments on one of his songs.[25]

Many of Shakur's raps seemed designed to inspire responsibility rather than violence. One of his most popular, "Dear Mama," was part thank-you letter to his mother for raising him on her own, and part explanation of bad choices he had made as an adolescent. "All along I was looking for a father—he was gone/I hung around with the thugs/And even though they sold drugs/They showed a young brother love," Shakur rapped. In another of his hits, "Papa'z Song," he recalled, all the more poignantly, having "had to play catch by myself/what a sorry sight."[26]

Shakur's songs, taken collectively, reveal "a complex and sometimes contradictory figure," as Jon Pereles, a music critic for the *New York Times,* wrote in an obituary. It was a key point missed by much of the media, which ran photos of the huge tattoo across Shakur's belly—"THUG LIFE"—but failed to pass along what he said it stood for: "The Hate You Give Little Infants Fucks Everyone." And while many mentioned that he had attended the High School of Performing Arts in Baltimore, few acknowledged the lasting impact of that education. "It influences all my work. I really like stuff like 'Les Miserables' and 'Gospel at Colonus,'" Shakur told a *Los Angeles Times* interviewer in 1995. He described himself as "the kind of guy who is moved by a song like Don McLean's 'Vincent,' that one about Van Gogh. The lyric on that song is so touching. That's how I want to make my songs feel."[27]

After Tupac Shakur's death a writer in the *Washington Post* characterized him as "stupid" and "misguided" and accused him of having "committed the unpardonable sin of using his immense poetic talents to degrade and debase the very people who needed his positive words most—his fans." To judge by their loving tributes to him in calls to radio stations, prayer vigils, and murals that appeared on walls in inner cities following his death, many of those fans apparently held a different view. Ernest Hardy of the *L.A. Weekly,* an alternative paper, was probably closer to the mark when he wrote of Shakur: "What made him important and forged a bond with so many of his young black (especially black male) fans was that he was a signifier trying to figure out what he signified. He knew he lived in a society that still didn't view him as human, that projected its worst fears onto him; he had to decide whether to battle that or to embrace it."[28]

Readers of the music magazine *Vibe* had seen Shakur himself describe this conflict in an interview not long before his death. "What are you at war with?" the interviewer asked. "Different things at different times," Shakur replied. "My own heart sometimes. There's two niggas inside me. One wants to live in peace, and the other won't die unless he's free."[29]

It seems to me at once sad, inexcusable, and entirely symptomatic of the culture of fear that the only version of Tupac Shakur many Americans knew was a frightening and unidimensional caricature. The opening lines from Ralph Ellison's novel, *Invisible Man,* still ring true nearly half a century after its publication. "I am an invisible man," Ellison wrote. "No, I am not a spook like those who haunted Edgar Allan Poe; nor am I one of your Hollywood-movie ectoplasms. I am a man of substance, of flesh and bone, fiber and liquids—and I might even be said to possess a mind. I am invisible, understand, simply because people refuse to see me."[30]

NOTES

1. Glenn Loury, "Unequalized," *New Republic,* 6 April 1998, pp. 10–11; Janet Hook, "Clinton Offers Plan to Close Health Gap," *Los Angeles Times,* 22 February 1998, p. A20; Pam Belluck, "Black Youth's Rate of Suicide Rising Sharply," *New York Times,* 20 March 1998, p. A1. See also David Shaffer et al., "Worsening Suicide Rate in Black Teenagers," *American Journal of Psychiatry* 151 (1994): 1810–12. On my selection and use of statistics see note 2 in the Introduction.

2. Caryl Rivers, *Slick Spins and Fractured Facts* (New York: Columbia University Press, 1996), p. 161; David Krajicek, *Scooped* (New York: Columbia University Press, 1998); Robert Elias, "Official Stories," *Humanist* 54 (1994): 3–8: Bill Kovach, "Opportunity in the Racial Divide," *Nieman Reports* 49 (1995): 2; Franklin Gilliam, Shanto Iyengar et al., "Crime in Black and White," Working Paper, Center for American Politics and Public Policy, UCLA, September 1995; Mark Fitzgerald, "Covering Crime in Black and White," *Editor and Publisher,* 10 September 1994, pp. 12–13; Carey Quan Gelernter, "A Victim's Worth," *Seattle Times,* 28 June 1994, p. E1; Suzan Revah, "Paying More Attention to White Crime Victims," *American Journalism Review* (1995): 10–11; Bruce Shapiro, "One Violent Crime," *Nation,* 3 April 1995, pp. 437, 445–52; Bruce Shapiro, "Unkindest Cut," *New Statesman* 8 (14 April 1995): 23; Gregory Freeman, "Media Bias?" *St. Louis Post-Dispatch,* 14 November 1993, p. B4; Debra Saunders, "Heeding the Ghost of Ophelia," *San Francisco Chronicle,* 4 September, 1995, p. A19.

3. Arnold Barnett, "How Numbers Can Trick You," *Technology Review* 97 (1994): 38–44; Karen Smith, "Tourism Industry Tries

to Reduce Visitors' Fears," *Ann Arbor News,* 16 January 1994, p. D5. See also Kim Cobb, "Media May Be Fanning a New Deadly Crime," *Houston Chronicle,* 18 September 1993, p. A1; Bill Kaczor, "Crimes Against Tourists Worry Florida Officials," *Ann Arbor News,* 24 February 1993, p. A7; James Bernstein, "Violence Threatens to Kill Florida's Winter Vacation Business," 2 November 1993, p. A1.

4. Robert Davis and Sam Meddis, "Random Killings Hit a High," *USA Today,* 5 December 1994, p. A1; Richard Moran, "Morning Edition," 18 April 1996. The FBI report was the Uniform Crime Report for 1993.

5. Jill Smolowe, "Danger in the Safety Zone," *Time,* 23 August 1993, pp. 28–33 (quote from issue's cover).

6. Ray Surette, "Predator Criminals As Media Icons," in G. Barak, ed., *Media, Process, and the Social Construction of Crime* (New York: Garland, 1994), pp. 131–58; Philip Jenkins, *Using Murder* (New York: Aldine de Gruyter, 1994), p. 156; Bureau of Justice Statistics, "Highlights from 20 Years of Surveying Crime Victims" (NCJ-144525), Washington, DC, 1993; National Center for Health Statistics, *Vital Statistics of the United States* (reports during early and mid-1990s), Washington, DC; Dave Shiflett, "Crime in the South," *The Oxford American* (Spring 1996): 136–41.

7. Krajicek, *Scooped,* p. 102. On how the news media perpetuates negative images of African Americans see also Mikal Muharrar, "Media Blackface," *Extra,* September 1998, pp. 6–8; Dennis Rome, "Stereotyping by the Media," in C. R. Mann and M. Zatz, eds., *Images of Color, Images of Crime* (Los Angeles: Roxbury, 1998), pp. 85–96.

8. Ted Rohrlich and Frederic Tulsky, "Not All L.A. Murders Are Equal," *Los Angeles Times,* 3 December 1996, pp. A1, 14–15; Gelernter, "Victim's Worth"; Shapiro, "Onn Violent Crime"; Gilliam, et al., "Crime in Black and White"; Jerome Skolnick, "Police Accountability and the Media," *American Bar Foundation Research Journal* (1984): 521–57; Renée Kasinsky, "Patrolling the Facts," in Barak, ed., *Media, Process, and the Social Construction of Crime,* pp. 203–34; Zhongdang Pan and Gerald Kosicki, "Assessing News Media Influences on Whites' Race Policy Preferences," *Communication Research* 23 (1996): 147–79. See also Van Jones, "Lessons from a Killing," *Extra,* May 1998, pp. 23–24.

9. Helen Benedict, *Virgin or Vamp: How the Press Covers Sex Crimes* (New York: Oxford University Press, 1992); Esther Madriz, *Nothing Bad Happens to Good Girls* (Berkeley: University of California Press, 1997), p. 155.

10. Scott Harris, "The Color of News," *Los Angeles Times,* 31 December 1995, p. B1. See also David Pritchard, "Race, Homicide and Newspapers," *Journalism Quarterly* 62 (1985): 500–507.

11. See Gilliam, et al., "Crime in Black and White."

12. Shaw made the comments during conversations in 1998. See also his "Minorities and the Press," *Los Angeles Times,* 11 December 1990.

13. Richard Goldstein, "What's Race Got to Do With It?" *Village Voice,* 9 April 1996, pp. 18–19.

14. Ibid. My depiction of the reporting relies on Goldstein's analysis of the *New York Post* and other outlets, coupled with my own review of articles on the shooting and trial published in the *New York Times, Newsday,* and *New York Daily News.*

15. Marna Walthall, "Jonesboro Teacher says Rap Music, School Killings May Be Linked," *Dallas Morning News,* 17 June 1998, p. A5; Timothy Egan, "From Adolescent Angst to Shooting Up Schools," *New York Times,* 14 June 1998, pp. A1, 20; ABC, "World News Tonight," 16 June 1998.

16. Steve Hochman, "Rap Artist Is Jailed over Anti-Police Lyrics," *Los Angeles Times* 4 March 1998, p. A3; Benjamin Adair, "Jailhouse Rap," *L.A. Weekly,* 13 March 1998, p. 18 (contains lyrics); Steve Hochman, "A Rapper's Risky Challenge," *Los Angeles Times,* 21 February 1998, pp. F1, 20.

17. Investment boycotts: Eric Boehlert, "Culture Skirmishes," *Rolling Stone,* 21 August 1997, pp. 29, 32; David Hinckley, "Rap Takes the Rap for Our Real Problems," *New York Daily News,* 4 June 1996, p. 33 ("civilization" quote). Tucker and Bennett Judith Weinraub, "Delores Tucker, Gangsta Buster," *Washington Post,* 29 November 1995, C1 (contains Tucker quote); William Bennett, "Reflections on the Moynihan Report," *American Enterprise,* January 1995, pp. 28–32; Frank Rich, "Hypocrite Hit Parade," *New York Times,* 13 December 1995, p. A23; Peter Range, "MM Interview; William J. Bennett," *Modern Maturity* (March 1995): 26–30.

18. Nelson George, *Buppies, B-Boys, Baps, and Bohos: Notes on Post-Soul Black Culture* (New York: HarperCollins, 1992), p. 156; Kevin Chappell, "What's Wrong (and Right) About Black Music," *Ebony,* September 1995, p. 25. For an example of the collaboration that was used for fundraising see William Bennett, Joe Lierberman, and C. DeLores Tucker, "Rap Rubbish," *USA Today,* 6 June 1996, p. A13, which ends with a toll-free telephone number. Those of us who dialed it got a recording that invited us to press 1 for information about the dangers of rap music, 2 for literature on a flat-rate tax proposal, or 3 to contribute money to Empower America. On political alliances against rap see Leola Johnson, "Silencing Gangsta Rap," *Temple Political & Civil Rights Law Review* (October, 1993): no pages listed.

19. George F. Will, "America's Slide into the Sewer," *Newsweek,* 30 July 1990, p. 64; Henry Louis Gates, Jr., "2 Live Crew, Decoded," *New York Times,* 19 June 1990, p. A23. "Laughing" quote in Kimberlé Williams Crenshaw, "Beyond Racism and Misogyny," in M. Matusda et al., *Words That Wound* (Boulder, CO: Westview Press, 1993), pp. 111–32. See also James Jones, "Gangsta Rap Reflects an Urban Jungle," *USA Today,* 2 January 1991, p. D13; Hinckley, "Rap Takes the Rap," p. 33; Nelson George, *Hip Hop America* (New York: Viking, 1998).

20. Crenshaw, "Beyond Racism." On the extent of sexism in rap and internal dialogues among rappers about the matter see Tricia Rose, *Black Noise* (Hanover, NH: Weslyan University Press, 1994), and Tricia Rose's review of *A Sister Without Sisters* by Sister Souljah, *Women's Review of Books,* June 1995, pp. 21–22. On overt homophobia and covert homoeroticism in rap see Touré, "Hiphop's Closet," *Village Voice,* 27 August 1996, pp. 59, 66. On the racist subtext in attacks on rap see Amy Binder, "Constructing racial rhetoric," *American Sociological Review* 58 (1993): 753–67; Tricia Rose, "Rap Music and the Demonization of Young Black Males," *USA*

Today Magazine, May 1994, pp. 35–36; Jon Pareles, "On rap Symbolism and Fear," *New York Times,* 2 February 1992, p. B1; Todd Boyd, "Woodstock Was Whitestock," *Chicago Tribune,* 28 August 1994, p. 36.

21. On Dole's remarks see Linda Stasi's column, *New York Daily News,* 5 June 1995, p. 3; "Dole Blasts 'Depravity' in Film, Music," *Facts on File World News Digest,* 8 June 1995.

22. Edward G. Armstrong, "The Rhetoric of Violence in Rap and County Music," *Sociological Inquiry* 63 (1993): 64–83; John Hamerlinck, "Killing Women: A Pop-Music Tradition," *Humanist* 55 (1995): 23.

23. Milwaukee and Texas incidents: Rogers Worthington, "Gangsta Rap Blamed for Cop's Killing," *Chicago Tribune,* 10 September 1994, p. 4; Elizabeth Sanger, "Change of Venue for Gangsta Rap Debate," *Newsday,* 28 June 1995, p. 31; Chuck Philips, "Texas Death Renews Debate over Violent Rap Lyrics," *Los Angeles Times,* 17 September 1992, p. A1; Jon Pareles, "Tupac Shakur, 25, Rap Performer Who Personified Violence, Dies," *New York Times,* 14 September 1996, pp. A1, 34. Other headline: David Van Biema, "'What Goes 'Round . . .'," *Time,* 23 September 1996, p. 40. Tucker continued to take on Shakur after his death: Johnnie Roberts, "Grabbing at a Dead Star," *Newsweek,* 1 September 1997, p. 48.

24. Ford and Cash songs quoted in Armstrong, "Rhetoric of Violence."

25. Quoted in "Obitnary: Tupac Shakur," *The Economist,* 21 September 1996.

26. Songs quoted in Christopher Farley, "From the Driver's Side," *Time,* 30 September 1996, p. 70; Donnell Alexander, "Do Thug Niggaz Go to Heaven?" *Village Voice,* 20 September 1996, p. 51.

27. Worthington, "Gangsta Rap"; Natasha Stovall, "Death Row," *Village Voice,* 24 September 1996, pp. 29–30 (contains definition of "THUG LIFE"); Chuck Philips, Q & A with Tupac Shakur, *Los Angeles Times,* 25 October 1995, p. F1. Songs quoted in Armstrong, "Rhetoric of Violence." Pereles quote from "Tupac Shakur." On rap being blamed see also Jon Pareles, "On Rap, Symbolism and Fear," *New York Times,* 2 February 1992, p. B1.

28. Kenneth Carroll, "A Rap Artist's Squandered Gift," *Washington Post* National Edition, 30 September 1996, p. 25; Ernest Hardy, "Do Thug Niggaz Go to Heaven," *L.A. Weekly,* 20 September 1996, p. 51. On the content and purposes of gangsta rap see also Eric Watts, "Gangsta Rap as Cultural Commodity," *Communication Studies* 48(1997): 42–58.

29. "All Eyes on Him," *Vibe,* February 1996.

30. Ralph Ellison, *Invisible Man* (New York: Random House, 1952), p. 1.

46

The Color of Sex

Postwar Photographic Histories of Race and Gender in National Geographic Magazine

CATHERINE A. LUTZ

JANE L. COLLINS

THE WOMEN OF THE WORLD

National Geographic photographs of the women of the world tell a story about the women of the United States over the post-World War II period. It is to issues of gender in White American readers' lives, such as debates over women's sexuality or whether women doing paid labor can mother their children adequately, that the pictures refer as much as to the lives of third world women. Seen in this way, the *National Geographic*'s women can be placed alongside the other women of American popular culture: the First lady, the woman draped over an advertisement's red sports car, the Barbie doll, the woman to whom the Hallmark Mother's Day card is addressed. Rather than treating the photos as simply images of women, we can set them in the context of a more complex cultural history of the period, with the sometimes radical changes it brought to the lives of the women who are the readers (or known to the male readers) of the magazine.

The photographs of *National Geographic* are indispensable to understanding issues of gender because the magazine is one of the very few popular venues trafficking in large numbers of images of Black women. While the photographs tell a story about cultural ideals of femininity, the narrative threads of gender and race are tightly bound up with each other. In the world at large, race and gender are clearly not separate systems, as Trinh (1989), Moore (1988), Sacks (1989), and others have reminded us.

For the overwhelmingly White readers of the *Geographic,* the dark-skinned women of distant regions serve as touchstones, giving lessons both positive and negative about what women are and should be (compare Botting 1988). Here, as else-where, the magazine plays with possibilities of the other as a flexible reflection—even a sort of fun-house mirror—for the self. The women of the world are portrayed in sometimes striking parallel to popular images of American womanhood of the various periods of the magazine's production—for instance, as mothers and beautiful objects. At certain times, with certain races of women, however, the *Geographic*'s other women provide a contrast to stereotypes of White American women—

they are presented as hard-working breadwinners in their communities.

As with American women in popular culture, Third World women are portrayed less frequently than men: one-quarter of the pictures we looked at focus primarily on women.[1] The situation has traditionally not been that different in the anthropological literature covering the non-Western world, and it may be amplified in both genres where the focus is on cultural difference or exoticism. Given the association between women and the natural world, men and things cultural (Ortner 1974), a magazine that aspires to describe the distinctive achievements of civilizations might be expected to highlight the world of men. But like the "people of nature" in the Fourth World, women have been treated as all the more precious for their nonutilitarian, nonrationalistic qualities. Photographs of women become one of the primary devices by which the magazine depicts "universal human values," and these include the values of family love and the appreciation of female beauty itself.[2] We turn to these two issues now, noting that each of them has had a consistent cultural content through the postwar period, during historical changes that give the images different emphases and form through the decades.

The motherhood of man. There is no more romantic set of photographs in the *Geographic* than those depicting the mothers of the world with their children. There is the exuberant picture showing the delight of a Kurd mother holding her infant. Filling much space, as an unusually high percentage of the magazine's mother-child pictures do, the photograph covers two pages despite the relative lack of information in it. Its classical composition and crisp, uncluttered message are similar to those in many such photos. They often suggest the Western tradition of madonna painting, and evoke the Mother's Day message: this relationship between mother and child, they say, is a timeless and sacred one, essentially and intensely loving regardless of social and historical context—the foundation of human social life rather than cultural difference. The family of man, these pictures might suggest, is first of all a mother-child unit, rather than a brotherhood of solidarity between adults.[3]

For the magazine staff and readers of the 1950s, there must have been even more power in these images than we see in them today. The impact of the photos would have come from the intense cultural and social pressures of middle-class women to see their most valued role as that of mother (Margolis 1984). The unusually strong pressure of this period is often explained as motivated by desires to place returning World War II veterans (and men in general) in those jobs available and by anxieties about the recent war horror and the future potential for a nuclear conflagration, which made the family seem a safe haven (May 1988). As a new cult of domesticity emerged, women were told—through both science and popular culture—that biology, morality, and the psychological health of the next generation required their commitment to full-time mothering. This ideological pressure persisted through the 1950s despite the rapid rise in female employment through the decade.

The idealization of the mother-child bond is seen in everything from the warm TV relationships of June Clever with Wally and the Beaver to the cover of a *Life* magazine issue of 1956 devoted to "The American Woman" showing a glowing portrait of a mother and daughter lovingly absorbed in each other; all of this is ultimately and dramatically reflected in the period's rapidly expanding birth rate. This idealization had its counterpoint in fear of the power women were given in the domestic domain. In both science and popular culture, the mother was criticized for being smothering, controlling, oversexualized, and, a bit later, overly permissive (Ehrenreich and English 1978, 1988).

The *National Geographic*'s treatment of children can be seen as an extension of these ideologies of motherhood and the family. As the "woman question" came to be asked more angrily in the late 1950s, there was a gradual erosion of faith in the innocence of the mother-infant bond and even in the intrinsic value of children (Ehrenreich and English 1978), centered on fears of juvenile delinquency and the later 1960's identification of a "generation gap." The *National Geographic,* however, continued to print significant numbers of photographs of children, perhaps responding to their increasingly sophisticated marketing information which indicated that photographs of children and cute animals were among their most popular pictures.

In the *National Geographic*'s pictures of mother and child, it often appears that the non-White mother is backgrounded, with her gaze and the gaze of the reader focused on the infant. The infant may in fact be an even more important site for dealing with White racial anxieties, by virtue of constituting an acceptable Black love object. A good number of pictures in the postwar period have the form of these two: one a Micronesian and the other an Iraqi infant, from 1974 and 1976 respectively, each peacefully asleep in a cradle with the mother visible behind. The peacefulness constitutes the antithesis of the potentially threatening differences of interest, dress, or ritual between the photographed adult and the reader.

Women and their breasts. The "nude" woman sits, stands or lounges at the salient center of *National Geographic* photography of the non-Western world. Until the phenomenal growth of mass circulation pornography in the 1960s, the magazine was known as the only mass culture venue where Americans could see women's breasts. Part of the folklore of Euramerican men, stories about secret perusals of the magazine emerged time after time in our conversations with *National Geographic* readers. People vary in how they portray the personal or cultural meaning of this nakedness, some noting it was an aid to masturbation, others claiming it failed to have the erotic quality they expected. When White men tell these stories about covertly viewing Black women's bodies, they are clearly not recounting a story about a simple encounter with the facts of human anatomy or customs; they are (perhaps unsuspectingly) confessing a highly charged—but socially approved—experience in this dangerous territory of projected, forbidden desire and guilt. Such stories also exist (in a more charged, ironic mode) in the popular culture of the African Americans—for example, in Richard Pryor's characterization of *National Geographic* as the Black man's *Playboy.*

The racial distribution of female nudity in the magazine conforms, in pernicious ways, to Euramerican myths about Black women's sexuality. Lack of modesty in dress places Black women closer to nature. Given the pervasive tendency to interpret skin color as a marker of evolutionary progress, it is assumed that White women have acquired modesty along with other characteristics of civilization. Black women remain backward on this scale, not conscious of the embarrassment they should feel at their nakedness (Gilman 1985: 114–15, 193). Their very ease unclothed stigmatizes them.

In addition, Black women have been portrayed in Western art and science as both exuberant and excessive in their sexuality. While their excess intrigues, it is also read as pathological and dangerous. In the texts produced within White culture, Haraway writes, "Colored women densely code sex, animal, dark, dangerous, fecund, pathological" (1989: 154). Thus for the French sur-realists of the 1930s, the exotic, unencumbered sexuality of non-Western peoples—and African women in particular—represented an implicit criticism of the repression and constraint of European sexuality. The Africanism of the 1930s, like an earlier Orientalism, evidenced both a longing for—and fear of—the characteristics attributed to non-Western peoples (Clifford 1988: 61). The sexuality of Black women that so entertained french artists and musicians in cafes and cabarets, however, had fueled earlier popular and scientific pre-occupation with the Hottentot Venus and other pathologized renditions of Black women's bodies and desires (Gilman 1985).

Cultural ambivalence toward women working outside the home has been profound during the postwar period, when women's waged employment grew from 25 percent in 1940 to 40 percent in 1960. More of this is accounted for by African American women, half of whom were employed in 1950, with their waged work continuing at high rates in the following decades. The ideological formulation of the meaning of women's work has changed. Working women in the fifties were defined as helpmates to their husbands. Only much later did women's work come to be seen by some as a means to goals of independence and self-realization (Chafe 1983), although even here, as Traube (1989) points out, messages were widely available that women's success in work was threatening to men. This ambivalence occasionally shows up in the *Geographic* when the laboring woman is presented as a drudge or when her femininity, *despite her working,* is emphasized. An example of the latter is found in a photograph of a Burmese woman shown planting small green shoots in a garden row (June 1974: 286). Retouching has been done both to her line of plants and to the flowers which encircle her hair. The sharpening and coloring of these two items lets the picture much more clearly tell a narrative about her femininity and her productivity and about how those two things are not mutually exclusive.

More often, however, the labor of women as well as other aspects of their lives are presented by the *Geographic* as central to the march of progress in their respective countries. Women are constructed as the vanguard of progress in part through the feminizing of the developing nation state itself (Kabbani 1986; cf. Shaffer 1988). How does this work? In the first instance, those foreign states are contrasted, in some Western imaginations, with a deeply masculine American national identity (Krasniewitz 1990; Jeffords 1989), a gendering achieved through the equation of the West (*in* the West, of course) with strength, civilization, rationality, and freedom, its other with vulnerability, primitivity, superstition, and the binds of tradition. Once this equation has been made, articles can be titled as in the following instance where progress is masculinized and the traditional nation feminized: "Beneath the surge of progress, old Mexico's charm and beauty live undisturbed" (October 1961).

Fanon (1965: 39) pointed out in his analysis of French colonial attitudes and strategies concerning the veil in Algeria that the colonialists' goal, here as elsewhere in the world, was "converting the woman, winning her over to the foreign values, wrenching her free from her status" as a means of "shaking up the [native] man" and gaining control of him. With this and other motives, those outsiders who would "develop" the Third World have often seen the advancement of non-Western women as the first goal to be achieved, with their men's progress thought to follow rather than precede it. In the nineteenth century, evolutionary theory claimed that the move upward from savagery to barbarism to civilization was indexed by the treatment of women, in particular by their liberation "from the burdens of overwork, sexual abuse, and male violence" (Tiffany and Adams 1985: 8). It "saw women in non-Western societies as oppressed and servile creatures, beasts of burden, chattels who could be bought and sold, eventually to be liberated by 'civilization' or 'progress,' thus attaining the enviable position of women in Western society" (Etienne and Leacock 1980: 1), who were then expected to be happy with their place.[4] The *Geographic* has told a much more upbeat version of this story, mainly by presenting other women's labors positively.

The continuation of these ways of thinking into the present can be seen in how states defined as "progressive" have been rendered by both Western media like the *National Geographic* and the non-Western state bureaucrats concerned. Graham-Brown (1988) and Schick (1990) describe how photographic and other proof of the progress of modernity of states like Turkey and pre-revolutionary Iran has often been found primarily in the lives of their women, and particularly in their unveiling.[5] Indeed, as Schick points out, "a photograph of an unveiled woman was not much different from one of a tractor, an industrial complex, or a new railroad; it merely symbolized yet another one of men's achievements" (1990: 369).

Take the example from the *Geographic*'s January 1985 article on Baghdad. Several photographs show veiled women walking through the city's streets. One shot shows women in a narrow alley. The dark tones of the photograph are a function of the lack of sunlight reaching down into the alley, but they also reproduce the message of the caption. Playing with the associations between veil and past that are evoked for most readers, it says, "In the shadows of antiquity, women in long black abayas walk in one of the older sections of the city." A few pages earlier, we learn about the high-rise building boom in the city and the changing roles of women in a two-page layout that shows a female electrical engineer in a hard hat and jeans organizing a building project with a male colleague. The caption introduces her by name and goes on: "Iraqi women, among the most progressive in the Arab world, constitute 25 percent of the country's work force and are guaranteed equality under Baath Party doctrine." On the opposite page, the modern buildings they have erected are captioned, "New York on the Tigris." The equation of the end point (Manhattan) with the unveiled woman is neatly laid out.

The celebration of simultaneous women's liberation and national progress is not the whole story, of course. The magazine also communicates—in a more muted way through the fifties and into the sixties—a sense of the value of the "natural," Gemeinshaft-based life of the people without progress. Progress can be construed as a socially corrosive process as it was in the late nineteenth century, when non-Western women were seen as superior to their Western counterparts because too much education had weakened the latter (Ehrenreich and English 1978: 114), sapping vitality from their reproductive organs. The illiterate woman of the non-Western world still lives with this cultural inheritance, standing for the woman "unruined" by progress.

An example of the contradictory place of progress is found in two photographs that draw attention to housewives. In the first, an Inuit woman wearing a fur trimmed parka stands in front of a washing machine: "Unfamiliar luxury" the caption says, "a washing machine draws a housewife to the new 'Tuk' laundromat, which also offers hot showers" (July 1968). This picture is explicitly structured around the contrast between the pre-modern and the modern, with the evaluative balance falling to the luxurious present. It might have still resonated for readers with the image from 1959 of Nixon and Khrushchev arguing over the benefits of capitalism next to a freshly minted washing machine and dryer at the American National Exhibition in Moscow. In those debates, Nixon could argue that the progress of American society under capitalism is found in its ability to provide labor-saving devices to women. "I think that this attitude toward women is universal. What we want is to make easier the life of our housewives," he said. In the gender stories told during the cold war, family life and commodities provided what security was to be found in the post-Hiroshima, post-Holocaust world (May 1988). The non-Western woman, too, could be deployed as proof of capitalism's value, of the universal desire for these goods, and of the role of women in the evolution of society.

From January 1971, however, an article titled "Housewife at the End of the World" documents the adventures of an Ohio woman settling in Tierra del Fuego, and congratulates her on adapting to local norms of self-sufficiency and simplicity. The last photo's caption articulates the theme of the whole article: "Life in this remote land spurs inventiveness. . . . My special interests keep me so busy I have little time to miss the conveniences I once knew." The North American woman chooses to forgo the benefits of progress in search of an authentically simple place, as her "younger sister" climbs the ladder in the other direction.

In stories of progress and/or decline, Western and non-Western women have often been played off of one another in this way, each used to critique the other in line with different purposes and in the end leaving each feeling inadequate. The masculine writer/image maker/consumer thereby asserts his own strength, both through his right to evaluate and through his completeness in contrast to women. Although non-Western men cannot be said to fare well in these cultural schemes, they are used less frequently and in other ways (Honour 1989) to either critique or shore up White men's masculinity.

In sum, the women of the non-Western world represent a population aspiring to the full femininity achieved in Western cultures, and, in a more secondary way, they are a repository for the lost femininity of "liberated" Western women. Both an ideal and thus a critique of modern femininity, they are also a measure to tell the Western family how far it has advanced. They are shown working hard and as key to their countries' progress toward some version of the Western consumer family norm. The sometimes contradictory message these pictures can send to middle class women is consistent with cultural ideologies in the United States that both condemn and affirm the woman who would be both mother and wage laborer. We can see the women of the *National Geographic* playing a role within a social field where the Cold War was being waged and where social changes in kinship structures and gender politics were precipitated by the entrance of White women into the paid labor force in larger and larger numbers.

NOTES

1. This proportion is based on those photos in which adults of identifiable gender are shown (N = 510). Another 11 percent show women and men together in roughly equal numbers, leaving 65 percent of the photos depicting mainly men.

2. The popularity of this notion in American culture, which *National Geographic* relies on as much as feeds, is also one wellspring for American feminism's focus on universal sisterhood, that is, its insistence, particularly in the 1970s, that Western and non-Western women will easily see each other as similar or sharing similar experiences.

3. Edward Steichen's *Family of Man* exhibition, first displayed in the United States in 1955, also included a substantial section devoted to mothers and infants, nicknamed "Tits and Tots" by the staff of photographers who organized it (Meltzer 1978). This exhibit was immensely popular when it toured, and the catalogue became a bestselling book.

4. Western feminism in the 1970s may have simply transformed rather than fundamentally challenged the terms of this argument as well when it argued that the women of the world were oppressed by men and to be liberated by feminism as defined in the West (see Amos and Parmar 1984).

5. Although feminist anthropology has analyzed and critiqued these kinds of assumptions, it has nonetheless often continued a basic evolutionary discourse in the assumption that Ong has identified: "Although a common past may be claimed by feminists, Third World women are often represented as mired in it, ever arriving at modernity when Western feminists are already adrift in postmodernism" (1988: 87).

REFERENCES

Amos, V., and Prathiba Parmar. 1984. Challenging Imperial Feminism. *Feminist Review* 17: 3–20.

Betterton, Rosemary, ed. 1987. *Looking On: Images of Femininity in the Visual Arts and Media.* London: Pandora.

Botting, Wendy. 1988. *Posing for Power/Posing for Pleasure: Photographies and the Social Construction of Femininity.* Binghamton, NY: University Art Gallery.

Canaan, Joyce. 1984. *Building Muscles and Getting Curves: Gender Differences in Representations of the Body and Sexuality among American Teenagers.* Paper presented at the Annual Meeting of the American Anthropological Association, Denver.

Carby, Hazel. 1985. "On the Threshold of Woman's Era": Lynching, Empire and Sexuality in Black Feminist Theory. In *Race, Writing and Difference,* ed. H. Gates, pp. 301–16. Chicago: University of Chicago Press.

Carson, Claybourne. 1981. *In Struggle: SNCC and the Black Awakening of the 1960s.* Cambridge: Harvard University Press.

Chafe, William. 1983. Social Change and the American Woman, 1940–70. In *A History of Our Time: Readings on Postwar America,* ed. William Chafe and Harvard Sitkoff, pp. 147–65. New York: Oxford University Press.

Clifford, James. 1988. *The Predicament of Culture: Twentieth-Century Ethnography, Literature and Art.* Cambridge, MA: Harvard University Press.

Collins, Patricia Hill. 1991. *Black Feminist Thought.* Boston: Unwin Hyman.

Ehrenreich, Barbara and Dierdre English. 1978. *For Her Own Good: 150 Years of the Experts' Advice to Women.* Garden City, NY: Anchor Press/Doubleday.

Fanon, Frantz. 1965. *A Dying Colonialism.* New York: Grove Press.

Gaines, Jane. 1988. White Privilege and Looking Relations: Race and Gender in Feminist Film Theory. *Screen* 29 (4): 12–27.

Gilman, Sander. 1985. *Difference and Pathology: Stereotypes of Sexuality, Race, and Madness.* Ithaca: Cornell University Press.

Graham-Brown, Sarah. 1988. *Images of Women: The Portrayal of Women in Photography of the Middle East, 1860–1950.* London: Quartet Books.

Haraway, Donna. 1989. *Primate Visions: Gender, Race, and Nature in the World of Modern Science.* New York: Routledge.

Honour, Hugh. 1989. *The Image of the Black in Western Art.* Vol. 4, From the American Revolution to World War I. New York: Morrow.

Jeffords, Susan. 1989. *The Remasculinization of America: Gender and the Vietnam War.* Bloomington: Indiana University Press.

Kabbani, Rana. 1986. *Europe's Myths of the Orient.* Bloomington: Indiana University Press.

Krasniewicz, Louise. 1990. *Desecrating the Patriotic Body: Flag Burning, Art Censorship, and the Powers of "Prototypical Americans."* Paper presented at the Annual Meeting of the American Anthropological Association, New Orleans.

Margolis, Maxine. 1984. *Mothers and Such.* Berkeley and Los Angeles: University of California Press.

May, Elaine Tyler. 1988. *Homeward Bound: American Families in the Cold War Era.* New York: Basic Books.

Meltzer, Milton. 1978. *Dorothea Lange: A Photographer's Life.* New York: Farrar Straus Giroux.

Moore, Henrietta. 1988. *Feminism and Anthropology.* Cambridge: Cambridge University Press.

Ong, Aihwa. 1988. Colonialization and Modernity: Feminist Re-presentation of Women in Non-Western Societies. *Inscriptions* 3/4: 79–93.

Ortner, Sherry. 1974. Is Female to Male as Nature Is to Culture? In *Woman, Culture and Society,* ed. M. Rosaldo and L. Lamphere, Pp. 67–88. Stanford: Stanford University Press.

Sacks, Karen. 1989. Toward a Unified Theory of Class, Race and Gender. *American Ethnologist* 16: 534–50.

Schaffer, Kay. 1988. *Women and the Bush: Forces of Desire in the Australian Cultural Tradition.* Cambridge: Cambridge University Press.

Tiffany, Sharon, and Kathleen Adams. 1985. *The Wild Woman: An Inquiry into the Anthropology of an Idea.* Cambridge, MA: Schenkman.

Traube, Elizabeth G. 1989. Secrets of Success in Post-modern Society. *Cultural Anthropology* 4: 273–300.

Trinh Minh-Ha. 1989. *Woman, Native, Other: Writing Postcoloniality and Feminism.* Bloomington: Indiana University Press.

Pp 504-507 in Gender Through the Prism of Difference.

47

Klaus Barbie, and Other Dolls I'd Like To See

SUSAN JANE GILMAN

For decades, Barbie has remained torpedo-titted, open-mouthed, tippy-toed and vagina-less in her cellophane coffin—and, ever since I was little, she has threatened me.

Most women I know are nostalgic for Barbie. "Oh," they coo wistfully, "I used to *loooove* my Barbies. My girlfriends would come over, and we'd play for hours . . . "

Not me. As a child, I disliked the doll on impulse; as an adult, my feelings have actually fermented into a heady, full-blown hatred.

My friends and I never owned Barbies. When I was young, little girls in my New York City neighborhood collected "Dawns." Only seven inches high, Dawns were, in retrospect, the underdog of fashion dolls. There were four in the collection: Dawn, dirty-blond and appropriately smug; Angie, whose name and black hair allowed her to pass for Italian or Hispanic; Gloria, a redhead with bangs and green eyes (Irish, perhaps, or a Russian, Jew?); and Dale, a black doll with a real afro.

Oh, they had their share of glitzy frocks—the tiny wedding dress, the gold lamé ball gown that shredded at the hem. And they had holes punctured in the bottoms of their feet so you could impale them on the model's stand of the "Dawn Fashion Stage" (sold separately), press a button and watch them revolve jerkily around the catwalk. But they also had "mod" clothes like white go-go boots and a multicolored dashiki outfit called "Sock It to Me" with rose-colored sunglasses. Their hair came in different lengths and—although probably only a six-year-old doll fanatic could discern this—their facial expressions and features were indeed different. They were as diverse as fashion dolls could be in 1972, and in this way, I realize now, they were slightly subversive.

Of course, at that age, my friends and I couldn't spell subversive, let alone wrap our minds around the concept. But we sensed intuitively that Dawns were more democratic than Barbies. With their different colors and equal sizes, they were closer to what we looked like. We did not find this consoling—for we hadn't yet learned that our looks were something that required consolation. Rather, our love of Dawns was an offshoot of our own healthy egocentrism. We were still at that stage in our childhood when little girls want to be everything special, glamorous and wonderful—and believe they can be.

As a six-year-old, I remember gushing, "I want to be a ballerina, and a bride, and a movie star, and a model, and a queen. . . ." To be sure, I was a disgustingly girly girl. I twirled. I skipped. I actually wore a tutu to school. (I am not kidding.) For a year, I refused to wear blue. Whenever the opportunity presented itself, I dressed up in my grandmother's pink chiffon nightgowns and rhinestone necklaces and paraded around the apartment like the princess of the universe. I dressed like my Dawn dolls—and dressed my Dawn dolls like me. It was a silly, fabulous narcissism—but one that sprang from a crucial self-love. These dolls were part of my fantasy life and an extension of my ambitions. Tellingly, my favorite doll was Angie, who had dark brown hair, like mine.

But at some point, most of us prima ballerinas experienced a terrible turning point. I know I did. I have an achingly clear memory of myself, standing before a mirror in all my finery and jewels, feeling suddenly ridiculous and miserable. *Look at yourself,* I remember thinking acidly. *Nobody will ever like you.* I could not have been older than eight. And then later, another memory: my friend Allison confiding in me, "The kids at my school, they all hate my red hair." Somewhere, somehow, a message seeped into our consciousness telling us that we weren't good enough to be a bride or a model or a queen or anything because we weren't pretty enough. And this translated into not smart enough or likable enough, either.

Looks, girls learn early, collapse into a metaphor for everything else. They quickly become the defining criteria for our status and our worth. And somewhere along the line, we stop believing in our own beauty and its dominion. Subsequently, we also stop believing in the power of our minds and our bodies.

Barbie takes over.

Barbie dolls had been around long before I was born, but it was precisely around the time my friends and I began being evaluated on our "looks" that we became aware of the role Barbie played in our culture.

Initially, my friends and I regarded Barbies with a sort of vague disdain. With their white-blond hair, burnt orange "Malibu" skin, unblinking turquoise eyes and hot-pink convertibles, Barbie dolls represented a world utterly alien to us. They struck us as clumsy, stupid, overly obvious. They were clearly somebody else's idea of a doll—and a doll meant for vapid girls in the suburbs. Dawns, my friend Julie and I once agreed during a sleepover, were far more hip.

But eventually, the message of Barbie sunk in. Literally and metaphorically, Barbies were bigger than Dawns. They were a foot high. They merited more plastic! More height! More visibility! And unlike Dawns, which were pulled off the market in the mid-'70s, Barbies were ubiquitous and perpetual bestsellers.

We urban, Jewish, black, Asian and Latina girls began to realize slowly and painfully that if you didn't look like Barbie, you didn't fit in. Your status was diminished. You were less beautiful, less valuable, less worthy. *If you didn't look like Barbie, companies would discontinue you.* You simply couldn't compete.

I'd like to think that, two decades later, my anger about this would have cooled off—not heated up. (I mean, it's a *doll* for chrissake. Get over it.) The problem, however, is that despite all the flag-waving about multiculturalism and girls' self-esteem these days, I see a new generation of little girls receiving the same message I did twenty-five years ago, courtesy of Mattel. I'm currently a "big sister" to a little girl who recently moved here from Mexico. When I first began spending time with her, she drew pictures of herself as she is: a beautiful seven-year-old with café au lait skin and short black hair. Then she began playing with Barbies. Now she draws pictures of both herself and her mother with long, blond hair. "I want long hair," she sighs, looking woefully at her drawing.

A coincidence? Maybe, but Barbie is the only toy in the Western world that human beings actively try to mimic. Barbie is not just a children's doll; it's an adult cult and an aesthetic obsession. We've all seen the evidence. During Barbie's thirty-fifth anniversary, a fashion magazine ran a "tribute to Barbie," using live models posing as dolls. A New York museum held a "Barbie retrospective," enshrining Barbie as a pop artifact—at a time when most human female pop artists continue to work in obscurity. Then there's Pamela Lee. The Barbie Halls of Fame. The websites, the newsletters, the collectors clubs. The woman whose goal is to transform herself, via plastic surgery, into a real Barbie. Is it any wonder then that little girls have been longing for generations to "look like Barbie"—and that the irony of this goes unchallenged?

For this reason, I've started calling Barbie dolls "Klaus Barbie dolls" after the infamous Gestapo commander. For I now clearly recognize what I only sensed as a child. This "pop artifact" is an icon of Aryanism. Introduced after the second world war, in the conservatism of the Eisenhower era (and rumored to be modeled after a German prostitute by a man who designed nuclear warheads), Barbies, in their "innocent," "apolitical" cutesiness, propagate the ideals of the Third Reich. They ultimately succeed where Hitler failed: They instill in legions of little girls a preference for whiteness, for blond hair, blue eyes and delicate features, for an impossible *über*figure, perched eternally and submissively in high heels. In the Cult of the Blond, Barbies are a cornerstone. They reach the young, and they reach them quickly. *Barbie, Barbie!* The Aqua song throbs. *I'm a Barbie girl!*

It's true that, in the past few years, Mattel has made an effort to create a few slightly more p.c. versions of its best-selling blond. Walk down the aisle at Toys-R-Us (and they wonder why kids today can't spell), and you can see a few boxes of American Indian Barbie, Jamaican Barbie, Cowgirl Barbie. Their skin tone is darker and their outfits ethnicized, but they have the same Aryan features and the same "tell-me-anything-and-I'll-believe-it" expressions on their plastic faces. Ultimately, their packaging reinforces their status as "Other." These are "special" and "limited" edition Barbies, the labels announce: clearly *not* the standard.

And, Barbie's head still pops off with ease. Granted, this makes life a little sweeter for the sadists on the playground (there's always one girl who gets more pleasure out of destroying Barbie than dressing her), but the real purpose is to make it easier to swap your Barbies' Lilliputian ball gowns. Look at the literal message of this: Hey, girls, a head is simply a neck plug, easily disposed of in the name of fashion. Lest anyone think I'm nit-picking here, a few years ago, a "new, improved" Talking Barbie hit the shelves and created a brouhaha because one of the phrases it parroted was *Math is hard.* Once again, the cerebrum took a backseat to "style." Similarly, the latest "new, improved" Barbie simply trades in one impossible aesthetic for another: The bombshell has now become the waif. Why? According to a Mattel spokesperson, a Kate Moss figure is better suited for today's fashions. Ah, such an improvement.

Now, I am not, as a rule, anti-doll. Remember, I once wore a tutu and collected the entire Dawn family myself. I know better than to claim that dolls are nothing but sexist gender propaganda. Dolls can be a lightning rod for the imagination, for companionship, for learning. And they're *fun*—something that must never be undervalued.

But dolls often give children their first lessons in what a society considers valuable—and beautiful. And so I'd like to see dolls that teach little girls something more than fashion-consciousness and self-consciousness. I'd like to see dolls that expand girls' ideas about what is beautiful instead of constricting them. And how about a few role models instead of runway models as playmates? If you can make a Talking Barbie, surely you can make a Working Barbie. If you can have a Barbie Townhouse, surely you can have a Barbie business. And if you can construct an entire Barbie world out of pink and purple plastic, surely you can construct some "regular" Barbies that are more than white and blond. And remember, Barbie's only a doll! So give it a little more inspired goofiness, some real *pizzazz!*

Along with Barbies of all shapes and colors, here are some Barbies I'd personally like to see:

Dinner Roll Barbie. A Barbie with multiple love handles, double chin, a real, curvy belly, generous tits and ass and voluminous thighs to show girls that voluptuousness is also beautiful. Comes with miniature basket of dinner rolls, bucket o'fried chicken, tiny Entenmann's walnut ring, a brick of Sealtest ice cream, three packs of potato chips, a T-shirt reading "Only the Weak Don't Eat" and, of course, an appetite.

Birkenstock Barbie. Finally, a doll made horizontal feet and comfortable sandals. Made from recycled materials.

Bisexual Barbie. Comes in a package with Skipper and Ken.

Butch Barbie. Comes with short hair, leather jacket, "Silence=Death" T-shirt, pink triangle buttons, Doc

Martens, pool cue and dental dams. Packaged in cardboard closet with doors flung wide open. Barbie Carpentry Business sold separately.

Our Barbies, Ourselves. Anatomically correct Barbie, both inside and out, comes with spreadable legs, her own speculum, magnifying glass and detailed diagrams of female anatomy so that little girls can learn about their bodies in a friendly, nonthreatening way. Also included: tiny Kotex, booklets on sexual responsibility. Accessories such as contraceptives, sex toys, expanding uterus with fetus at various stages of development and breast pump are all optional, underscoring that each young women has the right to choose what she does with her own Barbie.

Harley Barbie. Equipped with motorcycle, helmet, shades. Tattoos are non-toxic and can be removed with baby oil.

Body Piercings Barbie. Why should Earring Ken have all the fun? Body Piercings Barbie comes with changeable multiple earrings, nose ring, nipple rings, lip ring, navel ring and tiny piercing gun. Enables girls to rebel, express alienation and gross out elders without actually having to puncture themselves.

Blue Collar Barbie. Comes with overalls, protective goggles, lunch pail, UAW membership, pamphlet on union organizing and pay scales for women as compared to men. Waitressing outfits and cashier's register may be purchased separately for Barbies who are holding down second jobs to make ends meet.

Rebbe Barbie. So why not? Women rabbis are on the cutting edge in Judaism. Rebbe Barbie comes with tiny satin *yarmulke,* prayer shawl, *tefillin,* silver *kaddish* cup, Torah scrolls. Optional: tiny *mezuzah* for doorway of Barbie Dreamhouse.

B-Girl Barbie. Truly fly Barbie in midriff-baring shirt and baggy jeans. Comes with skateboard, hip hop accessories and plenty of attitude. Pull her cord, and she says things like, "I don't *think* so," "Dang, get outta my face" and "You go, girl." Teaches girls not to take shit from men and condescending white people.

The Barbie Dream Team. Featuring Quadratic Equation Barbie (a Nobel Prize—winning mathematician with her own tiny books and calculator), Microbiologist Barbie (comes with petri dishes, computer and Barbie Laboratory) and Bite-the-Bullet Barbie, an anthropologist with pith helmet, camera, detachable limbs, fake blood and kit for performing surgery on herself in the outback.

Transgender Barbie. Formerly known as G.I. Joe.

48

Sexuality and Gender Maneuvering

MIMI SCHIPPERS

It was just after midnight as Maddie and I approached The Empty Bottle. Maddie hated the first band scheduled to play, so we had hung out at Bryan's until she was confident they had finished their set. There were several people standing outside the bar in the doorway and on the sidewalk. As she scanned the faces, Maddie said, "Either they're still playing . . . and sucking . . . or we timed this perfectly. There's Colleen. She loves Munch. [This is a fictitious name for the opening band.] She wouldn't be outside if they were still playing."

As we came up to her, Colleen feigned a whisper to the man she was talking with, but said loudly enough so that we could hear, "Did you know she's a lesbian?" with a nod toward Maddie. She laughed and then said, "Not only that, but she's a bitch, too."

Maddie laughed and spat back, "And don't you wish you could be?"

"Hey, I'm a bigger bitch than you could ever dream of being."

Both Maddie and Colleen laughed, hugged, and continued a playful banter about who deserved membership in the "lesbian club" and "bitch club." By the tone of their exchange, it was clear that there was something admirable about being a lesbian and a bitch.

After chatting for a few minutes, Maddie said, "Well, we're going in. See you in there."

"Now be careful, she's a lesbian," Colleen said to me as we walked away.

Maddie quickly responded, "She knows. She's my girlfriend. Jealous?"

Colleen laughed and said, "Yeah, but I have my own girlfriend," and with a small gesture toward the man she was standing with triumphantly yelled, "*He* is really a *she!*" Everybody, including the man, laughed.

In this politicized, antiestablishment rock world, it is uncool to be a bigot, and alternative hard rockers include heterosexism as bigotry; being able to talk freely and openly about homosexuality is part of being cool. This cool pose translates into challenging, chastising, and making ridiculous derogatory talk about gay and lesbian people when it occasionally comes up. It also manifests as ironic performance, as when Colleen performed heterosexism and then, in the interactive process of face-to-face interaction, dismantled it. Alternative hard rockers engage in a lot of this kind of sexual play and sexual contact. There is a set of subcultural beliefs and practices about sexuality, just as there is about gender. The sub-culture has a gender order and a sexual order, and as alternative hard rock-

---

ers go about the business of rocking, they construct and maintain that sexual order.

Sexuality, like gender, is a system of beliefs and patterns of practice that structure or shape social life. We might call these patterns the *sexual order*. As conceptualized in queer theory, the contemporary, Western sexual order is partially based on the symbolic construction of sexuality as a hierarchical, binary relationship between heterosexuality and homosexuality. Like gender, sexuality is defined in terms of fixed identities, so there are assumed to be homosexual or heterosexual persons. These identities are believed to represent some internal, fixed characteristic of the individual person. There is an assumption that everybody has a sexual orientation, and that it is a central, defining feature of not simply a person's sexual desires and practices but also her personality. It is this understanding of sexuality that made the label *lesbian* significant in Maddie and Colleen's interaction. Within the meaning structure of sexuality, to call someone a lesbian is to identify what kind of person she is.

Further, within the dominant sexual order, heterosexuality is constructed as preferable, superior, and normal, while homosexuality is considered undesirable, inferior, and marginal or deviant. It was this assumption that homosexuality is inferior that gave Colleen's whisper meaning. Only within a larger cultural context that defines homosexuality in terms of a shameful secret would Colleen's actions make any sense.

Finally, sexuality not only defines and organizes identities, but is also an organizing feature of face-to-face interaction and of larger institutional and cultural settings. Like the gender order, the sexual order does not simply translate into assumptions about identities, but is also an organizing feature of social interaction and institutional relations more generally. At all levels of social organization—identities, practices, the structure of face-to-face interactions, and institutional structure—the norm is heterosexuality and there is an underlying assumption that everybody is heterosexual unless proven otherwise.

If we look at the interaction between Maddie and Colleen, we can identify the ways in which sexuality organizes the interaction and the subculture. While Colleen's, whisper about Maddie being a lesbian reproduced the identity hierarchy by suggesting there is something shameful about being a lesbian, in the ongoing process of this interaction, the meaning of that whisper as a parody of heterosexism was established. Meanings emerged from the interaction, and importantly, the sexual organization of the interaction itself emerged through the play of meanings. Colleen performed the role of homophobe, and through that performance set up a hierarchical relationship between herself and Maddie that reproduced the broader sexual order. With her own performance of sexuality Colleen set up and reproduced a heterosexist sexual organization for the interaction. However, rather than leaving heterosexism as the frame for the interaction, Colleen reconfigured the interaction as one that is critical of heterosexism. First, she overplayed her part by making sure the whisper was actually a public statement. It was clear that the meaning of the whisper was to expose and reject the secret of lesbian sexuality. Then Colleen said that Maddie was "a bitch, too." The women often called each other and themselves "bitch"; while sometimes it was used to put down particular other women, it was most often worn as a badge of honor, and like the label *slut* it was only used positively or affectionately in women's interpersonal exchanges with each other. Within this exchange, Maddie's and Colleen's insider knowledge about and understanding of the meaning of *bitch* shifted the meaning of *lesbian* to something positive through the fluid process of interaction. Maddie went along as they competed with each other over who was more lesbian and who was more bitchy, driving the antiheterosexist meaning and structure of the interaction home. Colleen and Maddie turned what first appeared to be heterosexism into a fairly scathing critique of heterosexism through a process of interactive moves or maneuvers. Further, they challenged compulsory heterosexuality by validating lesbianism through their competitive, interactive volley for the lesbian badge.

Through their interactive maneuvers they not only challenged the hierarchy that places heterosexuality above homosexuality, but also disrupted the hegemonic insistence on stable sexual identities. That is, they "queered" sexuality. Because the sexual order depends upon the construction of homosexuality and heterosexuality as stable identities, some queer theorists and activists suggest that one strategy for undermining heterosexism is to challenge the hegemonic construction of sexuality as consisting of two hierarchical fixed identities defined by the biological sex of one's object of desire. One way to destabilize the sexual order, then, would be to queer sexuality. To queer sexuality is to in some way step out of, blur, or challenge hierarchical, sexual identities that define individuals as homosexual or heterosexual. Sexuality can be queered through sexual practice and discourse about desire, identities, or sexual practices. I want to suggest that sexuality can also be queered through sexual maneuvering or by manipulating the meaning and performance of desire within any given interaction. Maddie and Colleen engaged sexual maneuvers in their interaction about being lesbians.

First, they disrupted the notion of stable sexual identities through their specific use of the identity label *lesbian.* As the two women engaged in their banter about who was more lesbian, they were reproducing the general belief that lesbians have a set of personality characteristics. While those characteristics were constructed as positive by Maddie and Colleen, there was still the underlying assumption that a lesbian is a particular kind of woman. This is very much characteristic of the sexual organization of the larger social structure. However, within the confines of this particular interaction, by invoking a language (and self-made claims) of being more lesbian, they suggested that lesbianism is a continuum, not a fixed category, and that one can move along this continuum through a set of behaviors, styles, and actions. This challenges the assumption that one either is or is not a lesbian, that *lesbian* is a fixed identity.

Likewise, Maddie and Colleen queered the sexual organization of the interaction as they manipulated the positions of everybody involved. When Maddie claimed that I was her girlfriend, Colleen responded by saying "I have my own girlfriend. . . . *He* is really a *she!*" Of course, the dominant sexual order has no room for women to have men as girlfriends. With an interactive maneuver to situate herself in a relation of erotic desire with her male companion, Colleen constructed herself as having a lesbian relationship with a man—very queer indeed. Also, Colleen's on-the-fly shift from the role of homophobe to that of lesbian within the same interaction challenges the sexual order's insistence on stable sexual identities. In other words, the sexual organization of the interaction, as it emerged, was queer to the extent that it disrupted or challenged the insistence on stable sexual identities that neatly match up with desire and practices. In the middle of the interaction, the sexual organization shifted and a different set of sexual arrangements emerged. That is, the sexuality of all involved emerged from negotiated social interaction as much as it framed the interaction.

Despite Colleen's move to mock this sort of heterosexism, and Maddie's and Colleen's collaborative construction of a rather queer structure for this interaction, within the context of the larger sexual structure of the subculture overall this interaction reflects the dominant sexual order more than it challenges it. Colleen had to have assumed Maddie was heterosexual for the banter about lesbians and bitches to have been not only funny but also effective as a cool, antiheterosexist pose. If Maddie was indeed a lesbian, this interaction probably would have backfired on Colleen, and she would have been chastised for being both heterosexist and sexist. Colleen would never have risked "outing" Maddie if there was any remote possibility that Maddie was a lesbian. Colleen must have safely assumed that people are heterosexual unless proven otherwise and, depending on that assumption, could construct herself, Maddie, and the meaning of the interaction as countercultural.

This interaction between Maddie and Colleen captures the sexual order of alternative hard rock. The women's subcultural practices and beliefs were grounded in a collective desire to not reproduce the old patterns of inequality in mainstream rock, including heterosexism and homophobia. While they were relatively successful at challenging compulsory heterosexuality and heterosexism in their talk and practices, there was still a rather heterosexist normative structure for the subculture overall.

THE SEXUAL ORDER OF MAINSTREAM ROCK

Mainstream rock is organized by sexuality. To reiterate, with the term *sexual organization* I mean that there are agreed-upon rules for thinking about, expressing, and acting on erotic desire. These collective beliefs about sex, sexual desire, and sexual identities, and expected patterns of sexual behavior structure or frame the activities, interactions, and expectations of people as they go about doing rock culture. For instance, the relationship between musician and groupie is sexualized as well as gendered, and this relationship is heterosexual. At the same time, there is much work done to mask or eliminate any homoeroticism in the relationship between musician and real fan. There have been very few rockers who have come out as gay or lesbian, and many rockers overtly express hostility toward homosexuality. No mainstream rocker, let alone a genre within mainstream rock, has publicly enacted intragender erotic desire as a central way of doing *rock musician.* While there have been some notable exceptions, the sexual meanings attached to the identity labels *rock musician, groupie, teenybopper,* and *real fan* set up a heterosexual structure for mainstream rock as an institutionalized cultural form. Within the world of mainstream rock, especially the mainstream rock of the 1980s that alternative hard rockers have more recently rejected, everyone is presumed straight until proven otherwise. As people performed rock in concert, on recordings, in videos, and in interviews, they simultaneously performed heterosexuality either by not explicitly situating their sexual desire or, more commonly, by compulsively expressing heterosexual desire.

THE SEXUAL ORDER OF ALTERNATIVE HARD ROCK

The sexual structure of mainstream rock parallels and reproduces the dominant sexual structure that both constructs sexuality as consisting of stable identities and defines homosexuality as inferior or, at best, marginal. While alternative hard rockers have rejected homophobic and heterosexist attitudes or behaviors in order to create a different form of rock, there are aspects of alternative hard rock that, like mainstream rock, parallel the dominant sexual order. For instance, the implicit assumption that everybody is heterosexual unless proved otherwise is a central feature of the organization of sexuality within alternative hard rock. This becomes apparent in the ways in which alternative hard rockers talk about gay people. As I discussed earlier, being comfortable talking about gay and lesbian people is considered "cool." The most common adaptation of this comfort with homosexuality manifests itself in talk about their gay, lesbian, or bisexual friends, roommates, family members, work colleagues, and so on. For example, in the first real conversation I had with Colleen, I asked her about her background. She told me about how strong her Catholic roots were. She even had two nuns in her family. Though we were not discussing sexuality, it came up in a story she told me about her aunts.

"Oh my god. This is hilarious. My roommate is gay. I'm like 'whatever' and don't really think about it. Well, when my aunts found out I had a man for a roommate, they sort of freaked out. I told them there was no way anything 'romantic' is going to happen. They were like, you know . . ."—here Colleen adopted an Irish accent—" 'Oh Colleen, my dear sweet child, you can never predict a man's behavior.' So I say, 'Don't worry. He's gay.' They covered their mouths and giggled. One of 'em said, 'Oh, do you mean he's happy?' I just rolled my eyes and said, 'Yeah. That's exactly what I mean. He's really happy.' They just can't wrap their heads around the fact that there are gay people. It's like, get over it." . . .

Despite alternative hard rockers' comfort in talking about the gay and lesbian people they know, I never heard anyone I spent time with in the subculture truly self-identify as gay, lesbian, homosexual, or bisexual. On a few isolated occasions people did talk about one woman in the subculture being a lesbian. Interestingly, I rarely saw this woman really interact with others, and I never saw her in the clubs unless her band was playing. I never heard of a man in the subculture being gay. For the most part, gay and lesbian people were constructed as people outside the subculture. And while they were deemed as deserving of all the rights, respect, and happiness of everyone else, homosexual people were nonetheless a marginalized "other." In this way, the overarching sexual organization of the subculture itself is very much in line with the dominant sexual order in that sexualities are assumed to be stable, identifiable personality traits, and it is heterosexist to the extent that nonheterosexual people were marginalized as outsiders.

Nonetheless, this overarching sexual organization for the subculture does not translate into straightforward heterosexual behavior, nor a simplistic heterosexual microorganization of face-to-face interaction. Like the gender order, the sexual order is not a fixed determinant of how people act and interact, but is instead a general set of rules. Those rules get reproduced and challenged as people go about their everyday lives. Through a process of *sexual structuration,* the sexual order simultaneously frames or guides behavior and interaction and is also an emergent feature of social interaction. . . .

Despite the construction of homosexual people as outsiders, often talk about gay and lesbian people reveals a conceptualization of sexuality that is somewhat more complex than the one offered by the dominant sexual order. For example, I was at an alternative hard rocker's house with several other people, including four men from a local band. These four were talking about whether or not it would be a good idea for them to take a gig opening for Tribe 8, a band out of San Francisco that consists of five women who are all very much out about their sexual desire for women and who make their sexual desire a central part of their performance. Joe, the singer and guitarist for the local band, was dubious about the whole thing.

"Man, I don't know if it would be such a good idea," he said. "It's going to be a bunch of lesbians who probably would not appreciate a bunch of aggressive guys up there." Egged on by everybody's laughter, Joe continued, "Shit, I don't want to get my ass kicked! There's no way they'd put up with us if they're waiting to see Tribe 8. I don't think we should."

Susan agreed: "And they *will* kick your ass!"

"And not because you're guys," Bryan added. "Because you fucking suck!"

Everybody except Joe laughed. While getting his ass kicked by lesbians for being a guy was pretty funny, someone kicking his ass for not being a good musician, even if it was a bunch of women, was serious business. Perhaps this was an expression of an underlying heterosexism, but the way he phrased this expression revealed at least some ambiguity. For instance, Joe did not say that he didn't want to open for Tribe 8 because *he* had something against lesbians. Instead, he expressed his concern in terms of what lesbians might expect. The problem was their legitimate rejection of him and his all-male band. Further, when he said he did not want to get his ass kicked, he was laying a fairly positive evaluation on the audience. Remember that, for alternative hard rockers, the notion of "kicking ass" has a positive connotation, especially when referring to women. As discussed earlier, this meant that a woman was exceptionally cool because she transgressed the requirements of femininity. Joe was implying that the women at the show would be tough, but also cool. In characteristic form for the subcultural norms, Joe constructed lesbians as deserving of respect, but also as outsiders. The combination of the sexual and gender display of Tribe 8 and the resulting gender and sexual dynamics of the audience would create a scene in which the presence of an all-male band would either not make sense or would possibly become a rallying point around which the women could express their feminism. Either way, the audience would be less than receptive. This was quite a daunting prospect for a group of guys whose self-worth is inextricable from their audience's adoration.

For our purposes, what is particularly interesting about Joe's characterization of the Tribe 8 show was that he said it was "going to be a bunch of lesbians." Later, attending the Tribe 8 show, I concluded that Joe's concerns about being aggressively rejected were well-founded, but the audience, even though it consisted mostly of women, could hardly be characterized as "a bunch of lesbians." There was more overt physical contact among women than I had seen at other shows, and many of the women were quite aggressive about keeping men out of the space in front of the stage. But I also noticed that—though there were some women there I did not know and who might self-identify as lesbians—there were also many women there who had regularly attended shows that Joe's band and other local bands had played, and these women did not self-identify as such. The women I had been spending time with in the alternative hard rock scene in Chicago were indistinguishable in their behavior from most of the women I did not recognize. These women did not become lesbians in the identity sense by attending nor by having sexual contact with other women at this show. They worked with other women to create a counter-hegemonic structure for sexual and gender display and interaction, but there is no reason to conclude that their sexual identities were or became lesbian. Joe did not have a language to identify the transformation of the normative structure, so he simply said that the audience would be "a bunch of lesbians"—including Maddie, Colleen, and others. It was the practices, interactions, and normative structure that differed at the Tribe 8 show, not the identities of the individuals who participated. When a group of women become "a bunch of lesbians" because of how they act and express desire, especially if there is an implicit assumption that these women do not limit their romantic and sexual relationships to women, the word *lesbian* gets somewhat dislodged from its hegemonic meaning.

This tension between sexual identity labels and sexual practices came through at a Hole show, when Courtney Love decided to reveal who her current sexual partner was.

"Guess who I'm fucking. If you can guess, I'll tell you. Come on, try to guess."

Several people in the audience, including both men and women, raised their hands. Someone from the crowd yelled, "Drew!" Eric Erlandson, the guitarist for Hole, was dating the actress Drew Barrymore at the time.

Love laughed and said, referring to Erlandson, "No. *He's* fucking Drew; I'm not. I'm not a lesbian. I'm only a part-time muff-muncher." Gesturing first to drummer Patty Schemel and then to bass player Melissa Auf der Maur, she continued, "She's a full-time muff-muncher, and she's a virgin." Schemel pounded out a quick power-thump while Auf der Maur looked down, shaking her head and smiling shyly.

When someone in the audience suggested Love was "fucking" Drew Barrymore, she responded by saying "I'm not a lesbian." What did that mean to Love? It meant that she is only a "part time muff muncher," referring to the act of cunnilingus. Although Love first used an identity label, and by doing so supported the dominant sexual order, she quickly shifted the emphasis to what one does in practice to define sexuality. That the bass player was a "virgin" in comparison to herself (a "part-time muff-muncher") and the drummer (a "full-time muff-muncher") meant that *not doing anything* defined one's sexuality. Sexuality was thus constructed as *what one did* and not so much as *who one was:* Love's immediate shift to who was a "muff-muncher" and who was not transformed sexuality from an identity to a set of practices. This is precisely what queer activists call for in their efforts to dismantle the heterosexist, sexual order—for sexuality to be defined as erotic desire and practices, not kinds of people. Through her talk, Love constructed the notion of lesbian not as some ontological state of being, but instead as a sort of becoming through sexual behavior: one *becomes* a lesbian when one limits her sexual practices to muff-munching full-time. There was still an underlying assumption that there *are* lesbians in the identity sense, but in her banter on stage, Love complicated or queered lesbianism's definition. . . .

Women would often engage in playful, sexualized interaction with each other. One evening, Maddie had a cigarette hanging from her lips and asked Carrie for a light. Carrie leaned in and put her mouth over Maddie's cigarette and pretended to bite it. When she pulled away, Carrie said, "Oh, I thought you said, "Can I have a bite?" I suppose I could give you a light, but I'd rather give you a bite."

Another time Maddie and Carrie were sitting a few seats away from each other at the bar. Carrie was looking at Maddie, winking and licking her lips. After ten or fifteen minutes, Carrie yelled to Maddie, "I'm leaving for a little while, will you miss me?" Maddie responded, "Of course, darling. But we're leaving anyway." Carrie exaggerated a pout and said, "Well then, there's no reason for me to come back." Though neither Carrie nor Maddie self-identified as lesbians, they often situated each other in an intragender erotic interaction.

Sometimes alternative hard rockers situate themselves as those who engage in intragender erotic behavior through storytelling. For instance, one time Maddie told me she had an especially fine time at a concert the night before because she "made out" with Colleen all night.

When I asked her what she meant, she said, "You know. I had my tongue down her throat. She had her tongue down my throat."

This story was told in the presence of other alternative hard rockers. Whether or not the story was true, when others went along and did not marginalize Maddie, they accepted and validated her position as a woman who "makes out" with other women. It is important to note that Carrie, Colleen, and Maddie had steady boyfriends. Though this sort of sexual play was a common feature of their relationships with each other at the rock shows, their steady partnerships were with men.

Interestingly, women's sexual desire is not in this instance limited to women and men but is extended to the sound of singers' voices, the sound of guitars, the syncopation of instruments, and other tonal or musical experiences. I heard women talk about wanting to "fuck the music" or about a singer's voice as "totally fuckable." When women particularly enjoy live or recorded music, a common expression they use to convey this is, "Just fuck me now"; sometimes they say "I need a cigarette" or "I'm spent" after a live performance. The sexual references are not addressed to any particular person or people, but instead are made toward and about the music as an object of desire and as sexually gratifying. As Lawrence Grossberg suggests, rock music, especially live rock music, is simultaneously an auditory and bodily experience. At these shows, the music is not only heard but also felt in the body. The rhythm and syncopation among the bass, drums, and guitars gives the bodily experience a sexual valence, which is thus expressed by the women. While this experience of the music is not limited to alternative hard rock, in this subculture it was common and expected for women to verbally express that feeling. It is entirely possible that women's "dirty dancing" together could be as much about sexualizing the music as it is about their sexual desire for each other. In other words, sexual desire, as expressed by the women in talk and through their actions, is far more diffused and fluid than the dominant sexual order would have it. This more diffused, fluid sexuality breaks down the relevance of sexual identity labels that reduce sexual desire to the biological sex of one's sexual object. For this reason, women's sexual desire cannot be simplified as bisexual or lesbian, but instead can be characterized as *queer* because it is opened up to include more than other women or even other individuals so that the sex category of the object of desire becomes irrelevant.

At the same time, it is uncommon at most of these shows to see men moving their bodies to the music, except for head-banging or playing "air guitar"; dancing is not something men in this sub-culture usually do. The men most often keep their eyes on the stage or each other while conversing between bands, so overtly "checking women out" is relatively uncommon. At least in the company of women at these shows, men do not usually express sexual desire for or attraction to a woman unless she is a musician and the attraction is couched in musical appreciation. On the rare occasions when men do appear to be expressing an overt sexual desire for women, others invariably make fun of them to keep the normative structure intact.

Though men in the audience do not engage in any sort of dirty dancing, some of the men on stage participate in some forms of intragender sexual contact. For instance, as part of their performances, men musicians sometimes publicly express sexual desire for other men. At one show the lead singer (a man) was wearing chaps with only a thong underneath. The drummer (also a man) had a microphone for backup vocals. At one point, the singer introduced the rest of the band. When he got to the drummer, the drummer then introduced the singer, saying, "Ass—I mean *voice*—of the gods." The singer then shook his ass toward the drummer. The drummer, expressing his admiration for the singer's voice, conflated that with a reference to the singer's body. That it was a reference to his ass put a fairly straightforward sexual valence on the compliment to the singer's vocal ability. . . .

The field of appreciation is not the limit to men's intragender erotic contact. Men on stage sometimes gyrate their hips against each other, kiss each other on the lips, roll around on the floor in a sexualized embrace, lick each other, and engage in various other overtly sexual behaviors. Interestingly, the only time I saw a woman and man doing anything close to dirty dancing, they were not re-producing anything like heteronormativity. It was at a Babes in Toyland show at Lounge Ax, and the man and woman were standing on a wooden ledge along the wall. The man was in front of the woman, who was holding on to the pipes that hung from the ceiling and grinding her hips into his ass. It looked like fucking, but if it was, *she* was fucking *him.*

On rare occasions, male musicians explicitly refer to having had sex with men. One singer talked about a journalist's evaluation of the band that suggested they were homophobic because the band had a song that included the word "faggot" in the lyrics. The singer had read and was referring to that article when he said,"So I guess I'm a homophobe. It's scary when some fucking critic can't tell his head from his ass and mixes up metaphor and reality. It's kind of hard to imagine how someone like me, someone who's given men head on several occasions, could be a homophobe. You know what I gotta say to that guy? Fuck you! Then again, no thank you."

Not only does this reflect the subcultural norm for confronting homophobia or heterosexism, but it also reveals something else about what was going on in this subculture. While people do not take on sexual identity labels for themselves but instead reserve them for people outside the subculture, people inside often talk about having sexual contact with others of the same gender, or actually do so as they rock. Like other alternative hard rockers, this singer did not say, "I'm gay" or "I'm bisexual"; he said he had "given men head on several occasions." In response to a charge of homophobia, this man responded by talking about his sexual experiences and behavior, not his identity. Rather than an expression of a sexual identity, sexual practices become an expression of a political stand in relation to heterosexism. Intragender sexual contact no longer reflects an internal essence or identity; it is a way to be "cool" and countercultural. In other words, the bodacious heterosexuality of mainstream rock is transformed in alternative hard rock into an audacious queer sexuality. . . .

Gender and sexuality are just two systems of inequality. One could just as easily focus on racial structuration and racial maneuvering in face-to-face interaction, or class structuration and maneuvering, or age, or ethnicity, and so on. In other words, future research might address the ways in which the meaning of social positions and the interpersonal power relations between people are negotiated through the manipulation of the relationships among racial, class, age, and/or ethnic positions. Similarly, an analysis of intersectionality might focus explicitly on the ways in which gender meanings and power are negotiated through a manipulation of the relationships among race, ethnic, class, and/or age positions, or how racial meanings and power are negotiated through a manipulation of the relationship between masculinity and femininity. In other words, *maneuvering,* as I've defined it, is not limited to negotiating gender, but might also apply to other systems of inequality as well. While my analytic interest and focus for this project is on resistive efforts to negotiate the gender and sexual order, it would have been equally possible to focus on class and race; sexuality and age; class, ethnicity, and sexuality; or any other configuration of intersecting systems of inequality in alternative hard rock. My hope is that the concept *gender maneuvering* provides enough analytic substance for other researchers to pick up and use for projects on racial, ethnic, class, and/or age maneuvering in rock and elsewhere. I also hope that people who are interested in challenging these systems of inequality might begin thinking about strategies of maneuvering more generally. What would it mean to *race maneuver?* In what ways can an individual or group disrupt the hierarchical relationships? . . .

Perhaps the most important question is, What is the relationship between maneuvering and larger systems of inequality? If our goal is to dismantle these systems of subordination, we must always keep an eye on not just the actions of individuals, groups, or subcultures but also on the broader political implications of those actions. For instance, alternative hard rockers seem committed to challenging homophobia and heterosexism. However, as I have demonstrated, they limit their understanding of heterosexism to individual attitudes and behaviors. There is no explicit subcultural awareness of nor efforts to transform heterosexism as a structural feature of rock or of social relations more generally. Sexual inequality is defined in terms of individual acts of homophobia, discrimination or bigotry, not as a characteristic of the social structure. . . .

This individualistic approach to sexual politics is characteristic of alternative hard rockers' approach to politics more generally, including feminist politics. In the end, gender maneuvering is the limit to feminist politics in alternative hard rock, and while this is quite effective in transforming the gender structure of the rock clubs in Chicago, the alternative hard rockers reproduce the sexual order. And, importantly, there are significant limits on their ability to impact gender relations more broadly.

49

"Oh No! I'm a Nerd!"

Hegemonic Masculinity on an Online Forum

LORI KENDALL

Every day, on an online forum called BlueSky,[1] a group of young people gather to chat, joke with each other, exchange work-related information, and "hang out." Starting at around 10:00 a.m. Pacific time and ending very late at night, people enter and leave the electronic space, exchanging greetings and taking their leave in the casual, friendly manner of people visiting their local pub. The conversation, on BlueSky ebbs and flows as people "go idle" to attend to work or other tasks, then return their attention to their computer screens and to more active participation in the ongoing electronic dialogue.

In this article, I present findings based on my research on BlueSky. I discuss BlueSky participants' online performances of gendered and raced identities. Participants interpret their own and others' identities within the context of expectations and assumptions derived from offline U.S. culture, as well as from their membership in various computer-related subcultures. Given the predominance of white men on BlueSky, such identity interpretations also rely on expectations concerning masculinity and whiteness. BlueSky identity performances provide information pertaining not just to online interaction but also to the social construction of gendered and raced identities more generally.

DOING RESEARCH ON BLUESKY

BlueSky is a type of interactive, text-only, online forum known as a "mud." Mud originally stood for Multi-User Dungeon (based on the original multiperson networked dungeons-and-dragons type game called MUD). As in other online chat programs, people connect to mud programs through Internet accounts and communicate through typed text with other people currently connected to that mud. There are hundreds of muds available on the Internet and through private online services. Many muds serve as gaming spaces for adventure or "hack-and-slash" games. Muds also operate as locations for professional meetings, classes, and other pedagogical purposes and as social spaces. Although participants have programmed various toys and games for use within BlueSky, BlueSky functions primarily as a social meeting space.

I began my research on muds after about a year of online experience (which did not include experience

Lori Kendall, "'Oh No! I'm a Nerd!' Hegemonic Masculinity on an Online Forum," from *Gender & Society,* Volume 14/2000, p. 256–274.

on muds). BlueSky was one of many muds I visited during the first few weeks of my research. I eventually focused the research solely on BlueSky, although still spending some time each week on other muds. From the beginning of my participation on BlueSky, I informed other participants that I was conducting research and often solicited comments from them regarding my interpretations.

I refer to my online research methodology as participant-observation despite the fact that my participation consisted largely of reading and writing online text. In contrast to studies of e-mail lists or newsgroups, the forum I studied involved near-synchronous communication (meaning that messages passed back and forth more quickly and in a more conversational style than in e-mail or bulletin board systems). During my participation, I experienced the online conversations just as the participants did, going through a learning process and acclimation to the medium like any other "newbie." My own experiences during this learning process provided me with important information about the nature of online textual communication. Unlike researchers studying previously produced online text, I had a stake in ongoing conversations. Joining the group and engaging in the same activities as other participants also allowed me to ask questions on the spot and to gain a feel for the timing and rhythm of communications.

Like participant-observers and ethnographers of other types of groups, I gradually became a member of the social group, learning both technical aspects of online communication and social norms that enabled me to continue my participation. While I was not able to observe facial and bodily gestures (except during offline group meeting and interviews), I did learn the social contexts for the text produced on BlueSky and also learned BlueSky participants' own methods for compensating for the lack of physical contact and "given-off" information.

I continued my participant-observation on BlueSky for more than two years, during which time I spent between 10 and 20 hours per week online. In addition to observing and participating in day-to-day conversations and interaction on BlueSky, I also conducted brief informal interviews with several participants online. Examples of online conversations in this article are taken from the thousands of pages of participation logs that I gathered while online through a feature of the program allowing me to record all text that appeared on my screen. Multiple conversations often occur simultaneously on the mud, making log segments long and confusing to read. I have therefore edited the log excerpts provided herein, removing portions of other conversations. However, I have left individual lines of text as originally expressed by participants. Each individual's contribution to a conversation begins with their online name. Since text from each participant only appears on other participants' screens when the participant finishes typing the line and hits the "enter" key, individual lines on muds tend to be short.

In addition to spending time with BlueSky people online, I've met them and other mudders offline for social activities and gatherings. I supplemented my participant-observation on BlueSky with many hours on several other social muds and by reading various online resources relating to muds, including Usenet newsgroup and e-mail list postings. In addition, I also conducted 30 in-depth, face-to-face interviews with BlueSky participants in several U.S. cities. As is common in ethnographic studies, my interview questions arose out of my experiences online. The interviews allowed me to more directly compare my understanding of BlueSky with that of other participants, to ask more detailed questions than is easily possible on the mud, to address sensitive and serious topics (sometimes difficult to bring up in the often raucous atmosphere of BlueSky), to obtain further information about participants' offline lives and relationships, and to compare my impressions of their offline identity performances with their online presentations of self.

Many of the people who connect to BlueSky have been mudding for more than seven years and have formed relationships with each other that often extend offline. Most are sophisticated computer users, many of whom work with computers as programmers or system administrators. Almost all come from middle-class backgrounds, and the majority are white, young, male, and heterosexual. While more than 300 people occasionally connect to BlueSky, I determined 127 to be "regulars," based on level of participation and participants' own understanding of who constituted regulars of the social space. Approximately 27 percent of these regulars are female, and approximately 6 percent are Asian American. Most participants are in their mid- to late 20s. I am able to state these demographics with confidence owing to several factors, including my own offline meetings with participants, participants' frequent offline meetings with each other, participants' length of acquaintance, and BlueSky norms regarding self-disclosure and congruity between online and offline presentations of self.

BlueSky, like many online forums, was established during the Internet's earlier years, when online participants were even more likely to be white, male, middle-class, and either associated with a university or working in a technical field. BlueSky participants have also resisted the entrance of newcomers into their group, especially in recent years. Thus, the percentage of women on BlueSky is even lower, at 27 percent, than that on the Internet generally. Like the Internet, BlueSky also remains predominantly white and middle class but may have a higher percentage of Asian American participants.[2]

STUDYING IDENTITY ONLINE

Text-based online communication, such as that which occurs on BlueSky, limits the communication of information about selves and identities to textual description only. Participants must learn to compensate for the lack of audio and visual cues and make choices about how to represent themselves. BlueSky participants use their years of experience with online communication and their familiarity with each other to compensate for the limitations of text-only communications. They have developed an elaborate subculture, using repeated patterns of speech and specialized features of the mud program to add the nuance and depth that such attributes as tone of voice and gesture provide in face-to-face communication. Now fully acclimated to the medium, they experience their online conversations as very similar to face-to-face interaction.

Researchers such as West and Fenstermaker (1995, 13) have emphasized the importance of understanding how "all social exchanges, regardless of the participants or the outcome, are simultaneously 'gendered,' 'raced,' and 'classed,'" (Such exchanges are also importantly characterized by other aspects of identity such as sexuality and age.) Despite frequent avowals to the contrary in various media, these aspects of identity characterize online social exchanges as well as face-to-face interaction. However, because taken-for-granted visual cues are unavailable in online text-based communication, people must make choices about what to reveal about themselves, how to describe themselves, and how to evaluate others' identity information and descriptions.

The limitations and special factors of online interaction can thus make participants more conscious of both their own identity performances and their evaluation of others' identity performances. Studying relations of dominance and difference online, where appearance cues are hidden, can yield further insights into the workings of the social processes by which identity understandings are created, maintained, and/or changed.

For instance, Omi and Winant (1994, 59) point out that "one of the first things we notice about people when we meet them (along with their sex) is their race," and that based on our cultural knowledge of racial differences, we make assumptions based on those appearances that we notice and classify as relating to race. "We expect differences in skin color, or other racially coded characteristics, to explain social differences" (Omi and Winant 1994, 60). One might expect, then, that in a social environment in which people encounter and interact with others without being able to see them, that online participants would not make gendered, raced, and classed assumptions about others whom they encounter. Certainly many online participants, in keeping with the predominance of the ideal of "color blindness" in our society, claim that this is the case.

Yet, gender and race are concepts "which signify and symbolize social conflicts and interests by *referring* to different types of human bodies" (Omi and Winant 1995, 55, emphasis added). The importance of such signification and symbolization continues in online interaction. The bodies of others may remain hidden and inaccessible, but this if anything gives references to such bodies even more social importance. As Omi and Winant explain, "Despite its uncertainties and contradictions, the concept of race continues to play a fundamental role in structuring and representing the social world" (p. 55). This remains true about race, as well as about gender, class, sexuality, and age, especially when that uncertainty is compounded by the lack of physical presence in online encounters. Online participants assume that other participants do have bodies and that those bodies, if seen, would reveal important information. The assumed congruence between certain types of bodies and certain psychological, behavioral, and social characteristics results in the expectation by online participants that aspects of the hidden bodies—of, in effect, other participants' "true" identities—can be deduced (if imperfectly) from what is revealed online.

BlueSky participants told me that they hold in reserve their evaluations of people online until able to check these through an offline meeting. In cases where offline identities do not match online identities, they also attempt to explain having been fooled as to someone's true identity. Individual cases of mistaken identity require adjustment and explanation, demonstrating participants' expectations that essential, consistent identities are rooted in and connected to distinctly classifiable bodies. They expect that in most cases, the truth of these identities will come through in online communication, at least for those experienced in evaluating online identity performances.

MASCULINITIES AND COMPUTER TECHNOLOGY

Masculinity does not constitute a single uniform standard of behavior but rather comprise a range of gender identities clustered around expectations concerning masculinity that Connell (1995) has termed *hegemonic masculinity.* Connell (1995, 77) defines hegemonic masculinity as "the configuration of gender practice which embodies the currently accepted answer to the problem of the legitimacy of patriarchy, which guarantees (or is taken to guarantee) the dominant position of men and the subordination of women." While few men actually embody the hegemonic masculine ideal, they nevertheless benefit from the patriarchal dividend of dominance over women. However, they must also negotiate their own relationship to that ideal.

This negotiation, as well as the performance of specific masculinities, occurs through interaction with others. As Messerschmidt (1993; 31) points out, "Masculinity is never a static or a finished product. Rather, men construct masculinities in specific social situations." Segal (1990; 123) also describes masculinity as emerging through relations with others and as relational by definition:

> As it is represented in our culture, "masculinity" is a quality of being which is always incomplete, and which is equally based on social as on a psychic reality. It exists in the various forms of power men ideally possess: the power to assert control over women, over other men, over their own bodies, over machines and technology.

Perhaps the most salient of these forms of masculine power for the men on BlueSky is that over technology. Not all BlueSky participants work with computers, but even most of those who do not work in computer-related fields have done so in the past. In addition to their socializing on BlueSky, many participants employ computers for other leisure uses, including playing computer games on their home computers and participating in networked games available on the Internet.

As such, BlueSky participants enact a form of masculinity congruent with computer culture, itself a largely masculine domain (Spertus 1991; Turkle 1984, 1988; Ullman 1995). Wright (1996, 86) discusses the particular style of masculinity in both engineering and computer culture as "requiring aggressive displays of technical self-confidence and hands-on ability for success, defining professional competence in hegemonically masculine terms and devaluing the gender characteristics of women." Many conversations on BlueSky revolve around topics relating to computers, including information concerning new software, planned purchases, technical advice, and so on. In my interviews, many participants stressed the importance of the computer work-related information they obtained on BlueSky. During the day, people frequently log on with a particular question or problem from work that the others on BlueSky help them solve. Through these interactions, participants demonstrate technical knowledge and reinforce a group identity connected to computer technology. This also connects the group identity to masculinity since, as Cockburn (1985; 12) states, "Technology enters into our sexual identity: femininity is incompatible with technological competence; to feel technically competent is to feel manly."

"How Did I Get So Nerdy?"

While their computer skills help BlueSky participants gain and maintain employment and their connections with computers have cultural cachet as well, U.S. culture regards computer expertise and those who hold it ambivalently. This ambivalence extends particularly to the perceived gender identity of people skilled in computer use. American ambivalence about computers centers on the figure of the "nerd." For instance, Turkle (1984, 197–98) discusses the self-perception of MIT students as nerds by virtue of their connection to technology; she argues that MIT computer science students are "the ostracized of the ostracized" and "archetypal nerds." However, in her discussion of Turkle's descriptions, Wajcman (1991, 144) points out that

> an obsession with technology may well be an attempt by men who are social failures to compensate for their lack of power. On the other hand, mastery over this technology does bestow some power on these men; in relation to other men and women who lack this expertise, in terms of the material rewards this skill brings, and even in terms of their popular portrayal as "heroes" at the frontiers of technological progress.

The growing pervasiveness of computers in work and leisure activities has changed many people's relationship to computers and thus has also changed some of the meaning of the term *nerd.* Its use as a pejorative term thus varies in meaning depending on the social context. As an in-group term, it can convey affection or acceptance. Even when used pejoratively to support structures of hegemonic masculinity, it can confer grudging respect for technical expertise.

Many BlueSky participants possess personal or social characteristics that fit the nerd stereotype. As represented in the Nerdity Test, available online, such characteristics include fascination with technology, interest in science fiction and related media such as comic books, and perceived or actual social ineptitude and sartorial disorganization.[3] BlueSky participants illustrate their recognition of the nerd as both a desirable and marginal masculine identity in their discussions about nerd identity, as exemplified by the following statements culled from several different conversations on blueSky. (Each of the lines below is presented as it appeared on my screen. Note that all caps in online discourse generally connotes shouting.)

> Ulysses looks in henri's glasses and sees his reflection, ad exclaims "Oh NO! I'm a NERD!"
> Mender says "when you punish please feel free to refer to me as 'nerdy but nice'" Jet says, "HOW DID I GET SO NERDY"
> Randy ←fits one of the standard nerd slots

In the above quotes, BlueSky participants humorously identify themselves as nerds and connect with each other through play with that identity. But they also indicate their understanding that this disqualifies them from a more hegemonic masculine identity. Ulysses's mock dismay at his nerdy looks and the "but" in Mender's phrase "nerdy but nice" indicate their evaluations of the nerd identity as not completely desirable.

"Didja Spike 'Er?": Heterosexual Masculinity Online

As Segal (1994; 268–69) points out, "'Gender' and 'sexuality' are at present conceptually interdependent" and "provide two of the most basic narratives through which our identities are forged and developed." understandings of one's own and others' gender identities include assumptions about sexuality. While not all BlueSky participants are heterosexual, heterosexuality is an important component of the particular style of masculinity enacted on BlueSky. However, in this forum in which relationships are based so heavily on "talk," talk about sex and about men and women not surprisingly becomes more important to acceptable masculine performance than avowed conformity to particular sexual desires, practices, or relationships.

For instance, two very active and well-respected BlueSky male regulars define themselves as bisexual.

One of these has never had a sexual relationship with a man. The other had a relationship with another male mudder (who only rarely appears on BlueSky), which was known about and accepted by most other BlueSky participants. Both of these BlueSky regulars currently live with women in long-term relationships. Neither is viewed by other BlueSky men as having strayed very far from heterosexuality. However, it is also worth nothing that they very actively participate in jokes and conversations depicting women as sexual objects as well as in other forms of BlueSky banter connected to the performance of masculinity.

In keeping with acceptable performance of hegemonic masculinity, both men and women on BlueSky distance themselves from femininity and, to some extent, from women in general. Conversations that refer to women outside the mud, particularly women in whom a male participant might have a romantic interest, bluntly depict such women as sexual objects. However, participants' allusions to sexual activity are so out of context to the circumstances described that these references incorporate a high degree of irony. Participants further enhance this irony through the use of formulaic joking patterns, as in the following variations on the question, "Didja spike her?" culled from three separate conversations.

> Mender says "did I mention the secretary babe smiled at me today"
> Roger Pollack WOO WOO
> Jet says "cool Mender"
> Jet says "did you spike 'er"
> Mender says "No, sir, I did not spike 'er."

> McKenzie wonders if he should continue this e-mail correspondence or just wait till he can meet her tomorrow
> McKenzie siigh
> Locutus says "meet whom"
> Locutus shouts into a microphone, "SPIKE HER"

> Locutus had a short conversation with a 50–55 year old wrinkly well dressed woman in the wine section of the grocery
> Mender says "didja spike 'er, Locutus?"
> Rimmer says "DIDJA SPIKE HER LOCUTUS"
> Locutus says "hell no"

In each of these conversations, mere mention of a woman provokes the formulaic question, "Didja spike her?" Such joking formulas constitute techniques of group identity construction. Through jokes regarding women's status as sexual objects, the men on BlueSky demonstrate support for hegemonic masculinity. As Lyman (1998, 173) explains, "The emotional structure of the male bond is built upon a joking relationship that 'negotiates' the tension men feel about their relationships with each other, and with women." The ironic sexism of much BlueSky discourse maintains "the order of gender domination" (p. 172), almost irrespective of other aspects of BlueSky men's activities and behaviors with and toward the women in their lives.

However, the joking quality of the "didja spike her?" conversations also suggests an uneasiness with hegemonic masculinity. During a period when several participants had read a piece I had written analyzing references to gender on BlueSky (which did not include a discussion of the term *spike*), Rimmer asked me about "spike her" references. (My online name is Copperhead in the following example.)

> Rimmer says "So if I now said to Locutus 'So did you SPIKE her?' would that be offensive?"
> Copperhead does find the "did you SPIKE her" stuff a bit offensive, actually
> Rimmer says "Wow; the SPIKE stuff wouldn't be funny if there was any chance in hell that anyone ever would"
> henri nods at rimmer
> Lucutus says "the 'didja spike her' joke brings up the whole 'women as conquest' idea"
> Rimmer says "Boy I don't think it's a woman as conquest thing at all"
> henri says "what you find offensive (and I agree) is people thinking any time a guy interacts with a woman they should ask if their pants fell off and they locked hips"
> Rimmer says "I think it's more of a 'Mudders never have sex' thing"
> McKenzie agrees with Rimmer, "asking 'didja SPIKE her' is more parody than anything else"
> Rimmer doesn't think he's ever asked "DIDJA SPIKE HER" and expected someone to actually say YES
> Rimmer says "It would be tacky as all hell in that case"

McKenzie says "actually everyone would say 'I HATE you'"

Rimmer points out the joking nature of the question, "Didja spike her?" His assertion that "the SPIKE stuff wouldn't be funny if there was any chance in hell that anyone ever would" specifically highlights the mildly mocking intent of the joke. Yet, as Locutus and henri recognize, "spike" references rely on the continuing portrayal of women as sexual objects. Women's unattainability as sexual objects to some men provides the sting in the self-deprecatory joke, leaving in place a normative expectation that masculinity involves the sexual possession of women and that this is a desirable norm to attain. Rimmer and McKenzie indicate this in their identification of "didja spike her" as a rhetorical question. Rimmer states that "mudders never have sex" and suggests that they would not talk about it if they did since the other "less fortunate" participants would, as McKenzie indicates, say, "I HATE you." The joke is intended to be on the participants themselves, regarding their nonhegemonic masculinity, but women are the true butts of the joke.

BlueSky participants' sexual practices also may diverge from the aggressive hegemonic model implied by "spike." The potential discrepancy between sexual practice and group identity practice demonstrates some of the dilemmas involved in negotiating masculinities. Like adolescent boys who feel compelled to invent sexual exploits about which they can brag, men in groups create sexual and gender narratives that may bear little resemblance to other aspects of their lived experience but that nevertheless comprise important elements of their masculine identities and their connections with other men.

"Blubbery Pale Nerdettes": Nerds, Gender, and Sexuality

BlueSky discussions also demonstrate the dilemma that nerd identity introduces into the connection between gender identity and sexuality. Nerdism in both men and women is held to decrease sexual attractiveness, but in men this is compensated by the relatively masculine values attached to intelligence and computer skills. In women, lack of sexual attractiveness is a far greater sin. This is demonstrated in the following excerpt of a conversation about attendance at science fiction fan conventions among several male BlueSky participants.

Mike Adams says "that's half the reason I go to cons. Sit and have these discussions with people"
Bob. o O (No it isn't)
Mike Adams says "well, okay it's to ogle babes in barbarian outfits"
Drog says "*BABES*?"
Drog says "you need new glasses"
Drog says "pasty skinned blubbery pale nerdettes"
Locutus laaaaaughs
Locutus says "ARRRRR 'tis the WHITE WHAAALE"
Drog wouldn't pork any women he's ever seen at gaming/other cons, not even with Bob's cock.
Perry says "that's because pork is not kosher, drog"
Locutus says "women-met-at-cons: the Other White Meat"
Perry LAUGHS
Drog HOWLS at locutus

While apparently quite misogynistic, the impetus for this conversation relates at least as much to the BlueSky love of wordplay (another nerdy pastime) as to negative attitudes toward women. The word choices and the source of the humor in the above banter also reveal some key assumptions about and perceptions of nerd identity. Besides the implication in Drog's description that female nerds, like their male counterparts, do not spend much time outdoors or engage in exercise, his and Locutus's statements also represent nerds as white. While the term *nerd* may be applied to nonwhite males who meet other nerd identity criteria (see, e.g., Cheng 1996), the ideal-typical nerd is white. Similarly, nerds are presumed male, as evidenced by the term *nerdette.* This term, like use of the phrase "lady doctors," defines the normative case of nerd as not female.

This connection between nerdism and masculinity may be what makes a nerd identity so damaging to women's potential and perceived sexual desirability. The participants express the assumption that nerdettes who would attend science fiction conventions by definition lack sexual desirability and quickly join the joke set by Drog's critique of Mike Adams's potentially transgressive desire. Mike Adams, on the other hand, ceased further participation in the conversation until the topic of cons had passed.

Heterosexual "Dropouts"

Some of the ways in which BlueSky participants enact and express heterosexual identities suggest that in examining connections between sexualities and masculinities, we need to problematize notions of heterosexuality as a single, uniform sexual identity. A standard Kinsey-style spectrum of straight to gay identities based on sexual behaviors or feelings does not adequately describe sexual identity on BlueSky, as it leaves out important information concerning affectional connections and orientation toward sexuality in general. As Segal (1994, 257) states, "It is men's fear of, or distaste for, sex with women, as well known as it is well concealed, that the heterosexual imperative works so hard to hide." Discussions of sexuality on BlueSky sometimes reveal this distaste, as well as the unorthodox solutions some men find for the dilemma imposed on them by the tension between distaste and hegemonic masculine identity, including its heterosexual component.

For instance, several of the straight men on BlueSky report that they have "given up" on women and/or on romantic relationships and have been celibate more or less by choice for several years. In discussions on BlueSky such as the one below, these men complain of rejection based on their nonhegemonic status.

> Stomp has problems with dating and women and stuff, but also has serious reservations about the accepted male-female dynamic in the USA, to the point where he's never felt much point in getting over the first set of problems.
> Drog says "Sides, women LIKE scumbags; it's been proven"
> Ulysses nods at Drog
> Drog should have been gay, he can relate to other guys
> Stomp says "as far as I've been able to observe, abusing women (subtly) is one of the fastest and most efficient ways of getting laid."
> Drog will agree with that
> Stomp says "Once I realized this, I just sort of went: Well, forget it, then."
> Drog says "guys get to be assholish and abusive cause that kinda attitude is richly rewarded"
> Ulysses says "Nice guys end up being the friends to whom those women say, 'You're such a good listener, let me tell you about the latest horrible thing my inconsiderate sweetie did to me' "
> Stomp says "Expressing interest in a way that isn't assholish invites getting cut down brutally."
> Ulysses says "We tried opening our mouths a few times, and got laughed at"
> Ulysses says "End of experiment"
> Stomp says "You get seen as weak."
> Ulysses says "self-assurance and confidence are not options for me. I'd have to go back to infancy and start over"
> Drog says "this mud is full of 'nice guys.' it's also full of guys who haven't been laid in epochs if ever"

The male participants in the above conversation express considerable ambivalence toward predominant standards of masculinity, portraying themselves as "nice guys" left out of the standard (in their understanding) heterosexual dynamic of violent conquest. Yet, although they designate more sexually successful men as (by definition) "jerks," their discussion implies that the real problem is not with "assholish" men but rather with the women who like the abuse they get from such men. Rather than merely rejecting a heterosexuality they view as abusive, they represent themselves as reacting to having been "cut down brutally," "laughed at," and "seen as weak," as well as used as a sympathetic ear without regard for their own potential desires. Drog, Stomp, and Ulysses still represent themselves as heterosexual, despite their avowed lack of heterosexual activity. Heterosexuality remains an important component of their identities, interconnected as it is with hegemonic masculinity. In their retreat from heterosexual activity. Drog, Stomp, and Ulysses do not opt to ally themselves in friendship or identification with women. Instead, as Drog says, they "relate to other guys." BlueSky provides them with a sympathetic forum in which most other participants are men and the few women are less obviously women both because they cannot be seen and because they conform to

BlueSky standards and expectations of behavior set by the men in the group.

The rather stereotypical depiction of women, as not only tolerating but also desiring abuse, points to some potential interpretations of the male angst expressed. Hegemonic masculinity's requirement of heterosexuality contains an inherent contradiction. As Lyman (1998; 178) points out,

> The separation of intimacy from sexuality transforms women into "sexual objects," which both justifies aggression at women by suspending their relationships to the men and devalues sexuality itself, creating a disgust of women as the sexual "object" unworthy of intimate attention.

While the hegemonic gender order thus depicts women as inferior and not acceptable identity models, it nevertheless requires that men desire these inferior (even disgusting) creatures. The men in the conversation above represent casualties of this contradiction. Their discomfort blends a rejection of perceived expectations regarding hegemonic masculinity—especially those involving violence toward women—with a more hegemonically congruent discomfort with women themselves.

"Mov[ing] Well in Caucasian Spaces"

Given online demographics, participants tend to assume that others they encounter online are white. As RaveMage, a Filipino American participant, stated, "All the males [on BlueSky] are caucasian or move well in caucasian spaces," implicitly recognizing BlueSky itself as a "caucasian space." Whiteness thus becomes the "default" identity. In addition, as revealed in the discussion of nerdettes above, whiteness is connected to the particular subcultural nerd identity. Aspects of nerdiness come to signify whiteness as well.

For instance, Jet, a very active regular on BlueSky for several years, complicates his Chinese American identity by often referring to himself online as white. Other BlueSky participants know that his parents emigrated from China, and discussions of his Chinese heritage also occur. When I asked Jet about his self-defining as white, he talked about how whiteness marks a cultural identity as well as a racial distinction. (Our conversation occurred through "whispers," meaning that the online text was viewed only by Jet and I and not by other participants on the mid.)

> Copperhead whispers "several times when questions of ethnicity or race have come up you've made the statement that you're white; I'm wondering what you mean by that."
>
> Jet whispers "I mean that I am essentially an american clothed in a chinese body. I hardly know how to speak chinese, I hardly know anything about the culture, and I don't associate with orientals a lot by choice, unlike many immigrant children. So I feel 'white,' i.e. american"
>
> Copperhead whispers "so if 'american' = 'white' is BlueSky a white space? And what does that mean for people who aren't white here?"
>
> Jet whispers "no no, american != white.[4] i use 'white' in the sense of the martin mull stereotype; very bland, whitebread; obviously i'm not. it's a sort of irony."
>
> Jet whispers "mudding transcends ethnicity. i don't consider blue sky 'white' or 'american' or any ethnicity, i just consider it a place to hang out, if you were all asian and had the same personalities, so be it"

While Jet refers to his own "cultural whiteness," he denies cultural effects of race or ethnicity through his suggestion that it would be possible for BlueSky participants to be "all asian" and yet have "the same personalities." This elision of the cultural aspects of race, which his ironic labeling of himself as white both contradicts and highlights, enables him to claim that "mudding transcends ethnicity." On one hand, Jet suggests that the physical characteristics associated with race do not determine identity. Although acknowledging his ethnic heritage in some ways (at one point during this conversation, he stated, for instance, that he would prefer to marry another Asian American) and labeling his body Chinese, Jet labels himself white based on the cultural affinities that he finds more salient. However, in calling himself white, he still gives his (cultural) identity a racial label. Although he denies that American equals white, he nevertheless labels his American-ness "white." Jet's representation of himself as white serves as a "racial project," which, in Omi and

Winant's (1994, 56) words, forms both "an interpretation, representation, or explanation of racial dynamics, and an effort to reorganize and redistribute resources along particular racial lines." In Jet's case, his representation of himself as white reinforces the dominant order in which benefits accrue to those who are white. But he also attempts to reposition himself as entitled to those benefits because beneath the "clothing" of his Chinese body, he is "really" white.

In recognition of the ironic contradictions involved in his self-identity, Jet associates true whiteness with "bland, whitebread." White participants on BlueSky also make this association. For instance, Peg, a white female regular, classified herself as "pretty white, but not wonder-bread, [my] father's family are eastern europeans." By referring to "real" whiteness as "wonder-bread" (bland, nonnutritious, over-processed), Peg distances herself from hegemonic white identity. This sets up a hierarchy of whiteness in which only full-blooded WASPs qualify as "really" white. Those who, like her, have other European ancestry are only "pretty" white. Jet's similar reference to "bland white-bread" allows him to be white too, even though he is not "really" white.

Both participants mark themselves with an ironically detached white-but-not-white identity. However, they arrive at this identity formulation from very different offline physical realities. Peg is short and petite, with very pale skin and light reddish-brown hair. Jet is more than six feet tall and thin with light brown skin and almost black hair. That I can so describe them, and experience their similar self-identification as ironic, points to assumptions concerning the physical nature of racial identity that I, like the other BlueSky participants, have internalized from the surrounding culture.

In the following conversation, several participants, drawing on this physical understanding of race, contest Jet's self-definition as white.

Jet rather enjoyed the LA riots in a sick way
Jet went to Canter's 3 days afterwards, and there was us, 4 white guys, and 12 cops
Jet says "That's it."
Jet says "(we were the 4 white guys)"
Mender . o O (Jet's a white guy!)
Ichi giggles at Jet
Jet . o O (oh i am)
Jet says "You've met me, you know I'm white"
Mender says "not as white as I am, bucko"
Pyramid says "HOW WHITE ARE YOU?"
McKenzie says "Mender gets waspy"
Jet says "I'm pretty white"
Jet says "no joke"

Mender's claim to be whiter than Jet provokes an accusation of "waspiness" from McKenzie. As with Peg's definition of herself as only "pretty white," this stance labels the aggressive assertion of white identity as waspiness, again relying on an understanding that white Anglo-Saxon protestants represent hegemonic whiteness. Just as male participants on BlueSky distance themselves in some ways from hegemonic masculinity, white participants distance themselves from hegemonic white identity. Like the ironic references to hegemonic masculinity contained in the "didja spike 'er" jokes, BlueSky discussions of whiteness disavow identification with the very top of the dominance chain, yet ultimately leave intact the taken-for-granted workings of racial dominance found in American society.

These discussions about racial identity online emphasize both the absence and the presence of race online. Gilroy (1987, 24) argues that race and racism are processes and that the meanings of race "are unfixed and subject to the outcomes of struggle." We learn to classify people by skin color and other physical identifiers and learn to associate these identifiers with race. Hence, I can easily point to Peg and label her white and to Jet and label him Asian. But the meanings of these designations vary and are sites of struggle, as both Jet and Peg indicate in their self-identifications. When these struggles are brought online, some of their parameters change.

Jet's self-identification of white is challenged by other BlueSky participants. Having met him, they rely on their understanding of the physical nature of race to classify him based on bodily characteristics. Thus, participants bring their assumptions about race with them to online interactions. However, online participants perform racial identities under slightly different rules. For instance, nonwhite participants can benefit from the predominant presumption of whiteness online. Spontaneity, a Chinese American, indicates that online interactions free him from fears of harassment.

Spontaneity whispers "I've noticed a lack of harassment on line in general."
Copperhead whispers "that's interesting; less harassment online than off?"
Spontaneity whispers "Yah, Now, it may just be that people are able to be more subtle online, but I don't think so. For example, it's fairly common for me to get shouted at on the streets."

The high percentage of whites online combines with a U.S. discourse of "color blindness," making direct references to race taboo (Frankenberg 1993, 14). This enables whites to assume that other online participants are also white. Since the space this potentially opens up for harassment-free speech from nonwhites remains defined as white, the advantage to nonwhites constitutes a form of "passing" for white rather than a true dissolution of racial difference and hierarchy. However, the lack of visual cues in text-based online spaces makes passing more feasible online than off. This does constitute some degree of "leveling the playing field" (although the type of game and its rules remain unquestioned).

CONCLUSION

The masculinities performed on BlueSky demonstrate the convergence and interaction of several important facets of identity, including class, gender, sexuality, race, age, and relationships to technology. U.S. cultural expectations regarding technology usage converge with stereotypes concerning race and gender, resulting in a white nerd masculine identity congruent with related forms of masculinity found in computing and engineering fields. In enacting this form of masculinity, BlueSky participants demonstrate both its divergence from and convergence with hegemonic masculinity. Participants recognize their lack of hegemonic status poke fun at some aspects of hegemonic masculinity. However, they also distance themselves from women and from femininity and engage in a style of interaction congruent with hegemonic masculinity. The coupling of expectations of technological competence with this predominant interfactional mode of obnoxious bantering strengthens connections between computer technological competence and masculinities.

BlueSky participants diverge somewhat from hegemonic masculinity in their discussions of various aspects of sexuality. Several participants find their homosexual or bisexual orientation accepted within the group. However, both heterosexual and nonheterosexual men (and women) participate in conversations that depict women as sexual objects. This may indicate that at least for some men, distance from women comprises a more important component of masculine identity than sexual distance from men. Inclusion of homosexual and bisexual men who perform aspects of heterosexual masculinity (in that they also sexually objectify women) creates a social environment in which homosociality takes precedence over attitudes toward homosexuality.

This more inclusive stance may be particularly possible for men online. In text-based online communication, the lack of physical presence and awareness of each other's male bodies decreases the likelihood that gestures or utterances will be misconstrued as sexual advances or interest. Under such circumstances, heterosexual men may be able to more safely "pal around" with nonheterosexual men, at least as long as those men continue to perform a masculine identity congruent in the main with that of the heterosexual men.

Conversations on BlueSky concerning men, women, relationships, and sexuality also demonstrate some of the variation within heterosexual male identities. Heterosexual men may like or dislike the women they theoretically desire. They may spend time socially with women or mostly with other men. As in the examples of several of the BlueSky men, some heterosexual men also maintain a heterosexual identity without engaging in heterosexual relationships. For men such as Ulysses and Stomp, changing norms of masculinity have failed to resolve the contradiction inherent in hegemonic masculinity's relationship to women as both desired and disgusting objects. Such men view hegemonically masculine males as jerks, thereby distancing themselves from that ideal. However, they also view women as people who like those jerks. In this way, they distance themselves from women, representing them as foreign beings who unfathomably like abuse. This leaves these heterosexual dropouts with no company but their own and that of other, similarly not-quite-hegemonic men (and a few women who perform congruent identities). Through wryly ironic jokes about men, women, and sexuality, BlueSky participants create and enact a culture that continually reiterates this pattern of distancing from both other men and most women.

BlueSky's culture, formed by a predominantly white group, also draws from and reenacts white cultural norms of masculine behaviors. Here again, BlueSky participants distance themselves from the hegemonic ideal ("waspy" or "true" whiteness) but also continue to distance themselves from oppressed groups. The whiteness of BlueSky is reinforced by the larger cultural contexts in which it is embedded, including U.S. and Internet cultures. The predominance of whites online, combined with U.S. norms of color blindness, leads to assumptions that online participants are white unless stated otherwise. Thus, Asian Americans on BlueSky must either take a distinctly oppositional stance to the predominant norm of whiteness or themselves perform versions of white masculinity to fit in with the group. For some, such as Spontaneity, presumptions of whiteness, combined with the unavailability in interaction of the physical markers of race, provide greater freedom from harassment. However, given BlueSky participants' knowledge of both online and offline identity information, Asian American men's status as "one of the white boys" can be challenged, as Jet found.

The relative inclusiveness of BlueSky is predicated in the continuation of a social structure in which white middle-class men continue to have the power to include or not to include people whose gender, sexuality, or race marks them as other. BlueSky's regulars include a few women, nonheterosexuals, and Asian Americans who fit themselves into BlueSky's cultural context through their performances of white masculinities. The text only nature of much online communication can facilitate greater inclusiveness. However, as on BlueSky, many online groups also make offline connections with each other and bring knowledge from those meetings to their online interactions. The predominance of white men online can also limit that inclusiveness to "others" who can fit themselves into a culture formed by and for those white men.

NOTES

1. I have changed all names in this article, including the name of the mud and character names. I have replaced character names with names drawn from similar sources and references to retain some of the flavor of the originals. I refer throughout to BlueSky participants by these character names because, for the most part, they also refer to each other using character names rather than real-life names.

2. I conducted two online searches for information regarding Internet demographics. In 1995, two sites provided information abut race, listing white participants at 83 percent and 87 percent, respectively; both showed Black participation at 5 percent and Asian at 3 percent. Neither of those sites still exists, and none of the sites I reviewed during my later search (28 November 1997) provided information regarding race. That 1997 search indicates that approximately half of Internet users are age 35 or younger, and most have at least some college experience. More than 60 percent hold some form of professional, technical, managerial, or other white-collar job, with incomes clustering in the $30,000 to $90,000 range. Estimates of the percentage of women online vary from 31 percent to 45 percent. The following is a partial list of sites I reviewed for my November 1997 search: http://www2.chaicenter.org/otn/aboutinternet/Demographics-Nielsen.html;http://www3.mids.org/ids/index.html; http://thehost.com/demo.htm; http://www.scruzner.com/%7Eplugin01/Demo.html;http://www.cyberatlas.com/demographics.html; http://www.cc.gatech.edu/gvu/user???surveys/survey-1997-04; and http://www.ora.com/research/users/results.html. Most of the surveys reported at these sites are done by commercial organizations that do not always reveal their methodology. They also often reserve details and/or the most recent information for paying customers. Therefore, I cannot vouch for the reliability of these statistics.

3. The Nerdity Test is available on the World Wide Web at, among other places, http://165.91.72.200/nerd-backwards.html.

4. The exclamation point and equals sign in this phrase come from programming languages in which != means "not equal to."

REFERENCES

Cheng, C. 1996. "We choose not to compete": The "merit" discourse in the selection process, and Asian and Asian-American men and their masculinity. In *Masculinities in organizations,* edited by C. Cheng. Thousand Oaks, CA: Sage.

Cockburn, C. 1985. *Machinery of dominance: Women, men and technical know-how.* London: Pluto.

Connell, R. W. 1995. *Masculinities.* Berkeley: University of California Press.

Frankenberg, R. 1993. *The social construction of whiteness: White women, race matters.* Minneapolis: University of Minnesota Press.

Gilroy, P. 1987. *"There ain't no black in the Union Jack:" The cultural politics of race and nation.* Chicago: University of Chicago Press.

Lyman, P. 1998. The fraternal bond as a joking relationship: A case study of the role of sexist jokes in male group bonding. In *Men's lives,* edited by M. S. Kimmel and M. A. Messner. 4th ed. Boston: Allyn & Bacon.

Messerschmidt, J. W. 1993. *Masculinities and crime: Critique and reconceptualization of theory.* Lanham, MD: Rowman & Littlefield.

Omi, M., and H. Winant. 1994. *Racial formation in the United States from the 1960s to the 1990s.* 2d ed. New York: Routledge Kegan Paul.

Segal, L. 1990. *Slow motion: Changing masculinities, changing men.* New Brunswick, NJ: Rutgers University Press.

———. 1994. *Straight sex: The politics of pleasure.* London: Virago.

Spertus, E. 1991. Why are there so few female computer scientists? ???Al Lab Technical Report [Online]. Available: http://www.ai.mit.edu/people/ellens/Gender/why.html.

Turkle, S. 1984. *The second self: Computers and the human spirit.* New York: Simon & Schuster.

———. 1988. Computational reticence: Why women fear the intimate machine. In *Technology and women's voices: Keeping in touch,* edited by C. Kramarae. New York: Routledge Kegan Paul.

Ullman, E. 1995. Out of time: Reflections on the programming life. In *Resisting the virtual life: The culture and politics of information,* edited by J. Brook and I. A. Boal. San Francisco: City Lights.

Wajcman, J. 1991. *Feminism confronts technology.* University Park: Pennsylvania State University Press.

West, C., and S. Fenstermaker. 1995. Doing difference. *Gender & Society* 9:8–37.

Wright, R. 1996. The occupational masculinity of computing. In *Masculinities in organizations,* edited by C. Cheng. Thousand Oaks, CA: Sage.

PART IX

CHANGE AND POLITICS

Lesbians and gays flock to San Francisco to participate in marriage, an institution once denounced as a bastion of sexism by the early feminist and gay liberation movements. Young men in college "rush" to join gay fraternities, seemingly subverting homophobia by going straight into the heart of masculinist hegemony. A group of mothers take to the streets on behalf of their children, demanding that politicians invest in job creation and safe streets. Women organizing handloom weavers in India use the internet to further their goals. Activities such as these challenge the idea that change in the prism of gender inequalities comes about principally through voting, lobbying, or other more orthodox means of politics. The chapters in this section examine how social change is emerging in the daily practices of individuals and communities, through social movement organizations and in renegotiated institutions and in the forward-looking visions of the future. Change in multifaceted and comes from unlikely candidates and in unlikely places.

College fraternity culture is widely recognized and portrayed in popular films such as *Animal House* as one of the stalwarts of homophobic masculinist culture. Yet no institution is immune to change, and as King-To Yeung and Mindy Stombler show, gay men on college campuses are embracing fraternities as their own, innovating Delta Lambda Phi as a gay fraternity. Becoming simulateously gay and Greek does involve some tightrope tensions, and the men of Delta Lambda Phi negotiate these tensions, Yeung and Stombler observe, by desexualizing and defeminizing their fraternity activities and interactions. This strategy can be seen as either capitulation to conformity with gender norms, or as the assimilation of a heterosexual institution to homosexual culture. Social change, we learn from this article, is rarely uniformly simple or unidirectional; it is often contradictory and messy.

The next chapters challenge traditional assumptions about women's participation in social and political movements. Mary Pardo's study reveals how Mexican-American women's identities as mothers helped to fuel grassroots political mobilization, which in turn sparked political transformations and expanded meanings of motherhood. Radhika Gajjala and Annapurna Mamidipudi suggest that internet technologies and cyberfeminism can bridge—or perhaps erode—the differences between poor women in the south (formerly known as the third world) and the affluent in the north. Poor women of color living in developed, industrial societies or in developing nations are not generally recognized as feminist activists, but both of these studies suggest how the diversity of these women's experiences fuels a more expansive range of feminist political activities.

Is sexism a static, permanent, and unyielding characteristic? Are men so committed to retaining patriarchal privileges that they are unable to change and support justice and equality in gender relations? The last chapter by Kevin Powell, suggests that the answer to these question is a resounding no. In his poignant and candid confession of the dilemmas he has faced as a recovering misogynist, Powell opens the door to a world based on new consciousness and newly negotiated relations of race and gender. Together, the authors in this final section of the book show us that embracing the prism of difference is a vital step toward building a more democratic future.

50

Gay and Greek

The Identity Paradox of Gay Fraternities

KING-TO YEUNG
MINDY STOMBLER

. . . Our research will examine the tensions faced by a group of self-identified gay men as they sought both to emulate and change the oppressive majority culture. We examine how the collective identity of a particular organization, a gay fraternity, emerged as members negotiated their precarious location with one foot placed in one of the most traditionally heterosexist cultures in straight society, the college fraternity culture (Martin and Hummer 1989; Moffatt 1989; Stombler 1994) and the other placed in an oppositional gay culture. Current gay identity research tends to focus on identity construction as an act of activism against mainstream culture. By concentrating research efforts on this subset of the gay population, sociologists learn more about oppositional strategies than "mainstreaming" strategies in gaining legitimization from the dominant culture. Given the heterosexist nature of the traditional fraternity, this research juxtaposes how assimilation into and subversion of the dominant order can co-exit in paradoxical ways.

The national gay fraternity, Delta Lambda Phi (DLP)—consisting of sixteen chapters across the United States—served as a social alternative for gay college men. DLP modeled itself after traditional fraternities and retained the traditional features of brotherhood, rituals, and group hierarchical structure.[1] Its members shared straight fraternity goals such as involvement in campus social life, enhanced prestige on campus, networking opportunities and alumni connections, and, although not explicitly stated, achieving power over women and other men[2] (c.f. Martin and Hummer 1989; Sanday 1990; Stombler 1994; Stombler and Padavic 1997; Stombler and Martin 1994). Yet, based on our observations at the national convention and within the observed chapter and our interview and archival data, DLP rejected some traditional fraternity practices such as hazing, promoting single-race membership, encouraging sexual coercion, and enforcing individual conformity (Stombler, Wharton, and Yeung, 1997). We contend that DLP's choice to emulate the organizational structure of straight fraternities was not arbitrary, allowing DLP members to relate to both the gay and straight worlds. Using a fraternity model provided DLP members an opportunity to subvert the heterosexist fraternal tradition and potentially achieve legitimacy within the college campus community. A frater-

King-To Yeung and Mindy Stombler, "Gay and Greek: The Identity Paradox of Gay Fraternities," from *Social Problems,* Volume 47, Number 1, pp. 134–152.

nity model that stressed brotherhood also allowed members to embrace and criticize aspects of the gay culture that they found unfulfilling. In both ways, adopting the fraternity model was a unique vehicle for members to restate what it meant to be gay and Greek. In doing so, however, DLP was faced with dilemmas that demanded that members choose between incompatible group strategies and ideologies. We will discuss not only how members constructed a collective identity within the gay fraternity, but also how the gay fraternity's placement, straddling both the gay and straight worlds, affected this development, creating a paradox of identity.[3]

METHODS AND DATA

This paper is part of a larger research project on gay fraternities (Stombler, Wharton, and Yeung 1997). Data for the project came from 42 open-ended in-depth interviews, participant observation, official manuals, and archival data.

The project was divided into two phases. In the first phase Stombler conducted participant observation for a year in the mid-1990s in a DLP chapter-in-formation. She attended all fraternity chapter meetings, social events, rituals, and community service projects. In addition she conducted in-depth face-to-face interviews with fraternity members (all members volunteered to be interviewed). Stombler also attended the National Gay Fraternity (Diva Las Vegas) where she observed interaction among members across the nation, interviewed members who responded to her research project announcement, and solicited additional interview volunteers for in-depth phone interviews.

In the second phase Yeung and Wharton joined the project and interviewed the previously recruited members from various chapters by telephone.[4] They also contacted chapter presidents and asked them for a list of additional interview volunteers. We also used the deviant cases sampling technique that involves seeking out respondents who are atypical to a setting such as straight or bisexual men in the case of the gay fraternity. Interviews—which were tape recorded and transcribed—averaged two hours. When the emergent concepts became "saturated" (Glaser and Strauss 1967), we ended the interview component of the project.[5] . . .

CONSTRUCTING A GAY IDENTITY

Gay organizations as communities of identity are self-reproducing (c.f., Melucci 1989) in two ways. First, the organization depends on a membership that includes individuals who identify themselves as gays or lesbians. This individual identification makes it possible for the organization to exist. Second, by participating in a gay organization, members are able to authenticate their sexual identity and reproduce the gay identity collectively. Gay identity is a point of entry for both the individual members and the organization to place sexual identity in the foreground while relegating other social identities to the background. In this section, we illustrate the dynamics of personal and collective reproduction of the gay identity by examining the ways DLP helped members to come out of the closet, bringing them into the gay community, and draw a collective boundary that challenged the traditional straight fraternity institution.

Coming Out and Moving Into the Gay World

Coming out of the closet represents the experience that gay men and lesbians have when first acknowledging their sexual orientation, identifying themselves as gay, acting on their sexual desire, disclosing this desire to other, and publicly entering the gay community (Dank 1971; Herdt 1992; Rhoads 1994; Troiden 1988). Some members of the gay fraternity reported that joining DLP marked their first coming out experience. In the observed chapter, many men used the fraternity rush event as their first function in the gay community. For instance, one member said he was so nervous that he was shaking during the rush party. Too scared to dress for the party in his dorm for fear of repercussions, he left in workout clothes and went to the mall where he purchased an outfit for the formal event and then changed into it before going to rush. The rush events often turned out to be the first time isolated gay college men met other gay men as a group.

For many members of DLP, the gay fraternity was the first site where they experienced their sexual identity in a structured form. The fraternity activities such as parties, rituals, and community service provided opportunities for new gay members to share their experiences and realfirm their commonalities as members of the gay community:

> [During pledging] we have sort of a process where we go around and get signature from all the active brothers and you talk about whatever. I went and talked with everyone about their coming out experience. . . . I feel like what brings us together is the experience of the fear of coming out. . . . I was so amazed that I was suddenly able to make connections with people who I had never felt like I could make them with before. (B08)

DLP also used formal programming to explicitly bring forth the cultural aspect of gay sexual identity. For instance, one chapter held workshops on "how to do fabulous drag" and "how to deal with HIV-AIDS when it affects you or someone you love" (B07). Another chapter included the "essential gay history" in its coming out support program:

> There's a reason why [gay men] idolize Joan Crawford: there's a reason why they love Marilyn Monroe. . . . We teach gay history in the coming out group. Everybody is supposed to know the gay history [and id tested on it on fraternity pledge tests]. (B22)

Besides transmitting a stock of knowledge about gayness, DLP also used cultural resources regarding gayness to bind its members, constructing a microcosm of the larger gay sub-cultural community. On movie nights, for instance, members often chose gay-theme movies such as "Jeffrey," or watched movies popular within gay culture:

> Instead of watching a regular old hit movie, [they] would seek out campy movies like "Breakfast at Tiffany's," "Mommy Dearest," and anything with Bette Davis [a gay icon] . . . [then, we went to the park] to play croquet and [it was] really campy. I'm like, "oh my god, my god, this is so gay, I love it!". (B30)

In another event, members played a game called "Gay Monopoly," which included "having discos instead of railroads, as well as locations and resorts popular among the gay community" (Hahn 1995). Through these events, members learned and created the cultural meaning of being gay.

Ultimately, DLP worked to redefine the meaning of being gay and helped members to recover from the fear, shame, or guilt they had experienced. Since the organization structured itself with an emphasis on brotherhood and mutual support among its members as a main goal (see below), the autonomy to become "who you are" found a structural support within the organization:

> One of our fraternity brothers was still in the closet. He didn't want to tell his family, but Pete [another brother] helped him along. He said, "Don't be ashamed of who you are. If your parents don't approve of you, fine, this is who you are." He told him, "You take it easy. Tell your parents individually or together, but you take it slowly. We'll work with you." He come out just fine even though his parents didn't approve of it at first. [His parents] kicked him out, but we found him a place to live. (B27, observed chapter)

The secure environment that DLP fostered allowed members to identify, reaffirm, and celebrate their sexual identity as gay men, incorporating them into the larger gay community. These processes of identity formation were often grounded in group work and interaction within the organization. The processes of coming out as a group and as an individual were intertwined and reinforced one another:

> It's nice to belong to a group whose motto is "making your presence known" and to know that when you go out as a group, you are going out with the intention of letting people know you are there. You are not going to hide. It's very important to me when I came out to make people know. It was part of my battle to accept my sexuality and it is nice to be with a group of men. When go out, we wear our shirts and you know we are there. You can't miss us. (B32)

Group Boundaries in the Straight World

The extent to which members as individuals, and DLP as group, could openly be out in the public, nonetheless varied according to DLP chapters' external social environments. The group boundary DLP established within the straight world was a contentious one, challenging the traditional fraternity institution on two levels. On one hand, the gay fraternity was striving to gain recognition within one of the most heterosexist institutions in American college life—the fraternity. On the other hand, DLP actively modified the traditional model by prohibiting hazing and other practices that were deemed "homophobic." At either level, DLP reconfigured its relations with the traditional institution by drawing a collective boundary that framed gayness as it core.

As a gay group, DLP demanded the right to enter the fraternity institution: "We feel if straight men can have the 'traditional' Greek experience, gay men should be able to have it as well" (DLP web site). DLP's existence as an openly gay fraternity had the potential to "shock" the traditionally homophobic fraternity institution that encourages a "macho image" (Martin and Hummer 1989). Since the word fraternity "and the word gay are not usually associated" (B36) within this system, establishing a gay fraternity was particularly meaningful for campuses located in conservative regions:

> I think by virtue of calling ourselves the gay fraternity was making a statement nationally, especially down here. In San Francisco or Washington, D.C. or New York, gay fraternities might not be such a huge statement, but in the Bible Belt, forming any kind of gay organization is making a statement. (B21)

By coming out as a group, DLP demanded recognition: "It is making a statement to colleges and campuses saying, 'Hey, you need to recognize that you do have gay students; you have large group of them.'" (B09)

DLP also challenged the traditional fraternity model by prohibiting hazing. In official statements and group interaction, gay members claimed that hazing was unacceptable. This rejection reflected DLP's acknowledgment of oppression as part of the collective gay identity: "We feel that gays have been hazed enough by society" (DLP Web site). Unlike straight fraternities that have similar policies but often fail to follow them in practice (Nuwer 1990), DLP strictly followed the no-hazing policy, even at the local level. . . .

. . . Men in straight fraternities tend to define masculinity narrowly, emphasizing sexual conquest, competition, ability to consume alcohol, and a devaluing of the feminine (Martin and Hummer 1989; Moffatt 1989). Members of DLP did not embrace this narrow definition of masculinity. For example, gay members did not stigmatize effeminate behaviors; indeed, DLP members encouraged expressions of femininity. One member explained that "one thing in the gay fraternity that you don't see in the straight fraternities is that we don't have to play out our masculinity. You know, like prove our masculinity in certain ways" (B03). Member desiring to dress up on drag found the fraternity a safe place to practice "femaling" (Ekins 1977) and to express their individuality.

Embracing this gender fluidity and resisting hegemonic masculinity have been major components of gay identity (see Norton 1996). DLP's organizational events frequently structured (both intentionally and unintentionally) an arena for members to transgress gender boundaries. One member described how, at an initiation party, the "butch" members who had never though of doing drag, attempted "border-crossing":

> The thing that sticks out the most from that evening is that we had what we call the Drag in the Bag Contest, which I think is unique to our chapter. . . . Without our knowledge, the little pledges got together all sorts of female and other paraphernalia . . . basically dress-up clothes, mostly female, but other things were in there also. You would see some of these really butch men dress up in drag and basically just have a good time with it. They were taking picture. (B23) . . .

THE PARADOX OF MAINSTREAMING

The group goals of DLP were inconsistent: although attempting to contest the traditional practices of straight fraternities, members also sought to construct a "normal," comparable fraternity image:

> We have a national [organization]; we have the same type of criteria that we all go through year after year. We're all men, and even though we are gay men, there's really not anything that really differentiates us

> from other men down the block in the other [straight] fraternities. (B13)

Mainstreaming was thus a way for DLP to seek legitimacy in the straight world.[6] This process involved the fraternity seeking to build respectability and to emphasize sameness over difference vis-à-vis traditional fraternities. Downplaying differences to integrate into the mainstream was contradictory for an organization that was based on a gay membership. In order to reestablish what the fraternity thought was the appropriate image for gay men, primarily by defying sterotypes through desexualization and defeminization, DLP implicitly reaffirmed the negative stereotypes imposed by the straight world. We will discuss these strategies to illustrate how DLP sought to downplay the gay identity in paradoxical ways.

Desexualizing

The gay fraternity was well aware of the misconceptions that members of the Greek system and the campus community had about gay men, in general, and DLP, specifically. Members found it particularly disturbing that outsiders associated being gay exclusively with sexual behavior. One member complained: "Here at the university they think we are the biggest sex club in the world. People have that viewpoint because you see gay and you see sex and that is all they think. We are not like that" (B27, observed chapter).

One way DLP members promoted the desexualizing goal (and group solidarity in case of failed relationship) was to formally discourage casual sex and ingroup dating (especially between pledges and brothers whose relationships leaders defined as inherently unequal and therefore potentially exploitative). DLP was more tolerant of long-term monogamous relationships between brothers, especially considering that some brothers joined as couples. Even with a formal ban, some casual relationships and encounters did occur. We noted pledges interested in joining the fraternity to meet and date men, pledges dating brothers, brothers casually dating brothers, and rare incidences of open casual sex. Either way, intra-fraternity dating was more often a consequence of the men's proximity to one another than a characteristic of the fraternal form, and fraternity leaders explicitly discouraged it, promoting ideologies of familial relationships as opposed to sexual ones. Clearly by adopting the fraternal organization form with its pseudo-familial kinship network of "brothers," and stressing the ideal of brotherhood over romance, DLP leaders made a strong statement against an overtly sexualized gay identity.

While DLP members did not always succeed in their desexualizing goal, their levels of sensitivity and reflexivity were reflected in how they dealt with problematic situations regarding the sexual image of DLP. During one gay pride event, a DLP chapter sold snow cones with "gay theme flavors" such as "lesbian lime." When "Gilbert's grapes"—referring to male genitals—appeared as a flavor, it triggered serious criticism from some members of the chapter:

> I mean because children attend the event and some straight people attend the event, and to me, I am really quite tired of the sexual stereotype that straight people have of gays, and to me, I just thought that this strengthened the impression that other people have of us, and I think at a public event that there was no need to use that. . . . I don't want to belong to an organization that promotes or encourages sexual innuendo or the perception that straight people may have of us. (B02)

This member successfully brought the issue to a vote where brothers decided their behavior was inappropriate and should be avoided in the future, thus reaffirming the desexualizing goal.

Public presentation of a non-sexualized image of DLP was paradoxical. It was impossible for DLP to address its own existence as a fraternity without also addressing the sexuality of its members. While desexualizing strategies presented DLP members as "normal" in the straight world, this strategy also interfered with another major goal, the celebration of sexual diversity. At the very least, we observed destigmatization of homosexuality only occurring in the back-stage of fraternity interaction. For example, members welcomed private conversation and jokes packed with sexual innuendo (see Wharton 1998). Such a distinction between the public and private sphere reflected DLP's paradoxical efforts to establish both their identities as legitimized Greek members and as non-stigmatized gay males.

Defeminizing

Although some fraternity members enjoyed acting feminine within the private space of the fraternity, they were aware that, in order to gain acceptance on campus and in the general public, members could not act like "flaming queens." Feminine behavior was a concern for DLP and its public image, particularly in interfraternity functions:

> The queeny guys sometimes don't want to tone it down, you know? It becomes really uncomfortable . . . to the more butch guys. I guess it's because [the butch guys] don't mind, but they don't want to be stereotyped as queeny. So when we're in pubic, it becomes a problem when the queeny guys just go off: "Girl Friend! Oh he's got a nice ass." And the straight-acting guys are like: "Uh-oh . . . let's, let's tone it down there. We don't want to draw too much attention to ourselves. We just like to keep a low profile. (B18)

In this instance, the concern over feminine behavior appeared to be an issue only for the "butch" members who felt uncomfortable with the "queens." Butch members perceived that acting "queenly" reinforced the stereotypes the straight population had about gay people. Indeed, straight-acting brothers often won such public controversy. When asked to "tone down" their queeniness, the queeny brothers usually complied.

By defining feminine behavior as inappropriate in public, many members co-opted the conventional prejudice that defined femininity as negative. In one chapter, the fraternity designed a specific program to ascribe gender-appropriate behavior. While the fraternity promoted tolerance of "flaming" behavior, one member, nevertheless, admitted that tolerance of flaming behavior was bounded. "Flaming queens" were required to learn appropriate behavior from the chapter's "True Gentlemen Program," aimed at preparing members for the real world:

> [The program taught] what to do etiquette-wise when you are going out to dinner and when you are doing this or doing that. It is not appropriate in the business setting or in a meeting to turn around and snap your fingers and queen out. If we are in a social setting [i.e., within the chapter], you can do that all you want. It is just learning appropriateness. (B09)

Prescribing and proscribing behaviors through member interaction and organizational practice also contradicted the group ideology of celebrating individuality that emphasized "being who you are." One member complained about this inconsistency:

> I got very aggravated at the brothers who, in a large group, act all butch and put others down for being nelly.[7] Then, in private, or when they get drunk, they turn into the biggest queens this side of Branson, Missouri. (B10)

Concentrating on how straight people might reach toward gay people through self-sanctioning. DLP shifted their group orientation from gay-focused to straight-referencing. The gay fraternity achieved this shift by clearly distinguishing between private space and the public sphere, thus splitting the public self from the private self (c.f. Goffman 1959) as described by the above brother. This split also resulted in different identity "markedness" (Brekhus 1996) according to the situation in which members were acting and interacting.

In the private fraternity space, the gay identity was salient both to the individual brothers and the fraternity as a collective. One brother explained that being feminine "was the standard pattern in the gay community, [such as] using feminine pronouns, and even by [calling one another] feminine names. It's very normal" (B19). Descried in the previous section, we also observed that the fraternity structured certain levels of gender fluidity, allowing members to pursue their individual preference of self-presentation.

In the public sphere, however, brothers often downplayed the stereotypical gay image, essentially reaffirming the negative connotation commonly attached to gay people.[8] Furthermore, by configuring a "normal" mainstream image, the gay fraternity restructured the gay identity at the collective level. Despite that essentially all of them were gay men, DLP used its group structure and group culture of brotherhood to reclaim their connection to the traditional fraternity institution in the hope of recognition. Rather than completely denying their gayness, members of DLP viewed mainstreaming as a way to reconstruct a new, more palatable gay image, if not a more realistic one, Yet DLP's decisions regarding how to operate in both the straight and gay worlds led to their public collective mainstreaming goal contradicting their private organizational goal of celebrating individuality, gay culture, and an uncompromised gay identity.

GAY BROTHERHOOD: CREATING AN ALTERNATIVE GAY SPACE

Just as mainstreaming strategies of the gay fraternity restated what it meant to be gay in the straight world, the formalization of a non-sexually defined brotherhood reshaped the meaning of membership in the larger gay community. Just as DLP utilized gay culture to challenge and modify the traditional fraternity model, it adopted the traditional fraternity ideal of brotherhood to create an alternative space in the gay community, attempting to improve a culture they found alienating and unfulfilling.

Despite their incorporation of aspects of the gay culture, many DLP members remained critical of aspects of the larger gay community. The founders of DLP recognized that while the larger gay community supported a plethora of clubs, most were either primarily motivated toward political or service goals or involved in "deviant" activities (Chapter Handbook). Current members of DLP also viewed the gay culture as over-sexualized, filled with destructive behaviors, lacking depth, and too appearance-oriented. One member complained that:

> A big part of the gay culture is the culture of sex and all the rituals that surround it—from the bar scene to social things. . . . People are doing things that ostensibly are just fun and they are doing it because it is SO MUCH FUN. But if you think about it, there is really nothing all that fun about it; it is kind of self-destructive. (B05)

Members also felt that the gay culture, as a whole, emphasized the "outside rather than the inside," because of its focus on appearance, youth, and power. Referring to Los Angeles, known as a gay hub, one member described a "pervasive superficiality":

> There is this competition to look like a model, to have the best looking [penis], the perfect body with all these muscles, a perfect looking face, clothes and cars, and all this stuff." (B12)

The members also judged the gay culture to be lacking cohesion:

> Gay men are very alienated from each other. We go around; we walk around on the streets and see each other, but at the same time, there seems to be a lack of a real . . . there is just this lack of feeling that we are a community. . . . There is a substantial amount of rejection of gay men toward each other. (B21)

Other members found that gay men were too opinionated, that they tended to judge each other critically, and that lacked trust toward one another and "put each other down a lot."

Drawing on the traditional fraternity model, the gay fraternity promoted a bond among its members using mythical ideals of brotherhood (see Clawson 1989; Clemens 1996). Brothers used shared symbols and rituals to foster a collective identity, creating a semblance of close relationships and connectedness:

> We all go through the same ritual and education process. The common things that we all know are the same handshake; we all know the same signs; we know what letters stand for; we all wear the same letters. It is an opportunity to have something that links us and when we go out and see somebody and we talk about an event like the Night of Madness Party, everybody knows what a Night of Madness Party is. If they talk about the exam or learning the song or singing the song or doing the cheer, everybody knows it. (B04)

. . . Some members told how others who came from different backgrounds, had divergent political views, or had "extreme" personalities accepted each other and developed long-term friendships because, as one member put it, "in the end, brotherhood won out" (B24). The ideal of brotherhood was both a myth and an actual way for members to accomplish intimate relationships with one another.

Formalized rituals were particularly important for DLP members' expression of intimacy, especially for members who felt the need to get close to other gay men without the presence of any sexual connotations. Rituals such as the "warm fuzzy" helped achieve this goal:

> In our warm fuzzy exercise, we have a ball of yarn, or we have a warm, fuzzy pillow or something. And then one person starts and throws the pillow at somebody and gives that person a warm fuzzy. Like, "oh, thank you for helping me out, you're one of the nicest people I've seen." And that person has to throw it to somebody else in the fraternity. We did this like for two hours, until we're all like really comfortable and tired. Its all sappy, and then a box of Kleenex gets passed around. It's like, "boo hoo [weeping sound] you're so wonderful to me." You know, a big drama, but it's great; it really pulls us all together. (B18)

This organization practice produced "emotion work" (Hochschild 1985) through which DLP members realized the ideal of brotherhood. Emotion work facilitated solidarity and allowed this non-conventional group to "create and legitimize new emotion norms that include expectations about how members should feel about themselves" (Taylor and Whittier 1996: 177). By fostering intimacy and emotional expression among gay men, the gay fraternity broke the conventional norms that detach masculinity from emotional expression for men in general (Cancian 1987) and for gay men in the particular clone culture (Blachford 1981; Levine 1998).[9] Thus, the brotherhood that DLP cultivated was both a brotherhood for men and also uniquely "gay" in the sense that it was a direct response to the need of young, college, gay men who sought an alternative site for interaction and support. Using the traditional fraternity model, whose quasi-familial nature facilitated the desexualizing strategy that allowed DLP to both mainstream its image and redefine the meaning of gay male relationships in the gay world, helped DLP brothers address their dissatisfaction with the gay culture. Being gay and being brothers were two forms of collective identity that helped members of DLP connect themselves together in transcendental unity, downplaying all types of social differences. This collective identity also reflected the placement of the fraternity in two worlds, as it simultaneously emulated and resisted the straight world and reproduced and criticized the gay world. . . .

CONCLUSION

. . . By emulating the organizational structure and drawing upon cultural resources such as the ideal of brotherhood from traditional fraternities, members of DLP were able to formalize intimate relations between gay men, thus addressing their dissatisfaction with a gay culture they considered too alienating and too sexual. At the same time, the gay fraternity drew upon cultural resources from the gay world, realized in policies that prohibited hazing, celebrated diversity, and supported in-group actions like performing gender fluidity, in order to resist the institutional oppression of the traditional fraternity system.

Gay fraternity group strategies included a mix of contradictory elements that frequently placed its collective identity in question. Mainstreaming strategies and downplaying gayness in public space created a paradoxical situation, similar to closeting, that contradicted DLP's goal of "making our presence known." This assimilation strategy was clearly limiting for a group that sought recognition in both the college and gay communities. In addition to the mainstream straight fraternity institution, the cultural configuration of the larger gay community shaped the way DLP organized its boundaries. Arguing for an alternative space that valued non-sexual intimacy, members' support of a men-only ideology based on the fraternity model also came into conflict with a gay culture that, to a great extent, advocates gender inclusivity. DLP thus operated in relative isolation compared to other gay organizations in the gay community and other fraternities in the collegiate Greek system. Consequently, DLP failed to become a full member of either world. . . .

NOTES

1. While DLP modeled itself after the traditional college fraternity, only one chapter had a fraternity house.

2. See Wharton and Stombler (1999) for a discussion of DLP's reproduction of hegemonic masculinity.

3. By "paradox" we mean something with seemingly contradictory qualities in reference both to being gay and to being involved in a fraternity (where masculinity has traditionally been defined hegemonically as not-gay and not-female) and to claiming simultaneous oppositional and mainstream identities. This understanding of the paradoxical nature of sexual identity is closer to that of Weeks (1995).

4. The respondents either signed consent forms ensuring confidentiality or gave their verbal consent to participating. We use a number system in this paper to identity individual members (e.g., "B 23").

5. Saturation refers to the point in the process of data collection and analysis where incidents of a particular category becomes repetitive and additional data no longer elaborate upon the meaning of the category (Charmaz 1983).

6. DLP's group strategies were similar to the early Homophile movement in the pre-Stonewall era when activists engaged in mainstreaming to "normalize" the gay identity by establishing respectability in the public sphere (D'Emilio 1983). But unlike the early Homophiles, the post-Stonewall cultural and institutional configuration no longer provided DLP an environment in which the fraternity could seek normalization without also addressing itself as a transgressive "agent." The strategic use of public and private presentation, which we will discuss below, was a reflection of this dilemma.

7. According to DiLallo (1994). "nelly" refers to gay men being effeminate.

8. This public/private distinction was far from an intentional group goal for DLP. Downplaying the gay identity in public was a consequence and potentially a reconciliation of DLP's contradictory attempts at both legitimization and transgression.

9. According to Levine's (1998) ethnographic study, the gay clone culture, which emerged in the 1970s and gradually retreated in the mid-1980s, was a subset of the gay culture that parodied the presentational style of heterosexual working class men—a tough macho image—and favored anonymous sexual relations as a way of displaying "real" masculinity.

REFERENCES

Blachford, Gregg 1981 "Male dominance and the gay world." In *The Making of the Modern Homosexual,* ed. Kenneth Plummer, 184–210. Totowa, NJ: Barnes & Noble.

Brekhus, Wayne 1996 "Social marking and the mental coloring of identity: Sexual identity construction and maintenance in the United States." *Sociological Forum* 11(3):497–522.

———. 1998 "A sociology of the unmarked: Redirecting our focus." *Sociological Theory* 16(1):34–51.

Bryan, William A. 1987 "Contemporary fraternity and sorority issues." In Fraternities and Sororities on the Contemporary College Campus, eds. R. B. Winston, Jr., W. R. Nettles III, and J. H. Opper, Jr., 37–56. *New Directions for Student Services* 40 (Winter). San Francisco: Jossey-Bass.

Cancian, Francesca M. 1987 *Love in America: Gender and Self-Development.* Cambridge, UK: Cambridge University Press. *Chapter Handbook*

Delta Lambda Phi. (archival data).

Charmaz, Kathy 1983 "The grounded theory method: An explication and interpretation." In *Contemporary Field Research,* ed. R. Emerson, 109–126. Boston: Little Brown.

Clawson, Mary Ann 1989 *Constructing Brotherhood: Class, Gender, and Fraternalism.* Princeton, NJ: Princeton University Press.

Clemens, Elisabeth S. 1996 "Organizational form as framer Collective identity and political strategy in the American Labor Movement, 1880–1920." In *Comparative Perspectives on Social Movements: Political Opportunities, Mobilizing Structures, and Cultural Framings,* eds. Doug McAdam, John D. McCarthy and Mayer N. Zald, 205–226. Cambridge, MA: Cambridge University Press.

Dank, Barry M. 1971 "Coming out in the gay world." *Psychiatry* 34(2).180–197.

D'Emilio, John 1983 *Sexual Politics, Sexual Communities: The Making of a Homosexual Minority in the United States,* 1940–1970. Chicago: University of Chicago Press.

DiLallo, Kevin 1994 *The Unofficial Gay Manual: Living the Lifestyle (or at Least Appearing to).* New York: Doubleday.

DLP Web site http://members.aol.com/dlpalpha/faq.html (archival data).

Ehrhart, Julie D., and Bernice R. Sandler 1985 *Campus Gang Rape: Party Game?* Washington, DC: Association for American Colleges.

Ekins, Richard 1997 *Male Femaling: A Grounded Theory Approach to Cross-Dressing and Sex Changing.* London: Routledge.

Epstein, Steven 1996 "A queer encounter: Sociology and the study of sexuality." In *Queer Theory/Sociology,* ed. Steven Seidman, 145–167. Cambridge, MA: Blackwell.

Garrett-Gooding, J., and Robert Senter, Jr. 1987 "Attitudes and acts of aggression on a university campus." *Sociological Inquiry* 57:348–372.

Glaser, Barney, and Anselm Strauss 1967 *The Discovery of Grounded Theory.* Chicago: Aldine.

Goffman, Erving 1959 *The Presentation of Self in Everyday Life.* Garden City, NY: Doubleday.

Greenberg, David F. 1988 *The Construction of Homosexuality.* Chicago: University of Chicago Press.

Hahn, Shannon 1995 "Gay frat first in U.S. to get house." *The Minnesota Daily,* October 24 (archival data).

Herdt, Gilbert 1992 "Coming out as a rite of passage: A Chicago study." In *Gay Culture in America: Essays from the Field,* ed. Gilbert Herdt, 29–67. Boston: Beacon Press.

Hochschild, Arlie Russell 1985 *The Managed Heart: Commercialization of Human Feeling.* Berkeley: University of California Press.

Levine, Martin P. 1998 *Gay Macho: The Life and Death of the Homosexual Clone.* New York: New York University Press.

Martin, Patricia Yancey, and Robert A. Hummer 1989 "Fraternities and rape on campus." *Gender and Society* 3(4):457–473.

——— . 1986 "Grounded theory and organizational research." *Journal of Applied Behavioral Science* 22(2): 141–157.

Melucci, Alberto 1989 *Nomads of the Present: Social Movements and Individual Needs in Contemporary Society.* London: Century Hutchinson.

Moffatt, Michael 1989 *Coming of Age in New Jersey: College and American Culture.* New Brunswick: Rutgers University Press.

Norton, Rictor 1996 *The Myth of the Modern Homosexual: Queer History and the Search for Cultural Unity.* London: Cassell.

Nuwer, Hank 1990 *Broken Pledges: The Deadly Rite of Hazing.* Atlanta: Longstreet Press.

O'Mara, Kathleen 1997 "Historicising outsiders on campus: The re/production of lesbian and gay insiders." *Journal of Gender Studies* 6(1):17–31.

Rhoads, Robert A. 1994 *Coming Out in College: The Struggle for a Queer Identity.* Westport, CT: Bergin and Garvey.

Sanday, Peggy Reeves 1990 *Fraternity Gang Rape: Sex, Brotherhood, and Privilege on Campus.* New York: New York University Press.

Stombler, Mindy 1994 "'Buddies' or 'slutties': The collective sexual reputation of fraternity little sisters." *Gender and Society* 8(3):293–296.

Stombler, Mindy, and Irene Padavic 1997 "Sister acts: Resisting men's domination in black and white fraternity little sister programs." *Social Problems* 44(2):257–275.

Stombler, Mindy, and Patricia Yancey Martin 1994 "Bringing women in, keeping women down: Fraternity 'little sister' organizations." *Journal of Contemporary Ethnography,* 23(2):150–184.

Stombler, Mindy, Renee Wharton, and King-To Yeung 1997 "A house with no closets: Exploring the structure of and dynamics within gay fraternities." Paper presented at the Annual Meeting of the Society for the Study of Social Problems, Toronto. (August 10).

——— . 1990 *Basics of Qualitative Research: Grounded Theory Procedures and Techniques.* Newbury Park, CA: Sage.

——— . 1994 "Grounded theory methodology: An overview." In *Handbook of Qualitative Research,* eds. Norman K. Denzin and Yvonna S. Lincoln, 273–287. Thousand Oaks, CA: Sage.

Swidler, Ann 1986 "Culture in action: Symbols and strategies." *American Sociological Review* 51:273–286.

Taylor, Verta, and Nancy E. Whittier 1996 "Analytical approaches to social movement culture: The culture of the Women's Movement." In *Social Movements and Culture. Social Movements, Protest, and Contention,* Vol. 4, eds. Hank Johnston and Bert Klandermans, 163–187. Minneapolis, MN: University of Minnesota Press.

Troiden, Richard R. 1988 *Gay and Lesbian Identity: A Sociological Analysis.* Dix Hills, NY: General Hall.

Vaid, Urvashi 1995 *Virtual Equality: The Mainstreaming of Gay & Lesbian Liberation.* New York: Doubleday.

Wharton, Renee 1998 *Hegemonic Masculinity in Gay Fraternities: Reproduction or Resistance?* Master's Thesis. Lubbock, TX: Texas Tech University.

Wharton, Renee, and Mindy Stombler 1999 "Making men in gay fraternities: Reproducing and resisting hegemonic masculinity." Unpublished manuscript. Texas Tech University.

Windmeyer, Shane L., and Pamela W. Freeman 1998 *Out on Fraternity Row: Personal Accounts of Being Gay in a College Fraternity.* New York: Alyson Books.

51

Mexican American Women, Grassroots Community Activists

"Mothers of East Los Angeles"

MARY PARDO

The following case study of Mexican American women activists in "Mothers of East Los Angeles" (MELA) contributes another dimension to the conception of grassroots politics. It illustrates how these Mexican American women transform "traditional" networks and resources based on family and culture into political assets to defend the quality of urban life. Far from unique, these patterns of activism are repeated in Latin America and elsewhere. Here as in other times and places, the women's activism arises out of seemingly "traditional" roles, addresses wider social and political issues, and capitalizes on informal associations sanctioned by the community. Religion, commonly viewed as a conservative force, is intertwined with politics. Often, women speak of their communities and their activism as extensions of their family and household responsibility. The central role of women in grassroots struggles around quality of life, in the Third World and in the United States, challenges conventional assumptions about the powerlessness of women and static definitions of culture and tradition.

In general, the women in MELA are long-time residents of East Los Angeles; some are bilingual and native born, others Mexican born and Spanish dominant. All the core activists are bilingual and have lived in the community over thirty years. All have been active in parish-sponsored groups and activities; some have had experience working in community based groups arising from schools, neighborhood watch associations, and labor support groups. To gain an appreciation of the group and the core activists, I used ethnographic field methods. . . . The following discussion briefly chronicles an intense and significant five-year segment of community history from which emerged MELA and the women's transformation of "traditional" resources and experiences into political assets for community mobilization.[1]

THE COMMUNITY CONTEXT: EAST LOS ANGELES RESISTING SIEGE

. . . MELA initially coalesced to oppose the state prison construction but has since organized opposition to several other projects detrimental to the quality of life in the central city.[2] Its second large target is a toxic waste incinerator proposed for Vernon, a small city adjacent to East Los Angeles. This incinerator would worsen the already debilitating air quality of the entire county and set a precedent dangerous for other communities throughout California.[3] When MELA took up the fight against the toxic waste incinerator, it became more than a single-issue group and began working with environmental groups around the state.[4] As a result of the community struggle, AB58 (Roybal-Allard), which provides all Californians with the minimum protection of an environmental impact report before the construction of hazardous waste incinerators, was signed into law. But the law's effectiveness relies on a watchful community network. Since its emergence, "Mothers of East Los Angeles" has become centrally important to just such a network of grassroots activists including a select number of Catholic priests and two Mexican American political representatives. Furthermore, the group's very formation, and its continued spirit and activism, fly in the face of the conventional political science beliefs regarding political participation. . . .

. . . All the women live in a low-income community. Furthermore, they identify themselves as active and committed participants in the Catholic Church; they claim an ethnic identity—Mexican American; their ages range from forty to sixty; and they have attained at most high school educations. However, these women fail to conform to the predicted political apathy. Instead, they have transformed social identity—ethnic identity, class identity, and gender identity—into an impetus as well a basis for activism. And, in transforming their existing social networks into grassroots political networks, they have also transformed themselves.

TRANSFORMATION AS A DOMINANT THEME

. . . First, women have transformed organizing experiences and social networks arising from gender-related responsibilities into political resources.[5] When I asked the women about the first community, not necessarily "political," involvement they could recall, they discussed experiences that predated the formation of MELA. Juana Gutiérrez explained:

> Well, it didn't start with the prison, you know. It started when my kids went to school. I started by joining the Parents Club and we worked on different problems here in the area. Like the people who come to the parks to sell drugs to the kids. I got the neighbors to have meetings. I would go knock at the doors, house to house. And I told them that we should stick together with the Neighborhood Watch for the community and for the kids.[6] . . .

Part of a mother's "traditional" responsibility includes overseeing her child's progress in school, interacting with school staff, and supporting school activities. In these processes, women meet other mothers and begin developing a network of acquaintanceships and friendships based on mutual concern for the welfare of their children.

Although the women in MELA carried the greatest burden of participating in school activities, Erlinda Robles also spoke of strategies they used to draw men into the enterprise and into the networks:

> At the beginning, the priests used to say who the president of the mothers guild would be; they used to pick 'um. But, we wanted elections, so we got elections. Then we wanted the fathers to be involved, and the nuns suggested that a father should be president and a mother would be secretary or be involved there [at the school site].

Of course, this comment piqued my curiosity, so I asked how the mothers agreed on the nuns' suggestion. The answer was simple and instructive:

> At the time we thought it was a "natural" way to get the fathers involved because they weren't involved; it was just the mothers. Everybody [the women] agreed on them [the fathers] being president because they worked all day and they couldn't be involved in a lot of daily activities like food sales and whatever. During the week, a steering committee of mothers planned the group's activities. But now that I think about it, a woman could have done the job just as well!

So women got men into the group by giving them a position they could manage. The men may have held the title of "president," but they were not making day-to-day decisions about work, nor were they dictating the direction of the group. Erlinda Robles laughed as she recalled an occasion when the president insisted, against the wishes of the women, on scheduling a parents' group fund-raiser—a breakfast—on Mother's Day. On that morning, only the president and his wife were present to prepare breakfast. This should alert researchers against measuring power and influence by looking solely at who holds titles.

Each of the confounders had a history of working with groups arising out of the responsibilities usually assumed by "mothers"—the education of children and the safety of the surrounding community. From these groups, they gained valuable experiences and networks that facilitated the formation of "Mothers of East Los Angeles." . . .

Second, the process of activism also transformed previously "invisible" women, making them not only visible but the center of public attention. From a conventional perspective, political activism assumes a kind of gender neutrality. This means that anyone can participate, but men are the expected key actors. In accordance with this pattern, in winter 1986 an informal group of concerned businessmen in the community began lobbying and testifying against the prison at hearings in Sacramento. Working in conjunction with Assemblywoman Molina, they made many trips to Sacramento at their own expense. Residents who did not have the income to travel were unable to join them. Finally, Molina, commonly recognized as a forceful advocate for Latinas and the community, asked Frank Villalobos, an urban planner in the group, why there were no women coming up to speak in Sacramento against the prison. As he phrased it, "I was getting some heat from her because no women were going up there."

In response to this comment, Veronica Gutiérrez, a law student who lived in the community, agreed to accompany him on the next trip to Sacramento.[7] He also mentioned the comment to Father John Moretta at Resurrection Catholic Parish. Meanwhile, representatives of the business sector of the community and of the 56th assembly district office were continuing to compile arguments and supportive data against the East Los Angeles prison site. Frank Villalobos stated one of the pressing problems:

> We felt that the Senators whom we prepared all this for didn't even acknowledge that we existed. They kept calling it the "downtown" site, and they argued that there was no opposition in the community. So, I told Father Moretta, what we have to do is demonstrate that there is a link (proximity) between the Boyle Heights community and the prison.[8]

The next juncture illustrates how perceptions of gender-specific behavior set in motion a sequence of events that brought women into the political limelight. Father Moretta decided to ask all the women to meet after mass. He told them about the prison site and called for their support. When I asked him about his rationale for selecting the women, he replied:

> I felt so strongly about the issue, and I knew in my heart what a terrible offense this was to the people. So, I was afraid that once we got into a demonstration situation we had to be very careful. I thought the women would be cooler and calmer than the men. The bottom line is that the men came anyway. The first times out the majority were women. Then they began to invite their husbands and their children, but originally it was just women.[9]

Father Moretta also named the group. Quite moved by a film, *The Official Story,* about the courageous Argentine women who demonstrated for the return of their children who disappeared during a repressive right-wing military dictatorship, he transformed the name "Las Madres de la Plaza de Mayo" into "Mothers of East Los Angeles."[10]

However, Aurora Castillo, one of the cofounders of the group, modified my emphasis on the predominance of women:

> Of course the fathers work. We also have many, many grandmothers. And all this IS with the support of the fathers. They make the placards and the posters; they do the security and carry the signs; and they come to the marches when they can.

Although women played a key role in the mobilization, they emphasized the group's broad base of active supporters as well as the other organizations in the "Coalition Against the Prison." Their intent was to counter any notion that MELA was composed exclusively of women or mothers and to stress the "inclusiveness" of the group. All the women who assumed lead roles in the group had long histories of volunteer work in the Boyle Heights community; but formation of the group brought them out of the "private" margins and into "public" light.

Third, the women in "Mothers of East L.A." have transformed the definition of "mother" to include militant political opposition to state-proposed projects they see as adverse to the quality of life in the community. Explaining how she discovered the issue, Aurora Castillo said,

> You know if one of your children's safety is jeopardized, the mother turns into a lioness. That's why Father John got the mothers. We have to have a well-organized, strong group of mothers to protect the community and oppose things that are detrimental to us. You know the governor is in the wrong and the mothers are in the right. After all, the mothers have to be right. Mothers are for the children's interest, not for self-interest; the governor is for his own political interest.

The women also have expanded the boundaries of "motherhood" to include social and political community activism and redefined the word to include women who are not biological "mothers." At one meeting a young Latina expressed her solidarity with the group and, almost apologetically, qualified herself as a "resident," not a "mother," of East Los Angeles. Erlinda Robles replied:

> When you are fighting for a better life for children and "doing" for them, isn't that what mothers do? So we're all mothers. You don't have to have children to be a "mother."

At critical points, grassroots community activism requires attending many meetings, phone calling, and door-to-door communications—all very labor-intensive work. In order to keep harmony in the "domestic" sphere, the core activists must creatively integrate family members into their community activities. I asked Erlinda Robles how her husband felt about her activism, and she replied quite openly:

> My husband doesn't like getting involved, but he takes me because he knows I like it. Sometimes we would have two or three meetings a week. And my husband would say, "Why are you doing so much? It is really getting out of hand." But he is very supportive. Once he gets there, he enjoys it and he starts in arguing too! See, it's just that he is not used to it. He couldn't believe things happened the way that they do. He was in the Navy twenty years and they brainwashed him that none of the politicians could do wrong. So he has come a long way. Now he comes home and parks the car out front and asks me, "Well, where are we going tonight?" . . .

Working-class women activists seldom opt to separate themselves from men and their families. In this particular struggle for community quality of life, they are fighting for the family unit and thus are not competitive with men.[11] Of course, this fact does not preclude different alignments in other contexts and situations.[12]

Fourth, the story of MELA also shows the transformation of class and ethnic identity. Aurora Castillo told of an incident that illustrated her growing knowledge of the relationship of East Los Angeles to other communities and the basis necessary for coalition building:

> And do you know we have been approached by other groups? [She lowers her voice in emphasis.] You know that Pacific Palisades group asked for our backing. But what they did, they sent their powerful lobbyist that they pay thousands of dollars to get our support against the drilling in Pacific Palisades. So what we did was tell them to send their grassroots people, not their lobbyist. We're suspicious. We don't want to talk to a high-salaried lobbyist; we are humble people. We did our own lobbying. In one week we went to Sacramento twice.

The contrast between the often tedious and labor-intensive work of mobilizing people at the "grassroots" level and the paid work of a "high-salaried lobbyist" represents a point of pride and integrity, not a deficiency or a source of shame. If the two groups were to construct a coalition, they must communicate on equal terms.

The women of MELA combine a willingness to assert opposition with a critical assessment of their own weaknesses. At one community meeting, for example, representatives of several oil companies attempted to gain support for placement of an oil pipeline through the center of East Los Angeles. The exchange between the women in the audience and the oil representative was heated, as women alternated asking questions about the chosen route for the pipeline:

> "Is it going through Cielito Lindo [Reagan's ranch]?" The oil representative answered, "No." Another woman stood up and asked, "Why not place it along the coastline?" Without thinking of the implications, the representative responded, "Oh, no! If it burst, it would endanger the marine life." The woman retorted, "You value the marine life more than human beings?" His face reddened with anger and the hearing disintegrated into angry chanting.[13] . . .

People living in Third World countries as well as in minority communities in the United States face an increasingly degraded environment.[14] Recognizing the threat to the well-being of their families, residents have mobilized at the neighborhood level to fight for "quality of life" issues. The common notion that environmental well-being is of concern solely to white middle class and upper class residents ignores the specific way working-class neighborhoods suffer from the fallout of the city "growth machine" geared for profit.[15] . . .

Mexican American women living east of downtown Los Angeles exemplify the tendency of women to enter into environmental struggles in defense of their community. Women have a rich historical legacy of community activism. . . .

But something new is also happening. The issues "traditionally" addressed by women—health, housing, sanitation, and the urban environment—have moved to center stage as capitalist urbanization progresses. Environmental issues now fuel the fires of many political campaigns and drive citizens beyond the rather restricted, perfunctory political act of voting. Instances of political mobilization at the grassroots level, where women often play a central role, allow us to "see" abstract concepts like participatory democracy and social change as dynamic processes.

The existence and activities of "Mothers of East Los Angeles" attest to the dynamic nature of participatory democracy, as well as to the dynamic nature of our gender, class, and ethnic identity. The story of MELA reveals, on the one hand, how individuals and groups can transform a seemingly "traditional" role such as "mother." On the other hand, it illustrates how such a role may also be a social agent drawing members of the community into the "political" arena. Studying women's contributions as well as men's will shed greater light on the networks dynamic of grassroots movements. . . .

NOTES

1. During the last five years, over 300 newspaper articles have appeared on the issue. Frank Villalobos generously shared his extensive newspaper archives with me. See Leo C. Wolinsky, "L.A. Prison Bill 'Locked Up' in New Clash," *Los Angeles Times,* 16 July 1987, sec. 1, p. 3; Rudy Acuña, "The Fate of East L.A.: One Big Jail," *Los Angeles Herald Examiner,* 28 April 1989, A15; Carolina Serna, "Eastside Residents Oppose Prison," *La Gente UCLA Student Newspaper* 17, no. 1 (October 1986): 5; Daniel M. Weintraub, "10,000 Fee Paid to Lawmaker Who Left Sickbed to Cast Vote," *Los Angeles Times,* 13 March 1988, sec. 1, p. 3.

2. MELA has also opposed the expansion of a county prison literally across the street from William Mead Housing Projects, home to 2,000 Latinos, Asians, and Afro-Americans, and a chemical treatment plant for toxic wastes.

3. The first of its kind in a metropolitan area, it would burn 125,000 pounds per day of hazardous wastes. For an excellent article that links recent struggles against hazardous waste dumps and incinerators in minority communities and features women in MELA, see Dick Russell, "Environmental Racism: Minority Communities and Their Battle against Toxics," *The Amicus Journal* 11, no. 2 (Spring 1989): 22–32.

4. Miguel G. Mendívil, field representative for Assemblywoman Lucille Roybal-Allard, 56th assembly district, Personal Interview, Los Angeles, 25 April 1989.

5. Karen Sacks, *Caring by the Hour.*

6. Juana Gutiérrez, Personal Interview, Boyle Heights, East Los Angeles, 15 January 1988.

7. The law student, Veronica Gutiérrez, is the daughter of Juana Gutiérrez, one of the confounders of MELA. Martín Gutiérrez, one of her sons, was a field representative for Assemblywoman

Lucille Roybal-Allard and also central to community mobilization. Ricardo Gutiérrez, Juana's husband, and almost all the other family members are community activists. They are a microcosm of the family networks that strengthened community mobilization and the Coalition Against the Prison. See Raymundo Reynoso, "Juana Beatrice Gutiérrez: La incansable lucha de una activista comunitaria," *La Opinion,* 6 Agosto de 1989, Acceso, p. 1, and Louis Sahagun, "The Mothers of East L.A. Transform Themselves and Their Community," *Los Angeles Times,* 13 August 1989, sec. 2, p. 1.

8. Frank Villalobos, Personal Interview.

9. Father John Moretta, Resurrection Parish, Personal Interview, Boyle Heights, Los Angeles, 24 May 1989.

10. The Plaza de Mayo mothers organized spontaneously to demand the return of their missing children, in open defiance of the Argentine military dictatorship. For a brief overview of the group and its relationship to other women's organizations in Argentina, and a synopsis of the criticism of the mothers that reveals ideological camps, see Gloria Bonder, "Women's Organizations in Argentina's Transition to Democracy," in *Women and Counter Power,* edited by Yolanda Cohen (New York: Black Rose Books, 1989): 65–85. There is no direct relationship between this group and MELA.

11. For historical examples, see Chris Marín, "La Asociación Hispano-Americana de Madres Y Esposas: Tucson's Mexican American Women in World War II," *Renato Rosaldo Lecture Series 1: 1983–1984* (Tucson, Ariz.: Mexican American Studies Center, University of Arizona, Tucson, 1985) and Judy Aulette and Trudy Mills, "Something Old, Something New: Auxiliary Work in the 1983–1986 Copper Strike," *Feminist Studies* 14, no. 2 (Summer 1988): 251–69.

12. Mina Davis Caulfield, "Imperialism, the Family and Cultures of Resistance."

13. As reconstructed by Juana Gutiérrez, Ricardo Gutiérrez, and Aurora Castillo.

14. For an overview of contemporary Third World struggles against environmental degradation, see Alan B. Durning, "Saving the Planet," *The Progressive* 53, no. 4 (April 1989): 35–59.

15. John Logan and Harvey Molotch, *Urban Fortunes* (Berkeley: University of California Press, 1988). Logan and Molotch use the term in reference to a coalition of business people, local politicians, and the media.

52

Cyberfeminism, Technology, and International "Development"

RADHIKA GAJJALA
ANNAPURNA MAMIDIPUDI

The simplest way to describe the term "cyberfeminism" might be that it refers to women using Internet technology for something other than shopping via the Internet or browsing the world-wide web.[2] One could also say that cyberfeminism is feminism in relation to "cyberspace." Cyberspace is "informational data space made available by electrical circuits and computer networks" (Vitanza 1999, 5). In other words, cyberspace refers to the "spaces," or opportunities, for social interaction provided by computers, modems, satellites, and telephone lines—what we have come to call "the Internet." Even though there are several approaches to cyberfeminism, cyberfeminists share the belief that women should take control of and appropriate the use of Internet technologies in an attempt to empower themselves. The idea that the Internet can be empowering to individuals and communities who are under-privileged is based on the notion of scientific and technological progress alleviating human suffering, offering the chance of a better material and emotional quality of life. In this article, we make conceptual links between "old" and "new" technologies within contexts of globalisation,[3] third-world development, and the empowerment of women. We wish to question the idea of "progress" and "development" as the inevitable result of science and technology, and develop a critique of the top-down approach to technology transfer from the Northern to the Southern Hemisphere. There are two questions of central importance: First, will women in the South be able (allowed) to use new technologies under conditions that are contextually empowering to them, because they are defined by women themselves? Second, within which Internet-based contexts can women from the South truly be heard? How can they define the conditions under which they can interact on-line,[4] to enable them to form coalitions and collaborate, aiming to transform social, cultural, and political structures?

THE INTERNET AND "DEVELOPMENT"

Cyberfeminists urge women all over the world to learn how to use computers, to get "connected,"[5] and to use the Internet as a tool for feminist causes and individual empowerment. However, ensuring that women are empowered by new technology requires us to investigate issues which are far more complex than merely provid-

Radhika Gajjala and Annapurna Mamidipudi, "Cyberfeminism, Technology, and International 'Development,'" from *Gender & Development* Volume 7, Number 2, p. 8–16.

ing material access to the latest technologies. The Internet has fascinated many activists and scholars because of its potential to connect people all across the world in a way that has never been possible before. Individuals can publish written material instantaneously, and broadcast information to remote locations. Observers predict that it will cause unprecedented and radical change in the way human beings conduct business and social activities. In much of the North, as well as in some materially privileged sections of societies in the South, the Internet is celebrated as a tool for enhancing world-wide democracy. The Internet and its associated technologies are touted as great equalisers, which will help bridge gaps between social groups: the "haves" and the "have-nots," and men and women.

Since the Second World War, development—in the sense of transferring and "diffusing" northern forms of scientific and technological "progress," knowledge, and modes of production and consumption, from the industrialised north into southern contexts—has been seen by many as the one over-arching solution to poverty and inequality around the world. Much of the current literature, as well as media representations of the so-called under-developed world, reinforces this discourse of "development" and "under-development." As scholars such as Edward Said (1978) have pointed out, this process is also apparent in the context of colonialism, when the production of knowledge about the colonised nations served the colonisers in justifying their project.

What, then, does it mean to say that the Internet and technology are feminist issues for women in developing nations, when the project of development in itself is saddled with colonial baggage? In order to examine whether women in these contexts are indeed going to realise empowerment through the use of technology, we need to understand the complexity of the obstacles they face, by considering the ways in which the conditions of their lives are determined by unequal power relations at local and global levels.

THE FORM OF THIS ARTICLE

In the following, we each describe our engagement with cyberfeminisms, development, and new technology, and discuss some of the problems that we encounter in our efforts. Both of us have interacted quite extensively using the Internet, where our interactions occasionally overlap when we engage in discussions and creative exchanges with others.[6] One of us, Annapurna Mamidipudi, is also involved with an NGO working with traditional handloom weavers in south India. The other, Radhika Gajjala, works within academia, and creates and runs on-line "discussion lists"[7] and websites from her North American geographical location, aiming to create spaces that enable dialogue and collaboration among women with access to the internet all over the world. This paper was written via the Internet, across a fairly vast geographical distance of approximately 10,000 miles. We have written the article as a dialogue, to make our individual voices and locations apparent. This unconventional form and method seems appropriate for our subject matter: a belief in the possibilities of dialogue and collaboration across geographical boundaries offered by this medium of the future. We do not consider either of us to represent the North or the South, "theory" or "practice," each of us will use her professional and personal experience of technology within both "first world" and "third-world" contexts. We share caste, class, national, and religious affiliations, but once again, neither of us are representative Indian women.

Annapurna Mamidipudi:

As a field-worker in an organisation which focuses on the development and use of environment-friendly dyes for textile production, I am part of a team that has been successfully introducing and transferring the technology of non-chemical natural dyes to clients. The course we offer is comprehensive; it includes training in botany and dye-material cultivation patterns, concepts of eco-friendly technology, actual dyeing techniques and tools, specific methodology for further research, aesthetics, and market research. While the service we provide is similar to that of any professional consultancy, a crucial difference is that we cater solely to traditional handloom weavers; our trainees, sponsors and manufacturers are all artisans, men and women from traditional weaving communities.

The craft of traditional natural dyeing is based on sophisticated knowledge that has been passed down from generation to generation of artisans. The end-product created by these artisans is exquisite hand-loomed cloth, woven of yarn hand-spun from local cotton by women in remote Indian villages, dyed in the vibrant colours of indigo and madder. This has been exported all over the world from pre-colonial times onwards. One might well ask, why should a skill that has been passed down successfully over so many generations suddenly need technical consultants like me for training?

Radhika Gajjala:

I am a producer, first, of theory concerned with culture, post-colonialism, and feminism. I am in continuous dialogue with women from non-privileged and non-western locations, examining the experience of activists like Annapurna, and collaborating with men and women from the South. I rely to a large extent on having access to knowledge through Northern technology and power structures, but I am not blind to the fact that these power structures oppress women and men living in poverty in both North and South.

My second role as a producer is in creating electronic "spaces" which are used by people of different identities to express themselves and talk to each other.[8] The Spoon Collective,[9] started in 1994, is "dedicated to promoting discussion of philosophical and political issues" (http://lists.village.virginia.edu/~spoons). The Spoon Collective was started in 1994, and I entered it in 1995, volunteering to co-moderate two "discussion lists." I set up two further discussion lists in 1995 and 1996, which I will mention later in this article.

While members of the Spoon Collective have different individual aims in belonging to the Collective, I believe that all of us are interested in the possibilities of activism through electronic communications. All of us have set up, and continue to moderate, discussion lists that implicitly question the global status quo, in one way or another. One member of the collective said, "One way in which we conceptualise what we do is by talking about thinking [and writing/speaking on-line] as a civic, public activity." As is characteristic of much Internet-based activity (whether activist, personal, or commercial), our goals and our actual output are constantly evaluated. We ceaselessly discuss their impact on society and culture. For example, what determines whether a list "works" or not? The volume of messages exchanged? The quality of information or discussion? But how would "quality" be defined? Do we determine the success of the list by the number of members who subscribe to it? Or by the number of members who participate by sending messages? By the number of websites that have links to our list-archives or the Spoon Collective website? How can we tell from this how many people we really reach?

In order to start up discussion lists, and construct websites, I had to teach myself sufficient programming and computer-related skills to be able to manage the technical side. My background as creative writer and student in the humanities had not trained me for the technical aspects of being an active producer on-line, and my knowledge is mostly self-taught. Later in this article, I will discuss my e-mail lists as part of an effort to try and facilitate collaborations between feminists across vast geographical boundaries. What scope is there for them to discuss and assert their differences on an equal basis, within these electronic social spaces which are themselves based in unequal economic, social and cultural relations? In a sense I suppose my on-line ventures could be called "cyber-feminist" investigations.

Annapurna:

Until the nineteenth century, most of the weaving industry in the area where I work was shaped by the demands of local consumers. Chinnur is a little village in Adilabad, in an interior region of the Deccan plateau in South India. There used to be a large concentration of weavers with a reputation for excellence in this area. Their reputation was based on three things: the skill of the farmers in producing different varieties of cotton, the ability of different groups of people to work together and process the cotton; and, finally, the wealth of knowledge of dyes and techniques that added aesthetic value to utility. Different castes and communities were inter-linked in occupational, as well as social relationships, exchanging services and materials, creating a strong local market economy which was entrenched in the traditions and rituals of daily life. For example, during specific seasons or events, women of leisure from non-weaving communities spun, exchanging spun yarn for sarees (Uzramma 1995).

However, the development of chemical dyes almost 100 years ago in Europe had a calamitous effect on traditional Indian dyeing practices. Processes which were the pride of the textile industry of this country were abandoned and replaced by chemical dyes. Even in remote Chinnur, the spreading wave of modern science changed people's perceptions of traditional technology; they now saw it as outmoded, and this resulted in almost total erasure of knowledge of the traditional processes within these communities.

Europeans had started to document the local dyeing and weaving activities in the eighteenth century; Indians themselves continued this up to the early twentieth century, in a bid to preserve knowledge. But this process meant that knowledge which had been firmly in the domain of practice of the artisans was now converted into textual information, and shifted the ownership of the knowledge to those able to "study," rather than those who "do."

As the outside world mutated into a global village, the organic processes of the traditional artisan weaver turned full cycle, back to popularity when the colour of neeli (indigo) caught the imagination of ecology-conscious consumers in the late 1970s. But even while the self-congratulatory back-patting went on among the nationalists and intellectuals, the weavers had internalised information about "modern" chemical technology. Just as they had begun to find a footing in the market, their practical knowledge was again found wanting. The only available information about vegetable dyes was documented in the language of the colonisers, codified, and placed in libraries or museums, inaccessible to the traditional practitioners from whom the information had been gathered in the first instance. Thus, although it looked as if a demand had been created for their product, in reality this further reinforced the image of weavers' technology as needful of input from outside experts, in the weavers' own minds as well as in those of others.

Today, in most descriptions of the hand-loom industry, the traditional weaver is seen as an object of charity, who can survive only through government handouts or patronage from social elites. Yet their "sunset" industry—as it was referred to by a top official in the Department of Hand-loom and Textiles in charge of formulating strategy for this industry (personal communication, 1999)—has the second largest number of practitioners in India, farming employing the greatest number. For the men and women engaged in weaving in villages across India, the journey from traditional neeli (indigo) to modern naphthol (chemical) dyes has meant a journey from self-sufficiency to dependence, self-respect to subordination; in short, a journey to "primitivity."

Radhika:

Most highly-educated women from the third world, whether or not we live in the North, experience a parallel journey to "primitivity" in the sense Annapurna uses above. In part, this happens through acquiring western-style education and professional status, which is not often an autonomous personal choice. No woman of the third world has the luxury of not choosing to be westernised if she aspires to be heard, or even simply to achieve a level of material freedom, comfort, and luxury within global structures of power. Many of us have "made it" within westernised professional systems, and have enjoyed the status of the representative third-world woman within global structures of power. Yet, as a result of our education and professional status, we are not representative, although we are of the third world, and our stories are not those of many truly under-privileged women in third-world locations.

Often, we meet other people's expectations by taking on the role of victims of third-world cultures, or, alternatively, victors who have "survived" our backgrounds. Yet, when we refuse these roles allotted to us, some feminists from Northern backgrounds suggest our experiences don't "count," since we are not "real" third-world women. Even as we demonstrate our potential by attaining the level of education and "westernisation" required to become powerful within global structures we are silenced once again.

Annapurna:

Outside the house of one of the weavers in the village of Chinnur is a chalk-written address board in English. It says: "Venkatesh U.S., Weavers' Colony, Chinnur." The initials U.S. after this man's name stand for "Unskilled Labour": a powerful statement on how an expert weaver chooses to categorise himself. This classification in the government records, he hopes, will make him eligible for a low-grade job in a government office.

I first came here as one of a team of field workers from an NGO which offered marketing support to craft groups. Natural dyeing seemed an option which would add value to the cotton cloth, and which would also eventually decrease weavers' dependence on a fickle market and centralised raw material supply systems. We ourselves did not know the technology, but we were optimistic about the chance of reviving it, provided there was active participation on the part of producer groups.

Transferring the technology of natural dyeing to the field presented many challenges. The sources of information available were texts—some of them 300 years old—noting original processes of artisan practice. Some scholars had researched fragments of the old processes, and some practitioners recalled parts of them. We needed historians to access information from libraries where the documentation was kept; we then needed dyeing experts to interpret the recipes, botanists to participate in the process of identifying materials, engineers to create appropriate technology to ensure fastness and brightness in colours, and chemical technologists to interpret the techniques and demystify processes that had been inter-linked with ways of life that were sometimes centuries old. Making scientists of the weavers, we had to help them reinterpret information to suit their changed environment and resources. We did not want to impose on them—in the name of traditional technology—processes that would place demands on them which would be more oppressive than toxic chemical dyes. The innate capability and skill of the weavers made this seemingly impossible task feasible, and success came five years later, when we produced a range of colours and dyeing techniques that withstood the most stringent of quality tests. A group of dyer-weavers now acted as resource people in workshops held by us to train other groups.

Our clients today are confident weavers who come back to us time and again, to participate in the effort to empower more and more artisan groups by sharing information on a technology that has emerged from their efforts on the field.

In Chinnur lives Venkatavva, whose husband is one of a group of six weavers who decided that they would take the risk of inviting an outside agency to help them become self-sufficient. When we first visited Chinnur eight years ago, Venkatavva was unable to offer us any hospitality. Her three-year-old daughter's staple drink was weak coffee, drunk without milk. There was no food to be offered to visitors who turned up once the morning meal was past. Today, she entertains buyers from Europe, while listening to her husband tell the story of his successes. Her eyes are bright with laughter when she remembers less successful experiments which resulted in pale and fugitive colours, and irate customers. She points proudly to the shirt that her husband Odellu wears today, which he himself has woven. The journey from chemical technology to the indigo vat, from dearth to bounty, from apathy to laughter—this is her journey. In this context, which technology is traditional and which modern? Who is to decide which one is the road to empowerment and self-respect?

Radhika:

My journey to "modernity" began with an increasing awareness of my own ignorance, and of the contradictions and injustices which exist within the Northern educational system. I refuse to be either a "victim" or a "victor," and continue to hope that through dialogue, women, men and children from different backgrounds throughout the world can work together to overcome injustice.

In late 1995, when I started my first Internet discussion list, access to the Internet was limited mainly to men and women from the North. (This is the case even now, although there are more men and women from the South who use the Internet.) I started the third-world women discussion list partly as a result of my frustration with what I saw as a lack of political commitment and exchange within some women-centred lists. I was frustrated with the way in which topics were discussed. Even in those instances where women and men from the South had access, they came from a particular class background. I was also frustrated with the way people represented themselves. In my opinion, some were too eager to be "ideal native informants" for Northern audiences. Southern participants used the

Internet as an opportunity to perform to a Northern audience and receive favours for sufficiently western, or appropriately exotic, performances. Even discussion lists and web-sites that claimed to be critical and feminist sometimes fell into this trap (possibly, my own lists and websites do so, too).

It was important to me at the time I started the third-world-women list, and continues to be now, that a conscious effort should be made to be critical and self-reflexive. My second list, Sa-cyborgs, was started with a similar goal in mind, but the focus of this list is an interactive exchange of creative writing in relation to gender, race, class and geographical location. Both lists were formed in the recognition that acts of representation are political.

One of the main purposes of both my Internet discussion lists is to facilitate connections between third-world activists and scholars located within, and outside, US academic institutions. I hope that this dialogue will result in collaborative work by and for women living in under-privileged and oppressive conditions, in North and South. My lists are humble efforts which form a small section of the larger efforts being made by women all over the world. Whether they have been successful in any sense is not for me to say. There are many feminists and activists using the Internet in far more effective ways, and examples of these can be seen all over the world-wide web (see http://www.igc.apc.org/vsister/res/index.html for some examples).

Annapurna:

Women who tussle with the question of how to define their class and Northern or Southern identity on the Internet are a privileged few. Questions relevant to women to whom Internet technology is being touted as the route to empowerment, might ask: "but who has the Internet empowered? How has this happened? How relevant is this process for women like Venkatavva?".

Venkatavva has seen the advent of roads, cars, telephones, and television in the short 30 years of her life, and understands the advantages, the disadvantages, and the illusion of access that these give her. In a land of faulty cables and unpredictable electricity supply, her children only drink milk on the days that the bus doesn't run, because on those days the milk in the village can't be taken to the city to be sold, and isn't worth any money. Modem technology holds no bogies for her; she has choices that many women in the north don't have access to. On days the electricity fails she watches the traditional story-telling enacted in the village square instead of the distant Santa Barbara on television. The quality and quantity of the choices available to her are based as much on the failure of technology, as on its success. So would modern technology be working towards more quality and quantity in choice, or less?

As an activist working in developing technology for her I can only say this: let her have access to the Internet—why should this be barred when other aspects of modern life are imposed, from Western consumer goods, to twentieth-century diseases such as HIV/AIDS. But let it not be assumed that the Internet will empower her. Otherwise this too will do what other imposed technology has done: the exact opposite of what it purports to do.

The Internet will be a more colourful, exotic place for us with women like Venkatavva flashing their gold nose pins, but what good will it do them? As it is at present, the Internet reflects the perceptions of Northern society that Southern women are brown, backward, and ignorant. A alternative, kinder, depiction of them which is also widespread is that they are victims of their cultural heritage. Is being exposed to such images of themselves going to help Southern women by encouraging them to fight in dignity and self-respect, or will it further erode their confidence in their fast-changing environment?

What, then, is the process by which a woman like Venkatavva could be empowered by the Internet?

Radhika:

Venkatavva should be free to decide how the Internet and other related technologies might be used to benefit and empower her and her community. The tools and access should be provided unconditionally, not as a way of selling a so-called superior life-style modelled on the "civilised" and urban centres of the world. Women like Ventakavva are perfectly capable of making the decisions needed to empower themselves according to their everyday needs. Policies designed to be empowering should aid and enable, not impose and preach while fostering further inequalities and inadequacies.

I would like to paraphrase (not without reservations similar to those voiced by Annapurna in her rejoinder) a contribution made to the Gender and Law thematic group[10] at the World Bank. For Spivak, the speaker, the key question that emerges in the context of her work with women in Bangladesh is "How do we approach the bottom?". That is, "How can we learn from below?". The idea is to enter into a society and learn its traditions from inside, seeing what traditions can be worked with to slowly improve the situation, and to ensure that new developments are initiated from the inside so that the changes are accepted. Spivak sees a need to do "invisible mending" of the native fabric, by weaving in the different positive threads which exist in the fabric (moderatorgl@worldbank.org, 20 April 1999).

Annapurna:

How do we resolve the contradictory sentiments of seeing the Internet as a panacea to the problems of the south; of thinking that on the contrary, it may even be bad for us; and of asserting that this doesn't mean we don't want it? We need to study processes of empowerment and work out how it is to be done in the context of the Internet. While case studies abound for the failure of this process, development workers in particular would not regard it as fair (or politically correct) to down-play the potential of the Internet to empower many women like Venkatavva in South and North. We cannot say, "I won't give you the Internet, for your own good."

Radhika:

My experience of observing the development of the Internet, and using this mode of communication, is that while there are hierarchies of power embedded in the very construction and design of Internet culture, there is still potential for using it in ways which might subvert these and foster dialogue and action on various unexpected fronts, in unpredictable ways. However, it remains true that the NGOs who speak with and for women living in poverty throughout the world, as well as the women themselves, have to negotiate and engage in dialogue with the powerful in the North from positions of lesser power. This situation of unequal economic and social power relations between the North and the South presents challenges for people such as myself who are trying to design electronic spaces of dialogue and activism.

Therefore I reiterate the questions central to our discussion in this article, and ask readers to think deeply and honestly about the issues they raise, beyond those we have addressed here. Will women all over the world be able (allowed) to use technologies under conditions that are defined by them, and therefore potentially empowering to them? Within which Internet-based contexts will women of lesser material and cultural privilege within "global" power relations be able to develop collaborative work, and coalitions, to transform social, cultural, and political structures?

These questions cannot be addressed only in relation to women of the third world. Women from the first world need answers to these questions too. The Internet has its "headquarters" in the first world, but this does not mean that it is contextually empowering to all women in that context. Whether located in the Northern hemisphere or the South, whether rich or poor, global structures of power (through their "invisible" control of the market, Internet service providers, software design, language and so on) clearly determine women's use of the Internet. If cyberfeminists want to ensure that the Internet is empowering, it is not enough to "get connected" and set up websites and maintain e-mail-discussion lists. The latter tasks, while necessary, are only a miniscule part of the battle.

NOTES

1. The writers thank Dr. Melissa Spirek, Dr. A Venkatesh, and the editor of *Gender and Development,* Caroline Sweetman, for commenting on several drafts of this article. Radhika Gajjala also wishes to thank all the Spoon Collective members as well as the members of the various lists that she (co-)moderates. They contribute significantly to our understanding of on-line existence. Several "real-life" bodies also commented on this article, including family members of both writers.

2. The Internet is a world-wide network of computers which communicate via an agreed set of Internet protocol. The world-wide web is a subset of the Internet which uses a combination of text, graphics, audio and video material to provide information on many subjects.

3. I use this term to denote "the rapidly developing process of complex inter-connections between societies, cultures, institutions and individuals worldwide. It is a process which involves . . . shrinking distances through a dramatic reduction in the time taken—either physically or representationally—to cross them, so making the world smaller and in a certain sense bringing human beings 'closer' to one another. But it is also a process which 'stretches' social relations, removing the relationships which govern our everyday lives from local contexts to global ones" (Tomlinson 1997).

4. The term "on-line" refers to activities carried out via the Internet or e-mail.

5. Getting "connected" means acquiring the necessary technology (computer, Internet browsing software, telephone modem, connection to an Internet Service Provider) to access the Internet.

6. Even as we collaborate on projects such as this article, we are exchanging non-traditional creative writing, in relation to our personal/professional/political conflicts and dilemmas, on sa-cyborgs. For information on sa-cyborgs and third-world women, see http://lists.village.virginia.edu

7. Electronic networks whose participants discuss a particular topic or topics.

8. See http://ernie.bgsu.edu/~radhik

9. The Spoon Collective is operated through the Institute for Advanced Technology in the Humanities at the University of Virginia.

10. Quoted from a post to the gender-law discussion list, gender-law@jazz.world bank.org, received on 29 April 1999.

REFERENCES

Said, E (1978) *Orientalism,* Pantheon Books, New York.

Tomlinson, J (1997) *'Cultural globalisation and cultural imperialism' in Mohammadi,* A (1997) International Communication and Globalisation, Sage, London.

Uzramma (1995) *'Cotton handlooms -industry of the future',* paper presented at a seminar on Indian textiles in 1995.

Vitanza, V (1999) *Cyberreader,* Allyn and Bacon, Boston.

53

Confessions of a Recovering Misogynist

KEVIN POWELL

I am a sexist male.

I take no great pride in saying this. I am merely stating a fact. It is not that I was born this way; rather, I was born into this male-dominated society, and, consequently, from the very moment I began forming thoughts, they formed in a decidedly male-centered way. My "education" at home with my mother, at school, on my neighborhood playgrounds, and at church all placed males at the center of the universe. My digestion of 1970s American popular culture in the form of television, film, ads, and music only added to my training, so that by as early as age nine or ten I saw females, including my mother, as nothing more than the servants of males. Indeed, like the Fonz on that TV sitcom *Happy Days,* I thought I could snap my fingers and girls would come running.

My mother, working poor and a product of the conservative and patriarchal South, simply raised me as most women are taught to raise boys: The world was mine, there were no chores to speak of, and my aggressions were considered somewhat normal, something that we boys carry out as a rite of passage. Those "rites" included me routinely squeezing girls' butts on the playground. And at school boys were encouraged to do "boy" things: work and build with our hands, fight each other, and participate in the most daring activities during our gym time. Meanwhile, the girls were relegated to home economics, drawing cute pictures, and singing in the school choir. Now that I think about it, school was the place that spearheaded the omission of women from my worldview. Save Betsy Ross (whom I remember chiefly for sewing a flag) and a stoic Rosa Parks (she was unfurled every year as an example of Black achievement), I recall virtually no women making appearances is my American history classes.

The church my mother and I attended, like most Black churches, was peopled mainly by Black women, most of them single parents, who dragged their children along for the ride. Not once did I see a preacher who was anything other than an articulate, emotionally charged, well-coiffed, impeccably suited Black man running this church and, truly, these women. And behind the pulpit of this Black man, where he convinced us we were doomed to hell if we did not get right with God, was the image of our savior, a male, always White, named Jesus Christ.

Not surprisingly the "savior" I wanted in my life was my father. Ten years her senior, my father met my mother, my father wooed my mother, my father impregnated my mother, and then my father—as per *his* socialization—moved on to the next mating call. Responsibility was about as real to him as a three-dollar bill. When I was eight, my father flatly told my mother, via a pay phone, that he felt she had lied, that I was not his child, and that he would never give her money for me again. The one remotely tangible image of maleness in my life was gone for good. Both my mother and I were devastated, albeit for different reasons. I longed for my father's affections. And my mother longed to be married. Silently I began to blame my mother for my father's disappearance. Reacting to my increasingly bad behavior, my mother turned resentful and her beatings became more frequent, more charged. I grew to hate her and all females, for I felt it was women who made men act as we do.

At the same time, my mother, a fiercely independent and outspoken women despite having only a grade-school education and being poor, planted within me the seeds of self-criticism, of shame for wrongful behavior—and, ultimately, of feminism. Clear that she alone would have to shape me, my mother spoke pointedly about my father for many years after that call, demanding that I not grow up to "be like him." And I noted the number of times my mother rejected low-life male suitors, particularly the ones who wanted to live with us free of charge. I can see now that my mother is a feminist, although she is not readily familiar with the term. Like many women before and since, she fell hard for my father, and only through enduring immense pain did she realize the power she had within herself.

I once hated women, and I take no pride in this confession.

I entered Rutgers University in the mid-1980s, and my mama's-boy demeanor advanced to that of pimp. I learned quickly that most males in college are some variety of pimp. Today I lecture regularly, from campus to campus, all over the country, and I see that not much has changed. For college is simply a place where we men, irrespective of race or class, can—and do—act out the sexist attitudes entrenched since boyhood. Rape, infidelity, girlfriend beat-downs, and emotional abuse are common, and pimpdom reigns supreme. There is the athlete pimp, the frat boy pimp, the independent pimp, and the college professor pimp. Buoyed by the antiapartheid movement and the presidential bids of Jesse Jackson, my social consciousness blossomed along racial lines, and behold—the student leader pimp was born.

Blessed with a gift for gab, a poet's sensibility, and an acute memory for historical facts, I baited women with my self-righteousness by quoting Malcolm X, Frantz Fanon, Machiavelli, and any other figure I was sure they had not studied. It was a polite form of sexism, for I was always certain to say "my sister" when I addressed women at Rutgers. But my politeness did not lend me tolerance for women's issues, nor did my affiliation with a variety of Black nationalist organizations, especially the Nation of Islam. Indeed, whenever women in our African Student Congress would question the behavior and attitudes of men, I would scream, "We don't have time for them damn lesbian issues!" My scream was violent, mean-spirited, made with the intention to wound. I don't think it is any coincidence that during my four years in college I did not have one relationship with a woman that lasted more than three or four months. For every friend or girlfriend who would dare question my deeds, there were literally hundreds of others who acquiesced to the ways of us men, making it easy for me to ignore the legitimate cries of the feminists. Besides, I had taken on the demanding role of pimp, of conqueror, of campus revolutionary—there was little time or room for real intimacy, and even less time for self-reflection.

Confessions are difficult because they force me to visit ghettos in the mind I thought I had long escaped.

I was kicked out of college at the end of my fourth year because I drew a knife on a female student. We were both members of the African Student Congress, and she was one of the many "subversive" female leaders I had sought to purge from the organization. She *had* left but for some reason was in our office a few days after we had brought Louis Farrakhan to speak at Rutgers. Made tense by her presence, I ignored her and turned to a male student, asking him, as she stood there, to ask her to jet. As she was leaving, she turned and charge toward me. My instincts, nurtured by my inner-city upbringing and several months of receiving anonymous threats as the Farrakhan talk neared, caused me to reach into my pocket and pull out a knife I had been carrying.

My intent was to scare her into submission. The male student panicked and knocked the knife from my hand, believing I was going to stab this woman. I would like to believe that that was not the case. It did not matter. This woman pressed charges on and off campus, and my college career, the one I'd taken on for myself, my undereducated mother, and my illiterate grandparents, came to a screeching halt.

It is not easy for me to admit I have a problem.

Before I could be readmitted to school I had to see a therapist. I went, grudgingly, and agonized over my violent childhood, my hatred of my mother, my many problems with women, and the nauseating torment of poverty and instability. But then it was done. I did not bother to try to return to college, and I found myself again using women for money, for sex, for entertainment. When I moved to New York City in August 1990, my predator mentality was still in full effect. I met a woman, persuaded her to allow me to live with her, and then mentally abused her for nearly a year, cutting her off from some of her friends, shredding her peace of mind and her spirit. Eventually I pushed her into the bathroom door when she blew up my spot, challenging me and my manhood.

I do not want to recount the details of the incident here. What I will say is that I, like most Black men I know, have spent much of my life living in fear: fear of White racism, fear of the circumstances that gave birth to me, fear of walking out my door wondering what humiliation will be mine today. Fear of Black women—of their mouths, of their bodies, of their attitudes, of their hurts, of their fear of us Black men. I felt fragile, as fragile as a bird with clipped wings that day when my ex-girlfriend stepped up her game and spoke back to me. Nothing in my world, nothing in my self-definition prepared me for dealing with a woman as an equal. My world said women were inferior, that they must at all costs be put in their place, and my instant reaction was to do that. When it was over, I found myself dripping with sweat, staring at her back as she ran barefoot out of the apartment.

Guilt consumed me after the incident. The women I knew through my circle of poet and writer friends begged me to talk through what I had done, to get counseling, to read the books of bell hooks, Pearl Cleage's tiny tome *Mad at Miles,* the poetry of Audre Lorde, the many meditations of Gloria Steinem. I resisted at first, but eventually I began to listen and read, feeling electric shocks running through my body when I realized that these women, in describing abusive, oppressive men, were talking about me. Me, who thought I was progressive. Me, who claimed to be a leader. Me, who still felt women were on the planet to take care of men.

During this time I did restart therapy sessions. I also spent a good deal of time talking with young feminist women—some friends, some not. Some were soothing and understanding, some berated me and all men. I also spent a great deal of time alone, replaying my life in my mind: my relationship with my mother, how my mother had responded to my father's actions, how I had responded to my mother's response to my father. I thought of my education, of the absence of women in it. How I'd managed to attend a major university affiliated with one of the oldest women's colleges in America, Douglas College, and visited that campus only in pursuit of sex. I thought of the older men I had encountered in my life—the ministers, the high school track coach, the street hustlers, the local businessmen, the college professors, the political and community leaders—and realized that many of the ways I learned to relate to women came from listening to and observing those men. Yeah, I grew up after women's studies classes had appeared in most of the colleges in America, but that doesn't mean feminism actually reached the people it really needed to reach: average, everyday American males.

The incident, and the remorse that followed, brought about something akin to a spiritual epiphany. I struggled mightily to rethink the context that had created my mother. And my aunts. And my grandmother. And all the women I had been intimate with, either physically or emotionally or both. I struggled to understand terms like *patriarchy, misogyny, gender oppression.* A year after the incident I penned a short essay for *Essence* magazine called, simply, "The Sexist in Me," because I wanted to be honest in the most public forum possible, and because I wanted to reach some men, some young Black men, who needed to hear from another male that sexism is as oppressive as racism. And at times worse.

I am no hero. I am no saint.
I remain a sexist male.

But one who is now conscious of it and who has been waging an internal war for several years. Some days I am incredibly progressive; other days I regress. It is very lone-some to swim against the stream of American male-centeredness, of Black male bravado and nut grabbing. It is how I was molded, it is what I know, and in rejecting it I often feel mad naked and isolated. For example, when I publicly opposed the blatantly sexist and patriarchal rhetoric and atmosphere of the Million Man March, I was attacked by Black men, some questioning my sanity, some accusing me of being a dupe for the White man, and some wondering if I was just "trying' to get some pussy from Black women."

Likewise, I am a hip-hop head. Since adolescence I have been involved in this culture, this lifestyle, as a dancer, a graffiti writer, an activist, a concert organizer, and most prominently a hip-hop journalist. Indeed, as a reporter at *Vibe* magazine, I found myself interviewing rap icons like Dr. Dre, Snoop Dogg, and the late Tupac Shakur. And although I did ask Snoop and Tupac some pointed questions about *their* sexism, I still feel I dropped the ball. We Black men often feel so powerless, so sure the world—politically, economically, spiritually, and psychologically—is aligned against us. The last thing any of us wants if for another man to question how we treat women. Aren't we, Black men, the endangered species anyhow? This is how many of us think.

While I do not think hip-hop is any more sexist or misogynist than other forms of American culture, I do think it is the most explicit form of misogyny around today. It is also a form of sexism that gets more than its share of attention, because hip-hop—now a billion-dollar industry—is the sound track for young America, regardless of race of class. What folks don't understand is that hip-hop was created on the heels of the Civil Rights era by impoverished Blacks and Latinos, who literally made something out of nothing. But in making that something out of nothing, many of us men of color have held tightly to White patriarchal notions of manhood—that is, the way to be a man is to have power. Within hip-hop culture, in our lyrics, in our videos, and on our tours, that power translates into material possessions, provocative and often foul language, flashes of violence, and blatant objectification of and disrespect for women. Patriarchy, as manifested in hip-hop, is where we can have our version of power within this very oppressive society. Who would want to even consider giving that up?

Well, I have, to a large extent, and these days I am a hip-hopper in exile. I dress, talk, and walk like a hip—hopper, yet I cannot listen to rap radio or digest music videos without commenting on the pervasive sexism. Moreover, I try to drop seeds, as we say, about sexism, whenever and wherever I can, be it at a community forum or on a college campus. Some men, young and old alike, simply cannot deal with it and walk out. Or there is the nervous shifting in seats, the uneasy comments during the question-and-answer sessions, generally in the form of "Why you gotta pick on the men, man?" I constantly "pick on the men" and myself because I truly wonder how many men actually listen to the concerns of women. Just as I feel it is Whites who need to be more vociferous about racism in their communities, I feel it is men who need to speak long and loud about sexism among ourselves.

I am a recovering misogynist.

I do not say this with pride. Like a recovering alcoholic or a crack fiend who has righted her or his ways, I am merely cognizant of the fact that I have had some serious problems in my life with and in regard to women. I am also aware of the fact that I can lapse at any time. My relationship with my mother is better than it has ever been, though there are days when speaking with her turns me back into that little boy cowering beneath the belt and tongue of a woman deeply wounded by my father, by poverty, by her childhood, by the sexism that has dominated her life. My relationships since the incident with my ex-girlfriend have been better, no doubt, but not the bomb.

But I am at least proud of the fact I have not reverted back to violence against women—and don't ever plan to, which is why I regularly go to therapy, why I listen to and absorb the stories of women, and why I talk about sexism with any men, young and old, who are down to rethink the definitions we've accepted so uncritically. Few of us men actually believe there is a problem, or we are quick to point fingers at women, instead of acknowledging that healing is a necessary and ongoing process, that women *and* men need to be a part of this process, and that we all must be willing to engage in this dialogue and work if sexism is to ever disappear.

So I fly solo, and have done so for some time. For sure, today I count among my friends, peers, and mentors older feminist women like bell hooks and Johnnetta B. Cole, and young feminists like Nikki Stewart, a girls' rights advocate in Washington, D.C., and Aishah Simmons, who is currently putting together a documentary on rape within the Black community. I do not always agree with these women, but I also know that if I do not struggle, hard and constantly, backsliding is likely. This is made worse by the fact that outside of a handful of male friends, there are no young men I know whom I can speak with regarding sexism as easily as I do with women.

The fact is, there was a blueprint handed to us in childhood telling us this is the way a man should behave, and we unwittingly followed the scrip verbatim. There was no blueprint handed to us about how to begin to wind ourselves out of sexism as an adult, but maybe there should have been. Every day I struggle within myself not to use the language of gender oppression, to see the sexism inherent in every aspect of America, to challenge all injustices, not just those that are convenient for me. I am ashamed of my ridiculously sexist life, of raising my hand to my girlfriend, and of two other ugly and hateful moments in college, one where I hit a female student in the head with a stapler during the course of an argument, and the other where I got into a punch-throwing exchange with a female student I had sexed then discarded like an old pair of shoes. I am also ashamed of all the lies and manipulations, the verbal abuse and reckless disregard for the views and lives of women. But with that shame has come a consciousness and, as the activists said during the Civil Rights Movement, this consciousness, this knowing, is a river of no return. I have finally learned how to swim. I have finally learned how to push for ward. I may become tired, I may lose my breath, I may hit a rock from time to time and become cynical, but I am not going to drown this time around.